Routledge Revivals

Religion and American Law

Originally published in 2000, the *Encyclopedia of Religion and American Law*, comprehensively describes and analyses important cases and legal controversies between religion and state. The book has contributions from numerous distinguished history and law professors and practicing attorneys of the period. It provides short and articulate encyclopedic style entries which capture the colour, richness and complexity of the topics covered. The book's multidisciplinary approach will make it an ideal library reference resource for scholars and students of law, as well as a valuable addition to any legal collection.

I0894731

Religion and American Law

An Encyclopedia

Edited by Paul Finkelman

Routledge
Taylor & Francis Group
Routledge Revivals

First published in 2000
by Garland Publishing Inc.

This edition first published in 2018 by Routledge
2 Park Square, Milton Park, Abingdon, Oxon, OX14 4RN
and by Routledge
711 Third Avenue, New York, NY 10017

Routledge is an imprint of the Taylor & Francis Group, an informa business

Publisher's Note

The publisher has gone to great lengths to ensure the quality of this reprint but points out that some imperfections in the original copies may be apparent.

Disclaimer

The publisher has made every effort to trace copyright holders and welcomes correspondence from those they have been unable to contact.

A Library of Congress record exists under LCCN: 99057222

ISBN 13: 978-0-8153-6531-0 (hbk)
ISBN 13: 978-1-351-26184-5 (ebk)
ISBN 13: 978-0-8153-6535-8 (pbk)

Religion and American Law

Garland Reference Library of the Humanities (Vol. 1548)

Religion and American Law: An Encyclopedia

Editor
Paul Finkelman

Chapman Distinguished Professor
University of Tulsa College of Law

GARLAND PUBLISHING, INC.
A MEMBER OF THE TAYLOR & FRANCIS GROUP
New York & London
2000

Published in 2000 by
Garland Publishing Inc.
A Member of the Taylor & Francis Group
19 Union Square West
New York, NY 10003

10 9 8 7 6 5 4 3 2 1

Library of Congress Cataloging-in-Publication Data is available from the Library of Congress

I dedicate this book to the memory of
Rose Sobel Finkelman and Hyman Finkelman
and
Mashah Yourkowsky Dobbis and Isadore Dobbis
who came to the United States seeking religious liberty and found it.

Contents

Introduction

"We are a religious people whose institutions presuppose a Supreme Being." So wrote Justice William O. Douglas in *Zorach v. Clausen* in 1952. He was, of course, right. We announce our trust in God on our money. We proclaim our allegience to our flag and our Republic, in the same sentence that we declare our nation is "under God." Our Supreme Court begins each term with a plea that "God save the United States and this honorable Court." Almost every president has invoked God in his inaugural address as well as in moments of national crisis or celebration.

We are equally a diverse people, who worship in different ways, to different cadences, and indeed to different Gods. Our holy texts — the Gospels, the Pentateuch, the Koran, the Book of Mormon, the Granth Sahib, the Bhagavad Giti, and Science and Health with Key to the Scriptures — tell different stories, proclaim different values, and reflect the cultures of the world. Our holy languages are varied, and we pray in the German of Luther, the English of King James I, Paul of Tarsus's Greek, the Latin of Constantine, the Hebrew of Moses, the Aramaic of the Sages of the Talmud as well as Jesus of Nazareth, the Arabic of Muhammad, and the Sanskrit of Sri Ramakrishna.

We pray to the sounds of music and we pray in silence. Our sounds of worship include the organ, the piano, guitar, the horn of a ram, the jazz band, and most often, that most elegant and divine of all instruments, the human voice. We pray with heads covered and uncovered, knees bent and straight, standing, sitting, kneeling, and prostrate on a prayer rug. We pray next to our families and separated by age and gender. We attend synagogues, mosques, churches, temples, Kingdom Halls, cathedrals, meeting houses, and gurdwaras. A holy place may be a building consecrated by an ordained member of the clergy or for Native Americans a mountain, waterfall, or volcano. We are led in prayers by imams, priests, ministers, preachers, shamans, rabbis, santeros, bishops, and yogis. Scattered throughout the nation are many who believe in no supreme being, and actively reject religion in any form or context.

Our rituals and our beliefs are as varied as our faiths. Some faiths abstain from alcohol while others require it. Catholicism believes that wine has been transformed by ritual into the blood of Christ through the incantations of a priest. Some faiths protect the lives of animals while others require the sacrifice of animals. Some Americans are pacifists, others are required by their faith to symbolically carry a weapon. Some declare abortion under any circumstances to be a sin; others do not; and some declare that it is a sin not to have an abortion if the mother's life is at risk. Some faiths and churches have endowed and supported important hospitals and medical schools, but some of faiths reject intervention by modern medical science, refusing medical aid even at the cost of lives.

A religious people of many faiths and practices, we are also a democractic people, governed by the will of the majority and the rule of law. But we are also a people governed by a Constitution and a body of laws that protect individual liberty, including the right to worship our religion as we please. Central to our Constitution is the First Amendment, which begins: "Congress shall make no law respecting an establishment of religion, or prohibiting the free exercise thereof."

There are, of course, great tensions between these aspects of the United States. When our institutions "presuppose a Supreme Being," they also threaten to establish the majority's view of what that Supreme Being might be or how that Supreme Being should be honored or even worshiped. Thus, any governmental institutionalization of the Supreme Being — any governmental establishment of religion — threatens to undermine the protection for religious minorities. On the other hand, to respect or protect the unique and unusual practices of minority faiths may lead to a kind of establishment for those religions by exempting their members from the rules the rest of society must follow.

The problem of church and state remains vibrant and meaningful in our culture. The Supreme Court has heard more than three hundred cases that touch on these issues. State and lower federal courts have heard thousands more. The jurisprudence of religion in complicated and often confusing. It highlights the tensions of our political culture and our democratic society. Two examples illustrate this complex relationship:

In *Engle v. Vitale* (1962) and *School District of Abington v. Schempp* (1963) the Supreme Court unambiguously held that schools could not sponsor prayer or Bible readings and that teachers, principals, and other school officials and employees could not lead prayers. To do so, according to the Court, was to establish religion in a government institution. Despite these cases, state legislatures have passed numerous acts to circumvent the Supreme Court ruling. State lawmakers pass such laws because they are popular with constitutents and are often excellent campaign issues. Time after time the federal courts have struck down such laws, but legislatures never seem to get the message. Meanwhile, we know that in numerous school districts teachers lead prayers and students say them every day, simply ignoring the law of the land. Parents and students who object to such prayers are often afraid to complain because of social pressure. The issue of school prayer illustrates the tension beween democracy and constitutional government. The continuations of school prayers in some schools—and the intimidation of those who object to such prayers—is a modern-day example of the "tyranny of the majority" that the French scholar Alexis de Tocqueville identified in the 1830s.

The flip side of the tyranny of the majority can be seen in the Religious Freedom Restoration Act (RFRA). In *Employment Division, Department of Human Resources of Oregon v. Smith* (1990) the Supreme Court ruled that states did not need to justify burdens on religious exercise with a compelling state interest. Instead, the Court ruled that religious exemptions to generally applicable laws are not constitutionally required. In 1993 Congress tried to reverse this ruling and bring back the compelling state interest test in cases involving the free exercise of religion. In passing this act Congress did not try to impose a "tyranny of the majority," but rather tried to get all majorities to protect minority religions. The law was passed "to restore the compelling interest test" as it had exised before *Oregon v. Smith,* and "to provide a cause of action to persons whose religious exercise is burdened by government." The law declared that "Government shall not burden a person's exercise of religion even if the burden results from a rule of law of general applicability" except "if it demonstrates that the application of the burden to the person . . . (1) is essential to further a compelling state interest; and (2) is the least restrictive means of furthering that compelling governmental interest." Rarely has Congress tried to reign in its own powers, and that of other branches of government, to protect minorities. But, this admirable goal could not pass constitutional scrutiny. In *City of Boerne v. Flores* (1997) the Supreme Court overturned RFRA on the ground it violated the separation of powers. Congress cannot dictate to the Supreme Court what theory of law the Court must adopt in its jurisprudence.

These examples show the complexity of the intersection between law and religion in our Constitutional democracy. This encyclopedia examines the issues surrounding religion and American law. The questions are in part historical and in part very modern. The entries cover a wide range of issues, events, and people. Some deal with individuals who had a profound affect on the development of religion and law, such as Roger Williams, James Madison, and a number of Supreme Court justices. Other entries focus on certain faiths and sects, particularly those that have often had confrontations with the American legal system. There are also discussions of various legal theories and historical developments of the law of church and state. The entries focus on the adoption of the U.S. Constitution and the Bill of Rights and the way the people of the new nation struggled to define the relationship between church and state. Finally, there are entries of all the major legal decisions that touch on religions and American law.

This book was possible only because of the hard work and patience of the contributors. I began this project in 1990, while teaching a course in Church and State at Brooklyn Law School. Colleagues there, and at Virginia Tech, Chicago-Kent College of Law, Hamline Law School, and the University of Akron School of Law encouraged the project and contributed to it. All of the contributors have worked hard in this difficult collaborative enterprise. However, I owe special thanks to William Ross, Walter Pratt, Patrick O'Neil, Bette Novitt Evans, William Funk, and David Gregory, who took on numerous articles and with great humor bailed me out on more than one occasion. Conversations and advice from Douglas Laycock, Sanford Levinson, Richard Aynes, Michael Kent Curtis, and Michael McConnell have vastly improved this book. A number of my students and former students have worked as research assistants on this project, and many have also written for it. I want to particularly thank Aimee Burnett, Mical Kapsner, David Meek, Mora Lowry, Philip Presby, Renee Redman, Jordan Tamagni, Rob Osberg, and Melissa Day. I especially want to thank Dawn Kostiak, whose work on this project went above and beyond the call of a research assistant. I also wish to thank Richard Steins of Garland Publishing for all his terrific work on this project.

Contributors

José Julián Alvarez-González
University of Puerto Rico Law School

John Arthur
State University of New York at Binghamton

Richard Aynes
University of Akron School of Law

Jonathan R. Baer
Yale University

James T. Baker
Western Kentucky University

Lance Banning
University of Kentucky

J. Jackson Barlow
Juniata College

Michal R. Belknap
California Western School of Law

Thomas Berg
Cumberland Law School

Joanne C. Brant
Ohio Northern University Claude W. Pettit College of Law

Alan E. Brownstein
University of California, Davis School of Law

Angela C. Carmella
Seton Hall Law School

Natasha Leigh Chefetz, Esq.
New York City

Brian E. Comerford
Brooklyn Law School

Daniel O. Conkle
Indiana University School of Law

Thomas J. Curry
Archdiocese of Los Angeles

Michael Kent Curtis
Wake Forest University School of Law

Stewart Davenport
Yale University

Melissa Day, Esq.
Cleveland, Ohio

Neal Devins
William and Mary School of Law

Norman Dorsen
New York University

Davison M. Douglas
William and Mary School of Law

Michelle Dye Neumann, Esq.
Gainesville, Florida

Bette Novit Evans
Creighton University

Paul Finkelman
University of Tulsa College of Law

Edwin B. Firmage
University of Utah School of Law

Edward B. Foley
Ohio State University School of Law

Tony Freyer
University of Alabama

William Funk
Lewis and Clark Law School

Sheldon Gelman
Cleveland-Marshall College of Law

W. Clark Gilpin
University of Chicago Divinity School

Laurilyn A. Goettsch, Esq.
Kansas City, Missouri

Leigh Hunt Greenhaw
Widener University Law School

David L. Gregory
St. John's University School of Law

Kermit L. Hall
North Carolina State University

Susan N. Herman
Brooklyn Law School

Steven J. Heyman
Chicago-Kent College of Law, Illinois Institute of Technology

Timothy Huebner
Rhodes College

L. Sue Hulett
Knox College

Calvin Jillson
University of Colorado, Boulder

Herbert A. Johnson
University of South Carolina School of Law

Barbara M. Jones
Union College

Beryl R. Jones
Brooklyn Law School

Catherine Kau, Esq.
Native Hawaiian Legal Corporation

Todd Kerstetter
University of Nebraska-Kearney

Andrew King
University of Maryland School of Law

Bryan F. LeBeau
Creighton University

F. Graham Lee
St. Joseph's University

James K. Lehman, Esq.
Washington, D.C.

Brian P. Levack
University of Texas

Sanford Levinson
University of Texas School of Law

Leonard W. Levy
Professor Emeritus, Claremont Graduate School

Melody Kapilialoha MacKenzie, Esq.
Hawaiian Claims Office

Joan Mahoney
Wayne State University Law School

Richard Collin Mangrum
Creighton University School of Law

William Marshall
Case Western Reserve University School of Law

Michael McConnell
University of Utah

Margaret E. Newell
Ohio State University

Donald G. Nieman
Bowling Green State University

William Offutt
Pace University

Patrick O'Neil
Broome College

Peter S. Onuf
University of Virginia

Rob Osberg
Reston, Virginia

Josephine F. Pacheco
George Mason University

J. Wilson Parker
Wake Forest University School of Law

Walter F. Pratt Jr.
School of Law University of Notre Dame

Phillip Presby, Esq.
Brooklyn, New York

Renee C. Redman, Esq.
New York City

Norman L. Rosenberg
Macalester College

William G. Ross
Cumberland School of Law

Jack Sahl
University of Akron School of Law

Richard B. Saphire
University of Dayton School of Law

Jeff D. Schultz
Cleveland, Ohio

Stephen K. Schutte, Esq.
Denver, Colorado

Thomas A. Schweitzer
Jacob D. Fuchsberg Law Center of Touro College

Amy Shapiro, Esq.
Binghamton, New York

Jennifer L. Sherman, Esq.
Livonia, Michigan

Cathy Shipe, Esq.
San Diego, California

Stephen A. Siegel
DePaul University College of Law

Peter Silver
Priceton University

John Y. Simon
Southern Illinois University at Carbondale

Rodney K. Smith
University of Little Rock School of Law

Nadine Strossen
New York Law School and President, American Civil Liberties Union

Mark Tushnet
Georgetown University Law Center

Melvin I. Urofsky
Virginia Commonwealth University

Lea Vandervelde
University of Iowa School of Law

Jon M. Van Dyke
University of Hawaii School of Law

Thomas Viles, Esq.
New York City

Peter Wallenstein
Virginia Tech

Spencer Weber Waller
Brooklyn Law School

Carol Weisbrod
University of Connecticut Law School

John Wertheimer
Davidson College

John G. West
Seattle Pacific University

Bryan H. Wildenthal
Thomas Jefferson School of Law

John R. Wunder
University of Nebraska-Lincoln

Barry L. Zaretsky
Brooklyn Law School

A

Abington v. Schempp
See SCHOOL DISTRICT OF ABINGTON TOWNSHIP V. SCHEMPP.

Adoption, Custody, and Visitation: Religion in the Context of Broken and Blended Families

At early English common law, feudalism and the patriarchal orientation of Christianity and antiquity firmly established the father as the legal head of the family who had absolute control over, among other things, his children's religious training. Paternal control over religious training, *religio sequitur patrem,* followed naturally from the more general rule of *patriae potestas,* the "empire of the father," and extended even after the father's death. In contrast, the mother had virtually no legal powers over the children, although she was entitled to respect. The Crown held limited power to intervene in family affairs under the doctrine of *parens patriae* but initially exercised that power only against pauper parents who were unable to care for their children. Consequently, the father's religious views controlled in the event of adoption or disputes about custody and visitation.

From Status-Oriented to Discretionary Standards

Although early pronouncements on the American law of child custody echoed the rules of *patriae potestas* and *religio sequitur patrem,* U.S. courts never applied the rules as rigorously as English courts had. During the latter part of the nineteenth century, states began adopting legislative standards for deciding adoption, custody, and care issues in favor of the general welfare of the child or the child's best interest.

Nonetheless, as a matter of due process rights, U.S. courts preserved a certain amount of parental autonomy against the state's view of the child's best interest. In *Meyer v. Nebraska* (1923), for example, the Supreme Court in the tradition of *Lochner v. New York* (1905) held that certain governmental deprivations of family autonomy—whether in the name of best interest of the children or of the public—violate fundamental liberties guaranteed by the Fourteenth Amendment. Similarly the Court in *Pierce v. Society of Sisters* (1925) and the companion case *Pierce v. Hill Military Academy* (1925) invalidated compulsory public education school laws on the basis of substantive due process and parental rights. Again in *Wisconsin v. Yoder* (1972) the Supreme Court invalidated a state compulsory high school education statute as violative of the fundamental rights of Amish parents to raise their children in accordance with the Amish tradition.

However, there are obvious limits to parental autonomy over family affairs. In *Prince v. Massachusetts* (1944), for example, the Court held that neither free exercise claims nor due process family rights will override the state's police and *parens patriae* authority to protect children from illegal conduct. There the Court stated the qualifying principle that, although the "custody, care and nurture of the child reside first in the parents," "it does not follow [that parents] are free . . . to make martyrs of their children before they have reached the age of full and legal discretion when they can make that choice for themselves."

The further question arises concerning whether parental rights continue in the fractured family. In *Palmore v. Sidoti* (1984) the Court held that the best-interest standard, by itself, provides an inadequate basis for overriding parental rights even in a post-divorce family. Thus the fact that the Caucasian custodial wife was then cohabitating with a black man, whom she later married, could not constitutionally state a basis for modifying custody on the reasoning that the child would be stigmatized by the interracial relationship.

Religious Beliefs and Parental Disputes

An examination of the historical, sociological, and constitutional factors involved in determining the role of religion in child custody, adoption, and visitation cases suggests the following points.

First, the religious preferences of the respective parents as well as of the child may be considered in custody, visitation, and adoption cases. In the case of adoption, most states by statute or constitutional proscription require, wherever possible, the religious matching of parents and adoptive children. In *Dickens v. Ernesto* (N.Y., 1972) the New York courts upheld against an Establishment Clause attacking New York's religious matching law, and the U.S. Supreme Court dismissed the appeal. The courts in this country for some time have also regarded the religious preferences of a mature child as a factor to be considered in the context of a child custody dispute incident to a divorce. Examples of this are found in *Matter of Vardinakis* (N.Y., 1936) and *Martin v. Martin* (N.Y., 1954). Sometimes the state specifies by statute "religious needs" as a factor to be included in a best-interest analysis. The court in *Bonjour v. Bonjour* (Alaska, 1979) relied on the statutorily based "religious needs" of a mature child as a factor in awarding custody to the "religious" father, rather than to the nonchurchgoing mother. Similarly, the court in *T. v. H.* (N.J., 1968) held that the capacity of a Jewish father who lived in New Jersey near Jewish temples and Jewish schools to service the child's religious needs could be taken into consideration where the mother had moved to "gentile" Idaho, where the nearest temple was eighty miles away.

The religious needs of the child may also justify time, place, and manner restrictions on visitation for the noncustodial parent. Thus the court in *Williamson v. Williamson* (Mo., 1972) modified the visitation order in aid of the mother's efforts at religious training. Similarly, the court in *Lee v. Gebhardt* (Mont., 1977) modified the weekly, weekend visitation to one weekend per month in aid of the custodial parent's opportunity to participate in the child's religious growth. To the same effect the court in *Pogue v. Pogue* (Pa., 1954) permitted a modification of a visitation award to require a Jehovah's Witness father to return the child to the Catholic mother on Sundays so that she could attend Mass with the child.

On the other hand, courts also have refused to tailor visitation orders in aid of either the child's or the custodial parent's preference. In *Angel v. Angel* (Ohio, 1956), for example, the court refused to modify the visitation order to allow the custodial father, a Catholic, to retain custody on Sundays so that the child could be brought up in the Catholic Church. Similarly, the court in *Matthews v. Matthews* (S.C., 1979) refused to reduce the mother's visitation rights with her son to only one day of visitation every two weeks in order to enhance the custodial parent's ability to attend church with his child more regularly. Again the court in *Wagner v. Wagner* (N.J., 1979) refused to modify the regular visitation schedule to accommodate the children's Hebrew school training.

Second, *Prince v. Massachusetts* (1944) established the principle that religious beliefs or practices which are illegal will not generally be protected by family rights. Thus custodial, adoption, and visitation orders may take into account the prospects of a guardian who aids and abets illegal activities. *Wisconsin v. Yoder* (1972), however, suggests that religiously inspired "illegal" conduct which poses neither a substantial threat "to the physical or mental health of the child" nor presents harm "to the public safety, peace, order, or welfare" of the child is constitutionally protected.

Third, religious beliefs or practices—even though not illegal—which pose an imminent and substantial threat to the physical or emotional well-being of the child may justify custodial, visitation, or adoption restrictions. Probably the most-oft-cited examples of this limitation are the blood transfusion cases. In cases such as *Battaglia v. Battaglia* (N.Y., 1958), *Levitsky v. Levitsky* (Md., 1963), and *State v. Perricone,* (N.J., 1962) the courts held that, where the religious convictions of Jehovah's Witness parents threatened the very survival of the children at risk, the courts had an obligation under the doctrine of *parens patriae* to intervene in favor of the children's well-being. However, the court in *Osier v. Osier* (Me., 1980) held that the mother's beliefs as a Jehovah's Witness disapproving of blood transfusions could not be relied on as a basis for a custody award without a showing that the belief posed an "imminent" and "substantial" threat to the healthy child. Along similar lines, the court adopted a less restrictive alternative in *Stapley v. Stapley* (Ariz., 1971) by upholding the custody award to a Jehovah's Witness mother while vesting the authority to make medical decisions in the noncustodial father.

Where the child's best interest is threatened merely by the unorthodoxy of the parent's religious beliefs, however, the due process and free exercise rights of the parent should prevail. In *Quiner v. Quiner* (Calif., 1967), for example, the court of appeals—refusing to open the Pandora's box of choosing between religions—reversed when the trial court awarded custody to the father on the speculative grounds that the mother's membership in a separatist religious group called the "Exclusive Brethren" was not in the best interest of the child.

Other courts, however, have been willing to open that Pandora's box. For example, the court in *In re Marriage of Hadeen* (Wash., 1980) held that a lesser "requirement of a reasonable and substantial likelihood of immediate or future impairment best accommodates the general welfare of the child and free exercise of religion by the parents." Even less evidence of potential harm was required in *Burnham v. Burnham* (Neb., 1981), in which the Nebraska Supreme Court reversed the trial court's custody award on the ground that the mother's ultraconservative Catholic and anti-Semitic beliefs as a member of the Tridentine Church would not be in the child's best interest.

Fourth, although the custodial parent generally has the primary right to control the religious training of the child, in the absence of a showing of substantial and imminent threat to the child's emotional well-being, courts under the guise of "best interest" may not interfere with the noncustodial parent's attempts to communicate variant religious beliefs. Thus in *Lewis v. Lewis* (Ark., 1976) the court, in reversing the trial court's religious-based visitation limitations, stated that visitation rights could not be refused on religious grounds without some showing of demonstrable harm to the children. Similarly, the respective courts in *In re Mentry* (Calif., 1983), *Munoz v. Munoz* (Wash., 1971), *Robertson v. Robertson* (Wash., 1978), *Khalsa v. Khalsa* (N.M., 1988), and *Hanson v. Hanson* (N.D., 1987) rejected the argument that a showing of speculative psychological harm is constitutionally sufficient to order a noncustodial parent not to discuss religion during visitation.

However, some courts, under best-interest auspices, have required minimal evidence of a threat to justify visitation restrictions. In *Ledoux v. Ledoux* (Neb., 1990), for example, the court—based on a minimal harm record—upheld a decree that ordered the noncustodial father, a Jehovah's Witness, "to refrain from exposing or permitting any other person to expose his minor children to any religious practices or teachings inconsistent with the Catholic religion" of the children's custodial mother.

Balancing Best Interest and Parental Autonomy

In conclusion, the role of religion in adoption, custody, and visitation cases has evolved from the status-oriented rules of *patriae potestas* and *religio sequitur patrem,* which vested nearly absolute authority in the father, to a discretionary standard of best interest hedged up by constitutional constraints that preserve a certain amount of parental autonomy even in fractured and blended families.

Richard Collin Mangrum

Bibliography

Baskin, Stuart J., "State Intrusions into Family Affairs: Justifications and Limitations," 26 *Stanford Law Review* 1383–1409 (1974).

Comment, "Child Custody: Best Interest of Children v. Constitutional Rights of Parents," 81 *Dickinson Law Review* 733–754 (1977).

Mangrum, Richard Collin, "Exclusive Reliance on Best Interest May Be Unconstitutional: Religion As a Factor in Child Custody Cases," 15 *Creighton Law Review* 25–82 (1982).

———, "Religious Constraints during

Visitation: Under What Circumstances Are They Constitutional?" 24 *Creighton Law Review* 445–494 (1991).

Otobac, Jennifer Ann, "For the Sake of the Children: Court Consideration of Religion in Child Custody Cases," 50 *Stanford Law Review* 1609 (1998).

Cases Cited

Angel v. Angel, 74 Ohio L. Abs. 531, 140 N.E. 2d 86 (1956).

Battaglia v. Battaglia, 9 Misc. 2d 1067, 172 N.Y. S. 2d 361 (Sup. Ct. 1958).

Bonjour v. Bonjour, 592 P. 2d 1233 (Alaska 1979).

Burnham v. Burnham, 208 Neb. 498, 304 N.W. 2d 58 (1981).

Dickens v. Ernesto, 30 N.Y. 2d 61, 281 N.E. 2d 153, 330 N.Y. S. 2d 346, appeal dismissed, 407 U.S. 917 (1972).

Hanson v. Hanson, 404 N.W. 2d 460 (N.D. 1987).

In re Marriage of Hadeen, 27 Wash. App. 566, 619 P. 2d 374 (1980).

In re Mentry, 142 Cal. App. 3d 260, 190 Cal. Rptr. 843 (1983).

Khalsa v. Khalsa, 107 N.M. 31, 751 P. 2d 715 (Ct. App. 1988).

Ledoux v. Ledoux, 234 Neb. 479, 452 N.W. 2d 1 (1990).

Lee v. Gebhardt, 173 Mont. 305, 567 P. 2d 466 (1977).

Levitsky v. Levitsky, 231 Md. 388, 190 A. 2d 621 (1963).

Lewis v. Lewis, 260 Ark. 691, 543 S.W. 2d 222 (1976).

Lochner v. New York, 198 U.S. 45 (1905).

Martin v. Martin, 308 N.Y. 136, 123 N.E. 2d 812 (1954).

Matter of Vardinakis, 160 Misc. 13, 289 N.Y. Supp. 355 (1936).

Matthews v. Matthews, 273 S.C. 130, 254 S.E. 2d 801 (1979).

Meyer v. Nebraska, 262 U.S. 390 (1923).

Munoz v. Munoz, 79 Wash. 2d 810, 489 P. 2d 1133 (1971).

Osier v. Osier, 410 A. 2d 1027 (Me. 1980).

Palmore v. Sidoti, 466 U.S. 429 (1984).

Pierce v. Hill Military Academy, 268 U.S. 510 (1925).

Pierce v. Society of Sisters, 268 U.S. 510 (1925).

Pogue v. Pogue, 89 Pa. D.&C. 588 (1954).

Prince v. Massachusetts, 321 U.S. 158 (1944).

Quiner v. Quiner, 59 Cal. Rptr. 503 (1967).

Robertson v. Robertson, 19 Wash. App. 425, 575 P. 2d 1092 (1978).

Stapley v. Stapley, 15 Ariz. App. 64, 485 P. 2d 1181 (1971).

State v. Perricone, 37 N.J. 463, 181 A. 2d 751 (1962).

T. v. H., 102 N.J. Super. 38, 245 A. 2d 221 (1968).

Wagner v. Wagner, 165 N.J. Super. 553, 398 A. 2d 918 (1979).

Williamson v. Williamson, 479 S.W. 2d 163 (Mo. Ct. App. 1972).

Wisconsin v. Yoder, 406 U.S. 205 (1972).

African Methodist Episcopal Church v. the City of New Orleans
15 La. 441 (1860)

Students of African American history have long recognized the centrality of organized religion to African American institutional life. The ruling class of the antebellum South recognized this, too, and responded by seeking to stamp out African American religious autonomy. A prime example of this is the 1860 Louisiana Supreme Court case *African Methodist Episcopal Church v. New Orleans*. The facts of the case follow.

In April 1858 the New Orleans Common Council, believing assemblages of "colored persons" to be "an evil which requires correction," adopted an ordinance mandating that no such person, free or slave, would be allowed to "address any assembly or deliver any public discourse" without prior mayoral permission. The measure also ordained that no such "colored persons" would henceforth be allowed to assemble for worship except "under the supervision and control of some recognized white congregation or church."

On passage of this oppressive ordinance, the black-run African Methodist Episcopal Church (A.M.E.) of New Orleans closed its doors and went to court. The A.M.E. Church had been active in New Orleans since 1848, when ten free blacks, acting according to the terms of Louisiana's incorporation statute of 1847, organized themselves into a "private corporation having a religious object." Under their corporate name, the directors of the A.M.E. Church went on to acquire three church buildings in New Orleans—property whose value totaled about twenty-one thousand dollars. In these buildings the church's expanding membership assembled freely for worship.

The ordinance of 1858 made continued free worship impossible. In court A.M.E. leaders claimed that the measure had driven off "each and every member of the[ir] large congregations." By preventing A.M.E. congregants from assembling, church leaders argued, the city had effectively "taken illegal possession and unauthorized control of the whole of their property." This, they maintained, constituted a violation of the Louisiana Constitution's Article 105, which prohibited both laws passed ex post facto and laws impairing the obligation of contracts. The A.M.E. Church urged the judges to declare the ordinance unconstitutional and to force the city to pay damages—rent for each month that the church was unable freely to use its property.

Although victorious in district court, the church was unable to persuade the judges of the state's highest bench. Supreme Court Justice Alexander Buchanan's majority opinion of 1860 held that the New Orleans ordinance overstepped neither the Louisiana Constitution nor the "legitimate bounds of police administration." Buchanan reversed the district court and held for the city.

With the legislative passage and subsequent judicial upholding of the 1858 ordinance, the A.M.E. and other black churches in New Orleans became invisible, though not extinct. Congregants continued to worship, but they did so clandestinely. This arrangement, however, proved to be short-lived. Within a year of the *A.M.E.* decision the slave South was at war. Within a few more years the Confederacy had been defeated; the Thirteenth, Fourteenth, and Fifteenth Amendments had been ratified; and African American religious autonomy had become a central feature of life in the postemancipation South.

The *A.M.E.* case casts light on at least three aspects of life in the late-antebellum South. First, it testifies to the lengths to which whites were willing to go to suppress African American autonomy. Second, it suggests that, notwithstanding this oppression, free blacks, like those who led the A.M.E. Church, retained enough faith in the legal system to seek (although perhaps not fully to expect) protection in court.

Finally, the *A.M.E.* case illustrates how nineteenth-century constitutional culture was quite different from its twentieth-century descendant. Whereas twentieth-century lawyers would look at the New Orleans measure and see blatant violations of religious, assembly, and speech freedoms, as well as the measure's invidious racial classifications, A.M.E. lawyers saw something quite different. They argued that the ordinance amounted to an unauthorized taking of property and an unallowable impairment of their 1848 contract with the state. The A.M.E. made no mention of the speech or religion clauses of the federal Constitution, probably because the U.S. Supreme Court had previously ruled, in *Barron v. Baltimore* (1833) and *Permoli v. First Municipality of New Orleans* (1845), that the First Amendment, like the rest of the Bill of Rights, constrained only the federal government and not the individual states. The A.M.E.'s courtroom approach suggests the extent to which property and contractual rights—and not civil liberties in the modern sense—dominated nineteenth-century American constitutional thought.

For African Americans in 1860, however, the niceties of legal strategy hardly seemed to matter. As Justice Buchanan, echoing *Dred Scott v. Sandford* (1857), declared in his *A.M.E.* opinion: "The African race are strangers to our Constitution, and are the subjects of special and exceptional legislation." Against this sort of judicial reasoning, no constitutional argument—no matter how clever—offered on behalf of African American litigants seemed to stand much of a chance.

John Wertheimer

Bibliography

Bucke, Emory S. (ed.), *The History of American Methodism,* vol. II (New York: Abingdon, 1964).

Walker, Clarence E., *A Rock in a Weary Land: The African Methodist Episcopal Church during the Civil War and Reconstruction* (Baton Rouge: Louisiana State University Press, 1982).

Cases Cited

African Methodist Episcopal Church v. the City of New Orleans, 15 La. 441 (1860).

Barron v. Baltimore, 7 Pet. (32 U.S.) 243 (1833).

Dred Scott v. Sandford, 19 How. (60 U.S.) 393 (1857).

Permoli v. First Municipality of New Orleans, 44 U.S. 589 (1845).

Agostini et al. v. Felton et al. 521 U.S. 203 (1997)

In *Agostini et al. v. Felton et al.* (1997) the U.S. Supreme Court by a 5-to-4 margin overturned *Aguilar v. Felton* (1985), which prohibited public schoolteachers from teaching federally mandated remedial classes on the grounds of parochial schools, and its companion case *Grand Rapids School District v. Ball* (1985), which determined that shared-time programs also violated the Establishment Clause.

In *Aguilar* the Court ruled that New York City's program, which sent public schoolteachers into parochial schools to provide remedial education, was unconstitutional. New York City's program was designed to meet the requirements of Title I of the Elementary and Secondary Education Act of 1965. In that original case Justice William J. Brennan, writing for the majority, asserted that the program constituted an excessive entanglement in violation of the First Amendment's Establishment Clause. Relying on *Lemon v. Kurtzman* (1971) the Court applied the three-pronged test to determine a violation of the Establishment Clause. If any one of the three prongs is met, the act is declared unconstitutional. These three prongs are

1. Is there a secular purpose for the act?
2. Does the act give the effect of advancing religion?
3. Is there an excessive entanglement with government?

The Court concluded that there was an excessive entanglement between church and state because of the need to have ongoing inspections to ensure that the inculcation of religion did not take place as part of the remedial instruction provided by the state. In order to protect against inculcation, the state had to have "a permanent and pervasive . . . presence in the sectarian schools" infringing on the Establishment Clause. The majority came to this conclusion despite the fact that the program's nineteen-year history did not show a single allegation of attempted religious indoctrination. As noted constitutional law scholar Leonard W. Levy wrote, "the decision adversely affected disadvantaged parochial school children who needed special auxiliary services."

More than a decade later, petitioners filed motions seeking relief from the injunction under Federal Rule of Civil Procedure 60(b)(5), which states that "the court may relieve a party . . . from a final judgment . . . [when] it is no longer equitable that the judgment should have prospective application." The petitioners argued that the cost of complying with *Aguilar*—an estimated $100 million—and the post-*Aguilar* decisions in cases including *Board of Education of Kiryas Village School District v. Grumet* (1994), *Zobrest v. Catalina Foothills School District* (1993), and *Witters v. Washington Department of Services for Blind* (1986) justified the reversal of the injunction.

Although the Court rejected the petitioner's use of Rule 60(b) because it would have the effect of eroding the integrity of the Court, the majority did agree that *Aguilar* could not be squared with many of the intervening cases. Justice Sandra Day O'Connor, who dissented in the *Aguilar* case, wrote the majority opinion in *Agostini.* Justice O'Connor—joined by Chief Justice William Rehnquist and Justices Antonin Scalia, Anthony Kennedy, and Clarence Thomas—decided that a federally funded program providing remedial and supplemental instruction on a neutral basis does not violate the Establishment Clause even if the program is given on the premises of sectarian schools by government employees.

The Court rejected the argument of the *Aguilar* Court that the programs violated the first prong (no secular purpose) and the second prong (the impermissible effect of advancing religion) and the third prong (excessive government entanglement with religion) of the *Lemon* test. In response to the *Aguilar* Court's second-prong claim, the *Agostini* Court, citing *Zobrest*—in which the Court permitted a deaf student to bring his state-employed sign language interpreter with him to his Roman Catholic high school—concluded that the presence of a public employee on the grounds of a parochial school does not constitute a symbolic union between church and state.

Further, the Court rejected the presumption that any public employee who works on a religious school's grounds inculcates religion. The Court relied on the fact that there was no evidence that any of the public teachers had attempted to inculcate religion in students. Citing *Witters*—a case which held that the

Establishment Clause did not bar a state from issuing a vocational tuition grant to a blind person who wished to attend a Christian college and become a pastor, missionary, or youth director—the majority ruled that not all government aid which benefits the educational functions of religious schools is invalid.

In response to the third-prong question, O'Connor's opinion noted that the New York City Title I Program does not give aid recipients any incentive to modify religious beliefs or practices in order to obtain access to the program. In fact, the aid is given in a neutral manner that neither favors nor disfavors religion. O'Connor concluded that

> any money that ultimately went to religious institutions did so only as a result of the genuinely independent and private choices of individuals and that based upon those cases *Aguilar* will not, as a matter of law, be deemed to have the effect of advancing religion through indoctrination.

In the end the majority decided that *Aguilar* was no longer good law.

Justices David Souter—joined by Justices John Paul Stevens, Ruth Bader Ginsburg and Steven Breyer—dissented in the case, stating

> the human tendency, of course, is to forget the hard lessons, and to overlook the history of governmental partnership with religion when the cause is worthy, and bureaucrats have programs. That tendency to forget is the reason for having the Establishment Clause (along with the Constitution's other structural and libertarian guarantees), in the hope of stopping the corrosion before it starts.

Souter went on to argue that

> what was true of the Title I scheme struck down in Aguilar will be just as true when New York reverts to the old practices with the Court's approval after today. There is simply no line that can be drawn between instruction paid for at taxpayers' expense and the instruction in any subject that is not identified as formally religious.

Critics of the decision argue that it has created a major crack in the wall of separation of church and state, while proponents believe that it will provide the Court with a set of decisions to uphold the constitutionality of school vouchers. Both views are probably overstated. However, the case does call into question the viability of the Court-established three-pronged *Lemon* test. The second prong of the test—the impermissible effect of advancing religion—has been reduced to mere legislative neutrality; i.e., as long as the practice has some religion-neutral goal, then it is permissible. The third prong of excessive entanglement has been a highly contentious and pivotal factor in the constitutionality of various practices. There can be little doubt that the third prong has been narrowed by *Agostini* by deemphasizing what "entanglement" entails. This case, in addition to overturning *Aguilar* and *Ball,* continues to mark the demise of the *Lemon* test in Establishment Clause jurisprudence.

Jeffrey D. Schultz

Bibliography

Eisgrubet, Christopher L., and Lawrence Sagat, "Congressional Power and Religious Liberty after *City of Boerne v. Flores,*" *1997 Supreme Court Review* 79 (1997).

Fallow, Richard H., "The Supreme Court, 1996 Term: Implementing the Constitution," 111 *Harvard Law Review* 54 (1997).

Cases Cited

Agostini et al. v. Felton et al., 521 U.S. 203 (1997).

Aguilar v. Felton, 473 U.S. 402 (1985).

Board of Education of Kiryas Village School District v. Grumet, 512 U.S. 687 (1994).

Grand Rapids School District v. Ball, 473 U.S. 373 (1985).

Lemon v. Kurtzman, 403 U.S. 602 (1971).

Witters v. Washington Department of Services for Blind, 474 U.S. 481 (1986).

Zobrest v. Catalina Foothills School District, 509 U.S. 1 (1993).

Aguilar

See UNITED STATES V. AGUILAR.

Aguilar v. Felton
473 U.S. 402 (1985)

The Supreme Court in this case held unconstitutional a New York City program that utilized federal funds to pay the salaries of public school employees who taught in the city's parochial schools. By a 5-to-4 vote, the Court invalidated the city program on the ground that it violated the Establishment Clause of the First Amendment, applicable to the states through the Fourteenth Amendment, that banned government establishments of religion.

In 1965 Congress enacted the Elementary and Secondary Education Act, Title I of which authorized the secretary of education to distribute financial aid to local schools to meet the special needs of "educationally deprived" children from low-income families by providing supplementary educational programs. Since 1966 New York City had used these federal funds to pay for auxiliary services to students on parochial school premises. Regular public school employees—including specialized teachers, guidance counselors, psychologists, psychiatrists, and social workers—taught English as a second language, remedial reading, and math, and offered guidance services. These professionals met in rooms devoid of religious symbols and worked under supervision similar to that which prevailed in the public schools; and the city monitored the instruction. The public school personnel were not accountable to parochial school officials, selected the students who needed their help, and used only materials and equipment supplied by secular authorities. They were under explicit instructions not to participate in any way in the activities of the parochial schools that they visited, to avoid religion in their own work, and to avoid collaboration with the parochial school staffs. Personnel of the city's department of education made at least one unannounced visit monthly and reported to supervisors who made occasional visits to monitor the operation of the program.

From these facts and without *any* evidence to warrant his conclusions, Justice William Brennan for the majority decided that the supervisory program for the administration of the city's Title I program "inevitably" resulted in "the excessive entanglement of church and state," making it unconstitutional. The majority Justices, all church members who respected religion, revealed a concern for the religious liberty of all citizens, including those not of the denomination with which the city had primarily become so enmeshed in the administration of the program. But the Court's good intentions were misdirected or far-fetched; not a particle of evidence showed a threat to anyone's religious liberty, least of all the children who benefited from the program. But the Court believed that the "ongoing inspection" of the secular authorities constituted "a permanent and pervasive State presence" in the parochial schools. "Agents of the State," said Brennan—who made that phrase sound like an Orwellian Big Brother—"must visit and inspect the schools regularly . . . in an attempt to guard against the infiltration of religious thought."

Thus, if government fails to provide some sort of surveillance to ward off such infiltration, it behaves unconstitutionally because it aids the religious mission of the church school; but if government does provide for monitoring—once a month plus occasional unannounced visits—it gets "excessively" entangled with religion. Either way, according to the Court, it behaves unconstitutionally. Its aid violates the Establishment Clause. Justice Lewis Powell, who provided the fifth vote for the majority, said in his concurring opinion that a forbidden entanglement became "compounded by the additional risk of political divisiveness stemming from the aid to religion here at issue." That, of course, assumed that the auxiliary services—such as teaching reading to children suffering from dyslexia—advanced the religious mission of the school, even though the children read from public school texts.

Of the four dissenting opinions, the one by Justice Sandra Day O'Connor made the most sense. She estimated that twenty thousand disadvantaged schoolchildren were adversely affected by the Court's decision against the city's program. For them the decision was "tragic." The majority, she argued—depriving the children of a program that might give them a chance at success—wrongly theorized that public school employees "are likely to start teaching religion because they have walked across the threshold of a parochial school." The records showed that almost three-fourths of the instructors in the program did not share the religious affiliation of any school they taught in. "The presumption—that the 'religious mission' will be advanced by providing educational services on parochial school premises—is not supported by the facts of this case." The voluminous evidence drawn from nineteen years of experience, she said, showed not one single incident in which a Title I instructor "attempted to indoctrine the students in particular religious tenets at public expense." O'Connor expressed her difficulty in understanding why auxiliary services on the school premises were any more entangling or advanced religion more than the same services provided in a mobile classroom parked near the school. Chief Justice Warren Burger, in a distempered dissent, remarked that it bordered on "paranoia" to see the pope lurking behind the program, and he absurdly stated that the Court (which was overconcerned with freedom of conscience) "exhibits nothing less than hostility toward religion and the children who attend church-sponsored schools."

Aguilar v. Felton (1985) was one of many Establishment Clause decisions which suggested that whether or not the Court discerned a violation of that clause, it had no clear or consistent idea of what constituted a law respecting establishment of religion.

Leonard W. Levy

Case Cited

Aguilar v. Felton, 473 U.S. 402 (1985).

Allegheny v. American Civil Liberties Union

See LYNCH AND ALLEGHENY RELIGIOUS SYMBOLS CASES AND THE DECLINE OF THE LEMON TEST.

Allen

See BOARD OF EDUCATION V. ALLEN.

Amos

See CORPORATION OF THE PRESIDING BISHOP OF THE CHURCH OF JESUS CHRIST OF LATTER-DAY SAINTS V. AMOS.

Atheism and Agnosticism

Doubt and disbelief about the existence of a deity have been part of Western culture since at least the Enlightenment of the eighteenth century. Although the point at which doubt shades into disbelief may be rather murky, our language recognizes the basic distinction between the two attitudes, calling doubters *agnostics* and disbelievers *atheists*. Both groups, however, can be distinguished from truly ardent believers, who have no doubt whatsoever that a deity exists. Even so, the line between belief and doubt is also a bit unclear, since someone who believes in God's existence can still harbor some doubt about the correctness of this belief.

When agnosticism and atheism began to acquire a sizable number of adherents, the question arose concerning what posture the state should adopt toward such doubt and disbelief. Should the state suppress agnosticism and atheism as essentially treasonous, since the legitimacy of the state previously had been thought ultimately to depend on the authority of God's law? Alternatively, may a new secular justification for the state's legitimacy be articulated, with the consequence that the state may tolerate agnosticism and atheism without fear of undermining its own legitimacy? Furthermore, if such a secular justification for the state is found, should the state then not merely *tolerate* agnosticism and atheism but instead treat them as *equally valid* as ardent faith, thereby maintaining a posture of *neutrality* among theism, atheism, and agnosticism?

These questions commanded the attention of eighteenth-century philosophers, and they remain relevant today. Thomas Jefferson, in his *Notes on the State of Virginia* (1784), expounded the then-new secular view that "[t]he legitimate powers of government extend to such acts only as are injurious to others." This view led Jefferson to claim that citizens have an equal right to espouse atheist opinions as orthodox theist beliefs because, as he put it, "it does me no injury for my neighbor to say there are twenty gods, or no god."

Jefferson believed that the state has no more right to establish religious orthodoxy than it does to establish scientific orthodoxy. He used the example of Galileo's persecution to illustrate his point: For the state to insist that Earth is flat does not make it so. The Enlightenment's favorite son, Jefferson argued that reason—not the state—is the arbiter of scientific truth and falsehood. Jefferson believed that reason is similarly the determinant of religious truth and falsehood.

Jefferson's views concerning the equal

rights of atheists became the law, first for Virginia and then for the United States. Jefferson wrote Virginia's Statute for Religious Freedom (enacted in 1786). The statute's operative language—"that all men shall be free to profess . . . their opinions in matters of religion"—is carefully phrased to extend equal rights to doubters and disbelievers as well as to all varieties of the ardently faithful.

Although Jefferson did not attend the Constitutional Convention in Philadelphia in 1787, that body adopted his view by including in the new Constitution the provision that "no religious Test shall ever be required as a Qualification to any Office or public Trust under the United States." This clause puts agnostics and atheists on an equal footing with believers for purposes of citizenship. Moreover, the Jeffersonian view also seems to have influenced the drafting of the First Amendment's Establishment Clause, since the language of the clause ("Congress shall make no law respecting an establishment of religion") is broad enough to prohibit a congressional preference for theism over atheism or agnosticism.

Many Americans, however, including George Washington, have rejected the Jeffersonian view and the philosophical premises underlying it. In particular, they have disputed Jefferson's claim that atheism is harmless. Believing instead that religious faith is the indispensable foundation for morality, they have contended that atheism breeds immorality and, therefore, that it is the duty of the government to promote piety.

This Washingtonian view was recently revived by Justice Antonin Scalia in a feverish dissent in *Lee v. Weisman* (1992). The case concerned the constitutionality of a nondenominational, theistic benediction at a public school graduation ceremony. The U.S. Supreme Court held the benediction unconstitutional, largely because it denied nonbelieving students an equal right to attend their graduation ceremony without being subjected to religious opinions they do not share. Justice Scalia dissented because he considered it imperative that the state be permitted to acknowledge God as the ultimate authority for its laws.

Thus, the debate between the Jeffersonian and Washingtonian views continues to the present, with little hope that either side will abandon its position. The impasse exists because the two camps have such different degrees of conviction about their own theological views. The Washingtonians hold their religious beliefs with a certitude that the Jeffersonians do not share. Even those Jeffersonians who are themselves religious believers have some doubt about the ultimate truth of their beliefs. (Jefferson himself believed in the existence of a deity, but he thought reason someday might prove him incorrect.) In short, Jeffersonians demand equal rights for atheists because they consider it plausible that atheism may prove true in the end and because they instinctively oppose persecution based on belief.

Thus, modern Jeffersonians, like their namesake, are children of the Enlightenment, believing in the power of reason to distinguish truth from falsehood. But contemporary Jeffersonians differ from him in one important respect: Unlike Jefferson himself, they do not equate scientific and religious opinions for the purposes of defending equal rights for atheists.

Contemporary Jeffersonians insist that public schools remain steadfastly impartial between theism and atheism, but they do not insist, for example, that the public schools remain neutral between believing Earth round and believing it flat. This is so because contemporary Jeffersonians do not consider the flat-Earth belief to be at all reasonable. Thus, the contemporary defense of equal rights for atheists is dependent on the proposition that the debate between theism and atheism is an epistemologically open issue—in contrast to the debate between round-Earthers and flat-Earthers, which is epistemologically closed.

This distinction between open and closed issues raises an important question: Does the contemporary defense of equal rights for atheism elevate agnosticism to a preferred position? In other words, must the state adopt agnosticism as its official position in order to maintain neutrality between theism and atheism? This question merits considerable attention, since contemporary Jeffersonians do seem to require that the state harbor a considerable degree of doubt about the ultimate correctness of any position on issues of theology. It would be ironic, however, if the Jeffersonian effort to secure equal rights for theists, atheists, and agnostics necessarily resulted in the state's adopting agnosticism as the official point of view.

Edward B. Foley

Bibliography

Dorsen, Norman, "The Religion Clauses and Nonbelievers," 27 *William & Mary Law Review* 863–873 (1986).

Foley, Edward B., "Tillich and Camus, Talking Politics," 92 *Columbia Law Review* 954–983 (1992).

Noonan, John T., *The Believer and the Powers That Are: Cases, History, and Other Data Bearing on the Relation of Religion and Government* (New York: Macmillan, 1987).

Peterson, Merrill D., and Robert C. Vaughan (eds.), *The Virginia Statute for Religious Freedom: Its Evolution and Consequences in American History* (Cambridge, Eng.: Cambridge University Press, 1988).

Rawls, John, *Political Liberalism* (New York: Columbia University Press, 1993).

Taylor, Charles, "Religion in a Free Society," *Articles of Faith, Articles of Peace: The Religious Liberty Clauses and the American Public Philosophy* (Washington: Brookings Institution, 1990).

Case Cited

Lee v. Weisman, 505 U.S. 577 (1992).

Autopsies and Religious Belief

Autopsies involve the inspection and partial dissection of dead bodies to discern the cause of death. The occasions and conditions under which autopsies are performed are prescribed by statute in most jurisdictions. Sometimes autopsies are performed at the request and with the consent of surviving relatives. But often autopsies are performed by, or at the order of, government officials, usually coroners or medical examiners. This is especially the case when death occurs under circumstances suggesting foul play or there is reason to believe that the circumstances or cause of death imply some significant public health concern.

The performance of autopsies may conflict with the belief systems of some religious communities. For example, the prohibition of autopsies is a basic tenet of Orthodox Jews and members of the Hmong faith community. The question arises whether those who oppose autopsies on religious grounds can successfully claim that the performance of an autopsy without consent violates the First Amendment's Free Exercise Clause, which guarantees the right to the free exercise of religion.

This issue arose in *You Vang Yang v. Sturner* (D. R.I., 1990). In this case, Neng Yang, the 23-year-old son of You Vang Yang and Kue Yang, U.S. citizens who resided in Rhode Island, suffered a seizure and lost consciousness. He was rushed to the hospital, where he died three days later, never having regained consciousness. The doctors who attended Neng could not determine the cause of his seizure or of his death. Because of the unexplained nature of the death, the doctors contacted the state medical examiner's office, as required by state law. On the day of Neng's death, his body was transferred to the medical examiner's office, where State Medical Examiner William Q. Sturner performed an autopsy.

Dr. Sturner acted under a state law that authorized medical examiners to conduct autopsies when the cause of death occurred under specified conditions. Included among those conditions was death that was "due to an infectious agent capable of spreading an epidemic within the state." Dr. Sturner also acted under regulations promulgated by his office that required autopsies when the cause of death could not be established with a reasonable degree of certainty. In such circumstances, the regulations authorized the performance of autopsies "without requiring permission of next of kin or legal representative."

Indeed, Dr. Sturner did not contact Neng's mother or father before the autopsy was performed. After the Yangs learned of these events, they filed suit in federal district court, alleging that the nonconsensual performance of an autopsy violated the family's constitutional right to religious freedom. In his initial decision, Judge Pettine agreed, describing the case as "sad" and "tragic." Applying criteria established by the U.S. Supreme Court, he found that the Yangs' religious belief against the performance of autopsies was sincere and that the autopsy in question violated that belief. Recognizing that free exercise rights are not absolute, he then applied the test of "compelling interest," which asks whether performance of the autopsy on Neng Yang was the least restrictive way available for the state to further its legitimate and compelling interests. Judge Pettine found that the state had established neither of these requirements. He therefore found that Dr. Sturner had violated the Yangs' First Amendment right and that he was liable for damages.

Unfortunately for the Yangs, the case did not end there. Shortly after Judge Pettine's initial decision, the U.S. Supreme Court decided the case of *Employment Division, Department of Human Resources of Oregon v. Smith* (1990). This case involved the question of whether Oregon's denial of employment compensation benefits to two Native American state employees violated the Free Exercise Clause; the employees had been fired because they used peyote as part of their church's religious sacraments. In *Smith,* Justice Antonin Scalia's majority opinion rejected the First Amendment claim. In the process of doing so, the Court significantly curtailed the circumstances in which the test of compelling state interest—applied by the district court in the Yangs' case—would be appropriate. In its analysis, which has since been widely criticized, the Court held that where the state enacts a regulation of general applicability, the fact that the regulation operates to burden, even significantly, an individual's ability to engage in religiously motivated conduct does not make the regulation actionable under the Free Exercise Clause. In other words, as a general rule, unless the state singles out religiously motivated activity for special regulation not applicable to similar nonreligious activity, the Free Exercise Clause simply does not apply. This means not only that the compelling-interest test would not be applicable in such situations, but also that *no* inquiry would be appropriate under the First Amendment.

While he was considering what damages to award the Yangs against Dr. Sturner, Judge Pettine learned of the Supreme Court's decision in *Smith.* Writing of his sympathy for the Yang family's grief and travail, the judge, "with deep regret," felt compelled to conclude that *Smith* required a reversal of his prior decision. Since the Rhode Island autopsy law was a law of general applicability—authorizing autopsies under prescribed circumstances regardless of the religious beliefs of those to whom the law was applied—the fact that the law profoundly impaired the Yang's religious freedom was constitutionally irrelevant.

The *Smith* decision, as Judge Pettine ultimately concluded, does seem quite clearly to remove any Free Exercise Clause infirmity from the operation of generally applicable, mandatory autopsy laws to those who would object on religious grounds. In addition to *Yang,* at least one other federal court, in *Montgomery v. County of Clinton Michigan* (Mich., 1990), has interpreted *Smith* as foreclosing a First Amendment religiously based challenge to the nonconsensual performance of autopsies. This does not necessarily mean, however, that religious believers can obtain no relief from such laws. The *Smith* decision purports to interpret only the First Amendment to the U.S. Constitution. It is conceivable that state courts could interpret religious freedom provisions of *state* constitutions more broadly and, as a matter of state law, impose the test of compelling state interest or something similar.

Another method by which relief might be obtained from laws such as that challenged in the *Yang* case is through a statutory exemption from the enacting legislature. In *Smith* the Supreme Court suggested that states could explicitly grant nondiscriminatory religious-practice exemptions from statutes which had the effect of burdening religious freedom. Indeed, in his first decision in *Yang,* Judge Pettine noted that several states—including California, New Jersey, and Ohio—require medical examiners to refrain from performing autopsies over the religious objections of the next of kin. Such laws reflect an effort to accommodate religious believers, and *Smith* suggests that they may be constitutionally permissible.

Finally, it should be noted that mandatory autopsy laws might have been challenged under the Religious Freedom Restoration Act of 1993 (RFRA), a federal law enacted in response to the *Smith* decision with the goal of restoring pre-*Smith* constitutional protections governing religious freedom. However, in June 1997, the Supreme Court, in *City of Boerne v. Flores,* invalidated RFRA as an unconstitutional exercise of congressional power.

Richard B. Saphire

Bibliography

McConnell, Michael, "Free Exercise Revisionism and the Smith Case," 57 *University of Chicago Law Review* 1109–1153 (1990).

———, "The Origins and Historical Understanding of Free Exercise of Religion," 103 *Harvard Law Review* 1409–1517 (1990).

Tribe, Laurence, *American Constitutional Law* 1154–1301, 2d ed. (Mineola, N.Y.: Foundation Press, 1988).

Cases Cited

City of Boerne v. Flores, 521 U.S. 507 (1997).

Employment Division, Department of Human Resources of Oregon v. Smith, 494 U.S. 872 (1990).

Montgomery v. County of Clinton, Michigan, 743 F. Supp. 1253 (W.D. Mich. 1990).

You Vang Yang v. Sturner, 728 F. Supp. 845, opinion withdrawn and case dismissed, 750 F. Supp. 558 (D. R.I. 1990).

Avitzur v. Avitzur
58 N.Y. 2d 108, 446 N.E. 2d 136, 459 N.Y. S. 2d 573 (1983)

The *Avitzur v. Avitzur* (1983) decision arose in the aftermath of a divorce decree entered in 1978. Susan Avitzur sued her former husband, Boaz Avitzur, for enforcement of that provision of the Ketubah—the marriage contract required under Orthodox Jewish religious law—by which the parties bound themselves to appear when summoned to the Beth Din, the rabbinical tribunal having the authority to make judgments concerning traditional Jewish religious law. On appeal, New York's Appellate Division found the Ketubah unenforceable in civil law because of its religious character. By a 4-to-3 decision the New York Court of Appeals reversed the Appellate Division's decision, holding, in an opinion written by Chief Judge Sol Wachtler, the relevant provisions of the Ketubah to be civilly enforceable.

Jewish religious law has always accepted divorce, although the Talmud and the Mishnah make clear that divorce is at the discretion of the husband, who is required to provide his wife a bill of divorce before sending her away from his house. Indeed, the prophet Malachi denounced the frequency of divorce in fifth-century-B.C.E. Judea.

In current Jewish religious law a husband is obliged to provide a "get"—a bill of divorce—to his wife, with few exceptions, when they separate. Without a "get" the wife becomes an "agunah"—a woman neither married nor unmarried, enjoying none of the normal benefits of the married state but unable to marry again.

The *Avitzur* decision rested on the contention of the court's majority that the right of the Beth Din to summon the respondent was civilly enforceable because of the contractual obligations under which the respondent had placed himself by signing the Ketubah. Furthermore, the relevant contractual obligations created by the Ketubah, although recognized by the court to have religious purposes, were held to be of such a nature as to be enforceable civilly without obliging the court to determine matters of theology and sectarian doctrine.

New York's Appellate Division had held that the Ketubah was a liturgical agreement and thus unenforceable by the state. The lower court concluded that, having granted a civil divorce, the state had no further interest in the marital status of the couple. The court of appeals specifically rejected this interpretation.

The court of appeals placed great emphasis on the fact that the Ketubah did not require the husband to grant a "get" but only to appear before the Beth Din. The court analogized this to an arbitration clause in a contract whereby parties bind themselves to refer certain matters to a nonjudicial forum. The court cited ample precedents to uphold the positions that an agreement to refer a matter concerning marriage to arbitration suffered no inherent invalidity; that the termination of the marriage did not affect the validity of the appropriate clause of antenuptial agreements; and, finally, that the agreement would be enforceable unless its enforcement violated the law or the public policy of the state.

The fact that Jewish religious law regards the Ketubah as the marriage contract does not in itself invalidate the court's conception of it as an antenuptual agreement. Civil law treats all marriages as involving the same obligations qua marriage. Since the Ketubah is actually signed before the marriage ceremony, those civilly enforceable conditions in excess of the common obligations of civil marriage may logically be construed as an antenuptual agreement irrespective of the theological interpretation of Jewish religious law.

The court recognized that the separation of church and state required the courts to avoid absolutely the enforcing of any agreement whose enforcement would necessitate the courts' resolving matters of religious dogma or orthopraxy.

The appeals court specifically invoked the U.S. Supreme Court standard developed in *Jones v. Wolf* (1979), which held that a state may adopt any approach to resolving religious disputes, providing only that it does not entail consideration of doctrinal matters. The High Court specifically endorsed the use of the "neutral principles of law." In this case, the New York Court of Appeals saw the issue as involving the neutral principles of contract law, which could be invoked without any reference to religious doctrine; the fact that the principles of the Ketubah itself were based on religious belief and practice did not in itself exclude the enforcement of a contract based on it.

The dissenting opinion, written by Judge Hugh R. Jones, rested on two major arguments—one strong, the other problematic. The weaker argument arose from the dissenting judges' questioning of the intent of the parties who subscribed to the Ketubah to have it enforced by civil proceedings. However, if the Ketubah otherwise met the criteria for an antenuptial agreement as the majority held and as the dissenting opinion did not challenge, then a presumption of an intent to civil enforceability would seem to be appropriate, since contracts do not need to specify civil enforceability and generally do so only when they purport to alter some aspect of that enforceability. Civil enforceability is one of the primary purposes for entering into a contract. The dissenters, however, argued:

> That no such civil enforcement of the obligation to appear before the Beth Din was contemplated either by the drafter of the Ketubah or by the parties as its signatories is evident from the inclusion of explicit authorization to the Beth Din "to impose such terms of compensation as it may see fit for failure to respond to its summons or to carry out its decision."

Clearly, the weight that the dissenting opinion places on the provisions for the Beth Din's enforcement of its own rights under the Ketubah are greater than can be sustained. In an arbitration agreement, the arbitrator is often given powers to enforce decisions by fines or other measures, even though, in the case of complete noncooperation, the civil courts would have to be utilized to enforce the original agreement as well as any subsequent penalties imposed. The enumeration of intermediate steps of compulsion open to the Beth Din would not seem by its mere presence in the contract to exclude civil enforcement of the Ketubah.

The stronger argument of the dissenters involved the possibility that enforcement of one part of the Ketubah would involve the court in the due consideration of other, prior violations of the contract—which consideration would necessitate involvement of the court in theological controversy. The respondent, for example, alleged that before the divorce he had requested a meeting of the Beth Din and had been denied. Did such a denial nullify the contractual elements of the Ketubah? To resolve such a question, the courts would seem to be forced into the troubled waters of doctrinal obligations.

The majority opinion did not acknowledge the husband's claim for the nullity of the contract based on the failure of the Beth Din to meet as he had requested, but one may suppose that the majority held *per curiam* that, since the Beth Din was not directly a party to either the contract or the suit, a simple failure of that body to discharge its duty in this one instance (if that were the case) would not nullify the contract between these signatory parties.

In the Domestic Relations Law (Article 13, Section 253), passed in 1983 and amended in 1984, New York State's legislature attempted to solve the type of problem posed by the *Avitzur* case by providing that no final judgment of annulment or divorce could be granted until the plaintiff filed a sworn statement:

> (i) that, to the best of his or her knowledge, he or she has, prior to the entry of such a final judgment, taken all steps solely within his or her power to remove all barriers to the defendant's remarriage following the annulment or divorce; or (ii) that the defendant has waived in writing the requirements of the subdivision.

Questions of the constitutionality of the "Get" Statute, as DRL 253 has become known, arose immediately. The governor's memorandum of approval, for example, raised such questions but left them to the courts for final resolution.

Civil courts have regularly enforced separation agreements that have contained requirements related to a "get." In *Margulies v. Margulies* (N.Y., 1973), for example, a husband was fined for failure to supply a "get" as per the separation agreement, and in *Matter of "Rubin" v. "Rubin"* (N.Y., 1973) enforcement of a foreign divorce decree was withheld until a wife accepted the "get" as required by the agreement.

This statute goes well beyond both these cases and *Avitzur,* however, because it would (even in the absence of a contractual obligation) attempt to compel a party to civil proceedings to submit to religious proceedings or practices under the compulsion of the withholding of civil relief. On those grounds this law is most probably in violation of the First Amendment to the U.S. Constitution by erecting an establishment of religion.

Patrick M. O'Neil

Bibliography

Breitowitz, Irving, *Between Civil and Religious Law: The Plight of the Agunah in American Society* (Westport, Conn.: Greenwood, 1993).

"Divorce," *Encyclopedia Judaica,* ed. Cecil Roth (New York: Macmillan, 1972).

Finkelman, Paul, "A Bad Marriage: Jewish Divorce and the First Amendment," 2 *Cardozo Women's Law Journal* 131–172 (1995).

Cases Cited

Avitzur v. Avitzur, 58 N.Y. 2d 108, 446 N.E. 2d 136, 459 N.Y. S. 2d 572 (1983).

Jones v. Wolf, 443 U.S. 595 (1979).

Margulies v. Margulies, 42 A.D. 2d 517, 344 N.Y. S. 2d 482 (1st Dept. 1973), appeal dismissed, 33 N.Y. 2d 894, 352 N.Y. S. 2d 447, 307 N.E. 2d 562 (1973).

Matter of "Rubin" v. "Rubin," 75 Misc. 2d 776, 348 N.Y. S. 2d 61 (Family Court Bronx County, 1973).

B

Badoni v. Higginson

638 F. 2d 172 (10th Cir. 1980), cert. denied, 452 U.S. 954 (1981)

The schism between the Establishment Clause and the Free Exercise Clause of the First Amendment often renders courts powerless in protecting Native American rights. There is an inherent complexity in trying to determine the existence of an Establishment Clause violation when the government responds to a free exercise claim. The conflict between the religion clauses was evident in *Badoni v. Higginson* (1980).

In 1963 the U.S. government finished constructing the Glen Canyon Dam on the Colorado River; on its completion, water built up behind the dam on what was once desert land, ultimately forming Lake Powell. By 1970 the lake entered the Rainbow Bridge National Monument, home to 160 acres of government-owned property and surrounded by a Navajo reservation. Within the national monument is Rainbow Bridge, an enormous sandstone arch. Along with a nearby spring and prayer location, the bridge was critically important to the religious practice of the Navajos.

By 1977 the dam had created over twenty feet of water directly under the bridge. Before the emergence of Lake Powell, the bridge was in a relatively remote and inaccessible area. Expansion of the lake eased access to the monument and encouraged tourists, who began visiting on tour boats and private pleasure boats. Tourism was augmented by government construction of docking facilities near the bridge, and the increasing numbers of tourists significantly hindered Native Americans from performing ceremonies essential to their religion. Moreover, the Navajos believed that when humans tampered with the earth near the bridge, prayers would not be heard by the gods, and ceremonies would be rendered ineffective in preventing evil and disease. As a result, individual members of the Navajo Tribe and three chapters of the Navajo Nation brought suit, arguing that the government's actions infringed on their ability to practice their religion. The interference, they argued, violated the Free Exercise Clause of the First Amendment. Simply stated, the tribe demanded, in the name of religious freedom, preferential use of the government's land and resources.

Using the Free Exercise Clause the Navajos argued that by allowing—even encouraging—tourists to visit the Rainbow Bridge area, the government allowed for the desecration of a sacred location. The effect of the government's actions prevented the Navajos from performing their rituals. They requested that the government actively prevent desecration of the area by, for example, prohibiting the consumption of alcohol at the monument. They further requested that the government, with reasonable notice from the Navajos, forbid tourists access to the monument when religious ceremonies were scheduled to take place there.

The Court of Appeals for the Tenth Circuit denied both requests. The court acknowledged that "[t]ourists visiting the sacred area have desecrated it by noise, litter and defacement of the Bridge itself. Because of the flooding and the presence of the tourists, plaintiffs no longer hold ceremonies in the area of the Bridge." Despite the inconvenience of performing the sacred ceremonies, however, the court asserted that any corrective action by the government would violate the Establishment Clause. "What plaintiffs seek in the name of the Free Exercise Clause is affirmative action by the government which implicates the Establishment Clause of the First Amendment." The court referred to the test created in *School District of Abington Township v. Schempp* (1963), which concludes that the government does not violate the Establishment Clause if its action entails a secular purpose and primary effect, and further, neither advances nor inhibits religion. Relying on *Schempp* the Tenth Circuit concluded that the "[i]ssuance of regulations to exclude tourists completely from the Monument for the avowed purpose of aiding plaintiffs' conduct of religious ceremonies would seem a clear violation of the Establishment Clause."

Badoni suggests that the Free Exercise Clause is experiencing constitutional limitations, further witnessed in later Supreme Court cases such as *Employment Division, Department of Human Resources of Oregon v. Smith* (1990). Government is generally free to regulate conduct, even if the prohibition or regulation happens to interfere with a person's religious practices, if the law is of general applicability and is not motivated by a desire to interfere with religion.

Conversely, if a government program prefers certain religious sects over others, the law will be held invalid unless it is narrowly tailored to promote a compelling interest. If there is no "sect preference," the *Schempp* methodology is used. The latter standard, and one easier to satisfy than a test of compelling interest, appears to provide some hope in protecting Native American rituals.

Stephen K. Schutte

Bibliography

Johnson, Alvin W., *Separation of Church and State in the United States* (Minneapolis: University of Minnesota Press, 1948).

Levy, Leonard William, *The Establishment Clause: Religion and the First Amendment* (New York: Macmillan, 1986).

Morgan, Richard E., *The Supreme Court and Religion* (New York: Free Press 1972).

Cases Cited

Badoni v. Higginson, 638 F. 2d 172 (10th Cir. 1980), cert. denied, 452 U.S. 954 (1981).

Employment Division, Department of Human Resources of Oregon v. Smith, 494 U.S. 872 (1990).

School District of Abington Township v. Schempp, 374 U.S. 203 (1963).

Ball

See SCHOOL DISTRICT OF THE CITY OF GRAND RAPIDS V. BALL.

Ballard

See UNITED STATES V. BALLARD.

Bankruptcy and Religion

American bankruptcy law is intended to provide an individual debtor with a "fresh start" by discharging his or her debts. It also seeks to maximize amounts recovered by creditors of individuals receiving bankruptcy discharges.

In general, an individual may enter a liquidation bankruptcy under Chapter 7 of the federal Bankruptcy Code or may pay debts out of future income under Chapter 12 or 13 of the code. In a Chapter 7 bankruptcy, the individual surrenders to a trustee all property not necessary for the fresh start and receives a discharge of any debt remaining after the property is distributed. In a Chapter 12 or 13 bankruptcy, the individual retains the property and instead proposes a plan that devotes all income beyond that necessary for the maintenance and support of the debtor and dependents to paying creditors over a three- or five-year period, receiving a discharge from any debts not repaid during that time.

Bankruptcy law has intersected with religion in two ways. First, as a means of maximizing the property available to creditors, the bankruptcy law permits the trustee to recover property transferred by the debtor before the bankruptcy if the debtor was insolvent at the time and did not receive reasonably equivalent value in exchange for the transfer. These transfers are called "fraudulent transfers," even though the debtor may not have intended any fraud.

Trustees have sought to recover as "fraudulent" those contributions to religious institutions made during the year before the bankruptcy case was commenced. Typically, the trustee argues that the contribution was a transfer of money, made while the debtor was insolvent and for which the debtor received nothing in return other than the satisfaction of supporting a religious institution. The religious institution typically maintains that the debtor received services or standing in the institution in exchange for the contribution. Moreover, religious institutions have asserted that the practice of tithing is a matter of necessity—much as food, clothing, and housing are necessities—to debtors with strong religious beliefs.

Although cases have been decided both ways, the trend among them seems to be in favor of permitting recovery of contributions made within the year before the bankruptcy case. For example, in *In re Young* (D. Minn., 1993), the court held that a bankruptcy trustee could recover contributions made by the debtors to their church while they were insolvent. The court found that although the church taught that people should make regular financial contributions, it did not require such contributions as a condition for membership or for attending worship services. Therefore, the debtors did not receive value in exchange for their contributions. In any event, according to the court, the services provided by the church bore no relation to the amount of money contributed. Therefore, it found that the debtors did not receive reasonably equivalent value in exchange for their contributions and, because the debtors were insolvent at the time, that the contributions could be recovered by the bankruptcy trustee.

The church in *Young* argued that permitting recovery of contributions violates the First Amendment of the U.S. Constitution, which protects free speech and religious practices. It maintained that recovery of religious contributions denies debtors the right to freely practice their religion and to disseminate their religious views. The court, however, rejected this First Amendment argument, finding that the fraudulent-transfer provisions of the Bankruptcy Code represent a neutral statute of general applicability. The court suggested that because the statute was not designed to regulate religious beliefs or conduct and is intended merely to enlarge the pool of assets available to creditors, it has only an incidental effect on the practice of religion and does not violate the First Amendment. Moreover, the court found that recovery of religious contributions entails, at most, only a minor interference with a contributor's ability to engage in free and open communication and does not violate the free speech right accorded by the First Amendment.

The second area in which bankruptcy law has intersected with religion also involves religious contributions. Under Chapters 12 and 13 of the Bankruptcy Code, an individual debtor may propose a plan for paying creditors over time, out of future income, instead of devoting current assets to the satisfaction of creditor's claims. The debtor proposes a plan that essentially devotes all disposable income for a three- to five-year period to payment of creditor's claims. "Disposable income" is that income remaining after the debtor's expenditures for support and maintenance of the debtor, his or her dependents, and, if the debtor is in business, the debtor's business. A question that has arisen with some frequency is whether religious contributions, or tithing, is one of the debtor's necessary expenditures that can be deducted from disposable income in formulating the debtor's plan.

Again, as with the fraudulent-transfer issue, courts have been divided on the question of whether the debtor can consider religious contributions as a necessary support or maintenance expenditure. Some courts have held that a debtor may include in the budget plan amounts for religious contributions as long as the amounts are not excessive. Those courts have expressed concern that a refusal to recognize such contributions as necessary expenditures would represent an undue interference with debtors' rights to practice their religions and express their religious views. For example, in *In re McDaniel* (Bankr. D. Minn., 1991) the court recognized that a Chapter 13 debtor should be permitted to include in his or her budget an expense for religious contributions, but it declined to approve a debtor's plan that called for contributions which were almost equal in amount to the payments that were due to creditors. In *In re Stottlemyre* (Bankr. W.D. Mo., 1992), the court approved a debtor's plan and budget which provided for church contributions that totaled less than 3 percent of the debtor's gross income.

Other courts have held that religious contributions should not be recognized as necessary expenses and have refused to confirm debtors' plans that provided for continued contributions notwithstanding that creditors were not being fully paid. For example, in *In* re Packham (Bankr. D. Utah, 1991) the court held that a plan paying creditors less than 100 percent could not be confirmed over a creditor's objection when the plan provided for regular contributions to the debtors' church. The court pointed out that the debtors could continue to practice their religion even if they discontinued contributions. Therefore, in the court's view, a refusal to include contributions in the debtors' budget would not deprive the debtors of their ability to practice their religion. Moreover, the court suggested that to permit such contributions to be included in the debtors' budget would, in effect, force creditors to be contributing to the religious institutions of the debtors' choosing.

Barry L. Zaretsky

Bibliography

Kosub, Bruce, and Susan Thompson, "The Religious Debtor's Conviction to Tithe As the Price of a Chapter 13 Discharge," 66 *Texas Law Review* 873–903 (1988).

Price, Donald R., and Mark C. Rahdert, "Distributing the First Fruits: Statutory and Constitutional Implications of Tithing in Bankruptcy," 26 *University of California at Davis Law Review* 853–934 (1993).

Cases Cited

In re McDaniel, 126 B.R. 782 (Bankr. D. Minn. 1991).

In re Packham, 126 B.R. 603 (Bankr. D. Utah 1991).

In re Stottlemyre, 146 B.R. 234 (Bankr. W.D. Mo. 1992).

In re Young, 152 B.R. 939 (D. Minn. 1993).

Baptists in Early America and the Separation of Church and State

A key to understanding the Baptist mind—and thus to Baptist contributions to the doctrine of the separation of church and state—is that the early Baptists were (and perhaps Baptists still are) a sect, not a church.

Envisioning the American System

Early in their development Baptists, forced by historical circumstances, adopted the defensive strategies and philosophies of a minority, a sect. They were by necessity and desire (cause and effect may be debated) driven to a minority mentality. Being themselves nonestablished, they fought the establishment of other groups, which they believed caused their own persecution. Persecuted, they sought ways to prevent those who persecuted them from holding the power to control and thus to persecute. Because they were forced to live on the exhilarating but precarious borderlands of society, because they were a "free" church, they sought to make other groups free as well: free of government support and free of the power to make free churches subservient to established ones. Freedom permeated every cell of their being: freedom of religious choice (volunteerism), freedom of conscience (the priesthood of all believers), and freedom of all churches and sects from clerical or political dictation (the separation of church and state).

As a sect and not a church—such as the established Roman Catholic, the established Lutheran, and the established Anglican churches—Baptists were never recipients of privilege. They were, in fact, victims of established churches and their various forms of discrimination. They turned their suffering into a thing of pride and drew from it a philosophy and model of church–state relations that envisioned a society where neither a state nor a church could dictate religious choice to them or to any other group. They envisioned the American system. They also helped devise, adopt, and secure it. When Baptists go astray from their historic support for separation of church and state, as often happens, it is usually because they have lost sight of and touch with their original vision.

Baptists have said from the beginning of their development that their churches approximate the ecclesial pattern of New Testament churches. They have always considered themselves pre-Constantinian—the Christian faith operating outside state control, without state support. This self-image, first imposed on them and later freely embraced, led some Baptists in the nineteenth century to claim an unbroken line of succession, akin to Roman Catholic apostolic succession, from first-century churches to their own. It certainly kindled in them a passion for the disestablishment of their powerful rivals.

In truth, however, Baptists emerged in the early seventeenth century from the overflow of the Lutheran Reformation, almost a century earlier, as a fringe element of the radical-left Protestant movement known as Ana-baptism, specifically from Dutch

Mennonites and English Separatists. The socially respectable sect founded by Menno Simons, which developed a branch in the Netherlands, is credited with saving the Anabaptist movement from its own extremism. These Dutch Mennonites helped a small body of expatriate English Separatists become Baptists.

In 1607 a Cambridge graduate and outspoken dissenter named John Smyth led to Amsterdam one of two bodies of Lincolnshire Separatists, the other body settling in Leyden and a decade later heading for Plymouth to become the American Pilgrim Fathers. In Amsterdam Smyth and his small congregation were deeply influenced by the doctrines of the Mennonites; and when in 1612 Thomas Helwys led back to England a remnant of this congregation, they had all the earmarks of future Baptists.

Helwys and his brood began meeting for worship in Spitalfield, a district just outside the eastern wall of London, and almost immediately encountered opposition. Helwys himself died in prison for preaching his peculiar brand of dissident separatism. But the tiny band survived and grew, and by 1644 they could claim forty-seven congregations scattered through southern and central England, loosely united by a common heritage and set of principles and in frequent contact with the Dutch Mennonites yet now calling themselves Baptists.

They were probably given this name first by their detractors, who linked them with continental Anabaptism and found their doctrine of baptism—immersion, for adults only—their most distinguishing characteristic. Superficially this was indeed what they represented, but on a deeper level they also represented a doctrine that would eventually have a much more profound influence on history, one that would help mold the American system of church–state relations. They were rapidly becoming England's most aggressive "free" church. They embodied a "minority mentality" that would persist, through persecution and triumph, until it affected world history.

Since they rejected clerical dictation and creedal conformity, they experienced a number of theological feuds and even some minor schisms. Eventually, at the end of a debate over the nature of the Atonement, an Arminian theology (General Atonement) won out over a Calvinist one (Particular Atonement), and the Baptists became even more open to converts than they had originally been. Eventually for the sake of clarity and unity they agreed to write "confessions of faith," which they insisted were not creeds; but through all their theological crises they stood for freedom of choice, freedom of conscience, and freedom of religion from state or state-church control. While the doctrine of General Atonement made them see all persons as capable of redemption, the doctrine of Particular Atonement persisted in their opposition to human control over Baptist souls. Man may be able to receive the grace of goodness; but he is just as surely corrupted by power.

As Baptists were coming of age, England was engulfed in civil war, and they were given a chance to make their voices heard. Conflict broke out in 1642 between the forces of King Charles I, who had long pressed for Anglican conformity, and supporters of a Parliament composed largely of Puritans and other dissenters. English Baptists supported the parliamentary side. Since they were not pacifists like their Mennonite cousins, they joined the New Model Army of Oliver Cromwell and fought for the side which they believed, if victorious, would give England freedom of religious thought and practice.

They made it clear from the start and continued to stress after Charles was captured and beheaded in 1649 that they opposed all religious establishments, Puritan as well as Anglican. They differed with Cromwell's Puritan followers about the nature of the church. To the Baptists the church was a congregation of "visible saints" without ties to a church or a state. They advocated, after victory, an absolute separation of church and state, of religion and politics. They said that no church body, not even their own, should dictate religious policy or doctrine to any other group. They served in the army with such distinction and in such numbers that most historians agree they helped prevent the establishment of a Puritan state church in Great Britain during the Commonwealth.

Baptists were uncomfortable with the Protectorate Cromwell established, but they strongly resisted the Restoration of King Charles II in 1660. Their fears that religious conformity would be reimposed by the restored Stuart monarchy were confirmed when Charles II and his Episcopal Parliament moved to exclude nonconformists from public office and universities and when attendance at Anglican services was required and nonconformist preaching was banned. The most revered seventeenth-century Baptist "saint," the indomitable John Bunyan, spent the years from 1660 to 1672 in Bedford jail for violating such restoration laws. Restrictions and punishments were eased in subsequent years, and Baptists praised King James II because he advocated freedom of choice for nonconformists as well as for Roman Catholics. But the price for being a minority in a nation with a state church continued to be high, and all the disadvantages were not erased until well into the twentieth century.

Defending and Shaping the American System

Baptists in North America, who arrived quite early in the Baptist experiment, brought their English experience with them. They advocated disestablishment and the separation of church and state not because of advanced political theory or Enlightenment humanism but because of their bitter experience as a religious minority. Their American experience only confirmed their British one. In Massachusetts they first settled near Puritan congregations, hoping that these Protestant cousins would grant them tolerance. Soon they found, however, as the Puritan Congregationalist Church sought and gained established status, that their hopes had been in vain. Little tolerance toward nonconformists came from former nonconformists who were now elevated to the position of an established religious power. Baptists learned once again that no one, no group, can be trusted with such power.

Eventually a majority of the thirteen colonies had established churches—in New England, Congregationalist; in Virginia and further south, Anglican. Baptists ran into trouble in all these places. In New England it had to do mostly with their refusal to pay taxes to support state churches, and there the penalty was most often loss of property. In the American South it had to do mostly with the refusal or inability to get official licenses to preach, and the penalty was most often imprisonment. Less trouble developed in the middle colonies because of the more balanced religious mixture and the absence of religious establishment there, and so Baptists flourished, proving to their own satisfaction the superiority of disestablishment.

Early American Baptists counted as their American founder and guiding light the New England nonconformist leader Roger Williams. Williams typified their struggle because he was banished from Puritan Massachusetts for his outspoken views on the separation of church and state. He founded the Rhode Island Colony as a refuge for dissidents. He helped found what Baptists considered their first church in the New World, the First Baptist Church of Providence, in 1639. They conveniently failed to mention that after a brief membership in the Baptist movement Williams withdrew and for the rest of his life referred to himself as a Seeker. The Baptists, however, did go on without him to help achieve religious toleration in Rhode Island and other colonies.

At the beginning of the eighteenth century the American colonies experienced the First Great Awakening. A spirit of religious revival swept north to south, awakening and causing both expansion and controversy in all the denominations. The movement was marked by great emotional outbursts, and response to the enthusiasm tended to divide the various religious bodies: Presbyterian, Congregational, and even Baptists. "New Lights" favored and profited from the revival, while "Old Lights" of each denomination disapproved and found themselves outnumbered by all the new converts. New Light Baptists—in general not so well educated, more open to emotionalism, and calling themselves "Separate Baptists"—embraced the Awakening theology and soon outdistanced Old Light Baptists, who were better educated and called themselves "Regular Baptists." The emphasis on personal salvation, emotion, and lay evangelism by what became the majority Baptists helped them attract large numbers of new converts and establish missions that a more educated clergy could never have hoped to serve. Baptists—now advocates of General Atonement for all, ready and willing to appeal more to the heart than to the intellect—became expert evangelists, and the denomination grew rapidly.

By 1770 they had become a significant religious and even social force in colonial America. They still lived in a land, however, where state churches held sway. Despite their growth and evidence that they might one day be the largest single group in certain colonies, they continued to hold firmly to the principles of disestablishment and the separation of church and state. This stand would at times be sorely tried after the Second Great Awakening of the nineteenth century, when they would grow so numerically strong, especially in the South and Southwest, that they could wield great power and influence. In modern times their support of disestablishment is often challenged by their fellow churchmen who see a chance to use their numerical strength (their "moral majority" strength) to enforce Baptist moral opinion on local, regional, and even national laws. They are at their best when they study their own history and understand what being a Baptist has meant to their nation. They have produced leaders like Harry Truman, Jimmy Carter, and Bill Clinton as well as Jerry Falwell.

Just as Baptists fought with Cromwell, so they fought on the Patriot (independence) side in the American Revolution. Some Baptists initially questioned the wisdom of involving themselves in what was clearly a political movement, but by 1776 Baptist laymen were volunteering as soldiers, and their ministers came forth as chaplains. Massachusetts Baptist leader Issac Backus made it clear in sermons and in published articles that the Patriots were fighting the very political and social evils which Baptists had been attacking for years. While Baptists might not trust their fellow Americans completely, knowing human nature, they believed they should trust the English even less.

As a result of their enthusiastic support for the war effort, which they were happy to see succeed, Baptists became immensely popular. They would gain more membership between 1770 and 1800 than during the years of the Great Awakening; and by 1800 they would be the largest single religious denomination in the United States. They had an enthusiastic, evangelistic membership and leaders, and they held principles approved by most Americans. As Anglicans (thought of as English) and Quakers (pacifists) lost ground, Baptists gained. Baptists were in tune with the times and seemed to be pointing toward the future. As historian Winthrop Hudson has written, they "needed to make no concessions to the popular mood. They typified it."

They used their new strength and influence to press their demands for reform on the new Republic. They began, even in the 1780s, to call for the states to disestablish their churches. One of their most articulate advocates was John Leland of Culpepper County, Virginia. Thomas Jefferson was his close friend, and Jefferson not only occasionally worshipped in Leland's church but also spent many evenings discussing public policy with him. Leland became a committed Jeffersonian Republican and lived long enough to be a Jacksonian Democrat. He doubtless made the point to Jefferson privately, as he did to the public at large, that the Lockean social compact did not imply that people must surrender their religious consciences to the state.

Baptists in Leland's Virginia were shocked in 1784, when their state, as a member of the loose Confederation, granted incorporated status to the Anglican-descended Protestant Episcopal Church, in effect making it the established church of Virginia. Baptists hotly and loudly claimed that this act contradicted both the Virginia Constitution and the state's Bill of Rights. In 1785 Leland's friend Jefferson introduced to the Virginia legislature his famous Bill for Religious Freedom, and in 1787 the Virginia Protestant Episcopal Church was effectively disestablished. It would be 1833 before Baptists and other advocates of the separation of church and state succeeded in the disestablishment of the Congregationalist Church of Massachusetts, but a pattern had been formed.

The "Baptist Clause"

As the Confederation demonstrated ever more clearly its inherent weaknesses, more and more American statesmen began calling for a convention to create "a more perfect union." Baptists petitioned Virginia's Revolutionary War hero George Washington, who presided over the Constitutional Convention and would serve as first president of the United States, to help provide a constitutional guarantee of the separation of church and state. Washington agreed to do so, and although this guarantee was not written into the Constitution of 1789, it was added by the First Congress in 1791 as the first sentence of the first constitutional amendment, the opening statement of the Bill of Rights: "Congress shall make no law respecting an establishment of religion, or prohibiting the free exercise thereof. . . ."

A battle had been won, but the war was not over. This amendment, this right, guaranteed that there would be no national church, but it did not prohibit states from having established churches, despite Madison's futile attempts to have it apply to the states as well as to the national government. The amendment did not immediately build the "wall" of separation between church and state, an image that Jefferson later used when writing to Baptists in Danbury, Connecticut, but it did guarantee that no church could legally enjoy special state privilege or dictate theology or practice to any other church. It paved the way for true pluralism.

Baptists did not write this amendment, and they needed a great deal of help getting it passed; but their experience as a disestablished minority and their fierce determination to end religious privilege are what fueled the movement toward the American separation of church and state. They are not completely wrong when they call the first part of the First Amendment the "Baptist clause" of the Constitution and boast that disestablishment is their contribution to the shape of the American Republic.

Since 1791 Baptists have had to deal with the implications of their achievement. If the state cannot control religion, can a religious group accept gifts from the state in the form of tax exemptions, so long as such gifts come to all religious groups equally? If church and state are separate, if a wall of some type stands between them, should religion try to influence political deliberations when they are perceived to be dealing with moral issues? In places where Baptists are an effective majority or plurality of the population, should they try to impose their will on what might be seen as a dissident, irresponsible, or immoral minority? Their victory in 1791 won for the Baptists more disturbing questions to answer and problems to solve. They are still dealing with them.

Baptist "Civil Wars"

Because Baptists so emphasized the doctrine of religious freedom, rejecting creedal formulas and clerical authority, they were throughout the nineteenth century prone to dissention and division. For the most part they had sufficient numbers to permit splintering without major injury to the denomination; but the controversies that buffeted them were painful and left scars. They fought over the mission enterprise, the Masonic Lodge, millenialism, and Landmarkism, in most cases finally coming down on the side of broad orthodoxy, practical reason, and freedom of choice. But on one issue—slavery—they were unable to resolve their conflict and ultimately split into two bodies, north and south.

As early as 1789 John Leland, who saw slavery as a moral issue and an institution incompatible both with Christianity and with republicanism, persuaded the Baptist General Committee—the nearest thing they had to a central representative body—to adopt a resolution calling for gradual abolition. The resolution, hated by the slave-owning South and neglected by Northern Baptists who feared that such action constituted a violation of the separation of church and state, was generally ignored and allowed to die.

The issue of slavery, however, moved to center stage in political discourse of the 1830s and 1840s, and in the end Baptists found that they could not avoid it. As Baptists in the North grew more vocal in their opposition, Baptists in the South stiffened their defenses. The former called slavery an affront to God, who the Northern Baptists said was no respecter of persons; while the Southern Baptists said that freedom of conscience meant freedom to choose whether to grant slaves their freedom.

The simmering controversy came to a boiling point when it began to involve foreign missions, which Baptists had come to believe was their primary purpose in the world. Believing that slave-owning Southern Baptists were hurting the cause of winning the world to Christ, both in 1841 and 1844 the Baptist Triennial Convention, which operated the Baptist mission enterprise, tried to deal with the issue, both times deciding that the denomination could not speak for its individual members. In 1845 Alabama Baptists asked the convention a hypothetical question: Would it appoint a missionary who owned slaves? The answer shook the denomination: No.

Later that year Baptists from the slave states met in Augusta, Georgia, and founded the Southern Baptist Convention. Not only was it to be a regional denominational organization, composed of and serving the interests of Southern Baptists, but it also was to be organized along lines significantly different from the earlier national denomination. It named boards to cover various assignments dictated by the convention—a system more centralized than anything Baptists in America had seen before. A century and a half later, the Southern Baptist Convention, controlled by leaders more conservative than anytime in its past, exercises more authority over its member churches than any other Baptist body in the world.

Cordial but Separate

During the Civil War each branch of the divided denomination supported its region's cause—Northern Baptists, the Union; Southern Baptists, the Confederacy. Only along the border were there controversies over affiliation. After the war had ended and the South was defeated, the two groups found it impossible to reconcile their differences. Not only were their feelings raw and tense, but over twenty years each group had developed different institutional patterns; and during the next few years those differences grew more pronounced. Northern and Southern Baptists agreed to remain cordial but separate—brothers in heritage, appearance, and ideology but alienated by history. The principles for which they originally stood were thus weakened but not abandoned. Baptists north and south, at their best, still work to implement them.

James T. Baker

Bibliography

Gaustad, Edwin S., *Dissent in American Religion* (Chicago: University of Chicago Press, 1973).

Hudson, Winthrop, *Religion in America* (New York: Scribner's, 1973).

Stokes, Anson P., *Church and State in the United States,* 3 vols. (New York: Harper and Row, 1950).

Torbet, Robert G., *A History of the Baptists* (Valley Forge, Pa.: Judson, 1969).

Tull, James E., *Shapers of Baptist Thought* (Valley Forge, Pa.: Judson, 1972).

Wood, James E. (ed.), *Baptists and the American Experience* (Valley Forge, Pa.: Judson, 1976).

Barron v. Baltimore

7 Pet. (32 U.S.) 243 (1833)

In *Barron v. Baltimore* (1833) the Supreme Court ruled that the Fifth Amendment guarantee against taking private property for public use without just compensation did not apply to state or local governments. Because of the decision in *Barron,* and early interpretations of the Fourteenth Amendment (ratified in 1868) following *Barron,* the religious freedom and establishment guarantees of the First Amendment were not applied to the states until the 1920s.

Barron claimed that, as a result of street repair, the City of Baltimore had dumped dirt and fill around his wharf so that ships could no longer dock. He claimed that the Takings Clause ("nor shall private property be taken for public use without just compensation") of the Fifth Amendment guaranteed him the right to be compensated for his loss.

Chief Justice John Marshall, speaking for a unanimous Court, denied Barron's claim and indicated that none of the guarantees of the federal Bill of Rights limited state or local governments. Marshall's interpretation had its problems. The text of the Fifth Amendment was general and was not explicitly limited to the federal government. Furthermore, in *Fletcher v. Peck* (1810) Chief Justice Marshall had suggested that some guarantees for private property could be read into the Constitution even in the absence of an explicit textual provision.

Still in *Barron,* Marshall explained that the Constitution was ordained by the "the people of the United States . . . for their own government, and not for the government of the individual states." States had their own constitutions with limits on state power. Generally phrased limitations of power set out in the federal Constitution, Marshall insisted, should be read to limit only the federal government. Marshall supported this argument by pointing out that limits on federal power (such as the prohibition on bills of attainder or ex post facto laws) contained in Article I, Section 9, were intended to limit only the federal government. These same limits were repeated in Article I, Section 10, and prefaced with the words "no state shall." Had the Framers of the Bill of Rights intended to limit the states, Marshall insisted, they would have followed the "no state shall" pattern of the original Constitution. Finally Marshall appealed to history. The federal Constitution had been opposed by those claiming its new national powers might be dangerous to liberty. The Bill of Rights had been intended to quiet those fears of excessive federal power. At the time the Bill of Rights was ratified, some New England states had religious establishments and others had religious tests for officeholding.

In the years following *Barron* the Court held that other guarantees of the Bill of Rights, including the religion clauses, limited only the federal government. *Permoli v. New Orleans* (1845), for example, held that the guarantee of free exercise of religion did not limit the states. While most state courts followed the decision in *Barron,* some held that rights set out in the federal Bill of Rights limited state power.

There is significant historical support for Marshall's argument. James Madison, who introduced the proposed amendments for a Bill of Rights in the First Congress, had suggested that the limits be inserted in the body of the original Constitution. The limits that have become the Bill of Rights Madison planned to put in Article I, Section 9, with other limits on federal power. Madison also advocated explicit limits on states to prohibit them from denying freedom of the press, equal rights of conscience, or trial by jury in criminal cases. Madison said that the states were as likely to invade these "invaluable privileges" as the federal government was and that a double security (federal as well as state guarantees) was crucial. Significantly, Madison prefaced his limits on the states with the words "no state shall," and he planned to put them in Article I, Section 10, with other limits on state power. Congress eventually placed the guarantees at the end of the document. Madison's plan to place explicit limits on states' power was defeated in the Senate.

While there are textual, structural, and historical explanations for the decision in *Barron,* the decision also reflects the changed political climate of the 1830s. Slavery had become an increasingly profitable institution, and Southern states were deeply suspicious of federal power as a threat to the South's peculiar institution. They were especially concerned that antislavery speech and press might raise the threat of slave revolts. Southern states passed laws designed to silence such expression. Because Southerners saw Northern free blacks as potential couriers for antislavery tracts, several provided for imprisonment of free black Northern sailors while in Southern ports. In *Elkison v. Deliesseline* (S.C., 1823) Justice Johnson on circuit held that South Carolina's law imprisoning Negro seamen violated the exclusive federal power to regulate commerce, but his decision was ignored. Chief Justice Marshall had a similar case, but he dodged the central issue. In a letter to Justice Story dated September 26, 1823, Marshall explained that he was not fond of butting his head against a wall in sport.

In *Barron* as in other, later Marshall Court decisions, Chief Justice Marshall tempered his earlier nationalism in recognition of political reality. The decision allowed the Court to avoid many issues of civil liberty raised by Southern attempts to suppress antislavery speech, press, religion, and political activity.

In 1866, after the Civil War, Congress proposed and the states subsequently ratified the Fourteenth Amendment. John Bingham, the primary author of the amendment's first section, insisted that, in light of *Barron,* an amendment was essential to deal with state denials of individual rights and denials of equal treatment to newly freed slaves and Southern Unionists. Bingham and Senator Jacob Howard, who presented the amendment to the Senate on behalf of the Joint Committee on Reconstruction, explained that the amendment was designed to require states to obey the commands of the Bill of Rights and to abrogate the decision in *Barron.*

Following Chief Justice Marshall's blueprint in *Barron,* the Fourteenth Amendment provided "No state shall . . . abridge the privileges or immunities of citizens of the United States" or deny due process or equal protection of the laws to any person. Bingham and Howard read the word "privileges" to refer to basic constitutional guarantees of liberty, including those in the Bill of Rights. Using the word in this way was similar to the way James Madison used it in the debate on the original Bill of Rights, and similar to the way the Revolutionary generation had used it.

Still the rule of *Barron* proved exceptionally resilient. Only in the twentieth century did the Court substantially depart from *Barron* and hold that most of the guarantees of the Bill of Rights limited the states. Having long since liquidated the Privileges or Immunities Clause in the *Slaughter-House Cases* (1872), the Court used the Due Process Clause of the Fourteenth Amendment to apply selected Bill of Rights guarantees to the states. In doing so the Court read the Due Process Clause to protect against state denial many of the "process" guarantees of the Bill of Rights (such as the privilege against self-incrimination and the right to a jury trial in criminal cases). It also read the Fourteenth Amendment's Due Process Clause to protect substantive rights to liberty such as free speech, free press, and free exercise of religion. Decisions incorporating Bill of Rights guarantees as limits on the states produced scholarly and political criticism. In the 1980s some "conservative" scholars and politicians advocated, in effect, a return to the rule of *Barron.* As of this writing, while the Court has read some Bill of Rights guarantees quite narrowly, it has not followed the suggestion that it free the states from the guarantees of the federal Bill of Rights.

Michael Kent Curtis

Bibliography

Amar, Akhil Reed, "The Bill of Rights and the Fourteenth Amendment," 101 *Yale Law Journal* 1193–1284 (1992).

Berger, Raoul, *The Fourteenth Amendment and the Bill of Rights* (Norman: University Oklahoma Press, 1989).

Curtis, Michael Kent, *No State Shall Abridge: The Fourteenth Amendment and the Bill of Rights* (Durham, N.C.: Duke University Press, 1986).

Nelson, William E., *The Fourteenth Amendment: From Political Principle to Judicial Doctrine* (Cambridge, Mass.: Harvard University Press, 1988).

Cases Cited

Barron v. Baltimore, 7 Pet. (32 U.S.) 243 (1833).

Elkison v. Deliesseline, 8 F. Cas. 493 (1823).

Fletcher v. Peck, 6 Cranch (10 U.S.) 87 (1810).

Permoli v. New Orleans, 3 How. (44 U.S.) 589 (1845).

Slaughter-House Cases, 16 Wall. (83 U.S.) 36 (1872).

Bestiality and Sodomy Prosecutions in Early America

Bestiality, sodomy, and "sodomitical" (male same-sex activity) prosecutions were rare but significant events in early America. Before the Revolution there were at least twenty-one sodomy and sodomitical accusations that came to the attention of colonial authorities, and at least seventeen bestiality accusations. Seven convicted of sodomy were executed, as were five bestiality convicts, with a sixth defendant avoiding death by "escaping." Although Puritan New England showed the greatest interest in eliminating such "deviant" sexuality, six non-Puritan colonies recorded such prosecutions as well. These cases, especially bestiality, possessed tremendous symbolic importance because they focused attention on the complex interaction of religion, law, community standards, and actual behavior.

Before 1533 bestiality and sodomy were ecclesiastical offenses in England, but Henry VIII removed them to law courts as capital offenses without benefit of clergy. With the exception of Virginia's brief experiment with martial laws in 1609, the colonies from Maryland south incorporated this part of English law without any statutory modification. However, New England's colonial legislatures passed eleven separate statutes on bestiality and sodomy, while the middle colonies added seven others. The Puritan statutes tracked biblical language: for bestiality, "if a man lie with a beast, he shall surely be put to death: and ye shall slay the beast" (Leviticus 20:15–16); for sodomy, "if a man also lie with mankind, as he lieth with a woman, both of them have committed an abomination; they shall surely be put to death" (Leviticus 20:13). Yet, in the absence of a confession, Puritan prosecutions faced difficult evidentiary hurdles imposed by laws that required two witnesses to the act (adopted from Deuteronomy 17:6). These laws further deviated from Leviticus to follow English law, which excused those who were forced into sodomy or were younger than fourteen. In contrast, Pennsylvania's Quakers made bestiality and sodomy noncapital offenses as part of their overall reform of criminal law. Their 1682 criminal sanction of whipping, forfeiture, and six months' imprisonment was the shortest American sentence before, astoundingly, 1961. Pennsylvania hardened the sanction for whites to life imprisonment and castration of married men in 1700 (castration was removed in 1706 at the Crown's demand), and it returned the offenses to the capital list for blacks. Colonial American denominations clearly were not uniform in this area.

Bestiality accusations shared some common features with sodomy. Both offenses were sins—violations against God, the family, the work ethic, and posterity. Governor William Bradford of Plymouth feared both had the possibility of "infecting" others. Those accused tended to be young, often teenagers, and servants, slaves, unbelievers, or otherwise on society's fringes. Both offenses generally went unprosecuted unless the violations were flagrant, as was the case when Bradford reported Thomas Granger's buggery of "a mare, a cow, two goats, five sheep, two calves and a turkey." Granger and his menagerie were executed, as was a New Haven man named Potter who had been practicing bestiality for fifty years (his wife had known for ten) and who saw eight of his animals killed from the scaffold. The conviction and execution of William Plaine rested on two instances of sodomy in England and more than a hundred masturbations of youths in New Haven, which authorities felt they could not ignore.

However, bestiality evoked more intensity because, unlike sodomy, bestiality dehumanized the sinner and, in Puritan folk wisdom, had the potential to produce monstrously deformed animal births. These were signs of visible betrayal of community ethics and stained the land with blood that could only be cleansed by execution. One-eyed New Haven servant George Spencer, on whom suspicion fell when a deformed one-eyed piglet was born, confessed under pressure and was executed. Thomas Hogg, whose hernia exposed his genitals, faced accusation when a "monster" piglet's eyes resembled his scrotum. Though imprisoned, Hogg refused to confess, and—without another witness against him (the piglet counted for one)—he escaped with a whipping. Because of the scarcity of witnesses to such private acts, others accused were freed, while some were convicted of attempted buggery and, like Hogg, were whipped instead of executed. All death sentences for bestiality came from New England except one in Quaker West Jersey of a slave named Harry for buggering a cow in 1692. The crowd in the courtroom surged forward, demanding a different punishment; the court put off execution, and three months later Harry could not be found. Quakers and other colonists further south apparently did not need to purge their land with blood.

The specific crime of sodomy required more than homosexual attraction. The underlying sin was lust, which could be polymorphous, and men could have it for other men (as Michael Wigglesworth had for his students) without being labeled as permanent deviants. Although the Bible and statutes defined the offense as "men lying with other men," only actual penetration constituted a capital crime. "Sodomy" prosecutions subject to the two-witness rule for penetration were difficult cases to win. Given the private nature of the act, even Nicholas Sension's thirty years of approaches to teenage boys were insufficient to convict him of "sodomy" because his one alleged lover died in King Philip's war before testifying. Sension's case revealed long-term community tolerance of nonflagrant activity. "Lewd" behavior and mutual masturbation between men brought charges and whippings for behavior that was "sodomitical" or "tending to sodomy," but they did not lead to executions. New England colonies also avoided cases, as when Plymouth returned to England "5 beastly Sodomitical boys" just arrived on the *Talbot.* When authorities could prove sodomy per se, however, executions usually followed. New England reserved capital punishment for flagrant offenders like Plaine or Mingo, a slave accused of forcible sodomy. Virginia, New Netherlands (twice), and Georgia also executed men for sodomy, and another Georgia sodomy conviction ended in three hundred lashes. Both sodomy and bestiality prosecutions declined in the eighteenth century as colonial criminal law retreated from biblical influence and focused on property and public order.

William Offutt

Bibliography

Godbeer, Richard, "'The Cry of Sodom': Discourse, Intercourse, and Desire in Colonial New England," *William and Mary Quarterly* (3rd ser.) 52 (1995) 259–286.

Katz, Jonathan Ned, *Gay/Lesbian Almanac* (New York: Harper and Row, 1983).

Oaks, Robert, "'Things Fearful to Name': Sodomy and Buggery in Seventeenth-Century New England," in *The American Man,* ed. Elizabeth H. Pleck and Joseph H. Pleck (Englewood Cliffs, N.J.: Prentice-Hall, 1980), pp. 53–76.

Bible in American Constitutionalism

The role of the Bible in influencing American constitutional thought has only recently begun to attract significant scholarly attention. Ironically, the Bible has long been recognized as a significant (perhaps as the single most significant) influence on American thought both in the colonial and in the early post-Revolutionary periods.

There can be little doubt that some biblical doctrines would have had profound effects on the psychological orientations of the Framers of the Constitution—even those Framers who might more accurately be classified as deistic or agnostic rather than as Christian. The story of the Fall of Man in Genesis with its attendant dogma of Original Sin was something that would have lent strong weight to the notion of the need for checks and balances in government, because the best of statesmen would be seen as flawed and imperfect beings who should not be trusted with unlimited power. The *Federalist* No. 51, for example, spoke in a semitheological vein when it said, "If men were angels, no government would be necessary."

In the case of the myth of the Fall and the doctrine of Original Sin, the Founders would have found the biblical viewpoint reinforced by the classical notion of the tragic flaw in man, as well as by the long historical record of the crimes and follies of humankind.

Also finding support in the Scriptures was the concept that the structure and procedures of government are open to human wisdom and human innovation. In most cultures of the ancient world (except for the Greek, Roman, and Hebrew civilizations), a society's particular form of government was believed to have been the direct creation of the gods and, therefore, immune to human transformation. Pharaoh was the incarnation of the god Horus, for example, and the Sumerian kings were the chief priests of the gods.

Two of the more famous biblical incidents which support the notion that questions of political forms and procedures are independent from theological issues occurred in the Old Testament. For example, when the corrupt judges had been removed, the people of Israel demanded of the prophet Samuel that he anoint for them a king, as other nations had over them. God demurred, arguing through Samuel the demerits of establishing a monarchy. When the people persisted in their demand, however, God relented and commanded Samuel to anoint Saul as king.

Likewise, during the wandering of the Israelites in the desert after their deliverance from Egyptian bondage, Moses became exhausted hearing all the disputes of his people in his capacity as their judge and ruler. Moses' father-in-law, Jethro, suggested the creation of what was, in effect, the first system of appellate jurisdiction: Moses adopted Jethro's plan whereby he appointed a judge for each of the twelve tribes and each of these judges referred to Moses only those disputes which were too complex for their own judgment. Moses set up this system without divine sanction, after merely human consultation.

The Framers would also have found in the biblical tradition much to instruct them about the need for flexibility in the interpretation of law and much concerning the dangers of unalterability in statute or in constitutional law. Indeed, even the Ten Commandments—given directly to Moses by God on Mt. Sinai—were reinterpreted in some aspects by Christ in the New Testament. The book of Mark records how, to the horror of the Pharisees, Jesus set aside the overly rigorous interpretations of the Sabbath rules that would have defeated the spirit of the law by excessive regard for its letter.

The unalterability of the law of the Medes and Persians twice was exposed in the biblical texts as leading to unintended consequences—especially consequences exactly opposed to the wishes of the sovereign who proclaimed those laws. In the Book of Daniel, Daniel must be saved from death by God's closing of the lions' mouths because he has been caught up in the consequences of the king's unalterable decree. In the Book of Esther, the Jews faced annihilation under an unalterable royal decree, but they were saved when a second decree allowed them to assemble and to defend themselves.

The final major role that the Bible played in American constitutionalism was an ambiguous one in regard to the separation of church and state. But the Constitution itself was ambiguous about that separation for, although it forbade religious tests for federal office and, by the First Amendment, proscribed a national establishment of religion as well as any federal interference with religious freedom, it left the states free to erect and to sustain established churches and otherwise to regulate religions under their manifold police powers.

Biblical support for religious establishment would be seen in the manifest theocratic nature of the Jewish state—with the kings anointed by priests or prophets, the law of God enforced by the state, and the priesthood supported by a system of tithing.

In a subtle way, however, both Old and New Testament distinguished between the state and the religious establishment of Israel. In the New Testament, of course, the forcible inclusion of Judea and Israel into the Roman Empire had somewhat vitiated that issue, but Christ's injunction in Matthew to "render unto Caesar that which is Caesar's and unto God the things that are God's" suggests the separability of the secular interests of the state from the religious duties of its subjects. In addition, the Jewish religious establishment as portrayed in the four gospels and in the Book of Acts—as embodied in the council of the Sanhedrin and the parties of the Pharisees, Sadducees, and Scribes—is generally portrayed as self-serving and hypocritical, and in some evangelical accounts it is even linked to the condemnation of Jesus.

In the Old Testament, any complete identity of church and state was undercut by the separation of the patriarchate from the priesthood, when during the Exodus the priestly duties passed from Moses the Patriarch to his brother Aaron and to Aaron's sons. Later, King Ozias/Uzziah was struck with leprosy in punishment for attempting to perform the priestly function of incensing the altar in the Holy of Holies.

Clearly, many of the ideas central to American constitutionalism were heavily influenced by, or reinforced by, the biblical knowledge of the Framers of the U.S. Constitution.

Patrick M. O'Neil

Bibliography

McDonald, Forrest, "A Founding Father's Library," *Literature of Liberty* (1978) 1.

Vile, John R., *The Constitutional Amending Process in American Political Thought* (New York: Praeger, 1992).

Bible in American Law

The Bible has played an enormous role in American law from the colonial period up to the present, but its role has been altered significantly over time.

A Source for American Law

In the early era of the formation of American law the Bible acted as an important source for law, especially in New England and Long Island, where the Mosaic Law was regarded as part of the law of the land. A claim of direct applicability of the Mosaic Law can be overstated, however, for even in Puritan New England only portions of that law were actually enforced in courts, and those portions were often enforced after filtration through colonial legislation, common law, or colonial judicial interpretations.

Fairly strict laws regulating work on Sunday were the rule in the American colonies, but even in New England the Sabbatarian Command of the Decalogue required explication, and there appears no equivalent of the sabbatical year of Exodus. Although slavery was more common in the southern colonies, no trace of the sabbatical-year freeing of slaves who adhered to the true faith can be found anywhere, nor can one find the debt-forgiveness and emancipation of the jubilee year of Leviticus.

The colonial manner of execution for consorting with witches was not stoning as was commanded in Leviticus, nor did a conviction for murder necessarily require more than one witness as provided by biblical law in the book of Numbers. Likewise, colonial children do not appear to have been subject to execution for lack of filial obedience, nor does the charging of interest seem to have been generally proscribed as in Deuteronomy.

The more pervasive and enduring influence of the Bible on American law, however, was in the indirect but vital influence of its moral teachings on customary law, the English common law, and the statutory law of England, the colonies, and the post-Independence American Republic. It is impossible to list all these indirect influences which Scripture has had on the minds of judges, lawmakers, and the electorate, but the laws regulating marriage and sexual conduct have clearly been strongly shaped by the popular understanding of biblical morality.

Despite the practice of polygamy by the Old Testament patriarchs, the rule of New Testament monogamy has prevailed in American law, as in the Christian West generally. Interestingly, in *Reynolds v. United States* (1878) the U.S. Supreme Court held that the fact that persons practiced or advocated illegal actions—polygamy in this case—based on their sincere biblically held beliefs did not extend First Amendment protection to that practice.

Sodomy and, particularly, male homosexuality were once universally and severely punished in American law. Although in recent years the tendency has been toward the repeal of such statutes, in *Bowers v. Hardwick* (1986) the Supreme Court refused to strike down a Georgia sodomy statute. The major legal issue in the case involved the question of whether the right of privacy extended to protect such activities, but various justices mused on whether the religious origins of the prohibition affected its status vis-à-vis the First Amendment's Establishment Clause. The majority proved unmoved by such claims, holding that, whatever its origins, a secular purpose could easily be imputed to such a statute.

Other forms of sodomy were also subject to harsh punishment, such as zoophilia, or bestiality, which was originally punishable by death, as the book of Exodus commanded: "Whoever lies with a beast shall be put to death." In the case of Thomas Granger—a Plymouth colonist who was convicted on the testimony of witnesses of multiple couplings with diverse animals—was put to death, and William Bradford, the governor, remarked that the death sentence handed down and carried out was done in conformity with the biblical injunctions on the matter.

Mosaic Law severely punished adultery, properly understood as sexual intercourse by which one or both partners violate their marital vows. Although Christ mitigated the punishment when he prevented the stoning of the woman caught committing adultery, most of the colonies prohibited adultery, as did most states. Although they are little enforced, several states keep antiadultery statutes on their law books, and the purpose appears to be more than pure symbolism, since such laws, in effect, permit aggrieved spouses to seek official assistance in pursuing grants of divorce.

Divorce itself, of course, has gone through various stages of acceptance in American law, even as it did at various stages in biblical history. At an early stage in Jewish history, divorce was a simple matter for the husband, who could obtain a divorce simply by putting aside his wife and granting her a bill of divorcement. The prophet Malachi lamented the frequency of divorce in fifth-century-B.C.E. Judea. Christ seems to have condemned divorce for any cause but adultery or, depending on the interpretation, to have ruled it out utterly.

In early American law, no court was authorized to grant a divorce, and divorce required a special enactment of the legislature—usually granted under only the most extraordinary circumstances. In the latter part of the nineteenth and early part of the twentieth centuries, many states not only provided for judicial decrees of divorce but also slowly broadened the grounds for such decrees from abandonment and adultery to cruelty, mental cruelty, and incompatibility. Throughout much of this period the state was not abandoning the religious view about marriage so much as tracking the changing attitudes of the mainstream Protestant churches, whose view about divorce altered radically over the century from 1850 to 1950.

Although the Catholic, Orthodox, and Anglican churches did not accept the new tolerance for divorce, the liberalization of American divorce law was in line with the general trend toward liberalization of doctrine and biblical interpretation within the dominant Protestant denominations, at least up until the widespread adoption of no-fault divorce in the 1960s and 1970s.

Another area of the influence of biblical morality on law was the criminalization of premarital intercourse—what theologians would term "simple fornication." From colonial times, simple fornication was a punishable offense at law, but the degree of the punishment was a good deal more lenient than that reserved for other lapses of sexual chastity. A classic of American literature, Nathaniel Hawthorne's *Scarlet Letter* (1850) conveys the atmosphere surrounding the Puritan sexual ethic and its social enforcement. In general, the milder treatment of fornication was in line with biblical prescriptions that set lesser punishments on it in Exodus.

In his *Criminal Justice in Colonial America,* Bradley Chapin opined that 11 percent of colonial laws were directly based on biblical texts, although that figure varied significantly by colony, ranging from 0 percent in Virginia (which adhered strictly to

English law), and 0.9 percent in Rhode Island (with its Separatist beginnings) to 40 percent in Connecticut and 38.8 percent in Massachusetts.

Finally, in considering the imposition of biblical sexual morality as a model for biblical influence on American law in general, it would be a serious oversight to ignore enactments against birth control. There are no direct injunctions against artificial birth control in Holy Writ, but God's command to Adam and Eve—"Be fruitful and multiply, fill the earth and subdue it. . . ."—was often cited, as was the sin of Onan, who spilled his seed on the ground rather than impregnate his brother's widow under the law of the levirate as set out in Genesis. Even apocryphal sources, such as the deuterocanonical Book of Tobias, were often cited in support of what was primarily Catholic natural law philosophy that had been incorporated into Protestant doctrine.

In *Griswold v. Connecticut* (1965), a case arising out of that state's anti–birth control statute—one of the few surviving acts of its kind—Justice William O. Douglas expounded the concept of a constitutional "right to privacy." But in none of the opinions in *Griswold* did any justice take judicial notice of the biblical and theological origins of the statute under review. The Court later used the privacy doctrine in the 1973 abortion cases, *Roe v. Wade* and *Doe v. Bolton.* Once again the Court avoided the issue of the original religious character of the legislation and looked to a different rationale for its invalidation. This scarcely seems surprising, since many laws framed before the middle of the nineteenth century evince a distinctly biblical cast of mind.

Courts and the Bible

Few political-legal movements in America have been unaffected by such biblical morality—and often both sides of such disputes have sought the sanction of Scripture: The pro- and antislavery movements, the pro- and anti-Prohibition parties, the segregationist forces and those battling for civil rights have all quoted Holy Writ for their own purposes.

Given the wide-ranging influence of religion, and especially of the Bible, on U.S. law, the courts have had to adopt a position of ignoring (in most instances) the inner motivation of legislators in order to consider instead the plausibility of an after-the-fact secular purpose in enactments. Clearly, also, another consideration for the courts has been whether particular instances of biblical morality represent merely a popular acceptance of the divine revelation of the Bible or represent instead a demonstration of the deep moral commitment of our culture to certain principles. Chief Justice Earl Warren himself utilized this latter approach in *Miranda v. Arizona* (1966), where he cited, in footnote 27, the principle of halakah (Jewish oral law tradition) and the commentary of Maimonides on the Mishnah Torah—itself a commentary on Scriptures—that nobody was to be declared guilty on his own admission alone.

In a similar manner, Justice Douglas used the erotic sensuality of the seventh and eighth chapters of Solomon's Song of Songs in his dissent from the pornography conviction in *Ginzberg v. United States* (1966). Using an allusion to the Book of Genesis for virtually the opposite effect of Douglas in *Ginzberg,* Chief Justice William Rehnquist in *Barnes v. Glen Theatre* (1991) remarked that, since Adam and Eve's expulsion from Eden, the deliberate exposure of nakedness has been viewed negatively and has been subject to regulation.

Ironically, dissenters from the majority opinion in *Bowers v. Hardwick,* the Georgia sodomy case, cited the State of Georgia's own citations of the Book of Leviticus, Paul's Epistle to the Romans, and the writings of St. Thomas Aquinas in its legal briefs to undermine the state's claim of a secular purpose to the statute.

In *Perin v. Carey* (1861) the Court noted positively that charities had their origins in the great command in the Book of Mark, "To love thy neighbor as thyself." In *Robinson v. California* (1962), however, the Court used biblical allusions in a negative way, claiming that California's criminalization of drug addiction was rooted in primitive notions not unlike the Old Testament concept of disease as a punishment for sin.

In *Fontain v. Ravenel* (1854), another suit involving charitable trusts, the Court alluded to the Jewish law of the Old Testament, which provided for the fields to be left fit for gleaning by the needy and the stranger. A dissenter in *Holmes v. Jennison* (1840)—a case involving the extradition of a criminal to Quebec—lamented that in light of the majority decision, citizens could no longer look on the Constitution of the United States and on their state constitutions as their "political bibles" pointing the way to their "political salvation."

In *M' Ilvaine v. Coxe's Lessee* (1804) the Court sought to establish a free right of expatriation in counterdistinction to the English common law's view of the matter. The common law principle, the court maintained, was not based on divine law, the law of nature, or the law of nations, and the Court cited Roman and Greek law as well as the Bible, "the most venerable book of antiquity." From the biblical sources the Court mentioned Jacob's immigration to Egypt, Moses' departure from Egyptian bondage, and David's escape from the realm of King Saul. The Court failed to mention the flight of the Holy Family into Egypt to escape the predation of King Herod, perhaps because it regarded three examples as sufficient or, alternatively, because the flight of Mary, Joseph, and the baby Jesus constituted a movement within the Roman Empire between different local jurisdictions.

In *Hickory v. United States* (1896) the Court held that attempting to conceal a murder was legitimate evidence in support of the guilt of the defendant. The decision claimed this as an ancient principle of law and of human psychology, dating back to Cain's denial of knowledge of the whereabouts of Abel when questioned by God after his act of fratricide.

Still other cases have focused on bibles as physical objects. *American Bible Society v. Grove* (1880) alluded to federal bankruptcy rules that exempted family Bibles from executions of seizure for debt. In *Jimmy Swaggart Ministries v. Board of Equalization of California* (1990) the Supreme Court upheld the constitutionality of California's imposition of its standard sales tax on religious items including bibles; and in *Texas Monthly, Inc. v. Bullock* (1989) Justice Antonin Scalia found it impossible to believe that the state is constitutionally prohibited from taxing *Texas Monthly* magazine as much as it taxes the Holy Bible. In *South Carolina v. Gathers* (1989), furthermore, the Court ordered a new penalty phase of a murder trial because the state prosecutors, in the course of obtaining the death penalty, had laid great emphasis on the presence of bibles in the belongings of the homicide victim, testifying to his moral worthiness.

Many modern involvements of the High Court with the Bible have concerned some aspect of biblical doctrine, teaching, or recitation as an instance of unconstitutional establishment of religion. Two of the more famous of such cases were *Doremus v. Board of Education of Borough of Hawthorne* (1952), wherein the Court rejected the legal standing of taxpayers of the district to bring suit on the matter; and *School District of Abington Township v. Schempp* (1963), where the Court finally forbade recitation of biblical passages as a devotional exercise in the public schools, although the Court was at pains to emphasize the legitimacy of the study of the Bible as literature or in the context of classes on comparative religion.

The attempt of the state to enforce orthodox biblical belief has also found its way into the federal judicial branch, with the Supreme Court striking down an Arkansas statute against the teaching of evolution in the schools in *Epperson v. Arkansas* (1968) and a Louisiana law mandating balanced treatment in high school biology between the theory of evolution and the doctrine of creation, in *Edwards v. Aguillard* (1987).

Finally, the Bible has been used in innumerable cases as a justification for particular practices, with varying degrees of success. In *Wisconsin v. Yoder* (1972) the Court exempted the Amish from school truancy laws, based on their belief that the Bible commands simplicity and that this excludes education beyond the eighth-grade level. The Court found for the Amish, not on the grounds of any absolute right to follow one's religious conscience—which would rapidly lead to anarchy in modern society—but on the state's lack of a compelling interest in forcing high school education on the Amish in light of their lifestyle.

Most such appeals have been quite unsuccessful. In *Hotema v. United States* (1902) the defendant's belief in the reality of witchcraft, based on biblical teachings, resulted in his killing of a reputed witch. The defense attempted to argue this belief in mitigation against the charge of first-degree murder with premeditation, but this legal strategy was a failure.

In *In re Summers* (1945) an attorney objected to his exclusion from the Illinois State bar, but the Court upheld the right of Illinois to exclude him because his biblical pacifism prevented him from taking a requisite oath to defend the Illinois Constitution, by force if necessary. In *Musser v. Utah* (1948) preaching in favor of plural marriage was treated as criminal incitement, rather than mere advocacy, despite the biblical basis of these beliefs.

In *Bob Jones University v. United States* (1983) biblical convictions against interracial dating and marriage were found insufficient to preserve tax-exempt status for a religious college that was held to practice racism by the IRS. Similarly, biblical beliefs did not justify sex discrimination in educational employment, according to the Court in *Ohio Civil Rights Commission v. Dayton Christian Schools* (1986).

In *Hamilton v. Regents of University of California* (1934) Bible-based pacifism was held insufficient to excuse a student in the California state university system from mandatory participation in ROTC. The Court reasoned that attendance in the state university was optional.

In general, the holding of religious beliefs has never been found sufficient grounds for the Court to invoke First Amendment rights. At a minimum, religious beliefs have had to be combined with the holding that the state lacked a compelling interest in the regulation of the matter—as was the case in *Yoder* (above). Sometimes, of course, the cause of religious freedom has been furthered by an appropriate approach to the interpretation of statute. In *Church of the Holy Trinity v. United States* (1892), for example, the Court found that a statute forbidding the prior contracting of foreign labor for U.S. employment was never designed by Congress to cover a church's arranging for a pastor from abroad.

Conclusion

The Bible, then, has had a protean existence in American law: Sometimes it has appeared as a simple physical object being taxed by a sales tax or being exempted from debt execution by federal bankruptcy law, and at other times it has been the very fountainhead of statutory and common law. Sometimes it has stood in the dock accused of being accessory to a governmental establishment of religion in contravention of First Amendment guarantees, and at others it has been called forth as a defense witness to attempt to exonerate a defendant or to hold blameless an alleged tortfeasor on the grounds that he or she had acted out of deeply held religious belief—often arising out of a reading of the Scriptures.

In addition the Bible has appeared at the side of judges, supplying evidence of the dominant moral feelings of Western civilization and even of the principles of ancient law. Finally, it has served as a rich source of literary allusions to embellish and enliven the dull prose of judicial rhetoric.

Patrick M. O'Neil

Bibliography

Bradford, William, *Of Plymouth Plantation, 1620–1647,* ed. William T. Davis (New York: Barnes and Noble, 1964).

Chapin, Bradley, *Criminal Justice in Colonial America, 1606–1660* (Athens: University of Georgia Press, 1983).

Levy, Leonard W., *Blasphemy: Verbal Offense against the Sacred, from Moses to Salman Rushdie* (New York: Knopf, 1993).

Cases Cited

American Bible Society v. Grove, 101 U.S. 610 (1880).

Barnes v. Glen Theatre, 501 U.S. 560 (1991).

Bob Jones University v. United States, 461 U.S. 574 (1983).

Bowers v. Hardwick, 478 U.S. 186 (1986).

Church of the Holy Trinity v. United States, 143 U.S. 457 (1892).

Doe v. Bolton, 410 U.S. 959 (1973).

Doremus v. Board of Education of Borough of Hawthorne, 342 U.S. 429 (1952).

Edwards v. Aguillard, 482 U.S. 578 (1987).

Epperson v. Arkansas, 393 U.S. 97 (1968).

Fontain v. Ravenel, 17 How. (58 U.S.) 369 (1854).

Ginzberg v. United States 382 U.S. 803 (1966).

Griswold v. Connecticut, 381 U.S. 479 (1965).

Hamilton v. Regents of University of California, 293 U.S. 245 (1934).

Hickory v. United States, 160 U.S. 408 (1896).

Holmes v. Jennison, 14 Pet. (39 U.S.) 540 (1840).

Hotema v. United States, 186 U.S. 413 (1902).

In re Summers, 325 U.S. 561 (1945).

Jimmy Swaggart Ministries v. Board of Equalization of California, 493 U.S. 378 (1990).

M' Ilvaine v. Coxe's Lessee, 2 Cranch (6 U.S.) 280 (1804).
Miranda v. Arizona, 384 U.S. 436 (1966).
Musser v. Utah, 333 U.S. 95 (1948).
Ohio Civil Rights Commission v. Dayton Christian Schools, 477 U.S. 619 (1986).
Perin v. Carey, 24 How. (65 U.S.) 465 (1861).
Reynolds v. United States, 98 U.S. 145 (1878).
Robinson v. California, 370 U.S. 660 (1962).
Roe v. Wade, 410 U.S. 113 (1973).
School District of Abington Township v. Schempp, 374 U.S. 203 (1963).
South Carolina v. Gathers, 490 U.S. 805 (1989).
Texas Monthly, Inc. v. Bullock, 489 U.S. 1 (1989).
Wisconsin v. Yoder, 406 U.S. 205 (1972).

Black Churches in the Antebellum South

In the wake of the religious revivals that swept the South in the late eighteenth and early nineteenth centuries, Christianity became central to the lives of most black Southerners. Although many whites encouraged the spread of Christianity among African Americans, most viewed black-controlled religious organizations as nurseries of insurrection, and they sought to suppress them. Despite guarantees of religious liberty contained in the national Bill of Rights and most state constitutions, whites established mechanisms to bar independent black worship and to subject the religious activities of free blacks as well as slaves to white supervision.

In the rural South, where the vast majority of slaves lived, whites were especially vigilant and intrusive. Slaveowners sometimes required slaves to attend white churches or brought white ministers to their plantations to conduct services for the slaves, thereby ensuring that religion reinforced black subordination. However, many planters permitted slave preachers to conduct services, and on occasion some slave preachers became so renowned for their spirituality and speaking abilities that they conducted services for whites. In Washington County, Texas, for example, a slave preacher named John Mark was so popular that, when his owner prepared to move from the county, several whites purchased him and deeded him to the Methodist Church. Although planters often permitted slave preachers to conduct services, they generally kept a watchful eye on the proceedings. Restive under white supervision and restrictions, many slaves sought the privacy necessary for free exercise of religion by worshipping clandestinely, often seeking refuge in "brush-arbor" churches in the woods. However, these gatherings were vulnerable to the patrols that policed the Southern countryside at night and enjoyed broad authority to break up unlawful assemblies of slaves and to beat slaves whom they found off their plantations without passes.

In Southern cities and towns, where most free blacks lived and where slaves enjoyed greater independence, African Americans made a strong bid for religious independence. During the late eighteenth century, black membership in urban Baptist and Methodist congregations grew rapidly. However, African Americans grew dissatisfied in these white churches, where they were generally denied a voice in church governance and where segregation was rigidly enforced. Beginning in the 1780s and continuing through the first two decades of the nineteenth century, many African Americans withdrew from white urban churches. Led by free blacks, they established large, independent black churches in towns and cities throughout the South.

Yet in the cities, as in the countryside, African Americans' religious freedom existed at the sufferance of whites. When whites became apprehensive about the growth of black churches, they had little trouble finding legal means to curb it. For example, in 1817 Morris Brown led over four thousand Charleston blacks out of the city's white Methodist church and established a flourishing congregation that soon developed formal ties with the African Methodist Episcopal (A.M.E.) Church in Philadelphia. Whites were alarmed by black Methodists' display of independence and by their increasingly close relationship with Northern blacks. Local authorities soon began to harass members of the congregation, arresting hundreds on charges of disorderly conduct. In 1822, in the wake of the Denmark Vesey conspiracy, Charleston officials moved from harassment to suppression. Found guilty of violating a law that barred free blacks from leaving and subsequently reentering the state, Brown and Henry Drayton, another leader among the black Methodists, were banished from the state. The city council then declared the church building itself a nuisance and ordered it destroyed.

The repression that began in Charleston spread to the rest of the South in the aftermath of the Nat Turner insurrection (1831). From Maryland to Mississippi, states adopted laws to bar blacks from preaching and to prohibit more than a handful of African Americans from gathering without white supervision. As a consequence, independent black churches that had blossomed earlier in the century and had experienced rapid growth in the 1820s either ceased to exist or went underground.

As the fear aroused by Nat Turner (himself a slave preacher) ebbed in the late 1830s and early 1840s, Southern towns and cities experienced a revival of black churches. Indeed, the two decades preceding the Civil War witnessed a steady growth of black congregations in the urban South. In most cities, however, these new black churches operated under the supervision of whites. As in the case of Richmond's First African Church, which boasted the largest place of worship in the city on the eve of the Civil War, they were typically established under the sponsorship of a white congregation, controlled by white trustees, and headed by a white minister, thus reassuring nervous whites that they would not become dens of antislavery activity.

The two decades preceding the Civil War also saw a renewed growth of independent black churches, especially in cities in the border states of Maryland, Kentucky, and Missouri, where black populations were smaller than in the Deep South and where whites' fear of slave insurrection was correspondingly diminished. Nevertheless, independent black churches, especially the few that emerged in the Deep South, enjoyed a precarious existence. During the 1840s New Orleans blacks organized three A.M.E. churches, obtaining charters for them in 1848 under the state's general incorporation law. In 1850 the Louisiana legislature adopted a statute prohibiting blacks from forming corporations for religious purposes, and eight years later the city council passed an ordinance requiring all black churches to place themselves under supervision of a white church. Although the black Methodists challenged the ordinance, claiming that it deprived them of vested rights, the state supreme court, in *African Methodist Episcopal Church v. New Orleans* (La., 1860), supported the city. "The African race are strangers to our Constitution," the court explained, "and are the subject of special and exceptional legislation."

The court's stark statement aptly summarized the position of African Americans in the antebellum South. Living beyond the guarantees of constitutional protection, free blacks as well as slaves were hemmed in by a constantly shifting set of laws and by arbitrary law enforcement practices whose aim was to protect slavery and white supremacy at all costs. In such an environment, such basic rights as freedom of speech and assembly—which were essential to religious liberty—proved chimerical.

Donald G. Nieman

Bibliography

Berlin, Ira *Slaves without Masters: The Free Negro in the Antebellum South* (New York: Pantheon, 1974).

Boles, John B. (ed.), *Masters and Slaves in the House of the Lord: Race and Religion in the American South, 1740–1870* (Lexington: University of Kentucky Press, 1988).

Finkelman, Paul (ed.), *Religion and Slavery* (New York: Garland, 1989).

Geneovese, Eugene D., *Roll, Jordan, Roll: The World the Slaves Made* (New York: Pantheon, 1974).

Raboteau, Albert J., *Slave Religion: The Invisible Institution in the Antebellum South* (New York: Oxford University Press, 1978).

Case Cited

African Methodist Episcopal Church v. New Orleans, 15 La. An. 441 (1860).

Black, Hugo Lafayette (1886–1971)

Justice Hugo L. Black's impact on the Constitution owed much to his decisions concerning religion. In the history of the Supreme Court no justice influenced more than Black the interpretation of the First Amendment's provisions establishing freedom of religion. The extent of such influence, however, opened the justice and his opinions to criticism and misunderstanding. Locating those decisions within the values that Black inherited from his Southern rural upbringing and his career as an elected politician helps to clarify the relationship between religion and his larger jurisprudence.

Religion was central to Black's formative years. Born in Clay County, a mountain region of eastern Alabama, Black learned early that various Protestant congregations—particularly those of numerous evangelical Baptist sects—reflected and shaped the community's hopes and fears. Martha, Black's mother, insisted that her sons and daughters attend services every Wednesday night and Sunday. For as long as he could remember, Black felt that public testimonials which regarded individual weakness—known as "speaking in tongues," associated with those services and given among a significant segment of a small rural town's population—harmed reputations, caused personal pain, and reduced self-respect. Probably the most significant factor influencing Black's beliefs, however, was that his father and two beloved uncles were publicly expelled from a Baptist congregation because they drank alcoholic beverages.

Undoubtedly, the expulsion of Fayette Black from the Baptist church created tensions for the family. Small, rural places like Justice Black's hometown, Ashland, cherished respectability, believing that it was vital to social stability and responsible individual behavior. They were committed to personal independence and moral accountability. Ideally, the unity of the community and the rights of the individual reinforced one another. Respectability was integral to this balance, because it liberated individuals from material or social dependency. Such independence was profoundly significant in a society intimately familiar with slavery and racial segregation. Thus Fayette Black's antisocial indulgence threatened the community's vital moral order. The stigmatization of his father's reputation strengthened Hugo's conviction that adherence to evangelical Christianity's moral code was necessary to the respectable individual conduct on which the well-being of family and the community depended.

Yet Black's encounter with religion as a youth instilled an ambivalent regard for individualism. Anxieties arising from the ambiguous social standing of his family intensified Black's sensitivity to the individual's status *within* the community. Although he accepted the small-town code of moral and religious respectability, he rejected it as a basis for condemning his father and other family members. Nor could he condone the code when it potentially tarnished the personal reputations of innocent members of his family, including himself. As a result, Black developed an inner strength to determine for himself how and to what extent he would apply community values to his own life. As he achieved professional success as a lawyer and elected public official, his conviction grew that, to the fullest extent consistent with a stable community, everyone should have the same right.

Black's small-town Southern heritage made him sensitive, then, to the interdependency between democratic community and individual freedom. Yet this sensitivity engendered actions that could easily appear to be contradictory. Black's success as a trial lawyer and his election to local office in Birmingham and the United States Senate owed much both to support for the advocacy of equal justice for African Americans and ethnic minorities such as Jews and Catholics, on the one hand, and to support for the xenophobic values of the white Protestant majority, on the other. Black strained to the limits the interdependence of individual and community values during his brief but professionally significant membership in the Ku Klux Klan. Nevertheless, Black just as readily defended religious, ethnic, and racial minorities by appealing to the community's regard for self-respect based on faith in equality before the law.

Still, for Black these contradictions did not exist, because he believed that human behavior remained constant. A lifelong study of the classics and ancient history convinced Black that, fundamentally, human conduct had not changed since earliest times. This conviction shaped his assumptions regarding religion, self-respect, and the interdependency between community and individual conscience. Black superimposed his constitutional faith on the presumption of the constancy of human behavior. Thus, according to Black, the principles of one age, such as those expounded by the Framers, were applicable to govern another. His conviction that human nature was changeless, moreover, led to an unswerving reliance on prescriptions and literalism as the surest guides to the application of the Supreme Court's authority.

Accordingly, cases following such standards would sooner or later receive sufficient public approval.

As a member of the Court, Black relied on his heritage to shape his approach to religious freedom. Americans' attitudes toward religious minorities underwent a change during the 1940s. Initially, religious intolerance pervaded the nation; but as World War II progressed, becoming a crusade against the totalitarian theories associated with Nazism and fascism, respect for religious diversity increased. Accordingly, many Americans perceived a connection between preserving democratic community and the acceptance of an individual's self-respect based on freedom of religious conscience. Black and the Court reflected the emerging shift of opinion in the unanimous decision of *Cantwell v. Connecticut* (1940), which struck down a law prohibiting solicitation as a violation of the First Amendment's guarantees of religious liberty incorporated into the Due Process Clause of the Fourteenth Amendment.

The Supreme Court reflected this change most clearly in cases involving Jehovah's Witnesses. In *Minersville School District v. Gobitis* (1940) an 8-to-1 majority, which included Black, rejected the claim of the Jehovah's Witnesses that the Fourteenth and First Amendments exempted their children from Pennsylvania's mandatory flag salute. But after the war began, the Witnesses fought on. In 1942 the Court upheld ordinances in Arkansas and Alabama requiring the religious group to pay a tax in order to sell denominational literature in local communities. In the Alabama case, *Jones v. Opelika* (1942) four justices dissented, including Black and William O. Douglas, who specifically repudiated their votes in *Gobitis.* The following year the dissenters became a majority. First, in a series of cases the Court struck down the tax ordinances as violations of the First and Fourteenth Amendments; finally, in *West Virginia v. Barnette* (1943) it overruled *Gobitis,* upholding the right of the Witnesses' children to exercise freedom of conscience.

Black's concurring opinion in *Barnette* explained the shift. Initially, he thought the flag salute seemed vital to community unity during a time of growing world struggle. But as Hitler justified authoritarian government and conquest by repudiating freedom of conscience, Black realized that "Love of country must spring from willing hearts and free minds" and, therefore, that state laws should "permit the widest toleration of conflicting view points consistent with a society of free men."

Black worked until he died to reconcile this tension between religious liberty and community values. In *Everson v. Board of Education* (1947) a New Jersey law authorized local school boards to reimburse parents for bus fares their children paid to attend either public or Catholic schools. A local taxpayer charged that the school board's plan violated the strict "wall of separation" between church and state required by the First Amendment's Establishment Clause. Equating the expenditure of tax dollars to ensure children's safe transport to both public and Catholic schools with the use of such funds to support police protection for all children, Black rejected the taxpayer's claim. According to Black, what the history of the Establishment Clause required in order to preserve the "wall of separation" was *neutrality.* In this case it was neither public nor Catholic schools but the children and their parents who benefited from the law—without regard for religious preference. There was vigorous dissent, but Black insisted that the principle of governmental neutrality where safety was at stake successfully preserved the inviolability of the Establishment Clause.

The limits of Black's neutrality principle became more apparent the next year, in *McCollum v. Board of Education* (1948). A state law permitted religious instruction within school buildings during regular school hours. Under a "released time arrangement" pupils whose parents signed "request cards" attended classes taught by outside teachers representing various religious faiths. Black's opinion for the Court held that "beyond all question" the policy violated the Establishment Clause as interpreted in the *Everson* decision. Yet in *Zorach v. Clauson* (1952) the Court sustained a New York law permitting released time from public school for religious instruction, because that instruction was carried on in separate buildings not supported by tax funds. Black dissented, arguing that it was only "by wholly isolating the state from the religious sphere and compelling it to be completely neutral, that the freedom of each and every denomination and of all non-believers can be maintained."

Black remained consistent on the Establishment Clause. *Engel v. Vitale* (1962) involved a New York law establishing in public school classrooms daily observance of a brief nondenominational prayer, with voluntary individual participation. Several parents challenged the law as a violation of the First Amendment. Black's majority opinion declared the law invalid, for it mandated a clear religious preference. The support of government thus created "indirect coercive pressure upon religious minorities to conform to the prevailing officially approved religion." The Framers based the Establishment Clause "upon an awareness of the historical fact that governmentally established religions and religious persecutions go hand in hand." Religion was "too personal, too sacred, too holy, to permit its unhallowed perversion by a civil magistrate."

Critics argued that Black's opinion was an unwarranted exercise of judicial activism. Black responded that he had preserved the welfare of the community by protecting the rights of religious minorities. He remained consistent in this view by dissenting when the Court in *Board of Education v. Allen* (1968) upheld a New York law providing free textbooks to children in both public and private schools. In *McGowan v. Maryland* (1961) and *Braunfeld v. Brown* (1961) Black joined the majority upholding the constitutionality of Sunday closing laws, despite claims of certain Protestant sects and Jews, respectively, in the two suits that the laws violated the First Amendment. When a South Carolina statute governing various labor practices was used as a basis to refuse employment to a Seventh-Day Adventist who declined to work on Saturday because it was her Sabbath, however, the Court with Black in the majority overturned the law. Meanwhile, in *Torasco v. Watkins* (1961) Black's majority opinion struck down a Maryland state constitutional provision that made employment as notary public dependent on a declaration of a belief in God.

Yet in a larger sense the critics missed the point. Black's commitment to religious freedom rested on neither a zealous attachment to judicial activism nor an unequivocal liberal preference for individual rights. Instead, a rural Southern heritage and the lifelong presumption that human conduct was changeless shaped Black's constitutional faith, which used prescriptions and literalism to establish the interdependency between individual freedom and democratic community. As the twentieth century draws to a close, Black's decisions in the field of religious liberty remain influential. His personal vision may not have led him too far astray after all.

Tony Freyer

Bibliography

Ball, Howard, and Phillip J. Cooper, *Of Power and Right: Hugo Black, William O. Douglas, and America's Constitutional Revolution* (New York: Oxford University Press, 1992).

Dunne, Gerald T., *Hugo Black and the Judicial Revolution* (New York: Simon and Schuster, 1977).

Freyer, Tony, *Hugo L. Black and the Dilemma of American Liberalism* (Glenview, Ill.: Scott Foresman, 1990).

Levy, Leonard W., *The Establishment Clause Religion and the First Amendment* (New York: Macmillan, 1986).

Cases Cited

Board of Education v. Allen, 392 U.S. 236 (1968).

Braunfeld v. Brown, 366 U.S. 599 (1961).

Cantwell v. Connecticut, 310 U.S. 296 (1940).

Engel v. Vitale, 370 U.S. 421 (1962).

Everson v. Board of Education, 330 U.S. 1 (1947).

Jones v. Opelika, 316 U.S. 584 (1942).

McCollum v. Board of Education, 333 U.S. 203 (1948).

McGowan v. Maryland, 366 U.S. 420 (1961).

Minersville School District v. Gobitis, 310 U.S. 586 (1940).

Torasco v. Watkins, 367 U.S. 488 (1961).

West Virginia State Board of Education v. Barnette, 319 U.S. 624 (1943).

Zorach v. Clausen, 343 U.S. 306 (1952).

Blaine Amendment

On December 14, 1875, Congressman James G. Blaine of Maine proposed an amendment to the United States Constitution to guarantee religious freedom and separation of church and state at the state level. Known as the Blaine Amendment, it provided:

> No State shall make any law respecting an establishment of religion, or prohibiting the free exercise thereof; and no money raised by taxation in any State for the support of public schools, or derived from any public fund therefor, nor any public lands devoted thereto shall ever be under the control of any religious sect or denomination; nor shall any money so raised or lands so devoted be divided between religious sects or denominations.

The proposed amendment passed in the House of Representatives, 180 to 7. Although it commanded a 28-to-17 majority in the Senate, two more votes were needed to meet the two-thirds majority required by the Constitution.

It is disputed whether the concern motivating the proposal was to protect the fund for state-supported public schooling from being divided for partial use by parochial schools or whether this was simply a cynical attempt by Republicans to mobilize anti-Catholic support after losing control of the House of Representatives in 1874. Public discussion of the proposal seems to have been generated by President Ulysses S. Grant.

In September 1875, while attending a reunion of soldiers in Iowa, Grant asked that they "resolve that neither State nor Nation shall support any institution save those where every child may get a common-school education, unmixed with any atheistic, pagan or sectarian teaching; leave the matter of religious teaching to the family altar, and keep Church and State forever separate." Grant made the same appeal in his State of the Union Address of December 7, 1875.

One week later Blaine introduced the proposed amendment into the House. When reported out from the Senate Judiciary Committee, its amendments included a clause indicating that the proposed amendment would not "prohibit the reading of the Bible in any school or institution."

The introduction of this amendment has been used by some to argue that the Fourteenth Amendment did not incorporate the Bill of Rights. At the time the Blaine Amendment was introduced, Blaine and twenty-four other members of Congress had also served at the adoption of the Fourteenth Amendment; two had been on the Joint Committee on Reconstruction, which drafted the amendment; and over fifty members had served in the legislatures of states that were called on to ratify the amendment from 1866 to 1868. The argument is that, if these individuals had known the Fourteenth Amendment to incorporate the entire Bill of Rights, the Blaine Amendment would not have been necessary.

The difficulty with this argument is that intervening decisions in the *Slaughter-House Cases* (1873), *United States v. Cruikshank* (1876), and *Walker v. Sauvinet* (1876) had indicated that the Supreme Court would not interpret the Fourteenth Amendment to enforce the Bill of Rights against the states. Indiana senator Oliver Morton, who had been a member of the Thirty-Ninth Congress, supported the Blaine Amendment while lamenting that the Fourteenth and Fifteenth Amendments "have, I fear, been very much impaired by construction, and one of them in some respects, almost destroyed by construction."

The force of this interpretation can been seen from the conduct of Republican senator Frederick Frelinghuysen of New Jersey. In 1874, after the *Slaughter-House Cases,* Frelinghuysen indicated that he was aware of the majority opinion but that Justice Bradley's lower court opinion—which included application of the Bill of Rights against the states—stated the "true construction" of the amendment. In the United States Circuit Court that initially heard the case *Live-Stock Dealers' & Butchers' Ass'n. v. Crescent City Live-Stock Landing & Slaughter-House Co.* (1870), Justice Bradley and District Judge Woods had indicated that state police regulations "cannot interfere with liberty of conscience, nor with the entire equality of all creeds and religions before the law." In his Supreme Court dissent, Bradley made it clear that the privileges and immunities of the Fourteenth Amendment included the rights protected by "the early amendments" to the Constitution and made specific references to portions of the First, Fourth, and Fifth Amendments, including the Free Exercise and Establishment Clauses. Yet during the debate on the Blaine Amendment, Frelinghuysen said that it would prevent "the states, for the first time, from the establishment of religion from prohibiting its free exercise."

Thus, like some of the framers of the Thirteenth Amendment who initially thought it gave all the protection eventually enacted into the Fourteenth Amendment, supporters of the Blaine Amendment may have accepted the decisions of the Supreme Court as binding and sought to achieve at least a part of their initial Fourteenth Amendment objectives in Blaine.

There is mounting specific evidence that the Thirty-Ninth Congress, which drafted the Fourteenth Amendment, intended the new amendment to enforce the Bill of Rights against the states and that this was the understanding of the public at the time of its adoption. Thus, it is highly unlikely that the Blaine amendment has any interpretative value for the Fourteenth Amendment.

Richard Aynes

Bibliography

Curtis, Michael K., *No State Shall Abridge.* (Durham, N.C.: Duke University Press, 1986).

Green, Steven K., "The Blaine Amendment Reconsidered," 36 *American Journal of Legal History,* 38–69 (1992).

O'Brien, F. William, "The Blaine Amendment 1875–1876" 41 *University of Detroit Law Review* 137–164 (1963).

Smith, Joseph P., *History of the Republican Party in Ohio* (Chicago: Lewis Publishing, 1898).

Cases and Statutes Cited

Live-Stock Dealers' & Butchers' Ass'n v. Crecent City Live-Stock Landing & Slaughter-House Co., 15 F. Cas. 649 (1870).

Slaughter-House Cases, 83 U.S. (16 Wall.) 36 (1873).

United States v. Cruikshank, 92 U.S. 542 (1876).

Walker v. Sauvinet, 92 U.S. 90 (1876).

Blaine Amendment, 4 Cong. Rec. 5453 (1876).

Blasphemy in American Law

Blasphemy represents an almost universal concept in religion and in law. In the ancient world, Roman and Greek law punished blasphemy: According to Plutarch, Alcibiades had his goods confiscated by Athens for mocking the rites of Ceres, and one might easily conclude that the trial of Socrates was, in part at least, a trial for blasphemy.

In the Bible, which has deeply influenced Anglo-American law, the Old Testament decreed death by stoning as the punishment for blasphemy (Leviticus 24:15–6). In the *Corpus Juris Civilis* of Justinian, where Roman law met Christian theology, blasphemy became a capital offense—specifically because of the danger that its toleration would bring the wrath of God upon the state, with "famine, earthquake, and pestilence."

Blasphemy in England

From the time of the Norman Conquest until the late Middle Ages, ecclesiastical courts in England, operating under canon law, dealt with blasphemy as with a wide range of other religious offenses including heresy, sacrilege, witchcraft, and the like. The parliamentary act of 1401, *De Haeretico Comburendo* ("On the Burning of Heretics"), seems to have been more a legislative support to Crown and miter rather than a drive by the Commons to usurp the traditional royal and ecclesiastical prerogatives in such matters.

In the aftermath of Henry VIII's break with the Roman Catholic Church (1533), the jurisdiction of ecclesiastical courts was greatly reduced, and secular courts began to prosecute blasphemy, heresy, and witchcraft as crimes against the state, through whose power the church was by law established.

The reign of Elizabeth I (1558–1603) was more tolerant, declaring that the government should not inquire about personal beliefs or, as the queen put it, "seek windows into mens souls." Under Elizabeth's policy of "latitudinarianism," heresy moved back into the jurisdiction of the weakened ecclesiastical courts, but blasphemy remained under the jurisdiction of the civil authorities. The state continued to see the crime of blasphemy as a fourfold threat against the state—making it liable to divine wrath, undermining public morality, subverting religious support for the state, and threatening severe breaches of the peace.

In English law, blasphemy ultimately became indictable both under common law and under statute, but English law did not make the ordinary distinction between sacrilege and blasphemy that has been made by traditional Christian moral theology; it instead treated sacrilege as a mere subcategory of blasphemy. As William Blackstone made clear in his eighteenth-century *Commentaries on the Law of England*, "blasphemy against the Almighty" consisted in denying his being or providence, in reproaches against Christ, or in scoffing at Holy Writ.

Throughout the two centuries before Blackstone's recapitulation of the common law of blasphemy, English courts persecuted numerous of the religious unorthodox, employing both common law and antiblasphemy statutes such as those of 1648, 1650, and 1699 to harass antitrinitarians, antinomians (including the Ranters), Quakers, and all who professed the "indwelling of divinity."

In the two centuries following Blackstone's encapsulation of the common law concerning blasphemy, indictments for this crime greatly decreased in Britain, but they have never entirely ceased. As late as 1978 the British Court of Appeals upheld the blasphemy conviction in the *Gay News* case, where a graphic poem by James Kirkup portrayed Christ as a homosexual, in *Reg. v. Lemon* (G.B., 1978).

Blasphemy in the Colonies

In America today the blasphemy laws remain on the books in many states, but they have become dead letters; it was not always so. From earliest colonial times blasphemy was a punishable offense at common law, but as in the mother country, colonial lawmakers found it necessary to supplement the common law with statutory enactments that broadened the definitions of or deepened the penalties for ungodly speech.

Virginia, the first British colony in mainland America, was first with a blasphemy statute. In its 1610 law code Virginia provided the death penalty for any who spoke impiously against the Trinity or "the knowne Articles of the Christian faith." Massachusetts did likewise in 1641, followed the next year by neighboring Connecticut.

The Connecticut legislature in 1642 enacted an antiblasphemy ordinance imposing the death penalty against all who blasphemed against God, the Trinity, the Christian religion, or Holy Scripture. With the exception of the supreme penalty, that statute remained in place with little alteration well into the twentieth century.

In drawing up this law, the legislators of Connecticut may have been influenced by the experience of Massachusetts with Roger Williams and Anne Hutchinson. In 1635 Massachusetts authorities decided to banish Williams because of his religious and political views. The Massachusetts magistrates had interpreted the blasphemy law to involve not only direct attacks on the inerrancy of Scripture but also significant denials of particular revelations contained therein. Williams advocated religious toleration and the separation of church and state. Since the Bible was alleged to teach intolerance and theocracy, Williams was held to have blasphemed against the Holy Word. Williams avoided banishment when he escaped across Narragansett Bay, where he established Rhode Island Colony in 1636.

Anne Hutchinson was examined by Governor John Winthrop and the General Court in November 1637 and was sentenced to exile from the colony. Before her expulsion from Massachusetts, she was tried by Boston's First Church in an ecclesiastical proceeding that ended in her excommunication. Her trial before the General Court amounted to a trial for heresy and blasphemy, and blasphemy was specified as one of her offenses in the pronouncement of excommunication against her by the ecclesiastical proceeding of the First Church.

Hutchinson was condemned at least in part for her "unwomanly" behavior in claiming the role of a prophetess and in challenging the authority of the clergy of the established church. The diverse heresies attributed to Hutchinson included antinomianism, by which the moral and civil law were held not to be binding on the true Christian; and mortalism, which held that the soul is not by nature immortal.

Her teaching of the indwelling and personal enlightenment by the Holy Spirit was taken to be a brand of religious enthusiasm, and her Covenant of Grace was so radically opposed to the Covenant of Works that she denied even the need of the saved to accept salvation by their will. Further, it was maintained that she preached that the letter of Scripture was but a part of the Covenant of Works, implying that sections of the Bible did not have to be accepted in their literal sense by believing Christians. She was alleged to have denied the resurrection of the body and to have held that this was but a scriptural metaphor for union in Christ.

Hutchinson, along with several of her followers, went into exile in Rhode Island, where she and her family were killed by Mohegans. Some scholars believe the elders of Massachusetts Bay Colony had encouraged the Mohegans to attack Hutchinson.

Despite the nominal existence of the death penalty for blasphemy in many of the colonies, it was only in Massachusetts where executions actually took place, and then primarily against Quakers who had defied judicial decrees of banishment. In general, to enforce the blasphemy laws colonial courts used warnings, fines, imprisonment, whippings, the pillory, and banishment in preference to death.

Rhode Island, where the complete separation of church and state prevailed from its foundation, provides the sole example of a colony without such a statute, although Quaker-influenced Pennsylvania had extremely lenient penalties. Ironically, Maryland—a kind of sanctuary for Catholics and for all trinitarian Christians—threatened death to all nontrinitarians and imposed lesser penalties for other blasphemy by the provisions of the 1648 Act of Toleration. An unnamed sea captain who blasphemed in that sanctuary of tolerance when boiling pitch burned his foot suffered a fine of twenty pounds, boring through his tongue, and a year in jail.

Blasphemy in Early America

After the adoption of the U.S. Constitution the law of blasphemy underwent no appreciable change—not least because the Establishment Clause of the First Amendment, like all of the Bill of Rights, did not apply to the states. State establishments of religion continued. Massachusetts, for example, did not abolish its establishment until 1833. Nevertheless, a subtle change of mood entered into the tenor of judicial considerations of blasphemy in both American and British court decisions in the early nineteenth century.

Perhaps as an effect of the Age of Enlightenment, the fear of divine vengeance seems to have disappeared as a rationale for the law, and the effect on the sentiments of the community now came to dominate judicial thinking about the nature of blasphemy. Now the contents of the suspect statement alone were no longer the key element; the focus shifted to the opprobriousness of the manner of its assertion.

In *People v. Ruggles* (N.Y., 1811) Chancellor James Kent upheld the conviction of the defendant who had claimed that Jesus Christ was a bastard and that his mother was a whore. Recognizing the need to reconcile the blasphemy statute with Article 38 of the New York State Constitution, which declared that "the free exercise and enjoyment of religious profession and worship, without discrimination or preference, should for ever thereafter be allowed within this state, to all mankind," Chancellor Kent relied heavily on a proviso appended to that section for his particular interpretation of this constitutional guarantee: ". . . the liberty of conscience hereby granted shall not be so construed as to excuse acts of licentiousness, or justify practices inconsistent with the peace and safety of the state."

Kent believed that the recognition by the law of the general role of the Christian faith in the society and in the maintenance of that public morality on which the operations of the law and the public safety depends was not a preferential establishment of religion, but only a codification of the actual state of affairs in New York. In this regard he cited the famous maxim from Cicero's *De Legibus* in support of his view: *Jurisprudentia est divinarum atque humanarum rerum notitia* ("Jurisprudence is the recognition of divine and human things").

The Massachusetts case of *Commonwealth v. Kneeland* (Mass., 1838) presents an exception to the new general rule of blasphemy's residing in the manner of presentation rather than in the statement's substance. Abner Kneeland, a pantheist who was convicted of blasphemy for denying God's existence, had published his claims in a journal called the *Boston Investigator* in the course of a piece contrasting his views with those of the Universalist Church.

The published piece was virtually academic in style, as the court acknowledged in the majority opinion written by Chief Justice Lemuel Shaw. Nevertheless, Shaw held that in the specific case of the complete denial of the divine existence, unlike other positions of doctrinal skepticism, the theological position need not be expressed offensively to be criminal—the simple advocacy of radical atheism was, *eo ipso,* blasphemous.

Shaw provided instances where the admission of atheism would not be criminal, such as in response to questions in a court under oath or in a private discussion among friends seeking spiritual enlightenment, but the chief justice insisted that its maintenance in what amounts to a proselytizing context was perforce blasphemy.

In a manner common to most of the nineteenth-century cases, Justice Shaw reconciled the Massachusetts blasphemy statute with the provisions of the state's constitution, which guaranteed religious rights, freedom of speech, and liberty of conscience. What is unique in the *Kneeland* case is the absolute insistence of the defendant that his writings had been misinterpreted and that he was, in fact, a believer in God.

The specific statement at issue read: "Universalists believe in a god which I do not; but believe that their god, with all his moral attributes (aside from nature itself) is nothing more than a mere chimera of their own imagination." In order to show the atheistic intent of the first statement, the indictment cited three additional articles appended to the first that denied Christ, miracles, the resurrection of the dead, and all forms of immortality.

In fact, Kneeland was well known to be a pantheist, not an atheist, and therefore his construction of his own statement may be presumed to be appropriate: He denied the god of the Universalists, not the existence of any god at all. For the court, however, acceptance of Kneeland's claim might have produced extreme legal difficulties, because—while pantheism was quite distinct from the proscribed atheism—the purposes of the state that were to be served by the blasphemy statute were as assaulted alike by pantheism as by atheism. Also, whereas atheism might be denied status as a religious conviction, pantheism could scarcely be so dismissed.

The god of the pantheists was not a personal god, and he did not judge human actions and assign rewards and punishments either in this world or in the next (there being no afterlife in pantheist dogma); therefore, the pantheistic belief system would not (it might be argued) uphold public morality by the twin goads of piety and fear of the Lord.

Other nineteenth-century decisions of interest include Justice Thomas Duncan's opinion in the *Updegraph Case* (Penn., 1824) and Chief Justice John M. Clayton's in *Chandler's Case* (Del., 1837). In *Updegraph,* for example, the trans-Atlantic legal fiction was rigorously maintained: Offensive expression and not subject matter dictated the presence of blasphemy.

Certain of the so-called Mormon cases arising out of federal prosecutions in the Utah Territory in the 1880s can be viewed as involving blasphemy. Criminal prosecutions for actually indulging in polygamy are not significant in the present context, but prosecutions for preaching or teaching the doctrine of the righteousness of polygamy—although not called blasphemy prosecutions—raised many of the same issues. In *Davis v. Beason* (1890) and *Mormon Church v. United States* (1890) the U.S. Supreme Court held that publications teaching or advocating the practice of polygamy were overt acts against peace and good order although done from religious opinions.

The Supreme Court avoided certain thorny issues by treating the abstract theological advocacy of polygamy as a criminal incitement to particular acts of multiple marriage, thus skirting the issue of First Amendment freedom to teach any religious doctrine.

Blasphemy and the Religion Clauses

In the twentieth century, the few cases involving blasphemy that were brought to trial usually ended in acquittal either initially or on appeal to a higher court. Michael X. Mochus, a Free Thought lecturer, had the distinction of being prosecuted for blasphemy by the State of Connecticut in 1916 and by the State of Illinois in 1917. The Connecticut case was never fully resolved because the defendant disappeared before retrial in 1918. The 1917 Illinois case was dismissed on a motion in the lower court before Judge Perry L. Persons on grounds that state and federal constitutional guarantees had annulled the common-law crime of blasphemy in America, and the appeal of the dismissal was denied by the circuit court on similar grounds.

The last prosecutions for blasphemy in the United States were in 1968. *Maryland v. West* (Md., 1970) involved a youth charged by a magistrate with blasphemy under a 1723 statute after the young man told a policeman to "keep your God damn hands off me." On appeal the Maryland appellate court ruled that the antiblasphemy law violated the First Amendment's Establishment Clause, despite attempts by the state to claim a secular purpose.

In 1968 authorities arraigned two Wilmington, Delaware, students for blasphemy after they called Jesus a bastard in an underground high school newspaper. The Delaware attorney general's office did not press the charges, perhaps influenced by the Maryland ruling.

The issue of blasphemy has never been squarely before the U.S. Supreme Court for a number of obvious reasons. The incorporation doctrine, which holds elements of the Bill of Rights to have been applied to the states via the Fourteenth Amendment, was not announced by the Court until *Gitlow v. New York* (1925). It was not until 1940, furthermore, in *Cantwell v. Connecticut,* that the Court applied the First Amendment's Free Exercise Clause to citizens of the various states. Since the elaboration of the incorporation doctrine by the Court, only a handful of blasphemy prosecutions have been undertaken, and none survived to the stage at which an application for certiorari would have been entertained.

There was, however, one modern Supreme Court decision that came close to the blasphemy issue. In *Burstyn, Inc. v. Wilson* (1952) the High Court struck down as an unconstitutional abridgment of free speech a New York State statute that allowed a state film censorship board to deny permission for the public showing of films held to be "sacrilegious." In an aside in his concurring opinion, Justice Felix Frankfurter observed that "blasphemy" was an even broader and more vague concept than "sacrilege," which a majority of the Court had held to be too subjective. Frankfurter's opinion contained an appendix listing definitions of the terms "blasphemy" and "sacrilege" in English dictionaries from the seventeenth century until the mid–nineteenth century.

Given the *Burstyn* decision, it is reasonable to assert that no blasphemy statute would survive judicial review by the federal bench. In recent years the protections of free speech and free press have been widely expanded by court decisions, and the "wall of separation" between church and state has been heightened and widened by the outcomes of numerous cases.

In addition to this, the makeup of the United States has changed radically from when Protestant Christianity was the faith of an overwhelming preponderance of the American public. Waves of immigration have made Catholicism, Eastern Orthodoxy, and Judaism significant factors in our present culture, and the newest immigrations bring Islam, Buddhism, Sikhism, Hinduism, and a dozen other non-Western faiths to our shores. Furthermore, cults, atheism, agnosticism, humanism, and New Age variants of older faiths compete with Wicca, witchcraft, and Santería in the new marketplace of religious ideas.

The religious conformity of the early nineteenth century—which had its own problems with Unitarianism, Universalism, Transcendentalism, Mormonism, Spiritualism, Millerism, etc.—has faded so completely that we may say that one person's blasphemy has become another person's creed.

Although blasphemy is extremely unlikely to come before the Supreme Court in the guise of a test case involving one of the extant antiblasphemy statutes, it may appear tangentially in any of a number of other issues including the "fighting-words" doctrine, incitement to riot, harassment, or one of the state statutes outlawing the disruption of religious ceremonies, which have become common in recent years.

Patrick M. O'Neil

Bibliography

Hall, David D. (ed.), *The Antinomian Controversy, 1636–1638: A Documentary History,* 2nd ed. (Durham, N.C.: Duke University Press, 1990).

Levy, Leonard W., *Blasphemy: Verbal Offense against the Sacred from Moses to Salman Rushdie* (New York: Knopf, 1993).

———, *The Establishment Clause: Religion and the First Amendment* (New York: Macmillan, 1986).

———, *Treason against God: A History of the Offense of Blasphemy* (New York: Schocken, 1981).

———, (ed.), *Blasphemy in Massachusetts: Freedom of Conscience and the Abner Kneeland Case—a Documentary History* (New York: Da Capo, 1973).

Schroeder, Theodore, *Constitutional Free Speech Defined and Defended—in a Case of Blasphemy* (New York: Da Capo, 1970).

Cases Cited

Burstyn, Inc. v. Wilson, 343 U.S. 495 (1952).
Cantwell v. Connecticut, 310 U.S. 296 (1940).
Chandler's Case, 2 Harr. 553 (Del., 1837).
Commonwealth v. Kneeland, 37 Mass. 206 (1838).
Davis v. Beason, 133 U.S. 333 (1890).
Gitlow v. New York, 268 U.S. 652 (1925).
Maryland v. West, 9 Md. App. 270 (1970).
Mormon Church v. United States, 136 U.S. 1 (1890).
People v. Ruggles, 8 Johns. 5 Am. Dec. 335 290 (N.Y., 1811).
Reg. v. Lemon, 3 *Weekly Law R.* 404-23 (Aug. 11, 1978).
Updegraph Case, 11 Serg. and R. 394 (Penn., 1824).

Board of Education v. Allen 392 U.S. 236 (1968)

In 1965 the New York legislature amended its education laws to require public school boards to purchase textbooks with public funds and lend the books without charge to students enrolled in any high school that complied with the state's compulsory education laws. This amendment required the school boards to supply free textbooks to private religious schools as well as public schools. Two school boards challenged the law, claiming that it required them to violate the Establishment Clause of the state and federal constitutions by providing direct government aid to religion.

Writing for a five-justice majority, Justice Byron R. White held that the statute was constitutional. The majority opinion relied on *Everson v. Board of Education* (1947), in which the Court had upheld a New Jersey law allocating tax monies toward the bus fares of students in private and public schools. *Everson* held that the law was a valid exercise of the state's police power, because its purpose was to ensure the safe transportation of schoolchildren. Although the textbook loans at issue in *Board of Education v. Allen* (1968) could not be justified under the state's police power, Justice White found that the New York statute had the secular purpose of furthering educational opportunities for the young and that any benefits to religion were, as in *Everson,* incidental in nature.

The majority also relied on *Pierce v. Society of Sisters* (1925), in which the Court acknowledged that religious schools provide both secular and religious education. Justice White found that the secular function of religious schools was not so intertwined with their religious function that the provision of secular textbooks could be presumed to further the school's religious mission. Justice White emphasized that the Court was proceeding on the assumption that only secular textbooks would be approved by the school board for use in sectarian schools.

The majority summarily dismissed the free exercise challenge to the statute because plaintiffs failed to show that the law had a coercive effect on them as individuals in the practice of their religion.

Justice Harlan filed a separate opinion concurring in the judgment. He found that the law was constitutional because it had a nonreligious purpose that was within the power of the state and because it did not generate political divisiveness.

Justice Black, who wrote the majority opinion in *Everson,* vigorously dissented. Black distinguished the power of the state to provide police or fire protection for all schoolchildren, including those in religious schools, from the use of tax-raised funds to purchase schoolbooks. The former, according to Black, was a valid exercise of the state's police power. Funding schoolbooks, however, lent the support of the state to "the most essential tool of education" and must "inevitably tend to propagate the religious views of the favored sect." Justice Black suggested that the rationale of *Allen* could easily be extended to justify the use of state funds to buy property on which to erect religious schools or to pay the salaries of religious schoolteachers.

Justice Douglas also dissented, noting that the statute provided for the initial selection of texts by the religious school, subject to veto by the school board. Douglas found that this arrangement would necessarily engender conflict. If the school board approved religious textbooks, the wall between church and state would be breached; and if the board limited its approval to secular texts, the state might come to dominate the church by determining what could be taught in church schools. Justice Douglas emphasized the difficulty of drawing lines between secular and sectarian influences in education, quoting passages from school texts on embryology and economics to illustrate how sectarian dogma could influence even nondenominational textbooks. Even textbooks that did not contain the "imprimatur" of a particular faith, Douglas suggested, might have "certain shadings" that would lead a parochial school to prefer one text over another. Douglas concluded that local school boards should not be in the business of approving or disapproving textbook choices made by religious schools.

Justice Fortas dissented, agreeing with Douglas that the right of religious schools to select the texts to be purchased by the state distinguished the New York program from *Everson,* where all schools, public and private, had received the same services from the state. Fortas concluded that because the books to be used in religious schools were "specially, separately and particularly chosen by religious sects," the law clearly mandated the unconstitutional use of public funds to support religion.

The Establishment Clause analysis performed by the Court in *Allen* has been modified over the years. The requirements of secular purpose and a primary effect that neither advances nor inhibits religion have remained, but in *Lemon v. Kurtzman* (1971) the Court added a third prong to its test by prohibiting excessive entanglement between government and religion. Justice Harlan's suggestion that a law should not generate political controversy enjoyed a brief period of support, but it was abandoned as an independent basis for an Establishment Clause violation in *Lynch v. Donnelly* (1984).

The Supreme Court has gone on to strike down most forms of government aid to religious schools. Types of aid found impermissible include: reimbursement for teachers' salaries and secular textbooks, struck down in *Lemon;* textbook loans to private schools with racially discriminatory policies, struck down in *Norwood v. Harrison* (1973); auxiliary services and instructional materials, found unconstitutional in *Meek v. Pittenger* (1975); transportation for field trips related to secular courses, struck down in *Wolman v. Walter* (1977); and shared time and community education programs, rejected by the Court in *Grand Rapids School District v. Ball* (1985). In *Committee for Public Education v. Nyquist* (1973) the Court also prohibited state tuition assistance to the parents of parochial students, either by direct grant or through state income tax benefits. However, in *Tilton v. Richardson* (1971) the Court permitted the states greater leeway in financing church-related institutions of higher education.

Joanne C. Brant

Cases Cited

Board of Education v. Allen, 392 U.S. 236 (1968).
Committee for Public Education v. Nyquist, 413 U.S. 756 (1973).
Everson v. Board of Education, 330 U.S. 1 (1947).
Grand Rapids School District v. Ball, 473 U.S. 373 (1985).
Lemon v. Kurtzman, 403 U.S. 602 (1971).
Lynch v. Donnelly, 465 U.S. 668 (1984).
Meek v. Pittenger, 421 U.S. 349 (1975).
Norwood v. Harrison, 413 U.S. 455 (1973).
Pierce v. Society of Sisters, 268 U.S. 510 (1925).
Tilton v. Richardson, 403 U.S. 672 (1971).
Wolman v. Walter, 433 U.S. 229 (1977).

Board of Education of Kiryas Village School District v. Grumet

See KIRYAS JOEL SCHOOL DISTRICT V. GRUMET.

Board of Education v. Mergens 496 U.S. 226 (1990)

In *Board of Education v. Mergens* (1990) the Court resolved several important elements of the controversial "equal-access" issue, which had divided the lower courts: When a public high school allows voluntary, student-initiated nonreligious student groups to meet on school premises, should it grant equal access to voluntary, student-initiated religious student groups? This issue encompasses two difficult constitutional inquiries: Are schools compelled to grant equal access by the Free Speech Clause? Or are they prohibited from doing so by the Establishment Clause?

In the absence of guidance from the Supreme Court, in 1984 Congress enacted the Equal Access Act to govern this issue. The act prohibits public secondary schools from denying equal access to "any students who wish to conduct a meeting . . . on the basis of the religious, political, philosophical, or other content of the speech" at the meeting, so long as the school has a "limited open forum."

Such a forum exists whenever the school allows one or more "noncurriculum related student groups to meet on school premises during noninstructional time."

The act raised a number of statutory interpretation issues, including the question of when a student group was "noncurriculum related," thus triggering the equal-access requirement. It also raised the same constitutional issues that existed in its absence; if the act either compelled or denied access when the Constitution would require the opposite result, it would be to that extent unconstitutional.

In *Mergens* the Court interpreted the phrase "noncurriculum related student group" broadly, as applying to any group that does not *directly* relate to the school's courses. The Court held that several such clubs at the school in question—a scuba diving club, a chess club, and a service group that worked with special education classes—were "noncurriculum" groups. Because the school allowed each of these groups to meet on school premises, the Court held that the Equal Access Act applied, and thus the school was required to allow a Christian club also to meet on its premises.

In addition, the Court ruled that the act does not violate the Establishment Clause. To reach this conclusion, Justice Sandra Day O'Connor, in a portion of her opinion joined by three other justices, essentially found the case controlled by *Widmar v. Vincent* (1981), in which the Court had rejected an Establishment Clause challenge to a public university's equal-access grant to a student religious group, applying the *Lemon* test. Justices Anthony Kennedy and Antonin Scalia reached this conclusion based on a narrower understanding of Establishment Clause requirements. They viewed the act as mandating a neutral "accommodation" of religion, which they argued would only violate the Establishment Clause under two conditions that were not present: if it tended to establish a state religion or if it coerced any student to participate in a religious activity.

Justices William J. Brennan, Thurgood Marshall, and John Paul Stevens cautioned that the other justices' Establishment Clause analysis lacked the special care that the Court traditionally had taken to protect public school students from a reasonable perception that the school endorses religion. In giving this caution, Justice Marshall, joined by Brennan, concurred in the judgment, while Justice Stevens dissented. Such a perception is especially likely in a high school, they explained, because students are there pursuant to compulsory attendance laws; because it is a highly structured environment; and because most high schools—including the one at issue—have only a narrow spectrum of student groups, rather than truly open forums, thus increasing the appearance that the clubs are school-sponsored. Accordingly, while recognizing that the Christian club meeting in the case at bar *might* survive Establishment Clause scrutiny, Justice Marshall's opinion concurring in the judgment concluded that the school must take additional steps to *ensure* that result, by fully disassociating itself from the Christian club's religious speech. A major question in the Establishment Clause analysis of the equal-access issue is the extent to which *Widmar*'s reasoning should apply to secondary students. *Widmar*'s pivotal holding was that, within the context of a student forum open to clubs on a nondiscriminatory basis—which was, in fact, used by a wide array of clubs—no reasonable student should perceive the university as endorsing any student group's message. The *Widmar* Court suggested, however, that this holding might not apply to a high school student forum, stating that "[u]niversity students . . . are less impressionable than younger students and should be able to appreciate that the [u]niversity policy is one of neutrality."

Consistent with the foregoing dictum in *Widmar,* in two subsequent decisions, *Hazelwood School District v. Kuhlmeier* (1988; involving student newspaper stories about divorce and teenage pregnancy) and *Bethel School District v. Fraser* (1986; involving a student speech, as part of a student government election, that contained sexual innuendoes), the Court rejected free speech claims by high school students precisely on the ground that, because of their youth, such students are particularly vulnerable to potential harms from exposure to speech about potentially upsetting or controversial subjects. In *Hazelwood* the Court reasoned that the school could censor student-written stories from the school newspaper because these stories might be upsetting to student readers, who might infer that the school endorsed them.

Notwithstanding the *Widmar* dictum and the intervening decisions involving high school students' nonreligious speech that were consistent with that dictum, the *Mergens* majority espoused a very different view about the presumed maturity of such students. Directly contrary to the *Hazelwood* rationale, *Mergens* asserted that high school students *were* sufficiently mature to distinguish between the school's neutral protection of students' free speech rights and the school's actual endorsement of the content of student speech.

The upshot of *Bethel, Hazelwood,* and *Mergens* is a double standard, under which students' access to religious speech is more protected than is their access to other speech. This discrepancy raises troubling Establishment Clause concerns. While that clause prohibits actual or apparent government endorsement of religious speech by nongovernmental speakers, the Constitution imposes no equivalent barrier with respect to nonreligious speech. Therefore, constitutional scholars have plausibly argued that organized student religious speech in public schools should be *less* protected than student speech about other subjects. At the very least, though, it is difficult to defend the status quo, under which organized student religious speech is *more* protected than other student speech.

Nadine Strossen

Bibliography

Laycock, Douglas, "Equal Access and Moments of Silence: The Equal Status of Religious Speech by Private Speakers," 81 *Northwestern University Law Review* 1–67 (1986).

Strossen, Nadine, "A Constitutional Analysis of the Equal Access Act's Standards Governing Public School Student Religious Meetings," 24 *Harvard Journal of Legislation* 117–190 (1987).

Teitel, Ruti, "The Unconstitutionality of Equal Access Policies and Legislation Allowing Organized Student-Initiated Religious Activities in the Public High School: A Proposal for a Unitary First Amendment Forum Analysis," 12 *Hastings Constitutional Law Quarterly* 529–595 (1985).

Cases Cited

Bethel School District v. Fraser, 478 U.S. 675 (1986).

Board of Education v. Mergens, 496 U.S. 226 (1990).

Hazelwood School District v. Kuhlmeier, 484 U.S. 260 (1988).

Widmar v. Vincent, 454 U.S. 263 (1981).

Board of Education v. Minor
23 Ohio St. 211 (1873)

In *Board of Education v. Minor* (Ohio, 1873) the Ohio Supreme Court unanimously held that there was no requirement that the Bible be read in Ohio's public schools. This case was the culmination of what was popularly known as "the Cincinnati Bible War."

The public school system in Cincinnati, Ohio, was established in 1829. By 1852 the traditional practice of opening each day of school with the reading of passages of the King James version of the Bible had been reduced to a written policy. The policy also provided that the students could read "such version of the sacred scriptures as their parents or guardians prefer."

In 1869 the school board, by a vote of 22 to 15, repealed this regulation and passed a resolution prohibiting "the reading of religious books, including the Holy Bible." This resolution had first been proposed to facilitate the merger between the pubic schools and the parochial schools of the Catholic Church in Cincinnati. Although the plans for merger had terminated, many saw the adoption of the resolutions as the result of the influence of the Catholic Church. In an era that saw widespread nativist opposition to providing any public funds to parochial schools, opposition to the resolution involved not only those who opposed it on the merits but also those who were motivated by anti-Catholic animus.

Consideration of this resolution resulted in the largest mass meeting Cincinnati had seen since the Civil War, to protest against the adoption of the resolution. The day after the resolution was adopted, John D. Minor and thirty-six others filed suit in the Cincinnati Superior Court claiming that the Northwest Ordinance of 1787 and the Ohio Constitution required Bible reading, and they sought an injunction to require the same.

The case involved some of the most prominent attorneys and judges in Cincinnati and attracted national attention. The three-judge panel to which the case was presented consisted of Marcellus B. Hagans, Bellmany Storer, and Alphonso Taft. Storer had prior service in the U.S. Congress, on the Ohio Supreme Court, and as president of the board of trustees of the Cincinnati public schools. Taft was a prominent local lawyer who went on to be U.S. Secretary of War, U.S. Attorney General, and the American ambassador to Austria-Hungary and Russia.

The court, with Hagans and Storer in the majority, issued the injunction, concluding that the state constitution required that the Bible be used in the public schools. Judge Taft dissented, finding that the state constitution required equality "of all religious opinion and sects" and that the government "must be neutral." The public interest in the case was keen. One indication of this was that in 1870, the same year as the Superior Court decision, a local publisher issued a book of over four hundred pages containing the arguments of counsel and the opinions of the judges. Writing two days after the court's decision, the *Nation* noted: "We are now fairly in for one of the most exciting questions the country has ever had to deal with. . . ."

The case was appealed to the Ohio Supreme Court, which unanimously reversed the appellate court. In doing so, it held only that Ohio's Constitution did not require Bible reading and that the management of the school system had been placed within the discretion of the school board.

This result parallels that reached a century later under the United States Constitution by the Supreme Court in *School District of Abington Township v. Schempp* (1963).

Richard Aynes

Bibliography

The Bible in the Public Schools, *Arguments before the Superior Court of Cincinnati in the Case of Minor v. Board of Education of Cincinnati* (1870; 1967 reprint with introduction by Robert G. McCloskey).

Fairman, Charles, *Reconstruction and Reunion, 1864–88* (New York: Macmillan, 1971).

Cases Cited

Board of Education v. Minor, 23 Ohio St. 211 (1873).

School District of Abington Township v. Schempp, 374 U.S. 203 (1963).

Bob Jones University v. United States 461 U.S. 574 (1983)

Governmental antidiscrimination objectives and religious liberty concerns were pitted against each other in *Bob Jones University v. United States,* a 1983 U.S. Supreme Court decision holding that educational organizations eligible for federal tax-exempt status may not discriminate on the basis of race. In addition to recognizing this antidiscrimination requirement, the Court rejected Bob Jones University's claim that racially discriminatory practices rooted in religious belief should be exempted from Internal Revenue Service antidiscrimination regulations. In the context of the Court's earlier decision in *United States v. Lee* (1982) and subsequent decisions such as *Bowen, Secretary of Health and Human Services, et al. v. Roy* (1986), *Lyng v. Northwest Indian Cemetery Protective Association* (1988), and *Employment Division, Department of Human Resources of Oregon v. Smith* (1990), the Supreme Court's refusal to grant a special exception from a generally applicable eligibility scheme to a religious organization was to be expected. What made the *Bob Jones University* decision especially noteworthy was the political firestorm that surrounded the decision, thanks to Reagan administration efforts to moot the *Bob Jones University* litigation by rescinding the IRS's antidiscrimination requirement.

Bob Jones University calls itself "the world's most unusual university." Although unaffiliated with any established church, the university is dedicated to the teaching and propagation of fundamentalist religious beliefs. In pursuit of these goals the university dictates strict rules of conduct for its students. To enforce one such rule forbidding interracial dating and marriage, the university denies admission to applicants engaged in or known to advocate interracial dating and marriage.

The Bob Jones University controversy began in November 1970, when the U.S. District Court for the District of Columbia in *Green v. Kennedy* (D.C., 1970) enjoined the IRS from according tax-exempt status to racially discriminatory private schools in Mississippi. The *Green* court suggested that the IRS would not be permitted to grant tax-exempt status to institutions that violate the government's public policy of nondiscrimination. The IRS then reversed its position of granting tax exemptions to racially discriminatory institutions and notified the university that it intended to challenge the tax-exempt status of private schools that maintain racially discriminatory admissions policies. In response, the university in 1971 sought to enjoin the IRS from revoking its tax-exempt status. That suit culminated in *Bob Jones University v. Simon,* a 1974 Supreme Court decision that "prohibited the University from obtaining judicial review by way of injunctive action before the assessment or collection of any tax."

The IRS in January 1976 formally revoked the university's tax exemption. After paying a portion of the federal unemployment taxes due, the university filed suit for a refund, contending that it was statutorily and constitutionally entitled to reinstatement of its tax exemption. In April 1981 the U.S. Court of Appeals for the Fourth Circuit upheld the revocation of the exemption. The Supreme Court granted certiorari in *Bob Jones University* and in *Goldsboro Christian Schools, Inc. v. United States,* cases presenting identical issues. On January 8, 1982, the Justice Department petitioned the Court to vacate these cases as moot in light of the Reagan administration's decision to reinstate the tax-exempt status of racially discriminatory private schools. Because of a related court order that prevented the administration from reinstating the tax-exempt status, however, the administration withdrew its request that the Court declare the cases moot. On May 24, 1983, the Supreme Court, by a vote of 8 to 1, denied tax exemptions to the two petitioner schools. In its decision the Court made certain general pronouncements, both on the meaning of the Internal Revenue Code's exemption provision and on the IRS's authority to issue rulings in accordance with its own interpretation of the code. The majority, in an opinion written by Chief Justice Warren Burger, held that a tax-exempt institution must confer some "public benefit" and that its purpose must not be at odds with the "common community conscience." The Court further held that the IRS has broad authority to interpret the code and to issue rulings based on its interpretation.

The Court also considered the religious liberty claims of Bob Jones University and Goldsboro Christian Schools. Noting that the "Government has a fundamental overriding interest in eradicating racial discrimination in education," the Court concluded that this governmental interest "substantially outweighs whatever burden denial of tax benefits" places on the exercise of religious belief. By holding that equality of treatment on the basis of race is the Constitution's most essential protection, and that the government's broad interest in racial discrimination in education was at issue, the Court had little difficulty in disposing of the religious liberty claims of Bob Jones University and Goldsboro Christian Schools. In fact, the Court devoted only three pages of its thirty-page opinion to the religious liberty issue.

The Court, however, overstated the government interest as it applied to Bob Jones University. Racial discrimination in education (or public support of such discrimination) was not the precise government interest at issue. More accurately, the government interest is a much more limited one, focusing on discriminatory policies applied by a religious school for religious reasons. Moreover, unlike Goldsboro Christian Schools, Bob Jones University admitted both minority and nonminority students.

The Court's failure to treat Bob Jones University's religious liberty claim seriously or to distinguish the religious liberty interests of the two schools can probably be attributed to the justices' efforts to make *Bob Jones University* a case of great symbolic value. Although the case initially was perceived as a religious liberty lawsuit, the Reagan policy shift transformed it into a socially significant racial discrimination lawsuit. Indeed, although several religious groups (including the American Baptist Churches, United Presbyterian Church, and National Association of Evangelicals) supported Bob Jones University's religious liberty claim, the vast majority of amicus curiae filings—sometimes joined by religious interests such as the American Jewish Committee—were by civil rights organizations that strenuously opposed Bob Jones University. Under these circumstances, the Court may have thought it best to keep the focus of the case narrow and to make the language about the evils of racial discrimination universal.

The Court should not be faulted too much for this interpretation. Between nondiscrimination in education and religiously inspired discrimination, the Court's endorsement of nondiscriminatory objectives is hardly surprising. To give substantial attention to religious liberty concerns would—by making the case appear more complex—indirectly limit the forcefulness of the Court's embrace of equal educational opportunity. In other words, the Court seemed to recognize the political impact of the decision and thus spoke in general terms about the meaning of the tax-exemption provision of the Internal Revenue Code and the evils of racial discrimination.

Neal Devins

Bibliography

Laycock, Douglas, "Tax Exemptions for Racially Discriminatory Religious Schools," 60 *Texas Law Review,* 259–277 (1982).

Neuberger, Thomas S., and Thomas C. Crumplar, "Tax Exempt Religious Schools under Attack: Conflicting Goals of Religious Freedom and Racial Integration," 48 *Fordham Law Review* 229–276 (1979).

Rabkin, Jeremy A., "Taxing Discrimination: Federal Regulation of Private Education by the Internal Revenue Service," in Neal E. Devins, ed., *Public Values, Private Schools* 133–157 (Stanford and London: Stanford Series on Education and Public Policy and Falmer Press, 1989).

Cases Cited

Bob Jones University v. Simon, 416 U.S. 725 (1974).

Bob Jones University v. United States, 461 U.S. 574 (1983).

Bowen, et al. v. Roy, 476 U.S. 693 (1986).

Employment Division, Department of Human Resources of Oregon v. Smith, 494 U.S. 872 (1990).

Green v. Kennedy, 309 F. Supp. 1127 (D. D.C. 1970).

Lyng v. Northwest Indian Cemetery Protective Association, 485 U.S. 439 (1988).

United States v. Lee, 455 U.S. 252 (1982).

Boerne v. Flores

See City of Boerne v. P. F. Flores, Archbishop of San Antonio, and the United States.

Bowen, Secretary of Health and Human Services, et al. v. Roy
476 U.S. 693 (1986)

Federal law requires persons who receive certain forms of welfare assistance, including Aid to Families with Dependent Children and food stamps, to furnish Social Security numbers. The purpose is to reduce multiple, fraudulent filings.

Roy and Miller, the parents of a 2-year-old child, Little Bird of the Snow, refused to provide a Social Security number for their daughter, arguing that it would violate their Native American beliefs. Accordingly, the Pennsylvania Department of Public Welfare terminated benefits for the child.

Roy prevailed in the district court. Acknowledging that he, his wife, and his 5-year-old son had Social Security numbers, Roy explained that now

> [b]ased on recent conversations with an Abenaki chief [he] believe[d] that technology is "robbing the spirit of man"; [that i]n order to prepare his daughter for greater spiritual power . . . he must keep her person and spirit unique; and, that the uniqueness of the Social Security number as an identifier, coupled with the other uses of the number . . . will serve to "rob the spirit of his daughter. . . ."

Therefore, he refused to obtain a number for his daughter.

On the last day of the trial, however, it was revealed that a Social Security number existed for Little Bird. Roy returned to the stand and now argued that his beliefs would still be violated by the very use of the number.

Using the standard developed in *Thomas v. Review Board of Indiana* (1981), the District Court for the Middle District of Pennsylvania ordered the benefits to be restored and continued until Little Bird turned 16. Both Roy's attorney and the solicitor general employed the *Thomas* "compelling governmental interest" standard in their briefs to the Supreme Court.

The Court reversed the lower court's decision. Speaking for the Court, Chief Justice Warren Burger distinguished two free exercise issues raised by Roy. The first was a novel claim: that the government's use of the Social Security number to identify Little Bird violated her free exercise. Although Justice Harry Blackmun in his concurrence allowed that this assertion had "some facial appeal," Burger more caustically dismissed the lower-court ruling as one only "libertarians and anarchists will . . . applaud" and concluded: "The Free Exercise Clause simply cannot be understood to require the Government to conduct its own internal affairs in ways that comport with the religious beliefs of particular citizens." All but Justice Byron White, who dissented, joined with Burger on this point.

A comment in the 1987 *University of Pennsylvania Law Review* by Jamie Alan Cole points out that there are now three categories of free exercise claims: those involving beliefs, which are absolutely protected; those involving government regulations that infringe on behavior, where there must be a balancing of interests; and those claims against how government runs its own business, which enjoy no constitutional protection.

Burger proceeded then to address the second issue: whether the requirement that applicants must provide a Social Security number passes constitutional muster. He did this despite the fact that both Blackmun and John Paul Stevens, in their concurrance, felt that the existence of a Social Security number for Little Bird rendered this issue nonjusticiable.

Burger's opinion set the stage for the complete emasculation of the *Thomas* standard by the Rehnquist Court in the 1990 landmark decision of *Employment Division, Department of Human Resources of Oregon v. Smith*. Burger rejected the claim that government must meet the strict standard the lower court used:

> [T]hat standard required the Government to justify enforcement of the use of Social Security number requirement as the least restrictive means of accomplishing a compelling state interest.

Instead, Burger claimed that

> [a]bsent proof of intent to discriminate . . . , the Government meets its burden when it demonstrates that a challenged requirement for governmental benefits, neutral and uniform in its application, is a reasonable means of promoting a legitimate public interest.

According to Burger, the standard in *Sherbert v. Verner* (1963) and *Wisconsin v. Yoder* (1972) was not neutral. Burger was able to secure only the votes of Powell and Rehnquist for this test. Blackmun and Stevens, as noted above, felt the controversy had evaporated when it was discovered that a Social Security number existed for Little Bird. Justice Sandra Day O'Connor, joined by William Brennan and Thurgood Marshall, dissented, arguing for adherence to precedent and the requirement that government demonstrate "a compelling state interest."

Although *Goldman v. Weinberger* (1986), decided during the same term, attracted the greater attention, *Roy* truly seems to have represented the more serious blow to free exercise. *Goldman* and *O'Lone v. Shabazz* (1987) could be distinguished as being exceptions fashioned because of the peculiar circumstances, respectively, of the military and of prisons. No such argument can be made in *Roy*. The problem caused by waiving the requirement for Little Bird seems minimal, unlike *United States v. Lee* (1982). In that case members of the Amish faith failed in their attempt to avoid paying Social Security taxes on the grounds that members of their faith never accepted Social Security payments. Avoiding taxes could make believers of many. But, it is unclear what advantage could be had by avoiding a Social Security number. Surely no person with fraud in mind would want to attract the attention that would follow a refusal to provide a Social Security number based on religious scruple.

F. Graham Lee

Bibliography

Bloostein, Marc J., "The 'Core' –'Periphery' Dichotomy in First Amendment Free Exercise Doctrine," 72 *Cornell Law Review* 827–858 (1987).

Cole, Jamie Alan, "A New Category of Free Exercise Claims: Protection for Individuals Objecting to Government Actions That Impede Their Religion," 135 *University of Pennsylvania Law Review* 1557–1590 (1987).

Kamenshine, Robert D., "Scrapping Strict Review in Free Exercise Cases," 4 *Constitutional Commentary* 147–154 (1987).

Vicko, Steve, "The Supreme Court and the Free Exercise Clause in the 1986 Term," 23 *Williamette Law Review* 135–177 (1987).

Cases Cited

Employment Division, Department of Human Resources of Oregon v. Smith, 494 U.S. 872 (1990).

Goldman v. Weinberger, 475 U.S. 503 (1986).

O'Lone v. Shabazz, 482 U.S. 342 (1987).

Sherbert v. Verner, 374 U.S. 398 (1963).

Thomas v. Review Board of Indiana, 450 U.S. 707 (1981).

United States v. Lee, 455 U.S. 252 (1982).

Wisconsin v. Yoder, 406 U.S. 205 (1972).

Bradfield v. Roberts
175 U.S. 291 (1899)

In this decision the Supreme Court held that a federal contract to construct a hospital on land owned by a religious group and to give the completed structure to the group in return for a promise to hold a percentage of the beds for use by poor patients did not violate the Establishment Clause.

Bradfield v. Roberts (1899) was the first Establishment Clause case decided by the Supreme Court. The case had its origins in Congress's efforts during the last quarter of the nineteenth century to restructure the government for the District of Columbia. For most of those years, Congress provided for the needy through appropriations given directly to private, charitable organizations in the District.

During those same years there was a growing nativist movement in the United States, fueled by groups such as the American Protective Association (APA), which was noted for its opposition to public aid for sectarian organizations. One of the movement's first goals was to defeat federal grants to Catholic schools for Indians. Those efforts soon spread to all public funding for secular activities. The debate in Congress reached a peak in 1896 with a bar on spending for sectarian purposes being added to the appropriations bill for the District of Columbia. As a compromise, the same amount of money went directly to the commissioners for the District, leaving them discretion about the final recipients. There was a similar debate in 1897, with speakers continuing to make constitutional as well as prudential arguments. Although the opponents of spending mustered considerable support, they did not succeed. Congress postponed the bar on grants to secular activities and added thirty thousand dollars for two isolation hospitals in the District, with the commissioners again having discretion to spend the money. The new buildings would provide a service unavailable in the District—the ability to isolate patients who had contagious diseases, a lack that had been felt most recently during the smallpox epidemic of 1894–1895.

Previous efforts to build a hospital had been thwarted by opposition to any new site from neighbors who did not want to live near an isolation ward. The commissioners therefore contracted to construct one of the buildings on the grounds of Providence Hospital, owned by the Sisters of Charity of Emmitsburg, Maryland. The 1864 act incorporating the hospital contained no reference to the religious nature of the organization; the sisters even used their birth names in signing the articles of incorporation. From its beginning, the hospital had received grants from the federal government, with congressmen such as Thaddeus Stevens sponsoring the grants.

Joseph Bradfield, representing himself, challenged the contract between the commissioners and the Sisters of Charity. He pleaded that he would suffer irreparable damage as a taxpayer of the United States if funds were spent in violation of the First Amendment. No one raised more than a fleeting objection to Bradfield's standing, contrary to what would become the Court's doctrine in such cases as *Frothingham v. Mellon* (1923) and *Flast v. Cohen* (1968). Neither did anyone seriously challenge the fact that Bradfield had not impleaded (sued) the proper parties. Ellis Roberts was the treasurer of the United States; he was not a party to the contract between the commissioners and the Sisters of Charity. The trial judge in *Bradfield v. Roberts* (D.C., 1898) enjoined the expenditure of money, because it created a joint ownership between the government and a religious organization. The Court of Appeals for the District of Columbia reversed in *Roberts v. Bradfield* (D.C., 1898).

On appeal, the Supreme Court held that Bradfield had failed to state a cause of action. Justice Rufus Peckham's opinion for a unanimous Court also ignored the standing and procedural issues. He considered only the constitutionality of the agreement between the commissioners of the District of Columbia and the directors of the hospital. Peckham had himself once been a member of the National League of Protection of American Institutions, an organization opposed to the appropriation of public funds for sectarian or denominational purposes. Nevertheless, he could find nothing wrong with the statute. He emphasized that the act of incorporation said nothing about religion. The hospital's purposes were also not sectarian, since there was never any religious test for admission. Thus, even though the commissioners had contracted with a religious establishment, they had done nothing to establish a religion.

Peckham's treatment of the constitutional issue was cavalier at best. Even though later courts would reach the same conclusion, few would have said that the fact of ownership and operation by the Catholic Church was "wholly immaterial." Nevertheless, the opinion did establish that more was required to violate the First Amendment than merely to contract with an entity owned by a church.

Walter F. Pratt, Jr.

Bibliography

Ambrosius, Paul W., "The End of Welfare As We Know It and the Establishment Clause: Government Grants to Religious Organizations under the Personal Responsibility Act of 1996," 28 *Columbia Human Rights Law Review* 135–163 (1996).

Esbeck, Carl H., "Government Regulation of Religiously Based Social Services: The First Amendment Considerations," 19 *Hastings Constitutional Law Quarterly* 343–412 (1992).

Kelley, Dean M., "Religious Access to Public Programs and Government Funding," 8 *Brigham Young Journal of Public Law* 417–438 (1994).

Laycock, Douglas, "A Survey of Religious Liberty in the United States," 47 *Ohio State Law Journal* 409–451 (1986).

Cases Cited

Bradfield v. Roberts, 175 U.S. 291 (1899).

Bradfield v. Roberts, 26 Wash. L.Rep. 84 12 App. D.C. 453 (1898).

Flast v. Cohen, 392 U.S. 83 (1968).

Frothingham v. Mellon, 262 U.S. 447 (1923).

Roberts v. Bradfield, 12 App. D.C. 453 (1898).

Brennan, William Joseph (1906–1997)

As an associate justice of the United States Supreme Court from 1956 to 1990, William J. Brennan, Jr., played a key role in deciding the appropriate place of religion in American public life. Born to Irish Catholic parents in Newark, New Jersey, in 1906, the second of eight children, the young Brennan developed a devout Catholic faith as well as a desire to pursue a legal career. After graduating from Harvard Law School in 1931, he practiced law in Newark, served in the Army during World War II, accepted an appointment to the New Jersey Superior Court in 1949, and was elevated to the New Jersey Supreme Court in 1952. Four years later, President Dwight D. Eisenhower appointed him to the Supreme Court of the United States. Brennan joined an emerging majority of liberal justices, under the leadership of Chief Justice Earl Warren, who actively fostered change in a number of areas of American law and society, including religious life.

Throughout his Supreme Court career, Brennan staunchly defended the principles of religious freedom and toleration, which he believed to be deeply rooted in the nation's past. In cases involving the First Amendment's Free Exercise Clause, for example, Brennan upheld the rights of religious minorities to practice freely their beliefs, often in the face of laws favoring the nation's Protestant Christian majority. Similarly, in cases arising under the First Amendment's Establishment Clause, Brennan questioned the constitutionality of specific laws or government actions that promoted cooperation between church and state. Despite Brennan's general consistency in upholding these principles, the changing composition of the Court during his thirty-three years of service forced a gradual shift in the justice's thinking. As the Court took a conservative turn and its senior associate justice neared the end of his career, Brennan advocated a stricter separation of religion from public life than he had in his earlier years on the Court. The new conservative majority, which permitted an increasing degree of accommodation between the state and the nation's dominant religious traditions, often forced the aging justice to articulate his "separationist" views in dissent.

Early Career: The Warren Court

Brennan's appointment came at an important time in the history of the constitutional debate over religion. Although only a handful of cases involving religious issues had come before the Supreme Court during its first 150 years, the decade and a half before Brennan's appointment produced a pair of key decisions in *Cantwell v. Connecticut* (1940) and *Everson v. Board of Education* (1947) that applied the First Amendment's guarantees of religious freedom against the states. At Brennan's arrival in 1956, the Court stood poised to advance significant changes in American religious life.

Brennan set the tone for the Warren Court's interpretation of the Free Exercise Clause in his first opinion in a religion case. *Braunfield v. Brown* (1961) involved a group of Orthodox Jewish merchants who charged that a Pennsylvania Sunday Closing Law prohibited them from making profits on one of their best business days and infringed on their rights of free exercise of religion. As Orthodox Jews, the business owners closed their operations on Friday nights and Saturdays and depended on Sunday's business to make up for lost profits. Although the Court's majority held that the law did not infringe on the merchants' rights, Brennan claimed otherwise. In dissent, he contended that religious freedom "has classically been one of the highest values of our society" and noted "the honored place of religious freedom in our constitutional hierarchy." Further criticizing the majority for allowing "any substantial state interest" to justify infringing on the religious freedom of the individual, Brennan concluded that the Sunday Closing Law was unconstitutional.

Brennan's *Braunfield* dissent had a lasting effect. The majority of the Court adopted his broad reading of the Free Exercise Clause just two years later in *Sherbert v. Verner* (1963), a case involving the rights of a Seventh-Day Adventist in South Carolina. After being fired from her job for refusing to work on Saturday and after declining other employment that would not permit her to adhere to the tenets of her church, the appellant filed for unemployment benefits from the state. Under a South Carolina law, however, the state denied her application for assistance because of her refusal to accept employment, even though doing so would have been contrary to her beliefs. This time writing for the majority, Brennan concluded that the law, upheld by the state's supreme court, violated the church member's free exercise rights: "The ruling [of the South Carolina Supreme Court] forces her to choose between following the precepts of her religion and forfeiting benefits, on the one hand, and abandoning one of the precepts of her religion in order to accept work, on the other hand." Brennan argued that government's imposition of such a choice was akin to penalizing the appellant for her Saturday worship practices. In short, absent any compelling interest on the part of the state, South Carolina could not infringe on the free exercise rights of its citizens.

Aside from these free exercise rulings, Brennan's most significant opinion during his early career involved a case arising under the Establishment Clause. The Court's decision in *School District of Abington Township v. Schempp* (1963), issued the same day as *Sherbert,* struck down a Pennsylvania law that provided for prayer and Bible reading in public school classrooms, thereby reiterating an earlier Court decision that had banned such state-sponsored religious activities as violative of the Constitution's prohibition of an establishment of religion. In *Schempp,* Brennan filed a lengthy concurring opinion that elaborately set forth his views of the First Amendment's religion clauses.

Invoking the intentions of the Founders, Brennan argued for the historical importance of both religious freedom and the separation of church and state in American life. In prohibiting laws "respecting the establishment of religion," Brennan claimed, the Framers of the Constitution not only intended to prevent the establishment of a state church but also sought to remove religious matters from the domain of legislative power. "The Establishment Clause," he asserted, "withdrew from the sphere of legitimate legislative concern and competence a specific, but comprehensive, area of human conduct: man's belief or disbelief in the verity of some transcendental idea and man's expression in action of that belief or disbelief." By preventing official involvements in religion, the Founders hoped neither to foster nor to inhibit the individual exercise of religion.

Yet Brennan noted that "an awareness of history and an appreciation of the aims of the Founding Fathers do not always resolve concrete problems," and he gave a number of reasons for rejecting a jurisprudence of original intention on the issue of religion. First, he contended, the historical record on this particular issue was ambiguous; partisans on either side of the question might find statements in support of their position. Second, Brennan observed, because both the American educational structure and the nation's religious composition had changed dramatically since the eighteenth century, any statements by the Founders would have little current value. Finally, he argued, an important link existed between the American experiment in public education and the nation's growing religious diversity. "The public schools," Brennan wrote, "serve a uniquely public function: the training of American citizens in an atmosphere free of parochial, divisive, or separatist influences of any sort—an atmosphere in which children may assimilate a heritage common to all American groups and religions."

Thus in *Schempp* Brennan both accepted and rejected a historical understanding of the Constitution's religious clauses. In championing the cause of religious freedom, Brennan relied on the American tradition of religious toleration and embraced the nation's history of diversity. On the other hand, in rejecting original intent as a guide for constitutional interpretation, Brennan looked suspiciously on those who favored a strict adherence to historical experience. By taking this approach to interpreting the religion clauses, Brennan allowed himself and the Court a degree of flexibility in dealing with future cases.

Indeed, although Brennan viewed organized prayer and Bible reading as clear violations of the Constitution, he nevertheless refused to declare the unconstitutionality of every vestige of cooperation between church and state and left the door open for the Court to decide future cases on their individual merits. "There may be myriad forms of involvements of government with religion," he wrote, "which do not import such dangers and therefore should not, in my judgment, be deemed violative of the Establishment Clause." Among such constitutionally permissible accommodations of religion listed by Brennan were the awarding of public welfare benefits to those whose eligibility rested on religious considerations (as in *Sherbert*), the saying of invocational prayers in legislative chambers, the appointment of legislative and military chaplains, the nondevotional use of the Bible in public schools, and the availability of uniform tax exemptions for religious institutions. Seven years later, Brennan stuck to this formulation in upholding tax exemptions for religious groups in *Walz v. Tax Commission* (1970). Although the focus of Brennan's early opinions in religion cases remained on religious freedom and diversity, he nonetheless showed a willingness to accommodate a minimal degree of cooperation between religion and the state.

Late Career: The Burger and Rehnquist Courts

During the 1970s and 1980s the flow of religion cases to the Supreme Court increased at the same time the Court's personnel changed. The retirement of Chief Justice Warren and his replacement by Warren Burger in 1969 initiated a slow ideological change on the Court that accelerated during the 1980s, when President Ronald Reagan appointed three new conservative justices and elevated William Rehnquist to the position of chief justice. These developments seemed to strengthen Brennan's convictions about the importance of both religious freedom and the separation between church and state.

In 1971 the Burger Court established a three-pronged test for assessing the constitutionality of laws that involved the state in religious affairs or institutions. In *Lemon v. Kurtzman* (1971)—a case involving two state statutes that provided for direct subsidies of public funds for activities carried on by sectarian educational institutions—Chief Justice Burger held that in order for a law to pass constitutional muster, the act needed to have a secular legislative purpose, could neither advance nor inhibit religion, and could not promote excessive government entanglement with religion. Applying the *Lemon* test to a Rhode Island law that provided for government assistance to nonpublic schoolteachers and to a Pennsylvania law that offered reimbursement to nonpublic schools for various instructional costs, the Court held both statutes to be unconstitutional. Brennan concurred in the decision.

In an opinion issued the same day, however, Brennan foreshadowed the differences he would encounter with his fellow justices over the interpretation of the Establishment Clause by dissenting in *Tilton v. Richardson* (1971). *Tilton* involved a federal law that provided construction grants for college and university facilities, excluding those "to be used for sectarian instruction or as a place for religious worship." Although four church-related colleges and universities in Connecticut received building funds under the act, the Court sustained the constitutionality of the law after applying the *Lemon* test. Brennan vigorously dissented, claiming that the federal law's provision that no "sectarian instruction" or "religious worship" take place in the facilities threatened the religious freedom and autonomy of the church-related colleges. Moreover, Brennan asserted, "the Establishment Clause forbids the Federal Government to provide funds to sectarian universities in which the propagation and advancement of a particular religion are a function or purpose of the institution."

In a series of similar cases during the 1970s Brennan continued to dissent from the majority and to reject any form of government aid to nonpublic schools of any kind. While his fellow justices often were more willing to uphold laws providing for government involvement with sectarian postsecondary institutions or laws that directly benefited children as opposed to schools, Brennan made no exceptions to his belief in the strict separation of government and nonpublic education. His reasoning on this issue, however, varied from case to case. In a 1973 dissent, for example, he repudiated a South Carolina law providing assistance to a Baptist college based on criteria he had articulated in *Schempp*. Any involvement of religious and secular institutions that "serve[d] the essentially religious activities of religious institutions; employe[d] the organs of government for essentially religious purposes; or use[d] essentially religious means to serve government ends, where secular means would suffice," was unconstitutional. In *Meek v. Pittenger* (1975), in contrast, Brennan employed the *Lemon* test, but only after asserting that the Court had implicitly, yet unknowingly, "added a significant fourth factor to the test." Any law, Brennan reasoned from his reading of *Lemon*, that caused political divisions along religious lines could not withstand constitutional muster. By this standard, Brennan deemed state laws unconstitutional in both *Meek* (1975) and *Wolman v. Walter* (1977).

Brennan's views on the proper association between religion and the state, however, were not always in the minority. Even during the 1980s, amid a growing tide of conservatism, Brennan's views continued to influence other justices. He wrote for the majority, for example, in *Grand Rapids School District v. Ball* (1985), striking down two Michigan educational programs in which public school systems paid their teachers to conduct special classes in nonpublic schools. "Our cases have recognized that the Establishment Clause guards against more than direct, state-funded efforts to indoctrinate youngsters in specific religious beliefs," Brennan wrote. "Government promotes religion just as effectively when it fosters a close identification of its powers and responsibilities with those of any—or all—religious denominations as when it attempts to inculcate specific religious doctrines." Also writing for the majority in *Edwards v. Aguillard* (1987), Brennan rejected a Louisiana law mandating the teaching of creation science in public school classrooms where the theory of evolution was taught. And in *Texas Monthly v. Bullock* (1989) Brennan for the majority declared a Texas tax exemption for religious periodicals to be unconstitutional. All these cases demonstrated Brennan's unyielding commitment to the separation of religion from public life.

Brennan's strict separationism, however, was less popular among his fellow justices when it involved practices wrapped in tradition—practices such as prayer at the opening of legislative sessions, the issue before the Court in *Marsh v. Chambers* (1983). Twenty years before, Brennan himself had all but affirmed the constitutionality of such prayers in dicta in his concurring opinion in *Schempp*. Dissenting in *Marsh*, however, Brennan repudiated his previous position and held Nebraska's legislative prayer to be violative of the Establishment Clause. "After much reflection," he wrote, "I have come to the conclusion that I was wrong then and that the Court is wrong today." In contrast to the majority, who had upheld legislative prayer on historical grounds, Brennan rigorously applied the *Lemon* test and forcefully asserted the practice's unconstitutionality. "It intrudes on the right to conscience. . . . It forces all residents of the State to support a religious exercise that may be contrary to their own beliefs. It requires the State to commit itself on fundamental theological issues. It has the potential for degrading religion by allowing a religious call to worship to be intermeshed with a secular call to order. And it injects religion into the political sphere." Brennan's powerful argument against legislative prayer illustrated the subtle change in his position on the relationship between church and state. Although during his early career Brennan seemed willing to accept accommodation of such traditional practices, by the 1980s he increasingly and passionately argued for separation.

Brennan's separationist position was also evident in Establishment Clause cases involving religious displays on government property. In *Lynch v. Donnelly* (1984) the Court upheld the display in Pawtucket, Rhode Island, of a nativity scene as part of the town's annual holiday decoration. Again Brennan vehemently disagreed with the majority, both for its "less-than-vigorous application of the *Lemon* Test" and its "fundamental misapprehension of the proper uses of history in constitutional interpretation." The majority opinion made much of the federal government's general historical recognition of the vital role of religion in American society. Brennan's dissent, however, analyzed the specific issue of the public celebration of Christmas, citing historical evidence of Puritan and evangelical hostility to the elaborate celebration of Christmas. "[T]he Religion Clauses," Brennan concluded, "were intended to ensure a benign regime of competitive disorder among all denominations, so that each sect was free to vie against the others for the allegiance of its followers without state interference. The historical record, contrary to the Court's uninformed assumption, suggests that, at the very least, conflicting views toward the celebration of Christmas were an important element of that competition at the time of the adoption of the Constitution." Brennan reiterated these views in *County of Allegheny v. American Civil Liberties Union* (1989), a similar case involving a holiday display in Pittsburgh in which a nativity scene, a 45-foot Christmas tree, and an 18-foot Hanukkah menorah were at issue. Even the display of the tree and menorah, Brennan contended, connoted an unconstitutional official endorsement of religion.

Although most of the significant religion cases during his late career involved the Establishment Clause, in free exercise claims Brennan consistently expressed his belief in individual religious freedom. In *Goldman v. Weinberger* (1986) Brennan disagreed with the majority's decision that the military could punish an Orthodox Jewish serviceman for wearing a yarmulke, a small skullcap traditionally worn to cover the head in God's presence. In dissent, Brennan criticized the Court for neglecting its "constitutionally mandated role" and for deferring to the judgment of military officials. Similarly, writing for a four-person minority in *O'Lone v. Estate of Shabazz* (1987), Brennan rebuked the majority for deferring to a prison's decision to forbid Muslim inmates from participating in a religious ceremony. "Incarceration by its nature denies a prisoner participation in the larger human community," Brennan concluded. "To deny the opportunity to affirm membership in a spiritual community, however, may extinguish an inmate's last source of hope for dignity and redemption." Finally, Brennan stood up for the religious rights of Native Americans in his dissent in *Lyng v. Northwest Indian Cemetery Protective Association* (1988) and by joining Justice Harry Blackmun's dissent in *Employment Division, Department of Human Resources of Oregon v. Smith* (1990). In *Lyng* Brennan criticized the U.S. Forest Service for its attempt to build a road through an area integral to the practice of Native American religion; Brennan applied the reasoning from his first religion opinion, *Braunfield.* Because the believers had shown that the proposed road would essentially prevent them from practicing their religion, Brennan believed that the government had violated the Free Exercise Clause. Again, as he had throughout his judicial tenure, Brennan sought to protect the rights of religious minorities who encountered potential threats to their religious liberty.

Conclusion

Brennan's interpretation of the religion clauses in many ways reflected his career as a whole. While some justices and constitutional scholars advocated a jurisprudence of original intention, in which judges sought to discover the aims of the Founders as guide for deciding key constitutional questions, Brennan employed a less mechanical, more flexible way of viewing the law. Like some of his fellow justices, Brennan looked to history for support of the principles in which he deeply believed—in Brennan's case, religious freedom, toleration, and diversity. On the other hand, he feared the misuse of history in either of two forms: a dogmatic adherence to the literal aims of the Founders or the circumvention of established precedents by devotion to time-honored religious traditions. By embracing the notion of a Constitution rooted in historical tradition yet adaptable to the changing conditions of society, Brennan allowed himself to interpret the religion clauses with an eye on the past, yet with a vision firmly focused on both the present and the future.

Kermit L. Hall
Timothy Huebner

Bibliography

Adams, Arlin M., "Justice Brennan and the Religion Clauses: The Concept of a 'Living Constitution,'" 139 *University of Pennsylvania Law Review* 1319–1331 (1991).

Ariens, Michael, "On the Road of Good Intentions: Justice Brennan and the Religion Clauses," 27 *California Western Law Review* 311–338 (1990).

"The Brennan Legacy: A Roundtable Discussion," 77 *American Bar Association Journal* 52–61 (1991).

Cases Cited

Braunfield v. Brown, 366 U.S. 599 (1961).
Cantwell v. Connecticut, 310 U.S. 296 (1940).
County of Allegheny v. American Civil Liberties Union, 49 U.S. 573 (1989).
Edwards v. Aguillard, 482 U.S. 578 (1987).
Employment Division, Department of Human Resources of Oregon v. Smith, 494 U.S. 872 (1990).
Everson v. Board of Education, 330 U.S. 1 (1947).
Goldman v. Weinberger, 475 U.S. 503 (1986).
Grand Rapids School District v. Ball, 473 U.S. 373 (1985).
Lemon v. Kurtzman, 403 U.S. 602 (1971).
Lynch v. Donnelly, 465 U.S. 668 (1984).
Lyng v. Northwest Indian Cemetery Protective Association, 485 U.S. 439 (1988).
Marsh v. Chambers, 463 U.S. 783 (1983).
Meek v. Pittenger, 421 U.S. 349 (1975).
O'Lone v. Estate of Shabazz, 482 U.S. 342 (1987).
School District of Abington Township v. Schempp, 374 U.S. 203 (1963).
Sherbert v. Verner, 374 U.S. 398 (1963).
Texas Monthly v. Bullock, 489 U.S. 1 (1989).
Tilton v. Richardson, 403 U.S. 672 (1971).
Walz v. Tax Commission, 397 U.S. 664 (1970).
Wolman v. Walter, 433 U.S. 229 (1977).

Burger, Warren Earl (1907–1995)

Chief Justice Warren Burger participated in forty-four cases involving the religion clauses. His interest in the issues, as well as his sense of their importance, is evident from the fact that he assigned himself to write the Court's opinion in fourteen of the cases, almost one-third of the total. He announced the Court's judgment in two other, plurality opinions. Burger wrote the opinion for or announced the judgment of the Court in the first seven religion clause cases to receive plenary treatment after he joined the Court. Thereafter, he found himself in a shifting minority as the Court fractured over drawing lines between permissible and impermissible conduct. In spite of Burger's interest, his opinions defy easy characterization. But that is what he would have wanted, for if there was a theme to his opinions, it was, as he said in *Committee for Public Education and Religious Liberty v. Nyquist* (1973), that the "fundamental principle . . . in this difficult and sensitive field of law, . . . is premised more on experience and history than on logic."

Sympathy for Tradition

Experience and history convinced Burger that diverse groups should be able to accommodate each other's differences. His patricianlike conviction, however, was one formed from the viewpoint of mainstream Anglo-American history. Within that normative view, the religion clauses did not stand alone; they existed alongside tradition, the family, and even an occasional new value, such as opposition to racial discrimination. Taken together the values constituted, as Burger wrote in *Wisconsin v. Yoder* (1972), "the very concept of ordered liberty." He could not support claims or institutions which threatened that order. Even the Court itself threatened the proper order when it became entangled with logic rather than attending to the lessons of history.

Burger's first opinion concerning the religion clauses was the majority opinion in *Walz v. Tax Commission of the City of New York* (1970). The case involved a challenge to the constitutionality of New York City's exemption of religious properties from taxes. He accepted that the exemption benefited churches; indeed, he even praised the exemption for having assisted the free exercise of religion. Nevertheless, Burger concluded that the exemption did not transgress the Establishment Clause. The reason was "an unbroken practice [dating from colonial times] of according the exemption to churches, openly and by affirmative state action, not covertly or by state inaction." That practice, Burger wrote, was "not something to be lightly cast aside." In maintaining his emphasis on experience and not constitutional doctrine, he added that "the purpose [of the religion clauses] was to state an objective, not to write a statute." For Burger the objective was "to insure that no religion be sponsored or favored, none commanded, and none inhibited."

Those initial warnings seemed to be cast aside in *Lemon v. Kurtzman* (1971), Burger's second opinion for the Court. Ironically, *Lemon* articulated what would become the Court's preferred test for the remainder of his tenure. *Lemon* involved a challenge to reimbursing private schools for teachers' salaries. The Court held the practice unconstitutional. Although Burger began with an allusion to history, he seemed to depart quickly by crafting a three-pronged test: "First, the statute must have a secular legislative purpose; second, its principal or primary effect must be one that neither advances nor inhibits religion . . . ; finally, the statute must not foster 'an excessive government entanglement with religion.'" The third test, excessive entanglement, was one that Burger had introduced in *Walz*. Although others would come to treat the tests as constitutional algorithms, Burger himself did not suggest that they were to be the sole inquiry. Indeed, in *Lemon* experience showed that the state was caught in a conundrum. On the one hand, by aiding teachers directly the state risked advancing religion, given the vital role teachers play in the schools. On the other hand, to avoid impermissible aid would require such supervision of the teachers that the state would become entangled with the religious education.

Lemon was therefore different from *Walz* because there was no "virtually universal practice imbedded in our colonial experience and continuing into the present." Direct aid for teachers was largely a development of the 1960s. Thus, in the absence of a bloodline, the aid in *Lemon* was impermissible. Likewise, in *Levitt v. Committee for Public Education and Religious Liberty* (1973), Burger wrote the Court's opinion to explain why New York could not constitutionally reimburse private schools for the expenses of teacher-prepared, but state-mandated, tests.

The nature of Burger's sympathy for tradition became clearer in *Yoder* (1972), his third opinion for the Court. The issue was whether Wisconsin's compulsory school attendance law violated the Free Exercise Clause. Members of two Amish religious groups objected to the state's requirement that their children attend school after the eighth grade. They argued that exposing the children to worldly ways threatened the Amish way of life. Burger's opinion in support of the Amish pointed to "almost 300 years of consistent practice, and strong evidence of a sustained faith pervading and regulating respondents' entire mode of life." Burger empathized with the Amish tradition of family because he could locate it in the "history and culture of Western civilization [which] reflect a strong tradition of parental concern for the nurture and upbringing of their children." With that reference, he rejected Douglas's dissent, which argued for an examination of the rights of children. He praised the Amish for reflecting "many of the virtues in Jefferson's ideal of the 'sturdy yeoman' who would form the basis of what he considered as the ideal of a democratic society." For such a traditional practice, "[a] way of life that is odd or even erratic but interferes with no rights or interests of others is not to be condemned because it is different." In *Thomas v. Review Board of the Indiana Employment Security Division* (1981) Burger expressed similar admiration for a Jehovah's Witness who objected to being assigned to fabricate turrets for military tanks: "[R]eligious beliefs need not be acceptable, logical, consistent, or comprehensible to others in order to merit First Amendment protection."

The sympathy, however, was not unlimited. The "but" clause in *Yoder* had said as much: An "odd or erratic" practice remained merely quaint so long as it did not interfere with the "rights or interests of others." The intimation in *Lemon* became explicit in *Yoder:* "It cannot be overemphasized that we are not dealing with a way of life and mode of education by a group claiming to have recently discovered some 'progressive' or more enlightened process for rearing children for modern life." Indeed, in *Cruz v. Beto* (1972), when the Court held that state prisons had to grant Buddhists rights equal to those of other religions, Burger wrote a separate opinion concurring in the result, with the comment that Texas prisons could not be required to "provide materials for every religion and sect practiced in this diverse country."

Nowhere was Burger's Blackstone-like satisfaction with the status quo more evident than in his majority opinion in *Marsh v. Chambers* (1983), upholding the right of the Nebraska legislature to employ a chaplain to open each session with a prayer:

> The opening of sessions of legislative and other deliberative public bodies with prayer is deeply embedded in the history and traditions of this country. From colonial times through the founding of the Republic and ever since, the practice of legislative prayer has coexisted with the principles of disestablishment and religious freedom.

He concluded with a familiar refrain, but one which also pointed to the chief difficulty with his base in history—those practices with a sufficiently long historical pedigree tended also to be the ones with the least-fervent religious content. Time tended to sap their verve:

> In light of the unambiguous and unbroken history of more than 200 years, there can be no doubt that the practice of opening legislative sessions with prayer has become part of the fabric of our society. To invoke Divine guidance on a public body entrusted with making the laws is not, in these circumstances, an "establishment" of religion or a step toward establishment; it is simply a tolerable acknowledgment of beliefs widely held among the people of this country.

The starkest example of this demystification of religion came in *Lynch v. Donnelly* (1984). In that case, Burger wrote the Court's opinion to explain why there was no violation of the Establishment Clause in a city's use of a crèche in its Christmas display. In one of his longest accounts of the history of religion and government, he pointed to the use of chaplains as well as to formal declarations of thanks and of prayer, concluding that there was "pervasive" "evidence of accommodation of all faiths and all forms of religious expression, and hostility toward none." Most important, he noted that all levels of government had "taken note of a significant historical religious event long celebrated in the Western World." He rejected the *Lemon* test, preferring to focus "on the crèche in the context of the Christmas season." He conceded that the crèche was a religious symbol, but he minimized its significance, preferring to persevere with his defense of a "celebration acknowledged in the Western World for 20 centuries, and in this country by the people, by the Executive Branch, by the Congress, and the courts for 2 centuries. . . ." To forbid the use of this one passive symbol, he continued,

> would be a stilted overreaction contrary to our history and to our holdings. . . . We are unable to perceive the Archbishop of Canterbury, the Bishop of Rome, or other powerful religious leaders behind every public acknowledgment of the religious heritage long officially recognized by the three constitutional branches of government.

Thus, from his earliest opinions, Burger based his conclusions on traditional relationships that constituted the "ordered liberty" he so valued. His vocabulary was not that of a syllogism originating in a constitutional phrase. Instead, he looked to Anglo-American history to show that in the field of religion the state must not intrude into certain relationships; neither should religious institutions intrude into the proper sphere of the state. As Burger explained in *Lemon,*

> Under our system the choice has been made that government is to be entirely excluded from the area of religious instruction and churches excluded from the affairs of government. The Constitution decrees that religion must be a private

matter for the individual, the family, and the institutions of private choice, and that while some involvement and entanglement are inevitable, lines must be drawn.

Threats to "Ordered Liberty"

Two of his later opinions well illustrate the twin exclusions Burger mentioned. In *National Labor Relations Board v. Catholic Bishop of Chicago* (1979) he invoked the "area of religious instruction" to explain why the NLRB could not assert jurisdiction over lay faculty members at Catholic high schools. Although that opinion purported to be based on the legislative history of the National Labor Relations Act, the constitutional import was clear. Burger had first emphasized the "impressionable age of the pupils" in *Lemon;* he repeated the image in *Tilton v. Richardson* (1971) and in *Yoder.* In *Catholic Bishop* he now returned to that theme by recalling that "[t]he key role played by teachers in such a school system has been the predicate for our conclusions that governmental aid channeled through teachers creates an impermissible risk of excessive governmental entanglement in the affairs of the church-operated schools." Seen in that light, it was inevitable that "the Board's inquiry will implicate sensitive issues that open the door to conflicts between clergy-administrators and the Board, or conflicts with negotiators for unions."

In *Larkin v. Grendel's Den Inc.* (1982). He invoked the other exclusion, that of churches "from the affairs of government," to explain why churches could not be given a veto over the grant of liquor licenses. "The Framers did not set up a system of government in which important discretionary governmental powers would be delegated to or shared with religious institutions."

The argument from "experience and history" did not always lead Burger to support a statute. For example, in *McDaniel v. Paty* (1978) he wrote to explain why a Tennessee statute violated the Free Exercise Clause when it barred ministers from being delegates to the state's constitutional convention. In that case, the history showed that Tennessee had come to stand almost alone in its prohibition, with the result that "the American experience provides no persuasive support for the fear that clergymen in public office will be less careful of anti-establishment interests or less faithful to their oaths of civil office than their unordained counterparts."

Likewise, history provided little security for a religious practice that challenged a principle vital to ordered liberty. Thus, when an Amish farmer claimed an exemption from Social Security taxes, Burger rejected the claim in *United States v. Lee* (1982). "To maintain an organized society that guarantees religious freedom to a great variety of faiths requires that some religious practices yield to the common good." In his view, Social Security was a valuable part of the organized society; to permit exceptions threatened both the Social Security system and the society itself. See also *Bowen, Secretary of Health and Human Services, et al. v. Roy,* (1986) for Burger's opinion that the Free Exercise Clause is not violated by requiring Native Americans to provide a Social Security number.

Similarly, not even a claim of free exercise could protect discrimination on the basis of race. The claim was a small part of a private school's attempt to retain its tax-exempt status. Nevertheless, Burger rejected it and all other attempts. The basis for his majority opinion in *Bob Jones University v. United States* (1983) was again history—the history of the concept of "charity": "Tax exemptions for certain institutions thought beneficial to the social order of the country as a whole, or to a particular community, are deeply rooted in our history, as in that of England. The origins of such exemptions lie in the special privileges that have long been extended to charitable trusts." In turning to the requirement that there be a public benefit, Burger resorted to a standard he had ostensibly rejected in *Walz.* In fact, in *Bob Jones* he found it unnecessary to inquire into the university's contribution to society. He implicitly reasoned that the university's discriminatory practices were so beyond the norm of acceptable conduct that no public benefit could rescue it. "A corollary to the public benefit principle is the requirement, long recognized in the law of trusts, that the purpose of a charitable trust may not be illegal or violate established public policy." Burger found that the strong public policy against discrimination sufficed to deny the schools' claims to be tax exempt.

Thus the religion Burger favored was not the one he described in *Walz*—one that took "strong positions on public issues [and engaged in] vigorous advocacy of legal or constitutional positions." Instead Burger supported claims of religious freedom that contributed to "ordered liberty." The churches in *Walz* fostered "moral or mental improvement"; the Amish in *Yoder* recalled a simpler, more ordered time; the prayers in the Nebraska legislature were part of a rich tapestry of experience. Buddhists in a Texas prison were not part of the tapestry; opponents of nativity scenes in Christmas displays challenged the proper order, as did annual debates about public funding for religious schools. The religion protected by the First Amendment was one that could be accommodated because it had reached its own accommodation. It was the "substantial yeoman" who knew his place in the order of things.

Walter F. Pratt, Jr.

Bibliography

Kobylka, Joseph F., "Leadership on the Supreme Court of the United States: Chief Justice Burger and the Establishment Clause," 42 *Western Political Quarterly* 545–568 (1989).

Kohler, Mark F., "Compromise and Interpretation: A Case Study of the Burger Court and the Religion Clauses," 23 *Tulsa Law Journal* 379–427 (1988).

Kurland, Philip B., "The Religion Clauses and the Burger Court," 34 *Catholic University Law Review* 1–18 (1984).

Pfeffer, Leo, *Religion, State and the Burger Court* (Buffalo, N.Y.: Prometheus, 1984).

Redlich, Norman, "Separation of Church and State: The Burger Court's Tortuous Journey," 60 *Notre Dame Law Review* 1094–1149 (1986).

Cases Cited

Bob Jones University v. United States, 461 U.S. 574 (1983).

Bowen, Secretary of Health and Human Services, et al. v. Roy, 476 U.S. 693 (1986).

Committee for Public Education and Religious Liberty v. Nyquist, 413 U.S. 756 (1973).

Cruz v. Beto, 405 U.S. 319 (1972).

Larkin v. Grendel's Den, Inc., 459 U.S. 941 (1982).

Levitt v. Committee for Public Education and Religious Liberty, 413 U.S. 472 (1973).

Lynch v. Donnelly, 465 U.S. 668 (1984).

Marsh v. Chambers, 463 U.S. 783 (1983).

McDaniel v. Paty, 435 U.S. 618 (1978).

National Labor Relations Board v. Catholic Bishop of Chicago, 440 U.S. 490 (1979).

Thomas v. Review Board of the Indiana Employment Security Division, 450 U.S. 707 (1981).

Tilton v. Richardson, 403 U.S. 672 (1971).

United States v. Lee, 455 U.S. 252 (1982).

Walz v. Tax Commission of the City of New York, 397 U.S. 664 (1970).

Wisconsin v. Yoder, 406 U.S. 205 (1972).

C

Cantwell v. Connecticut
310 U.S. 296 (1940)

Chief Justice Harlan Fiske Stone once described the Jehovah's Witnesses as "pests," yet at the same time noted that they "ought to have an endowment in view of the aid which they give in solving the legal problems of civil liberties." In the early 1940s a series of cases involving Jehovah's Witnesses forced the Supreme Court to confront a host of speech and religion questions, and in doing so it rewrote much of First Amendment jurisprudence.

The Witnesses are and always have been a small group within the larger religious community, but the group is a proselytizing sect that calls on its adherents to go into the community and preach the Word of God as they see it. The Witnesses, however, not only advocated their faith but also insisted that all other faiths were false; they would stop whomever they could on the street to inform them of the error of their ways and to try to convert them. Beyond that, the Witnesses took the biblical injunction against bowing down to graven images to include any form of secular symbol, such as the nation's flag, since they viewed patriotism as a form of secular religion. With World War II already under way in Europe, and the United States being drawn into the fray, Americans had little sympathy for either Jehovah's Witnesses or any other group whose patriotism might be in doubt.

The Witnesses regularly solicited from door to door, tried to sell their publications on the streets, and held parades and public meetings to gain new adherents to their sect. None of these activities by themselves seemed noxious to local authorities, but all of them fell under either state or local regulations that had long been considered legitimate exercises of the police power. Although the Witnesses could have secured the necessary permits or licenses, many of which required no more than registration with a clerk, they refused to do so on religious grounds, since they interpreted such registration as bowing to a temporal authority that they did not recognize as superior to divine authority.

The cases that came before the Court would have been difficult in any event, given the state of First Amendment jurisprudence at the time. It was unclear whether the objections raised by the Witnesses came under the Freedom of Speech Clause or the Free Exercise Clause: Were local authorities trying to stifle the Witnesses because they disagreed with their religious views, or were they muzzling them because of their alleged disloyalty? Moreover, state and local governments insisted that seeking donations or attempting to sell religious pamphlets on the street constituted nothing more than regular solicitation or a commercial transaction, both of which should be subject to the valid regulations that applied to others seeking funds or selling goods.

Ever since *Palko v. Connecticut* (1938), in which Justice Cardozo had announced the doctrine of selective incorporation of parts of the Bill of Rights to the states, the Witnesses had been trying to convince the courts to nationalize the Free Exercise Clause to protect them from regulation by the states. The Witnesses had brought this claim before the High Court twice, in *Lovell v. Griffin* (1938) and in *Schneider v. Irvington* (1939). In both instances they had won rulings setting aside convictions for violating local solicitation ordinances. But the Court, in both cases, had refused to accept the religious freedom arguments put forth by the Witnesses instead deciding the cases on more accepted interpretations of the Freedom of Speech Clause.

Then came the arrest of Newton Cantwell and his two sons, Jesse and Russell, each of whom claimed to be an ordained minister of the Witnesses, in New Haven, Connecticut. The Cantwells had set up a small table on Cassius Street in a heavily Catholic section of the city; on it they had a portable record player as well as a number of Witness publications. They would ask passersby whether they could play the record, which was entitled "Enemies" and which attacked all other religions, but especially Catholicism. Jesse approached two men and asked them whether they would listen to the record; they agreed, but when they heard the anti-Catholic message, they grew angry and warned Cantwell that he had better move on or be prepared to face the consequences. The Cantwells left, but police later arrested them, and they were tried and convicted on five counts, including soliciting without a license and the common-law offense of inciting a breach of the peace. The Connecticut Supreme Court upheld the convictions on appeal (*State of Connecticut v. Russell Cantwell et al.* [Conn., 1939]).

The Witnesses appealed to the U.S. Supreme Court, which heard oral argument on March 29, 1940. Hayden C. Covington represented Jesse Cantwell, while the attorney general of Connecticut, Francis A. Pallotti, defended the state's position.

The unanimous decision, delivered for the Court by Justice Owen J. Roberts on May 20, 1940, invalidated the convictions on free exercise grounds and finally gave the Witnesses the victory they had been seeking. Moreover, the Court incorporated the Free Exercise Clause of the First Amendment and applied it to the states.

Roberts agreed that state and local authorities could require licenses for religious or other types of solicitation, but he found the statute deficient because of the arbitrary authority it placed in the hands of the secretary of the public welfare council. The secretary could, without any restraints, choose to find that a particular group did not meet the requirements of a religious body and thus withhold issuance of the necessary permits. This was no mere time, place, or manner regulation, which the state could impose on any would-be speaker provided it did so in a content-neutral manner; the statute was too vague in providing guidance to the secretary about what constituted a legitimate religious group.

In a similar manner Roberts found the old common-law crime of inciting a breach of the peace to be too vague in definition when compared with the mandate of the First Amendment. But the essential part of the decision came in Roberts's avowal that the Fourteenth Amendment's Due Process Clause applied the strictures of the Free Exercise Clause to the states:

> The fundamental concept of liberty embodied in [the Fourteenth] Amendment embraces the liberties guaranteed by the First Amendment. The First Amendment declares that Congress shall make no law respecting an establishment of religion or prohibiting the free exercise thereof. The Fourteenth Amendment has rendered the legislatures of the states as incompetent as Congress to enact such laws.

Roberts went on to discuss the problem of the dichotomy between belief and conduct, and he reiterated the holding from *Reynolds v. United States* (1879) that, although belief is protected from any governmental interference, conduct "remains subject to regulation for the protection of society." However, that power to regulate "must be so exercised as not, in attaining a permissible end, unduly to infringe the protected freedom." In this case, the power had gone too far.

Cantwell is significant primarily for two reasons. First, it continued the process of incorporation that would ultimately bring most of the protections of the Bill of Rights into play against the states as well as the federal government. Second, the Court began to differentiate between the speech and religion clauses of the First Amendment, although that process would take several more years before a clear religion—as opposed to a speech—jurisprudence appeared. Until *Cantwell* the Court had made no distinction in treating claims under the speech and religion clauses, and in the next Witness case, in which the Gobitis children were expelled from school for refusing to salute the flag (*Minersville*

School District v. Gobitis [1940]), the Court retreated to a speech test. But by the second flag salute case (*West Virginia State Board of Education v. Barnette* [1943]), attention shifted back to delineating religious exercise from speech.

Melvin I. Urofsky

Bibliography

Pfeffer, Leo, *Church, State and Freedom* (rev. ed. 1967).

Cases Cited

Cantwell v. Connecticut, 310 U.S. 296 (1940).
Lovell v. Griffin, 303 U.S. 444 (1938).
Minersville School District v. Gobitis, 310 U.S. 586 (1940).
Palko v. Connecticut, 302 U.S. 319 (1938).
Reynolds v. United States, 98 U.S. 145 (1879).
Schneider v. Irvington, 308 U.S. 147 (1939).
State of Connecticut v. Russell Cantwell et al., 126 Conn. 1, 8 A.2d 533, (1939) rev'd 310 U.S. 296 (1940).
West Virginia State Board of Education v. Barnette, 319 U.S. 624 (1943).

Catholicism in America

The original Catholic population of the United States in the colonial period was minuscule and was concentrated primarily in Maryland and Pennsylvania. A few Catholics also trickled into the New Netherlands Colony during the Dutch period. In his report to the Vatican in 1785, John Carroll, who would become the first American bishop, estimated the total Catholic population at no more than twenty-five thousand.

The Colonies and Catholicism

Colonial America had little liking for Roman Catholicism, and the bulk of colonial charters and religious legislation discriminated against its creed and penalized its practice. The hatred and distrust of the Catholic Church in the American colonies had a long pedigree. From Henry VIII's break with Rome (1533) through the persecutions of Bloody Mary's reign (1553–1558) to the plots of Elizabethan and Jacobean England (such as the Babbington Conspiracy and the Gunpowder Plot of Guy Fawkes), Catholics were seen as opponents of religious liberty and traitors to England.

Foreign policy issues further undermined tolerance for Catholics. During the entire colonial period the primary foreign enemies of Great Britain—Spain and France—were continental Catholic powers. Irish uprisings, with their incredible brutalities, were often blamed on Catholicism, and many in England and the colonies firmly associated Catholicism with the unconstitutional plottings of James II (1685–1688) before the Glorious Revolution. Indeed, many Anglo-Americans saw a direct tie between Catholicism and despotism.

The heavily Puritan population of New England, furthermore, believed Roman Catholicism to be the Whore of Babylon and the papacy to be the very Antichrist, who had been prophesied. Massachusetts Bay Colony was a center of anti-papist agitation, and within the first year of the colony's existence Sir Christopher Gardiner was expelled on suspicion of Catholic belief. A 1647 law decreed banishment for any priest found in the colony—and death for any who returned from banishment. The legal prohibition on the celebration of Christmas was yet another of the antipopery devices of the Puritan colonial establishment.

An exception was Maryland, which was a proprietary colony under a 1632 charter granted to the Catholic peer Sir George Calvert, Lord Baltimore, who enjoyed the patronage of all churches within the colony. Fear of reaction both in England and in neighboring colonies precluded the possibility of making Catholicism the official religion of Maryland. In addition, because few English Catholics were willing to settle in America, the colony had a Protestant majority throughout its history. In 1649, with that majority growing rapidly, Lord Baltimore secured the Act of Toleration to protect the Catholic minority. In the wake of the Puritan Revolution, or English Civil War, Lord Baltimore was banished from his own colony, the Act of Toleration was repealed, and Catholics were banned from officeholding.

Later, in New York, no-popery agitation was ignited by James II's appointment of Thomas Dongan, a Catholic, as royal governor. The Glorious Revolution permitted the colony the opportunity to replace Dongan with Jacob Leisler and to enact a series of penal laws that disenfranchised Catholics, denied them office, and ordered their arrest.

Only Pennsylvania and Rhode Island proved havens for Catholics, and, in the former, London forced the Quaker-dominated assembly to deny officeholding to the adherents of Rome.

With the threat to the colonies coming from France and Spain in a series of wars between 1690 and 1763, fear of papist treachery increased, and various colonies—especially Georgia, Virginia, and Maryland—moved to disarm Catholics, forbid their acting as guardians or witnesses, exclude them from militia companies, and so forth.

Maryland in 1755 passed a double assessment on the lands of Catholics. With the outbreak of the Seven Years' War, Pennsylvania disarmed Catholics, expelled them from the militia, and increased their taxes as well as listing them publicly so that they might be kept under observation.

New York, beginning in 1698, disarmed Catholics, required them to post a bond for their good behavior, and later denied them the franchise and threatened their priests with life imprisonment.

Connecticut denied office to Catholics in 1724 and, in 1743, revoked all protections that Catholics had enjoyed, effectively eliminating all Catholic churches from the colony. New Hampshire in 1752 required an oath against Catholicism by members of the legislature.

The Revolution and Catholicism

The era of the American Revolution was not without its own special anti-Catholicism. Reaction in America to the Quebec Act of 1774—which provided for the establishment of the Catholic Church in the conquered colony of Quebec—was severe, with rumors spreading of George III's alleged secret conversion to Rome.

In general, however, the era of the Revolution saw an improvement in the condition of Catholics. Symbolically, Charles Carroll, of the prominent Maryland Catholic family, signed the Declaration of Independence. Of greater significance, the wartime alliance with France and Spain and the need to keep internal harmony in the colonies led to concern over Catholic sentiment. General George Washington wrote to several state legislatures to urge an end to Guy Fawkes Day celebrations, which in the colonies had ordinarily culminated with the burning of the pope in effigy.

The liberalizing of state constitutions brought some degree of relief to Catholics in some areas during the Revolution. For example, in 1776 Pennsylvania and Maryland included specific grants of religious liberty in their new organic laws that were broad enough to protect Catholics.

When the new Constitution of the United States was proposed to supersede the Articles of Confederation, it included a clause in Article VI guaranteeing that the federal government could never impose religious tests for office. And when the Bill of Rights was adopted subsequent to the Constitution's ratification in 1789, the First Amendment seemed to promise governmental neutrality among the denominations—at least on the federal level—but neither of these clauses affected state control of religious matters. Many states (including New Jersey, which kept its religious restrictions until the decade after the Civil War) reserved public office to Protestants, since the Establishment and Free Exercise Clauses, like all of the Bill of Rights, did not originally apply to the states.

The more liberal stance of the federal government and the liberalizing conditions in the country from 1790 through the 1820s helped to produce better conditions for Catholics. Vermont dropped its penal laws in 1786, as did South Carolina in 1790 and New Hampshire in 1792. Delaware adopted general white adult male suffrage, while Georgia abolished its religious test for office. Connecticut disestablished the Congregational Church in 1818; Massachusetts did likewise in 1833.

New York had allowed residency by Catholics but had denied naturalization to anybody who refused an oath abjuring all loyalty to foreign princes (including the pope). In 1822 it abolished that requirement.

This period of liberalization was marred only by minor events, such as the popular hostility to Rome's consecration of an American bishop, John Carroll, in 1790, and the simultaneous creation of an American diocese—the Diocese of Baltimore—which was coterminous with the boundaries of the new Republic. In part, at least, this opposition spread as much from hostility to hierarchy and "feudal" forms as from anti-Catholic hysteria.

During the early era of creation and reform in the new Republic, the Federalist Party was the locus of anti-Catholic suspicions. Partly, the New England roots of the

Federalists were reflected in this prejudice, but the events of the French Revolution and its aftermath led to an intensification of that bias. Although the Catholic Church was persecuted by the Jacobin radicals, this detested revolution arose in a nominally Catholic populace. The Irish Rebellion of 1798 added fuel to the fire, for Irish Catholics and Irish Jacobins fought side by side—with the French supplying material aid—against the Anglo-Irish Protestant establishment.

Furthermore, the Concordat between Napoleon and Pope Pius VII seemed to confirm the worst of Federalist fears. The most anti-Catholic measure enacted on the federal level at this time was the Alien Act, which extended the probationary period before naturalization from five to fourteen years, and which was passed along with the Sedition Act. Not coincidentally, these acts were passed in 1798, the year of the great Irish Rebellion.

Rising Nativist Sentiments

Federalist opposition to Catholics was not exclusively ideological, however, for Catholics, like most of the new immigrants, flocked in disproportionate numbers to the Democratic-Republican Party of the Jeffersonians. When the representatives of the New England states (with New York in observer status) met in the closing days of the War of 1812, at the Hartford Convention, one proffered amendment to the U.S. Constitution proposed that naturalized citizens be banned from all offices, just as the Constitution already banned them from the presidency (Article II, Section 1).

With the rise in European immigration during the 1820s and 1830s, anti-Catholicism increased. In part, a general nativist feeling was arising, springing from the reaction to the influx of paupers and the lowering of wages through the increased competition for jobs. But old biases also seemed to be reignited by the Papal Jubilee of Leo XII in 1827, with its splendid pomp, and by the meeting of the Provincial Council of Catholicity in America in 1829, with its call for the establishment of parochial schools and its denunciation of "corrupt translations of the Bible."

A simmering controversy of the 1820s flared up in various cities—including Baltimore, New Orleans, Philadelphia, and Charleston—over the question of the rights of trustees of churches to control funds and to appoint their own pastors. Laws designed specifically to fit Protestant habits and doctrines were ill suited to the customs and beliefs of the Catholic Church in regard to ecclesiastic structure and control. Most state laws provided for lay boards to oversee church funds and church property.

In the South, Bishop John England of Charleston quickly persuaded the legislatures of North and South Carolina and Georgia to amend their statutes to provide for alternative forms of control. In Philadelphia, Baltimore, and other places in the North, the struggle over control was more prolonged and more bitter, with the church often being stereotyped as hostile to democracy, authoritarian, and elitist.

The trustees controversy, combined with Pope Leo XII's Jubilee and the Provincial Council, created a smoldering resentment of Catholicism. Rising immigration, especially from Ireland and the Catholic areas of Germany—spurred by the Irish Potato Famine (1845–1849) and by the suppression of the continental rebellions of 1848—supplemented the ranks of Catholics in America.

During the same general period, the Anti-Masonic Party was launched. Ironically, Masonry and Catholicism were old enemies; but in the reaction against secrecy, ritual, and supposed elitism, the two organizations became linked in the public mind with un-American ideas and practices.

Combining with these factors was the new spirit in Protestantism. The period of the New Measures (sometimes called the Second Great Awakening)—associated with such preachers as the Reverend Charles G. Finney—saw a rise in fundamentalist theology, revivalism, and a general religious excitement.

A widespread and large-circulation religious press was active in producing both tracts and periodic newspapers—including the Boston *Recorder,* the *Christian Watchman,* and the New York *Observer*—and this press became a pillar of the nativist movement.

Reaction against Catholic emancipation in Britain was stimulated by the spread of protesting pamphlets from English Protestant sources and fueled the fires of American nativist anti-Catholicism. Especially effective in the new campaign was a salacious emphasis on alleged sexual immorality by the celibate Catholic nuns and clergy. Such works as Scippio de Ricci's *Female Converts: Secrets of Nunneries Disclosed* and Maria Monk's

Aweful Disclosures aroused Protestant ire with lurid tales.

In Boston, Philadelphia, and elsewhere, anti-Catholic and anti-Irish riots began to occur, and Irish homes and Catholic churches were primary targets. In one of the most famous incidents, the Ursaline convent at Mount Benedict outside Boston was torched by a mob in August 1834. Other attacks on Catholic property occurred in other cities, including New York and Philadelphia, but increasing vigilance by the forces of law and the threat by Catholics to arm to protect their religious establishments limited the extent of such violence.

From Bigotry to Acceptance

Political opposition to Catholicism increased with the fortunes of the so-called Know-Nothing Party, or American Party (1854–1856), which was organized specifically to oppose immigration and Catholicism—the two were rapidly becoming synonymous in the public mind. The new Republican Party, of course, became the political organization into which merged a large number of the older, single-issue parties. The remnants of the Whigs and the Free-Soilers combined with the Anti-Masonic and the American parties in the body of the Republican Party, which therefore became a center of anti-Catholic feeling; the Democratic Party thus received the political loyalties of most immigrants.

In the years immediately following the Civil War, the last remaining states that placed civil disabilities on Catholics rescinded such laws—as when New Hampshire and New Jersey in the 1870s abolished its ban on Catholic officeholding. In these postwar years, anti-Catholicism usually took the form of attempts to restrict immigration, although before the 1920s the only restrictions adopted were anti-Asian measures such as the Chinese Exclusion Act and the Gentlemen's Agreement with Japan.

In domestic affairs the drive to prevent public funding for parochial schools was the central manifestation of anti-Catholic bias; to forbid such aid, states including New York adopted the Blaine Amendment in their state constitutions. In addition, theological positions taken by the church under Pope Pius IX—such as the proclamation of the doctrines of the Immaculate Conception and of papal infallibility, as well as his promulgation of the Syllabus of Errors, which seemed to attack the most central beliefs of liberal democracy—drew hostile attention. The syllabus was utilized by the critics of Catholicism to maintain that the church was inherently opposed to democracy and that its adherents would not make suitable citizens for a democratic republic.

Anti-Catholic rhetoric played some role in Populism, in the campaign for Prohibition, and in support of certain feminist causes, such as the birth control movement; but the rhetoric was strongest in the movement to restrict immigration, which achieved significant success in the acts of 1921 and 1923. Quotas on immigration were based on the prior ethnic composition of the United States and would, therefore, favor national groups from northern Europe and the British Isles over those from southern and eastern Europe, who would tend to be Catholic.

Jewish immigration aroused even greater hostility than Catholic immigration, and opposition to these new immigrants was not solely on religious grounds; complexion, habits, politics, and poverty also contributed.

Nativism was in the ascendancy during the isolationist period of the 1920s, and the Ku Klux Klan, revived in 1915, led in the attempted intimidation of blacks, Jews, and Catholics. A memorable Supreme Court decision, *Pierce v. Society of Sisters* (1925), arose in response to an Oregon law, pushed by the Klan and its political allies, which required that all children attend public schools. The obvious object of the law was to close all parochial schools, but the court found the law unconstitutional.

Perhaps no event demonstrated the depth of anti-Catholic bigotry more than the reaction to the 1928 presidential campaign of Alfred E. Smith—Democratic candidate, governor of New York, and a devout Catholic. Rumors spread of a plot for an armed Catholic takeover or of papal plans to move into the White House after Smith's election. When the candidate traveled across Oklahoma by train, crosses were burned at every junction.

In the 1930s, with the coming of President Franklin Roosevelt's New Deal and the forging of the FDR coalition, the so-called Catholic ethnics had a secure place in the halls of power. Although Catholics had served on the Supreme Court before—most notably, Chief

Justice Roger B. Taney (1836–1864)—people began to speak of a "Catholic seat." Associate Justices Frank Murphy (1940–1949), William Brennan, Jr. (1956–1990), and Antonin Scalia, (1986–present) provide the examples.

The nomination and election of President John F. Kennedy in 1960 represented the new acceptance of Catholics in American life. During the late 1940s, the 1950s, and the early 1960s the politics of Roman Catholicism became popular. Its stern anti-communism, strict sexual morality, and moderate economic liberalism with a strong commitment to private property enhanced the church's image both with the U.S. government and with much of the population.

The ecumenical council Vatican II and its attendant liturgical reforms seemed to bring Catholicism more into line with Protestantism, as did its repudiation of any guilt of "deicide" against the Jews in regard to the crucifixion of Christ and its viewing of other religions as positive in their holding a portion of the truth rather than as roadblocks to the reception of the whole truth. In the intellectual sphere, furthermore, scholars such as John Courtney Murray, S.J., in his *We Hold These Truths,* reconciled traditional Catholic political philosophy to modern liberal democracy.

Catholicism and the Courts

A cloud appeared on the horizon in 1947, however, with the decision in *Everson v. Board of Education.* In that case, the Supreme Court upheld a state's busing of parochial school students, but in doing so it applied the criterion of "separation of Church and State" and a "wall of separation" between church and state, based on the Establishment Clause of the First Amendment. The so-called school prayer decisions followed in the early 1960s, with such cases as *School District of Abington Township v. Schempp* (1963), *Murray v. Curlett* (1963), and *Engel v. Vitale* (1962) holding that official prayers and other religious exercises, such as bible readings, were unconstitutional establishments of religion. To Catholic sensibilities this smacked of hostility to religion by the state. On the practical side a long series of decisions, culminating in *Lemon v. Kurtzman* (1971), precluded most forms of state aid to Catholic schools.

Supreme Court decisions beginning in the late 1950s effectively struck down most antipornography, antiobscenity, and antiblasphemy laws—to a chorus of denunciations by Catholic clergy and lay leaders. The sexual revolution of the 1960s saw the repeal of many local and state laws against fornication, adultery, sodomy, and birth control. Pope Paul VI's encyclical *Humanae Vitae,* restating traditional Catholic opposition to artificial birth control, placed the church at odds with much of Protestantism and Judaism and with governmental efforts to restrict world population growth. In *Griswold v. Connecticut* (1965) the Supreme Court struck down the last state statute banning birth control devices.

With the two abortion decisions in *Roe v. Wade* and *Doe v. Bolton* (1973) opposition between the secular culture, governmental policy, and the majority of American churches, on the one hand, and Catholicism, on the other, reached its zenith. The church regards the fetus as a moral and spiritual person and considers the medical procedure of abortion to be murder of the unborn. With nonabortifacient birth control along with illicit sexual relations, Catholics who were willing to make accommodation between their theology and the circumstances of a pluralistic society could point out that all those who participated in these evils were consenting to them.

Just as with the church's fervent opposition to the liberalization of divorce laws in the 1950s and 1960s, its opposition to abortion became extremely unpopular with the mainstream Protestant churches—although it helped to build bridges to the fundamentalist community, which had been historically most hostile to Catholicism.

The rise of feminism has also put pressures on the church. Radical feminists, both within and outside the church, have demanded not only an end to opposition to abortion but also ordination of women, an end to clerical celibacy, elimination of male imagery and terminology for God, acceptance of lesbian and homosexual marriage, and a deemphasis on traditional family roles in the church's moral theology.

During the Reagan administration the United States extended diplomatic recognition to the Vatican City for the first time since 1848, although President Franklin Roosevelt had a personal representative to the Holy See during World War II. It would appear, however, that U.S.–Catholic relations will remain strained for some time over a variety of complex moral issues and their vital legal implications.

Patrick M. O'Neil

Bibliography

Billington, Ray Allen, *The Protestant Crusade, 1800–1860: A Study of the Origins of American Nativism* (Gloucester, Mass.: Peter Smith, 1963).

Cases Cited

Doe v. Bolton, 410 U.S. 113 (1973).
Engel v. Vitale, 370 U.S. 421 (1962).
Everson v. Board of Education, 330 U.S. 1 (1947).
Griswold v. Connecticut, 381 U.S. 479 (1965).
Lemon v. Kurtzman, 403 U.S. 602 (1971).
Murray v. Curlett, 374 U.S. 203 (1963).
Pierce v. Society of Sisters, 268 U.S. 510 (1925).
Roe v. Wade, 410 U.S. 113 (1973).
School District of Abington Township v. Schempp, 374 U.S. 901 (1963).

Chaplinsky v. New Hampshire 315 U.S. 568 (1942)

Although best known to students of the Constitution as a free speech case, *Chaplinsky v. New Hampshire* (1942) may also be seen as a complex controversy involving religious freedom.

One of a long and important series of cases brought to the Supreme Court during the 1930s and 1940s on behalf of the constitutional liberties of Jehovah's Witnesses, *Chaplinsky* grew out of the conviction against a street-corner pamphleteer in Rochester, New Hampshire. While distributing literature for the Witnesses, Walter Chaplinsky attracted a hostile crowd; at one point during a heated exchange with bystanders, he characterized "organized religion" as a "racket." As police officers were leading Chaplinsky to safety, he confronted the city marshal, who had previously warned him to temper his rhetoric. Angrily, Chaplinsky denounced the officer as a "racketeer" and "a damned Fascist" and condemned the entire government of Rochester as "Fascist" for failing to protect his liberties. The marshal arrested Chaplinsky.

Chaplinsky's political comments not only ended that day's proselytizing but also began several years of protracted constitutional litigation. Charged under a state law that criminalized "offensive, derisive, or annoying" language in public places, Chaplinsky was convicted, and the state supreme court affirmed. In reaching this result, the New Hampshire courts excluded, as immaterial, the defense's contentions that Chaplinsky was only following his constitutionally protected religious calling "to preach the true facts of the Bible" and that the city marshal had failed to protect the free exercise of Chaplinsky's religious convictions from suppression by a hostile crowd. Chaplinsky appealed to the U.S. Supreme Court, claiming that the New Hampshire law violated his freedoms of speech, press, and religion.

Justice Frank Murphy, who had been appointed to the High Court by Franklin Roosevelt in 1940, wrote the unanimous opinion rejecting Chaplinsky's appeal. Before announcing his famous "two-tier theory" of speech—which held that certain categories of expression, such as libel or Chaplinsky's "fighting words," fall outside the zone of constitutional protection—Murphy also rejected Chaplinsky's other First Amendment claims, including his argument that New Hampshire had violated his constitutionally protected right to the free exercise of his chosen religion.

Murphy gave Chaplinsky's religious argument short shrift. Even if the Court were to view Chaplinsky's actions *before* his confrontation with the marshal and with the mob as entitled to protection as a religious activity, Murphy argued, this "would not cloak him with immunity for the legal consequences" of all *subsequent* actions. The Court, wrote Murphy, "cannot conceive that cursing a public officer is the exercise of religion in any sense of the term."

In one sense, given the political-constitutional context of the early 1940s, Murphy's *Chaplinsky* opinion seems unsurprising. In 1940, for example, Murphy had joined the Court's majority—which had included Justices William O. Douglas and Hugo L. Black—in holding that school officials could expel a school student for his refusal, on the basis of doctrines of Jehovah's Witnesses, to salute the American flag (*Minersville School District Board of Education v. Gobitis* [1940]). Indeed, *Chaplinsky* was only one of eight cases heard by the Supreme Court between 1940 and 1942 in which members of Jehovah's Witnesses failed to win even *one* favorable vote from *any* member of the High Court.

From another perspective, however, Murphy's blunt 1942 opinion in *Chaplinsky* seems troubling. Murphy himself had agonized a great deal over the earlier flag salute case, and it had required the personal entreaties of Chief Justice Charles Evans Hughes to keep the then-first-term justice from joining the eloquent dissent of Justice Harlan Fiske Stone. The *Gobitis* decision had been followed by many attacks on members of Jehovah's Witnesses, especially in small towns such as Rochester, New Hampshire. *Chaplinsky* simply ignored the hostile-audience issue and any questions relating to the practices of an unpopular religious minority. The actions of the marshal, for example, would seem to raise difficult questions about the neutrality of government officials, an issue made more glaring by the fact that New Hampshire specifically charged Chaplinsky with directing his "fighting words" toward the marshal himself, an officer of the state. Rather than acknowledging difficult issues such as these, Murphy's *Chaplinsky* opinion dismissed any free exercise problem out of hand.

Although *Chaplinsky* has never been formally overruled and is still an often-cited case for the proposition that not all First Amendment liberties are absolute, subsequent decisions have helped to right its strongly pro-state, anti–free exercise tilt. Little more than a year after *Chaplinsky*, in *Murdock v. Pennsylvania* (1943), the Court struck down the conviction of a member of Jehovah's Witnesses for violating a local ordinance proscribing distribution of handbills. Justice Black grounded the majority opinion in free speech and free press doctrines, but Justice Murphy wrote his own concurrence stressing the free exercise problem he had ignored in *Chaplinsky*. "[N]othing enjoys a higher estate in our society than the right given by the First and Fourteenth Amendments freely to practice and to proclaim one's religious convictions," a liberty enjoyed by "the aggressive and disputatious as well as the meek and acquiescent." Such a characterization of protected religious practice, it could well be argued, might have covered the activities of Walter Chaplinsky.

Norman Rosenberg

Bibliography

Fine, Sidney, *Frank Murphy: The Washington Years* (Ann Arbor: University of Michigan Press, 1984).

Gard, Stephen W., "Fighting Words As Free Speech," 58 *Washington University Law Quarterly* 536–564 (1980).

Manwaring, David R., *Render unto Caesar: The Flag Salute Controversy* (Chicago: University of Chicago Press, 1962).

Cases Cited

Chaplinsky v. New Hampshire, 315 U.S. 568 (1942).

Minersville School District Board of Education v. Gobitis, 310 U.S. 586 (1940).

Murdock v. Pennsylvania, 318 U.S. 748 (1943).

Chase v. Cheney
58 Ill. 509 (1871)

In this early case touching on church–state relations, the Illinois Supreme Court ruled that an Episcopal clergyman's complaint of bias and procedural irregularities in an Episcopal disciplinary court—appointed and organized according to the rules of the Episcopal Church—was not the business of the civil courts unless civil or property rights were abused. This case illustrates the way state courts dealt with intrachurch issues before the U.S. Supreme Court incorporated (applied) the Free Exercise and Establishment Clauses of the First Amendment to the states through the Fourteenth Amendment.

The Reverend Cheney had been charged with habitually and deliberately altering or omitting key doctrinal directions and phrases from the Episcopal *Book of Common Prayer* in the performance of activities such as infant baptism. His bishop, after warning Cheney, formed a commission of inquiry and judgment—essentially an ecclesiastical court—which found that Cheney had violated his office by these alterations. Cheney sued in the Superior Court of Chicago, which restrained the ecclesiastical court from firing Cheney. The ecclesiastical court then appealed the case to the Illinois Supreme Court.

The Illinois court ruled that the church's judicial body was largely in compliance with its own rules and canons. The court ruled that the minister, a voluntary member of the

Episcopal association who accepted with his ordination the disciplines and laws of that association, was thus properly charged, tried, and fired. Justice Anthony Thornton asserted that the Supreme Court of Illinois has

> no right, and therefore, will not exercise the power, to dictate ecclesiastical law. . . . We shall not inquire whether the alleged omission is any offense. This is a question of ecclesiastical cognizance. This is no forum for such adjudication. The Church should guard its own fold; enact and construe its own disciplines; and thus will be maintained the boundary between temporal and spiritual power.

In assessing Cheney's "right to preach," the court held that the right to preach "in any organized church, with written or printed rules," is a "qualified" right contingent on the preacher's following the rules of the church. And the civil courts must also follow the rules of the constitutional game to "maintain the boundary between church and state, and let each resolve in its respective sphere." The state must avoid interference in

> not only each man's religious faith, but his membership in the church, and the rites and disciplines which might be adopted. . . . Freedom of religious profession and worship cannot be maintained, if the civil courts encroach upon the domain of the church, construe its canons and rules, dictate its discipline and regulate its trials.

Since the clergyman's civil rights were not endangered and since the civil courts must refrain from judging, overturning, or enforcing the rules of church entities, unless they are "acts of licentiousness" or "practices inconsistent with the peace and safety of the state," Cheney's complaint was dismissed.

The Illinois Supreme Court was unanimous in supporting this result. But Chief Justice Charles Lawrence and Justice Benjamin Sheldon in a separate opinion rejected the principle that "a spiritual court is the exclusive judge of its own jurisdiction." The concurring justices argued that an "unlawfully constituted" private court would violate civil rights and therefore that civil courts should examine the question of jurisdiction "and if they find such tribunal has been organized in defiance of the laws of the association . . . they should furnish such protection as the laws of the land will give." In other words, although the justices did not find the tribunal in this case unlawfully constituted, they believed that it was the duty of secular courts to determine whether or not the spiritual court were "exercising a merely usurped and arbitrary power."

The principle that the state should excuse itself from interference in internal church affairs has faced a rocky road since 1871. In recent years courts have generally tried to avoid involvement in the internal workings of churches and disputes involving departure from doctrine. Of particular note, in *Serbian Eastern Orthodox Diocese v. Milivojevich* (1976), the U.S. Supreme Court ruled that it would not interfere with the decisions of an ecclesiastical court on matters involving doctrine, polity, and the right of individuals to be members of the clergy of a particular faith.

L. Sue Hulett

Bibliography

Stokes, Anson P., *Church and State in the United States,* 3 vols. (New York: Harper and Row, 1950).

Cases Cited

Chase v. Cheney, 58 Ill. 509 (1871).

Serbian Eastern Orthodox Diocese v. Milivojevich, 426 U.S. 696 (1976).

"Christian Nation" As a Concept in Supreme Court Jurisprudence

At various points during its history the U.S. Supreme Court has characterized the United States as a "Christian nation." Although the Court has not made such a claim in more than half a century, the issue reemerged in 1988, when a letter from Justice Sandra Day O'Connor characterizing three of the Court's decisions as holding the United States to be a Christian nation was utilized in a political effort by Arizona Republicans to secure a party resolution proclaiming America to be a Christian country.

During the nineteenth century, the Supreme Court issued many opinions containing references to the United States as a Christian nation. In *Vidal v. Girard's Executors* (1844), for example, a case involving a challenge to a will on the grounds that it devised property for a purpose "hostile to the Christian religion," the Court rejected the will challenge but did characterize the United States as a "Christian country." Similarly, in two slave trade cases, *The Antelope* (1825) and *The Slavers* (1864), the Court characterized the United States as one of the "Christian nations" of the world. Confronted with the question of the scope of American consulate jurisdiction, the Supreme Court in *Dianese v. Hale* (1875) and *In re Ross* (1891) resolved the issue by distinguishing between the "Christian countries" and non-Christian countries of the world. Similarly, the Court repeatedly legitimated broad congressional control over the property rights of Indian tribes, noting in *Beecher v. Wethersby* (1877) that Congress would be constrained by "such considerations of justice as would control a Christian people in the treatment of an ignorant and dependent race." During the last quarter of the nineteenth century, the Supreme Court decided a number of cases adverse to the interests of the Mormon religion, relying on the fact, as it said in *Mormon Church v. United States* (1890), that certain Mormon practices such as bigamy were contrary to the "spirit of Christianity." In *Davis v. Beason* (1890) the Court asserted that such practices were contrary to the "laws of all civilized and Christian countries."

Perhaps the Court's most forthright discussion of the notion of the United States as a Christian nation was in Justice David Brewer's opinion in *Church of the Holy Trinity v. United States* (1892). In that opinion Brewer set forth a lengthy argument for his claim that the United States is a religious—and specifically Christian—nation in the context of interpreting legislative intent behind a congressional statute. Brewer quoted several colonial charters, state constitutions, and state supreme court decisions that referred to the central importance of Christian belief in the life of the American people; cited the practice of various legislative bodies of beginning their sessions with prayer; and noted the large number of churches and Christian charitable organizations that exist in every community in the country as evidence that the United States is a Christian nation. In 1905 Justice Brewer expanded on his *Holy Trinity* decision in a series of lectures at Haverford College entitled "The United States Is a Christian Nation"; the lectures were also published as a book by the same title. Brewer's contemporaries made similar observations about the American polity. For example, British observer Lord Bryce commented in his 1888 two-volume study of the United States, *The American Commonwealth,* that "Christianity is in fact understood to be, though not the legally established religion, yet the national religion."

Since its *Holy Trinity* decision the Supreme Court has much less frequently characterized the United States as a Christian nation. In *United States v. Macintosh* (1931) the Court rejected an application for citizenship on the grounds that the applicant, claiming religious objections, had refused to pledge his unconditional support for this nation's future war efforts. Justice George Sutherland, writing for a narrow majority, noted that "[w]e are a Christian people . . . acknowledging with reverence the duty of obedience to the will of God" and that obedience to the nation's military endeavors was "not inconsistent with the will of God."

The *Macintosh* decision was the last time that the Court expressly characterized the United States as a Christian nation. Nevertheless the Court has continued on occasion to recognize the religious—if not explicitly Christian—nature of the American people. In *Zorach v. Clauson* (1952), for example, Justice William Douglas wrote for a Court majority that "[w]e are a religious people whose institutions presuppose a Supreme Being" in upholding a New York law permitting public schools to release students for religious instruction, notwithstanding compulsory school attendance laws. Similarly, in *McGowan v. Maryland* (1961) Justice Felix Frankfurter, writing for the Court, noted the religious nature of the American people in upholding a state Sunday closing statute.

Most recently, at least some justices have attempted to distance the Court from its "Christian nation" heritage. Justice William Brennan, for example, in *Lynch v. Donnelly* (1983), criticized the Court's modern Establishment Clause jurisprudence, characterizing it as "a long step backwards to the days when Justice Brewer could arrogantly declare for the Court that 'this is a Christian nation.'"

Davison M. Douglas

Bibliography

Borden, Morton, *Jews, Turks, and Infidels* (Chapel Hill: University of North Carolina Press, 1984).

Brewer, David J., *The United States Is a Christian Nation* (Philadelphia: Winston, 1905).

Bryce, James, *The American Commonwealth*, 3 vols. (New York: Macmillan, 1888).

"The 'Christian Nation' Controversy," 11 *American Lawyer* 70 (1989).

Cases Cited

Beecher v. Wethersby, 95 U.S. 517 (1877).
Church of the Holy Trinity v. United States, 143 U.S. 457 (1892).
Davis v. Beason, 133 U.S. 333 (1890).
Dianese v. Hale, 91 U.S. 13 (1875).
In re Ross, 140 U.S. 453 (1891).
Lynch v. Donnelly, 465 U.S. 668 (1984).
McGowan v. Maryland, 366 U.S. 420 (1961).
Mormon Church v. United States, 136 U.S. 1 (1890).
United States v. Macintosh, 283 U.S. 605 (1931).
Vidal v. Girard's Executors, 43 U.S. 127 (1844).
Zorach v. Clauson, 343 U.S. 306 (1952).
The Antelope, 23 U.S. 66 (1825).
The Slavers, 69 U.S. 350 (1864).

Church of the Holy Trinity v. United States 143 U.S. 457 (1892)

One of the strongest nineteenth-century statements about the role of Christian religion in American public life came from Justice David Brewer in the U.S. Supreme Court's 1892 decision in *Church of the Holy Trinity v. United States*. Brewer wrote for a unanimous Court that "no purpose of action against religion can be imputed to any legislation, state or national, because this is a religious people. . . . [T]his is a Christian nation." The context of Brewer's statement was the Court's consideration of whether, as a matter of statutory interpretation, a federal immigration statute prohibited entry to the United States of an English (Anglican) priest who was under contract to serve a New York church. The Court concluded that Congress did not intend the immigration statute to exclude clergy from entering the country and that any other interpretation would be inconsistent with the religious principles of this country.

The 1885 federal immigration statute in question prohibited any person or entity from paying the cost of passage to the United States of any immigrant who had agreed to perform labor in exchange for the passage. The purpose of the statute was to stem the tide of cheap, unskilled labor into the United States by barring those immigrants who were too poor to pay their own transportation costs. The concern expressed in Congress was that many such laborers did not assimilate into American culture and disrupted the American labor market by depressing wages.

At issue in this case was a decision by the Church of the Holy Trinity, an Episcopal church in New York City, to hire an Englishman and to pay his passage to New York so that he could serve as the church's rector. The U.S. government brought a civil action against the church to recover civil penalties provided for under the immigration statute; the lower court granted the government's request.

The Supreme Court conceded that the literal language of the statute appeared to cover the English rector. The Court concluded, however, that the statute must be construed in light of congressional purpose as well as its literal language. The Court cited convincing legislative history accompanying the statute to support the conclusion that Congress had intended the statute to cover only laborers, not professionals such as clergymen. This was one of the earliest uses of legislative history by the Court.

Justice Brewer, however, was not content to rest his argument merely on what appeared to be the clear legislative purpose of Congress. Brewer proceeded to spend the bulk of the opinion setting forth evidence for the proposition that the United States is a religious—and specifically Christian—nation and that therefore Congress would not have enacted a statute that had an adverse effect on Christian religion. Brewer, the son of a Congregationalist missionary to Asia Minor, quoted several colonial charters, state constitutions, and court decisions that referred to the importance of Christian belief in the affairs of the American people; cited the practice of various legislative bodies of beginning their sessions with prayer; and noted the large number of churches and Christian charitable organizations that exist in every community in the country as evidence that this is a Christian nation. In so doing, Brewer expressed the prevailing nineteenth-century Protestant view that America is a Christian nation.

Brewer expounded on the influence of Christianity on American life in other opinions, such as *Fong Yue Ting v. United States* (1893), and in a book, *The United States Is a Christian Nation,* based on a series of lectures that he delivered at Haverford College.

Davison M. Douglas

Bibliography

Brewer, David J., *The United States Is a Christian Nation* (Philadelphia: Winston, 1905).

Bryce, James, *The American Commonwealth,* 3 vols., (New York: Macmillan, 1888).

Kurland, Philip, *Religion and the Law: Of Church and State and the Supreme Court* (Chicago: Aldine, 1962).

Cases Cited

Church of the Holy Trinity v. United States, 143 U.S. 457 (1892).

Fong Yue Ting v. United States, 149 U.S. 698 (1893).

Church of the Lukumi Babalu Aye, Inc. and Ernesto Pichardo v. City of Hialeah 508 U.S. 520 (1993)

Religious liberty is often regarded as one of the cornerstones of the freedom enjoyed by Americans. Indeed, many of those who first came to settle America were motivated by a desire to escape the religious intolerance and persecution that pervaded the political and social institutions in much of Europe and the rest of the world. But even in a culture that professes a strong commitment to the values of religious freedom and religious pluralism, pressures toward conformity have arisen to challenge the scope and depth of that commitment.

Enforcing Conventional Norms

When religious individuals or communities have sought to engage in rituals that have been perceived to run counter to conventional norms, they have frequently been met by public criticism, hostility, and repression. One example of such reactions can be found in efforts by the City of Hialeah, Florida, to prevent the Church of the Lukumi Babalu Aye from establishing a church and practicing the ritual of animal sacrifice.

The Church of the Lukumi Babalu Aye and its congregants practice the Santería religion (the Lukumi religion, sometimes referred to as Yoba or Yoruba), which originated almost four thousand years ago with the Bantu people of Africa. During the sixteenth through eighteenth centuries many Santería practitioners were enslaved and brought to the eastern region of Cuba. As slaves and later as free people they were subjected to pervasive discrimination and social stigma because of their religious beliefs and practices, which were forbidden until they began to be syncretized with Catholicism. Adherents of Santería largely remained "underground" when they began to emigrate to the United States from Cuba in the 1950s and 1960s. A principal reason for the failure of Santería to receive significant social acceptance in the United States—and especially in South Florida, where as many as sixty thousand adherents now live—is widespread public disapproval or suspicion of some of its central tenets and rituals. One of the most controversial of these rituals is the practice of animal sacrifice.

In the Santería faith, animals—including chickens, goats, sheep, and turtles—are sacrificed as an integral part of religious ceremonies. The sacrifice is performed by a priest and an apprentice. The animals are killed in a usually brief ceremony; an animal is placed on a table, and a priest punctures its neck with a knife. Sometimes the animals are consumed following a ceremony; sometimes—for example, when the sacrifice is part of a healing rite—they are not consumed.

In June 1987 the church leased land in the City of Hialeah and decided to establish a house of worship as well as a school, cultural center, and museum on the property. Church members, led by their president and priest, Ernesto Pichardo, began the process of applying to the local zoning authorities for the appropriate licenses and approvals, and they made other arrangements to prepare the property for the construction of the planned facilities. Although the church encountered a number of obstacles in obtaining the necessary permits and approvals, by early August 1987 most of these had been secured. But final, legal approval to build the place of worship was not easily obtained. As noted, Santería incorporates a number of practices and rituals of which many citizens of Hialeah disapproved.

When the church announced its intention to come out into the open and practice its religious rituals, including animal sacrifice, it met with considerable hostility and opposition. The city council held an emergency public session at which residents, members of the council, and city officials made impassioned arguments against permitting the church to operate within the city. The crowd that attended the emergency council session interrupted statements that were critical of Santería with cheers; the brief comments made on behalf of the church by Pichardo, its leader and priest, were met with taunts. The city attorney commented, "This community will not tolerate religious practices which are abhorrent to its citizens," and Councilman Cardoso said that the Santería adherents were "in violation of everything this country stands for." The council's president, Councilman Echevarria, asked, "What can we do to prevent the Church from opening?"

The answer to this question came in the form of a number of ordinances that the city council adopted in September 1987. Four ordinances specifically addressed the practice of animal sacrifice. The first noted the residents' "great concern regarding the possibility of public ritualistic animal sacrifices" and declared the city policy "to oppose the ritual sacrifice of animals" within Hialeah. It also announced the intent to prosecute any person or corporation engaging in such a practice. A second ordinance prohibited animal sacrifice, defined as "to unnecessarily kill, torment, torture, or mutilate an animal in a public or private ritual or ceremony not for the primary purpose of food consumption," and it prohibited owning or possessing an animal "intending to use such animal for food purposes." It limited its application to the sacrifice of animals for "any type of ritual" and contained an exemption for slaughtering by "licensed establishment[s]" of animals "specifically raised for food purposes." A third ordinance—declaring that animal sacrifice was contrary to the public health, safety, and morals of Hialeah—provided that "[i]t shall be unlawful for any person, persons, corporations or associations to sacrifice any animal within the corporate limits of the City of Hialeah, Florida." The fourth ordinance provided an exemption to the prohibition against slaughtering animals for the slaughter or processing of "small numbers of hogs and/or cattle per week in accordance with exemption provided by state law." All these ordinances were passed by unanimous vote. Violations were punishable by fines of up to $500 and by up to sixty days in jail.

In addition, the city adopted an ordinance which incorporated a Florida statute that prohibited cruelty to animals. Although this statute was limited to the "unnecessary" or "cruel" killing of animals, according to an opinion solicited by Hialeah officials from the Florida attorney general's office, the ritual sacrifice of animals was considered unnecessary and thus was subject to the law's prohibition.

Violation of Free Exercise?

All these ordinances prohibited the church from obtaining the necessary official permission to begin operations at its facility—at least, as long as it intended to perform animal sacrifices there. In response, the church and Ernesto Pichardo filed suit in federal court seeking a declaration that the city's efforts to prevent the church from establishing its place of worship and to prevent its devotees from practicing the rituals of Santería violated the federal constitutional guarantee of religious liberty. Specifically, the plaintiffs claimed that the city's actions violated the Free Exercise Clause of the First Amendment to the U.S. Constitution. They sought an injunction to block the enforcement of the ordinances described, along with damages for the violation of their constitutional rights.

In 1989 the federal district court rejected the free exercise challenge. Stating that constitutional protection for religious freedom was not absolute and noting that the ordinances regulated religious conduct instead of beliefs, the court held that the ordinances did not represent efforts to target religious activity as such. Instead, the court found that the ordinances were animated by secular purposes and that they had secular effects—including the prevention of cruelty to animals, protection of the public from potential health hazards associated with the maintenance and disposal of animals used for sacrifice, and the protection of children from any psychological trauma that might be associated with observing animal sacrifices. The court found these secular purposes and effects to be "compelling" and held that they outweighed any burdens which the prohibition of sacrifices might impose on Santería adherents. The court refused to grant the plaintiffs an exemption from the ordinances, finding that "a religious exception for Santería practitioners is simply unworkable." The Court of Appeals for the Eleventh Circuit affirmed the district court's decision in a one-paragraph decision, and so the case proceeded on appeal to the U.S. Supreme Court in *Church of the Lukumi Babalu Aye, Inc. and Ernesto Pichardo v. City of Hialeah* (1993).

The Supreme Court's Framework

In a unanimous decision the Court reversed the lower courts and held that the Hialeah ordinances did indeed violate the First Amendment's guarantee of religious liberty. In an opinion delivered by Justice Anthony Kennedy the Court rejected the argument that the challenged ordinances could be justified in terms of secular purposes or effects. The Court applied the analytical framework that had been established in *Employment Division, Department of Human Resources of Oregon v. Smith* (1990). According to that framework, the free exercise guarantee comes into play only when the government regulates religious beliefs or enacts (or applies) regulations aimed at religiously motivated conduct. When a regulation is neutral with respect to religion and is generally applicable both to religious and to nonreligious conduct, the fact that it imposes obstacles to religious conduct is of no constitutional consequence.

The Court concluded that the challenged ordinances were not neutral with respect to religion and that they were not laws of general application. None of the ordinances explicitly referred to the Santería religion or its rituals, but the Court's analysis of their structure (e.g., the nature of the activity regulated, the nature of the activity left unregulated, and the scope of the prohibitions in light of the secular purposes offered in their defense by the city)—along with the legislative history leading up to the ordinances' enactment—led the Court to conclude that the ordinances constituted "religious gerrymandering." The Court noted, for example, that the ordinances' exemption of the killing of animals for the primary purpose of food consumption allowed almost all killings of animals *except for* religious sacrifice. The Court took special note of the fact that the ordinances did not prohibit the kosher slaughter of animals—a fact of particular significance given the large Jewish population in South Florida. Noting that "[t]he Free Exercise Clause protects against governmental hostility [toward religion] which is masked, as well as overt," the Court concluded that "[t]he record in this case compels the conclusion that suppression of the central elements of the Santería worship service was the object of the ordinances."

Having found Hialeah's ordinances to have been enacted for the purpose of prohibiting Santería animal sacrifice, the Court applied "strict judicial scrutiny." According to this test, the city was required to show that the ordinances advanced "interests of the highest order" and that they were "narrowly tailored in pursuit of those interests." The Court noted that only in "rare cases" could a law withstand this test, and it found that this was not such a case. Most often, when the Court applies strict scrutiny, it invalidates laws because they are not narrowly tailored to further the interests advanced on their behalf. This was the case here: The Court found that the ordinances were both too broad and too restrictive in terms of furthering such interests as public health and prevention of cruelty to animals. Only religious conduct that implicated these interests was prohibited, and only religious rituals of Santería were affected (whereas kosher slaughter was not affected). The Court went on to conclude that the ordinances were also unconstitutional because they did not advance legitimate and compelling government interests, in part because any legitimate interests were furthered only marginally, if at all.

In addition to Justice Kennedy's majority opinion, three justices filed concurring opinions. Justice Antonin Scalia (joined by Chief Justice William Rehnquist) wrote separately to argue that the Hialeah ordinances were unconstitutional because their purpose or object was to disfavor the religion of Santería. But he objected to that part of Justice Kennedy's opinion which found that the city council was subjectively motivated by animosity or disapproval of Santería, and that this religious motivation was a reason for finding the ordinances to be unconstitutional. According to Scalia, whether or not religious motivation exists is simply irrelevant in analyzing First Amendment religion clauses.

Justice David Souter also wrote a concurring opinion, largely devoted to criticizing the Supreme Court's 1990 decision in the *Smith* case and arguing that the Court's conclusion there—that the First Amendment does not apply to neutral laws of general applicability—should be reexamined.

Finally, Justice Harry Blackmun wrote a concurring opinion (joined by Justice Sandra Day O'Connor), which also criticized the First Amendment analysis adopted by the Court in *Smith*. Justice Blackmun also made a point that is worth emphasizing: He agreed that the Hialeah ordinances were unconstitutional because they singled out Santería sacrificial practice for disadvantageous treatment; however, he noted that this does not necessarily mean that the government is powerless to enact laws whose purpose is clearly secular—say the prevention of cruelty to animals—and to apply such laws in ways that burden or even prohibit religiously motivated conduct. As long as such a law is generally applicable to both religiously and nonreligiously motivated conduct, it would probably be upheld against constitutional challenge under the *Smith* analysis. And even those justices who have expressed disagreement with *Smith* might well also find that such a general law could constitutionally be applied to religiously motivated animal sacrifice. As Justice Blackmun noted: "[T]he question whether the Free Exercise Clause would require a religious exemption from a law that sincerely pursued the goal of protecting animals from cruel treatment" is one that the Court was not required to reach in this case. Therefore, that question is still open.

Richard B. Saphire

Bibliography

Annotation, "Development in the Law: Religion and the State," 100 *Harvard Law Review* 1606–1781 (1987).

McConnell, Michael W., "The Origins and Historical Understanding of Free Exercise of Religion," 103 *Harvard Law Review* 1409–1517 (1990).

Cases Cited

Church of the Lukumi Babalu Aye, Inc. and Ernesto Pichardo v. City of Hialeah, 508 U.S. 520 (1993).

Employment Division, Department of Human Resources of Oregon v. Smith, 494 U.S. 872 (1990).

Church of the New Song

From the confines of a federal prison in Atlanta, Georgia, Harry Theriault created the "Church of the New Song." After obtaining his Doctor of Divinity certification through a mail-order application, Theriault appointed himself Bishop of Tellus, and he ordained fellow inmate Jerry Dorrough to be First Revelation Minister of the Church of the New Song. Theriault based the organization's religious component on the Book of Revelation, claiming belief in the existence of a supreme being, the "Eclat." Theriault testified that, even though he began the church as a game, he became serious about it after noticing the sincere effect it had on many of his fellow inmates. Prison chaplains, however, denied his requests to hold religious services on the basis that the Church of the New Song was not a "recognized" religion. Theriault responded with threats of violence and bloodshed. As a result, prison officials placed him in solitary confinement.

In *Theriault v. Carlson* (N.D. Ga., 1972) (*Theriault I*) Theriault filed suit in federal court against five parties including Norman A. Carlson, Director of the Bureau of Prisons; Reverend Frederick Silber, Director of Chaplaincy Services; the prison warden; and the chaplains employed by the prison. Theriault claimed that the denial of his requests to hold his own religious services was a violation of the First Amendment's Establishment and Free Exercise Clauses. The court disposed of the Establishment Clause claim, finding that the prison satisfied its responsibility to provide for all inmates. The Bureau of Prisons hired professionals to effectuate necessary programs. This particular Atlanta prison employed both a Catholic and a Protestant chaplain, and they served the religious needs of all the inmates, regardless of their denominations. The court found this accommodation reasonable, because the prison could not feasibly provide for the individual religious needs of each inmate. The other option would be to ban all religious services; however, the court held that this would be an impermissible intrusion on the free exercise rights of the prisoners.

Turning to the free exercise claim, the court looked at the chaplains' denial of Theriault's requests to hold religious services on the basis that Church of the New Song was not a "recognized" religion. The court found that this clearly violated the Free Exercise

Clause, which prohibits the imposition of standards on one's religion. Respondents contended that Theriault's religion was illegitimate, but the court found itself without authority to define religion. Yet the record demonstrated that the members of the Church of the New Song believed in the existence of a supreme being, the Eclat; therefore, the court held that the church met one accepted concept of religion. Because respondents failed to demonstrate the substantial and compelling interest necessary to intrude on a person's First Amendment rights, the court ordered that Theriault and his fellow members be allowed to hold religious services in the prison. In addition, the court ordered that Theriault be released from solitary confinement.

Only days after the court rendered its decision, Theriault was transferred to a prison in LaTuna, Texas, where he was again placed in intermittent solitary confinement for disregarding security regulations and for using physical violence to insist on using the prison chapel for religious services without the prior approval of the prison chaplain. Theriault filed suit in the Western District of Texas (*Theriault II*) to request an evidentiary hearing on allegations that prison officials were denying his right to practice religion. His petition was dismissed on the day it was filed, and he appealed.

Because he was never released from solitary confinement during the few days before the Georgia court's decision in Theriault I and his transfer to Texas, Theriault filed another suit, *Theriault v. Carlson* (N.D. Ga., 1973) (*Theriault III*), asking the court to find defendants Carlson and Silber in contempt of court. Theriault also claimed that the Texas officials wrongfully placed him in solitary confinement during his first four days in Texas. The Georgia court found Carlson and Silber in contempt of court but deferred punishment until the appeal of the case was concluded. In addition, the court found itself without jurisdiction to consider the complaints against the Texas officials.

The two Georgia district court cases and the Texas district court case were consolidated on appeal in *Theriault v. Carlson* (5th Cir. 1974). Here the Fifth Circuit admonished the Georgia district court in *Theriault I* for failing to give adequate consideration to the government's claim that the movement was nothing more than a game by Theriault. Because "First Amendment freedoms are not absolute," the court held that an important governmental interest justified restrictions. The appellate court then remanded the case to the Texas district court for further findings to decide whether petitioners' beliefs were sincere. In addition, the appellate court reversed, annulled, and set aside the court's finding of contempt by Carlson and Silber in *Theriault III*.

To determine whether petitioners' First Amendment rights had been infringed, the Texas district court, in *Theriault v. Silber* (W.D. Tex., 1975), referred to the test created in *United States v. Seeger* (1965), which looked at whether the beliefs are sincerely held and whether these beliefs, in the minds of the petitioners, are religious. Applying this test to the facts, the Texas district court held that the Church of the New Song was not a religion but instead was "a masquerade designed to obtain First Amendment protection for acts which otherwise would be unlawful and/or reasonably disallowed by the various prison authorities." As a result, Theriault and his followers were not entitled to First Amendment protection.

Theriault responded by filing suit again. In this case, *Theriault v. Silber* (W.D. Tex., 1978), Theriault submitted additional evidence in an attempt to prove that the Church of the New Song was a religious organization. The Texas district court affirmed its 1975 finding that the church was not a religion and, therefore, was not protected under the First Amendment. In addition, the court found that because of his prisoner status, Theriault did not have unrestricted use over a prison chapel even if his church were entitled to First Amendment protection. The court held that his status as an inmate takes away his right of freedom and subjects him to rules and disciplinary restraints. As a result, prisoners' First Amendment rights are uniquely limited, and the state may restrict their religious acts if it shows both a substantial threat to the public and a compelling state interest.

Two years later Theriault brought another suit, *Church of the New Song v. the Establishment of Religion on Taxpayers' Money in the Federal Bureau of Prisons* (7th Cir. 1980), claiming prison officials were unconstitutionally infringing on the organization's right to practice religion freely. The court dismissed the case under the doctrine of res judicata.

Laurilyn A. Goettsch

Bibliography

Mueller, Michael J. "Abusive pro se Plaintiffs in the Federal Courts: Proposals for Judicial Control," 18 *Michigan Journal of Law Reform* 93–164 (1984).

Senn, Stephen, "The Prosecution of Religious Fraud," 17 *Florida State University Law Review* 325–252 (1990).

Cases Cited

Church of the New Song v. the Establishment of Religion on Taxpayers' Money in the Federal Bureau of Prisons, 620 F. 2d 648 (7th Cir. 1980).

Theriault v. Carlson, 339 F. Supp. 375 (N.D. Ga. 1972) vacated 495 F. 2d 390 (1974).

Theriault v. Carlson, 353 F. Supp. 1061 (N.D. Ga. 1973) vacated 495 F. 2d 390 (1974).

Theriault v. Carlson, 495 F. 2d 390 (5th Cir. 1974).

Theriault v. Silber, 391 F. Supp. 578, 582 (W.D. Tex. 1975).

Theriault v. Silber, 453 F. Supp. 254 (W.D. Tex. 1978).

United States v. Seeger, 380 U.S. 163 (1965).

Church Property after the American Revolution

After the Revolutionary War the Anglican Church was a target of efforts by newly independent states to seize property owned by loyalists. In cases such as *Terrett v. Taylor* (1815) and *Society for the Propagation of the Gospel in Foreign Parts v. New-Haven* (1823) the Supreme Court held that the Revolution had not changed property rights. The more difficult question was whether a state could deprive a religious corporation of its property as part of the state's disestablishment of religion. Courts generally protected the religious corporation, although the reasoning was not always clear and the surviving churches did not always have corporate status under state law. The best illustration of the perplexing responses is Justice Joseph Story's opinion in *Terrett.*

Terrett grew out of a Virginia statute of 1802—one in a series of enactments aimed at eliminating special privileges given to the Episcopal Church. The 1802 act provided that all property belonging to the Episcopal Church on the dissolution of the British government had devolved on the citizens of Virginia. To exercise the rights of the people of Virginia, the statute authorized the overseers of the poor to sell *glebe land* when it became vacant and to use the proceeds to pay the debts of the parish or for any other nonreligious purpose. (Glebe land is land owned by a church but not used specifically for church buildings. The glebe often included a house for the Anglican priest, farmland, and possibly rental property. Most Anglican churches in Virginia had some—and often substantial—glebe lands at the time of the Revolution.)

The Episcopal Church challenged the statute, first in the Virginia courts, where an evenly divided court upheld the statute in *Turpin v. Locket* (1804). The church then turned to the federal circuit courts, where it met with greater success in *Terrett.*

In *Terrett,* the vestry of the Fairfax parish Episcopal Church sought to enjoin the overseers and the church wardens from asserting a claim to church property, which the vestry wanted to sell. The particular property was 516 acres of glebe land that the vestry had purchased in 1770; by the time of the Virginia statute, however, the land was in the District of Columbia. Thus the church initially sued in the federal circuit court for the District of Columbia. That court was evenly divided, and thus the case went to the U.S. Supreme Court.

Justice Joseph Story's sweeping opinion for the Supreme Court sided with the vestry on a number of grounds, no one of which was clearly a federal constitutional point. He might well have written no more than that Virginia lacked the power to deal with the land after it had become part of the exclusive jurisdiction of the District of Columbia. But Story ranged far from that narrow point. He began with a reference to Virginia's guarantee of the free exercise of religion. That guarantee, according to Story, meant that Virginia could not establish a church; but churches could own property. Once churches owned property, they were protected from loss by such principles as the common law, "common sense," and "eternal justice."

Anticipating his opinion in *Dartmouth College v. Woodward* (1819), Story also reasoned that "principles of natural justice" as well as "the spirit and the letter of the constitution of the United States" barred the state from interfering with the rights of a private corporation. Although Story offered no explanation in *Terrett* of why the church was a private corporation, his opinion was the basis for argument in *Dartmouth College.*

Terrett was also the basis for a later decision in which religion played a less prominent role, *Society for the Propagation of the Gospel.* (1823). The society challenged a 1794 Vermont statute which declared that lands previously granted to the society were transferred to town governments for support of schools. Justice Bushrod Washington closely followed both *Terrett* and *Dartmouth College* in upholding the challenge. Washington rejected the state's contention that the Revolution had deprived the society of its capacity to hold property. He reasoned that a corporation had the same rights as an individual; and neither right was altered by a revolution. He then read the equation of "individual" with "corporation" into the 1783 peace treaty between the United States and Britain. The treaty prohibited the confiscation of land in the United States based on the side taken by its owner during the Revolutionary War. Justice Washington concluded that the Vermont statute contravened the treaty insofar as it transferred lands based on the fact that the owner was an alien.

Terrett and other similar cases, therefore, represent the courts' beginning efforts to redefine the public and private spheres in the early nineteenth century, while at the same time attempting to safeguard the religious content of American law.

Walter F. Pratt, Jr.

Bibliography

Buckley, Thomas E., S.J., "Evangelicals Triumphant: The Baptists' Assault on the Virginia Gelbes, 1786–1801," 45 *William and Mary Quarterly,* 3rd ser., 33–69 (1988).

Cases Cited

Dartmouth College v. Woodward, 17 U.S. (4 Wheat.) 518 (1819).

Society for the Propagation of the Gospel in Foreign Parts v. New-Haven, 21 U.S. (8 Wheat.) 464 (1823).

Terrett v. Taylor, 13 U.S. (9 Cranch) 43 (1815).

Turpin v. Locket, 6 Call 113, 10 Va. 113 (1804).

City of Boerne v. P. F. Flores, Archbishop of San Antonio, and the United States 521 U.S. 507 (1997)

The Supreme Court's 1997 decision in *City of Boerne v. P. F. Flores, Archbishop of San Antonio, and the United States* (1997) declared the Religious Freedom Restoration Act (RFRA) unconstitutional on separation of power grounds. The RFRA's enactment was in direct response to the Court's ruling in *Employment Division, Department of Human Resources of Oregon v. Smith* (1990), which dramatically changed how the Court interpreted free exercise claims under the First Amendment. By enacting the statute, Congress intended to grant individuals more protection than the Constitution required as interpreted by *Smith.*

In *Smith,* Oregon had a criminal statute that outlawed the use of numerous forms of narcotics—including peyote, even when used for religious purposes—and that allowed the state to deny unemployment benefits for those who were dismissed from their jobs because of religious-inspired use of narcotics. The Court stated that the precedent of *Sherbert v. Verner* (1963) had only invalidated governmental action in cases which dealt with the denial of unemployment compensation. Furthermore, in recent years the Supreme Court has refused to apply the test outside the unemployment field. (See *Bowen, Secretary of Health and Human Services, et al. v. Roy* [1986].) The effect of this case was to bring the test for free exercise back to the standard used in *Reynolds v. United States* (1879). There the Court stated that to exempt an individual from a law because it did not coincide with the person's religious beliefs would permit the person to "become a law unto himself" and that such an interpretation went against constitutional tradition and common sense.

The 103rd Congress passed the RFRA with a unanimous vote in the House and only three dissenters in the Senate. President Clinton signed it into law in November 1993. The statute states Congress's finding that "laws neutral toward religion may burden religious exercise as surely as laws intended to interfere with religious exercise." The Supreme Court's decision in *Smith* "virtually eliminated the requirement that the government justify burdens on religious exercise imposed by laws neutral towards religion."

Congress determined that the compelling interest test before *Smith* was "a workable test for striking sensible balances between religious liberty and competing prior governmental interests." The purposes of the statute are to "restore the compelling interest test as set forth in *Sherbert* and *Wisconsin v. Yoder* (1972)" and to guarantee its application and to "provide a claim or defense to those whose religious exercise is substantially burdened by government."

Under the statute the "government shall not substantially burden a person's exercise of religion even if the burden results from a rule of general applicability" except when the government can "demonstrate that application of the burden to the person is (1) in furtherance of a compelling governmental interest; and (2) is the least restrictive means of furthering that compelling governmental interest." Under section 6(a) the statute applies to all federal and state law whether adopted before or after the enactment of the RFRA. Section 7 specifically states that "nothing in this Act shall be construed to affect, interpret, or in any way address that portion of the First Amendment prohibiting laws respecting the establishment of religion." It specifically excludes the granting of funds, benefits, or exemptions to the extent permissible under the Establishment Clause as not constituting a violation of the act. In addition to providing a cause of action or a defense, the statute provides for legal fees.

In *City of Boerne v. Flores* the Archbishop of San Antonio, in response to a growing congregation, had applied for a building permit for the expansion of a church located in Boerne, Texas. The local zoning board denied the permit based on a city ordinance governing the preservation of buildings located in a designated historic district. This, according to the city, included the church building in question. The archbishop brought suit in federal district court challenging the denial of the permit under the RFRA, claiming that the ordinance placed a "substantial burden" on the church's free exercise of religion.

The district court found that Congress violated the separation of powers doctrine by displacing the authority of the judiciary to say "what the law is" as established in *Marbury v. Madison* (1803). On appeal, however, the Fifth Circuit reversed and found that Congress had the authority to enact the statute under the precedent set forth in *Katzenbach v. Morgan* (1966) and interpretation of Section 5 of the Fourteenth Amendment.

The Supreme Court reversed and found the statute unconstitutional on separation of power grounds. In its majority opinion written by Justice Kennedy and joined by Chief Justice Rehnquist, Justice Ginsburg, and Justice Thomas, the Court focused solely on the question of Congress's authority to enact the RFRA under the Enforcement Clause in Section 5 of the Fourteenth Amendment. The Court stated that Congress does have the authority to enact legislation to enforce the religion clauses. This authority, however, is limited to enforcement that "is only preventive or remedial" *(South Carolina v. Katzenbach* [1966]). The Court found that, in this case, Congress had made a substantive decision about the meaning of the religion clauses and then had used the statute to enforce that interpretation. "Legislation which alters the Free Exercise Clause's meaning cannot be said to be enforcing the clause. Congress does not enforce a constitutional right by changing what the right is."

By comparing the RFRA with the Voting Rights Act, the Court stated that, although Congress does have the right to enact preventative measures, they are only appropriate "when there is reason to believe that many of the laws affected by congressional enactment have significant likelihood of being unconstitutional." In comparing the legislative records, the Court pointed to the documentation about voting rights that was presented in Congress in 1965. Sufficient evidence showed that the states were using literacy tests in an intentionally discriminatory manner in order to prevent African Americans from voting. With the RFRA, Congress had no evidence on which to claim that the states were writing generally applicable laws with the intention of harming religious minorities. The only incidents pointed to in the legislative record were laws that put only an incidental burden on religion and that showed no hostility or animus.

In addition to the lack of support, the RFRA's "most serious shortcoming" is that the law is so sweeping in its coverage that it cannot be understood "to be responsive to, or designed to prevent, unconstitutional behavior." The statute intrudes on every level of federal and state government, displaces laws regardless of subject matter, applies to all law adopted before or after the statute, and has no termination date or mechanism. The RFRA is not designed to identify and counteract specific laws that are likely to be unconstitutional, and thus it severely intrudes into the states' traditional "prerogatives and general authority to regulate for the health and welfare of their citizens."

Three Justices—Breyer, O'Connor, and Souter—dissented from the majority opinion.

Justice Souter dissented solely on procedural grounds, feeling that the writ of certiorari should be dismissed as being improvidently granted. He felt that the case should be sent down for reargument in order to review the principles of *Smith,* since there was no hearing, briefing, or argument before the Court on the *Smith* decision.

Justice O'Connor wrote the main dissent but stated, "if I agreed with the Court's standard in *Smith,* I would join the opinion." Because the majority assumed that the precedent of *Smith* is correct, she could not agree with their findings. She used her opinion to state that the precedent of *Smith* was wrongly decided in light of the historical background and precedent and should thus be revisited by the Court.

Breyer concurred in O'Connor's opinion, agreeing that the Court should set the case for reargument to determine the validity of *Smith.* Yet he did not find it necessary to consider the question of whether Section 5 would authorize Congress to enact the legislation.

Concurring with the majority's decision, Justice Scalia (joined by Justice Stevens in part) wrote a separate opinion to respond to Justice O'Connor's claim that history supports a result contrary to the one reached in *Smith.* Scalia felt that the historical enactments which O'Connor cited are in fact more consistent with *Smith*'s interpretation of free exercise. In addition, he stated that, while the dissent has great public support and attraction, the issue in *Smith* was whether the people or the courts should control the outcome of such cases. The people through their representatives, not the courts, have the power to determine who should be exempted from general laws such as zoning. Justice Stevens added to Scalia's opinion by stating that he felt the RFRA violated the Establishment Clause of the Constitution by giving governmental preference to religion over irreligion. He is the only justice who made a reference to the religious issues involved in the case.

Melissa Day

Bibliography

Mangrum, R. Collin, "The Falling Star of Free Exercise and Substantive Due Process Entitlement Claims in City of Boerne v. Flores," 31 *Creighton Law Review* 693–710 (1998).

McConnell, Michael, "Comment: Institutions and Interpretations: A Critique of *City of Boerne v. Flores,*" 111 *Harvard Law Review* 153–195 (1997).

"Symposium: Reflections on *City of Boerne v. Flores,*" 39 *William and Mary Law Review* 597–960 (1998).

Cases Cited

Bowen, Secretary of Health and Human Services, et al. v. Roy, 476 U.S. 693 (1986).

City of Boerne v. P. F. Flores, Archbishop of San Antonio, and the United States, 521 U.S. 507 (1997).

Employment Division, Department of Human Resources of Oregon v. Smith, 494 U.S. 872 (1990).

Katzenbach v. Morgan, 384 U.S. 641 (1966).

Marbury v. Madison, 5 U.S. 137 (1803).

Sherbert v. Verner, 374 U.S. 398 (1963).

South Carolina v. Katzenbach, 383 U.S. 301 (1966).

Reynolds v. United States, 98 U.S. 145 (1879).

Wisconsin v. Yoder, 406 U.S. 205 (1972).

Religious Freedom Restoration Act, Pub. L. 103–141, 107 Stat. 1488 (1993).

Civil Religion

Sociologist Robert Bellah, in reflecting on the role of religion in the United States, is generally credited with coining the concept of "civil religion"; for him it consisted of the myths, rituals, and beliefs that constitute, describe, and justify a society's political and social order to itself. Bellah argued that, in an increasingly secularized society, American civil religion began to play the kind of role that true religions play elsewhere and had played in earlier periods in the United States.

Civil religion intersects with the law in two ways. First, legal documents are among the most important in the American civil religion. According to Irving Kristol, "The Flag, the Declaration [of Independence, and] the Constitution . . . constitute the holy trinity" of American civil religion. Like many sacred documents, the Constitution is a reference point for arguments by partisans of nearly every position on public policy. Even when partisans concede that the Constitution does not speak directly to their concerns, they often attempt to invoke the "spirit" of the Constitution, or the "values" it embodies, to justify their proposals. Another legal document that is often posited as part of American civil religion is the Virginia Statute on Religious Liberty, which serves as a reference point for discussions of separation of church and state.

Law professor Sanford Levinson uses theological terms to suggest how the Constitution, as part of civil religion, resembles other sacred texts. Examining controversies over constitutional interpretation, he distinguishes between "Protestant" and "Catholic" traditions of constitutional interpretation. These traditions differ in two ways, according to Levinson. The first difference involves whether there is a single authoritative interpreter of the Constitution or whether every person has equal standing to interpret it. Based on the analogy to the ultimate authority of the pope, a "Catholic" interpreter insists that Supreme Court constitutional interpretations exclude contrary interpretations. Pursuant to this view, Governor Orval Faubus's resistance to school desegregation in Little Rock, Arkansas, was wrong simply because the Supreme Court had definitively determined that school segregation was unconstitutional—even though no specific decision regarding Little Rock had yet been made.

A "Protestant" interpreter, in contrast, insists that every citizen, including public officials, has an obligation to interpret the Constitution personally. In this view, the mere fact that the Supreme Court has made a decision is not enough. Abraham Lincoln's response to the decision in *Dred Scott v. Sandford* (1857), during his debates with Stephen Douglas, exemplifies a "Protestant" stance. Lincoln conceded that the decision was legally binding on the parties to the case, but he refused to take the Court's decision as making it anticonstitutional for him and his political allies to propose legislation that, on a fair analysis of the decision, the Court was likely to hold unconstitutional.

The second difference between the traditions, according to Levinson, involves the sources for constitutional interpretation. Recalling the divisions between Protestants and Catholics in the fifteenth and sixteenth centuries, Levinson argues that the "Protestant" tradition in constitutional interpretation regards the Constitution's text as the nearly exclusive source, whereas the "Catholic" tradition looks more broadly to the principles articulated over time in Supreme Court decisions, and to society's values as reflected in its social decisions ratified through law.

Levinson notes that, when we examine discourse about the Constitution, we will find people taking a "Protestant" position on the exclusive authority of the Supreme Court and a "Catholic" one on the relevance of precedents, traditions, and the like; and similarly we will find people taking a "Catholic" position on authority and a "Protestant" one on the exclusive relevance of constitutional text. Importantly, these divisions do not align neatly with differences between "liberals" and "conservatives" or between proponents of "judicial restraint" and defenders of "judicial activism," and yet they provide illuminating insights into those differences as well.

Civil religion enters constitutional law more directly when the Supreme Court is asked to consider whether religious practices that implicate aspects of civil religion violate the constitutional ban on establishment of religion. Secularization, in depriving some religious symbols of their religious distinctiveness, makes the symbols more relevant, though less important, to a larger number of people. This has two consequences. First, invoking those symbols in public life becomes less contentious because the symbols are less divisive. Second, popular support for invoking the symbols grows to a point where majorities are willing to use them in government's actions. At that point Establishment Clause issues arise.

The modern Supreme Court confronted establishment questions about aspects of civil religion in two sets of cases. In *Engel v. Vitale* (1962) and *School District of Abington Township v. Schempp* (1963) the Court held unconstitutional the practice of having public schoolteachers conduct voluntary prayers for their students. Illustrating the way in which secularization leads to reducing the distinctively religious content of religious practices, the Court's first school prayer decision held impermissible a prayer—drafted by the state's education agency—that read, "Almighty God, we acknowledge our dependence upon Thee, and beg Thy blessings upon us, our parents, our teacher, and our Country." The second decision held unconstitutional a law requiring that ten verses from the Bible be read aloud each day.

These decisions, which barred the states from having school prayers, should be contrasted with the Court's flag salute decision in *West Virginia Board of Education v. Barnette* (1943). There the Court held it unconstitutional to compel children to salute the flag, but it did not bar school systems from conducting flag salute exercises for those who chose to participate. Seen from the perspective of civil religion, the contrast between the flag salute case and the school prayer cases suggests that, in the Court's view, government can support American civil religion when it is truly "civil" (that is, secular) but cannot support those aspects of civil religion that continue to be religious—even if the specifically religious content is much weaker than the sort of religion that takes place in houses of worship.

A generation later the Supreme Court returned to the problems posed by religious practices embedded in American civil religion in two cases involving public support for crèches and menorahs. In *Lynch v. Donnelly* (1984) the Court allowed a city to maintain a crèche as part of a larger Christmas display that included reindeer, Santa Claus, and clowns. In *County of Allegheny v. American Civil Liberties Union* (1989) a fractured Court upheld government support for a large menorah situated next to the city of Pittsburgh's Christmas tree and a statement declaring the city's "salute to liberty," but it barred the county from displaying a crèche, standing alone, in the central stairwell of a county courthouse.

In both cases the Court was sharply divided; there was a strong dissent in *Lynch*, and there was no majority opinion in *County of Allegheny*. The divisions show how difficult a problem the religious dimensions of civil religion pose in constitutional law. By emphasizing in *Lynch* the association of the crèche with the larger celebration of the season and in *County of Allegheny* the "salute to liberty" that the menorah symbolized, the decisions strive to minimize the strictly religious content of the displays. But in minimizing the religious content of the displays, the Court failed to acknowledge what proponents, and perhaps everyone else, understands: that the displays remain religious no matter how diluted the religious content. The constitutional difficulty is that, were the Court to acknowledge the religious content, it would not be easy to explain why government support for this religious display is not an establishment of religion.

American civil religion offers powerful public support for the idea of constitutionalism in the United States and provides some support for the Supreme Court's constitutional decisions no matter what they are. Deference to the Court, which some "Protestant" interpreters dislike, nonetheless supports constitutionalism as a whole. Yet the Court and the Constitution have difficulty dealing with the religious dimensions of civil religion. In this way, by taking the Constitution to be part of civil religion—and by understanding that the Establishment Clause is part of the Constitution—civil religion embodies a contradiction with which the Court continues to struggle.

Mark Tushnet

Bibliography

Levinson, Sanford, *Constitutional Faith* (Princeton, N.J.: Princeton University Press, 1988).

Richey, Russell E., and Donald G. Jones, eds., *American Civil Religion* (New York: Harper & Row, 1974).

Cases Cited

County of Allegheny v. American Civil Liberties Union, 492 U.S. 573 (1989).

Dred Scott v. Sandford, 19 How. (60 U.S.) 393 (1857).

Engel v. Vitale, 370 U.S. 421 (1962).

Lynch v. Donnelly, 465 U.S. 668 (1984).

School District of Abington Township v. Schempp, 374 U.S. 203 (1963).

West Virginia Board of Education v. Barnette, 319 U.S. 624 (1943).

Classical Legal Thought and Religious Perspectives

Classical legal thought, or legal formalism, is the jurisprudence that dominated American law from the second half of the nineteenth century until the 1930s. Its hallmark was the use of abstract concepts, definitions, and principles to resolve legal disputes. Classical legal thought rigorously modeled law on the natural sciences, which in the nineteenth century attained enormous prestige. It conceived of adjudication as the scientific discovery of preexisting, nonpolitical, and nondiscretionary solutions to matters of social controversy.

Classical jurists studied law empirically, primarily by parsing the decisions of appellate courts. To classicists, appellate reports were the juridical analog of observable phenomena in the physical sciences. Jurists studied judicial precedent to uncover fundamental principles of national law, much as scientists studied planetary motion to uncover fundamental principles of physical law. Inspired by Newton's accomplishments in celestial mechanics and optics, classicists envisioned a legal system in which the myriad rules of law were the elaboration of a few initial principles—principles that were themselves discovered in adjudicated cases whose outcome they governed. In classical law, most controversies had "right" answers dictated by (and deduced from) a small number of abstract principles; "right" answers were those which were logically consistent with legal precedent and legal principles.

Classical legal thought was a complex intellectual enterprise that served multiple needs and aspirations of the nineteenth-century bar. Classical jurisprudence found order and harmony among the welter of American decisional law whose unity was collapsing under the stress of contradictory decisions in over thirty courts of last resort. It justified the prestige and authority of the legal profession by depicting law as a learned endeavor. It stressed that law was reason and knowledge rather than will and politics, encouraging American courts to resist the tide of social welfare laws that legislatures were just then beginning to enact. Classical legal thought was the jurisprudence of the generation of judges who read laissez-faire into the Constitution's Due Process Clause, rendering decisions like *Lochner v. New York* (1905), which voided legislation forbidding bakers from working more than ten hours a day.

Historians have emphasized classicism's focus on science to depict it as the jurisprudence of America's first generation of secular jurists. Before the advent of classicism, legal thought blended religious tradition and common-law precedent to present law as a morally based system of rules. Law was a branch of moral science and thus conformed to its norms. In this account, classical jurists—whose lot it was to come to grips with the Darwinian revolution in social theory—substituted a belief in empirical science for religious conviction, assuaging the dread of their emergent agnosticism.

Yet this historiography overstates classical orthodoxy's secularism. Some classical jurists were secularists, particularly those associated with the Harvard Law School of Christopher Columbus Langdell. But most classicists were mainstream, nineteenth-century Protestants, and religious belief was among the most important sources of classicism's appeal. For these classicists, religious conviction provided the normative force behind the otherwise-arbitrary rules that empirical analysis discovered in common-law precedent.

Along with many nineteenth-century Americans, most classical jurists maintained a belief in a transcendent, Christian God who created a universe endowed with physical and moral law. The problem faced by these classicists was to connect the body of American law with God's moral ordinances. Although classical jurists prided themselves on adopting modern empirical methods of study, many also met—rather than abandoned—the challenge of crossing the boundary between the "is" discovered by positive study and the "ought" propounded by moral discourse.

Religiously informed classicists drew from two theories that enabled them to cross the "is/ought" boundary and to make classical law both a scientific and a deontological study. One theory derived from "the Scottish philosophy," also known as the "philosophy of common sense," which substantially influenced teaching at America's seminaries, colleges, and universities throughout the nineteenth century. Premised on a psychological theory that traces back to Aristotle, the Scottish philosophy taught that God endowed the human mind with a faculty of moral sense which perceived the difference between good and evil in human actions. By this theory, a judge hearing a case intuited its morally appropriate outcome without necessarily understanding the supporting reasons. Through the moral sense, said Joel Bishop,

> "Almighty God"appears in the midst of the tribunal . . . and reveals the right way to the understandings of the judges, as surely as he appears in the tempest on the ocean, and teaches each water-drop where to lie when the wind goes down. . . . And, as the ocean-drops do not know the philosophy of this; so, oftentimes, the judges do not apprehend the true reasons of their decisions. (Bishop 1868)

Legal scholars, however, could observe the pattern of decisional outcomes and could infer their underlying abstract principles. In this regard, judicial decisions functioned as physical events which legal scientists observed and from which they induced unseen governing principles.

The other theory, exemplified by the writings of Francis Wharton, drew from the newly emergent philosophy of historicism. This theory posited that God endowed each race and nationality with differing innate principles of action. The behavior of judges as well as ordinary people was strongly influenced by their inborn propensities. By studying the historic record of action and decision of each society, legal scholars could infer the appropriate rules of behavior for that society. This theory taught that the expression of a race's or nation's immanent spirit interacted with the changing external circumstances of the race or nation. National law was particularistic, in that some rules were appropriate for some societies and not for others; and it was evolutionary, in that appropriate rules for the same society changed as that society's circumstances changed. Undoubtedly influenced by Darwin's teachings, this theory was not fully Darwinian because it did not view human evolution as random and amoral. It postulated that divinely implanted, permanent principles of growth and order guided the process of cultural change.

Thus classical legal thought was a jurisprudence whose single analytic technique masked multiple, conflicting philosophical perspectives. These philosophical perspectives mirrored the diverse perspectives of late-nineteenth-century intellectual life. In nineteenth-century America, most social theorists blended the religious and the secular dimensions of life. Religious perspectives and assumptions permeated secular thinking, supporting and being supported by its increasing empiricism. Classicism was, in part, the jurisprudence of the last generation of Americans in which evangelical beliefs were part of high culture. It was the last time in which many secular theorists studied mundane events to demonstrate God's presence in the world and to understand the world as an expression of God's nature.

Classicism dominated American law during a period of fundamental transition in social theory. In the late nineteenth century, fully secular approaches to the study of nature, human nature, and society initiated their ultimately successful challenge to the fusion of science and religion. Classical legal thought's widespread appeal and longtime influence over American law rested on its being part of this progression in social science and on its ability to straddle both sides of this pivotal change in American social thought. Classical legal thought was a multifarious discipline that bridged the movement of Western intellectual life from traditional, static, natural-law theories to modern, dynamic, positivistic theories of human society.

Stephen A.Siegel

Bibliography

Bishop, Joel, *The First Book of Law* (Boston: Little, Brown, 1868).

Friedman, Lawrence, *A History of American Law,* 2nd ed. (New York: Simon and Schuster, 1985).

Grey, Thomas, "Langdell's Orthodoxy," 45 *University of Pittsburgh Law Review* 1–53 (1983).

Horwitz, Morton, *The Transformation of American Law, 1870–1960* (New York: Oxford University Press, 1992).

Siegel, Stephen, "Joel Bishop's Orthodoxy," 13 *Law and History Review* 215–259 (1995).

Wharton, Francis, *Commentaries on Law* (Philadelphia: Kay, 1884).

Case Cited

Lochner v. New York, 198 U.S. 45 (1905).

Clergy Privilege in Civil and Criminal Litigation

The clergy privilege is an exception to the rule that, when called to do so by a court, people should testify about facts within their knowledge. The clergy privilege, like the better-known attorney-client or doctor-patient privilege, is designed to encourage socially desirable relationships by fostering frank and open confidential communication with members of the clergy acting in their religious capacities by protecting those communications from disclosure in a court of law.

The clergy privilege derives from the ancient belief in the secrecy of the seal of the confessional; it was first recognized by an apostolic church father, Tertullian, in the third century A.D. Since Tertullian, the duty to protect communications under the seal of the confession has been recognized by the papacy and by the Lutheran, Eastern, Methodist, Mennonite, Anabaptist, and Baptist churches. The challenge in defining a modern clergy privilege has been not only to accommodate the changing role of clergy in providing counseling but also to protect the role of clergy in religions, such as Judaism, which have no tradition of confession.

The American priest-penitent privilege does not descend from English common law, which had abolished the privilege in the sixteenth century, around the time of the Reformation. Rather, the privilege is a product of federal and state constitutional protections of the free exercise of religion, state statutory protections, and the Federal Rules of Evidence.

The first reported case in the United States concerning the clergy privilege was *People v. Phillips* (N.Y., 1813), which involved a Roman Catholic priest who returned stolen property to the rightful owner but refused to testify in the grand jury, or at trial, about the identity of the person who gave him the goods. The court upheld the privilege not to testify based on New York State's constitutional provision guaranteeing free exercise of religion. Much of the record of this landmark case was reprinted in *Catholic Lawyer* in 1955. However, only four years later, in *People v. Smith* (1817), New York courts failed to uphold a claim of privilege by a Protestant minister, because the Roman Catholic requirements of confession and secrecy were absent.

In 1828 New York resolved this potential inconsistency and enacted the first statute concerning priest-penitent privilege. Other states soon followed with similar laws, which generally required that the communication must be made (1) in the course of a duty imposed by the church, (2) to a clergyman in his professional capacity, (3) where the communication was intended as confidential, and (4) the communication was penitential in nature.

Currently all fifty states plus Puerto Rico, the Virgin Islands, and the District of Columbia have statutes providing for some form of clergy privilege. The modern statutes differ from each other in terms of whom the statute protects, in what capacity, and whether the privilege may be waived. The legislatures and the courts have broadened or construed statutes to protect rabbis, nuns, intrafaith communications between ecclesiastical officials made in furtherance of a church duty, and Presbyterian Church elders. Some state statutes also protect lay employees of the clergy, or extend the privilege to nonministers who are reasonably perceived to be a minister. In the vast majority of states a priest may not testify unless the confessor waives his or her privilege. The remaining states, with the exceptions of Alabama and Colorado, hold that the priest may never testify, regardless of whether the confessor waives the privilege. In Alabama and Colorado both the penitent and the priest must waive the privilege before the priest can testify.

The scope of the privilege under state law has expanded from confession to a broad range of functions including draft and marriage counseling. However, communications outside the clergyperson's specific capacity generally are not privileged. An example of such a holding is found in *State v. Motherwell* (Wash., 1990).

Currently twenty-seven priest-penitent statutes specifically use the term "rabbi." However, in states where the statute does not refer to rabbis, narrow construction tends to preclude protection of communications with rabbis; for example, a California court reached this conclusion in *Simrin v. Simrin* (Calif., 1965).

The scope of the privilege under state law is critical because of the wording of Rule 501 of the Federal Rules of Evidence, which requires federal courts to apply the state's privilege law whenever state law provides the rule of decision for the merits of the case. In all other matters Rule 501 calls for the development of a federal common law of privilege.

Even before the adoption of Rule 501, federal common law tacitly acknowledged a priest-penitent privilege. In *Totten v. United States* (1876) the U.S. Supreme Court held that public policy forbids any trial which would inevitably lead to the disclosure of matters that the law regards as confidential, referring explicitly to the confidences of the confessional.

Only two modern Supreme Court cases have dealt explicitly with the priest-penitent privilege. In *United States v. Nixon* (1974), while discussing the scope of a president's executive privilege, the Supreme Court noted that "generally, an attorney or priest may not be required to disclose what has been revealed in professional confidence." Although *Trammel v. United States* (1980) directly dealt with the waiver of the spousal privilege, the Supreme Court also stated in dicta that "the priest-penitent privilege recognizes the human need to disclose to a spiritual counselor, in total and absolute confidence, what are believed to be flawed acts or thoughts and to receive priestly consolation and guidance in return."

The courts have yet to address definitively whether the clergy have an affirmative duty to protect innocent third parties. For example, all states require certain persons to report suspected cases of child abuse and to testify in court concerning that abuse. Fifteen states require anyone with reasonable cause to report suspected cases of child abuse regardless of whether the communication that gave rise to the suspicion is protected by law. Only five states—Florida, Kentucky, Oregon, South Carolina, and Wyoming—expressly protect the priest-penitent privilege in this context. In contrast, statutes often distinguish between reporting and testifying. Some go further. For example, the Mississippi statute appears to abrogate the privilege entirely, providing that "any . . . minister . . . or any other person having reasonable cause to suspect that a child . . . is a neglected child or an abused child . . . [must] cause an oral report to be made immediately." However, a 1990 amendment to that statute also expressly preserved the clergy privilege in actual child abuse proceedings. The Arkansas code imposes civil liability on those who fail to report abuse. This presumably includes clergypeople.

The proper interpretation of these statutes raises the same question courts face in any question of privilege. The courts will continue to struggle with assessing the values protected by preserving claims of the clergy privilege and balancing those benefits against the harm to society of not disclosing often-vital information needed to fairly decide questions of secular law.

Spencer Weber Waller
Natasha Leigh Chefetz

Bibliography

Annotation, "Matters to Which the Privilege Covering Communications to Clergymen or Spiritual Adviser Extends," *American Law Reports,* 3rd. ed. (Rochester, N.Y.: Lawyers Co-operative, 1976), 794–838.

Bush, John C., and William Harold Tiemann, *The Right to Silence,* 3rd ed. (Nashville, Tenn.: Arlington, 1989).

Coleman, Phyllis, "'Shrinking' the Clergyperson Exemption to Florida's Mandatory Child Abuse Reporting Statute," 12 *Nova Law Review* 115–145 (1987).

Mitchell, Mary Harter, "Must Clergy Tell? Child Abuse Reporting Requirements versus the Clergy Privilege and Free Exercise of Religion," 71 *Minnesota Law Review* 723–825 (1987).

Note, "Privileged Communications to Clergyman," 1 *Catholic Lawyer* 199–213 (1955).

O'Brien, Raymond, and Michael T. Flannery, "The Pending Gauntlet to Free Exercise: Mandating That Clergy Report Child Abuse," 25 *Loyola Los Angeles Law Review* 1–56 (1991).

Cases and Statutes Cited

People v. Phillips [N.Y., 1813], reprinted in 1 *Western Law Journal* 109 (1843), reprinted in 1 *Catholic Lawyer* 199 (1955).

People v. Smith, 2 *City Hall Recorder* (Rogers) 77 (N.Y. 1817).

Simrin v. Simrin, 233 Cal. App. 2d 90, 43 Cal. Rptr. 376 (5th Dist. 1965).

State v. Motherwell, 114 Wash. 2d 353, 788 P. 2d 1066 (1990).

Totten v. United States, 92 U.S. 105 (1876).

Trammel v. United States, 445 United States 40 (1980).

United States v. Nixon, 418 United States 683 (1974).

Ark. Code Ann. §12-12-504(b) (Michie Supp. 1991).

Mississippi Code Ann. §43-21-353(1) (1972 & Supp. 1991); Miss. Code Ann. §13-1-22 (Supp. 1990).

New York Rev. Stat., para. 72, pt.3, c. VII, art.8 (1828).

Rule 501, Federal Rules of Evidence.

Cleveland v. United States
329 U.S. 14 (1946)

Federal authorities prosecuted Heber Kimball Cleveland and others under the Mann Act (1910), which made it a federal crime to transport across state lines "any woman or girl for the purpose of prostitution or debauchery, or any other immoral purpose." Cleveland and the other defendants were polygamist members of a religious sect, known as Fundamentalists, which broke off from the Mormon Church as the result of the church's discontinuance in 1890 of the practice of polygamy. Each petitioner either transported or aided in the transportation of at least one woman across state lines for the purpose of facilitating a plural marriage to a member of the Fundamentalist religious community. For these religiously inspired activities they each were convicted of violating the Mann Act's prohibition of interstate traffic for "immoral purposes."

In interpreting the Mann Act, the justices relied on at least four interpretivist perspectives: (1) original intent, (2) plain meaning, (3) stare decisis, and (4) public interest or sociological consequences.

With respect to the original intent argument, the majority, concurring, and dissenting opinions all agreed that the Mann Act was aimed "primarily" at the business of interstate commercialized sex. The justices expressed conflicting views of the "plain meaning" of whether the act's proscription against transporting in interstate commerce "any woman or girl for the purpose of prostitution or debauchery, or for any other immoral purpose" reasonably could be interpreted to apply to polygamy. Speaking for the Court, Justice William O. Douglas admitted that, although under the "*ejusdem generis* rule of construction the general words are confined to the class and may not be used to enlarge it," the fact that the common meaning of debauchery includes a variety of lustful indulgences reasonably suggests that the scope of the proscription extends beyond "commercialized sex." Justice Frank Murphy, in dissent, reasoned to the contrary that, because "polygyny, like other forms of marriage, is basically a cultural institution rooted deeply in the religious beliefs and social mores of those societies in which it appears," it cannot be reasonably associated with the genus associated with prostitution and debauchery.

Sensing the weakness of his original intent and plain meaning arguments, Justice William O. Douglas relied heavily on the stare decisis effect of *Caminetti v. United States* (1917). The majority in *Caminetti,* over a strong dissent urging that the Mann Act applied only to "commercialized vice," upheld three convictions where the defendants had either traveled with or transported women across state lines for purposes of transient extramarital affairs. Justices Hugo Black and Robert Jackson, dissenting in *Cleveland,* stated that "the correctness of that rule [*Caminetti*] is so dubious that it should be restricted to its particular facts." Justice Wiley Rutledge, concurring, conceded that "[m]uch may be said for this view [that *Caminetti* was wrongly decided and should be overruled]" but concluded that because the facts in the instant case were indistinguishable from *Caminetti* he would "acquiesce in the Court's decision." Justice Murphy, dissenting, opined that, notwithstanding the principle of stare decisis, *Caminetti* should be overruled to avoid the prospect that "individuals, whatever may be said of their morality, are fined and imprisoned contrary to the wishes of Congress."

Faced with little analytical support for the majority opinion, Justice Douglas quoted extensively from the questionable sociological evidence against polygamy presented in the nineteenth-century Mormon polygamy cases, *Reynolds v. United States* (1878), *The Late Corporation of the Church of Jesus Christ of Latter-day Saints v. United States* (1890), and *Davis v. Beason* (1890). In these cases—decided in an era when the federal government was involved in a concerted "war on polygamy"—the Court stated that polygamy "has always been odious" and has been "treated as an offense against society," "a return to barbarism," and "contrary to the spirit of Christianity and of the civilization which Christianity has produced in the Western world." Based on this sociological evidence

Justice Douglas in *Cleveland* opined that polygamy remains more of "a notorious example of promiscuity" than the "isolated transgressions involved in the *Caminetti* case."

In dissent, Justice Murphy observed that the majority's reliance on the justices' own moral predilections as a valid basis for affirming Mann Act prosecutions would "make the federal courts the arbiters of the morality of those who cross state lines in the company of women and girls. They must decide what is meant by 'any other immoral purpose' without regard to the standards plainly set forth by Congress."

Apart from the interpretivist issue of whether polygamy falls within the ambit of the Mann Act, the Court in *Cleveland* gave short shrift to both the free exercise and the federalism issues, without even directly acknowledging any free exercise claim. Citing *Reynolds,* and therefore the belief/conduct dichotomy, Justice Douglas simply stated that polygamous practices "have long been outlawed in our society." With respect to the federalism issue, Justice Douglas stated that the "power of Congress over the instrumentalities of interstate commerce is plenary; it may be used to defeat what are deemed immoral practices; and the fact that the means may have the 'quality of police regulations' is not consequential."

Justice Douglas's majority opinion in *Cleveland* ignored legislative history, misconstrued the plain meaning of the Mann Act, and extended admittedly dubious precedent to criminalize religiously inspired polygamous marriages. What makes this opinion particularly interesting is that this moral assault on polygamy is led by the same justice who, in *Griswold v. Connecticut* (1965)—announcing for the first time the constitutional right of privacy—would later characterize marriage as a relationship "intimate to the degree of being sacred" and as "an association for as noble a purpose as any involved in our prior decisions."

Richard Collin Mangrum

Bibliography

Jaasma, Keith, "The Religious Freedom Restoration Act: Responding to Smith, Reconsidering Reynolds, 16 *Whittier Law Review* 211–299 (1995).

Cases and Statutes Cited

Caminetti v. United States, 242 U.S. 470 (1917).

Cleveland v. United States, 329 U.S. 14 (1946).

Davis v. Beason, 133 U.S. 333 (1890).

Griswold v. Connecticut, 381 U.S. 479 (1965).

The Late Corporation of the Church of Jesus Christ of Latter-day Saints v. United States, 136 U.S. 1 (1890).

Reynolds v. United States, 98 U.S. 145, 164 (1878).

Mann Act, 36 Stat. 825, 18 U.S.C. §398.

Cochran v. Louisiana State Board of Education 281 U.S. 370 (1930)

Cochran v. Louisiana State Board of Education (1930) arose out of the controversies of Huey P. Long's first term as governor in Louisiana. Before Long's election in 1928, the parents of children enrolled in both public and parochial schools purchased the schoolbooks their children used. Long's campaign promises included providing free textbooks to all school-age children. This was a critically important pledge in Louisiana, with its substantial Catholic population and numerous private religious schools.

Because the Free Exercise Clause of the First Amendment was not held to apply to the states through the Fourteenth Amendment until 1940 (*Cantwell v. Connecticut* [1940]) and the Establishment Clause was not held to apply until 1947 (*Everson v. Board of Education* [1947]), Long's proposal did not cause any federal Establishment Clause concerns. But the Louisiana Constitution had a provision that prohibited use of state funds for "sectarian" purposes. The proposal Governor Long submitted to the legislature attempted to surmount this difficulty by providing that the books were to be given directly to all school-age children; the schools were merely to be the distributors of the books.

At the time, Long's proposal was considered "radical" for Louisiana and resulted in a suit by two local school boards seeking to prevent the state's school board from distributing the books to schools within their local districts. At the same time they sought to strike down the provisions for funding books for students in private schools and to divert all the money thus appropriated into the local public school board budgets.

The Louisiana Supreme Court ultimately upheld Long's plan in *Borden v. Louisiana State Board of Education* (1928). But in the intervening time between the trial proceedings and the appeal, Long personally campaigned for the reelection of Supreme Court Justice John R. Land, whose support vote was later found to be necessary in the 4-to-3 vote sustaining the act. In treating the religious issues the Court held that no appropriation was made to help any school, religious or otherwise, and that the purpose was for "the use of the school children."

The added cost for the state to purchase the books was to be paid by a severance tax on oil. Simultaneously with the local school board suit, Standard Oil Company brought suit to declare unconstitutional the tax that was to fund the purchase of books. It was this case that reached the U.S. Supreme Court as *Cochran v. Louisiana State Board of Education* (1930). Chief Justice Charles Evans Hughes, speaking for a unanimous U.S. Court, upheld the Louisiana plan. In response to a republican form of government claim under Article IV, Section 4, the Court held that it was a political question that should not be resolved by the Court. In response to the Fourteenth Amendment claim that this was a "taking" without any public purpose, the Court quoted extensively from the opinion of the Louisiana Supreme Court and concluded that taxing power had been "exerted for a public purpose."

Although *Cochran* was not, itself, an Establishment Clause case, it has been important in the development of that clause's application to the states. In *Everson,* which was the first case to explicitly apply the Establishment Clause against the state, the majority cited *Cochran* for the proposition that there is a public purpose in children's receiving an education. Similarly, the dissent cited *Cochran* as the "first crack" in the wall of separation between church and state.

A similar provision to the one upheld in Louisiana was involved in New York, which required school authorities to lend textbooks free of charge to all students aged 7 to 12, even in private schools. In *Board of Education v. Allen* (1967) the Supreme Court, with a 5-to-4 majority, upheld New York's law. Both the majority and the dissent cited *Cochran.*

The basic strategy devised by Long and upheld in Louisiana seems to be a precursor of the modern "voucher" movement, under which parents receive a voucher from the government that can be "spent" at a school of their choice, whether public or private.

Richard L. Aynes

Bibliography

Hair, William Ivy, *The Kingfish and His Realm* (Baton Rouge: Louisiana State University Press, 1991).

Long, Huey P., *Everyman a King* (New Orleans, La.: National Book Co., 1933).

Williams, T. Harry, *Huey Long* (New York: Knopf, 1969).

Cases Cited

Board of Education v. Allen, 392 U.S. 236 (1968).

Borden v. Louisiana State Board of Education, 123 So. 655 (La. 1928).

Cantwell v. Connecticut, 310 U.S. 296 (1940).

Cochran v. Louisiana State Board of Education, 281 U.S. 370 (1930).

Everson v. Board of Education, 330 U.S. 1 (1947).

"Coercion" Test

During the 1980s an increasing number of judges and legal commentators began to express dissatisfaction with the test that the Supreme Court was using to evaluate claims under the First Amendment's Establishment Clause. That test, set forth most fully in 1971 in *Lemon v. Kurtzman,* forbids, among other things, any law whose "primary effect" is to "advance" religion. The Court employed variations on the *Lemon* test in striking down prayer and other religious exercises in public schools, as well as many forms of aid to church-related schools. Critics of *Lemon,* convinced that the test is both analytically incoherent and in practice hostile to religion, have proposed a number of alternatives. Among them is the suggestion that government may benefit, favor, or endorse religion, without violating the Establishment Clause, unless it *coerces* someone to assent to a religious belief or participate in a religious activity.

The distinction between "advancement" or "endorsement" of religion and "coercion" in favor of religion has primarily been raised in cases involving government sponsorship of religious exercises (such as official prayers) or religious symbols (such as Christmas crèches or Hanukkah menorahs). For example, in the original school prayer case, *Engel v. Vitale* (1962), the state argued that teacher-led prayers in public school classrooms were permissible because dissenting students were not required to participate. The Supreme Court, however, stated (without further explanation) that "the Establishment Clause, unlike the Free Exercise Clause, does not depend upon any showing of direct governmental compulsion." In later cases the Court relied on this statement to hold that other practices—posting the Ten Commandments in classrooms, instituting a "moment of silence" designed to encourage students to pray—were forbidden establishments because they "advanced" religion even though they involved no "coercion."

Similarly, cases involving publicly sponsored religious symbols have produced a division between justices supporting and opposing the coercion test. In *County of Allegheny v. American Civil Liberties Union* (1989) Justice Kennedy and three others would have permitted both a menorah and a crèche in public buildings because these symbols were not coercive—passersby were "free to ignore them"—but served only "to participate in [the] citizens' celebration of a holiday." The majority, however, invalidated the display of the crèche despite its noncoercive nature, saying that government may not "celebrate Christmas . . . in a way that endorses Christian doctrine."

The status of the coercion test in the Supreme Court remains unclear, but the test seems unlikely to command a majority of the current Court. Four sitting justices (Kennedy, Rehnquist, Scalia, and Thomas) have indicated approval of the test. But three other members of the Court (O'Connor, Souter, and Stevens) are firmly on record against it. The two newest justices (Ginsburg and Breyer) have not spoken specifically on the coercion test; but in *Rosenberger v. Rectors of University of Virginia* (1995) they expressed fairly strict separationist views that do not fit well with the coercion test's relative tolerance for government support of religion.

Even if a general "coercion" analysis were adopted, proponents probably would not agree on all its specifics. The Court in *Engel,* after stating that the Establishment Clause did not reach only "direct coercion," noted that classroom prayer involved subtle, informal, and "indirect" kinds of coercion even if participation in the exercise was not officially required. When *Lee v. Weisman* (1992) raised the question of prayers in the less controlled atmosphere of a school graduation ceremony, Justice Kennedy's majority opinion struck down the practice on the ground that there was still "social pressure" to participate in the prayers. *Weisman* also held that there was improper coercion even though audience members merely had to listen silently to the prayer, rather than join in reciting it. In contrast to this fairly broad notion of coercion, Justice Scalia and the other *Weisman* dissenters would limit the Establishment Clause to cases of coercion "by force of law and threat of penalty."

The coercion test provides even less guidance in cases involving government financial assistance to schools and social services that are religiously affiliated. Such cases involve coercion either way: Tax-supported aid coerces taxpayers to support religion, but government subsidization of secular entities and not religious ones arguably pressures or coerces citizens to forgo receiving their education or social services in a religious setting. Justice Kennedy modified his formulation of the coercion test in *County of Allegheny* in an apparent effort to address this question; but he did little more than restate the test, saying only that government could not "give direct benefits to religion in such a degree that it in fact 'establishes a [state] religion or religious faith, or tends to do so.'"

The arguments for and against the coercion test involve both history and logic. Proponents of the coercion analysis (including Justice Kennedy and, at one time, Professor Michael McConnell) point to the long history of government actions endorsing or favoring religion. Many of these traditions were adopted or approved by the First Congress, the body that framed the First Amendment: for example, presidential proclamations of prayer and thanksgiving, invocations at legislative and court sessions, and the appointment of congressional chaplains. Such practices, it is argued, can be explained only by the principle that the First Congress intended to allow noncoercive endorsements of religion.

Opponents of the coercion test (including Justice Souter and Professor Douglas Laycock) offer several responses concerning the history.

First, they assert, the whole range of historical practices cannot determine the scope of a constitutional principle, for sometimes even the drafters fail to live up to their ideals: Just as the Reconstruction Congress ran segregated schools in the District of Columbia, the First Amendment's Framers permitted some government-sponsored religious exercises supporting generalized Protestantism, largely because there were few non-Protestants to object. Moreover, opponents of the coercion test argue that the state-level disputes that played the greatest role in the development of the First Amendment show that the "establishments" the Framers had in mind were not limited to coercive schemes but included any support for religion. For example, in Virginia and Maryland, bills requiring taxpayers to support churches were rejected as establishments in the 1780s—"even," in Professor Laycock's words, "with the right to designate the recipient of the tax, to pay the tax to secular uses, and in Maryland, to escape the tax altogether by declaring unbelief." Proponents of the coercion test, such as Professor Michael Stokes Paulsen, respond that the arrangements in Virginia and other states did have coercive elements and were disapproved on that basis. Scholars thus remain divided on the historical issue.

Turning to analytical arguments, proponents of the coercion test, including Justice Kennedy, claim that because government can endorse or favor many other ideas, permitting noncoercive endorsements of religion is necessary to avoid "hostility to religion." For example, if government can celebrate the secular aspects of Christmas but not the religious ones, government will arguably contribute to the secularization of Christmas. Opponents of the coercion test respond that for the government to be "secular" does not mean it is antireligion and that there remain ample means to advance religion, and counteract the secularization of society, through activities and displays sponsored by private groups.

Opponents also argue that requiring "coercion" under the Establishment Clause would make the clause redundant, for the Free Exercise Clause itself prohibits governmental pressure on the right not to exercise religion. This line of argument poses little worry for most proponents of the coercion test, who regard the Free Exercise Clause as a protection for religion rather than for nonreligion. To many such proponents, the two clauses do indeed overlap: Both are aimed at protecting religious liberty against governmental compulsion—the Establishment Clause forbidding laws that compel religious practices, and the Free Exercise Clause forbidding laws that impede such practices.

More powerfully, opponents of the coercion test argue that permitting noncoercive endorsements of religion is difficult to harmonize with another, central principle underlying the Establishment Clause: that government may not give a preference to one denomination, or one religion, over another. (Chief Justice Rehnquist, and probably the other judicial proponents of the coercion test, accept this principle of "no preference between religions.") The conflict arises because any government acknowledgment of religion, however noncoercive, inevitably acknowledges a particular religion: Even generalized references to God—the staple of most public prayers—represent an "ecumenical" brand of religion that may be objectionable to adherents of more particularized faiths. A possible answer for proponents of noncoercive endorsements would be for government to endorse many faiths—for example, both the menorah and the crèche during the winter holidays—but whether such government actions could ever capture the range and subtlety of American religious identities remains questionable.

Thomas Berg

Bibliography

Laycock, Douglas, "'Noncoercive' Support for Religion: Another False Claim about the Establishment Clause," 26 *Valparaiso Law Review* 37–69 (1991).

———,"'Nonpreferential Aid' to Religion: A False Claim about Original Intent," 27 *William and Mary Law Review* 875–921 (1986).

McConnell, Michael W., "Coercion: The Lost Element of Establishment," 27 *William and Mary Law Review* 933–941 (1986).

Paulsen, Michael Stokes, "*Lemon* Is Dead," 43 *Case Western Reserve Law Review* 795–863 (1993).

Cases Cited

County of Allegheny v. American Civil Liberties Union, 492 U.S. 573 (1989).

Engel v. Vitale, 370 U.S. 479 (1962).

Lee v. Weisman, 505 U.S. 577 (1992).

Lemon v. Kurtzman, 403 U.S. 602 (1971).
Rosenberger v. Rectors of University of Virginia, 515 U.S. 819 (1995).

Committee for Public Education and Religious Liberty v. Nyquist 413 U.S. 756 (1973)

One of the greatest continuing First Amendment establishment controversies in the nation has revolved around the degree, if any, of constitutionally permissible public aid to parochial schools. Approximately 90 percent of all private schools are religiously affiliated. Public aid to private schools would not pose a constitutional problem. The constitutional controversy arises because of the religious affiliation of most of the nation's private schools. The decision underlying *Committee for Public Education and Religious Liberty v. Nyquist* (1973) exemplifies the strict separation jurisprudence of the Court in the early 1970s, a view that two decades later is no longer adhered to by the majority of its members.

In the *Nyquist* decision the Court found unconstitutional New York State's tuition reimbursement program for parents of children attending private parochial elementary or secondary schools. The majority meticulously applied the standards it had enunciated two years earlier, in *Lemon v. Kurtzman* (1971), to determine that government programs of financial assistance to religious institutions generally violated the Establishment Clause of the First Amendment of the U.S. Constitution. During the early 1970s, the first years of the tenure of Chief Justice Warren Burger, the Court diligently adhered to the jurisprudential principle of separation of church and state. During this period, Chief Justice Warren E. Burger and Justice William Rehnquist—both appointed to the Court by President Richard Nixon and both of whom favored governmental accommodation of religion—were frequently in dissent. Otherwise, the majority of then-sitting justices were veterans from the tenure of Chief Justice Earl Warren. These two camps within the Supreme Court did not significantly change until a decade later, when, in *Mueller v. Allen* (1983), the Court sustained partial indirect governmental tuition support for the parents of children in private schools in Minnesota. But throughout the 1970s and into the 1980s the Court consistently held that governmental financial assistance to private, religious-affiliated schools was an unconstitutional violation of the Establishment Clause of the First Amendment. *Nyquist* was a cornerstone case during the separationist era of the Supreme Court throughout the 1970s.

In 1972 New York State enacted several amendments to its education and tax laws, establishing three financial aid programs for nonpublic elementary and secondary schools. That year, in *Committee for Public Education and Religious Liberty [PEARL] v. Levitt* (S.D.N.Y., 1972), also known as *Levitt I*, PEARL sued the state commissioner of education, the comptroller, and the commissioner of taxation and finance for violations of the First Amendment's guarantee against governmental establishment of religion. The district court ruling was then appealed to the United States Supreme Court, in what became *Committee for Public Education and Religious Liberty v. Nyquist* (1973).

The New York law provided for direct money grants from the state to qualifying nonpublic schools to be used for maintenance and repair of school facilities and to ensure the health, welfare, and safety of the enrolled students. Qualifying schools were determined on the basis of the concentration of low-income students attending the schools.

The state law provided tuition reimbursements to parents of $50 per grade school child and $100 per high school student—but not to exceed one-half the total tuition actually paid, and only if the parents' annual taxable income was less than $5,000. The law also provided a tax relief program to provide aid to those parents who did not qualify for tuition reimbursement. The amount of the deductions allowed was determined on the basis of the parents' income, up to $25,000 per year.

With respect to the maintenance and repair provisions of the New York law, the Court found that the Establishment Clause had been violated because the essential effect was to subsidize and advance the religious mission of sectarian schools. There was no guarantee that the grants would not be utilized to foster the religious activities of the parochial schools. The tuition reimbursement grants also violated the Establishment Clause because their effect was to provide aid to sectarian institutions.

With respect to the maintenance and repair provisions, it would be possible for a secretarian elementary or secondary school to finance its entire maintenance and repair budget from state-raised tax funds. There were no statutory restrictions on the manner in which the money could be spent by the schools. "Nothing in the statute, for instance, bars a qualifying school from paying out of state funds the employees who maintain the school chapel, or the cost of renovating classrooms in which religion is taught, or the cost of heating and lighting those same facilities."

The tuition reimbursement program to the parents of the parochial school students even more clearly violated the First Amendment Establishment Clause and the "effects" prong of the *Lemon* test. Justice Lewis Powell summarized for the Court: "In the absence of an effective means of guaranteeing that the state aid derived from public funds will be used exclusively for secular, neutral and nonideological purposes, it is clear from our cases that direct aid in whatever form is invalid." Chief Justice Burger and Justices White and Rehnquist concurred in part and dissented in part.

Nyquist was strengthened by the Court's complementary decision in *Sloan v. Lemon* (1973), which struck down Pennsylvania's tuition scheme that likewise provided funds to reimburse parents for a portion of expenses incurred in sending their children to nonpublic schools.

Plaintiff taxpayers, at least one of whom was the parent of a child attending a Pennsylvania public school, sued the state treasurer. Plaintiffs alleged that the state law violated the Establishment Clause of the First Amendment because their tax monies were being used to finance the tuition aid program.

Under the Pennsylvania law, parents who paid tuition for their children to attend the state's nonpublic elementary and secondary schools were entitled to receive $75 for each child in elementary school and $150 for each child in secondary school, unless these amounts exceeded the total amount of tuition actually paid to educate each child. The funding for the program was derived from the state's cigarette sales tax proceeds. The program was to be administered by a five-member committee appointed by the governor. In an attempt to avoid an "entanglement" problem, the Pennsylvania legislation specifically precluded this committee from having any control whatsoever over the targeted nonpublic schools. Similarly, there were no restrictions or limitations placed on the use of funds received by parents under the law.

In striking down the Pennsylvania law as unconstitutional, the Court noted that "more than 90 percent of the children attending nonpublic schools . . . are enrolled in schools that are controlled by religious organizations or that have the purpose of propagating and promoting religious faith."

The Court examined the *Nyquist* issue of whether the way in which parents spent the monies reimbursed to them had an effect on whether the grants would be constitutional. The Court disregarded the speculative argument by plaintiffs regarding how the money would be spent. Again the Court focused on the "effects" portion of the *Lemon* test, concluding that "[t]he State has singled out a class of its citizens for a special economic benefit" and that the program's "intended consequence is to preserve and support religion-oriented institutions." Pennsylvania's tuition grants were direct benefits and thus violated the constitutional mandate against the "sponsorship" or "financial support" of religion or religious institutions.

Significantly, however, the Court made it clear that some other forms of aid may be acceptable in future plans. "We think that it is plain that this is quite unlike the sort of 'indirect' and 'incidental' benefits that flowed to sectarian schools from programs aiding all parents by providing bus transportation and secular textbooks for their children."

David L. Gregory

Bibliography

Gedicks, Frederick Mark, and Roger Hendrix, *Choosing the Dream: The Future of Religion in American Public Life* (New York: Greenwood, 1991).

Pfeffer, Leo, *Religion, State and the Burger Court* (Buffalo, N.Y.: Prometheus, 1984).

Cases Cited

Committee for Public Education and Religious Liberty v. Nyquist, 413 U.S. 756 (1973).

Committee for Public Education and Religious Liberty v. Levitt, 342 F. Supp. 439 (S.D. N.Y. 1972).

Lemon v. Kurtzman, 403 U.S. 602 (1971).
Mueller v. Allen, 463 U.S. 388 (1983).
Sloan v. Lemon, 413 U.S. 825 (1973).

Committee for Public Education and Religious Liberty v. Regan 444 U.S. 646 (1980)

During the period from 1970 through the early 1980s the Supreme Court dealt with religious issues in a seemingly schizophrenic fashion. The problem stems from the inherent difficulty in balancing the Establishment and Free Exercise Clauses of the First Amendment. The former seeks to prevent government from endorsing or supporting religion, while the latter forbids the government from seriously burdening a person's pursuit of whatever religion he or she chooses. The changing composition of the Court and a discernible evolution in thinking about religion among the justices also contributed to this vacillation.

In 1970 New York injected itself into the midst of this transformation when its state legislature enacted a law that appropriated public funds to reimburse both church-sponsored and secular nonpublic schools for performing services mandated by the state, namely, the "administration, grading and the compiling and reporting of the results of tests and examinations." Under this law, funds would be provided for both state-prepared and teacher-prepared exams. The tests dealt only with secular academic subjects, and the schools had no control over the contents of the tests, although the tests were graded by school personnel. Additionally, the statute did not provide for auditing of the funds received by the schools to ensure that the funds were applied to advance exclusively secular purposes. The comptroller became the target of a lawsuit that eventually was argued before the Supreme Court.

In *Levitt v. Committee for Public Education* (1973), known as *Levitt I,* the Court found that the comptroller's plan violated the Establishment Clause, because some religiously affiliated private schools were reimbursed for costs associated with the administration of teacher-prepared tests. The Court found that it was constitutionally impossible under such a statutory scheme to monitor whether such tests would be free from the influences of religious instruction. The Court stated that "the potential for conflict inheres in this situation, and because of that the state is constitutionally compelled to assure that the state supported activity is not being used for religious indoctrination." Thus the Court held that the statute was an impermissible aid to religion. The most troublesome aspect of the law was the financial support for teacher-prepared exams. Although the Court had earlier allowed the use of government monies to supply textbooks to sectarian schoolchildren, it was careful to distinguish that holding. The Court explained, "in terms of potential for involving some aspect of faith or morals in secular subjects, a textbook's content is ascertainable, but a teacher's handling of a subject is not."

During the early 1970s the separationist majority of the Court rigorously applied the three prongs of its *Lemon v. Kurtzman* (1971) test to find unconstitutional most forms of government aid to parochial schools. *Lemon* mandated that government action (1) have a secular purpose, (2) not have the primary effect of advancing religion, and (3) not excessively entangle the government in the internal affairs of the religion. Unless all three "prongs" of this test are met, a violation of the Establishment Clause exists.

Responding to *Lemon* and *Levitt I,* the New York State legislature altered its statute in 1974 by eliminating the reimbursements for teacher-prepared tests and by providing a means by which payment of state funds would be audited, thus ensuring that only the actual costs incurred would be reimbursed.

It is possible that, without the intervening decision of *Meek v. Pittenger* (1975), these changes would have been sufficient. Relying on *Meek,* however, a federal district court in *Committee for Public Education and Religious Liberty v. Levitt* (S.D.N.Y., 1976), known as *Levitt II,* invalidated the amended law. The *Meek* decision had struck down a Pennsylvania statute that provided auxiliary services such as lab equipment to nonpublic schools. Although the services provided were nonreligious in nature, the Court reasoned that the government, by providing schools with such materials, "had the primary and direct effect of advancing the religious mission of the sectarian school enterprise as a whole," which, hence, amounts to a forbidden establishment of religion.

By the time *Levitt II* reached the Supreme Court, there was more precedent to contend with. *Wolman v. Walter* (1977) found constitutional an Ohio statute that authorized, among other things, the expenditure of state funds to supply pupils who were attending nonpublic schools with the same standardized tests and scoring services used in the public schools. The Court vacated and remanded *Levitt II,* holding that, under *Wolman,* "state aid may be extended to a sectarian school's educational activities if it can be shown with a high degree of certainty that the aid will only have a secular value of legitimate interest to the State and does not present any appreciable risk of being used to aid the transmission of religious views." On remand, the Federal District Court for the Southern District of New York found that the statute did not violate the Establishment Clause.

When Edward Regan replaced Arthur Levitt as New York's comptroller, he became the defendant in the renamed *Committee for Public Education and Religious Liberty v. Regan* (1980). This time the Court, in a 5-to-4 decision written by Justice Byron White, held that *Wolman* was controlling and stated that there was no substantial risk that the tests could be used for religious education purposes since no school, public or private, had any control over the content or application of the tests. Because the tests were a state-mandated graduation requirement, the Court found a clearly secular purpose in their administration and grading. The auditing procedures were found sufficient to ensure that state funds would not be used in a constitutionally impermissible manner, without creating excessive governmental entanglement in the internal affairs of religiously affiliated schools. Joining White were Chief Justice Warren E. Burger and Justices Potter Stewart, Lewis Powell, and William Rehnquist. Justice Harry Blackmun filed a dissenting opinion, joined by Justices William Brennan and Thurgood Marshall. Justice John Paul Stevens filed a separate dissenting opinion.

The *Regan* decision thus marked an important transition toward the accommodationist jurisprudence of the Burger Court. Those justices who, less than a decade earlier, had championed *Lemon*-style separationist thinking now found themselves in the increasingly frustrated minority. The new majority refused to apply the *Lemon* test as stringently. Therefore, carefully crafted forms of indirect governmental aid to religiously affiliated schools received support from the Court in the 1980s. The *Regan* majority, in explaining the decision not to apply any "litmus-paper test to distinguish permissible from impermissible aid to religiously oriented schools," recognized that the Court members were divided among themselves "perhaps reflecting the different views on this subject of the people of this country."

David L. Gregory

Bibliography

Ivers, Gregg, *Lowering the Wall: Religion and the Supreme Court in the 1980s* (New York: Anti-Defamation League, 1991).

Cases Cited

Committee for Public Education and Religious Liberty v. Levitt, 414 F. Supp. 1174 (S.D.N.Y. 1976) (*Levitt II*).

Committee for Public Education and Religious Liberty v. Regan, 444 U.S. 646 (1980).

Lemon v. Kurtzman, 403 U.S. 602 (1971).

Levitt v. Committee for Public Education, 413 U.S. 472 (1973) (*Levitt I*).

Meek v. Pittenger, 421 U.S. 349 (1975).

Wolman v. Walter, 433 U.S. 229 (1977).

Commonwealth v. Kneeland 37 Mass. 206 (1838)

Commonwealth v. Kneeland (Mass., 1838) is the leading American case on the law of blasphemy, largely because of the formidable reputation of Chief Justice Lemuel Shaw of Massachusetts, who wrote the opinion of the Supreme Judicial Court of Massachusetts. Although Shaw, in the view of Oliver Wendell Holmes, was "the greatest magistrate" in American history, his opinion in *Kneeland* is one of his worst among 2,200 opinions.

The *Kneeland* case was saturated in politics. But for politics, Kneeland probably never would have been prosecuted. His blasphemy consisted of merely a temperate denial of God, Christ, and miracles, not a reviling or ridiculing of any of them. He did not, for example, say something as shocking or as offensive as the defendant in the first American blasphemy case, *People v. Ruggles,* decided in 1811 by Chief Justice James Kent of New York. In that case Ruggles had said,

"Jesus Christ was a bastard, and his mother must be a whore." Kneeland had written, "Universalists believe in a God which I do not." He thought too that the story of Christ was "fable and fiction" and that his miracles were the result of "trick and imposture." A state statute penalized blaspheming the holy name of God by willfully denying, cursing, or reproaching him or any person of the Trinity or the Bible. Kneeland's words were far more moderate than those of Tom Paine, Elihu Palmer, and many others whose books sold freely. Unitarians—who controlled Harvard, the Supreme Judicial Court, and most of Boston's Congregational churches—freely denied the divinity of Christ.

Kneeland, however, was a radical—a dangerous one—because he had a large audience among the working classes. He depicted the clergy as hypocrites, the rich as tyrants, and the legal profession as knavish; and he incited class hatred by advocating a union of farmers and workers, by castigating high prices, and by savaging corporate property. He even taught sex education. The worst of it all was that he was a leader of the left-wing Jacksonians. His lectures attracted thousands, and his newspaper, the *Investigator,* sold cheaply to the poor. The prosecutor declared that the newspaper was "a lava stream of blasphemy and obscenity which blasts the vision and gangrenes the very soul of the uncorrupted reader." Although Kneeland was convicted at his first trial, he won a retrial—and by no coincidence the dissentient juror who hung the jury was a Jacksonian journalist. Moreover, Kneeland's counsel was a high-ranking member of the state Democratic Party. When Kneeland's third trial was pending, the boss of the party, David Henshaw, wrote a tract exposing the bias of the trial judges and maintaining that no case more vitally affected "the civil liberties of the country" than Kneeland's, because it struck at "the root of the liberty of conscience, and the freedom of the Press." Nevertheless Kneeland was convicted and was sentenced to sixty days in jail; he appealed to Chief Justice Shaw's court.

His counsel having died, Kneeland represented himself in opposition to the state attorney general. He contended that he had not committed a crime. Even his Whig trial judges had admitted that an atheist might propagate his opinions in temperate language and that the truths of the Bible might be denied. He had spoken moderately, with none of the ferocity so common to theological arguments. Moreover, he had not even denied God, let alone express a disbelief in him; he merely expressed a disbelief in the creed of Universalists. "I do say," Kneeland declared, "and shall until my dying breath, I never intended to express a disbelief in, much less a denial of, God." He was no atheist, but a pantheist. He contended, further, that the blasphemy statute was unconstitutional because it violated the state constitution's protection of religious liberty. Kneeland relied on Jefferson's maxim that error of opinion may be safely tolerated when reason is left free to combat it. Freedom of speech and press, as well as freedom to express unpopular religious opinions, were constitutionally protected by the state's Bill of Rights.

Four Whig jurists sustained the conviction; Marcus Morton, the one Jacksonian on Shaw's court, dissented. Shaw revealed, as Richard Henry Dana noted, that he was a conservative Whig with "intense and doting biases." He was sure that Kneeland had blasphemed, because although the law permitted a temperate denial of God, Kneeland had willfully denied him. The statute punished willful denial, which Shaw defined as "purposely using words concerning God, calculated and designed to impair and destroy the reverence, respect, and confidence due to him." Blasphemy, he added, is a "willful and malicious" denial—a definition with which Kneeland did not disagree. After the jury's verdict and in the absence of proof of a mistake in the direction given to the jury, "it is to be taken as proved," Shaw declared, that Kneeland's language constituted blasphemy. Thus the fundamental question—whether Kneeland had blasphemed—was settled without reasoned consideration. It was "taken as proved" by the verdict, although the court had agreed to hear the case on the "whole indictment and all the circumstances." Shaw's opinion transcended the facts.

He next confronted the question of whether the statute conflicted with the Massachusetts Constitution. Shaw cited with approval Kent's opinion in the *Ruggles* case, where it was held that blasphemy was a common-law crime not abrogated by a constitution guaranteeing unlimited toleration. The point was reprehensible, because it implied, first, that the judge-made common law overrode the fundamental law of the state consitution and, second, that Kneeland was guilty of blasphemy at common law, because Christianity was part and parcel of the common law. This was an English doctrine that may have made sense in England, which maintained an established church and merely exempted dissenters from criminal penalties. But in a constitutional system that outlawed preference of one religion above others, as in New York and Massachusetts, Kent's adoption of the English common law violated freedom of conscience and the quality of religions. As he himself declared in *Ruggles,* "imposter" religions could be reviled but not Christianity. The prejudice that bottomed Kent's opinion tainted Shaw's opinion.

Notwithstanding his reliance on Kent, Shaw examined the provisions of the state constitution that Kneeland claimed had been violated. Freedom of the press, Shaw ruled, merely meant that individuals were at liberty to publish as they pleased without prior censorship, subject to responsibility for the criminality of their language. That was a definition of freedom of the press that accorded with the English common law. Shaw found that Kneeland had abused his freedom by engaging in licentiousness.

Thus freedom of the press did not constitutionally protect blasphemy. Nor did religious liberty, which allowed the fullest and freest advocacy of religious opinions, including denials and disbelief, but not if made willfully or with "a bad purpose." Although the statute and the case involved the criminality of mere words, not acts, Shaw concluded his point by saying that the statute was constitutional because it merely punished "acts" that would have a "tendency to disturb the public peace." If that were true, Kneeland should have been editing his paper, not facing jail. He had not been accused of acts tending to breach the peace, only of words that blasphemed. This section of Shaw's opinion endorsed the remote bad-tendency test of the criminality of speech, which subverted its freedom. As Jefferson had written in the preamble to his great Bill for Establishing Religious Freedom, to permit a magistrate to intrude his powers "into the field of opinion and to restrain the profession or propagation of principles, on the supposition of their ill tendency is a dangerous fallacy, which at once destroys all religious liberty," because the judge determines that tendency, making his opinion "approve or condemn the sentiments of others only as they shall square with or differ from his own." Jefferson concluded that the proper purposes of government are served when it can act only against principles that "break out into overt acts against peace and good order." Kneeland had not been charged with inciting to crime.

Justice Marcus Morton, the sole dissenter, considered as dangerous to freedom Shaw's doctrine that the constitutional guarantee extended only to religious professions and not to irreligious ones. To Morton religious truths required no assistance from government. An individual was responsible only to God for his or her opinions about religion. The state blasphemy statute, Morton believed, could survive constitutional scrutiny only if it allowed the expression of Kneeland's opinions. Shaw's emphasis on "willful denial" struck Morton as wrong, because "willful" merely meant "purposely" or "obstinately," not "maliciously." "I cannot agree that a man may be punished for willfully doing what he has a legal right to do."

Although Shaw had authority to suspend Kneeland's sentence and bind him to good behavior, he did not. Kneeland served his time. As Theodore Parker, the universal reformer, observed, "Abner was jugged for sixty days; but he will come out as beer from a bottle, all foaming, and will make others foam." Abner Kneeland did, and with much protest from the intellectual community in Boston. A petition was addressed to the governor requesting a pardon for Kneeland "because opinion should not be subjected to penalties." The names of the signatories read like a Who's Who among the reformers and intellectuals. William Ellery Channing's name headed the list, which included Parker, Emerson, Garrison, Alcott, and 163 others. The petition meant little to Governor Edward Everett, whose rival in the past four elections had been Marcus Morton. Everett rejected the petition. Shaw's opinion succeeded Kent's as the most authoritative and most cited American authority on the law of blasphemy. Today, because of the broad scope of the First Amendment as construed by the U.S. Supreme Court, no blasphemy prosecution could survive an appeal.

Leonard W. Levy

Bibliography

Commager, Henry Steele, "The Blasphemy of Abner Kneeland." 7 *New England Quarterly* 29–41 (1935).

Levy, Leonard W. (ed.), *Blasphemy in Massachusetts: Freedom of Conscience and the Abner Kneeland Case: A Documentary Record* (New York: Da Capo, 1973).

Stuart, French Roderick, *The Trials of Abner Kneeland: A Study in the Rejection of Democratic Secular Humanism,* Ph.D. dissertation (Ann Arbor, Mich.: University Microfilms, 1971).

Cases Cited

Commonwealth v. Kneeland, 37 Mass. 206 (1838).

People v. Ruggles, 8 Johns. (N.Y.) 290 (1811).

Conscientious Objection and the Free Exercise Clause

The philosophical basis for conscientious objection to governmental service or regulation dates back to 500 B.C.E. Historical examples of conscientious objectors include Jews who were exempted from Roman military service because they were Sabbatarians and early Christians who objected to military service because of their opposition to bloodshed and because the service was too closely connected to worshipping idols and the emperor.

The United States has a long tradition of accommodating conscience. By 1784 the constitutions or bills of rights of five states, as well as the militia statutes of a majority of states, exempted religious pacifists from required militia service. The exemption is not surprising, given that many early immigrants to America fled military conscription or conflict abroad. This tradition also includes successful conscientious objections to governmental conduct concerning sanctuaries, taxes, juries and oaths, pictures and reflectors, and autopsies.

The notion of religious freedom provides the basis for the accommodation between individual conscience and governmental power. Conscientious objections are traditionally based on the First Amendment's Free Exercise Clause, which provides that "Congress shall make no law respecting an establishment of religion, or prohibiting the free exercise thereof. . . ."

In evaluating free exercise challenges to governmental regulation, the U.S. Supreme Court has generally presumed that religious-exercise interests outweigh the government's interest in regulation unless the government can show a compelling reason for the regulation. The Court has rejected, however, claims of religious freedom to engage in overt acts that "pose some substantial threat to public safety, peace or order" (*Sherbert v. Verner* [1963]). For example, in *Reynolds v. United States* (1879) the Court rejected a free exercise challenge to a law criminalizing polygamy. Congress had determined that polygamy posed a threat to public morality and welfare, but the Court expressed concern about making "doctrines of religious belief superior to the law of the land, and in effect . . . permit[ing] every citizen to become a law unto himself." In 1963 the Court decided *Sherbert,* which established a three-part test for determining when a statute can be enforced against those who object to it on religious grounds. Two years after this seminal decision, the Court decided the well-known conscientious objection case of *United States v. Seeger* (1965). *Seeger* involved the most common and most public conflict between government and conscience—compulsory military service versus the religious belief that warfare is wrong under God's law that condemns violence.

Before *Seeger* the Court had summarily rejected conscientious objectors' free exercise challenges to Congress's power to draft citizens into military service (*Selective Service Draft Law Cases* [1918]). In a similar fashion the Court had also in dictum rejected any notion that the Constitution required conscientious objector exemptions for pacifists who sought citizenship under the Naturalization Act but who refused to promise to bear arms in defense of the country (*United States v. Macintosh* [1931]). Although the Court reversed its position on citizenship for conscientious objector aliens and found that conscientious objectors were covered by certain statutory exemptions to the draft, the Court has never held that the Constitution alone requires religiously based conscientious objector exemptions (*Girouard v. United States* [1946]).

In *Seeger* the appellant struck the words "training and" and put quotations around the word "religious" on the conscientious exemption application required under the Universal Military Training and Service Act. Seeger also refused to affirm or deny his belief in a supreme being, stating only that he held deep "conscientious scruples against . . . wars." His was a "belief in and devotion to goodness and virtue for their own sakes, and a religious faith in a purely ethical creed." Seeger argued that the act's requirement that conscientious objection be based on "religious training and belief," including the "belief . . . [in a] Supreme Being," violated the Free Exercise Clause.

The Court began by noting the "richness and variety of spiritual life in our country" and mentioned modern theologians, like Paul Tillich, who offered definitions of God that differed from traditional theism. The Court then unanimously concluded that when Congress amended the act and used the term "Supreme Being" instead of "God," it intended to exempt those whose beliefs were "sincere and meaningful and occup[ied] a place in the life of [their] possessor[s] parallel to that filled by the orthodox belief in God [in the life of a traditionally religious person]" (*Seeger,* 380 U.S. at 166). Although the Court mentioned the Free Exercise Clause only briefly, it held that the key "task [was] to decide whether the registrant's beliefs were "sincerely held and, . . . in his own scheme of things, religious." Furthermore, the government could not confine either the "source or [the] content" of those beliefs "to traditional or parochial concepts of religion." Thus a nontheistic claimant could qualify for conscientious objector status.

Concurring and citing *Sherbert,* Justice Douglas noted that if the Court construed the act differently, it would subject "those who embraced one religious faith rather than another . . . to penalties; [a] kind of discrimination [that] would violate the Free Exercise Clause of the First Amendment." In response to the Court's decision in *Seeger,* in 1967 Congress deleted the act's reference to a supreme being. Three years later the Court in *Welsh v. United States* (1970) reaffirmed the *Seeger* interpretation of the statute and stressed its application to avowedly secular beliefs.

The Court reviewed another conscientious objection challenge to the draft in *Gillette v. United States* (1971). The appellant, Gillette, conscientiously opposed fighting in the Vietnam War but did not oppose participating in "just" wars, such as a United Nations peacekeeping operation. Noting that Congress intended to exempt only conscientious objectors opposed to war "in any form," the Court held—in an opinion by Justice Marshall—that selective conscientious objectors like Gillette had no statutory recourse. After devoting most of its attention to Gillette's Establishment Clause claim, Justice Marshall and the majority rejected his argument that Congress "interfer[ed] with the free exercise of religion by conscripting persons opposed to particular wars on the grounds of conscience and religion." Justice Marshall noted that the Free Exercise Clause bars "governmental regulation of religious beliefs as such, interference with the dissemination of religious ideas," and even neutral regulatory laws with secular aims if the burden they impose on First Amendment values is not justified by the government's interest.

Justice Marshall observed that the act was "not designed to interfere with any religious . . . practice, and [did] not work a penalty against any theological position." Instead, it was a neutral regulation designed to "procur[e] the manpower necessary for military purposes" and to "[maintain] a fair system for determining 'who serves when not all serve.'" Any "incidental burdens on the religious practices of selective objectors [were] "justified by substantial governmental interests" in military readiness. The Court in *Gillette* therefore limited the status of conscientious objection to those who oppose participation in all wars. Moreover, the Court expressed a willingness to uphold neutral regulations that protected substantial governmental interests; it left unsettled the question of whether the Free Exercise Clause implicitly provides a constitutional right to an exemption.

In 1972 the scope of the Free Exercise Clause seemed very broad as the Court opined in *Wisconsin v. Yoder* that in some cases it prohibits even neutral regulations that interfere with religious activity. Between 1972 and 1995, however, the law of religious freedom changed significantly. Except for three unemployment cases that followed *Yoder,* the Court never again applied the test of compelling state interest in order to uphold a free exercise claim against a neutral and generally applicable law (*Employment Division, Department of Human Resources of Oregon v. Smith* [1990]).

In other cases, the Court increasingly avoided applying the standard of compelling state interest in reviewing free exercise challenges, and it often deferred to the government's interests. For example, in *Goldman v. Weinberger* (1986) the Court rejected the Free Exercise Clause challenge of an orthodox Jew who objected to Air Force uniform regulations that forbade him to wear a yarmulke. In *Bowen, Secretary of Health and Human Services, et al. v. Roy* (1986) the Court rejected a claim that a state welfare agency's use of Social Security numbers violated the Free Exercise Clause. The Court held in *O'Lone v. Estate of Shabazz* (1987) that prison officials are not constitutionally required to adjust prison work schedules to Muslim inmates' religious observances. In *Lyng v. Northwest Indian Cemetery Protective Association* (1988) the majority concluded that the Free Exercise Clause does not prohibit governmental authorization of timber harvesting and road construction in a national forest traditionally used by Indians for religious purposes.

By 1990 it was clear that some justices disagreed with the view that the Free Exercise Clause required exemptions from generally applicable laws for conscientious objectors. That year the Court decided *Smith* and abandoned the compelling interest test. The Court held that "the right of free exercise does not relieve an individual of the obligation to comply with a 'valid and neutral law of general applicability on the ground that the law proscribes (or prescribes) conduct that his religion prescribes (or proscribes).'"

The *Smith* decision focused renewed attention on religiously based conscientious objection and the Free Exercise Clause. In repudiation of *Smith,* Congress passed the Religious Freedom Restoration Act (RFRA), which became effective in November 1993. The RFRA's express purpose is "to restore the compelling interest test as set forth in *Sherbert v. Verner* and *Wisconsin v. Yoder.*" RFRA prompted debate, which focused on arguable ambiguities, constitutionality, and the ultimate impact on the adjudication of Free Exercise Clause claims. As a result of the overturning of RFRA in 1997, the law regarding conscientious objectors under the Free Exercise Clause remains unsettled. Regardless of their specific beliefs, however, commentators generally agree that the adjudication of religiously based conscientious objections to government activity will become more—and not less—challenging for the courts.

Jack Sahl

Bibliography

Berg, Thomas C., "What Hath Congress Wrought? An Interpretive Guide to the Religious Freedom Restoration Act," 39 *Villanova Law Review* 1–75 (1994).

Carter, Stephen L., *The Culture of Disbelief: How American Law and Politics Trivialize Religious Devotion* (New York: Basic Books, 1992).

Davis, Spencer E., "Constitutional Right or Legislative Grace? The Status of Conscientious Objection Exemptions," 19 *Florida State University Law Review* 191–208 (1991).

Eisgruber, Christopher L., and Lawrence G. Sager, "The Vulnerability of Conscience: The Constitutional Basis for Protecting Religious Conduct," 61 *University of Chicago Law Review* 1245–1315 (1994).

Flowers, Ronald B., "Government Accommodation of Religious-Based Conscientious Objection," 24 *Seton Hall Law Review* 695–735 (1993).

Landskroener, Paul M., "Not the Smallest Grain of Incense: Free Exercise and Conscientious Objection to Draft Registration," 25 *Valpariso University Law Review* 455–503 (1991).

Laycock, Douglas, "The Religious Freedom Restoration Act," 1993 *Brigham Young University Law Review* 221–258 (1993).

Marshall, William P., "In Defense of Smith and Free Exercise Revisionism," 58 *University of Chicago Law Review* 308–332 (1991).

———,"The Case against the Constitutionally Compelled Free Exercise Exemption," 40 *Case Western Reserve Law Review* 357–412 (1990).

McConnell, Michael W., "Free Exercise Revisionism and the Smith decision," 57 *University of Chicago Law Review* 1109–1153 (1990).

Satow, Michael S., "Conscientious Objectors: Their Status, the Law and Its Development," 3 *George Mason Civil Rights Law Journal* 113–139 (1992).

Cases Cited

Bowen, Secretary of Health and Human Services, et al. v. Roy, 476 U.S. 693 (1986).

Employment Division, Department of Human Resources of Oregon v. Smith, 494 U.S. 872 (1990).

Gillette v. United States, 401 U.S. 437 (1971).

Girouard v. United States, 328 U.S. 61 (1946).

Goldman v. Weinberger, 475 U.S. 503 (1986).

Lyng v. Northwest Indian Cemetery Protective Association, 485 U.S. 439 (1988).

O'Lone v. Estate of Shabazz, 482 U.S. 342 (1987).

Religious Freedom Restoration Act, Pub. L. 103–141, 107 Stat. 1488 (1993).

Reynolds v. United States, 98 U.S. 145 (1879).

Selective Service Draft Law Cases, 245 U.S. 366 (1918).

Sherbert v. Verner, 374 U.S. 398 (1963).

United States v. Macintosh, 283 U.S. 605 (1931).

United States v. Seeger, 380 U.S. 163 (1965).

Welsh v. United States, 398 U.S. 333 (1970).

Wisconsin v. Yoder, 406 U.S. 205 (1972).

Universal Military Training and Service Act, 81 Stat. 104, 50 App. U.S.C. A. s 456 (j) (1964 ed., Supp. IV).

Consumer Protection and Religion

Judaism, Islam, Catholicism, and other religions set strict standards concerning goods used by their adherents, that is, what foods may be eaten, how religious articles must be prepared, what clothes may be worn, and so on. A buyer of such items, therefore, must depend on the seller's representation that the goods comply with religious requirements—that, as the Jewish tradition puts it, they are "kosher."

The Federal Trade Commission Act and consumer protection acts in force in most states generally prohibit false and fraudulent advertisements and misrepresentation to induce sales. In addition, statutes and regulations in more than one-third of the states—including those like Kentucky and Louisiana, where Jews make up less than 1 percent of the population—have enacted laws specifically regulating kosher food.

New York enacted the nation's first kosher-food antifraud law in 1915. The New York law prohibits falsely representing that food is "prepared under the Orthodox Hebrew religious requirements." Michigan defines "kosher" as "prepared or processed in accordance with Orthodox Hebrew religious requirements by a recognized Orthodox Rabbinical Council," and Maryland states that food is kosher only if it is "prepared under and consisting of products sanctioned by the code of Jewish laws, namely in the Shulchan Aruch," a medieval European codification of Jewish law.

It is not clear whether such statutes, with their inevitable entanglement with religious observance, are constitutional. The constitutional issue arises because these statutes and regulations typically incorporate a religious standard to determine whether the law has been followed. Early judicial challenges contended that the statute's terms were so vague that they violated the Due Process Clause of the Fourteenth Amendment to the United States Constitution. In 1925, in *Hygrade Provision Company v. Sherman,* the United States Supreme Court held that the New York statute did not violate the Due Process Clause because it only punished intentional fraud and, therefore, "whatever difficulty there may be in reaching a correct determination as to whether a given product is kosher," merchants were required only to "exercise their judgment in good faith."

In *Everson v. Board of Education* (1947) the Court held that the Fourteenth Amendment prohibited state governments from "establishing" religion. Not until 1972, however, were kosher fraud statutes challenged as establishing religion. In *Ran-Dav's County Kosher, Inc. v. State* (1992) the New Jersey Supreme Court overturned that state's regulations regarding kosher food, finding them unconstitutional because they "impose substantive religious standards for the kosher-products industry and authorize civil enforcement of those religious standards with the assistance of clergy, directly and substantially entangling government in religious matters." The U.S. Supreme Court declined to hear an appeal from this decision.

As Mark A. Berman noted in an excellent and very thorough discussion of the laws and their constitutionality, it is possible to draft kosher fraud statutes that avoid constitutional problems. Such statutes require disclosure of the nature of religious supervision of preparation of the product, giving the consumer information to decide whether, in his or her view, it is indeed kosher. A 1982 New York statute, General Business Law Article 39-A, known as the "Torah Merchants Statute," follows this form. It regulates the sale of Torah scrolls by requiring Torah dealers to disclose to purchasers the source of the Torah, any identifying marks, and the authority of the merchant to sell the particular scroll. "Torah scroll" is defined merely as "an edition of the Pentateuch handwritten on parchment," a definition that contains no religious test, such as requiring that the scroll be written in accordance with Jewish law.

Amy Shapiro

Bibliography

Berman, Mark A., "Kosher Fraud Statutes and the Establishment Clause: Are They Kosher?" 26 *Columbia Journal of Law and Social Problems* 1–75 (1992).

Cases and Statutes Cited

Everson v. Board of Education, 330 U.S. 1 (1947).

Hygrade Provision Company v. Sherman, 266 U.S. 497 (1925).

Ran-Dav's County Kosher Kitchen, Inc. v. State, 608 A. 2d 1353 (N.J. 1992), cert. denied, 507 U.S. 952 (1993).

"Torah Merchants Statute," New York statute, General Business Law Article 39-A (1982).

Copyright and Suppression of Religious Dissent

Traditional copyright theory asserts that the copyright monopoly is desirable because it encourages literary creation and thereby expands public debate. In some instances, however, the monopoly has been used to stifle debate by limiting access to important works. One problematic instance of this occurs when the monopoly is used to stifle religious dissent. So far, there has been no clear and explicit consideration of the problem, although in a number of cases it is clear that a copyright has been used to aid a participant in a religious dispute.

Very briefly, copyright law provides an author with the exclusive rights to control the reproduction and distribution of a work and to produce different versions of the work. The monopoly is available to any author regardless of the content of the work, including authors who claim to have written a work with divine assistance or who claim that they themselves have divine qualities. As a result, copyright protection can be invoked to prevent the unauthorized reproduction of religious scriptures. (Many religious scriptures are not protected by copyright because either copyright law did not exist when the works were written or their copyrights have expired. Recent translations of these works may be copyrighted.) Under the traditional view, public debate about controversial ideas is not stifled because the underlying ideas in a protected work can be copied; the copyright extends only to the author's particular mode of expression. The limits of this theory can be plainly seen, however, when applied to religious texts. For many, the particular words of a religious document reverberate with meaning and nuance. Fierce doctrinal debates have centered on which particular version of a religious text is correct. In these instances, control of a particular text may yield control over religious doctrine. Moreover, if a copyright owner denies a dissenting group access to a copy of a religious scripture, that dissenting group may be unable to practice its religion.

This fact has not escaped religious communities embroiled in factional disputes. Two cases in which copyrights have been invoked in religious disputes are *United Christian Scientists v. Christian Science Board of Directors, First Church of Christ, Scientist* (1987) and *Religious Technology Center v. Scott* (1987). In both cases, the copyright owner was a religious entity that sought to bar the use of religious scripture by a group with which it had doctrinal disputes.

The first case involved a dispute between the First Church of Christ, Scientist and the United Christian Scientists. The First Church of Christ was founded by Mary Baker Eddy, author of *Science and Health with Key to the Scriptures. Science and Health* is the central theological text of the Christian Scientist religion. During her lifetime Eddy made several revisions of *Science and Health.* The First Church of Christ held all the copyrights obtained by Eddy for the different editions, but by 1971 all the versions had either fallen into the public domain or were in the last years of copyright protection. The United Christian

Scientists was formed by a group of Christian Scientists who differed with the First Church of Christ on a number of doctrinal matters, including which version of *Science and Health* was the authoritative statement of Eddy's teachings.

In 1971, at the urging of the First Church of Christ, the U.S. Congress passed Private Law 92-60, which granted the First Church of Christ extended copyright protection for *Science and Health*. Copyright protection was restored to those versions which had fallen into the public domain; protection was extended for the version still under copyright; and future protection was extended to any version that had not yet been published.

The legislative history makes it abundantly clear that the bill's principal advocates, including the First Church of Christ, supported the bill so that the wording of the text could be controlled for doctrinal reasons. One of their officials testified before a House Committee in support of the bill, "Changes of wording . . . are extremely important to members of our church. . . . Words, of course, stand for religious positions of vast significance in the lives of thousands of believers." The First Church of Christ wanted to control which version of *Science and Health* would be used by Christian Scientists, and the bill aided that effort. If all the versions of *Science and Health* were protected by copyright, only versions produced with the permission of the First Church of Christ could be printed. The legislation was adopted, although its constitutional infirmities had been pointed out by both members of Congress and many who testified at the hearings.

The United Christian Scientists brought suit challenging the constitutionality of Private Law No. 92-60 on the ground that it violated the Establishment and Free Exercise Clauses of the First Amendment. In a lengthy and thorough opinion in *United Christian Scientists v. First Church of Christ* the D.C. circuit court sustained the challenge, concluding that the law had the "unmistakable effect of advancing the [First] Church [of Christ]'s cause."

The length and detail of the court's legal analysis is somewhat surprising. There was no secular purpose to the bill, and thus clearly it could not have been sustained under *Lemon v. Kurtzman* (1971). In *Lemon* the U.S. Supreme Court set forth a three-pronged test for deciding whether government action violates the First Amendment. Under the first prong of the test a "statute must have a secular legislation purpose." Public Law 92-60 did not. It was adopted to aid the First Church of Christ's dispute with the United Christian Scientists. The bill's supporters had attempted to characterize their efforts as secular in nature, casting their concerns in the form of truth in advertising. They argued that only one version of *Science and Health* was the accurate statement of Eddy's teachings, and if the First Church of Christ could not prevent publication of other versions, consumers would be misled by purchasing or reading inaccurate statements. Even that argument, however, fails the first prong of the *Lemon* test, because it is intertwined with the necessarily religious judgment about what is or is not an accurate statement of Eddy's teachings. Private Law 92-60 was thus declared unconstitutional. Different versions of *Science and Health*—all of whose copyrights have now expired—can be freely distributed.

Not present in the *United Christian Scientist* case, but closely related, are the issues raised when a dissenting group is denied permission to use religious scriptures that are protected by the regular copyright statute. In *Religious Technology Center v. Scott* (1987) the principal parties were the Church of Scientology and a splinter group, the Church of the New Civilization. According to the teachings of the Church of Scientology, an individual's behavior and well-being can be improved through the process of "auditing," the techniques of which are described in a series of works written by L. Ron Hubbard, the founder of the Church of Scientology. Under the doctrines of the Church of Scientology, the works describing advanced auditing techniques—New Era Dianetics for Operating Thetans materials (NOTs)—were to be held in confidence and used only by certain individuals. Improper exposure would lead to spiritual injury.

Following a dispute, an associate of Hubbard established the Church of the New Civilization, which embraced beliefs and counseling techniques similar to those of the Church of Scientology. Learning that the Church of the New Civilization intended to use and perhaps make public the procedures described in the NOTs, the Church of

Scientology went to court in an effort to halt the use and dissemination of these materials. One basis for the suit was the allegation that, in violation of federal copyright law, the Church of New Civilization had reproduced in its *Advanced Ability V* materials substantial portions of the particular expression of the NOTs—not merely the underlying ideas. The Church of the New Civilization responded with a standard copyright defense: It was necessary to copy the particular expression of the ideas in the NOTs in order to convey the underlying ideas; therefore, the copying was not prohibited. Further, it argued that any inquiry into the need to duplicate the text would entail impermissible judgments about religious tenets.

Asserting "that [t]he inquiry is one of linguistic, not theological, interpretation," the district court in *Scott* found that the vast majority of the Church of the New Civilization's copying was necessary in order to convey the underlying ideas. It concluded further, however, that some of the copying might not have been necessary, and it permitted the case to proceed to trial. Despite the court's statement to the contrary, it is far from clear that the judicial consideration involved no theological interpretation. Any determination about whether particular statements or components of the protected works need to be reproduced would have to consider the importance of the statements or components to the auditing process. For example, the works apparently shared a similar sequence of presentation, a factor that normally would support an argument for infringement. An argument that doctrinal concerns required that auditing be presented in a particular sequence would certainly involve a theological inquiry. Indeed, the court itself stated, "Whether the sequence is dictated by the demands of the subject matter is not clear." To be sure, as the court noted, some inquiry had to be made. If no inquiry were permissible, any text would be placed outside the protection of the copyright law by the simple claim that the copying was necessary for religious purposes. Moreover, it would be problematic if the copyright law refused to extend protection to religious works.

The *Scott* decision is disappointing, however, because of the court's rather simplistic treatment of complex and difficult issues. The court failed to note the complexity of the problem and only superficially discussed cases in which claims of impermissible religious evaluations were made. Further, the court never fully resolved the Church of the New Civilization's claims. The *Scott* decision was written in response to a motion for a preliminary injunction. The court denied the preliminary injunction on the ground that the balance of hardships tipped in favor of the defendants, and it never resolved the legal question of whether the copying was necessary.

The interplay of copyright and religion raises complex and difficult problems about the separation of church and state that have never really been explored in the courts. These cases, like others involving disputes about religious scriptures, at best merely begin the effort to resolve these problems.

Beryl R. Jones

Bibliography

Colby, Richard, "The Road to a Copyright Term of Life Plus Fifty Years," 3 *Communications and the Law* 12–17 (1984).

Hearings on S.1866 before Subcomm. No. 3 of the House Comm. on the Judiciary, 92d Cong., 1st Sess. (1971).

Nimmer, Melville, 1 Nimmer on Copyright, §1.05 [A] n. 7 (1990).

Cases and Statutes Cited

Lemon v. Kurtzman, 403 U.S. 602 (1971).

Religious Technology Center v. Scott, 660 F. Supp. 515 (C.D. Cal. 1987). Rev'd 869 F. 2d 1306 (1989).

United Christian Scientists v. Christian Science Board of Directors, First Church of Christ, Scientist, 829 F. 2d 1152 (D.C. Cir. 1987).

Private Law 92-60, 85 Stat. 857 (December 15, 1971), §1866.

Corporation of the Presiding Bishop of the Church of Jesus Christ of Latter-Day Saints v. Amos 483 U.S. 327 (1987)

The Supreme Court in *Corporation of Presiding Bishop of the Church of Jesus Christ of Latter-Day Saints v. Amos* (1987) addressed the serious issue of whether the religious organization exemption from Title VII of the Civil Rights Act of 1964 violates the

Establishment Clause. The case involved a claim filed by appellee Mayson, who had worked at the Deseret Gymnasium in Salt Lake City, Utah, a nonprofit public facility owned and operated by the Church of Jesus Christ of Latter-Day Saints. When the church discharged him in 1981 because he failed to qualify for a "temple recommend"—a worthiness standard for determining whether members are eligible to attend church temples—he, along with others, brought a civil rights class action against the church, under Section 703, for discriminating in employment on the basis of religion. The church defended on the ground that Section 702 of the Civil Rights Act exempted religious organizations from the act. At trial Mayson successfully argued that Section 702 of the Civil Rights Act violates the second part of the *Lemon* test in that the provision as applied to a secular activity has the primary effect of advancing religion.

Justice White, writing for the Court in reversing the district court's judgment, held that the statutory exemption constitutionally accommodated religious practices without violating the Establishment Clause. Indeed, all the justices—although offering variant rationales—concluded that the Establishment Clause does not bar all religious exemptions from general regulatory laws.

The majority held that a religious exemption must pass the three-pronged *Lemon* test to avoid conflicting with the Establishment Clause. As applied to the facts, the majority held that under *Lemon*'s secular purpose test, "it is a permissible legislative purpose to alleviate significant governmental interference with the ability of religious organizations to define and carry out their religious missions." In response to Mayson's argument that Section 702 went too far in exempting more than the religious organization's "religious activities," the Court stated that limiting the exemption to only "religious activities" would unduly burden the religious organization's ability to define and carry out its religious mission. The Court did note that the questioned activities involved nonprofit activities, and it declined to answer whether the result would have been the same if the activity had been for profit.

Lemon's secular effect test presented the most difficult challenge for the Court. The majority held that this test is violated only where "the *government itself* has advanced religion through its activities and influence." Because the incidental advancement of the church could not reasonably be attributable to the government, the exemption did not have an impermissible religious effect. Similarly, the breadth of the exemption diminishes, rather than enhances, entanglement.

Justice Brennan, with whom Justice Marshall joined, wrote that the legislature may have a constitutional secular purpose of allowing churches—consistent with the Free Exercise Clause—to identify and carry out their religious missions. This definitional process is complicated, because a religious "community represents an ongoing tradition of shared beliefs, an organic entity not reducible to a mere aggregation of individuals." Thus, although the secular purpose should be limited "ideally" to protecting only "religious activities," the distinction between religious and secular activities of the church "is not self-evident." If an exemption required a showing that the activity fit the "religious" rather than the "secular" category, then interpretive confusion would necessarily have a chilling effect on "the community's process of self-definition. . . ." For Justice Brennan, this "risk of chilling religious organizations is most likely to arise with respect to nonprofit activities," because nonprofit entities have "historically been organized specifically to provide certain community services, not simply to engage in commerce," and he, therefore, would have decided otherwise had the activity been for profit.

Justice O'Connor, in a concurring opinion, offered an endorsement test as an alternative to the *Lemon* analysis. She wrote that the *Lemon* test makes no sense, because any exemption has a legislative purpose beneficial to religion; yet not all exemptions can be invalid, because some are required as a matter of free exercise. O'Connor suggested that an improved establishment analysis would first admit that the lifting of a generally applicable regulatory burden necessarily "does have the effect of advancing religion." The next step then would be to determine whether the accommodation may "provide unjustifiable awards of assistance to religious organizations."

To resolve this issue, Justice O'Connor suggested that the test ought to ask "whether government's purpose is to endorse religion and whether the statute actually conveys a message of endorsement." To ascertain whether the statute conveys a message of endorsement, the relevant issue is how it would be perceived by an objective observer who is acquainted with the text, the legislative history, and the implementation of the statute.

As applied to the facts, Justice O'Connor concluded that "[b]ecause there is a probability that a nonprofit activity of a religious organization will itself be involved in the organization's mission, in my view the objective observer should perceive the Government action as an accommodation of the exercise of religion rather than as a Government endorsement of religion." Justice O'Connor noted that her analysis may have been otherwise had the activities been for profit.

Amos has since been cited repeatedly for two line-drawing propositions: (1) that the state may have as a proper secular purpose the lifting of a regulation which burdens the exercise of religion and (2) that such an "accommodation" purpose has constitutional limits perhaps best explained by Justice O'Connor's endorsement-test alternative to *Lemon.*

Richard Collin Mangrum

Bibliography

Gedicks, Fredrick Mark, "Toward a Constitutional Jurisprudence of Religious Group Rights," 1989 *Wisconsin Law Review* 99 (1989).

McClure, Scott D., "Religious Preferences in Employment Decisions: How Far May Religious Organizations Go?" 1990 *Duke Law Journal* 587 (1990).

Case Cited

Corporation of the Presiding Bishop of the Church of Jesus Christ of Latter-Day Saints v. Amos, 483 U.S. 327 (1987).

County of Allegheny v. American Civil Liberties Union

See LYNCH AND *ALLEGHENY* RELIGIOUS SYMBOLS CASES AND THE DECLINE OF THE *LEMON* TEST.

Crane v. Johnson 242 U.S. 339 (1917)

Various religious sects with members living in the United States either reject the practice of modern medicine or recommend, as an alternative to conventional medical treatment, the use of prayer or faith healing. Often the tenets of these faiths have come into conflict with state statutes regulating the practice of medicine. In the late 1800s and early 1900s, Christian Science practitioners of one such form of spiritual healing challenged state medical regulations in state courts and legislatures, seeking exemptions from medical licensing requirements and other legal impediments to the practice of their faith. In response, legislatures often enacted or amended regulatory statutes to accommodate these religious practices.

The petitioner in *Crane v. Johnson,* (1917) P. L. Crane, was a nonreligious "drugless practitioner" who used the power of faith, hope, and mental suggestion to treat his patients. California law required that individuals who were engaged in the practice of "drugless" medical treatment must first be licensed, a condition that required the completion of a prescribed course of study and examination. However, the licensing requirement explicitly did not "regulate, prohibit or apply to any kind of treatment by prayer." Crane claimed that this exemption for treatment by prayer discriminated in favor of certain religious faiths—specifically, the Church of Christian Science—to the prejudice of individuals who employed other forms of religious and nonreligious faith healing. Crane argued that this discrimination violated the Equal Protection Clause of the Fourteenth Amendment.

The Supreme Court, in a unanimous opinion by Justice Joseph McKenna, upheld the statute. Because Crane himself was involved only in nonreligious faith healing, the Court refused to consider the claim that California's statute discriminated among religious practices. Thus the only issue to be resolved was whether a state could legitimately distinguish between "treatment by prayer" and the kind of nonreligious mental healing practiced by the petitioner. That distinction was easily justified. By his own admission, Crane's practice was grounded on years of study and experience. Accordingly, it was reasonable for the state to require that individuals providing such treatments must possess the necessary knowledge and skill to do so competently. Treatment by prayer, on the other hand, was a matter of religion and required neither skill nor knowledge. As the California Supreme Court had stated in upholding the same law in *People v. Jordan*

(Calif., 1916), there is no reason to believe that "the prayer of an illiterate person may . . . be more productive of harm or less beneficial than that of one possessing the learning and skill of an educated physician."

The U.S. Supreme Court found *Crane* to be a simple case, but that conclusion must be understood in its historical context. In 1917 the Supreme Court had not applied the First Amendment and the rest of the Bill of Rights to state governments; the incorporation of the Bill of Rights into the Fourteenth Amendment had not yet been recognized. The Equal Protection Clause did apply to state governments, but the standard of review courts used to implement this provision was a weak and differential one. Virtually any discriminatory classification would be upheld in 1917 as falling within the legislature's discretion.

Moreover, the exemption challenged in *Crane* provided relatively limited benefit to practitioners engaged in treatment through prayer. Certainly it did not clearly entitle them to substitute their spiritual healing for medication or surgery to the detriment of the patient. The law at issue merely permitted faith healers to engage in prayer healing without a license. The issues raised by *Crane* would receive more rigorous consideration today. If an exemption from general regulations was provided to certain religious faiths, but not to others, the exemption would be successfully challenged as violating the Establishment Clause of the First Amendment. In *Larson v. Valente* (1982) the Supreme Court emphatically explained that the "clearest command of the Establishment clause is that one religious denomination cannot be officially preferred over another." Thus, for example, statutes accepting treatment through prayer "in accordance with the tenets of a recognized religious body," as fulfilling state-mandated parental obligations for the care of one's children, have been held to violate the Constitution in that these laws discriminate between recognized and nonrecognized faiths. Although some courts in these circumstances ground their holdings on both Establishment Clause and equal protection grounds—such as the Ohio court did in *State v. Miskimens* (Ohio, C.P. 1984)—most judges base their opinions on Establishment Clause requirements, as did the courts in *Walker v. Superior Court* (Calif., 1988) and *Newmark v. Williams* (Del., Super. Ct. 1991). This conforms with the general tendency of courts today to subsume equal protection issues relating to religion under the rubric of the Establishment Clause.

A different issue arises if the exemption for treatment through prayer is extended to all religious faiths but not to the nonreligious individual whose belief system is in conflict with general health and medical regulations. Generally speaking, as *Hanzel v. Arter* (S.D. Ohio, 1985) and *Clonlara, Inc. v. Runkel* (E.D. Mich., 1989) illustrate, exemptions exclusively for religious believers are not held to violate equal protection principles. The criteria for determining when an exemption from general regulations for religious individuals will violate the Establishment Clause remains indeterminate and is a matter of controversy at this time.

Alan E. Brownstein

Bibliography

Gekas, JoAnna A., "California's Prayer Healing Dilemma," 14 *Hastings Constitutional Law Quarterly* 395–419 (1987).

Laughran, Catherine W., "Religious Beliefs and the Criminal Justice System: Some Problems of the Faith Healer," 8 *Loyola Los Angeles Law Review* 396–431 (1975).

Cases Cited

Clonlara, Inc. v. Runkel, 722 F. Supp. 1442 (E.D. Mich. 1989).

Crane v. Johnson, 242 U.S. 339 (1917).

Hanzel v. Arter, 625 F. Supp. 1259 (S.D. Ohio 1985).

Larson v. Valente, 456 U.S. 228, 244 (1982).

Newmark v. Williams, 588 A. 2d 1108 (Del. Super. Ct. 1991).

People v. Jordan, 172 Cal. 391 (1916).

State v. Miskimens, 490 N.E. 2d 931 (Ohio C.P. 1984).

Walker v. Superior Court, 763 P. 2d 852 (Cal. 1988) cert. denied 491 U.S. 965 (1989).

Cults and the Law

Religious cults pose many difficult problems for the legal system, often involving the constitutionality of government efforts to regulate proselytizing and recruiting by such religious groups and to control the conduct of their members. But cults have also generated litigation that raises difficult issues of tax, tort, and criminal law. Sometimes they have gone to court to defend themselves against official persecution or to challenge the tactics used by parents and "deprogrammers" to "rescue" recruits from their organizations. In other cases cultists have been the aggressors, using litigation as a weapon to attack those they consider their enemies.

Not a Legal Concept

Whether modern cults are, as they often claim, oppressed "new religious movements" or simply effective means by which charismatic leaders accrue power and wealth, there is no doubt that they have met vigorous resistance when they attempted to claim for themselves the same rights as more traditional religions. The Holy Spirit Association for the Unification of World Christianity (the Unification Church), led by Rev. Sun Myung Moon, offers a case in point. This organization has fought in court over such issues as whether facets of its aggressive political and economic agendas are bona fide religious practices and whether its foreign members can legitimately seek permanent residence in the United States in order to continue their proselytizing. Victimized by an allegedly discriminatory Minnesota statute that subjected only religious groups such as theirs to certain reporting requirements that received more than 50 percent of their contributions from nonmembers, the "Moonies" had to go to the Supreme Court to get that law struck down as a violation of the Establishment Clause in *Larson v. Valente* (1981).

The legal problems and approach to litigation of the Unification Church are not necessarily representative. Generalizing about cults and the law is extremely difficult, in large part because "cult" is not a legal concept. Indeed, it is not even a word with a clear definition. The term has often been employed pejoratively by members of mainstream religions to stigmatize new groups or ones that merely hold views strikingly different from their own. Thus one treatise on cult law devotes much of its attention to Christian Science. Sociologists have tried to achieve greater precision by identifying common features of groups that give rise to similar social problems, but their efforts have yielded a plethora of definitions, none of them particularly helpful to lawyers and judges. For those whose concern is the law, the term "cult" is most usefully applied to organizations that exhibit certain distinctive and problematic qualities giving rise to legal questions not normally associated with mainstream religious groups. These include (1) the swearing of total allegiance to an all-powerful leader; (2) the leadership's discouraging or forbidding of rational thought; (3) the use of deceptive recruitment techniques; and (4) the tendency of the group to discourage independence and to goad adherents into submission, thus producing a state of total dependence on the organization. There is, however, no legal definition of the word "cult."

Nor does the law distinguish between cults and legitimate religious groups. Indeed, any attempt to do so would violate the First Amendment. In *United States v. Ballard* (1944) the Supreme Court took the position that the First Amendment's religious clauses forbid government from inquiring into the truth or falsity of religious beliefs. At most a court may seek to determine whether someone's views are sincerely held—and then probably only if that individual is seeking some benefit from the government, such as a tax exemption or classification as a conscientious objector. Whether or not a cult's creed is acceptable, logical, consistent, or even comprehensible, it enjoys the protection of the Free Exercise Clause. Indeed, government may not even distinguish between groups that believe in a supreme being and those that do not. As long as an organization's dogma occupies in the life of its adherents a place parallel to that filled by God in more conventional religions—the Supreme Court has intimated—its members' beliefs and practices are protected by the First Amendment.

Because that amendment prohibits the federal government from distinguishing between legitimate and illegitimate religions, the Internal Revenue Service (IRS) has little choice but to grant even unpopular cults lacking any commitment to traditional spiritual values the benefit of the income tax exemption Congress has conferred on religious groups. Under at least one provision of the Internal Revenue Code, "any organization claiming to be a church" *is* a church. The IRS has identified fourteen criteria to help determine whether an organization qualifies as a church, one of them being whether it has a "distinct religious history." The courts, however, have applied these guidelines only haphazardly, and the

IRS, bound by the code itself, has avoided evaluating the legitimacy of organizations claiming to be religious in nature.

Instead the IRS has concentrated on determining whether groups that seek tax-exempt status satisfy the criteria set forth in section 501(c)(3) of the Internal Revenue Code. That provision requires (1) that an organization operate exclusively for religious purposes, (2) that no part of its revenue inure to the benefit of any private individual, (3) that no substantial portion of its activities involve the use of propaganda or attempts to influence legislation, and (4) that it not participate in any political campaign. In addition, courts have imposed a requirement that a group claiming to be an exempt religious organization serve a valid public purpose and confer a public benefit. The IRS revoked the tax-exempt status of the Church by Mail and the Church of Scientology because they failed to comply with the requirements of section 501(c)(3); in 1993, however, it later restored the Scientologists' status. In addition, under legislation enacted by Congress in 1976, religious groups that engage in commercial enterprises, such as manufacturing, must pay taxes on their "unrelated business income."

Cults and Laws of General Applicability

Cults enjoy even less immunity from criminal statutes than from the tax laws. The Free Exercise Clause forbids punishing anyone for religious beliefs. The Supreme Court has held, however, that the clause does not relieve a person of the obligation to comply with valid and neutral laws of general applicability that regulate or prohibit conduct in which the religion requires the person to engage or that commands the person to do something which the religion forbids. Thus, in *Employment Division, Department of Human Resources v. Smith* (1990), the Supreme Court affirmed the right of a state to enforce its drug laws against members of a Native American church who used peyote in religious ceremonies. It adopted a position already staked out by lower courts. In *United States v. Kuch* (D.C., 1968), for example, the U.S. District Court for the District of Columbia had held that it was not a violation of the Free Exercise Clause to punish a self-styled "ordained minister of the Neo-American Church" for possessing and distributing LSD and marijuana—even though members of that "church" professed to consider psychedelic substances the "true Host" and to believe that it was "the Religious duty of all members" to ingest the substances regularly under the guidance of a religious leader called a "Boo Hoo." In *Randall v. Wyrick* (Mo., 1977) a federal district court in Missouri upheld the drug-possession conviction of the leader of the Aquarian Brotherhood Church, despite his insistence that the use of hashish, marijuana, and cocaine was considered sacrament by that religion. The court took the position that freedom of belief was entirely protected but that freedom of religious actions was limited by the state's interest in protecting the public from the dangers posed by drugs. Although government can punish drug use and other dangerous conduct that some claim is required by their religion, prohibiting conduct *because* it is religious does—at least in the absence of a compelling governmental interest—violate the Free Exercise Clause. For that reason, in *Church of Lukumi Babalu Aye, Inc. and Ernesto Pichardo v. City of Hialeah* (1993) the Supreme Court struck down municipal ordinances banning the ritual sacrifice of animals practiced by followers of the Santería faith. As long as government does not engage in this sort of targeting of religion and only legislates in general terms, however, it may constitutionally punish religiously motivated behavior, whether this be the snake handling practiced by some southern sects, such as the Holiness Church, or the polygamy once expected of Mormons.

Cults and First Amendment Protections

Although the First Amendment does not shield criminal conduct, it does protect the distribution of literature by cultists and probably their efforts to recruit and indoctrinate new members. In *Lovell v. Griffin* (1938) the Supreme Court held that a city had violated the amendment's guarantees of freedom of expression by requiring a Jehovah's Witness who wanted to hand out religious material to obtain permission from an official, who had complete discretion about whether to grant or withhold the required authorization. In *Murdock v. Pennsylvania* (1943) the Court held unconstitutional the punishment of Jehovah's Witnesses for selling religious books without first paying a municipal license tax. *Prince v. Massachusetts* (1944) sanctions the application of child labor laws to prevent minors from hawking religious literature, and *Heffron v. International Society for Krishna Consciousness* (1981) holds that government may impose reasonable time, place, and manner restrictions on literature distribution and the solicitation of funds by religious groups when these activities take place in areas that have been opened up for the exchange of ideas, such as state fair grounds. Such restrictions may not, however, discriminate against some views and in favor of others. In another Hare Krishna case, the Court declared that it was permissible to forbid the repetitive solicitation of money within airport terminals. *Lee v. International Society for Krishna Consciousness, Inc.* (1992) also held, however, that the Constitution protects both the collection of money on public sidewalks outside airport terminals and the distribution of literature within them. In *Larson v. Valente* (1981) the Supreme Court took the position that a state law which imposed registration and reporting requirements on some religious groups that solicited money from nonmembers but not on others violated the Establishment Clause.

It is doubtful that the justices would tolerate much interference with cults' recruiting and indoctrination. Beginning with *Cantwell v. Connecticut* (1940) the Court invalidated a number of statutes that obstructed the dissemination of religious views on the ground that these laws interfered with freedom of expression. Groups commonly identified as cults often go beyond merely preaching their message to potential converts, however; they often engage in an extreme form of indoctrination which critics view as thought manipulation and compare to the "brainwashing" that the Chinese practiced on American prisoners during the Korean War. Unlike the evangelism of conventional churches, contends law professor Richard Delgado, cult recruiting is deceptive; potential members never give informed consent to affiliation with the organization, because they are not provided with complete information about the group until their will is no longer free. The deception to which cults resort justifies government intervention to protect the targets of their recruiting efforts, Delgado maintains. Such intervention would not violate the Free Exercise Clause, he insists, because that constitutional provision was designed to protect self-determination in religious matters and because the use of deception and coercion to impart belief is the antithesis of self-determination. Although Delgado is the leading legal expert on cults—and many people find his argument persuasive—there is little case authority to support his position.

Cults and Other Legal Questions

There is a similar shortage of judicial opinions about other legal questions enkindled by cult practices, and especially about issues related to deprogramming. Parents, convinced that their children have been "brainwashed" into joining deviant religious groups, have increasingly resorted to legal and extralegal means to wrest their offspring from the control of such organizations so that they can be "deprogrammed." Generally carried out by professional deprogrammers (or "exit counselors"), the goal of that process is to restore freedom of thought; once this has been accomplished, it is assumed, the youthful recruit will no longer wish to be affiliated with a cult.

Because deprogramming is practiced on a person who is at least initially an unwilling participant, the first step is to obtain physical control of the subject. The legal way to accomplish this is by securing a conservatorship order from a court. In some states a relative may be able to obtain one of these during an ex parte proceeding in which the cult member does not even participate. If the deprogramming works, by the time a full hearing is held both parties are in complete agreement, and there is nothing to litigate. This procedure smacks of judicially sanctioned kidnapping, and both a state court of appeals in *Katz v. Superior Court* (Calif., 1977) and a federal court of appeals in *Taylor v. Gilmartin* (10th Cir. 1982) have ruled against the use of state conservatorship laws for deprogramming purposes. But those are narrow decisions which focus on the language of the particular statutes in question and fail to address the fundamental issues posed by this approach to deprogramming.

Rather than seeking conservatorship, some parents resort to extralegal methods. The cult member is coaxed, tricked, or physically coerced into leaving the group and going with a deprogrammer to an isolated location where he or she is confined while deprogramming is carried out. Those who resort to this method often commit both the crime of kidnapping and the tort of false imprisonment. Yet prosecutors have proved reluctant to file charges in such cases, and when they do, public sympathy for the parents has frequently made it impossible to persuade grand juries to indict or trial juries to convict. Tort suits are also rare. If the deprogramming works, the former cult member does not want to litigate. Unsuccessfully deprogrammed cult members have sued for both false imprisonment and the intentional infliction of emotional distress, but judges sympathetic to parents and deprogrammers have often dismissed such actions. Even when successful, suits of this type have yielded only modest damage awards. Victims of deprogramming have also sued under two federal civil rights statutes, 42 U.S.C., sections 1983 and 1985(3). There are, however, serious doubts about whether either of these laws can constitutionally be applied to deprogramming, and such actions have also proved unsuccessful.

Former members have enjoyed greater success when suing the cult to which they once belonged. Some of these cases have resulted in the award of substantial damages. Yet the degree to which cult "brainwashing" is actionable is a question the courts have not fully resolved. Generally, where indoctrination is preceded by deceit regarding the nature of the organization or by other fraud, the victim may sue in tort because of the lack of informed consent. On the other hand, in *Weiss v. Patrick* (D.R.I. 1978) and *Ward v. Conner* (4th Cir. 1981) federal courts took the position that if someone's association with a cult is knowing and voluntary at the outset, the group will not be liable for damages because of the means it subsequently employs to procure the person's loyalty.

Besides having to establish that one has a legal claim, a former member who sues a cult faces serious constitutional obstacles. If the complaint is based on the defendant's protected religious activity, it will fail. In *Paul v. Watchtower Bible and Tract Society* (9th Cir. 1987), for example, a woman sued for defamation, fraud, and outrageous conduct after being subjected to "shunning" (a procedure under which loyal Jehovah's Witnesses are instructed to ignore former members of that organization). The federal court which decided the case held that shunning is protected by the First Amendment and that requiring the church to pay damages would "restrict the Jehovah's Witnesses' free exercise of religion." On the other hand, a cult cannot avoid liability merely by claiming that its activity is religious in nature, and thus some courts have upheld damages based on harassment of former members.

Suits involving cults often raise difficult legal issues. So do governmental actions designed to control cult conduct. Some of the activities of deviant religious groups—such as the stockpiling of military weapons by the Church Universal and Triumphant and the Branch Davidians—are extremely dangerous. Other cult behavior—such as the aggressive panhandling in which Hare Krishnas engage—is merely annoying to persons who do not share their views. The proselytizing of Jehovah's Witnesses is as clearly protected by the First Amendment as is that of Baptists, but the recruiting and indoctrination techniques utilized by some cults raise legitimate concerns that those of mainstream religious groups do not. On the other hand, so does deprogramming, which, however nobly motivated, is often accomplished through methods that are illegal. This is an area of the law where even a definition of the most basic concept is elusive and where there are few easy answers and many hard questions.

Michal Belknap
Cathy Shipe

Bibliography

Aronin, Douglas, "Cults, Deprogramming, and Guardianship: A Model Legislative Proposal," 17 *Columbia Journal of Law and Social Problems* 163–286 (1982).

Bacus, Andrew P., "The Adjudication of Religious Beliefs in Section 1985(3) Deprogramming Litigation," 11 *Oklahoma City University Law Review* 413–436 (1986).

Blum, Andrew. "Church's Litany of Lawyers," *National Law Journal,* 1, 36–38 (June 14, 1993).

Broadus, Joseph E., "Use of the 'Choice of Evils' Defense in Religious Deprogramming Cases Offends Free Exercise While Ignoring the Right to Be Free from Compelled Treatment," 1 *George Mason University Civil Rights Law Journal* 171–205 (1990).

Delgado, Richard, "Cults and Conversion: The Case for Informed Consent," 16 *Georgia Law Review* 533–574 (1982).

Heins, Marjorie, "'Other People's Faiths': The Scientology Litigation and the

Justiciability of Religious Fraud," 9 *Hastings Constitutional Law Quarterly* 153–197 (1981).
Moore, Joey Peter, "Piercing the Religious Veil of the So-Called Cults," 7 *Pepperdine Law Review* 685–710 (1980).
Morken, Paul J., "Church Discipline and Civil Tort Claims: Should Ecclesiastical Tribunals Be Immune?" 28 *Idaho Law Review* 93–165 (1991–1992).
"Note: Cults, Deprogrammers, and the Necessity Defense," 80 *Michigan Law Review* 271–311 (1981).
Rubenstein, I. H. *A Treatise on the Law on Cults,* 2nd ed. (Chicago: Ordain, 1981).
Rudin, Marcia R., "The Cult Phenomenon: Fad or Fact?" 9 *New York Review of Law and Social Change* 17–32 (1980–1981).
Shaller, Wendy Gerzog, "Churches and Their Enviable Tax Status," 51 *University of Pittsburgh Law Review* 345–364 (1990).
Whalen, Charles M., "'Church' in the Internal Revenue Code: The Definitional Problems," 45 *Fordham Law Review* 885–928 (1977).
"Who Represents the Church?" *National Law Journal* 36 (June 14, 1993).

Cases Cited

Cantwell v. Connecticut, 310 U.S. 296 (1940).
Church of Lukumi Babalu Aye, Inc. and Ernesto Pichardo v. City of Hialeah, 508 U.S. 520 (1993).
Employment Division, Department of Human Resources v. Smith, 494 U.S. 872 (1990).
Heffron v. International Society for Krishna Consciousness, 452 U.S. 640 (1981).
Katz v. Superior Court, 73 Cal. App. 3d 952, 141 Cal. Rptr. 234 (1977).
Larsen v. Valente, 456 U.S. 228 (1982).
Lee v. International Society for Krishna Consciousness, Inc., 505 U.S. 830 (1992).
Lovell v. Griffin, 303 U.S. 444 (1938).
Murdock v. Pennsylvania, 319 U.S. 105 (1943).
Paul v. Watchtower Bible and Tract Society, 819 F. 2d 875 (9th Cir. 1987).
Prince v. Massachusetts, 321 U.S. 158 (1944).
Randall v. Wyrick, 441 F. Supp. 312 (W.D. Mo. 1977).
Taylor v. Gilmartin, 686 F. 2d 1346 (10th Cir. 1982). cert. denied, 459 U.S. 147 (1983).
United States v. Kuch, 288 F. Supp. 439 (D.D.C. 1968).
United States v. Ballard, 322 U.S. 78 (1944).
Ward v. Conner, 657 F. 2d 45 (4th Cir. 1981).
Weiss v. Patrick, 453 F. Supp. 717 (D.R. I. 1978).

Cummings v. Missouri 71 U.S. (4 Wall.) 277 (1866)

In this 5-to-4 post–Civil War decision the U.S. Supreme Court invalidated several provisions of the Missouri Constitution of 1865, which required voters, state employees, jurors, lawyers, teachers, corporate officers, and clergypersons to take a loyalty oath on pain of disenfranchisement and relinquishment of their offices. These people were required to swear that they had not taken arms against the United States, nor had in any way aided or sympathized with those who had done so. John A. Cummings, a Catholic priest, was convicted of practicing his calling without taking the oath. He appealed to the Supreme Court, which in *Cummings v. Missouri* (1866) held that this requirement infringed the constitutional bans against bills of attainder and ex post facto laws.

Speaking for the Court, Justice Stephen J. Field held that the Missouri scheme constituted punishment for past acts which were legal when committed and which had no relation to a person's fitness for office. The Court added that Missouri unlawfully presumed Cummings's guilt until he purged himself by taking the oath. Justice Samuel F. Miller dissented. Joining him were Chief Justice Salmon P. Chase and Associate Justices David Davis and Noah H. Swayne. Miller did not write a dissent in *Cummings,* however. Instead, he wrote his dissent in a companion case, *Ex parte Garland* (1867), arguing that a law which requires an oath for all practitioners of a profession could not be considered an ex post facto law: "a statute, then, which designates no criminal, either by name or description—which declares no guilt, pronounces no sentence, and inflicts no punishment—can in no sense be called a bill of attainder."

The broad interpretation of the bill of attainder and ex post facto clauses in *Cummings* have since been partly repudiated. But, concerning law and religion, the holding in *Cummings* is on even firmer ground today. In 1867, one year before the adoption of the Fourteenth Amendment, the religion clauses of the First Amendment did not limit state power. In *Cummings,* Missouri argued that nothing in the federal Constitution precluded state licensing of the clergy, and the Court did not hold otherwise. However, since *Cantwell v. Connecticut* (1940) and *Everson v. Board of Education* (1947) it has been settled that the religion clauses apply to the states through the Due Process Clause of the Fourteenth Amendment. Under current standards—developed in such cases as *Gonzalez v. Roman Catholic Archbishop of Manila* (1929) and *Serbian Orthodox Diocese v. Milivojevich* (1976)—it seems clear that, as applied to the specific facts of *Cummings,* the Missouri loyalty oath would violate both religion clauses.

José Julián Alvarez-González

Bibliography

Adams, Arlin M., and William R. Hanlon, "*Jones v. Wolf:* Church Autonomy and the Religion Clauses of the First Amendment," 128 *University of Pennsylvania Law Review* 1291–1339 (1980).

Swisher, Carl B., *Stephen J. Field: Craftsman of the Law* (Hamden, Conn: Archon, 1963; reprint of 1930 edition).

Cases Cited

Cantwell v. Connecticut, 310 U.S. 296 (1940).

Cummings v. Missouri, 71 U.S. (4 Wall.) 277 (1866).

Everson v. Board of Education, 330 U.S. 1 (1947).

Ex parte Garland, 71 U.S. (4 Wall.) 333 (1867).

Gonzalez v. Roman Catholic Archbishop of Manila, 280 U.S. 1 (1929).

Serbian Orthodox Diocese v. Milivojevich, 426 U.S. 696 (1976).

D

"Dale's Laws"

"Dale's Laws" (as they were popularly known), or *Lawes Divine, Morall and Martiall* (as they were properly titled), were the first written legal codes of Virginia and were enforced, in some form or another, from May 1610 to April 1619. Originally adopted under the governorship of Sir Thomas Gates in 1610, these laws were meant to bring strict military order to the then-moribund colony. When Sir Thomas Gates arrived in Virginia in May 1610, only a handful of colonists had survived what was known as the "starving time" of the winter of 1609–1610. Promoters of the Virginia Company attributed the colony's problems to the moral degeneracy and lack of discipline of its colonists. Gates's responsibility as governor was to turn the situation around through the implementation of martial law. Three days after his arrival he posted a list of twenty-one articles that the colonists were to obey. It is unclear whether Gates himself or someone in England wrote these original articles, but Gates did add to them as necessity within the colony dictated.

The misnomer "Dale's Laws" comes from the fact that this list of articles was compiled, enlarged, and printed in 1612 by Sir Thomas Dale, then the acting deputy governor and high marshal of Virginia. Dale, who was governor from 1611 to 1616, when Gates returned, really only supplemented Gates's list of offenses and punishments with laws designed to protect the Virginia Company and with instructions regarding the duties of the colony's military officers.

Under "Dale's Laws" life in colonial Virginia was more like a penal colony than a place to gain one's fortune. All colonists were organized into labor gangs that were summoned to work by "the beating of the Drum." They were ordered to keep their houses "sweete and cleane" and were forbidden to run away. Furthermore, deference had to be paid to all superiors, work had to be conducted with diligence, and all mischief was forbidden. Infractions of any of these rules incurred severe punishments, often including death.

In the effort to bring discipline back to the colony "Dale's Laws" made religious observance and religious moral behavior central to the maintenance of order. Under article 33 of the laws, for example, there was a colony-wide screening in which every man and woman had to "give an account of his and their faith" to a local minister. If such faith were found lacking, the wayward colonist was then required to meet regularly with the minister and, if failing to meet those obligations, was reprimanded by whipping and public confession. Likewise all settlers were forced, by threat of losing their allowances or being flogged, to attend church services two times a day. As with work in the labor groups, colonists were regularly summoned to these services by "the first towling of the Bell." The *Lawes* also strongly encouraged the settlers to prepare for church "at home with private prayer, that they may be better fitted for the public."

"Captaines and Officers," who were no doubt ubiquitous in this small and strict military regime, were also required to attend to their religious duties. The first article of the *Lawes Divine* established that they "diligently frequent Morning and Evening prayer" at which, every time, they were required to read aloud the six-page-long prayer printed at the end of the *Lawes.* This prayer, incidentally, was a jeremiad, emphasizing how sinful the colonists were, asking God for forgiveness, and, at the end, asking protection from "mutinies and dissentions" and other internal disorders.

In addition to forcing people to attend religious services regularly, the *Lawes* established a strict code of morality about matters of personal behavior. Sodomy and adultery, for example, were punishable by death. Taking an oath untruly, or bearing false witness (i.e., lying), was also punishable by death, as was the offense of sacrilege, or "violating and abusing any sacred ministry." Blasphemy was an offense punishable by having a "bodkin thrust through [the offender's] tongue," and colonists could also be punished for failing to hold their local minister "in all reverend regard, and dutiful intreatie."

Apparently these strict rules were enforced. Sir Thomas Dale, who was a veteran soldier before coming to Virginia, had a particular reputation as a taskmaster. He did put people to death—often in cruel ways, such as burning them or breaking them on the wheel—and he made life so generally miserable that some colonists committed suicide or ran away. Dale maintained order, for the most part, through the numerous soldiers who patrolled the colony, but the *Lawes* also established an ecclesiastical policing network—what some historians have called an early form of a vestry. Under article 7 every church was to have a board of four church members that would keep up the church and, more important, "inform of the abuses and neglects of the people in their duties" and then reprimand them accordingly.

Colonial Virginia under the *Lawes Divine,* like the Puritan colonies of New England, was a place in which church and state were one and the same. The laws did not tolerate religious dissent of any sort and strongly enforced the inculcation of the state-supported religion. The laws also established strict standards of behavior that were enforced even more strictly. In April 1619 martial law under the *Lawes Divine* was repealed, and a more representative style of government was established; but the stricter elements of the *Lawes* remained. Sabbath observance was still mandatory, morally questionable behavior was still punishable, and local clergymen still had the authority to act as agents of the state.

Stewart Davenport

Bibliography

Diamond, Sigmund, "From Organization to Society: Virginia in the Seventeenth Century," in Stanely N. Katz, *Colonial America, Essays in Politics and Social Development,* 2nd ed. (New York: Knopf, 1976).

Force, Peter, *Tracts and Other Papers, Relating to the Origin, Settlement, and Progress of the Colonies in North America: From the Discovery of the Country to the Year 1776,* vol. III, tract II (Washington, D.C.: Pete & Force, 1836–1846).

Lippy, Charles H., Robert Choquette, and Stafford Poole, *Christianity Comes to the Americas, 1492–1776* (New York: Paragon House, 1992).

Rutman, Darrett B., "The Virginian Company and Its Military Regime," in Darrett B. Rutman, *The Old Dominion: Essays for Thomas Perkins Abernathy* (Charlottesville: University Press of Virginia, 1964).

Woolverton, John Fredrick, *Colonial Anglicanism in North America* (Detroit: Wayne State University Press, 1984).

De Facto Establishments of Religion

In his seminal *The Garden and the Wilderness* (1965) Mark De Wolfe Howe wrote that the social reality of the United States is one which demands "the advancement of religious interest." This reality was coined by Howe as the nation's "de facto establishment" of religion.

As Howe makes clear, there are two aspects of this de facto establishment. The first are the nonlegal social forces that shape the culture, including the nation's religious traditions and its commitment to religious freedom. The second are the religious traditions and tributes that enjoy the benefit of government support, such as the names of cities (e.g., St. Paul and Corpus Christi), the national motto ("In God We Trust"), and the observance of national holidays that have religious significance (e.g., Thanksgiving and Christmas). Even the U.S. Supreme Court begins its sessions with the invocation "God Save the United States and the Honorable Court."

The existence of this second aspect of the de facto establishment—i.e., government acknowledgment and support of the society's religious tradition—has proved to be problematic in the development of Establishment Clause doctrine under the First Amendment. How does one reconcile the existence of Thanksgiving as an official holiday with the notion that government should not endorse religion? How does one reconcile the existence of the Christmas holiday or Sunday closing laws with the notion that government must remain neutral toward all religions? How does one reconcile Justice Douglas's observation in *Zorach v. Clauson* (1952) that "[w]e are a religious people whose institutions presuppose a Supreme Being" with the notion that government should be free of religious influence?

The suggestion that all such governmental acknowledgements and tributes to religion are unconstitutional is, of course, not plausible. Religion is too much a part of the public culture to be excised. It is, therefore, not surprising to note, as the Court did in *Lynch v. Donnelly* (1984), that "there is an unbroken history of official acknowledgment in all three branches of government of the role of religion in American life from at least 1789." Indeed, there is a strong argument that excluding every facet of religion in the public culture would not be desirable even if it were possible. As Justice Anthony Kennedy noted in his opinion in *Lee v. Weisman* (1992), "A relentless and all-pervasive attempt to exclude religion from every aspect of public life could itself become inconsistent with the Constitution."

With the option of a full exclusion therefore unavailable, the Supreme Court has struggled when issues surrounding the legality of purported de facto establishments have arisen. In *Marsh v. Chambers* (1983) the Court's solution to a constitutional challenge to the practice of legislative prayer was simply to create an ad hoc exception to the Court's normal establishment doctrine. Relying on a historical/traditional test apparently intended only to apply to the facts of the case at hand, the Court upheld the challenged practice while virtually admitting that legislative prayer would not otherwise survive settled Establishment Clause inquiry.

In other cases the Court has attempted to resolve challenges by inquiring whether or not the religious practice involved has been significantly "secularized." For example, in *McGowen v. Maryland* (1961) the Court upheld the legality of Sunday closing laws, relying principally on this approach. More recently, in *Lynch* v. Donnelly (1984) and *County of Allegheny v. American Civil Liberties Union* (1989), the Court applied this inquiry to Establishment Clause challenges to government-sponsored nativity scenes, holding that their legality would depend on the context in which the display appeared. If the nativity scene appeared as part of a broad display, it could survive constitutional scrutiny (*Lynch*); if, on the other hand, "nothing in the context of the display detracts from the crèche's religious message," the practice would be found unconstitutional (*County of Allegheny*).

A third approach—which has not been formally relied on by the Supreme Court but has occasionally been alluded to in some opinions—is to apply a *de minimus* scrutiny to the challenged action. Under this approach culturally ingrained de facto establishments could be upheld as not presenting any serious constitutional concern.

None of these approaches is analytically satisfying. Ad hoc decisionmaking, such as that applied in *Marsh,* is exactly that—ad hoc. It provides no guides for future cases, nor does it place itself in an existing analytic framework. The secularization approach taken in *McGowan, Lynch* and *County of Allegheny* also has its infirmities. First, it may be criticized as employing no more than a "we know it when we see it" test, since it depends so much on the perception of the person reviewing the Establishment Clause claim. Second, the conclusion that religious matters may become, or have become, secularized has been fairly criticized as an attack on the integrity of the religious practice involved. The *McGowan*, *Lynch*, and *County of Allegheny* cases therefore have been soundly criticized from all sides. Those who search for workable legal standards have found the secularization approach unsatisfactory because of its fluidity; those seeking a strong separationist position criticize the decisions as allowing for too much public acknowledgement of religion; and those who hold strong beliefs regarding the inviolacy of religious belief and practice criticize the decisions for their purported "secularizing" of what to them are fundamentally religious matters.

The *de minimus* approach, as well, is not without its problems. As with the secularization approach, it is equally demeaning to characterize a religious matter as *de minimus.* More broadly, even the notion that there can be *de minimus* constitutional violations is itself problematic.

A better approach than those taken by the Court might be simply to address the problem of the de facto establishments in a more straightforward manner. Concede that there is such a class of establishments that should avoid strict scrutiny, and then set about the business of identifying that class. This approach, moreover, is not without its First Amendment analogy. The Court has used a similar classification approach in determining that some forms of expression (obscenity, fighting words, etc.) are not properly understood as falling within the protection of the Freedom of Speech Clause.

Nevertheless, even this classification approach is likely to be problematic because of the inherent difficulty in resolving the underlying definitional issue. For example, how is the Court to determine whether the national celebration of Christmas should be classified as an appropriate de facto establishment? Further, assume that the national celebration of Christmas fits the appropriate de facto establishment definition. Does that mean that nativity scenes at city hall should come within this definitional ambit? Similarly, to use the example in *Marsh*, how is it to be determined whether legislative prayer is an appropriate de facto establishment? And assuming that it is to be found constitutional under this approach, should graduation convocations be upheld as well? There is little to suggest that these definitional issues can be easily resolved.

Undoubtedly, then, the existence of de facto establishments will continue to lead to confusing judicial decisions and tortured doctrine. These results, however, may be inevitable; the existence of an antiestablishment prohibition combined with unremovable vestiges of religion in the culture can lead only to a confused mosaic.

William Marshall

Bibliography

Bellah, Robert N., "Civil Religion in America," 96 *Daedalus* 1–21 (1967).

Howe, Mark de Wolfe, *The Garden and the Wilderness* (Chicago: University of Chicago Press, 1965).

Marshall, William P., "'We Know It When We See It': The Supreme Court and Establishment," 59 *Southern California Law Review* 495–550 (1986).

Note, "Developments in the Law: Religion and the State," 100 *Harvard Law Review* 1606–1781 (1987).

Cases Cited

County of Allegheny v. American Civil Liberties Union, 492 U.S. 573 (1989).
Lee v. Weisman, 505 U.S. 577 (1992).
Lynch v. Donnelly, 465 U.S. 668 (1984).
Marsh v. Chambers, 463 U.S. 783 (1983).
McGowan v. Maryland, 366 U.S. 420 (1961).
Zorach v. Clauson, 343 U.S. 306 (1952).

Definitions of Religion in Constitutional Law

The very first words of the U.S. Bill of Rights protect religious liberty: "Congress shall make no law respecting an establishment of religion, or prohibiting the free exercise thereof; . . ." These magnificent words mask a perplexing dilemma. Preventing government establishment of religion and protecting religious exercise require an ability both to recognize a religion and to distinguish legitimate religious claims from spurious ones. But every effort to make such distinction infuses the Constitution with some particular notion of a legitimate religion or religious practice, and that is precisely what the First Amendment should forbid.

The solution to this dilemma cannot be found in any search for a "neutral" definition: Words are never neutral. Hence, no "neutral principles" are available for ascertaining when a *religious* belief, practice, institution, or identity is genuinely at stake. J. E. Barnhart describes the problem thus:

> A definition of religion which does not exclude any tradition that is already within the general assortment of religious phenomena (Geertz) is a diluted definition pleasing no one. Many who are recognized as strongly religious will protest that a lowest common denominator definition cannot capture the 'essence' of religion. . . . Any attempt to expand the definition of religion in order to save it

from remaining the diluted lowest common denominator will run into the problem of exclusiveness. . . . The problem here becomes a kind of paradox. If we try to gain depth in our definition of religion, we lose scope and breadth. But if we seek breadth, we lose depth. . . .

> It seeks to be impossible to find a neutral definition that, while enjoying depth, will not offend great numbers of people. We seem to be forced to conclude that no single definition of religion can do the job required by it.

When nontraditional convictions are asserted to be religions, courts have the awkward task of deciding what credibility to give to those assertions. This task is particularly difficult when the claim is made by individuals whose faith is not grounded in some institutionalized religious group or when the religious sincerity of the claimant is in question.

The fact that there are two religion clauses complicates the problem. The Free Exercise Clause has traditionally been considered the protection of religious dissenters; free exercise arguments often occur when nontraditional churches or their members attempt to convince a court that their religious beliefs or practices are indeed religious and thus deserving of constitutional protection. In contrast, the Establishment Clause prevents the politically dominant majority from enacting its own religious agenda into public policy; hence, conventional definitions shared by the community are more appropriate than those of the individual. From time to time, constitutional scholars have suggested that the two clauses require different definitions of religion. Broad definitions seem necessary to protect a wide range of individual religious exercises. However, definitions broad enough to include educational, social service, and patriotic activities would leave many ordinary governmental functions vulnerable to the charge of violating the Establishment Clause. Hence, narrow definitions of religion seem appropriate under the Establishment Clause. Kent Greenawalt, for example, has suggested that the Free Exercise Clause should protect anything that is "arguably religious," while the Establishment Clause should not preclude government from engaging in activities that are "arguably not religious."

Employing different conceptions of religion would have important policy consequences. As Judge Arlin Adams pointed out in *Malnak v. Yogi* (1979), such a bifurcated definition inevitably favors new religions and disfavors traditional ones. Overall, most First Amendment scholars prefer to seek a unified definition of religion, pointing out that the very language of the First Amendment suggests a single understanding. Justice Wiley B. Rutledge, dissenting in *Everson v. Board of Education* (1947), noted that the word "religion"

> governs two prohibitions and governs them alike. It does not have two meanings, one narrow to forbid "an establishment," and another, much broader, for securing "the free exercise thereof." "Thereof" brings down "religion" with its entire and exact content, no more and no less, from the first into the second guarantee. . . .

The dual nature of the religion clauses highlights our dual understanding of religious phenomena. Religion is both an individual spiritual experience and a social bond. To conceive of religion totally in terms of the individual believer fails to appreciate the fact that religion is not a purely individual phenomenon, but a social one. For many Americans, religion is experienced more in terms of a commitment to a people, a congregation, or an institution than as a personal spirituality. Definitions that focus on individual beliefs give a somewhat Protestant theological tinge to the characterization of religious experience and, hence, underemphasize its institutional and communal elements. On the other hand, social and institutional definitions of religion may inadequately protect individual believers as well as new or noninstitutionalized religious movements. Any adequate understanding of religion must take into account protection for both kinds of religious experiences.

The search for constitutional definitions of religion demands that we think seriously about the phenomenon of religion itself. Is it to be understood as a particular kind of belief, or as a particular kind of motivation within an individual? Or is the defining characteristic of religion the ceremonial and other practices that provide a sense of coherence and identity for a group? Sociologists of religion disagree among themselves about whether religion should be characterized by the nature of substantive belief or by a key concept such as sacredness, or by function, or by particular kinds of activities. The legal literature parallels these approaches with remarkable correspondence; proposed legal definitions have focused on (1) the content of belief, (2) the issues addressed and the function of belief for the believer, and (3) the sociocultural characteristics of religion—as well as on combinations of all three.

Belief in a Creator, a Supreme Being, a Christian God

For the men who wrote the First Amendment, and for the judges who interpreted it during most of our history, religion meant a theistic belief, based on faith in a deity as understood in Christianity and Judaism. Hence, the core notion of a religion was belief, and the distinguishing feature of the belief was its *content*: belief in a supreme being. James Madison's famous 1785 *Memorial and Remonstrance against Religious Assessments* referred to religion as "the duty we owe to our Creator."

Characteristic is the definition offered by the Supreme Court in the Mormon case of *Davis v. Beason* (1890):

> [T]he term "religion" has reference to one's own views of his relations with his Creator, and to the obligations they impose of reverence for his being and character and of obedience to his will. One cannot speak of religious liberty, without proper appreciation of its essential and historical significance, without assuming the existence of a belief in supreme allegiance to the will of God.

The narrowest belief-based definitions insisted that religion meant the Christian religion—and mainstream Christianity, at that. An extreme example of this kind of reasoning is a statement of the Georgia Supreme Court in *Wilkerson v. Rome* (Ga., 1922), upholding a statute requiring public schools to begin each day with a prayer and a reading from the King James Bible. Assuming that "Christianity is the only religion known to American law," the court concluded that the Free Exercise Clause was breached only if the state "gives one Christian sect a preference over others."

Although few courts have followed this example, most have understood religion within the Western tradition, which places belief in the existence of a supreme being at the heart of the religious experience. Thus the statutes providing for conscientious objection to military service specifically provided exemptions only for those whose objections stemmed from "belief in a Supreme Being." Nevertheless, by the middle of the twentieth century, the United States was becoming too religiously plural for such a definition to encompass the extent of religious experience. In *Torcaso v. Watkins* (1961) the U.S. Supreme Court recognized nontheistic religions when it struck down a Maryland law requiring that public officials affirm a belief in God. In the Court's words, ". . . neither can [government] aid those religions based on a belief in the existence of God as against those religions founded on different beliefs." (A footnote to this statement lists a number of religions in this country that do not teach what would generally be considered "a belief in God.") By the time the conscientious objection statutes were interpreted during the Vietnam War era, the Court recognized that relying on belief in a supreme being to define religion risked violating the Establishment Clause by preferring one kind of religious experience over others.

Definitions that focus on the content or substance of religious belief pose a particularly egregious First Amendment problem. Defining religion in terms of what is believed gets government perilously close to considering the veracity of religious beliefs. The tragic history of the Mormon Church in the nineteenth century illustrates the pitfalls of making distinctions between truth and falsity in religion. In *Davis* the Court said that Mormon tenets regarding polygamy were not religious tenets according to "the common sense of mankind," and in *Presiding Bishop of the Church of Jesus Christ of Latter-Day Saints v. United States* (1890) the Court upheld the repeal of the church's charter, asserting that the church's teaching of polygamy was not a religious tenet but a "pretense." Implicit in these decisions was that there were objectively "true" and "false" beliefs and that courts could appropriately determine which beliefs were false and exclude them from First Amendment protection.

Defining religion in terms of what is believed entails another serious problem. When people claim constitutional protection for acts that stem from their religious beliefs, the sincerity of their convictions may be in question. The Supreme Court faced this problem in *United States v. Ballard* (1944), which arose from charges of fraud by religious leaders who claimed special visions and powers. The Ballards were charged with making claims that "they well knew" were false. The Supreme Court majority, in an opinion written by Justice William O. Douglas, ruled that the veracity of the Ballards' religious claims could not be judged but that their sincerity could. Three concurring justices argued that both veracity and sincerity were appropriate for courts to consider. Justice Robert Jackson, dissenting, argued that veracity and sincerity were inseparable. His reasoning is particularly important: Because judges cannot avoid evaluating what people believe on the basis of what is considered believable, Jackson concluded that both sincerity and veracity be nonjusticiable. In general, however, most courts have followed the majority position; when religious sincerity is in question, courts are generally willing to receive evidence that beliefs are sincerely held.

In spite of the inadequacy of the "Supreme Being" definition, it is difficult to jettison the notion that religion is a special kind of belief. Shifting the focus from a deity to "the sacred" provides a broad understanding of religion while keeping cognitive content—belief—as its central defining characteristic.

Beliefs about the Sacred

Some of the broadest content-based definitions of religion are drawn from the classical nineteenth-century works in the sociology of religion. Central to these definitions is the notion of the *sacred*. Émile Durkheim, among the founding thinkers in the sociology of religion, defines religion as "a unified system of beliefs and practices relative to sacred things." Theologian Rudolf Otto describes the sacred as "wholly other," "beyond the sphere of the usual, intelligible, and the familiar." Anthropologist Clifford Geertz understands religion as positing an "inherent structure of reality" in which values are rooted. At the root of these and other discussions of the sacred is the sense of another reality that not only exists but also impacts on us in our everyday reality.

The sacred implies something that is set aside, separated from ordinary reality. Ancient Hebrew rituals concerning the tabernacle provide a striking prototype, and they are carried through in the sacredness of the ark in contemporary Jewish synagogues. Likewise, the tabernacle in Catholic churches is a sacred place; under normal conditions certain rituals cannot be performed anywhere else. Recognizing the notion of the sacred would likely make free exercise interpretation more sensitive to certain kinds of claims. To take seriously the concept of the sacred, courts would have to understand that people could believe that some things, places, times, or actions could be imbued with transcendent, other-worldly reality. Such a focus would likely encourage more sympathetic consideration of Native American claims for protection of sacred lands, in contrast to the cavalier treatment it received in such cases as *Lyng v. Northwest Indian Cemetery Protective Association* (1988). Likewise, sabbatarian claims, which have fared better, would be grounded more firmly in theological understanding: For some people, *time* is sacred. The sabbath, to believers, is not simply a time for rest and religious reflection, or even for worship; it is a holy time, which, in a sense, belongs to the deity.

Like the "Supreme Being" definitions, those based on beliefs about the sacred understand religion in cognitive terms. But this approach offers no justification for the special status of religion under the First Amendment. Focusing purely on the cognitive content of belief—without reference to the moral obligations that these beliefs entail—does not explain why one kind of ontological position should receive special protection, unless one assumes (as surely government must not) that certain ontological beliefs are "true." An adequate definition of religion must at least suggest why the actions that stem from beliefs are to be especially protected. Clearly, it is not just the nature of the beliefs but also the kinds of motivations that the beliefs engender which must be at the heart of the phenomenon.

Obligations of Conscience

An adequate definition of religion must at least suggest why the actions that stem from beliefs warrant special protection. One constant answer is that religion is valuable because it is a singularly important source of normative values. An impressive set of definitions stems from the premise that religion is distinguished, above all, as a system of moral obligations.

An intriguing but unsatisfying approach has been offered by Jesse Choper, arguing that religious belief could be characterized by belief in "extratemporal consequences." Choper reasons that the underlying insight of the religion clauses is to protect people from the agonizing choices between the commands of government and the dangers to their immortal souls. This characterization quite clearly excludes religions that do not rest on belief in an afterlife, or belief in eternal reward and punishment; furthermore, it offers no protection for religious practices that do not take the form of divine commands backed by threats. Moreover, Choper's definition does little to protect the institutional and identity interests of communities of believers; nor does it offer protection even for individual practices where eternal damnation is not at stake. Still, Choper has approached something critical. It is not just belief in the existence of a supernatural reality that makes religion special; it is the belief that reality impinges on the human in a certain way. Religions posit not only that an external reality exists, but also that it is normative, prescriptive, and authoritative for human beings. It imposes *duties* on human beings that are "higher" or more authoritative than the duties humans set for each other. This attribute has led many thoughtful observers to argue that *obligation* is the crucial characteristic of a religion.

This definition shifts our focus from the cognitive content of the belief to the fact that it is both prescriptive and authoritative. In sociologist Milton Yinger's words, "it is not the nature of belief, but the nature of believing that requires our study." In the same vein, political philosopher Michael Sandel has made a powerful critique of free exercise thinking and has suggested a significant reformulation of traditional First Amendment thinking. If we accept the dominant view that the religion clauses protect *voluntary* choice, we miss the fact that religious activities for most people are not acts of free choice, as consumers' choices are. Religious commands are powerful precisely because they are felt to be obligatory. Indeed, if religious practices were matters of choice, there would be far less powerful reasons for protecting them; it is their obligatory character that makes the protection of these acts seem so compelling.

Several hybrid definitions combine both a cognitive element and a prescriptive one. Chief Justice Charles E. Hughes, dissenting in *United States v. MacIntosh* (1931), captured both the theistic belief and the obligations it entails: "The essence of religion is belief in relation to God involving duties superior to those arising from any human relation."

Legal scholars have tried to capture this combination of cognitive and prescriptive elements. Ben Clements has suggested a definition that includes both the content and the functional elements of the "ultimate concerns" approach. He suggests defining religion as that which addresses fundamental questions of human existence *and* gives rise to obligations of conscience. The second part of the definition encompasses a justification for the religion clauses; it is there to prevent agonizing conflict between the obligations of government and the obligations to higher authority.

Steven Gey has proposed an intentionally narrow definition of religion that focuses on the conjunction of the sacred and the obligatory:

> (1) religious principles are derived from a source beyond human control, (2) religious principles are immutable and absolutely authoritative, and (3) religious principles are not based on logic or reason, and therefore, may not be proved or disproved.

Gey's narrow definition is intended specifically to encompass authoritatively obligatory religious behavior but to exclude others:

> Religious principles that are neither immutable nor absolutely authoritative would not lead to a conflict between secular and religious obligations because, by definition, mutable and non-absolute religious obligations can be modified or ignored by the adherent in order to comply with secular duties.

Powerful as the obligation definitions are, however, they remain inadequate. If we confine religion and, hence, religious protection only to those practices believed to be obligatory, we cannot adequately comprehend nonobligatory religious acts such as the celebration of holidays or festivals. These definitions ultimately fail to encompass the communal and symbolic, nonobligatory aspects of religious practice; hence, they offer little protection for institutions, identities, and non-conscience-based practices. Under this characterization, an act of government that did not require a person to violate religious conscience would not be deemed a violation of the Free Exercise Clause, no matter how damaging it might be in other ways. For example, the Supreme Court majority ruled in *Lyng* that destruction of Native American sacred lands did not literally require any individual to do something which his or her religion forbade. Similarly, in *Jimmy Swaggart Ministries v. Board of Equalization of California* (1990), the majority found no constitutional violation in requiring religious booksellers to pay a sales tax on the sale of religious items, since doing so did not violate religious obligations. Similarly, public religious holiday symbols, voluntary school prayers, or public support for religious schools do not require anyone to violate the commands of conscience. Yet they may infringe the Establishment Clause in other ways. Clearly, defining religion in terms of obligations of conscience, taken alone, would greatly constrict our understanding of both religion clauses. In short, such definitions give little protection to the social function of religion for communities of believers or to the religious practices that bind groups but do not stem from divine commands.

Ultimate Concerns and Functional Definitions

Theologian Paul Tillich's characterization of religion as "ultimate concerns" has been immensely influential in American legal thinking. This focus directs attention not to any specific content but to the *kinds of issues addressed by* a putative religion. Tillich's works have been extremely helpful in broadening the concept of religion to be inclusive of a greater range of expressions; at the same time, they have been easily misunderstood.

Tillich defines religion, most simply, as that which concerns "the depths of your life, of the source of your being, of your ultimate concern, of what you take most seriously without any reservation." In this view everyone has a religion. This rather simple interpretation of Tillich's gave rise to the "functional approach" in legal definitions, an approach that looked to the depth of a person's motivations as the defining characteristic. This was the approach the Supreme Court used in the Vietnam-era conscientious objector cases.

Congress has long granted exemptions from compulsory military service for persons who have religious objections to war. To invoke the conscientious objector exemption, one must be able to show that the objection is a genuinely *religious* one. The case *United States v. Kauten* (1943) relied on a conception of religion that foreshadowed the cases of a generation later. Here, the Second Circuit used functional language in describing religious conscience:

> [Conscientious objection] may justly be regarded as a response of the individual to an inward mentor, call it conscience or God, that is for many persons at the present time the equivalent of what has always been thought of as an religious impulse.

This decision provided to the Supreme Court a precedent for expanding the theistic definition of religion when it confronted the Vietnam-era conscientious objector cases. In these cases, the Court expanded religious exemptions from military service to include those whose moral and philosophical beliefs served for them the same *function* as the belief in God did for traditional religious believers.

In *United States v. Seeger* (1965) the Court was asked to interpret a provision of the Selective Service Act that exempted from combat any person

> who, by reason of religious training and belief, is conscientiously opposed to participation in war in any form. Religious training and belief in this connection means an individual's belief in relation to a Supreme Being, involving duties superior to those arising from any human relation, but does not include essentially political sociological, or philosophical views or a merely personal moral code.

Congress had explicitly used the term "Supreme Being" in defining religious belief, but the courts were aware, in the post-*Torcaso* era, that this kind of preference for one kind of religion over others seemed to violate the Establishment Clause. Seeger had applied for conscientious objector status, but his answers to questions concerning his religious beliefs were ambiguous. His application left the Court in an awkward position. To deny his application would have limited "religion" to a belief in a supreme being—something difficult to do in light of *Torcaso*. Furthermore, to interpret the statute literally would have risked a violation of the Establishment Clause by granting a privilege for one kind of religious belief and denying it to others. Holding the Selective Service Act unconstitutional on these grounds was a result no one wanted. The Court found its solution in Paul Tillich's *Shaking of the Foundations,* which defined religion as "the source of your being, of your ultimate concern, of what you take most seriously without any reservation." Citing Tillich, the Court reinterpreted the statute, stretching the definition of religion in order to grant Seeger's application. The Court

> concluded that Congress, in using the expression "Supreme Being" rather than the designation "God," was merely clarifying the meaning of religious training and belief so as to embrace all religions. . . . [T]he test of belief "in relation to a Supreme Being" is whether a given belief that is sincere and meaningful occupies a place in the life of its possessor parallel to that filled by the orthodox belief in God of one who clearly qualifies for the exemption.

Seven years later, in *United States v. Welsh* (1972), the Court continued this expansion, granting conscientious objector status to one who unambiguously rejected labeling his motivations as "religious":

> [I]f an individual deeply and sincerely holds beliefs which are purely ethical or moral in source and content but that nevertheless impose upon him a duty of conscience to refrain from participation in any war at any time, those beliefs certainly occupy in the life of that individual "a place parallel to that filled [by] God in traditionally religious persons."

Although the *Seeger* and *Welch* cases were important expansions of First Amendment protection, the policy of defining anyone's ultimate concern—or anything that functions parallel to a belief in God—as a religion bothered many critics. Despite the expansiveness of the definition, it raises embarrassing problems for the judicial process. Ought judges to probe what is of "ultimate concern" to a complainant? And if they do, then football, family, income, political ideology, or sex might well have to qualify. Moreover, as Kent Greenawalt has observed, most individuals lack lexical orders of motivations and do not have "ultimate concerns."

In truth, these objections may be based on an oversimplification of Tillich's point. His own notion of religion is not entirely open-ended; his explanation of "ultimate" is immersed in the notion of transcendence and holiness. Tillich's theory includes both the motivation and the cognitive content of belief, as James McBride explains:

> Influenced by [Rudolf] Otto's phenomenology of religion, Tillich's "ultimate concern" cannot be reduced to an affective attitude alone. . . . "[U]ltimate concern" indicates, on the one hand, *our* being ultimately concerned—the subjective side—and on the other hand, the *object* of our ultimate concern. Hence, the concept of "ultimate concern" involved by the Court cannot be reduced merely to an affective attitude as legal scholars and justices have implied. If Tillich's notion is to be spared violence, the court must recognize that there exist two poles in "ultimate concern," objective as well as subjective. Does that suggest that this legal notion may be characterized by both affective attitude and cognitive content? But if cognitive content is recognized as an inherent element of "ultimate concern," does that not violate *Ballard*'s prohibition against probing the truth and falsehood of religious claims?

The aspect of Tillich's definition that McBride terms "objective" is a more important characteristic of religion than is sometimes recognized. It reminds us that not every personal obsession is a religion. Religion is "ultimate" in that it addresses the questions of life for which every human being is presumed to need answers. Many sociologists of religion recognize the comprehensiveness of religious explanations as one of the cross-cultural characteristics of religion. Yinger, for example, writes that "[r]eligion . . . can be defined as a system of beliefs and practices by means of which a group of people struggles with the ultimate problems of human life." And Geertz understands religion as a system of symbols that help one interpret the meaning of life itself by "formulating conceptions of a general order of existence."

Judges who are persuaded that religion implies an attempt to answer the "ultimate questions" of life look for evidence that a belief system is comprehensive as well as deeply held. The focus on ultimate questions proved to be the downfall in the attempt by prisoner Frank Africa to declare his allegiance to the organization MOVE to be religious and to receive dietary accommodations in the Pennsylvania prison. Judge Arlin Adams found his beliefs to be sincere and even ultimate in his life, but he ruled that they were not a comprehensive system. In *Africa v. Pennsylvania* (3rd Cir. 1981), the Third Circuit held that however "deep" a sincerely held belief system might be, it does not qualify as a religion if it is not sufficiently "comprehensive."

The criterion of an ultimate and comprehensive belief system raises some serious legal problems. First, it is not clear how one would distinguish religion from theoretical physics, ontology, or any comprehensive philosophical system by this criterion. Any attempt to do so would involve judges in the wholly inappropriate role of religious censors, deciding which beliefs are ultimate and which are derivative. Furthermore, to conceive of religion as about "ultimate questions" makes it almost a totally cognitive phenomenon. Theologically inclined or introspective people might raise questions like: Why are we here? Why is there something rather than nothing? Why is there suffering and evil? Why is one thing more valuable than another? Why must we behave in certain ways? But many "religious" people are unable, or at least disinclined, to ponder these kinds of questions at all; for them, religion is ritual, identity, and some rules to live by. Such a cognitive definition might well deny First Amendment protection to those who cannot articulate profound religious philosophy. Furthermore, there may be a certain intellectual bias in defining religion in terms of ultimate concerns, which may disadvantage religions, or religious persons for whom reflection as opposed to doing or being is at the heart of the religious experience.

In both functional and content-based definitions the nature or function of the beliefs is the defining element; the practices that follow from them are considered derivative. The implicit model here is that religious *actions* flow from religious *beliefs*. But perhaps this reasoning is backward. Durkheim, argued that considering only states of mind as intrinsically valuable misunderstands the phenomenon; actions and practices may in fact be crucial in *creating* beliefs. In short, we believe *as a result of* what we do. The focus on belief may be bad social psychology; in addition, it could have dangerous constitutional consequences. If courts focus on belief, they may give far too little protection to social practices, institutions, and identities—which, Durkheim argues, are the heart of the religious experience.

Communal and Institutional Definitions

Whether we consider religion to be a kind of belief, the commands and motivations it generates, or the function of a belief system, religion is understood with reference to the individual adherent. The entire sociological tradition of religious thought directs attention to an entirely different set of phenomena: the shared symbols, practices, and identity that create and sustain a community. Earlier, a segment of Durkheim's definition of religion was quoted; the remainder of his explanation bears quoting here:

> A religion is a unified system of beliefs and practices relative to things sacred. . . beliefs and practices which unite into a single moral community called a Church and all those who adhere to them.

For Durkheim, the sense of the sacred is not an individual phenomenon but essentially a communal and institutional one: "In all history, we do not find a single religion without a Church." This focus on group practices, identities, and institutions—and on their social functions—is typical of most sociological definitions. Yinger, for example, insists that religion is a social phenomenon, that "it is shared and takes on many of its most significant aspects only in the interaction of the group." Notice again his definition:

> Religion, then, can be defined as a system of beliefs and practices by means of which *a group of people* struggles with these ultimate problems of human life.

Stephen Carter's definition emphasizes "group worship" while including the cognitive and conscience elements we observed earlier:

> When I refer to religion, I will have in mind a tradition of group worship (as against individual metaphysics) that presupposes the existence of a sentience beyond the human and capable of acting outside the observed principles and limits of natural science, and further, a tradition that makes demands of some kind on its adherents.

The significance of these definitions is that they understand religion not only as a source of individual meaning but also as encompassing the collective behaviors which create and support that system of meaning. Whereas the earlier definitions focused on individual faith and its function for the believer, social definitions direct our attention to the community created by shared faith and ritual and to the ways that social actions sustain faith.

The strength of this focus lies in protecting communal and institutional practices and the manifestations of group identity. For example, we noted that the emphasis on obligations of conscience would fail to protect nonobligatory religious acts, such as singing in the church choir. Focus on belief—whether in a supreme being or whether any comprehensive system of belief—fails to appreciate the importance of religious institutions and identity in the life of ordinary people.

A very practical problem remains. In concrete cases, how are judges and other public decisionmakers to distinguish *religious* communities and institutions from other kinds of group associations? Some identifying characteristic is needed to turn the sociological insight to a criterion useful in legal decisionmaking. One of the most promising solutions to this problem directs our attention not to any single characteristic but to a family of indicators that characterize religion.

Indicia and Analogies

A final type of attempt to distinguish religion seeks to avoid a single indicator and instead gathers together a family of indicia that, cross-culturally, capture the religious experience. No single element is strictly necessary; a combination of them produce what the ordinary person would recognize as a religion. These kinds of definitions encompass religion understood not only as a matter of individual meaning but also as the collective behaviors which create and support that system of meaning.

Greenawalt suggests that judges seek analogies between the putative religion and that which is indisputably religious. Analogies to the external manifestations of religion—such as ceremonies, clergy, or institutional practices of religion—would, of course, disadvantage new or noninstitutionalized religions; Greenawalt prefers analogies to the kinds of concerns and motivations included in traditional religions.

This effort was most notable in *Malnak,* in which the public school teaching of the techniques of transcendental meditation was challenged as the state inculcation of a religion in violation of the Establishment Clause. Concurring in the Third Circuit's sustaining of the challenge, Judge Arlin Adams developed a lucid attempt to describe the family of characteristics by which most people understand the word "religion":

> There appear to be three useful indicia that are basic to our traditional religions and that are themselves related to the values that undergird the first amendment.
>
> The first and most important of these indicia is the nature of the ideas in question. This means that a court must, at least to a degree, examine the content of the supposed religion, not to determine its truth or falsity, or whether it is schismatic or orthodox, but to determine whether the subject matter it comprehends is consistent with the assertion that it is, or is not, a religion. . . . Expectation that religious ideas should address fundamental questions is in some ways comparable to the reasoning of the Protestant theologian Dr. Paul Tillich, who expressed his view on the essence of religion in the phrase "ultimate concern." . . .

> [T]he element of comprehensiveness [is] the second of the three indicia. A religion is not generally confined to one question or one moral teaching; it has a broader scope. It lays claim to an ultimate and comprehensive "truth."
>
> A third element to consider in ascertaining whether a set of ideas should be classified as a religion is any formal, external, or surface signs that may be analogized to accepted religions. Such signs might include formal services, ceremonial functions, the existence of clergy, structure, and organization, efforts at propagation, observation of holidays and other similar manifestations associated with traditional religions. Of course, a religion may exist without any of these signs, so they are not determinative, at least by their absence, in resolving a question of definition. But they can be helpful in supporting a conclusion of religious status given the important role such ceremonies play in religious life.

Because it has proved much easier to observe the external manifestations of religious practice than the first two indicators, this approach places considerable weight on the social practices of the institution, rather than on the conscience of the believers.

A judicial approach requiring all the indicia as necessary components of a religion would be too narrow in free exercise cases, excluding from protection religions that are lacking in formal structures. Conversely, however, the approach may prove to be too broad in Establishment Clause cases. A strikingly unsuccessful attempt at a composite definition was attempted by U.S. District Court Judge Brevard Hand in the Alabama textbook case *Smith v. Board of Commissioners of Mobile County* (Ala., 1986). Judge Hand used such a composite to declare secular humanism to be a religion. His unwieldy composite was unable to distinguish religious questions from philosophical discourse into metaphysics, ontology, and ethics. The conclusions Judge Hand drew in this case reaffirm the method's shortcomings. Although the language suggested an effort to protect nontraditional religions, its effect was to protect traditional fundamentalist Christianity against the "establishment" of the "religion" of humanism. Judge Hand's opinion demonstrates how easy it is to draw analogies and to find indicia; it is not surprising that this decision was quickly reversed. It is worth noting that in both Establishment Clause cases—in *Malnak* and in *Smith*—ideas were declared to be religions *against* the arguments of their adherents, who denied that their ideas constituted a religion. In most free exercise cases, adherents attempt to claim religious status for their beliefs or practices.

Despite some difficulties in applying the indicia, or analogies, approach to defining religion, it remains a promising insight. Better than any of the others, it focuses attention on the dual nature of religion as both an individual and a collective phenomenon. Furthermore, the "family of resemblances" idea seems to offer the most promising practical solution to the concrete problems that judges most often confront.

Conclusion

None of the attempts at defining religion surveyed here is entirely satisfactory. Yet the absence of an objective and comprehensive definition of religion is not as serious as it might seem. In practice, courts rarely are faced with the broad inquiry of "What is a religion?" Constitutional questions are generally more limited. Was a religious belief burdened? Was a religious practice penalized? Was the autonomy of a religious institution undermined? The questions that courts must answer, hence, are smaller ones, which do not absolutely require encompassing definitions. Although less intellectually satisfying, an adequate approach would simply focus on the nexus between the challenged aspect of religion and the religious exercise being threatened. Thus, if someone claims that government has burdened his or her beliefs, it is appropriate to ask whether the beliefs that the person wants protected are *religious* beliefs. Here, sincerity, content, and ultimate concerns might well be appropriate. However, if the person claims that some aspect of religious *practice* is being threatened, then courts might focus on the relation of the practice to religious doctrine or its function for the community of believers. If institutional concerns are raised, the kinds of issues suggested by Judge Adams's third indicium are appropriate: Does the institution function in ways that most people, cross-culturally, expect of religious institutions?

The most frequent controversies over the nature of religion arise in free exercise cases, when an individual or group complains that government has interfered with a religious practice. Defining a religious practice raises its own problems. Religious practices range from liturgical or ceremonial activities done inside religious institutions to secular practices motivated by religious faith; they range from those which are institutionally obligatory (such as confession for Catholics) to those which are optional (social service ministries); they range from those which are authoritatively sanctioned by recognized "churches" to those which are based on the private conscience of an individual believer.

Because there is no "bright line" between a religious practice, belief, or institution and a nonreligious one, there seems little hope of conclusively resolving these definitional issues. As theological insights, cultural practices, and governmental programs evolve, the understanding of religion under the two religion clauses of the Bill of Rights promises to raise continuing challenges for American constitutional law.

Bette Novit Evans

Bibliography

Barnhart, J. E., *The Study of Religion and Its Meaning: New Explorations in Light of Karl Popper and Émile Durkheim* (The Hague: Mouton, 1977).

Carter, Stephen, *The Culture of Disbelief* (New York: Basic Books, 1993).

Choper, Jesse, "Defining Religion in the First Amendment," 1982 *University of Illinois Law Review* 579–613 (1982).

Clements, Ben, "Defining Religion in the First Amendment: A Functional Approach" 74 *Cornell Law Review* 532–558 (1989).

Galanter, Marc, "Religious Freedom in the United States: A Turning Point?" 1966 *Wisconsin Law Review,* 217–296.

Gey, Steven, "Why Is Religion Special: Reconsidering the Accommodation of Religion under the Religion Clauses of the First Amendment," 52 *Pittsburgh Law Review* 75–187 (1990).

Greenawalt, Kent, "Religion As a Concept in Constitutional Law, 72 *California Law Review* 753–816 (1984).

Hall, Timothy, "The Sacred and the Profane," 61 *Texas Law Review* 139–173 (1982).

Ingher, Stanley, "Religion or Ideology: A Needed Clarification of the Religion Clauses," 41 *Stanford Law Review* 233–333 (1989).

Madison, James, "A Memorial and Remonstrance against Religious Assessments," (circa June 20, 1785), in 8 *The Papers of James Madison,* ed. W. Hutchinson and W. Rachel (Chicago: University of Chicago Press, 1973), pp. 298–304.

McBride, James, "Paul Tillich and the Supreme Court: Tillich's 'Ultimate Concern' As a Standard in Judicial Interpretation," 30 *Journal of Church and State* 245–272 (1988).

Moon, Craig A., "Secular Humanism and the Definition of Religion: Extending the Modified 'Ultimate Concern' Test to *Mozert v. Hawkins County Public Schools* and *Smith v. Board of School Commissioners,* 63 *Washington Law Review* 445–468 (1988).

Note: "Toward a Constitutional Definition of Religion," 91 *Harvard Law Review* 1056–1089 (1978).

Sandel, Michael, "Religious Liberty: Freedom of Conscience or Freedom of Choice?" 1989 *Utah Law Review* 597–615 (1989).

Tillich, Paul, *The Shaking of the Foundations* (New York: Scribner's, 1948).

Whitehead, John, and John Conlan, "The Establishment of the Religion of Secular Humanism and Its First Amendment Implications," 10 *Texas Tech Law Review* 1–66 (1978).

Cases Cited

Africa v. Pennsylvania, 662 F. 2d 1025 (3rd Cir. 1981), cert. denied 456 U.S. 908 (1983).

Davis v. Beason, 133 U.S. 333 (1890).

Everson v. Board of Education, 330 U.S. 1, (1947).

Jimmy Swaggart Ministries v. Board of Equalization of California, 493 U.S. 378 (1990).

Lyng v. Northwest Indian Cemetery Protective Association, 485 U.S. 439 (1988).

Malnak v. Yogi, 592 F. 2d 197 (3rd Cir. 1979).

Presiding Bishop of the Church of Jesus Christ of Latter-Day Saints v. United States, 136 U.S. 1 (1890).

Smith v. Board of Commissioners of Mobile County, 655 F. Supp. 939 (S.D. Ala. 937,

1986), overruled 827 F. 2d 648 (11th Cir. 1987).
Torcaso v. Watkins, 367 U.S. 488 (1961).
United States v. Ballard, 322 U.S. 78 (1944).
United States v. Kauten, 133 F. 2d 703 (1943).
United States v. Seeger, 380 U.S. 163 (1965).
United States v. MacIntosh, 283 U.S. 605 (1931).
Welsh v. U.S., 398 U.S. 333 (1970).
Wilkerson v. Rome, 152 Ga. Rep. 762 (1922).

Departure from Doctrine: Judicial Resolution of Ecclesiastical Disputes

Throughout American history, religious organizations that were embroiled in internal conflicts have on occasion turned to secular courts to resolve their disputes. Courts have differed with regard to the appropriate standard to apply in resolving the disputes of religious organizations. At issue is the conflict between the need to settle with finality civil disputes—particularly those that relate to the title and ownership of real property—and the concerns contained in the First Amendment's prohibition against governmental intrusion into religious matters.

During the nineteenth century, state courts took various approaches to the question of how to resolve the internal disputes of religious organizations. Some courts, primarily those in New England, adopted a "majority rule" doctrine pursuant to which the court simply resolved the dispute in favor of the majority of the local church body, even if that majority had abandoned the traditional tenets or doctrines of the denomination.

State courts outside New England generally did not accept this principle. Particularly in the mid-Atlantic and southern states, courts favored an "implied trust" theory of resolving church disputes. Pursuant to this theory, courts held that church property was subject to an implied trust in favor of the established hierarchy of the church. Accordingly, these courts resolved local church disputes by identifying the group that represented the church hierarchy and granting the property to that group, even if the majority of the local congregation differed with the views of the hierarchy.

A few American courts adopted a variation of this implied trust doctrine, borrowing from the English decision in *Attorney General v. Pearson* (G.B., 1817). Pursuant to this English version of the implied trust theory, church property was deemed to be held in implied trust for the propagation of certain doctrines favored by the founders of the church. Thus, when these courts confronted a dispute between competing factions, they sought to determine the true and original doctrine of the church in question and then to ascertain which faction in the dispute most closely embraced that doctrine. This "departure from doctrine" test required courts to engage in a searching and often difficult inquiry into the "correct" doctrines of the church, as opposed to an inquiry attempting merely to identify which faction in a local dispute was aligned with the current church hierarchy.

The U.S. Supreme Court first addressed the question of the proper role of the courts in the resolution of internal religious disputes in *Watson v. Jones* (1871). The *Watson* case arose when a faction of a Presbyterian church congregation in Louisville, Kentucky—which objected to the denomination's antislavery position—seized control of the local church and sought to affiliate with the Presbyterian Church of the Confederate States. The proslavery majority of the local congregation ultimately took the matter to the Supreme Court for resolution.

The Court in the *Watson* case set forth several principles that had a profound effect on subsequent jurisprudence surrounding the issue of judicial resolution of church property disputes. First, the Court concluded that, if property had been given to a church on the express condition that the property be used for a specific purpose and the church departed from that directed purpose, civil courts could order the local church to return the property to the donor. Absent the creation of an express trust, however, courts would not inquire into the question of whether there had been a departure from the doctrine of the church founders; this was a rejection of the English implied trust theory.

Second, the Court held that if the church from which the dispute arose were one of congregational polity, whereby each local church independently governed its own affairs in all regards, then such dispute should be resolved in accord with the principles that govern voluntary associations, such as majority rule. Finally, the Court held that if the church from which the dispute arose were one of hierarchical polity, whereby the local church was subordinate to a broader church structure, then the civil court should defer to the position of the church hierarchy.

Thus, in the aftermath of *Watson,* church disputes would be resolved by deferring to the highest appropriate authority in the church; such authority would differ, depending on whether the church was of congregational or hierarchical polity. The Court rejected the view that courts should adjudicate disputes by reference to a determination of which party most closely adhered to a particular religious doctrine. The clear effect of *Watson* was to limit the role of the courts in the resolution of disputes over church property. Although the *Watson* opinion technically applied only to church property disputes brought in federal courts, the dictates of the decision were widely followed by state courts.

The *Watson* Court did not explicitly consider whether the religion clauses of the First Amendment to the United States Constitution in any way limited the ability of civil courts to adjudicate religious disputes. In the early decades of this century, the Supreme Court began to clarify the parameters of the religion clauses of the First Amendment; subsequently, in *Cantwell v. Connecticut* (1940), the Court held for the first time that the clauses applied to the actions of state governments. Thereafter, in *Kedroff v. Saint Nicholas Cathedral* (1952) and in *Kreshik v. Saint Nicholas Cathedral* (1960), the Supreme Court concluded that courts could resolve church property disputes in accord with the principles set forth in the *Watson* case without violating the First Amendment. Both the *Kedroff* and the *Kreshik* cases involved disputes between the Soviet-supported hierarchy of the Russian Orthodox Church and that church's North American diocese. The dispute centered on which entity had actual authority to appoint the archbishop of North America, with the Supreme Court favoring the hierarchy.

At the same time, however, the Supreme Court held in *Kedroff* and in *Serbian Eastern Orthodox Diocese v. Milivojevich* (1976) that the First Amendment sharply limits the ability of courts to adjudicate ecclesiastical disputes that do not involve property rights. To be sure, the Supreme Court initially appeared to contemplate some limited role for the courts in resolving church disputes that did not involve property claims. In *Gonzales v. Roman Catholic Archbishop* (1929) the Supreme Court noted that a court could properly review a decision of a church tribunal on non-property matters if the decision were accompanied by "fraud, collusion or arbitrariness." Subsequently, however, in *Milivojevich* the Court concluded that such an inquiry would infringe the First Amendment. In that case, the Holy Synod of the Serbian Orthodox Church defrocked a bishop, appointed a successor, and reorganized the bishop's diocese into three separate dioceses. The defrocked bishop sued to enjoin the Holy Synod's actions on the grounds that it had acted arbitrarily by failing to comply with the church's internal regulations and had exceeded its jurisdiction. The Supreme Court expressly rejected the "arbitrariness" exception of the *Gonzales* case, holding that the First Amendment prevented a civil court from reversing an ecclesiastical court for failing to abide by its own procedures. Similarly, the Court concluded that the First Amendment requires a civil court to defer to an ecclesiastical tribunal's exercise of jurisdiction over a church matter.

As a result, civil courts have consistently declined to resolve church disputes that do not involve property claims but that do require an evaluation of the correctness of church doctrine or compliance with church bylaws or other internal regulations. For example, on several occasions courts have declined to adjudicate disputes involving the removal of ministers or the expulsion of church members where no property claims were present.

During the last few decades the Supreme Court has attempted to clarify the proper role of civil courts in adjudicating disputes over property owned by religious organizations. First, in *Presbyterian Church in the United States v. Mary Elizabeth Blue Hull Memorial Presbyterian Church* (1969), the Court reaffirmed the principle of *Watson* that courts must resolve property disputes without attempting to resolve underlying controversies over religious doctrine. In that case, two Georgia churches had sought to leave the Presbyterian Church in the United States (PCUS) and a Georgia court had awarded the local congregations the church property on the grounds that the national denomination had departed from the traditional doctrines of the church. The Supreme Court reversed, concluding that a determination by a civil court that a church denomination had significantly departed from prior doctrine infringed the First Amendment.

The Court in the *Hull* case stated without explanation that civil courts must follow "neutral principles of law" in adjudicating disputes concerning church property. Thereafter, in *Jones v. Wolf* (1979), the Court elaborated on this approach in considering another effort by a local Georgia church to leave the PCUS over doctrinal differences. Under the "deference principle" articulated in *Watson* the denomination would likely have prevailed over the local church congregation on the grounds that the Presbyterian Church is organized with a hierarchical polity granting final authority over doctrinal and property disputes to denominational church courts. Yet pursuant to its neutral principles approach—which the Court majority legitimated as an acceptable alternative to the *Watson* deference approach—the Court remanded the case to the Georgia Supreme Court to determine whether the local congregation was entitled to the church property; the Georgia Supreme Court ultimately found that it was so entitled. Under this approach the lower courts are permitted to use accepted principles of trust and property law to determine who actually has title to the local property. If various documents such as the deed to the church property, the constitution of the denomination, and the charter of the local church establish that the local congregation has title to the church property, then the presumption of ownership rests with the congregation, notwithstanding the fact that the church's ecclesiastical structure permits the denominational courts final authority in resolving such disputes. As a result of the *Jones* decision some denominations have amended denominational canons to state explicitly that local church property is held in trust for the denomination, not for the local congregation.

In the wake of the *Jones* decision lower state and federal courts have adopted various approaches to the question of the manner in which civil courts should resolve disputes over church property. Some courts have continued to follow the deference principle initially articulated in the *Watson* case, giving deference to the position of the highest appropriate authority in the church in resolving disputes. Other courts have followed the neutral principles test or some variation of that test most fully developed in the *Jones* decision and have sought to determine ownership of the local property by reference to general principles of property and trust law. Under the Supreme Court's decisions, either means of resolving disputes over church property is acceptable under the First Amendment.

Davison M. Douglas
James K. Lehman

Bibliography

Adams, Arlin M., and William R. Hanlon, "*Jones v. Wolf*: Church Autonomy and the Religion Clauses of the First Amendment," 128 *University of Pennsylvania Law Review*, 1291–1339 (1980).

Ellman, Mark, "Driven from the Tribunal: Judicial Resolution of Internal Church Disputes," 69 *California Law Review* 1375–1444 (1981).

Gerstenblith, Patty, "Civil Court Resolution of Property Disputes among Religious Organizations," 39 *American University Law Review* 513–572 (1990).

Rotunda, Ronald, and John Nowak, *Treatise on Constitutional Law*, 2nd ed. (St. Paul, Minn.: West, 1992), vol. 4, sec. 21.12.

Sirico, Louis J., Jr., "The Constitutional Dimensions of Church Property Disputes," 59 *Washington University Law Quarterly* 1–79 (1981).

Note, "Judicial Intervention in Disputes over the Use of Church Property," 75 *Harvard Law Review*, 1142–1186 (1962).

Cases Cited

Attorney General v. Pearson, 36 Eng. Rep. 135 (Ch. 1817).

Cantwell v. Connecticut, 310 U.S. 296 (1940).

Gonzales v. Roman Catholic Archbishop, 280 U.S. 1 (1929).

Jones v. Wolf, 443 U.S. 595 (1979).

Kedroff v. Saint Nicholas Cathedral, 344 U.S. 94 (1952).

Kreshik v. Saint Nicholas Cathedral, 363 U.S. 190 (1960).

Presbyterian Church in the United States v. Mary Elizabeth Blue Hull Memorial Presbyterian Church, 393 U.S. 440 (1969).

Serbian Eastern Orthodox Diocese v. Milivojevich, 426 U.S. 696 (1976).

Watson v. Jones, 80 U.S. 679 (1871).

Dion, Dwight, Sr.

See UNITED STATES V. DWIGHT DION, SR.

Disestablishment of State Churches

The movement for religious freedom has, from the beginning of U.S. history, focused on the individual states. The Constitutional Convention in Philadelphia in 1787 paid limited attention to the issue, because much of the battle then was being pursued in the state legislatures. Many religious leaders also supported freedom of religion—some because they belonged to a minority sect not recognized in their state. However, at least one early American leader, Roger Williams, opposed establishment for philosophical reasons. Banished from Massachusetts Bay Colony in 1635 for his outspoken views on religion, Williams founded Providence, Rhode Island, as the first colony with complete religious freedom. Williams believed separation of church and state to be beneficial for religion, writing that "[t]he civil sword may make a nation of hypocrites and anti-Christians, but not one true Christian." Williams himself was mostly forgotten by the 1780s. However, such religious leaders as the Baptists Rev. George Eve and Elder John Leland continued to influence the fight for disestablishment in the states.

Rhode Island was unique among the original colonies in not having an established church. But by 1833 all the states had officially secured the disestablishment of state churches. This accomplishment is notable and in some ways surprising, considering that in the eighteenth century the majority of the American population (like the rest of the world) still believed that church and state should maintain their traditional cooperation.

The creation of the United States involved a unique situation that provided the elements necessary for a move toward freedom of religion. From its inception in the early eighteenth century, the United States contained a multitude of religious sects including Anglicans, Amish, Baptists, Catholics, Congregationalists, Jews, Lutherans, Methodists, Presbyterians, Quakers, and Unitarians. In states that originally maintained an established church, these religious dissenters were a major force in the push for disestablishment.

As the American Revolution approached, a few very influential religious and political leaders also advocated religious freedom. Thomas Jefferson, James Madison, and George Mason led the debate on the subject in the political arena. The Founders who pushed for religious freedom had many reasons for their avid support of separation of church and state. Many of them held a deep-seated distrust of established churches based on their dealings with England. They believed that the interaction of church and state would result only in the corruption of both. The Founders also recognized the practical considerations necessitated by pluralism. Others, like Jefferson, were deists who did not follow all the tenets of Christianity.

Virginia was the earliest site of the fight for disestablishment, and it is instructive because it shaped the debate and thought about religion and the state for the rest of the United States. Virginia was established as a colony with the Anglican Church as the official church. Ministers were required to show ordination from an English bishop, and the church was given large land holdings and special financial favors. Other sects were restricted and could not preach in public or after dark or perform legal marriages. Furthermore, Virginians, including members of other religious sects, were assessed a tax that supported the Anglican Church and its ministers. Although the Anglican Church held a great deal of power in Virginia, by the mid-1700s Anglicans were a minority sect in the state. Dissenters, the most vocal of whom were the Baptists, began petitioning for religious freedom as early as 1772. In the Virginia legislature George Mason and James Madison pushed for the passage of several bills that would decrease the powers of the Anglican Church.

In 1779 Thomas Jefferson proposed a "Bill for Establishing Religious Freedom" in the Virginia legislature. Finally enacted in 1786, the law begins:

> Well aware that Almighty God hath created the mind free: that all attempts to influence it by temporal punishments or burdens, or by civil incapacitations, tend only to beget habits of hypocrisy and meanness, and are a departure from the plan of the Holy Author of our religion, who being Lord both of body and mind, yet chose not to propagate it by coercions on either, as was in his Almighty power to do.

In the preamble Jefferson stated that it is not for fallible men to dictate the beliefs of others. The personal beliefs of every man are his own. He should not be restricted or punished for his views. After this statement of general philosophy the bill asserts:

> No man shall be compelled to frequent or support any religious worship, place or ministry whatsoever, nor shall be enforced, restrained, molested, or burthened in his body or goods, nor shall otherwise suffer on account of his religious opinions or belief; but that all men shall be free to profess, and by argument to maintain, their opinions in matters of religion, and that the same shall in nowise diminish, enlarge, or affect their civil capacities.

Jefferson composed the bill in 1779 while a member of the General Assembly of Virginia. However, it was not until 1785 that the bill was finally passed, as a result of the hard work and expert political manipulation of Madison. While Jefferson was busy in Europe, Madison pushed the bill through, despite the adamant opposition of Patrick Henry and other major political figures. Jefferson's Bill for Establishing Religious Freedom was extremely influential both in the disestablishment movement in other states and in the historical development of religious freedom in the United States.

Like Virginia, the Carolinas also had been colonized with an established Anglican Church. The territory that became North Carolina had a non-Anglican majority which was eager for disestablishment because it had suffered through a period from 1730 to 1773 when Carolina had adopted many of the same oppressive laws against religious dissenters as had England. After the separation from Britain in 1776 the new State of North Carolina adopted a bill of rights which declared "[t]hat all men have a natural and unalienable right to worship Almighty God according to the dictates of their own consciences." In reaction to past abuses of power by Anglican Church officials, the North Carolina Constitution included a provision forbidding clergymen from holding office.

North Carolina as well as New Jersey, Delaware, Pennsylvania, and Maryland all included guarantees of religious freedom in their state constitutions, adopted in 1776. However, these states maintained religious tests for political offices. New Jersey required that officeholders be Protestants—a limitation not dropped until 1874. Delaware limited eligibility to Trinitarian Christians, removing the restriction in 1792. The Pennsylvania Constitution included a religious test for office that excluded non-Christians. Although this test was modified in 1790, the Pennsylvania Constitution continued to exclude atheists and agnostics from holding public office (this provision remains in the constitution but is no longer enforceable). Maryland also barred non-Christians from office until 1826. North Carolina finally eliminated all vestiges of religious tests for officeholding in 1868, when the "radicals" were in power.

The New York Constitution, adopted in 1777, includes a clause declaring "that the free exercise and enjoyment of religious profession and worship, without discrimination or preference, shall forever hereafter be allowed, within this State, to all mankind." Significantly, New York's constitutional clause providing for religious freedom condemned religious "bigotry." The New York Constitution was greatly influenced by the debate that had occurred in Virginia, but New York went beyond Virginia in explicitly prohibiting a religious test for officeholding. New York made "ministers of the gospel" ineligible for public office. Five other states—Virginia, North Carolina, Delaware, Maryland, and South Carolina—had similar provisions prohibiting ministers from holding office.

In Connecticut and in Massachusetts the process of disestablishment continued well after independence was achieved. Connecticut did not realize religious freedom until 1818. The new constitution, ratified in 1818, provided "[t]hat the exercise and enjoyment of religious profession and worship without discrimination, shall forever be free to all persons in this State."

The separation of church and state in Massachusetts was precipitated by a fight for dominance by the two leading religious sects in the state. Until 1821 Massachusetts prohibited non-Protestants from holding public office. Massachusetts, dominated by the established Congregationalist Church from its beginnings, did not completely separate church and state until 1833. Until that time

Massachusetts retained a provision in its constitution that required all towns and villages to support monetarily "public Protestant teachers of piety, religion and morality." In the early nineteenth century the Congregationalist Church in Massachusetts split over a doctrinal debate into two sects, the Unitarians and the Trinitarians. A series of court battles over ownership of church property erupted when Unitarians split from the Trinitarians to form their own parishes. In *Baker v. Fales* (1820) and *Stebbins v. Jennings* (1830) a predominantly Unitarian Massachusetts Supreme Court subordinated the church to the parish. The two cases had the result of making the choice of sects in a parish subject to majority vote. The decisions led to increased plurality by allowing democratic control over state–church relations. A constitutional amendment adopted in 1833 eliminated the legal requirement for local support of the church and provided for complete freedom of religion.

New Hampshire was the last of the original states to have full separation. Its 1792 Constitution contained a confusing set of provisions about religion. Although the Constitution guaranteed the right of conscience and religious freedom for all individuals, there was no separation of church and state, and there was a clear preference for Protestant Christianity. The Constitution allowed the state to authorize local governments to hire "public protestant teachers of piety, religion and morality." The same clause endorsed "evangelical principles" and asserted that "every denomination of Christians, demeaning themselves quietly and as good subjects of the State, shall be equally under the protection of the law." However, religious dissenters had to pay to support ministers and teachers of other faiths. Other sections of New Hampshire's Constitution provided that only a person of "the Protestant religion" could serve in the state legislature or be elected governor. In 1850 the state's voters rejected a constitutional change that would have allowed non-Protestants to hold office. New Hampshire finally changed this in 1877, although the Constitution continued to allow for public support of "protestant" teachers until 1968.

New Hampshire's clinging to a Protestant establishment was clearly anomalous, even in the first five decades of the nation. The new states that were carved out of the West guaranteed religious freedom from the beginning. The Northwest Ordinance of 1787, after laying out a governmental structure for the new states to be created in the West, enacted six "Articles of Compact between the Original States and the people and States in the said territory." The first of these promised that "[n]o person demeaning himself in a peaceable and orderly manner shall ever be molested on account of his mode of worship or religious sentiments." However, in what would seem to be a contradiction today, Article III of the Northwest Ordinance also provided that land be set aside for public schools, "[r]eligion, morality, and knowledge being necessary to good government and the happiness of mankind. . . ."

Although the circumstances of America's colonization were conducive to religious freedom, it was by no means an inevitable result. Most of the Western world at that time still believed strongly in the maintenance of an established national religion. The pluralistic nature of the American colonies—combined with the work of such men as Thomas Jefferson and Roger Williams—resulted in freedom of religion for most people in the United States by the end of the eighteenth century. Although non-Christians were discriminated against both officially and unofficially as late as the 1960s, the foundations for religious freedom were laid in the individual states at the time of the Revolution.

Michelle J. Dye Neumann
Paul Finkelman

Bibliography

Bordon, Morton, *Jews, Turks and Infidels* (Chapel Hill and London: University of North Carolina Press, 1984).

Carmody, Denise Lardner, and John Tully Carmody, *The Republic of Many Mansions* (New York: Paragon House, 1990).

Castelli, Jim, *A Plea for Common Sense* (San Francisco: Harper and Row, 1988).

Finkelman, Paul, "Religious Liberty and the Quincentennary: Old World Intolerance, New World Realities, and Modern Implications," 7 *St. Johns Journal of Legal Commentary* 523–559 (1992).

Kurland, Phillip B., and Ralph Lerner (eds.), *The Founders' Constitution* (Chicago: University of Chicago Press, 1987).

Stokes, Anson Phelps, *Church and State in*

the United States (New York: Harper and Brothers, 1950).
Wood, Gordon S., *The Creation of the American Republic, 1776–1787* (New York: Norton, 1969).

Cases Cited

Baker v. Fales, 16 Mass. 488 (1820).
Stebbins v. Jennings, 10 Pick. (Mass.) 172 (1830).

Disturbance of Public Worship

During the early nineteenth century, as the Second Great Awakening swept the nation and Americans flocked to Protestant churches, gatherings for public worship became an increasingly significant part of American life. Over the course of the century, state courts and legislatures began to grant religious meetings legal protections by explicitly forbidding individuals from disrupting or interfering with public worship. In a series of decisions continuing until the mid–twentieth century, courts not only repeatedly found a constitutional basis for laws prohibiting such disturbances but also usually sustained the convictions of those found guilty under these measures.

The earliest such cases held that disturbing a religious assembly was an indictable offense at common law. The South Carolina Supreme Court's decision in *Bell v. Graham* (S.C., 1818) ranked the right to assemble for worship with the most fundamental guarantees of the common law, even though the case involved a public worship service attended by blacks and whites that had been interrupted by slave patrollers. "It is a principle so clear," the court concluded, "that those who unlawfully disturb the devotion of a religious assembly, by any indecency or violence, may be punished by indictment, that authorities are unnecessary to support it" (p. 281). North Carolina Chief Justice Thomas Ruffin presented a more extensive rationale for deeming disturbance of public worship an indictable offense. In *State v. Jasper* (N.C., 1833), a case involving a man accused of "talking and laughing in a loud voice" during worship, Ruffin argued that "the guaranty of religious freedom" demanded that religion "may be safely professed, and sincerely exercised in public assemblies" (p. 325). Citing a Massachusetts case involving a disturbance of a town meeting, Ruffin noted that such behavior constituted a breach of the peace. "Not less certainly," he reasoned, "does the public worship of Almighty God involve the good order of political society, and its disturbance produce wrath and violence" (p. 327). The following year Judge William Cranch of the U.S. Circuit Court of the District of Columbia echoed these arguments in *United States v. Brooks* (D.C., 1834), where he held that "the disturbance of public worship is an act tending to destroy the public morals and to excite a breach of the peace" (p. 1245).

By midcentury a number of states—mostly in the South—had enacted statutes that prohibited disturbance of public worship and categorized the crime as a misdemeanor. Several of these laws required that the disruption be "willful" in nature, and state appellate courts generally adhered to a strict interpretation of this standard. For example, a few men were convicted under an Alabama statute after they walked out of a worship service, engaged in some "loud talking" outside the church, broke a bottle against a tree, and returned to the service. The Alabama Supreme Court, however, overturned the conviction in *Brown v. State* (Ala., 1871), holding that in order for the disturbance to be willful, "it must be something more than mischievous—it must be in its character vicious and immoral" (p. 183). Similarly, the Texas Supreme Court repeatedly held that convictions under that state's statute had to be based on a "willful intent" to disrupt (*Richardson v. State* [Tex., 1879], *Wood v. State* [Tex., 1884], *Prucell v. State* [Tex., 1892]). Courts, however, defined more broadly the types of assemblages covered under these laws. North Carolina's statute, according to the state supreme court, protected "a congregation of people assembled for divine service," even though they did not worship in a church or chapel (*State v. Swink,* [N.C., 1839]). Likewise, the Tennessee Supreme Court ruled that the state's law against disturbance of worship applied to Sunday school meetings (*Martin v. State,* [Tenn., 1873]).

The most significant matter of judicial interpretation was the question of exactly what behavior constituted a disturbance of a religious service. Answers to that question varied widely. The Tennessee Supreme Court ruled in *Wright v. State* (Tenn., 1881) that one voluntarily engaging in a fight outside the door of a church during worship violated that state's statute. The Supreme Court of Texas, in a series of colorful decisions, held that "the cracking and eating of nuts" (*Hunt v. State* [Tex., 1877]), "groaning aloud and giggling during a prayer" (*Friedlander v. State* [Tex., 1879]), and "talking and beating on a tin can" (*Cantrell v. State* [Tex., 1895]) during worship services all constituted disruptions and violated the law. And the Indiana Supreme Court, presumably less tolerant of any sort of disturbance, held in *Hull v. State* (Ind., 1889) that a man could be convicted under state law for entering a Salvation Army meeting with a cigar in his mouth and refusing to remove his hat when requested! At the same time, state courts held that neither a disturbance in a churchyard after the dismissal of the congregation nor a fight engaged in near a church during a worship service (where the congregation could not hear the fight) constituted a disruption of public worship (*State v. Jones* [Mo., 1873], *State v. Kirby* [N.C., 1891]).

By the middle of the twentieth century, appellate court cases involving disturbance statutes were rare. As the rural and Protestant America of the nineteenth century gave way to an increasingly urbanized and secularized society, convictions under these laws became less and less frequent. Still, the attention that both legislatures and courts gave to such matters during the nineteenth century clearly demonstrates Americans' preoccupation with protecting their religious liberty.

Timothy Huebner

Bibliography

Tommasino, Joseph A., "Crimes: Disruption of Religious Meetings," 26 *Pacific Law Journal* 377–379 (1995).

Cases Cited

Bell v. Graham, 1 Nott and McC. 278 (S.C. 1818).
Brown v. State, 46 Ala. 175 (1871).
Cantrell v. State, 29 S.W. 42 (Tex. 1895).
Friedlander v. State, 7 Tex. App. 204 (1879).
Hull v. State, 120 Ind. 153 (1889).
Hunt v. State, 3 Tex. App. 116 (1877).
Martin v. State, 65 Tenn. 234 (1873).
Prucell v. State, 19 S.W. 605 (Tex. 1892).
Richardson v. State, 5 Tex. App. 470 (1879).
State v. Jasper, 15 N.C. 323 (1833).
State v. Jones, 53 Mo. 486 (1873).
State v. Kirby, 108 N.C. 772 (1891).
State v. Swink, 20 N.C. 358 (1839).
United States v. Brooks, F. Cas. No. 14,655 (4 Cranch, C.C. 427) (1834).
Wood v. State, 16 Tex. App. 574 (1884).
Wright v. State, 76 Tenn. 563 (1881).

Douglas, William Orville (1898–1980)

Before William O. Douglas's appointment to the bench in 1939, there had been relatively few religion clause cases decided by the U.S. Supreme Court. But soon thereafter the Court's docket shifted from cases dealing primarily with economic issues to questions of individual rights, and Establishment and Free Exercise Clause cases became a staple item in each term. Douglas originally had no set philosophy regarding these clauses, but over the years he emerged as the Court's strongest advocate of an absolutist interpretation of the Constitution's religious guarantees.

In his memoirs, written toward the latter part of his life, Douglas took a particularly harsh view toward organized religion. Himself the son of a Presbyterian preacher (who died when Douglas was only 5), and raised by a mother devoted to a strict, God-fearing religion, Douglas gradually came to resent organized religion. The churches, he charged, did little more than justify the exploitation of the poor and weak by the rich and powerful. In his travels around the world, however, Douglas also came to know and appreciate different varieties of religious culture. Moreover, his own love of nature convinced him that nothing short of a divine power could have created the great mountains, lakes, and forests. Over the years both this knowledge and tolerance of diversity as well as a sensitivity to individual beliefs manifested themselves in his opinions.

In both establishment and free exercise cases, Douglas moved from a moderate to an absolutist position. In his first opinion for the Court in an establishment case, *Zorach v. Clauson* (1952), he took a decidedly accommodationist approach, declaring that "[w]e are a religious people whose institutions presuppose a Supreme Being." The state could, therefore, encourage religious enterprise without running afoul of the First Amendment. But from then on, Douglas moved to a far more rigid and absolutist interpretation and came to argue that the Establishment Clause forbade any connection between religion and the state. In a concurrence in the school prayer case, *Engel v. Vitale* (1962), he listed activities that he believed are forbidden by the

First Amendment, including items he had originally described as permissible in his *Zorach* opinion. In two of the last Establishment Clause cases he heard, *Walz v. Tax Commission of City of New York* (1970) and *Wheeler v. Barrera* (1974), Douglas was the only dissenter; no other member of the Court, including Hugo Black and William Brennan, shared his absolutist view.

Douglas supported his view with three basic arguments. First, he believed that even minimal government involvement in religion would lead to greater and more invasive policies later on. Second, Douglas argued that only complete separation of church and state could ensure religious equality among all sects. Finally, he claimed that any government aid would have adverse affects on both the state (by engendering religious divisiveness) and religion (by fostering dependence on government support).

In the free exercise cases, Douglas also moved from a moderate position to an absolutist one. In an early case, *Cleveland v. United States* (1946), he spoke for the majority in affirming a Mormon's conviction under the Mann Act for interstate transportation of women to maintain polygamous marriages, casually dismissing the free exercise claim on the grounds that polygamy was inconsistent with American values. However, by then he had already begun questioning such assumptions. Although he had voted with the majority in the first flag salute case, *Minersville School District v. Gobitis* (1940), the wartime Jehovah's Witness cases bothered him, and by the second flag salute case, *West Virginia Board of Education v. Barnette* (1943), he had begun his journey. In his opinion in *United States v. Ballard* (1944) Douglas argued that the state never had a right to inquire into the truth of any individual's convictions. After 1946 Douglas never wrote a majority opinion for the Court in a free exercise case, and in his last terms he was the sole dissenter in several cases, including *Wisconsin v. Yoder* (1972).

Douglas's underlying philosophy in religion cases derived at least in part from his exposure to different religions as he traveled around the world, and his opinions draw widely on nonlegal sources. Moreover, his religion clause views related directly to his growing advocacy of a constitutionally based right of privacy. "The right to be let alone," he declared in his dissent in *Public Utilities Commission v. Pollak* (1952), "is indeed the beginning of all freedom." As Douglas developed his views on privacy, he came to believe that it encompassed an individual's right to be free from any form of governmental intrusion or compulsion, including any policy that sought to influence an individual's religious beliefs or actions. The right to privacy included the right to choose one's religious belief. As Thomas Emerson has noted, Douglas saw the entire First Amendment as helping individuals realize their full potential by ensuring "freedom of lifestyle, and freedom to expand, grow, and be oneself."

The absolutism he evidenced in religion cases mirrored the absolute view of individual rights that Douglas came to expound. In terms of religion this meant that one not only had the right to believe and practice the religion of choice but also to forgo any religion or even adopt an antireligious posture, free from fear of the state. Although he never retracted his condemnation of polygamy in the *Cleveland* case, he later wrote that public discomfort with unfamiliar religious beliefs did not justify government restrictions.

Many commentators have noted an inherent tension between the two religion clauses; and the more stringently one interprets these clauses, the greater the potential for conflict. Douglas only adverted to this tension once, in his concurrence in *Sherbert v. Verner* (1963), and there he missed the main issue. If a state must make an exception to a law of general applicability in order to accommodate one person's religious beliefs, this in some ways gives that religion a favored position vis-à-vis other sects. Since, in Douglas's view, the Establishment Clause prohibited any and all government assistance to religion, an exemption from a general law would violate the Constitution.

This tension can also be seen in the conscientious objector cases, and Douglas ignored it there as well. He did, however, insist that the government must grant conscientious objector status to people who did not subscribe to particular formal religions, as long as they believed in pacifism and opposed war. The government could not limit this benefit only to adherents of organized religion.

Douglas, despite his occasional contemptuous remarks about organized religion, was not antireligious. In fact, he valued religious beliefs highly, which is why he took such an absolutist approach to protecting belief from the government. He occasionally wrote about the basic tenets of freedom in near-reverential terms; he described the individual mind as a "sacred precinct" and claimed that protecting liberty would give the nation "spiritual strength." But the state could not interfere with religion, nor promote it in any way; religious beliefs belonged to an individual's private realm, and the best thing the government could do to promote religious belief, Douglas believed, was to protect that right of privacy and stay out of any entanglement with religious enterprises.

Melvin I. Urofsky

Bibliography

Ball, Howard, and Phillip J. Cooper, *Of Power and Right: Hugo Black, William O. Douglas, and America's Constitutional Revolution* (New York: Oxford University Press, 1992), chap. 10.

Emerson, Thomas I., "Justice Douglas's Contribution to the Law," 74 *Columbia Law Review* 353–357 (1974).

Powe, Lucas A., Jr., "Evolution to Absolutism: Justice Douglas and the First Amendment," 74 *Columbia Law Review 371–411 (1974)*.

Strossen, Nadine, "The Religion Clause Writings of Justice William O. Douglas," in Stephen L.Wasby (ed.), *"He Shall Not Pass This Way Again": The Legacy of Justice William O. Douglas* (Pittsburgh: University of Pittsburgh Press, 1990), pp. 91–107.

Cases Cited

Cleveland v. United States, 329 U.S. 14 (1946).

Engel v. Vitale, 370 U.S. 421 (1962).

Minersville School District v. Gobitis, 310 U.S. 586 (1940).

Public Utilities Commission v. Pollak, 343 U.S. 451 (1952).

Sherbert v. Verner, 374 U.S. 398 (1963).

United States v. Ballard, 322 U.S. 78 (1944).

Walz v. Tax Commission of City of New York, 397 U.S. 664 (1970).

West Virginia Board of Education v. Barnette, 319 U.S. 624 (1943).

Wheeler v. Barrera, 417 U.S. 402 (1974).

Wisconsin v. Yoder, 406 U.S. 205 (1972).

Zorach v. Clauson, 343 U.S. 306 (1952).

Drugs, Religion, and the Law

Religious sacraments—ways to relate to the "sacred" dimension of experience—may include ingesting substances that can alter physical behavior and mental states. For instance, certain Christian churches drink an alcoholic beverage, wine, when members gather; the Native American Church ingests peyote buttons, a mild hallucinogen; Rastafarians and the Ethiopian Zion Coptic Church use marijuana extensively. When such substances are legally controlled—as they have been in the United States—conflicts arise between the commitments to religious liberty and to the rule of law. Solutions to such conflicts are both legislative (statutory exemptions for the religious use of controlled substances) and judicial (constitutionally compelled religious exemptions).

During the Prohibition Era, Congress exempted the sacramental use of wine from the general prohibition of alcoholic beverages. (The Eighteenth Amendment was in force from January 1919 to its repeal by Amendment Twenty-One in December 1933.) The Code of Federal Regulations exempts bona fide ceremonies by the Native American Church from legal controls on the use, possession, and distribution of peyote, which is listed in Schedule I of the Controlled Substances Act. Several states have similar exemptions from their criminal drug laws for the sacramental use of peyote. Unless required by the U.S. Constitution's Free Exercise Clause, legislative accommodation of religious drug use is subject to challenge under the Establishment Clause and the Equal Protection Clause of the Fourteenth Amendment as being a governmental preference for religion. Whereas the peyote exemptions would probably pass constitutional muster, the U.S. Supreme Court has left establishment and equal protection limits on legislative exemptions unclear.

In the absence of legislative provisions, religious drug users have at times successfully invoked the protection of state and federal constitutional religious liberty provisions in the courts. However, a 1990 decision of the Supreme Court in *Employment Division Department of Human Resources of Oregon v. Smith* (1990) ended judicial relief under the Free Exercise Clause of the First Amendment. The Religious Freedom Restoration Act of 1993 (RFRA) may provide a statutory defense in certain cases, but legislative exemptions are the main protection for the sacramental use of controlled substances.

Free Exercise Exemptions from Drug Laws

Before *Employment Division, Department of Human Resources of Oregon v. Smith* (1990) courts in some states without a sacramental use exemption in their drug laws held that the Free Exercise Clause protected the use of peyote in religious ceremonies of the Native American Church from criminal prosecution. The reasoning followed the "strict scrutiny" or "compelling interest test" developed by the Supreme Court for high judicial protection of the fundamental interest in freedom of religious exercise.

In *Reynolds v. United States* (1878) the Court denied a Free Exercise Clause exemption to a practicing Mormon who was convicted of the criminal offense of polygamy. It reasoned that while the Free Exercise Clause deprived Congress of power over "mere opinion," it left Congress "free to reach actions which were in violation of social duties or subversive of good order." From this minimal protection the Court gradually increased its independent review of legislative compliance with the Free Exercise Clause. In *Cantwell v. Connecticut* (1940) the Court held that criminal conviction of Jehovah's Witnesses under broad licensing and breach of the peace ordinances for evangelizing, literature distribution, and solicitation of funds "unduly [infringed] the protected freedom."

Through the cases of *Sherbert v. Verner* (1963) and *Yoder v. Wisconsin* (1972) the Court firmly established the highest judicial protection of religious liberty, the strictest scrutiny of any government actions shown to burden religious exercise. *Sherbert* held that South Carolina could not deny unemployment benefits to a Seventh-Day Adventist who refused employment on Saturday, her Sabbath. *Yoder* held that Wisconsin could not criminally punish Amish parents for their child's truancy, caused by the Amish practice of ceasing formal schooling after age 14. Only government interests of "the highest order and those not otherwise served" could justify impinging on the fundamental rights and interests protected by the Free Exercise Clause.

California, in *People v. Woody* (Calif., 1964), applied the *Sherbert* standard to the Native American Church's use of peyote. It reasoned that peyote was the theological heart of the church and that its use was enforced by religious beliefs and controlled by the church's practices. To justify criminalizing it, therefore, California had to demonstrate that it had no other way of achieving its compelling interest in avoiding fraudulent "religious" drug use or preventing even minimal drug use that could lead to abuse or more dangerous drugs. The state failed to meet the burden. Arizona and Oklahoma held similarly. Montana indicated that it would render the contrary holding in a 1920s decision, however, and North Carolina refused an exemption for a peyotist with Buddhist leanings in 1967.

Federal courts had few occasions to rule on whether the Free Exercise Clause compelled an exemption for the Native American Church's use of peyote, because of the exemption in the federal Controlled Substances Act. Courts uniformly rejected free exercise defenses by religious groups seeking exemptions for religious use of other drugs, however. An early case was *United States v. Leary* (1969), which upheld convictions for violation of federal marijuana laws over the Free Exercise Clause defense that the marijuana was used as an "aid to illumination" in the Hindu sect of which the defendant was a member. The Supreme Court distinguished *Sherbert,* finding earlier Court precedents in which free exercise defenses to child labor and compulsory vaccination laws were rejected more apposite. It reasoned that Congress had found that marijuana posed a substantial threat to public safety, peace, and order. It also distinguished *Woody,* because marijuana is not a "formal requisite" to the Hindu religion, as peyote is to the Native American Church.

Several courts of appeal rejected Free Exercise Clause claims by the Ethiopian Zion Coptic Church to sacramental use of marijuana, and lower federal courts and state courts rejected similar claims by the Neo-American Church, Rastafarianism, the Aquarian Brotherhood Church, and followers of Tantric Buddhism. Some of the latter cases—for instance, *United States v. Kuch* (D.C., 1968) and *Randall v. Wyrick.* (Mo., 1977)—followed the *Leary* rationale, namely, that the *Sherbert* and *Yoder* compelling interest test was not applicable when the laws in question protected against a substantial threat to the public health and safety. Although the facts in *Sherbert* and in *Yoder* did not involve substantial threats to public health and safety, the opinions articulated a general standard of judicial review for free exercise exemption claims. The better reasoning, therefore, was application of the strict scrutiny standard.

A good example is the decision of the U.S. Court of Appeals for the District of Columbia in *Olsen v. Drug Enforcement Administration* (D.C., 1989). It held that the government had justified denial of a religious exemption to the Ethiopian Zion Coptic Church, even though the church's use of marijuana is a sincere religious practice and the request was restricted to use in certain times and places. Not only was the interest of the government in controlling marijuana use compelling, but the government could not achieve that control if an exemption were granted. The restrictions on marijuana use in the requested exemption were not self-enforcing by the teachings of the church, and they would entail governmental monitoring. The exemption would also require the government to make large quantities of marijuana available.

The 1990 *Smith* decision dramatically revised Free Exercise Clause protection of religious practices. It held that Oregon's limitation of eligibility for unemployment benefits to those who did not lose their employment as a result of misconduct—as applied to two men who were fired for ingesting peyote in a ceremony of the Native American Church—did not violate the Free Exercise Clause. The opinion was not based on the *Sherbert* case or its progeny, although it involved denial of unemployment benefits for religious conduct; the Court focused instead on the underlying employee conduct, the sacramental use of peyote, which was not exempted statutorily from Oregon's criminal drug laws.

Smith distinguished both *Sherbert* and *Yoder*, but it overruled the strict standard of review that they had applied. Under the *Smith* rule, if the challenged governmental action or law does not target religion and is generally applicable, it does violate the Free Exercise Clause by incidentally burdening religious exercise. Because Oregon's criminal drug laws were neutral with regard to religion and were generally applicable to any use of peyote, the Court concluded that their application to members of the Native American Church would not violate the Free Exercise Clause and that, therefore, denial of unemployment benefits did not either.

Smith removes Free Exercise Clause defenses to criminal prosecutions under otherwise valid and generally applicable drug laws. Such laws may criminalize a practice central to a religious community, and the government has no constitutional obligation to articulate or demonstrate substantial justification for refusing an exemption. After *Smith* statutory accommodation of sacramental use of controlled substances is not compelled by the Free Exercise Clause. Dicta in *Smith* indicate that such legislative accommodation is nevertheless constitutionally permissible.

Permissive Legislative Accommodation of Religious Drug Use

The Establishment Clause prohibits government preferences for one religion over another or for religion over nonreligion. In this aspect it is similar to the guarantee of equal treatment in the Equal Protection Clause of the Fourteenth Amendment. Legislative exemptions for religious drug use appear to prefer religion, and the exemptions for the Native American Church's use of peyote appear to prefer one religion over another. Other religious groups have challenged their exclusion from such exemptions under the Establishment and Equal Protection Clauses of the Constitution, albeit with limited success.

In *Corporation of the Presiding Bishop of the Church of Jesus Christ of Latter-Day Saints v. Amos* (1987) the Supreme Court held that legislative exemption of religious employers from the federal law forbidding religious discrimination in employment did not violate the Establishment Clause. However, if an exemption is not arguably required by the Free Exercise Clause (as the employment discrimination exemption might be, because it has to do with the internal affairs of a religious body), however, it should not single out religion for preferential treatment. For instance, in *Texas Monthly v. Bullock* (1989) the Court held that an exemption from state sales and use taxes for religious publications violated only the Establishment Clause.

Statutory exemptions for the use of peyote by the Native American Church are justified not only by Free Exercise Clause considerations but also by the relatively limited use and availability of peyote and by the church's traditional enforcement of strictures against the use of peyote and other drugs or alcohol outside religious ceremonies. Several courts have noted as well that the federal exemption is also justified by the special fiduciary relationship of the federal government to Native American peoples. In other words the government can justify the peyote use exemption for the Native American Church as serving substantial purposes other than the advancement of religion, thus withstanding establishment or equal protection analysis.

Exemptions that are specific to one religion are also susceptible to attack under the Establishment Clause for favoring one religion over another. The court in *Olsen* held that the above-listed characteristics of the Native American Church made its sacramental use of peyote sufficiently dissimilar from marijuana use by the Ethiopian Zion Coptic Church to justify the specific federal exemption. If courts construe such exemptions to include other groups similarly situated to the Native American Church, they also should withstand attack on the grounds that they prefer that church.

The Religious Freedom Restoration Act of 1993 (RFRA)

Congress responded to the *Smith* decision with the Religious Freedom Restoration Act of 1993. The RFRA created a statutory free religious exercise claim, and it specifies that the claim is to be assessed by the courts under the *Sherbert* and *Yoder* standard. After *Smith*, drug use as part of a sacramental act does not constitute constitutional grounds to dismiss an indictment under otherwise valid and generally applicable drug laws, but after passage of the RFRA, it does state a statutory defense. The act does not, and could not, overrule the *Smith* constitutional holding: The guarantee of free exercise of religion does not protect those who sincerely use drugs as a central sacrament of their religion from prosecution under otherwise valid and generally applicable drug laws. The act does, however, provide a statutory claim and/or defense, which may obtain the same result for the person who uses controlled substances as part of a religious sacrament.

Under the RFRA, if the defendant demonstrates that the conduct at issue is central to the sincere exercise of religion, the *Sherbert* and *Yoder* standard applies, and the government has to justify its refusal to accommodate the religious conduct in terms of a compelling government interest that could not otherwise be served. Inasmuch as the facts of *Smith* included peyote use in Native American Church ceremonies and a criminal drug law that did not exempt sacramental use of peyote, it argues against a religious exemption under the RFRA for the Native American Church's use of peyote. However, *Smith* was not a criminal prosecution and did not apply the *Sherbert* and *Yoder* standard. It is therefore not mandatory case authority against a religious exemption under the act for the use of peyote in ceremonies of the Native American Church. The federal legislative exemption supports the finding that such use is central to the religion; if sincere in the individual case, it therefore could not be prohibited unless the government can demonstrate the necessity of such a prohibition to achievement of a compelling interest. The reasoning of *Woody*—that under the *Sherbert* standard, the government did not justify refusing an exemption to peyote use by the Native American Church—could be a persuasive argument under the RFRA.

Leigh Hunt Greenhaw

Bibliography

Finkelman, Paul "The Second Casualty of War: Civil Liberties and the War on Drugs," 66 *Southern California Law Review* 1389–1452 (1993).

Cases and Statutes Cited

Cantwell v. Connecticut, 310 U.S. 296 (1940).

Corporation of the Presiding Bishop of the Church of Jesus Christ of Latter-Day Saints v. Amos, 483 U.S. 327 (1987).

Employment Division, Department of Human Resources of Oregon v. Smith, 494 U.S. 872 (1990).

Olsen v. Drug Enforcement Administration, 878 F. 2d 1458 (D.C. Cir. 1989).

People v. Woody, 61 Cal. 2d 716, 40 Cal. Rptr. 69, 394 P. 2d 813 (1964).

Randall v. Wyrick, 441 F. Supp. 312 (W.D. Mo. 1977).
Reynolds v. United States, 98 U.S. 145 (1878).
Sherbert v. Verner, 374 U.S. 398 (1963).
Texas Monthly v. Bullock, 489 U.S. 1 (1989).
United States v. Kuch, 288 F. Supp. 439 (D. D. C. 1968).
United States v. Leary, 383 F. 2d 851 (5th Cir.), rev'd other grounds, 395 U.S. 6 (1969).
Wisconsin v. Yoder, 406 U.S. 205 (1972).
Religious Freedom Restoration Act, Pub. L. 103–141, 107 Stat. 1488 (1993).

E

***Employment Division, Department of Human Resources of Oregon v. Smith* 494 U.S. 872 (1990)**

Decisions of the U.S. Supreme Court sometimes characterize particular Courts, or eras in judicial interpretation. Such expansive landmarks as *Sherbert v. Verner* (1963) and *Wisconsin v. Yoder* (1972) characterize the dominant understanding of the free exercise of religion between the early 1960s and the 1970s. Similarly, *Employment Division, Department of Human Resources of Oregon v. Smith* (1990) seemed to characterize the jurisprudence of the conservative Supreme Court as the 1990s began. In this case, a 6-to-3 majority held that a state law prohibiting the use of peyote could constitutionally be applied to ritual peyote use by members of the Native American Church, and it upheld the denial of unemployment compensation benefits for two members of the church who had been fired from their jobs for ritual peyote use. More significantly, a five-member majority (Justice Sandra Day O'Connor concurred on other grounds) rejected the need to justify burdens on religious exercise by compelling state interest, and it ruled that religious exemptions to generally applicable laws are not constitutionally required. *Smith* was one of the most controversial religion clause cases since the school prayer cases of the 1960s. The decision immediately spawned a broadly supported petition to the Court to reconsider its decision—as well as a congressional effort to reverse its impact.

Narrowing the Scope of Free Exercise Protections

Alfred Smith and Galen Black, recovered alcoholics, were employed in a private drug rehabilitation program. Both were fired when it was discovered that they used peyote as part of religious ritual of the Native American Church, of which they were members. They applied for unemployment compensation, but their application was denied on the grounds that they had been fired for work-related misconduct. Smith and Black appealed the denial of state benefits, and both the appellate and state supreme court decided in their favor. In 1986 in *Smith v. Employment Division* the Oregon Supreme Court ruled that religious exercises could not be considered as misconduct for purposes of denying state benefits, citing a consistent pattern of U.S. Supreme Court decisions (beginning with *Sherbert*) on this point. The state petitioned for certiorari to the U.S. Supreme Court, which, in *Employment Division v. Smith* (1988) (*Smith I*), vacated the state judgments and remanded the case to the Oregon courts to determine whether state law prohibited sacramental use of peyote and whether the Oregon Constitution protected sacramental peyote use. The Court reasoned that, if a state could punish by criminal law ritual use of the drug, it could justify the lesser penalty of denying unemployment benefits for its use. It is important to recall that *Smith* is not a criminal case. Neither Smith nor Black—nor anyone else for that matter—had been prosecuted in Oregon for peyote use in a religious ritual.

On remand, the Oregon Supreme Court, in *Smith v. Employment Division* (1988), concluded (unlike twenty-three other states and the federal government) that Oregon law "makes no exception for the sacramental use"; but the court also noted that, if the state should ever attempt to enforce the law against religious practice, that prosecution would violate the Free Exercise Clause of the U.S. Constitution.

The U.S. Supreme Court again granted certiorari. In April 1990 it overturned Oregon's decision that the application of the criminal statute to religious practices would be unconstitutional. Both Justice Harry Blackmun's dissent and many of the Court's critics have pointed out that the majority was thus ruling on a purely hypothetical issue—and resting a major constitutional precedent on an issue that had never arisen and that the highest state court had ruled to be irrelevant in any case.

Majority Opinions

Beyond the specific ruling about peyote use, the significance of this case lies in the majority's significant narrowing of the scope of free exercise protection. According to Justice Antonin Scalia, the Free Exercise Clause is breached when laws specifically target religious practice for unfavorable treatment. Generally applicable laws, neutral in intent, do not in this view raise First Amendment problems. This requirement is met simply by a formal neutrality; it requires only that a law be religion-blind and not on its face discriminate against religion; it does not require religious-based exemptions. In effect, as Douglas Laycock has noted, this reasoning understands the Free Exercise Clause as merely an adjunct to the equal protection guarantee. Religion may not be treated more disfavorably than any other activity.

Moreover, the *Smith* majority ruled that the Free Exercise Clause does not require that laws burdening religious exercise be justified by a compelling state interest. As enunciated in *Sherbert,* the "compelling state interest" standard requires that, when religious practices are burdened by acts of government, the government must demonstrate that the burden is necessary to achieve a compelling state interest which can be achieved in no less burdensome way. Perhaps the single clearest statement of this doctrine is in *Yoder:* ". . . only those interests of the highest order and those not otherwise served can overbalance legitimate claims to the free exercise of religion." The compelling state interest test—like the earlier "preferred position" test or the "strict scrutiny" required to evaluate racial classifications—poses a very heavy burden on government. In contrast to other litigation where the party challenging a law bears a burden of proof, in these instances the burden is reversed, and the state must establish that burdens on fundamental rights are justified by extremely important state interests that could not be achieved in any less objectionable way.

Both parties in *Smith* assumed the compelling state interest standard to be the appropriate standard of review. Neither party had challenged the use of that standard in its briefs. Thus, when the majority rejected this standard, it made a significant reversal in constitutional policy about an issue that was neither raised nor argued by the litigants. Because the Court's majority did not believe that the application of generally applicable laws to religious practices required justification, it did not question either the state's interest in a drug policy that prohibited sacramental peyote use or the closeness of fit between this law as enforced and the state's interests.

Whether or not this decision signals a reversal in the Court's long-standing approach to free exercise is a matter of some controversy. Justice Scalia took great pains in this case to suggest that the doctrine of compelling state interest was itself an aberration, applicable only in unemployment compensation cases but not in other circumstances, and most certainly not in cases involving the criminal law. "We have never held that an individual's religious beliefs excuse him from compliance with an otherwise valid law prohibiting conduct the state is free to regulate."

Justice Scalia's critics note that, in support of his argument, he relies heavily both on discredited doctrines (such as the distinction in *Reynolds v. United States* [1878] between beliefs and actions) and on long-overruled decisions (such as *Minersville School District Board of Education v. Gobitis* [1940]). Furthermore, critics point out that the compelling state interest doctrine *has,* in fact, been given at least lip service most of the time—although it is true that, except in unemployment compensation cases, courts have almost always found the burden to have been met by the state.

Furthermore, the majority opinion suggests that a threat to free exercise of religion alone is not a sufficient danger to invoke the heightened scrutiny of the compelling interest test. Such scrutiny, Justice Scalia argues, is appropriate only when both religious exercise and some additional constitutional guarantee are threatened. "The only decisions in which we have held that the First Amendment bars application of a neutral generally applicable law to religiously motivated action have involved not the free exercise clause alone, but the free exercise clause in conjunction with other constitutional protections, such as freedom of speech and of the press. . . ." Critics of the opinion have found nothing in precedents or in constitutional doctrine to support this novel approach to the First Amendment. This new category of what Scalia calls "hybrid situations" has left critics wondering why religion is not sufficiently important to warrant constitutional protection by itself. This cavalier treatment of religious rights has been the focus of the enormous criticism the decision generated.

Justice Scalia invokes an image of anarchy that religious exemptions would create. Quoting *Reynolds* he argues that "to make an individual's obligation to obey . . . a law contingent upon the law's coincidence with his religious beliefs, except where the State's interest is 'compelling,'" would permit him "to become a law unto himself."

This danger is all the more troubling, he argues, because "we are a cosmopolitan nation made up of people of almost every conceivable religious preference." Hence, "we cannot afford the luxury of deeming *presumptively invalid,* as applied to the religious objector, every regulation of conduct that does not protect an interest of the highest order." He then recounts what critics term a "parade of horribles" to illustrate the disarray of governmental policy—from child welfare and labor laws to taxation and public health measures—that would result from such a doctrine.

In light of this limited judicial protection of religious exercise, Justice Scalia recognizes that the majority approach leaves religious liberty within the political process. "Values that are protected against government interferences through enshrinement in the Bill of Rights are not thereby banished from the political process." He readily admits that "leaving accommodation to the political process will place at a relative disadvantage those religious practices that are not widely engaged in; but that unavoidable consequences of democratic government must be preferred to a system in which each conscience is a law unto itself. . . ."

Justice Sandra Day O'Connor's concurring opinion has received considerable attention. Like the dissenters, she would maintain the compelling state interest test; unlike them, however, she believed that Oregon had shown a compelling state interest in maintaining the consistency of its antidrug policy. Rejecting the majority's position, Justice O'Connor understands the First Amendment to be invoked by any law that burdens a religious exercise. "Because the First Amendment does not distinguish between religious belief and religious conduct, conduct motivated by sincere religious belief, like the belief itself, must therefore be at least presumptively protected by the Free Exercise clause." Further, she argues, "The First Amendment . . . does not distinguish between laws that are generally applicable and laws that target particular religious practices." "There is nothing talismanic about neutral laws of general applicability or general criminal prohibitions, for laws neutral toward religion can coerce a person to violate his religious conscience or intrude upon his religious duties just as effectively as laws aimed at religion."

Very little of our First Amendment history has concerned laws specifically targeting religious practices; to construe the Free Exercise Clause to cover only these instances would render it a minimal protection indeed. Justice O'Connor would restore the broader understanding of the clause, protecting religious exercise both from laws specifically targeting religion and from generally applicable laws. Furthermore, she would retain the compelling state interest test, which she finds not an anomaly but "a fundamental part of our First Amendment doctrine." Without serious judicial scrutiny the fate of minority religions would indeed be left up to the political process, which is precisely what the Bill of Rights is intended to prevent. "The very purpose of a Bill of Rights was to withdraw certain subjects from the vicissitudes of political controversy, to place them beyond the reach of majorities and officials and to establish them as legal principles to be applied by the courts."

Having defended the compelling state interest standard, Justice O'Connor spends the remainder of her opinion applying it to the ritual use of peyote. Doing so, she ultimately reaches the same conclusion as the majority. Recognizing both the burdens that the law places on the ability of people to exercise their religion and the state's interest in combating illicit drugs, she understands the critical question as "whether exempting respondents from the state's general criminal prohibition will unduly interfere with fulfillment of the governmental interest." She concludes that "uniform application of Oregon's criminal prohibition is essential." Hence, by applying the compelling interest test, Justice O'Connor concludes that Oregon has shown sufficiently overriding interest to justify applying the law to religious uses of peyote.

Dissenting Opinions

Justices Harry Blackmun, William Brennan, and Thurgood Marshall joined Justice O'Connor in the first two sections of her concurring opinion—those in which she challenged the majority's free exercise doctrine. They departed from her judgment that the state had shown a compelling interest in refusing to exempt sacramental peyote use. Justice Blackmun wrote a strongly worded dissent, with which Justices Brennan and Marshall joined. A striking footnote early in the opinion rejects the majority's claim to judicial restraint: "The members of the majority have been outspoken advocates both of judicial restraint and of the autonomy of state courts; nevertheless, in this case, they reached for an issue which had not been raised, on a problem that was hypothetical, to decide the constitutionality of a law the State had chosen not to enforce, and which the highest state court had declared to be irrelevant to the State law it was interpreting."

The dissenters' point of departure is Justice O'Connor's forceful defense of the compelling state interest argument, with which they agree. Their disagreement centers on what is to be balanced and on how the balancing is to be done. Citing Roscoe Pound, one of the originators of the balancing of interests approach to jurisprudence, Justice Blackmun reminds the majority that individual interests are not to be balanced against the general purpose of the law; clearly, general public purposes would always prevail over individual interests. "It is not the State's broad interest in fighting the critical 'war on drugs' that must be weighted against respondents' claim, but the State's narrow interest in refusing to make an exception for the religious, ceremonial use of peyote." From this perspective the dissenters conclude that virtually nothing is lost by granting the exemption. In contrast to Justice O'Connor's emphasis on the need for uniform applicability of drug laws, the dissenters point out that both the United States and twenty-three states exempt sacramental use of peyote from criminal prosecutions, without reported problems. Peyote use is quite unpleasant—causing nausea—and has virtually no attraction for recreational use. There is almost no illicit market in peyote, and neither the federal government nor states that permit its religious use have experienced any enforcement problems with illicit peyote use. Furthermore, Justice Blackmun notes that the Native America Church itself carefully controls the use of the drug and that it strongly supports abstention from alcohol and other drugs. Moreover, Blackmun notices, Oregon itself provided no evidence of the alleged dangers of peyote use; hence, he notes, the majority argument "rests on no evidentiary foundation at all."

The dissenters develop at some length the religious context of peyote use, with citations to scholarly literature on the subject. They conclude that "the values and interests of those seeking a religious exemption in this case are congruent, to a great degree with those the State seeks to promote through its drug laws. . . . Not only does the Church's doctrine forbid non-religious use of peyote; it also generally advocates self-reliance, familial responsibility, and abstinence from alcohol." Finally, the dissenters note the particular weight that falls on Native American and other minority religions by the majority's approach. While agreeing with the majority that courts ought not delve into the "centrality" of religious acts, they note that peyote rituals are "an integral part of the life process." "Respondents believe, and their sincerity has *never* been in doubt, that the peyote plant embodies their deity, and eating it is an act of worship and communion. Without peyote, they could not enact the essential ritual of their religion." The dissenters note the "devastating impact" of prosecuting them for an act of worship—an impact all the more troubling in view of Congress's policy of protecting the religious freedom of Native Americans as symbolized in the American Indian Religious Freedom Act.

The Effects of *Smith*

Shortly after the *Smith* decision the state of Oregon amended its controlled substances laws to exempt ritual peyote use from prosecution. Moreover, the decision produced the unusual effect of creating "strange bedfellows" among its critics; mainstream religious groups, the fundamentalist right, and the libertarian left were uncharacteristically united in decrying not only the specific outcome but also the implications of Justice Scalia's jurisprudence for religious rights within a religiously plural society. Shortly after the decision, a diverse number of religious advocacy groups and constitutional scholars petitioned the Court for a rehearing on the issue of the compelling state interest doctrine, but the petition was denied. In 1992 the Court revisited the controversy over compelling state interest, albeit inconclusively. In *Church of the Lukumi Babalu Aye, Inc. v. City of Hialeah* (1993) the Court unanimously struck down a local ordinance that prohibited ritual animal sacrifice, which quite obviously targeted a religious practice for disfavorable treatment. In concurring opinions Justices Souter and Blackmun (the latter joined by Justice O'Connor) urged the Court to reject the *Smith* majority's distinction between neutral laws and those targeting religion and to reinstate the compelling state interest standard.

At the same time, religious interest groups and constitutional scholars mounted a significant campaign to urge Congress to adopt legislation reversing the effects of the *Smith* decision. In November 1993 Congress enacted the Religious Freedom Restoration Act (RFRA), with the intention of restoring the compelling state interest test. The key section of the bill states that government may restrict a person's free exercise of religion only if government can show that such a restriction "(1) is essential to further a compelling governmental interest; and (2) is the least restrictive means of furthering that compelling governmental interest" standard. A constitutional challenge to this law reached the Supreme Court in June 1997 in the case of *City of Boerne v. P. F. Flores, Archbishop of San Antonio, and the United States.* A Court majority struck down the RFRA as reaching beyond the powers of Congress. The majority ruled that, whereas the Fourteenth Amendment grants Congress the power to enforce a constitutional right, the new law goes beyond enforcement and, in fact, alters the meaning of the right, thus infringing on the power of the judiciary and on the traditional prerogatives of states. Hence, at this writing, the *Smith* decision—and its rejection of the compelling state interest test—remains the constitutional standard for free exercise jurisprudence.

Bette Novit Evans

Bibliography

Epps, Garrett, "To an Unknown God: The Hidden History of *Employment Division v. Smith*," 30 *Arizona State Law Journal* 953–1024 (1998).

Gordon, James D., III, "Free Exercise on the Mountaintop," 79 *California Law Review* 91–116 (1991).

Laycock, Douglas, "The Remnants of Free Exercise," 1990 *Supreme Court Review* 1–68 (1990).

Marin, Kenneth, "*Employment Division of Human Resources v. Smith.* The Supreme Court Alters the State of Free Exercise Doctrine" (case note), 40 *American University Law Review* 1431–1476 (1991).

Marshall, William P., "In Defense of *Smith* and Free Exercise Revisionism," 58 *University of Chicago Law Review* 308–328 (1991).

McConnell, Michael, "Free Exercise Revisionism and the *Smith* Case," 57 *University of Chicago Law Review* 1109–1153 (1990).

Rawlings, Tom C., "*Employment Division of Human Resources v. Smith:* The Supreme Court Deserts the Free Exercise Clause" (case note), 25 *Georgia Law Review* 567–593 (1991).

Sherwin, Richard K., "Rhetorical Pluralism and the Discourse Ideal: Countering *Division of Employment v. Smith*: A Parable of Pagans, Politics, and Majoritarian Rule," 85 *Northwestern University Law Review* 388–441 (1991).

Tepker, Harry F., Jr., "Hallucinations of Neutrality in the Oregon Peyote Case," 16 *American Indian Law Review* 1–56 (1991).

Cases and Statutes Cited

City of Boerne v. P. F. Flores, Archbishop of San Antonio, and the United States, 521 U.S. 507 (1997).

Church of the Lukumi Babalu Aye, Inc. v. City of Hialeah, 508 U.S. 520 (1993).

Employment Division v. Smith (Smith I), 485 U.S. 660 (1988).
Employment Division, Department of Human Resources of Oregon v. Smith, 494 U.S. 872 (1990).
Minersville School District Board of Education v. Gobitis, 310 U.S. 586 (1940).
Reynolds v. United States, 98 U.S. 145 (1878).
Religious Freedom Restoration Act, Pub. L. 103–141, 107 Stat. 1488 (1993).
Sherbert v. Verner, 374 U.S. 398 (1963).
Smith v. Employment Division, 301 Or 209, 721 P. 2d 445 (1986).
Smith v. Employment Division, 307 Or 68, 763 P. 2d 146 (1988).
Wisconsin v. Yoder, 406 U.S. 205 (1972).

Engel v. Vitale
370 U.S. 421 (1962)

Engel v. Vitale (1962), the Supreme Court's seminal school prayer decision, has remained one of the most controversial decisions in American constitutional law. In *Engel* the Court ruled that the State Board of Regents of New York violated the Establishment Clause in mandating the daily recitation of a particular, state-composed prayer. The prayer at issue read as follows: "Almighty God, we acknowledge our dependence upon Thee, and we beg Thy blessings upon us, our parents, our teachers and our country." This daily ceremony was adopted on the recommendation of the board of regents and was said aloud at the beginning of each school day, in every classroom, in the presence of a teacher.

The lawsuit was brought in the Supreme Court, Special Term, Nassau County, by five plaintiffs—parents of children in Union Free schools and taxpayers within that district. The plaintiffs included members of the Jewish faith, of the Society for Ethical Culture, of the Unitarian Church, and one nonbeliever. The defendants represented the Board of Education of Union Free School District Number Nine.

The lawsuit challenged the constitutionality of the practice on two separate grounds. First, the plaintiffs argued that the use of the official prayer in public schools was contrary to their religious beliefs and practices and, thus, infringed on their free exercise rights. Second, they alleged that both the state law authorizing the use of prayer in the public schools and the school district's regulation ordering the recitation of the prayer violated the Establishment Clause.

The state supreme court upheld the prayer recitation based on its conclusions that the practice did not amount to religious instruction and was permissible as an "accepted" practice. This latter holding rested in large part on the lower court's reasoning that—because at the time of the adoption of the First Amendment it was the accepted practice to have prayer in schools—it would, therefore, be proper to continue this practice today. (In so holding, the trial court did not consider that, at the time of the adoption of the First Amendment, public schools were virtually nonexistent; if prayer in schools was, in fact, the "accepted" practice, it was a practice that occurred in the private schools.) The trial court, however, did direct the school board to take measures to ensure that students would not be subject to any compulsion to recite the prayer. The Supreme Court Special Term's ruling was affirmed on appeal by the Supreme Court, Appellate Division, Second Department. The Court of Appeals of New York also affirmed, holding that, because the recitation of the prayer did "not amount to religious education nor was it the practice of or establishment of religion," there was no constitutional violation.

On December 4, 1961, the U.S. Supreme Court granted certiorari. Because the petitioners had dropped the free exercise claim, only the establishment issue was presented to the Court. In arguing that the prayer was unconstitutional, the petitioners primarily relied on *McCollum v. Board of Education* (1948), in which the Court invalidated in-school "released-time" programs for religious instruction. According to the plaintiffs, *McCollum* stood for the proposition that the Establishment Clause forbids any state aid to religion in the form of religious instruction.

The respondents countered with two separate contentions. First, although conceding that the school prayer was religious, they argued that it was constitutional because state prayer had traditionally been accepted. Second, they relied on *Zorach v. Clauson* (1952), in which the Court upheld the "released-time" programs for religious instruction when those programs were occurring off-campus. The respondents read *Zorach* for the proposition that the government can aid all religions without violating the Establishment Clause. The regent's prayer, therefore, was constitutional as a permissible accommodation.

Engel was argued on April 3 and 6, 1962. In a 6-to-1 decision, with neither Justices Felix Frankfurter nor Byron White participating, the U.S. Supreme Court reversed, holding the daily recitation of the regent's prayer to be in violation of the Establishment Clause.

Justice Hugo L. Black, writing for the Court, held that "the Establishment clause . . . is violated by the enactment of laws which establish an official religion whether those laws operate directly to coerce nonobserving individuals or not. . . ." The Court explicitly ruled that neither the nondenominational character of the prayer nor the fact that students could be excused from the ceremony would allow this legislation to circumvent the restrictions of the Establishment Clause.

The actual test the Court applied, however, was not clear. The Court did not rely on, nor did it require, a finding of coercion in order to find that the prayer was in violation of the Establishment Clause. Further, the Court did not find that the prayer had the effect of promoting a belief of any kind. Rather, the Court generally focused on the state's promotion of religious practices in the public schools and concluded that this promotion alone was constitutionally prohibited. More narrowly, the Court focused on the fact that the prayer was state-composed, holding that, "it is no part of the business of the government to compose official prayers for any group of American people to recite as a part of a religious program carried on by the government."

Justice William O. Douglas filed a concurring opinion, which focused on the problem of a government-sponsored religious activity. In his view the violation of the Establishment Clause was entrenched in the government's financing of a religious exercise, and not in the actual "establishment" of a religion through the daily recitation of the regent's prayer.

Justice Potter Stewart wrote the sole dissent in *Engel*. In a scathing opinion he asserted that the Court had violated the free exercise rights of the other students in the district, and he vigorously asserted the position that the students who wished to say the prayer should be permitted to do so. Justice Stewart pointed to the "total lack of evidence of any coercion" and for that reason argued that the Court had misapplied the Establishment Clause. To Stewart, the school exercise did not amount to the establishment of religion.

The *Engel* opinion, delivered on June 25, 1962, was met with a tremendous public furor. The controversy surrounding the decision was so extensive that Justice Tom C. Clark—one of the *Engel* majority—broke with tradition by agreeing to explain this decision in a public speech in which he emphasized the narrowness of the decision. First, he emphasized that the prayer, which was recited daily by students in a public school, had been composed by the state. Second, he commented that the legislation required that a state-employed teacher be present during the recitation. Third, he noted that the prayer was recited aloud in unison, not individually. He also seemed particularly concerned with the public's misconception of the reach of the *Engel* holding. He pointed to the fact that the Court did *not* expressly prohibit silent meditation or all forms of prayer in public schools.

Despite Justice Clark's attempt to explain the decision, *Engel* continues to be misunderstood and/or is still resisted. The central objection is derived not from *Engel*'s narrow ruling invalidating state-composed prayers but, rather, from its broader holding that any state-endorsed prayer in public schools would be unconstitutional. This latter conclusion was made explicit the following year in *Schempp,* where the Court struck down Bible readings in the public schools.

The school prayer controversy has not abated. Despite the decision in *Engel,* the incidence of school prayer has not ceased. Many schools continue to engage in various religious practices, including homeroom devotional exercises, prayer over the loudspeaker, prayer before lunch, and formal Bible instruction. Similarly, although some states may appear to have acquiesced to the prohibition against school prayer, attempts to "run around" the *Engel* decision remain prevalent. For example, the Court recently addressed the constitutionality of prayer at a public school graduation and promotion, and in *Lee v. Weisman* (1991) it held this practice to be in violation of the Establishment Clause. Last, but not least, numerous amendments have been proposed to overturn *Engel* and to allow prayer in public schools; as of yet, these efforts have not succeeded.

Prayer in public schools has remained—and probably will continue to remain—an emotionally charged issue. This is undoubtedly so because the issue involves two highly sensitive matters: religious freedom, which is one of the most precious of individual liberties; and the public schools, which compose the most visible and the most important institution in setting our national goals and values. The Court is to be commended for following the wisdom of James Madison, who first warned that "it is proper to take alarm at the first experiment on our liberties." Perhaps, as Professor Kurland predicted, *Engel* (along with *Schempp*) will eventually come to be "recognized as one of the bulwarks of America's freedom."

Jennifer L. Sherman

Bibliography

Dierenfield, Richard B., "The Impact of the Supreme Court Decisions on Religion in the Public Schools," 62 *Religious Education* 445 (1967).

Dolbeare, Kenneth M., and Phillip E. Hammond, *The School Prayer Decisions* (Chicago: University of Chicago Press, 1971).

Graham, Kristin J. "The Supreme Court Comes Full Circle," 42 *Buffalo Law Review* 147 (1994).

Hudgins, H. C., Jr., *The Warren Court and the Public Schools* (Danville, Ill.: Interstate Printers and Publishers, 1970).

Kurland, Philip B., "The Regent's Prayer Case: 'Full of Sound and Fury, Signifying . . .,'" 1962 *Supreme Court Review* 1.

Laycock, Douglas, "Formal, Substantive, and Disaggregated Neutrality toward Religion," 39 *DePaul Law Review* 993 (1990).

Marshall, William P., "'We Know It When We See It': The Supreme Court and Establishment," 59 *Southern California Law Review* 495 (1986).

Muir, William K., *Prayer in the Public Schools* (Chicago: University of Chicago Press, 1967).

Smith, Rodney K., *Public Prayer and the Constitution* (Wilmington, Del.: Scholarly Resources, 1987).

Stone, Geoffrey R., "In Opposition to the School Prayer Amendment," 50 *University of Chicago Law Review* 823 (1983).

Cases Cited

Engel v. Vitale, 370 U.S. 421 (1962).

Lee v. Weisman, 505 U.S. 577 (1992).

McCollum v. Board of Education, 333 U.S. 203 (1948).

School District of Abington Township v. Schempp, 374 U.S. 203 (1963).

Zorach v. Clauson, 343 U.S. 306 (1952).

English Toleration Act

In 1689 the Convention Parliament, summoned at the time of the Glorious Revolution, passed an act granting freedom of worship to Protestants who dissented from the Church of England. This statute (1 William and Mary, c. 18), known as the Toleration Act, exempted certain Protestant dissenters from the penal laws that had been enacted during the reigns of Elizabeth I (1558–1603); James I (1603–1625), and Charles II (1660–1685). Those dissenters—who took an oath of allegiance to William and Mary, swore that the pope could not depose kings or exercise jurisdiction in England, and made a declaration against the Roman Catholic doctrine of transubstantiation—were allowed to worship separately in their own meeting houses, provided the doors of those houses remained unlocked. The act specifically exempted these persons from the penalties enumerated in the Elizabethan statute of 1593 and the Conventicles Act of 1670, both of which had been directed against Protestant sectaries, and it freed them from the liability of prosecution for nonconformity in the English ecclesiastical courts.

The Toleration Act declared further that dissenting ministers who subscribed to all but three of the Thirty-Nine Articles of Religion (those dealing with homilies, the tradition of the church, and the consecration of bishops) were exempted from the penalties of the Act of Uniformity of 1662 and the Five-Mile Act of 1665, both of which had been intended to prevent the growth of Protestant nonconformity in the aftermath of the Puritan Revolution. Baptist ministers were also exempted from subscription to the section of Article 27 regarding infant baptism. Quakers, who would not take oaths, were allowed to substitute affirmations for the oaths required by the act, a procedure that was extended to include testimony in civil (but not in criminal) trials in the Act of Solemn Affirmation (1695).

The Toleration Act specifically excluded Roman Catholics and Unitarians, and it did not remove the civil disabilities imposed on Protestant dissenters by the Corporation Act (1661) and the Test Act (1673), which limited political and military office to those who took the Anglican communion. Dissenters continued to be required to pay tithes in support of the Church of England, and attendance at Anglican service was still required of all who did not resort to a dissenting meeting house. The act also required the registration of all dissenting meeting places before the bishops, archdeacons, or J.P.s who had jurisdiction in the localities where the meetings were held.

The Toleration Act was an integral part of the Revolution Settlement of 1689. It originated in the efforts of the Anglican Church to win the support of Protestant dissenters after James II, a Roman Catholic, had granted a broad toleration to both Catholic and Protestant dissenters in his Declarations of Indulgence (1687 and 1688). The Toleration Act of 1689 was therefore intended to achieve Protestant unity in the face of the threat from Rome. In their petition to James II in May 1688, the Anglican bishops had promised Protestant dissenters true liberty of conscience, but during the Puritan Revolution Anglican commitment to accommodating Protestant dissent weakened. The earl of Nottingham introduced two bills in the Convention Parliament of 1689—one to comprehend moderate dissenters within the Anglican Church and the other to tolerate only the most obdurate sectaries. The bill for comprehension was dropped, however, after William III revived Anglican fears by proposing the repeal of the sacramental test for all dissenters. This left all dissenters, moderate as well as radical, with only the limited form of toleration provided in Nottingham's second bill.

The limited nature of the toleration granted in the act of 1689 and the grudging manner of its concession perpetuated tensions between Anglicans and dissenters well into the eighteenth century. Dissenters feared the repeal of the act, and in fact it was modified by passage of the Occasional Conformity Act of 1711, which threatened dissenters with fines and removal from office if they attended nonconformist services after having taken the Anglican communion in order to qualify for political office. In similar fashion the Schism Act of 1714 required dissenting schoolmasters to take the sacramental test and to obtain a license from a bishop; this act provided for the revocation of their license if they should subsequently attend a meeting of dissenters. Neither the Occasional Conformity Act nor the Schism Act was consistently enforced, and both statutes were repealed in 1719. The Corporation and Test Acts, however, remained on the statute book until 1828—although annual Indemnity Acts, beginning in 1727, effectively allowed nonconformists to hold public office.

The nature of the Toleration Act and its failure to provide political benefits for dissenters became central issues in *Rex and Regina* v. *Larwood,* which was decided by the court of King's Bench in 1694. Larwood, a Protestant dissenter, having been elected sheriff of Norwich (an onerous position) and being required to take the Anglican communion in order to qualify himself for that post, claimed that he was excused from that requirement, and from assuming the office itself, by the terms of the Toleration Act. The judges decided, first, that the Toleration Act was a private statute, since it had not been extended to all dissenters but only to those who made their declaration at quarter-sessions, or assizes. The Toleration Act was not made a public statute until 1779. The judges also decided that the Corporation Act—which Larwood had refused to comply with and had originally pleaded as the basis of his exemption—had been intended to discourage dissenters, not to favor them, and that no man could take advantage of his own disability when he has the power to remove it. Judgment therefore was given against Larwood. In 1767, however, the House of Lords decided against the Corporation of London for fining Allen Evans, a dissenter, because he had refused to take the communion test after being nominated as sheriff of London. In that case Lord Mansfield ruled that the policy of the city, which was intended to raise money by means of such fines, violated the principles of religious liberty as enforced by the Toleration Act.

The Toleration Act was the first statute to give legal recognition to Protestant dissenters in England. As the judges wrote in the Larwood case, "the law took no notice of the Dissenters until this Act." The Anglican Church remained established by law, but it was no longer the only lawful church within the kingdom. The passage of the Toleration Act thus constituted an admission that uniformity of religious belief and practice, which had been one of the main goals of English religious legislation since the Reformation, could not be achieved. Consequently the theory of comprehension, by which all English subjects were considered to be members of one state church, finally had to be abandoned.

On the basis of the Toleration Act more than 2,500 dissenting places of worship were licensed between 1691 and 1710. The Tories, who generally opposed the dissenting interest in Parliament, were convinced that the statute had encouraged the growth of dissent, along with heresies like Deism and Socinianism. The dissenters' numerical strength, however, actually declined during that period. Their membership had begun to drop in the 1680s, and that trend continued into the early eighteenth century. Having formed 5 percent of the population in 1670, the dissenters were reduced to a mere 2 percent by 1710. The majority of their adherents in the eighteenth century came from the ranks of the urban middle class. At the same time the members of the landed class, who were reluctant to adopt forms of worship that would disable them politically, became overwhelmingly Anglican.

Although the Anglican Church remained established by law, the loss of its monopoly over the religious life of the nation undermined its clergy's self-confidence. The Toleration Act also made it difficult for Anglicans to enforce ecclesiastical discipline. Churchwardens were reluctant to present individuals for nonattendance, in effect perpetuating the greater latitude provided by James II's Declarations of Indulgence. Nonattendance became especially prevalent in the cities and towns; in the large urban parishes of Yorkshire fewer than 10 percent of the potential churchgoers made their Easter communion in 1743.

The substance of the Toleration Act was extended to the North American colonies by instructions to colonial governors, inclusion in new colonial charters, or legislation by colonial assemblies. In Pennsylvania, New York, New Jersey, and Rhode Island this extension had little effect, since those colonies had already passed more liberal religious legislation than the act demanded. The predominantly dissenting New York Assembly actually used the terms of the English act to exclude Catholics from office for the first time and to deny them liberty of conscience. In Massachusetts, where the Congregational Church could consider itself both as a dissenting sect that benefited from the English act and as the established church in the colony, the new charter of 1691 granted "liberty of conscience . . . in the worship of God to all Christians (except Papists)." Although the leaders of the colony professed a theoretical commitment to toleration and publicly praised the English act, they only reluctantly and grudgingly tolerated Baptists, Quakers, and Presbyterians. As late as 1708 Samuel Sewall refused to sign a warrant for a Quaker meetinghouse.

In Connecticut, where the Congregational Church was also established, the application of the English act did not become an issue until the first decade of the eighteenth century. A law passed in 1702 against the entertainment of "any Quaker, Ranter, Adamite or other notorious heretic" was disallowed by Queen Anne in 1705 on the grounds that it violated the liberty of conscience granted both by the Toleration Act and by the colony's charter of 1662. Three years later, in response to petitions from Baptists and Anglicans and out of fear that the queen might abrogate the colony's charter, the General Assembly passed its own Toleration Act. Intended "for the ease of such as do soberly dissent from the way of worship and ministry established by the ancient laws of this government," the Connecticut law allowed dissenting congregations to "qualify themselves" for freedom of worship according to the provision of the English Toleration Act.

In Maryland toleration was not achieved until 1700 as part of the act establishing the Church of England in the colony. Four years earlier the Privy Council had invalidated another act of the colony, which required ministers to read the Book of Common Prayer, on the grounds that the law violated the English Toleration Act. Legislation passed in South Carolina was likewise nullified for imposing stricter requirements on dissenters than did the English statute. In Virginia, where the legislature recognized the application of the English act to the colony in 1699, efforts were made throughout the eighteenth century to restrict the toleration that dissenters were allowed by law. During the 1740s authorities tried to check the spread of Presbyterianism in

Virginia by confining itinerant preachers to designated places of worship. This led the Presbyterian preacher Samuel Davies to take his case to London and to secure from the Lords Commissioners of Trade and Plantations a declaration that "toleration and a free exercise of religion should ever be held sacred in his Majesty's colonies." As late as 1773 Baptists were being arrested and imprisoned in western Virginia.

Despite the belated achievement of toleration in some of the American colonies—and the occasional violation of the policy—Protestant dissenters in eighteenth-century America fared better than their counterparts in England did. All who took the loyalty oath were eligible for public office, and no sacramental test excluded them from an American college. By the middle of the eighteenth century, the principle of toleration had become widely accepted in virtually all political and intellectual circles. The concept, however, implied condescension on the part of the established church toward those outside it, and at the time of the American Revolution it was replaced by a concept of religious liberty shared equally by all. Article 16 of the Virginia Bill of Rights (1776), which originally called for "the fullest toleration in the exercise of religion," was amended by James Madison to declare that "all men are equally entitled to a full and free exercise of religion." This article served as one of the main sources of the First Amendment to the United States Constitution.

Brian P. Levack

Bibliography

Barlow, Richard B., *Citizenship and Conscience: A Study in the Theory and Practice of Religious Toleration in England during the Eighteenth Century* (Philadelphia: University of Pennsylvania Press, 1963).

Butler, Jon, *Awash in a Sea of Faith: Christianizing the American People* (Cambridge, Mass.: Harvard University Press, 1990).

Curry, Thomas J., *The First Freedoms: Church and State in America to the Passage of the First Amendment* (New York: Oxford University Press, 1986).

McLoughlin, William G., *New England Dissent, 1630–1833* (Cambridge, Mass.: Harvard University Press, 1971).

Watts, Michael, *The Dissenters: From the Reformation to the French Revolution* (Oxford, England: the Clarendon Press, 1978).

Cases and Statutes Cited

Rex and Regina v. Larwood, 91 English Rep. 155 (1694).

Act of Solemn Affirmation, 7 Statutes of the Realm 152 (7 and 8 William, c. 34).

Occasional Conformity Act of 1711, 9 Statutes of the Realm 551–53 (10 Anne, c. 6).

Schism Act of 1714, 9 Statutes of the Realm 915–17 (13 Anne, c. 7).

Toleration Act of 1689, 6 Statutes of the Realm 74–76 (1 William and Mary, c. 18).

Equal Access Act
20 U.S.C. Secs. 4071–4074 (1988)

Congress enacted the Equal Access Act in 1984 to govern the controversial "equal access" issue: When a public high school allows voluntary, student-initiated nonreligious student groups to meet on school premises, should it grant equal access to voluntary, student-initiated religious student groups? This issue encompasses two difficult constitutional inquiries, which the Supreme Court had not yet addressed when the act was passed: Are schools compelled to grant equal access by the Free Speech Clause? Or are they prohibited from doing so by the Establishment Clause?

The Equal Access Act applies to all public secondary schools that receive federal financial assistance. It prohibits them from denying equal access to "any students who wish to conduct a meeting . . . on the basis of the religious, political, philosophical, or other content of the speech" at the meeting, so long as the school has a "limited open forum." Such a forum exists whenever the school allows one or more "noncurriculum related student groups to meet on school premises during noninstructional time."

The act raised a number of statutory interpretation issues, including when a student group was "noncurriculum related," thus triggering the equal access requirement. It also raised the same constitutional issues that existed in its absence; if the statute required a school either to grant or to deny access to a student club when the Constitution would compel the opposite result, the act would to that extent be unconstitutional.

In *Board of Education v. Mergens* (1990) the Supreme Court resolved two important issues about the Equal Access Act. First, it interpreted the term "noncurriculum related student group" broadly, as applying to any group that does not *directly* relate to the school's courses. Second, the Court ruled that the act does not violate the Establishment Clause.

In seeking to resolve the tension between Free Speech and Establishment Clause values that are posed by the equal access issue, the act leaned in favor of free speech. Thus, under the act, students have more statutory free speech rights than they do under recent First Amendment jurisprudence. Conversely, the act was less sensitive to Establishment Clause concerns than were the Court's previous rulings in the public school setting. Many critics charge that the act was originally designed as a vehicle for evading Establishment Clause constraints on the role of religion in the public schools. Consistent with these charges, earlier versions of the act had expressly singled out religious speech for special protection.

The Court's past cases involving state-sanctioned religious expression on public school premises had invalidated nearly all such expression, even where individual student participation was at least arguably voluntary. In support of these rulings the Court had repeatedly expressed the fear that, because of young people's particular impressionability, they might be more likely than adults to perceive any religious expression on school premises as manifesting the school's approval of religion. However, in *Mergens* the Court asserted that secondary students are sufficiently mature to understand that a school does not endorse student speech but that it merely permits such speech on a neutral, nondiscriminatory basis.

In *Mergens* the Court also rejected the dissenters' arguments that other aspects of high schools create special dangers that might make students perceive a student religious group as school-endorsed: the compulsory attendance requirement, the highly structured school environment, and the fact that at most high schools the range of student groups is relatively narrow and does not include any advocacy-oriented organizations.

In response, the Court's plurality opinion stressed provisions in the Equal Access Act that are designed to minimize the risk of perceived school endorsement. Most importantly, the act forbids any school officials from participating in meetings of student religious groups, other than in a custodial capacity, and it forbids any such meetings during "instructional time." The Court also stressed that, ultimately, "the school itself has control over any impressions it gives its students," and it suggested that schools could take steps to emphasize their nonendorsement of student religious speech (as well as other student speech), such as the issuance of disclaimers. The Court's dissenters would have made this suggestion into a requirement.

The dissenters' approach is more consistent with the fact-specific, contextual nature of the Court's previous Establishment Clause rulings, which suggest the relative inutility of per se rules. Standing alone, the rules imposed by the Equal Access Act certainly reduce the danger that reasonable students would understand religious clubs to bear the school's imprimatur, but they do not guarantee such a result in any particular case. In addition to complying with the act, each school should take any other steps that are warranted, in light of its particular circumstances, to avoid the appearance of sponsoring religion.

Nadine Strossen

Bibliography

Laycock, Douglas, "Equal Access and Moments of Silence: The Equal Status of Religious Speech by Private Speakers," 81 *Northwestern University Law Review* 1–67 (1986).

Strossen, Nadine, "A Constitutional Analysis of the Equal Access Act's Standards Governing Public School Student Religious Meetings," 24 *Harvard Journal of Legislation* 117–190 (1987).

———, "A Framework for Evaluating Equal Access Claims by Student Religious Groups: Is There a Window for Free Speech in the Wall Separating Church and State?" 71 *Cornell Law Review* 143–183 (1985).

Teitel, Ruti, "The Unconstitutionality of Equal Access Policies and Legislation Allowing Organized Student-Initiated Religious Activities in the Public High School: A Proposal for a Unitary First

Amendment Forum Analysis," 12 *Hastings Constitutional Law Quarterly* 529–595 (1985).

Case and Statute Cited

Board of Education v. Mergens, 496 U.S. 226 (1990).

Equal Access Act, 20 U.S.C. Secs. 4071–4074 (1988).

Equal Employment Opportunity Commission v. Kamehameha Schools/Bishop Estate

900 F. 2d 458 (9th Cir. 1993), cert. denied, 510 U.S. 963 (1993)

The Bishop Estate—established in 1884 by the will of Princess Bernice Pauahi Bishop—plays a central role in Hawaii because it owns 337,000 acres of land, controls $1.2 billion in assets, and runs the important Kamehameha Schools and other educational programs for children of Hawaiian ancestry. In the 1993 case, *Equal Employment Opportunity Commission v. Kamehameha Schools/Bishop Estate,* the U.S. Court of Appeals for the Ninth Circuit reversed a district court ruling, and agreed with the U.S. Equal Employment Opportunity Commission (EEOC) that the Kamehameha Schools' policy of hiring only Protestant teachers violated Title VII of the 1964 Civil Rights Act. Title VII prohibits discrimination in employment on the basis of religion, but it exempts religious organizations from this prohibition. The Ninth Circuit's opinion was based on the court's view that the Kamehameha Schools are not sufficiently religious in character to justify an exemption from the general rule against discrimination. This decision is troubling because the court has assumed the role of determining what is and what is not a bona fide religion.

In *Equal Employment Opportunity Commission v. Kamehameha Schools/Bishop Estate* (1991), Judge Alan Kay of the U.S. District Court had upheld the Protestant-only restriction because of the "religious purpose and character" of the Kamehameha Schools, ruling that requiring teachers to be Protestant was a bona fide occupational qualification. Certainly there can be no doubt that Princess Pauahi desired that the schools have a Protestant orientation, although she did not require that the students themselves be Protestant.

It is intriguing to compare the Ninth Circuit's decision with *Corporation of the Presiding Bishop of the Church of Jesus Christ of Latter-Day Saints v. Amos* (1987). In that case, the U.S. Supreme Court upheld the decision of the Mormon Church to fire a janitor working at a gymnasium it owned and operated (as a nonprofit facility open to the public) because he had failed to qualify as a "temple recommend." To be a "temple recommend," and thus to be eligible to attend the church's temples, one must observe the church's standards involving church attendance, tithing, and abstinence from coffee, tea, alcohol, and tobacco. The janitor had argued that his work had nothing to do with religion and that his firing violated his First Amendment rights. The Court unanimously rejected his claim, stressing that the government should not interfere "with the ability of religious organizations to define and carry out their religious missions." Justice William Brennan wrote a sensitive and eloquent concurring opinion stressing that many religions feel that the ability to create an exclusive community of believers is an essential component of their religion: For many individuals, religious activity derives meaning in large measure from participation in a larger religious community. Such a community represents an ongoing tradition of shared beliefs, an organic entity not reducible to a mere aggregation of individuals. Determining that certain activities are in furtherance of an organization's religious mission, and that only those who are committed to that mission should conduct them, is thus a means by which a religious community defines itself.

The Bishop Estate and the Kamehameha Schools had argued similarly that Princess Pauahi wanted to create a school with a religiously oriented Protestant community for its students and employees. The Ninth Circuit rejected this argument, concluding that the schools are not sufficiently religious to qualify for the exemption. The appellate court stressed that no religious test is required of the teachers (they simply certify that they are Protestants), that students are accepted from all religions, and that no attempt is made to convert the non-Protestant students. According to the Ninth Circuit, the "generic" Protestant religion community at the Kamehameha Schools was not sufficiently religious to qualify for a religious exemption, even though the more rigorous Mormon religious community does qualify.

It is troubling to have a court determine what a true religious community is and how elaborate its belief system must be. Can it not be legitimate for a group to want to operate within a loosely defined and spiritually flexible Protestant community? On the other hand, if such "generic" religious communities are able to discriminate against members of minority religions, the result might be to eliminate all teeth to the prohibition against religious discrimination. Once Congress provided a religious exemption in Title VII to the 1964 Civil Rights Act, it was inevitable that courts would have to undertake the assignment of interpreting what religion is sufficient to qualify. And it is natural for a court to interpret this exemption narrowly to ensure that the general norm of religious nondiscrimination is adhered to.

Jon M. Van Dyke

Bibliography

Van Dyke, Jon M., "The Kamehameha Schools/Bishop Estate [*EEOC v. Kamehameha Schools/Bishop Estate,* 990 F. 2d 458 (9th Cir., 1993] and the Constitution," 17 *University of Hawaii Law Review* 413–425 (1995).

Cases Cited

Corporation of the Presiding Bishop of the Church of Jesus Christ of Latter-Day Saints v. Amos, 483 U.S. 327 (1987).

Equal Employment Opportunity Commission v. Kamehameha Schools/Bishop Estate, 990 F. 2d 458 (9th Cir. 1993).

Equal Employment Opportunity Commission v. Kamehameha Schools/Bishop Estate, 780 F. Supp. 1317 (D. Haw. 1991).

Equal Protection Clause and the Free Exercise of Religion

The principle that people of all religious faiths should be treated as equals by the government is a core premise underlying many U.S. Supreme Court decisions relating to religious freedom. Yet the application of this basic principle in constitutional doctrine remains complex and uncertain.

In one sense, to paraphrase Chief Justice Harlan Fiske Stone in *Hirabayashi v. United States* (1943), "distinctions between citizens" solely because of their religious faith "are by their nature" as "odious to a free people" as are distinctions based on race or national ancestry. State discrimination against Jews, Catholics, Jehovah's Witnesses, or other minority religions with regard to access to public employment or the distribution of government largess will invoke rigorous constitutional scrutiny and almost certainly will be struck down. Yet—despite this apparent constitutional commitment to exorcising invidious religious discrimination from governmental decision making—there have been few Supreme Court cases applying the Equal Protection Clause to alleged acts of disparate treatment among religions, and there has been no decision formally invalidating a religious classification on equal protection grounds. Instead, claims of religious favoritism or mistreatment are regularly reviewed as possible violations of the Free Exercise Clause or of the Establishment Clause of the First Amendment.

This apparent anomaly has both a historical and a conceptual explanation. From a historical perspective the Equal Protection Clause, as originally understood and applied, was limited in its scope. It did not prohibit discrimination based on classifications other than race and national origin. Indeed, until the seminal decision of *Brown v. Board of Education of Topeka* (1954), even blatant racial discrimination was often upheld as constitutional. It was not until the late 1960s and early 1970s that the scope of the Equal Protection Clause was extended to prohibit discrimination against women, aliens, and nonmarital children. Religious discrimination might reasonably be added to that list, but by 1970 the Court had already interpreted the Establishment Clause of the First Amendment to prohibit both government favoritism toward majority religions and the imposition of unfair burdens on the members of minority faiths. When the Court explicitly declared, in *Larson v. Valenti* (1982), that the "clearest command of the Establishment Clause is that one religious denomination cannot be officially preferred over another," it was reciting accepted doctrine that had been recognized as controlling authority years earlier.

The conceptual difficulties with using equal protection doctrine to prohibit religious discrimination are more complicated. In one sense religious groups easily fit most of the criteria used by courts to determine which classes need to be protected against prejudice and unfair legislation. Members of minority faiths are to a degree "discrete and insular." They have been historically victimized by discrimination and prejudice. They are politically vulnerable. Although one's religious affiliation is technically mutable, religion plays such a fundamental role in a person's identity that it is ludicrous to expect that individuals may easily transform their religious beliefs in order to escape legislative burdens. Finally, one's religion does not determine a person's abilities or his or her behavioral propensities. Therefore, religion is seldom a rational proxy for the state to employ in drafting laws that distinguish among individuals.

On the other hand, most of the classifications that the courts rigorously scrutinize under the Equal Protection Clause (e.g., those based on race or national ancestry) involve personal attributes that the state can safely ignore in furthering the government's objectives without threatening to abridge other constitutionally recognized interests. This is not the case with regard to religious beliefs and practices, however. Both free exercise principles and considerations of fairness and respect for religious conscience require the state to consider religion in performing governmental functions. Thus, Quaker pacifists may avoid military service as conscientious objectors, the Amish need not comply with compulsory school attendance requirements, and those who consider Saturday to be their Sabbath must be provided unemployment compensation benefits even if they turn down employment offers that would require them to work on their day of rest. Thus, whereas racial minorities are more likely to receive equal treatment if government ignores their race and acts in a color-blind fashion, religious minorities may find religion-blind decisions by the state to be hurtful and oppressive.

If, however, the state does recognize freedom of religious conscience and permits people to perform religiously motivated activities that are prohibited to the general public, it may be criticized as favoring religious individuals over nonbelievers. By exempting certain individuals because of their faith from regulations experienced as burdensome by most citizens—such as taxes or military conscription—the state appears to provide the religious person preferential treatment. Thus there is an undeniable tension between traditional equality concerns and the fundamental right of religious freedom.

Difficult questions arise even when courts attempt to ensure that the freedom to practice one's religion is equally available to the members of all religious faiths. If the religious practice or institution at issue is essentially fungible, careful review of inequality of treatment among religious faiths constitutes a useful tool that courts may employ to implement free exercise guarantees. Thus in *Islamic Center of Mississippi v. Starkville, Mississippi* (5th Cir. 1988), a Mississippi city had granted exceptions from its zoning ordinances to nine Christian churches seeking to locate houses of worship in restricted residential areas, but it denied an exception to a similarly situated Islamic religious center. This disparate treatment substantially undermined the city's claim that it was necessary to bar the Muslim house of worship in order to promote the legitimate interests of traffic control and public safety. Accordingly, the court found that the plaintiff's free exercise interests outweighed the city's unpersuasive zoning justifications, and it prohibited the city from interfering with the Islamic Center's worship services.

Yet this kind of objective equality of treatment cannot always be provided to diverse religious faiths, because the impact on society of one religion's rituals and practices may be more substantial than that of other creeds. Congress, for example, has exempted the religious use of the hallucinogenic drug peyote by members of the Native American Church from the restrictions of the Controlled Substances Act (1987). Another faith, the Ethiopian Zion Coptic Church, uses marijuana as its sacrament, but the federal courts in *Olsen v. Drug Enforcement Administration* (D.C. Cir. 1989) and other cases have consistently rejected the Coptic Church's "establishment clause–equal protection challenge" that a similar exemption from federal narcotics laws must be provided to their religion. The different social problems associated with the use of marijuana and peyote, the courts held, justify the sectarian distinction drawn by the government with regard to exemptions for the religious use of these substances.

Equality concerns are relevant to the state's treatment of religious practices and religious groups. The Establishment Clause, in particular, is informed by equal protection doctrine and, properly understood, operates to prevent government from engaging in religious favoritism or discrimination.

Religion, however, raises sufficiently unique problems with regard to the constitutionality of state action that an independent doctrinal framework must be utilized by the courts to reconcile the Free Exercise Clause and the Establishment Clause. The functional compatibility of these two important constitutional principles—freedom of religious practice and equality among religious groups—cannot be achieved by looking to equal protection doctrine alone.

Alan E. Brownstein

Bibliography

Brownstein, Alan E., "Harmonizing the Heavenly and Earthly Spheres: The Fragmentation and Synthesis of Religion, Equality, and Speech in the Constitution," 51 *Ohio State Law Journal* 89–174 (1990).

Lupu, Ira C., "Reconstructing the Establishment Clause: The Case against Discretionary Accommodation of Religion," 140 *University of Pennsylvania Law Review* 555–612 (1991).

Cases and Statutes Cited

Brown v. Board of Education of Topeka, 347 U.S. 483 (1954).

Hirabayashi v. United States, 320 U.S. 81 (1943).

Islamic Center of Mississippi v. Starkville, Mississippi, 840 F. 2d 293 (5th Cir. 1988).

Larson v. Valenti, 456 U.S. 228 (1982).

Olsen v. Drug Enforcement Administration, 878 F. 2d 1458 (D.C. Cir. 1989).

Controlled Substances Act, 21 C.F. R. Sec. 1307.31 (1987).

Establishment Clause: Background and Adoption

Of all the clauses of the Bill of Rights none generates more controversy among scholars today concerning its original meaning and intent than the opening statement: "Congress shall make no law respecting an establishment of religion. . . ." At the time, however, the term "establishment of religion" caused no controversy. Americans understood it to mean a government preference for a single church, sect, or religion, and virtually every statement about establishment—in the writings of individuals, in provisions of state constitutions, and in public petitions—pointed to such an understanding. Although individuals and states differed diametrically over whether religion should receive public financial support, they all shared a single definition of "establishment" as a preference on the part of government for one religion over all others. They also universally agreed that the Establishment Clause, together with the Free Exercise Clause, constituted a formal proclamation of a meaning already implied in the Constitution—that the new federal government had no power in religious matters.

It is equally clear that when these same Americans described an establishment as a preference for one religion, they were not implying approval of nonpreferential or nonexclusive government support for religion. Nothing in the history of the time warrants such a conclusion, and here again the utterances of individuals and the enactments of the states overwhelmingly demonstrate that even those who opposed any kind of government support—even support that was proposed to assist more than one religion—still defined an establishment as a government preference for one religion. Americans adhered to this definition of establishment because that is what their experience and history told them an establishment was, even though over the years they had witnessed and, for the most part, rejected arrangements that would seem to have modified this understanding by providing for a more broadly based nonpreferential government support for religion.

Separationists and Accommodationists

Although Americans generally agreed that the federal government held no power in the area of religion, they differed over the need for that fact to be formally set forth, as they did about the other elements of the Bill of Rights. Some Federalists, such as Madison and Hamilton, argued that such protection for individual liberties was unnecessary, because the federal government possessed only those powers actually specified in the Constitution. They argued, moreover, that a bill of rights could be harmful, because either the government or the people might assume that the government had power over any area of life not specifically excluded from its purview. In the ratifying conventions, however, four states asked for protection for religious rights, and three of these—New York,

Virginia, and North Carolina—specifically requested a stated prohibition of an establishment of religion. Moreover, groups such as Baptists in Virginia complained that the new Constitution did not provide sufficient guarantees for religious liberty. Consequently, many Federalists feared that, without the promise of a bill of rights, the Constitution might not be ratified; thus James Madison, who was elected to the House of Representatives for the First Congress, committed himself to securing one. In fulfillment of his promise he introduced a series of amendments, including one stating that no "national religion" should be established. The House discussion of the proposal proved desultory—a result primarily of the fact that many members considered a prohibition against an establishment or religion to be redundant. The discussion did show clearly, however, that James Madison, the amendment's sponsor, thought of an establishment in terms of a preferential national church. Eventually, the House sent to the Senate the statement: "Congress shall make no law establishing religion. . . ." The Senate refused to accept this wording, and its members proposed several substitutions along the lines of "Congress shall make no law establishing any particular denomination of religion in preference to another . . ." before settling on "Congress shall make no law establishing articles of faith or a mode of worship. . . ." The House, in turn, refused to accept that wording, and a conference committee produced the final statement: "Congress shall make no law respecting an establishment of religion. . . ." By 1791 the Establishment Clause of what became the First Amendment had been ratified by a sufficient number of states. Massachusetts, Connecticut, and Georgia were not among them, but the reasons for this had nothing to do with the amendment's content.

This history has become the source of severe polarization among modern scholars—a division in thinking that dates from the decision handed down by the Supreme Court in *Everson v. Board of Education* (1947), its first interpretation of the Establishment Clause. In that decision the Court held the Establishment Clause to mean that government could not "pass laws which aid one religion, aid all religions, or prefer one religion over another. . . ." According to the Court, the original purpose of the clause was to erect "a wall of separation between Church and State." This interpretation soon came to be known as the separationist position. Critics of the Court, on the other hand, argued that, although the Establishment Clause forbade government from giving a preference to one religion, it did not forbid assistance to all religions on a nonpreferential basis or to religion in general—a position generally referred to as accommodationist.

Both separationists and accommodationists can cite considerable supportive evidence, but neither can account for the historical anomalies in their respective positions, a fact that has resulted in a good deal of confusion and skepticism about the value of history or its ability to provide much insight into the meaning of the Establishment Clause.

Ahistorical Assumptions

Both separationists and accommodationists, however, argue from the same completely ahistorical assumption, and therein lies the modern problem of interpretation. Both are wedded to the hypothesis that those involved in the enactment of the Establishment Clause conceived of and differentiated between preferential and nonpreferential government assistance to religion. Both assume that in defining an establishment of religion as a preference for one particular sect, Americans at the same time saw a distinction between a narrow establishment favoring one religion and a more broadly based nonpreferential government support for several religions or religion in general. Accommodationists hold that those who enacted the Establishment Clause rejected only the former (i.e., a narrow preference for one religion) but approved of a more broadly based nonpreferential support for religion. Separationists hold that the same populace understood and rejected all government support for religion, whether preferential or nonpreferential.

One sequence of events in particular—the debate in the Senate—appears to ground such a distinction between preferential and nonpreferential aid in a solid historical foundation. In place of the House proposal that "Congress shall make no law establishing religion, . . ." senators proposed four alternatives—all to the effect that Congress shall make no law establishing "any particular denomination of religion in preference to another . . ."—before agreeing on the statement "Congress shall make no law establishing articles of faith or a mode of worship. . . ." Logically and on its face, the Senate debate would appear to prove that a majority of its members favored prohibiting only government preference for a single religion, thus leaving the door open to general nonpreferential government assistance to religion, which position the House rejected. This logical interpretation, however, gives rise to several historical contradictions. It presumes that the Senate, at least, wanted to bestow on the federal government the power to assist religion in general; yet all the members agreed that the amendment's purpose was to make explicit the already-existing understanding that the government possessed no jurisdiction in matters of religion. No evidence at all has ever surfaced to prove that any division existed among the members of the House or Senate regarding the power of the federal government to assist religion. Moreover, the assumption that Americans distinguished between preferential and nonpreferential government assistance to religion renders James Madison's role in the formation of the Establishment Clause inexplicable, in that his utterances in the First Congress would show him as advocating only a ban on a narrow, preferential, or "national" establishment, as he repeatedly described it. Yet Madison clearly opposed all government assistance to religion.

In reality, then, Americans in 1789 did not, when they referred to an establishment of religion, think in terms of preferential and nonpreferential government assistance to religion. Those who vehemently opposed any government financial assistance to religion, even when such assistance would purportedly benefit multiple religious groups, nevertheless defined an establishment as a government preference for one group. Similarly, several states—New Jersey, Delaware, North Carolina—that specifically forbade government aid to religion on any basis defined and prohibited an establishment of religion as a government preference for one religion. History provides not a speck of evidence to show that, in accepting a definition of establishment of religion as a government preference for one religion over others, Americans signaled a willingness to accept the idea of government assistance to religion on a broader, nonpreferential basis—that, although government could not prefer one religion, it could support all religions. The logical argument adhered to by modern scholars, namely, that Americans in banning an exclusive government preference for one religion implied that government could assist religion in a nonexclusive fashion, must give way before overwhelming historical evidence to the contrary.

The additional belief adhered to by modern scholars—that people in the several colonies and states either experienced or debated the merits of nonpreferential, nonexclusive, or multiple establishments of religion—gives further credence to the idea that Americans at the time of the adoption of the Bill of Rights recognized two different types of establishment. However, what appears to have been an American variation on the traditional system of establishment as preference was in reality no new invention but, rather, a result of historical circumstances.

The history of the New England colonies and states (always exempting Rhode Island, which never provided public financial support for religion) seems to provide an example of a considerably broader and more inclusive form of establishment of religion than a traditional government preference for a single religion. Until well after the formation of the United States, New England provided public financial support for ministers and churches in accord with the choices of its individual towns. In theory, a town could establish any one of many Christian Protestant groups; but this was neither the intent nor the effect of the system.

The Puritans who settled New England arrived there determined to set up what they believed to be true religion, free from the corruptions of the Anglican Church in England, which they were convinced was turning back to Rome. They enjoyed great success in the initial decades of colonization, inasmuch as their experiment coincided with the Puritan Revolution in England. In 1660, however, the Restoration of the monarchy ended that English revolution and reestablished the Anglican Church. New England Puritans, now called Congregationalists, found themselves classified as dissenters, subject to a religiously hostile mother country. Despite this setback, they remained intent on maintaining their religious dominance and, with remarkable ingenuity and tenacity, succeeded in doing so until long after the formation of the United States.

The New England colonies, and Massachusetts in particular, continued the religious dominance of Congregationalism by way of a decentralized system. Each town was required to maintain a minister at taxpayers' expense, and, since Congregationalists predominated in the population, the minister was invariably Congregationalist. At first, non-Congregationalists were taxed for the support of these ministers. But early in the eighteenth century, under pressure from England, the New England colonies were obliged to modify the system and to grant exemptions for Baptists and Quakers and to allow Anglicans to designate their taxes for the support of their own clergy.

Massachusetts and New Hampshire incorporated this system into their state constitutions, and when the First Amendment was enacted, the New England states—Rhode Island again excepted—all provided public financial support for ministers selected by local towns.

Nevertheless, to posit that in 1789 the inhabitants of the New England states saw the church–state system in that region as a new kind of establishment is to misread the historical record. The idea that Baptists and Quakers could be part of the New England establishment—religiously equal to Congregationalists—would have been absurd and repugnant to each of those groups. For their part, Anglicans in New England sometimes argued that the established church of England followed the king's dominion and that they were the only legitimate establishment of the empire. However, they never conceived of themselves as part of a nonpreferential or multiple establishment of religion in New England simply because they were allowed to designate their taxes for support of their own ministers. Like other Americans, they believed that Congregationalism was the preferred and established religion in the New England colonies and states.

Congregationalists, on the other hand, were ambivalent about the system. Their reaction depended on circumstances. Before the American Revolution, when Anglicans claimed that theirs was the established church of the whole empire, Congregationalists asserted that they represented the true original established religion of New England. They claimed also that theirs was a truly mild and equitable system, hardly to be called an establishment, as John Adams noted. After independence, they sometimes denied that the system constituted an establishment at all; but, for the most part, they focused on its equity and fairness and did describe it in terms of an establishment. The Massachusetts Constitution of 1780 did not refer to the system of public support of religion as an establishment of religion, nor did the law that eventually dismantled it make any reference to disestablishment. When non-Congregationalists, such as Baptists, argued against an establishment of religion, they had in mind what they were experiencing in New England, as well as the English establishment. When Congregationalists argued against an establishment of religion, whether on the state or federal level, they were referring only to the kind of establishment represented by the established Church of England.

Colonial New York also produced a good deal of discussion about establishment of religion, because royal governors there, at the request and with the support of the English government, attempted to impose an Anglican establishment of religion on a largely non-Anglican populace. The ensuing discussion resulted from the determination of the populace to frustrate this plan, not from any attempt to devise a new understanding of establishment of religion. After the American Revolution removed the threat of Anglican dominance, the arguments about establishment that had been prevalent in colonial times never surfaced again.

The General Assessment Debate

During the American Revolution several states abolished or suspended establishments of religion. In reaction to this development some groups proposed that, because religion was the basis of civility and public virtue, government should support it on an equitable rather than a preferential basis. In Virginia in the 1780s a proposed general assessment—by which churches and ministers would receive tax support only as designated by individual taxpayers—produced a most noteworthy debate. James Madison galvanized the opposition with his famous *Memorial and Remonstrance,* and, as a result, the assessment proposal was defeated; Jefferson's *Bill for Religious Freedom,* which decreed that religion would be supported only voluntarily, was enacted in its stead.

The general assessment debate seems to provide another clear example of Americans, before the passage of the First Amendment, discussing a nonpreferential or multiple establishment of religion. That was not how contemporaries saw it, however. Throughout the debate, the description of establishment as preferential—as a system of religious oppression dating back to Constantine—predominated among those who opposed the proposal. In the historical context, their failure to distinguish a general assessment as a new kind of establishment becomes very understandable.

To opponents of a general assessment, their opposition constituted only one episode in a long struggle to destroy the old privileges that they felt the Anglican Church in Virginia continued to enjoy. Immediately after the Revolution they had succeeded in suspending public tax support for the Anglican Church. Then they fought to deprive that church of the exclusive right to perform marriages. Next they worked successfully to repeal that church's legal incorporation, and finally, after a prolonged campaign, they stripped it of the public lands it had acquired during its establishment in the colonial years. Many Virginians saw a general assessment as only another effort to assist or restore public support for the Anglican Church; they had little reason or motivation to view it as a new nonpreferential establishment, and they did not do so. Maryland, too, proposed a similar system of public support for religion, but even more than the populace of Virginia, the people of Maryland saw in it a method of assisting the Anglican Church, and they firmly rejected it.

Neither in the colonies nor in the states did Americans invent a new kind of nonexclusive, nonpreferential establishment of religion. They experienced systems of, or proposals for, public support for religion as preferential, and they associated these with the traditional concept of establishment, which they understood as a government preference for one religion over others.

What America did invent—or, at least, successfully demonstrate to be feasible—was voluntary support of religion. In this regard, although Rhode Island had earlier inaugurated such a system, Pennsylvania provided the most influential example of a society's not only surviving but also prospering on the basis of voluntary support, thereby disproving the prevailing conception that, without official public assistance to religion, social decency and even civilization itself would disintegrate.

From the beginning of colonization, religious evangelicals had argued that state support for religion only controlled and corrupted it. Over the course of the colonial period this thinking spread, as more and more people came to identify free exercise of religion with voluntary support of religion. Ultimately, many Americans became convinced that even a minimal tax imposed for the support of religion was coercive, violated the right of free exercise, and constituted an establishment. The influence of the Enlightenment as it penetrated America provided secular support for this idea of liberty.

During the American Revolution and even beyond the formation of the federal government, public support for religion was the single church–state issue over which Americans were divided. New England Congregationalists, in particular, held such support essential to the preservation of morality. Throughout all the states, however, increasing numbers of Americans contended that both civil and religious liberty demanded that religion be supported voluntarily. By the time of the enactment of the Establishment Clause, the great majority of them adhered to the principle of voluntary support. Of the states that ratified the Bill of Rights, only New Hampshire of the original thirteen provided public tax support for religion. Thus, when they considered church–state systems, Americans did not contrast government preference for one religion with government assistance for all religions. Rather, they thought in terms of government preference for a single religion as opposed to voluntary support for all religions.

Only those groups which were or had been the beneficiaries of specific systems of public tax support for religion, such as New England Congregationalists, continued to argue that such support was fair and equitable. Moreover, since the historical experience of most Americans had been either that of voluntary support or that of a preferential establishment of religion, most of them, when confronted with the idea of a general assessment, decided that its intent was, and its result would be, state support for one religion.

The members of the First Congress all shared a similar definition of establishment of religion as a government preference for one sect, regardless of their individual views on state support for religion. Had they dealt more intensely with the term, some argument would doubtless have arisen among them. Representatives from New England, for example, would have maintained that a state tax for the support of religion was fair and equitable as long as no one was taxed for a religion other than one's own. Other delegates would have disagreed, claiming that such a tax constituted an establishment of religion and violated the free exercise of religion. This kind of division did not surface, however, because the delegates' task, as they saw it, was simply to make a formal declaration that the federal government was not empowered to deal with religious matters.

The Religion Clauses

Modern courts treat the Establishment and the Free Exercise Clauses as applicable to separate functions, dealing with government support for religion under the Establishment Clause and with claims against government regulation under the Free Exercise Clause. The Framers of the First Amendment, however, made no such distinction. For them establishment and free exercise were correlative and coextensive. They believed that religious liberty entitled them to believe and practice any religion they wished, short of causing civil disturbance. They further believed that religion had to be supported voluntarily and that mandated state support, even for the religion of one's choice, was coercive, was a violation of the free exercise of religion, and was an establishment of religion. Together, the two clauses doubly guaranteed a single freedom, which either one of them would have sufficed to guarantee.

The historical fact remains, however, that, although the members of the First Congress agreed that the federal government had no power in religious matters, they nevertheless enacted provisions involving religion. They provided for a day of prayer and thanksgiving, and they appointed chaplains to both houses of Congress and to the armed forces. Accommodationists have argued that these actions by the federal government and many similar ones by state governments demonstrate that the intent of the Establishment Clause was to prohibit a preferential establishment of religion but not to prohibit nonpreferential assistance to the various religions or religion in general.

Again, these actions must be seen in their historical context. At the time of the enactment of the Bill of Rights, the inhabitants of the states were overwhelmingly Christian and Protestant. Although they belonged to many different denominations, they all shared many of the same religious beliefs and practices. These common religious practices, such as Bible reading and days of prayer, were so indigenous to and intertwined with the general culture as to be an accepted part of it. The great majority of citizens at that time could not even imagine how such religious customs, which to them formed an integral part of civilization itself, could possibly be coercive. Therefore, they did not examine their motives in approving government support for such practices. In thus supporting particular religious traditions so linked with their own common culture, however, they gave no indication that they wished in principle to support other religions or religion in general.

Most Americans at the time disapproved of Roman Catholicism or feared it greatly, and they had little knowledge of or sympathy for non-Christian religions. Several states excluded Catholics or non-Christians from voting or from holding public office. Nothing in contemporary history would indicate that the members of the First Congress or Americans generally wanted to assist these religious groups, and indeed the history of America both preceding and following the enactment of the First Amendment lends strong support to the argument that they did not.

Therefore, when Americans at both the federal and state levels provided government support for the commonly accepted cultural religious practices of the time, they were not looking beyond the largely unexamined, noncontroversial, and familiar religious customs of their own society. To argue, as accommodationists do, that, by approving government support for the particular religious practices acceptable to them, Americans were asserting in principle the power of government to assist all religions or religion in general in a nonpreferential way is to make an unwarranted leap from practice to principle and to attribute to them clarifications that they did not attempt to make. Similarly, to argue, as separationists do, that, by enacting the Establishment Clause, the First Congress intended to forbid all assistance to religion and to create a "wall of separation" between church and state is to ignore historical evidence and to attribute to Americans at the time principles far more sweeping than they had worked out for themselves.

Both sides in the modern controversy about the meaning of the Establishment Clause claim too large a role for history, and neither side is able to ground its arguments solidly in the historical understanding of those who enacted the clause. Those Americans enunciated definite principles about church–state relations, but they applied them only to a limited extent. In enacting the Establishment Clause they proclaimed that the federal government had no power in religious matters. For the people in virtually all the states that ratified the clause, a lack of power in religious matters meant primarily two things: (1) that citizens had the right to practice whatever religion they chose, provided, as Jefferson wrote, principles did not "break out into overt acts against peace and good order," and (2) that religion had to be supported voluntarily. They regarded any other method of public support as coercive and as an establishment of religion, which they continued to define as a government preference for one religion over others. Apart from these specific applications, they did not define in practice their principles regarding church and state. Despite their stated principle that government had no power in religious matters, they persisted in allowing it to support the familiar religious forms and customs acceptable to them. They did so because they could not imagine how these commonly accepted practices could be coercive to anyone. When they thought of prohibiting government power in religious matters, they thought primarily of the power of government to coerce. They thought of establishment as coercion, because that is how they had experienced establishment and that is what they wished to eliminate. To Americans at the time, then, coercion was the central ingredient of an establishment of religion. They traced such coercion back to the Emperor Constantine, through the establishments they had experienced in America, and especially through the contemporary English establishment of religion. The depth of their fear of the English establishment had manifested itself in the late 1760s, in reaction to a proposal that Anglican bishops be introduced into the colonies. Although supporters of that proposal argued that the bishops in question would fulfill only a religious role for the members of the Anglican Church, Americans, including Anglicans, went into a frenzy of opposition and produced one of the largest bodies of controversial literature that had appeared on any subject before the Revolution. The prospect of bishops triggered fears that in their wake would come forced subscription to particular beliefs, the obligation to pay tithes, and the introduction of ceremonies reminiscent of Roman Catholicism. John Adams considered the Bishops Controversy one of the principal causes of the American Revolution, and it provides a clear insight into Americans' attitude toward establishment of religion. A grasp of their fear of the established English church is essential to understanding their approach to the issue of establishment of religion. Their concept of establishment of religion as exclusive and coercive dominated their thinking, and they would have found incomprehensible the argument of the Supreme Court in *School District of Abington Township v. Schempp* (1963)—that religious coercion is not an essential ingredient of an establishment of religion.

Over a period of two hundred years, culture and sentiment in America have changed radically, and so has the notion of coercion in religious matters. The religious practices that Americans of two centuries ago found unexceptionable, and for which they provided government support, would seem to later generations highly exceptionable. In one area particularly, that of public tax support for religion, those who enacted the Establishment Clause illustrated principle in practice. In other areas of church and state they experienced little division or dissent and thus left few practical examples of how the principles they enunciated worked out in practice. It has remained to subsequent generations to apply the principles enunciated by the Founders to situations neither experienced nor even imagined by them.

Originally only Congress was bound by the Establishment Clause. However, by way of the Fourteenth Amendment, the Supreme Court has applied the clause to government at all levels. As a result, the clause has assumed an immediacy and scope utterly unanticipated by those who enacted it. To argue, as some scholars tend to do, that the history of the formation of the Establishment Clause will provide answers to the specific church–state problems our society is encountering at the present time is to overburden history. However, those who enacted the clause did hand down principles of enduring value: that government had no power in religious matters; that it was forbidden above all to engage in any kind of religious coercion; that anything other than a voluntarily supported religion amounted to coercion; and that government was forbidden to promote religion as, in James Madison's words, "an engine of Civil policy."

The application of these principles to varying situations will no doubt continue to be a source of controversy, and doubtless the history surrounding the Establishment Clause will continue to be invoked to support varying interpretations about its application today. However, in considering such applications and invocations, scholars need to interpret the relevant history in a way that integrates all the historical evidence, rather than to abstract selective historical items in order to buttress modern positions that few if any Americans could have anticipated at the time the Bill of Rights was adopted.

Thomas J. Curry

Bibliography

Adams, Arlin M., and Charles J. Emmerich, "A Heritage of Religious Liberty," 137 *University of Pennsylvania Law Review* 1559–1617 (1989).

Antieau, Chester J., Arthur L. Downey, and Edward C. Roberts, *Freedom from Federal Establishment: Formation and Early History of the First Amendment Religion Clauses* (Milwaukee: Bruce Publishing, 1964).

Curry, Thomas J., *The First Freedoms: Church and State in America to the Passage of the First Amendment* (New York: Oxford University Press, 1986).

Finkelman, Paul, "James Madison and the Bill of Rights: A Reluctant Paternity," 1990 *Supreme Court Review* 301–347 (1991).

Howe, Mark D., *The Garden and the Wilderness* (Chicago: University of Chicago Press, 1965).

Laycock, Douglas, "'Nonpreferential' Aid to Religion: A False Claim about Original Intent," 27 *William and Mary Law Review* 875–923 (1986).

Levy, Leonard W., *The Establishment Clause: Religion and the First Amendment* (New York: Macmillan, 1986).

McLoughlin, William G., *New England Dissent, 1630–1833: The Baptists and the Separation of Church and State,* 2 vols. (Cambridge, Mass.: Harvard University Press, 1971).

Miller, William Lee, *The First Liberty: Religion and the American Republic* (New York: Knopf, 1986).

Cases Cited

Everson v. Board of Education, 330 U.S. 1 (1947).

School District of Abington Township v. Schempp, 374 U.S. 203 (1963).

Establishments of Religion Created through Free Exercise Exemptions

Nowhere is the well-known tension between the Free Exercise Clause and the Establishment Clause documented more clearly than in cases where exemptions from general rules are urged by legislatures or by the courts in defense of free exercise values. Those who favor the strict separation of law and religion have suggested that any exemption from general regulatory laws would unconstitutionally endorse religion in violation of the Establishment Clause. Accommodationists, in comparison, have suggested that free exercise values may require or permit special exemptions for religiously inspired conduct. Justice Antonin Scalia, dissenting in *Texas Monthly v. Bullock* (1989), and quoting *Thomas v. Review Board* (1981), described the choices as being like traveling between "the Scylla [of what the Free Exercise Clause demands] and the Charybdis [of what the Establishment Clause forbids] through which any state or federal action must pass in order to survive constitutional scrutiny." Perhaps the narrowness of that passage explains why the cases appear contradictory and why the justices often write separate opinions with no principle unifying the results.

Exemptions Upheld

The U.S. Supreme Court in certain cases has upheld legislative exemptions aimed at religious activities as serving, among other things, the secular purpose of respecting free exercise values. In conscientious objector cases, for example, the Court has considered the constitutionality of legislation that exempts from the military draft those who "by reason of religious training and belief" oppose "participation in war in any form" (Military Selective Service Act, 1988). In *United States v. Seeger* (1965) the Court, to avoid establishment concerns, expanded the "religious training and belief" category to include anyone whose "claimed belief occup[ies] the same place in the life of the objector as an orthodox belief in God. . . ." In *Welsh v. United States* (1970) the Court extended the exemption even further to include those who oppose war on the basis of "political, sociological, or philosophical views," contrary to the literal wording of the statute. Justice John Marshall Harlan, II, in a concurrance, reasoned that limiting the exemption in accordance with congressional intent would violate the Establishment Clause. In comparison, the Court in *Gillette v. United States* (1971) permitted a denial of a conscientious objector status to an applicant who opposed only the Vietnam War. There the Court held, with Justice William O. Douglas dissenting, that the statutory exemption did not violate the Establishment Clause despite the fact that the statute benefited only specific religious or functionally religious beliefs.

In *National Labor Relations Board v. Catholic Bishop of Chicago* (1979) the Court rejected establishment clause challenges to statutory exemptions from NLRB jurisdiction for religious employers. In *Corporation of the Presiding Bishop of the Church of Jesus Christ of Latter-Day Saints v. Amos* (1987) the Court exempted a religious employer from Title VII employment discrimination. These cases follow *Walz v. Tax Commission of New York City* (1970), which upheld a New York property tax exemption that applied to properties owned by nonprofit entities generally, including religious entities.

The Court has judicially recognized exemptions, on free exercise grounds, to door-to-door solicitation licensing fees as applied to religious literature in *Follett v. Town of McCormick* (1944) and *Murdock v. Pennsylvania* (1943).

The Court also has created free exercise exemptions in the area of Social Security benefits. The Court first considered the issue in *Sherbert v. Verner* (1963). Although unemployment compensation rules required that an employee accept available work as a condition for receiving unemployment compensation, the Court held that the Free Exercise Clause required that the Sabbatarian applicant be exempted from any Saturday work requirement. The Court reinforced this result under similar facts in *Hobbie v. Unemployment Appeals Commission* (1987). Similarly, the Court in *Frazee v. Illinois Department of Employment Sec.* (1989) exempted a "Christian" from a Sunday work requirement as a condition for receiving unemployment compensation. In a related case, *Thomas v. Review Board* (1981), the Court held that a conscientious objector did not have to accept employment in a weapons plant as a condition for receiving unemployment compensation.

The most important free exercise exemption case is *Wisconsin v. Yoder* (1972), in which the Court exempted Amish children from compulsory school laws after they have completed eighth grade. *Yoder* requires that, if free exercise rights are implicated, the state must establish a compelling state interest and must have no less restrictive alternative.

Exemptions Denied

The Court has invalidated several legislative exemptions that were passed in deference to free exercise values. In *Estate of Thornton v. Caldor, Inc.* (1985) the Court invalidated a Connecticut statute that prohibited an employer from requiring an employee to work on his or her Sabbath, on the grounds that the exemption violated the Establishment Clause because it benefited Sabbath observers "no matter what burden or inconvenience this imposes on the employer or fellow workers."

The Court in *Texas Monthly, Inc. v. Bullock* (1989) also invalidated a Texas sales tax exemption for religious periodicals. There the Court held that "when confined exclusively to publications advancing the tenets of a religious faith, the exemption runs afoul of the Establishment Clause. . . ." Justice William Brennan's opinion, joined by Justices Thurgood Marshall and John Paul Stevens, explained that the Establishment Clause proscribes all legislation "that constitutes an endorsement of one or another set of religious beliefs or of religion generally." Justice Brennan distinguished cases such as *Widmar v. Vincent* (1981), *Mueller v. Allen* (1983), and *Walz*—all of which upheld exemptions benefiting religion—because

> In all of these cases . . . we emphasized that the benefits derived by religious organizations flowed to a large number of nonreligious groups as well. Indeed, were those benefits confined to religious organizations, they could not have appeared other than as state sponsorship of religion; if that were so, we would not have hesitated to strike them down for lacking a secular purpose and effect.

Thus, according to Justice Brennan's rationale, "when government directs a subsidy exclusively to religious organizations that is not required by the Free Exercise Clause and that burdens nonbeneficiaries markedly or cannot be seen as removing a significant state-imposed deterrent to the free exercise of religion," then the state has impermissibly endorsed religion in violation of the Establishment Clause.

Justice Scalia, joined by Chief Justice William Rehnquist and Justice Anthony Kennedy, wrote a scathing dissent highlighting the irreconcilable conflict that the majority opinion creates:

> As a judicial demolition project, today's decision is impressive. The machinery employed by the opinions of Justice Brennan and Blackmun is no more substantial than the antinomy that accommodation of religion may be required but not permitted, and the bold but insupportable assertion (given such realities as the text of the Declaration of Independence, the national Thanksgiving Day proclaimed by every President since Lincoln, the inscriptions on our coins, the words of our Pledge of Allegiance, the invocation with which sessions of our Court are opened and come to think of it, the discriminatory protection of freedom of religion in the Constitution) that government may not "convey a message of endorsement of religion."

Referencing "'undeviating acceptance' throughout the 200-year history of our Nation," and quoting *Walz,* Justice Scalia stated:

> Few concepts . . . are more deeply embedded in the fabric of our national life, beginning with pre-Revolutionary colonial times, than for the government to exercise at the very least this kind of benevolent neutrality toward churches and religious exercise generally so long as none was favored over others and none suffered interference.

Without question the most significant recent case addressing the issue of whether the courts must craft judicial exemptions to general laws if they conflict with free exercise practices is *Employment Division, Department of Human Resources of Oregon v. Smith* (1990). *Smith* involved two Native Americans who had been fired from their jobs because they had taken the drug peyote as part of a religious ceremony and then were denied unemployment compensation. They sued, arguing that they had a First Amendment right to take peyote and that the state thus had no right to deny them unemployment compensation. Justice Scalia's majority opinion, which rejected these arguments, eviscerates the Court's prior free exercise jurisprudence. Quoting in part *United States v. Lee,* Scalia wrote: "[T]he right of free exercise does not relieve an individual of the obligation to comply with a 'valid and neutral law of general applicability on the ground that the law proscribes (or prescribes) conduct that his religion prescribes (or proscribes).'" Justice Scalia explained away the significance of prior free exercise cases, such as *Yoder,* on the questionable grounds that in each other case the free exercise claim had been connected with another substantive right, such as free speech or the right of parents to control the upbringing of their children. Accordingly, Justice Scalia rejected the notion that the state must prove a compelling state interest and no less restrictive alternative if a free exercise claim is present.

Justice O'Connor, concurring, rejected the majority's diminished view of free exercise but nonetheless held that the state had an "overriding interest" under the facts of the case in preventing the use of peyote by drug rehabilitation counselors. Thus, despite the fact that the denial of unemployment compensation has traditionally been the one consistent area where free exercise claims have been deemed sufficient to overrule the state's interest in administering unemployment benefits, Justice O'Connor concurred with the result reached by the majority. The three dissenting justices would have required, on free exercise grounds, the recognition of an exemption for religious consumption of peyote as not qualifying as work-related "misconduct" that justified the denial of unemployment compensation.

The Court, in other cases, has refused to recognize a free exercise exemption to general regulatory laws. The landmark cases remain *Reynolds v. United States* (1878) and *Prince v. Massachusetts* (1944), where the Court respectively refused religious exemptions from antibigamy laws and child labor laws. More recently the Court in *Goldman v. Weinberger* (1986) held that the Air Force's compelling interest in maintaining uniformity with its dress codes was sufficient to override an Orthodox Jewish officer's religious duty to wear a yarmulke. Again in *Braunfeld v. Brown* (1961) the Court refused a Sabbatarian shop owner's request for a Sunday closing exemption, despite the fact that his honoring of Sabbatarian religious beliefs coupled with Sunday closing laws rendered him less competitive with other shop owners. Similarly, the Court in *O'Lone v. Estate of Shabazz* (1987) refused a Friday work exemption for Islamic inmates on the grounds of administrative convenience at the prison.

Exemptions Unreconciled

In the area of Social Security claims—where the Court has repeatedly recognized free exercise exemptions in other cases—the Court has sporadically refused exemptions for "compelling reasons." For example, the Court in *United States v. Lee* (1982) held that the state's interest in a sound tax system outweighed an Amish employer's claim for an exemption on the ground that the Amish refuse for religious reasons to take advantage of Social Security benefits. To the same effect, the Court in *Bowen, Secretary of Health and Human Services, et al. v. Roy* (1986)—despite the fact that her father stated that taking a Social Security number would "'rob the spirit' of his daughter and prevent her from attaining greater spiritual power"—upheld the agency's number requirement as a condition precedent for receiving Social Security benefits on the grounds that the number system served the compelling interest of administrative convenience and accuracy.

The status of religious-based statutory and judicial exemptions remains a perplexing constitutional issue. The Court's cases cannot be reconciled with any principled analysis. On the one hand, the *Smith* case makes it unlikely that the present Court will judicially create free exercise exemptions from neutral and uniform statutes; on the other hand, cases such as *Amos* and *Texas Monthly* suggest that the Court will uphold free exercise statutory exemptions unless they appear to endorse religion. Of course the Free Exercise Clause appears to endorse religion. Thus under present establishment reasoning the courts are left with the conundrum that religious exemptions may be required by the Free Exercise Clause even as they may be prohibited by the Establishment Clause.

Richard Collin Mangrum

Bibliography

Kurland, Philip B., "The Irrelevance of the Constitution: The Religion Clauses of the First Amendment and the Supreme Court," 24 *Villanova Law Review* 3–27 (1978).

Note, "Religious Exemptions under the Free Exercise Clause: A Model of Competing Authorities," 90 *Yale Law Journal* 350–376 (1980).

Steinberg, David E., "Religious Exemptions As Affirmative Action," 40 *Emory Law Journal* 77–139 (1991).

Cases and Statutes Cited

Bowen, Secretary of Health and Human Services, et al. v. Roy, 476 U.S. 693 (1986).

Braunfeld v. Brown, 366 U.S. 599 (1961).

Corporation of the Presiding Bishop of the Church of Jesus Christ of Latter-Day Saints v. Amos, 483 U.S. 327 (1987).

Employment Division, Department of Human Resources of Oregon v. Smith, 494 U.S. 872 (1990).

Estate of Thornton v. Caldor, Inc., 472 U.S. 703 (1985).

Follett v. Town of McCormick, 321 U.S. 573 (1944).

Frazee v. Illinois Department of Employment Sec. 489 U.S. 829 (1989).

Gillette v. United States, 401 U.S. 437 (1971).

Goldman v. Weinberger, 475 U.S. 503 (1986).

Hobbie v. Unemployment Appeals Commission, 480 U.S. 136 (1987).
Mueller v. Allen, 463 U.S. 388 (1983).
Murdock v. Pennsylvania, 319 U.S. 105 (1943) (1944).
National Labor Relations Board v. Catholic Bishop of Chicago, 440 U.S. 490 (1979).
O'Lone v. Estate of Shabazz, 482 U.S. 342 (1987).
Prince v. Massachusetts, 321 U.S. 158 (1944).
Reynolds v. United States, 98 U.S. 145 (1878).
Sherbert v. Verner, 374 U.S. 398 (1963)
Texas Monthly, Inc. v. Bullock, 489 U.S. 1 (1989).
Thomas v. Review Board, 450 U.S. 707 (1981).
United States v. Lee, 455 U.S. 252 (1982).
United States v. Seeger, 380 U.S. 163 (1965).
Walz v. Tax Commission of New York City, 397 U.S. 664 (1970).
Welsh v. United States, 398 U.S. 333 (1970).
Widmar v. Vincent, 454 U.S. 263 (1981).
Wisconsin v. Yoder 406 U.S. 205 (1972).
Military Selective Service Act, 50 U.S.C. app. §456(j) (1988).

Everson v. Board of Education 330 U.S. 1 (1947)

At least since World War II the pressure to introduce religion into public education followed two broad courses. The first sought to make religious teachings and observances part of the public school curriculum. The other worked to obtain public tax dollars for aid and support of various private religious schools. A contrary trend resisted these pressures in defense of the principle that the First Amendment's Establishment Clause required preserving a "wall of separation" between church and state. Before the war ended the Court had declared that the Free Exercise Clause and, by implication, the Establishment Clause applied to the state as well as to the federal government. The first attempt to formulate a standard prescribing just what this meant occurred in *Everson v. Board of Education* (1947).

The Court's opinion established the basic criteria governing the meaning of the Establishment Clause. Accepting the correctness of these criteria, the four dissenters nonetheless profoundly questioned whether Justice Hugo Black's opinion was in fact consistent with their logic. The conflict within the Court reflected the tension in the wider society.

At issue was a New Jersey law authorizing local school boards to reimburse parents for bus fares their children paid to attend either public or Catholic schools. The New Jersey law allowed reimbursements for children going to public schools or to *all* not-for-profit private schools, including parochial schools. In *Everson* the only nonpublic schools were Catholic schools. Since the program specifically aided the children and their parents, any benefit accruing to the sectarian schools themselves was indirect. Nevertheless, a local taxpayer charged that the school board's plan violated the Establishment Clause. After winning in the trial and appellate courts, the taxpayer lost on review by the state's highest tribunal, whereupon he appealed to the U.S. Supreme Court.

The case was of interest to a number of groups. The American Civil Liberties Union, the General Conference of Seventh-Day Adventists, and the Junior Order of United American Mechanics of New Jersey sided with the taxpayer in amici curiae briefs. The attorneys general of Illinois, Indiana, Louisiana, Massachusetts, Michigan, and New York—along with the National Council of Catholic Men—supported the New Jersey law. The broad issue involved whether the state should breach the "wall of separation" created by the Establishment Clause. The compelling power of that simple proposition obscured, however, the narrower and more correct question: Did the reimbursement program itself constitute such a breach?

The question, moreover, was not as uncomplicated as it may have seemed. State courts divided evenly; five sustained and five overturned the constitutionality of laws similar to New Jersey's. The courts either accepted or rejected the rationale that the beneficiaries were children or their parents, not sectarian schools. A few of the courts which invalidated the laws took the absolutist position that any aid whatsoever constituted an establishment of religion. Undercutting such absolutism was the fact that as early as 1930 the Supreme Court had held that a state's appropriation of taxes to purchase books for private schoolchildren was constitutional. This was done on the basis of the "child benefit" theory: The children, rather than the sectarian schools, gained from a state's action.

The child benefit theory involved the larger question of the scope of the public purpose doctrine. In many cases the Court had held that the use of a state's tax funds to support public services such as police and fire departments did not violate the Fourteenth Amendment's due process clause. Arguably, New Jersey's reimbursement program provided the means for children to attend school by means safer than hitchhiking, long walks, or riding bicycles. Accordingly, the state's monies were funding a public purpose not unlike that served by the fire department or the police. The counterargument, of course, was that the purpose of the reimbursement program involved education more directly than safety. The preservation of safety was never considered to have involved the Establishment Clause. Education, however, always had a direct relation to the Establishment Clause, usually by forbidding the connection. Again the problem was—short of maintaining a position of absolute prohibition—where the Court should draw a line permitting a "public purpose."

A final issue involved what weight, if any, the Court might give to the history surrounding the Establishment Clause. James Madison and Thomas Jefferson formulated the original theory of the need for an absolute separation between church and state. At the time of the framing of the Establishment Clause, only a few states, principally in New England, favored some sort of state aid to religion. All the other states opposed any direct use of government funds to support religion. There was no agreement among these states, however, about which aid constituted indirect assistance; hence arose the gradual development of the child benefit programs on the state level. Until the rise of the incorporation theory, of course, the Establishment Clause of the First Amendment applied only to the federal government. But when the Supreme Court extended the incorporation doctrine to the Establishment Clause in 1940, the issue of original purpose became relevant in cases involving the states. Even so the original intent of the Framers provided little or no guidance regarding whether some line could be drawn between direct and indirect uses of public aid of the sort established in the child benefit programs.

Justice Black wrote the majority opinion in *Everson.* The issue was, he said, whether the state could provide this particular public service without violating the First Amendment's Establishment Clause. He equated the expenditure of tax dollars to ensure children's safe transport to both public and Catholic schools with the use of such funds to support police protection for all children. Black reviewed the history of the nation's experience with religious establishment, concluding that the First Amendment required the "state to be a neutral in its relations with groups of religious believers and unbelievers." In support of this neutrality principle, he drew on a number of documents familiar to the First Amendment's Framers, including the Virginia Bill of Religious Liberty and Madison's *Memorial and Remonstrance.* In this case the state neither contributed money nor otherwise supported the parochial schools; it merely provided a "general program to help parents get their children, regardless of their religion, safely and expeditiously to and from accredited schools." Finally, Black affirmed, the wall separating church and state "must be kept high and impregnable. We could not approve the slightest breach. New Jersey has not breached it here."

Justice Black linked the emphasis on neutrality and the ringing affirmation of the "wall of separation" to another, subsequently famous statement: "The 'establishment of religion' clause of the First Amendment means at least this: Neither a state nor the Federal Government can set up a church. Neither can pass laws which aid one religion, aid all religions, or prefer one religion over another."

The dissents took somewhat different paths. Justice Robert Jackson dissented, with Justice Felix Frankfurter joining him. The "undertones of the opinion, advocating complete and uncompromising separation of Church from State," Jackson said, "seem utterly discordant with its conclusion yielding support to their commingling in educational matters." Exhibiting the zeal and yet self-consciousness of a convert, Jackson buttressed his assessment of Black's opinion with poetic allusion: "The case which irresistibly comes to mind as the most fitting precedent is that of Julia who according to Byron's reports, 'whispering "I will ne'er consent,"—consented.'" Jackson had in fact initially supported Black's opinion, until persuaded by Justice Wiley Rutledge that an absolutist position was most appropriate. Rutledge's dissent—which Justices Frankfurter, Harold Burton, and Jackson joined—had pushed Black to sharpen the linkage between the public purpose–child benefit doctrine and the principle of neutrality. Ultimately the dissenters rejected the possibility that any public purpose was consistent with an absolute separation between church and state.

The elegant simplicity of the dissenters' position obscured the comparative complexity of Black's logic. He could simultaneously adhere to the absolutist wall of separation and the neutrality principle because they were constitutionally distinct doctrines that independently defined the scope of the Establishment Clause. Black's opinion, accordingly, formulated the neutrality principle as an interpretive prescription. Essentially, this resort to prescription was no different from Black's attempt to distinguish speech from conduct or advocacy and overt act in other areas involving the First Amendment. The prescription established the meaning, which should be applied as a consistent rule of interpretation.

Thus the critics underestimated Black's attempt to articulate principles governing the establishment of religion. Black was no more willing than Rutledge or Jackson to breach the wall separating church and state. At the same time he was certain that establishing the principle of governmental neutrality where safety was at stake successfully preserved the inviolability of the Establishment Clause. After all, New Jersey's legislature had conferred the reimbursement authority on local school officials to assist without preference both the public school majority and the Catholic school minority.

Justice Black's *Everson* opinion established the basic interpretation of the Establishment Clause as it related to education. In the years to come the Court accepted with little question the principle that the Establishment Clause applied to the states through the Fourteenth Amendment's Due Process Clause. Eventually, both defenders of absolutism and advocates of accommodation found in the decision principles supporting their views. These views in turn were spun into doctrinal theories of remarkable complexity, until the meaning of the "wall of separation" became quite obscure, and the principle of neutrality was virtually ignored. Even so, as late as 1979, in *School District of Pittsburgh v. Pennsylvania Department of Education,* the Court dismissed for want of a federal question a case involving a state law that required school districts to provide bus transportation for all schoolchildren. Thus, even though the pressures for injecting religion into public education have not abated during the half-century since World War II, Black's *Everson* opinion has remained a constant.

Tony Freyer

Bibliography

Ball, Howard, and Phillip J. Cooper, *Of Power and Right: Hugo Black, William O. Douglas, and America's Constitutional Revolution* (New York: Oxford University Press, 1992).

Dunne, Gerald T., *Hugo Black and the Judicial Revolution* (New York: Simon and Schuster, 1977).

Freyer, Tony, *Hugo L. Black and the Dilemma of American Liberalism* (Glenview, Ill.: Scott Foresman/Little, Brown, 1990).

Levy, Leonard W., *The Establishment Clause, Religion and the First Amendment* (New York: Macmillan, 1986).

Cases Cited

Everson v. Board of Education, 330 U.S. 1 (1947).

School District of Pittsburgh v. Pennsylvania Department of Education, 443 U.S. 901 (1979).

Evolution, the Public Schools, and the Courts

To some religious groups—most notably, fundamentalist Christians—Charles Darwin's theories about evolution have no place in public schools. They argue that public schools should not expose students to views that conflict with or ignore the teachings of the Bible. At a minimum, they contend that equal time should be given to theories about the origins of life that incorporate a religious perspective. Although a significant number of state legislatures have taken steps to address these concerns, the Supreme Court has shown little sympathy with their efforts.

The Butler Act and Scopes

The Scopes "monkey trial" (1925) was the first and remains the most widely known of these cases. Although the case never reached the U.S. Supreme Court, it was immortalized in theatrical and cinematic venues under the title *Inherit the Wind.* The case arose when John Scopes, a public schoolteacher in Dayton, Tennessee, agreed to participate in a test case to determine the legality of the recently enacted Butler Act. The Butler Act applied to all teachers in Tennessee public schools, and it prohibited them from teaching "any theory that denies the story of the Divine Creation of man as taught in the Bible and teaches instead that man has descended from a lower order of animals." The penalty for violating this law was a fine of at least $100 but no more than $500 for each offense.

Scopes's 1925 trial drew national attention, largely because of the stature of the attorneys involved: Clarence Darrow represented John Scopes, and William Jennings Bryan, Jr., argued for the State of Tennessee. As a matter of legal precedent, the case is thoroughly outdated. The trial court found Scopes guilty of having taught evolution and fined him $100. Scopes appealed, challenging the constitutionality of the Butler Act on both state and federal grounds. In *Scopes v. Tennessee* (Tenn., 1927) the state's Supreme Court upheld the act, primarily because the protections of the federal Bill of Rights had not yet been extended to state employees. One justice thought that the statute was unconstitutional, on the grounds that it was too vague to provide fair notice.

Addressing the state law issue, the court found that the Establishment Clause of the Tennessee Constitution—which prohibited only laws affording a preference to a religious establishment or mode of worship—did not conflict with the Butler Act. The court reasoned that, because some proponents of evolutionary theory were religious and some opponents of the theory were nonreligious, then the act "preferred" no religion. The superficiality of this analysis has not commended it to modern courts or commentators.

The Tennessee Supreme Court frustrated Clarence Darrow on two counts: It upheld the constitutionality of the Butler Act, and it reversed Scopes's conviction. The $100 fine had been imposed by the trial judge, but the statute provided that the fine be imposed by a jury. Based on that rather-technical procedural defect, the court put an end to what it characterized as a "bizarre case" and directed the state attorney to enter a *nolle prosequi* against Scopes (a declaration that the state no longer prosecute the defendant). Although Darrow's client had "gotten off," this ruling foreclosed Scopes from appealing to the U.S. Supreme Court and obtaining a definitive ruling on the statute.

The Rotenberry Act and *Epperson*

The *Scopes* case provided encouragement to antievolutionists in Tennessee and other states. Although Scopes's conviction had been vacated, the state's Supreme Court had upheld the Butler Act against a constitutional challenge. This success inspired the Arkansas legislature to pass the Rotenberry Act in 1928. This act prohibited any teacher in a state-supported school from teaching the "theory or doctrine that mankind ascended or descended from a lower order of animals." The act also prohibited the use or adoption of any textbooks that included evolutionary doctrine. Violation of the act was a misdemeanor that subjected teachers to dismissal and a fine of up to $500.

The Rotenberry Act languished for nearly forty years, unenforced and unchallenged. During that time, the fundamentalist cause was taken up by proponents of "creation science" (teaching the biblical story of the creation of the world as though it were science), and the U.S. Supreme Court changed the ground rules of constitutional analysis. The Court made a substantial portion of the Bill of Rights binding on the states by incorporating those guarantees into the Due Process Clause of the Fourteenth Amendment. Public employers became subject to the Establishment Clause of the First Amendment when the Supreme Court decided *Everson v. Board of Education* (1947), which upheld a program providing publicly financed transportation to parochial students against an Establishment Clause challenge. These changes in constitutional doctrine proved critical to the Supreme Court's first decision involving the constitutionality of antievolution laws.

The State of Arkansas hired Susan Epperson in the fall of 1964 to teach tenth-grade biology. She was provided with a textbook that included a chapter setting forth the evolutionary thesis. She thus faced the dilemma of being directed to use a text that would apparently violate state law and that would subject her to criminal charges and dismissal from her position.

Epperson sought a declaratory judgment that the Rotenberry Act was unconstitutional. In *Epperson v. Arkansas* (1968) the Supreme Court, in an opinion by Justice Abe Fortas, unanimously held that the act violated the Establishment Clause of the First Amendment. A six-member majority found that, because the act "selects from the body of knowledge a particular segment which it proscribes for the sole reason that it is deemed to conflict with a particular religious doctrine," the act lacked a proper secular purpose. Based on the absence of secular purpose on the part of the enacting legislature, the Court concluded that the Rotenberry Act violated the Establishment Clause.

Epperson also contended that the act was unconstitutionally vague because it was unclear whether it prohibited the mere mention of evolutionary doctrine or only teaching the doctrine as an established scientific fact. However, the majority declined to resolve the vagueness argument, since it found that the absence of a secular purpose provided sufficient reason to strike down the act under the Establishment Clause.

Justice Hugo Black concurred separately, indicating that he had serious doubts whether there was a case or controversy, since Arkansas had neither brought suit nor threatened to enforce the Rotenberry Act against any teacher for almost forty years. Assuming the presence of a justiciable controversy, Black stated that he would find the act void for vagueness. He agreed with Epperson that ordinary teachers would be unable to determine whether the law prohibited them from mentioning Darwin's theory or left them free to discuss the doctrine as long as they did not contend that it was true.

Justice Black disagreed with the Court's majority about the absence of secular purpose on the part of the Arkansas legislature. He suggested that the legislature might have been motivated by the desire to remove a controversial subject from the public schools. Black also noted that, insofar as proponents of creation science considered evolution to be an "anti-religious doctrine," a ruling that the federal Constitution required the states to permit its exposition in public schools raised its own Establishment Clause concern. Such a ruling, suggested Black, might violate the principle of neutrality between religious and nonreligious views that the Establishment Clause is thought to embody.

"Equal Time" and "Balanced Treatment"

In the 1960s the ghost of the *Scopes* case reemerged in Tennessee. In 1967 the Tennessee legislature repealed the Butler Act. Six years later, however, it drafted a second antievolution law which sought to avoid the Constitutional shortcomings of the Arkansas statute that had been struck down in *Epperson*. This statute required any biology textbook containing the evolutionary thesis to contain a disclaimer stating that evolution was "a theory . . . and not scientific fact." Teachers of biology were required to give equal time to the Genesis version of creation, and the Bible was described as a "reference work" that did not have to carry any disclaimer. The act's most unusual feature was its specific exclusion of "the teaching of all occult or satanical beliefs of human origin." It was unclear whether this exclusion was intended to forbid the teaching of such theories entirely or merely to exclude them from the disclaimer and equal-time requirements set out in the remainder of the statute.

The Tennessee statute was challenged by biology teachers and parents, and in *Daniel v. Waters* (6th Cir. 1975) the Sixth Circuit Court of Appeals found that the statute violated the Establishment Clause. Rather than relying on *Epperson*, which looked to the purpose of the enacting legislature, the Sixth Circuit found that the statute would involve Tennessee's State Textbook Commission in theological disputes (in an effort to identify "occult" or "satanical" theories of human origin), thus creating excessive government entanglement with religion. The court also found that the requirement of equal time for the Genesis account of human origins amounted to preferential treatment for a particular faith in violation of the Establishment Clause.

Efforts to pass equal-time laws continued to flourish after *Daniel v. Waters*. In 1981 Louisiana passed the Balanced Treatment Act, which forbade the teaching of evolution in public schools unless equal time were given to the teaching of creation science. Seeking to improve the constitutional footing of this bill and to distinguish it from the *Epperson* statute, the legislature provided in the text of the act that its purpose was to support academic freedom. A legal challenge was promptly filed by the parents of public schoolchildren, teachers, and religious leaders. The plaintiffs sought a court order that would declare the statute unconstitutional and prohibit its enforcement.

In *Edwards v. Aguillard* (1987) the U.S. Supreme Court ruled in favor of the plaintiffs and struck down the Balanced Treatment Act under the Establishment Clause. Justice William J. Brennan, writing for the majority, applied a three-pronged test that the Court had developed in *Lemon v. Kurtzman* (1971). Under this test, (1) a statute must have a secular purpose, (2) its primary effect may neither advance nor inhibit religion, and (3) it may not result in excessive entanglement between government and religion. Violation of any of the three prongs of the *Lemon* test is sufficient to make out a violation of the Establishment Clause.

The Secular Purpose Inquiry

Justice Brennan found that, even though the articulated purpose of the Balanced Treatment Act was the furtherance of academic freedom, the act was not designed to further that goal, and therefore judicial deference to the stated legislative purpose was inappropriate. Reviewing the legislative history of the act, he noted that its sponsor had indicated that neither evolution nor creation science should be taught in public schools—a statement that tended to undermine the goal of academic freedom. The majority also noted that the act eliminated the freedom to provide instruction about evolutionary theory without also teaching creation science, an option which teachers had enjoyed before passage of the act. Accordingly, the majority held that the stated purpose of academic freedom was not advanced by the statute's provisions.

Justice Brennan concluded that the articulated legislative purpose of the act had little to do with the legislature's real intent and goals. He thus went on to consider the real purpose of the Balanced Treatment Act. Brennan determined that the predominant purpose was "to advance the religious viewpoint that a supernatural being created mankind" and to restructure the science curriculum to conform with that religious viewpoint. Since the primary purpose of the act was to endorse a particular religious doctrine, the act failed the secular purpose prong of the *Lemon* test and therefore violated the Establishment Clause.

Justice Lewis Powell, joined by Justice Sandra Day O'Connor, concurred. Their opinion reviewed the language and legislative history of the act in greater detail and concluded, with the majority, that the purpose of the act was, in fact, the promotion of a particular religious belief. Powell emphasized that mere coincidence or harmony between subjects taught in public schools and the tenets of a religion would be insufficient to make out an Establishment Clause violation, since the specter of the latter arises only when the purpose of the instruction is to advance a particular religious belief.

Justice Byron White concurred separately, noting that the Court traditionally defers to the judgments of state courts regarding the intent of their state legislature. He pointed out that Louisiana judges sitting on both the federal district court and the court of appeals had concluded that the legislative purpose in this case was the furtherance of religious belief.

Justice Antonin Scalia, joined by Chief Justice William Rehnquist, dissented. Scalia expressed reservations about the wisdom of invalidating legislation based on the motivation of the enacting legislature. Absent strong evidence of insincerity, which he found to be lacking in this case, he concluded that the Court should defer to the legislature's articulated statement of purpose.

Both *Epperson* and *Aguillard* were careful to emphasize that states have the right to prescribe public school curricula; they simply may not do so in a manner that "aids or opposes" any religion. As the Court noted in *Epperson,* it would be permissible for a public school curriculum to survey various religions or to study the Bible from a literary or historic viewpoint, as long as the material was presented "objectively as part of a secular program of education."

Epperson and *Aguillard* are two of only four cases in which the Supreme Court has struck down a statute under the Establishment Clause because of the absence of secular purpose. In *Stone v. Graham* (1980) the Court struck down a law requiring public schools to post the Ten Commandments, and in *Wallace v. Jaffree* (1985) the Court found unconstitutional, on similar grounds, a law requiring a minute of silence for "silent meditation or voluntary prayer." In fact, the Court has elsewhere sustained government action despite an express finding of a nonsecular purpose. For example, in *Zorach v. Clausen* (1952) the Court upheld a "released time" program that allowed students to attend religious classes away from their public school during school hours.

Some commentators agree with Scalia that the secular purpose inquiry should be insufficient, standing alone, to render a statute unconstitutional. These critiques rely on the difficulty of determining the subjective intent of a legislative body, and on the fact that a law may be passed for any combination of permissible and impermissible reasons, yet have only secular effects.

Other commentators have identified numerous legislative initiatives—including abolition, Prohibition, women's suffrage, and civil rights—that arose from explicitly religious motivations. Should the secular purpose inquiry prohibit a legislature from making religiously informed judgments or from passing laws that draw on the religious values of their constituents? Such an interpretation, as Professor Michael McConnell has noted, suggests that those whose understanding is derived from religious sources are "second-class citizens" who may not lobby for their principles in the public sphere.

Tension between the Religion Clauses

In *Epperson,* Justice Black pointed out yet another difficulty with invalidating government action based on the absence of secular purpose. This difficulty arises from the underlying tension between the Free Exercise Clause and the Establishment Clause. The Free Exercise Clause sometimes obliges the government to act with a nonsecular purpose—to afford a preference to religion—in order to facilitate the unburdened exercise of religious rights. It may be necessary, in other words, for the government to act in a manner that offends the first prong of the *Lemon* test in order to comply with the directives of the Free Exercise Clause.

The Court has been responsive to this tension in other contexts. In *Corporation of the Presiding Bishop of the Church of Jesus Christ of Latter-Day Saints v. Amos* (1987) the Court appeared to tolerate the absence of a secular purpose where the legislature did not intentionally promote the perspective of a particular religious organization. *Amos* held that an exemption to Title VII employment discrimination which permitted a religious employer to require employees to adhere to the employer's religious beliefs did not violate the Establishment Clause. *Amos* suggests that the Court will not always find religious purpose to be a sufficient basis for invalidating a statute, at least where the law does not further a particular religious belief.

Balanced treatment legislation has been proposed in at least twenty states, and *Aguillard* in no way suggests that the majority of these laws would be found unconstitutional. Proponents of such legislation are likely to learn from *Aguillard* and to do a better job of keeping evidence that undermines an articulated secular purpose out of the legislative record. By second-guessing the motivation of the legislature and deciding the case on a summary judgment record, the *Aguillard* majority opened itself to charges of insufficient respect for representative assemblies and for the trial process. Had *Aguillard* proceeded to trial, the evidence would probably have shown that the primary effect of teaching creation science was to advance religion. The Louisiana law would have been struck down under the second prong of the *Lemon* test, and the case could have been decided on a more complete record.

Neither *Aguillard* nor *Epperson* considered one of the more telling objections to balanced treatment laws. By reducing the field of inquiry regarding human origins to only two competing theories, these laws posit a false duality that excludes by implication the beliefs of other, often non-Christian religions. Contrary to the suggestion of the Tennessee Supreme Court in *Scopes,* such laws do promote certain religions at the expense of others. This goes to the heart of the Establishment Clause prohibition. By failing to address this issue and resting their decisions on the shifting sands of the secular purpose inquiry, *Epperson* and *Aguillard* ensured that the battle between antievolutionists and the public schools is far from over.

Joanne C. Brant

Bibliography

Carter, Stephen, "Evolutionism, Creationism, and Treating Religion As a Hobby," 1987 *Duke Law Journal* 977–996 (1987).

Ginger, Ray, *Six Days or Forever? Tennessee v. John Thomas Scopes* (Chicago: Quadrangle, 1969).
Larson, Edward J., *Summer for the Gods: The Scopes Trial and America's Continuing Debate over Science and Religion* (New York: Basic Books, 1997).
———, *Trial and Error: The American Controversy over Creation and Evolution* (New York: Oxford University Press, 1985).
McConnell, Michael, "Religious Freedom at a Crossroads," 59 *University of Chicago Law Review* 115–194 (1992).
Note, "Leading Cases: Teaching Creationism—Louisiana's Balanced Treatment Act," 101 *Harvard Law Review* 189–199 (1987).
Rosen, Lawrence, "Continuing the Conversation: Creationism, the Religion Clauses and the Politics of Culture," 1988 *Supreme Court Review* 61–84 (1988).
Strossen, Nadine, "'Secular Humanism' and 'Scientific Creationism': Proposed Standards for Reviewing Curricular Decisions Affecting Students' Religious Freedom," 47 *Ohio State Law Journal* 333–406 (1986).
Wills, Garry, *Under God: Religion and American Politics* (New York: Simon and Schuster, 1990).

Cases Cited

Corporation of the Presiding Bishop of the Church of Jesus Christ of Latter-Day Saints v. Amos, 483 U.S. 327 (1987).
Daniel v. Waters, 515 F. 2d 485 (6th Cir. 1975).
Edwards v. Aguillard, 482 U.S. 578 (1987).
Epperson v. Arkansas, 393 U.S. 97 (1968).
Everson v. Board of Education, 330 U.S. 1 (1947).
Lemon v. Kurtzman, 403 U.S. 602 (1971).
Scopes v. Tennessee, 154 Tenn. 105, 289 S.W. 363 (1927).
Stone v. Graham, 449 U.S. 39 (1980).
Wallace v. Jaffree, 472 U.S. 38 (1985).
Zorach v. Clausen, 343 U.S. 306 (1952).

F

First Federal Congress and Religion

The First Congress under the Constitution of the United States convened on March 4, 1789, and confronted staggering tasks, including a number that had substantial religious dimensions.

The most pressing of these tasks with religious dimensions was the ratification, as part of a general bill of rights, of a constitutional amendment ensuring religious liberty. Many of the states had ratified the Constitution on the understanding that amendments composing a bill of rights would be proposed by the new Congress at the earliest moment feasible.

On June 8, 1789, James Madison proposed that the House of Representatives go into a committee of the whole to consider amendments to the new Constitution. When several speakers opposed this motion, Madison read a series of proposed amendments for consideration by a select committee. Among these proposals were the following: "Fourthly. That in Article 1st, section 9, between clauses 3 and 4, be inserted these clauses, to wit: The civil rights of none shall be abridged on account of religious belief or worship, nor shall any national religion be established, nor shall the full and equal rights of conscience be in any manner, or on any pretext, infringed."

On August 18 the House of Representatives proposed twelve amendments, the third of which read, "Congress shall make no law respecting an establishment of religion, or prohibiting the free exercise thereof, or abridging the freedom of speech, or of the press, or the right of the people peaceably to assemble, and to petition the government for a redress of grievances"; and on September 28, 1789, the Congress sent these amendments to the states for ratification. By December 12, 1791, the third through the twelfth of the proposed amendments received the necessary ratifications by state legislatures.

The changed wording of the First Amendment (the third of the proposed amendments) reflected the incorporation of certain other key liberties such as speech, press, assembly, and petition into the religious liberty amendment, rather than retaining them as separate amendments. It also reflected the dropping of the right-of-conscience provision, which many thought too broad and too vague a grant of exemption to governmental authority.

The creation of this amendment ranks as the single greatest religion-related action of the First Congress, and although its precise meaning has long been a matter of dispute, no serious scholar disputes that, at a minimum, it proscribed the creation of a national church.

Some of the other actions of the First Congress in relation to religious issues are surprising, however, for they were scarcely in line with any of the major interpretative theories of church–state relations that have held sway with modern scholars.

On June 14, 1790, Congress was presented with the petition of the Reverend Joseph Willard on behalf of the Congregationalist clergy of Massachusetts, who desired Congress to establish an official version of Scripture—as the British Parliament had done with the King James Version of the Bible—in order to protect the public from the allegedly unreliable translations of Holy Writ under production by printers in the various states. Congress declined to create such a federal imprimatur for scriptural translations.

On April 22, 1789, the House of Representatives opened nominations for chaplains for the House and the Senate. Under the rules that were eventually adopted, each legislative chamber chose its own chaplain, each clergyman was to receive compensation for his services, but at any given time the chaplains must not be from the same denomination.

In 1983 the case of *Marsh v. Chambers* was resolved by the Supreme Court in a 6-to-3 decision in which Chief Justice Warren E. Burger wrote the opinion of the court's majority, with Associate Justices John Paul Stevens, William J. Brennan, and Thurgood Marshall dissenting.

The suit challenged, under the concept of the separation of church and state from the First Amendment's Establishment Clause, the constitutionality of Nebraska's practice of providing a paid chaplain for the legislature—a practice of the vast majority of states and of the U.S. Congress.

Chief Justice Burger upheld the practice by refusing to apply the tripartite test of *Lemon v. Kurtzman* (1971, 1973) and by defending the practice as one that preceded the Constitution; its origins went back to the First Continental Congress (1774). Burger further emphasized that the First Congress, which had proposed the Bill of Rights, was, in fact, responsible for reinstituting this practice under the new charter of government. Recitation of prayers by tax-supported legislative chaplains had become, in the chief justice's phrase, "part of the fabric of our society."

Justice Stevens's dissent focused on the fact that the Nebraska legislature's sixteen-year tenure of a Presbyterian minister gave preference to one denomination over the others, while Justices Marshall and Brennan dissented based on the traditional objections to the entanglement of government with religion and the sponsorship of religious worship by government.

Burger's majority opinion in part rested on a historical argument. The chief justice insisted on creating an exemption for a practice on the basis of its pedigree, dating from the First Federal Congress.

In a different arena, chaplaincies arose again when the U.S. Senate on March 4, 1791, advised and consented to the officers nominated by President Washington to fill positions in the third regiment, a new unit created under the Military Establishment Act of March 3, 1791. Among the officers nominated and approved was John Hunt, who was to serve as regimental chaplain, which office had been created by the fifth section of the act.

Interestingly, the Militia Act of 1790 dropped a section requiring that states appoint regimental chaplains for their militias on the ground that morality and religion are useful for the promotion of discipline and good behavior in military forces, which had earlier been proposed. The elimination of this section appears to have been intended simply to leave this option to the discretion of each state.

Also, it should be noted that on September 25, 1789, the House proposed, "[t]hat a joint committee of both Houses be directed to wait upon the President of the United States to request that he would recommend to the people of the United States, a day of public thanksgiving and prayer to be observed, by acknowledging, with grateful hearts, the many signal favors of Almighty God, especially by affording them the opportunity peaceably to establish a Constitution of government for their safety and happiness." Ultimately, this resolution was adopted by the Senate and was implemented by President Washington, who issued such a proclamation to the general public, creating what would become a tradition from the earliest days of the Republic.

On August 7, 1789, the House of Representatives passed an "Act to Provide for the Government of the Territory North-West of the River Ohio." This act essentially readopted the Northwest Ordinance of 1787, which had been invalidated (as were all laws of the Confederation) by the ratification of the Constitution. In reenacting the Ordinance, the Congress altered minor provisions to bring it into conformity with the new organic law. However, Congress left in place provisions for public lands to be set aside in each township to support churches and schools. The statute asserted that such land use would promote morality and fitness for self-government.

Finally, on June 1, 1789, the Oath Act, which provided for the administration of oaths to all officials of the federal government and of the states, became law. The oath for which the act provided kept the option of swearing or affirming, stating simply, "I, . . . , do solemnly swear or affirm (as the case may be) that I will support the Constitution of the United States." This oath adhered closely to the constitutional prohibition on religious tests by omitting all religious references, including the traditional, ". . . so help me God," which had (and has been) a fixture in many state oaths for judicial witnesses, etc.

The diverse actions of the First Congress may be made sense of, perhaps, if one realizes that these national legislators were firmly committed to the avoidance of any establishment of religion—hence the congressional support for the First Amendment, for the refusal to create an official Bible, and for the avoidance of any religious test in oaths for office. On the other hand, however, these early legislators saw little danger of an establishment of religion where no preference was extended to any particular denomination and/or where outlays of funds were one-time grants or involved *de minimis* amounts.

Presidential thanksgiving proclamations had no compulsory power within them and involved virtually no expenditure of public funds. Military and legislative chaplaincies involved small expenditures, but were, in theory, open to all denominations and involved no compulsion of belief or of liturgical practice. Finally, the provision of land in the territories for the support of churches might seem the closest to an establishment of religion, but in addition to its nonpreferential nature, this legislative act could be construed as an act of the government not *qua* national government but as the municipal authority of the territory—the equivalent of a state government, in effect—and in that sense it was arguably unrestricted by the First Amendment.

Patrick M. O'Neil

Bibliography

Bickford, Charlene Bangs, and Kenneth R. Bowling, *Birth of the Nation: The First Federal Congress, 1789–1791* (Washington, D.C.: First Federal Congress Project/George Washington University, 1989).

Documentary History of the First Federal Congress, 1789–1791, 14 vols., ed. Linda Grant DePauw, Charlene Bangs Bickford, Lavonne Siegel Hauptman, Kenneth R. Bowling, Helen E.Veit, and William Charles DiGiacomantonio (Baltimore: Johns Hopkins University Press, 1974–1995).

Kurland, Philip B., and Ralph Lerner (eds.), *The Founders' Constitution,* 5 vols. (Chicago: University of Chicago Press, 1978).

Cases Cited

Lemon v. Kurtzman 403 U.S. 602 (1971) [I], 411 U.S. 192 (1973) [II].

Marsh v. Chambers 463 U.S. 783 (1983).

Flag Salute Cases

Minersville School District v. Gobitis et al. (1940) and *West Virginia State Board of Education v. Barnette* (1943)—commonly referred to as the "flag salute cases"—are among the most peculiar in American constitutional history. At issue in both was the right of a state to require public school students to salute the flag and say the Pledge of Allegiance. The plaintiffs were Jehovah's Witnesses who refused, on religious grounds, to salute the flag. In 1940, in *Gobitis,* the U.S. Supreme Court upheld the school district's attempt to force students to salute the flag. Three years later, in *Barnette,* the Court reversed course, implicitly siding with the claims of religious freedom made by the Jehovah's Witnesses.

These cases must be understood in the light of the evolution of the Jehovah's Witness faith, the emergence of a "Roosevelt Court," and the issues of patriotism and national unity surrounding American entrance into World War II.

Alienated from Mainstream America

The Jehovah's Witness movement (members of the faith are emphatic that it is not a "church") began in the 1870s under the leadership of Charles Taze Russell, but it did not become widespread until the 1920s and 1930s, when Joseph F. Rutherford became the head of the movement. Rutherford organized a proselytizing, aggressively millennial movement. The Jehovah's Witnesses publicly bear "witness" against what they believe are the three major allies of Satan: the "false" teachings of most other churches and the Catholic church in particular, human government, and capitalism and business.

In addition to denouncing "false" churches, the faith rejects patriotic exercises.

Starting in 1935 American Witnesses refused to salute the flag, asserting that doing so violated the biblical injunction against worshipping graven images.

Already unpopular because of their aggressive proselytizing, their heated denunciations of other faiths, and their uncompromising stands on scriptural interpretation, the Witnesses' hostility to political authority and their refusal to salute the flag further alienated them from mainstream America and from political and police officials. This set the stage for the flag salute cases.

Minersville School District v. Gobitis (1940) resulted from the refusal of 12-year-old Lillian Gobitis and her 10-year-old brother, William, to say the Pledge of Allegiance in the public schools of Minersville, Pennsylvania. The father of these children, Walter Gobitis, had grown up in Minersville and was raised in a Roman Catholic family and had saluted the flag as a child. In 1931 Gobitis became a Witness. The Gobitis children continued to salute the flag until November 1935. In 1935 Witnesses in Germany refused to salute the Nazi flag. Ultimately, more than ten thousand German Witnesses would be sent to concentration camps for their affront to Nazi authorities. In 1935 the leader of the Witnesses in America declared that followers of the faith "do not 'Heil Hitler' nor any other creature." After this, American Witnesses refused to take part in flag saluting ceremonies.

In a more cosmopolitan community the refusal of the Gobitis children to salute the flag might have gone unnoticed. But neither Gobitis nor his faith were popular in Minersville, where 80 percent of the population was Roman Catholic. Rather than ignoring an act that was neither defiant nor disruptive, School Superintendent Charles E. Roudabush took steps that led to the expulsion of the Gobitis children and one other Witness sixth-grader. Gobitis then sent his children to a private Jehovah's Witness school.

Eighteen months later Gobitis sued the school district in *Gobitis v. Minersville School District* (E.D., Pa., 1937). United States District Court Judge Albert B. Maris, a recent Roosevelt appointee to the federal bench, heard the case. As a Quaker, Judge Maris was probably more sympathetic to the Witnesses than most Americans. Although he had a distinguished military record during World War I, as a member of a faith once persecuted for its pacifism, Maris doubtless understood the nature of prejudice and religious persecution that the Jehovah's Witnesses faced.

During the trial Superintendent Roudabush was openly hostile to the Witnesses and plaintiffs, claiming that the children were "indoctrinated," thereby implying that their actions were not based on sincerely held religious beliefs. Judge Maris rejected Roudabush's contentions, asserting that "[t]o permit public officers to determine whether" religious views were "sincerely held . . . would sound the death knell of religious liberty." Rebuffing this "pernicious and alien doctrine," Maris reminded the school officials that Pennsylvania itself had been founded "as a haven for all those persecuted for conscience' sake."

Judge Maris doubted that failing to salute the flag could "prejudice or imperil the safety, health or morals" of other students, and he concluded that, "although undoubtedly adopted from patriotic motives," the flag salute requirement "appears to have become in this case a means for the persecution of children for conscience' sake."

Finally, Maris noted that "religious intolerance is again rearing its ugly head in other parts of the world" and that thus it was of "utmost importance that the liberties guaranteed to our citizens by the fundamental law be preserved from all encroachment." Although the point was not central to his decision, Maris placed the controversy over the Jehovah's Witnesses in the context of the rise of Nazism and the likelihood of another world war.

Maris ordered the children readmitted to the public schools, and eighteen months later a unanimous three-judge panel upheld his ruling. By this time many other states had also begun to prosecute Jehovah's Witnesses for their refusal to salute the flag. In his opinion Judge William S. Clark denounced the "eighteen big states" that "have seen fit to exert their power over a number [at least 120 nationwide] of little children" who sought to worship God in their own way and to also attend the public schools. Clark also tied the controversy to the specter of Nazism in Europe, quoting in a footnote Adolf Hitler's 1935 declaration dissolving the Jehovah's

Witnesses in Germany and confiscating their property. Clark also argued that refusing to salute the flag created no "clear and present danger" to the government and that thus the religious freedom of the children should be protected.

A "Symbol of National Unity"

Initially the Minersville school officials did not plan to appeal to the Supreme Court. Such an appeal cost more than this rural school district cared to spend. But patriotic groups, including the American Legion, helped finance the appeal. Before the Supreme Court, Harvard Law School Professor George K. Gardner argued Gobitis's case on behalf of the American Civil Liberties Union. He was joined by the national leader of the Jehovah's Witnesses, Joseph Rutherford, who was also an attorney. Joseph W. Henderson, a lawyer from Philadelphia, continued to represent the school board as he had in the lower courts.

Writing for an 8-to-1 majority in the Court, Justice Felix Frankfurter reversed the lower courts. Frankfurter was a former Harvard Law School professor, a liberal activist recently appointed by President Roosevelt, and a Jewish immigrant from Austria. Given his background, one might assume that Frankfurter would have been sensitive to those who were persecuted for their religious beliefs and who at that very moment were being sent to concentration camps alongside the Jews in Germany, Austria, and elsewhere in Europe. Instead, he used this background to bolster his support for the flag salute laws.

Justice Frankfurter conceded that "the affirmative pursuit of one's convictions about the ultimate mystery of the universe and man's relation to it is placed beyond the reach of law. Government may not interfere with organized or individual expression of belief or disbelief." However, Frankfurter noted that there were no absolute guarantees of religious freedom. He found that the task of the Court was to "reconcile two rights in order to prevent either from destroying the other." He found that

> conscientious scruples have not, in the course of the long struggle for religious toleration, relieved the individual from obedience to a general law not aimed at the promotion or restriction of religious beliefs. The mere possession of religious convictions which contradict the relevant concerns of a political society does not relieve the citizen from a discharge of political responsibilities.

Put simply, Frankfurter argued that the First Amendment's guarantee of religious freedom extended only to protection from laws that were overtly religious in nature. Frankfurter rejected the findings of the lower court that the enforcement of the Pledge of Allegiance was overt religious discrimination.

In a hyperbolic analogy Justice Frankfurter compared the dilemma of the Jehovah's Witnesses to that of Lincoln's query during the Civil War: "Must a government of necessity be too *strong* for the liberties of its people, or too *weak* to maintain its own existence?" Frankfurter argued that the flag was a "symbol of national unity, transcending all internal differences," and, as such, he implied that failure to salute it somehow threatened the existence of the nation. He further argued that the states should be given great latitude in determining how best to instill patriotism in children and to "awaken in the child's mind considerations as to the significance of the flag contrary to those implanted by the parent." He ended by noting that judicial review was "a limitation on popular government" which should be used sparingly. He urged that issues of liberty be fought out in the state legislatures and "in the forum of public opinion" in order to "vindicate the self-confidence of a free people."

In dissent Justice Harlan Fiske Stone (later to become chief justice) noted that "by this law the state seeks to coerce these children to express a sentiment which, as they interpret it, they do not entertain, and which violates their deepest religious convictions." Stone dismissed Frankfurter's appeals to patriotism and his unrealistic suggestion that the issue be decided "in the forum of public opinion" by appeals to the wisdom of the legislature. Stone pointed out that "[h]istory teaches us that there have been but few infringements of personal liberty by the state which have not been justified, as they are here, in the name of righteousness and the public good, and few which have not been directed, as they are now, at politically helpless minorities." Finally, Stone argued that the Constitution was more than just an outline for majoritarian government; it was "also an expression of faith and a command that freedom of mind and spirit must be preserved, which government must obey, if it is to adhere to that justice and moderation without which no free government can exist."

Justice Stone conceded the importance of instilling patriotism in future citizens. He declared that the state might "require teaching by instruction and study of all in our history and in the structure and organization of our government, including the guarantee of civil liberty, which tend to inspire patriotism and love of country." But forcing children to violate their religious precepts was, in Stone's mind, not the way to teach patriotic values. He thought it far better that the schools find "some sensible adjustment of school discipline in order that the religious convictions of these children may be spared" than to approve "legislation which operates to repress the religious freedom of small minorities."

Reactions to *Gobitis*

Gobitis helped unleash a wave of political, legal, and physical attacks on Jehovah's Witnesses. Immediately following the decision, there were hundreds of assaults on Jehovah's Witnesses and their property. In Kennebunk, Maine, a Jehovah's Witnesses' temple was burned; in Maryland the police helped a mob break up a Jehovah's Witnesses' meeting; in at least thirteen other states mobs—which often included police officials—beat, mobbed, and kidnapped Witnesses. In Odessa, Texas, for example, the police arrested seventy Jehovah's Witnesses for their own "protection," held them without charges when they refused to salute the flag, and then released them to a mob of over a thousand people who chased them for five miles. In Wyoming Witnesses were tarred and feathered, in Arkansas some were shot, and in Nebraska one Witness was castrated.

Witnesses also faced official violence and persecution. Throughout the country they were arrested without charges or on bogus charges. Sometimes the police tortured them. In Richwood, West Virginia, the police arrested a group of Jehovah's Witnesses who sought protection; the police forced the Witnesses to drink large amounts of castor oil, tied them up, and paraded them through the town.

State legislatures and school boards responded to *Gobitis* with new flag salute laws. By 1943 over two thousand Jehovah's Witnesses had been expelled from schools in all forty-eight states. This was the nationwide answer to Justice Frankfurter's unrealistic suggestion that the Jehovah's Witnesses appeal to the state legislatures for relief.

The nation's intellectual community responded to *Gobitis* in quite a different way. Overwhelmingly, law review articles condemned the decision. The law reviews at Fordham, Georgetown, and Notre Dame and other Catholic schools unanimously denounced *Gobitis,* even though the Jehovah's Witnesses had traditionally vilified the Roman Catholic Church. Catholic scholars clearly understood that the issue here was civil liberties, not theology. Members of the Supreme Court soon came to doubt the wisdom of *Gobitis.* In *Jones v. Opelika* (1942) the Court affirmed the convictions of Jehovah's Witnesses for distributing their pamphlets without proper licenses from various towns in Alabama, Arkansas, and Arizona. The laws in question were similar to other repressive laws passed in the wake of *Gobitis.* Significantly, however, four justices dissented, arguing that the statutes unconstitutionally restricted freedom of the press, freedom of speech, and the free exercise of religion. One of the dissenters was Justice Stone, recently promoted to Chief Justice. Also dissenting were three members of the *Gobitis* majority: Justices Frank Murphy, William O. Douglas, and Hugo Black. All three specifically concurred with Stone's dissent. Black wrote an exceedingly short dissent, designed to make one simple point: "Since we joined in the opinion in the Gobitis Case, we think this is an appropriate occasion to state that we now believe that it was also wrongly decided." The dissenters declared: "The First Amendment does not put the right freely to exercise religion in a subordinate position."

Equally important, the *Opelika* majority conspicuously failed to rely on *Gobitis* for its result. This was probably because the recently appointed Justice Robert Jackson, one of the majority justices, disagreed with the reasoning and result in *Gobitis.* Just as *Gobitis* served as an invitation for the states to suppress the Jehovah's Witnesses, the dissents in *Opelika*—combined with the failure of the majority to cite *Gobitis*—served as an invitation to challenge that recent precedent.

A New Court, a New Case

The final step before a reversal of *Gobitis* was a change in the membership of the Court. In October 1942 Justice James F. Byrnes, one of the majority in *Opelika,* resigned. In February 1943 District Judge Wiley Rutledge joined the Court. On the district court Rutledge had dissented in a case very similar to *Opelika;* his dissent indicated that he would also oppose *Gobitis.* It now appeared that a majority of the Court wished to overturn *Gobitis.* All that was lacking was a test case to bring the issue back to the Supreme Court.

In January 1942 West Virginia's state school board adopted a strict flag salute requirement. The preamble to the board's resolution quoted at length from Frankfurter's *Gobitis* opinion. Shortly after the adoption of this resolution, school officials in Charleston expelled a number of Jehovah's Witnesses, including the children of Walter Barnette.

In August 1942—two months after the decision in *Opelika*—Barnette's attorneys asked a three-judge panel to permanently enjoin state school officials from requiring Jehovah's Witnesses to salute the flag. Writing for a unanimous court in *Barnette v. West Virginia State Board of Education* (S.D., West Virginia, 1942), Judge John J. Parker, of the Fourth Circuit Court of Appeals, granted the injunction. Parker acknowledged that "ordinarily" the lower court would "follow an unreversed decision of the Supreme Court of the United States, whether we agreed with it or not." However, in the light of the dissents in *Opelika,* Parker expressed doubt that *Gobitis* was still binding. He noted that three justices had explicitly announced their disagreement with *Gobitis* and that the majority opinion distinguished *Opelika* from *Gobitis.* Because the three-judge panel believed that the West Virginia regulation violated "religious liberty when required of persons holding the religious views of the plaintiffs," Parker declared that the panel members would be "recreant to our duty as judges, if through a blind following of a decision which the Supreme Court itself has thus impaired as an authority, we should deny protection to rights which we regard as among the most sacred of those protected by constitutional guaranties."

In the rest of his opinion Judge Parker made three important points. First, he noted that the flag salute controversy had become another episode in the history of religious persecution, and that those who defended it differed little from past persecutors. "There is not a religious persecution in history that was not justified in the eyes of those engaging in it on the ground that it was reasonable and right and that the persons whose practices were suppressed were guilty of stubborn folly hurtful of the general welfare."

Second, Judge Parker noted that religious freedom had its limits. "He [who belongs to the minority religion] must render to Caesar the things that are Caesar's as well as to God the things that are God's. He may not refuse to bear arms or pay taxes because of religious scruples, nor may he engage in polygamy or any other practice directly hurtful to the safety, morals, health or general welfare of the community."

Finally, Judge Parker confronted Justice Frankfurter's deference to the state legislatures. He argued that the "suggestion that the courts are precluded by the action of state legislative authorities in deciding when rights of religious freedom must yield to the exercise of a police power would of course nullify the constitutional guarantee." Indeed, the guarantee of religious freedom "would not be worth the paper it is written on if no legislature or school board were bound to respect it except in so far as it might . . . choose" to respect it. If the courts were "to abdicate the most important duty which rests on them," Parker continued, then the "tyranny of majorities over the rights of individuals or helpless minorities" would continue to be "one of the great dangers of popular government."

The circuit court found that to "force" someone to salute the flag "is petty tyranny unworthy of the spirit of this Republic." Thus the judges granted the injunction, and for the most part West Virginia's authorities obeyed. No more Jehovah's Witnesses were expelled from the schools, and even the Barnette children returned to their classes. Meanwhile the state's school board appealed to the Supreme Court.

Before the Supreme Court the attorney for the board of education unimaginatively relied almost entirely on *Gobitis.* His brief was supported by a weak amicus brief from the American Legion. Attorneys for Barnette attacked *Gobitis,* comparing it to the decision in *Dred Scott v. Sandford* (1857). Amicus briefs for Barnette came from the American Civil Liberties Union, written by Osmond K. Fraenkel and Arthur Garfield Hays; and the

American Bar Association's Committee on the Bill of Rights, written by Harvard Law School Professor Zachariah Chafee, Jr.

Gobitis Reversed

On June 14, 1943—which ironically was Flag Day—the Court upheld the lower court and reversed the *Gobitis* precedent. Justice Jackson wrote for the six-justice majority, while Justice Frankfurter wrote a bitter dissent.

Oddly, the issue of freedom of religion was virtually absent from Jackson's majority opinion. Jackson accepted, without question, that the Witnesses' sincerely held beliefs made it impossible for them to conscientiously salute the flag. But Jackson offered no analysis of the importance of that belief or, even, of the role of religious freedom in striking down the mandatory flag salute. Indeed, he linked the freedom to worship with other Bill of Rights protections, noting that the "right to life, liberty, and property, to free speech, a free press, freedom of worship and assembly, and other fundamental rights may not be submitted to vote; they depend on the outcome of no elections." Jackson found that the "freedoms of speech and of press, of assembly, and of worship may not be infringed" on "slender grounds."

Rather than grounding his opinion in freedom of religion, Justice Jackson analyzed the case as one of freedom of speech and expression. Jackson argued that the flag salute—or the refusal to salute the flag—was "a form of utterance" and thus was subject to traditional free speech analysis. He noted that the flag was a political symbol and that, naturally, saluting the symbol was symbolic speech:

> Symbolism is a primitive but effective way of communicating ideas. The use of an emblem or flag to symbolize some system, idea, institution, or personality, is a short cut from mind to mind. Causes and nations, political parties, lodges and ecclesiastical groups seek to knit the loyalty of their followings to a flag or banner, a color or design. The State announces rank, function, and authority through crowns and maces, uniforms and black robes; the church speaks through the Cross, the Crucifix, the altar and shrine, and clerical raiment. Symbols of the State often convey political ideas just as religious symbols come to convey theological ones.

The question for Justice Jackson was rather simple: Did the "speech" of the Jehovah's Witnesses threaten the rights of any individuals or the peace and stability of the government? If either threat were present, then Jackson might have allowed the mandatory flag salute. But if the Witnesses' "speech" did not threaten the rights of others or threaten the government, then there was no valid reason to suppress it.

Jackson noted that the conduct of the Jehovah's Witnesses "did not bring them into collision with rights asserted by any other individuals." The Court was not being asked "to determine where the rights of one end and another begin." It was, rather, a conflict "between [governmental] authority and rights of the individual."

Justice Jackson compared the flag salute with the issues in *Stromberg v. California* (1931), which had allowed protesters to carry a red flag. This case and others supported the "commonplace" standard in free speech cases "that censorship or suppression of expression of opinion is tolerated by our Constitution only when the expression presents a clear and present danger of action of a kind the State is empowered to prevent and publish. It would seem that involuntary affirmation could be commanded only on even more immediate and urgent grounds than silence." But no one claimed that the silence of the children "during a flag salute ritual creates a clear and present danger." Jackson pointed out the irony that "[t]o sustain the compulsory flag salute we are required to say that a Bill of Rights which guards the individual's right to speak his own mind, left it open to public authorities to compel him to utter what is not in his mind."

Justice Jackson's shrewd analysis had turned the case inside out. It was no longer one of freedom of religion but one that, in part, took the form of an establishment of religion on the part of the government through its "flag salute ritual." Jackson correctly saw that the Jehovah's Witnesses were not trying to force their views on anyone else but, rather, that the government was trying to force its views and beliefs on the Jehovah's Witnesses. He noted that in *Gobitis* the Court had "only examined and rejected a claim based on religious beliefs of immunity from general rule." But, Jackson pointed out, the correct question was "whether such a ceremony so touching matters of opinion and political attitude may be imposed upon the individual by official authority . . . under the Constitution." In other words, did the government have the power to force anyone, regardless of religious beliefs, to participate in any ceremony or "ritual"? What Jackson might have asked was, Did the Constitution allow for the establishment of a secular national religion with the flag as the chief icon?

In *Gobitis* Justice Frankfurter had noted Lincoln's "memorable dilemma" of choosing between civil liberties and maintaining a free society. Jackson had little patience for "such oversimplification, so handy in political debate." He "doubted whether Mr. Lincoln would have thought that the strength of government to maintain itself would be impressively vindicated by our confirming power of the state to expel a handful of children from school." Here Jackson revealed the fundamental weakness of Frankfurter's assertion in *Gobitis* that somehow the safety of the nation depended on whether Jehovah's Witnesses were forced to salute the flag in the public schools.

Justice Jackson noted that even Congress had made the flag salute optional for soldiers who had religious scruples against such ceremonies. This act "respecting the conscience of the objector in a matter so vital as raising the Army" contrasted "sharply with these local regulations in matters relatively trivial to the welfare of the nation."

"The Right to Differ"

At the time of *Gobitis* the nation was not at war, but war seemed imminent. By *Barnette* the nation had been at war for over a year. Jackson agreed that in wartime "national unity" was necessary and was something the government should "foster by persuasion and example." But could the government gain national unity by force? Jackson made references to the suppression of the early Christians in Rome, to the Inquisition, to "the Siberian exiles as a means of Russian unity," and to the "fast failing efforts of our present totalitarian enemies." He warned that "those who begin coercive elimination of dissent soon find themselves exterminating the dissenters. Compulsory unification of opinion achieves only the unanimity of the graveyard."

During a war against Nazism, Justice Jackson's opinion was a plea for the nation to avoid becoming like its enemies. He argued that the test of freedom was "the right to differ as to things that touch the heart of the existing order." This led him to a ringing defense of individual liberty: "If there is any fixed star in our constitutional constellation, it is that no official, high or petty, can prescribe what shall be orthodox in politics, nationalism, religion, or other matters of opinion or force citizens to confess by word or act their faith therein."

Justice Felix Frankfurter was unmoved by Jackson's powerful defense of individual liberty and by his condemnation of oppressive "village tyrants" who expelled small children from school because of their religious beliefs. At a time when millions of Jews (and thousands of Jehovah's Witnesses) were perishing in German death camps, Frankfurter used his ethnicity to justify his support for the suppression of a religious minority in the United States. He began: "One who belongs to the most vilified and persecuted minority in history is not likely to be insensible to the freedoms guaranteed by our Constitution." But he argued that he could not bring his personal beliefs to the Court, because, "as judges we are neither Jew nor Gentile, neither Catholic nor agnostic." He then defended judicial self-restraint and recapitulated and elaborated on his *Gobitis* opinion.

Justice Frankfurter argued that "saluting the flag suppresses no belief nor curbs it," because those saluting it were still free to "believe what they please, avow their belief and practice it." In making this point, Frankfurter failed to explain how one could "practice a belief" by doing what that belief prohibited. Nor did he explain how forcing children to say and do one thing—while encouraging them to believe secretly that what they were doing was a violation of God's commandments—would inspire patriotism in them.

Frankfurter conceded that the flag salute law "may be a foolish measure" and that "patriotism cannot be enforced by the flag salute." But he argued that the Court had no business interfering with laws made by democratically elected legislatures and that, because a total of thirteen justices had found the flag salute laws to be constitutional, the state laws "can not be deemed unreasonable." Because the state legislators had relied on the recent decision in *Gobitis,* Frankfurter felt that it was unfair to strike down their legislation.

Frankfurter condemned "our constant preoccupation with the constitutionality of legislation rather than with its wisdom. . . ." Yet he refused to strike down the West Virginia law, which he conceded was unwise, not because it passed all constitutional tests but because of judicial restraint and respect for stare decisis. He argued that the "most precious interests of civilization" were to be "found outside of their vindication in courts of law," and thus he urged that the Court not interfere in the democratic process but wait for a "positive translation of the faith of a free society into the convictions and habits and actions of the community." What would happen to the Witnesses in the meantime seemed of little concern to Frankfurter.

There was some minor resistance to *Barnette* in a few localities; the Supreme Court heard a few cases in which various local decisions were overturned. After 1946, however, the Court heard no more cases on the flag salute issue as *Barnette* became an important precedent for other free speech and freedom of religion cases.

Paul Finkelman

Bibliography

Curtis, Michael Kent, *The Constitution and the Flag* (New York: Garland, 1990).

Irons, Peter, *The Courage of Their Convictions* (New York: Free Press, 1988).

Manwaring, David, *Render unto Caesar: The Flag Salute Controversy* (Chicago: University of Chicago Press, 1962).

Roenme, Victor W., and G. F. Folsom, Jr., "Recent Restrictions upon Religious Liberty," 36 *American Political Science Review* 1053–1067 (1942).

Cases Cited

Dred Scott v. Sandford, 19 Howard (60 U.S.) 393 (1857).

Gobitis v. Minersville School District, 21 F. Supp. 581 (1937).

Jones v. Opelika, 316 U.S. 584 (1942).

Minersville School District v. Gobitis et al., 310 U.S. 586 (1940), reversing *Minersville School District v. Gobitis et al.,* 108 F. 2d 683 (1939).

Stromberg v. California, 283 U.S. 359 (1931).

West Virginia State Board of Education v. Barnette, 319 U.S. 624 (1943), reversing *Barnette v. West Virginia State Board of Education,* 47 F. Supp. 251 (1942).

Flast v. Cohen 392 U.S. 83 (1968)

In *Flast v. Cohen* (1968) the U.S. Supreme Court upheld the right of citizens to sue the federal government in what are known as "taxpayer's suits." This overturned a barrier against such suits that was imposed by the Court forty-five years earlier, in *Frothingham v. Mellon* (1923). The *Frothingham* Court had ruled that a federal taxpayer was without standing to challenge the constitutionality of a federal statute. In *Flast* the Court reexamined this holding, looking at whether an intrusion on First Amendment rights justified an exception to the *Frothingham* standard. Seven plaintiffs, in their capacity as taxpayers, sued Mr. Wilbur Cohen—the Secretary of Health, Education and Welfare—to enjoin the allegedly unconstitutional expenditure of federal funds to finance textbooks and instruction in religious schools. They claimed that these expenditures made pursuant to the Elementary and Secondary Education Act of 1965 violated the Establishment and Free Exercise Clauses of the First Amendment.

The district court, relying on *Frothingham,* dismissed the plaintiffs' complaint for lack of standing. The Supreme Court reversed, holding that the plaintiffs did satisfy the U.S. Constitution's Article III requirements for standing to sue. The Court distinguished *Flast* from *Frothingham,* noting that the taxpayer in *Frothingham* was denied standing because her relatively minor interest in the Treasury's funds was not enough to constitute a "direct injury," a necessary component under Article III. In addition, the Court found that the *Frothingham* analysis was based largely on an outdated policy of judicial restraint. As a result, the Court undertook a new examination of the standing limitations on taxpayers.

In an opinion written by Chief Justice Earl Warren, the Court created a two-part "nexus test" to determine whether the taxpayers in *Flast* demonstrated a sufficient stake in the outcome to satisfy Article III standing requirements. First, there must be a logical link between the status asserted by the plaintiff and the legislation attacked. Second, there must be a connection (nexus) between the status of the litigant and the nature of the constitutional infringement.

The plaintiffs in *Flast* met both these criteria. As taxpayers, they were challenging the disbursement of funds under the Taxing and Spending Clause of Article I, Section 8, of the Constitution, thereby asserting a sufficient relationship between themselves and the challenged legislation. However, the Court warned that a taxpayer would not be allowed to challenge spending merely incidental to a regulatory program; instead, the challenge must be to an expenditure made directly pursuant to the Taxing and Spending Clause. The second and more difficult part of the test required a specific constitutional limitation on the exercise of the power asserted. The Court found such a limitation on the taxing and spending power imbedded in the history of the Establishment and Free Exercise Clauses of the First Amendment. Historical analysis revealed that the Framers intended to provide a check against majoritarian abuse of the taxing and spending power in aid of religion. Because the Establishment Clause specifically limits the taxing and spending power under Article I, Section 8, and because the plaintiffs challenged a breach of this limitation, the Court found that the plaintiffs met the second part of its nexus test. The Court specifically declined comment on the substantive merits of the appellants' claims.

Three justices filed concurrences in *Flast.* Justice William O. Douglas argued for complete rejection of the *Frothingham* standard, rather than simply making an exception when a taxpayer is able to demonstrate the necessary criteria. Justice Stewart confined his analysis to the facts of the case, i.e., where a federal taxpayer has standing to challenge the validity of a specific expenditure on the ground that it violates the Establishment Clause of the First Amendment. Justice Fortas agreed with Justice Stewart that the case should not be used "as a launching pad for an attack upon any target other than legislation affecting the Establishment Clause." Justice Harlan dissented. He found the majority's reasoning erroneous and urged that the Court not abandon the *Frothingham* prohibition against federal taxpayers' suits.

The Court's decision in *Flast* provided a necessary modification in the doctrine of standing. If the Court had ruled that a plaintiff in his or her capacity as taxpayer could never demonstrate a direct injury from unconstitutional expenditures of federal funds, all "unconstitutional" appropriations under the taxing and spending power would be immune from judicial review. The two-part test developed by the *Flast* Court creates a useful balance. The *Flast* test grants standing only to certain taxpayers, preventing an overflow of taxpayer suits in federal court while preserving the Framers' intent to keep religion and government appropriations separate. As Lawrence Tribe has noted, "The only way to understand . . . the Court's conclusion in *Flast v. Cohen,* is to recognize in the religion clauses a fundamental personal right not to be part of a community whose official organs endorse religious views that might be fundamentally inimical to one's deepest beliefs."

Laurilyn A. Goettsch

Bibliography

"Recent Cases, Constitutional Law—Standing—Federal Taxpayer Has Standing to Challenge Federal Expenditures Violating Specific Constitutional Prohibition." 21 *Vanderbilt Law Review* 850–854 (1968).

"The Supreme Court, 1967 Term," 82 *Harvard Law Review* 63–317 (1968).

Tribe, Lawrence, *American Constitutional Law,* 2nd ed. (Mineola, N.Y.: Foundation Press, 1988).

Cases Cited

Flast v. Cohen, 392 U.S. 83 (1968).

Frothingham v. Mellon, 262 U.S. 447 (1923).

Founders and Religion

The federal Constitutional Convention met in Philadelphia in 1787 from May 25 through September 17. During the nearly four months of debate the subject of religion was brought up only a few times, and in no instance did a member propose a national religious establishment. In fact, after observing on June 28 that "4 or five weeks of close attendance & continual reasonings" on the issue of representation had produced so thorough a deadlock that the convention itself seemed threatened, Benjamin Franklin proposed that "prayers imploring the assistance of

Heaven, . . . be held . . . every morning before we proceed to business." Following a brief discussion in which "only three or four persons" spoke in support of Franklin's motion, members adjourned without voting. The idea was never mentioned again.

Most delegates seemed to agree with South Carolina's Charles Pinckney, who, in a speech on June 25, described the opportunity before the convention in the following words: "Our situation appears to me to be this—a new, extensive country containing within itself, the materials of forming a government capable of extending to its citizens all the blessings of civil & religious liberty." The Founders' unwillingness to use the federal Constitution to protect or establish religion in the new nation is explained by the role of religion during the colonial history of the country, by the way in which religion had been treated in the state constitutions since the Revolution, and by the founding generation's visions of both religion and government.

America's geographic isolation and the initial isolation of each community within America were partly responsible for preventing the establishment of a national religion. John Winthrop and his Puritan coreligionists left England specifically to get beyond the reach of the Church of England. These early colonists were as firmly dedicated to the idea of governing their own churches as they were to governing their own communities. Although they initially were quite willing and even eager to establish close and supportive relations between church and state, the increasing secularization and advancing diversity of colonial society during the eighteenth century weakened these ties markedly.

The American Revolution—although fought for many different reasons—brought demands for enhanced political, economic, and religious rights and liberties to the fore. Not surprisingly, then, when the newly independent states turned to writing constitutions in the summer and fall of 1776, virtually every one contained a bill of rights that promised religious freedom to citizens. Virginia led the way in its June 12, 1776, *Declaration of Rights.* Section 16 read: "That religion, or the duty which we owe to our CREATOR, and the manner of discharging it, can be directed only by reason and conviction, not by force or violence; and therefore all men are equally entitled to the free exercise of religion, according to the dictates of conscience; and that it is the mutual duty of all to practice Christian forbearance, love, and charity, toward each other." Five other states—Delaware, Maryland, New Jersey, Pennsylvania, and North Carolina—enacted similar provisions before the year was out, and most others followed soon thereafter.

Section 2 of Delaware's *Declaration of Rights and Fundamental Rules* read: "That all men have a natural and unalienable Right to worship Almighty God according to the Dictates of their own Consciences and Understanding." The *Declaration of Rights* contained in the Maryland Constitution of 1776 read: "That, as it is the duty of every man to worship God in such a manner as he thinks most acceptable to him; all persons, professing the Christian religion, are equally entitled to protection of their religious liberty." New Jersey provided "[t]hat no person shall ever, within this Colony, be deprived of the inestimable privilege of worshipping Almighty God in a manner agreeable to the dictates of his own conscience." North Carolina promised "[t]hat all men have a natural and unalienable right to worship Almighty God according to the dictates of their own consciences."

Very similar language appeared in almost every state constitution that was written in 1776 and 1777. Established state religions that sought actively to prohibit the practice of other religions were rapidly becoming a thing of the past in the new nation.

Nonetheless, most of the same state constitutions that proclaimed religious liberty also contained provisions that limited full religious freedom to—in the words of the Delaware and Maryland declarations—"Persons professing the Christian religion." The New Jersey Constitution, for example, declared "[t]hat there shall be no establishment of any one religious sect in this Province." However, it then went on to say "that all persons, professing a belief in the faith of any Protestant sect, . . . shall be capable of being elected into any office of profit or trust." The North Carolina Constitution, just before declaring "no establishment," declared "[t]hat no person, who shall deny the being of God or the truth of the Protestant religion, or the divine authority of either of the Old or New Testaments . . . shall be capable of holding any office or place of trust or profit in the civil department within this State." The Pennsylvania Constitution contained similar language.

Therefore, the issue before the Constitutional Convention was never whether to establish a national religion in America. Rather, the question was whether religious tests of any kind—even of adherence to Protestantism broadly understood—would be permitted under the national Constitution. Not surprisingly, concerned Catholics and Jews waited nervously as the convention deliberated. After more than three months of silence, Jonas Phillips, on behalf of "the people called Jews of the City of Philadelphia," wrote to the president and members of the convention to plead that "the natural and unalienable Right To worship almighty God according to the dictates of their own Conscience and understanding" be fully respected in the new Constitution. Although this plea came too late to affect the work of the convention, it did reflect the concern that all non-Protestants felt about how a more powerful national government might treat their still-unrealized right to religious liberty free from political discrimination.

Of all the delegates attending the convention, Charles Pinckney and James Madison were most determined to ensure that a religious test would not be permitted. On Monday, August 20, 1787—three months into the debates of the convention—the members unanimously passed and sent to the Committee of Detail a long list of propositions authored by Charles Pinckney. Included among Pinckney's proposals was one requiring that "[n]o religious test or qualification shall ever be annexed to any oath of office under the authority of the United States." With the Constitution nearly finished, the Committee of Detail was charged to put the resolutions accepted to date in appropriate form and to report to the full convention about issues that remained unresolved. The report of the Committee of Detail did not contain Pinckney's prohibition against religious tests. Therefore, Pinckney proposed on August 30 that Article XX of the Committee of Detail report, which declared that "[t]he Members of the Legislatures, and the executive and judicial officers of the United States, and of the several States, shall be bound by oath to support this Constitution," be amended to add the clause "no religious test shall ever be required as a qualification to any office or public trust under the authority of the United States." The only debate that followed Pinckney's suggestion was a remark by Roger Sherman that this prohibition was "unnecessary, the prevailing liberality being a sufficient security against such tests." Nonetheless, Pinckney's motion was approved without a recorded vote, and it now appears nearly verbatim as part of Article VI of the U.S. Constitution.

Following the convention's final adjournment, Maryland's Luther Martin, a disgruntled former member of the convention, commented on the sparse attention given to the explicit protection of religion in the proposed Constitution; his extensive critique was entitled *Genuine Information.* In Section 100 of this broadside against the convention's work, Martin admitted that "[t]he part of the system which provides, that *no religious test* shall ever be required as a qualification to any office or public trust under the United States, was adopted by a great majority of the convention, and without much debate." He went on to complain that a few members, himself included, had wanted a restriction to Christians, such as that commonly found in the state constitutions. Martin wrote that "there were some members *so unfashionable* as to think, that *a belief of the existence of a deity,* and of a *state of future rewards and punishments* would be some security for the good conduct of our rules, and that, in a Christian country, it would be *at least decent* to hold out some distinction between the professors of Christianity and downright infidelity or paganism."

Yet no antiestablishment clause—no explicit statement separating religion from the federal government—was written into the Constitution. The reason for this seeming oversight is the same reason that prominent Founders often used to deny the need for a bill of rights. Many thought that explicit protection for religion from the national government was simply unnecessary. The Constitution provided for a limited government of enumerated powers. The Constitution never gave the national government power over religion, and so any protection from abuses of that power was considered to be redundant. Edmund Randolph, in answer to an allegation by Patrick Henry that the

Constitution did not provide for the protection of religious freedom, replied that nowhere in the Constitution was the national government given any power to legislate on religious matters. James Madison, the future father of the national Bill of Rights, also felt that Congress had no power over religious matters. The establishment of the national government did not alter the power of the state constitutions. Because the state constitutions and bills of rights were still in operation, the insertion of a religious freedom clause in the Constitution was felt by many to be unnecessary.

In addition, many Americans felt there was no need to worry about a national establishment of religion because of the plurality of religious sects in the country. America included dozens of different Christian sects and a small population of Jews. This plurality made an established national religion impractical as well as improbable. Randolph employed precisely this argument to assuage doubts expressed in Virginia's ratifying convention that the Constitution did not do enough to secure freedom of religion. Randolph said: "I am a friend of a variety of sects, because they keep one another in order. . . . And there are so many now in the United States that they will prevent the establishment of any one sect in prejudice to the rest, and will forever oppose all attempts to infringe religious liberty."

Thus the Founders arrived at the Constitutional Convention with no intention to give the national government power over religion. Although religion played a major role in most of the Founders' lives, they did not intend for the national government to interfere with it. They believed also that to combine religion and government would belittle and corrupt both. The Constitution was based on separating power to prevent its misuse, and the absence of any religious establishment is merely a logical extension of that system. Thus, the aim of the men who attended the Constitutional Convention was to join the states into a viable government. Neither restraining nor establishing religion was seen as the proper role for government; that role was to be left with the states and, ultimately, with the people.

Calvin Jillson
Michelle Dye Neumann

Bibliography

Alley, Robert S., *James Madison on Religious Liberty* (New York: Prometheus, 1985).

Bradley, Gerard V., *Church–State Relationships in America* (New York: Greenwood, 1987).

Farrand, Max, *The Records of the Federal Convention of 1787* (New Haven, Conn.: Yale University Press, 1966).

Finkelman, Paul, "Religious Liberty and the Quincentennary: Old World Intolerance, New World Realities, and Modern Implications," 7 *St. Johns Journal of Legal Commentary* 523–559 (1992).

———, "James Madison and the Bill of Rights: A Reluctant Paternity," 1990 *Supreme Court Review* 301–347 (1991).

Hunter, James D., and Os Guiness, *Articles of Faith, Articles of Peace* (Washington, D.C.: Brookings Institution, 1990).

Lee, Francis Graham, *Wall of Controversy: Church–State Conflict in America* (Malabar, Fla.: Krieger Publishing, 1986).

Levy, Leonard W., *Essays on American Constitutional History* (Chicago: Quadrangle, 1972).

Lieberman, Jethro K., *The Enduring Constitution* (New York: Harper and Row, 1987).

York, Neil L., *Toward a More Perfect Union: Six Essays on the Constitution* (New York: State University of New York Press, 1988).

Free Exercise Clause in Historical Perspective: The "New" American Philosophy of Religious Pluralism

In modern legal thinking, freedom of religion tends to be assimilated into the familiar framework of Lockean liberal individualism. This denies the singularity of religion in life and, more particularly, in political life. Under this view, the Free Exercise Clause of the First Amendment presents a puzzle: Why should religion receive special protection? Is this not an unjustified preference for religion and, hence, a violation of the Establishment Clause itself?

This prevailing understanding of religious liberty, however, is ahistorical. It ignores the important role of religious ideas and evangelical religious movements in the framing of the Free Exercise Clause. An understanding of the historical roots of the Free Exercise Clause suggests a conception of the relation between religion and government that emphasizes the integrity and diversity of religious life rather than the secularism of the state.

Religious Freedom in the Colonies

There were four main approaches to religious liberty in the American colonies. At one extreme were the Puritans of New England. Their system was profoundly democratic, based on their congregational organization, but it was also rigid and intolerant. Dissenters, including Baptists Roger Williams and Anne Hutchinson, were expelled from the colony. Dissenters who persisted in returning to Massachusetts were flogged and, as with four Quakers, sometimes executed. Although the Puritans stopped violent repression of religious dissenters by 1680, the established church and the hostility to religious diversity continued in New England well into the nineteenth century.

In Virginia the Church of England was established by order of the Crown and was maintained, in large part, as an instrument of social control by the governing authorities and the local gentry. Both New England and Virginia, then, combined church and state, but there the similarity ends. In New England the primary impetus was theological, and the state was in service of true religion; in Virginia the primary impetus was political and economic, and the church was in service of the social order. For the first century of its existence the Virginia establishment required little overt coercion, since few dissenters ventured into the colony. In the eighteenth century, however, waves of newcomers—Presbyterians, at first, but Baptists and a few Quakers, later—began to stream into the colony, which in response became more intolerant. During the eighteenth century, Virginia was the most intolerant of the colonies; its model spread to Maryland and throughout the southern colonies, albeit in less intolerant forms.

The third approach to religious liberty might be described as benign neglect. In New York and New Jersey a policy of de facto religious toleration evolved, primarily because of the area's extraordinary religious diversity.

Finally, there were those colonies which were explicitly established as havens for religious dissenters: Maryland (Roman Catholic), Rhode Island (Baptist), and Delaware and Pennsylvania (Quaker). In addition, Carolina provided a haven for religious dissenters because of its founders' commitment to enlightenment and Lockean concepts of toleration.

Maryland, founded by the Catholic nobleman Lord Baltimore, was the first haven for dissenters. After 1689, however, the proprietor was removed, and the Protestant majority in Maryland established the Church of England and initiated a program of discrimination and intolerance toward dissenters, particularly Roman Catholics, for whose benefit the colony was originally founded. In the eighteenth century, in fact, Maryland rivaled Virginia in its repression of religious dissenters.

Charters obtained by the proprietors or founders of the Rhode Island, Carolina, and New Jersey colonies were almost identical and were the most expansive of the day. The language of these early free exercise provisions did not survive in North Carolina, South Carolina, or New Jersey—it was superseded by later (and more limited) religious freedom provisions—but the substance of these provisions later reemerged as the most common pattern in the constitutions adopted by the states after the Revolution.

The Rhode Island Charter of 1663 was the first to use the formulation "liberty of conscience." The depth and breadth of Rhode Island's commitment to religious freedom was unparalleled until after the American Revolution, but it is unlikely that the colony's provisions had much direct influence on subsequent developments of the free exercise principle. The writings of its founder, Roger Williams, were lost until 1773. Moreover, Rhode Island was the pariah among the colonies, with a reputation for disorder and instability.

In practice the most influential examples of religious pluralism were the middle colonies, where no church was established (except in the four counties of metropolitan New York) and where the widest range of religious persuasions lived in relative harmony. William Penn's colonies were particularly associated with religious freedom and harmony because of Penn's widely read work *The Great Case of Liberty of Conscience* (1670). Under his 1701 Charters of Privileges, Pennsylvania and Delaware protected the religious profession of all theists, although they confined public office to Christians. This example caught the eye of statesmen in other colonies. Pennsylvania's promise of toleration contributed to the highest level of immigration of any of the colonies, and with immigration came prosperity.

The movement for freedom of religion in the 1780s was part of a broad reaction against the dominant but uninspired religious cultures represented by the Congregationalists in New England and by the Anglicans in the south. It is a mistake to read the religion clauses under the now-prevalent assumption that deism or natural law dominated the intellectual scene in the late eighteenth century. Quite the contrary, America was in the wake of a great religious revival, and the drive for religious freedom, at both the state and federal levels, was part of this evangelistic movement.

Religious Freedom in the States

The Revolution inspired a wave of constitution writing in the new states. Eleven of the thirteen states (plus Vermont) adopted new constitutions between 1776 and 1780. Of those eleven, six (plus Vermont) included an explicit bill of rights; three more states adopted a bill of rights between 1781 and 1790. With the exception of Connecticut, by 1789 every state, with or without an establishment, had a constitutional provision protecting religious freedom, although two states confined their protections to Christians, and five others confined protections to theists. A number of states had religious tests for office, reflecting the widespread view that toleration required an equality of civil but not of political rights.

There was no discernible difference between the free exercise provisions adopted by states that had an establishment and those without one. The free exercise clauses of Massachusetts and New Hampshire were almost identical to those of New Jersey, Pennsylvania, and Delaware. Freedom of religion was universally said to be an inalienable right; the status of other rights commonly found in state bills of rights—relating to property or trial by jury, for example—was more disputed and was often considered derivative of civil society.

Because it is reasonable to infer that those who drafted and adopted the First Amendment assumed that the term "free exercise of religion" meant what it had meant in their states, these state constitutional provisions provide the most direct evidence of the original understanding. Each of the state constitutions first defined the scope of the free exercise right in terms of the conscience of the individual believer and the actions that flow from that conscience. None of the provisions confined the protection to beliefs and opinions (as Jefferson advocated), nor to expression of beliefs and opinions. Indeed, the language appears to have been drafted precisely to refute those interpretations. Nor did these constitutions follow the British political philosophy of John Locke in defining the scope of free exercise negatively, as a sphere of otherworldly concern that does not affect the public interest. The free exercise provisions defined the free exercise right affirmatively, based on the scope of duties to God perceived by the believer.

Although the free exercise right plainly extends to some forms of conduct, the scope of protected conduct in these clauses is less clear. The provisions fall into two categories. Four states (Virginia, Georgia, Maryland, and Rhode Island) protected all actions stemming from religious conviction, subject to certain limitations. The Virginia Declaration of Rights (1776)—the model for three of the state proposals for the First Amendment and presumably the greatest influence on Madison—is especially clear on this point. It provides that "all men are equally entitled to the free exercise of religion, according to the dictates of conscience," and it defines "religion" as "the duty which we owe to our Creator, and the manner of discharging it." In the biblical tradition, "duties" to God included actions, perhaps all of life, and not just speech and opinion. So, according to Virginia, the right of free exercise extended to all of a believer's duties to God and included a choice of means as well as ends. By contrast, eight states (New York, New Hampshire, Delaware, Massachusetts, New Jersey, North Carolina, Pennsylvania, and South Carolina) and the Northwest Ordinance confined their protection of conduct to acts of "worship."

The limitation to acts of worship, however, was not carried over into the federal Free Exercise Clause, which imitated the most expansive models among the states. No direct evidence suggests whether the adoption of the broader formulation was deliberate, but this seems consistent with the general theological currents of Protestant America, which were "low church" and antiritualistic and thus were less likely to view religious obligation in terms of "worship," narrowly understood. The ready availability of narrow models in the recently enacted Northwest Ordinance and in the Constitution of Massachusetts (the home state of Fisher Ames, the final drafter of the federal Free Exercise Clause) makes it likely that the choice of broader language was deliberate.

Indeed, even in the states that apparently limited free exercise to acts of worship, it is not clear that the limitation had any actual effect. In none of the state free exercise cases during the early years of the Republic did the lawyers argue or the courts hold that religiously motivated conduct was unprotected because it was not "worship." Since the scope and nature of religious duty were contested issues among religions, it seems unlikely that the state provisions intended to interject a judicial discrimination among forms of religious practice—and especially unlikely that this interjection would favor ritual over pious conduct.

In any event, it would be difficult on this evidence to conclude that the Framers of the Free Exercise Clause intended it to be confined to acts of worship. That would require the assumption that Fisher Ames and the First Congress accidentally failed to use familiar language that would have precisely expressed their meaning and adopted instead new language that went beyond their intentions. Either the broader meaning was intended, or no thought was given to the matter at all.

Another common element in state free exercise provisions is that the provisions limited the right by particular, defined state interests. Typical was Article LVI of Georgia's Constitution of 1777: "All persons whatever shall have the free exercise of their religion; provided it be not repugnant to the peace and safety of the State." New York, New Hampshire, Georgia, Delaware, Maryland, Massachusetts, New Jersey, Rhode Island, and South Carolina limited the free exercise right to actions that were "peaceable" or that would not disturb the "peace" or "safety" of the state. New York, Maryland, Rhode Island, and South Carolina also expressly disallowed acts of licentiousness or immorality; New Hampshire and Massachusetts forbade acts that would interfere with the religious practices of others; Rhode Island forbade the "civil injury or outward disturbance of others"; Maryland added acts contrary to "good order"; and Delaware disallowed acts contrary to the "happiness" or which "disturb the Peace, the Happiness or Safety of Society."

These provisos are the most revealing and important feature of the state constitutions. They strongly suggest that the free exercise provisions themselves contemplated religiously compelled exemptions from at least some generally applicable laws (those not needed to protect the public "peace and safety," or other particularly important types of laws). Because even according to the Lockean no-exemptions view religious persons cannot be prohibited from engaging in otherwise legal activities, the provisos would only have effect if religiously motivated conduct violated the general laws in some way. The "peace and safety" provisos can be seen as roughly equivalent to the modern constitutional formulation that a burden on the free exercise of religion may be justified only by a "compelling governmental purpose."

Some historians dispute this interpretation of the "peace and safety" provisos, maintaining that they authorized a complete withdrawal of free exercise rights from any religious denomination whose teaching was deemed to be contrary to the public peace or safety. Although this is linguistically plausible, there is no evidence of actual practice consistent with this interpretation, whereas the practice of conferring religious exemptions was relatively common.

The principal sources of conflict between civil law and religious conviction at this time centered on oath requirements, military conscription, and religious assessments. In each of these contexts, religious minorities struggled and eventually succeeded in winning exemptions in many of the states. The right of religious exemption from compulsory military service is a particularly telling example. Not only was this right recognized by almost every state, but it also was protected by the Continental Congress during the Revolution and was almost included in the proposals for a federal bill of rights passed by the House of Representatives (only to be rejected by the Senate).

Of course, the general congruence between religious beliefs and general social mores meant that the occasions when religious conscience came into conflict with generally applicable secular legislation were few. But the resolution of these conflicts suggests that exemptions were seen as natural and legitimate responses to the tension between law and religious convictions. Rather than making oaths, military service, and tithes voluntary for everyone, and rather than coercing the consciences of otherwise loyal and law-abiding citizens who were bound by religious duty not to comply, the colonies and states wrote special exemptions into their laws. The wording of the early state constitutions suggests—though it does not dispositively prove—that the idea of exemptions was part of what was meant by "free exercise of religion."

Religious Freedom in the Republic

The original Constitution drafted by the convention in 1787 and ratified by the states in 1788 contained no provisions protecting the general freedom of religion. It was not, however, entirely silent about religion. Two provisions of the Constitution reflect a spirit and purpose similar to that of the Free Exercise Clause: the prohibition on religious tests for office (Article VI) and the allowance of affirmations in lieu of oaths (Articles I, II, and VI). Both provisions were designed to prevent restrictions hostile to particular religions and thus to make the government of the United States more religiously inclusive. Neither provision, however, used the device of a religion-specific exemption, nor was either sufficient to assuage the concerns of America's religious sects, for whom only a bill of rights would do.

If the principal danger to religious liberty was the deliberate oppression of religious minorities by the majority, then James Madison's vision of a large republic with competing groups holding one another in check offered a powerful answer to those who demanded a free exercise clause. This is because in a nation of many different religious groups, each jealous of the others, it would be difficult if not impossible for any group to impose its beliefs on the others. Thus the Federalists argued that no bill of rights and no free exercise clause was necessary.

The Federalists' argument, however, did not carry the day. This is perhaps because Madison's large republic model did not satisfy the concerns of those who feared the unintended effects of legislation passed without regard to the religious scruples of small minorities, rather than deliberate oppression. The multiplicity of sects itself provides no protection against ignorance or indifference. Indeed, the position of religious minorities might have been much worse. Because settlements of minorities tended to be concentrated in particular regions, most sects had greater influence at the state than at the national level. The same extended republic that might protect minority faiths against oppression also might make them more vulnerable to thoughtless general legislation.

Whatever the reason, the religious minorities of America—especially the "enthusiastic" Protestant sects, such as the Baptists—pressed for express constitutional protection. In response, Madison wrote to the Baptist leader George Eve in January 1789, pledging to his Baptist constituents that he would work for "the most satisfactory provisions for all essential rights, particularly the rights of Conscience in the fullest latitude." Lawmakers in other states responded to similar public pressure and drafted proposals for amendments. Five of the state ratifying conventions (plus the minority report in Pennsylvania) urged protection for religious freedom. These conventions, with one exception, employed the language free "exercise" of "religion," borrowing from the Virginia Declaration of Rights.

The recorded debates in the House over these proposals centered on establishment questions and thus cast little light on the meaning of the Free Exercise Clause. Instead we must rely primarily on successive drafts of the clause during its passage through the First Congress. Rejecting the model of the state proposals, Madison drafted the following formulation: "The civil rights of none shall be abridged on account of religious belief or worship [n]or shall any national religion be established, nor shall the full and equal rights of conscience be in any manner, nor on any pretext, infringed."

Three aspects of this proposal are suggestive. First, the formulation "full and equal rights of conscience" implies that the liberty has both a substantive and an equality component: The rights must be both "full" and "equal." Hence, the liberty of conscience is entitled not only to equal protection but also to some absolute measure of protection apart from mere governmental neutrality.

Second, the formulation that the rights in question shall not "in any manner nor on any pretext be infringed" suggests protection from infringements in any form, even those not expressly directed at religious practice.

Third, Madison favored the formulation "rights of conscience" over the formulation "free exercise of religion." This choice of language was ultimately reversed by the House and the Senate.

Rather than debating Madison's proposal, the Select Committee proposed a much shorter version: "no religion shall be established by law, nor shall the equal rights of conscience be infringed." The committee deleted Madison's reference to "civil rights," probably because it was redundant, and shortened his "full and equal rights of conscience" to "equal rights of conscience." If this change was more than stylistic, it emphasizes equal treatment rather than full substantive protection.

The Select Committee language ran into trouble in the House, largely because of concerns that its establishment provision might interfere with the ability of states to support religion. After a brief flirtation with language proposed by New Hampshire ("Congress shall make no laws touching religion, or to infringe the rights of conscience"), the House adopted a formulation proposed by Fisher Ames of Massachusetts: "Congress shall make no law establishing religion, or to prevent the free exercise thereof, or to infringe the rights of conscience." The House approved the amendment as proposed by Ames without recorded debate or discussion. Both the House and the Senate journals record that the House passed and sent to the Senate a proposed amendment slightly different from the Ames proposal using the verb "prohibiting" instead of Ames's actual term, "prevent." This was the version that was considered by the Senate and that ultimately was employed in the First Amendment.

In the Senate the debate was not recorded, but various versions of the religion clauses were adopted and rejected in succession. Each of these versions used either the phrase "rights of conscience" or the phrase "free exercise of religion" (not both, as in the Ames proposal). The Senate ultimately adopted a version that read: "Congress shall make no law establishing articles of faith or a mode of worship, or prohibiting the free exercise of religion."

The House rejected the Senate's version, presumably because of its narrow provision on establishment. A Conference Committee, on which Madison served, proposed the version of the religion clauses that was ultimately ratified. The Free Exercise Clause itself was unchanged from the final Senate bill: "Congress shall make no law respecting an establishment of religion or prohibiting the free exercise thereof."

Free Exercise: Pluralism *and* Stability

Of the many linguistic changes made during the drafting of the First Amendment, the most significant was the substitution of "free exercise of religion" for "liberty of conscience." It is theoretically possible that this had no substantive meaning, for in many of the debates in the preconstitutional period the concepts of "liberty of conscience" and "free exercise of religion" were used interchangeably, and there were no recorded debates concerning the choice of language. The fact that the Ames proposal contained both and that the Senate oscillated between drafts containing the two different terms, however, strongly suggests that the linguistic decision was understood as important. There are three principal differences between the terms.

The least ambiguous difference is that the term "free exercise" makes clear that the clause protects religiously motivated conduct as well as belief. This casts doubt on the U.S. Supreme Court's later insistence on a belief–conduct distinction, with conduct receiving only secondary protection. A second important difference is that "conscience" emphasizes individual judgment, whereas "religion" also encompasses the corporate or institutional aspects of religious belief. The third, and most controversial, difference between the "free exercise of religion" and the "rights of conscience" is that the latter might seem to extend to claims of conscience based on something other than religion, such as belief systems based on political ideology or secular moral philosophy. By deleting references to "conscience," in other words, the final version of the First Amendment singles out religion for special treatment.

The textual insistence on the special status of "religion" is rooted in the prevailing understandings, both religious and philosophical, of the difference between religious faith and other forms of human judgment. Not until the second third of the nineteenth century did the notion that the opinions of individuals have precedence over the decisions of civil society gain currency in American thought. In 1789 most would have agreed with Locke in *A Letter Concerning Toleration* (1689) that "the private judgment of any person concerning a law enacted in political matters, for the public good, does not take away the obligation of that law, nor deserve a dispensation."

Religious convictions were of a different order. Conflicts arising from religious convictions were conceived of not as a clash between the judgment of the individual and of the state but as a conflict between earthly and spiritual sovereigns. The believer was not seen as the instigator of the conflict; the believer was simply caught between the inconsistent demand of two rightful authorities. Not only were the spiritual and earthly authorities envisioned as independent, but in the nature of things the spiritual authorities also had a superior claim. As Madison put it in *Memorial and Remonstrance against Religious Assessments* (1785):

> It is the duty of every man to render to the Creator such homage and such only as he believes to be acceptable to him. This duty is precedent both in order of time and degree of obligation to the claims of Civil Society. The duties to God are precedent both in time and also in importance. Before any man can be considered as a member of Civil Society, he must be considered as a subject of the Governor of the Universe: And if a member of Civil Society who enters into any subordinate Association, must also do it with a reservation of his duty to the general authority; much more must every man who becomes a member of any particular Civil Society do it with a saving of his allegiance to the Universal Sovereign.

The Free Exercise Clause accords a special, protected status to religious conscience not because religious judgments are better, truer, or more likely to be moral than nonreligious judgments are but because the obligations entailed by religion transcend the individual and are outside the individual's control. As John Locke wrote in his third letter on toleration, the "magistrates of the world" thus have no authority to coerce individuals on account of religious opinion, for in this sphere they can have no basis for action other than "their own belief, their own persuasion," which is as likely to support the false as the true religion.

In contrast to Jefferson, Madison grasped that the United States was not amenable to Enlightenment solutions: Religious sectarianism will not go away, nor should it. Madison's contribution was to understand factions, including religious factions, as a source of peace and stability. If there are enough factions, they will check and balance one another and frustrate attempts to monopolize or oppress—no matter how intolerant or fanatical any particular sect may be. This position is consistent with an aggressive interpretation of the Free Exercise Clause, which protects the interests of religious minorities in conflict with the wider society and thereby encourages the proliferation of religious factions. In other words, as the organizing principle of church–state relations, the Madisonian perspective points toward pluralism rather than toward assimilation, ecumenism, or secularism. The happy result of the Madisonian solution is to achieve *both* the unrestrained practice of religion in accordance with conscience (the desire of the religious "sects") *and* the control of religious warfare and oppression (the goal of the Enlightenment).

In this sense, the Free Exercise Clause may well be the most philosophically distinctive feature of the American Constitution. Viewed in its historical light—as the product of religious pluralism and intense religious sectarianism in the American states and colonies, with some influence from the rationalistic Enlightenment—the Free Exercise Clause represents a new and unprecedented conception of government and its relation to claims of higher truth and authority. Government is understood as a subordinate association in the most profound sense, for the Constitution recognizes the authority of the divine will while also recognizing that government is incompetent to determine what particular conception of the divine is authoritative. Even the democratic will of the people is, in principle, subordinate to the commands of God, as heard and understood in the individual conscience. In such a nation, with such a commitment, totalitarian tyranny is a philosophical impossibility.

Michael McConnell

Bibliography

Adams, Arlin, and Charles Emmerich, "A Heritage of Religious Liberty," 137 *University of Pennsylvania Law Review* 1559–1671 (1989).

Berns, Walter, *The First Amendment and the Future of American Democracy* (New York: Basic Books, 1976; Chicago: Gateway reprint, 1985).

Cobb, Sanford H., *The Rise of Religious Liberty in America* (New York: Macmillan, 1902).

Curry, Thomas J., *The First Freedoms: Church and State in America to the Passage of the First Amendment* (New York: Oxford University Press, 1986).

Finkelman, Paul, "Religious Liberty and the Quincentennary: Old World Intolerance, New World Realities, and Modern Implications," 7 *St. Johns Journal of Legal Commentary* 523–529 (1992).

———, "James Madison and the Bill of Rights: A Reluctant Paternity," 1990 *Supreme Court Review* 301–347 (1991).

Hamburger, Philip A., "A Constitutional Right of Religious Exemption: An Historical Perspective," 60 *George Washington Law Review* 915–948 (1992).

Howe, Mark De Wolf, *The Garden and the Wilderness* (Chicago: University of Chicago Press, 1965).

Kurland, Philip B., "The Origins of the Religion Clauses of the Constitution," 27 *William and Mary Law Review* 839–861 (1986).

Malbin, Michael J., *Religion and Politics: The Intentions of the Authors of the First Amendment* (Washington, D.C.: American Enterprise Institute for Public Policy Research, 1978).

McConnell, Michael W., The Origins and Historical Understanding of Free Exercise of Religion, 103 *Harvard Law Review* 1409–1517 (1990).

Friedman v. Board of County Commissioners of Bernalillo County 781 F. 2d 777 (1985)

Friedman v. Board of County Commissioners of Bernalillo County (N. Mex., 1985) involved the issue of whether the official seal of a New Mexico county violated the First Amendment's Establishment Clause. The Bernalillo County seal included a Latin cross beneath the Spanish motto "Con Ésta Vencemos" ("With This We Conquer" or "With This We Overcome"). Set against a blue background representing the sky, the motto and the cross stood above four darker-blue mountains and a green plain; eight white sheep stood on the plain. Although the precise origins of the symbol were unknown, the county used the seal as early as 1925 on some documents, and beginning in 1973 the seal appeared on all official records, stationery, motor vehicles, and sheriffs' uniforms. After residents filed an action seeking an injunction to prevent use of the seal, a U.S. district court ruled that the emblem violated neither the Establishment Clause nor the Free Exercise Clause of the First Amendment. A three-judge panel of the Tenth Circuit Court of Appeals affirmed the lower court's decision, but the entire seven-member court subsequently reheard the case.

The full court reversed the panel's earlier decision and held that the county's use of the seal did indeed violate the Establishment Clause. Writing for the majority, Judge James K. Logan, appointed by President Jimmy Carter in 1977, applied the three-pronged *Lemon* test to determine whether or not the county's use of the seal constituted an Establishment Clause violation. Under this test—established by the U.S. Supreme Court in *Lemon v. Kurtzman* (1971)—if the governmental action in question has a secular purpose, if its principal or primary effect "neither advances nor inhibits" religion, and if the action does not foster excessive government entanglement with religion, then the measure does not violate the Establishment Clause. Failure to satisfy all three of these requirements renders the action unconstitutional.

According to Judge Logan, the key in the *Friedman* case was the district court's finding on the second prong of the *Lemon* test—the so-called effect test. In interpreting this aspect of *Lemon,* Logan followed Justice Sandra Day O'Connor's concurring opinion in *Lynch v. Donnelly* (1985), a case involving a local government's Christmas display of a crèche, or nativity scene. In *Lynch* Justice O'Connor contended that the second prong of the *Lemon* test rendered impermissible any governmental action that an average observer perceived as an endorsement of religion. "If the challenged practice is likely to be interpreted as advancing religion," Logan reasoned, echoing O'Connor, "it has an impermissible effect and violates the Constitution, regardless of whether it actually is intended to do so" (p. 781). The advancement of religion, continued Logan, "need not be material or tangible." Rather, "an implicit symbolic benefit" to religion was enough to render a judgment against the action in question" (p. 781). "The seal as used conveys a strong impression to the average observer that Christianity is being endorsed," Logan concluded (p. 782). The appeals court held that Bernalillo County's use of the cross and motto in its official seal advanced the Christian faith, and the judges thus reversed the district court's ruling.

The majority opinion provoked strong dissent. Two judges openly disagreed; a third, who had written the original opinion for the three-judge panel, no doubt shared their views, although he did not file a dissenting opinion. Judge James E. Barrett, a 1971 appointee of President Richard Nixon, made his objections most clear, contending that the *Lemon* test is useful only if it is applied with "common sense," taking into account the nation's rich religious heritage (p. 785). Paradoxically, the dissenters also looked to *Lynch* to support their position, for the Supreme Court had upheld the display of the crèche because of its historical and cultural importance. "Here, too, the display of the Christian symbol of the Cross," Barrett argued, "in combination with the secular symbols, has deep historical and cultural significance to Bernalillo County." Citing various forms of permissible interaction between church and state—including opening prayers at public school graduations and sessions of the U.S. Congress—Judge Barrett criticized the majority's "easy bright-line approach for addressing constitutional issues." "We have repeatedly cautioned that *Lemon* did not establish a rigid caliper capable of resolving every Establishment Clause issue," he concluded, "but that it sought only to provide 'signposts'" (p. 786).

Friedman represented the increasingly uncertain nature of the constitutional interpretation of the religion clauses during the 1980s. Although a more conservative U.S. Supreme Court grew amenable to religious accommodation, especially with its decision in *Lynch*, at least some members of the federal judiciary felt that the justices were perhaps moving too far in this direction. The decision in *Friedman*, therefore, stood as a clear effort by the Tenth Circuit Court of Appeals to narrow the conceivably broad implications of the Supreme Court's opinion in *Lynch*. Despite the potential conflict between these two decisions, however, the Supreme Court decided not to hear an appeal of *Friedman*.

Timothy S. Huebner

Bibliography

Cropper, Gregory, "*Friedman v. Board of County Commissioners*: Toward Rebuilding Jefferson's Wall of Separation between Church and State," 1987 *Utah Law Review* 59–78.

Posselius, Edward J., "Hiding behind the Wall: *Friedman v. Board of County Commissioners*," 64 *Denver University Law Review* 81–100 (1987).

Cases Cited

Friedman v. Board of County Commissioners of Bernalillo County, 781 F. 2d 777 (1985).

Lemon v. Kurtzman, 403 U.S. 602 (1971).

Lynch v. Donnelly, 465 U.S. 668 (1984).

Fundamental Constitutions of Carolina

In the summer of 1669 Anthony Ashley Cooper (Baron Ashley) and his secretary, the now-esteemed philosopher John Locke, drafted the Fundamental Constitutions of Carolina. Formally adopted by the Lords Proprietors of the Carolina Colony on March 1, 1670, the Fundamental Constitutions had a significant impact on the political and religious history of the proprietary province of Carolina and on the continued vitality of the royal colonies and states of North and South Carolina. The document established toleration for all religious opinion that met a tripartite test:

> (1) That there is a God.
>
> (2) That God is publicly to be worshipped.
>
> (3) That it is lawful and the duty of every man, being thereunto called by those that govern, to bear witness to truth; and that every church or profession shall in their terms of communion, set down the eternal way whereby they witness a truth as

> in the presence of God, whether it be by laying hands on or kissing the bible, as in the church of England, or by holding up the hand, or any other sensible way.

The last portion of the test was to facilitate affirmations to the truth when required in court proceedings or other occasions. Quakers, prohibited from taking an oath, would otherwise be excluded from participation in public life.

Stating the need to maintain peace despite diversity of religious opinions, the Fundamental Constitutions provided that "Jews, Heathens and other dissenters from the purity of the Christian religion" should have an opportunity to learn "the reasonableness of its doctrines" while living among Christian believers. In addition, "no person whatsoever shall disturb, molest, or persecute another, for his speculative opinions in religion, or his way of worship."

Any seven individuals meeting the three-part standard might form a church or "profession," and the terms of admission to membership and participation in worship should be set forth in a book to be kept by the public registrar of the area in which the group was formed. All residents over the age of 17 were required to belong to one such group before receiving protection of the law or access to public office. Membership in a religious group was evidenced by signing its terms of communion as maintained by the local registrar; an individual might resign from membership by striking his signature from the official registry. Religious groups that were established under these provisions were prohibited from disturbing any other group, from speaking irreverently about another group, and from uttering sedition about the government during meetings.

Before approving the Cooper-Locke draft of the Fundamental Constitutions, the proprietorial board insisted that a provision be inserted making the Church of England the established church of Carolina. The final draft therefore established the Anglican Church in the province, but it recognized and tolerated all other religious beliefs. As a consequence, individuals who were not members of the Church of England might hold public office in the colony, and dissenting congregations enjoyed legal status. Because the three-part test was the only standard to be met by a religious group, and because the test was neither Christian nor trinitarian in its requirements, the Carolina province was second only to Rhode Island in its tolerance of divergent religious opinions.

Growing numbers of Anglican settlers precipitated a crisis in regard to religious qualifications for holding office. This was the "Exclusion Crisis" of 1706, which centered on a colonial law that required membership in the Church of England as a qualification for holding public office. In the course of the dissenting party's efforts to secure repeal, a pamphlet entitled *Party-Tyranny; or, An Occasional Bill in Miniature, as Now Practiced in Carolina* was published in England. It attacked the exclusionary law as a breach of the political compact—the *Pacta Conventa*—contained in the Fundamental Constitutions. The author argued that tolerance of religious belief and the access to public office were part of the inducement that brought dissenters to the colony. Since the proprietors had breached their part of the agreement, the colony should revert to the possession of the Crown. Bowing to pressure from Carolina and from royal officials at home, the Lords Proprietors disallowed the offending statute. Thus the Fundamental Constitutions—despite its general lack of implementation as a governmental instrument—nevertheless gained prestige as a "higher law" document guaranteeing religious toleration and freer access to public office than existed in contemporary England.

Although the Church of England gained establishment in colonial South Carolina, toleration of dissenting religious belief continued. The 1778 state Constitution imposed the requirement that those who otherwise were qualified to vote should meet the broad religious requirement that they believed in God and in a future state of rewards and punishments. Although all religious groups acknowledging the existence of God and a future state of rewards and punishments were tolerated, access to office was limited to "Protestants." The 1778 South Carolina Constitution continued the Fundamental Constitutions provisions concerning the formation of independent churches and religious professions; it also perpetuated the 1670 document's provision that Quakers and others might depart from the traditional oath when their conscience required.

Herbert A. Johnson

Bibliography

Johnson, Herbert A., "The Palmetto and the Oak: Law and Constitution in Early South Carolina, 1670–1800," in Kermit L. Hall and James W. Ely, Jr. (eds.), *An Uncertain Tradition: Constitutionalism and the History of the South* (Athens: University of Georgia Press, 1989), pp. 83–101.

Sirmans, M. Eugene, *Colonial South Carolina: A Political History, 1663–1763* (Chapel Hill: University of North Carolina Press, 1966).

G

***Gay Rights Coalition of Georgetown University Law Center et al. v. Georgetown University et al.,* 536 A. 2d 1 (D.C. App. 1987)**

The Free Exercise Clause and statutorily created civil rights came into direct confrontation in *Gay Rights Coalition of Georgetown University Law Center et al. v. Georgetown University et al.* (D.C., 1987), a case in which student gay rights groups challenged the decision of Georgetown University (a private institution affiliated with the Catholic Church) not to grant the student groups official recognition.

Gay student groups at Georgetown University and the Georgetown Law Center applied for "university recognition," a status that would have allowed the groups to have a campus mailbox, to use campus services for computerized labels and mailing, and to apply for funding from the university. Both groups previously had been granted "student body endorsement" by the student government at Georgetown, a status that enabled the groups, among other things, to use the university's facilities, including campus advertising, and to apply for lecture-fund privileges. During academic years 1978–1979 and 1979–1980, the gay student groups were denied university recognition by various officials in the administration. On both occasions Georgetown—which was founded by Jesuits in 1789 and maintains an ongoing relationship with the Roman Catholic Church—reasoned that, although it did not discriminate against gay and lesbian students and would continue to make the university's facilities available to the groups for meetings and other events, it could not, consistent with the teachings of the Catholic Church that homosexual acts are morally wrong, "endorse" gay student organizations by granting them university recognition.

The student groups brought suit against Georgetown under the District of Columbia's Human Rights Act, which forbade any educational institution from denying use of its facilities or services on the basis of, among other things, sexual orientation. Georgetown offered two defenses: (1) that it was not denying university recognition "on the basis of" sexual orientation but, rather, because of the group's purposes and activities; and (2) that even if the denial were based on the sexual orientation of the students in the groups, the Free Exercise Clause of the First Amendment protected Georgetown from being forced to act contrary to its religious beliefs. The trial court ruled that, although Georgetown had violated the terms of the Human Rights Act, the Free Exercise Clause precluded the act from being applied to Georgetown.

After a panel of the District of Columbia Court of Appeals reversed the trial court and ruled that Georgetown must recognize the student groups, the complete court heard the appeal and issued seven separate opinions, none of which garnered a majority. The lead opinion, written by Judge Mack, used a Solomonic approach, severing the "tangible" benefits of university recognition (e.g., to have a campus mailbox, to use the computerized label and mailing services, and to apply for funding from the university) from the "intangible" benefit of endorsement by Georgetown. She interpreted the District of Columbia's Human Rights Act as applying only to tangible benefits, reasoning that reading the statute to require endorsement would jeopardize the constitutionality of the statute under both the Free Speech and the Free Exercise Clauses. This effectively dropped the endorsement issue out of the case. Judge Mack then found a violation of the Human Rights Act insofar as Georgetown had denied the tangible benefits to the gay student groups based on the sexual orientation of the members. Only then did she consider the university's free exercise defense.

In doing so, Judge Mack used the U.S. Supreme Court's familiar three-part test for religious accommodation cases—dating back to *Sherbert v. Verner* (1963) and *Wisconsin v. Yoder* (1972), and as recently formulated in *Bob Jones University v. United States* (1983)—to determine whether the Free Exercise Clause required that Georgetown be exempted from the statute. First she found that forcing Georgetown to comply with the Human Rights Act by providing the tangible benefits to the gay student groups would be a sufficient burden on the university's religious practice so as to invoke First Amendment protection. Next Judge Mack tackled the "novel question" of whether the District of Columbia had a compelling governmental interest in eradicating discrimination based on sexual orientation. After an extensive survey of the literature on the causes of homosexuality and the extent and effects of discrimination against homosexuals, Judge Mack concluded that the District of Columbia "acted on the most pressing of needs" when it banned discrimination on the basis of sexual orientation under the Human Rights Act and, therefore, that the requirement of compelling governmental interest was met. She then weighed the "relatively slight" burden on Georgetown's religious practice (if it provided the tangible benefits to the gay students groups) against the District of Columbia's compelling interest in eradicating discrimination based on sexual orientation, and she concluded that the governmental interest outweighed the burden on Georgetown. Last, she concluded that the enforcement of the statute against Georgetown was indeed the least-restrictive means of eradicating discrimination based on sexual orientation.

Two judges on the appeals court concurred with Judge Mack's Solomonic result. Two other judges would have held that Georgetown also was required under the Human Rights Act to grant *all* the benefits conferred by university recognition; they concluded that Judge Mack's severance of the tangible from the intangible was impractical and that, since recognition did not equal endorsement, such a result would not run afoul of the First Amendment. The final two judges concurred with Judge Mack's conclusion that the Free Exercise Clause prevented the Human Rights Act from forcing Georgetown to "endorse" the student groups, but they dissented regarding the ability of the act to force Georgetown to provide the tangible benefits, because of free speech and free exercise concerns.

The import of *Gay Rights Coalition* is limited by its scope. The opinion is significant in holding that a statute backed by the compelling interest in eradicating discrimination based on sexual orientation outweighs the burden on a religious educational institution to provide services and facilities to groups whose beliefs are counter to the institution's moral teachings. However, Judge Mack's severing of the tangible benefits from the intangible endorsement enabled the court to sidestep the more difficult issue of whether a sincere religious belief can exempt a religious group from a law that is based on a compelling interest designed to eradicate the very belief which would exempt the religious group from the law.

Ironically, the decision may be as well known for its fallout as for its actual holding. After the court of appeals decision, Georgetown University and the student groups entered into a consent decree that abided by the court's decision but that still respected the university's religious beliefs. As part of the consent decree, both sides agreed not to appeal to the U.S. Supreme Court. At this point, however, Congress got involved, via a rider to the District of Columbia's appropriations act that would have denied the District government funding unless its council overturned the *Gay Rights Coalition* decision by exempting religiously affiliated educational institutions from the Human Rights Act. The council filed suit rather than abide by the terms of the rider, and in *Clarke v. United States* (D.C., 1989) the U.S. Court of Appeals for the D.C. Circuit held that the rider violated the free speech rights of the council members. However, the victory for the council was hollow; Congress subsequently amended the

Human Rights Act itself under its Article I power to oversee the District of Columbia.

Scott T. Schutte

Bibliography

Comment, "*Georgetown Rights Coalition v. Georgetown University:* Failure to Recognize a Catholic University's Religious Liberty," 32 *Catholic Lawyer* 170 (1988).

Dutile, Fernand N., "God and Gays at Georgetown: Observations on *Gay Rights Coalition of Georgetown University Law Center v. Georgetown University,*" 15 *Journal of College and University Law* 1 (1988).

Seidman, Louis Michael, "The Preconditions for Home Rule," 39 *Catholic University Law Review* 373 (1990).

Cases Cited

Bob Jones University v. United States, 461 U.S. 574 (1983).

Clarke v. United States, 886 F. 2d 404 (D.C. Cir. 1989).

Gay Rights Coalition of Georgetown University Law Center et al. v. Georgetown University et al., 496 A. 2d 567 (D.C. 1985), panel opinion modified by 536 A. 2d 1 (D.C. App. 1987).

Sherbert v. Verner, 374 U.S. 374 (1963).

Wisconsin v. Yoder, 406 U.S. 205 (1972).

***Goldman v. Weinberger* 475 U.S. 503 (1986)**

S. Simcha Goldman was a captain in the U.S. Air Force. An Orthodox Jew and rabbi, he worked on an air base serving as a clinical psychologist. Like other Orthodox Jews, Goldman was under a religious obligation to wear a yarmulke or some other form of head covering at all times. After Goldman testified as a defense witness in a court-martial, opposing counsel complained to the hospital commander that Goldman was in violation of Air Force regulations that forbid wearing "headgear" indoors. In *Goldman v. Weinberger* (1986) Goldman argued that, as applied to him, the military regulation was a violation of his First Amendment right to free exercise of religion.

Relying on *Sherbert v. Verner* (1963) Goldman asked the Court to apply strict scrutiny to the regulation, asking whether there is a compelling state interest that cannot be achieved by a less restrictive means than the one chosen by the military. Rejecting that approach, Justice William Rehnquist wrote for the majority, which included Chief Justice Burger and a concurring opinion by Justice Stevens with which Justices White and Powell joined. Justice Brennan wrote a dissenting opinion, joined by Justice Marshall. Justice Blackmun also wrote a dissenting opinion, as did Justice O'Connor, with whom Justice Marshall joined.

Justice Rehnquist held that the Court's "review of military regulations challenged on First Amendment grounds is far more deferential than constitutional review of similar laws or regulations designed for civil society." Unlike civilian officials, Rehnquist said, military officials need not encourage or even allow debate and discussion, much less protest. The mission of the military, he stressed, requires "obedience, unity, commitment and esprit de corps"; therefore, when courts review military regulations, they must give "great deference to the professional judgment of military authorities" concerning the needs and interests of the military. It was the military's judgment that allowing the yarmulke would "detract from the uniformity" sought by the dress regulations, and therefore, Rehnquist concluded, the regulation can be applied and Captain Goldman can be disciplined despite the fact that religious beliefs require wearing headgear.

In his concurring opinion Justice John Paul Stevens emphasized his concern that the military not be put in a position of choosing among different religious beliefs and practices to decide which ones are warranted exceptions and which are not. All military personnel, Stevens said, should be treated the same. Allowing Captain Goldman's demand to be made an exception could force the military to make distinctions that improperly discriminate against unconventional religions, he said.

In dissent Justice William Brennan attacked the Court's uncritical deference to the military. Although he thought the "special needs" of the military can be accommodated within the compelling interest approach, Justice Brennan also argued that, even if a more deferential test were used, Captain Goldman's wearing of his 5½-inch yarmulke is still constitutionally protected. He emphasized that when the military "burdens the free exercise rights of its members in the name of necessity," it should at least be required to provide a "credible" explanation of why the regulation is necessary in order for the military to meet its legitimate goals. Responding to the possibility that Goldman's yarmulke could lead to "turbans, saffron robes and dreadlocks," Justice Brennan suggested that courts require military rules at least to have a "reasoned basis." These might include functional utility, health and safety considerations, and a professional appearance. But it is "totally implausible," he said, that a yarmulke could threaten these interests, including the "group identity" of the military.

Justice Harry Blackmun, in a separate dissent, argued that, although he was concerned about the costs to the military of trying to accommodate religious exemptions, there had been no showing that a significant number of people would request such exemptions or that granting the requests would impair the image of the military. Also in dissent, Justice Sandra Day O'Connor stressed that she agreed with earlier cases holding that, whenever a free exercise claim is overridden by government, it must be for the sake of something like a "compelling" or "overriding" interest. Furthermore, the government must show that the means adopted to achieve its end (in this case, the rule banning headgear) are essential or, at least, are the least-restrictive means available. Using that approach, she concluded that the military is constitutionally required to "accommodate" Captain Goldman's sincere religious belief.

The degree of deference by the Court's majority to military authorities is striking. All the justices, including the dissenters, agreed that rules governing free exercise of religion for those in the military may differ from rules for civilians. But the majority did not stop there; it went on to argue, far less plausibly, that the Court not only should allow greater regulatory latitude but also should defer to the judgment of the military concerning the nature and extent of such regulations. Thus the military is treated in a doubly deferential way: It is not governed by the same constitutional requirements as civilian authorities, *and* courts are to defer to military officials when defining the extent of those extraordinary powers the military may exercise. The limits of that deference, if any, are not described; but it is perhaps ironic that the Court would so severely limit the rights of those who are expected to risk their lives defending a Constitution that provides them so little protection. As Captain Goldman said in the brief filed on his behalf, ". . . the symbolic significance of our Nation's military services and the educational role of the military in teaching the young defenders of our country the principles of liberty require acceptance of [Goldman's] religious observance."

John Arthur

Bibliography

Michelman, Frank, "Forward: Traces of Self-Government," 100 *Harvard Law Review* 4–77 (1986).

Sandel, Michael, "Religious Liberty—Freedom of Conscience or Freedom of Choice," 1989 *Utah Law Review* 597–615 (1989).

Cases Cited

Goldman v. Weinberger, 475 U.S. 503 (1986).

Sherbert v. Verner, 374 U.S. 398 (1963).

The Good Samaritan

A central problem in modern tort and criminal law is whether, and under what circumstances, the law should require individuals to act for the benefit of others—in particular, whether the law should impose a *duty* to rescue another person in danger. In approaching this issue, Anglo-American courts have often invoked the biblical image of the Good Samaritan.

In Luke 10:25–37 a lawyer asks Jesus what one must do to inherit eternal life. The answer is that, according to (Old Testament) law, one must love God with all one's heart, and love one's neighbor as oneself (see Deuteronomy 6:5 and Leviticus 19:18). When the lawyer pursues the matter by asking, "Who is my neighbor?" Jesus responds with the parable of the Good Samaritan, telling the story of a man who was going down from Jerusalem to Jericho. The man was ambushed by robbers, who took everything and beat him and left him for dead. A priest and later a Levite who were going down that road saw the man, but they passed by on the other side. When a Samaritan saw the man, however, he had compassion. He bound up the man's wounds, brought him to an inn, cared for him, and left money with the innkeeper for further care. Jesus concludes by asking the lawyer, "Which of these three, do you think, proved [literally, "became"] neighbor to the man who fell among the robbers?" When the lawyer replies, "The one who showed mercy to him," Jesus tells him, "Go and do likewise."

In the United States, England, and other common-law jurisdictions, courts hold that there is no legal duty to be a Good Samaritan. In a well-known opinion, *Buch v. Amory Manufacturing* Co. (N.H., 1897), the New Hampshire Supreme Court declared: "With purely moral obligations the law does not deal. For example, the priest and the Levite who passed by on the other side were not, it is supposed, liable at law for the continued suffering of the man who fell among thieves, which they might and morally ought to have prevented or relieved." As the British judge Lord Atkin expressed it in *Donoghue v. Stevenson* (Eng. 1932), "The rule that you are to love your neighbor becomes in law, you must not injure your neighbor; and the lawyer's question, Who is my neighbor? receives a restricted reply."

The use which these judicial opinions make of Good Samaritan imagery reflects the legal positivism that became dominant in the late nineteenth century. Positivism draws a fundamental distinction between legal and moral obligations. In this context, to characterize a duty to rescue in moral or religious terms lends rhetorical as well as conceptual force to the contention that civil law imposes no such obligation.

In addition to legal positivism the *Buch* opinion also appears to reflect a particular reading of the parable in the Book of Luke itself. In this reading the priest and the Levite represent the law of the Old Testament. By acting from a spirit of love, the Samaritan transcends the narrow requirements of the law. Such love is inherently boundless and cannot be reduced to any legal rule. Read in this way, the parable itself implies that rescue is not a proper subject for legal obligation.

This interpretation of the story, however, arguably overlooks the central issue in the dialogue between Jesus and the lawyer: the meaning of the law's commandment to love one's neighbor. The lawyer's question shows that he views this commandment as an abstract legal rule, giving rise to technical issues such as who is a neighbor for this purpose. In response Jesus reverses the question, asking not "Who is my neighbor?" but rather "Who *became* a neighbor?" to the victim. The effect is to shift the focus away from the formal rule, not merely to the love shown by the Samaritan but also to the concrete relationship of community that is created when one person recognizes another as a neighbor, as a fellow human being created in the image of God. The essence of this relationship is expressed in the law's commandment to love one's neighbor as oneself. In this interpretation the Samaritan's conduct represents not the negation but the fulfillment of the law. In this connection it should be observed that contemporary Jewish law did require that one assist another person in danger. This obligation was derived from Leviticus 19:16, "neither shalt thou stand idly by the blood of thy neighbor."

In this alternative reading the parable of the Good Samaritan points toward community as the basis of affirmative obligations toward others. In Luke, of course, this community is represented in religious terms. But the same insight may be applied to relationships within the secular society. For example, the courts have long recognized that affirmative duties may arise from special relationships, such as those among family members.

More generally, a strong argument for a duty to rescue can be based on the responsibilities of citizenship in a liberal community. This argument has roots in the traditional theory of the social contract, which has undergone a revival in recent years. According to this view, the state is a community constituted for the purpose of protecting the rights and promoting the welfare of its citizens. The state thus has a fundamental obligation to protect against criminal violence and to provide rescue in other emergency situations. Often, however, the state can perform these functions only through the action of citizens who are present at the scene of danger. Accordingly, it is appropriate for the law to provide that every citizen, in return for the benefits that he or she derives from the community, has a responsibility to act on its behalf to rescue a fellow citizen in peril. Because this obligation arises from the relationship among citizens, it is a duty owed to the particular individual in danger as well as to the state itself. Thus it is appropriate for the duty to be enforced not only through criminal sanctions but also through an action for civil compensation brought by the individual who suffers harm as a result of someone's failure to rescue.

In response to this argument it might be doubted whether contemporary society is characterized by the sort of community that could serve as the basis for a duty to rescue. A crucial insight from the Good Samaritan parable, however, is that it is action on behalf of others that *creates* a relationship of community among individuals. In the same way, adoption of a duty to rescue not only might reflect but also might promote a greater sense of community in contemporary society.

In recent years American law has gradually moved toward recognition of broader affirmative obligations that people owe to each other. Judicial decisions have steadily expanded the category of special relationships that give rise to such obligations. Through legislation several states have gone further, imposing affirmative duties on citizens in general. In 1967 Vermont became the first state to adopt a general duty to provide reasonable assistance to others who are exposed to grave physical harm; Minnesota and Rhode Island followed in the 1980s. Several other states—responding to such notorious incidents as the Catherine ("Kitty") Genovese murder in New York and the tavern rape in New Bedford, Massachusetts—have enacted laws requiring citizens to report violent crimes committed against others. Although most states continue to recognize no legal duty to assist strangers, they seek to encourage such assistance through statutes known as Good Samaritan laws, which grant those who voluntarily aid an injured person broad immunity from any liability for additional harm that may be caused by their actions.

Steven J. Heyman

Bibliography

Derrett, J., and M. Duncan, "Law in the New Testament: Fresh Light on the Parable of the Good Samaritan," 10 *New Testament Studies* 22–37 (1964).

Heyman, Stephen J., "Foundations of the Duty to Rescue," 47 *Vanderbilt Law Review* 673–755 (1994).

Ratcliffe, James M. (ed.), *The Good Samaritan and the Law* (Garden City, N.Y.: Anchor, 1966).

Weinrib, Ernest, "Rescue and Restitution," 1 *S'Vara: A Journal of Philosophy and Judaism* 59–65 (1990).

Cases Cited

Buch v. Amory Manufacturing Co., 44 A. 809 (N.H. 1897).

Donoghue v. Stevenson [1932], A.C. 562 (Scot.) [Great Britain].

Grand Rapids v. Ball

See SCHOOL DISTRICT OF THE CITY OF GRAND RAPIDS V. BALL.

Grant and General Orders Number 11

On December 17, 1862, Major General Ulysses S. Grant issued General Orders Number 11, Department of the Tennessee. It read:

> The Jews, as a class, violating every regulation of trade established by the Treasury Department, and also Department orders, are hereby expelled from the Department. Within twenty-four hours from the receipt of this order by Post Commanders, they will see that all of this class of people are furnished with passes and required to leave, and any one returning after such notification, will be arrested and held in confinement until an opportunity occurs of sending them out as prisoners unless furnished with permits from these Head Quarters. No permits will be given these people to visit Head Quarters for the purpose of making personal application for trade permits.

In February 1862 Grant had cracked the Confederate defense line in Tennessee, and by mid-December he had reached Oxford, Mississippi, steadily occupying portions of the rich cotton kingdom. As Northern armies advanced, trade followed—a policy designed to pacify Southerners and to benefit the North's economy. Confederate authorities urged planters to burn their bales, which otherwise were subject to seizure by the U.S. Army for sale to benefit the Treasury. Some traders crossed the lines to buy cotton from rebels with gold and then transported the bales to markets in the North. Grant knew that such deals benefited the enemy, cheated the Treasury, and demoralized soldiers who were bribed to smuggle cotton through the lines.

Like several of his subordinates, he blamed this odious practice on unscrupulous Jewish merchants.

Grant's smoldering anger ignited when his father arrived in Mississippi to buy cotton in partnership with a Jewish firm in Cincinnati. The relationship between father and son contained considerable ambivalence, but Ulysses wrote to his father throughout the war and craved his approval. When Jesse Grant arrived to capitalize on his son's high rank, Ulysses Grant struck out instead at the Jews.

Although composing only a small portion of cotton traders in the Mississippi Valley, Jews received a disproportionate share of abuse. References to "Jew traders" may have been intended to insult those who were not Jewish. Grant began to employ the term in correspondence in July 1862, but several months later he knew little about Jews. By referring to Jews "as a class," he apparently groped toward a category excluding religion. His orders showed no awareness of Jewish soldiers in his army and no understanding that his department—stretching to the Tennessee and Ohio Rivers—contained many Jewish civilians who were not involved in cotton trading. Indeed, the orders indicated as much ignorance as anti-Semitism.

Orders that referred to Jews "as a class" violating trade regulations confused subordinates about enforcement. The number of Jews expelled remains unknown, and the only evidence of strict enforcement came from Paducah, Kentucky—as far away from the front lines as any part of the department could be—where a zealous subordinate expelled entire families, including two Union veterans. Community leader Cesar F. Kaskel telegraphed a protest to President Abraham Lincoln and then set out for Washington, along the way rallying Jewish leaders against the order.

After listening to Kaskel, Lincoln directed General-in-Chief Henry W. Halleck to revoke the orders. Halleck explained to Grant that Lincoln had "no objection to your expelling traders & Jew peddlers, which I suppose was the object of your order, but as it in terms prescribed an entire religious class, some of whom are fighting in our ranks, the President deemed it necessary to revoke it."

Congressional action to condemn General Orders Number 11 soon degenerated into partisan politicking and ultimately failed because the orders had been revoked. The issue faded until 1868, when Democrats revived it after Grant's Republican presidential nomination. The unpolitical general normally declined to answer criticism, but accusations of anti-Semitism forced him to respond. "I do not sustain the order," he wrote, but "incensed by a reprimand" for tolerating gold smuggling by "Jews within my lines," he had telegraphed the order "the moment it was penned and without reflection." Grant's explanation, more defensive than apologetic, ended his public statements about the issue, which went unmentioned in two volumes of his *Memoirs*. He told his wife, however, that he deserved rebuke for "that obnoxious order" because he "had no right to make an order against any special sect."

John Y. Simon

Bibliography

Grant, Ulysses S., *The Papers of Ulysses S. Grant, Vol. 7: December 9, 1862–March 31, 1863* (Carbondale and Edwardsville: Southern Illinois University Press, 1979).

Korn, Bertram Wallace, *American Jewry and the Civil War* (Philadelphia: Jewish Publication Society of America, 1951).

H

Harlan, John Marshall (1899–1971)

During his sixteen-year tenure as an associate justice of the U.S. Supreme Court, John Marshall Harlan, II, steered a moderate course on matters relating to the Constitution's First Amendment religion clauses. Appointed by President Dwight D. Eisenhower in 1955 to replace the outgoing Justice Robert H. Jackson, Harlan is often characterized as a conservative justice who took a greater interest in preserving state power than in expanding the scope of civil liberties and the role of the federal judiciary. Nevertheless, Harlan, the grandson of the late-nineteenth-century justice by the same name, embraced many of the Warren Court's liberal opinions on church and state issues. Like the rest of his colleagues, Harlan attempted to strike a balance between First Amendment rights and the autonomy and power of the states.

Beginning in the early 1960s, with the coalescence of a new liberal majority of justices, the Supreme Court adopted an increasingly "separationist" stance toward the place of religion in American public life. The Presbyterian Harlan endorsed many of the Court's moves in this direction. He joined majority opinions that invalidated a requirement that state officials declare a belief in God (*Torasco v. Watkins* [1961]), prohibited state-sponsored prayer in public schools (*Engel v. Vitale* [1962]), and banned organized Bible reading during opening exercises in public schools (*School District of Abington Township v. Schempp* [1963]). Later he joined his colleagues in striking down two statutes allowing states to support directly the salaries of teachers of secular subjects in parochial and other nonpublic schools (*Lemon v. Kurtzman* [1971]). In all these instances, Harlan believed, state legislatures had violated the First Amendment's Establishment Clause.

Yet Justice Harlan proved more tolerant of state legislation when the connection to specific religious beliefs or practices was less apparent. He twice, for example, voted to sustain state Sunday closing laws. In *Braunfield v. Brown* (1961), in which Orthodox Jews claimed that a Pennsylvania law placed them at a competitive disadvantage and interfered with their rights under the Free Exercise Clause, Harlan concurred in upholding the measure as a valid exercise of state power. Two years later in *Sherbert v. Verner* (1963), although the Court seemingly reversed itself, Harlan remained consistent. In the case, a Seventh-Day Adventist who was fired from her job for refusing to work on Saturdays declined other employment that would not allow her to adhere to the tenets of her church and then applied for unemployment benefits from the State of South Carolina. When the state denied her application because of her refusal to accept work that required her to go against her beliefs, the Court held that the South Carolina law violated the woman's free exercise rights. In dissent, Harlan warned against the implications of the majority opinion. Under the ruling, he argued, states "must single out for financial assistance those whose behavior is religiously motivated, even though it denies such assistance to others whose identical behavior (in this case, inability to work on Saturdays) is not religiously motivated." It was this interference with the state's power to create its own rules and regulations for unemployment compensation that irked Justice Harlan. Given what he described as "the indirect, remote, and insubstantial effect" of the state's policy on the woman's religious liberty, Harlan rejected the idea that the Free Exercise Clause compelled South Carolina to alter its rules of eligibility (p. 423).

By the end of his career Justice Harlan had developed a clear conception of the scope and meaning of the religion clauses. In a pair of significant 1970 cases, he described the principles of voluntarism and neutrality as being at the "core" of the Constitution's religious provisions. *Walz v. Tax Commission of City of New York* (1970), the first of these cases, involved property tax exemptions for religious organizations in New York. In an extensive concurring opinion Justice Harlan held that, because the tax exemption policy in question "neither encourag[ed] nor discourag[ed] participation in religious life," it satisfied the First Amendment's voluntarism requirement (p. 696). The statute similarly met the criterion of neutrality. Under this standard, Harlan employed an "equal protection mode of analysis" to determine whether the law unduly favored religious individuals or organizations (p. 696). Because the New York law provided tax-exempt status to all nonprofit organizations devoted to the cultural and moral improvement of the community, rather than only to religious institutions, Harlan concluded that the measure was not violative of the Establishment Clause.

The second of these cases, *Welsh v. United States* (1970), involved the conscientious objector provisions of the Universal Military Training and Service Act. Under the law, conscientious objectors were exempted from military service if, because of "religious training and belief," they opposed participation in war. The act defined "religious belief" as "a relation to a Supreme Being involving duties superior to those arising from any human relation," but it specifically rejected "political, sociological, or philosophical views or a merely personal moral code" as grounds for exemption. Welsh, an opponent of war for nonreligious reasons who was convicted for refusing to be drafted, challenged the law as a violation of the Establishment Clause. The majority, unwilling to invalidate the section of the act in question, circumvented the issue by adopting a broad interpretation of the term "religious belief" to include Welsh's moral and philosophical stance. In other words, the Court reversed Welsh's conviction but sustained the law. Justice Harlan, although concurring in the result, accused his colleagues of living in "an Alice-in-Wonderland world where words have no meaning." He questioned how the Court could engage in such a loose construction of a statute that clearly mandated theistic religious belief. Because the law granted an explicit advantage to the "religious" and, moreover, disadvantaged those whose religious beliefs did not include the worship of a supreme being, Harlan viewed the statute as offensive to the principle of neutrality. In contrast to his colleagues, he therefore believed that the law violated the Establishment Clause.

Over the course of his career Justice John Marshall Harlan followed the general outlines of the Supreme Court's interpretation of the religion clauses. Although he dissented in nearly half of the 613 opinions he wrote during his tenure on the Court, this pattern did not apply in cases involving the religion clauses. He usually agreed with the Court's liberal wing about the necessity of a clear separation between church and state, but his strong belief in state power helps to explain his acceptance of lesser forms of religious accommodation, such as Sunday closing laws and tax exemptions.

Timothy S. Huebner

Bibliography

Dorsen, Norman, "John Marshall Harlan, II," in Melvin Urofsky (ed.), *The Supreme Court Justices: A Biographical Dictionary* (New York: Garland, 1994).

———, "John Marshall Harlan, Civil Liberties, and the Warren Court," 36 *New York Law School Review* 81 (1991).

———, "The Second Mr. Justice Harlan: A Constitutional Conservative," 44 *New York University Law Review* 249 (1969).

Shapiro, David L. (ed.), *The Evolution of a Judicial Philosophy: Selected Opinions and Papers of Justice John M. Harlan* (Cambridge: Harvard University Press, 1969).

Yarbrough, Tinsley E., *John Marshall Harlan: Great Dissenter of the Marshall Court* (N.Y.: Oxford University Press, 1992).

Cases Cited
Braunfield v. Brown, 366 U.S. 599 (1961).
Engel v. Vitale, 370 U.S. 421 (1962).
Lemon v. Kurtzman, 403 U.S. 602 (1971).
School District of Abington Township v. Schempp, 374 U.S. 203 (1963).
Sherbert v. Verner, 374 U.S. 398 (1963).
Torasco v. Watkins, 367 U.S. 488 (1961).
Walz v. Tax Commission of City of New York, 397 U.S. 664 (1970).
Welsh v. United States, 398 U.S. 333 (1970).

Harris v. McRae
448 U.S. 297 (1980)

In *Harris v. McRae* (1980) the U.S. Supreme Court upheld the constitutionality of the "Hyde Amendment," under which Congress prohibited the use of Medicaid funding to subsidize abortions. The Court decided two important constitutional issues concerning abortion. First, it reaffirmed its earlier ruling that the constitutional right to choose abortion did not require the government to fund abortions for indigent women. Second, and more important for general issues of law and religion, the Court rejected the argument that laws against abortion were unconstitutional establishments of religion because they enacted religious doctrines that abortion is sinful and that human life begins at conception.

Before 1976 the federal Medicaid program paid for the cost of indigent women's abortions (from 250,000 to 300,000 abortions a year) in states where abortion was legal. But in the mid-1970s opponents of abortion became politically galvanized by the invalidation of criminal abortion laws in *Roe v. Wade* (1973). In September 1976, after a proposed constitutional amendment to reverse *Roe* failed in the House of Representatives, Henry Hyde, a member of the House from Illinois, turned the offensive to public funding. Hyde introduced an amendment to the Medicaid appropriations bill prohibiting the use of any of the program's funds to pay for abortions except where necessary to save the mother's life.

The Hyde Amendment produced passionate debates in Congress. As the court summarized when reviewing the matter, in *McRae v. Califano* (S.D. N.Y., 1980):

> Both houses viewed the issue as a moral and not a financial issue [and] sharply debated the place [of] any restrictive legislation of therapeutic abortion, the importance of leaving to the woman the decision between childbirth and abortion, the question whether a constitutional right to choose abortion rather than childbirth implied a right in the indigent to have the abortion paid for from Medicaid, [and] the issue of discrimination against the indigent woman who decided upon abortion.

A pervasive feature in the arguments for the Hyde Amendment was "the premise that the human fetus was a human life that should not be ended."

The Hyde Amendment finally passed both houses and was implemented in August 1977. Similar limits were attached to Medicaid appropriations in later years, sometimes with additional compromise exceptions for documented cases of rape, incest, or "severe and long-lasting physical health damage to the mother."

In the meantime, a federal lawsuit was filed by two plaintiffs (a pregnant Medicaid recipient and a group of hospitals that performed abortions) challenging the funding restriction on several constitutional grounds. In the Southern District of New York a preliminary injunction blocking the funding restriction was entered, and then, on instructions from the U.S. Supreme Court, the matter was reconsidered in a full trial. The district court heard testimony concerning the effects of funding restrictions on the lives of indigent women as well as testimony from numerous theologians and religious leaders concerning the deep and divided feelings in religious communities concerning abortion. Ultimately the court ruled that the funding restriction unconstitutionally violated rights of bodily liberty, equal protection of the laws, and free exercise of religion.

The U.S. Supreme Court reversed and rejected all challenges to the Hyde Amendment. The Court held that the constitutional right to choose abortion—recognized as a basic "liberty" under the Due Process Clause in *Roe*—did not require the government to subsidize abortions even if it subsidized the alternative of childbirth. By denying funding, the Court said, the government "place[d] no obstacles" of its own to a woman's seeking an abortion; thus the government was free to make "a value judgment favoring childbirth over abortion." For similar reasons the Court refused to find that the Hyde Amendment violated equal protection because it discriminated against indigent women.

The plaintiffs argued that the Hyde Amendment violated the First Amendment's Establishment Clause because (in the Court's words) it "incorporate[d] into law the doctrines of the Roman Catholic Church concerning the sinfulness of abortion and the time at which life commences." They pointed to the active involvement of religious views and institutions, especially those of Roman Catholicism, in the antiabortion movement and in the congressional debates on the Hyde Amendment. This claim presented a potentially broad challenge to the historic ties between religious morality and the law and to the tradition of religious activism in politics—as the district judge recognized in rejecting the claim:

> [I]t is clear that the healthy working of our political order cannot safely forego the political action of the churches, or discourage it. The . . . spokesmen of religious institutions must not be discouraged nor inhibited by the fear that their support of legislation, or explicit lobbying for such legislation, will result in its being constitutionally suspect.

The Supreme Court agreed, although in less sweeping language, holding that a law is not an establishment merely "because it 'happens to coincide or harmonize with the tenets of some or all religions.'" The majority pointed out that laws against larceny are not invalid simply because "the Judaeo-Christian religions oppose stealing."

Recognizing the many instances in which laws are undergirded by religious tenets, the plaintiffs argued that antiabortion laws were unusual because there was not sufficient secular consensus against abortion to ground such laws in anything other than religious doctrine. The Court did not discuss whether this distinction, if proved, would indeed make antiabortion laws into forbidden establishments. Instead, it concluded that there were secular reasons to disfavor abortion: "[t]he Hyde Amendment . . . is as much a reflection of 'traditionalist' values toward abortion, as it is an embodiment of the views of any particular religion."

The plaintiffs also raised another religion clause issue, claiming that the Hyde Amendment impinged on the free exercise of religion of women who chose abortion for reasons of conscience. This claim would have required the Court to evaluate the extent to which the abortion decision could be a matter of religious command or conscience and whether protecting fetal life was a strong enough interest to overcome free exercise. But these issues were left unresolved; the Court ruled that none of the plaintiffs had legal standing because none of them as individuals had in fact made a religious decision to abort. More than a decade later, fear of such free exercise claims to abortion led antiabortion forces to fight and nearly block Congress's efforts to bolster free exercise rights generally through the Religious Freedom Restoration Act.

The plaintiffs' religion clause arguments presented tricky questions for mainline and liberal religious groups that supported abortion rights but were politically active on other issues and were thus uncomfortable with Establishment Clause limits on such activity. The National Council of Churches of Christ in the U.S.A., for example, filed an amicus curiae brief urging the justices "to avoid the establishment issues altogether" and "applaud[ing] the district court's reaffirmation of the right of religious groups to participate fully in the political process." Instead the council and several other groups argued that abortion was unusual because it involved the "conscientiously implemented religious convictions," and thus the free exercise rights, of pregnant women.

Since *Harris,* yearly Hyde amendments have continued to forbid federal funding of abortions. The Supreme Court decision is a cornerstone of the current constitutional edifice concerning abortion: Government may not forbid abortions but may regulate and disfavor them in various ways. More broadly, the decision assured religious groups of considerable latitude in influencing the political process. Although the Court did not resolve all questions in that area, it reaffirmed that a law does not "establish religion" simply because some religious views were prominent in its passage and because it coincides with the tenets of some or all churches.

Thomas C. Berg

Bibliography

Briefs in *Harris v. McRae,* reprinted in Philip Kurland and Gerhard Casper (eds.), *Landmark Briefs and Arguments of the Supreme Court of the United States,* vol. 115 (Washington: University Publications of America, 1981): Brief for Appellant, the Secretary of Health, Education and Welfare (pp. 2–45); Brief of Appellees (pp. 46–254); and Brief Amicus Curiae on Behalf of the National Council of Churches of Christ in the U.S.A. (pp. 599–633).

Wenz, Peter Z., *Abortion Rights As Religious Freedom* (Philadelphia: Temple University Press, 1992).

Cases Cited

Harris v. McRae, 448 U.S. 297 (1980).

McRae v. Califano, 491 F. Supp. 630 (S.D. N.Y. 1980).

Roe v. Wade, 410 U.S. 113 (1973).

Hawaiian Native Religion and American Law

The Free Exercise Clause of the First Amendment guarantees to Native Hawaiians the freedom to practice their religion. To Native Hawaiians this includes the freedom to practice a way of life that acknowledges the sacredness of certain places, beings, and natural forces. The scope of free exercise protection, however, depends on how the courts have interpreted the Free Exercise Clause. Such interpretation has a long and varied history. Most recently the scope of free exercise protection has been severely restricted by the U.S. Supreme Court in cases dealing with native religions, such as *Lyng v. Northwest Indian Cemetery Protective Association* (1988) and *Employment Division, Department of Human Resources of Oregon v. Smith* (1990).

Under these cases, religious minorities can claim protection under the Free Exercise Clause only if the government singled out or penalized specific religious practices. The 1978 American Indian Religious Freedom Act also has proved to be an empty promise to native peoples, providing no greater protection than the First Amendment itself. Similarly, in Hawai'i (the indigenous spelling of the state name) the state constitutional guarantee of free exercise of religion has been interpreted as virtually synonymous with the First Amendment. Although a separate state constitutional provision confirms customary and traditional rights of Native Hawaiian tenants, this provision has yet to be interpreted in the context of a religious freedom claim. Unfortunately, recent federal and state judicial developments do not bode well for the survival and continued practice of Native Hawaiian religion.

Native Hawaiian Religious Beliefs

In ancient Hawaiian thought, life was not confined to the physical world. Life continued after death, and physical life was viewed as a place of preparation for the afterlife. All human beings had, as R. K. Johnson noted in a state report on native Hawaiian religion, "spiritual origin, material birth, and spiritual eternity of complete unceasing existence. . . ." Thus, besides the physical body (*kino*), an individual also had a second separable spirit, which could move during sleep, and the eternal spirit (*'uhane*), which survived death.

Hawaiians regarded themselves as the younger siblings both of the land (*'_ina*) and of taro (*kalo*), their staple food. The first Hawaiian, the food *kalo,* and the Hawaiian islands themselves all descended from *W_kea,* sky-father, and *Papa,* earth-mother. Out of this familial relationship arose the concept of *m_lama '_ina*—caring for and serving the land, an essential pattern of Hawaiian life. It was the duty of Hawaiians to care for and serve the *'_ina,* and in turn the *'_ina* would feed and provide shelter for Hawaiians. This reciprocal relationship helped to create and preserve *pono,* a universe in balance or harmony.

Hawaiian religion rested on a basic belief in spirits and the realm of the spirit. Spirits, in the form of gods (*akua*) and family guardians (*'aum_kua*), were involved in every aspect of life. In farming, fishing, tapa making, dancing, sports, or any activity of Hawaiian life, Hawaiians were able to ask for the guidance and support of the appropriate *akua* or *'aum_kua.*

The four male gods of the Hawaiian religious system were *K_* (god of war and medicine); *K_ne* (god of life, fresh water, sunlight, and natural phenomena in the sky); *Lono* (god of peace, agriculture, and fertility); and *Kanaloa* (god of the ocean and ocean winds). Each of these gods personified the natural forces and governed a facet of Hawaiian life. Hawaiians also had numerous other gods, most of whom represented some aspect of nature. Chief among the other deities was *Pele,* goddess of fire and the volcano, who was also a feared sorceress.

In addition to the *akua,* Hawaiians also worshipped *'aum_kua*—personal gods unique to a particular family. Hawaiians not only worshipped their *'aum_kua* but also considered themselves to be related to them. Most *'aum_kua* had been respected and wise humans who, after death, continued to offer advice and guidance.

Akua and *'aum_kua* manifested themselves in earthly forms as animals, plants, or forces of nature. The *'aum_kua* especially could be called on for aid in difficult times. Many stories are told of the shark, owl, or lizard *'aum_kua* rescuing families from peril.

Hawaiian religion also encompassed a prescribed code of behavior and rituals in order to regulate *mana,* the animating force of all life forms. *Mana* was strongest in the gods, the high chiefs, and the priests (*k_huna*). However, all persons, places, and things had *mana* either as active or as dormant energy. *Mana* could increase or decrease and was transferable. Thus, many actions were performed in order to preserve or increase *mana. Mana* could be used for either good or evil, and the mere strength of one's *mana* did not guarantee eternal life. As R.K. Johnson has noted, "No spirit (*'uhane*) of man or woman ascends into the spiritual life guaranteed into eternity except by *pono,* which means duty, responsibility, justice, and righteousness. Without *pono* no good life for mankind either on earth or beyond earth develops."

One way of conferring *mana* was by performing ceremonies and rites. Through chanting, prayer, or human sacrifice the *mana* of the gods could exist in persons or objects. Priests directed *mana* by using ritual. Ritual preserved and protected the concept of *mana* to such a large extent that even after the overthrow of the early Hawaiian religious system, belief in the power of certain rituals remained. To the Native Hawaiian, ritual was a vital link to *mana* and therefore to the entire religious system.

The *kapu* system, a complex set of rules and laws, protected the *mana* of individuals and places and prevented *mana* from harming others. A major impact of the *kapu* system was manifested in the relationship between humans and the gods, whereby the various physical forms of the gods were forbidden to followers. Similarly, the physical forms of a family's *'aum_kua* were forbidden to family members. Another example of the *kapu* system involved the relationship between men and women, whereby members of the opposite sex were not allowed to eat together. John F. Mulholland and others have argued that the *kapu* system imposed severe hardships on Hawaiians, eventually leading to its abolishment. However, *kapu* also regulated the conservation of natural resources and undoubtedly served a vital function in preserving the Hawaiian social structure.

In 1819 the *kapu* system was abolished by the breaking of the law forbidding men and women to eat together, when the young king, Liholiho, publicly ate with the powerful chieftesses Ka'ahumanu and Ke_p_olani, widows of Kamehameha I. Subsequently Liholiho ordered the destruction of the temple images. Christian missionaries arrived a few months later.

Although the *kapu* system itself vanished, certain basic Hawaiian religious concepts have remained. These include the concept of *mana,* or sacredness of certain places, persons, or things; love and respect for the land and its natural resources (*m_lama '_ina);* and the reverence and honor due to the ancient gods of Hawai'i and to the *'aum_kua* of each family. Today these religious beliefs and practices continue to permeate Native Hawaiian life.

Native Hawaiian Religion and Federal Law

In Hawai'i, claims about Native Hawaiian religious freedom initially arose in the context of access to sacred lands. In *United States v. Mowat* (9th Cir., 1978) several members of the Protect Kaho'olawe 'Ohana were charged with trespassing on the island of Kaho'olawe. Federal statutes and regulations banned entry onto Kaho'olawe without advance consent by the Commandant of the Fourteenth Naval District. The defendants claimed access based on free exercise of religion. The Ninth Circuit Court of Appeals concluded, however, that requiring advance approval before entry was not unreasonable because Kaho'olawe was used as a bombing target and might contain live unexploded ordnance, thus putting trespassers at risk. This risk outweighed any burden on free exercise of religion. Citing the U.S. Supreme Court's decision in *Sherbert v. Verner* (1963), the appeals court balanced the burden placed on the defendants' free exercise of religion against the government's interests. The court concluded that "the compelling Government interest . . . in keeping outsiders off dangerous land . . . outweighs any burden on defendants' free exercise of religion."

Aluli v. Brown (D. Haw. 1977) also involved Kaho'olawe. Here the plaintiffs sought to stop military bombing of the island and to prevent further destruction of archeological sites of religious and historical significance to Native Hawaiians. Although the federal district court denied an injunction, it required the military to file annual environmental impact statements pursuant to the National Environmental Policy Act (NEPA). Even though the court did not support the plaintiffs on their religious exercise claim, it reminded the government that adverse effects on archeological sites could have adverse effects on the welfare of human beings. Noting that eighty-nine archeological sites of possible importance to Hawaiian history and culture had been found on Kaho'olawe, the court stated:

> [A]n adverse effect upon the archeological sites may have a direct effect upon human beings; for example the plaintiffs. Regardless, the court believes that an adverse effect upon the sites would be an adverse effect upon the environment which would have an indirect effect on human beings. . . . [D]efendants' . . . bombardment of Kahoolawe is a major federal action significantly affecting the quality of the human environment.

Native Hawaiians are specifically mentioned in the 1978 American Indian Religious Freedom Act (AIRFA), reiterating the federal policy to protect and preserve the right of Native Americans to believe, express, and exercise their traditional religions "including but not limited to access to sites, use and possession of sacred objects, and the freedom to worship through ceremonials and traditional rites."

The express purpose of the AIRFA was to require that federal policies comply with the constitutional mandate of free exercise of religion. The AIRFA, however, is simply a policy statement, with no enforcement mechanisms or penalty provisions. Indeed, in *Lyng* the U.S. Supreme Court stated that the AIRFA was not a source of legal rights or a cause of action. Consequently, despite its congressional directive to safeguard traditional religious practices, the AIRFA has afforded little protection and has rarely been used or cited in Hawai'i cases.

Native Hawaiian Religion and State Law

Hawai'i state courts have had limited opportunity to invoke Free Exercise Clause analysis. Article I, Section 4, of the Hawai'i Constitution reads, in part: "No law shall be enacted respecting an establishment of religion, or prohibiting the free exercise thereof. . . ." However, in *Medeiros v. Kiyoski* (Hawaii, 1970) and subsequent cases the Hawaiian state courts have declined to interpret the requirements of the state constitutional provision on free exercise of religion to extend greater protection than the federal provision does. For the most part, Hawai'i courts have applied the test developed by the U.S. Supreme Court in *Wisconsin v. Yoder* (1972) by examining the legitimacy of the religious belief involved, the burden on the religious belief, the impact on religious practices, and the existence of a compelling state interest. Such cases as *State v. Andrews,* (Hawaii, 1982) and *State v. Blake* (Hawaii, 1985) illustrate this trend.

In *State v. Lono* (Hawaii, 1985) members of the Temple of *Lono* were arrested and charged with camping without a permit at Kualoa Regional Park. Kualoa is a sacred site, the location of an ancient temple (*heiau*) dedicated to *Lono*. Temple members had entered and remained in the park for periods from three weeks to four months, in violation of park regulations, in order to perform various ceremonies. One of the religious practices involved sitting in a meditative state until experiencing *h'ike a ka p,* or night visions, which provide inspiration and guidance. In their defense, temple members challenged the park regulations as an infringement on religious freedom. The trial court determined that defendants' "religious interest in participating in dreams at Kualoa Regional Park are not indispensable to the Hawaiian religious practices, and further that the Defendants' practices in exercising their religious beliefs . . . are philosophical and personal and therefore not entitled to First Amendment protection." The Hawai'i Supreme Court also gave short shrift to the religious freedom argument, affirming the trial court in a memorandum opinion.

In the only fully articulated Hawai'i case dealing with the exercise of Native Hawaiian religion, *Dedman v. Board of Land and Natural Resources* (Hawaii, 1987), the Hawai'i Supreme Court applied the *Yoder* test. In *Dedman,* Native Hawaiians challenged a decision by the Board of Land and Natural Resources (BLNR) that permitted geothermal development in an area which is significant to native religious practitioners who honor the deity *Pele.* The *Pele* practitioners claimed that the proposed development would impinge on their right to free religious exercise, since geothermal development requires drilling into the body of *Pele* and taking her energy and lifeblood. According to Native Hawaiian religious belief, the area proposed for geothermal development is considered the home of *Pele.*

In *Dedman* the Hawai'i Supreme Court first acknowledged the sincerity of the religious claims at issue. It then considered whether the BLNR's approval of the proposed geothermal development would unconstitutionally infringe on Native Hawaiian religious practice. On this question, the court found controlling the absence of proof that religious ceremonies were held in the area proposed for development. Without evidence of a burden on the free exercise of native religion, the court did not reach the question of compelling state interest. Accordingly, it concluded that no Free Exercise Clause violation had occurred. Thus the *Dedman* court applied a narrow analysis of free exercise infringement, accounting for its failure to find any burden on Native Hawaiian religious practices. Any doubt concerning the Hawai'i Supreme Court's constitutional analysis of free exercise protection dissolved in 1988, when the U.S. Supreme Court denied review of *Dedman.*

In November 1978 the Hawai'i Constitution was amended to include a provision guaranteeing the traditional and customary rights exercised by Native Hawaiian tenants of an *ahupua'a* (a land unit extending from the mountains to the sea containing within its borders all the products needed for subsistence). The new Article XII, Section 7, states:

> The State reaffirms and shall protect all rights, customarily and traditionally exercised for subsistence, cultural and religious purposes and possessed by *ahupua'a* tenants who are descendants of native Hawaiians who inhabited the Hawaiian Islands prior to 1778, subject to the right of the State to regulate such rights.

As early as 1879, in *In re Boundaries of Pulehunui* (Hawaii, 1879), and as recently as *Palama v. Sheehan* (Hawaii, 1968), Hawaiian courts have recognized the *ahupua'a* as the principal Hawaiian land division. In *Pele Defense Fund v. Paty* (Hawaii, 1993), the Hawai'i Supreme Court held that Article XII, Section 7 may provide a legal basis for extending the gathering rights of Native Hawaiian tenants. However, although the constitutional provision includes protection of rights exercised for "religious purposes," the Hawai'i courts unfortunately have never interpreted this constitutional amendment in the context of a religious freedom claim. In *Dedman* the state constitutional amendment was not specifically implicated. This may have been because those challenging the BLNR action did not claim to live within the *ahupua'a* where the land was located nor to have such rights. However, given the fact that the Hawai'i Supreme Court in *Dedman* failed to give any greater protection to native religious practitioners under Hawai'i's own constitutional religious freedom provision, it would appear unlikely that the state supreme court would be sympathetic to an argument based on *ahupua'a* tenant rights.

Most recently, the Hawai'i Supreme Court has reviewed a group of trespass convictions arising out of Hawaiian protests over geothermal development in the Wao Kele 'O Puna rainforest. In a series of memorandum opinions issued in the fall of 1991 (*State v. Lee, State v. Kanahele, State v. Lee, State v. Luning, State v. Eaton, State v. Kaipo, State v. Kaleiwahea,* and *State v. Dedman*) the court gave little credence to arguments that the geothermal developer violated the defendants' free exercise of religion by prohibiting access to the development site. The defendants wished to conduct a religious ceremony at the site to heal damage to *Pele* caused by geothermal drilling. In *State v. McGregor* (Hawaii, 1991)—the most detailed of the memorandum opinions—the Court examined whether there was a sufficiently close nexus between the state and the challenged action, in this case prohibiting McGregor from entering the area of the geothermal well site to conduct a religious ceremony. If such a nexus existed, then the action of the geothermal developer could be treated as an action of the state itself. Not surprisingly, the court found that the defendant had not met her burden of showing by clear and convincing evidence that the state directed, encouraged, or supported the private developer in prohibiting access to the geothermal drill site. The court thus determined that there was no state action and that McGregor's arrest for trespassing did not violate her free exercise of religion.

Conclusion

Native Hawaiian religion lacks significant protection under traditional American law. The distinctiveness of Native Hawaiian religion—so different from traditional Judeo-Christian doctrines—makes it especially vulnerable and renders doubtful its continued protection under the Free Exercise Clause. Recent judicial interpretations of the Free Exercise Clause of the U.S. Constitution and of the equivalent provision in the Hawai'i Constitution indicate that a burden on the free exercise of religion exists when government action regulates or directly impinges on Native Hawaiian religious practices. Furthermore, only government conduct that compels irreverence of religious beliefs or that penalizes individuals for their religious actions would warrant free exercise protection. Certainly, few practitioners of native religion meet this standard. Such a constricted approach consigns free exercise protection to the far end of a rapidly diminishing spectrum of native rights.

Strengthening the American Indian Religious Freedom Act and enforcing the 1978 state constitutional amendment protecting rights customarily and traditionally exercised by *ahupua'a* tenants for religious purposes appear to offer Native Hawaiians only limited safeguards for their unique native religion.

Melody Kapilialoha MacKenzie
Catherine Kau

Glossary

'_ina: land, earth
ahupua'a: principal land unit, containing all the products needed for subsistence
akua: god, goddess, spirit
'aum_kua: family spirits or guardians
heiau: temple, Hawaiian place of worship
h'ike a ka p: night visions providing inspiration and guidance
k_huna: priests
kalo: taro, the staple food of Hawaiians
Kanaloa: god of the ocean and ocean winds
K_ne: god of life, fresh water, sunlight, and natural phenomena in the sky
kapu: taboo, prohibition; ancient system of rules and laws
kino: physical body
*K_*: god of war and medicine
Lono: god of peace, agriculture, and fertility
m_lama '_ina: practice of caring for and serving the land
mana: supernatural or divine power; animating force of life
Papa: earth-mother, female progenitor of the Hawaiian race
Pele: goddess of fire and the volcano
pono: balance or harmony; goodness, righteousness
'uhane: eternal spirit
W_kea: sky-father, male progenitor of the Hawaiian race

Bibliography

Emerson, Nathaniel B., *Pele and Hiiaka: A Myth from Hawaii* (Rutland, Vt.: C.E. Tuttle, 1978).

Johnson, R. K., "Native Hawaiian Religion," in Native Hawaiians Study Commission, *Report on the Culture, Needs, and Concerns of Native Hawaiians,* majority report (Washington, D.C., 1983), p. 226

L. Kame 'eleihiwa, *Native Lands and Foreign Desires-Pehea L_E Pono Ai?* 23–25 (Honolulu: Bishop Museum Press, 1992).

Mulholland, John F., *Hawaii's Religions* (Rutland, Vt.: C.E. Tuttle, 1970).

Pukui, Mary K., *Hawaiian Religion* (Honolulu: n.p., 1945).

Cases and Statutes Cited

Aluli v. Brown, 437 F. Supp. 602 (D. Haw. 1977).

Dedman v. Board of Land and Natural Resources, 69 Haw. 255, 740 P. 2d 28 (1987), cert. denied, 485 U.S. 1020 (1988).

Employment Division, Department of Human Resources of Oregon v. Smith, 494 U.S. 872 (1990).

In re Boundaries of Pulehunui, 4 Haw. 239 (1879).
Lyng v. Northwest Indian Cemetery Protective Association, 485 U.S. 439 (1988).
Medeiros v. Kiyoski, 52 Haw. 436, 478 P. 2d 314, (1970).
Palama v. Sheehan, 50 Haw. 298, 440 P. 2d 95 (1968).
Pele Defense Fund v. Paty, 73 Haw. 578, 837 P. 2d 1247 (1993).
Sherbert v. Verner, 374 U.S. 398 (1963).
State v. Andrews, 65 Haw. 289, 651 P. 2d 473 (1982).
State v. Blake, 5 Haw. App. 411, 413, 695 P. 2d 336 (1985).
State v. Dedman, Hawaii Supreme Court, No. 15092 (Dec. 18, 1991) (memorandum opinion).
State v. Eaton, Hawaii Supreme Court, No. 15279 (Dec. 18, 1991) (memorandum opinion).
State v. Kaipo, Hawaii Supreme Court, No. 15280 (Dec. 18, 1991) (memorandum opinion).
State v. Kaleiwahea, Hawaii Supreme Court, No. 15281 (Dec. 18, 1991) (memorandum opinion).
State v. Kanahele, Hawaii Supreme Court, No. 15069 (Oct. 15, 1991) (memorandum opinion).
State v. Lee, Hawaii Supreme Court, No. 14984 (Oct. 15, 1991) (memorandum opinion).
State v. Lee, Hawaii Supreme Court, No. 14877 (Oct. 16, 1991) (memorandum opinion).
State v. Lono, Hawaii Supreme Court, No. 9571 (Apr. 3, 1985) (memorandum opinion).
State v. Luning, Hawaii Supreme Court, No. 15063 (Dec. 18, 1991) (memorandum opinion).
State v. McGregor, Hawaii Supreme Court, No. 14984 (Sept. 26, 1991) (memorandum opinion).
United States v. Mowat, 582 F. 2d 1194 (9th Cir. 1978).
Wisconsin v. Yoder, 406 U.S. 205 (1972).
American Indian Religious Freedom Act (AIRFA), 42 U.S.C. §1996.
National Environmental Policy Act (NEPA), 42 U.S.C. §4321.

Historic Preservation of Religious Buildings

Many religious structures of historic or architectural significance have been designated as local, state, or national landmarks. The resulting restrictions on alteration and demolition have made it difficult or impossible for some religious communities to accommodate changing demographics, to address financial pressures, to redesign their worship environments, or to express beliefs through new architecture. The free exercise argument against landmark preservation has often been based on indirect economic burdens sustained by churches, such as (1) the diminution of property value and reduced marketability, (2) the diversion of funds away from religious purposes for the public enjoyment of aesthetics, and (3) interference with lucrative development plans intended to fund religious ministry. These economic-burden arguments have been unsuccessful. Churches have had greater success challenging historic preservation in cases that present examples of direct entanglement of landmarks commissions in religious affairs and direct involvement in the religious design statement.

In *Employment Division, Department of Human Resources of Oregon v. Smith* (1990) the U.S. Supreme Court replaced strict scrutiny with a rational basis standard of judicial review whenever neutral laws of general applicability burden religious exercise. Therefore, the government is required to justify its burdens on religion only when the action lacks religious neutrality or violates fundamental rights to speech, association, and equal protection claims (so-called hybrid rights of free exercise claims coupled with other constitutional protections). If historic preservation is considered to be facially neutral, generally applicable, and lacking a hybrid element, then the government action of landmark designation (and specific restrictions flowing from that designation) will be upheld as constitutional.

Such an analysis was adopted in *St. Bartholomew's v. City of New York* (2d Cir. 1990). In that case, the city refused to allow an Episcopal church on Park Avenue to demolish its landmarked community house. It had planned to replace the building with a forty-seven-story office tower that would house social services and produce income for church programs. In litigation the church argued that, in violation of the Free Exercise Clause, the landmark restrictions impaired its ability to carry on and expand the charitable works that are central to its religious mission. The Court of Appeals for the Second Circuit agreed that the landmark restrictions "drastically reduced the Church's ability to raise revenues for its religious activities," but the court held nonetheless that the Free Exercise Clause was not implicated because landmark preservation was a neutral law of general applicability, presumptively constitutional under *Smith.* Because the landmark regulation had not prevented the church from continuing its religious and charitable mission at its *current* level in its existing building, it was held constitutional.

Two state courts have taken very different approaches in order to strike down historic preservation as unconstitutional. In *Society of Jesus v. Boston Landmarks Commission* (Mass., 1990) the Jesuits challenged the authority of a landmarks commission to designate the *interior* of a church. The Jesuits proposed the renovation of a church (the interior of which was landmarked); the plans included the addition of a new free-standing altar and the removal of the main and side altars. Such changes were part of an effort to reflect architecturally those modifications made to the Roman Catholic liturgy during the Second Vatican Council. The commission granted permission for the installation of the new central altar, although it did reserve for itself a consultative role in the new altar's design. With respect to two of the three existing altars, however, the commission encouraged their screening, rather than their removal. The Jesuits revised their proposal, agreeing to screen the main altar, but they continued to request removal of the left side altar. At first the commission refused; it later reversed this decision and permitted the removal of the left side altar because of constitutional concerns.

In a summary judgment action the Jesuits challenged the constitutionality of the interior designation as a violation of free exercise and as a taking. In a pre-*Smith* decision the superior court had found the designation to be an invalid interference with the free exercise of religion under the First Amendment and had vacated the designation. After *Smith* the Massachusetts Supreme Judicial Court affirmed the facial invalidity of interior designation of houses of worship, but the invalidity was based on the *state* constitutional free exercise provision. Presumably this was done to avoid the effects of *Smith.*

In *First Covenant Church v. City of Seattle* (Wash., 1992) a church made a facial challenge to the city's landmark designation of the exterior of its house of worship. In 1990, before *Smith,* the Washington Supreme Court had held the designation unconstitutional under federal and state free exercise provisions, but the decision was later vacated by the U.S. Supreme Court and then remanded to the high state court for reconsideration in light of *Smith.* In 1992 the Washington Supreme Court reinstated its original holding. It held first that, under the Free Exercise Clause, *Smith*'s rational basis analysis did not govern in this case because the landmark designation of a specific building was not a generally applicable, facially neutral law. Furthermore, *Smith*'s minimal protection was inapplicable because the church's appearance was an architectural "proclamation" of religious belief within the free exercise–free speech hybrid. A specific non-neutral law burdening free speech in addition to free exercise requires a sufficiently compelling justification with no less-restrictive alternative. But because preservation relates to aesthetics, not to health or safety, it did not qualify as a compelling governmental interest. The Washington Supreme Court next held—much as did the Massachusetts high court in *Society of Jesus*—that even under an independent interpretation of its state constitution, interior designation of a church was unconstitutional.

A most interesting feature of the case was the "liturgical exemption" that had been written into the designating ordinance, which permitted the church to make changes to the building that were necessitated by changes in the liturgy. The state high court decided that this exemption would lead to impermissible governmental entanglement in religious affairs, because the city had the final authority to decide which proposed building alterations fell into the category of liturgical change.

Following *First Covenant,* the Seattle Landmarks Commission next landmarked a church but held the restrictions in abeyance until the building ceased to be used for "religious purposes," presumably to prevent a sale of the church building for private development. The Washington Supreme Court was concerned tht such a determination of the cessation of "religious purposes" would involve the government in a religious decision and in *First United Methodist Church v. Hearing Examiner* (Wash., 1996) struck the designation. The court reasoned further, contrary to the analysis employed in *St. Bartholomew's,* that the church has the right to sell its property and use the proceeds to advance its religious mission free from financial and administrative burdens of landmark restrictions. The high court continued to protect decisionmaking regarding church property when it held in *Munns v. Martin* (Wash., 1997) that a demolition permit ordinance applicable to older buildings providing for a waiting period of up to fourteen months was an unconstitutional burden on a religious ministry.

A Maryland church was denied permission to demolish a church building and monastery which were part of a historic district and replace it with smaller facilities. In *Keeler v. Mayor and City of Cumberland* (Md. Dist. Ct., 1996), the federal district court, citing *Society of Jesus* and *First Covenant,* reasoned that strict scrutiny continues to apply even after *Smith* because preservation is not accomplished by way of generally applicable laws. It held that the Free Exercise Clause allows a church to demolish and rebuild in order to improve worship, increase accessibility, and express its religious belief.

The U.S. Supreme Court's decision in *City of Boerne v. Flores* involved a dispute arising from the landmarking of a church building, but the issue before the court was only the constitutionality of the federal Religious Freedom Restoration Act (RFRA), which the city had raised in defense of the church's RFRA claim. The Court found RFRA unconstitutional. Thus, we have no statement by the Court on the underlying dispute: The church intended to demolish all but the facade of its house of worship to accommodate its rapidly growing parish; the designation prevented this action. The city has suggested that if the church needs more space, it should simply build another house of worship elsewhere—borrowing the "alternative location" analysis from zoning. Dicta in *City of Boerne* suggests that the Supreme Court was assuming that historic preservation laws are generally applicable, facially neutral zoning laws. One can only speculate whether the Supreme Court, in deciding the constitutionality of historic preservation ordinances under the Free Exercise Clause, would find them to be generally applicable and facially neutral as the *St. Bartholomew Keeler* court did, or whether it would reject this characterization as the *Keeler* court and Washington Supreme Court have done.

Angela C. Carmella

Bibliography

Babcock, Richard F., and David A. Theriaque, "Landmarks Preservation Ordinances: Are the Religion Clauses Violated by their Application to Religious Properties?" 7 *Journal of Land Use & Environmental Law* 165 (1992).

Carmella, Angela "Houses of Worship and Religious Liberty: Constitutional Limits to Landmark Preservation and Architectural Review," 36 *Villanova Law Review* 401 (1991).

Nunez, Felipe M., and Eric Sidman, "California's Statutory Exemption for Religious Properties from Landmark Ordinances: A Constitutional Policy Analysis," 12 *Journal of Law and Religion* 271 (1995–96).

Note, "Religious Landmarks, Guidelines for Analysis: Free Exercise, Takings, and Least Restrictive Means," 53 *Ohio State Law Journal* 211 (1992).

Note, "Free Exercise, Free Expression and Landmarks Preservation," 91 *Columbia Law Review* 1813 (1991).

Cases Cited

City of Boerne v. Flores, 521 U.S. 507 (1997).

Employment Division, Department of Human Resources of Oregon v. Smith, 494 U.S. 872 (1990).

First Covenant Church v. City of Seattle, 840 P. 2d 174 (Wash. 1992).

First United Methodist Church v. Hearing Examiner, 916 P. 2d 374 (Wash., 1996).

Keeler v. Mayor and City of Cumberland, 940 F. Supp. 879 (1996).

Munns v. Martin, 930 P. 2d 318 (Wash., 1997).

St. Bartholomew's v. City of New York, 914 F. 2d 348 (2d Cir. 1990), cert. denied 111 S. Ct. 1103 (1991).

Society of Jesus v. Boston Landmarks Commission, 564 N.E. 2d 571 (Mass. 1990).

History and Its Role in Supreme Court Decisions on Religion

The unique characteristic of the Supreme Court's use of history in First Amendment religion clause cases is its ubiquity. Driven by the arcane and absolutist language—"no law," "respecting," "establishment," and even "free exercise,"—the justices have repeatedly looked to the eighteenth century for instruction.

The Court's Uses of History

In seeking "instruction," the Court does not act as a historian, striving to understand an era. Instead, the Court looks to history as part of its task of adjudicating a dispute between particular parties. One consequence is that the Court's use of history has been referred to disparagingly as "law-office history": history written solely to support an argument. Equally superficial is a second use of history: as allegorical embellishment, with little actual reference to historical fact. For example, Justice Abe Fortas introduced his opinion in *Epperson v. Arkansas* (1968) with this sweeping statement: "The antecedents of today's decision are many and unmistakable. They are rooted in the foundation soil of our Nation. They are fundamental to freedom." Likewise, in *Lemon v. Kurtzman* (1971), Chief Justice Warren Burger made a wholesale reference to the "history of many countries [which] attests to the hazards of religion's intruding into the political arena or of political power intruding into the legitimate and free exercise of religious belief."

A third use of history is simply the working of stare decisis: The Court seeks guidance in its own history, its precedents. In most other areas of constitutional law those precedents soon provide a mediating layer of authority between the language of the Constitution and that of the Court's opinions. The religion clauses have resisted such a veneer of precedent. The justices did find in history one mediating metaphor for the Establishment Clause: Thomas Jefferson's "wall of separation." The phrase first appeared in a Supreme Court opinion when Chief Justice Morrison Waite quoted it in *Reynolds v. United States* (1878). According to Waite, the phrase had value because Jefferson had been "an acknowledged leader of the advocates" of the First Amendment. Over the next century, the phrase appeared regularly in the Court's decisions under the Free Exercise Clause. But the phrase never captured the justices' full allegiance, and more recently they have grown increasingly dissatisfied with it. For example, in *Gillette v. United States* (1971) Justice Thurgood Marshall has warned that the "metaphor of a 'wall' or impassable barrier between Church and State, taken too literally, may mislead constitutional analysis." Justice William Rehnquist went further in his dissent in *Wallace v. Jaffree* (1985), calling for a rejection, writing that the metaphor was "based on bad history" and had "proved useless as a guide to judging." Two decades earlier, Justice Potter Stewart had made a similar point in his dissent in *Engel v. Vitale* (1962).

Thus, in the absence of a mediating principle, the justices find themselves regularly combing the history of the religion clauses. In some instances, a historical exegesis seems more a rite of passage or an initiation ordeal, as when a justice makes a first substantial foray into the jurisprudence of the religion clauses. Among the better examples of this use are Justice Felix Frankfurter's separate opinion in *McGowan v. Maryland* (1961), to which he added two appendixes, one listing colonial statutes and the other listing current laws. Other examples of similar bibliographic efforts to gain respectability in the club include the opinions of both Justice Tom Clark and Justice William Brennan in *School District of Abington Township v. Schempp* (1963), of Justice Lewis Powell in *Committee for Public Education and Religious Liberty v. Nyquist* (1973), and of Justice Antonin Scalia in *Lee v. Weisman* (1992).

In other instances, however, the use of history is more substantial. Virtually all these more telling usages are rooted in a conviction that the founding era has a special relevance for the interpretation of the religion clauses. Part of that relevance comes from a sense of "original intent"—that is, a belief that the meaning of the Constitution was determined at its drafting. In the case of the religion clauses, however, there is an equally significant but less clearly articulated relevance for history: History cushions the clauses' threat to majoritarianism by offering the consolation of continuity. That is, the religion clauses are almost always invoked to challenge a statute. Whether the statute is upheld or not, history can be invoked to show that the outcome has the presumed wisdom of age, thereby lessening any insult to a momentary majority.

Two Views of Continuity

Within this shared belief in the persuasive power of continuity there are actually two different positions. One position seeks solace in institutional practices; the other appeals to what it sees as the continuity of purpose in the religion clauses. The former position is akin to the "originalist" who articulates beliefs in judicial self-restraint. Justices who hold this position tend to see practices that have continued since the founding era as having the approval of both the Founders and the intervening generations. The other position denies the value of continuity of practice, pointing instead to important discontinuities, especially those wrought by the Fourteenth Amendment. The justices who hold this position find in history the consoling principle that the religion clauses themselves were designed to ensure that differences did not become destructive.

Neither position was represented in the Court's earliest cases concerning religion—a time before the emergence of a generational gap that separated the Court from the founding era. There was then little use of history. Two examples of that fact come from opinions by Justice Joseph Story. In *Terrett v. Taylor* (1815) he appealed to "common sense" and "maxims of eternal justice," while in *Vidal v. Executors of Girard* (1844) he accepted that "the Christian religion is a part of the common law of Pennsylvania." Justice Story's view of a homogeneous nation continued through the late nineteenth century, persisting even when the Court began to see evidence of religious diversity. The first significant challenge to reach the Supreme Court came from the Mormons' claim that the Free Exercise Clause protected their right to practice polygamy. Faced with that challenge in *Reynolds,* in 1878, and without any significant judicial opinion on which to rely, Chief Justice Morrison Waite turned to history of two sorts. First, he looked to history for assistance in determining the meaning of "religion," which he noted was "not defined in the Constitution." He continued, "We must go elsewhere, therefore, to ascertain its meaning, and nowhere more appropriately, we think, than to the history of the times in the midst of which the provision was adopted. The precise point of the inquiry is, what is the religious freedom which has been guaranteed." Waite found his answer in Thomas Jefferson's letter to the Danbury Baptist Association. In Waite's view, however, the First Amendment "wall" protected only belief; it did not reach "actions which were in violation of social duties or subversive of good order." The second type of history was therefore that of permissible "actions." Waite limited his history to that of "the northern and western nations of Europe," where he found agreement that the practice of polygamy was "odious." He then summarized the history of prohibitions within the United States, concluding, "In the face of all this evidence, it is impossible to believe that the constitutional guaranty of religious freedom was intended to prohibit legislation in respect to this most important feature of social life." Chief Justice Waite's history was therefore that of legislative practice, which had the effect of supporting the legislative majority against a minority. Twelve years later, Justice Stephen Field expressed a similar view about bigamy, in his majority opinion in *Davis v. Beason* (1890).

The chaos of World War II brought a different view, influenced by the atrocities against religious minorities in Europe. With the United States in conflict with totalitarian governments, the Court could no longer limit its efforts to majority history, as Waite had done sixty years before. Even before the United States entered the war, the Court reflected the conflict. For example, in *Cantwell v. Connecticut* (1940) Justice Owen Roberts emphasized the religion clauses' continuity of purpose to protect diversity:

> The essential characteristic of these liberties is, that under their shield many types of life, character, opinion and belief can develop unmolested and unobstructed. Nowhere is this shield more necessary than in our own country for a people composed of many races and of many creeds.

Justice William Douglas echoed that sentiment when he later wrote, in *United States v. Ballard* (1944),

> The Fathers of the Constitution were not unaware of the varied and extreme views of religious sects, of the violence of dis-

agreement among them, and of the lack of any one religious creed on which all men would agree. They fashioned a charter of government which envisaged the widest possible toleration of conflicting views. Man's relation to his God was made no concern of the state.

Discontinuity and Debate

World War II also forced a kind of chaos within the Court, as the justices struggled to define their new role as protectors of individual liberties. Whether the Bill of Rights would apply to the states provoked a renewed interest in history, of the Fourteenth Amendment as well as of the First. For the first time there was genuine debate about the historical sources—sources that were now more readily available, thanks to professional historians who continued their publication of manuscript sources. *Everson v. Board of Education of Ewing Township* (1947) marked the beginning of the Court's most significant period for using history. Justice Hugo Black returned to Jefferson's "wall of separation" metaphor to support the conclusion that a state could reimburse parents for transporting their children to parochial schools. Justice Wiley Rutledge dissented, with the longest historical analysis to date. In this first significant Establishment Clause case, Rutledge penned an explanation which would become a refrain for those who turned to history:

> No provision of the Constitution is more closely tied to or given content by its generating history than the religious clause of the First Amendment. It is at once the refined product and the terse summation of that history. The history includes not only James Madison's authorship and the proceedings before the First Congress, but also the long and intensive struggle for religious freedom in America, more especially in Virginia, of which the Amendment was the direct culmination. In the documents of the times, particularly of Madison, who was leader in the Virginia struggle before he became the Amendment's sponsor, but also in the writings of Jefferson and others and in the issues which engendered them is to be found irrefutable confirmation of the Amendment's sweeping content.

Rutledge thus set the framework for the next wave of decisions, as the Court struggled to locate its opinions in the nation's history at the same time that it effected the great discontinuity brought on by applying the Bill of Rights to the states. For a time the Court struggled with its newly rediscovered metaphor. Justice Robert Jackson, in *Illinois ex rel. McCollum v. Board of Education* (1948), warned against making "the legal 'wall of separation between church and state' as winding as the famous serpentine wall designed by Mr. Jefferson for the University he founded." Likewise, Justice Stanley Reed, dissenting in *McCollum,* relied on other actions and statements of Jefferson to support his conclusion that "[a] rule of law should not be drawn from a figure of speech." Reed then set out what would become the opposing theme to Jefferson's "wall": "Well-recognized and long-established practices." And he concluded:

> This Court cannot be too cautious in upsetting practices embedded in our society by many years of experience. . . . The Constitution should not be stretched to forbid national customs in the way courts act to reach arrangements to avoid taxation. Devotion to the great principle of religious liberty should not lead us into a rigid interpretation of the constitutional guarantee that conflicts with accepted habits of our people. This is an instance where, for me, the history of past practices is determinative of the meaning of a constitutional clause, not a decorous introduction to the study of its text.

Not until the 1960s did the Court confront another series of religion clause cases. The two themes—continuity of practice and continuity of purpose—continued to dominate the opinions. But ironic subthemes also began to appear. Those who supported a continuity of practice found that the practice often robbed actions of their religious content. Those who supported a continuity of principle had to grapple with the discontinuity of the Fourteenth Amendment. Thus, in upholding Sunday "blue laws" in *McGowan,* in 1961, Chief Justice Earl Warren could write that "we find the place of Sunday Closing Laws in the First Amendment's history both enlightening and persuasive." But his conclusion was not that the juxtaposition supported a religious practice; instead,

> In light of the evolution of our Sunday Closing Laws through the centuries, and of their more or less recent emphasis upon secular considerations, it is not difficult to discern that as presently written and administered, most of them, at least, are of a secular rather than of a religious character, and that presently they bear no relationship to establishment of religion as those words are used in the Constitution of the United States.

Justice Douglas was the first to acknowledge the discontinuity, in *McGowan:*

> Those reasons would be compelling if the First Amendment had, at the time of its adoption, been applicable to the States. But since it was then applicable only to the Federal Government, it had no possible bearing on the Sunday laws of the States. The Fourteenth Amendment, adopted years later, made the First Amendment applicable to the States for the first time. That Amendment has had unsettling effects on many customs and practices—a process consistent with Jefferson's precept "that laws and institutions must go hand in hand with the progress of the human mind."

Justice Brennan would later echo that view in 1963, in his concurring opinion in *Schempp,* when he referred simply to the "ambiguity of history." More recently, Justice Harry Blackmun has explicitly linked the theme of continuity of purpose with a rejection of history. He referred to the "bedrock Establishment Clause principle that regardless of history, government may not demonstrate a preference for a particular faith" (*County of Allegheny v. American Civil Liberties Union* [1989]). Justice Anthony Kennedy disagreed, writing in the same case, "that the meaning of the [Establishment] Clause is to be determined by reference to historical practices and understanding."

Inherent Contradictions

The Court thus has found itself faced with contradictions inherent in the history of the religion clauses: The history of religious schisms that lay behind the clauses was the same history behind the continuity of certain practices, such as public prayer and reading of the Bible. Thus in 1962 Justice Black could invoke history to support his majority opinion in *Engel,* striking down a requirement that a prayer be recited in New York public schools:

> It is a matter of history that this very practice of establishing governmental composed prayers for religious services was one of the reasons which caused many of our early colonists to leave England and seek religious freedom in America.

Yet twenty years later, in *Marsh v. Chambers* (1983), Chief Justice Burger could invoke history in support of prayers at the opening of legislative sessions:

> The opening of sessions of legislative and other deliberative public bodies with prayer is deeply embedded in the history and tradition of this country. From colonial times through the founding of the Republic and ever since, the practice of legislative prayer has coexisted with the principles of disestablishment and religious freedom.

Walter F. Pratt, Jr.

Bibliography

Finkelman, Paul, "The Constitution and the Intentions of the Framers: The Limits of Historical Analysis," 50 *University of Pittsburgh Law Review* 349–398 (1989).

Healey, Robert M., "Thomas Jefferson's 'Wall': Absolute or Serpentine?" 30 *Journal of Church and State* 441–462 (1988).

Kelly, Alfred H., "Clio and the Court: An Illicit Love Affair," 1965 *Supreme Court Review* 119–158 (1965).

McConnell, Michael W., "The Origins and Historical Understanding of Free Exercise of Religion," 103 *Harvard Law Review* 1409–1519 (1990).

Wiecek, William, "Clio As Hostage: The United States Supreme Court and the Uses of History." 24 *California Western Law Review* 227–268 (1988).

H

Cases Cited

Cantwell v. Connecticut, 310 U.S. 296 (1940).
Committee for Public Education and Religious Liberty v. Nyquist, 413 U.S. 756 (1973).
County of Allegheny v. American Civil Liberties Union, 492 U.S. 573 (1989).
Davis v. Beason, 133 U.S. 333 (1890).
Engel v. Vitale, 370 U.S. 421 (1962).
Epperson v. Arkansas, 393 U.S. 97 (1968).
Everson v. Board of Education of Ewing Township, 330 U.S. 1 (1947).
Gillette v. United States, 401 U.S. 437 (1971).
Illinois ex rel. McCollum v. Board of Education, 333 U.S. 203 (1948).
Lee v. Weisman, 505 U.S. 577 (1992).
Lemon v. Kurtzman, 403 U.S. 602 (1971).
Marsh v. Chambers, 463 U.S. 783 (1983).
McGowan v. Maryland, 366 U.S. 420 (1961).
Reynolds v. United States, 98 U.S. 145 (1878).
School District of Abington Township v. Schempp, 374 U.S. 203 (1963).
Terrett v. Taylor, 13 U.S. (9 Cranch) 43 (1815).
United States v. Ballard, 322 U.S. 78 (1944).
Vidal v. Executors of Girard, 43 U.S. (2 How.) 127 (1844).
Wallace v. Jaffree, 472 U.S. 38 (1985).

Hull Memorial Church

See PRESBYTERIAN CHURCH IN THE UNITED STATES V. MARY ELIZABETH BLUE HULL MEMORIAL CHURCH.

Hutchinson, Anne

See TRIAL OF ANNE HUTCHINSON.

I

Immigration and Naturalization Law and Religion

The role that religion has played throughout the immigration history of the United States has often been contradictory. The United States has traditionally considered itself a haven for those fleeing religious persecution. However, although the U.S. Supreme Court has issued opinions and Congress has passed laws grounded in this legacy, a would-be immigrant's religion has often acted to bar entry into the United States. Since Congress began limiting the numbers of immigrants in the mid–nineteenth century, it has provided exceptions based on religious grounds but has also limited the admission of aliens based on their religion.

Immigration

Until the mid–nineteenth century, immigrants—whether or not they were refugees—were generally welcome because of the need for labor and population in the country. However, in the mid–nineteenth century, after a series of economic depressions, Congress began passing laws limiting certain classes of aliens.

One of the first cases decided by the U.S. Supreme Court involving immigration and religion emanated from one of these laws. The act of February 26, 1885, prohibited the "importation and migration of foreigners and aliens under contract or agreement to perform labor in the United States." It was intended to limit the numbers of uneducated laborers. But in *Church of the Holy Trinity v. United States* (1892) the Court held that this prohibition did not apply to a contract between an English alien and a religious organization that wished to hire him as its minister. The "religious organization" was an Episcopal church. The Court conceded that the contract in question was within the "letter" of the act. However, the Court believed that, because "this is a Christian nation," Congress could not have intended to prevent such a transaction from taking place.

The Immigration Act of 1917 introduced a literacy test for those wishing to enter the United States: Would-be immigrants had to prove that they were literate in at least one language by reading a passage in front of an examiner at the port of entry. The test was intended to curtail immigration of Catholics from southern and eastern Europe, Jews from eastern Europe, and immigrants from the Middle East. Ironically, the only people exempt from this requirement were those fleeing religious persecution.

Although the act of 1917 remained the basic law until the passage of the Immigration and Nationality Act of 1952, Congress added another restriction in 1921. The Immigration Act of 1921 instituted a quota system based on national origins, limiting immigration to 3 percent of the "number of foreign-born persons of such nationality resident in the United States as determined by the United States census of 1910"; Congress also put an annual cap for all immigration. Northern and western European immigrants were granted an annual quota of about 200,000; the quota for immigrants from southern and eastern Europe was set at about 155,000. Again, the system was specifically aimed at excluding Catholics, Jews, and other non-Protestants.

In response to ever-increasing levels of immigration of these "undesirables," Congress soon adopted a new, more restrictive quota system. The National Origins Act of 1924 lowered the nationality quota from 3 percent to 2 percent and lowered the cap to 164,667 immigrants per year. To further limit what Congress deemed were undesirable ethnic groups and religions, the benchmark year was pushed back from 1910 to 1890, when fewer U.S. citizens were descendants of southern and eastern Europeans. As intended, the reductions of quotas severely affected those from eastern and southern Europe—and did so at a time when masses of people were fleeing the pogroms and results of World War I. These quotas later served to limit the numbers of eastern Europeans admitted during the rise of Nazism in the 1930s and during World War II.

Although those escaping religious persecution remained exempt from the literacy test, they were not exempt from the quota restrictions. However, "ministers of religion" were exempt from the quota if they had practiced their vocation for the two years immediately preceding their application for a visa. In *Matter of M* (BIA 1941) and *Matter of B* (BIA 1948), the Board of Immigration Appeals reversed two decisions of the Board of Special Inquiry at Ellis Island. In both cases the board had excluded rabbis based on the fact they had not practiced their vocations for the two years before their applications. One refugee had spent three years in a concentration camp and over one year in a displaced persons camp; the other managed to escape from Poland and had spent World War II fleeing from the German army.

Current immigration policy continues to reflect the special status that religious practitioners have traditionally occupied. The Immigration Act of 1965 redefined the category of "ministers of religion" as "special immigrants" but maintained the exemption from numerical quotas. The Immigration Act of 1990 removed this exemption and limited the category to those seeking to enter the United States before October 1, 1994. Under this act an alien could immigrate if he or she was (1) a minister of a religious denomination, (2) entering to work for a religious organization in a professional capacity, or (3) entering to work for a religious organization in a religious vocation or occupation. The immigrant still had to have practiced his or her vocation for the two years immediately preceding the application.

However, as a result of extensive lobbying by religious groups, the Immigration Act of 1990 introduced a special nonimmigrant visa for temporary religious workers. The R-1 visa is available to ministers of religion, religious professionals, and "other religious workers." There are no numerical limitations, and, unlike "special immigrants," the applicant need not have performed his or her religious work for the two-year period preceding the application.

Refugees

Huguenots, Quakers, Mennonites, Amish, and Jews fleeing religious persecution in the seventeenth century; Jews escaping pogroms in the late nineteenth century; and Armenians fleeing Turkish pogroms during the first decades of the twentieth century all found refuge in this country with relatively few legal obstacles. However, by the 1930s and 1940s, when masses of Jews were fleeing Nazi-occupied Europe, immigration was severely limited by a strict quota system and other requirements. No exceptions from the quotas were made for people fleeing persecution of any kind.

However, although no right to asylum existed based on religious persecution until the adoption of the Refugee Act of 1980, the special status of those fleeing such persecution was previously recognized in immigration law in that such people were exempt from the literacy test. To be admitted, would-be immigrants had to prove that they were literate in at least one language by reading a passage in front of an examiner at the port of entry. Aliens were exempt from the test only if they could prove that

> they are seeking admission to the United States to avoid religious persecution in the country of their last permanent residence, whether such persecution be evidenced by overt acts or by laws or governmental regulations that discriminate against the alien or the race to which he belongs because of his religious faith. . . .

Aliens were not automatically admissible if they were found to be escaping religious persecution; they still had to meet the other requirements for admission. In addition, if they were merely fleeing racial or political persecution, they were not exempt from the literacy test. Therefore, this exception forced courts to define persecution based on religion.

Courts struggled throughout the 1920s with the definition of "religious persecution," and they often arrived at conflicting conclusions. For example, in *Johnson v. Tertzag; Ex parte Soghanalian* (1st Cir. 1924), a federal court admitted an illiterate Armenian woman on the grounds of religious persecution after she described how the Turks had killed her parents and all other Christians from her town and how she had been seized and kept in a harem for three and a half years until saved by Allied armies. However, in *United States ex rel. Azizian v. Curran* (2d Cir. 1923), another case involving an Armenian woman, the United States Circuit Court found that although

> common knowledge enables us to recognize in this most unfortunate woman a victim of what are too well known as "Armenian massacres," neither evidence nor common report enables us to say that what happened in Urmia in 1917 was religious persecution, as distinguished from robbery and banditry at a time and place of social dissolution, if not political revolution.

In 1942, in *Matter of M,* the Board of Immigration Appeals found that members of a Jewish Romanian family who had been denied admission because they could not read satisfactorily were exempt from the test because they were fleeing "Hitlerism," which the board declared was a state religion that subverted all other religions. The board believed that for the "Hebrew" people, "race and religion are one," but that the Nazi persecution was based on religious and not racial motives.

During the years immediately following World War II, Congress passed new legislation that provided for the admission of refugees created by the war. For example, the Displaced Persons Act of 1948 exempted war refugees from the quota restrictions. However, beginning in 1950, the definition of "persecution" had to be confronted with increasing frequency. In 1950 Congress amended the Immigration Act of 1917 to provide that an alien could avoid deportation if he or she would be subjected to physical persecution on the basis of race, nationality, religion, or political opinion. In the Immigration and Nationality Act of 1952, Congress further amended this provision to give the attorney general the discretionary power to withhold deportation based on the same grounds.

The Immigration Act of 1965 replaced the physical requirement with the requirement that the persecution be "on account of race, religion or political opinion." In 1966, in *Matter of Salama,* the Board of Immigration Appeals stopped the deportation of a Jewish man to Egypt because an official campaign of discrimination had already forced the departure of almost the entire Jewish population of Egypt. Section 203(a)(7) of the Immigration Act of 1965 also provided a procedure for paroling into the United States those who qualified as refugees under the claim of religious discrimination in their homeland. Although relief under this provision was available to people already in the United States, they still had to show that they had fled their country of citizenship "because of persecution." For example, in *Matter of Lalian* (BIA 1967), an Iranian Christian woman was denied refugee classification because she had entered the United States on a visitor's visa and because her subsequent actions indicated that she intended to return to Iran. She had received extensions of her visa and of her passport as well as two new passports from the Iranian authorities.

The Refugee Act of 1980 eliminated the discretion of the attorney general in withholding deportation, although the circumstances for doing so are quite narrow. The 1980 act also introduced asylum for anyone who qualified as a "refugee" as defined by the *Protocol to the United Nations Convention on Refugees.* An applicant's well-founded fear of persecution because of religion is one of the five grounds specified in the *Protocol* (the others are race, nationality, political opinion, and social group). However, the 1980 law allows the attorney general to retain discretion in whether asylum should be granted.

The definition of religious persecution has developed rapidly since the passage of the Refugee Act of 1980. To qualify, the applicant must show that he or she fears persecution and not merely personal threats, animosity, or simple discrimination. It also must be established either that the persecution is government-sanctioned or that the government is unable to stop it. For example, in *Matter of Chen* (BIA 1989) a man from a Catholic family in the People's Republic of China—whose family members experienced horrendous mistreatment during the Cultural Revolution—was found to have a well-founded fear based on this past persecution. Similarly, in *Doe v. Immigration and Naturalization Service* (6th Cir. 1989) a federal court held that a Chinese student who converted to Christianity while in the United States had a well-founded fear of persecution.

However, in *Gumbol v. Immigration and Naturalization Service* (6th Cir. 1987) a Christian Iraqi was found not to possess such a fear, even though he had been beaten by a member of the Baath Party because he was Christian and refused to join that party. The court found that he had not established that the beating was government-sanctioned, rather than merely an isolated incident.

In addition, the persecution must be *on account of* the applicant's religious beliefs or actions. This issue is especially contentious where army conscription is involved, because people have many reasons, including fear, for refusing to serve in their nation's army. For example, in 1988, in *Matter of Canas,* the Board of Immigration Appeals held that a Jehovah's Witness who refused to be conscripted into the Salvadorian army based on his religious beliefs did not qualify as a refugee because he had not established that the conscription laws were enacted with the intent of persecuting members of a certain religion. The Salvadorian government imprisoned everyone who refused to serve, regardless of their reasons.

On appeal, the circuit court in *Canas-Segovia v. Immigration and Naturalization Service* (9th Cir. 1992) attempted to accord persecution on account of religion greater deference than persecution on any of the other four grounds specified in the Immigration Act of 1980. The court based its opinion on U.S. constitutional law and on the *United Nations Handbook on Refugees.* It held that, where the alien's refusal to serve in the army was based on genuine religious beliefs and where such refusal, regardless of the reason, automatically subjects the alien to imprisonment, torture, or death, the alien qualifies as a refugee. The *Handbook*—which is generally considered a legitimate interpretive source—states that conscientious objectors may be eligible for refugee status if their government does not provide an exception for religious beliefs.

However, the appeals court's second basis, U.S. constitutional law, was more controversial because aliens do not enjoy the protections of the First Amendment's religion clauses. The court began by acknowledging the special place that religion holds in U.S. law and by recognizing that religious conscientious objectors are exempt from serving in the U.S. military. It then likened the aliens' situation to one where, under the freedom of religion clause in the First Amendment, a facially neutral statute is deemed unduly burdensome to a religious group. Applying this constitutional principle, it found that the fact that the Salvadorian conscription law was neutral on its face did not preclude it from being persecuted.

The U.S. Supreme Court did not address either ground when it heard the *Canas* case. Instead, it vacated the lower court's decision and remanded the case to the court of appeals for reconsideration in light of its own opinion in *Immigration and Naturalization Service v. Elias-Zacarias* (1992), where it had ruled that, to show persecution on account of political opinion, the persecutor's intent must be shown. On remand, the court of appeals held that, under the *Elias-Zacarias* precedent, Canas had to show the intent of his home government to persecute him because of his religious beliefs. But Canas was unable to establish that he would be imprisoned specifically because he refused to serve in the army for religious reasons, and thus the court of appeals concluded that he did not have a well-founded fear of persecution on account of his religion.

Naturalization

The major area where the Supreme Court has dealt with religion and immigration is that concerning the oath of citizenship. The Naturalization Act of 1906 required that, to become a citizen, an applicant had to "declare an oath in open court . . . that he will support and defend the Constitution and laws of the United States against all enemies, foreign and domestic, and bear true faith and allegiance to the same."

In *United States v. Schwimmer* (1929) the Court upheld the denial of a naturalization application of a 49-year-old woman who agreed to take the oath of allegiance but refused to take up arms in the defense of the United States because she was a pacifist. Two years later, in *United States v. MacIntosh* (1931), the Court held that a Baptist minister who agreed to take up arms only if he deemed the purpose justified could not be naturalized. The same day, in *United States v. Bland* (1931), the Court held that the application should be denied in the case of a woman who refused to take the oath of allegiance to defend the U.S. Constitution and laws unless she were allowed to add the words "as far as my conscience as a Christian will allow" and who refused to swear to bear arms in the defense of the United States.

In all three cases, the Court based its holdings on the principle that naturalization was a privilege. Even though Congress allowed for conscientious objector status based on religious scruples for those people who are already citizens, it was within Congress's power to deny such a privilege to prospective citizens. The Court found no constitutional right to refuse to bear arms in defense of the United States based on religious reasons; the privilege came from an act of Congress.

In *Girouard v. United States* (1946) the Court overruled all three decisions based on its rereading of congressional intent as expressed in the statute requiring the oath of allegiance. *Girouard* involved a Seventh-Day Adventist who refused to take up arms for religious reasons but who agreed to perform noncombatant military duty. The Court concluded that the statute did not expressly require aliens to promise to bear arms as long as there were other ways to defend the United States.

Although the case was not decided on constitutional principles, Justice Douglas reasoned that Congress had consistently upheld the freedom of religion of U.S. citizens to refuse to take oaths and should not, therefore, deny this important right to those wishing to become citizens. It could not have been congressional intent to require an alien to set aside religious beliefs in order to become a citizen but not to require the same in order to become a member of Congress. Inasmuch as religious freedom was firmly embedded in the country's traditions, if Congress wished to prevent conscientious objectors from becoming citizens, it had to do so by express statutory enactment.

In the Naturalization Act of 1952, Congress provided that, if the alien could prove by "clear and convincing evidence . . . that he is opposed to the bearing of arms . . . by reason of religious training and belief," he or she could still take the oath of allegiance and become a citizen of the United States.

The Sanctuary Movement

One modern phenomenon in immigration is the sanctuary movement that emerged during the 1980s. This was a movement of people who smuggled illegal refugees from Central America across the Mexican border to Arizona. They counseled the aliens about how to cross the border and directed them to churches that operated as sanctuaries. They acted out of humanitarian and religious motivations as well as with the intent to protest the involvement of the United States in what they believed to be illegal wars in Central America. Churches were used as refuges on the grounds that they have historically operated as sanctuaries from governmental authorities. In other words, supporters of the sanctuary movement believed that the Immigration and Naturalization Service could not legally raid the churches in their search for illegal aliens.

In *United States v. Aguilar* (9th Cir. 1989) appellants had been convicted of several crimes connected to the movement's smuggling activities. Many of their defenses centered on their religious motivations. For example, several had been convicted of transporting illegal aliens pursuant to Article 8, Section 1324, of the U.S. Code, which requires the government to show that the appellants transported the aliens "knowing or having reasonable grounds to believe that [their] last entry into the United States occurred less than three years prior thereto." One justification argued on appeal was that, because the appellants had transported the Central Americans out of religious motivations, the requisite intent was negated. The Ninth Circuit Court of Appeals simply stated that the appellants were "confusing motivation with intent."

These appellants also argued that the First Amendment protection of free exercise of religion prevented their conviction because their "sincere religious beliefs inspired them" to break the law. The Court, employing a strict scrutiny test, found that the immigration law did not unduly burden their free exercise of religion, because no Christian religion demands participation in the sanctuary movement. The Court noted not only that there are many ways to assist illegal aliens but also that Christian religious groups are not the only people who wish to provide such aid.

The Court also found that, even if the appellants were able to establish that enforcement of the law unduly interfered with their religious beliefs, the government obviously had a compelling interest in uniformly enforcing the immigration laws. It stated that a limited exemption in favor of the four churches involved would not be feasible. If it were granted, other religious and nonreligious groups would demand similar exemptions, rendering the immigration laws useless.

Renee C. Redman

Bibliography

Golden, Renny, and Michael McConnell, *Sanctuary: The New Underground Railroad* (Maryknoll, N.Y.: Orbis, 1986).

Gordon, Charles, and Stanley Mailman, *Immigration and Procedure,* rev. ed. (New York: Matthew Bender, 1994).

Cases Cited

Canas-Segovia v. Immigration and Naturalization Service, 902 F. 2d 717 (9th Cir. 1990).

Canas-Segovia v. Immigration and Naturalization Service, 970 F. 2d 599 (9th Cir. 1992).

Church of the Holy Trinity v. United States, 143 U.S. 457 (1892).

Doe v. Immigration and Naturalization Service, 867 F. 2d 285 (6th Cir. 1989).

Girouard v. United States, 328 U.S. 61 (1946).

Gumbol v. Immigration and Naturalization Service, 815 F. 2d 406 (6th Cir. 1987).

Immigration and Naturalization Service v. Canas-Segovia, 502 U.S. 1086 (1992).

Immigration and Naturalization Service v. Elias-Zacarias, 502 U.S. 478 (1992).

Johnson v. Tertzag; Ex parte Soghanalian, 2 F. 2d 40 (1st Cir., 1924).

Matter of B, 3 I&N Dec. 162 (BIA 1948).

Matter of Canas, 19 I&N Dec. 697 (BIA 1988).

Matter of Chen, Int. Dec. 3104 (BIA 1989).

Matter of Lalian, 12 I&N Dec. 124 (BIA 1967).

Matter of M, 1 I&N Dec. 147 (BIA 1941).

Matter of M, 1 I&N Dec. 280 (BIA 1942).

Matter of Salama, 11 I&N Dec. 536 (BIA 1966).

United States v. Aguilar, 883 F. 2d 662 (9th Cir. 1989), cert den., 498 U.S. 1046 (1991).

United States ex rel. Azizian v. Curran, 12 F. 2d 502 (2d Cir. 1926).

United States v. Bland, 283 U.S. 636 (1931).

United States v. MacIntosh, 283 U.S. 605 (1931).

United States v. Schwimmer, 279 U.S. 644 (1929).

Incorporation of the Bill of Rights in the Fourteenth Amendment and the Religion Clauses

When the Framers proposed the new Constitution in 1787, it lacked a bill of rights. In the battle over ratification, James Madison and some other supporters of the Constitution agreed that after ratification they would support amendments adding a declaration of rights to the Constitution. In the First Congress in 1789, true to his promise, Congressman Madison proposed amendments to declare basic rights. Madison's proposal for a declaration of rights included several that were explicitly designed to limit state governments: "No state shall violate the equal rights of conscience, or the freedom of the press, or trial by jury in criminal cases." Although Madison thought his provision securing these "privileges" against the states was the most important of all his proposals, Congress refused to recommend his limitations on state power.

Congress did propose, and the states ratified, a guarantee that "Congress shall make no law respecting an establishment of religion, or prohibiting the free exercise thereof; . . ." In *Barron v. Baltimore* (1833) the Supreme Court held that the guarantees of the Bill of Rights did not limit state or local governments. Chief Justice Marshall said that if the Framers of the Bill of Rights intended it to limit the states, they would have followed the example of the original Constitution and prefaced the limitations with the "no state shall" language used in Article I, Section 10, for limitations on state power. In *Permoli v. First Municipality of New Orleans* (1845) the Court explicitly held that the "Constitution makes no provision for protecting the citizens of the respective states in their religious liberties." The Court said that protection of such liberties was left to "state constitutions and laws."

The Court handed down the decision in *Barron* in 1833, during a growing crisis of civil liberty. In *Barron* the Court held that the guarantees of the Bill of Rights did not limit state government. In press, pulpit, pamphlets, and public assemblies, advocates of liberty for the slave had begun to demand the immediate abolition of slavery. Southern states had passed laws suppressing antislavery publications and speeches. Southern authorities directed these laws against both religious and secular critics of slavery. In 1850, for example, in North Carolina a minister was tried and exiled from the state for giving a young white woman a tract suggesting that slavery violated the Ten Commandments. In 1860 another antislavery minister was tried and convicted for disseminating a copy of the antislavery book (and Republican campaign document) *The Impending Crisis of the South: How to Meet It.* From the founding of the Republican Party in 1854 to the Civil War, laws and mobs made it impossible for Republicans to campaign in the South. Faced with widespread Southern denial of civil liberties to themselves and their allies, leading Republicans developed the unorthodox legal theory that a proper reading of the Constitution required states to obey the guarantees of liberty contained in the Bill of Rights.

When they proposed the Thirteenth Amendment abolishing slavery and the Fourteenth Amendment making African Americans citizens and securing basic rights to all American citizens, leading Republicans recalled that slavery had been characterized by violations of freedom of speech, press, and religion. A number of Republican congressmen and senators insisted that Southern state actions had violated federal constitutional guarantees of freedom of speech, press, and religion. In 1866 Republicans in Congress said that the South was again denying freedom of speech and the press.

The first section of the Fourteenth Amendment made persons born in the country citizens of the United States and of the state in which they lived. It provided that "[n]o state shall make or enforce any law which shall abridge the privileges or immunities of citizens of the United States; nor shall any state deprive any person of life, liberty, or property, without due process of law; . . ." Many Republicans read the word "privileges" literally so that it meant "rights." In Congress in 1866 Senator Jacob Howard, who reported the Fourteenth Amendment to the Senate on behalf of the Joint Committee on Reconstruction, said that the Privileges or Immunities Clause of the Fourteenth Amendment was designed to require states to obey the guarantees of the Bill of Rights. Congressman John Bingham who wrote most of Section 1 made similar suggestions in the House. No one contradicted them.

The Bingham-Howard plan to require state governments to respect the basic liberties in the federal Bill of Rights was soon liquidated by the U.S. Supreme Court. In the *Slaughter-House Cases* (1872) the Court deprived the Privileges or Immunities Clause of the Fourteenth Amendment of any significant meaning. Subsequently, some in Congress proposed a constitutional Amendment, known as the Blaine amendment, which would have prohibited state governments from establishing religion or prohibiting its free exercise and from aiding parochial schools. Some supporters noted that recent constitutional amendments had been deprived of their intended meaning. Congress did not pass the Blaine Amendment with the necessary two-thirds majority, and so it was never submitted to the states.

Some have argued that the Blaine Amendment proves that the Fourteenth Amendment was never intended to apply First Amendment freedoms to the states. If it had been, they argue, Congress would not have proposed a subsequent amendment to do the same thing. The Blaine Amendment was proposed after the *Slaughter-House* decision limited the Fourteenth Amendment's protections of federal rights to a very narrow class of rights, such as the right to protection on the high seas. Most of the debate about the amendment occurred after the Court had explicitly held that none of the guarantees of the Bill of Rights limited the states under the newly enacted Fourteenth Amendment.

Although the Court initially read the Fourteenth Amendment narrowly, it gradually began to read the word "liberty" in the Due Process Clause more broadly—at first, as a protection against government regulation of the economy, such as some laws about minimum wages and maximum hours. In *Pierce v.*

Society of Sisters (1925) the Court read the guarantee of liberty in the Due Process Clause expansively enough to void a state law that prohibited children from attending private or religious schools. The Court did not specifically rely on the guarantee of freedom of religion contained in the First Amendment, because that guarantee had not been "incorporated" into the Fourteenth Amendment—that is, had not been held to limit the states. The Court invoked the right of parents to raise their children and to teach them religion.

By the mid-1920s the Court first assumed and later held that free speech and some other guarantees of the Bill of Rights were encompassed in the "liberty" that was protected by the Fourteenth Amendment's Due Process Clause. In *Palko v. Connecticut* (1937) the Court sought to rationalize the selective application of Bill of Rights guarantees to the states. The Court said that "some of the privileges and immunities" in the Bill of Rights were so fundamental to liberty that states would not be permitted to abridge them. Other "privileges or immunities" in the Bill of Rights were less essential, and states could violate them. The reading was consistent with the Court's cases, but it was a curious way to deal with an amendment that said "no state shall . . . abridge the privileges or immunities of citizens of the United States." Still, the Court suggested that freedom of thought and of speech was within the circle of those fundamental "privileges and immunities" that were protected against state denial by the Due Process Clause.

In *Cantwell v. Connecticut* (1940) the Court held that the guarantee of free exercise of religion was applicable to state as well as federal power. And in *Everson v. Board of Education* (1947) the Court held that the prohibition against an establishment of religion was applicable to the states.

After the *Everson* decision the Court confronted controversial and emotional issues involving religion and state government. In *School District of Abington Township v. Schempp* (1963) the Court held that states could not require that the Bible or the Lord's Prayer be recited in schools, even if the schools made provision for excusing students from the exercises at the request of their parents. In the 1960s the Court also increasingly required states to abide by the criminal procedure guarantees of the Bill of Rights.

The school prayer and criminal law decisions, among others, sparked political protests that have continued to the present time. Increasingly, critics of the Court looked for methods of undoing what they saw as the damage it had done. One theory that critics suggested was that the Court should reverse the incorporation doctrine, by which it applies most guarantees of the Bill of Rights to the states under the Fourteenth Amendment. In the published version of a speech he delivered to the American Bar Association, Edmund Meese, President Reagan's attorney general, attacked the incorporation doctrine as an unwarranted assumption of power by the Court.

Jaffree v. Board of School Commissioners of Mobile County, a 1983 district court case in Alabama, was the most remarkable result of political and academic criticisms of the doctrine by which states were required to observe most of the limits on power set out in the Bill of Rights. In that case, the district court upheld teacher-led school prayers. It concluded that the framers of the Fourteenth Amendment had not intended to require the states to obey the guarantees of the First Amendment or, for that matter, other guarantees of the Bill of Rights. The district court followed what it thought were the teachings of the framers of the Fourteenth Amendment, not the decisions of the Supreme Court. The decision of the district court was promptly reversed, and in *Wallace v. Jaffree* (1985) the Supreme Court reaffirmed its decisions that the guarantees of the First Amendment limit state as well as federal power.

Although the argument for freeing the states from all the guarantees of the Bill of Rights was unsuccessful, some scholars soon suggested a second, subtler and more limited theory. By this analysis the Establishment Clause was merely a declaration that federal power did not extend to the subject of establishment of religion, whereas state power to establish religion remained intact. The conclusion was that the Establishment Clause, like the Tenth Amendment, could not intelligibly be incorporated as a limit on state power. In *Lee v. Weisman* (1922) the Court, by a 5-to-4 majority, upheld a challenge to state-sponsored prayer at high school graduation exercises. It also explicitly rejected the proposal to selectively disincorporate the

Establishment Clause as a limit on state power under the Fourteenth Amendment. Instead of broadly rejecting the incorporation doctrine or selectively disincorporating guarantees, the present Court seems more likely to read the religion guarantees more narrowly—whether the "government" that is affected is federal or state.

Michael Kent Curtis

Bibliography

Amar, Akhil Reed, "The Bill of Rights and the Fourteenth Amendment," 101 *Yale Law Journal* 1193–1284 (1992).

Berger, Raoul, *The Fourteenth Amendment and the Bill of Rights* (Tulsa: University of Oklahoma Press, 1989).

———, "Incorporation of the Bill of Rights in the Fourteenth Amendment: A Nine-Lived Cat," 42 *Ohio State Law Journal* 435–466 (1981).

Curtis, Michael Kent, *No State Shall Abridge: The Fourteenth Amendment and the Bill of Rights* (Durham, N.C.: Duke University Press, 1986).

———, "Further Adventures of the Nine-Lived Cat: A Response to Mr. Berger on Incorporation of the Bill of Rights" 43 *Ohio State Law Journal* 89 (1982).

Nelson, William E., *The Fourteenth Amendment: From Political Principle to Judicial Doctrine* (Cambridge, Mass.: Harvard University Press, 1988).

Cases Cited

Barron v. Baltimore, 32 U.S. (7 Pet.) 243, (1833).

Cantwell v. Connecticut, 310 U.S. 296 (1940).

Everson v. Board of Education, 330 U.S. 1 (1947).

Jaffree v. Board of School Commissioners of Mobile County, 554 F. Supp. 1104, rev.'d *Jaffree v. Wallace,* 705 F. 2d 1526 (11th Cir. 1983).

Lee v. Weisman, 505 U.S. 577 (1992).

Palko v. Connecticut, 302 U.S. 319 (1937).

Permoli v. First Municipality of New Orleans, 44 U.S. (3 How.) 589 (1845).

Pierce v. Society of Sisters, 268 U.S. 510 (1925).

School District of Abington Township v. Schempp, 374 U.S. 203 (1963).

Slaughter-House Cases, 83 U.S. 36 (1872).

Wallace v. Jaffree, 472 U.S. 38 (1985).

"In God We Trust"

In 1956 Congress adopted the phrase "In God We Trust" as the official motto of the United States. However, as early as 1865 Congress had given official recognition to the motto by authorizing that the inscription be placed on certain coins. Congress reaffirmed the use of this phrase on coins in 1908, and in 1955 it expanded the requirement to apply to all coins and currency. Moreover, one of the stanzas of "The Star-Spangled Banner," written in 1814 and adopted as the national anthem in 1931, contains the statement "And this be our motto: 'In God is our trust!'" Congress also considered as a possible motto the phrase "E pluribus unum," but "In God We Trust" was believed to be more inspirational, as well as in "plain, popularly accepted English," as the House and Senate committees noted in their reports on the bill.

The national motto and its inclusion on coins and currency have been challenged as violative of the First Amendment's religion clauses in two cases. In *Aronow v. United States* (9th Cir. 1970), the Ninth Circuit Court of Appeals affirmed the dismissal of a complaint alleging that the motto and the requirement to place it on coins and currency violated the Establishment Clause. The court stated that the use of the phrase is of "a patriotic or ceremonial character and bears no true resemblance to a governmental sponsorship of a religious exercise," relying on language in the Supreme Court decision of *Engel v. Vitale* (1962), distinguishing between New York's prescribed prayer for beginning school days and patriotic or ceremonial activities that might include references to God. In *O'Hair v. Blumenthal* (Tex., 1978) a district court in Texas dismissed the challenge brought by Madalyn Murray O'Hair, an activist atheist, by reference to the Ninth Circuit's decision in *Aronow.*

Numerous other courts, including the Supreme Court, have referred to the national motto and its inclusion on coins and currency as examples of ceremonial deism not rising to the level of an Establishment Clause violation.

William Funk

Bibliography

Stokes, Anson, and Leo Pfeffer, *Church and State in the United States* (New York: Harper and Row, 1964).

Cases Cited

Aronow v. United States, 432 F. 2d 242 (9th Cir. 1970).

Engel v. Vitale, 370 U.S. 421 (1962).

O'Hair v. Blumenthal, 462 F. Supp. 19 (W.D. Tex.), aff'd, 588 F. 2d 1144 (5th Cir. 1978).

J

Jacobson v. Massachusetts
197 U.S. 11 (1905)

In *Jacobson v. Massachusetts* (1905) Justice John Marshall Harlan upheld a Massachusetts statute that made it a crime to refuse a vaccination. Justices David Brewer and Rufus Peckham dissented but offered no opinion. *Jacobson* was the first Supreme Court decision to address questions of forcible, public intervention into a person's biological processes. Since *Jacobson* the Court has allowed similar interventions in *Buck v. Bell* (1927) (allowing forced sterilization of a retarded person); *Washington v. Harper* (1990) (allowing forced psychiatric drugging of prisoners); and *Skinner v. Oklahoma* (1942) (on equal protection grounds, invalidating forced sterilization of "habitual criminals").

Although frequently described as a case where someone refused vaccination on religious grounds—see, e.g., *Olsen v. Drug Enforcement Administration* (D.C. Cir. 1989)—*Jacobson* did not, in fact, involve a religious refusal. The defendant believed vaccinations to be ineffective and often damaging to health. In particular, he claimed that a childhood vaccination had caused him serious side effects. Religious belief had nothing whatever to do with his refusal to be vaccinated. The misapprehension of *Jacobson* as a religious refusal case probably began with *West Virginia State Board of Education v. Barnette* (1943). "Conduct . . . has often been compelled," the *Barnette* Court wrote, "in the enforcement of legislation of general applicability even though the religious consciences of particular individuals rebelled at the exaction."

First among the cases cited in support of that proposition was *Jacobson*. Although the *Barnette* decision never quite said that *Jacobson* had involved a religious refusal, it clearly suggested as much. Then, in *Prince v. Massachusetts* (1944), the Court completed its misreading of *Jacobson*. A parent "cannot claim freedom from compulsory vaccination for the child more than for himself on religious grounds," the Court said in *Prince,* again citing *Jacobson* as authority. This unmistakably portrayed *Jacobson* as a religious refusal case—perhaps even a case of a parent's refusing vaccination for a child on religious grounds.

Jacobson included a single reference to religion, in a dictum that was unnecessary to the decision and not part of the case's holding. In his concurring opinion in *Welsh v. United States* (1970) Justice John Marshall Harlan—the grandson of the first Justice Harlan, who had authored *Jacobson*—described *Jacobson*'s reference to religion as "dictum." "Liberty," the first Justice Harlan said in *Jacobson,* includes

> the right of a person to live and work where he will . . . yet he may be compelled, by force if need be, against his will and without regard to his personal wishes or his pecuniary interests, or *even his religious or political convictions,* to take his place in the ranks of the army of his country and risk the chance of being shot down in its defense. (Emphasis added)

Although the reference was to military service, it probably contributed to the mistaken idea of *Jacobson* as a religious refusal of vaccination case. After all, *Jacobson* said something about religious convictions, and it was a vaccination case. Linking those two attributes produces *Prince*'s misreading of *Jacobson.*

The Court cited military service and religious refusal only to make the point that liberty was not absolute. The justices did not take limitations on liberty for granted in 1905. *Lochner v. New York* (1905)—decided during the same term as *Jacobson*—ushered in an era when the Supreme Court struck down reform legislation in the name of "liberty." In the view of later commentators, this Court allowed the concept of liberty to run amok in its jurisprudence. And so Harlan's argument about "liberty"—he would dissent vigorously in *Lochner*—was hardly pro forma. The military service/religious refusal example culminated a three-page discussion; it also followed another example, involving the quarantine of travelers exposed to cholera, that had no religious dimension to it.

Taken on its own terms, *Jacobson*'s dictum means that a religious objection does not exempt someone automatically from laws of general application. The point seems obvious, and rather modest. Harlan did not say that religious objections never afforded exemptions; that question was simply not before the Court. Nor did *Jacobson* hold that liberty always yielded to the state's needs, just because it did so in the military example.

Of course, one may argue that submission to vaccination, like submission to military service, constitutes an essential element of social self-defense. If so, religious objections to both should receive the same treatment. Harlan's two examples—quarantine and military service—perhaps suggest as much. But the Court did not decide that point in *Jacobson.* Not until *Employment Division, Department of Human Resources of Oregon v. Smith* (1990) did the Court announce a rule against religious exemptions from general criminal laws.

Jacobson remains important as the first case to uphold compelled, state intervention into the biological processes of a person. And it established a precedent by refusing to accord those processes special constitutional protection. The Court deferred to the legislature, and it treated objections harshly. For example, it dismissed the defendant's arguments that vaccination had injured him as a child—and that it had also injured his son—with the observation that "absolute certainty" about vaccination's safety was impossible. Refusal would be permitted, the Court suggested, when vaccination was demonstrably "cruel and inhuman in the last degree."

Lochner took a different approach entirely. It dealt harshly with the state's arguments about the need for a law limiting hours of employment. *Lochner* independently evaluated the threat to health represented by long working hours, and it rejected the state's conclusions. In modern terms, the Court used "strict scrutiny" in *Lochner* and "ordinary scrutiny" in *Jacobson.* Subsequent events—including the sterilization edict of *Buck,* the Court's retreat from strict scrutiny of social and economic legislation after the crisis of the New Deal, and even the political acts of biological mayhem in our era—suggest that the Court in *Lochner* should have applied *Jacobson*'s level of scrutiny and that the Court in *Jacobson* should have applied *Lochner*'s.

Sheldon Gelman

Bibliography

Severyn, Kristine M., "*Jacobson v. Massachusetts*: Impact on Informed Consent and Vaccine Policy," 5 *Journal of Pharmacy and Law* 249–274 (1996).

Cases Cited

Buck v. Bell, 274 U.S. 200 (1927).
Employment Division, Department of Human Resources of Oregon v. Smith, 494 U.S. 872 (1990).
Jacobson v. Massachusetts, 197 U.S. 11 (1905).
Lochner v. New York, 198 U.S. 45 (1905).
Olsen v. Drug Enforcement Administration, 878 F. 2d 1458 (D.C. Cir. 1989).
Prince v. Massachusetts, 321 U.S. 158 (1944).
Skinner v. Oklahoma, 316 U.S. 535 (1942).
Washington v. Harper, 494 U.S. 210 (1990).
Welsh v. United States, 398 U.S. 333 (1970).
West Virginia State Board of Education v. Barnette, 319 U.S. 624 (1943).

Jefferson and Religion

Thomas Jefferson opposed established religion throughout his adult life. In 1777, as a young legislator in the Virginia General Assembly, he introduced the original version of the Statute of Religious Freedom, finally brought to passage by his friend James Madison in 1786. Along with drafting the

Declaration of Independence and founding the University of Virginia, authorship of the statute was one of the three great achievements Jefferson wanted listed on his tombstone. During his presidency, Jefferson continued to uphold the First Amendment's "wall of separation" between church and state, rebuffing clerical efforts to involve the federal government in national fasts and other religious observances. "[I believe] with you that religion is a matter which lies solely between man and his God," Jefferson wrote the Baptists of Danbury, Connecticut, in his famous letter of January 1, 1802.

Jefferson's extreme tolerationism grew out of his faith in the rationalistic precepts of natural religion. He was convinced that the enormous power of organized religion depended on the clergy's success in mystifying and obfuscating otherwise self-evident truths. In the Christian tradition, the doctrine of the Trinity—the idea that three equals one—constituted the most egregious example of mystification. Exploiting popular credulity and pretending privileged access to God's Word, clergymen demanded unquestioning faith and obedience from their flocks. For Jefferson the rule of "priestcraft" was the religious equivalent to the social and political tyranny of monarchy and aristocracy: In both cases, common folk were misled into believing that *inequality,* not equality, was man's natural state. The destruction of the old regime meant the elimination of all invidious distinctions and privileges. An end to superstition, bigotry, and intolerance was crucial to the success of this revolution. The moral foundation of republican self-government was the people's virtue, vigilance, and common sense.

Religion and ethics were virtually indistinguishable for Jefferson. Although raised as an Anglican, the young Jefferson was exposed to Enlightenment influences at William and Mary, including the revival of interest in the teachings of the Roman Stoic and Epicurean philosophers. Embracing this ethical framework, Jefferson believed that the pretensions of any religious sect could be determined by asking whether or not it provided a practical design and inspiration for the good life. The dangerously divisive effects of sectarianism were particularly conspicuous during Jefferson's formative years as a Revolutionary statesman, when evangelical "dissenters" struggled for religious freedom. In this case, of course, sectarian strife centered on the question of state support: Disestablishment promised to depoliticize religion and so enable the warring sects to live in peace and harmony. But if his fight for toleration in Virginia confirmed his lifelong reputation as a champion of the evangelicals, Jefferson had serious misgivings about the compatibility of evangelical Christianity and republican government. The dangers of a privileged religious establishment were obvious—and remediable. But how could freedom of thought be secured against an intolerant majority, carried away by sectarian fervor? This question troubled Jefferson increasingly in his later years as he sought to protect his privacy and peace of mind against the tyranny of "public opinion."

Jefferson's concerns about evangelical bigotry—grounded in his profound antipathy to "Calvinist" doctrine—dated back to his youth. Calvinists epitomized sectarian irrationality because in preaching salvation by faith alone they radically devalued "good works," or ethical behavior, as a means of securing eternal life. Jefferson believed that the doctrine of predestination, by emphasizing man's incapacity to determine his own fate, subverted personal morality and justified arbitrary power. Presbyterians were particularly noxious to Jefferson because their arbitrary and antiethical theology was combined with powerful institutional structures; in Massachusetts and Connecticut their Congregationalist allies continued to enjoy the benefits of state support. Not coincidentally, as partisan controversy escalated in the wake of the French Revolution, Presbyterian and Congregational preachers rallied to the Federalist cause, denouncing Jefferson for his infidelity and Jacobin tendencies.

Jefferson was ambivalent about the future of Christianity in America. Early in his career, he looked forward to the triumph of reason, hopeful that popular Christianity would eventually be stripped of the superstitious folk beliefs and clerically inspired mysteries that had accumulated over the centuries. If the clergy were no longer able to invoke the state's support in exploiting a credulous people, he believed, then their numbers and power would diminish. In a fair contest, reason would vanquish superstition. Jefferson's advocacy of religious freedom therefore was originally tactical, as a means of promoting a competition that would ultimately guarantee popular enlightenment; it was *not* premised on the idea that all versions of Christianity were equally "true" or that it was impossible to make judgments about their truth value. Ever the optimist, the antitrinitarian Jefferson could still, late in his life (1822), predict that "there is not a *young man* now living in the United States who will not die an Unitarian."

Jefferson's expectations were not realized—the rise of Unitarianianism notwithstanding. A free competition among Christian denominations, as many clergymen had long since recognized, created optimal conditions for effective proselytizing. The proliferation of new sects such as the Disciples of Christ during the so-called Second Great Awakening promoted a profound and far-reaching "democratization" of American Christianity. Many of Jefferson's most ardent admirers were drawn from the ranks of self-professed "primitive" evangelical Christians whose anti-establishment appeals and radical reformist impulses in religion mirrored Jeffersonian efforts to restore American politics to republican purity. Certainly these developments confounded Jefferson's hopes for a dawning age of reason. Far from prefiguring the future, Jefferson's Enlightenment faith became increasingly anachronistic and irrelevant. Yet Jefferson did not simply withdraw in confusion and consternation. To the contrary, in an effort to comprehend and accommodate to the Christianization of America, Jefferson undertook an arduous quest for religious enlightenment.

The key figure in Jefferson's later spiritual development was Joseph Priestley, the great English scientist and Unitarian theologian who settled in Pennsylvania. Priestley's *History of the Corruptions of Christianity* (1782) juxtaposed the uncorrupted ethical teachings of Jesus to the neo-Platonic mystifications of his self-proclaimed disciples. By conceiving of Jesus as a great moralist, Jefferson could reaffirm his belief in the unity of the Godhead while vindicating his authentic "Christianity" against partisan, sectarian assaults. The publication of Priestley's *Socrates and Jesus* (1803) prompted Jefferson to set forth the outlines of his mature faith in a letter to Benjamin Rush in April 1803. This "Syllabus . . . of the doctrines of Jesus, compared with those of others" was followed by his collections of extracts from the new Testament, "The Philosophy of Jesus" (1804), and by the much more elaborate "Life and Morals of Jesus," compiled late in his life. Imposing his own critical scheme on the Gospels, Jefferson excluded passages that introduced mysterious and miraculous elements into the record of Jesus' moral teachings. In this way, the rationalist Jefferson could enthusiastically embrace Christianity; he could also convince himself that Christian ethics, because they were premised on the unity of mankind, constituted a profoundly progressive improvement on Classical philosophy.

Once Jefferson had successfully distinguished "Primitive Christianity" from its doctrinal and institutional corruptions, he could envisage a positive and mutually reinforcing relationship between religion and republican government. As a philosophical materialist who rejected Platonic idealism, Jefferson always believed in some form of afterlife; as a practical moralist, he recognized that concern for future rewards and punishments represented an essential prop to social virtue. Yet because of his lifelong antipathy to religious establishments and evangelical irrationality, Jefferson was unwilling to compromise the purity of either church or state by permitting any sort of formal institutional relationship between the two spheres. His growing misgivings about the progress of reason also led Jefferson to a more modest conception of the benefits of toleration: Toleration was less important as a means toward popular enlightenment than as a means of securing private conscience against the tyranny of public opinion.

Ironically, even in retirement, when there were no longer any political risks in alienating more conventional Christians, Jefferson was unwilling to expose his own religious views. The mature Jefferson was much more interested in upholding the sanctity of conscience as the ground of private and public virtue than in promoting his own version of religious truth. To proselytize, even on behalf of what had seemed to the younger Jefferson to be self-evident truths, was to foment partisan and sectarian strife while threatening the sovereignty of individual conscience. Jefferson's spiritual quest may not have led either to a profoundly transforming conversion experience or to original philosophical formulations. But it did deepen his commitment to the principle of religious toleration. Late in his life Jefferson wrote that "I am of a sect by myself, as far as I know." For the young Revolutionary who had looked forward to the triumph of reason over sectarian irrationality, this was a remarkable conclusion, not the least for its nonpejorative use of the word "sect." It also represented the convergence between Jefferson's conception of toleration and that of earlier champions of Christian liberty such as Roger Williams—a radical Calvinist who also constituted a sect unto himself.

Peter S. Onuf

Bibliography

Conkin, Paul, "Jefferson's Religious Pilgrimage," in *Jeffersonian Legacies*, ed. Peter S. Onuf (Charlottesville: University Press of Virginia, 1993).

Sanford, Charles, *The Religious Life of Thomas Jefferson* (Charlottesville: University Press of Virginia, 1984).

Sheridan, Eugene R., Introduction, *Jefferson's Extracts from the Gospels: "The Philosophy of Jesus" and "The Life and Morals of Jesus,"* in *The Papers of Thomas Jefferson*, 2nd series, ed. Dickinson W. Adams (Princeton, N.J.: Princeton University Press, 1983).

Jehovah's Witnesses

Of all religious groups and sects, Jehovah's Witnesses have had the most profound impact on the U.S. Supreme Court's jurisprudence. The Supreme Court has decided at least thirty-seven plenary decisions involving the First Amendment rights of the Witnesses. Some cases rely on freedom of religion, others on freedom of speech and press, and still others on both. Jehovah's Witnesses provided the factual vehicle for the incorporation, via the Fourteenth Amendment's Due Process Clause, of the First Amendment's guarantee of free exercise of religion against state infringement; for the development of the "preferred position" theory of First Amendment jurisprudence; and for the least-restrictive-alternative analysis of limitations on First Amendment activities.

The Witnesses' Background and Beliefs

The group known as Jehovah's Witnesses was founded in 1868 by Charles Taze Russell, who, at age 16, decided that all religions were wrong and formed his own Bible study group in Pittsburgh, Pennsylvania. The group, initially known as "Russellites," centered their beliefs on the notion that Jehovah alone—not the Trinity—is the Almighty God and Creator. They found support for their beliefs in numerous biblical passages.

In 1875 Russell published fifty thousand copies of a pamphlet entitled *The Object and Manner of the Lord's Return,* which made a case for the end of the "Gentile Times," during which, in his opinion, Jehovah's sovereignty was not being expressed by any government on earth. It proclaimed that, in 1914, the invisible second coming of Christ would take place. The group eventually came to profess that the soul is mortal, that the dead will not be resurrected, and that punishment for "unrepented wickedness is not eternal torment but annihilation." They believed that their highest function was to disseminate their interpretation of the Bible and their religious beliefs. (In furtherance of these ends, in 1879 Russell began publishing a pamphlet entitled *Zion's Watchtower* that is now named *The Watchtower.*) These convictions and biblical interpretations continue to form the core of Witness beliefs.

In 1884 the organization was incorporated in Pennsylvania as the Watchtower Bible and Tract Society. Its stated purpose was "the dissemination of Bible truths in various languages by means of the publication of tracts, pamphlets, papers and other religious documents, and by the use of all other lawful means." The name was changed in 1896 to the Watch Tower Bible and Tract Society, and in 1909 a separate corporation was formed in New York named the People's Pulpit Association. This was changed in 1956 to the Watchtower Bible and Tract Society of New York, Inc. (the "Society"). The name "Jehovah's Witnesses" was finally adopted in 1931.

When Russell died in 1916, "Judge" Joseph Franklin Rutherford, formerly general counsel of the corporation, took over as president and remained in that position until his death in 1942. During Rutherford's tenure Jehovah's Witnesses were banned in many parts of the world and created a record of being one of the most persecuted religious groups in U.S. history. The catalyst for concerted attacks by the government and by Catholic and Protestant clergy on Jehovah's Witnesses was Russell's last book, *The Finished Mystery,* published in 1917. Among other things the widely distributed book contained the following passage:

> Nowhere in the New Testament is Patriotism a narrow-minded hatred of other peoples encouraged. Everywhere and always murder in its every form is forbidden: and yet, under the guise of Patriotism the civil governments of earth demand of peace-loving men the sacrifice of themselves and their loved ones and the butchery of their fellows, and hail it as a duty demanded by the laws of heaven.

As a result of this position, on May 7, 1918, Rutherford and other Society officials were arrested and quickly convicted for violation of the Espionage Act of June 15, 1917. In *Rutherford v. United States* (1919) the U.S. Court of Appeals upheld the seven men convicted of conspiring to cause "insubordination, disloyalty and refusal of duty in the military and naval forces of the United States of America when the United States was at war. . . ." They were sentenced to twenty years' imprisonment, but the case was later reversed and remanded. In 1920, well after World War I was over, the U.S. attorney general completely exonerated the defendants.

The initial trial of Rutherford precipitated the first occasion for the Witnesses to appear before the U.S. Supreme Court. During the trial a Jehovah's Witness, Agnes Hudgings, had refused to cooperate as a witness for the state and was held in contempt of court. In *Ex Parte Hudgings* (1919) the Supreme Court held that the district court had no power to adjudge a witness guilty of contempt solely because in the court's opinion she was willfully refusing to testify truthfully. Nor did it have the power to confine the witness until she gave testimony that the court deemed truthful.

While Protestant and Catholic clerics had encouraged the government's prosecution of Rutherford, a real campaign of condemnation by clergymen began when Rutherford was released from prison in 1919, and it continued between the two world wars. For example, in 1938, the Detroit-based priest, Father Charles E. Coughlin encouraged a mob attack on a Watchtower convention in New York City's Madison Square Garden. Shortly after, a Catholic boycott of Gimbel Brothers Department Store forced the store to cease its sponsorship of Rutherford's radio broadcasts.

Rutherford's already negative attitude toward other Christian churches and clergy (he was sympathetic to Jews and Zionism) blossomed into genuine personal, if not doctrinal, animosity. He began a campaign condemning commerce, politics, and religion as Satan's instruments. In his book *Enemies,* published in 1938, he wrote with respect to the clergy in Rome:

> The Kingdom of God under Christ, as proclaimed by Jehovah's Witnesses, is the only thing the Roman Catholic Hierarchy really fear. The old "harlot" is now very diligent to hide from the people her long and bloody record as inquisitionist and the many crimes she has committed, and when her activity and filthy record, as recorded in history, are mentioned and the truth of God's Word is told about her, she howls and with great crocodile tears says: "That speech is shocking to our religious Susceptibilities."

The playing of a recording of this book was the catalyst for the U.S. Supreme Court case of *Cantwell v. Connecticut* (1940), which led to the incorporation of the Free Exercise Clause of the First Amendment to the states through the Fourteenth Amendment.

The Witnesses before the Court

Immediately before and during World War II, cases involving Jehovah's Witnesses became regular features before the Supreme Court. Throughout this period the Court—eminently aware that these cases were part of a piece involving a group "marching to a different drummer"—was continually confronted with cases that demanded that the constitutional rights of the Witnesses be upheld. On May 3, 1943, alone, the Court decided thirteen cases, consolidated into four decisions, that involved Jehovah's Witnesses.

This enormous presence before the Supreme Court stemmed from the increased level of persecution experienced by Jehovah's Witnesses during World War II. The Society's continued discouragement of Witnesses from participation in politics and military service, as well as its proselytization activities, were ready sources of friction. Jehovah's Witnesses continued to attack all institutionalized churches as things of Satan, and they protested any form of religious or secular ceremony, including saluting the U.S. flag.

Their refusal to salute the flag during World War II led to significant persecution on a national scale. During the 1930s Jehovah's Witnesses had refused to salute not only because of their fundamental opposition to flag worship but also out of sympathy with the plight of Witnesses in Germany who had been among the first groups to suffer suppression when the Nazis came to power in 1933. Largely because of their refusal to salute the Nazi flag, over ten thousand Jehovah's Witnesses were sent to concentration camps, from which most never returned.

In *Minersville School District v. Gobitis et al.* (1940) the Supreme Court held that a local school board had a right to require flag saluting and that the expulsion of Witness children was within its power. Attacks on Witnesses began in earnest. The decision precipitated a slew of resolutions by local school boards that required flag saluting. Some towns passed ordinances specifically forbidding Witnesses from distributing literature. Others arrested Witnesses on sight "just in case." Kingdom Halls (Witness "churches") were burned, and congregations were attacked by mobs. Jehovah's Witnesses were regularly run out of small towns. Finally the Supreme Court explicitly overruled *Gobitis* in *West Virginia State Board of Education v. Barnette* (1943), based on the Witnesses' freedoms of speech and expression.

Although the *Gobitis* decision undoubtedly precipitated much of the persecution experienced by the Witnesses, their own proselytizing activities were also a significant catalyst. Charles Taze Russell had regarded the Society's members as the 144,000 chosen from birth to rule with Christ in Heaven after Armageddon. However, Rutherford invented a new doctrine: Those who had sinned out of ignorance could be saved only by forsaking their evil ways. It was the Witness's task to convince people to repent. Witnesses were to take literally the biblical command "Go ye into all the world and preach the gospel to every creature." This, of course, called for knocking on the doors of homeowners as well as preaching and passing out literature on street corners. The Society provided Witnesses with reams of literature, phonograph recordings of speeches, and even portable phonographs on which to play them. A Witness preaching on a street corner attracted a crowd and became a ready target because his beliefs were perceived to be unpatriotic.

Protests of Witnesses' proselytizing activities reached their peak in the 1940s. In efforts to thwart them, local authorities initially attempted to use peddling and solicitation ordinances as restraining mechanisms. The first arrest of a Jehovah's Witness for house-to-house preaching was in 1928, but arrests for selling literature without a license, disturbing the peace, and violating Sabbath blue laws increased from 268 in 1933 to 1,149 in 1936. It is the constitutionality of these local laws that was the focus of most of the Witness cases before the Supreme Court during this period.

The Witnesses were quite prepared to defend what they considered to be state infringement on their rights of free expression of religion and speech. In the 1930s the Society had published a pamphlet entitled *Order of Trial* to be used as an aid by Witnesses defending themselves. Initially most cases had lost at trial anyway, but Witness lawyers had continued to shepherd the cases through the judiciary system until they had finally begun to reach the Supreme Court in the late 1930s. Many of these cases are considered landmark decisions and are cited frequently.

By 1945 the Supreme Court had upheld the Witnesses' right to proselytize in public as well as in company-owned and government-owned towns. The only significant limit the Court placed on the Witnesses' First Amendment freedoms involving their proselytizing activities was when children were involved. In *Prince v. Massachusetts* (1944) the Court upheld the conviction, under child labor laws, of a Witness who allowed her 9-year-old niece to sell or pass out literature on the street.

During the same period that the Supreme Court was deciding Jehovah's Witness cases regarding their preaching activities and their refusal to salute the flag, it was also confronted with cases of Witnesses refusing to report for military duty. A total of eleven Selective Service cases eventually received plenary disposition by the Supreme Court.

The Society had not always discouraged Witnesses from joining the military. During World War I there was no Witness doctrine requiring Witnesses to resist conscription. In fact, many fought, while others sought conscientious objector exemptions, usually without success. They were similarly unsuccessful during World War II, as shown by the fact that this tiny sect produced over two-thirds of all the conscientious objectors in prison. At least 4,050 Witnesses were imprisoned between 1941 and 1946.

Under the Selective Service Act of 1940 "regular or duly ordained ministers of religion" were exempt from the draft. Such a "regular minister of religion" was defined as "a man who customarily preaches and teaches the principles of religion of a recognized church . . . without having been formally ordained as a minister of religion; and who is recognized by such church . . . as a minister." Jehovah's Witnesses were considered a recognized religious sect under the act. Hayden Covington, general counsel of the Watchtower Society, and General Lewis B. Hershey, deputy director of the Selective Service, arranged that all "pioneer" Witnesses (those who preached full time) would be exempt as "regular ministers of religion."

This privilege was a big step forward from the attitudes toward Jehovah's Witnesses during World War I, but those Witnesses who could not procure such status were relegated to conscientious objector status. This required them to report to national civil work camps, which completely prevented them from proselytizing.

Between 1939 and 1945 the number of "pioneer" Witnesses doubled. The government accused the Watchtower Society's publications of encouraging more Witnesses to engage in full-time proselytizing in order to evade the draft. Covington answered, truthfully, that the Society had *always* encouraged full-time preaching.

Under the Selective Service Act, local draft boards had discretion with respect to classification of Witnesses, who had no right of appeal. The boards had a thankless job because Covington and other Witness lawyers argued that each Witness was entitled to the exemption because each Witness was a minister of religion. After all, the raison d'etre of Witnesses was preaching.

All the Witness draft cases to reach the Supreme Court at this time were challenges to the lack of review of the classifications made by local draft boards. The Witnesses were successful in only two out of five decisions. In *Falbo v. United States* (1944), without acknowledging that the case involved a Jehovah's Witness, the Court held that Congress was not required to make available judicial review of the validity of a draft board's classification. However, in *Estep v. United States* (1946)—decided after the war ended—the Court reversed a conviction of a Witness who refused to report for induction because he was not allowed to challenge his local board's classification during his trial. This decision was extremely important for civil liberties because it prevented local draft boards from the unchecked enforcement of local prejudices. During the Korean War there were fewer convictions of Witnesses for draft violations, and those who were convicted were paroled earlier and treated better than other conscientious objectors were.

During the Vietnam War many Witnesses applied for conscientious objector status, got it, and then refused to report for alternative civilian duty. They reported when ordered by the courts because, as opposed to the draft boards, they believed courts were a "higher power" that Apostle Paul had commanded them to obey.

Internal Dissent, External Issues

By the beginning of the 1960s, cases involving Witness activities and beliefs dwindled. However, internal dissent and turmoil did not die away. In 1966 a book published by the Society entitled *Life Everlasting in Freedom of the Sons of God* indicated that 1975 was a likely date for Armageddon. The book contained a chronological "Chart of Significant Dates," including the self-fulfilling prophesy of the publishing date of the book and ending with 1975 as the "End of 6th the 1,000-year day of Man's existence (in early autumn)."

In preparation for Armageddon, Witnesses sold houses and businesses, gave up jobs, and delayed marriage, child birth, and even medical attention. They chanted "Make do till '72, Stay alive till '75." By the end of 1975 the Society's headquarters in Brooklyn, New York, was flooded with letters from disillusioned Witnesses.

A purge of "apostates" followed in 1977, when nearly thirty thousand Witnesses were "disfellowshipped"—completely ostracized from other Witnesses. Disfellowshipping is the most serious punishment of Jehovah's Witnesses. Since the 1950s, Witnesses who left the Society voluntarily were "disassociated," but other Witnesses were still permitted to associate with them. Only those who were found guilty of such things as smoking, oral sex, or challenging church doctrine were disfellowshipped. But since the 1970s any Witness who leaves, voluntarily or not, has been considered disfellowshipped. Witnesses who are charged with a disfellowshipping offense are considered guilty until proved innocent. Usually a judicial committee conducts a hearing with or without the presence of the accused; there is no right to appeal the committee's decision.

The effects of this practice can be devastating. Parents of a child who is disfellowshipped are told to care for the child's physical needs and discipline, but in other areas of life the wrongdoer must remain silent and not participate. In the case of a disfellowshipped spouse, all interaction is to be kept to a bare minimum, and all religious discussion must terminate.

At least one Witness has sued the Society for tort damages. In *Paul v. Watchtower Bible and Tract Society of New York, Inc.* (9th Cir. 1987) a disfellowshipped Witness sued for the common-law torts of defamation, invasion of privacy, fraud, and outrageous conduct. Janice Paul had disassociated herself from the Society in 1975, when her parents had been disfellowshipped. She had continued to associate with Witnesses until 1981, when the Society forbade any contact between a Witness and one disfellowshipped.

Noting that "shunning" is an old Christian practice, and based on the Witnesses' interpretation of canonical text, the Ninth Circuit held that disfellowshipping is protected under the First Amendment guarantee of free expression. The Court found that imposing tort liability for shunning would constitute a "direct burden on religion" and would have the effect of prohibiting the practice, causing the church to "abandon part of its religious teachings."

In the two major modern Supreme Court cases involving Jehovah's Witnesses—*Wooley v. Maynard* (1977) and *Thomas v. Review Board of the Indiana Employment Security Division* (1981)—the Court reaffirmed principles it had enunciated in past Witness cases. In *Maynard* the Court relied on its reasoning in *Barnette* to find a First Amendment protection for a Witness who refused to be a spokesman for the state's ideology and covered up the motto "Live Free or Die" on his car's license plate.

In *Thomas* the Court held that the state's denial of Thomas's unemployment compensation violated his First Amendment right of free expression. Thomas, a Jehovah's Witness, had quit his job at a roll foundry after he was transferred to a department that made turrets for military tanks. He had been denied unemployment compensation because the hearing referee found that he had not quit for a "good cause [arising] in connection with [his] work," as required by the state statute.

The Supreme Court reiterated that it felt no compulsion to question the genuineness of Thomas's beliefs but held that he could not be forced to choose between the free exercise of his religion and participation in an otherwise-available public program because this would constitute a burden on his constitutional right to freedom of religion.

The two major issues that occupied the Witnesses in lower courts during the 1980s and early 1990s involved zoning disputes and blood transfusions.

The zoning cases involved disputes between Jehovah's Witness congregations that wished to build Kingdom Halls (places of worship) and local authorities who sought to prevent their construction. Although the Supreme Court has never ruled on the issue, at least two federal courts have come to conflicting conclusions regarding the rights of Witnesses to freely exercise their religion as opposed to the right of local municipalities to prohibit construction of religious buildings in residential areas.

Similarly, courts have come to conflicting conclusions regarding the right of Witnesses to refuse blood transfusions. Jehovah's Witnesses have discouraged the giving of blood transfusions since the 1950s; transfusions became clear grounds for disfellowshipping only in 1971. Witnesses base their refusal on biblical admonishments against eating blood. Regardless of the fact that blood transfusions did not exist during biblical times, Witnesses find support in the Council of Jerusalem's admonishment to new Christian converts to "keep abstaining from things sacrificed to idols and from blood. . . ." In *How Can Blood Save Your Life?*—a Society pamphlet published in 1990—practical reasons for refusing blood transfusions (including the danger of AIDS and hepatitis) are given, along with biblical prohibitions against the eating of blood.

The use of a case-by-case balancing test by courts has not produced a uniform approach to the issue, and the degree of "compellingness" of the state's interest has varied from court to court. For example, in *John F. Kennedy Memorial Hospital v. Heston* (N.J., 1971) the state's interest in preserving life prevailed over the Witness's right to refuse a blood transfusion. In *In re Osborne* (D.C., 1972) the Witness's freedom of choice outweighed the state's interest. Using a *parens patriae* justification, courts have generally ordered transfusions for Witness children over their and their parents' objections. This result is often buttressed by reliance on the Supreme Court's holding in *Prince*.

Today most Witnesses carry a medical document card that is renewed annually and is signed by the Witness and a witness, often the next of kin. This relieves doctors and hospitals of legal liability. In addition, Hospital Information Services at the Society's Brooklyn headquarters trains and supervises elders to assist Witnesses in time of medical need.

Proselytizing: The Limits of Free Exercise

Proselytizing continues to be the raison d'etre for Jehovah's Witnesses. In 1991 there were 66,207 congregations in 211 countries with 4,278,820 "Peak Publishers" (members who proselytize full time) and 4,071,954 "Average Publishers" (members who preach part time). The legal department in Brooklyn had a staff of forty to assist members in legal matters associated with their membership. Although preaching activities are generally not obstructed in the United States, Witnesses continue to be persecuted in other parts of the world.

Proselytizing and the distribution of religious literature have existed in the United States from the time the continent was first settled. The spreading of Christianity was one avowed purpose of most early settlers in the New World. Both the first and second Virginia charters declared that a major objective was the spread of the Christian religion. The Pilgrims hoped to spread their religion among the natives. One purpose of William Penn's charter was to bring the native Indians into the Quaker fold. During the eighteenth century, the Jesuits preached among the Indians in New France.

Inevitably, this American tradition came into direct conflict with the rights found in the First Amendment. In a series of cases from the 1930s to the early 1950s, the proselytizing activities of the Jehovah's Witnesses provided the Supreme Court with opportunities to define the limits of the Free Exercise Clause with regard to this activity.

As noted earlier, Witnesses take literally the biblical command "Go ye into all the world and preach the gospel to every creature." This necessarily involves knocking on the doors of homeowners and giving speeches and passing out religious literature in public places. In the 1930s and 1940s local authorities passed and enforced licensing and solicitation ordinances in efforts to thwart these activities. The constitutionality of these local laws and ordinances has been the focus of over twenty cases before the Supreme Court.

In *Coleman v. City of Griffin* (1937) the Supreme Court dismissed an appeal of a Witness convicted of violating an ordinance requiring prior written permission from the city manager of Griffin, Georgia, before distributing literature of any kind. The city manager had complete discretion in deciding who would be permitted to distribute. The Court unanimously dismissed the appeal for want of a substantial federal question. However, five months later, in *Lovell v. City of Griffin* (1938), the Court unanimously reversed a conviction under the same ordinance as invalid on its face as a prior restraint of the freedom of the press. The Witness in both cases had refused, on religious grounds, to seek a permit before distributing religious literature. The Court avoided this issue by deciding that, because the ordinance was constitutionally void on its face, the Witness did not need to obtain a permit.

One year later the Court struck down another ordinance as an impermissible obstruction of the freedoms of speech and press. The ordinance at issue in *Schneider v. State* (1939) required the local police chief to deny a permit to distribute literature house-to-house should he decide that "the canvasser is not of good character or is canvassing for a project not free from fraud." In striking down the ordinance the Court noted that "streets are natural and proper places for the dissemination of information and opinions." Foreshadowing the least-restrictive-alternative test, the Court also noted that, although the prevention of litter in the streets and fraud are legitimate governmental concerns, where fundamental personal freedoms are infringed, the Court must "appraise the substantiality of the reasons advanced in support of the regulation."

In 1940 the Witnesses began their modern practice of standing on a downtown street corner to pass out literature and preach. The Society provided members with literature, recordings of speeches, and even portable phonographs. It was one of these phonographs that led to the case of *Cantwell,* where the Court held that a local permit requirement for solicitation for religious purposes was invalid on its face as a prior restraint and thus was censorship on the free exercise of religion.

In the next case before the Court regarding the Witness's proselytizing activities, *Cox v. New Hampshire* (1941), the Court rejected a right of assembly claim and upheld the convictions of sixty-eight Witnesses for parading without a statutorily required permit. The Witnesses had been marching on a sidewalk carrying placards that read "[r]eligion is a Snare and a Racket" and distributing leaflets. Even though the Witnesses had repeatedly asserted that the street is their church, this may have struck the Court as an improper religious practice. Justice Hughs wrote that "[n]o interference with religious worship or the practice of religion in any proper sense is shown, but only the exercise of local control over the use of streets for parades and processions."

In *Chaplinsky v. New Hampshire* (1942) the Court upheld the conviction of a Witness for violating a statute outlawing offensive language addressed to another in a public place. Mr. Chaplinsky had yelled at a city marshal who was arresting him for disturbing the peace: "You are a God damned racketeer" and "a damned Fascist and the whole government of Rochester are Fascists or agents of Fascists." The Court upheld the conviction of Chaplinsky, declaring that the First Amendment's guarantee of freedom of speech did not protect "fighting words."

The Jehovah's Witnesses also lost their next case, *Jones v. City of Opelika* (1942), which consolidated three cases of Witnesses who had been convicted for violating ordinances that imposed a license tax on the sale of printed material. The Court's majority upheld the ordinances as religiously nondiscriminatory and, therefore, as not infringing on the fundamental rights of freedom of speech, press, and religion. The opinion is significant for Justice Stone's dissent. He compared the tax to the stamp tax used by England to suppress colonial pamphleteers, and he concluded that First Amendment freedoms enjoyed a "preferred position." Because of this "preferred position," every form of taxation which, because it is a "condition of the exercise of the privilege, is capable of being used to control or suppress it" must be thwarted. The decision was vacated in a *per curium* decision less than a year later after the Court's decisions in *Murdock v. Pennsylvania* (1943) and *Martin v. City of Struthers* (1943).

On March 8, 1943, the Court decided two cases in the Witness's favor. In *Largent v. Texas* (1943) the Court invalidated an ordinance in Paris, Texas, that required a permit issued by the mayor, if he "deems it proper or advisable," for the selling of books in a residential neighborhood. The unanimous opinion recognized the ordinance as an abridgment of First Amendment privileges.

In *Jamison v. Texas* (1943) a Dallas ordinance forbidding handbill distribution, as applied to a Witness who was distributing fliers advertising a lecture, was held to violate the guarantees of both freedom of the press and freedom of religion. The fact that the fliers mentioned two books for sale for twenty-five cents did not diminish the religious status of the activity. It was still protected under the First and Fourteenth Amendments.

On May 3, 1943, the Court decided thirteen Jehovah's Witness cases that were consolidated into four decisions. *Murdock* concerned an ordinance that outlawed selling, by canvassing, any merchandise of any kind without a license. The Witnesses were convicted of the door-to-door distribution of books, sometimes selling them for the price of twenty-five cents but often giving them away for nothing. The Court recognized that door-to-door distribution was a religious activity that deserved constitutional protection regardless of the fact that the books were sometimes sold. It held that requiring religious distributors to pay a tax as a condition to the pursuit of their activities was a violation of their constitutional freedoms of the press, speech, and religion—rights that are in a "preferred position" and therefore cannot be so restricted.

In *Martin* a Witness was convicted of violating a "Green River" ordinance forbidding handbill distributors from ringing the doorbell or knocking on the door of a residence. Although the Witness claimed an infringement on her freedom of religion, the Court focused only on the freedoms of speech and press when invalidating the ordinance and found alternative methods for achieving the community's concerns about protection from annoyance.

On the same day, in *Douglas v. City of Jeanette* (1943), the Court denied a request for an injunction against threatened prosecutions under the same ordinance invalidated in *Murdock* because it found no reason to believe that the local authorities would not comply with the Supreme Court's decision in *Murdock.*

The next year, in *Follett v. Town of McCormick* (1944), the Court invalidated, as a violation of Follett's right to freedom of religion, an ordinance imposing a flat tax on book agents as applied to a Witness distributing religious literature. The Court reached this result by extending *Murdock*—even though, unlike in *Murdock,* the Witness in this case was a resident of the town, and this was his sole source of income. The Witnesses lost their next case, *Prince,* where the Court held that the freedom of religion was not absolute and that a state has a legitimate interest in preventing the exploitation of child labor.

In 1946 the Court extended the Witnesses' right to distribute literature. In *Marsh v. Alabama* (1946) the Court expanded its reasoning in *Martin* to hold that the First Amendment rights of a Witness passing out literature on the streets of a company-owned town had priority over the rights of the property owner. In *Tucker v. Texas* (1946) the Court upheld a Witness's right to distribute, regardless of the fact that the town was completely owned by the U.S. government. However, in 1948, the Court denied certiorari to a case where the New York Court of Appeals had refused to extend *Marsh* and *Tucker* to include the interior hallways of a privately owned apartment building.

In *Saia v. New York* (1948) the Court invalidated an ordinance on its face that required a permit from the chief of police for the use of sound amplification devices. Because the ordinance had no standards for decision, it was invalidated as a prior restraint of free speech.

In *Niemotko v. Maryland* (1951) the Court reversed a conviction of a Witness for holding Bible talks in a city park as an unconstitutional restraint of the freedoms of religion and speech. Again, the ordinance provided no standards for determining who could use the park or for what purpose. Two years later, in *Fowler v. Rhode Island* (1953), the Court unanimously reversed a conviction of a Witness pursuant to an ordinance that prohibited religious or political talks in public parks. However, in the same year, in *Poulos v. New Hampshire* (1953), the Court found that an ordinance forbidding the holding of a religious meeting in a public park without a license did not violate First Amendment principles because the local officials did not possess complete discretion in granting licenses.

Since the 1950s other "fringe" religious groups—such as the Hare Krishna movement, Jews for Jesus, and the Unification Church—have faced hostility and legal restrictions like those the Witnesses encountered earlier in the century. The Witnesses, however, are less likely to be the target of official sanction.

Renee C. Redman

Bibliography

Kurland, Philip B., *Religion and the Law of Church, State, and the Supreme Court* (Chicago: Aldine, 1967, 1962).

Manwaring, David, *Render unto Caesar: The Flag Salute Controversy* (Chicago: University of Chicago Press, 1962).

McAninch, William Shepard, "A Catalyst for the Evolution of Constitutional Law: Jehovah's Witnesses in the Supreme Court," 55 *University of Cincinnati Law Review* 997–1190 (1987).

"Religious Liberty," 36 *American Political Science Review* 1053–1072 (1942).

Rotnem, Victor W., and F. G. Folsom, Jr., "Recent Limitations upon Religious Liberty," 36 *American Political Science Review* 1053 (1936).

Cases Cited

Cantwell v. Connecticut, 310 U.S. 296 (1940).

Chaplinsky v. New Hampshire, 315 U.S. 568 (1942).

Coleman v. City of Griffin, 302 U.S. 636 (1937).

Cox v. New Hampshire, 312 U.S. 569 (1941).

Douglas v. City of Jeanette, 319 U.S. 157 (1943).

Estep v. United States, 327 U.S. 114 (1946).
Ex Parte Hudgings, 249 U.S. 378 (1919).
Falbo v. United States 320 U.S. 549 (1944).
Follett v. Town of McCormick, 321 U.S. 573 (1944).
Fowler v. Rhode Island, 345 U.S. 67 (1953).
In re Osborne, 294 A. 2d 372 (D.C. 1972).
Jamison v. Texas, 318 U.S. 413 (1943).
John F. Kennedy Memorial Hospital v. Heston, 279 A. 2d 670 (N.J. 1971).
Jones v. City of Opelika, 316 U.S. 584 (1942).
Largent v. Texas, 318 U.S. 418 (1943).
Larson v. Valente, 456 U.S. 228 (1982).
Lovell v. City of Griffin, 303 U.S. 444 (1938).
Marsh v. Alabama, 326 U.S. 501 (1946).
Martin v. City of Struthers, 319 U.S. 141 (1943).
Minersville School District v. Gobitis et al., 310 U.S. 586 (1940).
Murdock v. Pennsylvania, 319 U.S. 105 (1943).
Niemotko v. Maryland, 340 U.S. 268 (1951).
Paul v. Watchtower Bible and Tract Society of New York, Inc., 819 F. 2d 875 (9th Cir. 1987), cert. denied, 484 U.S. 926 (1987).
Poulos v. New Hampshire, 345 U.S. 395 (1953).
Prince v. Massachusetts, 321 U.S. 158 (1944).
Rutherford v. United States, 258 F. 855 (2d. Cir., 1919), reversing and remanding United States v. Rutherford, unreported (E.D., New York).
Saia v. New York, 334 U.S. 558 (1948).
Schneider v. New Jersey, 308 U.S. 147 (1939).
Thomas v. Review Board of the Indiana Employment Security Division, 450 U.S. 707 (1981).
Tucker v. Texas, 326 U.S. 517 (1946).
Watchtower Bible and Tract Society, Inc. v. Metropolitan Life Insurance Company, 297 N.Y. 339, 79 N.E. 2d 433, cert. denied, 335 U.S. 886 (1948)
West Virginia State Board of Education v. Barnette, 319 U.S. 624 (1943).
Wooley v. Maynard, 430 U.S. 705 (1977).

Jews and American Religious Liberty

Both individually and collectively, Jews have had a profound impact on American law. Until the recent ascendancy of Buddhism and Islam, Jews constituted the only numerically significant non-Christian group in the United States. As such, they have been among the most prominent beneficiaries of the Free Exercise and Establishment Clauses and have stood in the forefront of legal actions and social movements to advance the cause of American religious freedom. Their treatment by the Christian majority has provided a measuring rod of the limits of American religious toleration.

Since colonial times, Jews have regarded America as a haven from persecution and have generally enjoyed freedoms that were not available in the lands from which they emigrated. Even in this country, however, Jews have encountered various forms of legalized discrimination until relatively recent times. The small number of Jews who settled in the colonies encountered many forms of social and economic discrimination and a raft of legal disabilities. In what later became the world's most Jewish city (New York), Governor Peter Stuyvesant of New Amsterdam attempted to prevent the settlement of Jews. During the mid–seventeenth century, a Jew escaped death under Maryland's blasphemy law only by converting to Christianity. Although Jews gradually acquired freedom of worship, all the colonies—even the relatively tolerant Pennsylvania and Rhode Island—officially barred Jews from voting and from holding public office, even though these restrictions were not always enforced. In most of the colonies, Jews were forced to contribute to the financial support of established churches. The hope of full political emancipation under a republican government may help to explain why members of the nation's small Jewish community tended to favor independence during the American Revolution.

In the wake of the Revolution, most states enacted new constitutions that removed many disabilities from Jews. Several states, however, retained tax support for Christian religions well into the nineteenth century. Likewise, Jews did not acquire full political rights in many states until long after the Revolution. For example, Jews could not vote or hold public office in Connecticut until 1818, in Rhode Island until 1842, and in North Carolina until 1868. Likewise, restrictions on legal testimony by Jews persisted in many states until well into the nineteenth century. Although the First Amendment to the U.S. Constitution was regarded from its inception as barring any federal discrimination against Jews, its religion clauses were not made applicable to the states until the mid–twentieth century. Jews therefore had no federal protection against state and local discrimination until more than 150 years after the ratification of the Constitution. Discrimination against Jews was upheld by many state courts on the ground that Christianity was part of the common law.

Although the Jewish proportion of the American population increased steadily throughout the nineteenth century and grew markedly early in the twentieth century, Jews continued to encounter many painful and ominous reminders that their legal status was precarious in a country in which the overwhelming majority of people were gentile and Christian. In 1862, for example, General Ulysses Grant officially excluded Jews from the military district that he commanded in Tennessee until President Abraham Lincoln countermanded his order. Later in the nineteenth century, a movement for a constitutional amendment to declare the United States a Christian nation received the support of Supreme Court Justice William Strong. Another justice, David Brewer, declared in *Church of the Holy Trinity v. United States* (1892) that "this is a Christian nation."

Jewish insecurity was exacerbated by the continuation of persecution of Jews in many other nations and by the persistence of anti-Semitic prejudices throughout the United States. Until after World War II many major corporations maintained discriminatory hiring practices, while powerful social clubs routinely excluded Jews. Similarly, most prestigious universities imposed quotas on the admission of Jewish students and hired almost no Jewish faculty members. In addition to such forms of private discrimination, Jews also sometimes faced public discrimination in the form of police harassment and biased judicial proceedings.

Sunday closing laws, which imposed economic hardships on Jewish businesspeople (because they also were closed on Saturday, their Sabbath), were a special source of frustration throughout the nineteenth century and most of the twentieth. Although most legal challenges were unsuccessful, the ongoing campaigns against these so-called blue laws helped to forge a tradition of legal activism in support of religious freedom and strict separation of church and state.

Jewish opposition to Sunday closing laws culminated in two Supreme Court decisions, *Gallagher v. Crown Kosher Super Market of Massachusetts* (1961) and *Braunfeld v. Brown* (1961), in which the Supreme Court rejected the arguments of Orthodox Jewish merchants that the closing laws violated both the Establishment and the Free Exercise Clauses and constituted a denial of equal protection of the laws. A closely divided Court held that the statutes were primarily secular in purpose and that they advanced a legitimate state interest in encouraging a general day of rest. Exceptions, the Court contended, would confer unfair commercial advantages, engender fraudulent religious claims, and present difficult enforcement problems. In one of the dissents, Justice Potter Stewart declared that the Pennsylvania law "grossly violate[d]" the Free Exercise Clause by offering an Orthodox Jew "a cruel choice" between "his religious faith and his economic survival." Left largely intact by the courts, Sunday closing laws have subsequently been eroded by the legislatures in response to the growing secularism and commercialization of society.

Jews also have been particularly sensitive to Protestant Christian practices in the public schools. Believing that public schools offered a unique opportunity both for assimilation and for the erosion of anti-Semitism, Jews generally refused to follow the example of Roman Catholics by establishing separate schools. Jewish support for an 1869 ordinance prohibiting all religious instruction in public schools culminated in a landmark decision of the Ohio Supreme Court, *Board of Education v. Minor* (1873), that upheld the prohibition on grounds of religious freedom.

Starting in 1905 the Central Conference of American Rabbis conducted a campaign in opposition to Bible reading in the public schools that helped to prevent the enactment of compulsory reading laws in several states. Jewish opposition to religious exercises in the public schools contributed to the Supreme Court's decisions in the early 1960s prohibiting prayer and Bible reading in the public schools. Jewish individuals and groups were active in opposing the New York Board of Regents' prayer that the Court's decision in *Engel v. Vitale* (1962) found to violate the Establishment Clause. Two of the five plaintiffs in that case were Jewish, and amicus briefs were submitted to the Court by the National Jewish Community Relations Advisory Council (NJCRAC), the Synagogue

Council of America (SCA), the American Jewish Committee (AJC), and the Anti-Defamation League (ADL). The same organizations were the only religious organizations to submit briefs in *School District of Abington Township v. Schempp* (1963), in which the Supreme Court declared that a Pennsylvania Bible reading law violated the Establishment Clause. Jews have remained vigilant in their opposition to religious intrusions in public education.

Although Jews have often been the beneficiaries of judicial decisions about religious freedom, Jews have consistently lost cases before the Supreme Court concerning public accommodation of their special religious needs. In addition to ruling against Jews in the Sunday closing laws, the Court in *Goldman v. Weinberger* (1986) upheld an Air Force prohibition on unauthorized headgear that had been challenged by an Air Force psychologist who wore a yarmulke. Exercising special deference to the needs of the military, the Court held that the regulation did not violate the Free Exercise Clause. The 5-to-4 decision provoked sharp dissents. Dismissing as "totally implausible" the argument that the wearing of the yarmulke threatened group identity, Justice William J. Brennan declared that "a yarmulke worn with a United States military uniform is an eloquent reminder that the shared and proud identity of United States servicemen embraces and unites religious and ethnic pluralism." The Air Force later repealed its regulation.

In *Kiryas Joel School District v. Grumet* (1994) the Court invalidated a New York statute that had created a special public school district for the education of handicapped children who were members of the Satmar Hasidic sect. The state had created the school district because the Orthodox children were uncomfortable attending public schools with persons from different traditions. The Court held that the law violated the Establishment Clause by conferring government benefits and powers on a group that was defined in terms of religion, in a manner that did not necessarily prevent religious favoritism. The three dissenters emphasized that the statute involved no public aid to private schools and did not mention religion.

Despite the relatively small number of landmark cases involving Jews, Jewish organizations have been active participants in a broad spectrum of cases involving religious and moral issues. As early as 1925 the AJC submitted an amicus brief in *Pierce v. Society of Sisters* (1925) opposing the constitutionality of an Oregon law that required all children to attend public elementary schools. The NJCRAC—a coordinating organization that comprises the American Jewish Committee, four other national Jewish organizations, and more than one hundred Jewish community councils throughout the nation—has filed briefs on its own behalf and jointly with non-Jewish organizations such as the American Civil Liberties Union. Briefs submitted by Jewish organizations have won widespread acclaim for their superior quality. In cases involving the religion clauses, the Synagogue Council of America has been the most frequent intervenor as amicus curiae.

The SCA, however, has not participated in cases involving aid to parochial schools, because some Orthodox constituencies in the council have often favored such aid while Conservative and Reform elements have generally opposed it. Despite widespread Jewish support for rigid separation of church and state, many Jews have expressed fear that separationism will undermine all religions, erode public morality, and exacerbate interfaith conflict. Although misgivings about separationism have appeared in all branches of Judaism, hostility toward strict separation has been most pronounced among Orthodox Jews. Many Orthodox were particularly outspoken in opposition to the Supreme Court's prayer and Bible reading decisions, and others have supported public aid to parochial schools.

This division of opinion led in 1965 to the formation of the Jewish Committee on Law and Political Action (JCOLPA), which has worked with the Roman Catholic Church in cases involving parochial aid and has also followed an independent position on other issues of concern to Jews. The Lubbavich Hassidim have been particularly vocal in support of allowing menorahs on public property and using public funds for yeshivas. Orthodoxy's Rabbinical Council and the Union of Orthodox Jewish Congregations, however, have generally continued to adhere to a separationist position that has permitted cooperation with NJCRAC on many issues.

In addition to their participation in litigation, Jewish organizations and individual Jews have been at the forefront of major social movements that have expanded the scope of freedom in the United States. Early in the twentieth century, Reform Rabbi Stephen S. Wise was instrumental in establishing the Joint Committee on Social Action, and Conservative Judaism soon formed a counterpart. Jewish organizations were particularly active in demanding the dissolution of segregation and other barriers to equality for African Americans.

Jews have made major contributions to American law as lawyers, judges, and academics. Seven Jews have served as associate justices of the U.S. Supreme Court: Louis D. Brandeis (1916–1939), Benjamin N. Cardozo (1932–1938), Felix Frankfurter (1939–1962), Arthur J. Goldberg (1962–1965), Abe Fortas (1965–1969), Ruth Bader Ginsburg (since 1993), and Stephen G. Breyer (since 1994). In addition, Judah P. Benjamin was nominated to the Supreme Court in 1853 but refused to serve. Nominations of Abe Fortas to the chief justiceship in 1968 and Douglas H. Ginsburg to an associate justiceship in 1987 were withdrawn.

William G. Ross

Bibliography

Borden, Horton, *Jews, Turks, and Infidels* (Chapel Hill: University of North Carolina Press, 1984).

Cohen, Naomi W., *Jews in Christian America: The Pursuit of Religious Equality* (New York: Oxford University Press, 1992).

Dalin, David G. (ed.), *American Jews and the Separationist Faith: The New Debate on Religion in Public Life* (Washington, D.C.: Ethics and Public Policy Center, 1993).

Dinnerstein, Leonard, *Anti-Semitism in America* (New York: Oxford University Press, 1994).

Feldman, Egal, *Dual Destinies: The Jewish Encounter with Protestant America* (Urbana: University of Illinois Press, 1990).

Pfeffer, Leo, "Amici in Church–State Litigation," 44 *Law and Contemporary Problems* 83–110 (Spring 1981).

Sachar, Howard M., *A History of the Jews in America* (New York: Knopf, 1992).

Cases Cited

Board of Education v. Minor, 23 Granger (23 Ohio St.) 211 (1873).

Braunfeld v. Brown, 366 U.S. 599 (1961).

Church of the Holy Trinity v. United States, 143 U.S. 457 (1892).

Engel v. Vitale, 370 U.S. 421 (1962).

Gallagher v. Crown Kosher Super Market of Massachusetts, 366 U.S. 617 (1961).

Goldman v. Weinberger, 475 U.S. 503 (1986).

Kiryas Joel School District v. Grumet, 512 U.S. 687 (1994).

Pierce v. Society of Sisters, 268 U.S. 510 (1925).

School District of Abington Township v. Schempp, 374 U.S. 203 (1963).

Jones v. Wolf
443 U.S. 595 (1979)

In *Jones v. Wolf* (1979) the U.S. Supreme Court attempted to bring greater clarity to the perplexing tangle of law that has complicated the resolution of disputes in which competing religious factions have claimed the title to the property of congregations in which schisms have occurred. The Court broadened the so-called neutral principles doctrine that it had developed in earlier decisions, particularly *Presbyterian Church in the United States v. Mary Elizabeth Blue Hull Memorial Presbyterian Church* (1969) and *Serbian Eastern Orthodox Diocese v. Milivojevich* (1976). In those decisions the Court had suggested that church property disputes could be resolved through the application of common-law principles of property and contract. By undertaking a "neutral" examination of such documents as deeds and church constitutions, courts could avoid inquiries into religious doctrine that might violate the Establishment and Free Exercise Clauses of the First Amendment.

The Court in *Jones* vacated and remanded a Georgia Supreme Court decision upholding a trial court's award of church property to the majority faction in a congregation that had withdrawn from the Presbyterian Church in the United States (PCUS). Although the Georgia Supreme Court took a neutral principles approach and had examined Georgia statutes, the PCUS constitution, and title documents, the U.S. Supreme Court held that the Georgia court had not adequately explained the grounds for its decision.

In a forceful endorsement of the so-called

neutral principles doctrine, Justice Harry Blackmun's opinion for the Court explained that this approach to the resolution of church property disputes is "completely secular in operation, and yet flexible enough to accommodate all forms of religious organization and polity." Since "neutral principles" rely exclusively on objective, well-established concepts of trust and property law that are familiar to lawyers and judges, the Court believed that the approach "promises to free civil courts completely with entanglement in questions of religious doctrine, polity and practice."

Moreover, the Court stated that the neutral principles approach "shares the peculiar genius of private-law systems in general-flexibility in ordering rights and obligations to reflect the intentions of the parties." For example, it permits religious societies to use appropriate reversionary clauses and trust provisions to specify what will happen to church property in the event of a particular contingency. The Court cautioned that courts which apply neutral principles must take special care to scrutinize documents in purely secular terms and must eschew reliance on religious precepts. The Court concluded, however, that "the promise of nonentanglement and neutrality inherent in the neutral principles approach more than compensates for what will be occasional problems in application."

Despite its endorsement of neutral principles, the Court explained that a state may adopt any method of dispute resolution that involves no consideration of religious doctrine. The Court also stated that courts still must defer to authoritative ecclesiastical bodies when the interpretation of deeds, corporate charters, or church constitutions would require the civil courts to resolve a religious controversy. In dictum, the Court also suggested that a court could properly adopt a presumptive rule of favoring a majority faction, defeasible on a showing that the identity of the local church is to be determined by some other means.

In a dissenting opinion joined by three other members of the Court, Justice Lewis F. Powell warned that the Court's analysis was likely to encourage "intrusion into church polity forbidden by the First Amendment." Powell explained that the constitutional documents of churches "tend to be drawn in terms of religious precepts" and that any attempt to interpret them in "purely secular terms" is "more likely to promote confusion than understanding." Although Powell did not reject the concept of neutral principles, he contended that the Court's application would unduly restrict the scope of admissible evidence by permitting the courts to consider the form of church government only if the polity had been stated—in express relation to church property—in the language of trust and property law. Powell stated that courts should defer to the decisions reached within the polity chosen for dispute resolution by the members themselves.

During the years following the *Wolf* decision, a number of states have formally adopted the neutral principles approach. In several other states, however, courts have refused to use the neutral principles method and have continued to adhere to the so-called polity theory, in which the courts defer to the decisions of the church's own internal system of governance. Other states have handed down decisions that have not required a definitive selection of one theory or the other. The *Wolf* decision has encouraged religious denominations to draft constitutions, charters, and other legal instruments in a manner that clearly provides for the disposition of property in the event of a congregational schism.

William G. Ross

Bibliography

Adams, Arlin M., and William R. Hanlon, "*Jones v. Wolf*: Church Autonomy and the Religion Clauses of the First Amendment," 128 *University of Pennsylvania Law Review* 1291–1339 (June 1980).

Ross, William G., "The Need for an Exclusive and Uniform Application of 'Neutral Principles' in the Adjudication of Church Property Disputes," 32 *Saint Louis University Law Journal* 263–316 (1987).

Sirico, Louis J., Jr., "The Constitutional Dimensions of Church Property Disputes," 59 *Washington University Law Quarterly* 1–79 (1981).

Cases Cited

Jones v. Wolf, 443 U.S. 595 (1979).

Presbyterian Church in the United States v. Mary Elizabeth Blue Hull Memorial Presbyterian Church, 393 U.S. 440 (1969).

Serbian Eastern Orthodox Diocese v. Milivojevich, 426 U.S. 696 (1976).

K

Karcher v. May
484 U.S. 72 (1987)

In the past several decades the Supreme Court has decided hundreds of cases devoted to the issue of religious liberty. The justices sought to determine the extent to which an individual's inalienable right to the free exercise of religion supersedes the state's right to legislate for the common good. The Court has discovered new qualifications and entanglements that complicate the two-centuries-old question of what "establishment of religion" means. A big question for 1992 concerned the tradition of prayers at high school convocation ceremonies. The Court decided in *Lee v. Weisman* (1992) that a nondenominational blessing violated the principle of separation of church and state. The Bush administration argued that a prayer in the context of a commencement celebration was simply "acknowledgment of God and the role of God in our life as a nation." Justice Antonin Scalia agreed, remarking that such a prayer differed little from the traditional prayers at the opening of a court and was merely a reflection of "people, in a country that overwhelmingly believes in God, wanting to invoke God's blessing." Opponents of prayers in the schools, including five Supreme Court justices, argued that prayer is prayer and thus is unconstitutional in schools because it has the effect of state-sponsored religion. In response to Scalia's arguments, supporters of the majority opinion noted that there is a great difference between adults who voluntarily participate in prayer and prayer that is imposed on students, who are essentially a captive audience.

Ever since the Supreme Court banned prayer in school in *Engel v. Vitale* (1962), states have tested the limits of the First Amendment's waters. As of 1981, twenty-five states had statutes permitting observation of a moment of silence at the beginning of each high school day. By a 6-to-3 vote the Court ruled such moments unconstitutional in *Wallace v. Jaffree* (1985), because they served "no secular purpose." Chief Justice Warren Burger wrote, in dissent, that the notion that the Alabama statute is a step toward creating an established church borders on—if it does not trespass into—the ridiculous. The New Jersey legislature next tested the waters and again lost, in *Karcher v. May* (1987). However, Justice Sandra Day O'Connor, speaking for a unanimous Court, deftly avoided the establishment issue by throwing the appellees out of court on the grounds of mootness and lack of jurisdiction.

The issue in *Karcher* was a statute that required elementary and secondary public schools to permit students to observe a moment of silence at the beginning of school. A teacher and several students and parents brought suit against the New Jersey Department of Education for violating the Establishment Clause of the First Amendment. Alan Karcher and Carmen Orechio, presiding officers of the state legislature, intervened as defendants when neither New Jersey's attorney general nor the department of education chose to defend the statute. Both the district court and the court of appeals declared the statute unconstitutional because it lacked the secular purpose necessary, in the courts' opinions, according to the landmark Establishment Clause case, *Lemon v. Kurtzman* (1971). According to Chief Justice Warren Burger, who wrote the opinion of the

Court in *Lemon,* "First, the statute must have a secular legislative purpose; second, its principal or primary effect must be one that neither advances nor inhibits religion; finally the statute must not foster an excessive government entanglement with religion."

The appellees sought to defend the constitutionality of the statute. Before the case reached the Supreme Court in 1987, however, the appellees lost their positions as presiding state officers, and their successors withdrew New Jersey's appeal to the Court. Although Karcher and Orechio sought to continue the appeal as "individual legislators and as representatives of the majority of the 200th New Jersey legislature that enacted the minute of silence statute," the Supreme Court ruled that, "since they no longer hold those offices, they lack the authority to pursue this appeal on behalf of the legislature. Karcher and Orechio as individual representatives . . . are not 'parties' entitled to appeal the Court of Appeal's judgment."

Justice Byron White, who often favored government accommodation of religion as long as it did not prefer one religion over another, concurred in the judgment in *Karcher* that the plaintiffs lacked standing. However, he used a separate concurrence to lay the ground for an attack on the *Lemon* test. In *Karcher* he noted an avenue of future attacks:

> It bears pointing out, however, that we have now acknowledged that the New Jersey Legislature and its authorized representative have the authority to defend the constitutionality of a statute attacked in federal court. . . . It is also clear that because Karcher and Orechio did not seek to intervene as individual legislators in a non-representative capacity, we again leave for another day the issue of whether individual legislators have standing to intervene and [defend] legislation for which they voted.

Also left open is the Supreme Court's view on prayer and the Establishment Clause. The endless parade of related cases give testimony to the ferment in courts, schools, and legislatures over prayer in school. The Court's calendar after 1987 exploded with church–state issues that involved a contest between the guarantee of the free exercise of religion and the prohibition of the establishment of religion—not all of which can be avoided because appellees lose standing or jurisdiction.

L. Sue Hulett

Bibliography

Goldberg, Steven S., "The Supreme Court Remains Silent on Moments of Silence: *Karcher v. May,*" 43 *Educational Law Reporter* 849–853 (1989).

Johnson, Mary Ellen Quinn, "Comment: School Prayer and the Constitution: Silence Is Golden," 48 *Maryland Law Review* 1018–1044 (1989).

Cases Cited

Engel v. Vitale, 370 U.S. 421 (1962).
Lee v. Weisman, 505 U.S. 577 (1992).
Lemon v. Kurtzman, 403 U.S. 602 (1971).
Wallace v. Jaffree, 472 U.S. 38 (1985).

Kiryas Joel School District v. Grumet 512 U.S. 687 (1994)

Although the U.S. Supreme Court's decision in *Kiryas Joel School District v. Grumet* (1994) broke no new major ground in the law of the First Amendment's religion clauses, it did involve one of the most exotic fact situations to come before the Court in a First Amendment case. New York's legislature had created a public school district whose boundaries were drawn to encompass only members of the Satmar Hasidim—an insular and traditionalist Orthodox Jewish group—in order to permit the handicapped children of that sect to attend special education classes solely with other Satmar children. The Supreme Court held that the creation of the district constituted favoritism for the Hasidim in violation of the Establishment Clause; it rejected the claim that the district was a legitimate accommodation of the distinctive religious and cultural practices of the group.

The members of the Satmar sect fled persecution in eastern Europe in the 1940s and came to Brooklyn, New York. In the 1970s the group purchased a large tract of land in an upstate county, and members began moving there, forming the settlement of Kiryas Joel within a larger, existing town. The Satmar Hasidim are a highly insular and traditionalist people who speak primarily Yiddish, permit no television or radio, require distinctive clothing and hairstyles for both males and females, and educate their children in private schools segregated by sex and permeated by religious teaching. The Satmars' practices soon came in conflict with the customs of the surrounding majority. After a zoning dispute over the Satmars' use of their homes for schools and religious services, the Satmars seceded in 1977 and formed the separate village of Kiryas Joel, inhabited only by members of the sect.

The next conflict between the Hasidim and their neighbors came over the education of Kiryas Joel's handicapped children, who have disabilities ranging from deafness to mental retardation. Under federal and state laws these disabled children, like others, are entitled to publicly funded special education classes to meet their special needs. By law the duty fell on the local public school district, which at first provided its own staff to conduct classes in Kiryas Joel's religious schools. However, the district dropped that program after two Supreme Court decisions—*Grand Rapids v. Ball* (1985) and *Aguilar v. Felton,* (1985)—held that similar programs violated the First Amendment's Establishment Clause. The district required the Satmar children to come into the public schools for classes. But the Satmar parents reported that their children were mocked and were traumatized from being exposed to the unfamiliar language and customs of the outside world; and the parents withdrew the children from the classes.

Although the Satmars are a small group, they fought tenaciously for accommodation of their practices; and because they and other Hasidic groups in New York form disciplined voting blocs, they enjoy a certain influence with legislators. The parents and the public school authorities ultimately agreed to resolve this problem by going their separate ways: They successfully asked the New York legislature to pass a special statute creating a separate public school district for the Satmar, drawn along the village lines of Kiryas Joel. Thus the public schools were freed from the burden of educating these unusual children, and the Satmars were able to obtain state and federal funding and at the same time have their children educated in familiar surroundings. Although classes in the Kiryas Joel public district were almost entirely made up of Satmar children, the district was not permitted to teach religious tenets.

However, the statute was challenged in court by a state taxpayer on the ground that, by creating a district specifically for the Satmar sect, it violated the Establishment Clause's prohibitions on government assistance to religion. The state courts agreed and held the special district unconstitutional. The U.S. Supreme Court, by a 6-to-3 vote, reached the same result. The Court's ruling did not substantially break from its religion clause precedents. But identifying the precise rationale of the ruling is somewhat complicated, because there were several separate opinions.

A majority of the justices concluded that the statute creating the Kiryas Joel district failed the command that government be neutral toward religion. Justice Souter's opinion for four justices, joined in this part by Justice O'Connor, argued that the state had provided a unique benefit to the Satmars—the creation of a small school district tailored to the boundaries of the religious community—and that the Court could not be sure that the benefit was "one that the legislature will provide equally to other religious (and nonreligious) groups." If another group did seek to create its own school district, and if the legislature refused to create such a district as it had for the Satmars, the justices said, a court could not effectively review such a refusal to act. The Court indicated that the government could accommodate needs such as those of the Satmars, but not by a special statute enacted solely for them.

Justice Souter's opinion also concluded that, by drawing the lines of the school district to encompass only Satmars, the state had "defin[ed] a political subdivision and hence the qualification for its franchise by a religious test, resulting in a purposeful and forbidden 'fusion of governmental and religious functions.'" (Although Justice Souter did not mention it, his finding of a "fusion" of religious and civil authority may have been influenced by press reports of religious tension in the village. Dissidents assertedly had been harassed by followers of the chief rabbi, a religious figure who exercised a tremendous influence over the citizens of the village, including its political leaders. These claims were disputed, however, and were never put into evidence in the litigation.) Although this part of the opinion attracted only four votes, Justice Kennedy concurred on a related ground, arguing that "[t]he Establishment Clause forbids the government to draw political boundaries on the basis of religious faith."

The dissenting opinion, written by Justice Scalia and joined by Chief Justice Rehnquist and Justice Thomas, challenged every argument of the members of the majority. The dissenters argued that the benefit to the Satmars was not unique, because New York had created other special districts for other special children, such as those in orphanages. They also argued that there was no reason to think that the state would fail to respond to the needs of other groups whose handicapped children needed special treatment. Finally, they argued that the state had delegated power not to a religious group as such, but to the villagers of Kiryas Joel—and they pointed out that numerous communities across America were formed by, and even now are primarily composed of, members of one religious faith.

The *Kiryas Joel* decision did not end efforts to provide publicly funded special education for the Satmar children in their own community. Responding to the Supreme Court's "neutrality" rationale, as well as to explicit suggestions in the opinions of Justices O'Connor and Kennedy, the New York legislature immediately passed a new, general statute allowing the creation of a smaller school district out of any larger district as long as certain criteria were met. That statute was promptly challenged by the same plaintiffs, who argued that its purported generality was a sham and that its requirements were specially chosen so as to allow the Satmar, and no other group, to have their own district. In *Grumet v. Cuomo* (N.Y., 1997) the state's highest court struck down this statute as well.

The Kiryas Joel dispute provides a dramatic example of the difficulties that can arise as the government seeks to extend the benefits of public welfare programs to religious citizens and religious groups, to accommodate their religious and cultural distinctives, and at the same time to avoid unconstitutional favoritism for religion. The Supreme Court decision also shows a Court with a majority of justices suspicious of explicit legislative accommodations of religious practices. But the decision is unlikely to be highly influential or to provide much guidance for future cases (although church–state observers did take note that five justices expressed a willingness to overrule the *Aguilar* and *Grand Rapids* decisions that had prevented the Kiryas Joel students from receiving assistance in Satmar private schools in the first place). It is highly unusual for a state to draw political boundaries along religious lines, and relatively unusual for a state to make a legislative accommodation explicitly for only one religious group. The *Kiryas Joel* case seems likely to remain a "one-shot wonder."

Thomas C. Berg

Bibliography

Berg, Thomas C., "Slouching toward Secularism: A Comment on *Kiryas Joel School District v. Grumet,*" 44 *Emory Law Journal* 433–499 (1995).

Greene, Abner S., "*Kiryas Joel* and Two Mistakes about Equality," 96 *Columbia Law Review* 1–86 (1996).

Lupu, Ira C., "Uncovering the Village of Kiryas Joel," 96 *Columbia Law Review* 104–120 (1996).

Rosen, Jeffrey, "*Kiryas Joel* and *Shaw v. Reno*: A Text-Bound Interpretivist Approach," 26 *Cumberland Law Review* 387–406 (1996).

Cases Cited

Aguilar v. Felton, 473 U.S. 402 (1985).

Grand Rapids v. Ball, 473 U.S. 373 (1985).

Grumet v. Cuomo, 90 N.Y. 2d 57 (1997); 681 N.E. 2d 340 (1997).

Kiryas Joel School District v. Grumet, 512 U.S. 687 (1994).

Kneeland

See COMMONWEALTH V. KNEELAND.

L

Labor Law and Religion

The U.S. Supreme Court has consistently demonstrated a remarkable degree of judicial deference to institutional employers' interests at the expense of the employees' right to the free exercise of their religion in the workplace and of their right not to be discriminated against in employment on the basis of their religion. The Supreme Court dramatically subordinated employees' rights to the prerogatives of institutional employers in a series of important decisions beginning in 1977. As the tenure of Chief Justice Warren Burger evolved and matured, the activist, proinstitutional, statist jurisprudence of the Court became increasingly inimical to the debilitated First Amendment and Title VII rights of individual employees—rights that theoretically were designed respectively to protect free exercise of religion and to protect against employment discrimination on the basis of religion. After a decade passed, and as Chief Justice William Rehnquist succeeded Warren Burger in 1986, these initially sharply polarized cases of the late 1970s were unproblematically accepted, largely without dissent, by virtually all the members of the Court. Several cases that were decided between 1977 and 1987 powerfully exemplify these troubling jurisprudential diminutions of the free exercise and Title VII rights of employees.

Labor Contracts and Religious Practices

Trans World Airlines, Inc. v. Hardison (1977) marked the beginning of this trend in the Court's debilitation of employees' Title VII protections against discrimination on the basis of an employee's religion. Justice Byron White wrote for the seven-member Court majority, with Justices William Brennan and Thurgood Marshall in dissent.

Trans World Airlines (TWA) hired Larry G. Hardison to work in TWA's Stores Department. The Stores Department is crucial to TWA's operations and therefore must operate twenty-four hours a day, every day of the year. TWA employees had to be flexible. Hardison was subject to a seniority system designed through a collective bargaining agreement that TWA had negotiated with the union of the International Association of Machinists and Aerospace Workers. Under the agreement the most-senior employees had first choice for job and shift assignments.

In the spring of 1968 Hardison joined the Worldwide Church of God, which forbade work on the Sabbath (Saturday) and proscribed work on specified religious holidays. Hardison told his supervisor of the problem, which was temporarily resolved by moving Hardison to a different shift. However, Hardison subsequently transferred to a different area, where he did not have enough seniority to avoid working on his Sabbath. Hardison was asked to work, and he refused to report. After a hearing, Hardison was discharged for insubordination for refusing to work his designated shift.

Hardison sued both TWA and the union. He claimed that his discharge constituted unlawful religious discrimination in violation of Title VII of the federal Civil Rights Act of 1964. Hardison also claimed that the union discriminated against him by failing to represent him adequately in his dispute with TWA and by depriving him of his right to exercise his religious beliefs. Hardison's claim of religious discrimination was based on the 1967 guidelines of the federal Equal Employment Opportunity Commission (EEOC), which required employers "to make reasonable accommodations to the religious needs of employees whenever such accommodations do not constitute 'undue hardship.'"

The Supreme Court held that TWA's discharge of Hardison did not violate Title VII. The Court explained the requirements mandated by the EEOC guidelines. Under the guidelines an employer must make reasonable accommodations of employees' religious needs. The EEOC, however, did not suggest what sort of accommodations would be "unreasonable."

The Court opined that TWA made reasonable efforts to accommodate the employee's religious practices and Sabbath observance as required by Title VII and, in addition, that TWA had done all it reasonably could to accommodate the employee's religious practices within the bounds of the seniority system in the collective bargaining agreement. Therefore, stated the Court, the duty to accommodate Hardison's religious observance and refusal to work on Saturday did not require TWA to take steps inconsistent with the seniority system of the valid collective bargaining agreement.

The Court, placing great weight on the seniority system, agreed that religious observances are a reality. However, religiously observant employees cannot always get first choice of shifts. If there are not enough employees to work Saturdays, the seniority system made seniority the determinative factor. If not, then the senior person would be denied his or her rights under the collective bargaining agreement.

Title VII does not stand for the proposition that a company can deprive employees of labor contract rights in order to accommodate other employees' religious preferences. Neither the employer nor the labor union was required by Title VII to make special exception to the labor contract's seniority system in order to accommodate the employee's religious obligations. The Court found that "to require TWA to bear more than a *de minimis* cost in order to give Hardison Saturdays off is an 'undue hardship' not required by Title VII." The costs of giving certain employees days off to accommodate their religion—by abandoning the seniority system—would result in preferential treatment of employees on the basis of religion.

The dissent, written by Justice Marshall and joined by Justice Brennan, stated that the majority opinion was a fatal blow to the requirement to accommodate religious practices in the workplace. Notably, the dissent argued that accommodation should not be rejected simply because it involved unequal treatment. Title VII of the federal Civil Rights Act required employers to grant privileges as part of the accommodation process, and a huge carrier like TWA could have borne the burden of the extra costs without undue hardship.

With the *Hardison* decision, however, the employer's Title VII duty to reasonably accommodate the religious practices of the observant employee was utterly minimized by the Court. Any accommodation measure that resulted in more than a *de minimis* cost to the employer was an unreasonable "undue hardship" and thus was not required of the employer by Title VII, 42 U.S.C. §2000 e(j), §701(j). This effective judicial relief for the employer from its federal statutory duty to reasonably accommodate the employee's religious observance, practice, and belief was made even more complete by the Supreme Court in 1986. Chief Justice Rehnquist wrote for the seven-member majority in *Ansonia Board of Education v. Philbrook* (1986), with only Justices Marshall and Stevens filing opinions concurring in part and dissenting in part.

Philbrook had been employed by the Ansonia School Board since 1962 to teach business classes. In 1968 he was baptized into the Worldwide Church of God. The church required its members to refrain from working during designated holy days, which caused Philbrook to miss six school days per year.

Pursuant to the collective bargaining agreement between the school board and the teacher's union, teachers were granted three days of annual leave for observance of religious holidays, but they could not use any accumulated sick leave for religious observances. Philbrook used the three days granted for religious holidays each year. Since he needed three more days to observe his religion, he asked the school board either to adopt the policy of allowing use of three days for personal business or, in the alternative, to allow him to pay the cost of a substitute and to receive full pay for additional days off for religious observances. The school board rejected Philbrook's request. Philbrook sued, alleging that the prohibition on the use of "necessary personal business" leave for religious observance violated sections 703(a)(1) and (2) of Title VII. He sought both damages and injunctive relief.

Although the Supreme Court remanded the case for further factual findings and thus did not issue a dispositive decision, it reiterated that the employer met statutory obligations by offering a reasonable accommodation for religious practices, observances, and beliefs to the employee. Significantly, the employer is not required to acquiesce to the employee's most desired, most beneficial accommodation. As Chief Justice Rehnquist summarized:

> Thus, where the employer has already reasonably accommodated the employee's religious needs, the statutory inquiry is at an end. The employer need not further show that each of the employee's alternative accommodations would result in undue hardship. As *Hardison* illustrates, the extent of undue hardship on the employer's business is at issue only where the employer claims that it is unable to offer any reasonable accommodation without such hardship.

Through these two important decisions the Supreme Court essentially relieved the employer of its statutory duty to reasonably accommodate the religious employee; anything beyond *de minimis* cost caused by the accommodation will be an "undue hardship" to the employer, which is beyond the employer's Title VII duty of reasonable accommodation of the observations, practices, and beliefs of the religious employee.

Accommodating Religious Institutions

When the employer is a recognized, mainstream religious institution, the Supreme Court has been even more deferential to the employer—again at the expense of the rights of the employees. Indeed, those who advocate strict separation between church and state may see the Court's accommodation of the religious institutional employer as a violation of the Establishment Clause of the First Amendment. That, obviously, is not a perspective shared by the Supreme Court, which instead prefers to accommodate the prerogatives of the religiously affiliated institutional employer.

In *National Labor Relations Board v. Catholic Bishop of Chicago* (1979) Chief Justice Burger, writing for a bare five-member majority of the Court, asserted that the federal National Labor Relations Board (NLRB) did not have jurisdiction to investigate unfair labor practice charges brought against the Catholic bishop of Chicago. The bishop was the employer of the complaining faculty members who were employed in the schools operated under the auspices of the Catholic Church.

Although the prerogatives of this powerful institutional employer could have been constrained if it had been subject to the federal National Labor Relations Act, the Court majority was extremely sensitive to the Free Exercise and Establishment Clauses of the First Amendment. Chief Justice Burger summarized:

> Accordingly, in the absence of a clear expression of Congress' intent to bring teachers in church-operated schools within the jurisdiction of the Board, we decline to construe the Act in a manner that could in turn call upon the Court to resolve difficult and sensitive questions arising out of the guarantees of the First Amendment Religion Clauses.

The NLRB originally found that the Catholic bishop, as the institutional employer of the lay faculty members at the schools operated under auspices of the Catholic Church, had violated the National Labor Relations Act and had committed unfair labor practices by refusing to recognize or to bargain with the faculty union.

In 1974 and 1975 separate representation petitions were filed with the NLRB by the faculty union. The Catholic bishop challenged the board's assertion of jurisdiction. The U.S. Court of Appeals for the Seventh Circuit agreed with the Catholic Bishop. The Free Exercise and Establishment Clauses of the First Amendment of the Constitution precluded the NLRB from exercising jurisdiction over the schools of the Catholic Church and over the Catholic bishop as the institutional employer.

In a highly technical decision, which deliberately did not reach or address the underlying merits of the bishop's unfair labor practices of refusing to recognize or to bargain with the faculty unions, the Supreme Court affirmed the decision of the Seventh Circuit.

In his opinion for the majority of the Court, Chief Justice Burger pointed to the legislative history of the National Labor Relations Act, which revealed nothing to indicate that church-operated schools would be within the NLRB's jurisdiction. The chief justice referred specifically to the debate behind an amendment to the act, which reflected certain First Amendment guarantees, and argued, "the absence of an 'affirmative intention of the Congress clearly expressed' fortifies our conclusion that Congress did not contemplate that the Board would require church-operated schools to [recognize] unions as bargaining agents for their teachers." The Supreme Court, therefore, affirmed the Seventh Circuit. While the Court admitted that the NLRB's jurisdiction was broad in nature, it again pointed to the legislative history of the act. Finding nothing in the legislative history that would endorse the type of jurisdiction which the NLRB sought in this case, the Court decided that it had no alternative but to decline jurisdiction over labor law matters in church-operated schools. The alternative to that, noted the Court, would lead to "mandatory bargaining, which in turn would cause too many conflicts with church administrators."

In a powerful, sharp dissent Justice Brennan—joined by Justices White, Marshall, and Blackmun—characterized the majority opinion as a failed lesson in statutory construction. The dissent argued that the majority opinion failed to consider the federal National Labor Relations Act's language and history. Justice Brennan further asserted that the majority failed to consider the Court's own precedents, which held that the jurisdiction of the NLRB is extremely broad. The dissent plainly would have included church-operated schools within the board's jurisdiction.

Within less than a decade the increasingly accommodationist Court cavalierly sustained, without dissent, the religiously affiliated institutional employer's prerogative to terminate—summarily—competent, long-service employees in *Corporation of the Presiding Bishop of the Church of Jesus Christ of Latter-Day Saints v. Amos* (1987).

Christine J. Amos was an employee of Beehive Clothing Mills, a profit-making company. Frank Mayson was a custodian at the Deseret Gymnasium, a nonprofit facility open to the public. Both enterprises were owned and operated by the Corporation of the Presiding Bishop of the Church of Jesus Christ of Latter-Day Saints and by the Corporation of the President of the Church of Jesus Christ of Latter-Day Saints. Amos, three other Beehive Clothing Mills employees, and Mayson challenged their individual firings, which were based on their failure to obtain a temple recommend (a standard for determining members' eligibility to attend a temple). The individuals failed to have the district court declare them to be a class.

The defendant church and presiding bishop argued that a temple recommend was a legitimate requirement for working in what was essentially a religious institution. The Supreme Court felt that there were insufficient findings of fact at the district court regarding the religious or nonreligious character of the activities at Beehive Clothing Mills, but it proceeded to judgment concerning the activities at the Deseret Gymnasium, where Mayson worked. Thus, despite the fact that the employment status of Amos was not at issue, the Court retained Amos's name in the caption of the case.

Both the Corporation of the Presiding Bishop of the Church of Jesus Christ of Latter-Day Saints and the Corporation of the President of the Church of Jesus Christ of Latter-Day Saints are religious entities associated with an unincorporated religious association sometimes called the Mormon Church. Frank Mayson worked at the Deseret Gymnasium for approximately sixteen years, but he was discharged in 1981 because he failed to qualify for a temple recommend. Mayson then brought suit alleging unlawful discrimination on the basis of religion. The church moved to dismiss, maintaining that Section 702 of the federal Civil Rights Act of 1964 shielded it from liability. Mayson argued that the Civil Rights Act should not be construed to permit religious employers to discriminate on religious grounds in employment of persons for obviously nonreligious, secular jobs. Mayson believed that such an interpretation of Section 702 of Title VII would violate the First Amendment, as an establishment of a religion.

Without dissent, the Supreme Court reversed the decision of the lower federal court, which had found in favor of former employee Mayson. The Court examined whether Section 702 of Title VII of the federal Civil Rights Act of 1964—which exempts religious organizations from Title VII's prohibition of religious discrimination in employment—was unconstitutional in light of the Establishment Clause of the First Amendment. Specifically, did Section 702's statutory exemption from Title VII have the primary effect of unconstitutionally advancing religion, in violation of the Establishment Clause? The Court resolved the question in the negative.

The Court measured the facts and the statute against the Establishment Clause, according to the classic multipart test set forth in the landmark case of *Lemon v. Kurtzman* (1971). The *Lemon* test comprises three parts, or prongs: (1) Does the law at issue serve a "secular legislative purpose"? (2) Does the law in question have a "principal or primary effect that neither advances nor inhibits religion"? (3) Does the law in question "impermissibly entangle Church and State"?

The Court concluded that, under the first prong of the *Lemon* test, it was permissible for the Congress to attempt to minimize governmental "interference with the decision-making process in religions." Under the second prong, the Court stated that a law is not necessarily unconstitutional simply because it allows churches to advance religion. In order to violate this prong, the Court reasoned that it would be necessary to show that the government itself had advanced religion through its own activities and influence. Finally, under the third prong of the *Lemon* test, the Court concluded that there was no unconstitutional entanglement raised by Section 702 of Title VII.

Justice O'Connor suggested that a new approach be applied to the *Lemon* test: The inquiry should be "whether government's purpose is to endorse religion and whether the statute actually conveys a message of endorsement," as judged by an objective observer. This accommodationist thinking has proved increasingly influential among additional members of the Court since the *Amos* decision in 1987, but has yet to lead to the Court's repudiation of the *Lemon* test in its Establishment Clause jurisprudence.

Neither Labor Law nor Religion Enhanced

As a result of these salient cases neither labor law nor religion has been enhanced by the Supreme Court. Rather—on both conceptual and practical levels—labor law doctrine, the First Amendment religion clauses, and Title VII protections against discrimination in employment because of religion have all been debilitated by the Court. The only consistent winner in these cases has been the institutional employer, whereas employees have been thoroughly unsuccessful. Much more significantly, and ominously, the Supreme Court has moved inexorably to a pro-institutional, "statist" bias, effectuating an insidious calculus of interests that routinely subordinates individuals and employees who generally lack corporate institutional power and influence.

David L. Gregory

Bibliography

Gedicks, Frederick M., and Roger Hendrix, *Choosing the Dream: The Future of Religion in American Life* (New York: Greenwood, 1991).

Gregory, David L., "Catholic Labor Theory and the Transformation of Work," 45 *Washington and Lee Law Review* 119–157 (1988).

Laycock, Douglas, "Towards a General Theory of the Religion Clauses: The Case of Church Labor Relations and the Right to Church Autonomy," 81 *Columbia Law Review* 1373–1417 (1981).

Cases Cited

Ansonia Board of Education v. Philbrook, 479 U.S. 60 (1986).

Corporation of the Presiding Bishop of the Church of Jesus Christ of Latter-Day Saints v. Amos, 483 U.S. 327 (1987).

Lemon v. Kurtzman, 403 U.S. 602 (1971).

National Labor Relations Board v. Catholic Bishop of Chicago, 440 U.S. 490 (1979).

Trans World Airlines, Inc. v. Hardison, 432 U.S. 63 (1977).

Larson v. Valente
456 U.S. 228 (1982)

In 1978 the Minnesota legislature amended the Minnesota Charitable Solicitations Act to exempt only those "religious organizations" that received more than half their contributions from their own members or from affiliated organizations. The statute—which the legislature had enacted in 1961 to prevent organizations that were seeking registration as charities from defrauding contributors—had since its inception exempted all religious organizations. As amended, the act required religious organizations that received less than half their revenues from their own members or from affiliated organizations to submit annual reports detailing revenues and expenses to the Minnesota Department of Commerce, which would determine the submitting organization's eligibility to register as a charity.

On learning that their organization now fell within the act's reporting requirements, members of the Unification Church sued the Department of Commerce, seeking a declaration that the act as amended "constituted an abridgement of their First Amendment rights of expression and free exercise of religion. . . ." The Unification Church also sought to enjoin the act as it applied to the Unification Church; the members argued that the church emphasized "door-to-door and public-place proselytizing" as part of its religious mission, which the act's reporting requirements would impede.

The Minnesota Department of Commerce argued that the act's new reporting requirements did not abridge the church's First Amendment rights because the solicitation at issue "bore no substantial relationship to any religious expression." Therefore, such solicitation warranted no First Amendment protection. In addition, the state argued that the Unification Church did not qualify as a religion and that the solicitation of funds from nonmembers bore no relation to any religious purpose.

The magistrate who conducted the trial held that the act as amended was facially unconstitutional and that the reporting requirements which the act imposed favored some religious organizations over others: The amendment "inhibit[ed] religious organizations which received more than half of their contributions from nonmembers and thereby enhance[d] religious organizations which receive[d] less than half from non-members." The magistrate thus enjoined enforcement of the act regarding *any* religious organization.

The Eighth Circuit Court of Appeals agreed with the magistrate that the Charitable Solicitations Act unconstitutionally burdened those religious organizations which solicited more than half their funds from outside their membership. The proper remedy was to exempt all religious organizations from the act's reporting requirements. However, the Eighth Circuit vacated the magistrate's decision insofar as it enjoined the application of the act in its entirety to all religious organizations, and it questioned whether the Unification Church was a religious organization that would be eligible under the act's exemption clause.

The U.S. Supreme Court noted probable jurisdiction on the appeal. The principal question the Court faced on appeal was "whether [the act], imposing certain registration and reporting requirements upon only those religious organizations that solicit more than fifty per cent of their funds from non-members, discriminates against such organizations in violation of the Establishment Clause of the First Amendment." Justice William Brennan delivered the majority opinion, in which Justices Thurgood Marshall, Harry Blackmun, Louis Powell, and John Paul Stevens joined. Justice Stevens also wrote a separate concurring opinion. Justice Byron White wrote a dissenting opinion, in which Justice William Rehnquist joined. Justice Rehnquist wrote a separate dissent from the majority's resolution of the standing issue it faced. Chief Justice Warren Burger and Justices White and Sandra Day O'Connor joined in Justice Rehnquist's dissent.

Justice Brennan noted that Minnesota, in its arguments to the Supreme Court, no longer argued that the Unification Church was not a religion and therefore that its solicitation activities did not merit First Amendment protection. Rather, the state now argued that the Unification Church was not a "religious organization" within the act's meaning and therefore was not exempt from the act's requirements. Justice Brennan concluded that either formulation of the argument failed under Establishment Clause jurisprudence. He noted that the act had exempted the Unification Church until 1978, at which point it attempted to impose the act's reporting requirements on the Unification Church precisely because the act had been amended to cover certain "religious organizations."

Justice Brennan began his analysis noting that

> [t]he clearest command of the Establishment Clause is that one religious denomination cannot be officially preferred over

> another. . . . Free exercise . . . can be guaranteed only when legislators—and voters—are required to accord to their own religions the very same treatment given to small, new, or unpopular denominations. . . . In short, when we are presented with a state law granting a denominational preference, our precedents demand that we treat the law as suspect. . . .

Justice Brennan concluded, without extensive analysis, that the act's "fifty per cent rule . . . clearly grants denominational preferences of the sort consistently and firmly deprecated in our precedents." Therefore the Court's inquiry would be limited to whether the 50-percent rule was "closely fitted" to serve the "valid secular purpose"—which Justice Brennan assumed for the sake of argument was a "compelling interest"—of protecting the citizens of Minnesota from "abusive practices on the solicitation of funds for charity."

According to Justice Brennan:

> [The state's] argument is based on three distinct premises: that members of a religious organization can and will exercise supervision and control over the organization's solicitation activities when membership contributions exceed fifty per cent; that membership control, assuming its existence, is an adequate safeguard against abusive solicitations of the public by the organization; and that the need for public disclosure rises in proportion with the *percentage* of nonmember contributions.

Justice Brennan saw no merit in any of these premises of the state's argument. With regard to the first premise, Justice Brennan seemed to think that making distinctions based on the source of 50 percent of an organization's funds was arbitrary. There simply was no way to ensure that members of an organization would exert any greater control over the organization by virtue of the fact that those members are responsible for more than 50 percent of the organization's funds. With regard to the second premise, Justice Brennan indicated that it directly contradicts the very purpose of amending the act in the first place. That is, if, as the state suggests, membership control is a sufficient safeguard to protect the public, there is no need for the legislation in the first place—regardless of the source of the organization's funds. Finally, Justice Brennan noted the folly of using percentages to distinguish whether or not an organization comes under the act's requirements. Regulating according to percentage in no way diminishes the opportunity for a religious organization to defraud the public.

In summing up, Justice Brennan noted that the test which the Supreme Court had articulated in *Lemon v. Kurtzman* (1973) was not relevant to this case, because that test pertained to instances where legislation applied to all religions rather than distinguishing among religions, as the amendment to the act did. However, Justice Brennan did note that the amendment to the act "risked . . . politicizing religion." That is, the act as amended clearly presented an excessive entanglement between government and the religious institutions it would then monitor. Indeed, as amended, the act amounted to "religious gerrymandering."

Justice Stevens agreed with the Court's determination that the Unification Church had standing to challenge the act, but he indicated that a determination of the church's status as a religious organization was essential to the resolution of this controversy. Thus, it was inappropriate for the Court to be adjudicating the controversy, because the subsequent adjudication of outstanding issues in the lower courts would lead to more litigation. Justice Stevens reiterated his position in *United States v. Lee* (1982), that there is "an important interest in avoiding litigation of issues relating to church doctrine." The majority decision would only engender more litigation.

Justice White took issue with the majority decision in several aspects. The first area of contention was basically procedural: He faulted the majority for making what he described as factual determinations that should have been made by the magistrate at the trial level. In addition he criticized the majority for not applying the *Lemon* test as the magistrate had done at trial. Justice White then condemned the majority's finding that the act was not neutral with regard to all religious institutions. He seemingly based this criticism on the fact that the language of the act singled out no institution by name; rather, it distinguished among religious organizations based on their sources of funding.

Justice White also noted that there is a compelling state interest in safeguarding the public from the fraudulent fundraising practices by charitable organizations, and he accused the majority of substituting its own judgment for that of Minnesota's legislature. In addition, Justice White took issue with the majority's rejection of the legislature's finding that religious organizations which receive more than 50 percent of funding from their members are better able to monitor themselves and their fundraising. Justice White appeared to believe that the legislature was justified in imposing on a reasonably and well-defined class of religious organizations the same reporting requirements that applied to any religious organization.

Phillip Presby

Bibliography

Eisgruber, Christopher L. and Lawrence G. Sager, "Mediating Institutions: Beyond the Public/Private Distinction: The Vulnerability of Conscience: The Constitutional Basis for Protecting Religious Conduct," 61 *University of Chicago Law Review* 1245–1315 (1994).

Todres, Jacob L., "Internal Revenue Code Section 170: Does the Receipt by a Donor of an Intangible Religious Benefit Reduce the Amount of the Charitable Contribution Deduction? Only the Lord Knows for Sure," 64 *Tennessee Law Review* 91–153 (1996).

Cases Cited

Larsen v. Valente, 456 U.S. 228 (1982).
Lemon v. Kurtzman, 411 U.S. 192 (1973).
United States v. Lee, 455 U.S. 252 (1982).

Leahy v. District of Columbia 833 F. 2d 1046 (D.C. Cir. 1987)

Leahy v. District of Columbia (D.C., 1987) presented a First Amendment Free Exercise Clause challenge to the District of Columbia's requirement that applicants for driver's licenses provide the District with their Social Security numbers. John Leahy asserted a First Amendment right of religious freedom in refusing to have his application for a driver's license listed with his Social Security number.

The municipal regulations of the District of Columbia specified that each driver's license application would state the applicant's Social Security number. Asserting religious objections to the requirement, Leahy refused to supply his number and instead presented his passport and birth certificate; but the licensing examiner would not accept these substitutes. As a result, Leahy was not permitted to take the license examination and was not issued a driver's license.

Leahy asserted that he came to believe that the use of his Social Security number for any purpose not related to the administration of his Social Security account would "endanger his chances of being chosen for life after death." The theological roots of this belief were said to lie in the New Testament Book of Revelation, which refers to two beasts and prophesies that those who receive the mark of the second beast shall be condemned to eternal damnation. This mark is characterized as a number required for buying and selling.

Leahy averred that Social Security numbers have come to share many of the characteristics of the mark of the beast, and that they may be the mark of the beast. Therefore, he refused to provide his number for non–Social Security purposes when applying for a driver's license.

In an opinion written by Judge (now Justice) Ruth Bader Ginsburg, the U.S. Court of Appeals for the District of Columbia Circuit reversed the trial court's *sua sponte* ("without prompting") dismissal of the case, stating that the case needed to be examined on the basis of compelling state interest rather than on a less rigorous standard of scrutiny.

The court of appeals based its ruling on *Bowen, Secretary of Health and Human Services, et al. v. Roy* (1986). Applying the test of compelling state interest to the limited record before it, the court stated that the District of Columbia had not demonstrated that requiring a religious objector to provide his Social Security number in order to obtain a driver's license was the least-restrictive means of achieving the public safety objective at stake. The trial court's dismissal apparently occurred as a result of a misreading of *Roy* and a miscounting of the positions of the justices in *Roy*'s fragmented opinion. The court of appeals read *Roy* as having rejected the standard of "reasonable means of promoting a legitimate public interest." The reasonable means standard proposed by Chief Justice Warren Burger was joined by only two other justices, William Powell and William

Rehnquist. It was expressly rejected by five justices: Harry Blackmun, Sandra Day O'Connor, William Brennan, Thurgood Marshall, and Byron White. Instead of the reasonable means standard, the Court reiterated that for Free Exercise Clause jurisprudence the test continued to be the compelling state interest of *Sherbert v. Verner* (1963) and *Thomas v. Review Board of the Indiana Employment Security Division* (1981).

The Court of Appeals for the District of Columbia reversed the trial court as a matter of law and remanded the case to consider the sincerity of Leahy's belief as well as for a determination of any relief to which he may have been entitled.

Leahy was later cited to a contrary outcome in the case of *Piester v. State Department of Social Services* (Colo., 1992). In *Piester* the plaintiffs refused to supply their Social Security numbers in order to obtain pension benefits, because they asserted that to do so violated their religious beliefs. The court held that the burden of supplying the Social Security numbers was small and nondiscriminatory and that the system could not readily be altered to accommodate the plaintiffs' beliefs. In *Billman v. Commissioner of Internal Revenue* (D.C. Cir. 1988) the court denied the plaintiff's claim that the Internal Revenue Service's Form 1040 violated his religious freedom, because the court held that the plaintiff had never alleged that his refusal to supply the number would result in adverse consequences.

Lea Vander Velde

Bibliography

Cole, Jamie A., "A New Category of Free Exercise Claims: Protection for Individuals Objecting to Governmental Actions That Impede Their Religions," 135 *University of Pennsylvania Law Review* 1557–1590 (1987).

Pepper, Stephen, "Conflicting Paradigms of Religious Freedom: Liberty versus Equality," 1993 *Brigham Young University Law Review* 7–62 (1993).

Cases Cited

Billman v. Commissioner of Internal Revenue, 847 F. 2d 887 (D.C. Cir. 1988).

Bowen, Secretary of Health and Human Services, et al. v. Roy, 476 U.S. 693 (1986).

Leahy v. District of Columbia, 833 F. 2d 1046 (D.C. Cir. 1987).

Piester v. State Department of Social Services, 849 P. 2d 894 (Colorado 1992).

Sherbert v. Verner, 374 U.S. 398 (1963).

Thomas v. Review Board of the Indiana Employment Security Division, 450 U.S. 707 (1981).

Lee

See UNITED STATES V. LEE.

Lee v. Weisman
505 U.S. 577 (1992)

In *Lee v. Weisman* (1992) the Supreme Court held that the Establishment Clause of the First Amendment was violated when Rabbi Leslie Gutterman delivered an invocation and a benediction at the Nathan Bishop Middle School graduation ceremony in Providence, Rhode Island, on June 29, 1989. School principal Robert E. Lee, who invited Rabbi Gutterman to participate in the ceremony, was acting pursuant to long-standing school district policy. Lee furnished Rabbi Gutterman with a two-page leaflet issued by the National Conference of Christians and Jews, which contained guidelines for public prayers at nonsectarian civic ceremonies, and he advised the rabbi that the invocation and benediction should be nonsectarian.

Daniel Weisman, whose 14-year-old daughter was one of the graduates, sought an injunction to bar the prayers after school officials refused to delete them from the graduation ceremony. U.S. District Judge Francis J. Boyle denied preliminary injunctive relief, and Rabbi Gutterman delivered the prayers at the graduation ceremony. However, Judge Boyle later held that the prayers violated the Establishment Clause and permanently enjoined such invocations.

Since 1970 federal and state courts have adjudicated about ten challenges to the constitutionality of graduation prayer, with varying results—although most recent courts have held that the practice violated the Establishment Clause. Most courts had scrutinized the prayers under the three-pronged test of *Lemon v. Kurtzman* (1971) (i.e., in order to be held constitutional under the Establishment Clause, a challenged law or practice must have a secular purpose, must have a primary effect of neither advancing nor inhibiting religion, and must not foster excessive entanglement between the state and religion). One exception was *Stein v. Plainwell Community Schools* (6th Cir. 1987), where the court applied the Supreme Court's test in *Marsh v. Chambers* (1983). Although the High Court had applied the *Lemon* test in every Establishment Clause case involving public schools since 1971, in Marsh it ignored the test when it upheld the Nebraska legislature's practice of paying a chaplain to offer prayers.

Emboldened by the fact that at least five justices had criticized the *Lemon* test (Justices White, Rehnquist, O'Connor, Scalia, and Kennedy), the solicitor-general urged the Court to take this opportunity to discard or modify the *Lemon* test. The solicitor-general and supporters of the prayers argued that graduation prayers are more like legislative prayers than like prayers in the classroom, since they occur at most once a year, they last at most a few minutes, audience participation is not required, and attendance at graduation is not required to gain a diploma.

In his Opinion of the Court in *Lee,* Justice Kennedy—joined by Justices Blackmun, Stevens, O'Connor, and Souter—rejected the parallel with *Marsh* and concluded that the appropriate analogy was to "the classroom setting, where we have said the risk of compulsion is especially high." Teachers and principals retain close control over the graduation ceremony, and students are not free to leave, unlike the legislators in *Marsh.* Moreover, in this case the students stood during the rabbi's prayers, and the Court believed that for many, if not most, the act of standing or remaining silent signified participation in the prayers. Accordingly, *Engel v. Vitale* (1962) (outlawing recitation of New York's nondenominational "Regents Prayer" in public school classrooms) and *School District of Abington Township v. Schempp* (1963) (outlawing Bible reading and recitation of the Lord's Prayer in public school classrooms) were controlling, and so Rabbi Gutterman's prayers violated the Establishment Clause. Without applying it, the Court declined to reconsider the *Lemon* test.

Justice Kennedy's opinion was consistent with his position that coercion was required for an Establishment Clause violation. In *County of Allegheny v. Greater Pittsburgh American Civil Liberties Union* (1989) Justices Blackmun, O'Connor, and Stevens roundly criticized Justice Kennedy for this position. In *Lee* Justice Kennedy emphasized the fact that high school graduation "is one of life's most significant occasions," and he rejected as "formalism" the government's position that objecting students were free to remain absent. He concluded that "the State has in every practical sense compelled attendance and participation in an explicit religious exercise at an event of singular importance to every student, one the objecting student had no real alternative to avoid." This violated the Establishment Clause.

Justice Blackmun's concurrence reiterated his continued support for the *Lemon* test and his view that coercion was not required for an Establishment Clause violation. Justice Souter, in his first Establishment Clause opinion as a Supreme Court justice, revealed himself to be a staunch separationist. His scholarly concurring opinion also stressed that coercion was not required for an Establishment Clause violation, and it invoked the history of the clause's origin to refute "nonpreferentialism," i.e., the view that government can aid religion so long as it does not discriminate against or in favor of a particular religion.

Justice Scalia's caustic dissent, which Chief Justice Rehnquist and Associate Justices White and Thomas joined, ridiculed Kennedy's opinion, labeling it "incoherent," an exercise in "social engineering," an example of "psychology practiced by amateurs," a "psycho-journey," and a "jurisprudential disaster." In *Allegheny* Justice Kennedy had stated that the Establishment Clause's meaning had to be determined "by reference to historical practices and understandings" and that an Establishment Clause test which "would invalidate long-standing traditions cannot be a proper reading of the Clause." Scalia had concurred in Kennedy's *Allegheny* opinion. Graduation prayers were a long-standing American tradition, and Scalia now accused Kennedy of inconsistency with his *Allegheny* opinion.

Justice Scalia also derided Justice Kennedy's view that public pressure and peer pressure on students to stand during the prayers constituted "coercion," and he charged that the Court's psychological coercion test was "boundless, and boundlessly manipulable." In Scalia's view, unconstitutional establishments of religion should be limited to "coercion of religious orthodoxy and of financial support *by force of law and threat of penalty*" (emphasis in original).

Scalia regarded the graduation ceremony prayers as "utterly devoid of compulsion," since standing could signify either participation in the prayers or mere respect for the views of others. Moreover, those who objected could remain seated, and no student who failed to take part in the invocation or benediction was subject to any penalty or discipline. The situation, Scalia asserted, was thus totally different from that in *West Virginia Board of Education v. Barnette* (1943), in which schoolchildren were required by law to recite the Pledge of Allegiance; those who refused could be expelled and sent to a reform school, and their parents could be incarcerated for causing delinquency.

Lee will probably be seen by future legal historians not as a landmark but rather as a transitional decision. Ostensibly, the Supreme Court's separationist tradition survived, largely because of the emergence of a moderate centrist block—Justices Kennedy, O'Connor, and Souter—which also was pivotal five days later in upholding the fundamental right of women to an abortion, in *Planned Parenthood of Southeastern Pennsylvania v. Casey* (1992). However, for only the second time in thirty-two Establishment Clause decisions since 1971, the Supreme Court majority opinion did not apply the *Lemon* test, whose days appear to be numbered. Thus, Justice Kennedy was faithful to his objective of having the Court adhere to his "coercion test," which now commands five votes on the Court and appears to have prevailed over Justice O'Connor's endorsement test. Accordingly, Professor Jesse Choper appears to be accurate in his assessment that liberals who hailed *Lee* had won the battle but lost the war.

Thomas A. Schweitzer

Bibliography

DuPuy, Robert K., "Religion, Graduation, and the First Amendment: A Threat or a Shadow?" 35 *Drake Law Review* 323–364 (1986).

McAndrew, Gregory M., "Invocations at Graduation," 101 *Yale Law Journal* 663–683 (1991).

Schweitzer, Thomas A., "*Lee v. Weisman* and the Establishment Clause: Are Invocations and Benedictions at Public School Graduations Constitutionally Unspeakable?" 69 *University of Detroit Mercy Law Review* 113–210 (1992).

Cases Cited

County of Allegheny v. Greater Pittsburgh American Civil Liberties Union, 492 U.S. 573 (1989).

Engel v. Vitale, 370 U.S. 421 (1962).

Lee v. Weisman, 728 F. Supp. 68 (D.R. I. 1990), aff'd, 908 F. 2d 1090 (1st Cir. 1990), aff'd, 505 U.S. 577 (1992).

Lemon v. Kurtzman, 403 U.S. 602 (1971).

Marsh v. Chambers, 463 U.S. 783 (1983).

Planned Parenthood of Southeastern Pennsylvania v. Casey, 505 U.S. 833 (1992).

School District of Abington Township v. Schempp, 374 U.S. 203 (1963).

Stein v. Plainwell Community Schools, 822 F. 2d 1406 (6th Cir. 1987).

West Virginia Board of Education v. Barnette, 319 U.S. 624 (1943).

Leland, John (1754–1841)

John Leland fought against religious establishments throughout his long career. Born in Grafton, Massachusetts, in May 1754, Leland responded to "a sign from God" and sought a Baptist preacher's license in 1775. After a year-long stint as an itinerant, Leland and his new wife, Sarah Devine, moved to Virginia, where the fires of the New Light revivals still burned. They eventually settled in Orange County, where Leland became "the most popular [preacher] of any who ever resided in the state."

During Leland's fifteen-year residence, the Baptists matured from a beleaguered sect that was subjected to "mobs, fines, bonds and prisons" to a powerful denomination. Leland contributed to this institution building by holding successful revivals, serving on the Virginia Baptist General Committee (a policy-making body), and collecting materials for a church history, *The Virginia Chronicle* (1790). That same year he tried but failed to persuade the committee to adopt an antislavery resolution.

The most crucial aspect of the Baptists' program was their revolutionary attack on

Virginia's Episcopal establishment. Basing their arguments on the Virginia Declaration of Rights, the Baptists organized a petition campaign against the Incorporation Act of 1784, lobbied for the abolition of tithes and for the public confiscation of church glebe lands, and supported Thomas Jefferson's Statute for Religous Freedom. Leland participated actively in these successful efforts, serving as one of the committee's legislative agents in 1786 and 1790 and helping to secure the repeal of the Incorporation Act in 1787.

The Baptists' organization made them a potent political force, and both sides in the debate over the federal Constitution sought their backing. Like many dissenters, Leland initially opposed the Constitution because it lacked a bill of rights and failed to provide "for the secure enjoyment of religious liberty." Through his earlier lobbying efforts Leland had become acquainted with James Madison, who (according to tradition) met with Leland before the March 1788 elections and convinced him to rally behind ratification. In turn, Leland impressed on Madison the need for a bill of rights. With Baptist support, Madison handily won election to the ratifying convention and secured approval of the Constitution.

In 1791 Leland traveled to Connecticut, where non-Congregationalists faced a number of legal disabilities. Exemption from ecclesiastical taxes required dissenters to obtain certificates, to reside within five miles of their meeting house, and to submit to annual examinations of their faith. During his stay Leland published two pamphlets deriding the certificate laws. In *The Rights of Conscience Inalienable, and Therefore Religious Opinions Not Cognizable by Law; or, The High-Flying Churchman, Stript of His Legal Robe, Appears a Yaho* (1791), he used the Connecticut case as a springboard for a general examination of the antidemocratic character of religious establishments. In *Van Tromp* (1806), Leland contended that state coercion discouraged piety and morality, and he urged Connecticut's citizens to replace their charter with a constitution that protected freedom of conscience.

The Lelands eventually settled in Cheshire, Massachusetts, a small Baptist community in Berkshire County, where they encountered another "quasi-establishment." Article III of the 1780 Massachusetts Constitution mandated the collection of taxes to support public worship. Technically, dissenters could apply their taxes to the support of their preferred religious institutions, but towns often withheld revenues from dissenting churches, and non-churchgoers and members of small sects enjoyed no exemption. Worse, in 1810 the state's supreme court declared that unincorporated religious societies—which included the majority of Baptist congregations—were ineligible for state support under this law. In *The Yankee Spy* (1794) and *A Blow at the Root* (1801) Leland called for revision of the Massachusetts Constitution to eliminate Article III and to guarantee the separation of church and state.

An avid Jeffersonian, Leland also wrote for Phinehas Allen's Pittsfield *Sun* on subjects ranging from the evils of slavery, aristocracy, and federalism to the benefits of an elective judiciary. In 1801 he traveled to Washington and presented President Jefferson with a 1,235-pound "Mammoth Cheese" (the handiwork of the women of Cheshire), an incident that garnered him considerable publicity. Elected to the General Court in 1811, Leland helped spearhead a "Religous Freedom Act" to protect unincorporated churches. In the 1820s Leland became a strong supporter of Andrew Jackson—partly out of dismay over the Sabbatarian movement. Leland's convictions regarding the separation of church and state and his concern for the rights of non-Christians led him to oppose religious tests for office and Sabbath-observance blue laws. Circumstantial evidence suggests that Leland's anti-Sabbatarian writings influenced the 1830 Congressional Report on the question of Sunday mails.

Having lived to celebrate disestablishment in Massachusetts in 1833, Leland died in 1841 at age 86.

Margaret E. Newell

Bibliography

Butterfield, L.H., "Elder John Leland, Jeffersonian Itinerant," 62 *Proceedings of the American Antiquarian Society* 154–242 (1952).

Greene, L.F., *The Writings of the Late Elder John Leland* (New York: G.W. Wood, 1845).

L

Lemon v. Kurtzman

403 U.S. 602 (1971), 411 U.S. 192 (1973)

In *Lemon v. Kurtzman* (1971) the Supreme Court established the landmark test for determining whether legislation fosters excessive entanglement between church and state. Although prior case law had set forth some standards, there was no clear precedent for such evaluations. The so-called *Lemon* test requires courts to apply a three-pronged test to determine a statute's constitutionality under the First Amendment's religion clauses. The first prong of the test requires that the statute have a secular purpose. The test's second prong requires that the statute's "principal or primary effect must be one that neither advances nor inhibits religion." The court distilled these two prongs of the test from *Board of Education v. Allen* (1968). The *Lemon* test's third prong, derived from *Walz v. Tax Commission of City of New York* (1970), requires that the statute "not foster 'an excessive government entanglement in religion.'"

Lemon came from the appeals of decisions rendered by three-judge panels in district courts in Pennsylvania and Rhode Island. Essentially, faced with tremendous burdens on educational resources—and acknowledging the role of nonpublic, sectarian education—both states had enacted legislation whose primary effects would be to provide public funds to religious schools. Taxpayers in each state filed complaints seeking to enjoin operation of the statutes. A description of the district courts' holdings in each case and of the Supreme Court's decision follows.

The Rhode Island Case: *DiCenso v. Robinson* (D.R.I., 1970)

Rhode Island's legislature had determined that 25 percent of the state's student population attended nonpublic schools, which thus played a vital role in efforts to provide Rhode Island's youth with high-quality education. The vast majority of these nonpublic schools were Catholic schools, and financial problems plagued them as they began to rely more on lay teachers and as the costs of teachers' salaries threatened to compromise the quality of education that they could offer. To remedy this situation, Rhode Island's legislature passed the Salary Supplement Act in 1969.

In passing the act, the legislature acknowledged that nonpublic schools played a vital role in Rhode Island's educational mission. The Salary Supplement Act's specific purpose was "to assist nonpublic schools to provide salary scales which will enable them to retain and obtain teaching personnel who meet recognized standards of quality." The legislature set aside money, and nonpublic schools could apply for 15 percent of the cost of salaries paid to teachers of secular subjects. To qualify for funding under the statute, teachers had to have a teaching certificate, had to teach a course similar to one taught in public schools with state-approved textbooks, and had to agree not to teach a class in religion. In addition, the schools at which applicant teachers taught had to submit financial data to the state's commissioner of education for eligibility review.

At the time the complaint was filed in the District Court of Rhode Island, each of the approximately 250 teachers who had applied for aid under the statute taught at Catholic schools. Plaintiffs were citizens and taxpayers of Rhode Island who sought to enjoin the operation of the Salary Supplement Act on the grounds that it violated their First Amendment rights. Defendants were Rhode Island's commissioner of education and the state's treasurer and controller. In addition, a couple whose children attended parochial schools and several parochial schoolteachers intervened as defendants.

The District Court of Rhode Island concluded that, as a factual matter, the sectarian function of religious schools could not be separated from their secular function. Thus, as a legal matter, the statute could not withstand scrutiny under the Establishment Clause. The court based its decision on the Supreme Court's holdings in *Everson v. Board of Education* (1947), *School District of Abington Township v. Schempp* (1963), *Board of Education v. Allen* (1968), and *Walz v. Tax Commission of City of New York* (1970). The Court conceded that, on its face, the Salary Supplement Act had not been designed to aid religion. However, the act's "necessary effects" would be "not only substantial support for a religious enterprise, but also the kind of reciprocal embroilments of government and religion the First Amendment was meant to avoid."

The Pennsylvania Case: Lemon v. Kurtzman (E.D. Pa., 1969)

In 1968 Pennsylvania's legislature determined that increasing demands linked to rising population and costs had created a "crisis" in the state's elementary and secondary educational systems. The legislature also found that 20 percent of the state's students attended nonpublic schools. These nonpublic schools contributed to the public welfare by providing their students with both secular and nonsecular education. The legislature found that it was a duty of the state government to help the nonpublic schools fulfill their role in augmenting the public welfare. To this end, the legislature passed the Nonpublic Elementary and Secondary Education Act (Nonpublic Education Act), which the governor of Pennsylvania signed into law on June 19, 1968.

The Nonpublic Education Act enabled nonpublic schools, whether secular or nonsecular, to purchase "secular educational services" at actual cost in classes in mathematics, modern foreign languages, physical science, and physical education through contracts negotiated with the superintendent of public instruction. The statute specifically excluded funding for classes teaching "subject matter expressing religious teaching, or the morals or forms of worship of any sect." The superintendent of public instruction had authority to review the curricula of nonpublic schools that made purchases under the Nonpublic Education Act.

When it drafted the Nonpublic Education Act, Pennsylvania's legislature was conscious of the potential problems that public funding for nonsecular institutions could create. Thus, the statute reimbursed participating schools only if they complied with an elaborate accounting scheme that tracked the use of funds for nonsecular educational purposes. At the time litigation commenced, the statute had been in effect for a year, and 1,181 nonpublic schools in fifty-five counties had received payments, which came from a special fund collected from gambling proceeds.

Alton J. Lemon, the named plaintiff, was an African American parent of a child attending public school in Pennsylvania. The other individual plaintiffs brought suit in their capacity as citizens and taxpayers of Pennsylvania. In addition, national and state chapters of the National Association for the Advancement of Colored People filed complaints which were dismissed because the Court found that these organizations lacked standing. The complaint alleged that the Nonpublic Education Act violated the plaintiffs' First Amendment rights under the Establishment and Free Exercise Clauses, claiming that the purpose and primary effect of the Nonpublic Education Act were to aid religion. Plaintiffs also alleged that the act violated their equal protection rights under the Fourteenth Amendment. The district court rejected the plaintiffs' equal protection arguments, holding that the Nonpublic Education Act did not use religion or race as a basis to decide which applicants to fund.

David J. Kurtzman, the named defendant, was the Pennsylvania Superintendent of Public Instruction. The other defendants in the suit were the state's treasurer and seven sectarian schools of various denominations that had contracted to purchase services under the Nonpublic Education Act. The defendants moved to dismiss the complaint.

The question of law that the district court faced was "whether the purpose or primary effect of the Pennsylvania Education Act on its face or in the necessary effect of its administration is to advance or inhibit religion." Relying on the U.S. Supreme Court's decisions in *Everson* and *Allen,* the district court upheld the statute. The court observed that the statutes at issue in each of these decisions had the effect of "provid[ing] some indirect measure" of aid to parochial schools without the government's breaching its neutrality toward religion. Similarly, the Pennsylvania statute did not breach the government's duty of neutrality.

The district court dismissed the complaint, holding that the purpose and effect of the statute were the decidedly secular ones of "promot[ing] the welfare of the people of the Commonwealth of Pennsylvania" and "promot[ing] the secular education" of students attending nonpublic schools. Referring to Pennsylvania's overburdened public education system, the court acknowledged the importance of private education in general and of sectarian private education in particular. And while nonsecular private schools had the dual mission of teaching both secular and nonsecular subjects, the schools were capable of keeping the two roles separate. Thus funding secular subjects in nonsecular schools did not violate constitutional constraints.

Chief Circuit Judge Hastie dissented, stating that any benefit to the public welfare from the statute was "at best an incidental consequence." Judge Hastie agreed with the majority that the interests of the state and of religion often overlap and that such overlap could survive constitutional scrutiny. However, he did not agree that the Constitution permitted "direct financing of a religious enterprise because such aid also benefits the state." Indeed, the purpose of a sectarian school was primarily religious. Helping such an institution with direct subsidies for any purpose "is not essentially different from a payment of public funds into the treasury of a church." In addition, he pointed out that the majority's decision would force the government to play an impermissible role in monitoring the records and curricula of sectarian schools.

Lemon v. Kurtzman
403 U.S. 602 (1971)

The plaintiffs in *Lemon* and the defendants in *DiCenso* each appealed the district court decisions in their respective cases. The Supreme Court granted certiori in each case and combined the cases for the purposes of the decision. Arguments in these two cases and in *Tilton v. Richardson* (1971) took place on March 3, 1971. The Court delivered its opinion on June 28, 1971, with Chief Justice Warren Burger writing for the majority. Justices Hugo Black, John Marshall Harlan, Potter Stewart, Harry Blackmun, and Thurgood Marshall joined the chief justice's opinion. Justice William O. Douglas filed a concurring opinion in which Justice Black joined. Justice Marshall filed a separate statement concurring with Justice Douglas. Justice William Brennan filed a concurring opinion. Justice Byron White filed an opinion concurring in part and dissenting in part.

The Majority Opinion

After a brief exploration of the legislative findings leading to the passage of each of the statutes, Chief Justice Burger began his legal analysis with a discussion of *Everson,* noting Justice Hugo Black's warning that his decision in that case carried the law "'to the verge' of forbidden territory under the Religion Clauses." The chief justice then made the rather candid acknowledgment that "we can only dimly perceive the lines of demarcation in this extraordinarily sensitive area of constitutional law."

It is thus evident that the chief justice saw the decision in this case as a difficult one, particularly in light of the language of the religion clauses, which is "opaque at best." However, at least the first step of the analysis—which under *Allen* was to ensure that the statute have a "secular legislative purpose"—was straightforward. The chief justice found no basis to conclude that the statutes had any purpose other than to "enhance the quality of the secular education in all schools covered by compulsory attendance laws." The chief justice therefore deferred to the legislatures.

While conceding that the legislatures did not intend to advance religion in enacting these statutes, Chief Justice Burger called attention to the fact that each legislature took fairly elaborate precautions to ensure that state funds were not used for religious instruction. By doing so, the legislatures "recogniz[ed] that these programs approached, even if they did not intrude upon, the forbidden areas under the Religion Clauses." The chief justice refrained from deciding whether these precautions prevented the statutes from running afoul of the religion clauses. Instead, he indicated that the precautions themselves were an "excessive entanglement between government and religion." The statutes therefore failed the second prong of the *Allen* test: "This kind of state inspection and evaluation of the religious content of a religious organization is fraught with the sort of entanglement the Constitution forbids."

The opinion examines each state's program in detail. With regard to the Rhode Island program, Chief Justice Burger agreed with the lower court's finding that "[t]he various characteristics of the schools make them 'a powerful vehicle for the transmitting of the Catholic faith to the next generation.' . . . In short, parochial schools involve substantial religious activity and purpose." Although the Court in *Allen* allowed the state to provide textbooks to sectarian schools, the state could readily monitor the content of such books. But it could not readily monitor the content of the daily lessons that teachers in sectarian institutions taught to their students: "Inevitably, some of a teacher's responsibilities hover on the border between secular and religious orientation." Indeed, as the Rhode Island parochial school system's "Handbook of

School Regulations" itself pointed out, "'[r]eligious formation is not confined to formal courses; nor is it restricted to a single area."

The chief justice saw the Pennsylvania statute as having essentially the same effect as the Rhode Island statute. However, the Pennsylvania statute had the added detraction of providing that the state pay money directly to sectarian schools after reviewing the schools' accounting records. Quoting *Walz,* the Court described this direct payment of funds to religious schools as "a relationship pregnant with [government] involvement." Such a relationship could not withstand constitutional scrutiny.

Chief Justice Burger also noted that legislation of this type would lead to a "broader base of entanglement." In an appeal to history the chief justice proclaimed that "the Constitution's authors sought to protect religious worship from the pervasive power of government." Programs that provide state aid to religious institutions would lead religious institutions to engage in political lobbying. Such lobbying activities, in turn, would force legislators to vote on behalf of or against such aid, which would amount to the politicization of religion. The ultimate outcome of this type of legislation would be antagonism between government and religious institutions. Nor could such legislation be compared with exempting religious institutions from tax laws; such exemptions have a centuries-old history and do not present the threat of entanglement that the statutes at issue presented.

Justice Douglas's Concurrence

Justice Douglas's concurrence in *Lemon* reflects his scathing dissent from the Court's decision in *Tilton,* in which the Court upheld certain aspects of a federal statute providing aid to religious colleges and universities. Justice Douglas's concurrence shows little restraint, especially when compared with the majority's guarded tones. The statutes at issue required that the government place a "public investigator in every classroom," or else "the zeal of religious proselytizers promises to carry the day and make a shambles of the Establishment Clause." Douglas perceived government aid to religious schools as ushering in a new era of "policing sectarian schools"—a significant departure from the government's previous and well-defined role of accrediting sectarian schools. Such laws would lead to "vast governmental suppression, surveillance or meddling in church affairs."

Justice Douglas also pointed out the folly of the recordkeeping requirements which each statute imposed to ensure that religious schools used state funds for secular purposes. To allow the statutes to survive on this basis would be to make "a grave constitutional decision turn merely on cost accounting and bookkeeping entries." Any public funding would assist a sectarian school's religious mission: "It matters not that the teacher receiving taxpayers' money only teaches religion a fraction of the time. Nor does it matter that he or she teaches no religion. The school is an organism living on one budget."

Justice Brennan's Concurrence

Justice Brennan's concurrence adheres to the views he expressed in earlier cases involving the religion clauses. Justice Brennan reasoned that involvements between the secular and the sectarian violate the constitution if they "(a) serve the essentially religious activities of religious activities; (b) employ the organs of government for essentially religious purposes; or (c) use essentially religious means to serve governmental ends, where secular means would suffice." The statutes at issue that day all provided "a direct subsidy from public funds for activities carried on by sectarian educational institutions." However, Justice Brennan was not willing to join in the majority's reliance on *Everson* and *Allen;* rather, he felt that these particular statutes had to be examined in light of the "history of public subsidy of sectarian schools."

Justice Brennan noted that "subsidy of sectarian educational institutions became embroiled in bitter controversies very soon after the Nation was formed." By the beginning of this century, opponents of public subsidies of sectarian education had "largely won their fight." Today, only a few state constitutions fail to contain provisions that prohibit such subsidies. In addition to the history of antagonism of funding sectarian education with public funds, Justice Brennan noted that legislation such as that at issue in *Lemon* threatens the church as much as the state: The statutes "require too close a proximity of government to the subsidized sectarian institutions and in my view create the real dangers of the secularization of a creed."

Justice White's Opinion

Justice White dissented from the decision in *Lemon*, noting that parochial schools play the dual role of providing both secular and sectarian education. Justice White perceived the legislative intent behind the statutes as ending the issue; the statutes were not enacted to advance religion, and any aid they may have afforded religion was incidental to their primary purpose. Justice White took issue with the distinction that the other justices made between (1) elementary and secondary educational institutions and (2) colleges and universities, and he opined that the Court should have upheld the two state statutes as it had upheld the statute in *Tilton*.

Beyond *Lemon*

Although the Court's decision in *Lemon* resolved debate over the constitutionality of direct state subsidies for religious schools and those who taught in them, ancillary issues spawned by the Pennsylvania case came before the Court two years later. In implementing the Court's holding in *Lemon,* the federal district court in Pennsylvania enjoined future payments to church schools. However, it rejected the plaintiffs' motion for an injunction against payments to religious schools for services they had performed during the 1970–1971 school year. (These payments had not been made at the time the *Lemon* decision was announced in June 1971.) The plaintiffs appealed, asking the Supreme Court to block all payments under the act.

In *Lemon II,* (1973) a sharply divided Court affirmed the decision of the district court. Justices Harry Blackmun, Lewis Powell, and William Rehnquist joined Chief Justice Burger's opinion, with Justice Byron White concurring in the judgment. Burger pointed out that a final payment for services already rendered did not threaten the sort of ongoing state entanglement in religion that had led the Court to find the Pennsylvania statute unconstitutional in *Lemon I.* Moreover, he argued that religious schools had relied on the statute in good faith, undertaking programs with the expectation that the state would help defray their costs. As a matter of equity, he asserted, those expectations ought not be dashed simply because the Court subsequently found the statute unconstitutional.

In a dissent joined by Justices William Brennan and Potter Stewart, Justice William O. Douglas noted that *Lemon I* had announced no new rule of law but had merely affirmed the well-established principle that the First Amendment barred government from subsidizing religion. Those who relied on the constitutionality of the statute should have known better, he insisted, and "no considerations of equity . . . should allow them to profit from their unconstitutional venture."

The test adopted in *Lemon I* has been subjected to harsh criticism. Conservatives have denounced it, charging that it precludes incidental government aid to religious institutions and discriminates against religion in a manner that would appall the Framers of the First Amendment. Even some supporters of strict separation of church and state find the *Lemon* test wanting. Historian Leonard Levy, a leading First Amendment scholar, has argued that it is too vague. Because it relies on relative concepts like *excessive* entanglement, he suggests, it offers little guidance in deciding concrete cases, and it invites the justices to decide cases subjectively. In recent years a majority of current justices have indicated dissatisfaction with the *Lemon* test. In *Lee v. Weisman* (1992), for example, Justice Anthony Kennedy expressly declined to use *Lemon* as the basis for his majority opinion striking down prayer at a middle school graduation. Despite growing dissatisfaction, the Court has not repudiated *Lemon.* Indeed, it reaffirmed *Lemon* (albeit in passing) in its decision in *Lamb's Chapel v. Center Moriches Union Free School District* (1993), provoking sharp criticism from Justice Antonin Scalia: "Like some ghoul in a late-night horror movie that repeatedly sits up in its grave and shuffles abroad after being repeatedly killed and buried, *Lemon* stalks our establishment clause jurisprudence once again, frightening . . . little children and school attorneys. . . ."

Phillip Presby
Donald G. Nieman

Bibliography

Kahn, Ronald, "Polity and Rights Values in Conflict: The Burger Court, Ideological Interests, and the Separation of Church and State," 3 *Studies in American Political Development: An Annual* 279–293 (1989).

Levy, Leonard, *The Establishment Clause: Religion and the First Amendment* (New York: Macmillan, 1988).

Morgan, Richard E., "The Establishment Clause and Sectarian Schools: A Final Installment?" *Supreme Court Review* 57 (1973).

Cases Cited

Board of Education v. Allen, 392 U.S. 236 (1968).

DiCenso v. Robinson, 316 F. Supp. 112 (D.R.I. 1970).

Everson v. Board of Education, 330 U.S. 1 (1947).

Lamb's Chapel v. Center Moriches Union Free School District, 508 U.S. 384 (1993).

Lee v. Weisman, 505 U.S. 577 (1992).

Lemon v. Kurtzman, 310 F. Supp. 35 (E.D. Pa. 1969).

Lemon v. Kurtzman, 403 U.S. 602 reh'g denied, 404 U.S. 876 (1971).

School District of Abington Township v. Schempp, 374 U.S. 203 (1963).

Tilton v. Richardson, 403 U.S. 672 (1971).

Walz v. Tax Commission of City of New York, 397 U.S. 664 (1970).

Levitt v. Committee for Public Education and Religious Liberty 413 U.S. 472 (1973)

Levitt Committee for Public Education and Religious Liberty (1973) was a companion case to *Committee for Public Education and Religious Liberty v. Nyquist* (1973) and *Sloan v. Lemon* (1973), which were decided on June 25, 1973. The three cases held that various New York and Pennsylvania statutes which provided direct cash payments to private religious schools and tax benefits to parents of students at such schools violated the Establishment Clause of the First Amendment. Chief Justice Warren Burger stated that the Court's holding in *Nyquist* required affirmance of the district court in *Levitt,* and so his brief, eleven-page *Levitt* opinion—which all justices but Byron White joined—must be read together with Justice William Powell's forty-three-page opinion for the Court in *Nyquist.*

Chapter 138 of New York State's Laws of 1970 appropriated $28 million to reimburse nonpublic schools throughout the state for the expense of complying with certain state-mandated "services," including the administration and grading of tests, compiling test results and reporting them to the state's education authorities, and maintaining and reporting records about enrollment, personnel, and pupils' health. The most expensive mandated services, which were performed by teachers, consisted of administering and grading various examinations: the state-required "Regents' examinations," standardized evaluation tests, and teacher-prepared tests in subjects required to be taught by state law. Qualifying schools received $27 for each pupil in grades 1 through 6 and $45 for each pupil in grades 7 through 12.

A three-judge district court held that Chapter 138 violated the Establishment Clause and permanently enjoined its enforcement. The U.S. Supreme Court affirmed. The district court in *Levitt v. Committee for Public Education and Religious Liberty* (N.Y., 1973) had noted that teacher-prepared tests were "an integral part of the teaching process." Chief Justice Burger referred to the "substantial risk" that examinations which are prepared by teachers at religious schools "will be drafted with an eye, unconsciously or otherwise, to inculcate students in the religious precepts of the sponsoring church." Moreover, "no attempt is made under the statute, and no means are available, to assure that internally prepared tests are free of religious instruction," whereas under *Lemon v. Kurtzman* (1971) the state was "constitutionally compelled to assure that the state-supported activity is not being used for religious indoctrination." Since the aid devoted to secular functions "is not identifiable and separable from aid to sectarian activities," Chapter 138 constituted an impermissible aid to religion under *Nyquist.*

Chief Justice Burger reasoned that inability to monitor the possibly sectarian content of teacher-prepared tests distinguished Chapter 138 from the totally nonsectarian activities that the Court had upheld in *Everson v. Board of Education* (1947) (state-subsidized bus rides to religious schools) and *Board of Education v. Allen* (1968) (secular textbooks provided by the state to religious schools). In addition, Burger squarely rejected appellants' argument that the state should be permitted to pay for any activity "mandated" by state law, since that would frustrate scrutiny under the three-pronged *Lemon* test for constitutionality.

Justice Hugo Black had stated in *Everson* that "[n]o tax in any amount, large or small, can be levied to support any religious activities or institutions. . . ." In *Nyquist* the Court held that there must be "an effective means of *guaranteeing* that the state aid derived from public funds will be used *exclusively* for secular, neutral, and non-ideological purposes . . ." (emphasis added). The holding in *Levitt* seems compelled by this absolutist standard, particularly since the statute provided the religious schools with direct cash payments—the most constitutionally vulnerable form of government assistance. Nevertheless, after New York State carefully revised its statute providing reimbursement for testing services to meet the objections of the Court in *Levitt,* the Court upheld by 5 to 4 the constitutionality of the amended statute in *Committee for Public Education and Religious Liberty v. Regan* (1980). This was the only Supreme Court ruling to sanction direct cash payments to religious primary and secondary schools.

Thomas A. Schweitzer

Bibliography

Giacoma, James M., "*Committee for Public Education and Religious Liberty v. Regan:* New Possibilities for State Aid to Nonpublic Schools," 24 *St. Louis University Law Journal* 406–424 (1980).

Cases Cited

Board of Education v. Allen, 392 U.S. 236 (1968).

Committee for Public Education and Religious Liberty v. Nyquist, 413 U.S. 756 (1973).

Committee for Public Education and Religious Liberty v. Regan, 444 U.S. 646 (1980).

Everson v. Board of Education, 330 U.S. 1 (1947).

Lemon v. Kurtzman, 403 U.S. 602 (1971).

Levitt v. Committee for Public Education and Religious Liberty, 342 F. Supp. 439 (S.D.N.Y., 1972).

Levitt v. Committee for Public Education and Religious Liberty, 413 U.S. 472 (1973).

Sloan v. Lemon, 413 U.S. 825 (1973).

Lowrey v. Hawaii

See Overseas Possessions of the United States and Religious Liberty.

***Luetkemeyer et al. v. Kaufmann* 419 U.S. 888 (1974)**

In *Luetkemeyer et al. v. Kaufmann* (1974)—appealed from the U.S. District Court for the Western District of Missouri—the U.S. Supreme Court affirmed the judgment for the defendant Kaufmann by memorandum, with Justice Byron White and Chief Justice Warren Burger dissenting.

Urban Luetkemeyer, the chief plaintiff, was a Missouri taxpayer who sent his children to a Roman Catholic school in accordance with his religious conscience. He sued to overturn a Missouri statute that provided for bus transportation for public school students who lived a specified distance from their respective schools but provided no transportation for private school students, including students of religious schools. Luetkemeyer based his suit on the claim that the denial of bus transportation to children attending private religious schools violated the Due Process and the Equal Protection Clauses of the Fourteenth Amendment as well as the Free Exercise Clause of the First Amendment.

Specifically, the plaintiffs raised the issues that Catholic schoolchildren and their parents were forced to forgo the free exercise of their religion in order to enjoy a public benefit and were denied by an arbitrary and capricious classification the benefits deriving from certain constituent parts of the general tax revenue.

In *Luetkemeyer v. Kaufmann,* (W.D. Mo. 1973), a three-judge federal district court, by a vote of 2 to 1, upheld the constitutionality of the Missouri statute, denying the relief sought by plaintiffs. In the majority opinion, written by District Judge John W. Oliver and concurred in by Judge Collinson, the court found that Missouri had a legitimate state interest in providing a higher wall of separation between church and state than that required by the First Amendment of the U.S. Constitution.

Plaintiffs relied heavily in their arguments on the *Everson v. Board of Education* (1947) decision, in which the U.S. Supreme Court found the provision of bus transportation to parochial schoolchildren by school districts under a New Jersey state statute to be constitutional. Utilizing the child benefit theory found in decisions such as *Everson* and in *Board of Education v. Allen* (1968), the plaintiffs argued that the state had an obligation to provide assistance to private schools equivalent to that given to the public schools. Judge Oliver in the majority opinion cited *Norwood v. Harrison* (1973), wherein the Supreme Court upheld the right of a state to deny assistance to private schools that discriminate on racial grounds, and *Lemon v. Kurtzman* (1947), which by implication denied any absolute right to equal aid.

The district court emphasized that *Everson*'s finding of the constitutional permissibility of state-provided bus transportation for parochial school students must not be construed to require such provision.

A secondary argument of plaintiffs cited *Shapiro v. Thompson* (1969), which pronounced the doctrine that "any classification which serves to penalize the exercise of [a constitutional] right, unless shown to be necessary to promote a compelling governmental interest, is unconstitutional." This plaintiffs linked with *Pierce v. Society of Sisters* (1925), which held that attendance at a church-sponsored school was a constitutional right; but the district court countered this interpretation with Chief Justice Burger's distinction in *Norwood* that *Pierce* "said nothing of any supposed right of private or parochial schools to share with public schools in state largesse, on an equal basis or otherwise."

Relying on *San Antonio Independent School District v. Rodriquez* (1973), which held that education was not a federally protected right, the court held that the standard to be applied to judge the constitutionality of the Missouri statute was not the *Shapiro* doctrine but the doctrine refined in *McGowan v. Maryland* (1961): "The constitutional safeguard is offended only if the classification rests on grounds wholly irrelevant to the achievement of the State's objective."

The court found that the Missouri Constitution and the state's long-established tradition dictated a higher wall of separation between church and state than that mandated by the U.S. Bill of Rights and that maintaining this separation constituted a legitimate purpose of the state, reasonably advanced by the statute.

Finally, in the plaintiffs' collateral issue of the financial implications of the Missouri restriction, the court noted that *Braunfeld v. Brown* (1961) had established that the "economic effects of a statute is not an appropriate test for determining whether [it] violates the Constitution," and the court cited *Union Refrigerator Transit Co. v. Com. of Kentucky* (1905), which held that "a general tax cannot be dissected to show that, as to certain constituent parts, the taxpayer receives no benefit."

Circuit Judge Gibson in his dissenting opinion held that, in light of *Everson,* it was contradictory to hold that New Jersey's providing bus transportation to religious school attendees did not violate the separation of church and state and yet to hold in *Luetkemeyer* that Missouri's denying of such transportation was for the rational purpose of guarding that separation.

The key element in Judge Gibson's dissent would seem to lie in a belief that the U.S. Constitution's separation of church and state was relatively complete. If that separation were absolute, then, logically, state constitutions could not impose stronger restrictions on such relations without impinging free exercise. If, however, the federal wall of separation were high but not impenetrable, then states might erect stronger barriers against such entanglements.

On appeal to the U.S. Supreme Court, the decision of the district court was affirmed by memorandum, with Chief Justice Burger and Associate Justice White dissenting. Relying primarily on the *Everson* decision and the Free Exercise Clause of the First Amendment, the dissenters maintained that jurisdiction should have been noted and that the case should have been set for argument before the full tribunal.

Patrick M. O'Neil

Bibliography

Kelley, Dean M., "Religious Access to Public Programs and Government Funding," 8 *Brigham Young University Journal of Public Law* 417–438 (1994).

Cases Cited

Board of Education v. Allen, 392 U.S. 236 (1968).

Braunfeld v. Brown, 366 U.S. 599 (1961).

Everson v. Board of Education, 330 U.S. 1 (1947).

Lemon v. Kurtzman, 403 U.S. 602 (1971).

Luetkemeyer et al. v. Kaufmann, 419 U.S. 888 (1974).
Luetkemeyer et al. v. Kaufmann, 364 F. Supp. 376 (W.D. Mo., 1973).
McGowan v. Maryland, 366 U.S. 420 (1961).
Norwood v. Harrison, 413 U.S. 455 (1973).
Pierce v. Society of Sisters, 268 U.S. 510 (1925).
San Antonio Independent School District v. Rodriquez, 411 U.S. 1 (1973).
Shapiro v. Thompson, 394 U.S. 618 (1969).
Union Refrigerator Transit Co. v. Com. of Kentucky, 199 U.S. 194 (1905).

The *Lynch* and *Allegheny* Religious Symbols Cases and the Decline of the *Lemon* Test

In a series of cases during the 1980s the U.S. Supreme Court took a new approach to First Amendment Establishment Clause controversies. Previously the Court had been guided by *Lemon v. Kurtzman* (1971), which focused closely on the religious nature of a challenged government activity. But in *Marsh v. Chambers* (1983), *Lynch v. Donnelly* (1984), and *County of Allegheny v. American Civil Liberties Union* (1989) the Court stopped looking closely and started to require only that the government place its challenged activity in some sort of a secularizing "context" in order to be lawful. It has become much easier for a government practice involving religion to pass muster under the Establishment Clause. The Supreme Court's new stance embodies a variety of theories advocated by different justices. The theories all move away from *Lemon,* but they are often contradictory, and it is unclear where the law will settle.

Background to *Lynch v. Donnelly*

In *Lemon v. Kurtzman* (1971) the Supreme Court established a reasonably straightforward test for assessing whether a government action or practice violates the Establishment Clause. The act of a federal, state, or municipal government will be upheld if it can satisfy three requirements:

> First, the legislation must have a secular legislative purpose; second, its principal or primary effect must be one that neither advances nor inhibits religion; finally, the legislation must not foster "an excessive government entanglement with religion."

For more than a decade, without exception, the Supreme Court and lower federal courts used this three-pronged test to analyze Establishment Clause controversies. As the Court said in *Committee for Public Education and Religious Liberty v. Nyquist* (1973), "the *Lemon* test had to be satisfied for a law 'to pass muster under the Establishment Clause.'"

In the early 1980s, as the Supreme Court's composition changed, new standards started to creep into its thinking. For example, in *Larson v. Valente* (1982) members of a small new religion challenged a Minnesota law that had the effect of discriminating against their practices, but not against the practices of established churches, for it required that only religious groups which received most of their funding from nonmembers had to register with the state. The law was aimed at new religions, like the Unification Church and the Hare Krishnas, which are more likely to look to outsiders for funding. *Larson* held that the challenged law failed the *Lemon* test. Significantly, the Court also subjected the case to a new test, which it termed a "strict scrutiny" analysis and which previously had been unheard of in an Establishment Clause case.

A year after *Larson* the Court dealt a more serious blow to *Lemon*'s exclusive position in Establishment Clause cases. In *Marsh v. Chambers* (1983) the Court rejected a challenge to the Nebraska legislature's practice of opening its sessions with a prayer, delivered by a clergyman who was paid out of state funds. The Court made practically no effort to reconcile *Marsh* with earlier cases. Instead, it pointed to "the unique history" of chaplains in American legislatures and examined the challenged practice from the perspective of its context in history and tradition. Reflecting an "originalist" perspective, the *Marsh* Court examined Nebraska's practice in light of how it thought the Framers would have reacted. Reaching back to a similar enactment of the First Congress, the Court reasoned that the Framers could not have intended to prohibit the payment of a chaplain to open legislative sessions. In other words, the Court determined that, since the *drafters* of the Constitution did not restrain themselves from engaging in the contested practice, the Constitution *itself* could not be read to prohibit state governments from doing so now.

The *Marsh* Court also was influenced by the prayer's content. Since the chaplain's prayer was interdenominational, it could not be said to show official sectarian preference. Accordingly, the Court found that Nebraska's prayer simply marked an "acknowledgment" of the fact that many citizens held religious beliefs. Relying on *McGowan v. Maryland* (1961), a case upholding Sunday closing laws, the Court noted that the Nebraska prayer's text showed no preference for a particular religious denomination or sect; rather it "harmonize[d] with the tenets of some or all religions." The Court concluded:

> In light of the unambiguous and unbroken history of more than 200 years, there can be no doubt that the practice of opening legislative sessions with prayer has become part of the fabric of our society. To invoke Divine guidance on a public body entrusted with making the laws is not, in these circumstances, an "establishment" of religion or a step toward establishment; it is simply a tolerable acknowledgment of beliefs widely held among the people of this country.

The *Marsh* Court did not adequately take into account the preference of religion over nonreligion, which the legislature's address to a deity implies. Thirty-five years earlier, in *Everson v. Board of Education* (1947), the Supreme Court had recognized that the Constitution did not merely prohibit "an established church"; instead, it more broadly forbade "establishment of religion," including government "aid [to] all religions." In *Marsh* the Court showed that it was no longer offended by religious symbols or usage as long as they did not advance a particular faith. As will be seen, subsequent Supreme Court Establishment Clause cases have been similarly indifferent to the interests of nonbelievers. Further, *Marsh,* like *Larson,* showed that the *Lemon* test had ceased to be the exclusive one for Establishment Clause cases.

Lynch Takes *Lemon* Off Its Pedestal

Lemon was dealt another blow in *Lynch v. Donnelly* (1984). For forty years the Pawtucket, Rhode Island, city government had put up and maintained at public expense a Christmas display, prominently featuring a crèche, in its downtown shopping area. The crèche stood with an array of other holiday decorations, including depictions of Santa Claus, reindeer, carolers, and a Christmas tree. There also were hundreds of colored lights and festive images that were not associated with any religious holiday, including a clown, a teddy bear, and an elephant. Pawtucket citizens brought an Establishment Clause challenge to the use of public money to finance the display of a reenactment of the birth of Jesus Christ.

In *Lynch* the Supreme Court moved toward a reconfiguration of the relationship between church and state. Government "acknowledgment" of religious traditions, first indulged in *Marsh,* grew into an affirmative government duty to "accommodate" religion. The Court stated for the first time that the Constitution "affirmatively mandates accommodation, not merely tolerance, of all religions, and forbids hostility toward any." Writing for the Court, Chief Justice Warren Burger—joined by Justices Byron White, William Powell, William Rehnquist, and Sandra Day O'Connor—said that the Establishment Clause "never intended" that the state show "callous indifference" to the religious convictions of its citizens. In this way, *Lynch* transformed the principle of "accommodation"—which formerly had guided cases only where the state had inhibited religious practices—into a constitutional imperative governing official practices even where there is no obstacle to religious observances.

Like *Marsh, Lynch* began by adverting to the acts of the First Congress. But whereas *Marsh* spoke of the "unique" history of legislative prayers, *Lynch* observed that many American institutions traditionally have been imbued with religious symbols and practices, suggesting that to extirpate them would be to reject a significant part of American culture. The Court noted not only that American *legislatures* have traditionally used chaplains but also that *all* levels and branches of American government have "an unbroken history of official acknowledgment . . . of the role of religion in American life." Indeed, American history is "replete with official references to the value and invocation of Divine guidance and deliberations and pronouncements of the Founding Fathers and contemporary leaders." The Court referred to presidential proclamations of "Days of Thanksgiving" since the beginning of the Republic. It quoted Justice William

Douglas's statement in *Zorach v. Clauson* (1952) that "[w]e are a religious people whose institutions presuppose a Supreme Being." It pointed out that our national motto is "In God We Trust" and that the Pledge of Allegiance to the American flag contains the words "one nation under God." It relied on the facts that some federally funded art galleries display Renaissance religious paintings, that there were chapels in the Capitol building, and that Moses was depicted with the Ten Commandments in the Supreme Court chamber. In further support, it observed that the oft-quoted dictum of Thomas Jefferson, that there should be a "wall of separation" between church and state, was merely a "useful figure of speech [but] not a wholly accurate description of the practical aspects of the relationship that in fact exists between church and state."

Lynch's reliance on historical and customary practices was less persuasive than *Marsh*'s. It is far easier to argue, as the *Marsh* Court did, that the hiring of a chaplain for the First Congress—composed of the drafters of the First Amendment—justified Nebraska's having done the same thing. There is no comparable historical basis to justify a publicly funded glorification of the Christian Messiah—an act without roots in early national practice.

After discussing the "pervasiveness" of religious themes in American institutions, the Court recited a second ground for its decision, which seems at odds with the first: that the challenged symbols have little religious significance. Instead, the city's erection of the crèche was so imbued with secular motives that the crèche could not properly be viewed as much of a religious display:

> The city, like the congresses and presidents, . . . has principally taken note of a significant historical religious event long celebrated in the Western World. The crèche in the display depicts the historical origins of this traditional event long recognized as a National Holiday.

Quoting *McGowan v. Maryland* (1961), the Court noted that the nativity scene was viewed as something that "merely happens to coincide or harmonize with the tenets of some . . . religions." Because the message was only "coincidentally" religious, any benefit to religion is "indirect," "remote," or "incidental."

Like a word that loses meaning with constant repetition, the crèche lost its importance as a religious object by continuous deployment in civil life. Instead of celebrating a sacred event (the birth of the Christian Messiah), Pawtucket's display of the nativity scene—accompanied by a panoply of secular symbols—had reduced the crèche to something profane, a secular and often commercial symbol, like a Santa Claus or a Christmas tree, erected merely "to celebrate the Holiday and to depict the origins of that Holiday," not something that could advance religion.

In *Lynch* the Court also complained that the *Lemon* test was overused and too stringent: *Lemon*'s "focus exclusively on the religious component of any activity would inevitably lead to . . . invalidation under the Establishment Clause."

It is difficult to say why "focusing" on the crèche was inappropriate in *Lynch*. The crèche, after all, occasioned the lawsuit in the first place; the Santa Clauses and the Christmas trees were not controversial. Nor is it completely accurate to say that *Lemon* unreasonably forces courts to focus on the "religious component" of a challenged government act. As Norman Dorsen and Charles Sims have noted, the "exclusive focus on the religious component of an activity is often nonsensical" in many Establishment Clause cases. In school aid cases, for example, "what is the religious component of a bus ride?" But the crèche is intrinsically religious. Indeed, the facts of *Lynch* make the Court's disinclination to examine the crèche in isolation from other Christmas displays particularly puzzling. According to the case's record, Pawtucket's mayor had even announced that he wanted the crèche to be kept up to defy those who wanted to "take Christ out of Christmas." Such an explicitly religious motive renders perplexing if not bizarre the Supreme Court's description of the crèche as solely a depiction of "the historical origins of [a] traditional event long recognized as a National Holiday," one "long celebrated in the Western World." The Court's point, however, was clear: Henceforth the judiciary should focus less on the challenged symbol itself and more on its context, physical surroundings, or historical background.

In *Lemon*'s place, *Lynch* enunciated an analysis that is indulgent of intrusions by religion into the practices of civil government.

The *Lynch* Court held that the first prong of *Lemon,* the purpose test, no longer requires that the government's purpose be "exclusively secular." Instead, "a secular purpose"—that is, *one* arguably secular purpose, regardless of whether other overtly religious motives exist—is all that is required.

With respect to the second *Lemon* prong, the effects test, the Court excused the Pawtucket crèche on the ground that the activity was "indirect, remote, and incidental." It was "no more an advancement or endorsement of religion than the Congressional and Executive recognition of origins of the Holiday itself as 'Christ's Mass' or the exhibition of literally hundreds of religious paintings in government-supported museums."

Four justices dissented in *Lynch* in an opinion by Justice Brennan that condemned the Court's slide from *Lemon.* Brennan criticized the Court for ignoring the undeniably religious message of the crèche. The fact that Christmas is such a "familiar and agreeable" tradition does not exempt the government from the constitutional command that it remain strictly neutral toward the religious aspects of the celebration. The Brennan opinion observed that, under *Lemon,* "context" could secularize the government's use of religious symbols only when the government had taken pains to explain that it was not endorsing the religious message that the symbol conveyed. *Lemon* demanded no less. In the dissenters' view, *Lynch* was significant because the Pawtucket municipal government had "made no effort whatever to provide a similar cautionary message."

Justice Harry Blackmun also wrote a dissent, joined by Justices Thurgood Marshall and John Paul Stevens. He criticized the Court for secularizing the religious symbols involved, in order to permit Pawtucket to display them constitutionally. "The crèche has been relegated to the role of a neutral harbinger of the holiday season, useful for commercial purposes." Justice Blackmun deplored this as "a misuse of a sacred symbol."

Thus, by the mid-1980s, the Supreme Court's Establishment Clause doctrine had undergone significant changes. *Lemon* ceased to be the exclusive test for assessing whether an establishment of religion had occurred. With *Lynch* the Supreme Court started to take a holistic approach. Whether a government practice violates the Establishment Clause depended on "all the circumstances of the particular relationship" between religion and the government practice. The Court began to look for some sort of context—historical heritage or physical surroundings—for government-sponsored religious symbols. The more enduring a religious practice, or the more secular symbols surrounding it, the more likely that it comports with the Establishment Clause. This "unwillingness to be confined to any single test of a criterion in this sensitive area" condemned the Court to another round of litigation later in the 1980s.

Justice O'Connor's "Endorsement" Test

Although Justice O'Connor agreed with the outcome of the *Lynch* case, she took a different view of the Establishment Clause in a concurring opinion. She was comfortable with the continued primacy of *Lemon* but she advocated a radically new reading of that case.

In Justice O'Connor's view, the Establishment Clause forbids government "endorsement" of religion. "Endorsement" differs significantly from *Lemon*'s conception of the "advancement" of religion, which occurs whenever the government commits any of its resources to a religious message. Endorsement depends less on what the government does and more on the mental state of the officials involved and observers. Endorsement has occurred if citizens who are not members of the faith that is communicated feel like "outsiders, not full members of the political community."

Justice O'Connor's endorsement analysis and the purpose branch of *Lemon* are congruent. The government fails the purpose test in *Lemon* when it intends to advance a religious message; similarly, an impermissible endorsement of religion would occur whenever the government seeks to carry a religious message to its citizens. But the effects elements of *Lemon* and the O'Connor endorsement test diverge significantly. Whereas *Lemon* would forbid any form of government advancement, Justice O'Connor would prohibit only such acts of advancement that fairly and reasonably could be perceived by the public as approval of a religious point of view.

Thus, Justice O'Connor's endorsement analysis recasts the *Lemon* tests into two components: subjective and objective. A government act, such as putting up a crèche, would fail the subjective test only if it could be shown that the government intended to communicate a religious message. The objective test evaluates what an audience of citizens reasonably might think when they receive the government-sponsored message: "What is crucial is that a government practice not have the effect of *communicating* a message of government endorsement or disapproval of religion" (emphasis added). The government would fail the objective test only if it could be shown that one reasonably would understand that the government's message approves or disapproves of religion, thereby rendering some citizens "outsiders." Even if the government intends no such message, it can still fail the objective test.

According to O'Connor, the Pawtucket crèche was not unconstitutional because it did not "endorse" religion under either the subjective or the objective test. The crèche was no more than the "celebration of the public holiday through its traditional symbols." Public holidays "have cultural significance even if they also have religious aspects," and Pawtucket's purpose for maintaining the crèche was a secular one. Further, Justice O'Connor found that the crèche display celebrated a holiday, "and no one contends that declaration of that holiday is understood to be an endorsement of religion." Thus, the Pawtucket crèche passed the objective test too. Following *Marsh,* Justice O'Connor concluded that, although the crèche "acknowledges" a religious tradition, it does not "endorse" it. In her view, the crèche in no way "communicates government approval of Christianity."

County of Allegheny v. American Civil Liberties Union (1989)

Two religious symbols were disputed in *Allegheny.* First, there was a nativity scene that bore the banner Gloria in Excelsis Deo ("Praise to God on High"), which was erected on the main stairway of the Allegheny County Courthouse in Pittsburgh. The government provided the space and potted plants for the fence surrounding the crèche, although the crèche itself was owned by the local Catholic church. The second religious symbol in *Allegheny* was an 18-foot Hanukkah menorah "of an abstract tree-and-branch design." The menorah also was owned by a private religious group. The local government set it up next to a Christmas tree on public land adjacent to Pittsburgh's City-County Building, a block from the courthouse. A sign proclaimed that these "festive lights remind us that we are the keepers of the flame of liberty and our legacy of freedom." In *Allegheny* the Supreme Court held that the nativity scene's placement was unconstitutional but that the menorah's inclusion in the other display was not.

Most striking about the *Allegheny* case is the distinction that the fragmented Court made between these two religious symbols—reflecting the indeterminacy of its new contextual, or holistic, approach. A five-justice majority (O'Connor, Blackmun, Stevens, Marshall, and Brennan) held that the *crèche* was unconstitutional; Chief Justice Rehnquist and Justices White, Scalia, and Kennedy disagreed. Six justices (Rehnquist, Scalia, White, Kennedy, Blackmun, and O'Connor) concluded that the *menorah* display was lawful; Justices Brennan, Marshall, and Stevens disagreed with that finding.

Three ideological camps could be discerned: the justices who urged stricter adherence to *Lemon* (Brennan and Marshall); those who wanted the Court to permit the "traditional" government use of religious symbols (Rehnquist, Scalia, White, and Kennedy); and those who advocated a new middle ground in the endorsement analysis first enunciated in Justice O'Connor's *Lynch* concurrence (Blackmun and O'Connor). The remaining justice (Stevens) also was a member of the endorsement camp, although, unlike Justices Blackmun and O'Connor, he advocated a "strong presumption against the public use of religious symbols."

Justice Blackmun wrote the opinion of the Court with respect to the crèche and a plurality opinion on the menorah. He briefly referred to the *Lemon* test when he commented that *Lemon* "has been applied regularly in the Court's . . . Establishment Clause cases." But he said that subsequent decisions "refined" the effects branch of the *Lemon* test. This refinement turned out to be the virtual adoption of Justice O'Connor's endorsement test, with its dual emphasis on the government's subjective intentions and the reasonable, or objective, reactions of viewers. The opinion concluded that the Establishment Clause was written to prohibit government "endorsement" of religious ideas—that is, "favoritism," "preference", or "promotion." And it criticized the 1984 *Lynch* decision for its failure to work as an effective guide to Establishment Clause jurisprudence:

> The rationale of the majority opinion in *Lynch* is none too clear: the opinion contains two strands, neither of which provides guidance for decision in subsequent cases. First, . . . the opinion offers no discernible measure for distinguishing between permissible and impermissible endorsements. Second, the opinion observes that any benefit the government's display of the crèche gave to the religion was no more than "indirect, remote, and incidental," . . . without saying how or why.

By contrast, the O'Connor approach was considered a much more workable test of government endorsement, since it is based on "what viewers may fairly understand to be the purpose of the display."

Significantly, a majority of justices did not explicitly adopt Justice Blackmun's frontal attack on *Lynch*. But they did reject exclusive reliance on the history and "tradition" of a particular religious usage, and they favored standards measuring whether the government engaged in some form of religious preference. The Court rejected a "sweeping" reading of the *Marsh* case, "that all accepted practices 200 years old and their equivalents are constitutional today." Nevertheless, *Allegheny* accepted *Lynch*'s holistic analysis in finding that decisions on the use of religious symbols must be based on their "particular physical setting."

Noting that both the crèche in *Lynch* and the menorah in *Allegheny* were surrounded by secular symbols (Santa Clauses, Christmas trees, candy-striped poles, and the like), a majority of justices agreed that the municipal government's placement of a menorah on public property could not fairly be viewed as a government "endorsement" of Judaism or any other religion, at least within the meaning of Justice O'Connor's test.

In order to buttress this conclusion, Justice Blackmun emulated the *Lynch* Court by trying to secularize the symbol. He determined that the menorah is "the primary visual symbol for a holiday that, like Christmas, has both religious and secular dimensions." He described Hanukkah as a "cultural or national event, rather than as a specifically religious event," as an "expression of ethnic identity," and one "fairly low in religious significance"; and he said that it was unclear what relevance the Talmud's teachings had to the "subjective" intentions of the municipal government or its citizens about the display.

Justice O'Connor agreed with these conclusions, but she criticized Justice Blackmun for failing to apply the endorsement analysis more strictly. She also did not think it necessary to desanctify the Hanukkah holiday, saying that it was proper to find the menorah constitutional even though Hanukkah is "a religious holiday" and the menorah is the "central religious symbol" of that holiday. The two justices agreed that the religious significance of the menorah, as opposed to its "cultural" and "ethnic" meaning, was significantly reduced by its placement next to a Christmas tree and to the sign saluting "liberty"—a secular political ideal that was the theme of the display. Three justices (Brennan, Marshall, and Stevens) dissented from the view that the menorah simply celebrated a civil holiday, contending that the juxtaposition of secular images to religious ones does not necessarily remove the religious significance of the display. To the contrary, they asserted that the juxtaposition serves to heighten the religious significance of Christmas trees and other holiday images.

The Court concluded that the Pittsburgh nativity scene presented different problems from the menorah, which stood by itself on the courthouse steps, unattended by secular symbols or messages. Instead of a sign applauding the secular concept of freedom, the crèche's Latin motto praised God. The Court also found it offensive that the local government had decorated the crèche at public expense. "It is as if the county had allowed the [church] to display a cross on the Grand Staircase at Easter, and the county had surrounded the cross with Easter lilies." Referring to the "display of the crèche *in this particular setting,*" the court found that the "county sends an unmistakable message that it supports and promotes the Christian praise to God that is the crèche's religious method" (emphasis added). Accordingly, the *Allegheny* Court's close examination of the context and physical surroundings of two religious symbols yielded different outcomes.

Justice Kennedy's "Traditionalism"

The traditionalist approach did not expire

with *Allegheny*. In a separate opinion Justice Kennedy, joined by Chief Justice Rehnquist and Justices White and Scalia, agreed with the Court about the menorah but concluded that the crèche also was constitutional.

Justice Kennedy unleashed a frontal attack on *Lemon*'s persisting influence. He pointed out that "[p]ersuasive criticism of *Lemon* has emerged" and that Chief Justice Rehnquist and Justices White, Scalia, and O'Connor all have "question[ed] its utility in providing concrete answers to Establishment Clause questions." He added that "[s]ubstantial revision of our Establishment Clause doctrine may be in order."

Justice Kennedy's approach was a pronounced form of traditionalism: The government must be given "some latitude in recognizing and accommodating the central role religion plays in our society," or the result would "border on latent hostility toward religion." In his view, recent political history has shown the rapid expansion of the "administrative state" into all aspects of the lives of its citizens. Standing in the way of this "pervasive public sector" is the nation's traditionally pervasive "accommodation" of religion, as illustrated by legislative chaplains and other examples.

Justice Kennedy criticized the Court's recent tendency to recognize "only the secular aspect" of religious messages; to him that signified a "callous indifference toward religious faith that our cases and traditions do not require." In advocating a reversal of this trend, he found irrelevant what citizens might think of the religious symbols. If the government communicates offensive religious messages, the remedy for citizens is simply to ignore them, as in the case of any unappealing government speech. Otherwise, a citizen would be able to invalidate a government practice whenever "mere feelings of exclusion" are experienced.

Justice Kennedy's opinion went beyond rejection of *Lemon;* he also rejected the endorsement test, and any other test that gives weight to citizens' opinions about their government's use of religious symbols and practices. His opinion supported the government's right to engage in whatever religious practices it "traditionally" has engaged in, at the expense of the individual's right to a secular, religiously neutral government.

After *Allegheny*

Because of the recent changes and disagreements in the Supreme Court, and the decline of *Lemon,* lower courts have been confronted with a renewed round of controversies over religious symbols and rites in government business. Not surprisingly, there has been a variety of contradictory decisions.

For example, in *Jager v. Douglas County School District* (1989) a court of appeals in the South prohibited the use of a prayer before a high school football game and rejected *Marsh* as authority to the contrary. But in *Stein v. Plainwell Community Schools* (1987) a court of appeals in the Midwest held that no Establishment Clause violation occurred when an ecumenical prayer was offered at a public high school graduation. Yet a third court of appeals held in *North Carolina Civil Liberties Union Legal Foundation v. Constangy* (4th Cir. 1991) that it was unconstitutional for a North Carolina state judge to open court sessions with a nondenominational prayer. Another court found that student invocations and benedictions at ceremonies held in a Texas public high school were constitutional.

Religious symbols as well as practices have been hotly contested. The municipal seals of two Illinois towns were declared unconstitutional because they incorporated images of Christian crosses or churches. (See *Harris v. City of Zion* [7th Cir. 1991].) In another case, an appeals court sided with a Kansas public school administration that had ordered an elementary teacher not to display the Bible during school time. (See *Roberts v. Madigan* [10th Cir. 1990].) Another federal court declared unconstitutional a town's sponsorship of an Italian-language mass as part of a festival celebrating the ethnic heritage of some of its residents. (See *Doe v. Village of Crestwood* [7th Cir. 1990].) There also have been challenges to the government's display of a lighted cross in a war memorial and the use of the Christian cross in a police-force emblem. In a case challenging the erection of a 28-foot menorah in a Beverly Hills park, a federal judge ordered that a nearby tree be decorated with Christmas lights to secularize the display, much as the *Allegheny* menorah and the *Lynch* crèche were found to have been secularized by juxtaposed Christmas trees.

In 1992 the Supreme Court was offered an opportunity to clarify the law, but it declined to do so. In *Lee v. Weisman* (1992) a public junior high school had invited a rabbi to recite an ecumenical prayer at a graduation ceremony. A student and her parents challenged this action as an Establishment Clause violation, and they won in the lower courts. The Supreme Court affirmed.

Justice Kennedy's opinion for the Court avoided the "difficult questions" that divided the Court in recent cases, and it rejected "the invitation" of petitioners and the United States as amicus curiae to reconsider *Lemon.* Instead, he focused on the fact that the prayer was given in a public school ceremony. Tracing Supreme Court precedents, he found that special concerns arise when the religious consciences of schoolchildren are at stake. Reasoning that children are especially vulnerable to "public pressure" and "peer pressure," Justice Kennedy stated that the government must be especially vigilant in the primary and secondary schools against delivering messages favoring any point of view on religion. Even "subtle" or "indirect" government pressures in support of religion in the schools are forbidden. Justice Kennedy thus was able to find that government-sponsored prayer in a public school ceremony violated the Establishment Clause, without ever having to revisit the traditionalist arguments that he had championed in *Allegheny.*

Justices Blackmun, Stevens, O'Connor, and Souter joined Justice Kennedy's opinion, but in two concurring opinions (by Blackmun and Souter) they argued that this result was compelled as much by the endorsement analysis of *Allegheny* as by the "special" considerations articulated by Justice Kennedy.

The four dissenting justices—Chief Justice Rehnquist and Justices Scalia, White, and Thomas—restated the traditionalist argument in a forceful opinion by Justice Scalia. The dissenters sharply rejected Justice Kennedy's application of the coercion analysis to a schoolchild's elusive feelings of "pressure"; they branded it "psychology practiced by amateurs." And they maintained that the long history of government-sponsored religious usage in American society legitimated an ecumenical observance in an open graduation ceremony, even if the law forbade prayer in a closed classroom.

The continued vitality of the *Lemon* test is still much in doubt, and a principal question is whether the endorsement test or the traditionalist approach will prevail if *Lemon* is overruled. *Lee* showed that the Supreme Court is deeply and almost evenly divided on the issue. Until the Court is able to answer the question decisively, Establishment Clause law will continue in a confused state, and lower courts will continue to render divergent and contradictory decisions.

Norman Dorsen
Thomas Viles

Bibliography

Dorsen, Norman, and Charles Sims, "The Nativity Scene Case: An Error of Judgment," 1985 *University of Illinois Law Review* 837–868 (1985).

Karst, Kenneth, "The First Amendment, the Politics of Religion and the Symbols of Government," 27 *Harvard Civil Rights–Civil Liberties Law Review* 503–530 (1992).

Cases Cited

Committee for Public Education and Religious Liberty v. Nyquist, 413 U.S. 756 (1973).

County of Allegheny v. American Civil Liberties Union, 492 U.S. 573 (1989).

Doe v. Village of Crestwood, 917 F. 2d 1476 (7th Cir. 1990).

Everson v. Board of Education, 330 U.S. 1 (1947).

Harris v. City of Zion, 927 F. 2d 1401 (7th Cir. 1991).

Jager v. Douglas County School District, 862 F. 2d 824 (11th Cir.), cert. denied, 490 U.S. 1090 (1989).

Larson v. Valente, 456 U.S. 228 (1982).

Lee v. Weisman, 505 U.S. 577 (1992).

Lemon v. Kurtzman, 403 U.S. 602 (1971).

Lynch v. Donnelly, 465 U.S. 668 (1984).

Marsh v. Chambers, 463 U.S. 783 (1983).

McGowan v. Maryland, 366 U.S. 420 (1961).

North Carolina Civil Liberties Union Legal Foundation v. Constangy, 947 F. 2d 1145 (4th Cir. 1991).

Roberts v. Madigan, 921 F. 2d 1047 (10th Cir. 1990).

Stein v. Plainwell Community Schools, 822 F. 2d 1406 (6th Cir. 1987).

Zorach v. Clauson, 343 U.S. 306 (1952).

M

Madison and Religion

James Madison (1751–1836) vigorously defended the principle of freedom of conscience throughout his adult life. Beginning with his efforts in 1776 to strengthen provisions for religious toleration in the Virginia Declaration of Rights, Madison consistently opposed church establishment in his home state. He mobilized popular opposition to a proposed tax in support of Christian clergy (the General Assessment, in 1784) and successfully piloted Thomas Jefferson's Statute for Religious Freedom through the state legislature in 1785–1786. At the national level, Madison fought to secure "the rights of Conscience in the fullest latitude" by helping to draft the 1791 Bill of Rights; and as president he consistently blocked attempts to breach the "wall of separation" between church and state.

Personal Conviction and Natural Theology

Madison's early education helped shape his commitment to the principle of religious liberty. As a student at Princeton from 1769 to 1772, he studied under the Reverend John Witherspoon, the college's Edinburgh-educated Presbyterian president, who introduced Madison to the "Common Sense" works of Scottish Enlightenment philosophers Thomas Reid, Francis Hutcheson, and Dugald Stewart. These writers sought a middle ground between the two poles of late-eighteenth-century religion. On the one hand were evangelicals and champions of orthodoxy who viewed Enlightenment science as a threat to true religion; at the opposite extreme, skeptics like David Hume, David Hartley, and Rousseau questioned basic tenets of Christian faith. The Common Sense school defended the efficacy of human moral and inductive reasoning and encouraged its adherents to subject human institutions and beliefs to rigorous examination rather than relying on blind faith; ultimately, however, proponents contended that inquiry would uphold the truths of rational religion. Under Witherspoon's auspices, Madison embarked on his own investigation of church history, focusing on the relationship between ecclesiastical and civil authority.

From his studies Madison derived a set of religious beliefs that stressed the importance of personal conviction and natural theology rather than received truths and enforced orthodoxy. Madison did not doubt that "the belief in a God All Powerful wise & good, is . . . essential to the moral order of the World & to the happiness of man," but he contended that the most convincing proofs resided in the design of nature, not in theological dogma. "The course of reasoning . . . 'from Nature to Nature's God,'" he informed Frederick Beasley in 1825, "[w]ill be the more universal & more persuasive application." In addition, Madison's readings in church history convinced him that ecclesiastical establishments represented a danger to rational religion. He informed William Bradford in 1774 that "[r]eligious bondage shackles and debilitates the mind and unfits it for every noble enterprise [and] every expanded prospect." "Religion flourishes in greater purity without than with the aid of Govt," Madison concluded.

Madison in Virginia: The General Assessment

Madison's own observations of religious and political affairs in the colonies reinforced these convictions. Growing up in Orange County, where his father was an Anglican vestryman, Madison had witnessed the sometimes violent suppression of Baptist and Presbyterian dissenters. Returning from Princeton in 1773–1774, he was struck by the contrast between Virginia's Anglican conformity and Pennsylvania's religious pluralism. He expressed dismay that "well meaning men" suffered for their beliefs in his home colony, and he hoped that "Liberty of Conscience" would "revive among us." In addition to its theological consequences, however, Madison worried about the political impact of "[t]hat diabolical Hell conceived principle of persecution" in America. As an ardent Whig, he feared that Virginia's Anglican establishment reinforced clerical power, social hierarchy, and British tyranny and dulled the colonists' will to resist "slavery and Subjection." The question was not "Is Religion necessary?" he noted, but "[A]re Relig[ious] Establishments necessary?" Thus Madison upended conventional wisdom and asserted that established religion undermined rather than supported both piety and civil society in America.

Elected to the Virginia House of Delegates in June 1776, Madison's first opportunity to apply these ideas came during the debate over including the Declaration of Rights in the state Constitution. Its chief author, George Mason, had provided for religious toleration, but Madison contended that legal toleration failed to protect religious freedom as a natural, inalienable right prior to government and instead implied government's power to grant or rescind it. At Madison's prompting, the committee changed the declaration's wording: Mason's "Divine and omnipotent Creator" became merely "our Creator," while "toleration" became "the full and free exercise of [religion] accord[in]g to the dictates of Conscience." On two other key issues, however—prohibiting religious establishments and deleting specific references to Christianity in order to protect non-Christians—Madison failed to win the day. He supported Thomas Jefferson's proposed Statute for Religious Freedom in 1779 because it would have achieved both goals, but the General Assembly refused to enact it. Indeed, Madison himself reluctantly voted in 1784 to extend the right of incorporation to the Episcopal (Anglican) church in order to fend off growing pressure for establishment.

That same year, however, Virginians revisited the issue of religious establishment when Patrick Henry proposed the General Assessment, a tax in support of the established ministry. Henry's bill responded to public concern over the wartime impoverishment of the clergy, and initially it enjoyed the support of a majority of delegates. Even George Washington perceived merit in asking the inhabitants either to support their churches or to identify themselves as non-Christians in order to obtain exemptions. In addition, by extending the assessment's benefits to Presbyterians as well as to Episcopalians, the bill threatened to shatter the dissenting coalition of Mennonites, Quakers, Baptists, and Presbyterians that had previously opposed establishment. Madison mounted a masterly two-pronged counterattack to the General Assessment. First, he supported Henry's candidacy for governor in order to remove him (and his powerful oratory) from the assembly floor during debates, and he won a delay on the vote. Second, at the instigation of allies George Mason, George Nicholas, and Wilson Nicholas, in May 1785 Madison anonymously authored his *Memorial and Remonstrance against Religious Assessments,* which his supporters circulated throughout the state, collecting thousands of signatures and spawning parallel petition drives directed at the Assembly.

Memorial and Remonstrance offered fifteen objections to Henry's bill—the foremost being that the assessment violated Virginians' freedom of conscience under the Declaration of Rights. Here Madison first made the argument regarding minority rights that reappeared in *Federalist* No. 10: Even if a majority of Virginians supported establishment, the legislature lacked the power "to overleap the great Barrier which defends the rights of the people." "No man's right is abridged by . . . Civil Society," he declared, "and . . . Religion is wholly exempt from its cognizance." The petition reminded Virginians that the assessment's discriminatory treatment of dissenters, Catholics, and non-Christians posed a threat to the liberties of all: "Who does not see that the same authority which can establish Christianity, in exclusion of all other Religions, may establish with the same ease any particular sect of Christians?"

Memorial and Remonstrance raised other political, moral, and social objections to establishment. The inevitable contention accompanying such a bill would "tend to enervate the laws in general, and to slacken the bands of Society," endangering America's republican experiment with old-world-style religious conflicts and tyranny. Aside from endangering civil order, Madison predicted that a coercive tax would fail to achieve the object of advancing Christianity. He proffered historical examples which demonstrated that enforced conformity inhibited the diffusion of moral and religious values because it substituted "superstition, bigotry, and persecution" for the exercise of human reason. Coercion also weakened believers' "pious confidence in Christianity's innate excellence," since why would a true faith require the support of civil government? Nor did *Memorial and Remonstrance* ignore more practical socioeconomic concerns. Pointing toward the attraction that religious toleration held for European newcomers, Madison charged that the assessment would retard immigration and hasten out-migration, the latter of which was an issue of some concern in the House of Delegates.

By autumn of 1785, petitioners had collected over ten thousand antiassessment signatures, and Madison, Mason, and the Nicholas brothers eked out a narrow legislative victory over Henry's bill. Ironically, the near loss in the General Assessment battle reinvigorated the old antiestablishment coalition and mobilized new support. As a result, when Madison reintroduced the Statute for Religious Freedom, the Virginia Assembly enacted it in 1786. Again, Madison served as chief tactician, guiding the statute through the assembly, lobbying the Senate, and opposing efforts to exclude non-Christians from the bill's provisions.

Madison on the National Stage: The Bill of Rights

By 1787, however, Madison was displaying his political talents on the national stage as a key architect of the proposed federal Constitution and as coauthor of *The Federalist Papers*. Although his arguments for a federal government focused chiefly on protecting the rights of economic minorities—i.e., property owners—from the designs of majority-controlled state legislatures, and on controlling the excesses of faction-ridden local politics, the rights of religious minorities shaped his thinking as well. The failure of Virginia's Declaration of Rights to ensure freedom of conscience indicated that state bills of rights, mere "parchment barriers," offered insufficient protection against "overbearing" legislative attacks on the inhabitants' natural rights, he noted in an October 1788 letter to Jefferson (an argument that he employed in *Federalist* No. 48); only a national government could provide such security. In *Federalist* No. 10 Madison used religious pluralism as an analogy for political faction in a federal republic: In both cases, diversity precluded the dominance or establishment of any one sect or interest.

Despite his commitment to freedom of conscience, however, Madison strenuously opposed adding a formal bill of rights to the Constitution. Such a list was unnecessary, he insisted, and might be seen as a final, finite statement that delegitimized any rights not included. During Virginia's ratifying debates in June 1788 he derided Patrick Henry's contention that the Constitution failed to protect religious freedom. "It is better that this security should be depended upon from the general legislature," Madison declared; "A particular state might concur in one religious project. But the United States abound in such a variety of sects, that it is a strong security against religious persecution." Yet as it became clear that ratification even in his home state of Virginia depended on some compromise with Anti-Federalist opinion, Madison softened his stand on a bill of rights. Many of his former allies in the battle for disestablishment, including Baptist leader John Leland, were now ranged in opposition to the Constitution over the issue. In exchange for the dissenters' support in the ratification vote, Madison agreed to promote such a bill in the new federal Congress.

Once converted, Madison became a zealous advocate. Writing to Baptist minister George Eve in January 1789, he brushed aside his earlier opposition and expressed hope that a bill of rights would educate Americans, reconcile Anti-Federalists to the new Constitution, and secure "all essential rights, particularly the rights of Conscience." When the new Congress convened, he moved for the creation of a committee to draft a set of constitutional amendments. Concerned that an early version of the First Amendment failed to guard against abuses of the "implied powers" granted to Congress under the Constitution, Madison pushed the committee to change the bill's wording from "[n]o religion shall be established by Law" to "congress shall make no laws touching religion, or infringing the rights of conscience." Still, he remained convinced that local government represented the greatest threat to liberty. Madison clashed with fellow committee member St. George Tucker over whether the First Amendment should also apply to the states—a battle that Madison lost, resulting in the persistence of religious establishments and discrimination in several states.

Madison's Rigorous "Wall of Separation"

Although the Virginia contests from 1776 to 1786 and the debate over the Bill of Rights represented Madison's most crucial contributions to freedom of religion, he continued to address the issue both publicly and privately. After briefly retiring from public life in the late 1790s, Madison returned to pen the Virginia Resolutions, a response to the Federalist-sponsored Alien and Sedition Acts of 1798. While the acts struck most strongly against the rights of speech, press, and assembly, Madison contended that they violated the First Amendment with regard to freedom of conscience as well. In his address to the Virginia General Assembly in January 1799 Madison questioned the wisdom of permitting judicial and civil officers to evaluate the "licentiousness" of public speech. Under such a system "the judge as to what is licentious may escape through any constitutional restriction. . . . . [u]nder it men of a particular religious opinion might be excluded from office . . . under it Congress might denominate a religion to be heretical and licentious," creating a quasi-establishment.

During two terms as president (1808–1816) Madison had several opportunities to restate his position regarding the "wall of separation" between church and state. In 1811 he vetoed a bill that would have given the Episcopal church in Alexandria, Virginia, all responsibility for poor relief and education. Madison's veto message acknowledged that religious organizations were free to engage in private charity, but he contended that it was not the government's provenance to be "giving to religious societies as such a legal agency in carrying into effect a public and civil duty." A bill granting land to a Baptist congregation in the Mississippi Territory met with the same fate on the grounds that it misused federal moneys. Even the payment of congressional and military chaplains came in for censure. Indeed, Madison was so consistent and rigorous in his defense of the separation of church and state that he bridled at clerical requests for days of national fast and thanksgiving. Criticizing John Adams's presidential injunctions to "Christian Worship," Madison assured Edward Livingston in 1822 that as president he had taken care to make his proclamations "absolutely indiscriminate, and merely recommendatory."

Madison counseled vigilance because he believed his fellow citizens underestimated the continued threat of "silent accumulations & encroachments by Ecclesiastical Bodies." In private memoranda he criticized the states for their failure to guarantee this separation fully in their constitutions. Toward the end of his life he grew particularly concerned about the civil power and exemptions that wealthy, incorporated religious denominations enjoyed in America. Only the complete separation of civil and religious authority would secure freedom of conscience; "every provision for them [churches] short of this principle, will be found to leave crevices at least thro's which bigotry may introduce persecution." There was no middle ground—a truth that Madison's experiences in designing the curriculum at the University of Virginia bore out. Observing the sectarian battles that rocked institutions like Harvard in the 1820s, he commented that "there seems to be no alternative but between a public University without a theological professorship, and sectarian Seminaries without a University." For Madison the choice was obvious; theological appointments and public education were incompatible.

Despite these concerns, at the end of his life Madison reviewed the outcome of America's experiment in religious and political freedom with great satisfaction. The Republic's success had demonstrated "the great truth that Govts. do better without Kings & Nobles." But just as importantly in his mind, it proved that religion and morality could flourish in a secular state. Few contemporaries played a more significant role in both revolutions than James Madison.

Margaret E. Newell

Bibliography
Alley, Robert S., ed., *James Madison on Religious Liberty* (Buffalo, N.Y.: Prometheus Books, 1985).
Finkelman, Paul, "James Madison and the Bill of Rights: A Reluctant Paternity," 1990 *Supreme Court Review* 301–347 (1990).
The Papers of James Madison, ed. William T. Hutchinson et al. (Chicago and Charlottesville, Va.: University of Chicago Press and University Press of Virginia, 1967–).
Rutland, Robert Allen, *James Madison, the Founding Father* (New York: Macmillan, 1987).

Madsen v. Erwin
395 Mass. 715, 481 N.E. 2d 1160 (1985)

In *Madsen v. Erwin* (Mass., 1985) a gay employee of the *Christian Science Monitor* brought suit against her former employer for her discharge. Christine Madsen alleged wrongful discharge, defamation, invasion of privacy, intentional infliction of mental distress, sexual and affectional preference discrimination, and breach of fiduciary responsibilities under deeds of trust by the *Christian Science Monitor* and by a member of the Christian Science Church.

The Massachusetts Supreme Judicial Court reversed the trial court's denial of the defendants' motion for summary judgment on some of the claims, while leaving some of the claims still open for trial. Among the claims that the court foreclosed were Madsen's claims under the federal and state constitutions as well as her claims for breach of contract and for wrongful discharge. The court left open for further litigation many of the plaintiff's tort claims, including those claims for defamation, interference with advantageous relations, interference with the plaintiff's employment contract, invasion of privacy, and intentional infliction of emotional distress. Although the court found fault with the allegations of the complaint, the plaintiff was given the opportunity to replead her claims under guidelines set out in the opinion.

Under the facts of the case, the plaintiff had worked for the *Christian Science Monitor* for several years, beginning her employment as a "copygirl." Over the years Madsen had received successive promotions and salary increases. Beginning in September 1981 she held a writing position in the special sections department of the *Monitor.* Later that year Madsen learned that rumors concerning her sexual predilection were being circulated at the newspaper. Subsequently, she was informed that her superiors had learned of allegations that she was a homosexual, that she had entered into a "homosexual marriage," that she had attempted to entice a manager's wife into a homosexual relationship, that she attended meetings of homosexuals, and that she lived with a homosexual. Madsen was not told the name of the person who provided this information to her superiors at the newspaper.

In response, Madsen denied that she had entered into a "homosexual marriage," had attempted to entice a manager's wife into a homosexual relationship, attended meetings of homosexuals, and lived with a homosexual. She did state, however, that she was gay. Within a month, the *Monitor* terminated Madsen's employment. The plaintiff alleged that she was unable to obtain comparable employment since the termination; the defendants, she alleged, had caused her extreme mental distress, loss of earning capacity, loss of respect and reputation, and other injuries to body and mind.

The initial question that concerned the court was whether Madsen's employment by the *Christian Science Monitor* was actually employment by a church. The court concluded that the newspaper was an arm of the Christian Science Church, and that the plaintiff—although a writer for the *Monitor*—was, in fact, an employee of the church. Further evidence of her employment by the *Monitor* was the fact that the plaintiff wore a badge stating that she was a church employee.

The court appeared to finesse the issue of the connection between the newspaper and the church by highlighting the religious nature of the newspaper's decision to fire her. The court stated that the decision to fire Madsen because of her sexual preference "can only be construed as a religious one, made by a Church as employer. Thus, we must defer to that decision."

The court cited two other cases from lower state courts that involved the firing of homosexuals based on the proposition that the free exercise of religion allows religious employers' interests to trump the interests of employees of those institutions. These cases were *Walker v. First Presbyterian Church* (Calif., 1980), which involved a church organist, and *Lewis ex rel. v. Buchanan* (Minn., 1979), which involved a teacher in a parochial school.

Among the several lines of argument cited by the court for this result were the ideas that (1) entanglement of the defendants in such litigation would involve the court in a review of an essentially ecclesiastical procedure whereby the church reviews its employees' spiritual suitability for continued employment; and that (2) if the plaintiff were allowed to collect damages from defendants because she was discharged for being gay, the defendants would be penalized for their religious belief that homosexuality is "a sin for which one must repent." Requiring the defendants to pay damages to maintain their religious beliefs would constitute "a substantial burden on defendants' right to free exercise of religion.

In addition, the court ruled that the *Monitor* had the right to terminate Madsen's employment. Under then-current Massachusetts common law the fact that Madsen had no written employment contract meant that her only right to be free from termination would be if she had a basis for job protection under a constitutional provision or a statute or if she had a common-law claim for protection from her employer's bad faith. The court could find no basis for job protection under the U.S. Constitution, the Massachusetts Constitution, or in federal or Massachusetts statutes. Because there was no showing of bad faith as exemplified under *Fortune v. National Cash Register Co.* (Mass., 1977) and *RLM Associates v. Carter Manufacturing Corp.* (Mass., 1969), and because her discharge had not deprived her of future compensation for past service, Madsen had no protectible job interest.

Notwithstanding the court's dismissal of Madsen's complaint, the court allowed her to replead her several tort claims under several principles outlined in the opinion. The court began by stating two seemingly contradictory principles: "Without retreating for a moment from the foundational rule 'that the First Amendment prohibits civil courts from intervening in disputes concerning religious doctrine, discipline, faith, or internal organization,' we restate the equally important rule that the rights of religion are not beyond the reach of the civil law."

Particularly, the court stated that the First Amendment does not protect "a clergyman [from] defam[ing] a person, intentionally inflict[ing] serious emotional harm on a parishioner, or commit[ting] other torts." The structure of First Amendment religious provisions is different with regard to two concepts, "freedom to believe and freedom to act. The first is absolute but, in the nature of things, the second cannot be." Citing *Cantwell v. Connecticut* (1940), the Massachusetts court stated that "[c]onduct remains subject to regulation for the protection of society." Because the torts of which the plaintiff complained were "conduct" and not "belief," the court held that they were subject to regulation. The court noted that the defendant may be able to interpose defenses or qualified privileges, but that those defenses or qualified privileges would not be subject to a motion to dismiss.

The dissent by Massachusetts Supreme Court Justice Francis Patrick O'Connor took issue with the court's permitting the plaintiff to replead her tort claims as conduct not beyond the reach of civil law. The dissent questioned why the First Amendment would preclude the courts from imposing damages on the defendants for wrongful termination of contract but not for wrongful tortious conduct. The dissent maintained that there could have been no defamation in this case because the statements of the employer's personnel were conditionally privileged; because there was no suggestion that the defendants had abused their conditional privilege by speaking with "malice in fact"; and because there was no unnecessary, unreasonable, or excessive publication of the defamatory matters. The dissent maintained that there could be no claim for intentional infliction of emotional distress because the conduct fell short of the test, which was to be "so outrageous in character and so extreme in degree as to go beyond all possible bounds of decency and to be regarded as atrocious and utterly intolerable in a civilized community." Nor, according to the dissent, did the complaint allege that the actions were taken out of malevolence or with actual malice. Finally, as to invasion of privacy, the dissent maintained that there could have been no invasion. The dissent reasoned that, because the defendants could lawfully have discharged Madsen on the basis of her sexual preference, when allegations surfaced about Madsen's sexual preference, the defendants had a right to question her about it.

The dissent also took issue with the characterization of Madsen's employment as employment by a church or so deeply entangled in religious matters as to be protected. Although the dissent suggested that the constitutional question should best be avoided, the dissent maintained that the Supreme Court never held that civil courts cannot intervene in matters involving lay church employees. The dissent distinguished between ministers and religious leaders and other church employees. "While the beliefs and practices of a minister are of critical importance to the church in which the minister functions, making judicial involvement in decisions affecting a minister's tenure inappropriate, it is far from clear that the same is true with respect to a sportswriter on the staff of a church-affiliated newspaper." The dissent opined that the appropriate test in this case should have been a judicial balancing of the competing church and state interests.

Lea Vander Velde

Bibliography

Cicchino, Peter M., et al., "Sex, Lies and Civil Rights: A Critical History of the Massachusetts Gay Civil Rights Bill," 26 *Harvard Civil Rights–Civil Liberties Law Review* 549–631 (1991).

Grissum, Gayle A., "Church Employment and the First Amendment: The Protected Employer and the Vulnerable Employee," 51 *Missouri Law Review* 911–931 (1986).

Hayden, Paul T., "Religiously Motivated 'Outrageous' Conduct: Intentional Infliction of Emotional Distress As a Weapon against 'Other People's Faiths,'" 34 *William and Mary Law Review* 579–677 (1993).

Lupu, Ira C., "Free Exercise Exemption and Religious Institutions: The Case of Employment Discrimination," 67 *Boston University Law Review* 391–442 (1987).

Marshall, William P., and Douglas C. Blomgren, "The Tension between the Free Exercise Clause and the Establishment Clause of the First Amendment: Regulating Religious Organizations under the Establishment Clause," 47 *Ohio State Law Journal* 293–331 (1986).

Note, "Sexual Orientation and the Law: Employment Law Issues Affecting Gay Men and Lesbians," 102 *Harvard Law Review* 1554–1584 (1989).

Okamoto, Duane, "Religious Discrimination and the Title VII Exemption for Religious Organizations: A Basic Values Analysis for the Proper Allocation of Conflicting Rights," 60 *Southern California Law Review* 1375–1427 (1987).

Cases Cited

Cantwell v. Connecticut, 310 U.S. 296 (1940).

Fortune v. National Cash Register Co., 373 Mass. 96, 364 N.E. 2d 1251 (Mass. 1977).

Lewis ex rel. v. Buchanan, 21 Fair Employment Practices Cases (BNA) 696 (Minn. Dist. Ct. 1979).

Madsen v. Erwin, 395 Mass. 715, 481 N.E. 2d 1160 (1985).

RLM Associates v. Carter Manufacturing. Corp., 356 Mass. 718, 248 N.E. 2d 646 (Mass. 1969).

Walker v. First Presbyterian Church, 22 Fair Employment Practices Cases (BNA) 762 (Cal. Super. Ct. 1980).

Marsh v. Chambers 463 U.S. 783 (1983)

Marsh v. Chambers (1983) is a unique entry in the U.S. Supreme Court's religion clause jurisprudence. In *Marsh* the Court upheld the State of Nebraska's practice of employing a state-appointed chaplain to open each session of its unicameral legislature with a prayer. The prayer was led by the Reverend Palmer, a Presbyterian minister, who had served as the official chaplain of Nebraska's legislature for over sixteen years. His salary was paid by the state treasury. The prayers used by the Reverend Palmer were from the Judeo-Christian tradition and from time to time were collected and published in prayer books at state expense. The plaintiff, Ernest Chambers, was a member of the legislature.

Chambers filed his lawsuit in federal district court in Nebraska, seeking to enjoin both the practice of maintaining a state-paid chaplain and the practice of opening legislative sessions with a prayer. The district court held that the state practice of paying a chaplain with state funds violated the Establishment Clause, but it left undisturbed the practice of opening each session of the legislature with a prayer. Cross-appeals were taken. The Eighth Circuit held that the entire practice violated the Establishment Clause. In a 6-to-3 decision the U.S. Supreme Court reversed, holding the actions of Nebraska's legislature to be constitutionally valid except for the practice of publishing the prayers at state expense.

In choosing to hear *Marsh* the Court placed itself in a tenuous position. If it struck down Nebraska's legislative prayer, it would place in doubt the constitutionality of the U.S. Congress's 200-year-old practice of beginning its session with a prayer. The Court would then be in direct confrontation with Congress over a matter on which Congress was unlikely to compromise willingly. Moreover, such a decision would also cast doubt on the Court's own practice of beginning its sessions with the invocation "God save the United States and this Honorable Court."

On the other hand, a decision to uphold legislative prayer would seriously undercut existing Establishment Clause doctrine. Logically such a decision would necessitate that the Court alter, if not overrule, its own oft-stated Establishment Clause test announced in *Lemon v. Kurtzman* (1971), requiring that—in order to pass constitutional muster—a state practice (1) must have a secular purpose, (2) must have a primary effect that does not advance or inhibit religion, *and* (3) must not excessively entangle the state in religious matters. Legislative prayer, presumably, would fail all three prongs of the *Lemon* test.

Writing for the Court, however, Chief Justice Warren Burger avoided both pitfalls. In a decision of great political if not legal acumen, the Court resolved its dilemma by simply creating an ad hoc exception to *Lemon.* It was thus able to uphold the chaplaincy practice while leaving the *Lemon* test intact.

The Court's vehicle for its judicial sleight of hand was to create, out of whole cloth, a historical/traditional approach under which the Court was able to validate the practice of legislative prayer because of its "unique history." This historical/traditional analysis focused on the particular fact that the First Congress in 1789 passed the legislation creating the post of Congressional Chaplain three days before agreeing on the language of the Bill of Rights, which included the Establishment Clause prohibition. As the Court argued:

> It can hardly be thought that in the same week Members of the First Congress who voted to appoint and to pay a chaplain for each House and also voted to approve the draft of the First Amendment for submission to the states, intended the Establishment Clause of the Amendment to forbid what they had just declared acceptable.

This history regarding congressional prayer, according to the Court, then also meant that state legislative prayer must also be constitutional.

> In applying the First Amendment to the states through the Fourteenth Amendment, *Cantwell v. Connecticut,* 310 U.S. 296 (1940) it would be incongruous to interpret that Clause as imposing more stringent First Amendment limits on the states than the draftsmen imposed on the Federal Government.

The *Marsh* opinion, however, was notable for the care which it took to ensure that the approach it maintained in the case would not be construed as inviting a whole new approach to establishment issues. As the Court stated, "standing alone, historical patterns cannot justify constitutional guarantees." However, in this case, the Court felt that the Framers' contemporaneous actions "reveal their intent."

There were two dissents in *Marsh.* The first, written by Justice Brennan and joined by Justice Marshall, recognized the narrowness of the Court's holding:

> The Court today has written a narrow and, on the whole, careful opinion . . . and its limited rationale should pose little threat to the overall fate of the establishment clause.

On the other hand, Justice Brennan's opinion took note that the decision in *Marsh* could not be sustained under settled establishment doctrine. As Brennan wrote, "I have no doubt that, if any group of law students were asked to apply the principles of *Lemon* to the question of legislative prayer, they would nearly unanimously find the practice to be unconstitutional."

But Justice Brennan did not confine his criticism to doctrine. He criticized the decision as violating "the principles of neutrality and separation that are embedded within the establishment clause." He also levied two attacks against the Court's mode of historical analysis. First he argued that the contemporaneous action of the Framers in approving legislative prayer is not dispositive of their views on the establishment issue:

> Legislators, influenced by the passions and exigencies of the moment, the pressures of constituents and colleagues, and the press of business, do not always pass sober constitutional judgment on every piece of judgment they enact and this must be assumed to be true of the numbers of the First Congress as any other. Indeed the fact that James Madison, who voted for the bill authorizing the payment of the first congressional chaplains later expressed the view that the practice was unconstitutional is instructive on precisely this point.

Brennan cut to the heart of the historical analysis itself, claiming that the Court's approach was fundamentally misguided. To Brennan, "the Constitution is not a static document whose meaning on every detail is fixed for all time by the life experience of the Framers."

Justice Stevens's dissent was far briefer. To Stevens, the Nebraska chaplaincy practice was unconstitutional because the state had created a preference for one faith by employing the same chaplain for a period of over sixteen years.

There is much merit in the opinions of both Justice Brennan and Justice Stevens. On the other hand, in many ways *Marsh* is a difficult decision to criticize. The Court's admission that it is not applying current doctrine immunizes it from any criticism that the Court has misapplied or misconstrued precedent. Similarly the Court's assertion that its rationale is limited only to the case at hand and is not to be expanded into a general Establishment Clause methodology immunizes the decision from any claim that the methodology which the Court employed misunderstands or does not recognize important establishment principles. Indeed, the Court's holding is so narrow that it seems the only point of criticism available is whether one agrees or disagrees with the *result*. This issue, in turn, is so insignificant in the larger context of church–state relations that it may be that *Marsh* can avoid serious scrutiny entirely.

Yet it may be that the purported narrowness of the *Marsh* holding is its real flaw. True to its word, the Court has not applied *Marsh* in any subsequent cases, including those in which a historical analysis might arguably be available. Nevertheless, the decision has worked only to confuse lower courts. Believing that the *Marsh* decision extended beyond the facts of the case itself, a number of lower courts have attempted to apply its historical test, only to be reversed eventually by the U.S. Supreme Court on appeal. More fundamentally there is a legitimate question to be asked concerning whether or not it is an appropriate exercise of judicial power that a court carve out ad hoc exceptions to constitutional rules. The result is that *Marsh* more clearly resembles a product of political compromise than a reasoned result of judicial decisionmaking.

William P. Marshall

Bibliography

Cox, Kenneth M., "The *Lemon* Test Soured: The Supreme Court's New Establishment Clause Analysis," 37 *Vanderbilt Law Review* 1175–1203 (1984).

Mirsky, Yehudah, "Note: Civil Religions and the Establishment Clause," 95 *Yale Law Journal* 1237–1257 (1986).

Slovek, Robert M., "Legislative Prayer and the Establishment Clause: An Exception to Traditional Analysis," 17 *Creighton Law Review* 157–185 (1984).

Cases Cited

Cantwell v. Connecticut, 310 U.S. 296 (1940).

Lemon v. Kurtzman, 403 U.S. 602 (1971).

Marsh v. Chambers, 463 U.S. 783 (1983).

Maryland Toleration Act (1649)

The Maryland Toleration Act (officially titled "An Act Concerning Religion") was framed by Maryland Colony's Roman Catholic proprietor, Cecil Calvert (Lord Baltimore), and was adopted by the Maryland Assembly on

April 21, 1649. To the extent that it provided for religious toleration, the act was the most liberal of its time. Moreover, before its demise at the end of the seventeenth century, it exceeded England's Toleration Act of 1689 and was second only to Rhode Island's Charter of 1663 and Pennsylvania's "Great Law" of 1683.

The Maryland Toleration Act protected anyone who professed a belief in Jesus Christ (excluding nontrinitarians) from being "troubled, molested, or discountenanced" for his or her religion or in the "free exercise thereof" and from being "compelled to the belief or exercise of any other religion against his or her consent." Balancing such enlightened provisions were those which provided for the death penalty and confiscation of property for blasphemers against God, Christ, or the Trinity, as well as lesser penalties (e.g., fines, whipping, and imprisonment) for those who profaned the Sabbath; who made reproachful references to the Virgin Mary or the Apostles; or who, in referring to others, used derogatory terms such as "heretic," "schismatic," "idolater," or "Jesuited papist."

The Maryland Toleration Act was the first public act to use the phrase "free exercise of religion," later employed in the First Amendment to the U.S. Constitution. This suggests some recognition of the idea that religion involves more than belief. At that time, however, such phraseology was intended only to protect trinitarian Christians in their public worship. Provisions in the act that forbade the reproachful use of names or terms such as "heretic" or "popish priest," Leonard Levy has suggested, anticipated current group libel laws.

Cecil Calvert sought to establish a colony that would be both profitable and a haven for Catholics, where Catholics would be spared the statutory disabilities to which they were subjected in England (e.g., they could neither vote nor hold office). There was to be no established church, and Catholics and Protestants were to be free to worship openly without fear of state reprisal. By the charter granted to George Calvert, Cecil's father, the proprietor was given the power to license churches, provided that they were "dedicated and consecrated according to [the] ecclesiastical laws . . . of England." Such a provision would suggest that any churches which Calvert might establish should be of the Church of England. Calvert, however, established no churches and discouraged any attempt on the part of the Maryland legislature to do so. All churches and ministers were supported by voluntary contributions.

Before 1649 religious toleration was provided for by implication in the colonial charter, by proprietary edict, by the courts, and by popular consent. The only relevant legislation was "An Act for Church Liberties," adopted by the Maryland Assembly in 1639. It read that churches in the colony would have all their "rights, liberties, and immunities, safe, whole, and inviolable in all things." Many historians have suggested that, in this matter, the Maryland Assembly acted without Calvert's lead. Some have even suggested that, in doing so, the legislators were siding with the Jesuits in their attempt to gain preferments denied them by the proprietor. If that was the case, however, the act was easily circumscribed, and, judging by the legislation that followed, the Jesuits gained little from it.

Why Calvert deemed the Toleration Act of 1649 necessary is the subject of some debate. Calvert explained that historically the use of force over conscience in matters of religion had proved to be of "dangerous consequence" and that he offered the measure in order to preserve "mutual love and amity" among the colony's inhabitants. Historians such as John Krugler, however, have argued that the act was, in fact, a tacit admission that Calvert's policy before 1649 had failed. Calvert may have thought that the few measures he had taken were sufficient and that he could continue to avoid scrutiny in England by avoiding any other legal enactments. But in the face of his failure to attract any significant numbers of Catholic landowners, and as the proportion of Protestants—significantly augmented by a recently arrived group of Puritans from Virginia who were hostile to his policy of toleration for Catholics—increased, and in view of the growing hostility between the Puritan Parliament and Charles I in England, and when the appointment of a Protestant governor in 1648 failed to placate the governor's coreligionists, Calvert concluded that a more definitive measure was needed.

Along these lines, historians have argued that the Maryland Toleration Act added nothing new to, or that it was less liberal than, the policy it replaced and that its contrastingly liberal and conservative provisions constituted a compromise whereby Catholics secured toleration and Protestants were placated on all other issues. Some have suggested that Calvert authored the entire act, while others attribute its less liberal provisions to the Maryland legislature. It has been further argued that the act's more orthodox provisions were unworkable, in that, if they had been implemented and a Protestant had been punished—for calling someone a papist, for example—the resulting publicity would have jeopardized the very freedoms Calvert sought to protect in the first place. In fact, no Protestant was ever so charged.

The failure of the Maryland Toleration Act has been attributed to the limits within which colonial Americans understood such freedom. It was, after all, a century in which religious wars and rebellions continued unabated in Europe, and in England attitudes toward Catholics were much the same as they had been since the Reformation. Anglicans and dissenters alike were anti-Catholic. Maryland, unlike any other colony, faced the test of providing religious toleration for a large number of Catholics but had no precedent to guide it.

Some students of the period have suggested that the demise of the Maryland Toleration Act resulted from the Calverts' perception of themselves as absolute lords and of their lands in Maryland as feudal baronies. As Thomas Curry has pointed out, Cecil Calvert sought to achieve toleration for Catholics through fiat rather than persuasion. Opponents seemingly could not help but associate such tendencies with Catholics and with Catholic rule, which they feared was Calvert's objective all along. Not being able to divorce the two, they opposed both.

Others have attributed the failure of Maryland's experiment in religious freedom to the provocative actions of resident Catholics. The Calverts, it is argued, sought to establish a colony in which Catholics could worship freely, but unobtrusively. In his instructions to his brother Leonard, Maryland's first governor, Cecil Calvert specified that Catholics were to "suffer no scandal nor offence to be given to any of the Protestants, whereby any just complaint may hereafter be made, by them, in Virginia or in England." All "acts of Roman Catholic religion" were to be carried out as privately as possible, and all Catholics were "to be silent upon all occasions of discourse concerning matters of religion." The failure of Catholics, especially Jesuits, to heed Calvert's orders led to continued religious and political strife between Catholics and the Protestant majority and between the Calverts and Protestant leaders until both the Toleration Act and the proprietors' governing authority were revoked.

During the Puritan Commonwealth period, Parliament created a commission that sought to establish its authority over the colonies. Between 1652 and 1655 the commission and the governor of Maryland struggled for control of the colony. In 1654 the Maryland Assembly, which was already Puritan-controlled, repealed the Toleration Act and specifically excluded Roman Catholics from any protection under the law. The next year, the governor capitulated, and the commission and the colony's Puritan residents seized total control. Unexpectedly, however, Oliver Cromwell came to the support of the proprietor. In 1657 Cecil Calvert regained control of the colony and, in the following year, the Toleration Act of 1649 was restored.

The Glorious Revolution of 1688 precipitated the final threat to the Toleration Act. A delay on the part of the colony in recognizing the new king and queen, and the seeming reluctance on the part of the proprietor to force the matter, raised suspicions in certain quarters that the Calverts were Jacobites; there were even rumors of Indian-Catholic plots to overthrow British rule of the colony. In July 1689 the Protestant Association seized control of the government. King William sided with the rebels and revoked the Calverts' governing authority, although they kept their rights as proprietors of the land.

In 1692 the new governor of Maryland administered the English test oaths and oaths of office to all officeholders. Catholics could not comply. Although instructed to permit "a liberty of conscience" for all residents, the governor was also ordered to establish the Church of England, which after several false starts was accomplished in 1702. That act of the Maryland legislature extended the English Act of Toleration to the colony, but it also excluded Catholics from public office. In 1718 the legislature disfranchised Catholics altogether. In 1704 the legislature prohibited Catholic worship and forbade priests to make converts or to baptize the children of any but Catholic parents, but the act was later modified to allow

Catholic worship in private homes.

Bryan LeBeau

Bibliography

Curry, Thomas J., *The First Freedoms: Church and State in America to the Passage of the First Amendment* (New York: Oxford University Press, 1986).

Everstine, Carl N., "Maryland's Toleration Act: An Appraisal," 79 *Maryland Historical Magazine* 99–116 (1984).

Hanley, Thomas O'Brien, *Their Rights and Liberties: The Beginnings of Religious and Political Freedom in Maryland* (Westminster, Md.: Newman, 1959).

Krugler, John D., "Lord Baltimore, Roman Catholics, and Toleration: Religious Policy in Maryland during the Early Catholic Years, 1634–1649." 65 *Catholic Historical Review* 49–75 (1979).

———, "'With Promise of Liberty in Religion': The Catholic Lords Baltimore and Toleration in Seventeenth-Century Maryland, 1634–1692." 79 *Maryland Historical Magazine* 21–43 (1984).

Lasson, Kenneth, "Free Exercise in the Free State: Maryland's Role in Religious Liberty and the First Amendment," 31 *Journal of Church and State* 419–449 (1989).

Levy, Leonard W., "Maryland Toleration Act," *Encyclopedia of the American Constitution,* ed. Leonard W. Levy, 4 vols. (New York: Macmillan, 1986) vol. 3, p. 1222.

Mason, George

In the spring of 1776 the colony of Virginia, having declared its independence from Great Britain, began the process of establishing a government for the new state. A convention, meeting in Williamsburg, appointed a committee to draw up a constitution to be preceded by a statement of the rights of the individual. Although George Mason of Gunston Hall assumed a leadership role in preparing both documents, his fame rests on his draft of the Virginia Declaration of Rights, which found general acceptance in the convention. In his proposed declaration Mason called for recognition of the sanctity of life, liberty, and property; for the necessity of legal protections in court cases; for the denial of any hereditary right to officeholding; and for the separation of powers among branches of government. He wrote:

> That as Religion, or the Duty which we owe to our divine and omnipotent Creator, and the Manner of discharging it, can be governed only by Reason and Conviction, not by Force or Violence; and therefore that all Men shou'd enjoy the fullest toleration in the Exercise of Religion, according to the Dictates of Conscience, unpunished and unrestrained by the Magistrate, unless, under Colour of Religion, any Man disturb the Peace, the Happiness, or Safety of Society or of Individuals.

In a society where the Anglican Church was legally established, Mason's proposal demonstrated both a rational approach to religion and the recognition of a revolutionary change in the relationship of church and state. But James Madison believed that Mason's proposed statement was inadequate, for he feared that toleration left too much power in the hands of public authorities. Therefore, apparently with Mason's approval, Madison substituted a stronger statement of religious freedom:

> That Religion, or the duty which we owe to our Creator, and the manner of discharging it, can be directed only by reason and conviction, not by force or violence; and, therefore, all men are equally entitled to the free exercise of religion, according to the dictates of conscience.

The Virginia Declaration of Rights did not deny the primacy of Christianity. Mason's amended draft, which the convention approved, proclaimed: "It is the mutual duty of all to practise Christian forbearance, love, and charity towards each other." Nor did Mason—a lifelong Anglican and for many years a member of the vestry of his church—intend disestablishment. In his capacity as vestryman, he joined his neighbors in assisting the poor, chastising the sinful, and enforcing the norms of Virginia society as interpreted by the leading members of the community. Nevertheless, the growing strength of Baptist, Presbyterian, and Methodist congregations served to undermine the power and authority of the establishment.

As the War for Independence drew to a close, Americans lamented the decline of morality, a decrease in church attendance, and the disappearance of public virtue so essential for the maintenance of republican government. Patrick Henry responded to these concerns by proposing in 1784 "A Bill Establishing a Provision for Teachers of the Christian Religion," which implicitly replaced the Anglican establishment with state support for all churches. Both Mason and Madison saw in such a statute the potential for government interference in religion. At Mason's urging, Madison wrote and circulated his *Memorial and Remonstrance against Religious Assessments* as a warning against what they saw as "a dangerous abuse of power."

Mason had *Memorial and Remonstrance* printed at his own expense and disseminated it among his friends. He must have been disappointed that neither George Washington nor Richard Henry Lee would sign Madison's *Memorial.* Although Mason had written in the Virginia Declaration of Rights that representative government could not survive without a citizenry that practiced "justice, moderation, temperance, frugality and virtue," he had come to believe that neither enforced religious conformity nor government support of religion could create a virtuous Virginia. Clearly Mason had grown in his understanding of religious freedom and why it was essential for the survival of representative government.

At the same time he never wavered in his insistence on the necessity of protecting the rights of the individual against the power of government. For that reason, at the Philadelphia Convention of 1787 he urged the inclusion of a declaration of rights in the U.S. Constitution, and when he failed in this and other proposals for changes, he refused to sign the completed document. In order to justify his position, he wrote a list of objections that began with the important statement: "There is no Declaration of Rights, and the laws of the general government being paramount to the laws and constitution of the several States, the Declarations of Rights in the separate States are no security." Throughout the country this absence of a bill of rights became the most widely discussed reason for opposition to the new Constitution.

Mason carried the fight to the Virginia ratifying convention in the summer of 1788, insisting, as he had twelve years before, that government could not invade the rights of citizens and that those rights had to be spelled out: "There shall be a Declaration of Rights, asserting and securing from Encroachment the essential and unalienable Rights of the People." In debate he constantly reminded his fellow Virginians that there had to be a "barrier drawn between the government and the rights of the citizens." He proposed that additions to the Constitution should include the statement:

> That Religion, or the Duty which we owe to our Creator, and the Manner of discharging it, can be directed only by Reason and Conviction, not by Force or Violence, and therefore all Men have an equal natural and unalienable Right to the free Exercise of Religion, according to the dictates of Conscience. And that no particular religious Sect or Society of Christians ought to be favoured or established by Law, in Preference to others.

Mason's dogged insistence on a declaration of rights assuredly led Madison to accept its inevitability and to push through the First Congress the amendments that became known as the Bill of Rights.

Mason himself stated his contribution to American history when he said, in the Virginia ratifying convention, "I always fear for the rights of the people." Though he may have had a limited vision of "the people," later generations would use his words and his ideas to expand the concept to today's inclusiveness.

Josephine F. Pacheco

Bibliography

Copeland, Pamela C., and Richard K. MacMaster, *The Five George Masons: Patriots and Planters of Virginia and Maryland* (Charlottesville: University Press of Virginia, 1975).

Miller, Helen Hill, *George Mason; Gentleman Revolutionary* (Chapel Hill: University of North Carolina Press, 1975).

Rutland, Robert A. (ed.), *The Papers of George Mason, 1725–1792,* 3 vols. (Chapel Hill: University of North Carolina Press, 1970).

Massachusetts Body of Liberties (1641)

The Body of Liberties, Massachusetts's first published legal code, was the culmination of an eleven-year battle. In 1630 the settlers framed their government according to the Massachusetts Bay Company's charter, which provided for an elected governor and a council of assistants. Together the governor and assistants composed the General Court, which had both legislative and judicial functions. Key colonial leaders—notably, Governor John Winthrop—contended that a legal code or list of enactments beyond the charter was unnecessary. Instead, they wished to rely on judicial precedent and to allow magistrates wide discretion in deciding individual cases guided by the Bible. Winthrop also feared that, because of the Puritans' distinct social and religious goals, a formal code would necessarily include some laws contrary to English custom in violation of the charter.

The voting citizens, or freemen, remained dissatisfied. They charged that precedents would take too long to accumulate, permitting judges and officials to make arbitrary decisions. They "desired a body of laws," recalled Winthrop, "and thought their condition very unsafe, while so much power rested in the discretion of the magistrates." In 1634 the freemen demanded the right to elect representatives from the towns to the General Court. A year later these "deputies" demanded a body of laws for the colony "in resemblance to a Magna Charta," and the court appointed a committee to frame this new fundament.

The first committee failed to produce a code. A second committee convened in 1636, and one of its members, the Reverend John Cotton, prepared a list of laws called "Moses his Judicialls." Cotton's code provided for a system of local courts, taxation, military training, and the regulation of economic life—all supported by references to scripture. It identified fifty capital crimes, including moral lapses such as adultery. More controversially, Cotton proposed that the assistants, once elected, enjoy a life tenure on the General Court. "Judicialls" influenced the framers of New Haven's legal code, the "Fundamentals," but the Massachusetts deputies rejected it.

In 1638 the General Court created yet another committee, composed of Governor Winthrop and his key advisers (who still opposed the notion of a legal code) as well as Richard Bellingham and other deputies and ministers (who advocated a code). The divided committee turned the matter over to Nathaniel Ward of Ipswich, a former minister and Massachusetts Bay Company organizer. Ward had practiced law for ten years in London, honing his legal skills in the common-law courts. In 1639 he submitted a drafted code to the General Court. After presenting it first to the towns and church elders for revision and approval, Massachusetts adopted Ward's Body of Liberties in November 1641.

Ward drew in part on "Moses his Judicialls," declaring that "no custom or prescription shall ever prevaile amongst us . . . that can be proved to be morallie sinfull by the word of God." But ultimately he crafted not a compilation of Deuteronomic statutes but a bill of rights and a frame of government—a distinct document grounded in the common-law and the inhabitants' "sollemne consent."

The preamble and ninety-eight provisions of the Body of Liberties established the "liberties Immunities and privileges" of men, women, children, servants, foreigners, and even "the Bruite Creature" in Massachusetts Bay. Ward's list of "freedomes" included common-law traditions like the right of petition; the right to due process and trial by jury; the protection of persons and property against unjust arrest, distraint, or seizure; and prohibitions against self-incrimination and double jeopardy. "Strangers," the "unfree," and even those inhabitants under church censure enjoyed these privileges.

The Body of Liberties departed from English practice on several significant fronts. Articles 18 through 37 simplified judicial procedures, outlined defendants' rights and rules of evidence, and penalized frivolous lawsuits. The code forbade "Barbarous" punishments and limited physical correction to "forty stripes"—fewer than the common law permitted. Unlike English law, it protected married women against "bodilie correction or stripes by her husband." The list of "Capitall Laws"—apostasy, witchcraft, blasphemy, murder, sodomy, man-stealing, perjury, bestiality, adultery, and treason—followed John Cotton in citing the Bible rather than the common law in support of its provisions. But in this area, religious law offered a more humane alternative; although the Body of Liberties assigned the death penalty to sexual misdeeds that received lesser punishments in England, its list of twelve capital crimes remained far shorter than the mother country's, which recognized fifty crimes as capital in 1641—a number that doubled in the eighteenth century.

Articles 9 through 17 introduced a number of innovations regarding economic life. They prohibited feudal dues and eliminated courts of Wards and Liveries, confirming the inhabitants' freehold land tenure and corresponding right to alienate or assign their property to others. Article 9 outlawed monopolies—a measure that had long been part of the Puritans' parliamentary agenda in England.

In addition to privileges that all inhabitants shared, the Body of Liberties defined the specific rights of freemen and the framework of the "Civill State." It confirmed the right of freemen to elect annually the governor and all representatives to the General Court. The code also recognized the town as a unit of government, enjoining freemen to select "fitt men" to administer local affairs and to enact measures not in conflict with the laws of the colony. Article 95 established the "Liberties [of] . . . the Churches." Ward, who later published a tract decrying religious toleration, was unequivocal on this point: The Body of Liberties empowered the civil state to establish and advance the Congregational Way.

The final provision of the Body of Liberties called on the General Court to reevaluate the code within three years. This process began in 1644, and after considerable delay the magistrates published a revised code, the Laws and Liberties, in 1648. Connecticut modeled its 1650 code on this version, absorbing some passages verbatim. The Laws and Liberties retained the substance of Ward's document but appended additional materials, including a compilation of statutes, three new capital crimes, and provisions regarding the economy and education. It was revised and reprinted in 1660 and again in 1672.

Margaret E. Newell

Bibliography

Chapin, Bradley, *Criminal Justice in Colonial America, 1606–1660* (Athens: University of Georgia Press).

Gray, F. C., "Remarks on the Early Laws of Massachusetts Bay," Massachusetts Historical Society *Collections,* 3rd ser., VIII (Boston, 1838): 191–237 (includes a reprint of the Body of Liberties).

Morgan, Edmund, *The Puritan Dilemma* (Boston: Little, Brown, 1958).

Morison, Samuel Eliot, *Builders of the Bay Colony* (Boston: Publisher, 1930).

McCollum v. Board of Education 333 U.S. 203 (1948)

Religious instruction is considered by many parents to be an integral part of a child's educational development. The belief that this instruction belonged outside the doors of the public school resulted in the development of released-time programs. The first programs "released" children from school to attend religion classes in their own churches. No instruction took place on school grounds, and the school released the children only during times they would otherwise be enjoying recess, so as not to disturb their public school instruction. The Supreme Court addressed the constitutionality of a variation on this traditional released-time program in *People of State of Illinois ex rel. McCollum v. Board of Education* (1948). Applying the First Amendment, Justice Hugo Black, speaking for the Court, struck down the Illinois school district's program as a violation of the "establishment of religion."

McCollum marked the first time that the Court applied the Establishment Clause of the First Amendment to strike down state action. The case involved a program that provided religious instruction on public school premises during regular school hours. The program began in 1940, when volunteers of Jewish, Catholic, and several Protestant faiths formed an association called the Champaign Council on Religious Education. Members of this organization obtained permission from the board of education to teach religious classes to students in grades 4 through 9. If parents signed a card stating that they wanted their children to receive religious instruction, the children were excused from their secular classes for periods of thirty to forty-five minutes a week. The school allowed the religious instruction to take place in separate classrooms within the public school building. Children who did not participate in the religious instruction continued their secular work during this time.

Although the school district did not pay the religious teachers, they were supervised by the superintendent of schools. The superintendent judged the competency of the instructors and determined whether there were enough students of a particular sect to justify a class in that religion. In addition, the school maintained attendance records of the religious classes in the same manner it did for its secular classes. Finally, the school provided the physical setting for these classes—in public school buildings.

The petitioner, Vashti McCollum, an atheist, was the parent of a child attending a public school in this district. She brought suit, claiming that the release-time program violated the First and Fourteenth Amendments and asking the court to prohibit all religion instruction in public schools. The Circuit Court for Champaign County denied her petition for a writ of mandamus to compel the school district to cease providing religious education at taxpayers' expense and on public property. The Supreme Court of Illinois affirmed this ruling. In her appeal to the U.S. Supreme Court, McCollum was supported by amicus briefs from the American Civil Liberties Union, the American Ethical Cultural Union, the Joint Conference Committee on Public Relations of Several Baptist Conventions, the Synagogue Council of America, and the General Conference of Seventh-Day Adventists. The U.S. Supreme Court reversed, holding that the school system's incorporation of religious instruction into the school day constituted an impermissible action under the Establishment Clause.

Only one year earlier, in *Everson v. Board of Education* (1947), the Court had held that the Fourteenth Amendment incorporated the Establishment Clause, making it applicable to the states. The *Everson* Court, quoting Thomas Jefferson, found that the Establishment Clause was intended to erect "a wall of separation between Church and State." As a result, the Court held that "[n]o tax in any amount, large or small, can be levied to support any religious activities or institutions, whatever they may be called, or whatever form they may adopt to teach or practice religion." The *McCollum* Court applied this reasoning to determine that the use of tax-funded public school property to disseminate religious instruction violated the Establishment Clause doctrine of strict separatism. In addition, the Court found that the state gave impermissible aid to the religious groups by helping "to provide pupils for their religious classes through the use of the state's compulsory public school machinery." Although the Court criticized the extent of integration between the schools and the religious instructors, it failed to articulate the specific components of the Champaign program that it found unconstitutional.

Justice Felix Frankfurter, in a concurring opinion, felt that a discussion of the prohibition against "commingling of sectarian with secular instruction in the public schools" was necessary to understand the Court's decision. Frankfurter found that separatism in education was a concept accepted throughout the nation by 1875. History demonstrated, therefore, that the separation of religious instruction from the public schools came long before the Fourteenth Amendment subjected the states to the limitations of the First Amendment. Frankfurter concluded that the states had accepted the reasoning of the Framers of the U.S. Constitution, who had inserted this policy of separatism into the Constitution to accommodate "a people as religiously heterogeneous as ours." Even though most agreed that religious instruction belonged outside the public schools, religious people insisted on sectarian education for their children. One result was the development of released-time programs.

Although thousands of communities operated released-time programs, Frankfurter's opinion reached the Champaign program only. He recognized that judicial scrutiny was necessary only when the involvement of the public school became too great. Analyzing the close relationship between the school and the classes in this case, he found that the religious instruction was woven inextricably into the school. Frankfurter argued that this closely integrated program gave the religion classes an aura of authoritative acceptance, placing unconstitutional pressure on children to attend. In addition, because not all sects could be represented in the supplemental religion classes, he found that some children would feel alienated, a consequence that the Establishment Clause forbids in its policy of separation. Finding that "[i]n no activity of the State is it more vital to keep out divisive forces than in its schools," Frankfurter concluded that separatism was the best policy both for the state and for religion.

Justice Jackson, while joining Frankfurter's concurrence, also wrote a separate concurrence criticizing the failure of the Court to place bounds on its decision. He expressed concern that an elimination of everything people might find contrary to their religious beliefs would result in "leaving public education in shreds." Without a more precise articulation of what constituted a violation of the Establishment Clause, Jackson predicted that "the legal 'wall of separation between church and state'" would develop into a wall "as winding as the famous serpentine wall designed by Mr. Jefferson for the University he founded."

Justice Reed filed the sole dissent in the *McCollum* decision. Like Justice Jackson, he criticized the Court for its failure to articulate what made the Champaign plan unconstitutional. Reed interpreted the majority's opinions as prohibiting any religious instruction of public school children during school hours, regardless of whether the classes took place on or off the school grounds. He disagreed with the conclusion that releasing children from their secular work on a strictly voluntary basis constituted an aid to religion. Justice Reed thought that "aid to religion" should be defined only "as a purposeful assistance" to a religious organization "of such a character that it may fairly be said to be performing ecclesiastical functions."

Reed felt that history and tradition demonstrated that a close association between church and state did not mandate a violation of the Establishment Clause. He cited examples of past Court decisions upholding such associations. In *Everson* the Court allowed publicly funded transportation for parochial school students. In *Cochran v. Louisiana State Board of Education* (1930) the Court upheld a statute providing free textbooks to both public and private schools. Reed also noted that all churches receive "aid" from the government through their exemptions from taxation. On the basis of these past relationships between church and state, Reed concluded that a voluntary release program in which the teachers were paid for and provided by a separate religious organization did not constitute an aid to religion under the Establishment Clause.

The importance of *McCollum* lies in the end result—it was the first time the Court applied the Establishment Clause to invalidate state action. Nevertheless, the concerns of Justices Jackson and Reed proved prophetic. The Court in *McCollum* held that the Establishment Clause erected a wall between church and state, prohibiting the state from doing anything that would "aid" religion. The Court, however, failed to adequately define which actions created a break in this wall. Instead, it deferred the question of what constituted impermissible aid to later decisions.

Laurilyn A. Goettsch

Bibliography

"Religion and the State," 14 *Law & Contemporary Problems* 1–159 (1949).

Swancara, Frank, *The Separation of Religion and Government: The First Amendment, Madison's Intent, and the McCollum Decision* (New York: The Truth Seeker Co., 1950).

Note, "Tracing the 'Wall': Religion in the Public School System," 57 *Yale Law Journal* 1114–1122 (1948).

Cases Cited

Cochran v. Louisiana State Board of Education, 281 U.S. 370 (1930).

Everson v. Board of Education, 330 U.S. 1 (1947).

People of State of Illinois ex rel. McCollum v. Board of Education, 333 U.S. 203 (1948).

McDaniel v. Paty

See TORCASO V. WATKINS.

Meek v. Pittenger
421 U.S. 349 (1975)

Meek v. Pittenger (1975) examined whether a state law providing assistance to nonpublic, church-related, elementary and secondary schools was constitutional under the Establishment Clause of the First Amendment. The statute in question authorized the Commonwealth of Pennsylvania to provide what it called "auxiliary services" to all children enrolled in nonpublic elementary and secondary schools meeting Pennsylvania's compulsory attendance requirements. "Auxiliary services" included counseling, testing, and psychological services; speech and hearing therapy; and teaching and related services for exceptional children, remedial students, and the educationally disadvantaged. In addition, the statute defined auxiliary services as "such other secular, neutral, nonideological services as are of benefit to nonpublic school children and are presently or hereafter provided for public school children of the Commonwealth." Other parts of the statute in question authorized the state's secretary of education to lend textbooks without charge to children attending nonpublic elementary and secondary schools and to lend directly to the nonpublic schools other instructional materials and equipment that were useful to the education of nonpublic school children. The statute was challenged as violative of the Establishment Clause by several plaintiff individuals and organizations.

In an opinion written by Justice Potter Stewart, the Court held that all but the textbook loan provisions of the statutes in question violated the Establishment Clause. Justice Stewart cited the test developed by the Court in *Lemon v. Kurtzman* (1971) to determine whether there had been a constitutional violation. The three-pronged *Lemon* test to be applied to the statute was (1), that the statute must have a secular legislative purpose, (2) that it must have a "primary effect" that neither advances nor inhibits religion, and (3) that the statute and its administration must avoid excessive government entanglement with religion.

The Court had previously upheld a New York textbook loan program in *Board of Education v. Allen* (1968), and the Court found that the textbook loan provisions of the Pennsylvania statute were similarly unproblematic. The Court distinguished the loan of instructional material and equipment, however, on several bases. Although textbooks are lent only to students, the Pennsylvania statute authorized the loan of instructional material and equipment directly to qualifying nonpublic elementary and secondary schools.

In analyzing the loan of instructional material and equipment, the Court first found that the statute had a legitimate secular legislative purpose in that it ensured that present and future generations of schoolchildren would have an opportunity to develop their intellectual capacities. The Court found the statute constitutionally defective, however, in that the direct loan of instructional material and equipment had the primary effect of advancing religion because of the predominantly religious character of the schools benefiting from the act. The only requirement imposed on nonpublic schools to qualify for loans of instructional material and equipment was that they satisfy the Commonwealth's compulsory attendance law by providing, in the English language, the subjects and activities prescribed by the standards of the state board of education. Of the 1,320 nonpublic schools in Pennsylvania that met the requirements of the compulsory attendance law and thus qualified for aid under the statute, more than 75 percent were church-related or religiously affiliated educational institutions. Thus, the Court found that the primary beneficiaries of the statute's instructional material and equipment loan provisions were nonpublic schools with a predominant sectarian character, like the beneficiaries of the "secular educational services" reimbursement program considered in *Lemon* and the tuition reimbursement plan considered in *Sloan v. Lemon* (1973).

The Court also stated that, as part of general legislation made available to all students, a state may include church-related schools in programs providing bus transportation, school lunches, and public health facilities—secular and nonideological services unrelated to the primary, religion-oriented educational function of the sectarian school. The indirect and incidental benefits to church-related schools from those programs do not offend the constitutional prohibition against establishment, but the aid that was provided to the church-related nonpublic schools of Pennsylvania by the statute in question was "massive" and "neither indirect or incidental." The Court stated that it would simply ignore reality to attempt to separate secular educational functions from the predominantly religious role performed by many of the state's church-related elementary and secondary schools "Even though earmarked for secular purposes," the Court wrote, "when it flows to an institution in which religion is so pervasive that a substantial portion of its functions are subsumed in the religious mission, state aid has the impermissible primary effect of advancing religion."

With regard to the auxiliary services authorized to be provided by the statute, the Court rejected the view that one could rely entirely on the good faith and professionalism of the secular teachers and counselors functioning in church-related schools to ensure that a strictly nonideological posture was maintained. The Court found that these provisions of the statute could create serious administrative as well as political entanglement. Ensuring that teachers played a strictly nonideological role would necessarily give rise to a constitutionally intolerable degree of administrative entanglement between church and state. Particular features of the Pennsylvania statute—such as special provisions for remedial and exceptional students only—were held not to distinguish the legislation from other programs the Court had struck down. The fact that the teachers and counselors who provided auxiliary services were employees of the public school unit did not eliminate the need for continuing surveillance. And thus, although the potential for impermissible fostering of religion under the circumstances was reduced, it was still present because the state would have to impose limitations on the activities of the auxiliary personnel and then engage in some form of continuing surveillance to ensure that the limitations were being followed and enforced. Finally, the recurrent nature of the appropriation process and the prospect of repeated confrontation between proponents and opponents of the program provided successive opportunities for political fragmentation and division along religious lines. This potential for political entanglement was one of the principal evils against which the Establishment Clause was intended to protect.

Justice William Brennan, joined by Justices William Douglas and Thurgood Marshall, concurred in part and dissented from the parts of the opinion upholding the textbook loan provisions. Justice Brennan wrote that the approval of New York's textbook loan program was not the appropriate precedent for this case, because *Allen* had been decided before the Court recognized the factor of political divisiveness in the *Lemon* decision. Application of that factor would lead to a different result in the Pennsylvania case. Moreover, Justice Brennan wrote that it was fantasy to treat the textbook program as a loan to students rather than to schools.

Although Justices William Rehnquist and Byron White voted to uphold the textbook loan program as constitutionally indistinguishable from the program upheld in *Allen,* they took issue with the majority's use of the primary effect test, which they felt posed problems of arbitrariness in focusing unduly on the percentage of religious schools that benefited. "If the number of sectarian schools were measured as a percentage of all schools, public and private, then no doubt the majority would conclude that the primary effect of the instructional materials and equipment program is not to advance religion." Justice Rehnquist also took issue with the Court's position that entanglement would occur.

Meek was later cited favorably in *Roemer v. Board of Public Works of Maryland* (1976), *Wolman v. Walter* (1977), and *Committee for Public Education and Religious Liberty v. Regan, Comptroller of New York* (1980). In *Roemer* a Maryland statute that authorized paying state funds to any private institutions of higher learning which refrained from awarding "only seminarian or theological degrees" and required that the funds be used only for sectarian purposes was upheld as not involving excessive entanglement. In *Wolman* an Ohio statute authorized various forms of aid to nonpublic schools, most of which were sectarian; the Court again distinguished among different forms of aid authorized by the statute. In *Regan* the Court upheld a New York statute that directed payment to nonpublic schools for the costs they incurred in complying with certain state-mandated requirements, including the testing of pupils, reporting, and recordkeeping. The Court reasoned that the statute did not violate the Establishment Clause because its principal purpose was neither to advance nor inhibit religion but to prepare New York citizens for adult life, which was a legitimate state interest.

A recent case on the subject was *Zobrest v. Catalina Foothills School District* (1993), which has generated an enormous literature. In a 5-to-4 decision the Court ruled that the Establishment Clause does not preclude the public financing of a sign language interpreter at a sectarian school for a student who has a profound hearing impairment. The Court ruled that the fact that a public employee will be physically present in a sectarian school does not by itself make this the same type of aid that was disapproved in *Meek* and in *School District of Grand Rapids v. Ball* (1985). In those cases, the challenged programs gave direct grants of government aid—instructional equipment and material, teachers, and guidance counselors—which relieved sectarian schools of costs they otherwise would have borne in educating their students. In *Zobrest* the Court said that the child is the primary beneficiary and that the school receives only an incidental benefit. In addition, an interpreter—unlike a teacher or a guidance counselor—neither adds to nor subtracts from the sectarian school's environment but merely interprets whatever material is presented to the class as a whole. Thus there appears to be no absolute bar to the placing of a public employee in a sectarian school.

Lea Vander Velde

Bibliography

Lee, Rex E., "The Religion Clauses: Problems and Prospects," 1986 *Brigham Young University Law Review* 337–347 (1986).

Cases Cited

Board of Education v. Allen, 392 U.S. 236 (1968).
Committee for Public Education and Religious Liberty v. Regan, Comptroller of New York, 444 U.S. 646 (1980).
Lemon v. Kurtzman, 403 U.S. 602 (1971).
Meek v. Pittenger, 421 U.S. 349 (1975).
Roemer v. Board of Public Works of Maryland, 426 U.S. 736 (1976).
School District of the city of Grand Rapids v. Ball, 473 U.S. 373 (1985).
Sloan v. Lemon, 413 U.S. 825 (1973).
Wolman v. Walter, 433 U.S. 229 (1977).
Zobrest v. Catalina Foothills School District, 509 U.S. 1 (1993).

Memorial and Remonstrance against Religious Assessments (1785)

During the 1784 session of the Virginia General Assembly, Patrick Henry introduced "A Bill Establishing a Provision for Teachers of the Christian Religion." Without the state's support, the old Episcopal establishment was in precipitous decline. Many Virginians sensed a rising tide of immorality and vice, and an assessment that would free each individual to designate which church would get his taxes seemed to many an appropriate and equitable response. Opponents barely managed to postpone a final reading of the bill, insisting that a measure so important should not pass until the legislators could assess the sentiments of voters. In the spring of 1785 the brothers George and Wilson Carey Nicholas appealed to James Madison, the legislative leader of the opposition, to prepare a form for a petition to be circulated between assembly sessions as an instrument for shaping and expressing popular opinion.

Madison's anonymous *Memorial and Remonstrance against Religious Assessments* was more eclectic than inventive. It was an effort to arouse both evangelicals and skeptics, to appeal to those concerned about the purity of faith as well as to republicans who wanted to protect the state from religious passions and bigots. In the manner of John Locke, it opened by insisting that religious liberty was fundamentally "unalienable" by nature. Since opinion cannot be coerced, Madison insisted, it is the natural right of every individual "to render to the Creator such homage and such only as he believes to be acceptable to Him. This duty is precedent both in order of time and in degree of obligation to the claims of civil society. . . . And . . . every man who becomes a member of any particular civil society [does] it with a saving of his allegiance to the Universal Sovereign." "In matters of religion," Madison maintained, "no man's right is abridged by the institution of civil society, and . . . religion is wholly exempt from its cognizance."

As was often true, Madison carried the contractual philosophy to rigorous extremes, permitting none of the exceptions that Locke himself had made to his original insistence on the separate spheres of church and state. No one should be tempted, Madison believed, to see a bill that provided equal treatment for every Christian sect as a valid compromise between the rights of conscience and the interests of the state. "Who does not see that the same authority which can establish Christianity, in exclusion of all other religions, may establish with the same ease any particular sect of Christians in exclusion of all other sects? That the same authority which can force a citizen to contribute three pence only of his property . . . may force him to conform to any . . . establishment in all cases whatsoever?" Even nonbelievers were entitled to protection. If liberty of conscience were abused, Madison submitted that this would constitute "an offense against God, not against man: To God, therefore, not to man, must an account of it be rendered."

What theory taught, experience confirmed, and Madison moved neatly to a series of historical and practical objections. He argued, first, that Christianity did not require state aid, that it had prospered best and had attained its greatest purity "prior to its incorporation with civil policy," when its teachers had "depended on the voluntary rewards of their flocks." What, he asked, had been the fruits of nearly fifteen centuries of state support? "More or less, in all places, pride and indolence in the clergy, ignorance and servility in the laity, in both, superstition, bigotry, and persecution." Neither did the needs of government require establishments or general assessments. On the contrary, "Torrents of blood have been spilt in the old world by vain attempts of the secular arm to extinguish religious discord." Even the most liberal establishment "degrades from the equal ranks of citizens all those whose opinions in religion do not bend to those of the legislative authority. Distant as it may be in its present form from the Inquisition, it differs from it only in degree. The one is the first step, the other the last in the career of intolerance."

Completed by the end of June 1785, the anonymous *Memorial and Remonstrance* was circulated widely through Virginia's counties, obtaining some 1,700 signatures. Thousands of other Virginians signed Baptist or Presbyterian petitions opposing the assessment. When the legislature reassembled, no one tried to resurrect the bill of 1784, and Madison seized the occasion to win enactment of Thomas Jefferson's Statute for Religious Freedom, with which *Memorial and Remonstrance* is often paired by courts in attempting to determine the intentions of the principal framer of the religion clauses of the First Amendment. It has been calculated that Madison's opinions, expressed most fully in this classic, have been cited in at least forty federal and fifty-five state cases concerning church and state. *Memorial and Remonstrance* still stands among the documentary foundations of the libertarian tradition.

Lance Banning

Bibliography

Buckley, Thomas J., *Church and State in Revolutionary Virginia, 1776–1787* (Charlottesville, Va.: University Press of Virginia, 1977).

Hutchinson, William T. (ed.), *The Papers of James Madison,* vol. 8, 295–306 (Chicago and Charlottesville, Va.: University of Chicago Press and University Press of Virginia, 1967).

Peterson, Merrill D., and Robert C. Vaughan (eds.), *The Virginia Statute for Religious Freedom: Its Evolution and Consequences in American History* (Cambridge, Mass.: Harvard University Press, 1988).

Mergens

See BOARD OF EDUCATION V. MERGENS.

Meyer v. Nebraska
262 U.S. 390 (1923)

German American communities throughout the United States were subjected to widespread and sometimes violent hostility during World War I. Nativists and other proponents of so-called 100 percent Americanism particularly objected to the widespread use of the German language, which they alleged engendered subversion and impeded national unity. Government officials in many heavily German areas of the Middle West urged and sometimes ordered churches and parochial schools to abandon the use of the German language. German American clergy and congregations generally acquiesced to such pressure, even though the discontinuation of German in the churches and schools created many hardships and social dislocations.

During the period of social and political unrest that immediately followed Word War I, advocates of assimilation vowed to continue their campaign of "Americanization" of all ethnic groups. A principal result of this campaign was the enactment of more than twenty state statutes that prohibited the teaching of modern foreign languages in public, private, and parochial elementary schools. Although some public educators objected to the laws, the principal opponents of the statutes were Lutheran and Roman Catholic parochial schools. These schools taught foreign languages in order to help children participate in their community's church services and home devotions. Roman Catholics and Lutherans feared that the statutes presaged bolder assaults on parochial schools.

During 1919 and 1920 three teachers at Lutheran parochial schools in Nebraska, Iowa, and Ohio openly defied the laws by teaching German. They were convicted and fined. In 1921 state supreme courts upheld the convictions, and the Nebraska Supreme Court also denied a motion by a Lutheran synod and the father of a student at a Roman Catholic parochial school to enjoin enforcement of Nebraska's law. Opponents of the laws argued that the statutes infringed both property rights and personal rights, including freedom of religion. Rejecting these arguments, the state supreme courts upheld the statutes as valid exercises of the police power. The Nebraska and Iowa courts contended that the statutes did not violate religious liberty, because the doctrines of the churches could be taught in English, and the Ohio court ignored the religious issue. In a dissent joined by two other justices, Chief Justice William D. Evans of Iowa argued that the Iowa law infringed freedom of religion because "free exercise of religion is impossible without the free use . . . of such language as the worshipper may choose. . . . Ability to speak and read a language is essential to intelligent worship. Concededly, the parents had a right to worship in their own language. Necessarily, the children had a constitutional right to worship in the same language."

In its landmark decisions in *Meyer v. Nebraska* (1923) and related Iowa and Ohio cases, the U.S. Supreme Court held that the laws violated the Fourteenth Amendment because they deprived teachers and parents of their liberty without due process of law. Although the Court expressed sympathy with the legislative desire to "foster a homogenous people with American ideals," the Court stated that the statutes exceeded the power of the states because "[m]ere knowledge of the German language cannot reasonably be regarded as harmful."

While the Court explained that it was not necessary "to define with exactness" the liberties that are guaranteed by the Fourteenth Amendment, the Court could state "[w]ithout doubt" that the Fourteenth Amendment

> denotes not merely freedom from bodily restraint but also the right of the individual to contract, to engage in any of the common occupations of life, to acquire useful knowledge, to marry, establish a home and bring up children, to worship God according to the dictates of his own conscience, and, generally to enjoy those privileges long recognized at the common law as essential to the orderly pursuit of happiness by free men.

The Court stated that the Fourteenth Amendment protected the right of teachers to teach foreign languages and the right of parents to engage teachers to offer such instruction. The Court also suggested that the statute unconstitutionally interfered with the right of pupils to acquire knowledge and with the power of parents to control the education of their children. The Court's opinion ignored the religious dimensions of the case except for its dictum about the freedom to worship God. Although opponents of the statute did not emphasize the religious aspects of the case in their arguments before the Supreme Court, private documents make clear that they continued to regard religious freedom as a paramount issue. They regarded the decision as a great victory for religious freedom and correctly foresaw that it would chill a growing movement to require all children to attend public schools. The Supreme Court relied heavily on *Meyer* in its decision in *Pierce v. Society of Sisters* (1925), which struck down Oregon's compulsory public education law.

Justice Oliver Wendell Holmes, Jr., joined by Justice George Sutherland, reluctantly dissented from the Court's opinion, explaining that the statutes were reasonably calculated to facilitate the desirable goal of a common language. Although it may seem ironic that Holmes—known as a great civil libertarian—dissented in the case while the archconservative McReynolds delivered the majority opinion, Holmes's dissent was consistent with his belief in judicial deference to the legislature, and McReynolds's decision was consonant with his occasional judicial activism. Inasmuch as the decision favored conservative and generally law-abiding citizens, it is not necessarily inconsistent with other decisions of the same period in which McReynolds and other conservatives on the Court much more narrowly construed the scope of civil liberties in cases involving political radicals.

Despite the sweeping dicta of the majority opinion, the actual grounds for the Court's decision are enigmatic and have provoked controversy. Since the Court before *Meyer* often had invoked due process to strike down social and economic regulations that were opposed by private businesses, some scholars have seen *Meyer* as another case in which the Court was concerned only about property rights. *Meyer* seems at least partly to have been based on economic rights, since the Court indicated that the statute interfered with the livelihood of language teachers and with the contractual rights of parents. But the broad language of the Court concerning the freedoms that are protected by the Fourteenth Amendment suggests that the Court also believed that the statutes infringed personal liberties. Since the Supreme Court had not yet incorporated into state law any of the specific liberties—including freedom of religion—that are guaranteed by the First Amendment, the Court based its decision on substantive due process rights conferred by the Fourteenth Amendment. By recognizing that the Fourteenth Amendment protects a broad array of personal freedoms, the decision in *Meyer* presaged the process by which the Court later incorporated into state law the guarantees of the Bill of Rights, including the free exercise of religion.

Although many scholars believe that today the *Meyer* case would be decided under the Free Speech Clause of the First Amendment, the religious motivation for teaching German suggests that the Free Exercise Clause would be a more appropriate basis for the decision.

William G. Ross

Bibliography

Finkelman, Paul, "German Victims and American Oppressors: The Cultural Background and Legacy of *Meyer v. Nebraska*," in John R. Wunder, ed., *Law and the Great Plains: Essays on the Legal History of the Heartland* (Westport, Conn.: Greenwood Press, 1996), pp. 33–56.

Hanley, Thomas O'Brien, "A Western Democrat's Quarrel with the Language Laws," 50 *Nebraska History* 151–171 (1969).

Luebke, Frederick C., *Bonds of Loyalty: German Americans and World War I* (DeKalb: Northern Illinois University Press, 1974).

Ross, William G., "A Judicial Janus: *Meyer v. Nebraska* in Historical Perspective," 50 *University of Cincinnati Law Review* 125–204 (1988).

Cases Cited

Meyer v. Nebraska, 262 U.S. 390 (1923).

Pierce v. Society of Sisters, 268 U.S. 510 (1925).

Minnesota v. Hershberger Cases

In the *Minnesota v. Hershberger* cases (Minn., 1989, 1990) the Supreme Court of Minnesota held that a statute which required slow-moving vehicles to display an emblem—as applied in these cases—violated the free exercise rights of the Amish defendants under the First Amendment to the U.S. Constitution. The two *Hershberger* cases document a religious minority's appeal for constitutional guarantees of free exercise of religion in the face of what they consider burdensome government regulation. The ever-changing relation of state constitutions and appellate court decisions to the federal arena is a second and equally important issue addressed by these cases.

In the interest of public safety, Minnesota Statute 169.522 (1988) mandates that the back of slow-moving vehicles on the state's public highways display a reflective orange triangular warning symbol. This same statute authorizes a less gaudy emblem—a dull black triangle with a white reflective border— that can be used after obtaining a permit. In all situations, however, the standard orange triangle must be used between sunset and sunrise, or in inclement weather. Minnesota Rule 7440.350 explains that the permits for the alternative black triangle are for "persons who have sincerely held religious beliefs prohibiting their use of the standard emblem" and who drive horse-drawn vehicles.

These legal exceptions were fashioned for Minnesota's growing Amish population. The fourteen appellants of the *Hershberger* cases are Old Order Amish—ultraorthodox Protestants who retain an outward symbolism of prescribed plain dress and lifestyle to separate their community from the rest of the world and to remain obedient to the Amish church. Although the Amish are perhaps best known for their distinctive dress, they also educate their children in separate schools and refuse to use electricity or to operate motor vehicles. It is not surprising that the Amish, like other separatist religious groups in the United States, have often confronted the law in such areas as compulsory school attendance, conscription, compulsory "welfare" systems (Social Security), and vehicle traffic control.

The horse and buggy, in particular, has symbolized Amish affirmation of a slower-paced worklife and rejection of mechanized farming. It has also embodied the delicate balance between separation from and accommodation to the non-Amish world. By the 1920s state laws began requiring electric lights on the buggies as safety measures, and most Amish acquiesced. By the 1950s these laws preferred the orange triangle. Although this "loud" color offended the Amish sense of modesty, the Amish usually compromised on this issue.

In Minnesota's Fillmore County the Old Order Amish decided to observe the public safety intention of the Minnesota statute. Although they considered the sanctioned alternative antithetical to their faith and modesty, they were willing to outline their buggy backs with silver reflective tape and to carry a lighted red lantern. Nonetheless in 1988 each of the fourteen appellants received a traffic citation for displaying neither of the two sanctioned reflective triangles.

After convictions in the Fillmore County District Court for violation of the statute, the court certified the question of the federal and state constitutionality of the statute's application in this case to Minnesota appellate jurisdiction. In *Hershberger I* the Supreme Court of Minnesota held that the statute as applied violated the Amish defendants' free exercise rights under the First Amendment to the U.S. Constitution. The Minnesota Supreme Court vacated the trial court's order and dismissed charges. The court applied the three recognized factors from *Sherbert v. Verner* (1963) for evaluating a free exercise claim: The appellants' claim was a "sincerely held religious belief"; the Minnesota statute did "burden the exercise of that religious belief"; and although public safety was acknowledged by the court as a "compelling state interest," the burden on the appellants could be lightened by a "less intrusive alternative" such as silver tape and a red lantern. In-terestingly, the court did not address the appellants' claim in light of Article I, Section 16, of the Minnesota Constitution, which is a far stronger affirmative statement than the federal: "The right of every man to worship God according to the dictates of his own conscience shall never be infringed . . . nor shall any control of or interference with the rights of conscience be permitted. . . ."

The State of Minnesota petitioned the U.S. Supreme Court for writ of certiorari, which was granted on April 23, 1990. The Court vacated the judgment and remanded the case to the Supreme Court of Minnesota "for further consideration in light of *Employment Division, Deptartment of Human Resources of Oregon v. Smith*" (1990). In this landmark case about American Indian use of peyote in religious ceremonies, the U.S. Supreme Court abandoned the "compelling state interest" test and decided that a free exercise violation exists only when the state seeks to ban religious acts solely on a religious basis. Furthermore, the right of free exercise does not excuse a person from complying with a law that is valid and "neutral" in any direct application to religious practice. In his *Smith* dissent, Justice Harry Blackmun quoted *Wisconsin v. Yoder* (1972) for the point that "if Oregon can constitutionally prosecute them for this act of worship, they, like the Amish, may be 'forced to migrate to some other and more tolerant region.'" The Supreme Court of Minnesota now took up the unresolved issue of Minnesota state constitutionality, along with the applicability of *Smith*. Chief Justice Peter Popovich delivered the *Hershberger* decision on November 9, 1990. First, he echoed Justice Blackmun's dismay at the High Court's shift in *Smith*. But then he quickly moved to the Minnesota Constitution: "This language is of a distinctively stronger character than the federal counterpart . . . whereas the first amendment establishes a limit on government action at the point of *prohibiting* the exercise of religion, Section 16 precludes even an *infringement* on or an *interference* with religious freedom." Popovich traced Minnesota history in several state cases and concluded: "This court has long recognized that individual liberties under the state constitution may deserve greater protection than those under the broadly worded federal constitution . . . the early settlers of this region were of varied sects, may have endured religious intolerance in their native countries and were thus sensitive to religious differences among them." In a concurring opinion, Associate Justice John E. Simonett invoked the Northwest Ordinance's legacy.

Hershberger I and *II* thus remind us of the important role of state constitutions and courts in free exercise claims. Generally, states must guarantee to their citizens the "minimum" protection of the federal First

Amendment. However, they can still interpret the state's bill of rights independently of the U.S. Supreme Court and, in fact, prevent federal review by relying on separate and independent state grounds. The Supreme Court under Chief Justice Earl Warren in the 1950s and 1960s applied the federal Bill of Rights, not state constitutions, to civil liberties cases, with the effect that many people still perceive state constitutions to be inferior to the federal document in that area. But in the 1970s the Burger Court ushered in a more ambivalent interpretation of free exercise and related guarantees. States such as California began to regard their own constitutions as better protection for civil liberties.

Some scholars believe that in *Hershberger* the Supreme Court of Minnesota should have resolved the state claim first, not the federal. Then the decision would have had more impact; as it now stands, by vacating *Hershberger I* the U.S. Supreme Court effectively removed any precedential force from the Minnesota opinion. Also, while the Rehnquist Court is radically reinterpreting the Free Exercise Clause, states can avoid federal review and not become dependent on such U.S. Supreme Court decisions as *Smith*.

Barbara M. Jones

Bibliography

DeMeules, Rita C., "Minnesota's Variable Approach to State Constitutional Claims," 17 *William Mitchell Law Review* 163–198 (1991).

Hostetler, John A., "Government and the Amish," in *Amish Society*, 3rd ed. (Baltimore: Johns Hopkins University Press, 1980).

Kraybill, Donald B., *The Riddle of Amish Culture* (Baltimore: Johns Hopkins University Press, 1989).

Vogel, Howard J., "Minnesota's Forgotten Bill of Rights," 19 *Roots* 26–31 (1990).

Cases Cited

Employment Division, Department of Human Resources of Oregon v. Smith, 494 U.S. 872 (1990).

Minnesota v. Hershberger, 444 N.W. 2d 282 (Minn. 1989), *Hershberger I*.

Minnesota v. Hershberger, 495 U.S. 901 (1990).

Minnesota v. Hershberger, 462 N.W. 2d 393 (Minn. 1990) *Hershberger II*.

Sherbert v. Verner, 374 U.S. 398 (1963).

Wisconsin v. Yoder, 406 U.S. 205 (1972).

Minor

See BOARD OF EDUCATION V. MINOR.

Mormon Courts and the Civil Laws

The Mormons in the nineteenth century were devoted to Zion: They believed in a perfected community of "saints" organized in economic, political, and social affairs under priesthood direction and control and unified by love of God rather than by civil laws. For Mormons, vexatious lawsuits that were premised on "gentile" claims threatened the priority of the religious vision. Consequently, the Mormons in the nineteenth century established ecclesiastical courts that had jurisdictional priority among the saints over conflict resolution.

Priesthood leaders ensured the priority of the ecclesiastical courts by publicly condemning members for suing other saints "before the ungodly." This condemnation was not purely advisory. Indeed, a member who refused to dismiss a civil action in a gentile court in favor of ecclesiastical adjudication could be excommunicated for "un-Christian-like" conduct. Priesthood leaders established and maintained alternative real and personal property ownership rules, principles of family relationships, and tort and contract norms—all through the auspices of the Mormon ecclesiastical courts.

Perhaps the most radical substitution of ecclesiastical law for civil law was exhibited in the area of land acquisition. The Mormons arrived in the Great Basin in 1847, but the federal government did not extend its land laws to the Great Basin until 1869. Between 1847 and 1869 Mormon settlers could not obtain legal title to the lands they had settled. They were, in effect, squatters on the public domain. Nonetheless, under the leadership of Brigham Young the Mormons established a pattern of settlement that clustered the farmers into villages with their farms on the outskirts of the community. Priesthood leaders allocated each farmer a village lot for his residence and a farming lot of approximately 14 acres in a large field outside the village. Priesthood officials recorded these priesthood-directed and beneficial-use-oriented allocations for purposes of priority claims on disputed land. Two decades later, when the federal government first extended the federal preemption and homestead laws to the Great Basin, legal conflicts appeared inevitable because the federal acts provided for alternative methods of acquiring 160-acre parcels of land and required proof of residence on the land that was claimed and cultivated.

The Mormons overcame the initial entitlement claims to land through "priesthood intervention," reinforced by the church courts. Local priesthood leaders appointed "trustees" who would secure patents in compliance with federal land laws. Subsequently, these trustees would transfer portions of their legally acquired lands to claimants with church-recognized titles. In the event of conflict, the church courts would adjudicate title and boundary disputes. Bishop's courts would hear initial claims. If the parties were unsatisfied, they could appeal their stake claims to high-council courts. The final appeal rested in the hands of the first (highest) presidency of the church.

Priesthood directives, reinforced by the church courts, also resolved potential legal controversies involving resources, including water disputes. The common-law doctrine of riparian rights treated water law as incidental to the law of real property. Proprietors of land that adjoined streams had the "natural" right to use water in its natural flow, subject only to the correlative right of other riparians to coequal use. This right required no affirmative action by the property owner to legitimize use. The doctrine of riparian rights, however, made no sense in the desert regions of the Great Basin, where farming efforts depended on communal irrigation projects. Thus, on entering the Salt Lake Valley, Brigham Young announced that there would be no private ownership of the streams that come out of the canyons, nor of the timber that grows on the hills. Under his leadership church high councils directed the communal construction of canals and ditches to carry water from canyon rivers and streams to the various communities in the valleys. Again the principle of beneficial use controlled the allocation of water conveyed through the irrigation system. The church courts maintained exclusive jurisdiction over conflict resolution of water rights created under this system.

The ecclesiastical courts similarly provided exclusive jurisdiction over Mormons' domestic disputes. The jurisdiction of the church courts over family matters was essential for a variety of reasons. First, the fact that Mormons in the nineteenth century practiced polygamy made it impossible for polygamous families to receive adequate assistance in the civil courts, where polygamous marriages were illegal and therefore unrecognized. Thus a polygamous spouse who wanted a divorce had no available civil forum. Second, Mormons taught that temple marriages which were sealed by proper priesthood authority committed the spouses to the marriage for all time and eternity. Only a proper priesthood cancellation could effect a divorce. The civil court's traditional authority over divorce actions, therefore, was ineffectual for Mormon temple marriages. Third, Mormon leaders stressed reconciliation as the ideal solution to domestic disputes. The church courts allowed the priesthood leaders to counsel the spouses and to require patience and forgiveness where appropriate. A member could be excommunicated for bypassing the church court system and divorcing a spouse civilly. On the other hand, the parties were allowed to formalize ecclesiastical divorces in the civil courts—usually, the probate courts—to avoid subsequent polygamy prosecutions.

The Mormons deferred to their church courts for contract and tort disputes as well. In these areas the church courts refused to consider any claim to common-law-based rights but, rather, considered the equitable resolution of the issue to be as dictated by the priesthood leader's inspiration. Through invocation of theological principles in mundane commercial and social matters, the church reinforced the priority given to God's commands.

As the vision for building Zion here and now faded in the latter part of the nineteenth century under the weight of the federal assault on polygamy and the distinctive institutions of the church, the role of the ecclesiastical courts over temporal matters receded into the historical past. For a time, however, the Mormon church court system represented a remarkable system of alternate dispute resolution premised on communal values in furtherance of the holy commonwealth.

Richard Collin Mangrum

Bibliography

Firmage, Edwin, and Richard Collin Mangrum, *Zion in the Courts: A Legal*

History of the Church of Jesus Christ of Latter-Day Saints, 1830–1900 (Urbana: University of Illinois Press, 1988).

Leone, Mark, *Roots of Modern Mormonism* (Cambridge, Mass.: Harvard University Press, 1979).

Swenson, Raymond, "Resolution of Civil Disputes by Mormon Ecclesiastical Courts," 1978 *Utah Law Review* 573–595 (1978).

Mormon Free Exercise in Nineteenth-Century America

The history of the Mormons, the members of the Church of Jesus Christ of Latter-Day Saints, began in New York in the 1830s. Because of their belief in prophetic leadership, a theocratic social structure, and communal economics, the Mormons quickly came into conflict with their neighbors and were driven from New York to Ohio to Missouri to Nauvoo, Illinois; this saga culminated in the murder of Joseph Smith, the founder of Mormonism, and his brother Hyrum in 1844 at Carthage, Illinois. The Mormon exodus to the Great Basin of the American West followed, under the direction of Brigham Young, one of this nation's leading colonizers.

The choice of a largely uninhabited desert as the center place for the Mormon kingdom was primarily motivated by the desire of the members of the Church of Jesus Christ of Latter-Day Saints to be left alone so that they could establish a distinctive way of life that other communities had found so threatening and offensive. Because Utah was a federal territory, the Mormons now had to deal with the federal government and its laws. The federal government was initially cautious but soon hostile and bent on eradicating Mormon distinctiveness. The Mormons and the federal authorities were in direct conflict for more than forty years. In order to gain a measure of independence, the Mormons sought admission of much of the intermountain West as the State of Deseret. Congress refused. Repeated attempts to admit a much smaller area, the territory of Utah, were also turned down. Thus the Mormons were forced to fight the federal authorities in the territorial courts until Utah was finally granted statehood in 1896.

The Mormons found the courts less than receptive. Nineteenth-century America was radically different from the world we know today. Many Americans—and American courts, for that matter—thought that Americans shared a common understanding of God and religion. While the courts professed a belief in the free exercise of religion, many courts assumed that America was a Christian country; more particularly, many defined it as a Protestant Christian country. In 1854, for example, the Supreme Court of Maine in *Donahoe v. Richards* (Maine, 1854) upheld a decision to expel an Irish Catholic child from a school for refusing to participate in a Protestant religious exercise. In *People v. Ruggles* (N.Y., 1811), the highest state court in New York upheld an indictment for blasphemy and stated, "[W]e are a Christian people, and the morality of the country is deeply ingrafted upon Christianity."

This "Christian nation" attitude permeated the judiciary and sustained the religious views of the majority. Thus the early Mormon church had to contend not only with a national consensus defining America's religion by popular sentiment but also with a judiciary that was accustomed to intruding into the most sensitive aspects of church–state relations.

The clash point with the Mormons was over polygamy. Officially acknowledged as part of Mormon doctrine in 1852, the practice of polygamy soon became a national issue. The practice had begun in the 1830s and had been conducted openly in Utah since the Mormons arrived. The 1856 Republican Party platform called for the elimination of the "twin relics of barbarism: slavery and polygamy." Polygamy provided a clear rallying point for anti-Mormon forces. It was a practice so abhorrent to most nineteenth-century Americans that sophisticated constitutional arguments were not necessary to justify its eradication.

This essay will examine the Mormon conflict with the federal authorities first by setting forth the various nineteenth-century statutes aimed at the Mormons and second by focusing on the resulting court cases.

Congressional Actions

From 1862 to 1887 the Congress passed four major acts to curb Mormon polygamy.

The Morrill Act (1862)

In 1856 the antislavery Republican Representative Justin Morrill of Vermont had introduced legislation outlawing polygamy; six years later two bills named in his honor became law. The more famous was the Morrill Act of 1862, which provided for land grants for higher education in the territories. The day before the passage of that act, Congress adopted the Morrill Anti-Polygamy Act, which contained three sections directed at Mormon polygamy. The first section of the antipolygamy act provided that no person having a husband or wife living should "marry any other person, whether married or single, in a Territory of the United States." This offense was termed "bigamy" and was made punishable by fines of up to $500 and imprisonments for as much as five years. Exceptions were provided for annulments, divorces, and cases where a spouse had disappeared for at least five years and was believed to be dead. The second section revoked an 1855 act of the Utah territorial legislature incorporating the Church of Jesus Christ of Latter-Day Saints. The third section annulled all other acts of the territorial legislature that "establish, support, maintain, shield, or countenance polygamy."

The Poland Act (1874)

In 1874 the Congress placed the Utah judiciary under firm federal control by passing the Poland Act. The U.S. marshal was empowered to serve all process. Federal district courts were given exclusive original jurisdiction of all suits over $300. The U.S. Supreme Court was granted the right to review any error of law made by a Utah court, thus avoiding the previous requirement that federal law or a federal constitutional question be involved.

The Edmunds Act (1882)

In 1881 President Chester A. Arthur demanded that Congress pass new legislation to deal with "the difficulty of procuring legal evidence sufficient to warrant a conviction even in the case of the most notorious offenders." In 1882 the bill that finally passed was sponsored by a Vermont Republican, Senator George F. Edmunds.

The Edmunds Act imposed civil disabilities on polygamists and dramatically simplified the prosecution of polygamy. Supporters of the act claimed that the measure was necessary to ensure the effective prosecution of polygamists. The first section effected a cosmetic change by naming the Morrill Act offense of "bigamy" as "polygamy." The evidentiary problem of proving polygamous marriages that had hampered the Morrill Act was neatly solved by the creation of a new offense, unlawful cohabitation, for which no proof of marriage was required. The act of "cohabitating" with more than one woman was deemed a misdemeanor offense punishable by a maximum fine of $300 or six months' imprisonment or both. Nor did prosecutors have to decide which charge they would prove at trial, since the act allowed both polygamy and cohabitation to be charged in the same indictment.

Section 5 of the Edmunds Act restricted Mormons' ability to influence prosecutions by providing that potential jurors who were or had been polygamists could be questioned on that subject and excluded for cause. A juror's responses could not be used against him in criminal proceedings, but a juror who declined to answer questions about his polygamous activities could be rejected as incompetent. Finally, potential jurors who believed "it right to have more than one living and undivorced wife" could be rejected from jury duty. Thus, not only practicing polygamists but also all faithful church members could be excluded from jury duty under the Edmunds Act. The act also denied the right to vote and hold elective office to polygamists and those unlawfully cohabiting. To ensure that the Mormons' electoral power was broken, the Congress declared all Utah elective offices vacant and all voter registration invalid. A five-member commission was set up to re-register voters and supervise elections.

The Edmunds-Tucker Act (1887)

When Congress enacted its strongest anti-Mormon legislation, in 1887, the polygamy problem was confronted even more directly. Sections 1, 2, and 6 of the Edmunds-Tucker Act eliminated various evidentiary obligations to polygamy prosecutions. The common-law rule barring a wife from testifying against her husband was abrogated, if the wife agreed, in cases involving "bigamy, polygamy, or unlawful cohabitation." Witnesses were compelled to appear in court by the U.S. marshal. A Utah statute requiring polygamy prosecutions to be brought by a spouse was annulled. Also, in order to make proof of marriage easier, all marriages were required to be licensed and registered.

Section 20 disenfranchised Utah's women. Women had been granted the vote in Utah since 1870. Legislative redistricting was taken away from the control of the Mormon-dominated legislature and placed in the hands of the territorial governor, secretary, and the five members of the Utah Commission. Electors were required to take an oath that they would obey the antipolygamy laws and would not aid "directly or indirectly" those engaged in polygamous crimes. To satisfy concerns about the predominantly Mormon influence over the public schools, Utah's schools were placed under federal control.

Most important, along with dismantling much of Utah's government, the Congress dismantled the Mormon church. The Edmunds-Tucker Act directed that the unenforced provision of the Morrill Act which disincorporated the church be enforced and that the attorney general institute proceedings to "wind up the affairs of said corporation." Section 13 of the act directed the attorney general of the United States to institute proceedings, pursuant to the Morrill Act of 1862, to confiscate all church real estate in excess of $50,000 in value. The legislation specified that only the church's real property was subject to seizure; but because the Morrill Act arguably revoked the church's charter in its entirety, the church no longer existed as a body capable of holding property in the eyes of the law. Thus, such personal property as stocks, livestock, and furniture was left ownerless and was forfeited to the state. Also, church property was to be seized and the income used to foster the common schools.

Judicial Actions

The Mormons reacted to congressional attack by seeking protection from the courts. They were sorely disappointed.

The Reynolds Decision

George Reynolds was an English immigrant, private secretary to Brigham Young, and a polygamist. In October 1875 Reynolds was indicted for violating the Morrill Act. Reynolds was convicted and sentenced to two years' hard labor and a $5,000 fine. The Utah Supreme Court sustained his conviction.

Reynolds appealed to the U.S. Supreme Court. The bulk of the Court's opinion in *Reynolds v. United States* (1879) was devoted to Reynolds's claim that the trial court improperly failed to instruct the jury that a finding that Reynolds engaged in polygamy as a result of a sincere religious conviction would justify his acquittal. Reynolds argued that the First Amendment's guarantee of the free exercise of religion could excuse conduct that would otherwise be criminal. The Court's analysis of that issue made *Reynolds* a landmark case.

The *Reynolds* Court first attempted to define how the word "religion" fell within the ambit of the Free Exercise Clause. Finding no guide to the definition of religion in the Constitution itself, the Court turned to the writings of Jefferson to the effect that "religion is a matter which lies solely between man and his God; . . . the legislative powers of the government reach actions only, and not opinion." Adopting this demarcation, the Court concluded that "Congress was deprived of all legislative power over mere opinions, but was left free to reach actions which were in violation of social duties or subversive of good order."

Having established the belief–conduct distinction and determined that the First Amendment was no bar to outlawing religiously inspired conduct, the Court next concluded that polygamy was sufficiently "subversive of good order" to make it a crime properly. The Court conceded that polygamous sects might be well ordered, and it never examined whether polygamy degraded women. Instead the Court found subversion of the social order on the basis of an abstract syllogism that polygamy meant patriarchy, which meant despotism. To avoid this amorphous social evil, the Court invaded the right to marry. Reynolds's conviction was unanimously affirmed.

Underlying the entire decision in *Reynolds* was an assertion of the "Christian character" of the United States. Chief Justice Morrison Waite noted that polygamy had been confined to "Asiatic and . . . African people" and as such was inappropriate for the civilized, Christian United States.

The Prosecution of Cohabitation under the Edmunds Act

In 1882 Congress adopted the Edmunds Act, which gave federal officials a weapon for the prosecution of polygamists by creating the new offense of unlawful cohabitation. The act, however, did not say which conduct constituted cohabitation, nor does the

Congressional Record offer any evidence that Congress considered the question. The courts first confronted the issue of what constituted cohabitation in *United States v. Cannon* (1886). Angus Cannon, president of the Salt Lake Stake, had married three wives before passage of the Edmunds Act. Two of these wives, Clara and Amanda, lived with him in separate quarters in the same home. The third lived in a house nearby. Cannon was indicted for cohabitating with Amanda and Clara after the passage of the Edmunds Act. At trial, Cannon offered to prove that, after Congress had passed the Edmunds Act, he had told Clara, Amanda, and their families that he did not intend to violate the law and thereafter "did not occupy the rooms or beds of, or have any sexual intercourse with" Clara; but he could not afford a separate house for Clara and her family. The court excluded the evidence as irrelevant, and Cannon was convicted.

Cannon appealed to the Utah Supreme Court. His main objections were that "all cohabitation which the laws deal with is sexual cohabitation," of which he was innocent. The court concluded that "cohabitation meant dwelling together and not sexual intercourse." The U.S. Supreme Court affirmed the decision, concluding that cohabitation was established if Cannon "held [the two women] out to the world, by his language or conduct, or both, as his wives." Cannon's agreement to abstain from sexual relations with his plural wives was dismissed with the comment that "compacts for sexual non-intercourse, easily made and easily broken, when the prior marriage relations continue to exist . . . [are] not a lawful substitute for the monogamous family which alone the statute tolerates."

As the pace of polygamy prosecutions accelerated, the cohabitation statute was made more fearsome by prosecutorial interpretation that forced every defendant to face not one cohabitation charge but many. Thus, each year that a man cohabitated illegally could be the basis of a separate offense. A judicial test of this theory was attempted in *United States v. Snow* (1886). Lorenzo Snow was charged with cohabitation in three separate indictments, each one charging the same offense with the same women, except for different years. In separate trials Snow was convicted on each indictment and was given the maximum sentence for each conviction. Thus, by segregating the charges against Snow, the prosecution was able to triple his punishment. The Utah Supreme Court affirmed the convictions. The U.S. Supreme Court dismissed Snow's appeal on the ground that the Court did not have jurisdiction to hear it, because Snow did not question the validity of the federal statute but only its application.

Federal prosecutors swiftly began expanding their use of the segregation of offenses, testing how far the principle could be pushed. In *United States v. Groesbeck* (1886) the prosecution cut in half the period of each offense, charging the defendant with two counts of cohabitation, one for each of the two six-month periods. On appeal, the Utah Supreme Court sustained this innovation.

Meanwhile, Lorenzo Snow had served his first six-month sentence. He then applied to the U.S. Supreme Court for a writ of habeas corpus, claiming that his further detention was unlawful because the two remaining sentences were the result of an unlawful segregation of a single offense. This time the Court held that it had jurisdiction. Cohabitation, the Court stated in *In re Snow* (1887), was "inherently a continuous offense, having duration; and not an offense consisting of an isolated act." Therefore cohabitation was related to the relationship with more than one woman, not merely acts within a given time period.

But even after *In re Snow* the courts could still impose multiple punishments for what was in reality one offense. The Edmunds Act specifically allowed charges of polygamy and cohabitation to be brought together. Because the definitions of the offenses were different, a man could be convicted of marrying a polygamous wife and then be convicted again for living with her. The Supreme Court finally set limits on the combination of offenses in *Exparte v. Hans Nielsen* (1889). Nielsen was indicted for adultery and cohabitation. Nielsen pleaded guilty to the charge of cohabitation and was sentenced to three months' imprisonment. When arraigned on the adultery charge, Nielsen claimed that his conviction for cohabitation barred his further prosecution. Nielsen was tried and convicted for adultery and was sentenced to an additional 125 days' imprisonment. The U.S. Supreme Court granted Nielsen's petition for a writ of habeas corpus.

The Court managed to arrive at a sensible result. It reasoned that the proof that Nielsen and Caroline lived together as husband and wife carried with it an assumption of intercourse that was the essential element of the adultery charge. Thus, when Nielsen was convicted of cohabitation, he was convicted of all the elements of adultery and could not be convicted separately for that offense. *Nielsen* ended the attempts to make the polygamy laws more savage by piling offenses together or fracturing a single act into many separate offenses.

On another level, the Edmunds Act prosecutions also distorted the rules of evidence. Because the offense of cohabitation consisted of appearing to consort with two or more women, as long as a polygamist cohabited with only one woman, he seemingly could not cohabitate, regardless of whether that woman was the man's lawful wife. The judicial solution to this problem was a presumption, first announced in *Snow,* that a man could live only with his legal wife.

To comply with the law, Lorenzo Snow had established each of his older wives in a separate household and had refrained from almost all contact with them. He lived solely with his last wife, who still had infant children to raise. Nevertheless, he was convicted of cohabitation. The Utah Supreme Court upheld the conviction, not because he was cohabiting with more than one wife but because he was with the wrong wife. The court reasoned that the Edmunds Act was intended to protect the institution of monogamous marriage and should be construed directly to achieve that intent. Thus, the court presumed that a man cohabited with his lawful wife. At first this was offered as a rebuttal presumption, justified by society's policy of encouraging marital fidelity and by common experience as a factual generalization.

But in 1888 the Utah Supreme Court so diluted the amount of evidence required to prove the presumption of cohabitation with a legal wife that, in effect, the presumption became a conclusive presumption of law. In *United States v. Harris* (1888) the court approved jury instructions to the effect that if "the legal wife of the defendant lives in the same vicinity with him, bearing his name, in a household maintained by him; that is . . . absolutely and conclusively cohabitation with his legal wife." Under such a standard, it seemed unlikely that any polygamist could insulate himself from all contact with his lawful wife sufficiently to avoid a finding of cohabitation.

In loosening the rules of evidence to ensure the punishment of polygamy the courts undermined the elemental bases of judicial procedure and due process of law. The most basic assumption that an accused is presumed innocent and must be found guilty beyond a reasonable doubt by competent evidence was undermined. The courts were indeed accurate when they identified cohabitation as an offense of appearance or reputation, for under such evidentiary standards an accused's conduct seemed largely irrelevant.

Witnesses to Cohabitation

To convict Mormon men of polygamy offenses, certainly no more effective and knowledgeable witnesses could be found than their wives. Two obstacles, however, appeared to bar use of this pool of witnesses. First, most Mormon wives were unwilling to testify against their husbands. Second, even if they were willing to testify, at common law a person could not testify against his or her spouse. These problems were first confronted in *Miles v. United States* (1881), the only other Morrill Act case to reach the U.S. Supreme Court besides *Reynolds.*

From the evidence at trial it appeared that John Miles had married three women on the same day. Because Miles was charged with bigamy, under the Morrill Act, it was necessary to prove his marriages to the three women. Therein lay the difficulty, for the marriage ceremony was shrouded in secrecy. Miles's wife, Caroline, however, was willing to testify against him. Miles conceded his marriage to Caroline but denied his marriage to his first wife. Caroline's testimony was essential to the state's case, but if Caroline were Miles's lawful wife, under the common-law rule her testimony was inadmissible. But her testimony helped establish that, at the time Miles married her, he already had a lawful wife. And if Miles had a wife when he married Caroline, his marriage to her was invalid, and she was a competent witness. The trial court resolved this perplexing question by throwing the whole matter to the jury. Caroline was allowed to testify.

On appeal, the U.S. Supreme Court rejected the trial court's avoidance of the issue.

It concluded that a defendant's witness-wife must be treated prima facie as his lawful wife. The principle behind this ruling was that a witness who is "prima facie incompetent" cannot give evidence "to establish his competence, and at the same time prove the issue." The Court reached this ruling with apparent regret. The Court recommended two escapes from this predicament. First, eyewitnesses to a marriage were not necessary. Polygamous marriages could be proved like any other fact, by admissions of the defendant or by circumstantial evidence. Second, if under existing laws it was too difficult to prove polygamy, Congress could always change the laws. Miles's conviction was reversed.

Nearly six years after the *Miles* decision, Congress provided in the Edmunds-Tucker Act that a wife was a competent witness in polygamy, bigamy, and cohabitation trials. The law still provided that only a willing wife would be allowed to testify. However, Utah's judges did not always follow the law. A number of Mormon women were required to testify against their husbands or risked facing contempt charges. Judicial use of the contempt power in the polygamy cases presented many Mormon families with a cruel dilemma. If the wife who was called as a witness submitted and testified, her husband would almost surely be convicted and imprisoned. If she refused, her husband might escape conviction, but then she would be imprisoned. Perhaps the most egregious case of judicial conduct in this regard was that of Belle Harris in *Ex Parte Harris* (Utah, 1884). Mrs. Harris and her infant son ultimately spent three and one-half months in prison for her refusal to testify before a grand jury investigating polygamy charges against her husband.

The general pattern was that, under the guise of stamping out polygamy, the government systematically abridged Mormons' due process rights.

Exclusion of Mormons As Jurors, Electors, and Officeholders

The provision of the Edmunds Act that excluded Mormon jurors was predictably sustained by the Supreme Court in *Clawson v. United States* (1885). Clawson was indicted for cohabitation and polygamy, and Clawson argued that the exclusion of Mormons did not extend to grand juries. The Supreme Court, however, without considering the unique role of the grand jury in society, held that the term "juror" encompassed both grand and petit juries and that the Edmunds Act therefore must be read broadly to disable Mormons from service on any jury. In theory, Mormons were excluded from serving as jurors only in polygamy trials. But in Idaho—a hotbed of anti-Mormon sentiment—a statute provided that only qualified electors could serve as jurors; thus, Idaho law effectively barred Mormons from the jury. This disability was upheld by the Idaho Supreme Court in *Territory v. Evans* (Idaho, 1890).

The provision of the Edmunds Act that denied polygamists the right to vote disenfranchised Mormon women in particular. In 1870 Utah's territorial legislature had granted women the right to vote. Over time, enfranchised Mormon women came to be seen as an impediment to the elimination of polygamy and to the destruction of the Mormons' political power, because Mormon women were perceived as favoring the interest of the Mormon hierarchy.

The Edmunds Act also excluded Mormons from public office on the theory that eligibility for public office required eligibility to vote. To enforce these provisions, the Utah Territory's registration and election offices were declared vacant, and a five-man commission was appointed to oversee elections. During its first year the Utah Commission barred over twelve thousand Mormons from voting. This was nearly one-fourth of eligible Mormon voters, and it far exceeded the number of polygamists in Utah.

The Utah Commission's exclusion of Mormon voters met an immediate judicial challenge. In *Murphy v. Ramsey* (1884) the U.S. Supreme Court confined the Utah Commission to ensuring that elections in Utah were fairly conducted. Addressing the disenfranchisement of the polygamists, the *Murphy* Court again ruled that practicing polygamists could be disenfranchised.

In 1890 the Supreme Court reinforced its *Murphy* holding in *Davis v. Beason* (1890) by upholding an Idaho constitutional provision barring the vote to polygamists because that provision merely denied the franchise to a class of criminals. *Davis* had a more far-reaching effect, because the Court upheld the language of the Idaho statute that reached beyond those practicing polygamy to those who merely believed in polygamy or supported an organization that taught polygamous activity.

This substantially eroded the belief–action distinction of *Reynolds.* Justice Stephen J. Field also dismissed the argument that "the whole punitive power of the government for acts, recognized by the general consent of the Christian world in modern times as proper matters for prohibitory legislation, must be suspended in order that the tenets of a religious sect encouraging crime may be carried out without hindrance." The most interesting aspect of this quotation is that Justice Field noted that the "Christian world" determined appropriate behavior.

Assault on Mormon Economic Power

In 1851 the Assembly of the State of Deseret passed an ordinance incorporating the Church of Jesus Christ of Latter-Day Saints. By the terms of this charter the church was granted vast powers: It could acquire and sell property, regulate marriages, register births and deaths, and make all laws, rules, and adjudications it deemed necessary. It was also not subject to legal review.

Armed with these powers the church became deeply involved in members' economic lives. It established itself as a major business interest in Utah and—consistent with the church's communal doctrines—held a major portion of the Mormons' collective wealth. These policies made the church quite vulnerable to federal pressure. The seizure of church property would be a devastating blow to the entire Mormon community. The federal government did not hesitate long before it used the ultimate weapon. The Morrill Act of 1862 revoked the charter incorporating the Mormon church, at least insofar as that charter supported or aided polygamy. No attempt was made to enforce the forfeiture.

On July 30, 1887, the U.S. attorney for Utah initiated proceedings before the territorial supreme court to dissolve the church corporation and to recover all property held by the church except for any real property acquired before 1862 and valued at less than $50,000.

The Mormons argued that the territorial charter given to the church constituted a right that Congress could not constitutionally nullify. But in *The Late Corporation of the Church of Jesus Christ of Latter-Day Saints v. United States* (1890) the Court disagreed.

The Mormons argued for the sanctity of contract: Citing *Dartmouth College v. Woodward* (1819), they argued that the church's charter was a contract that Congress could not lawfully break. They suggested that in the Morrill Act and before, Congress had implicitly recognized the charter. In the alternative, even if Congress were to break the contract, the church's property should rightfully revert to the church's membership.

The Court rejected each piece of the argument in turn. The property held by the church was donated for public and charitable purposes. Instead, the church used it to promote polygamy. By depriving the church of its property, then, Congress directed that property to its proper end and furthered Congress's policy of blocking the spread of polygamy. As legal precedent the Court elaborately outlined the ancient doctrine of *cy pres;* under this legal principle, if a charitable trust could not be fulfilled according to its terms, the state would apply the property to those charitable uses that most nearly approximated the original purpose of the grant. By analogy, the Mormons' continued unlawful adherence to polygamy made a return of church property to the members improper.

The Supreme Court remanded the case to the territorial court. While the case was under consideration, the church officially renounced polygamy in October 1890. The seizure of the church's property—property inseparably connected to the church's social programs and the territory's economy—had brought terrible pressure to bear. On September 24, 1890, church president Wilford Woodruff issued the Manifesto, in which he declared "my intention [is] to submit to those laws, and to use my influence with members of the church over which I preside to do likewise." However, despite a vigorous dissenting opinion, the Utah Supreme Court refused to abandon the forfeiture proceedings and created a trustee to apply church property "to support and aid of the poor of the church, and to the building and repairing of its house of worship."

With the judiciary unwilling to return church property, Congress finally ended its confrontation with the Mormon church. In 1893 Utah's congressional delegate, Joseph L. Rawlins, introduced a resolution directing the return of the church's personal property. With minor amendments the resolution passed Congress, and on January 10, 1894, what was left of the church's personal property was returned. On June 8, 1896, the church's real estate was returned.

Aftermath

In the battle of wills between the Mormon church and the federal government, the government was victorious. It suppressed polygamy and crippled the church's political, social, and economic power in the territory. For Mormons the cost of the war against polygamy was high. By 1893, after the church had renounced polygamy, prosecutions had largely ceased: There had been 1,004 convictions for unlawful cohabitation and 31 for polygamy. The number of polygamy and cohabitation convictions, however, understates the impact of "the raid" on Mormon society. Not just any Mormon male was allowed to practice polygamy; only those who were morally worthy and financially able were permitted to take plural wives. Thus, by and large, the polygamists were also the Mormons' leaders. The conviction and imprisonment of polygamists served to paralyze Mormon society by removing its leadership. Mormon women were jailed for failing to testify against their husbands. Polygamous families were left fatherless, as Mormon men either went into hiding or obeyed federal law and abandoned wives and children. Federal spies tracking down polygamists disrupted Mormon communities and invaded the privacy of Mormon homes.

Of more long-lasting importance, the unique Mormon experience of founding a theocratic state with a communitarian economic structure and polygamous family organization ended. American pluralism could not tolerate that degree of diversity within the secular democratic society of the nineteenth century. In the final result, the civil and religious powers in Utah were clearly separated, and the Mormons became, by and large, indistinguishable from other Americans.

But anti-Mormon prejudice lingered for decades. Almost twenty years later an Idaho Mormon, Alfred Budge, was elected to the Idaho bench as a district judge. In 1906 a Mr. Toncray contested the seating of Budge in the Idaho courts on the ground that the Idaho constitution provided: "No person is permitted to . . . hold any civil office . . . who . . . is living in what is known as 'patriarchal or celestial marriage' . . . or who is a member of, or contributes to the support, aid, or encouragement of, any order, organization, association, corporation, or society, which teaches, advises, counsels, encourages or aids any person to enter to enter into bigamy, polygamy or such patriarchal or plural marriage."

Toncray v. Budge (Idaho, 1908) was unusual because the thrust of the case was not to stop polygamy but to target directly the Mormon belief in "celestial marriage." Practicing Mormons believed that a marriage which was performed in a Mormon temple not only was valid for the life of the parties involved but also was binding in the hereafter—and hence a "celestial marriage." Toncray asserted that Budge, a practicing Mormon, was living in a celestial marriage and "teaching, advising, counseling, and encouraging persons to enter" into celestial marriages.

The Idaho Supreme Court dispatched Toncray's argument by interpreting the phrase "celestial marriage" in the context of the constitutional section as a synonym for "polygamy," not any theological belief in the continuity of marriage into an afterlife. Idaho Justice Ailshie stated that "constitutions and statutes . . . protect a man in believing anything he wants to believe with reference to the future." Since the Mormon church had eliminated polygamy in the Manifesto of 1890, Budge was allowed to take his seat as an Idaho judge.

Toncray v. Budge is important because it shows that the effects of the Mormon war with the federal government extended beyond the nineteenth century. Toncray was able to bring the case only because of strong anti-Mormon feelings that still lingered in early-twentieth-century Idaho.

On a broader level the nineteenth-century Mormon cases reflect a refusal on the part of the federal judiciary, the Congress, and the executive branch to allow for a radically different vision of American society to coexist in a nation colored by the concept of traditional Protestant Christianity. The First Amendment's declaration that "Congress shall make no law respecting an establishment of religion, or prohibiting the free exercise thereof . . ." was confined to constituting a directive merely allowing the free exercise of religious beliefs that were generally accepted in Protestant Christian American society. People with odd or unusual creeds or doctrines were subject to the majority's disapproval and the use of legal force.

Edwin B. Firmage

Bibliography

Allen, James B., and Glen M. Leonard, *The*

Story of the Latter-Day Saints (Salt Lake City, Utah: Deseret, 1976).

Arrington, Leonard, *Brigham Young: American Moses* (New York: Knopf, 1985).

———, *Great Basin Kingdom: An Economic History of the Latter-Day Saints* (Cambridge, Mass.: Harvard University Press, 1958).

———, and Davis Bitton, *The Mormon Experience: A History of the Latter-Day Saints* (New York: Knopf, 1979).

———, Feramorz Y. Fox, and Dean May, *Building the City of God: Community and Cooperation among the Mormons* (Salt Lake City, Utah: Deseret, 1976).

Bushman, Richard L., *Joseph Smith and the Beginnings of Mormonism* (Urbana: University of Illinois, 1984).

Firmage, Edwin B., "Religion and the Law: The Mormon Experience in the Nineteenth Century," 12 *Cardozo Law Review* 765–803 (1991).

———, "Free Exercise of Religion in Nineteenth Century America: The Mormon Cases," 7 *The Journal of Law and Religion* 281–313 (1989).

———, and Richard C. Mangrum, *Zion in the Courts: A Legal History of the Church of Jesus Christ of Latter-Day Saints, 1830–1900* (Urbana: University of Illinois Press, 1988).

Hansen, Klaus J., *Mormonism and the American Experience* (Chicago: University of Chicago Press, 1981).

Larson, Gustive O., *The "Americanization" of Utah for Statehood* (San Marino, Calif.: Huntington Library, 1971).

Cases and Statutes Cited

Cannon v. United States, 116 U.S. 55 (1886), vacated 118 U.S. 355 (1886).

Clawson v. United States, 114 U.S. 477 (1885).

Dartmouth College v. Woodward, 17 U.S. 518 (1819).

Davis v. Beason, 133 U.S. 333 (1890).

Donahoe v. Richards, 38 Me. 379 (1854).

Ex Parte Harris, 4 Utah 5, 5 P. 129 (Utah 1889).

Ex Parte Hans Nielsen, 131 U.S. 176 (1889).

In re Snow, 120 U.S. 274 (1887).

The Late Corporation of the Church of Jesus Christ of Latter-Day Saints v. United States 136 U.S. 1 (1890).

Miles v. United States, 103 U.S. 304 (1881).

Murphy v. Ramsey, 114 U.S. 15 (1885).

People v. Ruggles, 9 Johns 290 (N.Y. 1811).

Reynolds v. United States, 98 U.S. 145 (1879).

Territory v. Evans, 23 P. 232 (Idaho 1890).

Toncray v. Budge, 95 P. 26 (Idaho 1908).

United States v. Cannon, 4 Utah 122, 7 P. 369 (Utah Terr. 1885); aff'd, 116 U.S. 55 (1886); vacated, 118 U.S. 355 (1886).

United States v. Groesbeck, 4 Utah 487, 11 P. 542 (1886).

United States v. Harris, 5 Utah 436, 17 P. 75 (1888).

United States v. Snow, 4 Utah 280, 313 P. 501; appeal dismissed, 118 U.S. 346 (1886).

Edmunds Act, Act of Mar. 22, 1882, c. 47, 22 Stat. 30.

Edmunds-Tucker Act, Act of Mar. 3, 1887, c. 397, 24 Stat. 635.

Morrill (Anti-Polygamy) Act, Act of July 1, 1862, c. 126, 12 Stat. 501.

Poland Act, Act of June 23, 1874, c. 469, 18 Stat. 253.

Mueller v. Allen
463 U.S. 388 (1983)

In recent years the interest and demand for public support for private schools has grown, in part as a response to the actual or perceived deterioration of public school systems in various parts of the country and in part because of concomitant increase in the demand for and the utilization of private educational alternatives. The turn toward private education has put legislative bodies under increasing pressure to provide alternatives. When they have, the programs they have enacted have been subject to constitutional challenge.

One such program was enacted in 1982 by the State of Minnesota. The State enacted a statute that allowed taxpayers, in computing their state income taxes, to deduct certain expenses incurred in the education of their children. Deductible expenses included tuition, transportation, and textbooks fees of up to $500 for each child in grades K through 6 and $700 for each child in grades 7 through 12. The deductions were available for any child attending any elementary or secondary school, whether public or private, in Minnesota and several other states, as long as the school satisfied the requirements of Minnesota's compulsory attendance laws. Approximately 820,000 students were enrolled in the state's public school system, while 91,000 students attended some 500 privately supported schools in the state. Crucially, 95 percent of the private school students attended schools that considered themselves sectarian.

A group of Minnesota taxpayers filed suit against the commissioner of the Minnesota Department of Revenue in federal district court alleging that this statutory scheme violated the First Amendment to the U.S. Constitution because it provided financial assistance to sectarian institutions. The district court upheld the constitutionality of the statute, and the U.S. Court of Appeals for the Eighth Circuit affirmed. The plaintiffs then appealed to the U.S. Supreme Court. In *Mueller v. Allen* the Court, by a vote of 5 to 4, affirmed the decisions of the lower courts.

The plaintiffs in *Mueller* based their challenge to the Minnesota statute on the Establishment Clause of the First Amendment. This clause provides that "Congress shall make no law respecting an establishment of religion, . . ." This provision, although in terms only applicable to the federal government ("Congress"), has been held by the Supreme Court to be binding on both the federal government and the states. It is the part of the Constitution that provides the basis for the principle commonly known as "the separation of church and state."

Like many of the Constitution's most important provisions, the language of the Establishment Clause has been the subject of a good deal of interpretive disagreement and debate. For example, while the text clearly contemplates that the government not "establish" a particular religion as the (or an) official state religion, it is less clear what the text means when it prohibits the making of laws "respecting" the establishment of religion. Were this language to be construed at its broadest, it could be understood to prohibit government from enacting laws that might in any way reflect endorsement of a particular religion or take any action which—even in relatively insignificant and indirect ways—could be said to benefit religion. Such a construction of the Establishment Clause would be problematic in a number of ways. For example, if the government is prohibited from doing anything that benefits religion, even in some small way, it might feel compelled to act in ways that are ultimately hostile or adverse to religious believers or institutions. Such a posture would create serious tension with that part of the First Amendment which prohibits government from "prohibiting the free exercise" of religion (the Free Exercise Clause.)

Given the ambiguity of the language of the Establishment Clause, courts have looked to the historical context in which the First Amendment was proposed and ratified for help in determining its proper meaning and scope. The assumption has been that textual uncertainties should and can be resolved by attempting to ascertain the "original understanding" or the "Framers' intentions" concerning the constitutional language. Although this historical context itself has been the subject of much discussion and debate, it has generally been agreed that, at a minimum, the clause was intended to prohibit the creation of a state church, governmental favoritism toward one or more sects or denominations, and the direct payment of public funds to one or more religious institutions. Beyond these specific concerns, and underlying them, the Establishment Clause has been thought to require the government to maintain a posture of neutrality with respect to religion in general, as well as among particular religious institutions, persons, and communities. The theory has been that a policy of government neutrality will minimize the risk of religious persecution and secular–sectarian strife.

Determining when these concerns are sufficiently implicated in legislation such as that at issue in *Mueller* has not been easy. The Supreme Court had previously adopted a three-part test in evaluating the constitutionality of such statutes. The test asks (1) whether the legislation was enacted for a secular purpose; (2) whether its principal or primary effect was to either advance or inhibit religion; and (3) whether the statute fostered an excessive government entanglement with religion. In previous cases this test had been applied to reach results that, to many, seemed inconsistent or even incoherent. Indeed (now Chief) Justice William Rehnquist's opinion for the Court in *Mueller* acknowledged that the Court's past decisions were not easy to apply and that they only "dimly" established guidelines for determining what was constitutionally permissible and what was not.

In *Mueller* the majority of the Court concluded that Minnesota's education tax deduction scheme satisfied each of the three inquiries discussed above. In the process the Court distinguished a prior case, *Committee for Public Education* v. *Nyquist* (1973), in which it had invalidated a New York statute that, among other things, provided certain "tax benefits" in the form of grants to low-income parents who sent their children to nonpublic schools. Because under the Minnesota law both public and private schoolchildren (and schools) were eligible for the tax deductions and because the state did not bestow the benefits directly on sectarian schools, Minnesota could not be said to have bestowed its imprimatur on any particular religion or on religion generally. Thus the law was not viewed as significantly implicating the "evils against which the Establishment Clause was designed to protect."

In a dissenting opinion Justice Thurgood Marshall—joined by Justices Brennan, Blackmun, and Stevens—argued that the Minnesota law was indistinguishable in principle from the New York law that had been struck down in *Nyquist.* Although he agreed with the Court that the Minnesota law could be said to further a secular purpose, he argued that it had the direct and immediate effect of subsidizing parochial school education and, thus, of advancing religion. Moreover, because the law did not confine the tax deduction to expenses associated with the secular educational programs of parochial schools, the Minnesota subsidy inevitably supported the religious missions of those schools.

Mueller typifies the dilemma the Supreme Court has faced in determining the constitutionality of public programs directed toward, or effectively benefiting, sectarian schools. As private sectarian schools have come to play a more significant role in the education of the nation's children, the state's legitimate interest—indeed, its stake—in the success of those schools becomes more difficult to question. But where states extend financial assistance to those schools, the assistance may have the effect, or be perceived to have the effect, of supporting or endorsing the religious mission or programs of the institutions in question. In trying to strike an appropriate accommodation between the Establishment Clause values and the secular educational interests at stake, the Court has rejected bright-line rules in favor of a more flexible analysis. Such an analysis, as was the case in *Mueller,* invites legitimate and serious disagreement among the justices concerning the proper outcome in individual cases. But unless the Court fundamentally reorients its establishment clause jurisprudence—something that the Rehnquist Court has hinted it may be prepared to do—the debate concerning the validity of state efforts to assist sectarian schools can be expected to continue.

Richard B. Saphire

Bibliography

Conkle, Daniel O., "Toward a General Theory of the Establishment Clause," 82 *Northwestern University Law Review* 1113–1194 (1988).

"Developments in the Law: Religion and the State," 100 *Harvard Law Review* 1606–1618 (1987).

Cases Cited

Committee for Public Education v. Nyquist, 413 U.S. 756 (1973).

Mueller v. Allen, 463 U.S. 388 (1983).

N

National Day of Prayer

In 1952 Congress passed a joint resolution establishing the National Day of Prayer. It requires that each year the president set aside and proclaim a day, other than a Sunday, as the National Day of Prayer on which people may "turn to God in prayer and meditation at churches, in groups, and as individuals." It was occasioned by a speech on February 3, 1952, by the Reverend Billy Graham on the steps of the Capitol asking Congress to pass such a law. The next day the resolution was introduced in the House with statements of support by leaders of both parties and a representation that President Harry Truman viewed it with extreme favor. Typical was a statement by Senator A. Willis Robertson of Virginia that the need for divine guidance was acute because the nation was "threatened at home and abroad by the corrosive forces of communism which seek simultaneously to destroy our democratic way of life and the faith in an Almighty God on which it is based."

This action followed a 1950 law designating Memorial Day as a day of prayer for permanent peace. This law requests the president to call on the people to observe Memorial Day by praying for peace, to designate a period during the day when all people may unite in prayer for peace, and to call on them to unite in prayer at that time.

The tradition of congressional resolutions, sometimes enacted into law, calling on the president to declare a day of prayer has long historical roots. The very day that the First Congress approved the First Amendment it requested President George Washington to proclaim "a day of public thanksgiving and prayer, to be observed by acknowledging with grateful hearts the many and signal favours of Almighty God." Washington acceded to this request and on at least one other occasion issued a thanksgiving proclamation during his presidency. President John Adams issued at least two such proclamations, and James Madison four.

The practice was not without its critics. For example, Representative Thomas Tucker of South Carolina opposed the first congressional resolution calling for a day of thanksgiving and prayer on the ground that it involved religious matters and therefore was proscribed to Congress. One of the most famous statements regarding the religion clauses was occasioned by the request of the Danbury Baptist Association in 1802 for a proclamation of a day of fast and prayer in thanksgiving for the welfare of the new nation. President Thomas Jefferson declined the request on the basis of the First Amendment, which he characterized as "building a wall of separation between church and state." Andrew Jackson, at some cost to his popularity, likewise refused to issue thanksgiving proclamations.

Nevertheless, the practice of officially recognizing Thanksgiving as a holiday became routine. During the Civil War, in order to raise morale, President Abraham Lincoln began the annual practice of declaring Thanksgiving a national holiday, and its religious underpinnings continue to be reflected in the modern presidential proclamations.

Although there is no recorded case of any person's challenging the constitutionality of any national day of prayer as an establishment of religion—and given the doctrine of standing, it might be difficult for anyone to raise such a challenge—several courts, including the Supreme Court, have referred to the practice of national days of prayer as harmless or positive acknowledgments or affirmations of the religious heritage of the United States. For instance, in *Lynch v. Donnelly* (1984) the Court used the National Day of Prayer as one of several examples in which government officially acknowledged religion in order to demonstrate that not all such acknowledgments violate the Establishment Clause. In *County of Allegheny v. American Civil Liberties Union* (1989), on the other hand, the majority in dictum distinguished the National Day of Prayer from the prayers by which legislatures open their sessions, which had been upheld in *Marsh v. Chambers* (1983). The former, the Court said, urges citizens to engage in religious practices, which is different from allowing legislators themselves to engage in prayer. Thus, the Court concluded, *Marsh* did not control the constitutionality of the National Day of Prayer. However, Justice Anthony Kennedy, in a partial dissent on behalf of himself and three other justices, included the National Day of Prayer in a list of examples of official government action that expressly endorses religion or religious activity. He deduced that such a list demonstrates that mere endorsement of religion should not be deemed to violate the Establishment Clause.

William Funk

Bibliography

Antieau, Chester, Arthur Downey, and Edward Roberts, *Freedom from Federal Establishment* (Milwaukee: Bruce, 1964).

Dreisbach, Daniel, *Real Threat and Mere Shadow* (Westchester, Ill.: Crossways, 1987).

Stokes, Anson, and Leo Pfeffer, *Church and State in the United States* (New York: Harper and Row, 1964).

Cases Cited

County of Allegheny v. American Civil Liberties Union, 492 U.S. 573 (1989).

Lynch v. Donnelly, 465 U.S. 668 (1984).

Marsh v. Chambers, 463 U.S. 783 (1983).

Native American Religious Rights

It is both difficult and hazardous to draw generalizations about the immensely diverse religious and quasi-religious beliefs that characterize the vast array of Native American (American Indian) cultures in North America. It seems safe to say, however, that religion has generally played as vital a role in Native American cultures as it has in the predominantly Christian cultures of the European settlers and their descendants. Religion has also played an important role in European–Indian relations, from the dawn of European exploration down to the present day. The European majority's attitude toward Native American religious rights has both highlighted and challenged the conceptual limits and cultural parochialism of religious freedom as a constitutional principle in the United States, and it has forced the expansion and refinement of that principle.

Native Religions: A Unique Legal Paradox

Pursuit of religious freedom was a chief cause of European migration to North America, and that concept became part of the early tradition of the English colonies. The example of the Puritans, however, who fled persecution in England only to impose a theocracy of their own in Massachusetts, illustrates a selective and hypocritical tendency in this tradition, which found especially virulent expression in policy toward the Indians. Indian religious beliefs were unfamiliar and often incomprehensible to the settlers with their Judeo-Christian frame of reference, and the reverse was also true from the Indian perspective. For many Europeans, spreading Christianity to the "heathen" natives was a sacred duty that both required and justified assuming a purportedly benevolent protectorship over the various Indian nations. The refusal of many natives to abandon their own religious beliefs and practices was viewed as satanic wickedness and was deemed to justify their dispossession, enslavement, and even extermination. With the establishment of the American Republic and the ratification of the U.S. Constitution and Bill of Rights—including the guarantee of free exercise and the related ban on establishment of religion in the First Amendment—Native American religions thus came to present a unique legal paradox.

Federal governmental support for missionary activities among the Indians conflicted most notably, early on, with the emerging principles of the Establishment Clause. Before the ratification of the Constitution or the First Amendment, for example, the Congress under the Articles of Confederation granted land to the Society of the United Brethren for Propagating the Gospel among the Heathen. This trend continued, surprisingly, even under President Jefferson, who had authored Virginia's 1786 Statute of Religious Freedom, which banned aid to Christian religious sects even on a nonpreferentialist basis and is widely viewed as a model for the Establishment Clause. In 1803 the Senate approved a treaty negotiated by the Jefferson administration with the Kaskaskia Indians under which the United States paid $100 annually for the maintenance of a Catholic priest to minister to the tribe. Similar grants of land or money for religious purposes were made to the Oneida, Tuscarora, and Stockbridge Indians under President Washington (1794), to the Wyandots under President Monroe (1817), to the Osage under President John Quincy Adams (1825), to the Kickapoo under President Jackson (1832), and again to the Oneida under President Van Buren (1838).

Chief Justice Marshall offered the first definition of the Native Americans' status under the American constitutional scheme in *Johnson v. McIntosh* (1823), *Cherokee Nation v. Georgia* (1831), and *Worcester v. Georgia* (1832), in which he held that Indian tribes constituted "domestic dependent nations" with limited sovereignty and title to their lands, which only the federal government, as a sort of trustee, could purchase or extinguish. This federal "protection" of the tribes against incursions by the states or freelance settlers proved famously impotent in the 1830s, when President Jackson, despite *Worcester,* endorsed Georgia's designs on Cherokee land and the removal of the Cherokees to what is now Oklahoma, in the infamous Trail of Tears. The pattern of intervention and removal was repeated many times over the next fifty years, often accompanied by violent warfare—two examples being the devastating Long Walk and temporary exile of the Dine (Navajo) from their southwestern desert homeland from 1864 to 1868, and the campaign against Chief Joseph and the Nez Perce in 1877, resulting in their permanent exile from Oregon's Wallowa Valley.

Efforts to "Christianize and Civilize"

The 1870s and 1880s saw profound changes in U.S. government policy toward the Indians, including the shifting of the Commissioner of Indian Affairs from the War Department to the Interior Department and, by an 1871 act of Congress, the abandonment of treaty making with the tribes and the move toward direct legislation and regulation. Most significantly for Native American religious rights, President Grant, under his "Peace Policy" of 1870, placed the government's local Indian agencies under various Christian religious denominations, to act as missionaries with the avowed goal to "Christianize and civilize the Indian." This began a sustained policy of forcible religious and cultural assimilation of Native Americans. For example, directives of the Commissioner of Indian Affairs in 1886–1887 forbade instruction in reservation schools, whether government- or missionary-run, in any language other than English. Boarding schools for Indian children were created, with the avowed purpose, as expressed by the military superintendent of one such school, to "kill the Indian in him and save the man." The Interior Department instituted "courts of Indian offenses" on the reservations, with rules promulgated in 1883 and 1892 prohibiting, among other things, Indian religious dances, polygamous marriages as practiced in many native cultures, and the "practices of medicine men" with "their barbarous rites and customs." The massacre of Lakota (Sioux) Indians at Wounded Knee in 1890 occurred largely because of governmental alarm over the revival of the religious Ghost Dance.

The policy of religious and cultural assimilation was accompanied by moves to abolish the Indian tribes as "domestic dependent nations." Under the General Allotment (Dawes) Act of 1887, Congress sought to coerce the Indian nations into "negotiating" the surrender of their remaining sovereignty, with communal tribal lands being broken up and distributed to individual Native Americans, who would receive U.S. citizenship. Despite the Fourteenth Amendment's grant of citizenship in 1868 to all people "born . . . in the United States and subject to the jurisdiction thereof" (which was understood to exclude natives "in a tribal relation"), the Supreme Court in *Elk v. Wilkins* (1884) had rejected the claim to citizenship and voting rights of an Indian who had left his tribe and fully subjected himself to ordinary state and federal jurisdiction. Justice Harlan dissented, objecting that the ruling created "a despised and rejected class of persons, with no nationality whatever." It was not until 1924 that Congress granted citizenship to all Native Americans, even those maintaining tribal relations.

Under the Curtis Act of 1898, Congress abandoned even the facade of negotiation and authorized the Dawes Commission to proceed with the goals of the Dawes Act without Indian consent. The goal of some supporters of the allotment policy was that the Indians would become private-property-owning farmers and adopt "civilized" European ways with the rights and responsibilities of ordinary American citizens. The desire to open up Indian lands for settlement, especially in the West, was a more potent factor—notably, in Oklahoma, where the Cherokee and affiliated tribes were effectively expropriated of most of the land reserved to them after the Trail of Tears. Senator Teller, speaking in opposition to one early allotment bill in 1881, prophetically predicted that the Native Americans "would [in 30 or 40 years] curse the hand that was raised professedly in their own defense . . . and if the people who are clamoring for [such legislation] understood Indian character, and Indian laws, and Indian morals, and Indian religion, they would not be here clamoring for this at all."

Reorganization, Assimilation (Again) and Self-Determination

In 1933–1934 the first of three major pendulum swings in twentieth-century federal Indian policy took place. Congress passed the Indian Reorganization (Wheeler-Howard) Act in 1934 at the instigation of President Roosevelt and his reformist Commissioner of Indian Affairs, John Collier. Under the Wheeler-Howard Act, the government abandoned the allotment policy (although much of the damage remained irreparably in place), sought to promote tribal self-government, and retreated from attempts to suppress native cultures and religions. Commissioner Collier, immediately on taking office in 1933, made clear that the Bureau of Indian Affairs would no longer interfere with Native Americans' exercise of their religious freedom and traditional ceremonies. Indeed, Collier actively promoted efforts to revitalize tribal cultures.

A second policy reversal occurred in 1953, however, with congressional passage of House Concurrent Resolution 108, which instructed the Interior Secretary to recommend legislation to terminate federal supervision of certain Indian tribes, with the long-range goal of disbanding the remaining native governments, revoking Native Americans' special status under federal law, and again attempting to assimilate them as ordinary citizens. This revival of the allotment philosophy proved relatively short-lived, though again with lasting damaging effects. A number of tribes underwent termination and then, realizing the costs, regained recognition only after lengthy legal battles, as happened with the Menominee in Wisconsin. Prompted by growing opposition, the executive branch began to passively resist Congress's mandate.

Finally, President Nixon's 1970 message to Congress on Indian policy strongly repudiated the 1953 termination approach and instead promoted self-determination and the right of tribes to administer federal support programs locally. Congress had already begun moving in this direction by making tribes the direct recipients of such support under President Johnson's Great Society programs, and this trend continued in the 1970s. Nixon's 1970 message, with its return to the spirit of the Roosevelt-Collier approach of the 1930s, remains the foundation of federal Indian policy today.

Congress, by Public Law 280 enacted in 1953, placed native reservations in several states under direct state criminal and civil jurisdiction and provided all other states the option of imposing jurisdiction (though tribal consent was required by the Indian Civil Rights Act of 1968), thus enhancing the risk of conflict between state laws and some practices associated with Native American religions. The California Supreme Court in *People v. Woody* (Calif., 1964) reviewed an attempt by the state to prosecute several Navajos for possession of peyote, a hallucinogen that they had used in a sacrament of central importance to the Native American Church. Applying the "compelling state interest" standard for free exercise of religion claims that was enunciated by the U.S. Supreme Court in *Sherbert v. Verner* (1963), the court reversed the convictions. Justice Tobriner's opinion held that the inconvenience of administering a bona fide religious exemption from the state's drug law was outweighed by the threat posed to the "theological heart" of the native religion at issue. It is noteworthy that an exemption was allowed under the National Prohibition (Volstead) Act of 1919 for the sacramental use of wine, such as in Roman Catholic or Jewish ceremonies. While religious peyote use *is* different, in that its mind-altering effects play a central role, that should not matter for constitutional purposes; if anything, peyote is arguably *more* essential to Native American Church ceremonies than, say, wine is to Catholic communion.

Some tribal governments themselves have come into conflict with native religious practices, as in *Native American Church v. Navajo Tribal Council* (10th Cir. 1959), in which the U.S. Court of Appeals for the Tenth Circuit upheld the Navajo Nation's ban on possession or use of peyote, even for ritual religious purposes. The tribe amended its criminal code in 1967, however, to permit religious use of peyote. The *Native American Church* decision is especially noteworthy because it relied on the principle—ultimately derived from Chief Justice Marshall's early trio of opinions—that the Indian tribes enjoy a residual sovereignty predating the Constitution and separate from that of either the states or the federal government. Full sovereignty was lost by conquest, treaty cession, or where affirmatively supplanted by U.S. law, but the residual sovereignty remains. As a result, tribal governmental actions are not directly subject to the limitations imposed by the Bill of Rights, the Fourteenth Amendment, and other constitutional guarantees on the federal and state governments. This principle was articulated by the Supreme Court as early as *Talton v. Mayes* (1896), which declined to apply the Fifth Amendment grand jury requirement to the Cherokee Nation, and it was reaffirmed in recent years by *United States v. Wheeler* (1978), which found no violation of the Fifth Amendment's double jeopardy clause in successive prosecutions in tribal and federal court for the same offense.

Imposing the Bill of Rights

This tribal immunity principle was challenged in cases such as *Colliflower v. Garland* (9th Cir. 1965), in which the U.S. Court of Appeals for the Ninth Circuit, while conceding that constitutional guarantees might not apply, held that a federal court had jurisdiction to issue a writ of habeas corpus to at least "inquire into the legality of the detention of an Indian pursuant to an order of an Indian court." Soon after, in the Indian Civil Rights Act of 1968, Congress took matters into its own hands and imposed most guarantees of the Bill of Rights on tribal governments, including the Free Exercise Clause. A notable omission was the Establishment Clause, imposition of which, it was thought, would have devastated many native religions integral to Indian cultures that remain heavily dependent on tribal governmental support.

Application of the Free Exercise Clause under the compelling interest standard led to numerous cases upholding religious exemptions from laws of general application, and cases involving native religious rights were no exception. In *Frank v. State* (Alaska, 1979), for example, the Alaska Supreme Court upheld the right of an Alaskan native to hunt a moose out of season for a funeral "potlatch," or feast required by Athabascan religious tradition. Likewise, Congress recognized the need for an Indian religious exemption from the Eagle Protection Act, which generally bans the hunting of bald and golden eagles. Congress amended the statute in 1962 to authorize the Interior Secretary to grant permits to natives to take eagles for bona fide religious purposes, such as the ceremonial use of feathers. In *United States v. Dion* (8th Cir. 1985), the U.S. Court of Appeals rejected a religious freedom claim by a Sioux Indian who killed several eagles without a permit, finding that he did so for commercial gain.

In *Teterud v. Burns* (8th Cir. 1975), the Eighth Circuit upheld a Native American prison inmate's right to a religious exemption from a prison regulation prohibiting long hair, finding that growing long hair was of great spiritual importance to many Indians and that the state's penological interests "could be served by viable, less restrictive means." The Supreme Court in *O'Lone v. Estate of Shabazz* (1987), however, established a far more deferential "reasonableness" standard for free exercise claims by inmates, resulting in the rejection of most subsequent religious claims by Native American prisoners, whether involving hair length, as in *Pollock v. Marshall* (6th Cir. 1988) and *Iron Eyes v. Henry* (8th Cir. 1990); use of a "sweat lodge," as in *Allen v. Toombs* (9th Cir. 1987); or wearing religious headbands, as in *Standing Deer v. Carlson* (9th Cir. 1987). Even after *O'Lone,* however, clearly discriminatory regulations were struck down. Illustrating how Indian claims have furthered the development of religious freedom principles to benefit all faiths, the Ninth Circuit in *Swift v. Lewis* (9th Cir. 1990) upheld the right of certain Christian prisoners to adhere to the "Vow of the Nazarite" by refusing to cut their hair or beards (in view of a hair-length exemption already permitted for Native Americans), and of Asian Indians to adhere to the Sikh religion. And in *SapaNajin v. Gunter* (8th Cir. 1988) the Eighth Circuit, enforcing a prior consent decree, held that a Sioux inmate's rights were violated when the prison gave him access only to a medicine man whose beliefs were contrary to those of most Sioux.

Ironically, in view of *Teterud,* the Tenth Circuit in *New Rider v. Board of Education* (1973) rejected the claim of three Pawnee junior high school students for a religious exemption from a school dress code forbidding boys from wearing hair below the collar. More recently, however, U.S. District Judge William Wayne Justice of the Eastern District of Texas struck down a similar school regulation on both free exercise and free expression grounds in *Alabama and Coushatta Tribes of Texas v. Big Sandy Independent School District* (Texas, 1993). Judge Justice stressed the importance of hair length to the Indian students' positive identification with their cultural and religious traditions, which is part of a nationwide revival of native cultures—a point apparently missed by the school board in its concern over a revival of "hippie" fashions. Although many Native Americans are Christian, Indian students who adhere to traditional native beliefs, have—like Jews and other religious minorities—raised important challenges under the Establishment Clause. In *Jager v. Douglas County School District* (11th Cir. 1989), in an opinion by Judge Johnson, the U.S. Court of Appeals for the Eleventh Circuit upheld a Native American high school band member's religious objection to the use of Christian prayers to open school football games.

Efforts to Promote Native Religious Rights

In the years following the adoption of the Indian Civil Rights Act of 1968, Congress continued to make some efforts to promote and protect native religious rights. In 1978 Congress enacted the American Indian Religious Freedom Act (AIRFA), which, despite its grandiose title, merely stated the sense of Congress that native religious rights (including access to sacred sites) should generally be respected; the act instructed the president and executive agencies to "evaluate" possible changes in governmental policies and procedures in that light and to report back to Congress. Yet Congress failed to act on the detailed legislative recommendations that were returned by President Carter's task force. The basically toothless and hortatory nature of the act was illustrated in *Sequoyah v. Tennessee Valley Authority* (6th Cir. 1980), in which the U.S. Court of Appeals for the Sixth Circuit rejected a challenge by two Cherokee bands to the completion of the Tellico Dam in Tennessee, which flooded various lands that were sacred to the Cherokee. Congress, following the Supreme Court's decision regarding the same dam in the "Snail Darter Case" of *Tennessee Valley Authority v. Hill* (1978), had ordered the dam completed without regard to the Endangered Species Act "or any other law," including the AIRFA. In *Badoni v. Higginson* (10th Cir. 1980) the Tenth Circuit rejected efforts by Navajos to prevent inundation by the Glen Canyon Dam Reservoir, and desecration by tourists, of sacred religious sites in Rainbow Bridge National Monument. And in *Wilson v. Block* (D.C. Cir. 1983) the U.S. Court of Appeals for the District of Columbia Circuit rejected efforts by both Hopis and Navajos to stop the expansion of a ski resort in the San Francisco Peaks, which are sacred to the religions of both tribes. The court held that government agencies satisfy any obligation under the AIRFA by merely "consider[ing] the views of Indian leaders" and "avoid[ing] unnecessary interference with Indian religious practices." The Supreme Court later held in *Lyng v. Northwest Indian Cemetery Protective Association* (1988) (discussed further below) that the AIRFA itself does not create any judicially enforceable right or cause of action.

The Indian Child Welfare Act, also enacted by Congress in 1978, has had a far more substantial effect in protecting Native American religion and culture. The act responded to long-standing abuses in the widespread adoption of Native American children by non-Indians. Not only did native communities have little control over such adoptions, or removals into foster care, but the adoptive or foster parents or institutions often raised the children in a Euro-American cultural milieu, cut off from any contact with Native American culture or religion. With some studies indicating that as many as a fourth to a third of all Native American children were ending up separated from their birth families in some manner, the potential deracinating effects of this trend recalled for many Native Americans the abuses of the old Indian boarding schools. The Child Welfare Act generally vests jurisdiction over Indian child custody proceedings in tribal courts, and it permits a child's Indian parents or the tribe itself to remove a proceeding from state court. Along with numerous other procedural safeguards regarding removal of children from their families or communities, the act establishes the right of Native American children, on reaching adulthood, to obtain information about their biological parents and tribal affiliation.

In passing the Native American Graves Protection and Repatriation Act of 1990, Congress also went far to remedy a long-standing grievance that has had profound religious overtones. Huge amounts of Native American human remains have languished for years in museums and research facilities, including the Smithsonian Institution, deeply offending the religious sensibilities of the affected tribes. Desecration of Indian burial sites in the name of anthropological research, or by treasure hunters, and theft of items found therein, has also been a perennial problem. The 1990 act vests ownership of any subsequently discovered Native American human remains and sacred, funerary, or other culturally significant objects found on federal or tribal lands in the descendants of such natives or their culturally affiliated tribes, where ascertainable. The act also imposes strict regulations on excavation or removal of such remains or objects on federal and tribal lands. The National Museum of the American Indian Act passed by Congress in 1989 imposes procedures and standards for the Smithsonian Institution to inventory and repatriate such remains and objects to appropriate native descendants or culturally affiliated tribes, where ascertainable, and the 1990 act extends this mandate to other federal agencies and all federally funded museums.

The Supreme Court and Native Free Exercise

In the 1980s and 1990s Native American claims began to dominate as never before the Supreme Court's jurisprudence on freedom of religion. The unusual nature of some of these claims, and the unfamiliar premises of native religions when viewed from a Western Judeo-Christian perspective, seemed to baffle the Court and ultimately led it to sharply restrict the protective scope of the Free Exercise Clause as applied to all religions. This in turn triggered a congressional response of epic importance.

In the first of three major cases, *Bowen, Secretary of Health and Human Services, et al. v. Roy* (1986), the Court confronted a religious objection by an Abenaki Indian (Roy) to the use of a Social Security number for his 2-year-old daughter, Little Bird of the Snow, as a condition for receipt of food stamps and welfare benefits. Roy believed that use of a number to identify the girl would "rob" her of her "spirit." He objected most strongly to any requirement that he himself provide or make use of the number in applying for benefits; more broadly, he objected to any use of the number by the government itself, even for its own internal recordkeeping purposes. The Court had little difficulty rejecting the latter claim; Chief Justice Burger wrote for an 8-to-1 majority on that point, with only Justice White dissenting in a brief, cryptic opinion finding the case controlled by *Sherbert.* The justices disputed whether the first claim was moot or unripe for decision, with Justice Stevens refusing to address it on the merits. The other justices split 5 to 3 in favor of Roy (assuming the merits were properly reached), though in separate opinions with the trial court left to sort out the issues on remand. Only Burger and Justices Powell and Rehnquist rejected Roy's first claim, arguing that the government need not accommodate such an idiosyncratic religious belief in enforcing "a facially neutral and uniformly applicable requirement" for receiving government benefits. Justice O'Connor's separate opinion, joined by Justices Brennan and Marshall (with the separate endorsement of Justice Blackmun and the implicit agreement of White), insisted on applying the traditional compelling interest standard. She found that a religious exemption for Roy would not significantly impair the government's ability to fulfill its concededly compelling interest in preventing welfare fraud, especially since the government had already assigned a Social Security number to Little Bird of the Snow and, pursuant to the Court's holding on Roy's second claim, could make internal use of it to process her benefits.

The Court finally addressed a sacred-site Native religious claim in the 1988 *Lyng* decision. In *Sequoyah, Badoni,* and *Wilson* the Sixth, Tenth, and D.C. Circuits had rejected sacred-site claims under both the AIRFA and the Free Exercise Clause. In *Lyng,* members of the Yurok, Karok, and Tolowa tribes of Northern California challenged the U.S. Forest Service's plans to build a road through a pristine wilderness area of the Six Rivers National Forest held sacred by the tribes. According to the uncontradicted evidence, the resultant traffic, noise, and logging (which the Forest Service planned to permit within half a mile of specific religious sites) threatened to render impossible the exercise of, and thus completely destroy, the plaintiffs' religion. In *Northwest Indian Cemetery Protective Association v. Peterson* (9th Cir., 1986), the Ninth Circuit, in a striking departure from prior case law, ruled in favor of the natives. Judge Canby, an acknowledged expert on Indian law, emphasized the central and indispensable religious role of the "high country" at issue and also discounted the government's claimed interest in building the road, which was part of the Forest Service's general policy of subsidizing excessive and uneconomical logging of public lands.

The Supreme Court, however, reversed. Justice O'Connor's 5-to-3 majority opinion professed an inability to distinguish the holding on the broader claim in *Roy,* despite the obvious differences between internal record-keeping practices of the government's own creation and the physical destruction of a landscape predating the government itself. As several commentators have noted, the majority's analysis seemed hobbled by an ethnocentric inability to recognize the essential character of most native faiths, or at least an unwillingness to flexibly refashion established doctrine to provide such faiths protection equivalent to that afforded more familiar Judeo-Christian beliefs. As Justice Brennan recognized in dissent, joined by Justices Marshall and Blackmun, the rituals that were threatened by the government's conduct in *Lyng,* unlike those of most Western religions, would have no meaning divorced from the land held sacred by the tribes: "Where dogma lies at the heart of Western religions, Native American faith is inextricably bound to the use of land. The site-specific nature of Indian religious practice derives from the Native American perception that land is itself a sacred, living being."

In response, the majority emphasized the practical implications of granting a religious "veto" over governmental development of "what is, after all, its land," at least where such action has some "neutral" justification and is not deliberately aimed at any particular religion. Indeed, the difficulties of fully protecting Native American religious beliefs within the Western premises of American law should not be underestimated. Most Native American languages have no word for "religion" as such, reflecting the lack of distinction in most native cultures between the sacred and the secular—a distinction central to Western thought and, specifically, to American constitutional law relating to religion. Similarly, the predominant native belief that humankind and its spiritual welfare cannot be separated from that of what non-Indians call "nature" or the land itself, although not unique to Native American thought, carries implications that, as suggested by Justice O'Connor in *Lyng,* may conflict with traditional Western legal notions of property. Since the Court's compelling interest analysis of free exercise claims already committed it, however, to the inherently difficult task of weighing, in a traditional evidentiary manner, the sincerity and character of various religious beliefs and the quantifiable impact of governmental action on them, it is difficult to see why the Court could not at least have made more of an effort to apply such analysis to the admittedly challenging Native American claims in cases like *Lyng.*

Instead, in the next major free exercise case it confronted, the Court abandoned compelling interest analysis and, in the view of many commentators, deprived the Free Exercise Clause of most of its independent constitutional significance. In *Employment Division, Department of Human Resources of Oregon v. Smith* (1990) the Court confronted the same peyote issue raised in *Woody.* Oregon had denied unemployment benefits to two Native American Church members who had been fired from their jobs for sacramental use of peyote, on the basis of Oregon's criminal prohibition of such conduct. Justice Scalia's majority opinion upheld the denial and effectively overruled *Sherbert*'s compelling interest test, at least as applied to a "neutral, generally applicable" criminal law. In the Court's view, so long as such a law is valid under other constitutional provisions, applies across the board, and does not discriminatorily target any particular religion, it should be sustained even though it directly conflicts with a central tenet or practice of a religious faith and even though the government's interests are minor or could easily be served by alternative less restrictive means. Justice O'Connor concurred in the judgment on the ground that the government's compelling interest in regulating drug use would be fatally undermined by an exemption for bona fide religious use of peyote, a conclusion seemingly refuted by the actual practice of the federal government and nearly half the states, which by 1990 had provided such an exemption from their drug laws. O'Connor vehemently disagreed with the majority's sweeping repudiation of the compelling interest test, however—a stance shared by Justice Blackmun, who, joined by Justices Brennan and Marshall, dissented outright for largely the same reasons expressed by the California Supreme Court in *Woody.*

Reactions to Native Free Exercise

There could hardly be a better illustration than *Smith* of the impact of Native American religious claims on the general law of religious freedom. The reaction to *Smith* was so strong and, almost universally, so negative that Congress, three years later, passed the Religious Freedom Restoration Act (RFRA), which attempted to restore *Sherbert*'s compelling interest test by statutory mandate. The Supreme Court recently struck down the RFRA as exceeding congressional power, in *City of Boerne v. P. F. Flores, Archbishop of San Antonio, and the United States* (1997), but a constitutional amendment along the same lines remains a distinct possibility. That such an amendment is even seriously debated—and would mark the first alteration of the Bill of Rights since its adoption in 1791—illustrates yet again the extraordinary ripple effects of the disputes over Native American religious practices. Interestingly, the Senate Judiciary Committee Report on the RFRA indicated that the act was also intended to overrule *O'Lone* and to restore the more rigorous "balancing test" previously used to adjudicate prisoners' religious claims. It appears dubious, however, whether the RFRA's standard, even if embodied in a constitutional amendment, would force a major overhaul of prisoners' religious rights cases. The Eighth Circuit, for example, in *Hamilton v. Schriro* (8th Cir. 1996), found a prison's institutional goals sufficiently compelling under the RFRA to reject a Choctaw inmate's claimed right to wear long hair and to use a sweat lodge. Judge McMillian, dissenting, argued that the RFRA would have required a return to the standard of *Teterud* rather than *Iron Eyes,* although, foreshadowing the Supreme Court's recent ruling, he concluded that the RFRA was unconstitutional in any event.

Although the RFRA itself did not expressly pass judgment on the specific result in *Smith,* as opposed to its broad reasoning, Congress amended the AIRFA in 1994 to prohibit the United States or any state or local government from banning the bona fide ceremonial use of peyote by Indians, or from discriminating against any Indian based on such use, while allowing for reasonable regulation. The invalidation of the RFRA casts some doubt on the constitutionality of the AIRFA amendment, though it would likely be upheld under Congress's power to regulate Indian affairs.

Commentators continue to debate the sufficiency of protection afforded to Native American religions, especially concerning sacred sites and especially given the uneven record of decisions even under the pre-*Smith* standard. The same 103rd Congress that enacted the RFRA and the peyote amendment to the AIRFA saw the introduction of several other bills to "put teeth" in the AIRFA, notably by providing greater protection for sacred sites. These were endorsed in general terms by President Clinton in an April 1994 meeting with Native American leaders, but none passed. The president issued an executive order in May 1996 that may go some way toward achieving the same goal, by requiring all federal agencies both to "accommodate access to and ceremonial use of Indian sacred sites" and to "avoid adversely affecting the physical integrity of such sacred sites." The order, however, was framed purely as a measure "to improve the internal management of the executive branch," and it specifically disclaimed any enforceability in court. However these particular issues are resolved, it seems safe to say, as the United States enters its third century under the

Constitution and Bill of Rights, that the religious beliefs of its original inhabitants will continue to challenge and inform the jurisprudence of religious freedom.

Bryan H. Wildenthal
Patrick M. O'Neil

Bibliography

Canby, William C., Jr., *American Indian Law in a Nutshell,* 2nd ed. (St. Paul, Minn.: West, 1988).

Debo, Angie, *And Still the Waters Run: The Betrayal of the Five Civilized Tribes* (Norman: University of Oklahoma Press, 1984; orig. pub. Princeton, N.J.: Princeton University Press, 1940).

———, *A History of the Indians of the United States* (Norman: University of Oklahoma Press, 1970).

Deloria, Vine, Jr., and Clifford M. Lytle, *The Nations Within: The Past and Future of American Indian Sovereignty* (New York: Pantheon, 1984).

———, and ———, *American Indians, American Justice* (Austin: University of Texas Press, 1983).

Ehle, John, *Trail of Tears: The Rise and Fall of the Cherokee Nation* (New York: Anchor Books/Doubleday, 1988).

Getches, David H., Charles F. Wilkinson, and Robert A. Williams, Jr., *Cases and Materials on Federal Indian Law,* 3rd ed. (St. Paul, Minn.: West, 1993).

Levy, Leonard W., *The Establishment Clause: Religion and the First Amendment* (New York: Macmillan, 1986).

O'Brien, Sharon L., "Freedom of Religion in Indian Country," 56 *Montana Law Review* 451–484 (Summer 1995).

Otis, D. S., *History of the Allotment Policy: Hearings on* H.R. 7902 before the House Committee on Indian Affairs, 73rd Cong., 2nd Sess. (1934).

Prucha, Francis Paul (ed.), *Documents of United States Indian Policy,* 2nd ed. (Lincoln: University of Nebraska Press, 1990).

Rhodes, John, "An American Tradition: The Religious Persecution of Native Americans," 52 *Montana Law Review* 13–72 (Winter 1991).

Shattuck, Petra T., and Jill Norgren, *Partial Justice: Federal Indian Law in a Liberal Constitutional System* (Oxford, Eng.: Berg, 1991).

Tapahe, Luralene D., Comment, "After the Religious Freedom Restoration Act: Still No Equal Protection for First American Worshipers," 24 *New Mexico Law Review* 331–363 (Spring 1994).

Thomas, David Hurst, Jay Miller, Richard White, Peter Nabokov, and Philip J. Deloria, *The Native Americans: An Illustrated History* (Atlanta: Turner, 1993).

Trope, Jack F., and Walter R. Echo-Hawk, "The Native American Graves Protection and Repatriation Act: Background and Legislative History," 24 *Arizona State Law Journal* 35–77 (Spring 1992).

Tyler, Lyman S., *A History of Indian Policy* (Washington, D.C.: U.S. Government Printing Office, 1973).

Wilkinson, Charles F., *American Indians, Time, and the Law: Native American Societies in a Modern Constitutional Democracy* (New Haven, Conn.: Yale University Press, 1987).

Williams, Robert A., Jr., *The American Indian in Western Legal Thought: The Discourses of Conquest* (Oxford and New York: Oxford University Press, 1990).

Wunder, John R., *"Retained by the People": A History of American Indians and the Bill of Rights* (Oxford and New York: Oxford University Press, 1994).

Cases and Statutes Cited

Alabama and Coushatta Tribes of Texas v. Big Sandy Independent School District, 817 F. Supp. 1319 (E.D. Tex. 1993), remanded without op., 20 F. 3d 469 (5th Cir. 1994).

Allen v. Toombs, 827 F. 2d 563 (9th Cir. 1987).

Badoni v. Higginson, 638 F. 2d 172 (10th Cir. 1980), cert. denied, 452 U.S. 954 (1981).

Bowen Secretary of Health and Human Services, et al. v. Roy, 476 U.S. 693 (1986).

Cherokee Nation v. Georgia, 30 U.S. (5 Pet.) 1 (1831).

City of Boerne v. P. F. Flores, Archbishop of San Antonio, and the United States, 521 U.S. 507 (1997)

Colliflower v. Garland, 342 F. 2d 369 (9th Cir. 1965).

Elk v. Wilkins, 112 U.S. 94 (1884).

Employment Division, Department of Human Resources of Oregon v. Smith, 494 U.S. 872 (1990).

Frank v. State, 604 P. 2d 1068 (Alaska 1979).

Hamilton v. Schriro, 74 F. 3d 1545 (8th Cir. 1996).

Iron Eyes v. Henry, 907 F. 2d 810 (8th Cir. 1990).

Jager v. Douglas County School District, 862 F. 2d 824 (11th Cir. 1989), cert. denied, 490 U.S. 1090 (1989).

Johnson v. McIntosh, 21 U.S. (8 Wheat.) 543 (1823).

Lyng v. Northwest Indian Cemetery Protective Association, 485 U.S. 439 (1988).

Native American Church v. Navajo Tribal Council, 272 F. 2d 131 (10th Cir. 1959).

New Rider v. Board of Education, 480 F. 2d 693 (10th Cir. 1973), cert. denied, 414 U.S. 1097 (1973).

Northwest Indian Cemetery Protective Association v. Peterson, 795 F. 2d 688 (9th Cir. 1986), rev'd, 485 U.S. 439 (1988).

O'Lone v. Estate of Shabazz, 482 U.S. 342 (1987).

People v. Woody, 61 Cal. 2d 716, 40 Cal. Rptr. 69, 394 P. 2d 813 (1964).

Pollock v. Marshall, 845 F. 2d 656 (6th Cir. 1988), cert. denied, 488 U.S. 897 (1988).

SapaNajin v. Gunter, 857 F. 2d 463 (8th Cir. 1988).

Sequoyah v. Tennessee Valley Authority, 620 F. 2d 1159 (6th Cir. 1980), cert. denied, 449 U.S. 953 (1980).

Sherbert v. Verner, 374 U.S. 398 (1963).

Standing Deer v. Carlson, 831 F. 2d 1525 (9th Cir. 1987).

Swift v. Lewis, 901 F. 2d 730 (9th Cir. 1990).

Talton v. Mayes, 163 U.S. 376 (1896).

Tennessee Valley Authority v. Hill, 437 U.S. 153 (1978).

Teterud v. Burns, 522 F. 2d 357 (8th Cir. 1975).

United States v. Dion, 762 F. 2d 674 (8th Cir. 1985), rev'd in part, 476 U.S. 734 (1986).

United States v. Wheeler, 435 U.S. 313 (1978).

Wilson v. Block, 708 F. 2d 735 (D.C. Cir. 1983), cert. denied, 464 U.S. 1056 (1984).

Worcester v. Georgia, 31 U.S. (6 Pet.) 515 (1832).

Act of Congress, ch. 120, 16 Stat. 544, 566 (1871), codified in relevant part at 25 U.S.C. §71 (1994).

American Indian Religious Freedom Act, Pub. L. 95-341, 92 Stat. 469 (1978), codified in part at 42 U.S.C. §1996 (1994).

American Indian Religious Freedom Act Amendments, Pub. L. 103-344, §2, 108 Stat. 3125 (1994), codified at 42 U.S.C. §1996a (1994).

Curtis Act, ch. 517, 30 Stat. 495 (1898).

Eagle Protection Act, ch. 278, 54 Stat. 250 (1940), amended by Pub. L. 87-884, 76 Stat. 1246 (1962), codified at 16 U.S.C. §§668–668d (1994).

General Allotment (Dawes) Act, ch. 119, 24 Stat. 388 (1887).

House Concurrent Resolution 108, 83rd Cong., 1st Sess., 67 Stat. B132 (1953).

Indian Child Welfare Act, Pub. L. 95-608, 92 Stat. 3069 (1978), codified at 25 U.S.C. §§1901–1963 (1994).

Indian Civil Rights Act, Pub. L. 90-284, tit. II, 82 Stat. 77 (1968), codified at 25 U.S.C. §§1301–1341 (1994).

Indian Citizenship Act, ch. 233, 43 Stat. 253 (1924), codified at 8 U.S.C. §1401(b) (1994).

Indian Reorganization (Wheeler-Howard) Act, ch. 576, 48 Stat. 984 (1934), codified at 25 U.S.C. §§461–494 (1994).

Menominee Restoration Act, Pub. L. 93-197, 87 Stat. 770 (1973).

Menominee Termination Act, Pub. L. 83-399, 68 Stat. 250 (1954).

Message from the President of the United States Transmitting Recommendations for Indian Policy, H.R. Doc. No. 363, 91st Cong., 2nd Sess. (July 8, 1970).

National Museum of the American Indian Act, Pub. L. 101-185, 103 Stat. 1336 (1989), codified at 20 U.S.C. §§80q to 80q-15 (1994).

National Prohibition (Volstead) Act, ch. 85, 41 Stat. 305 (1919).

Native American Graves Protection and Repatriation Act, Pub. L. 101-601, 104 Stat. 3048 (1990), codified at 25 U.S.C. §§3001–3013 (1994).

Navajo Tribal Council Res. CO-65-67 (1967), codified at Navajo Tribal Code tit. 17, §1201 (1978).

Presidential Executive Order 13007, 61 Fed. Reg. 26771 (May 24, 1996).

Public Law 83-280, 67 Stat. 588 (1953), codified in part at 18 U.S.C. §1162 and 28 U.S.C. §1360 (1994).

Religious Freedom Restoration Act, Pub. L. 103-141, 107 Stat. 1488 (1993), codified at 42 U.S.C. §§2000bb to 2000bb-4 (1994).

Senate Judiciary Comm. Rep. No. 103-111, 103rd Cong., 1st Sess. (1993), reprinted at 1993 USCCAN 1892.

Senate Report on Religious Freedom Restoration Act of 1993.

Treaty with the Kaskaskia, Aug. 13, 1803, 7 Stat. 78.

Treaty with the Kickapoo, Oct. 24, 1832, 7 Stat. 391.

Treaty with the Oneida, etc., Dec. 2, 1794, 7 Stat. 47.

Treaty with the Oneida, Feb. 3, 1838, 7 Stat. 566.

Treaty with the Osage, June 2, 1825, 7 Stat. 240.

Treaty with the Wyandot, etc., Sept. 29, 1817, 7 Stat. 160.

New Haven Colony's Fundamental Articles (1639)

The Reverend John Davenport and Theophilus Eaton, a merchant, led the move of Puritans to New Haven in 1638. Both men had arrived in Boston in 1637 with plans to settle in the Massachusetts Bay Colony; they soon became dissatisfied there, however, largely because of the controversy surrounding Anne Hutchinson. They then moved to a site on the Quinnipiac River in Connecticut. Although they claimed title to the land through purchase from the Indians, they had no charter. To alleviate the uncertainty caused by the lack of a charter, the free planters in the colony met on June 4, 1639, and accepted the Fundamental Agreement as the foundation for both civil and church government.

This rudimentary document recorded the planters' formal assent to each of six questions posed orally by Davenport. To each question the assembled planters indicated their unanimous assent. After each oral vote, a clerk wrote the question, then read it back to those assembled for a second vote.

The first of Davenport's six propositions was that the Scriptures provided the "perfect rule" for the duties which people were to perform in all areas of their lives: to God, to civil government, to family, and to church. From that first proposition followed the next three. For civil government, the planters reaffirmed the "plantation covenant," to which they had agreed when they first settled in the area. In addition, they agreed that a government "according to God" would best produce the civil order they desired. For ecclesiastical government, they indicated their desire to gather a church as soon as possible.

The two remaining actions were to create a way to select governmental officials and to start their church. The Reverend Davenport urged the planters to refer to the Scriptures for guidance in selecting members of government. After some discussion, the planters agreed that magistrates and other officials should be chosen from burgesses, who could be selected only from church members. Likewise, the church was to be started only by a select group of twelve whose reputations were untarnished. Once again the planters publicly discussed the matter before selecting only eleven men who were fit to begin a church; the twelfth would come later.

The Fundamental Agreement reflects the early congregational form of government—a characteristic Puritan joinder of church and state under the umbrella of God's law. "Agreement" is an apt title, for through it the colonists self-consciously bound themselves in a compact with God and with each other. The public act of assenting was vital to this formation of government. To emphasize that fact, those who joined later were required to affix their signatures to the document, to signify their personal acceptance of the fundamental order of the society.

In these halting, awkward procedures the colonists took early steps toward a written constitution. The excessive formality for recording responses reveals a society on the cusp between oral and written culture. The Fundamental Agreement also hints at a nascent sense of constitutionalism, with the colonists providing a written document for their own governance.

Walter F. Pratt, Jr.

Bibliography

Hoadly, Charles J. (ed.), *Records of the Colony and Plantation of New Haven* (Hartford, Conn.: Case, Tiffing and Co., 1857).

Lambert, Edward R., *History of the Colony of New Haven* (New Haven, Conn.: Hitchcock and Stafford, 1838).

N

New York Ministry Act of 1693

In September 1693, after nearly a year of urgent pleading by the province's royal governor, Benjamin Fletcher, the New York Assembly passed "An Act for Settling a Ministry and Raising a Maintenance for them." The act seemed to be straightforward, but its wording later proved to be so vague as to make its interpretation the cause of a series of bitter disputes. The act created new parishes for the support of "good sufficient Protestant Minister[s]" in New York City, Westchester, Rye, Richmond (Staten Island), and Hempstead and Jamaica on Long Island (communities where English settlement was densest).

The annual levies for the ministers were to range from 40 pounds in Richmond (where the salary could be paid "in Country produce") to 100 pounds in New York City. Their collection was to be overseen by two churchwardens and ten vestrymen, who were to be elected annually by all the freeholders, regardless of denomination, in each parish. In a similarly decentralized fashion, the ministers were to be "called to officiate in their respective precincts by the respective Vestry men and church wardens." Governor Benjamin Fletcher, an Anglican, however, in an inaugural squabble over the act's meaning, told the assemblymen that, if they thought that the local clergy could be hired without his approval, they were "far mistaken: for [he had] the power of collating . . . any minister in [his] government" by virtue of his royal commission.

One interpretation of the act, taken up by hopeful dissenting congregations, was that it simply restated with greater strength and specificity the provisions of the Duke's Laws of 1665. Vestries could call and subsidize clergymen of whatever denomination a local ministry favored, just as they had under the old "local option" plan. The provincial assembly infuriated Fletcher by backing this view in 1695, when it announced that the New York City vestry, which was elected under the Ministry Act's provisions, was entitled to call a non-Anglican "Dissenting Protestant minister" to what would later become Trinity Church.

Fletcher's own stridently advanced interpretation was that the act had exclusively established the Church of England in the six parishes. It was the opinion of at least one observer that Fletcher had allowed the act to be so "very loosely worded" precisely for the purpose of slipping an Anglican establishment past the almost wholly dissenting legislature. There were, however, not enough Anglican clergymen in the province to staff each of the proposed parishes (in 1693, for example, there was only one, the chaplain of the royal fort at Manhattan); nor were there enough Anglican parishioners to fill all the proposed churches. Still, Fletcher was determined to assert Anglicanism's special status in New York so far as he could. At one point he had to resort to denominational bribery to win the vestry contest—an action indicative of Anglican weakness in New York. Fletcher did incorporate a Dutch Reformed church in Manhattan, exempting it from government oversight only months before yet another elected vestry finally called an Anglican minister to the city. The Dutch were evidently grateful enough for their charter to clear the way at least for a publicly funded Anglican church in New York City.

Despite a few disputes surrounding attempts by Lord Cornbury, a later governor, to use his much-disputed collating power to plant Anglican ministers in dissenting pulpits, for much of the next half-century the church's establishment in New York was of necessity a provisional and compromising one. Dissenting Protestants were always tolerated; and though only Anglican clergy could be publicly supported in the six parishes, from 1699 onward, public funds could at least be levied for the construction and repair of dissenting local majorities' church buildings. The Ministry Act may have nudged New York away from a multiple establishment toward the establishment of the Church of England, but it did so only tentatively.

Peter Silver

Bibliography

Butler, Jon, *Awash in a Sea of Faith: Christianizing the American People* (Cambridge, Mass.: Harvard University Press, 1990).

Curry, Thomas J., *The First Freedoms: Church and State in America to the Passage of the First Amendment* (New York: Oxford University Press, 1986).

Henshaw, R. Townsend, "The Ministry Act of 1693," 10 *Quarterly Bulletin of the Westchester County Historical Society* 1–7 (1934).

Levy, Leonard W., *The Establishment Clause: Religion and the First Amendment* (New York: Macmillan, 1986).

New York State Statutory Revision Commission, *The Colonial Laws of New York from the Year 1664 to the Revolution,* vol. 1 (Albany, N.Y.: James B. Lyon, 1984).

O'Callaghan, E.B., *The Documentary History of the State of New York,* vol. 3 (Albany, N.Y.: Weed Parsons, 1850).

Pratt, John Webb, *Religion, Politics, and Diversity: The Church and State Theme in New York History* (Ithaca, N.Y.: Cornell University Press, 1967).

Northwest Ordinance

Article I of the Northwest Ordinance—enacted by the Confederation Congress of July 13, 1787—stated: "No person, demeaning himself in a peaceable and orderly manner shall ever be molested on account of his mode of worship or religious sentiments in the said territory." One of six "articles of compact" that were supposed to secure "the fundamental principles of civil and religious liberty," this guarantee of toleration was to "forever remain unalterable, unless by common consent" of the "Original States and the people and States in the said territory."

By later standards, the language of Article I is weak and permissive. Toleration was guaranteed under every state constitution, even where specific denominations retained their privileged position. For tactical reasons, however, the authors of the Northwest Ordinance defined religious freedom in minimalist terms and expected settlers to stake out more advanced positions when they drafted their own constitutions. This expectation was based on Congress's reservation of public lands "for the maintenance of public schools," but *not* of churches, in its Land Ordinance of May 20, 1785, organizing the survey and sale of the national domain.

For congressional policy makers, the crucial question was whether public resources would underwrite an establishment—presumably of several denominations—during the period of federal trusteeship. Federal interference in the religious life of the *states* was unlikely, even without the adoption of the Bill of Rights, but the situation of new *territories* that were subject to Congress's plenary authority was far more vulnerable. The challenge was to preempt the possibility that any denomination or denominations would gain a privileged position *before* statehood. Of course, religious diversity in Congress itself discouraged a favored position for any specific denomination. The more subtle danger was that the rapid devolution of public lands to local authorities would permit the emergence of a multiple establishment similar to the array of different church–state arrangements found in the original states. The 1785 Land Ordinance prevented such an outcome by securing federal control of all public lands, except those dedicated to schools, until they were transferred to private hands.

Congress's task was complicated by the need to attract orderly and industrious settlers. The most eligible recruits—as the rapid organization of the Ohio Company of Associates demonstrated—were New Englanders, who customarily expected new town lands to be set aside for the support of religion. But growing opposition to church establishments, even in New England, made provision for schools instead of churches in the 1785 ordinance an attractive alternative. In the words of James Madison, Congress thus banished the "antiquated Bigotry" of established religion. At the same time, however, it was not in Congress's interests to draw attention to this substitution. The weak language in Article I of the Northwest Ordinance—drafted by Nathan Dane of Massachusetts in consultation with Rev. Manasseh Cutler, the Ohio Company's lobbyist at Congress—reflected the ordinance's function as a device for promoting the sales of federal lands. Article III further demonstrated Congress's sensitivity to Yankee predilections: "Religion, Morality and knowledge being necessary to good government and the happiness of mankind, Schools and the means of education shall forever be encouraged." The premise here was that religion would flourish where schools enjoyed state (federal) support, where no denomination could claim a privileged position, and where settlers could worship without molestation.

The Land Ordinance of 1785 and the Northwest Ordinance of 1787 together guaranteed religious freedom in the new states of the West by asserting federal control over the settlement process and by precluding the use of public resources for the support of churches. Congress's intention was to recruit settlers from the entire union, including states such as Connecticut and Massachusetts, where church establishments survived the Revolution. The ultimate success of this policy—apparent in the mixed settlement of the Northwest—set the stage for more forthright statements of the principle of religious freedom in the constitutions of Ohio (1802) and subsequent new western states.

Peter S. Onuf

Bibliography

Onuf, Peter S., *Statehood and Union: A History of the Northwest Ordinance* (Bloomington: Indiana University Press, 1987).

Nyquist

See COMMITTEE FOR PUBLIC EDUCATION AND RELIGIOUS LIBERTY V. NYQUIST.

O

Officeholding Clause of Constitution and Religious Test for Officeholding

The U.S. Constitution's clause prohibiting religious tests as a qualification for officeholding represents a break with the practice of England and of most of the American states. With the exception of New York and Virginia, all English and American governments in 1787 limited officeholding to those who professed particular religious beliefs. By including this provision, the Constitutional Convention signaled its acceptance of the libertarian principles of Thomas Jefferson's Virginia Statute of Religious Freedom, as well as its practical judgment that the diversity of religious practice in America made sectarianism unlikely to threaten the civil order. The prohibition of religious tests points beyond the idea of "toleration" found in John Locke's *Letter Concerning Toleration* and toward the First Amendment's Free Exercise Clause.

The requirement of a religious test for holding public office in England, according to William Blackstone's *Commentaries,* was imposed "in order the better to secure the established church against perils from non-conformists of all denominations, infidels, turks, jews, heretics, papists, and sectaries." Following the Restoration, a series of test acts effectively limited officeholding to members of the Church of England. The Act of Toleration in 1689 lifted certain penalties for dissenting Protestants, but it kept in place the legal apparatus, including test oaths, that disqualified Catholics and dissenters from becoming members of Parliament or holding office.

Locke's *Letter Concerning Toleration,* published in 1689, found a receptive audience in Revolutionary America. The most famous of the founding-era documents concerning religious liberty, Jefferson's 1786 Virginia Statute of Religious Freedom, for example, draws heavily on Locke's arguments. The idea of religious freedom, of course, had been a part of the American political culture since the time of Roger Williams; the Revolution's rejection of British practices likewise undermined the religious establishments in the states. In most early state constitutions, religious tests were retained, but as Thomas Curry suggests, these tests were intended to ensure good government rather than to support an established church.

The Constitutional Convention spent very little time considering the prohibition on religious tests. The clause prohibiting test oaths was introduced by Charles Pinckney of South Carolina on August 20, 1787, and was committed without discussion or debate to the Committee of Detail. Ten days later Pinckney reintroduced it on the convention floor. The only recorded comment about the proposal is that of Roger Sherman, who "thought it unnecessary, the prevailing liberality being a sufficient security against such tests." Without revision, and with no further discussion, the motion passed unanimously.

In the debate over ratification, Federalists used the clause prohibiting test oaths to show that the Constitution gave Congress no power over religion and, moreover, ensured that Congress would stay out of that field. Oliver Ellsworth of Connecticut pointed to the practical problem that "[a] test in favour of any one denomination of Christians [i.e., Protestants] would be to the last degree absurd in the United States." Such a test "would incapacitate more than three-fourths of the American citizens for any publick office." Ellsworth concluded that "the true principle" was that "[c]ivil government has no business to meddle with the private opinions of the people."

Federalists also argued, as did Edmund Randolph in Virginia's ratifying convention, that the clause was an exception to a general power of Congress to impose oaths of office on federal officials, not an exception to a general power of Congress over religion. In North Carolina's ratifying convention, Anti-Federalists, like William Lancaster, made an issue of this inconsistency. In fact, the general sentiment favoring freedom of conscience and opposing religious tests led most interpreters to read the clause as Ellsworth did, as a prevention of religious establishments and a signal that the government should stay out of the private sphere. Even those who, like William Lancaster, deplored the possibility that "Papists" and "Mahometans" might occupy "the President's chair" did not object to the principle of abolishing tests.

Most of the dissatisfaction with the clause prohibiting religious tests concerned its failure to bar officeholding by non-Christians. Particularly vocal were New England Anti-Federalists, who objected to the clause as "a departure from the principles of our forefathers, who came here for the preservation of their religion; . . . it would admit deists, atheists, &c., into the general government . . . and, of course, a corruption of morals ensue." Another concluded his objections to the Constitution "by saying, that he shuddered at the idea that Roman Catholics, Papists, and Pagans might be introduced into office, and that Popery and the Inquisition may be established in America."

Despite the Anti-Federalists' misgivings, the separation of civil and religious duty that is implied by the clause is not absolute. It follows immediately the requirement that all officers in both the federal and the state governments should be bound "by oath or affirmation" to support the Constitution. Oliver Wolcott, in Connecticut's ratifying convention, noted that this oath is itself "a direct appeal to that God who is the avenger of perjury" and added—perhaps to reassure the Anti-Federalists—that this appeal "is a full acknowledgment of his being." Thus one of the amendments recommended by South Carolina's ratifying convention would have altered the clause to read: "but no *other* religious test shall ever be required. . . ." When this recommendation was put before Congress in 1789, Roger Sherman again offered the sole observation. In a letter signed "A Citizen of New Haven" in the *New York Packet,* Sherman described the South Carolina proposal as "an ingenious one, but not very important, because the Constitution as it now stands, will have the same effect, as it would have with that amendment." Thus far, the practice of requiring oaths of allegiance has not been challenged on the ground that it constitutes, even implicitly, an establishment of religion or an imposition on its free exercise. The Constitution's prohibition on religious tests has generally been accepted, instead, as an assurance of the free exercise of religion without fear of "civil incapacitations."

J. Jackson Barlow

Bibliography

Blackstone, William, *Commentaries on the Law of England,* 4 vols. (Oxford, Eng.: Clarendon, 1765–1769).

Borden, Morton, *Jews, Turks, and Infidels* (Chapel Hill: University of North Carolina Press, 1984).

Curry, Thomas J., *The First Freedoms: Church and State in America to the Passage of the First Amendment* (New York: Oxford University Press, 1986).

Kurland, Philip B., and Ralph Lerner, (eds.), *The Founders' Constitution,* 5 vols. (Chicago: University of Chicago Press, 1987).

Pfeffer, Leo, *Church, State, and Freedom,* rev. ed. (Boston: Beacon, 1967).

Officeholding: Religious-Based Limitations in Eighteenth-Century State Constitutions

Most of the American colonies originally followed the English practice of imposing religious tests on holders of public office. The nature of the tests, however, varied from colony to colony, according to the influence of the religious establishment, as did the extent to which tests were carried over into the first state constitutions. It is difficult, and perhaps ultimately misleading, to make generalizations about what the idea of a religious establishment meant to Americans of the eighteenth century. For example, one might expect that an element of any establishment would be a requirement that officeholders subscribe to its beliefs and that the requirement would disappear with the establishment. Yet many of the early state constitutions apparently saw no inconsistency in prohibiting establishments, on the one hand, and retaining a religious test, on the other.

In this respect Pennsylvania's Bill of Rights of 1776, reaffirmed in 1790, was typical: It abolished the religious establishment and yet provided that no man "who acknowledges the being of a God" could be deprived of civil rights. The flurry of state constitution writing in the 1770s did not produce immediate or convincing victories for the principle of religious liberty, however frequently invoked. Only two states, New York and Virginia, dropped the requirement of a religious test altogether. New York did so explicitly in its 1777 Constitution, declaring religious freedom and formally ending its religious establishment. Virginia's 1776 Constitution, prefaced by its influential Bill of Rights, passes over the issue of religious tests in silence. Not until the Statute of Religious Freedom a decade later were all religious limitations explicitly removed in Virginia.

Two states, Connecticut and Rhode Island, did not write new state constitutions but continued under their royal charters of 1662 and 1663, respectively. Connecticut, where the religious establishment remained after the Revolution, retained disabilities for "dissenters." Rhode Island's 1663 charter had gone further than any contemporary document in granting religious freedom, and it served as the state constitution until 1842, when the new constitution incorporated a religious liberty clause drawn almost verbatim from the Virginia statute.

The other nine states that wrote constitutions in the Revolutionary era imposed various forms of religious tests, either as a precondition for officeholding or as an oath to be taken on assuming office. The most common requirement, which appears in the constitutions of five states, is that officeholders be Protestants. The New Hampshire Constitution of 1784, for example, required that all officeholders "shall be of the Protestant religion," but it did not require them to swear to that fact. These restrictions stayed in place until 1877. Other states that limited officeholding to Protestants were New Jersey, North Carolina, South Carolina, and Georgia.

Massachusetts and Maryland, in a variation of this requirement, specified that officeholders must take an oath declaring a belief in "the Christian religion." Massachusetts further added an oath abjuring any allegiance to any "foreign power whatsoever" in "any matter, civil, ecclesiastical, or spiritual, within this commonwealth." These oaths were dropped in 1821, more than a decade before Massachusetts formally ended its religious establishment. In Maryland a bill to grant citizenship rights to Jews was first considered and defeated in 1802; similar "Jew Bills" were defeated in 1804, 1819, and 1823 before finally becoming part of Maryland's Constitution in 1826. The test became a general "declaration of belief in the existence of God" in the Constitution of 1867. This requirement persisted until the U.S. Supreme Court ruled it unconstitutional in *Torcaso v. Watkins* (1961).

The next most common feature was a prohibition on officeholding by members of the clergy. New York disqualified clergymen "of any denomination whatsoever," while North Carolina limited the disability to clergymen who were active. South Carolina not only excluded active clergy but also imposed a two-year waiting period after they left the ministry. Georgia's 1789 Constitution dropped the requirement of the 1777 Constitution that all representatives "be of the Protestant religion," instead prohibiting the clergy from holding office. Some states retained a similar prohibition well into the twentieth century; for example, the Supreme Court did not strike down Tennessee's provision until the 1978 case of *McDaniel v. Paty.*

Three states—Pennsylvania, Delaware, and North Carolina—required a belief in the divine inspiration of the Old and New Testaments. Pennsylvania's heritage of religious toleration was apparent in its 1776 Constitution, which prohibited ecclesiastical establishments. Yet it also required of public officials an oath affirming belief in "one God, the creator and governor of the universe" and acknowledging "the Scriptures of the Old and New Testaments to be given by Divine Inspiration." These provisions were dropped in 1790. Delaware replaced its requirement (together with that of a belief in the Trinity) in 1792 with a prohibition on religious tests.

North Carolina's 1776 Constitution went further than any other in imposing a religious test. Article 32 of the North Carolina Constitution barred from office anyone "who shall deny the being of God." It also excluded those who denied "the truth of the Protestant religion, or the divine authority either of the Old or New Testaments." Finally, to make sure that no one was overlooked, it banned those "who shall hold religious principles incompatible with the freedom and safety of the State." Despite Article 32, Jews were permitted to hold seats in North Carolina's legislature, and exclusion on religious grounds became an issue chiefly for constitutional conventions. In 1835, after intense debate, the article was changed only by substituting "Christian" for "Protestant." Not until 1868 was it replaced by a simple disqualification of "all persons who shall deny the being of Almighty God."

South Carolina's 1778 Constitution called for a religious establishment and described that establishment in unusual detail. In addition to the common requirement that senators and representatives be Protestant, this constitution also imposed the unique requirement that each voter acknowledge that he accepts "the being of a God, and believes in a future state of rewards and punishments." These tests were dropped in the 1790 Constitution, although a prohibition on clerical officeholding was retained.

Although some state religious tests remained even into the twentieth century, most had disappeared by the end of the eighteenth. The new state constitutions of the later 1780s and 1790s reflect the influence of the 1786 Virginia Statute of Religious Freedom and the U.S. Constitution of 1787, as well as the experience of the first decades of independence. In each case, the newer constitutions show a movement away from religious tests and toward greater freedom, as well as a greater consistency with state bills of rights guaranteeing religious liberty.

J. Jackson Barlow

Bibliography

Adams, Willi Paul, *The First American Constitutions* (Chapel Hill: University of North Carolina Press, 1980).

Borden, Morton, *Jews, Turks, and Infidels* (Chapel Hill: University of North Carolina Press, 1984).

Curry, Thomas J., *The First Freedoms: Church and State in America to the Passage of the First Amendment* (New York: Oxford University Press, 1986).

Levy, Leonard W., *The Establishment Clause: Religion and the First Amendment* (New York: Macmillan, 1986).

Thorpe, Francis Newton (ed.), *The Federal and State Constitutions, Colonial Charters, and Other Organic Laws* 7 vols. (Washington, D.C.: U.S. Government Printing Office, 1909).

Cases Cited

McDaniel v. Paty, 435 U.S. 618 (1978).

Torcaso v. Watkins, 367 U.S. 488 (1961).

Ohio Civil Rights Commission v. Dayton Christian Schools 477 U.S. 619 (1986)

In the circumstances leading up to this case a pregnant teacher was told that her employment contract with the religious school where she worked would not be renewed because of the school's religious doctrine that mothers should stay home with their preschool-age children. After the teacher had contacted an attorney, who threatened suit under state and federal sex discrimination laws, Dayton Christian Schools rescinded its nonrenewal decision but terminated the teacher because she had violated its doctrine of resolving disputes internally. That is, the Dayton Christian Schools also required that its teachers subscribe to a particular set of religious beliefs, including belief in the internal resolution of disputes through the "Biblical chain of command." As a contractual condition of employment, teachers must agree to present any grievance to their immediate supervisor and to acquiesce in the final authority of Dayton's board of directors, rather than to pursue a remedy in civil court.

The teacher then filed a charge with appellant Ohio Civil Rights Commission, alleging that under Ohio statutes Dayton's original nonrenewal decision constituted unlawful sex discrimination and that its termination decision unlawfully penalized her for asserting her rights.

Ohio Civil Rights Commission v. Dayton Christian Schools (1986) concerned the appropriateness of federal court intervention in this dispute. The Civil Rights Commission had initiated administrative proceedings against Dayton Christian Schools, which answered the complaint by asserting that the First Amendment prevented the commission from exercising jurisdiction over it, because its actions had been taken pursuant to sincerely held religious beliefs. While the administrative proceedings were pending, Dayton Christian Schools filed an action in federal district court seeking an injunction against the state administrative proceedings on the ground that any investigation of its hiring process or any sanctions for its nonrenewal or termination decisions would violate the religion clauses of the First Amendment. The federal district court refused the injunction, ruling instead that the Civil Rights Commission's actions would not violate the First and Fourteenth Amendments.

In an opinion by Justice William Rehnquist, the U.S. Supreme Court held that the district court should have abstained under the doctrine developed in *Younger v. Harris* (1971). *Younger* held that a federal court should not enjoin a pending state criminal proceeding except when necessary to prevent great and immediate irreparable injury. This doctrine was based on concerns for comity and federalism. The Supreme Court held that such concerns are equally applicable to other types of state proceedings, including administrative proceedings, judicial in nature, in which important state interests are vindicated, so long as in the course of those proceedings the federal plaintiff will have a full and fair opportunity to litigate his or her constitutional claim. The elimination of prohibited sex discrimination was deemed to be a sufficiently important state interest to bring the present case within the ambit of the *Younger* doctrine. Moreover, the Court held there was no reason to doubt that Dayton Christian Schools would receive an adequate opportunity to raise its constitutional claims. Even assuming that Ohio law is such that the Civil Rights Commission may not consider the constitutionality of the statute under which it operates, it is sufficient that under Ohio law constitutional claims may be raised in state court judicial review of the administrative proceedings.

The Supreme Court rejected the religious school's contention that the mere exercise of jurisdiction over it by the state administrative body would violate its First Amendment rights. The Court held that the commission violates no constitutional rights by merely investigating the circumstances of the teacher's discharge, if only to ascertain whether the ascribed religious-based reason was in fact the reason for the discharge. Justice Rehnquist was joined in this opinion by then–Chief Justice Warren Burger and Justices Byron White, Louis Powell, and Sandra Day O'Connor.

The remaining justices—John Paul Stevens, William Brennan, Thurgood Marshall, and Harry Blackmun—joined in a concurring opinion written by Justice Stevens. Stevens agreed with the majority that the investigation of the charges and the conduct of a hearing on those charges would not violate the First Amendment. He further agreed that a challenge to a possibly intrusive remedy would be premature at this point in the proceedings. The only difference taken by the concurrence appeared in a footnote; Justice Stevens disagreed with the majority on whether the *Younger* doctrine required the dismissal of the complaint:

> That disposition would presumably deny the School a federal forum to adjudicate the constitutionality of a provisional administrative remedy, such as reinstatement pending resolution of the complainant's charges, even though the constitutional issues have become ripe for review by the Commission's entry of a coercive order and the Commission refuses to address the merits of the constitutional claims. *Younger* abstention has never been applied to subject a federal-court plaintiff to an allegedly unconstitutional state administrative order when the constitutional challenge to that order can be asserted, if at all, only in state-court judicial review of the administrative proceeding.

Lea Vander Velde

Bibliography

"Government Regulation of Religious Organizations," 100 *Harvard Law Review* 1740–1781 (1987).

Lupu, Ira C., "Where Rights Begin: The Problem of Burdens on the Free Exercise of Religion," 102 *Harvard Law Review* 933–990 (1989).

——— "Free Exercise Exemption and Religious Institutions: The Case of Employment Discrimination," 67 *Boston University Law Review* 391–442 (1987).
Fiebler, David "Serving God or Caesar: Constitutional Limits on the Regulation of Religious Employers," 51 *Missouri Law Review* 779–791 (1986).
Wessels, Shelley K., "The Collision of Religious Exercise and Governmental Nondiscrimination Policies," 41 *Stanford Law Review* 1201–1231 (1989).

Cases Cited

Ohio Civil Rights Commission v. Dayton Christian Schools, 477 U.S. 619 (1986).
Younger v. Harris, 401 U.S. 37 (1971).

Overseas Possessions of the United States and Religious Liberty

In 1898 the United States annexed Hawaii pursuant to the Newlands Resolution and acquired Puerto Rico and the Philippines as war booty under the Treaty of Paris. The cases *Lowrey v. Hawaii* (1907 and 1910), *Ponce v. Roman Catholic Apostolic Church* (1908), and *Santos v. Holy Roman Catholic Apostolic Church* (1907) illustrate—as Chief Justice Melville Fuller said for a unanimous Court in *Ponce*—some of the problems that courts had to confront "incident to the transfer of sovereignty from a regime of union of church and state to the American system of complete separation." Those problems dealt mainly with issues of church property and of the juridical personality of the Catholic Church. In Puerto Rico and the Philippines the transfer of sovereignty to the United States immediately marked the disappearance of all government financing of the Catholic Church and its clergy, as had been practiced under Spanish rule. The Treaty of Paris, however, expressly preserved in Article 8 the right of the Catholic Church to retain the property it possessed before 1898, most of which it had obtained from government sources.

In *Lowrey* Justice Joseph McKenna, for a unanimous Court, enforced an 1850 agreement whereby a religious institution transferred a school to the Hawaiian government with the condition that religious training be continuously offered. In the event of nonfulfillment of that condition, the agreement provided for reversion of title to the grantor or payment of $15,000, at Hawaii's option. Hawaii's Organic Act prohibited governmental aid to sectarian institutions. However the Court implicitly rejected that this prohibition relieved the territory of the obligation accepted by its predecessor. The Court ordered Hawaii to exercise its option under the agreement.

In *Ponce* the Court faced a challenge by a Puerto Rican municipality to the Catholic Church's possession of two temples that had been built in the early 1800s with municipal funds. The Court affirmed the Puerto Rico supreme court and recognized, both under the treaty and under international law, the juridical personality of the Catholic Church and its right to retain title to property it had received from the Spanish government. The municipality forcefully argued that the Catholic Church had no legal personality, because it had not been incorporated under the laws of Puerto Rico, and thus it could not bring suit. The Supreme Court rejected this contention. It held that under Spanish law the Catholic Church had corporate existence and that the treaty and international law recognized its legal status.

The *Ponce* decision had two important consequences. First, it spurred a settlement of all pending lawsuits involving church property. This settlement included the federal government, which compensated the church for certain property reserved for military use by presidential order. Second, on the authority of *Ponce,* the Catholic Church in Puerto Rico has never incorporated, unlike other religious organizations.

Lastly, in *Santos* Justice Oliver Wendell Holmes, speaking for a unanimous Court, reiterated the *Ponce* holding and affirmed a Philippine judgment returning certain property to the Catholic Church, which owned it at the time of the transfer of sovereignty.

The transition in Hawaii, Puerto Rico, and the Philippines to a regime of separation of church and state was relatively smooth. In the Philippines most property disputes were settled without recourse to the courts. In Puerto Rico there was more litigation, but it quickly ended after the *Ponce* decision.

José Julián Alvarez-González

Bibliography

Colón-Rosado, Aníbal, "Relations between Church and State in Puerto Rico," 46

Revista del Colegio de Abogados de Puerto Rico 51 (1985).

Kauper, Paul G., and Stephen C. Ellis, "Religious Corporations and the Law," 71 *Michigan Law Review* 1499–1574 (1973).

Kerr, James, *The Insular Cases: The Role of the Judiciary in American Expansionism* (Port Washington, N.Y.: Kennikat, 1982).

Vivas, José G., "La Defensa de los Bienes Temporales de la Iglesia Durante los Años 1904–1908," 16 *Revista de Derecho Puertorriqueno* 395 (1977).

Cases and Statutes Cited

Lowrey v. Hawaii, 206 U.S. 206 (1907), 215 U.S. 554 (1910).

Ponce v. Roman Catholic Apostolic Church, 210 U.S. 296 (1908).

Santos v. Holy Roman Catholic Apostolic Church, 212 U.S. 463 (1908).

Newlands Resolution, 30 Stat. 750 (1898).

Treaty of Paris, 30 Stat. 1754 (1898).

P

Pacifists and Naturalization

The Naturalization Act of 1906 required an applicant for citizenship to declare under oath that he or she would "support and defend the Constitution and laws of the United States against all enemies, foreign and domestic. . . ." During World War I the Naturalization Service began to ask all applicants for citizenship whether they were willing, if necessary, "to take up arms" in defense of the nation. In 1927 Rosika Schwimmer, a well-known pacifist author and lecturer, stated in her application for naturalization that she could not in good conscience take up arms to defend the United States, although she was willing to take the oath of allegiance. In a 6-to-3 decision in *United States v. Schwimmer* (1929) the Supreme Court held that Schwimmer's refusal to say that she would bear arms constituted a valid ground for rejecting her application for citizenship. In his opinion for the Court, Justice Pierce Butler explained that "it is the duty of citizens by force of arms to defend our government against all enemies whenever necessity arises" and that "[w]hatever tends to lessen the willingness of citizens to discharge their duty to bear arms in the country's defense detracts from the strength and safety of the government." He warned that the "influence of conscientious objectors against the use of military force in defense of the principles of our government is apt to be more detrimental than their mere refusal to bear arms."

In a sharp dissent Justice Oliver Wendell Holmes, Jr., pointed out that Schwimmer, a 52-year-old woman, "would not be allowed to bear arms if she wanted to" and that she did not subscribe to subversive political views. Although Holmes acknowledged that some of her opinions "might excite popular prejudice," he declared that "if there is any principle of the Constitution that more imperatively calls for attachment than any other it is the principle of free thought—not free thought for those who agree with us but freedom for the thought we hate." Holmes further observed that pacifists had made significant contributions to the nation and that "I had not supposed hitherto that we regretted our inability to expel them because they believed more than some of us do in the teachings of the Sermon on the Mount."

The Court reaffirmed its decision in *Schwimmer* in two later decisions, *United States v. Bland* (1931) and *United States v. Macintosh* (1931). In those cases, the Court upheld the denial of naturalization to persons who were willing to bear arms in defense of the nation only if they felt that a war was morally justified. In his opinion for the Court in *Macintosh,* Justice George Sutherland stated that concessions which were made to conscientious objectors were privileges conferred by Congress rather than constitutional rights. In a dissent joined by Justices Holmes, Louis D. Brandeis, and Harlan Fiske Stone, Chief Justice Charles Evans Hughes argued that the naturalization statute did not clearly exclude conscientious objectors and that such an interpretation of the statute could not be implied, because it was "directly opposed to the spirit of our institutions and to the historic practice of the Congress."

The Supreme Court overruled its three earlier decisions in *Girouard v. United States* (1946). The Court in that case held that the court of appeals had improperly denied naturalization to James Girouard, a Seventh-Day

Adventist who had stated in his application for naturalization that he would not be willing to bear arms to defend the United States. Although Girouard contended that combatant military duty would violate his religious scruples, he had not claimed exemption from all military service, and he was willing to take the oath of allegiance to the United States that was required for naturalization.

In a decision written by Justice William O. Douglas the Supreme Court ruled that neither the text nor the legislative history of the naturalization statute indicated that Congress intended to bar from citizenship persons whose religious scruples prevented them from promising to bear arms in defense of the nation. The Court pointed out that the naturalization oath did not specifically require that naturalization candidates promise to bear arms and that the bearing of arms was not the only manner in which a naturalized citizen could fulfill the oath to "support and defend the Constitution and laws . . . against all enemies. . . ." The Court explained that

> [o]ne may adhere to what he deems to be his obligation to God and yet assume all military risks to secure victory. The effort of war is indivisible; and those whose religious scruples prevent them from killing are no less patriots than those whose special traits or handicaps result in their assignment to duties far behind the fighting front.

The Court contended that Congress traditionally had attempted to accommodate the rights of conscientious objectors, and Justice Douglas declared that the

> victory for freedom of thought recorded in our Bill of Rights recognizes that in the domain of conscience there is a moral power higher than the State. Throughout the ages men have suffered death rather than subordinate their allegiance to God to the authority of the State. Freedom of religion guaranteed by the First Amendment is the product of that struggle.

In dissent Justice Stone argued that Congress intended to prevent the naturalization of aliens who refused to promise to bear arms, because Congress had failed to make exceptions for conscientious objectors after the Supreme Court in its decisions in *Schwimmer, Bland,* and *Macintosh* had construed the law to prevent the naturalization of such aliens. Stone pointed out that Congress had declined to adopt various measures to overrule those decisions and in 1940 had enacted a new naturalization law that failed to reject those decisions and reenacted without change the same naturalization oath that the Court had construed in those cases. In response to Stone's arguments, Justice Douglas's opinion for the Court declared that the "history of the 1940 Act is at most equivocal" and that "[i]t is at best treacherous to find in Congressional silence alone the adoption of a controlling rule of law."

Although the Court based its decision on statutory construction rather than on constitutional interpretation, the Court strongly hinted that the naturalization law would violate the First Amendment's guarantee of religious freedom if it were construed to bar the naturalization of aliens who refused for religious reasons to bear arms. The Court's decision was consistent with other cases of the same period, such as *Cantwell v. Connecticut* (1940), *West Virginia State Board of Education v. Barnette* (1943), and *Everson v. Board of Education* (1947), in which the Court expanded the scope of the religion clauses. The decision also reflected the extraordinary self-confidence that prevailed in the United States during the spring of 1946, when there seemed to be little threat to national security; World War II had ended in 1945, the Cold War was only beginning, and the anticommunist campaigns of Senator Joseph McCarthy lay several years in the future. The ambiguity of the 1940 statute was eliminated by the Naturalization Act of 1952, which made clear that conscientious objectors are not required to pledge that they will bear arms. The statute (Article 8, Section 1448, of the United States Code) presently provides that a conscientious objector who can prove "by clear and convincing evidence . . . that he is opposed to the bearing of arms in the Armed Forces . . . by reason of religious training and belief" is not required to take an oath, required of other applicants, "to bear arms on behalf of the United States when required by the law." Such a person is required only to swear that he or she would be willing to perform noncombatant duty in the armed forces or "to perform work of national importance under civilian direction when required by the law." The statute states that the phrase "religious training and belief" means "an individual's belief in relation to a Supreme Being involving duties superior to those arising from any human relation, but does not include essentially political, sociological, or philosophical views or a merely personal code."

William G. Ross

Bibliography

Konvitz, Milton R., *Civil Rights in Immigration* (Ithaca, N.Y.: Cornell University Press, 1953); reprint (Westport, Conn.: Greenwood, 1977).

Cases Cited

Cantwell v. Connecticut, 310 U.S. 296 (1940).
Everson v. Board of Education, 330 U.S. 1 (1947).
Girouard v. United States, 328 U.S. 61 (1946).
United States v. Bland, 283 U.S. 636 (1931).
United States v. Macintosh, 283 U.S. 605 (1931).
United States v. Schwimmer, 279 U.S. 644 (1929).
West Virginia State Board of Education v. Barnette, 319 U.S. 624 (1943).

Penn's Frame of Government, "The Great Law," and Religion

William Penn's founding of Pennsylvania required the transformation of Quaker religious principles into legal form, a process that involved hundreds of Quakers, government officials, lawyers, and non-Quakers. While in England, Penn wrote at least twenty drafts of what became known as his Frame of Government, which, along with his Laws Agreed upon in England, were modified and adopted by the first Pennsylvania assembly in 1682 as "The Great Law." The resulting declaration of government policy balanced three sometimes contradictory goals: the establishment of religious tolerance, the enforcement of Christian laws of morality, and the entrenchment of Quakers as the ruling elite in a religiously plural settlement.

Religious toleration as a governing principle developed under the harsh persecution that Quakers suffered in England. Quakers—because of their belief in the primacy of conscience (the "Inner Light"); their practice of public preaching; and their refusal to take oaths, to doff hats, and to pay tithes to the Church of England—had been subject to repeated civil and criminal penalties. Penn, himself having been subject to persecution, had a personal as well as a denominational interest in ensuring that his colony preserved liberty of conscience; he also saw toleration as a way to increase the pool of settlers who were willing to settle in his colony, which would redound to his economic benefit. Penn rested his case for toleration not merely on the idea that one's conscience could not be coerced but also on empirical observations that England's vicious conflicts over religion had not united the nation in faith but rather had weakened it. Penn thus attempted to identify core Christian beliefs that could be allowed in the interest of peace to coexist, a definition that would be stretched to include Catholics but not heathens.

In his first draft Penn placed liberty of conscience in the first section, but by the time the revised Frame of Government was promulgated in England, such ideals were buried in Section 35 of the Laws Agreed upon in England. The Great Law returned this issue to Chapter 1, providing that those "who Shall Confess and acknowledge one Almighty God to be the Creator and Ruler of the World" and who lived peacefully under Penn's civil government would not be molested or prejudiced for their religious persuasion or practice. Although conscience had primacy, only those whose consciences adhered to certain core Christian beliefs were entitled to tolerance. Reinforcing this right, such believers would not have to frequent or support (financially or otherwise) any denomination, and anyone who would "abuse or deride any Other for his or her diferant Perswasion and practice" was deemed a disturber of the peace to be punished at law. Thus, Penn and the first settlers of Pennsylvania defined both the limits of religious behavior and the limits of toleration.

Religious tolerance was not religious indifference. Chapter 1 of the Great Law also required the maintenance of the Sabbath as a day of rest, following Penn's earlier drafts. Chapter 2 required that all who were appointed or elected to government had to believe that Jesus Christ was "Son of God the Savior of the World," thus imposing a religious test on officeholding. The most substantive additions to Penn's Laws Agreed upon in

England came in the area of criminal law. Penn had stated in Section 37 of the laws that "the Wildness and Looseness of the People provoke the Indignation of God against a Country," and then he proceeded to list over thirty "Offences against God." The Great Law drew on this list as well as on the Duke of York's laws, which had relied on Puritan sources, to create a morals code with specific penalties attached to particular offenses. Oaths not only were removed as legal requisites but also were made illegal as swearing by the name of God. Other verbal offenses including cursing, profane talking, spreading false news, scolding, and defaming entered the criminal code. Prohibited sexual activities included rape, incest, sodomy, whoredom, fornication, adultery, bigamy, and clandestine marriages. Recreational activities—such as drinking healths, drunkenness, stage plays, cards, dice, lotteries, bull baiting, and cockfighting—were all specifically forbidden.

In terms of punishment, Quakers followed law-reform ideals more than biblical mandates. Capital punishment was reserved for murder and treason only; incest, sodomy, and adultery received imprisonment, whipping, and property forfeiture under the Quaker code. In comparison with the draconian English criminal sanctions, the code drastically lightened penalties for crimes against property. This innovation reflected the Quaker emphasis on rehabilitation of the criminal and on recompensing the victim. Most minor moral offenders faced a fine (five shillings, usually) and/or a few days' imprisonment.

Penn's third religious purpose, that of ensuring Quaker control over his colony, was woven into the structure of power that his Frame of Government established. In the preamble Penn discoursed on the role of God and the need for laws among sinful men, but ultimately he rested his faith not in the "good laws" that he was then promulgating but in "good men" to administer them. By retaining powers of appointment over the magistrates (justices of the peace who controlled county government and courts) and by detailing reforms in both civil and criminal law designed to make justice simple, cheap, and quick, Penn and subsequent governors could ensure that Quaker principles of jurisprudence would be enforced. These justices of the peace—imbued with interlocking religious and legal principles—gave Quaker courts legitimacy and allowed Quakers to control a colony that was diverse both religiously and ethnically from the beginning.

Tolerance continued to attract a large number of religiously diverse settlers, and Quakers quickly became a minority, which threatened their control over the colony that Penn had planned as their sanctuary. Although morals prosecutions dwindled in the early 1700s, other Quaker law reforms—plus the behavior of Quaker justices in using fair processes—continued to legitimize the system, allowing the dwindling number of Quakers to maintain their hold on power well into the middle of the eighteenth century.

William Offutt

Bibliography

Beckman, Gail McKnight (ed.), *The Statutes at Large of Pennsylvania in the Time of William Penn,* vol. 1, 1680–1700 (New York: Vantage, 1976).

Frost, J. William, *A Perfect Freedom: Religious Liberty in Pennsylvania* (New York: Cambridge University Press, 1990).

Offutt, William M., Jr., *Of "Good Laws" and "Good Men": Law and Society in the Delaware Valley 1680–1710* (Champaign: University of Illinois Press, 1995).

People v. Ruggles
8 Johns (N.Y.) 290 (1811)

People v. Ruggles (N.Y., 1811) was the first reported state court case involving the common-law offense of blasphemy. In Salem, New York, in 1810, Ruggles loudly proclaimed in the presence of many, "Jesus Christ was a bastard, and his mother must be a whore." After a local court tried and convicted Ruggles, Judge Ambrose Spencer, a member of the Supreme Court of Judicature, sentenced him to three months' imprisonment and a fine of five hundred dollars. On appeal to New York's highest court, the justices had to decide whether Ruggles's remarks constituted a legal offense.

Counsel for Ruggles admitted that blasphemy was punishable under English common law but contended that it was not punishable by the laws of the State of New York. The distinction was important. In

England, Christianity was the established religion and was thus linked to the law of the land. In New York, however, no statute established Christianity as the state religion, and the state's constitution even guaranteed religious toleration. "For aught that appears," Ruggles's attorney concluded, "the prisoner may have been a Jew, a Mahometan, or a Socinian; and if so, he had a right, by the constitution, to declare his opinions." In contrast, counsel for the state argued that, because the New York Constitution of 1777 adopted the common law of England, the offense of blasphemy became a part of state law, even though no specific statute dealt with the matter. According to Blackstone, blasphemy included "denying the being or providence of God; contumelious reproaches of Christ; profane scoffing at the Holy Scripture, or exposing it to contempt or ridicule." By these standards, the state claimed, Ruggles's remarks were clearly illegal.

Chief Justice James Kent—regarded as one of the great judges in American history—held for a unanimous court that blasphemy did constitute a punishable offense in New York. Rejecting arguments made on behalf of Ruggles, Kent ruled that the crime of blasphemy existed "independent of any religious establishment or the rights of the church." Because nothing in New York's experience or institutions prevented the adoption of common law in this area, Kent claimed that English precedent and tradition prohibiting blasphemy were in full force. "Reviling is still an offense," he argued, "because it tends to corrupt the morals of the people, and to destroy good order." Kent saw blasphemy as analogous to obscenity or other behaviors that were viewed as injurious to public morality. The common law, he reasoned, served to promote "moreal discipline" and "those principles of virtue which help bind a society together."

Kent insisted that his decision neither undermined the principles of religious freedom nor constituted an establishment of religion. Constitutional guarantees of toleration remained intact, according to Kent, but Ruggles's "malicious" remarks were an "abuse" of his rights of religious expression. Further, Kent held that the crime of blasphemy could apply only to statements reviling Christianity, not to similar "attacks upon the religion of Mahomet or of the grand Lama." "The case assumes that we are a Christian people," Kent continued, "and the morality of the country is deeply ingrafted upon Christianity, and not upon the doctrines or worship of those impostors." Christianity, therefore, received special treatment under the laws, according to Kent, because it was the dominant religion of the people of New York. He adamantly maintained, however, that this special status did not constitute an establishment of religion. Rather, to construe the Constitution's Establishment Clause as eliminating all legal barriers "against licentious, wanton, and impious attacks upon Christianity" would surely pervert its meaning. Blasphemy laws, in short, in no way violated the Constitution.

Kent's opinion derived from his conservative Federalist background and his deep admiration for the common law, rather than from his own Christian convictions. he frequently praised, as he once put it, "the approved wisdom and sober sense of the English common law," which he viewed as the foundation of the American social order (*Yates v. People* [1810]). In contrast, he despised Catholicism, derided the enthusiasm of some Protestant sects, and once described Christianity in general as a "vulgar superstition." Still, Kent viewed the Christian religion as an essential underlying component of the laws of the state, and he thought that blasphemy struck "at the root of moral obligation and weaken[ed] the security of the social ties."

The decision in *Ruggles* did not initiate a wave of blasphemy convictions, but the opinion did prove controversial. At the New York constitutional convention of 1821, where delegates crafted a new constitution for the state, Kent's decision became a particular source of contention. Erastus Root, the leader of a movement to democratize the government and expand the franchise, proposed that New York's Constitution be amended to forbid the judiciary to "declare any particular religion the law of the land." He took specific aim at the *Ruggles* case, which he feared established Christianity as the state religion. Kent, also a member of the convention, responded that *Ruggles* had not established Christianity; the opinion simply provided that blasphemy with malicious intent violated public morals and decency. Kent succeeded in persuading Root to delete the reference to the judiciary from his amendment, and in its final form the motion stated that "it shall not be declared or adjudged that any particular religion is the law of the land." Judge Ambrose Spencer, Kent's judicial colleague who had presided at Ruggles's original trial, then joined the debate. He maintained that Christianity was indeed the established religion of the state. Though Spencer and Kent differed on the issue of the exact relationship between Christianity and the law of the land, as well as on the precise definition of blasphemy, the two jurists united to vote against Root's amendment, which went down to defeat.

The principles enunciated in *Ruggles* prevailed, and blasphemy—defined as indecent or reviling attacks against Christianity—remained a criminal offense in New York. *Ruggles* was the leading American case on the law of blasphemy during the early years of the nineteenth century. Kent's prestige and reputation gave tremendous authority to the opinion, however distasteful it might be to modern sensibilities. The decision in *Ruggles* paved the way for a later landmark Massachusetts decision with a similarly intolerant tone, *Commonwealth v. Kneeland* (1838) and, therefore, accurately represented judicial thinking about blasphemy at the time.

Timothy S. Huebner

Bibliography

Horton, John Theodore, *James Kent: A Study in Conservatism, 1763–1847* (New York: Da Capo, reprinted 1969; orig. pub., 1939).

Levy, Leonard W., *Blasphemy: Verbal Offense against the Sacred: From Moses to Salmon Rushdie* (New York: Knopf, 1993).

Stokes, Anson Phelps, and Leo Pfeffer, *Church and State in the United States* (New York: Harper and Row, 1964).

Cases Cited

Commonwealth v. Kneeland, 37 Mass. 206 (1838).

People v. Ruggles, 8 Johns (N.Y.) 290 (1811).

Yates v. People, 6 Johns (N.Y.) 229 (1810).

Permoli v. First Municipality of New Orleans

44 U.S. (3 How.) 589 (1845)

On November 9, 1842, Bernard Permoli, a Roman Catholic priest of New Orleans, was arrested and subsequently fined for performing an open-casket funeral in the church of St. Augustin in the French Quarter. This violated a city ordinance passed ten days earlier that prohibited funerals at any "Catholic churches" within the city other than a designated mortuary chapel on the outskirts of town. The case was appealed all the way to the U.S. Supreme Court, where *Permoli v. First Municipality of New Orleans* (1845) earned the distinction of being the Supreme Court's first case involving the Free Exercise Clause of the First Amendment.

The Supreme Court disposed of the constitutional argument in one sentence: "The Constitution makes no provision for protecting the citizens of the respective states in their religious liberties; that is left to the state constitutions and laws: nor is there any inhibition imposed by the Constitution of the United States in this respect on the states." In other words, the First Amendment does not apply to the states. This holding remained in force until well into the twentieth century, when it was held that the protections of the First Amendment had become applicable to the states through the medium of the Due Process Clause of the Fourteenth Amendment. The details of the *Permoli* case have therefore virtually been forgotten. But the case is interesting and important in its own right, independent of the "incorporation" question, for both doctrinal and historical reasons.

As a doctrinal matter, the *Permoli* case raised three issues, all of which remain important to First Amendment law today. The case suggests a surprising degree of continuity between the legal arguments of today and those of 150 years ago.

First, the New Orleans ordinance under which Father Permoli was prosecuted applied by its terms only to "priests" of the "Catholic churches of this municipality" leading counsel for the defendant to argue that this violated the principle of "[e]quality before the law," which he said to be "of the very essence of liberty, whether civil or religious." Counsel for the city responded that there was only one non-Catholic church within the municipality and that Protestant services for the dead were performed at cemeteries rather than within the churches, making it unnecessary for the city to pass an ordinance applicable to them. This can be understood as an argument between "formal neutrality" (the insistence that the law not be framed in such a way that singles out a particular religion, or religion in general) and "substantive neutrality" (the insistence that the law not have the effect of prohibiting or inducing a particular form of religious exercise, or religion in general).

Second, according to the testimony of Bishop Antoine Blanc in the case, the dogmas of the Catholic Church did not require that funerals be conducted in a church, but that this was a matter of church discipline only. This led counsel for the city to argue that an ordinance limiting funerals to a single location was not an infringement on religious liberty: "The place, then, for the mortuary ceremony not being sacramental, how is the faith or conscience of Catholics assailed, by designating a few places in which they could not be performed? The essence of the right consists in the thing that is to be done, and not in the place of performance." Counsel for the defendant responded that matters of church discipline, and not just mandatory doctrine, are exempt from secular control. This is an early instance of an argument still contested today: whether free exercise protects only explicit religious duties or whether it extends to other elements of religious life and practice.

Third, the ostensible rationale for the ordinance was to prevent the spread of yellow fever, the cause of which was at that time unknown. Counsel for the city argued that if the ordinance was "designed merely as a regulation of sanitary police, for the preservation of the public health, then the law of necessity pleads in its behalf; and all obituary rites and ceremonials which tend to frustrate its objects, or impair its efficacy, must yield to the supremacy of the public good." Counsel for the defendant made three responses (not in this order). First, he maintained that constitutional rights prevail over the police power, invoking the decision of *Willson v. Black Bird Creek Marsh Co.* (1829), in which the Court held that the federal rights of commerce prevail over the state's power to drain a marsh, even to protect the health of the inhabitants. Second, he argued that there is an "absolute immunity for religious worship so long as it is conducted in a peaceable and orderly manner." Much of the testimony in the case was to the effect that Catholic funerary rites contain "nothing calculated to disturb the public peace." Interestingly, counsel for the city acknowledged that it was an open question "how far religious, as well as civil rights and privileges, may be constrained to give way to the public necessities and the common good," urging that this question did not need to be resolved, because the choice of place to conduct funeral rites is not a matter of religious doctrine. This aspect of the *Permoli* controversy raises what is generally considered to be the most important question of modern free exercise law, which was brought to a head in *Employment Division, Department of Human Resources of Oregon v. Smith* (1990): whether generally applicable laws passed for a legitimate public purpose may be said to violate the Free Exercise Clause. Finally, counsel for the defendant argued, in effect, that the health rationale was pretextual, pointing out that no one other than a priest is subject to penalty for exposing a corpse to the air.

The historical context of the *Permoli* case strongly suggests that the justification *was* pretextual. Indeed, the New Orleans ordinance appears to have been an instance of municipal interference in one of the most significant internal disputes in the history of the American Catholic Church. In the late eighteenth and early nineteenth centuries, Roman Catholic hierarchical authority was weak, and lay boards—called "wardens" (and in New Orleans called "marguilliers")—effectively controlled church operations, including the appointment of parish priests. In the second quarter of the nineteenth century, bishops in many cities (including Buffalo, St. Augustine, Charleston, Norfolk, and throughout Louisiana) sought to wrest control over the appointment of priests, over the strenuous opposition of their boards of wardens. Such a controversy had simmered in the Archdiocese of New Orleans for many years and had broken out into public and vituperative controversy after the death of a long-standing and well-beloved curate of the cathedral in 1842. To replace him, Bishop Blanc appointed a foreign cleric, unknown to the wardens, and the wardens refused to recognize his authority. An attempted compromise then failed when the agreed-upon successor proved to be a supporter of the bishop's claim to control of the affairs of the church. With matters at a standstill, Bishop Blanc removed all clergy from the cathedral (as well as from the cathedral's mortuary chapel, which was under the control of the wardens), thus depriving the wardens of the revenues that come from funeral and other services; the bishop's actions also generated pressure from the sacrament-starved faithful for the wardens to come to terms. The wardens sued the bishop in state court for $20,000 in damages for dereliction of duty and libel and slander, leading to a major precedent in the Louisiana Supreme Court, which held that civil courts may not interfere in the internal operations of a church.

Compounding the ecclesiological controversy was the conflict between the Creole elite, who dominated both the board of wardens and the city council, and the newer Irish immigrants. The Irish, although mostly lower class and uneducated, were strict in their religious practices and considered the Creoles "pseudo-Catholics." In the struggle between Bishop Blanc and the wardens, the Irish sided with the bishop.

At the height of this controversy, on October 31, 1842, the city council passed the ordinance at issue in *Permoli,* preventing Bishop Blanc's priests from performing funerals anywhere other than in the mortuary chapel, which, according to the record in the case, was "under the administration of the said wardens." Two days later the bishop removed the clergy from the cathedral church, the next day the mayor approved the ordinance, four days later the ordinance was amended to apply sanctions only to priests, and two days later Father Permoli officiated at a funeral in defiance of the law. Counsel for the city referred to this controversy in his argument before the Supreme Court, noting that the sequence of events "leaves the inference fair that there was a necessary connection" between the quarrel between Bishop Blanc and the wardens and the enactment of the ordinance. "But this is not so," he told the Court. The "circumstances strongly repel all inferences that the First Municipality council could have designed any infringement upon, or impairment of, the privileges of Catholics. The great body of the constituency of that council is Catholic, and very frequently the whole of that council, are such as have been reared up in the Catholic faith."

However, counsel for the defendant (who also served as counsel for the archdiocese in the suit between the wardens and the bishop) described the ordinance as limiting the observances of religion "to a building in the possession of notorious schismatics, who might tax them to virtual prohibition, or apply the proceeds, at their own discretion, to the subversion of religion itself." Perhaps perceiving the seriousness of this charge, he tactfully amended his remarks to note that "[t]he point is stated *arguendo;* but borrowed from the facts which gave rise to this appeal to the court." In this context, it is evident that the fact that the city council was made up of Catholics did not refute his point, for the ordinance under which Father Permoli was prosecuted appears to have been an effort by the Creole city council to assist their fellow Creole wardens in the controversy against Bishop Blanc and his Irish supporters, by forcing the clergy to perform that most indispensable and lucrative of sacraments in a chapel under the control of the wardens.

Notwithstanding the Supreme Court's failure to intervene, the wardens' victory was short-lived. Bishop Blanc established his authority over the appointment of priests, and by the next decade the influx of Irish immigrants had shifted the balance of power permanently to designated hierarchical authorities.

Michael McConnell

Bibliography

Miller, Randall M., "A Church in Cultural Captivity: Some Speculations on Catholic Identity in the Old South," in *Catholics in the Old South: Essays on Church and Culture,* ed. Randall M. Miller and Jon L. Wakelyn (Macon, Ga.: Mercer University Press, 1983).

Cases Cited

Employment Division, Department of Human Resources of Oregon v. Smith, 494 U.S. 872 (1990).

Permoli v. First Municipality of New Orleans, 3 How (44 U.S.) 589 (1845).

Willson v. Black Bird Creek Marsh Co., 2 Pet. (27 U.S.) 245 (1829).

"Persecution on Account of Religion"

Pursuant to the Refugee Act of 1980, those fleeing "persecution on account of religion" may be granted asylum in the United States. For much of U.S. history such a category was unnecessary, because there were few obstacles to immigration. Masses of people fleeing religious persecution successfully sought haven in the United States. Huguenots, Quakers, and Mennonites fleeing religious persecution in the seventeenth century; Jews escaping pogroms in the late nineteenth century; and Armenians fleeing Turkish pogroms during the first decades of the twentieth century all found refuge in this country with relatively few legal obstacles. However, by the 1930s and 1940s, when masses of Jews were fleeing Nazi-occupied Europe, immigration was severely limited by a strict quota system and other requirements. No exceptions were made for people fleeing persecution of any kind.

Even though no right to asylum existed based on religious persecution until 1980, the special status of those fleeing such persecution was previously recognized in immigration law in that such people were exempt from the literacy test. Pursuant to the Immigration Act of 1917, to be admitted a would-be immigrant had to prove that he or she was literate in at least one language by reading a passage in front of an examiner at the port of entry. The 1917 act provided that aliens would be exempt from the test only if they could prove that

> they are seeking admission to the United States to avoid religious persecution in the country of their last permanent residence, whether such persecution be evidenced by overt acts or by laws or governmental regulations that discriminate against the alien or the race to which he belongs because of his religious faith . . . .

They were not automatically admissible if found to be escaping religious persecution; they still had to meet the other requirements for admission. In addition, if the aliens were merely fleeing racial or political persecution, they were not exempt from the literacy test. Therefore, this exception forced courts to define persecution based on religion.

Throughout the 1920s courts struggled with the definition of "religious persecution" and often arrived at completely conflicting conclusions. In 1924, in *Johnson v. Tertzag; Ex parte Soghanalian* (1924), an illiterate Armenian woman was found admissible on the grounds of religious persecution after she described how the Turks had killed her parents and all other Christians from her town, and how she had been seized and kept in a harem for three and a half years until saved by Allied armies. However, in *United States ex rel. Azizian v. Curran* (2nd Cir. 1926), another case involving an Armenian woman, the court found that although

> common knowledge enables us to recognize in this most unfortunate woman a victim of what are too well known as "Armenian massacres," neither evidence nor common report enables us to say that what happened in Urmia in 1917 was religious persecution, as distinguished from robbery and banditry at a time and place of social dissolution, if not political revolution.

In 1942, in *In the Matter of M* (BIA, 1942), the Board of Immigration Appeals found that a Jewish Romanian family who had been denied admission because they were unable to read satisfactorily were exempt from the test because they were fleeing religious persecution; they were fleeing "Hitlerism," which was a state religion that subverted all other religions. The BIA felt that, although for the Hebrew people "race and religion are one," Nazi persecution was based on religious and not racial motives.

The definition of religious persecution has developed since the passage of the Refugee Act of 1980, which provided for asylum for anyone who qualifies as a "refugee" as defined by the *Protocol to the United Nations Convention on Refugees.* A well-founded fear of persecution on account of the applicant's religion is one of the five grounds specified in the *Protocol.* To qualify, the alien must show that he or she fears persecution on account of those beliefs; personal threats, animosity, or simple discrimination are not sufficient. It also must be established either that the persecution is government-sanctioned or that the government is unable to stop it. For example, in *Matter of Chen* (BIA 1989) a man from a Catholic family in the People's Republic of China whose family members experienced horrendous mistreatment during the Cultural Revolution was found to have a well-founded fear based on this past persecution. Similarly, in *Doe v. Immigration and Naturalization Service* (6th Cir. 1989) a Chinese student who converted to Christianity while in the United States was found to have a well-founded fear of persecution.

However, in *Gumbol v. Immigration and Naturalization Service* (6th Cir. 1987) a Christian Iraqi was found not to possess such a fear, even though he had been beaten by a member of the Baath Party because he was Christian and had refused to join that party. The court found that he did not establish that the beating had been government-sanctioned and was not merely an isolated incident.

Whether or not an alien is required to make a showing that persecution is specifically on account of religion and not based on some other ground continues to be litigated. The issue is especially contentious where army conscription is involved, because people have many reasons, including fear, for refusing to serve in their nation's army. For example, in 1988 the Board of Immigration Appeals held that a Jehovah's Witness who refused to be conscripted into the Salvadorian army based on his religious beliefs did not qualify as a refugee because he did not establish that the conscription laws were enacted with the intent of persecuting members of a certain religion. The government imprisoned everyone who refused to serve, regardless of their reasons.

On appeal, the Circuit Court of Appeals for the Ninth Circuit attempted to give persecution on account of religion greater deference than persecution on any of the other four grounds specified in the Refugee Act of 1980. The Court based its opinion on U.S. constitutional law and on the *United Nations Handbook on Refugees.* It held that where the alien's refusal to serve in the army was based on genuine religious beliefs and where such refusal, regardless of the reason, automatically subjects the alien to imprisonment, torture, or death, the alien qualifies as a refugee. The *Handbook*—generally considered a legitimate interpretive source—states that conscientious objectors may be eligible for refugee status if their government does not provide an exception for religious beliefs.

However, the second basis, U.S. constitutional law, is more controversial because aliens do not enjoy the protections of the First Amendment religion clauses. The court of appeals began by acknowledging the special place that religion holds in U.S. law and recognizing that religious conscientious objectors are exempt from serving in the military in the United States. It then likened the aliens' situation to one where, under the Free Exercise Clause in the First Amendment to the U.S. Constitution, a facially neutral statute is deemed unduly burdensome on a religious group. Applying this constitutional principle, it found that the fact that the Salvadorian conscription law was facially neutral did not preclude it from being persecutive.

The Supreme Court did not address either ground but vacated the decision and remanded the case back to the court of appeals for redetermination in light of its opinion in *Immigration and Naturalization Service v. Elias-Zacarias* (1992), where it had ruled that, to show persecution on account of political opinion, some level of the persecutor's intent must be shown. On remand, the court of appeals held that, because the Supreme Court required at least some showing of the persecutor's intent and because the petitioner was unable to establish that, he would be imprisoned specifically because he refused to serve in the army for religious reasons; he did not have a well-founded fear of persecution on account of his religion.

Renee C. Redman

Bibliography

Hyland, St. George Kieran, *A Century of Persecution under Tudor and Stewart Sovereigns* (London, New York: Dutton K. Paul, T. Trubner, 1920).

Little, Lewis Peyton, *Imprisoned Preachers and Religious Liberty in Virginia* (Lynchburg, Va: J. P. Bell, 1938).

Myers, Gustavus, *History of Bigotry in the United States* (New York: Random House, 1943).

Cases Cited

Doe v. Immigration and Naturalization Service, 867 F. 2d 285 (6th Cir. 1989).

Gumbol v. Immigration and Naturalization Service, 815 F. 2d 406 (6th Cir. 1987).

Immigration and Naturalization Service v. Elias-Zacarias, 502 U.S. 478 (1992).

In the Matter of M, 1 I&N Dec. 280 (BIA 1942).

Johnson v. Tertzag; Ex parte Soghanalian, 2 F. 2d 40 (5th Cir. 1924).

Matter of Chen, Int. Dec. 3104 (BIA 1989).

United States ex rel. Azizian v. Curran, 12 F. 2d 502 (2nd Cir. 1926).

Pierce v. Society of Sisters
268 U.S. 510 (1925)

Pierce v. Society of Sisters (1925) was decided on June 1, 1925, in a unanimous opinion authored by Justice James C. McReynolds. The case arose out of the State of Oregon. Context for the decision is provided by understanding the fact that among the developments which followed World War I was the rise of the second Ku Klux Klan. This movement combined the appeals to racism of the first Klan with widespread nativism, anti-Semitism, and anti-Catholicism. Oregon was one of the states in which the Klan exercised considerable political power.

In 1922 the Klan supported a statewide initiative that required all children between the ages of 8 and 16 to attend the public schools. By allowing one to meet the compulsory attendance laws only by attending public schools, the statute, in effect, outlawed private schools. Parents who violated the statute were subject to penalties ranging from fines of $5 to $100 and imprisonment from two to thirty days for each day the child missed school. The purpose of the initiative was to have the public schools educate students in "Americanism" and to avoid the possibility that anti-American ideas might be taught in religious or elitist private schools.

Commentators on this era agree that—although the initiative was targeted against economic elites, immigrants, Jews, and Lutherans—the major concern of the proponents were the Catholic schools. This appears to have been part of a national campaign. Similar proposals were offered in several states at about this same time. One proposal had been defeated in Michigan. But the initiative was passed by the voters of Oregon in the November 1922 general election.

Although not designed to take effect until September 1, 1926, the Oregon law was almost immediately challenged in the courts. Money for the litigation was raised by the American Civil Liberties Union, the National Catholic Welfare League, and the Knights of Columbus. The plaintiffs were not the children or the parents who would be subjected to the penalty but two private schools, the Society of Sisters and Hill Military Academy. The defendant was Oregon Governor Walter M. Pierce. Although historian David Tyack indicates that Pierce's record on private schools was inconsistent, he also indicates that in 1919, when Pierce was a state senator, he had charged "that a teacher of German had poisoned the minds of his two daughters."

Relying on the Supreme Court's decision in *Meyer v. Nebraska* (1923), which struck down a prohibition against a private school's teaching German, a three-judge panel struck down the Oregon statute and issued a preliminary injunction on March 31, 1924.

Pierce was represented in the U.S. Supreme Court by George E. Chamberlain, a former U.S. senator and governor of Oregon. The plaintiffs were represented by William D. Guthrie, a Wall Street lawyer, Columbia Law professor, and renowned Supreme Court advocate.

The state argued that this compulsory attendance law was within its police power, that the state stood in loco parentis with its minors, that the statute did not interfere with religious liberty, and, indeed, that the statute helped ensure separation of church and state. The brief for the schools argued that the statute interfered with the "closely interrelated" freedoms of private and parochial schools, teachers, parents and guardians, and the freedom of students. The schools also argued against a "state monopoly" of education and likened the Oregon system to those of Plato's Republic, Sparta, and the Soviet Union.

Speaking for a unanimous court, Justice McReynolds's opinion relied on *Meyer* and stated that, under that decision, it was "entirely plain" that the Oregon act was unconstitutional. This was so because it "unreasonably interferes with the liberty of parents and guardians to direct the upbringing and education of children under their control." The most enduring language from Justice McReynolds's opinion is:

> The fundamental theory of liberty upon which all governments in this Union repose excludes any general power of the state to standardize its children by forcing them to accept instruction form public teachers only. The child is not the mere creature of the state; those who nurture him and direct his destiny have the right, coupled with the high duty, to recognize and prepare him for additional obligations.

The contemporary legal commentaries on *Pierce* were largely favorable. The legacy of

Pierce is the stuff over which modern intellectual battles are fought. While acknowledging the traditional view that *Pierce* stands for "pluralism [and] family autonomy," Barbara Bennett Woodhouse suggests that *Pierce* also stands for "the patriarchal family . . . a class-stratified society, and . . . a parent's private property rights in his children. . . ."

Nevertheless, *Pierce* continues to have vitality and influence. Because it was decided before the beginning of incorporation in *Gitlow v. New York* (1925), *Pierce* was clearly a substantive due process ("liberty") case and not a free exercise case. And yet the religious background and issues of *Pierce* have caused it to be utilized often in religious-related cases. For example, it is cited both in the majority opinion in *Everson v. Board. of Education* (1947) and in Justice Jackson's dissenting opinion, in which Justice Frankfurter joined.

Similarly, *Pierce* has played a supporting role in many of the Court's religious cases, such as *Wisconsin v. Yoder* (1972). *Pierce* has also played an important part in the jurisprudence in the area of "privacy" and "autonomy," including *Griswold v. Connecticut* (1965) (contraception), *Roe v. Wade* (1973) (abortion), and *Moore v. City of East Cleveland* (1977) (right to live as an extended family).

Richard L. Aynes

Bibliography

MacLean, Nancy, *Behind the Mask of Chivalry: The Making of the Second Ku Klux Klan* (New York: Oxford University Press, 1994).

Oregon School Cases: A Complete Record (Baltimore, Md.: Belvedere, 1925).

"State Control of Education," 74 *University of Pennsylvania Law Review* 77–79 (1925).

Stumberg, George W., Note, "State Supervision of Education and the Fourteenth Amendment," 4 *Texas Law Review* 93–97 (1925).

Woodhouse, Barbara Bennett, "'Who Owns the Child?': Meyer and Pierce and the Child As Property," 33 *William and Mary Law Review* 995–1122 (1992).

Cases Cited

Everson v. Board of Education, 330 U.S. 1 (1947).

Gitlow v. New York, 268 U.S. 652 (1925).

Griswold v. Connecticut, 381 U.S. 479 (1965).

Meyer v. Nebraska, 262 U.S. 390 (1923).

Moore v. City of East Cleveland, 431 U.S. 494 (1977).

Pierce v. Society of Sisters, 268 U.S. 510 (1925).

Roe v. Wade, 410 U.S. 113 (1973).

Wisconsin v. Yoder, 406 U.S. 216 (1972).

Pledge of Allegiance

The ceremony identified with saluting the United States flag began as part of a campaign in 1892 by the magazine *Youth's Companion* to celebrate the quadricentennial of Columbus's reaching the Americas. The campaign succeeded in having Congress authorize the president to proclaim October 12 a national holiday to be observed in public schools with appropriate exercises. Francis Bellamy, one of the editors of *Youth's Companion,* was named chair of the committee responsible for determining the "appropriate exercises." The program included an ode by Edna Dean Proctor, an original song by Hezekiah Butterworth, and a declaration on the "Meaning of the Four Centuries" written by Bellamy. While these aspects of the ceremony have been lost to posterity, the capstone of the ceremony was to be a salute to the flag spoken in unison by the public school students and teachers. It was Bellamy, perhaps with assistance from a co-editor, James B. Upham, who composed the Pledge of Allegiance for recital on that first Columbus Day.

As the twentieth century dawned, states had instituted flag salute ceremonies for the opening of the school day. It was, however, the American Legion, founded in 1919, that was really responsible for the pledge's adoption nationwide. At its first convention the Legion created a National Americanism Commission, which sponsored National Flag Conferences in 1923 and 1924. These conferences largely adopted the text first used in 1892. Their only change was to substitute the words "to the flag of the United States of America" for the simpler "my flag" in the original. The National Flag Conferences called on states to incorporate flag instruction into their public school curriculum, and in 1934 the American Legion's national convention passed a resolution urging states to require flag salutes in their schools. In the 1920s and 1930s such laws became widespread, often imposing duties on teachers as well as students to recite the pledge.

The Pledge and Judicial Restraint: *Gobitis*

As early as 1918, conflicts between the pledge requirement and the requirements of various religious sects became apparent, but it was not until the first Jehovah's Witnesses refused to recite the Pledge of Allegiance in 1935 that the issue came into national focus. According to Witness theology, pledging allegiance to any secular institution is the equivalent of pledging allegiance to Satan. At the same time, Witnesses were no strangers to the legal process. Their leader, Joseph Rutherford, was a former lawyer, and the organization maintained an active legal department to deal with the numerous prosecutions of Witnesses that arose from their missionary work. Hundreds of Witness children were expelled from schools in various states for refusing to recite the pledge, and prosecutions were brought against parents or children in Massachusetts, Georgia, New Jersey, California, Texas, New York, Florida, and Pennsylvania. With the support of the American Civil Liberties Union, defendants appealed several of these cases to the Supreme Court, arguing that the flag salute requirement interfered with the students' free exercise of religion as protected by the First Amendment to the Constitution. But between 1937 and 1939 federal courts dismissed four separate appeals for want of a substantial federal question.

In 1938, for the first time, a federal district court in Pennsylvania found in favor of the Witnesses, and the Third Circuit Court of Appeals agreed, essentially forcing the Supreme Court to address the issue on the merits. In *Minersville School District v. Gobitis* (1940), despite briefs on behalf of Gobitis by both the American Civil Liberties Union and the American Bar Association, the Court by an 8-to-1 margin reversed the court below. Justice Felix Frankfurter's opinion for the Court noted that the Court had consistently held that persons were not excused from compliance with secular laws because of their religious convictions, citing among others the case of *Reynolds v. United States* (1878), which upheld the prosecution of a Morman under an antipolygamy statute.

In his *Gobitis* opinion Justice Frankfurter argued that one of the most important governmental objectives was involved: the promotion of national unity by training children in patriotic ceremonies. It was not for courts, he said, to second-guess what the legislature had found necessary in order to achieve that unity or to create exceptions where the legislature had created none. The Court's opinion thus reflected the conception of judicial restraint, for which Justice Frankfurter is well known and which was a reaction to the judicial activism that had plagued the early New Deal. Justice Harlan Fiske Stone, the sole dissenter, suggested that where there are competing demands of the interests of the government and of liberty under the Constitution, there must be made a reasonable accommodation between them, if that is possible, in order to preserve both. Here, he indicated the irony of celebrating freedom by compelling children against their will to affirm beliefs they did not hold. As for judicial restraint, Justice Stone cited the Court's history of willingness to subject laws to special scrutiny if they restricted the liberties of racial or religious minorities.

Although Witnesses were hardly popular in America and the flag was, the *Gobitis* decision was roundly condemned from many quarters, including the legal, educational, and religious establishments. The fact that a court in Nazi Germany was reported to have recently convicted a Witness child for refusing to "Heil Hitler" helped to make the decision appear to authorize religious persecution. Nevertheless, the *Gobitis* opinion resulted in a number of new flag salute laws and stricter enforcement of old ones. It was during this time that Congress passed the first federal law codifying the Pledge of Allegiance and the flag salute ceremony. The West Virginia State Board of Education, quoting liberally from *Gobitis,* adopted a mandatory flag salute requirement in January 1942, and shortly thereafter Witness children were expelled from school throughout the state for refusal to participate. A class action was brought in federal district court to enjoin the board's rule, and a three-judge district court unanimously held that the board's rule was unconstitutional.

Ordinarily, a precedent as clearly on point as *Gobitis* would be binding on lower courts. Earlier in 1942, however, the Supreme Court, in *Jones v. Opelika* (1942), had indicated that it might be ready to reconsider the *Gobitis* decision. *Jones* involved a challenge to a license tax that was imposed on

Witnesses who distributed their religious literature. By a bare 5-to-4 vote the Court upheld the tax; but rather than rely on *Gobitis,* the majority distinguished it, and Justices Hugo Black, William O. Douglas, and Frank Murphy (who with Justice Stone dissented) wrote especially to indicate that they no longer concurred in *Gobitis.* The district court read *Opelika*'s reluctance to rely on *Gobitis* as an invitation to reconsider it.

High Hurdles to Limits on Speech: *Barnette*

On June 14, 1943, of all days—Flag Day—the Supreme Court decided *West Virginia State Board of Education v. Barnette* (1943) by a vote of 6 to 3 finding the compulsory flag salute unconstitutional and expressly overruling *Gobitis.* Justice Robert Jackson's opinion for the Court attacked the problem from a different perspective. Whereas all the earlier opinions had essentially assumed the power of the state to compel the flag salute generally and had focused on whether there was a duty to create an exception for those with religious objections, Jackson questioned the initial power of the state to make the salute a legal duty. Indeed, the issue did not "turn on one's possession of particular religious views or the sincerity with which they are held." Rather the issue was more fundamental, i.e., whether the state could compel *anyone* to declare a belief that he or she does not hold. In answering this question, Justice Jackson indicated that the policy behind judicial restraint where claims are founded on unarticulated rights that are protected, if at all, by substantive due process does not apply where the claim is based on the First Amendment. The First Amendment, he noted, imposed high hurdles to government limitations on a person's freedom to speak one's mind; it would be strange indeed if that same amendment "left it open to public authorities to compel him to utter what is not in his mind." Justice Jackson's conclusion has been often quoted for the ideas it expresses and the style with which it expresses them:

> The case is made difficult not because the principles of its decision are obscure but because the flag involved is our own. . . . But freedom to differ is not limited to things that do not matter much. That would be a mere shadow of freedom. The test of its substance is the right to differ as to things that touch the heart of the existing order.
>
> If there is any fixed star in our constitutional constellation, it is that no official, high or petty, can prescribe what shall be orthodox in politics, nationalism, religion, or other matters of opinion or force citizens to confess by word or act their faith therein. . . .
>
> We think the action of the local authorities in compelling the flag salute and pledge transcends constitutional limitations on their power and invades the sphere of intellect and spirit which it is the purpose of the First Amendment to our Constitution to reserve from all official control.

Justices Black and Douglas, concurring, wrote separately to discuss the role of the Free Exercise Clause when it collides with a secular law. They argued that, although the First Amendment does not absolve persons from complying with generally applicable laws "imperatively necessary to protect society as a whole from grave and pressingly imminent dangers," it is the solemn duty of the Court to decide whether a particular law that strikes at the heart and substance of a religious belief or practice is so necessary.

Justice Murphy, also concurring, emphasized his view that the benefits derived from the compulsory flag salute were insufficiently definite and tangible to justify the invasion of freedom and privacy involved or to compensate for the restraint on the freedom of the individual to be vocal or to be silent according to conscience or inclination.

Justices Stanley Reed and Owen Roberts dissented, merely noting their continued belief in *Gobitis.*

Justice Frankfurter wrote a lengthy and heated dissent. For a man who viewed himself as the leading intellect on the Court and as a skilled politician in winning votes for cases, the majority's opinion was triply humiliating. It turned in a few short years his majority opinion to a dissenting opinion. It decisively rejected each and every one of his arguments, and it made him look like the bastion of repression, a man who, in his own words, "belongs to the most vilified and persecuted minority in history" and who as a lawyer had defended the outcast. Nevertheless, he could not accept the Court's willingness to weigh for itself the need and efficacy of government regulations even against the express limitations of the Bill of Rights. His faith in majoritarian institutions and lack of trust in courts as institutions of "liberalism" set him apart from the newly developing Court.

Flag saluting in public schools did not die out with *Barnette,* and despite the Court's decision there were even attempts from time to time to enforce saluting as a compulsory requirement. As a precedent *Barnette* has had mixed success. Its ringing language did not prevail in various loyalty oath cases, and it was not cited affirmatively in a majority opinion until *Wooley v. Maynard* (1977). There, a Jehovah's Witness was prosecuted for taping over New Hampshire's motto, "Live Free or Die," on his automobile's license plate. Chief Justice Warren E. Burger, relying on *Barnette,* held that the state could not require a person to display on his personal property a statement of belief he did not hold. Justices William Rehnquist and Harry Blackmun dissented on the basis that the inclusion of a motto on a license plate did not require the owner of the vehicle to affirm that motto, nor did it reasonably suggest that the owner agreed with the motto. Therefore, they believed *Barnette* was distinguishable.

Justice Frankfurter's view that the Free Exercise Clause does not authorize courts to weigh the need for a secular law or to balance that need against an individual's interest in exercising his or her religion was largely readopted by the Supreme Court in *Employment Division, Department of Human Resources of Oregon v. Smith* (1990). *Barnette*'s holding, however, based on First Amendment free speech concepts, seems more secure.

The flag salute controversy again reached public attention during the 1988 presidential campaign, when the Republican candidate, George Bush, criticized the Democratic candidate, Governor Michael Dukakis of Massachusetts, for vetoing a bill requiring teachers in public schools to lead the Pledge of Allegiance recitation at the beginning of each school day. Governor Dukakis had taken this action after an advisory opinion from the Massachusetts Supreme Court concluded that the requirement was unconstitutional in light of *Barnette* and *Wooley.*

Constitutionally "Under God"

In 1954 Congress adopted its first amendment to the text of the Pledge of Allegiance to insert "under God" between the words "one Nation" and "indivisible." The author of the joint resolution, Senator Homer Ferguson of Michigan, stated that the idea for it came from a sermon given by the Reverend George M. Docherty of Washington, D.C. In that sermon the Reverend Docherty ruminated on the differences between the United States and the Soviet Union and indicated that one of greatest differences between the free world and communism is a belief in God. Yet, he noted, nothing in the Pledge of Allegiance highlighted that distinction.

In this period following the Korean War the nation was preoccupied with the domestic and international spread of communism. The Senate Judiciary Committee quoted with approval Senator Ferguson's statement that adding "under God" to the pledge "will strike another blow against those who would enslave us." The House Judiciary Committee similarly concluded that, in light of the attack on the principles of the American way of life by communists, adding "under God" to the pledge "would further acknowledge the dependence of our people and our Government upon the moral directions of the Creator [and] would serve to deny the atheistic and materialistic concepts of communism with its attendant subservience of the individual."

Both committees made reference to the long history of appeals to God in American life, from the Mayflower Compact, the Declaration of Independence, Lincoln's Gettysburg Address, and the inscription "In God We Trust" on U.S. coins, to Supreme Court statements, including the Court's assertion in *Zorach v. Clauson* (1952) that "We are a religious people whose institutions presuppose a supreme being."

Both committees also made passing reference to possible arguments that adding the phrase might run afoul of the Establishment Clause of the First Amendment to the Constitution. The committees found a distinction between establishing a church or religion as an institution and recognizing a belief in the sovereignty of God: "The phrase 'under God' recognizes only the guidance of God in our national affairs."

There is no reported court case challenging the law adding the words "under God" to the Pledge of Allegiance. In light of *Barnette*'s prohibition on requiring persons to make the pledge, it might be difficult under current doctrines of standing for any person to challenge the law. This has not stopped numerous courts from mentioning the provision, however, always in the context of a list of situations in which the federal government by statute or practice acknowledges God. In each circumstance the reference suggests that the Supreme Court believes the provision constitutional.

William Funk

Bibliography

Concannon, John J. III, "The Pledge of Allegiance and the First Amendment" 23 *Suffolk University Law Review* 1019–1047 (1989).

Curtis, Michael Kent (ed.), *The Flag and the Constitution,* vol. I, *Flag Salute and the Law* (New York: Garland, 1993).

Manwaring, David, *Render unto Caesar: The Flag Salute Controversy* (Chicago: University of Chicago Press, 1962).

Pfeffer, Leo, *Church, State, and Freedom* (Boston: Beacon, 1967).

Cases Cited

Employment Division, Department of Human Resources of Oregon v. Smith, 494 U.S. 872 (1990).

Jones v. Opelika, 316 U.S. 584 (1942).

Minersville School District v. Gobitis, 310 U.S. 586 (1940).

Reynolds v. United States, 98 U.S. 145 (1878).

West Virginia State Board of Education v. Barnette, 319 U.S. 624 (1943).

Wooley v. Maynard, 430 U.S. 705 (1977).

Zorach v. Clauson, 343 U.S. 306, (1952).

Ponce v. Roman Catholic Apostolic Church

See OVERSEAS POSSESSIONS OF THE UNITED STATES AND RELIGIOUS LIBERTY.

Presbyterian Church in the United States v. Mary Elizabeth Blue Hull Memorial Church

393 U.S. 440 (1969)

Presbyterian Church in the United States v. Hull Memorial Church (1969) arose out of the explosive theological, political, and social issues that split American churches in the 1960s: civil rights, the Vietnam War, and loyalty to the "faith of our fathers." By the end of the case, the U.S. Supreme Court announced a fundamental constitutional principle of religious freedom: Civil courts that resolve disputes within a religious group must refrain from deciding on the basis of their interpretation of religious doctrine.

The *Hull Memorial Church* case stemmed from divisions within the Presbyterian Church in the United States (PCUS), otherwise known as the Southern Presbyterian Church, which broke away from the national church at the outset of the Civil War. (The PCUS and most northern Presbyterians were eventually reunited in a series of mergers culminating in 1983.) For its first several decades the PCUS, reflecting the culture of Southern whites and the circumstances of its creation, was highly "conservative": strictly Calvinist in theology, suspicious of ecumenical cooperation with "liberal" Northern churches, focused on individual sins and "saving souls," and condoning or at least ignoring the region's racial segregation and other social evils. By the 1950s, however, denominational leaders in the PCUS had made important changes in each area. They endorsed critical biblical studies, joined ecumenical bodies, and began speaking on social issues—most controversially, condemning segregation and endorsing the Supreme Court's ruling in *Brown v. Board of Education of Topeka* (1954).

These changes in the PCUS produced a conservative reaction, and some unhappy local congregations considered breaking with the denomination. However, they were hampered by the PCUS's ecclesiastical structure, or "polity": Like other Presbyterian denominations, the PCUS was "hierarchical," with higher bodies exercising authority over local congregations. Because of this structure, the common law generally provided that title to church property, even though formally vested in the local church, was held in an "implied trust" for the denomination and would revert to the denomination if the local church broke away.

In 1966 two local congregations in Savannah, Georgia, voted to withdraw from the PCUS on the ground that the denomination had departed from its original confessions of faith and practice. Among the departures complained of, as later summarized by the Georgia Supreme Court in *Presbyterian Church in the United States v. Eastern Heights Presbyterian Church* (Ga., 1968), were "ordaining of women as ministers and ruling elders[;] making pronouncements and recommendations concerning civil, economic, social, and political matters[;] giving support to the removal of Bible reading and prayers by children in the public schools[;] . . . teaching neo-orthodoxy alien to the Confession of Faith[;] . . . causing all members to remain in the National Council of Churches of Christ[; and pronouncing on] international issues such as the Vietnam conflict." The denomination responded by taking possession of the local churches' property. The local churches then sued in state court to enjoin the denomination from "trespassing" on the property.

A jury awarded the property to the seceding congregations on the basis of a state-law condition on the "implied trust" doctrine: The general church would forfeit its interest if it had committed "a fundamental or substantial abandonment of [its] original tenets and doctrines." This "departure from doctrine" limit was designed, commendably, to prevent diversions of charitable contributions from the purpose intended by the donor; and in England, where it first developed, it made sense, given the tradition of state supervision of the church. In America, however, the tradition of separation of church and state raised serious questions about the legitimacy of a civil court's rendering a theological judgment on whether a development in church doctrine was a "substantial departure" from the original faith.

The *Hull Memorial Church* case presented such dangers in vivid form. In the angry climate of the 1960s, it was hardly surprising that a jury of average Southerners would sympathize with the conservative congregations and would view liberal trends among the churches as dangerous and misguided. Nor was it surprising that the largely Baptist jury—familiar with the Baptist principle of congregational autonomy—had little regard for the customs and practices of a hierarchically organized church. Nevertheless, despite these dangers of government intrusion through theological second-guessing, the Georgia Supreme Court affirmed the verdict awarding title to the local congregations.

The U.S. Supreme Court, however, unanimously reversed, holding that the "departure from doctrine" rule violated First Amendment guarantees of religious freedom by inhibiting religious doctrine and entangling church and state. Under the rule that the Court noted, a court or jury had to determine not only whether a "substantial" doctrinal departure had taken place but also whether the issue held "such importance in the traditional theology as to require that the trust be terminated." Thus the court or jury was required "to determine matters at the very core of a religion"—a role that the First Amendment "[p]lainly" barred civil courts from playing.

The Court, however, reemphasized that courts are not entirely barred from deciding intrachurch property disputes. Such a completely "hands-off" approach could have unhappy consequences. By removing a neutral arbiter, it would make it more difficult for contending religious factions to resolve their differences; and by completely refusing to police the actions of church leaders, it might actually discourage some religious activities such as charitable giving. In sending the *Hull Memorial Church* case back to the Georgia courts for further consideration, the Court reaffirmed that some kinds of rules for deciding church property disputes were permissible. The Court expressly endorsed the employment of "neutral principles of law, developed for use in all property disputes." Examples of these might include traditional rules for interpreting the language of conditions in a deed or a charitable bequest, or a state rule that awards property on religiously neutral terms—for example, to the majority of the congregation. (This neutral principles approach received an even greater boost from the Supreme Court ten years later in *Jones v. Wolf* [1979], which held that the question of which faction represented a congregation could be resolved by a state law of majority rule even if an authoritative tribunal in the hierarchical church had decided otherwise.)

Hull Memorial Church makes clear, however that no rule—whether set forth in a legal document or in a state law—can make the award of property turn on an interpretation or resolution of religious doctrine. That constitutional principle has proved relevant in other situations as well. For example, courts have consistently refused to hear cases in which ministers claim that they were wrongfully dismissed for allegedly violating church doctrine.

On remand, the Georgia Supreme Court still ruled for the local congregations, holding that the departure from doctrine limit was a crucial condition of the implied trust in favor of the PCUS and that, therefore, the invalidation of that condition meant the whole trust must fall. This time the U.S. Supreme Court declined to intervene, leaving the property still in the hands of the seceding congregations.

Thomas C. Berg

Bibliography

"Battle over Breakaways," 91:4 *Time* 62–63 (Jan. 26, 1968).

Kauper, Paul G., "Church Autonomy and the First Amendment: The Presbyterian Church Case," 1967 *Supreme Court Review* 349.

Smylie, James H., "Ecclesiological Storm and Stress in Dixie," 95 *Christian Century* 321–325 (Mar. 13, 1968).

———,"On Being Presbyterian in the South," 97 *Christian Century* 936–940 (Aug. 5, 1970).

Cases Cited

Brown v. Board of Education of Topeka, 347 U.S. 483 (1954).

Jones v. Wolf, 443 U.S. 595 (1979).

Presbyterian Church in the United States v. Eastern Heights Presbyterian Church, 224 Ga. 61, 159 S.E. 2d 690 (1968).

Presbyterian Church in the United States v. Mary Elizabeth Blue Hull Memorial Church, et. al., 393 U.S. 440, (1969).

Prince v. Massachusetts 321 U.S. 158 (1944)

Sarah Prince, a Jehovah's Witness, was convicted in the Plymouth County Superior Court under a Massachusetts statute prohibiting child labor for allowing her 9-year-old niece, Betty M. Simmons, to sell goods in a street or public place. At the time of the arrest the defendant's niece-ward was selling Jehovah's Witnesses religious tracts in the defendant's presence on a public street. "Both Mrs. Prince and Betty were ordained ministers" in the Witness movement. They were attempting to sell or even give away copies of *The Watchtower* and other Witness publications at night, when a school attendance official ordered Prince to take Betty home. Prince responded, "Neither you nor anybody else can stop me. . . . This child is exercising her God-given right and her constitutional right to preach the gospel, and no creature has a right to interfere with God's commands." Although Prince took Betty home that night, she was subsequently charged under the state's child labor laws.

The appeal in *Prince v. Massachusetts* (1944) was based on the claims (1) that the enforcement of the statute against the sale of religious literature created an unconstitutional abridgment of religious freedom, (2) that the statute ought not to be interpreted to include religious items and literature, (3) that this enforcement of the statute violated the freedom of conscience of both the defendant and her niece-ward, and (4) that the application of this statute to the activities in this case exceeded the legitimate police powers of the state.

The U.S. Supreme Court upheld the conviction in a decision written by Justice Wiley Rutledge. Numerous complex issues intersected in the Court's *Prince* decision. On the one hand, there was the freedom of religion, guaranteed by the First Amendment and recently extended to state actions through *Cantwell v. Connecticut* (1940). Complicating the application of religious liberty to the case was the minority of the child affected: Children's exercise of most constitutional rights is done through parental authority or guardianship, and the parental exercise of that authority is often subject to individual review or control by judicial authorities or to collective regulation through legislation. Furthermore, in the famous footnote 4 of *United States v. Carolene Products Co.* (1938) Chief Justice Harlan Fiske Stone announced the Court's newfound emphasis on political rights and those personal liberties—such as freedom of speech, press, petition, and assembly—which supplement the political process.

On the other hand, the authorities prosecuted Prince under legislation that was specifically framed as a child labor–child welfare law. From the 1880s through the mid-1930s the Supreme Court had used the doctrine of substantive due process or a restrictive notion of interstate commerce to strike down various state and federal acts attempting to regulate commerce and other economic activity. Commentators and politicians particularly criticized the Court for its decisions in

Lochner v. New York (1905) and *Hammer v. Dagenhart* (1918), which undermined the ability of the states or the national government to protect workers from market forces. In *Hammer* the Court had struck down the Keating-Owen Child Labor Act of 1916, a federal prohibition on child labor. In the mid-1930s, in decisions such as *Schecter Poultry v. United States* (1935), the Court struck down key programs of the New Deal, including the National Industrial Recovery Act and the Agricultural Adjustment Act. In the aftermath of President Franklin Roosevelt's attempt to institute his "court-packing plan," the High Court retreated from enforcement of the substantive due process doctrine.

In *Prince* the Court was asked, in effect, to set aside or to significantly narrow a child labor–child welfare statute on the grounds of its interference with the "preferred" freedoms; but for the majority of the Court, that action may have seemed uncomfortably close to a return to the abandoned doctrine of substantive due process. No one would suppose that the Court would question the sincerity of the legislature's intent in protecting the welfare of minor children through this law, because the prohibitions of the act were general, not specifically aimed at religious liberty—much less at the Jehovah's Witnesses per se. There was, furthermore, no claim of selective enforcement placed before the Court, and the Court itself rejected the expedient of reinterpreting the legislative intent of the statute to exclude religious literature, because the Court held that the state court's interpretation of a state statute is definitive.

The general unpopularity of the group involved in the case, the Jehovah's Witnesses, seems unlikely to have been a factor in the Court's motivations in *Prince,* because the Court had reversed itself in *West Virginia State Board of Education v. Barnette* (1943), a decision that aided the Witnesses.

Issues relating to freedom of the press and speech were not raised by the appellant, presumably because the claims for free exercise of religion were felt to be more precisely relevant to this case. Freedom of conscience was cited by the appellant, especially since the child and her aunt-guardian felt that the distribution of the literature was a serious religious duty. The Court, however, held that freedom of conscience in constitutional law did not extend beyond the specific freedoms guaranteed by the Constitution. In his opinion, Justice Rutledge, relying on *Reynolds v. United States* (1879) and *Davis v. Beason* (1890), asserted that "neither rights of religion nor rights of parenthood are beyond limitation." Similarly, the Court relied on *Jacobson v. Massachusetts* (1905), which allowed for compulsory vaccinations, to show that the state could limit religious freedom to protect children. Put simply, Rutledge held that "the state's authority over children's activities is broader than over like actions of adults."

Justice Robert Jackson, along with Justices Felix Frankfurter and Owen Roberts, concurred with the result, but on different grounds. They were troubled by the notion that children might have fewer rights to religious freedom than adults. Jackson believed that Rutledge's opinion laid a foundation "for any state intervention in the indoctrination and participation of a child in religion." Jackson would have upheld the conviction on much narrower grounds.

In dissent, Justice Frank Murphy argued that Betty Simmons was "engaged in genuine religious, rather than commercial, activity." He framed the question not as one of protecting children from labor but as "whether a state, under the guise of enforcing its child labor laws, can lawfully prohibit girls under the age of eighteen and boys under the age of twelve from practicing their religious faith insofar as it involves the distribution or sale of religious tracts on the public streets." Murphy considered this case just one more in the history of "persecution and intolerance" for religious reasons. With his usual passionate language, Murphy concluded: "Religious freedom is too sacred a right to be restricted or prohibited in any degree without convincing proof that a legitimate interest of the state is in grave danger." Murphy found no such danger in this case.

It appears that in *Prince* the repudiation of the substantive due process doctrine had reached a high-water mark, but the Court's new role as the especial protector of personal and political liberties had not yet reached its zenith. In addition, there had been a long tradition of the states' having greater rights of interference in constitutional rights when they are exercised through the guardianship relation, whether that of natural parents, adoptive parents, or legal guardians for minor children.

Because the guardianship relation implies by its very nature that the minor is incapable of making (unsupervised) those decisions, the parent or guardian is vested with that responsibility. Despite the theory of guardianship, however, the law recognizes the fact that guardians often imperfectly represent the interests of their minor wards. As a consequence of that realization, the state feels compelled and entitled to exercise a supervening role in certain guardianship judgments in its role as *parens patriae*. Minimum ages for alcohol consumption and for marriage, compulsory school attendance laws, and ordinary child labor laws are examples of the state's substitution of its own judgment for parental authority in ordinary areas of activity. There are limits even on such restrictions, of course, for the Court in *Pierce v. Society of Sisters* (1925) held that the child was not the creature of the state nor under its discretion solely.

Regularly, however, the courts and legislatures do intervene to substitute their judgments for those of parents in cases where specific religious orthopraxy imposes duties on children that the state believes might threaten grave injuries to their welfare. Members of the Bible-inspired snake-handling cults are regularly prosecuted for allowing their minor children to handle dangerous, poisonous reptiles during their worship ceremonies. The most common of these conflicts, perhaps, arise among Christian Scientists, Seventh-Day Adventists, Jehovah's Witnesses, and others whose beliefs forbid all or many medical procedures. The state regularly intervenes in order to secure medical treatment for such children.

Patrick M. O'Neil
Paul Finkelman

Bibliography

Witte, John, Jr., "The Essential Rights and Liberties of Religion in the American Constitutional Experiment," 71 *Notre Dame Law Review* 371–445 (1996).

———, "The Theology and Politics of the First Amendment Religion Clauses: A Bicentennial Essay," 40 *Emory Law Journal* 489–507 (1991).

Cases Cited

Cantwell v. Connecticut, 310 U.S. 296 (1940).
Davis v. Beason, 133 U.S. 333 (1890).
Hammer v. Dagenhart, 247 U.S. 251 (1918).
Jacobson v. Massachusetts, 197 U.S. 11 (1905).
Lochner v. New York, 198 U.S. 45 (1905).
Pierce v. Society of Sisters, 268 U.S. 510 (1925).
Prince v. Massachusetts, 321 U.S. 158 (1944).
Reynolds v. United States, 98 U.S. 145 (1879).
Schecter Poultry v. United States, 295 U.S. 495 (1935).
United States v. Carolene Products Co., 304 U.S. 144 (1938).
West Virginia State Board of Education v. Barnette, 319 U.S. 624 (1943).

Prison Inmates and the Free Exercise of Religion

Imprisonment engenders both a widespread need for the meaningful exercise of religion and formidable difficulties in meeting that need. Just as being in a foxhole is said to convert atheists, the experience of being imprisoned leads many to discover or rediscover religion. Those who have been incarcerated have ample reason to consider their spirituality and the direction of their lives, and they have ample time in which to do so. At various times in the history of prison, in fact, the connection between religion and incarceration has been more than coincidental. The Walnut Street Jail in Philadelphia, founded by the Quakers in 1789, was the first "penitentiary," where everything from architecture to attitudes to schedules was designed to encourage inmates to meditate about their fall into criminality and gradually to repent and be reaccepted into society. The goals of religion and incarceration were perceived to be commensurate.

Limits on Inmates' Free Exercise

But the isolation and dependency of prisoners, which perhaps promotes reflection, also has a profound impact on the ability of prisoners to observe the rituals and requirements that are a defining aspect of most organized religions. Group worship, whether in the form of the Catholic Mass or the Muslim Jumu'ah, is central to many religions. Some religions require a minimum number of people for certain observances, like the Jewish minyan. A prison may not contain enough coreligionists for an inmate to meet the requirements of group worship, particularly if the religion is not a popular one. Even if there are enough adherents to a particular religion in the prison, group worship may be rendered impossible by prison rules limiting free association or by prison schedules limiting the times at which inmates may attend chapel or gather together. Some religions require that certain services be conducted by a religious leader, like an imam, rabbi, or priest. Prisoners must depend on their wardens to allow these leaders to be brought into the prison at appropriate times if proper services are to take place.

Prisoners are also dependent on prison officials to meet their religious needs for a particular diet and for access to the headgear, prayer books, or artifacts required by their religion. In short, prisoners lack the freedom to freely exercise religion, and therefore they must demand that prison administrators actively accommodate their religious needs.

Perhaps because the goals of prison and religion are frequently compatible, prison administrators have historically been sympathetic to many of those demands. American prisons typically have provided chapels, where observers of the most prevalent religions could meet with a chaplain who could lead Catholic, Protestant, or sometimes Jewish worship services at critical times, like the Sabbath or major holidays. But these resources and cooperation were not always extended to those who observed other religions less popular in the United States: Buddhists, Muslims, Native Americans, Rastafarians, or adherents to newly created or reinterpreted faiths.

Prison administrators who declined prisoners' demands for assistance in their religious worship have typically cited one of two kinds of reasons. First is the issue of resources. Providing additional worship facilities and a variety of special diets could become expensive, and that expense has sometimes seemed to prison administrators to be unjustifiable if only a few inmates would be benefited. The second issue concerns security and order within the prison. To inmates who wish to wear religious headgear, like Muslim prayer caps or Jewish yarmulkes, some prison administrators have responded that it is too easy to hide contraband under a hat; to inmates who wish to grow beards or not cut their hair for religious reasons, some prison administrators have retorted that it is too easy for inmates to change their appearance by growing or removing facial hair, thus possibly compromising security. While prison administrators who are willing to honor inmates' religious claims have sometimes minimized or scoffed at such concerns about security or order, other prison administrators have declared themselves unwilling to take any action that might be perceived as risky.

Expanding Inmates' Free Exercise

The fact that some of the first inmates to demand expansion of prison officials' willingness to accommodate religion were Black Muslims, during the 1960s and 1970s, exacerbated the natural tension between the inmates' claims of rights and the prison administrators' practical concerns. Prison administrators—who may have perceived Judeo-Christian worship as a soothing and benign influence on potentially volatile inmates—saw the Muslim movement as a challenge to their authority and so tended to resist the demands of Black Muslim inmates. This was particularly true when an inmate was a recent convert to Islam, or when the inmate also challenged the prison on issues other than religion.

Thus, during the 1970s, prisoners, often Muslim, began to turn more frequently to the courts when they were dissatisfied with prison officials' responses. One outgrowth of the civil rights movement and of the Warren Court era was that the courts—at least the federal courts—were willing to entertain some of these complaints. In earlier eras, when prisoners had tried to complain to the courts about the callousness of prison officials, they were met with a "hands-off" policy. As the Virginia Supreme Court eloquently put it, in *Ruffin v. Commonwealth* (Va., 1871), prisoners were "slaves of the state" and had no rights to assert in court. Ironically, the Virginia court used this metaphor only six years after the Thirteenth Amendment had formally abolished slavery. A century later, however, the U.S. Supreme Court, perceiving prisoners to be another of the politically disadvantaged minorities that the Warren Court had set out to protect, began to reevaluate the notion that prisoners had no rights and that courts should not question what happened inside prison walls.

One of the earliest cases decided in favor of a prisoner plaintiff by the Supreme Court was *Cruz v. Beto* (1972). The Texas inmate in that case alleged that, as a Buddhist, he was denied the opportunity to practice religion that other inmates enjoyed—whereas Catholic, Protestant, and Jewish inmates were permitted to use the chapel, he was not; whereas those inmates had prison chaplains of their faith funded by the state, he did not. Part of Cruz's claim was that this state sponsorship improperly encouraged inmates to join particular religions—inmates were provided with free Jewish and Christian Bibles, for example, and not other religious books. Cruz submitted a pro se complaint (without counsel of an attorney) to the district court written on toilet paper.

The Supreme Court did not evaluate whether Cruz was a sincere Buddhist or whether he was denied a reasonable opportunity to pursue his faith, because the district court had dismissed his complaint. The Court ruled that if Cruz could prove what he alleged, he had been denied his constitutional right to a "reasonable opportunity" to exercise the religious freedom guaranteed him by the First and Fourteenth Amendments. The fact that the prison was allegedly discriminating against a particular religion was considered significant. Although the Court did note that not every religious sect or group regardless of number would be entitled to have identical facilities, prisons were put on notice that freedom of religion was a right that survived incarceration, a right that was not so fundamentally inconsistent with status as a prisoner as to be extinguished on imprisonment. While his litigation wended its way through the courts, Cruz was released, and so the prison was spared the challenge of accommodating his religious needs.

Cruz dovetailed with other decisions protecting the constitutional rights of prisoners. In *Procunier v. Martinez* (1974) the Court held a state scheme of censorship of prisoners' mail unconstitutional—although on the basis of the First Amendment rights of the prisoners' correspondents; and in *Wolff v. McDonnell* (1974) the Court declared that accommodation is required between prisoners' constitutional rights and legitimate penological objectives. These cases, along with *Cruz,* led to a proliferation of prisoners' rights claims in the lower federal courts, including numerous claims of religious rights, on behalf of Muslims and many others.

Approaches to "Reasonable Accommodation"

The lower courts struggled to give content to the Supreme Court's vague pronouncements: What was a "reasonable" opportunity to practice a religion? What was an appropriate "accommodation" between prisoner and prison, one that gave enough deference to prison administrators but did not allow them to prevail on the basis of "exaggerated concerns"? Some courts adopted the test of "compelling state interest," a method of analysis of constitutional claims typically used in First Amendment cases outside the prison context and used in *Procunier.* Under the compelling state interest test prison officials must justify a refusal to accommodate bona fide religious practices by showing that their actions are necessary to serve a legitimate and compelling governmental interest. Examples of this approach include *Walker v. Blackwell* (5th Cir. 1969), *Kennedy v. Meachum* (10th Cir. 1976), and *Barnett v. Rodgers* (D.C. Cir. 1969). This approach tended to lead to victories for prisoner plaintiffs. Other courts used a modified approach, requiring prison administrators to show only that their asserted interests were "important" (*Madyun v. Franzen* [7th Cir. 1983]), "legitimate" (*Walker v. Mintzes* [6th Cir. 1985]), or "substantial" (*Shabazz v. Barnauskas* [11th Cir. 1986])—tests that more frequently resulted in claims being denied.

An informative and lively debate about the relative merits of these different approaches took place in *St. Claire v. Cuyler* (3rd Cir. 1980). St. Claire, a Muslim inmate at Graterford Prison in Pennsylvania, complained of difficulties in practicing his faith; he was disciplined for wearing a kufi to the dining hall, and he was unable to convince prison officials to have a guard escort him from a segregated housing facility to attend worship services. In light of the fact that prison authorities had testified that headgear in the dining room could "interfere with decorum, conceal contraband, and serve as a means of group identification," and that assigning special guards to escort prisoners to worship services was not "feasible," a three-judge panel of the appellate court found no First Amendment problem, stressing that Supreme Court case law taught that "it is the informed discretion of the prison administrators that controls . . . and not 'a court's idea of how best to operate a detention facility.'" Here the Third Circuit quoted *Bell v. Wolfish* (1979). St. Claire asked the entire court to reconsider the case en banc, and the ten judges split evenly on whether to do so. Judge Arlin Adams, dissenting from the court's denial of the petition for rehearing, accused the other members of the court of adopting "a rule of complete deference to prison officials," in a manner inconsistent with the Supreme Court's statement that there must be an accommodation between the rights of inmates and legitimate penological objectives. "Under the test announced by the panel," he said, "there is no room for recognition or accommodation if a prison official is able to speculate that religious observance might implicate security interests. . . . [I]t would be an unimaginative prison official who could not conjure up a potential security concern underlying any particular restriction."

The *O'Lone* Standard: Overruling Earlier Decisions

The Supreme Court put this judicial debate to rest in *O'Lone v. Estate of Shabazz* (1987). Instead of applying usual First Amendment standards to the analysis of prisoners' religious claims, the Court applied the same accommodationist balancing test it had just adopted in *Turner v. Safley* (1987) to analyze prisoners' free expression claims. The lower courts were told to question only whether the prison regulation or action was reasonably related to a legitimate penological interest, and to consider four factors during that inquiry: (1) whether there is a valid, rational connection between the prison regulation and the interest asserted; (2) whether there are alternative means of exercising that right that remain open to inmates; (3) the impact that accommodation of the asserted constitutional right would have on guards, other inmates, and the allocation of prison resources generally; and (4) whether there are obvious, easy alternative means by which the prison might serve its interest without impinging on the inmates' First Amendment freedom. Under this malleable test, the Court reversed the lower court decision in *Shabazz v. O'Lone* (3rd Cir. 1985), which had required a prison to allow Muslim inmates who were assigned to a work detail outside the main prison building to attend a weekly congregational service. The Supreme Court held in *O'Lone* that the prisoners had not shown that the prison's regulation was an unreasonable means of promoting order in the facility. In its decision the Court stressed the need for courts to defer to decisions made by prison administrators, and it found that the fact that Muslims had an opportunity to observe other requirements of their religion was sufficient to satisfy the Free Exercise Clause.

The *O'Lone* standard, applied by the lower federal courts, led to increasingly one-sided results. Courts that had found prisons to have violated inmates' First Amendment rights before *O'Lone* understood this new standard to require new analysis and different results. In *Fromer v. Scully* (2nd Cir. 1989), for example, the Second Circuit overruled its earlier decision in *Fromer v. Scully* (2nd Cir. 1987) in favor of the prisoner plaintiff. Initially the court had struck down a prohibition on Orthodox Jews' wearing beards of more than one inch. After *O'Lone* the court allowed this prohibition. Similarly, in *Iron Eyes v. Henry* (8th Cir. 1990) the court allowed prison officials to prohibit Native American prisoners from wearing long hair. *Iron Eyes* overruled the same court's decision in *Teterud v. Burns*, (8th Cir. 1975) striking down a prohibition on Native Americans' wearing long hair. Although the courts had previously differed about the extent of prison administrators' obligations to accommodate religious practices, after *Turner* and *O'Lone* the courts tended to uphold not only prison grooming requirements but also other restrictions on prisoners' religious claims. In *Al Amamin v. Gramley* (7th Cir. 1990) the court approved a prison's refusal to provide special diets for Muslim inmates. Similarly, in *Kahey v. Jones* (5th Cir. 1988) another circuit held that prisons were not required to provide Muslim inmates pork-free diets. Muslims were not the only prisoners to face difficulties in practicing their religion. In *Friend v. Kolodzieczak* (9th Cir. 1991) a court allowed prisons to prohibit the possession of rosaries, while in *Young v. Lane* (7th Cir. 1991) the court upheld a prison's right to refuse to allow a Jewish inmate to wear a yarmulke.

Smith and the RFRA: Reactions to *O'Lone*

In *Employment Division, Department of Human Resources of Oregon v. Smith* (1990) the Supreme Court extended reasoning not unlike that of *O'Lone* to a case outside the prison context. In *Smith* the Court held that the right of free exercise does not relieve an individual of the obligation to comply with a valid and neutral law of general applicability on the ground that religion prohibits or requires certain conduct. Congress reacted to this decision, which had been almost universally condemned. In the Religious Freedom Restoration Act of 1993 (RFRA) Congress overruled *Smith*. Although Congress did not explicitly say so in the act, the legislative history shows that the act also overrode *O'Lone*. (This history is set out in H.R. No. 88, 103rd Cong., 1st Sess. at 7 [1993] and in S.R. No. 111, 103rd Cong., 1st Sess. at 9 [July 27, 1993].) Signed into law by President Clinton in November 1993, the RFRA conferred religious rights on prisoners and reinstated fairly traditional First Amendment analysis to prisoners' litigation concerning their right to the free exercise of religion. The law declared: "Government may substantially burden a person's exercise of religion only if it demonstrates that application of the burden to the person (1) is in furtherance of a compelling governmental interest; and (2) is the least restrictive means of furthering that compelling governmental interest." Under this statute the courts were once again required to reevaluate prisoners' claims of rights to everything from diets to worship services to possession of religious accouterments—this time, under a standard that put a thumb on the prisoner's side of the scale.

The RFRA provided no assistance to the courts about one of the thorniest issues concerning free exercise of religion in prison: What counts as a religion? Inmates who were Rastafarians, or members of the Church of Wicca, or who had simply declared their own belief systems have challenged the courts to define what it is that renders a system of beliefs a "religion" that is entitled to the solicitude of the First Amendment. In *Africa v. Commonwealth of Pennsylvania* (3rd Cir. 1981) the Third Circuit developed a frequently followed three-part test to define religion, questioning (1) whether the organization or belief system addresses fundamental and ultimate questions, (2) whether the beliefs are comprehensive in nature, and (3) whether the organization or belief system has defining characteristics like that of a traditional religion. Under this test, the Third Circuit found the MOVE organization to be a philosophy, not a religion. However, in *Dettmer v. Landon* (4th Cir. 1986) the Fourth Circuit found the Church of Wicca to be a religion.

The case that most plagued the federal courts involved an inmate-organized religion named the Eclatarian Faith, or the Church of the New Song (CONS). Harry Theriault, the chief architect of this purported religion, litigated the status of his organization almost endlessly in the federal courts. These cases included *Theriault v. Carlson* (N.D. Ga. 1972) (*Theriault I*); *Theriault v. Carlson* (N.D. Ga. 1973) (*Theriault II*); *Theriault v. Silber* (W.D. Tex. 1978) (*Theriault III*). Eventually the courts held that the Church of the New Song was not in fact a "religion." The credibility of Theriault's claim was not helped by one Eclaration who declared to prison administrators that the religion required, as a sacrament, a weekly meal of porterhouse steak and wine.

The RFRA did engender a new spate of cases in which all the claims that had been rejected almost routinely under the *O'Lone* test resurfaced and had to be reconsidered under the statute's new standards. Once again, the courts became sympathetic to many prisoners' claims that their ability to exercise their religion had been "substantially burdened." In the face of prison administrators' claims of security considerations, courts held that prisoners had to be allowed to exercise their religions in appropriate ways, even if those particular observances were not "required" by the religion. In *Sasnett v. Sullivan* (7th Cir. 1996), for example, prison officials prohibited the wearing of a cross as dangerous because, given the nature of its design, a cross can lacerate the skin; but the court hearing a claim from a prisoner who wished to wear a cross held that this prohibition violated the RFRA. Other courts, like the Hawaiian court in *Belgrade v. State* (D. Haw. 1995), required prisons to accommodate Native Americans' long hair or, as in *Lewis v. Scott* (E.D. Tex. 1995), to allow religiously inspired beards. But the legislative history of the RFRA also spoke of the need for courts to give deference to prison administrators, and so prisoners often failed in their claims under the statute. Some courts held, for example, that in analyzing whether there were less restrictive means for the prison to serve its goals (such as maintaining security), the court should give deference to the prison defendants' analysis of whether alternatives were feasible and risk-free. Under this reasoning, the court in *Hamilton v. Schriro* (8th Cir. 1996) allowed a prison to deny a Native American prisoner access to a sweat lodge and to require him to cut his hair, and the court in *Lawson v. Singletary* (11th Cir. 1996) allowed a prison to censor Hebrew Israelite literature that contained racially inflammatory material.

It had not seemed surprising when the Warren Court, with its dedication to promoting equality and the rights of minorities, led the federal courts in amplifying the religious rights of prisoners. The federal courts had long been the last resort for unpopular claimants seeking tolerance of their views or recognition of their humanity. It was also unsurprising when the increasingly conservative Supreme Court cut back, in cases like *O'Lone,* on what the earlier Court had promised. Chief Justice Rehnquist, who led the Court at the time of *O'Lone,* had been the sole dissenter in the watershed Supreme Court decision in *Cruz,* complaining that the federal courts should not be required to waste their time on frivolous matters like whether Cruz could exercise his religion. The great surprise was that Congress—democratically elected and presumed not to be overly sympathetic to the rights of prisoners or to the demands of non-mainstream religions—took on what had been seen as the job of the federal courts in enacting the RFRA and trying to restore those rights.

City of Boerne: Returning to *O'Lone*

But the passage of the RFRA did not end the story. In many of the cases brought by prisoners and others under the RFRA, defendants challenged the constitutionality of the act, on the ground that Congress was reinterpreting the First Amendment, in violation of the fundamental principle of judicial review (the right of the judiciary to interpret the Constitution). Those invoking the act pointed out that, because the Constitution generally aims to protect the rights of individuals against intolerant majorities, the courts had generally allowed Congress to increase individual rights through legislation; it was legislation that attempted to *decrease* rights that was viewed as constitutionally suspect. In the landmark case of *City of Boerne v. P. F. Flores, Archbishop of San Antonio, and the United States* (1997) the Supreme Court, still headed by Chief Justice Rehnquist, considered these arguments and invalidated the RFRA. Citing *Marbury v. Madison* (1803), a divided Court held that Congress had exceeded its powers by reinterpreting the First Amendment, as opposed to providing additional remedies for its violation.

After this decision the lower courts had to resign themselves to hearing yet another round of litigation between prisoners and prison officials, about the same range of claims about headgear, services, hair length, diet, etc. Once again, all recent case law became irrelevant. Cases would require reexamination under the new old rules. After *City of Boerne,* the *O'Lone* test will again rule in prisons, and prisoners' ability to exercise their religions in all the ways described above will be subject to the discretion, or sometimes whim, of those who run the prisons. Dostoyevsky once said that the quality of a civilization may be judged by looking at its prisons. The Warren Court and even the 1993 Congress tried to close the gap between the religious life of prisoners and nonprisoners. Now, without the attention of the federal courts, the quality of religious life in the American prison may become more strained.

Susan N. Herman

Bibliography

Blischak, Matthew, "*O'Lone v. Estate of Shabazz*: The State of Prisoners' Religious Free Exercise Rights," 37 *American University Law Review* 453–486 (1988).

Frankel, Geoffrey, "Untangling First Amendment Values: The Prisoner's Dilemma," 59 *George Washington Law Review* 1614–1646 (1991).

Giles, Cheryl Dunn, "*Turner v. Safley* and Its Progeny: A Gradual Retreat to the 'Hands Off' Doctrine," 35 *Arizona Law Review* 219–236 (1993).

Lupu, Ira, "Statutes Revolving in Constitutional Orbit," 79 *Virginia Law Review* 1–89 (1993).

Ryan, James, "*Smith* and the RFRA: An Iconoclastic Assessment," 78 *Virginia Law Review* 1407–1446 (1992).

Cases and Statutes Cited

Africa v. Commonwealth of Pennsylvania, 662 F. 2d 1025 (3rd Cir. 1981).

Al Amamin v. Gramley, 926 F. 2d 680 (7th Cir. 1991).

Barnett v. Rodgers, 410 F. 2d 995 (D.C. Cir. 1969).
Belgrade v. State, 883 F. Supp. 510 (D. Haw. 1995).
Bell v. Wolfish, 441 U.S. 520 (1979).
City of Boerne v. P. F. Flores, Archbishop of San Antonio, and the United States, 521 U.S. 507 (1997).
Cruz v. Beto, 405 U.S. 319 (1972).
Dettmer v. Landon, 799 F. 2d 929 (4th Cir. 1986).
Employment Division, Department of Human Resources of Oregon v. Smith, 494 U.S. 872 (1990).
Friend v. Kolodzieczak, 923 F. 2d 126 (9th Cir. 1991).
Fromer v. Scully, 874 F. 2d 69 (2nd Cir. 1989).
Hamilton v. Schriro, 74 F. 3d 1545 (8th Cir.), (1996).
Iron Eyes v. Henry, 907 F. 2d 810 (8th Cir. 1990).
Kahey v. Jones, 836 F. 2d 948 (5th Cir. 1988).
Kennedy v. Meachum, 540 F. 2d 1057 (10th Cir. 1976).
Lawson v. Singletary, 85 F. 3d 502 (11th Cir. 1996).
Lewis v. Scott, 910 F. Supp. 282 (E.D. Tex. 1995).
Madyun v. Franzen, 704 F. 2d 954 (7th Cir.) (1983).
Marbury v. Madison, 5 U.S. 137 (1803).
O'Lone v. Estate of Shabazz, 482 U.S. 342 (1987).
Procunier v. Martinez, 416 U.S. 396 (1974).
Ruffin v. Commonwealth, 62 Va. (21 Gratt.) 790 (1871).
Sasnett v. Sullivan, 91 F. 3d 1018 (7th Cir. 1996).
Shabazz v. Barnauskas, 790 F. 2d 1536 (11th Cir.) (1986).
Shabazz v. O'Lone, 782 F. 2d 416 (3rd Cir. 1985).
St. Claire v. Cuyler, 634 F. 2d 109, (3rd Cir. 1980).
Teterud v. Burns, 522 F. 2d 357 (8th Cir. 1975).
Theriault v. Carlson, 339 F. Supp. 375 (N.D. Ga. 1972); *Theriault v. Carlson,* 353 F. Supp. 1061 (N.D. Ga. 1973) (1974); *Theriault v. Silber,* 453 F. Supp. 254 (W.D. Tex. 1978).
Turner v. Safley, 482 U.S. 78 (1987).
Walker v. Blackwell, 411 F. 2d 23 (5th Cir. 1969).
Walker v. Mintzes, 771 F. 2d 920 (6th Cir. 1985).
Wolff v. McDonnell, 418 U.S. 539 (1974).
Young v. Lane, 922 F. 2d 370 (7th Cir. 1991).
Religious Freedom Restoration Act of 1993, 42 U.S. Code §2000bb (1993).

Privacy Rights and Religious Influences

Although the United States has a written constitution and a history of relative political and individual liberty, the laws regulating contraception, abortion, and private consensual sexual behavior that existed until fairly recently—some of which in fact still exist—are largely inconsistent with principles of individual freedom. Most western European countries, even those without the American tradition of free speech and political participation, are considerably less concerned with individual decisions regarding sexuality and reproduction than is the United States. Only in those countries in which organized religion plays a major role in politics, such as Italy and Ireland, do the same disputes regarding abortion and contraception arise.

What makes the United States unusual is that, unlike Ireland, for instance, where the role of the Catholic Church is incorporated into the constitution, the American Constitution specifically provides for the separation of church and state, prohibiting the establishment of religion but also guaranteeing its free exercise. Given those provisions, one might expect legislators in the United States, either state or federal, or the federal judges who are expected to pass on the constitutionality of state and federal laws, to be wary of passing or enforcing laws that appear to have no secular purpose and are instead fairly obviously consistent with—indeed, presumably propelled by—religious beliefs concerning the morality of certain sexual conduct or the existence of a soul before birth.

Nonetheless, it is clear that legislators on all levels are frequently motivated by their own religious beliefs or those of their constituents. In addition, the U.S. Supreme Court has been reluctant to reject laws that are arguably motivated only by religious philosophy and has, instead, made an effort to find an allowable secular purpose to uphold such statutes. Despite, therefore, an intuitive sense that laws regulating reproduction and private sexual behavior are religiously based—an intuition often supported by factual material such as legislative debates—neither the Establishment Clause nor the Free Exercise Clause of the First Amendment has ever been used to strike down such legislation.

In recent years the Supreme Court has relied primarily on the Due Process Clause of the Fourteenth Amendment to establish a right to privacy that has been used to overrule laws regulating contraception and abortion. It has done so without regard to the issue of religion. Arguably, the religious question is irrelevant, if the result is the same. The problem with the current approach is that the more conservative Supreme Court of recent years has been narrowing the Fourteenth Amendment right to privacy and may well determine in the near future that no such right exists. In that case, the Court is unlikely to adopt instead an approach rejecting legislation on Establishment Clause grounds. On the other hand, if the line of privacy cases had from the beginning recognized the religious basis of the laws that were found unconstitutional, perhaps that approach might have survived a more conservative Court.

Expanding Privacy Rights

The early cases in the privacy area concerned family integrity rather than "privacy" in any sense of the word. In *Meyer v. Nebraska* (1923) a teacher was convicted of teaching a class in German to a child under a certain age, contrary to state law. The Supreme Court held that it was up to parents to decide what their children could be taught, not up to the state. The interest of parents in making decisions about the education of their children was also upheld in *Pierce v. Society of Sisters* (1925), which struck down an Oregon statute requiring parents to send their children to public schools. Finally, in *Skinner v. Oklahoma* (1942) the Supreme Court struck down an Oklahoma law that required the compulsory sterilization of felons who were convicted of two or more crimes of moral turpitude. Although the decision was actually based on the Equal Protection Clause, the Court, for the first time, referred to a fundamental right of procreation.

The modern line of privacy cases begins with *Griswold v. Connecticut* (1965) in which the Supreme Court struck down a Connecticut statute prohibiting the use or sale of contraceptive devices. Rather than relying on the Fourteenth Amendment's Due Process Clause (an approach that had been discredited early in the century because of its use in protecting property rights), Justice William O. Douglas found that the penumbras of specific guarantees of the Bill of Rights create a zone of privacy that encompasses the decision of married couples to use contraceptives. Justices William Brennan and Arthur Goldberg concurred, with Earl Warren, Chief Justice, on the ground that the Ninth Amendment reserves unenumerated rights to the people and that the right to privacy is a liberty interest protected by fundamental concepts of justice.

Following *Griswold* there were a number of cases in which the Court expanded on the right of privacy and became clearer about where in the Constitution it could be found. In *Roe v. Wade* (1973) the Court determined that the decision regarding abortion should be left to a woman and her doctor, except as the state's interest becomes more significant late in a pregnancy. The Court found that the Fourteenth Amendment's concept of personal liberty was sufficient to protect the right, without making it clear where in the Fourteenth Amendment this was located. Subsequent decisions were more clearly based on the Due Process Clause of the Fourteenth Amendment.

In addition to *Roe* and to the other abortion cases in which the Court upheld the right of a woman to choose abortion free from state restrictions, the Court also established that family relationships were immune from state regulation. In *Moore v. City of East Cleveland* (1977) the Court rejected an ordinance that defined "family" for zoning purposes in a way that would preclude an extended family from living together. And in *Zablocki v. Redhail* (1978) a Wisconsin statute that prohibited marriage by state residents who were not in compliance with child support orders was struck down as interfering with the fundamental right to marry.

Contracting Privacy Rights

Although the concept of personal autonomy or privacy seemed almost infinitely expandable, in recent years the Court has declined to accept the invitation to continue to expand those rights. Although the Court has followed *Roe* (at least until the most recent decisions), it has narrowed the privacy right in other areas.

In *Bowers v. Hardwick* (1986) the Court rejected a challenge to the Georgia sodomy statute brought by a homosexual who had been arrested, although never tried or convicted, for an act of consensual sodomy within his own bedroom. The Court found that there was no connection between rights involving the family, marriage, and procreation with homosexuality, and it relied on the history of criminal statutes proscribing homosexual activity.

Similarly, in *Michael H. v. Gerald D.* (1989) the Court allowed California law to define paternity in such a way that the natural father of a child, who had acted as her social father as well, was precluded from legally establishing paternity. A plurality looked at history (as they had in *Bowers*) in order to determine the reach of the Due Process Clause.

Webster v. Reproductive Health Services (1989) was decided by a similarly divided Court and does very little to determine what limits a state may set on the abortion decision, except that there can be more limits than *Roe* would seem to indicate. Justice Sandra Day O'Connor, who has been the deciding vote in several of these cases, takes the position that states may impose regulations—even in the first trimester—so long as they do not unduly burden the abortion decision. That would seem to rule out criminal penalties or laws requiring that women establish cause before they could have an abortion, but it is not clear what else it rules out or whether there are now enough votes on the Court to overrule *Roe,* even without O'Connor.

Finally, in *Cruzan v. Director, Missouri Department of Health* (1990) the Court faced the first "right to die" case. *Cruzan* involved a young woman who had been in a persistent vegetative state for six years following a car accident. Her parents requested that the tube providing nutrition and hydration be disconnected—a decision with which the trial court agreed. The Missouri Supreme Court overruled the lower court, holding that the interest of the state in life is so strong as to require clear and convincing evidence before such action can be taken. The Supreme Court—again in a split decision—agreed that even if there is a fundamental right to refuse medical treatment (and only Justice Scalia was willing to say that there was no such *constitutional* right), the state could set the level of required evidence. Four dissenters argued that the state was deliberately trying to forestall the decision and that Nancy Cruzan ought to be allowed to exercise her constitutional right to refuse treatment (or to have her parents exercise it on her behalf) on the showing that was made—that is, the preponderance of the evidence.

Privacy Rights and the Religion Clauses

In contrast to the privacy area, the line of cases in which the Supreme Court has defined the scope of the Establishment Clause is not easy to describe briefly. As a rule, in challenges to prayer in public schools, such as *School District of Abington Township v. Schempp* (1963), the Court has found the practice unconstitutional, as it has in cases involving economic assistance to religious schools, such as *School District of the City of Grand Rapids v. Ball* (1985). On the other hand, where the government assistance or support of religion has not involved finances, the decisions have been less clear. In *McGowan v. Maryland* (1961) the Court upheld a Sunday closing law, on the ground that there were secular as well as religious purposes behind the statute; and in *Lynch v. Donnelly* (1984) the display of a crèche in a public park was upheld, based apparently on the presence of secular Christmas decorations in addition to the crèche itself.

In 1971 the Court adopted a test, in the case of *Lemon v. Kurtzman* (1971), to determine the validity of legislation when it was challenged as violative of the Establishment Clause. The test requires that the statute have a secular legislative purpose, that its principal effect be one that neither advances nor inhibits religion, and that the statute not foster excessive government entanglement with religion. Unfortunately, the *Lemon* test has not made the cases in this area easier to predict or understand. It has been used both to strike down a state statute requiring the teaching of "creation science," in *Edwards v. Aguillard* (1987), and to uphold tax credits for the parents of both public and parochial school students, in *Mueller v. Allen* (1983). In the *Lynch* case, the Court upheld the crèche display without reference to the *Lemon* test, although both decisions were written by Chief Justice Burger.

The most interesting aspect of the intersection between the privacy cases and the Establishment Clause cases is reminiscent of the dog in the Sherlock Holmes story that was notable because it did *not* bark. The Court has rarely even discussed the impact of religion on the laws regulating sexuality and reproduction and has steadfastly refused to use the Establishment Clause to protect the right to privacy.

One of the earliest of the privacy cases, *Pierce v. Society of Sisters* (1925), involved an Oregon law requiring parents to send their children to public school. One of the plaintiffs, the Society of Sisters, made the argument that parents have the right to guide their children religiously and intellectually, but the argument was made without reference to the First Amendment. The decision of the Court relies more on the property rights of the schools that would be forced to close as a result of the statute than on the exercise of religious liberty, although there is at least a reference to the rights of parents to direct the upbringing and education of their children.

In her article on the background to the *Griswold* case, Mary L. Dudziak states, "The central reason for the repeated inability of the Connecticut legislature to modify its birth control statutes was the role of religion in state politics." Dudziak goes on to document the significant role of the Catholic Church in Connecticut's politics generally and the role of the Catholic Church specifically in preventing reform of the laws on birth control. In spite of the religious significance of the Connecticut law, the Supreme Court twice refused to consider whether the law was unconstitutional, in *Tileston v. Ullman* (1943) and in *Poe v. Ullman* (1961). When the Court did reach the merits of the case in *Griswold,* it rejected the statute on privacy grounds, rather than deciding, or even considering, the Establishment Clause problem.

The Court in *Roe* was more willing to admit the religious issues underlying the abortion controversy and, indeed, held that the question of when life begins is primarily medical, theological, and philosophical. As Justice Blackmun stated, "We need not resolve the difficult question of when life begins. When those trained in the respective disciplines of medicine, philosophy, and theology are unable to arrive at any consensus, the judiciary, at this point in the development of man's knowledge, is not in a position to speculate as to the answer."

Although there have been a number of changes on the Supreme Court since the decision in *Roe,* the holding remained essentially undisturbed, at least until the *Webster* case. On the other hand, the Court was unwilling to extend the holding of *Roe* to guarantee access to abortion, restricting it instead to a prohibition on legislation that positively interfered with the abortion right. Starting in 1976 and continuing until the present, Congress has annually passed legislation prohibiting the use of Medicaid funds to reimburse states for the cost of abortions. That statute, known as the Hyde Amendment, was incorporated in Public Law 96-123, Section 109, 93 Stat. 926, when it was challenged in the Supreme Court. Earlier versions allowed an exception if the abortion was performed to save the life of the mother or if the pregnancy was the result of rape or incest that had been promptly reported. The 1989 version contains only the exception for preserving the woman's life.

The Hyde Amendment was challenged in *Harris v. McRae* (1980), where the plaintiffs argued that the provision violated both the due process and the equal protection principles as well as the Establishment Clause of the First Amendment. The Supreme Court rejected all three arguments, taking the position that the government is free to fund those activities it wishes to encourage (such as childbirth) while not funding those it seeks to discourage (such as abortion) without implicating constitutional concerns. Finally, the Court held that a statute does not violate the Establishment Clause simply because it "happens to coincide or harmonize with the tenets of some or all religions."

Indeed, the Court not only is unwilling to strike down legislation because it embodies a particular religious viewpoint but also has upheld laws based on the religious tradition behind them. In *Bowers* the Court upheld the Georgia statute criminalizing consensual sodomy despite the argument that private sexual activity should be protected by the same principles as those that protected decisions regarding abortion and contraception. Instead, the majority looked to historical tradition and determined that the right to engage in homosexual sodomy was neither deeply rooted in the nation's history nor implicit in the concept of ordered liberty. In his concurring opinion, Chief Justice Burger supported the Court's result by referring to "Judeao-Christian moral and ethical standards."

Recently, Justice John Paul Stevens has raised the argument that laws restricting abortion have no secular purpose but are instead based on a religious philosophy concerning the question of when life begins. In *Thornburgh v. American College of Obstetricians and Gynecologists* (1986) Justice Byron White, dissenting, distinguished between the minimal interest of the state in preventing conception and the greater interest in restricting abortion because of the existence of the fetus. He further argued that the decision to protect life is not an impermissible "religious" act merely because it coincides with the views of one or more religions. Justice Stevens, concurring, argued that the only basis for distinguishing between the state's interest in the moment before conception occurs and in the moment after is based on religion and is therefore impermissible.

Similarly, in *Webster* the majority found it unnecessary to determine the validity of the preamble to the Missouri abortion statute under consideration. The preamble stated that life begins at conception and that unborn children have protectable interests, but the majority found that the words were "merely precatory" and imposed no substantive restrictions on abortion. Justice Stevens, dissenting, argued that "the absence of any secular purpose for the legislative declarations that life begins at conception and that conception occurs at fertilization makes the relevant portion of the Preamble invalid under the Establishment Clause."

Justice Stevens is the only current member of the Court who is willing to confront the obvious intersection of the privacy cases and the religion clauses. Because the other members deny such a connection, the right to privacy will continue to exist or not, based on the interpretation of the Fourteenth Amendment, and the impact of organized religion on laws relating to sexual privacy and reproduction will continue to be denied.

Joan Mahoney

Bibliography

Dudziak, Mary L., "Just Say No: Birth Control in the Connecticut Supreme Court before *Griswold v. Connecticut,*" 75 *Iowa Law Review* 915–939 (1990).

Tribe, Laurence H., *American Constitutional Law,* 2nd ed. (Mineola, N.Y.: Foundation Press, 1988).

Cases Cited

Bowers v. Hardwick, 478 U.S. 186 (1986).
Cruzan v. Director, Missouri Department of Health, 497 U.S. 261 (1990).
Edwards v. Aguillard, 482 U.S. 578 (1987).
Griswold v. Connecticut, 381 U.S. 479 (1965).
Harris v. McRae, 448 U.S. 297 (1980).
Lemon v. Kurtzman, 403 U.S. 602 (1971).
Lynch v. Donnelly, 465 U.S. 668 (1984).
McGowan v. Maryland, 366 U.S. 420 (1961).
Meyer v. Nebraska, 262 U.S. 390 (1923).
Michael H. v. Gerald D., 491 U.S. 110 (1989).
Moore v. City of East Cleveland, 431 U.S. 494 (1977).
Mueller v. Allen, 463 U.S. 388 (1983).
Pierce v. Society of Sisters, 268 U.S. 510 (1925).
Poe v. Ullman, 367 U.S. 497 (1961).
Roe v. Wade, 410 U.S. 113 (1973).
School District of Abington Township v. Schempp, 374 U.S. 203 (1963).
School District of the City of Grand Rapids v. Ball, 473 U.S. 373 (1985).
Skinner v. Oklahoma, 316 U.S. 535 (1942).
Thornburgh v. American College of Obstetricians and Gynecologists, 476 U.S. 747 (1986).
Tileston v. Ullman, 318 U.S. 44 (1943).
Webster v. Reproductive Health Services, 492 U.S. 490 (1989).
Zablocki v. Redhail, 434 U.S. 374 (1978).

Public Aid to Parochial Education

Probably no area of American constitutional law is as confused and inconsistent as the jurisprudence of the First Amendment's Establishment Clause, which provides that "Congress shall make no law respecting an establishment of religion." This jurisprudence was spawned by *Everson v. Board of Education* (1947), in which the Supreme Court held for the first time that the states were bound by the Establishment Clause because it had been "incorporated" by the Fourteenth Amendment's Due Process Clause. *Everson* upheld a New Jersey act providing public funding of bus transportation to private schools, including Catholic schools.

Distinctions "Divorced from Common Sense"

From 1968 to 1986 the Court decided sixteen parochial school aid cases, which constitute the most important group of *Everson* progeny. One of these, *Lemon v. Kurtzman* (1971), gave rise to the prevailing three-pronged test, or *Lemon* test, for constitutionality under the Establishment Clause. To survive scrutiny under the *Lemon* test a challenged statute must (1) have a secular purpose, (2) not have the primary effect of advancing or inhibiting religion, and (3) not foster excessive entanglement between the government and religion. In *Lemon* the Court found unconstitutional, among other things, state reimbursement of part of the salaries of teachers of secular courses.

The Supreme Court has exhibited appropriate modesty about its work product in this area. Chief Justice Warren Burger admitted in *Lemon* that "we can only dimly perceive the lines of demarcation in this extraordinarily sensitive area of constitutional law." Justice Lewis Powell stated in *Wolman v. Walter* (1977) that "[o]ur decisions in this troubling area draw lines that often must seem arbitrary." Some commentators have been more caustic. Jesse H. Choper characterized the parochial school aid cases as "a conceptual disaster area," and Philip B. Kurland said that they constituted "a hodge-podge of decisions" which might seem "derived from Alice's Adventures in Wonderland."

The cases are replete with subtle distinctions that seem divorced from common sense. Thus, in *Everson* the Court upheld public funding of bus transportation to and from parochial schools, whereas in *Wolman* the Court held that public funding of bus transportation on parochial school field trips was unconstitutional. The Court held in *Board of Education v. Allen* (1968), *Meek v. Pittenger* (1975), and *Wolman* that state programs providing for lending state-approved secular textbooks to students at religious schools were constitutional, whereas in *Lemon* it held unconstitutional a Pennsylvania statute providing for state reimbursement to private elementary and secondary schools for costs of secular textbooks and instructional materials. It later held that lending such instructional materials as maps, films, movie projectors, or laboratory equipment was unconstitutional whether the recipients were schools *(Meek)* or students *(Wolman)*.

In *Levitt v. Committee for Public Education and Religious Liberty* (1973) the Court struck down a New York law authorizing state grants to parochial schools for the cost of preparing, administering, and grading teacher-prepared tests, whereas in *Wolman* it upheld the state's supplying of standardized tests and scoring services to parochial schools. In *Committee for Public Education and Religious Liberty v. Regan* (1980) the Court upheld state funding of the administration and grading by private schoolteachers of tests prepared by state officials.

In *Meek* the Court struck down the provision of remedial instruction, guidance counseling, and speech and hearing services on nonpublic school premises, whereas in *Wolman* it upheld the constitutionality of the state's providing speech and hearing and psychological diagnostic services on such premises. But the *Wolman* Court also held that remedial, therapeutic, and guidance services were constitutional only if provided by state employees off the premises of the nonpublic schools. And in *Aguilar v. Felton* (1985) the Court held that providing remedial and enrichment courses under Title I of the Elementary and Secondary Education Act of 1965 on nonpublic school premises was unconstitutional. In *School District of the City of Grand Rapids v. Ball* (1985) the Court invalidated a program that furnished parochial students with classes taught by public employees in classrooms leased from the parochial schools.

The Court in *Committee for Public Education and Religious Liberty v. Nyquist* (1973) concluded that a New York program providing tuition tax credits and outright grants to parents of nonpublic schoolchildren was unconstitutional. In *Mueller v. Allen* (1983), in contrast, the Court upheld Minnesota's conferring of a tax deduction on parents of both public and nonpublic schoolchildren for the cost of textbooks, instructional materials, school equipment, transportation to school, and tuition. In every case except *Regan,* direct grants to nonpublic elementary and secondary schools were fatal to a state statute's constitutionality, whereas in *Roemer v. Board of Public Works* (1976), *Hunt v. McNair* (1973), and *Tilton v. Richardson* (1971) the Court consistently upheld direct grants to church-affiliated colleges and universities as long as the funds were not spent on religious training. While the Court in *Nyquist* had struck down New York's program of maintenance and repair grants for the upkeep of nonpublic elementary and secondary school buildings, in *Tilton* it upheld a

1963 federal statute authorizing federal grants for the construction of buildings at religious colleges and universities, so long as the buildings were not used for sectarian instruction or religious worship.

In *Witters v. Washington Department of Services for the Blind* (1986), the Court held unanimously that it was constitutional for a state to provide a tuition grant to a blind man to attend a Christian college to prepare himself for a career as a pastor, missionary, or youth director. The Court emphasized that the financial benefit to the college was the result of Witters's free choice and that the statute did not provide greater benefits for recipients who applied their aid to religious education. It failed, however, to distinguish this form of aid from the tax benefits to parents of parochial schoolchildren, which it had struck down in *Nyquist*. Concurring opinions joined by five justices in this case seem clearly to support the constitutionality of voucher plans that permit students to use public funds to pay tuition at religious elementary and secondary schools.

Tradition of Opposing Parochial Aid

As indicated above, *Everson* inaugurated this area of federal constitutional law when the Supreme Court held for the first time that the Fourteenth Amendment's Due Process Clause "incorporated" the Establishment Clause and thereby made it binding on the states. A strong tradition of state law prohibitions on aid to parochial schools, however, predated *Everson* by a century. Connecticut in 1818 became the first state to bar explicitly the use of public funds for religious schools in its Constitution. It became a model for other states, all of which eventually enacted constitutional bans on such aid. For its part, Congress in 1876 nearly enacted the Blaine Amendment, which would have made unconstitutional the appropriation of state or federal funds to support religious schools. The amendment, which President Ulysses S. Grant supported, was unsuccessfully reintroduced twenty times (most recently in 1929). The federal government's practice, however, was different; for most of the nineteenth century, Congress appropriated funds for Catholic and other religious schools among the Indian tribes, and this practice ended only in 1897.

The history of the controversy over government aid to parochial schools is inextricably intertwined with the history of hostility to the Roman Catholic Church, whose schools were unquestionably the principal beneficiaries of the various aid schemes struck down by *Everson*'s progeny. Since the mid–nineteenth century, Catholic schools have made up the largest system of religious schools in the United States, and practically every pre-college-level school aid case since *Everson* has involved Catholic schools, even where other denominations also benefited. The Catholic school system's development, which was required by canon law, received a further impetus from the fact that, throughout the nineteenth century, American public schools were in effect nondenominational Protestant schools, teaching Protestant theology and employing readings of the King James Bible. Horace Mann, the leader of the public school movement, took it for granted that the schools would foster morality and nonsectarian Christianity.

In reaction, Catholics established their own parochial schools, and this provoked sometimes violent controversy. Although the Protestant-affiliated Public School Society had run public schools with public funds for New York City, for example, Protestant leaders insisted that the Catholic schools receive no government aid. As Douglas Laycock notes:

> We can trace the political origin of [the] tradition [of no public funds for religious schools], and it is not pretty. It traces not to any careful deliberation about constitutional principles or the proper relation of church and state. Rather, it traces to vigorous nineteenth century anti-Catholicism and the nativist reaction to Catholic immigration. The fact is that no one in America worried about religious instruction in schools before Catholic immigration threatened the Protestant hegemony.

In the absence of a federal constitutional prohibition against government aid to parochial schools, however, such aid was authorized by legislation in isolated instances and was upheld by the Supreme Court on two occasions. In *Quick Bear v. Leupp* (1908) the Court rejected a challenge by Sioux Indian plaintiffs to payments by the government out of a tribal trust fund to Catholic schools on the reservation; plaintiffs argued that the payments were illegal, but they apparently did not argue that the Establishment Clause was violated. And in *Cochran v. Louisiana State*

Board of Education (1930) the Court approved a Louisiana law similar to the New York statute later upheld in *Allen,* which authorized the state to furnish free textbooks to students at religious and other private schools. The taxpayer plaintiffs in *Cochran* did not invoke the Establishment Clause, arguing instead that the law constituted an unlawful taking of public property for private use.

Breaching the Wall of Separation

Thus, *Everson*—in which Justice Hugo Black for the Court embraced Thomas Jefferson's principle that a "high and impregnable wall" should separate church and state—signaled a sea change in Establishment Clause jurisprudence. As a precursor of things to come, however, the Court was sharply divided, not over the doctrine but over its application. Justice Wiley Rutledge, whose dissent garnered four votes, and Justice Robert Jackson charged that the Court's holding that busing subsidies were constitutional breached the wall of separation. Justice Black justified the holding by regarding the law as part of a general program of social legislation benefiting public and religious schools alike, which was "so separate and so indisputably marked off from the religious function" of the schools. He emphasized that the Establishment Clause required the state to be neutral between believers and nonbelievers, not to be their adversary.

The child benefit theory of *Everson* provides the principal rationale for subsequent holdings approving parochial school aid, and even the staunchest separationists on the Court in recent years—Justices William Brennan, Thurgood Marshall, Harry Blackmun, and John Paul Stevens—each have approved certain limited forms of aid on this basis. These justices took this position on a variety of cases, including *Allen* (Brennan); *Wolman* (Marshall, Blackmun, and Stevens); and *Witters* (Marshall, Brennan, Blackmun, and Stevens). Aid to parents through tax deductions or tax credits, in contrast, less frequently passes constitutional muster and has been allowed only in *Mueller.* Direct aid to religious schools is the most suspect of all, as *Lemon* and its progeny reveal, and has been upheld only in a single case: *Regan.* Aid in the latter case was justified in part on the grounds that it was to compensate the institutions for the cost of state-mandated reporting and other services.

Another consistent thread running through the case law is that the Court has been more ready to approve forms of aid which it deems less susceptible of being infused with sectarian content in the teaching process (e.g., bus transportation to and from school, and the loan of secular textbooks) than other forms of aid which are more closely related to teaching itself. In addition, certain forms of aid are more likely to be approved if they are delivered to parochial school students off campus than on campus, as in *Wolman* and *Aguilar.* Finally, although most forms of aid to primary and secondary parochial schools have been struck down on the grounds that such institutions are "pervasively sectarian," the Court has regarded most religiously affiliated colleges and universities as not "pervasively sectarian," and on that basis it has approved large-scale aid to them by Congress *(Tilton)* and by state legislatures *(Hunt* and *Roemer).* Yet the accuracy of the Court's conclusion that virtually all religiously affiliated institutions of higher education are not "pervasively sectarian" is doubtful. And as Chief Justice Burger himself acknowledged in *Nyquist,* the reasons for distinguishing between "direct" aid to parochial institutions and "indirect" aid (to students or parents) are "admittedly difficult to articulate."

While the Supreme Court has assumed that most state aid to parochial schools is unconstitutional, it has failed to address an argument—based on the "unconstitutional conditions" doctrine—that such aid is not merely permissible but constitutionally required. The modern era has witnessed a great expansion of the welfare state and of government intervention in society. If all that government touches must be secular, such an expansion inevitably shrinks the sphere of religious choice. Although compulsory school attendance laws have been held constitutional, it is also settled law, under the precedent of *Pierce v. Society of Sisters* (1925), that the government cannot eliminate private schools and impose a public monopoly over education. As Michael McConnell stated: "If the government offers a free education to those who are willing to forego a religious dimension to their schooling . . . but declines to support the secular aspects of the education of those who choose a religious alternative, religious choice is plainly constrained. The Court has been peculiarly inattentive to this side of the problem." Thus, in *Brusca v. Missouri* (E.D.

Mo. 1971) the district court rejected the argument that denying aid to religious schools while providing it to public schools deprived parochial schoolchildren of equal protection and violated their right to free exercise of religion; the Supreme Court summarily and without analysis also rejected this argument when it affirmed the district court decision without opinion in 1972.

The conceptual disarray in parochial school aid jurisprudence in large part reflects sharp disagreements among the justices themselves; these disagreements have not waned with time. As Justice Byron White noted in *Regan:* ". . . Establishment Clause cases are not easy; they stir deep feelings, and we are divided among ourselves, perhaps reflecting the different views on this subject of the people of this country." Much of the confusion in this field is no doubt traceable to the contradictions of *Everson* itself, in which the Court purported to erect a high and impregnable wall of separation between church and state even while approving bus subsidies to parochial schoolchildren. In *Everson* and its progeny the Court was content to substitute the barren "wall of separation" metaphor for reasoned analysis, and the confused and anomalous results of this approach appear to vindicate Justice Stanley Reed's protest in *McCollum v. Board of Education* (1948) that "[a] rule of law should not be drawn from a figure of speech."

Thomas A. Schweitzer

Bibliography

Choper, Jesse H., "The Establishment Clause and Aid to Parochial Schools: An Update," 75 *California Law Review* 5–14 (1987).

Kurland, Philip B., "Commentary: The Religion Clauses and the Burger Court," 34 *Catholic University Law Review* 1–19 (1984).

Laycock, Douglas, "Summary and Synthesis: The Crisis in Religious Liberty," 60 *George Washington Law Review* 841–856 (1992).

McConnell, Michael W., "Political and Religious Disestablishment," 1986 *Brigham Young University Law Review* 405–463 (1986).

Paulsen, Michael A., "Religion, Equality, and the Constitution: An Equal Protection Approach to Establishment Clause Adjudication," 61 *Notre Dame Law Review* 311–371 (1986).

Segall, Eric J., "Parochial School Aid Revisited: The *Lemon* Test, the Endorsement Test and Religious Liberty," 28 *San Diego Law Review* 263–290 (1991).

Sorauf, Frank J., *The Wall of Separation: The Constitutional Politics of Church and State* (Princeton, N.J.: Princeton University Press, 1976).

Cases Cited

Aguilar v. Felton, 473 U.S. 402 (1985).

Board of Education v. Allen, 392 U.S. 236 (1968).

Brusca v. Missouri, 332 F. Supp. 275 (E.D. Mo. 1971).

Cochran v. Louisiana State Board of Education, 281 U.S. 370 (1930).

Committee for Public Education and Religious Liberty v. Nyquist, 413 U.S. 756 (1973).

Committee for Public Education and Religious Liberty v. Regan, 444 U.S. 646 (1980).

Everson v. Board of Education, 330 U.S. 1 (1947).

Hunt v. McNair, 413 U.S. 734 (1973).

Lemon v. Kurtzman, 403 U.S. 602 (1971).

Levitt v. Committee for Public Education and Religious Liberty, 413 U.S. 472 (1973).

McCollum v. Board of Education, 333 U.S. 203 (1948).

Meek v. Pittenger, 421 U.S. 349 (1975).

Mueller v. Allen, 463 U.S. 388 (1983).

Pierce v. Society of Sisters, 268 U.S. 510 (1925).

Quick Bear v. Leupp, 210 U.S. 50 (1908).

Roemer v. Board of Public Works, 426 U.S. 736 (1976).

School District of the City of Grand Rapids v. Ball, 473 U.S. 373 (1985).

Tilton v. Richardson, 403 U.S. 672 (1971).

Witters v. Washington Department of Services for the Blind, 474 U.S. 481 (1986).

Wolman v. Walter, 433 U.S. 229 (1977).

Public Funding of Religious Education

The First Amendment to the U.S. Constitution provides that Congress shall make no law respecting the establishment of religion. In recent history the meaning of this Establishment

Clause as it applies to direct or indirect public funding of religious schools has been the subject of some dispute. As Justice Byron White noted in *Committee for Public Education and Religious Liberty v. Regan,* (1980), ". . . Establishment Clause cases are not easy; they stir deep feelings, and we are divided among ourselves, perhaps reflecting the different views on this subject of the people of this country." Earlier in the nation's history, however, the issue was much simpler.

The Early History of Parochial Aid

In the colonial period virtually all educational institutions were religious in nature. Even in New England—where the free, tax-supported public school had its origin in the mid-seventeenth century—the division between the state and church was so slight that the church effectively controlled the instruction. When control passed into civil hands, moreover, the curriculum and teaching materials still reflected the religious nature of the instruction. For example, the *New England Primer* used at the end of the seventeenth century included the Westminster Catechism, taught numerals by reference to Bible chapters and verses, and taught the alphabet with homilies such as "P—*Peter* denies His Lord and cries."

By the time of the Revolution, however, other attitudes began to be expressed. Perhaps most famous was the defeat in Virginia of "a bill establishing a provision for teachers of the Christian religion." Introduced by Patrick Henry in 1784, the bill would have established a property tax (with the rate uncertain) to support ministers or teachers of the Christian religion. In 1785 James Madison wrote his famous *Memorial and Remonstrance against Religious Assessments* in opposition to the bill. Nevertheless, general education, to the extent that it existed at all, remained integrally related to religious education.

The Continental Congress, as the preconstitutional instrument of the United States, reflected the then-prevailing view of identifying education with religious instruction, as is seen in the Northwest Ordinance of 1787, which stated: "Religion, morality and knowledge being necessary to good government and the happiness of mankind, schools and the means of education shall be forever encouraged." To carry this admonition into execution, the ordinance set aside tracts of land for schools and churches. The Congress also set aside some 10,000 acres of land in the area for the United Brethren (or Moravians) for "civilizing the Indians."

Even after the adoption of the First Amendment, Congress continued the practice of identifying education with religious education. This is reflected in its reenactment of the Northwest Ordinance by the First Congress and in its treatment of Indian education, one of the few areas in which the new federal government was involved in education. "Propagating the Gospel among the heathen" was viewed as a necessary part of bringing civilization to the Indians. This was to be accomplished both by treaty and by administration of reservations. For example, in 1803 President Thomas Jefferson entered into a treaty with the Kaskaskia Indians, which included a requirement that the United States support a Roman Catholic priest for seven years and erect a church for the tribe. More important, for almost a century Congress regularly appropriated funds providing for reservation schools run by missionaries from various religions.

A strong tradition of state law prohibitions on aid to parochial schools, however, predated the federal government's move toward educational secularization. Connecticut in 1818 became the first state to bar explicitly the use of public funds for religious schools in its constitution. It became a model for other states, all of which eventually enacted constitutional bans on such aid. For its part, Congress in 1876 nearly enacted the Blaine Amendment, which would have made unconstitutional the appropriation of state or federal funds to support religious schools. The amendment, which President Ulysses S. Grant supported, was unsuccessfully reintroduced twenty times (most recently in 1929).

It was not until 1895 that federal attitudes changed, and Congress included a rider to its appropriations providing that public monies "should not be used for education in sectarian institutions." Despite this limitation, the government continued to expend tribal trust funds, on the grounds that they were not "public monies," to pay for sectarian education of Indians in sectarian institutions. In *Quick Bear v. Leupp* (1908) the Supreme Court found this practice consistent with both the statute and the Constitution.

The history of the controversy over government aid to parochial schools is inextricably intertwined with the history of hostility to the Roman Catholic Church. Since the mid-nineteenth century, Catholic schools have made up the largest system of religious schools in the United States, and practically every pre-college-level school aid case has involved Catholic schools, even where other denominations also benefited. The Catholic school system's development, which was required by canon law, received a further impetus from the fact that, throughout the nineteenth century, American public schools were in effect nondenominational Protestant schools, teaching Protestant theology and employing readings of the King James Bible. Horace Mann, the leader of the public school movement, took it for granted that the schools would foster morality and nonsectarian Christianity.

In reaction, Catholics established their own parochial schools, and this provoked sometimes violent controversy. Although the Protestant-affiliated Public School Society had run public schools with public funds for New York City, for example, Protestant leaders insisted that the Catholic schools receive no government aid. As Douglas Laycock notes:

> We can trace the political origin of [the] tradition [of no public funds for religious schools], and it is not pretty. It traces not to any careful deliberation about constitutional principles or the proper relation of church and state. Rather, it traces to vigorous nineteenth century anti-Catholicism and the nativist reaction to Catholic immigration. The fact is that no one in America worried about religious instruction in schools before Catholic immigration threatened the Protestant hegemony.

The Supreme Court and the Establishment Clause

Thus, as American society became more heterogeneous, especially with large-scale immigration of Catholics and Jews, the movement to take religion out of the public classroom increased. Nevertheless, the extent of its eradication remains an issue today, whether in terms of prayers during graduation or sporting events, religious extracurricular groups, or the teaching of "Creationism," the so-called scientific belief that the universe was created in seven days.

The first modern Supreme Court case on the subject, *Everson v. Board of Education* (1947), confirmed the belief that the Establishment Clause of the First Amendment barred direct financial support to religious activities. *Everson* involved a New Jersey law that authorized local school boards to provide for the transportation of children to and from all schools, other than private schools run for profit. A particular local board provided for reimbursement of parents, including parents of children attending Catholic parochial schools, for the cost of buses operated by the public transportation system. In response to an Establishment Clause challenge, the Supreme Court, by a 5-to-4 vote, upheld the program, analogizing it to the public provision of fire, police, sewer, and water services to churches, rather than as financial support of religious activities. The majority, however, in an opinion written by Justice Hugo Black, affirmed a broad prohibition arising from the Establishment Clause, saying that it "means at least this: Neither a state nor the Federal Government can set up a church. Neither can pass laws which aid one religion, aid all religions, or prefer one religion over another. . . . No tax in any amount, large or small, can be levied to support any religious activities or institutions, whatever they may be called, or whatever form they may adopt to teach or practice religion. . . . In the words of Jefferson, the clause against establishment of religion by law was intended to erect 'a wall of separation between church and State.'" To the dissenters, this language suggested that the bus reimbursement program was unconstitutional, because it was, in the words of Justice Robert Jackson, the equivalent of a "subsidy, bonus or reimbursement of expense to individuals for receiving religious instruction and indoctrination."

This agreement about the nature of the Establishment Clause prohibition but sharp disagreement about its application in particular circumstances has characterized the Supreme Court decisions in the area of indirect support of religious education since *Everson*. For example, in *Lemon v. Kurtzman* (1971) the Court identified a three-pronged test by which to determine whether any particular law complies with the Establishment Clause. This test has become known as the *Lemon* test and has been routinely applied in various funding cases. First, the law must have a secular purpose. Second, its primary effect must not be to advance or inhibit religion. And third, the law must not cause excessive entanglement between government and religion. Laws routinely pass the first part of the *Lemon* test, because invariably governments can articulate a secular purpose for the funding or support that in some way redounds to the benefit of sectarian schools. In *Lemon* itself, for example, a statute from Rhode Island provided for a 15 percent salary supplement for teachers in nonpublic elementary schools, and a Pennsylvania statute authorized the state superintendent of instruction to "purchase" secular educational services from nonpublic schools. In both states, the motivation for the legislation was a financial crisis in the Catholic parochial schools within the states, which educated almost a quarter of all schoolchildren. The bankruptcy of the parochial schools would have had a devastating financial impact on the public schools, which would have had to increase enrollments accordingly with no corresponding new source of income. In both instances, however, the Court found that there was a secular purpose, because the statutes were aimed at trying to maintain or improve the secular education of children within the state.

The second prong of the *Lemon* test has impaled several laws. For example, in *Committee for Public Education and Religious Liberty v. Nyquist* (1973) the Court struck down a New York law that (1) made direct grants to nonpublic schools for "maintenance and repair" of facilities and equipment to ensure the students' "health, welfare, and safety"; (2) provided partial tuition reimbursement to low-income parents who sent their children to nonpublic schools; and (3) provided essentially a variable tax credit for higher-income parents based on the income of the parents and the number of children enrolled in nonpublic schools. Although each of these programs was found to have a secular purpose, each was found to have a primary effect that advanced religion. The Court unanimously found that the maintenance and repair program had that effect because there was no provision in the law that limited the use of the funds to buildings or equipment used for secular purposes. It distinguished *Tilton v. Richardson* (1971), where the Court had upheld federal financial support for the construction of buildings by private colleges, including sectarian schools, because the federal law had specified that no building constructed under the program could be used for any sectarian purpose.

By a 6-to-3 margin the Court in *Nyquist* found that the tuition reimbursement and tax credit had the primary effect of advancing religion because, in effect, they subsidized sectarian education by not ensuring that the state financial aid would support only secular education in the nonpublic schools.

Attempts to respond to this failure to oversee the use of the funds have implicated the third prong of the *Lemon* test, by entangling government authorities in the administration of religious schools. In *Lemon* itself, under the contracts authorized by the statute to purchase the secular services from the religious schools, the state would reimburse nonpublic schools for their actual expenditures on teachers' salaries, textbooks, and instructional materials, but only with respect to courses in the curricula of public schools and only with respect to books and materials approved by the superintendent. The law prohibited reimbursement for any course containing "any subject matter expressing religious teaching, or the morals or forms of worship of any sect." Although these provisions ensured that the primary effect of the aid was not to advance religion, the Court found that they fostered excessive entanglement between church and state because of the required oversight of the instruction provided to ensure that sectarian elements were not included. Accordingly, the laws were unconstitutional.

This "Catch-22"—having to ensure that any support does not further sectarian ends but not being allowed to monitor closely the activities underwritten—has doomed a number of attempts to further secular education within nonpublic schools. For example, in *Aguilar v. Felton* (1985) the Court split 5 to 4, finding that paying public schoolteachers to provide remedial instruction and guidance services to nonpublic school students (who overwhelmingly attended Catholic parochial schools) would create an excessive entanglement of church and state, because of the need for ongoing inspection to ensure the absence of a religious message, given the fact that the assistance would be provided in the pervasively sectarian environment of the parochial school.

A companion case, *School District of the City of Grand Rapids v. Ball* (1985), involved two programs offered in nonpublic schools: the Shared Time Program, which provided remedial and "enrichment" mathematics, reading, art, music, and physical education, taught during regular school hours by full-time public schoolteachers using public school materials; and the Community Education Program, which involved teaching arts and crafts, home economics, Spanish, gymnastics, yearbook production, drama, newspaper, chess, model building, nature appreciation, etc., after regular school hours to children and adults by nonpublic schoolteachers hired part time by the school board to teach these courses. The Court found that the primary effect of these programs was to advance religion, because there was inadequate assurance that subtle religious messages would not be transmitted either through the teachers or the physical setting in which the programs occurred.

Conflicts of the *Lemon* Test

Applications of the *Lemon* test have been characterized by differences in outcome that often seem difficult to justify on the basis of the facts of the cases. Thus, while tax credits for nonpublic school tuition in *Nyquist* were found unconstitutional, tax deductions for tuition and other expenses at public and nonpublic schools were upheld in *Mueller v. Allen* (1983). In *Board of Education v. Allen* (1968) the Court approved of state loans of textbooks to all schoolchildren, including those attending religious schools; but in *Meek v. Pittenger* (1975) the Court overturned a state law lending instructional materials and equipment, such as maps and laboratory equipment, to nonpublic schools; and in *Wolman v. Walter* (1977) the Court overturned a statute lending instructional equipment to nonpublic schools and reimbursing such schools for secular field trips. In *Wolman,* however, the Court upheld a provision authorizing the use of public school personnel to administer standardized tests and to provide diagnostic speech, hearing, and psychological services at nonpublic schools. And in *Regan* the Court upheld a law reimbursing nonpublic schools for the cost of administering state-mandated and state-composed tests. But in *Levitt v. Committee for Public Education* (1973) the Court struck down reimbursing nonpublic schools for their expenses in administering state-required but teacher-prepared tests.

Professor Lawrence Tribe, in his treatise *American Constitutional Law,* has tried to synthesize the cases as follows:

> First, if equipment [is] supplied [at] public expense, [it] must be supplied only to pupils or their parents and not to parochial schools themselves. [Second,] if services are to be supplied at public expense, they must be supplied by personnel not subject to parochial school control, and their content cannot be subject to specification by parochial schoolteachers or administrators. [Third,] publicly funded services cannot be provided [on] parochial school premises if they afford opportunity for anything beyond the most impersonal and limited contact with the child.

Most cases raising questions about government funding of religious education involve elementary and secondary education. The few cases involving higher education have more consistently allowed government financial support. Thus, in *Tilton* the Court upheld federal financial support of construction of college buildings at church-related colleges, so long as those buildings were used exclusively for secular purposes—although it struck down a provision which eliminated that restriction after twenty years. Similarly, in *Hunt v. McNair* (1973) the Court upheld a state statute authorizing bonds to assist in financing construction of buildings used for secular purposes at religious colleges. In *Roemer v. Board of Public Works* (1976) the Court approved a state program of annual noncategorical grants to state-accredited private colleges, including religious colleges, so long as the funds were not used for sectarian purposes and the college did not award only theological degrees. And in *Witters v. Washington Department of Services for the Blind* (1986) the Court upheld a grant under a state rehabilitation statute to a blind person to attend a Christian college to become a pastor, missionary, or youth director. The less rigorous application of the *Lemon* test with respect to higher education may be explained as reflecting a perception that even religiously affiliated colleges are not as pervasively religious as parochial schools and that older students are less likely to perceive government aid as constituting government identification with religion.

Several members of the Court have criticized the *Lemon* test, particularly in its application to Establishment Clause cases that do not involve government funding of religious education. For example, in *Lee v. Weisman* (1992), which involved a challenge to a prayer during a high school graduation ceremony, Justice Antonin Scalia—joined by Chief Justice William Rehnquist and Justices Byron White and Clarence Thomas—argued that the *Lemon* test "positively conflict[s] with our long-accepted constitutional traditions." They apparently would rely more on historical traditions as guides for the constitutional limitations contained in the Establishment Clause. Moreover, both Justices Anthony Kennedy and Sandra Day O'Connor have also found fault with the *Lemon* test. The failure of the Court to agree on a different formulation undoubtedly has helped to prolong the use of the *Lemon* test.

William Funk

Bibliography

Levy, Leonard, *The Establishment Clause* (New York: Macmillan, 1986).

Pfeffer, Leo, *Church, State, and Freedom* (Boston: Beacon Press, 1964).

Tribe, Laurence, *American Constitutional Law* 2nd ed. (Mineola, N.Y.: Foundation Press, 1988).

Cases Cited

Aguilar v. Felton, 473 U.S. 402 (1985).

Board of Education v. Allen, 392 U.S. 236 (1968).

Committee for Public Education and Religious Liberty v. Nyquist, 413 U.S. 756 (1973).

Committee for Public Education and Religious Liberty v. Regan, 444 U.S. 646 (1980).

Everson v. Board of Education, 330 U.S. 1 (1947).

Hunt v. McNair, 413 U.S. 734 (1973).

Lee v. Weisman, 505 U.S. 577 (1992).

Lemon v. Kurtzman, 403 U.S. 602 (1971).

Levitt v. Committee for Public Education, 413 U.S. 472 (1973).

Meek v. Pittenger, 421 U.S. 349 (1975).

Mueller v. Allen, 463 U.S. 388 (1983).

Quick Bear v. Leupp, 210 U.S. 50 (1908).

Roemer v. Board of Public Works, 426 U.S. 736 (1976).

School District of the City of Grand Rapids v. Ball, 473 U.S. 373 (1985).

Tilton v. Richardson, 403 U.S. 672 (1971).

Witters v. Washington Department of Services for the Blind, 474 U.S. 481 (1986).

Wolman v. Walter, 433 U.S. 229 (1977).

Public Proselytizing, Solicitation, and Sale of Religious Literature

The U.S. Supreme Court has included religious public meeting, speaking, leafleting, fundraising, and distribution and sale of literature among traditional "core" First Amendment activities. Governmental actions adversely affecting these activities receive the most exacting judicial scrutiny. Generally, government may not prohibit such activities, nor restrict them by criteria related to the message being proclaimed, in public places like parks, streets, sidewalks, or public university facilities otherwise open for expressive activities. It may do so only if the action is necessary to serve a compelling governmental interest and is narrowly drawn to achieve it.

On government-owned property *not* of the type traditionally open to the public for expressive activities nor so designated by the government, the government may more freely restrict proselytizing and religious solicitation on the basis of its message or the identity of the speaker. These "nonpublic" forums include U.S. mailboxes, school mail facilities, and central terminals of metropolitan airports. The First Amendment permits regulation that is reasonable in light of the purpose of the property but not an effort to suppress the activity merely because public officials oppose the speaker's viewpoint.

Today, these free speech and press principles invalidate unjustified government restriction related to the content of orderly expressive activities in public places, whether religious or secular. Public proselytizing and religious fundraising do not receive greater or independent protection as religious exercise under the Free Exercise Clause.

From 1938 to 1953, however, religious activities and Free Exercise Clause values shaped freedom of speech and press doctrine. The Court analogized proselytizing and solicitation on sidewalks and from house to house to more conventional sermon and collection-plate passing—activities assumed to be within the reach of the Free Exercise Clause—as being a "preferred freedom." It held that government prohibition or overly broad restriction of public speech, distribution and sale of literature, and solicitation when applied to such religious exercises violated the Free Exercise Clause as well as the speech and press clauses. Religious freedom was a persuasive factor in the gradual judicial extension of First Amendment protection to expressive activity in public places.

Development of the Case Law

The Jehovah's Witnesses' zealous proselytizing on sidewalks, parks, and from house to house were at stake in the large majority of early cases. Witnesses would testify or preach their beliefs, distribute handbills inviting the public to a meeting at which a Witness would speak, distribute or sell pamphlets and books describing the Witnesses' beliefs, and solicit contributions toward the printing of the literature or their ongoing work.

Based on the belief that all but the sect's members will be destroyed in a literal Armageddon, proselytizing to inform all people of an alternative is a Witness duty. Because the Witnesses believe other religions false, their evangelistic practices are often offensive to others. In the 1930s and 1940s Witness campaigns targeted particular towns, with as many as a hundred Witnesses coming to proselytize. These campaigns often led to arrests, special legislation, and violence against the Witnesses. Compounding hostility to the Witnesses was their objection to military service during both world wars and their refusal to salute the American flag (see *Flag Salute Cases*). In response to the proselytizing campaigns, many local governments enacted ordinances that seldom named the Witnesses but that prohibited the practices in which they engaged or required a permit and/or payment of a fee to engage in them.

The Court held that the Witnesses' practices are protected speech and press activities—a form of religious exercise that is protected by the Free Exercise Clause. Ordinances that simply prohibit handbill distribution on public streets and sidewalks or in house-to-house calling the Court held void on their face as violations of the freedoms of speech, press, and religion. The First Amendment protects expression in public streets and parks and includes leafleting as well as oral speech within its protection. The Court therefore reversed the convictions of Jehovah's Witnesses under such ordinances in *Jamison v. Texas* (1943) and *Martin v. Struthers* (1943). More recently, in *Board of Commissioners v. Jews for Jesus* (1987), the Court struck an outright prohibition on "First Amendment activities" in a metropolitan airport; it was too broad a prohibition on dissemination of ideas to be justified in either a public or a nonpublic forum.

Localities also tried to suppress the Jehovah's Witnesses through ordinances that required a permit to hold a public meeting, distribute literature, and solicit or sell literature in public places. If the ordinances gave the granting official overly broad discretion, the Court invalidated them as prior restraints on speech, press, and the exercise of religion. A local government could prohibit actual littering, fraud, or breach of the peace through ordinances less likely to be used to suppress a message. For instance, in *Cox v. New Hampshire* (1941) the Court upheld a nondiscretionary parade licensing system as it was applied to a Jehovah's Witnesses' informational march.

Cantwell v. Connecticut (1940) exemplifies the potential harm to First Amendment values inherent in allowing officials discretion in issuing permits. An ordinance required the mayor to determine, before issuing a permit to solicit money, whether the cause was a religious one or a bona fide object of charity or philanthropy. Members of the Cantwell family, Jehovah's Witnesses, engaged in typical Witness proselytizing and solicitation without a permit and were convicted of violating the ordinance. The Court held the ordinance void because it allowed the mayor to censor religious speech and to unreasonably obstruct or delay the collection of funds.

Discriminatory regulation of proselytizing and religious solicitation in public places violates not only freedom of speech and religion but also the Fourteenth Amendment's guarantee of equal protection. A permit ordinance and a ban, respectively, were unconstitutionally applied to deny Jehovah's Witnesses' use of public parks, when other religious and political groups were allowed to use the parks for similar services and meetings, in *Niemotko v. Maryland* (1951) and *Fowler v. Rhode Island* (1953). In the modern era the Court held in *Larson v. Valente* (1982) that Minnesota's Charitable Solicitation Act was unconstitutional because it applied only to denominations whose fundraising was largely from nonmembers and thus discriminated among religions and violated the Establishment Clause. The Unification Church brought this challenge.

Localities may restrict the time, place, and manner of public proselytizing and religious solicitation. The Supreme Court subjects such restriction to quite lenient review. In *Heffron v. International Society for Krishna Consciousness* (1981) the Court upheld a state fair regulation that restricted distribution of materials, including literature, to certain locations within the fairgrounds. Practitioners of *Sankirtan* had challenged this regulation of the public distribution and sale of religious literature and solicitation of donations to the Krishna religion. The regulation was a time, place, and manner restriction on expressive activity: It did not discriminate on the basis of content, did not allow arbitrary exercise of administrative discretion, and was applicable to all persons selling or distributing materials. It was valid because it served the purpose of crowd control, which is a significant purpose in state fairgrounds, and it left open ample communication alternatives, such as speaking with fairgoers throughout the fairgrounds.

Cantwell and other early cases protected the Witnesses' attempts to sell religious tracts or request contributions toward their printing—activities found by the state courts in each case to be solicitation. Government may not ban religious public solicitation incidental to proselytizing activity nor subject it to an arbitrary permit system. In *Jones v. Opelika* (1942) the Court upheld an Alabama law levying a tax on the religious tracts sold by the Witnesses. However, a year later, in *Murdock v. Pennsylvania* (1943), the Court reversed itself, holding that a flat license fee on solicitation—as applied to the Jehovah's Witnesses' literature ministry—violated freedom of speech and religion. A government could no more tax the Witnesses' proselytizing and soliciting than it could tax the delivery of a sermon and the passing of a collection plate. In *Jimmy Swaggart Ministries v. Board of Equalization* (1990) the Court limited *Murdock* to flat taxes operating as prior restraints on religious exercise, and it denied a religious group an exemption under the Free Exercise Clause from general state sales and use taxes for the sale of evangelistic religious literature and goods.

Fees on meetings, parades, or other First Amendment activities that are not flat license fees and are based on costs incident to policing the licensed activity are permissible. In *Cox v. New Hampshire* (1941) the Court upheld a sliding parade fee based on the size of the parade. In *Forsyth County v. The Nationalist Movement* (1992), however, the Court held that fees which were based on listeners' probable reactions to the licensed activity were impermissibly regulated by content.

Since the 1950s strict judicial scrutiny of content restrictions or bans on protected expressive activity in public forums has invariably resulted in holding the government action unconstitutional. First Amendment protection from content-based or discriminatory regulation, from overbroad administrative discretion, and from unreasonable time, place, and manner restrictions have been extended by the Court equally to secularly motivated activities and to religious proselytizing and soliciting. However, in *International Society for Krishna Consciousness v. Lee* (1992) and *Lee v. International Society for Krishna Consciousness* (1992) the Court held that the central terminal of a large, government-owned, metropolitan airport was not a public forum like bus or rail terminals or public streets and parks. Therefore, it did not subject a ban on repetitive, in-person solicitation in the airport terminal to strict scrutiny. The ban was valid if merely reasonable in light of the purposes of the airport terminal. As it helped prevent delays and decreased the risk of duress and fraud in face-to-face encounters, the Court upheld it as applied to the religious ritual of *Sankirtan*. In the latter of the two companion cases, a different majority struck a ban on distribution of free literature in the airport terminal, without agreeing on a rationale. The opinions indicate that five members of the Court may uphold a similar ban on the face-to-face sale of religious literature in airports.

Conclusion

Protection of proselytizing and religious solicitation as a form of expression under speech and press principles eclipsed its early protection as religious exercise. In *Heffron* the Court said that religious speech, literature distribution, and solicitation in public places does not merit protection preferential to that afforded similar, secular activities. Both the *Heffron* and the *Lee* opinions analyzed restrictive regulation of *Sankirtan*—which admittedly is a religiously mandated rite—under speech principles, without reference to freedom of religion exercise. *Jimmy Swaggart Ministries* similarly rejected Free Exercise protection for a religious organization's evangelistic sale of religious literature and articles otherwise subject to generally applicable taxes.

When nonreligious expressive activities enjoy high judicial protection, inclusion of proselytizing and religious fundraising under the broader speech rubric does not harm religious groups. They may benefit by avoiding the charge that religious activities are given preferential treatment. However, the *Lee* opinion used public forum speech doctrine not to protect religious solicitation but to legitimatize government designation of where and when to accommodate it. The *Jimmy Swaggart Ministries* opinion precludes recourse to an argument based on the Free Exercise holdings of the 1940s and 1950s: that the Free Exercise Clause independently protects religious proselytizing, sale of literature, and solicitation. Such religious exercises may therefore be more vulnerable to hostile or indifferent governmental regulation today than they were fifty years ago.

Leigh Hunt Greenhaw

Bibliography

Regan, Richard J., *Private Conscience and Public Law* (New York: Fordham, 1972).

Rotunda, Ronald D., and John E. Nowak, *Treatise on Constitutional Law: Substance and Procedure,* 2nd ed. (St. Paul, Minn.: West, 1992).

Stevens, John D., *Shaping the First Amendment* (Beverly Hills, Calif.: Sage, 1982).

Cases Cited

Board of Commissioners v. Jews for Jesus, 482 U.S. 569 (1987).

Cantwell v. Connecticut, 310 U.S. 296 (1940).

Cox v. New Hampshire, 312 U.S. 569 (1941).

Forsyth County v. The Nationalist Movement, 505 U.S. 123 (1992).

Fowler v. Rhode Island, 345 U.S. 67 (1953).

Heffron v. International Society for Krishna Consciousness, 452 U.S. 640 (1981).

International Society for Krishna Consciousness v. Lee, 505 U.S. 672 (1992).

Jamison v. Texas, 318 U.S. 413 (1943).

Jimmy Swaggart Ministries v. Board of Equalization, 493 U.S. 378 (1990).

Jones v. Opelika, 316 U.S. 584 (1942).

Larson v. Valente, 456 U.S. 228 (1982).

Lee v. International Society for Krishna Consciousness, 505 U.S. 830 (1992) (per curiam).

Martin v. Struthers, 319 U.S. 141 (1943).

Murdock v. Pennsylvania, 319 U.S. 105 (1943).

Niemotko v. Maryland, 340 U.S. 268 (1951).

Public School Curricula and Free Exercise Challenges

In *Pierce v. Society of Sisters* (1925) the U.S. Supreme Court upheld the right of parents to send their children to private rather than public schools. In so doing, the Court recognized the "fundamental right" of parents to direct the education of their children. One of the more troublesome issues in the jurisprudence of the religion clauses concerns the scope of this "parental right" in the public school context. Do parents have a free exercise right to remove their children from particular classes or to avoid specific texts that are part of the public school curriculum?

In each of the following cases, the right of parents to direct the education of their children conflicts with the well-established power of the state to control public school curricula. Although the Supreme Court has not yet addressed a Free Exercise Clause challenge to public school curricula, a number of lower federal courts have grappled with this issue. The general trend has been to deny free exercise challenges to "core curriculum" courses and textbooks but to permit students to avoid courses or requirements that the courts deem less central to the educational mission of the public school.

The early cases involved free exercise challenges to public school requirements that were clearly incidental to the educational mission of the school. These challenges were generally successful. For example, in *Spence v. Bailey* (6th Cir. 1972) the Sixth Circuit exempted on religious grounds a high school student from participation in an ROTC course (Reserve Officers' Training Corps). Similarly, in *Davis v. Page* (D. N.H. 1974) a federal district court in New Hampshire exempted on religious grounds elementary schoolchildren from audiovisual programs intended for entertainment. The court refused, however, to extend the exemption to audiovisual programs intended for general or health-related education. In *Moody v. Cronin* (C.D. Ill. 1979) an Illinois federal court exempted religious students from coeducational gym classes. In *Church of God v. Amarillo Independent School District* (N.D. Tex. 1981) a federal district court in Texas held that a school district policy limiting absences for religious holidays violates free exercise. Finally, in *Ware v. Valley Stream High School* (N.Y., 1989) New York's highest court remanded for further determination whether the state's interest in mandatory AIDS education was compelling and thus outweighed a burden on the plaintiff's free exercise objection to such education. These cases were rather straightforward for the courts because they presented instances of coerced conduct, did not seek to exclude children from core curriculum courses, and did not present a conflict with the statutory duties of the public schools.

In *Wright v. Houston Independent School District* (S.D. Tex. 1972), a Texas district court refused to excuse students from classes about evolution on the basis of their religious objections. With minimal analysis the court found that the students had failed to state a free exercise claim because the offending material was "peripheral to the matter of religion." The court also rejected plaintiffs' claims based on establishment and equal protection of the laws.

A subsequent effort to mount a free exercise challenge to a public school textbook was equally unsuccessful. In *Grove v. Mead School District* (9th Cir. 1985) the parent of a high school sophomore brought suit against the school, arguing that the use of *The Learning Tree* in an English literature class offended her religious beliefs. Upholding summary judgment for the school board, the Ninth Circuit noted that the student was permitted to read an alternate book and to absent herself from class discussion of the offensive text. The court concluded that no free exercise issue was presented because the element of coercion necessary to establish a burden on free exercise rights was lacking. However, in an aside that set the stage for things to come, the concurring opinion suggested that if the student had been required to remain in the classroom while the offensive text was read and discussed, a free exercise issue "probably" would have been presented.

While the appeal was pending in *Grove,* a similar case was building in eastern Tennessee. In December 1983 a group of parents and children brought suit against the Hawkins County Board of Education, alleging that the school's use of the Holt, Rhinehart and Winston publishing house's basic reading series in grades 1 to 8 violated their religious beliefs. The parents sought a court order permitting their children to "opt out" of reading classes that utilized the offensive texts and to study alternative texts at home. The district court ruled in favor of the parents, finding that mandatory use of the Holt series violated the plaintiffs' religious beliefs and that the First Amendment required the school to accommodate the parents by permitting the use of alternative texts during home study. The school board appealed this decision. In *Mozert v. Hawkins County Board of Education* (6th Cir. 1987) the Sixth Circuit Court reversed, finding that accommodation was not required by the First Amendment because "mere exposure" to religiously offensive material did not amount to an unconstitutional burden on the free exercise rights of the plaintiffs. The Supreme Court denied certiorari in this case.

Proving a Burden: From *Sherbert* to *Mozert*

Both *Mozert* and *Grove* were decided under the Supreme Court's traditional Free Exercise standard, as set forth in *Sherbert v. Verner* (1963). Under this test, plaintiffs must establish that the state has substantially burdened their religious practices in order to demonstrate a prima facie violation of the Free Exercise Clause. The government must then prove, in order to prevail, a compelling state interest furthered by narrowly tailored means. The plaintiffs in both *Mozert* and *Grove* failed to convince the court that use of the challenged textbooks burdened their religious interests. Without proof of a substantial burden on religious exercise, the respective school boards never had to make what would have been a difficult showing, namely, that their use of the challenged texts amounted to a narrowly tailored means of achieving a compelling state interest.

The Supreme Court has never clearly enunciated what plaintiffs must show in order to meet the threshold requirement of a burden on their free exercise rights. However, there are some general indicators. In the cases where the Supreme Court has recognized a burden on free exercise, there has generally been a state-sponsored compulsion to act in a way that is contrary to one's religious beliefs. For example, in *West Virginia State Board of Education v. Barnette* (1943) the Supreme Court held that a mandatory flag salute and Pledge of Allegiance violate the free speech and free exercise rights of Jehovah's Witnesses. Three decades later, in *Wisconsin v. Yoder* (1972), the Court upheld the free exercise claim of Amish parents to remove their children from public schools before the age of 16. However, the Supreme Court has refused to hold that state action which is "merely offensive" to religious beliefs amounts to a burden on free exercise. Thus, in *Epperson v. Arkansas* (1968) the Court stated that the First Amendment does not permit the state to tailor its curriculum to the principles or prohibitions of any religious group.

In *Mozert* the Sixth Circuit held that requiring children to read offensive texts did not amount to government compulsion to engage in conduct contrary to the plaintiff's expressed religious beliefs. The court reasoned that the students were not compelled to act in a manner contrary to their religious beliefs or to affirm a belief that was forbidden by their religion. In other words, the students were free to read the offensive texts critically and to reject any concepts that conflicted with their religious beliefs. In fact, the school contended that "critical reading" was an essential skill taught by its reading program and that the students were not required to accept their reading texts at face value. To establish a burden on free exercise, plaintiffs would have to prove that they were required to affirm or deny a religious belief or to engage or refrain from engaging in a practice contrary to their sincerely held religious beliefs, such as the flag salute that was found unconstitutional in *Barnette.* Since the plaintiffs' proof failed to satisfy this requirement, the court denied their free exercise claim.

Mozert has been criticized for three reasons. First, the case is often read as reintroducing a requirement that the plaintiff prove "coercive intent" by the government in order to satisfy the threshold requirement of a burden on their religious beliefs. The principal objection here is that a coercion requirement unduly constricts the scope of constitutionally protected religious exercise.

A second and related argument is that the school's requirement that the plaintiffs' children read the offensive texts amounts to government compulsion to act in a manner contrary to the plaintiffs' religious beliefs. The Sixth Circuit addressed this concern, although not to the satisfaction of all observers, by noting that the plaintiffs' church had taken the position that reading the challenged texts did not contravene its tenets; the court also found that the parents' positions on offensive materials were inconsistent. However, as the Supreme Court noted in *Thomas v. Review Board* (1981), plaintiffs' religious views need not be internally consistent nor ratified by their church in order to warrant the protection of the First Amendment.

The Sixth Circuit went on to find that the parents had failed to present any evidence that reading the texts was forbidden by their religion. Under this reading, *Mozert* does no more than establish a pleading requirement; if plaintiffs had clearly alleged that the act of reading offensive texts was conduct prohibited by their religion, then the burden test would be satisfied. Had this been the case, then the outcome of *Mozert* would have turned on the issue raised by Judge Anthony Kennedy, who wrote a separate concurrence arguing that the burden on plaintiffs' free exercise rights was justified by compelling state interests. Judge Kennedy found that the state had demonstrated a compelling interest in teaching critical reading skills, avoiding disruption in the classroom, and avoiding religious divisiveness.

The most troubling objection to *Mozert* is that the Sixth Circuit gave insufficient weight to the argument that there is no such thing as "mere exposure." The parents contended that simply reading the offensive textbooks was likely to teach or inculcate values that would undermine or confuse their children's religious beliefs. This argument points up the central moral dilemma raised by *Mozert.*

The Tennessee legislature charged its

public schools with an obligation to provide an education that encompassed moral values; yet the plaintiffs contended that any discussion of moral or social issues that did not recognize the primacy of a biblical perspective violated their religious beliefs. In short, the school district officials had three choices, none of which was satisfactory. They could attempt to remove all controversial moral or social issues from their curriculum, which would arguably conflict with their statutory mandate. They could provide moral education from a biblical perspective, which would raise Establishment Clause problems. Finally, they could do as they did and require their students to engage in critical reading and thinking about controversial moral and social issues, thereby offending the plaintiffs' religious beliefs. The issue, once again, was whether that offense was sufficient to amount to a constitutionally significant burden on the plaintiffs' free exercise, and the Sixth Circuit concluded that it was not.

Mozert offers no easy answers. Any subject taught in a public school may communicate values to students that conflict with the students' or parents' religious beliefs. The solution is not value-free public education, which is simply impossible, but careful attention to the admittedly fine line between "mere offensiveness" and "coerced conduct or belief." Although *Mozert* may not, in the end, make it any easier to distinguish which cases fall on the prohibited side of this line, it strikes a balance and offers a fairly straightforward test to determine when a plaintiff has made out a constitutional burden on free exercise rights.

The Burden after *Smith*: "Hybrid" Cases

The Supreme Court has shown no inclination to clarify this aspect of free exercise jurisprudence since *Mozert*. In *Employment Division, Department of Human Resources of Oregon v. Smith* (1990) the Court held that a state may prohibit a religious communion ceremony involving peyote consumption under generally applicable drug laws—a striking restriction of free exercise rights. Justice Antonin Scalia, writing for a five-justice majority, stated that the *Sherbert* test which had been applied in *Mozert* and most other Free Exercise Clause cases would not apply in cases where the religious claimant sought to challenge a neutral, generally applicable criminal law. In such cases, the Court found that unless the plaintiff could invoke another constitutional right in addition to free exercise, the plaintiff could not maintain a constitutional challenge to the law. In "hybrid cases," where the plaintiff challenges a generally applicable law based on the infringement of free exercise together with another constitutional right, traditional *Sherbert* analysis would still apply.

Justice Scalia characterized *Barnette* (free speech) and *Pierce* and *Yoder* (parental control) as hybrid cases, in which the application of the *Sherbert* test was appropriate. Scalia also suggested that the First Amendment right to freedom of association might be joined with free exercise rights to create a hybrid claim.

The scope of *Smith* is widely disputed. In *Salvation Army v. Department of Community Affairs* (3rd Cir. 1990); *Rector, Wardens and Members of the Vestry of St. Bartholomew's Church v. City of New York* (2nd Cir. 1990); and *Intercommunity Center for Justice and Peace v. Immigration and Naturalization Service* (2nd Cir. 1990) federal courts have found that the decision applies to generally applicable civil as well as criminal laws. If these decisions are correct, then free exercise challenges to curricula may now be evaluated under a different standard than that applied in *Mozert*, and plaintiffs may be required to demonstrate infringement of another constitutional right in addition to free exercise.

Plaintiffs may choose to invoke *Pierce* and *Yoder* as the basis for their "additional" constitutional right, since the *Smith* Court specifically reaffirmed the "right of parents to direct the education of their children." However, that reference may simply mean that those decisions are still good law. Some of *Smith*'s critics read both *Yoder* and *Pierce* as straightforward free exercise cases, which do not establish an independent constitutional right.

The Sixth Circuit recently applied *Smith* in a public school setting. In *Vandiver v. Hardin County Board of Education* (6th Cir. 1991) a public school required a high school student to pass equivalency exams in order to obtain credit for a religious home study program. The court found that the school's policy amounted to a "valid and neutral law of general application within the meaning of *Smith*," and it rejected the plaintiff's free exercise challenge, finding that no other constitutional right had been infringed by the test-taking requirement. The plaintiff in *Vandiver* was not a minor, and so reliance on *Pierce* was not attempted. *Vandiver* strongly suggests that free exercise challenges to public curricula may need to be coupled with another constitutional right in order to survive *Smith*.

An observation by Justice Jackson in *McCollum v. Board of Education* (1948) remains timely and compelling. In the course of striking down an Illinois program that provided for the religious instruction of consenting students in public school classrooms he stated: "If we are to eliminate everything that is objectionable to any of these warring sects or inconsistent with any of their doctrines, we will leave public education in shreds." Inasmuch as the future of free exercise challenges to public school curricula will depend on judicial interpretations of *Smith* and its progeny, Justice Jackson may yet have the last word.

Joanne C. Brant

Bibiliography

Dent, George W., Jr., "Religious Children, Secular Schools," 61 *Southern California Law Review* 863–944 (1988).

Harkins, James C., IV, "Of Textbooks and Tenets: *Mozert v. Hawkins County Board of Education* and the Free Exercise of Religion," 37 *American University Law Review* 985–1012 (1988).

Lupu, Ira, "Where Rights Begin: The Problem of Burdens on the Free Exercise of Religion," 102 *Harvard Law Review* 933–990 (1989).

Yerby, Winton, III, "Toward Religious Neutrality in the Public School Curriculum," 56 *University of Chicago Law Review* 899–934 (1989).

Cases Cited

Church of God v. Amarillo Independent School District, 511 F. Supp. 613 (N.D. Tex. 1981).

Davis v. Page, 385 F. Supp. 395 (D. N.H. 1974).

Employment Division, Department of Human Resources of Oregon v. Smith, 494 U.S. 872 (1990).

Epperson v. Arkansas, 393 U.S. 97 (1968).

Grove v. Mead School District, 753 F. 2d 1528 (9th Cir. 1985).

Intercommunity Center for Justice and Peace v. Immigration and Naturalization Service, 910 F. 2d 42 (2nd Cir. 1990).

McCollum v. Board of Education, 333 U.S. 203 (1948).

Moody v. Cronin, 484 F. Supp. 270 (C.D. Ill. 1979).

Mozert v. Hawkins County Board of Education, 827 F. 2d 1058 (6th Cir. 1987).

Pierce v. Society of Sisters, 268 U.S. 510 (1925).

Rector, Wardens and Members of the Vestry of St. Bartholomew's Church v. City of New York, 914 F. 2d 348 (2nd Cir. 1990).

Salvation Army v. Department of Community Affairs, 919 F. 2d 183 (3rd Cir. 1990).

Sherbert v. Verner, 374 U.S. 398 (1963).

Spence v. Bailey, 465 F. 2d 797 (6th Cir. 1972).

Thomas v. Review Board, 450 U.S. 707 (1981).

Vandiver v. Hardin County Board of Education, 925 F. 2d 927 (6th Cir. 1991).

Ware v. Valley Stream High School, 550 N.E. 2d 420 (N.Y. 1989).

West Virginia State Board of Education v. Barnette, 319 U.S. 624 (1943).

Wisconsin v. Yoder, 406 U.S. 205 (1972).

Wright v. Houston Independent School District, 366 F. Supp. 1208 (S.D. Tex. 1972).

Public Schools and Controversies over Religion during the Nineteenth Century

The development of universal public education in the United States during the middle of the nineteenth century created inevitable religious conflicts that often provoked political and legal controversies. Although the newly created public schools were officially nonsectarian, most schools fostered generically Anglo-American Protestant religious beliefs and practices that were objectionable to Roman Catholics, Jews, and many Protestants, particularly Lutherans. The controversies over the place of religion in the public schools stimulated the growth of parochial schools and helped to hasten the process of secularization of the public schools.

The idea of a wholly secular school was alien to the nineteenth-century mind, since education historically had been conducted under the auspices of religious institutions in Europe and America. Even the so-called public schools of the colonial and early national periods in America were generally joint ventures of the government and various churches. The so-called common school movement of the early decades of the nineteenth century was ostensibly nonsectarian. Proponents of universal public education, however, were unwilling to banish all religious instruction from the schools. In accordance with their Calvinist heritage, they viewed religion in instrumental terms, believing that the inculcation of basic moral and ethical values would help to ensure the development of the type of educated citizenry that was necessary for the success of both democracy and the Industrial Revolution.

As the tide of immigration rose during the mid–nineteenth century, many middle-class Protestants became convinced that the public schools would provide a critical role in adapting the immigrants to American political ideals and work patterns. Since they regarded the values of hard work, discipline, thrift, and self-reliance as dependent on religious faith, they generally encouraged biblical instruction and prayer in the schools. The erosion of denominational distinctions during this period facilitated the creation of generically Protestant devotions and instruction. As Carl Kaestle has explained, the "homilies of native Protestant belief became both the justification and message of the common schools." Even Horace Mann, the principal advocate of universal public education, contended that the schools could and should teach a common core of nonsectarian Christian beliefs.

What seemed nonsectarian to the Unitarian Mann and many Protestants, however, seemed quite sectarian to many other Christians as well as Jews. In attempting to instill "American" virtues in the immigrants who were coming to America in ever-increasing numbers, the public schools often relied on religious lessons and practices that contravened the religious heritage of many students. Roman Catholics—still a small and beleaguered minority—felt particularly vulnerable to what they perceived as Protestant proselytizing in the public schools. Catholics were offended by the many blatantly or tacitly anti-Catholic passages in textbooks, and they objected to the use of Protestant hymns and prayers in the officially nonsectarian schools. They also vehemently opposed the widespread practice of instruction in the King James version of the Bible. Riots over Bible reading in the Philadelphia public schools that left dozens of persons dead in 1844 were merely the most dramatic manifestation of a controversy that erupted in many other places throughout the mid–nineteenth century.

Outnumbered on most of the nation's school boards, Roman Catholics began to reinforce their parochial school system during the 1840s. Although the Roman Catholic hierarchy in the United States always had encouraged parochial schooling, it initially was tolerant of parents who could not afford to send their children to church institutions. The First and Second Plenary Councils of Baltimore, in 1852 and 1866, urged bishops to establish parochial schools throughout their dioceses, as did the Vatican's Congregation of Propaganda in 1876. Universal parochial education finally became the official goal of the Roman Catholic Church in 1884, when the Third Plenary Council of Baltimore decreed that every parish must maintain its own school. The council also declared that parents must send their children to their parish school in the absence of extenuating circumstances.

Like the Roman Catholics, many Lutherans feared that religious instruction in the public schools would expose their youth to heterodox beliefs that would erode their distinctive doctrines or encourage conversion to Anglo-American sects. Although Scandinavian Lutherans tended to accept the public schools, several German synods established parochial schools. During the 1840s the Missouri Synod began a network of parochial schools that today is second in size only to the Roman Catholic system. Like the Lutherans, Episcopalians and Presbyterians also adhered to distinctive doctrines and liturgies, and they too attempted to establish a network of parochial schools during the mid–nineteenth century. Apathy, however, doomed these efforts. Despite a few short-lived attempts during this period to establish Jewish day schools, most Jews likewise attended public schools.

Since parochial education eased the financial burden of the state, many Roman Catholics believed that the government should subsidize parochial schools. In 1840 Governor William H. Seward of New York proposed a plan for state aid to parochial schools. Although Roman

Catholics enthusiastically endorsed the basic outlines of Seward's proposal, Protestant opposition ensured its defeat. Instead of Seward's proposal, the legislature enacted statutes that prohibited the distribution of public monies to schools that inculcated sectarian doctrines, and it forbade public school boards to exclude the reading of scriptures.

The New York controversy presaged similar conflicts in other states that likewise resulted in various laws that prohibited state aid to sectarian schools. The dispute over state aid to parochial schools was revived shortly after the Civil War, when William M. "Boss" Tweed attempted to win Democratic support among Roman Catholic voters in New York City by advocating public support for sectarian schools. After the New York legislature repulsed Tweed's plan, several other states rejected similar proposals and enacted constitutional amendments to prohibit state aid to parochial school. In 1875 President Ulysses S. Grant advocated a federal amendment sponsored by Republican Representative James G. Blaine of Maine that would have prohibited any state legislature from appropriating any funds to any religious institution for any purpose. Opponents of the amendment emphasized that it would unduly impinge on the prerogatives of the states, on which the First Amendment's religion clauses were not yet binding. The amendment also was opposed by members of Congress who viewed it as an expression of religious bigotry or were fearful of offending ethnic voters. Despite the failure of the movement of the amendment, the widespread public outcry against public funding for parochial schools caused Roman Catholics to discontinue their calls for public support for their schools.

During the early postwar period, the question of Bible reading in the public schools flared up again in many parts of the nation. The most intense controversy occurred in Cincinnati, where the school board in 1869 voted to exclude the Bible from the public schools. By a vote of 2 to 1, the Superior Court of Cincinnati enjoined the enforcement of the order, but the state supreme court in *Board of Education of Cincinnati v. Minor* (1873) unanimously held that the board had acted within its authority.

The increase of parochial schools precipitated a nativistic campaign against them during the late nineteenth century. Attempting to exercise greater control over the parochial schools, some nativists advocated legislation to establish state inspections of parochial schools and to require them to use the English language for instruction in the basic academic subjects.

In Massachusetts, nativists in 1889 sponsored legislation for the imposition of fines against any person who encouraged a parent to withdraw a child from public school or who attempted to influence a parent to send a child to a parochial school by threatening social or ecclesiastical disabilities. After bitter and protracted hearings, Roman Catholics and liberal Protestants joined forces to defeat the measure.

Meanwhile, critics of parochial education in Wisconsin and Illinois proposed legislation that tightened state control over parochial school curricula and required parochial schools to teach the common subjects in the English language. Although swift and vigorous opposition among Roman Catholics and Lutherans ensured the defeat of these measures, the controversy presaged growing public regulation of parochial schools and anticipated later disputes over the use of foreign languages in parochial schools.

William G. Ross

Bibliography

Cremin, Lawrence A., *American Education: The National Experience, 1783–1876* (New York: Harper and Row, 1980).

Jorgenson, Lloyd P., *The State and the Non-Public School, 1825–1925* (Columbia: University of Missouri Press, 1987).

Kaestle, Carl, *Pillars of the Republic: Common Schools and American Society, 1780–1860* (New York: Hill and Wang, 1983).

Tyack, David, Thomas James, and Aaron Benavot, *Law and the Shaping of Public Education, 1785–1954* (Madison: University of Wisconsin Press, 1984).

Case Cited

Board of Education of Cincinnati v. Minor, 23 Granger 211 (Ohio 1873).

Puerto Rico's Christian Action Party

In 1960 a political party called the "Christian Action Party" was founded in Puerto Rico. It was patterned after European and Latin American "Christian Democratic" parties, but Catholic Church influence and participation exceeded that found in the European and Latin American models. Its creation was actively promoted by the Roman Catholic hierarchy in Puerto Rico, which at the time was headed by two American bishops. The party flag was yellow and white and closely resembled the Vatican's.

The two bishops were locked in a squabble with then-Governor Muñoz-Marín over public aid to parochial schools—a battle the Catholic Church had lost once already, when in 1952 Puerto Rico adopted a Constitution which expressly resolved the issue against that church, in language that went beyond that of the First Amendment. The bishops went so far as to write, distribute, and read from the pulpit a pastoral letter that denounced the ruling Popular Democratic Party and claimed that it would be a sin for any Catholic to vote for that party.

The Christian Action Party competed in two elections, in 1960 and 1964, and then disappeared. In 1960 it garnered 6.5 percent of the vote and elected two legislators. Both legislators were refused their seats, however, after a legislative investigation revealed that the party's registration had been tainted by fraud. In 1964 the party again competed in the general elections. This time it received $145,000 in public funding under the local election law, although participation in the electoral fund was never tested in the courts. However, its electoral support had dwindled to 3.3 percent. By 1964 the two American bishops who spurred the party's creation had been transferred back to the United States. The relationship between the Popular Democratic Party and the Catholic Church in Puerto Rico, now headed by two Puerto Rican bishops, had improved significantly.

This short-lived experiment was an embarrassment to the Catholic Church, which has since shied away from partisan politics, albeit not from public issues. However, this episode produced an unexpected result. The Catholic Church hierarchy, led by American bishops since shortly after the American invasion in 1898, passed on to the hands of natives of Puerto Rico.

The Puerto Rican Christian Action Party was not formally affiliated with the Catholic Church and was under secular rule. Its receipt of public funding probably would have resisted constitutional attack under the Establishment Clause. United States courts have never had to face the issue of a religiously based political party competing in an election and receiving public funding. However, *McDaniel v. Paty* (1978), which held it unconstitutional to disqualify clergy from public office, suggests that such a party would not run afoul of constitutional principles. Although there was no majority opinion in *McDaniel*—and a plurality opinion by four justices expressly left open the possibility that a showing could be made "of the dangers of clergy participation in the political process"—Justice William Brennan's separate concurrence seems correct in suggesting that the Establishment Clause would prevent efforts "to justify repression of religion or its adherents from any aspect of public life." Discrimination against a political party because of its religious tint seems precisely the type of repression that Justice Brennan considered offensive.

José Julián Alvarez-González

Bibliography

Anderson, Robert W., *Party Politics in Puerto Rico* (Stanford, Calif.: Stanford University Press, 1965).

Greenawalt, Kent, *Religious Convictions and Political Choice* (New York: Oxford University Press, 1988).

Ramos de Santiago, Carmen, *El Gobierno de Puerto Rico,* 2nd ed. (1970), pp. 300–341.

Case Cited

McDaniel v. Paty, 435 U.S. 618 (1978).

Q

Quebec Act of 1774

On June 22, 1774, the British Parliament passed the Quebec Act, vesting the government of Quebec in a governor and council and guaranteeing the use of French civil law in Quebec. Although Quebec was a British colony, it consisted of a largely French population. The act further ensured the French Canadians' right to practice the Roman Catholic religion, and it allowed the Catholic Church to collect a tax from its members.

Great Britain passed the act to settle fast-emerging issues of law and government in Quebec. The confusion over Quebec governance resulted from the English attempt to make the Canadian French colony a province of the British Empire in North America. The question of whether an assembly should be called was hotly debated. Most of the population of the Province of Quebec were Roman Catholics, and because of the Test Act, they would be excluded from serving as representatives. Also unresolved was whether followers of Roman Catholicism should be permitted to exercise their faith at all and, if so, under what conditions. Finally, there was the question of whether French or English law should decide matters in the courts.

In response, the Quebec Act placed the power to legislate in the hands of governor and council. Roman Catholics were permitted to practice their faith, and the church was allowed to continue collecting its tithe. Further, Roman Catholics were permitted to serve as representatives, thereby waiving the Test Act, and were required to take only an oath of allegiance, thus permitting them to hold office. French civil law continued, but English criminal law was used. As a whole, the accommodating provisions of the act reflect an attempt to deal with the peculiar conditions of the province.

As a territorial matter, the act enlarged Quebec to include much of what is now Quebec, Ontario, and the midwestern United States. Because no effective means existed to regulate Indian affairs or to help oversee French settlers along the Ohio and Mississippi Rivers, the act had to extend the land granted in the Proclamation of 1763. Thus, territory between the two rivers was placed under the governor of Quebec, and the boundaries of Quebec extended southward to the junction of the Ohio and Mississippi Rivers and northward between the Great Lakes and Hudson Bay.

Although the act is often touted as an attempt to resolve questions of law and government in Quebec, some have suggested a different reason for its adoption. Britain was certainly aware of a potential revolution among the increasingly disgruntled American colonies to the south. Britain may have passed the Quebec Act to assuage French support if a revolution did result—or at least to limit French participation. Ironically, British actions may have actually provoked the American Revolution. The massive land declaration coupled with a recognition of the Roman Catholic religion was seen as a threat to the security of the American colonies, where many feared a resurgent French Empire. Colonists viewed the act as coercion, thus serving as a catalyst in the Revolution and ultimately provoking the American colonies to invade Quebec in 1775.

The Quebec Act of 1774 was instrumental in forming the basis of French Canada's religious and legal rights. Quebec's governor, Guy Carleton, is generally held responsible for the language of the act recognizing the Roman Catholic Church and French civil law. Some scholars argue that the act was inspired by a spirit of liberalism, yet many historians argue that it was designed to create French Canadian loyalty if an American revolt ensued. Indeed, many Americans of the new colonies south of Quebec labeled the Quebec Act as one of the Intolerable Acts.

Stephen K. Schutte

Bibliography

Coupland, Reginald, *The Quebec Act: A Study in Statesmanship* (New York: Oxford University Press, 1968).

Neatby, Hilda, *The Quebec Act: Protest and Policy* (New York: Prentice-Hall, 1972).

Quick Bear v. Leupp

See REUBEN QUICK BEAR [ET AL.] V. FRANCIS E. LEUPP, COMMISSIONER OF INDIAN AFFAIRS.

R

Ratification of the Constitution and Religion

The struggles over the ratification of the Constitution of the United States were, in several states at least, bitter and intense. Different economic interests, the contesting ambitions of state officeholders, the visions of national patriots versus the hopes of state patriots—all contributed to the passions of these conflicts.

Religion played a significant role in these battles too, so that when James Madison took up the problem of factions in *Federalist* No. 10, he listed in his catalog of the causes of faction a "zeal for different opinion" in religion as uppermost of these. Again, in *Federalist* No. 51, in defending the role of the federal principle in palliating the baneful effects of faction, Madison used religious liberty as his analogy for political liberty. Just as multiplicity of religious sects works to prevent one denomination from gaining ascendancy in order to impose its creed and its practices on the general population, so the variety and countervailing tendencies of factions based on secular interests within the broad expanse of a federal union can prevent the prolonged and oppressive domination of a single faction.

In *Federalist* No. 52, furthermore, Madison mentions the ban on religious test for federal office under Article 6, Paragraph 3, of the Constitution as part of the positive opening to talent virtually regardless of wealth, age, or naturalized status. Again, in *Federalist* No. 57 Madison proclaims that "[n]o qualification of wealth, of birth, of religious faith, or of civil profession is permitted to fetter the judgment or disappoint the inclination of the people," but he failed to resolve the issue of the right of states to impose further limitations on qualifications for service in the House of Representatives. For many decades after the Constitution was ratified, several states continued to require additional qualifications for the office of U.S. representative, including in some instances, religious qualifications.

Finally, in *Federalist* No. 69 Alexander Hamilton, in attempting to refute the charge that the presidency of the United States is like the kingship of Great Britain, cites among the contrasts the fact that "[t]he one has no particle of spiritual jurisdiction; the other is the supreme head and governor of the national church!"

For some, of course, the absence of an invocation or other acknowledgment of deity was an obvious sign of the new Constitution's irreligious nature. The Declaration of Independence, after all, had mentioned God three times—speaking of "the Laws of Nature and of Nature's God," of the unalienable rights by which all men are "endowed by their Creator," and of "appealing to the Supreme Judge of the world."

Not too much could be made of the absence of references to God in the Constitution, however, for the Articles of Confederation had also lacked any specific dedication or petition to God, and state constitutions were a mixed bag in this regard. The Virginia Constitution of 1776 lacked reference to God, although the Virginia Declaration of Rights, adopted several weeks prior, spoke of "religion, or the duty which we owe to our Creator," and the Massachusetts Constitution of 1780, in its preamble, spoke of "the goodness of the Great Legislator of the Universe."

The contrast between the Declaration's multiple references to God and the Constitution's silence, however, may have no significance beyond the fact that the Declaration, in its necessary appeal to natural law concepts (filtered through Lockean interpretations) in justifying the revolt against Britain would naturally have recourse to notions of the divine, while the Constitution, as a practical blueprint of government, concerned itself more with rules and definitions.

The general silence of the Constitution also threatened, in the view of many of the Anti-Federalists, to provide a loophole by means of which the national government might create an official national church, interfere with state establishments of religion, or regulate religious practices within a state.

For this reason the Anti-Federalist minority at Pennsylvania's ratifying convention, after their loss in the ratification vote, issued a report that, among other things, demanded a number of amendments be made to the Constitution. They listed first of all an amendment protecting freedom of conscience and forbidding federal interference with provisions of state constitutions that were designed to preserve religious freedom.

The critics of the Constitution often saw the prohibition on religious tests for federal office as hostile to religion, but the Federalist Oliver Ellsworth in his "Letters from a Landholder" (No. 7, published in the *Connecticut Courant* of December 17, 1787) responded that the only purpose of the ban was to exclude persecution and so help establish religious liberty. Ellsworth went on to argue the futility of test laws in the United States, given its great variety of sects, no one of which came close to commanding the allegiance of a majority of citizens. He cited the usurpation by a minority in Pennsylvania who had instituted a Test and Abjuration Act that had excluded over half the citizens of the commonwealth from the franchise and from officeholding. In addition, Ellsworth argued, the experience of Britain had demonstrated that a test act was useless, because the unprincipled would swear to it without hesitation, despite their lack of belief.

Approval of the ban on religious tests was scarcely universal, however, and Luther Martin in his Anti-Federalist pamphlet, "The Genuine Information," which reprinted his pieces from the *Maryland Gazette* (Baltimore), condemned the proscription of tests most vigorously. He rejected denominational tests but thought it unwise to forbid a test to ensure belief in a deity and in post-mortem rewards and punishments, so as to ensure trustworthiness in public officials and in their oath taking.

In an ironic situation, the Massachusetts ratifying convention saw an exchange on January 31, 1788, between the Reverend Daniel Shute and Colonel William Jones concerning the inability to impose religious tests for office in the Constitution. The clergyman defended the ban on both the grounds of religious liberty and public policy considerations, while the military man expressed the belief that one could not be a good man unless one were a good Christian. Several days later, the Reverend Isaac Backus spoke to convention delegates, reminding then that religion is a matter between God and the individual soul.

Not all dissent concerning a clause about religious tests arose among Anti-Federalists. William Williams, a Federalist, wrote to the *American Mercury* (Hartford, Conn.) on February 11, 1788, in defense of the Constitution. Concerning the role of religion within the document, however, he readily admitted defects but argued that its faults were not fatal. Mr. Williams avowed that he would have favored prefixing the following words to the Preamble and to have permitted no test but the affirmation of these principles:

> We the people of the United States, in a firm belief of the being and perfections of the one living and true God, the creator and supreme Governour of the world, in his providence and the authority of his laws: that he will require of all mortal agents an account of their conduct, that all rightful powers among men are ordained of, and mediately derived from God, therefore in a dependence on his blessings and acknowledgment of his efficient protection in establishing our Independence. . . .

In North Carolina's ratifying convention the Reverend David Caldwell and Samuel Spencer debated adding a test clause, with Caldwell lamenting that such a provision would serve as an open invitation "for Jews, and Pagans of every kind" to immigrate to America. Spencer, on the other hand, warned that test oaths tend to exclude only the conscientious, because people of no principle can easily swear falsely. Spencer concluded his remarks by answering an Anti-Federalist pamphlet which claimed that in the absence of a religious test the pope might be elected president of the United States with the observation that a pope would have to be a native-born American in order to qualify.

In many instances, of course, the debates about a test clause became intertwined with arguments about the protection of religious liberty. Joseph Spencer conveyed to James Madison on February 28, 1788, the objections of John Leland, a leading Virginia Baptist. Among Leland's many objections was his conviction that a test clause would provide insufficient guarantees for religious liberty, because if, for example, the president and a majority of Congress were to be from one denomination, they might combine to force all to pay taxes for the support of the favored church. The only remedy, in Leland's view, was a bill of rights.

Samuel Bryan in his "Centinel" (No. 2, published on October 24, 1787, in the *Freeman's Journal* of Philadelphia) expressed the standard Anti-Federalist fear that the Constitution supplied no guarantee to the "unalienable right to worship Almighty God, according to the Dictates of [one's] own conscience[. . .] and understanding." Jefferson, writing to Madison from Paris on December 20, 1787, also cited this absence of a bill of rights with specific guarantees for religious freedom. Number 4 (November 8, 1787) of the "Letters from a Federal Farmer," which were published in *The Republican* (New York), gave the same objections from an Anti-Federalist perspective.

Very few persons seemed to have favored a denominational test for federal office, but many Anti-Federalists, and not a few Federalists, expressed their preference for a test against atheism or a test for general Christianity. On the other hand, many who supported a clause banning tests held it to be an inadequate rampart to defend religious liberty. Not surprisingly, perhaps, some who objected to the ban on religious tests also favored an amendment for the protection of religious liberties.

Clearly, religious questions played a significant role in the thinking of many who supported and many who opposed the ratification of the Constitution.

Patrick M. O'Neil

Bibliography

The Documentary History of the Ratification of the Constitution, ed. Merrill Jensen (Madison: State Historical Society of Wisconsin, 1976–1978).

Regan

See COMMITTEE FOR PUBLIC EDUCATION AND RELIGIOUS LIBERTY V. REGAN.

Rehnquist, William (1924–)

William Hubbs Rehnquist became an associate justice of the U.S. Supreme Court in 1971 and chief justice in 1986. He has been among the most consistently conservative voices on the Court during his 23 years of service. As the Court overall has become more conservative, his votes have moved steadily from minority to majority positions. Throughout his tenure, however, he has been consistent in his judicial philosophy, favoring governmental power over constitutional claims, narrow rather than broad roles for the federal courts, and state sovereignty over federal power. These same positions (especially the first two) are reflected in his narrow construction of both the Establishment Clause and the Free Exercise Clause, producing considerable deference to the government in matters of religion.

Rehnquist has consistently voted to reject Establishment Clause challenges to government-sponsored prayers, government-sponsored religious symbols, and government funding of religious organizations. He also wrote the majority opinion in *Valley Forge College v. Americans United for Separation of Church and State* (1982), denying taxpayers access to federal courts to challenge government support for religion unless the government has affirmatively expended funds.

Rehnquist's positions, however, have not been driven by solicitude for religious activity. He has been an equally reliable vote to reject challenges based on the free exercise of religion. He has consistently joined in votes finding that government interests justified infringements on religious freedom; and he further joined in the Court's broader holding in the "peyote case," *Employment Division, Department of Human Resources of Oregon v. Smith* (1990)—that religious claimants seldom if ever have a constitutional right to be free from a "neutral law of general applicability," no matter how severely it restricts their religious freedom.

In at least two cases involving the religion clauses of the Constitution, Rehnquist cast the lone vote to uphold government action. His dissent in *Larkin v. Grendel's Den* (1982) argued that a city ordinance giving churches the right to veto the licensing of any nearby liquor establishment was a legitimate attempt to protect churches from "incompatible" activities. And his dissent in *Thomas v. Review Board* (1981) argued that a state should be free to deny unemployment benefits to a Jehovah's Witness whose pacifist religious convictions led him to refuse available work in a factory that produced tanks.

As an associate justice, Rehnquist was a conservative maverick on a generally moderate Court. From time to time, he explicitly advocated new overall standards for the religion clauses that would give greater deference to the government than existing law did. Among his prime concerns in this area, as in others, has been to restrain constitutional interpretation to fairly strict readings of the Framers' intent. In dissent in *Wallace v. Jaffree* (1985) he canvassed the history surrounding Congress's passage of the Establishment Clause and argued that it did not create a "wall of separation" between church and state, as the Court had claimed since *Everson v. Board of Education* (1947). Instead, he argued, the clause only "prevent[ed] the establishment of a national religion or the governmental preference of one religious sect over another"; thus, government was free to "aid all religions evenhandedly."

Rehnquist based his argument for "nonpreferentialism" primarily on early proposed versions of the Establishment Clause that prohibited Congress from establishing "a national religion" or favoring any "particular religious sect or society." Surprisingly, his was the first serious analysis of the congressional debates to appear in any Supreme Court opinion; it thus helpfully focused attention on the specific history of the Establishment Clause. Rehnquist's reading of the history, however, has been challenged. As Professor Douglas Laycock has observed, the First Congress rejected the proposals on which Rehnquist focused and adopted the broader language forbidding any law "respecting an establishment of religion," thus implying a restriction broader than Rehnquist's "no preference for one sect." Since *Jaffree,* neither Rehnquist nor any other justice has advocated the nonpreferentialism theory.

As an associate justice, Rehnquist also proposed substantial cutbacks in free exercise protection. His primary concern has been to preserve the government's discretion to act even if its actions happen to impose severe restrictions on religiously motivated conduct. In a lone dissent in *Thomas* he attacked the Court's then-existing doctrine that a religious believer must be exempted from a general law that significantly infringes on religious exercise unless the law is necessary to serve a "compelling state interest." Rehnquist argued powerfully that religious exemptions were inconsistent with the Court's Establishment Clause test (the "*Lemon* test"), which forbids actions with the purpose or "primary effect" of "advancing" religion. He was concerned to eliminate this "tension" between free exercise and nonestablishment and to "restore what was surely intended to have been a greater degree of flexibility to the Federal and State governments." To do so, Rehnquist advocated cutting back judicial review on both sides: The government should usually be free to exempt religion from general laws, but it should not be constitutionally required to do so. In recent cases, most notably *Smith,* the Court has essentially shifted to Rehnquist's position.

Free exercise exemptions are just one example of how the recent Supreme Court has adopted Rehnquist's positions of deference to government in matters of religion. Indeed, in recent years Rehnquist, as chief justice and a leader of the Court's conservatives, has written frequent majority opinions in religion cases. In these opinions, however, he has seemed to prefer moving the law to the right in incremental rather than dramatic steps (perhaps under the constraint of keeping five votes). This is shown in several cases where he has written to uphold government assistance to religious organizations.

In *Bowen v. Kendrick* (1988), for example, Rehnquist wrote for the Court in upholding a federal statute that provided funds to religious social service agencies, among other agencies, to combat teenage pregnancy. The opinion, however, did not jettison the three-part test of *Lemon v. Kurtzman* (1973) and give broad approval to funding of religious entities, as Rehnquist's earlier theory of nonpreferentialism would have done. Instead, he applied the *Lemon* test but distinguished earlier cases in which the test had been used to strike down the provision of funds to religiously affiliated schools. Rehnquist seized on the asserted distinction that church-related welfare agencies were generally less "pervasively sectarian" than church related schools; because of this, his opinion said, the Court could not assume that funds provided to such agencies would be used to teach religious doctrine. As Justice Blackmun pointed out in dissent, Rehnquist's opinion seemed to ignore the deeply religious nature of issues concerning teenage sexuality. The *Kendrick* decision also cut narrowly, however, for it stated only that the provision of funds to religious agencies was not void in all cases. The Court indicated that funding would be unconstitutional in those particular cases in which the funds were actually used to teach religion.

Similarly, Rehnquist has been a leader in approving programs that give financial benefits to parents and allow them to use the benefits at religious schools among other schools; but even here he has moved cautiously. In *Mueller v. Allen* (1983) he wrote the Court's opinion upholding tax deductions for private school tuition, even though most families taking the deduction would do so at Roman Catholic schools. But the opinion emphasized the legislature's "broad latitude" over tax matters and thus seemed to leave open the constitutionality of affirmative aid such as vouchers—a question later at least partially settled in favor of such aid in *Witters v. Washington Department of Services for the Blind* (1986).

Similarly, in *Zobrest v. Catalina Foothills School District* (1993), Rehnquist had an attractive set of facts by which to remake the law to give broad permission to parochial aid: A deaf student had been denied a sign language interpreter, to which he was otherwise entitled under federal disabilities law, solely because he attended a Catholic high school. The *Zobrest* opinion followed *Mueller* and *Witters* in permitting such "neutral" aid to individuals, but it included reasoning that might be used to limit the decision's scope. For example, Rehnquist noted that the provision of a sign language interpreter, unlike some other forms of aid, was not "central to the school's educational process" and would not add any religious content to the teaching that was not already present.

Whether operating under the constraints of a majority opinion or with the freedom of a dissenting opinion, Rehnquist has been a consistent and effective voice for his philosophy of judicial deference to the democratic majority in matters of religion. It must be pointed out, however, that such deference is a questionable posture for interpreting the two phrases in the First Amendment that specifically limit government's power over religion.

Thomas C. Berg

Bibliography

Davis, Derek, *Original Intent: Chief Justice Rehnquist and the Course of American Church/State Relations* (Buffalo, N.Y.: Prometheus, 1991).

Davis, Sue, *Justice Rehnquist and the Constitution* (Princeton, N.J.: Princeton University Press, 1989).

Shapiro, David, "Mr. Justice Rehnquist: A Preliminary View," 90 *Harvard Law Review* 293–357 (1976).

Cases Cited

Bowen v. Kendrick, 487 U.S. 589 (1988).

Employment Division, Department of Human Resources of Oregon v. Smith, 494 U.S. 872 (1990).

Everson v. Board of Education, 330 U.S. 1 (1947).

Larkin v. Grendel's Den, 459 U.S. 116 (1982).

Lemon v. Kurtzman, 411 U.S. 192 (1973).

Mueller v. Allen, 463 U.S. 388 (1983).

Thomas v. Review Board, 450 U.S. 707 (1981).

Valley Forge College v. Americans United for Separation of Church and State, 454 U.S. 464 (1982).

Wallace v. Jaffree, 472 U.S. 38 (1985).

Witters v. Washington Department of Services for the Blind, 474 U.S. 481 (1986).

Zobrest v. Catalina Foothills School District, 509 U.S. 1 (1993).

Religious Freedom Restoration Act of 1993

In April 1990 the U.S. Supreme Court decided *Employment Division, Department of Human Resources of Oregon v. Smith* (1990). This case is one of the most important and controversial modern Supreme Court decisions dealing with the so-called Free Exercise Clause—that part of the First Amendment of the U.S. Constitution which prohibits the government from making any law "prohibiting the free exercise" of religion.

In *Smith* the Court rejected the constitutional claims of two members of the Native American Church who had argued that their use of peyote as part of the church's sacraments could not be the basis for the denial of their claim to state unemployment compensation benefits. The claimants had argued that the denial of benefits based on their sacramental use of peyote failed to satisfy the Supreme Court's principal free exercise test, which asked whether government regulations that burdened religiously motivated conduct could be justified as "necessary" to the furtherance of a "compelling government interest." But in a majority opinion written by Justice Antonin Scalia, the Court refused to apply this test. Instead, the Court announced a new test for evaluating free exercise claims: Where the government enacts a law "of general applicability," and one that is "neutral" with respect to religion (in the sense that the law does not discriminate against some or all religiously motivated conduct), the law simply will not implicate the Free Exercise Clause.

In other words, even if the actual operation of a neutral and generally applicable law significantly burdens or even prohibits conduct motivated by sincere religious beliefs, those whose conduct is adversely affected cannot even assert a free exercise claim. Unless there is some independent constitutional claim (for example, free speech or constitutional privacy) available to the religious believer, any claim to immunity or exemption from the regulation in question must be addressed to the relevant legislative or executive officials responsible for the enactment and enforcement of the law in question. (The Court in *Smith* indicated that at least some legislative accommodations of religion—in the form of exempting religious conduct from the requirements of general regulations—would be permissible.)

The reaction to the *Smith* decision in both the religious and academic communities was swift and, for the most part, extremely critical. In a statement before a congressional committee considering potential legislative responses to *Smith,* Congressman Stephen Solarz of New York claimed that the Supreme Court "virtually removed religious freedom from the Bill of Rights." Law Professors Edward Gaffney, Douglas Laycock, and Michael McConnell, writing in the magazine *First Things,* described *Smith* as "a sweeping disaster for religious liberty" because it essentially deprived the courts of any role in protecting religious believers from the vicissitudes of the political process and because it placed minority religions and religious believers in peril of majoritarian abuses.

Shortly after *Smith* was decided, an extraordinarily diverse national coalition of religious groups, calling itself the "Coalition for the Free Exercise of Religion," mobilized with the goal of getting federal legislation enacted that essentially would restore free exercise doctrine to its potentially more religion-protective, pre-*Smith* state. This legislation, known as the Religious Freedom Restoration Act (RFRA), was finally passed by Congress in November 1993 and was signed into law by President Clinton on November 16, 1993.

The RFRA's stated purpose was "to restore the compelling interest test" as set forth in pre-*Smith* case law and "to provide a cause of action to persons whose religious exercise is burdened by government." It goes on to state that "[g]overnment shall not burden a person's exercise of religion even if the burden results from a rule of law of general applicability" except "if it demonstrates that the application of the burden to the person . . . (1) is essential to further a compelling state interest; and (2) is the least restrictive means of furthering that compelling governmental interest." The RFRA is made applicable to federal, state, and local governments, and it explicitly provides for judicial relief.

Notwithstanding the broad support it garnered among religious groups and in Congress, concern was expressed in some quarters about whether the RFRA might be beyond Congress's constitutional powers to enact. As a general principle, Supreme Court decisions on constitutional matters cannot be overturned by regular legislation. The Court's decisions are the law of the land until such time as the Court overrules itself or until a constitutional amendment effectively overruling a decision is proposed and adopted according to the process set forth in Article 5 of the Constitution. Although Congress has the power under Section 5 of the Fourteenth Amendment to "enforce, by appropriate legislation, the provisions of this article" (which, given past Court decisions, includes the power to enforce the Free Exercise Clause of the First Amendment), some scholars maintained that the RFRA amounted to an overruling of the *Smith* decision and thus exceeded Congress's power. Other scholars maintained that the RFRA, by subjecting much state and local legislation to federal court review, exceeded the constitutionally prescribed balance of power between the federal government and the states. Still others argued that the RFRA, by extending special protection to religiously motivated activity, violated the principles of church–state separation prescribed by the First Amendment's Establishment Clause. Given these concerns, the constitutionally of the RFRA was certain to be challenged.

Such a challenge was presented to the Supreme Court in *City of Boerne v. P. F. Flores, Archbishop of San Antonio, and the United States* (1997) in which a 6-to-3 majority of the Court held that the RFRA was indeed unconstitutional. The case involved a suit brought under the RFRA by the Catholic archbishop of San Antonio. The suit challenged the failure of local officials in Boerne, Texas, to issue a zoning permit allowing a local Catholic church to enlarge its facilities. The city officials relied on a general ordinance governing historic landmarks and districts. The plaintiff claimed that the application of the zoning ordinance imposed an impermissible religious burden under the RFRA that could not be justified as the "least restrictive means" of furthering a "compelling governmental interest." The federal district court held that the RFRA was an unconstitutional exercise of Congress's power; the U.S. Court of Appeals for the Fifth Circuit, finding the RFRA to be constitutional, reversed.

The Supreme Court, in an opinion written by Justice Anthony Kennedy (and joined in large part by Chief Justice Rehnquist and Justices Stevens, Thomas, Ginsburg, and Scalia), reversed the court of appeals and held that the RFRA was indeed unconstitutional. The Court's opinion relied on its interpretation of Section 5 of the Fourteenth Amendment, as well as on constitutional principles pertaining to the separation of powers. Relying on its analysis of the history of the Fourteenth Amendment and its past decisions, the Court conceded that Congress had significant authority under Section 5 to "remedy" and "prevent" unconstitutional conduct engaged in by state and local governments. But the RFRA, according to the Court, went beyond this authority. Instead of "enforcing" the Free Exercise Clause as interpreted in *Smith,* the RFRA purported to "make a substantive change" in, or to "alter the meaning of," the clause; and this Congress could not do.

The Court acknowledged that Congress had considerable flexibility to interpret the Free Exercise Clause in light of *Smith.* It also endorsed congressional power to determine how best to remedy government conduct that violates the clause (again, as interpreted by the Court itself). But congressional action had to be both "congruent" and "proportional" to plausibly unconstitutional injury. Since the RFRA would extend to a wide range of state and local regulations that could not plausibly be viewed as unconstitutional under *Smith,* it failed these requirements. According to the Court, "RFRA cannot be considered remedial, preventive legislation, if those terms are to have any meaning." In the final analysis, the Court concluded that the RFRA represented an effort by Congress finally and authoritatively to determine what the Constitution means, thus usurping the power that our constitutional tradition has placed in the Supreme Court itself.

Justice Stevens wrote a separate concurring opinion, in which he expressed the view that the RFRA was also unconstitutional as a "law respecting an establishment of religion" under the First Amendment's Establishment Clause. Justice Scalia felt compelled to write a concurring opinion as well, in which he attempted to refute Justice O'Connor's extensive argument, in dissent, that *Smith* itself was unsupported by historical evidence and should thus be overruled. Justices Souter and Breyer also wrote brief, dissenting opinions.

The reaction to *City of Boerne,* as was true with *Smith,* has been characterized by significant criticism. And efforts to reinstate the broad principles of religious liberty that were embodied in the RFRA are already under way. These efforts have been undertaken at both the federal and state levels. At the federal level, Congress has responded by holding hearings in the fall of 1997 to explore what, if any, legislative action might be taken to restore the protections of the RFRA while respecting the limits on congressional powers set out by the Supreme Court in *City of Boerne*. The options proposed by constitutional scholars include the adoption of a constitutional amendment to nullify *Smith* and/or *City of Boerne;* reenacting an RFRA-like statute in a way that would meet the Supreme Court's concerns about the limits of Congress's Section 5 (Fourteenth Amendment) powers; enacting an RFRA-like statute, but relying on Congress's power under some other provision of the Constitution, like the Commerce Clause or the power to make treaties; and trying to accomplish the RFRA-like goals by Congress's attaching restrictions on the availability and use of federal funds. At the state level, efforts have been undertaken to persuade state legislatures to enact statutes, or even state constitutional amendments, that would accomplish the RFRA-like goals. Since states could rely on their general lawmaking authority, they would presumably be free of many of the federal constitutional constraints on congressional authority identified in the *City of Boerne* decision.

In retrospect, one can view the *Smith* decision and the enactment of the RFRA as extraordinary, if not unparalleled, modern constitutional events. They represent the beginning of an important conversation among the Supreme Court, Congress, and the American people. By adopting a restrictive view of constitutionally protected religious freedom in *Smith,* the Court catalyzed broad segments of the American people to move Congress to take swift and decisive action. Congress's response, in the form of the RFRA in 1993, prompted the Court, in *City of Boerne,* to address a set of profound questions, not only about the scope of religious freedom but also about the fundamental nature of, and relationship between, the legislative and judicial power established by the Constitution. The legislative responses to the *City of Boerne* represent a continuation of this important constitutional conversation.

Richard B. Saphire

Bibliography

Conkle, Daniel O., "The Religious Freedom Restoration Act: The Constitutional Significance of an Unconstitutional Statute," 56 *Montana Law Review* 39 (1995).

Durham, W. Cole, Jr., Edward McGlynn Gaffney, Douglas Laycock, and Michael W. McConnell, "A Declaration: For the Religious Freedom Restoration Act," First Things (March 1992), p. 42; "How to Restore Religious Freedom: A Debate," *First Things* (April 1992) p. 37.

McConnell, Michael W,. "Comment: Institutions and Interpretation: A Critique of *City of Boerne v. Flores,"* 111 *Harvard Law Review* 153 (1997).

Ryan, James E., "*Smith* and the Religious Freedom Restoration Act: An Iconoclastic Assessment," 78 *Virginia Law Review* 1407 (1992).

Cases Cited

City of Boerne v. P. F. Flores, Archbishop of San Antonio, and the United States, 501 U.S. 507 (1997).

Employment Division, Department of Human Resources of Oregon v. Smith, 494 U.S. 872 (1990).

Religious Garb

The religious garb debate began in the 1890s, when Roman Catholic sisters taught in parochial and public schools. The schools sometimes shared the same facility. Though economically advantageous, this arrangement understandably led to conflicts over separation of church and state. The sisters' wearing religious garb while teaching public schoolchildren aroused public disapproval, partly fueled by strong anti-Catholic sentiment during certain times in U.S. history.

The religious garb cases reveal a classic civil liberties conflict within the federal First Amendment as well as many state constitutions: the teacher's freedom to exercise religious choice versus the freedom of students from an established religion in the public schools. Also relevant are Article 6 of the U.S. Constitution and similar clauses in state constitutions prohibiting a religious test for holding public office. The most recent cases also raise claims under Title VII of the 1964 Civil Rights Act, which protects public employees against religious discrimination on the job.

When a religious garb case reaches the courts, it typically falls into one of two scenarios. In states with statutes prohibiting teachers from wearing religious garb in the public schools, the court must decide whether the statute or administrative regulation is "reasonable," usually within the context of providing a religiously neutral learning environment. Historically, the statutes have usually been upheld with the reasoning that wearing particular garb is no more an absolute right than the student's right to be free from the influence of possible sectarianism. The U.S. Supreme Court has never ruled on the constitutionality of these state anti-garb laws, except to dismiss an appeal in *Cooper v. Eugene School District* (1987).

In the absence of a statute the court must decide whether wearing religious garb violates the state or federal constitutional guarantees against sectarianism in publicly supported institutions. In almost all cases since the 1890s, the courts have looked for an "aggregate" of violations: full holy-water fonts, rosaries, religious instruction in public classrooms during regular school hours, and proximity to churches or convents. In such cases, all sectarian practices are enjoined; but usually the courts have ruled that the wearing of religious garb by itself does not violate any constitutional provisions.

Hysong v. School District of Gallitzin Borough (Pa., 1894), the first garb case in Pennsylvania, illustrates the early litigation that led to the first garb laws. It is cited in all subsequent garb cases. In *Hysong* the Pennsylvania court ruled that religious sisters could not be enjoined from wearing their religious habits if that was the only display of their religious belief. The religious sisters in question were not teaching religious subjects during the school day. Almost immediately the Pennsylvania legislature, clearly responding to strong public anti-Catholic sentiment, passed an anti-garb statute in 1895. This statute was upheld in *Commonwealth v. Herr* (Pa., 1910), and it was reenacted in 1949.

By 1946 a National Education Association survey showed that, out of thirty-eight states reporting, sixteen allowed, and twenty-two did not allow, religious garb to be worn by public schoolteachers. Six states had anti-garb laws on the books.

If a state had no anti-garb statute, the court's task was to decide whether the practice was subject to any constitutional inhibitions. Over the next fifty years one set of decisions upheld the *Hysong* majority, claiming that to deprive religious sisters of their habit is an infringement of their constitutionally guaranteed religious freedom. *Gerhardt v. Heid* (N.D., 1936) involved six North Dakota sisters who taught in their habits without rosary or crucifix and who contributed a portion of their earnings to their order. In the absence of an anti-garb statute, the state supreme court found no evidence that the sisters had used the habit to impose religious beliefs on the students or that the practice had converted the public school into a sectarian one. Judge A.M. Christianson wrote in the opinion: "Whether it is wise or unwise to regulate the style of dress to be worn by teachers in our public schools or to inhibit the wearing of dress or insignia indicating religious belief is not a matter for the courts to determine. The limit of our inquiry is to determine whether what has been done infringes on and violates the provisions of the Constitution."

Other cases finding that religious garb alone did not constitute sectarian teaching are *City of New Haven v. Town of Torrington* (Conn., 1945) and *State v. Boyd* (Ind., 1940). Neither of these involved state anti-garb statutes. In *Boyd* the Supreme Court of Indiana ruled on the constitutionality of a Depression-era agreement between the Vincennes City School Board and a group of Roman Catholic priests who could no longer afford to operate their parish schools. The city assumed administrative and instructional obligations for the parochial schoolchildren but kept them in the parochial school buildings, with no sectarian instruction allowed. Religious pictures, holy fonts, voluntary religious instruction before school, and religious garb were allowed. The court decided that the agreement did not allow undue sectarian influence and that the wearing of religious robes did not constitute sectarian teaching.

Rawlings v. Butler (Ky., 1956) affirmed a decision that wearing religious garb while teaching in a public school does not alone violate state or federal constitutional guarantees of freedom of religion. The majority decided that dress denoting membership in a religious order "do[es] not deprive them of their right to teach in public schools, so long as they do not inject religion or the dogma of their church. The garb does not teach. It is the woman within who teaches. . . ." The court quoted extensively from the *Hysong* opinion. *Rawlings* drew a great deal of attention from legal scholars, most of whom recommended that states adopt statutes to avoid this kind of decision.

Another set of cases rejected *Hysong,* in support of state constitutional guarantees of freedom *from* religion for public school students. In these cases there were no state anti-garb laws, and when religious garb was part of an aggregate of sectarian influences, all such influences were found unconstitutional and were enjoined. In *Knowlton v. Baumhover* (Iowa, 1918) the court ruled unconstitutional an arrangement between the local school board and a Roman Catholic priest who was renting out the second floor of the Maple River Township's parochial school for public school classrooms. In this case the evidence shows that administratively the public and parochial school had become intertwined: A religious sister was put in charge of the entire school building, the student statistics were not maintained separately, and daily instruction included religion. Here the court clearly rejected the authority of *Hysong* and quoted Judge Henry W. Williams's *Hysong* dissent: "It is not holding an ecclesiastical office or position that disqualifies them, for it does not. It is the introduction into the schools of persons who are by their striking and distinctive ecclesiastical robes necessarily and constantly asserting their membership . . . in a religious order within that church, and the subjection of their lives to the direction and control of its officers." Williams's dissent remains one of the most comprehensive analyses of the power of one's appearance to influence others.

Zellers v. Huff (N.M., 1951) was a taxpayers' class action against numerous New Mexico public school districts and the Roman Catholic brothers and sisters who taught in them. Throughout the 1940s priests had taught religion and conducted prayer during regular school hours. School bus schedules followed the sectarian class schedule, so that in inclement weather a non-Catholic child was sometimes forced either to attend religious instruction or to stand in the rain. In a very complex case, the Supreme Court of New Mexico ruled in favor of the plaintiffs in most instances. While the case was before the New Mexico high court, the state board of education adopted an anti-garb resolution in 1951. The court still made a point of declaring that by its nature religious garb introduced sectarianism into the public schools.

In two recent decisions the changing religious profile of the United States is evident. In *Cooper v. Eugene School District No. 4J* (Ore., 1986), Oregon's anti-garb statute was challenged by a Sikh.

Janet Cooper wore white clothing and a turban while teaching her sixth- and eighth-grade special education classes. After Cooper persisted in wearing this garb despite warnings of suspension, her teaching certificate was revoked. The Oregon Court of Appeals found this action to be an "excessive sanction." The Supreme Court of Oregon reversed, and the appeal was dismissed by the U.S. Supreme Court. Justices William Brennan, Thurgood Marshall, and Sandra Day O'Connor dissented.

The case gives a clear explanation of the difference between deciding a case on constitutional guarantees or on the validity of a statute designed to protect such guarantees. In Oregon, Associate Justice Hans A. Linde reasoned, the legislature made a policy choice to guarantee religious neutrality in the public schools. Unlike *Rawlings,* this case accentuates the twofold power of religious garb: "'religious dress' must be judged from the perspective both of the wearer and of the observer."

United States v. Board of Education for the School District of Philadelphia (3rd Cir. 1990), involved Alima Reardon, an observant Muslim who wore a head covering and robe-like garment while a substitute teacher for the school board of Philadelphia. In 1984 Reardon reported to schools and was told she could not teach, though she was given the option of going home to change clothes. School officials acted under the anti-garb statute of 1895, which was passed on the heels of *Hysong,* reenacted in 1949, and still in effect. Reardon refused to change her clothing and filed charges with the Equal Employment Opportunity Commission (EEOC). On behalf of Reardon the Justice Department contended that the actions taken by school administrators to enforce the garb law violated Title VII of the Civil Rights Act of 1964. Under that law an employer cannot "fail or refuse to hire or to discharge any individual . . . because of such individual's . . . religion," though there is an exception for "undue hardship" on the part of the employer.

The U.S. District Court decided in favor of the United States; of the two appellants, it decided against the school board and for the Commonwealth of Pennsylvania. In appeal and cross-appeal of that judgment, the U.S. Court of Appeals, Third Circuit, reversed in part and affirmed in part. Judge Walter K. Stapleton held that accommodating religious garb imposed undue hardship on the school board, but he affirmed that the government did not show that the commonwealth had a "pattern or practice of resistance" in enforcing employee's rights under Title VII. The decision was heavily based on the U.S. Supreme Court's summary disposition of *Cooper.* Judge Stapleton also noted that the Pennsylvania Garb Law was passed in 1895, when there was significant anti-Catholic sentiment; but the court decided that, because the law was reenacted in 1949 with clear motivation toward religious neutrality, its anti-Catholic history was irrelevant.

In an important concurring opinion, Judge Harold Ackerman rejected the court's heavy reliance on *Cooper* because the Oregon Supreme Court *declined* to comment on violation of Title VII. Instead, he invoked Justice Brennan's guidelines as set out in *Edwards v. Aguillard* (1987) and *Lemon v. Kurtzman* (1971), and he sought to determine whether state action had violated the Establishment Clause. Ackerman found that the state statute had a secular purpose, did not to advance or inhibit religion, and did not result in "entanglement" with religion. Ackerman then concluded that wearing of religious garb sends the message that "the state prefers religion over nonreligion" and should be enjoined.

Ackerman's analysis illuminates the Title VII issues far more clearly than the majority opinion does. In recent cases, Justices Brennan and Marshall despaired over the Court's broad application of "undue hardship" in favor of the employer and predicted the demise of the Title VII religious protections. Holly Bastian argues that one could use Brennan's analysis to reach a view *opposing* Ackerman's: Accommodating religious garb achieves the secular purpose of complying with Title VII; we cannot assume that children perceive garb as approval or disapproval of their own religious beliefs (might they not see Reardon's being sent home as disapproval of her religion?); and, finally, accommodation relieves the state's bureaucratic burden of monitoring dress.

Currently only Nebraska, North Dakota, Pennsylvania, and Oregon have religious garb statutes. With the growing multicultural makeup of urban public schools in particular, free exercise of religious belief will become an increasingly volatile issue for both teachers and students.

Barbara M. Jones

Bibliography

Bastian, Holly M., "Religious Garb Statutes and Title VII: An Uneasy Coexistence," 80 *Georgetown Law Journal* 211–232 (1991).

Choper, Jesse, "The Free Exercise Clause," in Jesse Choper, Yale Kamisar, and Lawrence Tribe, *The Supreme Court: Trends and Developments 1982–83* (Minneapolis: National Practice Institute, 1984), pp. 79–84.

"Religious Garb in the Public Schools: A Study in Conflicting Liberties," 22 *University of Chicago Law Review* 888–895 (1955).

Cases Cited

City of New Haven v. Town of Torrington, 43 A. 2d 455 (Conn. 1945).

Commonwealth v. Herr, 78 A. 68 (Pa. 1910).

Cooper v. Eugene School District No. 4J, 723 P. 2d 298 (Or. 1986), appeal dismissed, 480 U.S. 942 (1987).

Edwards v. Aguillard, 482 U.S. 578 (1987).

Gerhardt v. Heid, 267 N.W. 127 (N.D. 1936).

Hysong v. School District of Gallitzin Borough, 30 A. 482 (Pa. 1894).

Knowlton v. Baumhover, 166 N.W. 202 (Iowa 1918).

Lemon v. Kurtzman, 403 U.S. 602 (1971).

Rawlings v. Butler, 290 S.W. 2d 801 (Ky. 1956).

State v. Boyd, 28 N.E. 2d 256 (Ind. 1940).

United States v. Board of Education for the School District of Philadelphia, 911 F. 2d 882 (3rd Cir. 1990).

Zellers v. Huff, 236 P. 2d 949 (N.M. 1951).

Reuben Quick Bear, Ralph Eagle Feather, Charles Tackett, and All Other Members of the Sioux Tribe of Rosebud Agency, South Dakota v. Francis E. Leupp, Commissioner of Indian Affairs
210 U.S. 50 (1908)

Quick Bear v. Leupp arose from a dispute over government funding of schools on the

Rosebud Sioux Indian Reservation in South Dakota. By the Sioux Treaty of 1868, the United States agreed to provide a school and a teacher for every thirty children who could be induced to attend. In some cases, Congress authorized agreements with existing mission schools to fulfill this obligation. On Rosebud, Congress contracted with the St. Francis Mission Boarding School.

Beginning in 1876 Congress paid for these schools with a combination of public money, money taken from treaty payments, and a trust fund established for the Sioux from the sale of Sioux lands. By the 1890s, however, a movement arose opposing the use of public funds to pay for education in sectarian Indian schools. In response, Congress in 1895 began phasing out public funding of sectarian schools, making its final Indian education appropriation of public funds in 1899. On Rosebud, this left tribal funds as the sole source of payments to St. Francis Mission.

Against this background Reuben Quick Bear, a Protestant Sioux, and other residents of Rosebud asked for a permanent injunction against the use of treaty and trust fund monies to pay for school costs. They believed it violated the government's policy of not using public funds for sectarian education as stated in the 1897 Indian Appropriations Act that read in part, "[I]t is hereby declared to be the settled policy of the government to hereafter make no appropriation whatever for education in any sectarian school." The plaintiffs also argued that the tribe had not requested the use of tribal funds to pay St. Francis Mission. It was the Department of Interior not the Rosebud Sioux that authorized such expenditures, which would diminish treaty payments and the trust fund. The United States was required by treaty to provide educational services to the Sioux, but because Congress had restricted direct federal payments for Indian education, tribal trust funds were used. Consequently, Quick Bear believed that the federal government's action changed Indian monies into public funds that were used to establish a religion, thus constituting a violation of the First Amendment.

In its defense the federal government argued that tribal funds were separate and distinct from public funds and could be used at the discretion of the Secretary of the Interior to fulfill the government's treaty obligations to provide educational opportunities for the Sioux. The government also presented a petition bearing 212 signatures of the 4,986 enrolled Rosebud Sioux who requested the use of tribal funds to pay for educational services at St. Francis, and it stipulated that these signatures represented 669 shares of the annual treaty and trust fund payments—more than enough to cover the cost of the St. Francis contract.

Chief Justice Melville W. Fuller, writing for the U.S. Supreme Court, affirmed the ruling of the Federal Court of Appeals of the District of Columbia, finding that treaty funds and trust funds were not public monies but were funds belonging to the Sioux. Fuller found that Indians should be able to spend their money as the federal government saw fit in educating their children.

Fuller, however, went one step further. He found that by preventing the use of Indian funds for sectarian education, the federal government would effectively prohibit the free exercise of religion among the Indians and missionaries. By this reasoning, denial of the subsidization of Roman Catholic schools by the federal government using Sioux funds would be a denial of free exercise religious rights. Although Chief Justice Fuller did not attempt to overrule the emerging case law, which held that Native Americans were not covered by the Bill of Rights, including the First Amendment, he did come closer to reaching this result than had any Supreme Court jurist up to this time.

Todd Kerstetter and John R. Wunder

Bibliography

Deloria, Vine, Jr., and Clifford M. Lytle, *The Nations Within: The Past and Future of American Indian Sovereignty* (New York: Pantheon, 1984).

——— and ———, *American Indians, American Justice* (Austin: University of Texas Press, 1983).

Prucha, Frances Paul, *The Great Father: The United States Government and the American Indians*, 2 vols. (Lincoln: University of Nebraska Press, 1984).

Wilkinson, Charles F., *American Indians, Time, and the Law: Native Societies in a Modern Constitutional Democracy* (New Haven, Conn.: Yale University Press, 1987).

Wunder, John R., *"Retained by the People": A History of American Indians and the*

Bill of Rights (New York: Oxford University Press, 1993).

Case Cited

Reuben Quick Bear, Ralph Eagle Feather, Charles Tackett, and All Other Members of the Sioux Tribe of Rosebud Agency, South Dakota v. Francis E. Leupp, Commissioner of Indian Affairs, 210 U.S. 50 (1908).

Reynolds v. United States
98 U.S. (8 Otto) 145 (1879)

Joseph Smith, the founder of Mormonism, grew up in the burned-over district of upstate New York. After founding the Church of the Latter-Day Saints of Jesus Christ, also known as the Mormons, he and his followers went west to Nauvoo, Illinois. After persecutions and finally Smith's murder in Carthage, Illinois, Brigham Young organized the Latter-Day Saints and led them on a trek farther west, to an area then outside the United States. The present state of Utah began as the independent state of Deseret in 1847. The land became a territory in 1850, after Mexico ceded the area to the United States.

In 1852 the Latter-Day Saints revealed to the world that they were practicing plural marriage under an earlier, secret revelation to Joseph Smith concerning the "order of Jacob." Public opposition—illustrated, for example, by a reference in the Republican platform of 1856 to polygamy and slavery as the twin relics of barbarism—resulted in the Morrill Act (1862), a federal statute outlawing bigamy in the territories.

In 1862, responding to national agitation over the notorious revival of polygamous marriage within the United States, Congress passed the first of several antipolygamy statutes. The Morrill Act provided that "every person having a husband or wife living, who shall marry any other person, whether married or single, in a Territory of the United States, or other place over which the United States [has] exclusive jurisdiction, shall . . . be adjudged guilty of bigamy. . . ." At about the same time, Utah made a third application for statehood. The litigation over the constitutionality of the statute—called a test case in some accounts—involved George Reynolds, secretary to Brigham Young.

The case, *Reynolds v. United States* (1879), was decided by the Supreme Court, in an opinion by Chief Justice Morrison R. Waite. Justice Steven J. Field concurred, except on one point relating to evidence concerning the nature of Mormon plural marriage.

The Latter-Day Saints, committed to the idea that the American Constitution is divinely inspired, apparently believed also that the First Amendment would protect them. Reynolds had been denied a jury instruction to the effect that if he had committed bigamy "in pursuance of and in conformity with what he believed at the time to be a religious duty, that the verdict must be 'not guilty.'" The judge in fact instructed the jury that: "if the defendant, under the influence of a religious belief that it was right—under an inspiration, if you please, that it was right—deliberately married a second time, having a first wife living, the want of consciousness of evil intent—the want of understanding on his part that he was committing a crime—did not excuse him; but the law inexorably in such case implies the criminal intent." In their brief, the Mormons had argued that Reynolds lacked specific criminal intent.

In his opinion Chief Justice Waite rejected the idea that a religious claim could justify an illegal act. Polygamy was not protected by the First Amendment's Free Exercise Clause. Waite's opinion is significant for three different aspects of its analysis: (1) its treatment of the history of the First Amendment, (2) its treatment of the idea of an exemption under the Free Exercise Clause, and (3) its general perspective on marriage and the state.

First Serious Review of Free Exercise

Although not the first case dealing with church and state to reach the Supreme Court, *Reynolds* is the first serious Supreme Court consideration of the Free Exercise Clause. The opinion contains an early and influential review of its history, which included a discussion of the issue in Virginia; and references to Madison's *Memorial and Remonstrance,* which was included as an appendix to *Everson v. Board of Education of Ewing Township* (1947); and Jefferson's statute on religious freedom, which states first that opinion is free and second that "it is time enough for the rightful purposes of civil government for its officers to interfere when principles break out into overt acts against peace and good order." "In these two sentences," Chief Justice Waite wrote, "is found the true distinction between what properly belongs to the church and what to the State." Waite also quoted Thomas Jefferson's 1802 letter to the Baptists of Danbury, Connecticut, repeating the distinction between belief and action and saying that the First Amendment erected "a wall of separation between church and State."

Congress was authorized to bar polygamy, because it was "left free to reach actions that were in violation of social duties or subversive of good order." Polygamy was clearly such action. "Polygamy has always been odious among the northern and western nations of Europe, and, until the establishment of the Mormon Church, was almost exclusively a feature of the life of Asiatic and of African People."

According to Waite's biographer, the chief justice referred to the *Reynolds* opinion as his "sermon on the religion of polygamy." For centuries polygamy had been viewed as an offense against society that was cognizable by the civil courts. Congress was clearly entitled to act to protect monogamy. "Laws are made for the government of actions," the Court said, "and while they cannot interfere with mere religious belief and opinions, they may with practices." The Court related polygamy, human sacrifices, and suttee. "Suppose one believed that human sacrifices were a necessary part of religious worship, would it be seriously contended that the civil government under which he lived could not interfere to prevent a sacrifice? Or if a wife religiously believed it was her duty to burn herself on the funeral pyre of her dead husband, would it be beyond the power of the civil government to prevent her carrying her belief into practice?" To permit religiously mandated polygamy in the face of a criminal statute "would be to make the professed doctrines of religious belief superior to the law of the land, and in effect to permit every citizen to become a law unto himself. Government could exist only in name under such circumstances."

The Court's discussion of monogamous marriage is a staple in America's treatment of domestic relations:

> Marriage, while from its very nature a sacred obligation, is nevertheless, in most civilized nations, a civil contract, and usually regulated by law. Upon it society may be said to be built, and out if its fruits spring social relations and social obligations and duties, with which government is necessarily required to deal. In fact, according as monogamous or polygamous marriages are allowed, do we find the principles on which the government of the people, to a greater or less extent, rests. Professor Lieber says, polygamy leads to the patriarchal principle, and which, when applied to large communities, fetters the people in stationary despotism, while that principle cannot long exist in connection with monogamy.

In the reference to Professor Lieber, Waite invoked the name of a contemporary academic luminary who is remembered today mostly by academics. Francis Lieber, a German émigré who made his career ultimately at Columbia University and who died in 1872, had for some time agitated against polygamy and against Utah's admission to the Union as a polygamous state, with such articles as "The Mormons: Shall Utah be Admitted into the Union?" The 1873 edition of James Kent's *Commentaries on American Law* had cited Lieber to support a proposition to the effect that polygamy could be seen as "exclusively the feature of Asiatic manners and a half-civilized life" and was "incompatible with civilization, refinement and domestic felicity." The link between Mormonism and a tendency hostile to republicanism was a nineteenth-century commonplace. This was expressed in such books as Josiah Strong's *Our Country: Its Possible Future and Its Present Crises* (1885). The Mormon kingdom, he said, was "an *'imperium in imperio'* ruled by a man who is prophet, priest, king and pope, all in one. . . ."

The conviction of George Reynolds stood, and he served nineteen months in prison. Welcomed home as a "living martyr," he married for a third time in 1885.

The Woodruff Manifesto and Statehood

The difficulty of proving plural marriage in Utah—because of the secrecy of the ceremony—underlies a second case under the 1862 statute, *Miles v. United States* (1880), reversing a bigamy conviction based on testimony of an (admitted) second wife on the grounds that, under Utah law, until the first marriage was shown, the second wife was the lawful wife and could not testify against her husband. Partly because it was so difficult to prove polygamy, several other congressional enactments followed the original antibigamy statutes. The last of these, which involved a disincorporation of the Mormon Church and confiscation of its property, resulted in a formal declaration known as the Woodruff Manifesto (Sept. 25, 1890), under which the Mormon Church officially abandoned polygamy. The manifesto, issued by Wilford Woodruff, the president of the Mormon Church, stated:

> We are not teaching polygamy or plural marriage, nor permitting any person to enter into its practice....
>
> In as much as laws have been enacted by Congress forbidding plural marriages, which laws have been pronounced constitutional by the court of last resort, I hereby declare my intention to submit to those laws, and to use my influence with the members of the Church over which I preside to have them do likewise.
>
> ... And I now publicly declare that my advice to the Latter-day Saints is to refrain from contracting any marriage forbidden by the law of the land.

B. Carmon Hardy in *Solemn Covenant* (1992) argues that, even after the Woodruff Manifesto, leaders of the Mormon Church continued to sanction polygamous marriages while publicly denying their existence.

Following the formal abandonment of polygamy, Congress admitted Utah to the Union under a state constitution providing that "perfect toleration of religious sentiment shall be secured, and that no inhabitant of said State shall ever be molested in person or property on account of his or her mode of religious worship: *Provided,* That polygamous or plural marriages are forever prohibited."

Supreme Court's Hostility to Polygamy

The Supreme Court's hostility to polygamy was carried forward by later cases. In *Mormon Church (Late Corporation of the Church of Jesus Christ of Latter-Day Saints) v. United States* (1889) the Supreme Court said that polygamy was "a return to barbarism . . . contrary to the spirit of Christianity and of the civilization which Christianity has produced in the Western world." Justice Stephen J. Field in *Davis v. Beason* (1890) stated that bigamy and polygamy are crimes, tending "to destroy the purity of the marriage relation, to disturb the peace of families, to degrade woman and to debase man." In contrast to *Davis,* the rhetoric of *Reynolds* may be seen as moderate. Thus Leo Pfeffer, in *Church, State, and Freedom* (1953), suggested that the opinion in *Reynolds* was essentially consistent with the ideas of Jefferson and Madison. The opinion "did not deny that the practice of polygamy may be a tenet of religion; nor did it imply that it is the function of civil courts to protect orthodox Christianity from less conventional sects." Rather, Pfeffer concluded that *Reynolds* "was based on the fact that marriage is a relationship created, regulated and protected by civil authority, and that the preservation of the monogamous family unit is more important to American society than the unrestrained religious liberty of believers in polygamy." Although the Mormons are the usual example of religiously based polygamy, it may also be noted that an individual's free exercise of religion in connection with bigamy was raised (and rejected) in *Long v. State* (Ind., 1922).

In litigation over the conviction of a polygamist under the Mann Act, the issue of polygamy was again discussed. Justice William O. Douglas, writing the majority opinion in *Cleveland v. United States* (1946), upheld the application of the Mann Act to the interstate transportation of a plural wife. Douglas said that "[t]he establishment or maintenance of polygamous households is a notorious example of promiscuity." Justice Frank Murphy dissented in *Cleveland,* urging that polygamy was a legitimate form of marriage:

> There are four fundamental forms of marriages: (1) monogamy; (2) polygyny, or one man with several wives; (3) polyandry, or one woman with several husbands; and (4) group marriage. The term "polygamy" covers both polygyny and polyandry. Thus we are dealing here with polygyny, one of the basic forms of marriage. Historically, its use has far exceeded that of any other form. It was quite common among ancient civilizations and was referred to many times by

> the writers of the Old Testament; even today it is to be found frequently among certain pagan and non-Christian peoples of the world. We must recognize, then, that polygyny, like other forms of marriage, is basically a cultural institution rooted deeply in the religious beliefs and social mores of those societies in which it appears.

Reynolds itself continues to be reaffirmed. As recently as 1985 the 10th Circuit reaffirmed it in *Potter v. Murray City* (10th Cir. 1985). At another level, however, in a child custody case, *Sanderson v. Tryon* (Utah, 1987), the Utah Supreme Court noted that "polygamous practices should only be considered as one among many other factors regarding the children's best interests."

The history of *Reynolds* as a matter of constitutional doctrine is complex. On the one hand, *Reynolds* was never overruled and was sometimes reinforced. In the language of Justice Frankfurter, writing in *Minersville School District v. Gobitis* (1940): "[c]onscientious scruples have not, in the course of the long struggle for religious toleration, relieved the individual from obedience to a general law not aimed at the promotion or restriction of religious beliefs." Justice Scalia, writing for the Court in *Employment Division, Department of Human Resources of Oregon v. Smith* (1990), referred to *Reynolds* as the first case in which that principle had been asserted.

On the other hand—*Gobitis* and even *Smith* notwithstanding—an idea of exemption from valid laws based on the Free Exercise Clause did develop and continues to exist, to the extent that the leading citation, *Wisconsin v. Yoder* (1971), has not been overruled. Writing in a separate opinion in *Yoder*, Justice Douglas thought that the polygamy case might be rejected. The exemption that was granted to the Amish, he wrote, "opens the way to give organized religion a broader base than it has ever enjoyed; and it even promises that in time *Reynolds* will be overruled." As noted, that did not happen.

As is true today in the international context, where polygamy is closely associated with the subordination and oppression of women, the nineteenth-century American polygamy cases are often understood with reference to issues relating to the status of women. In nineteenth-century America the degradation of women was not seen in quite the same way by those in the women's suffrage movement who saw that polygamous women voted in Utah while monogamous women were denied the vote in the United States generally. But George Bernard Shaw's observation in *The Revolutionist's Handbook and Pocket Companion,* appended to *Man and Superman* (1930)—that Mormon polygamy was polygamy under "modern democratic conditions"—was not widely held. The debate over the criminalization of bigamy/polygamy is summarized by a comment to the Model Penal Code §230.1, (1980): "Although the punishment of bigamy as a crime is of relatively recent origin, it enforces an ancient religious scruple. Even today, punishment of plural marriage reflects a desire to redress an affront to established social customs reinforced by religious belief." The comment noted that "[m]ost prior law seemed to rest on the largely unexamined assumption that this rationale has continued validity in modern society." The comment notes that a secular harm must be established, because "in the absence of perceived secular harms, it could be argued convincingly that the enforcement of religious scruple by the criminal law is misplaced."

Typical issues of bigamy (fraud or desertion, for example) may not arise in the case of religiously motivated plural marriage. Rather, the secular harm alleged in, for example, modern fundamentalist polygamy in Utah (for neither *Reynolds* and its successors nor the Woodruff Manifesto destroyed polygamous marriage in Utah) involves the argument that young girls are married to much older men in a culture which considers women as property. Thus in a June 11, 1989, editorial the *Salt Lake Tribune* argued that the "State has [a] primary obligation to bar exploitive polygamy."

Both a Wall and a Linkage between Church and State

Reynolds is cited in several fields of law. It is a basic citation in the field of church and state for the proposition that there can be no free exercise exemption from a generally valid law. In the field of criminal law it is discussed in the context of criminal "offenses against the family"—more accurately, offenses against the monogamous family. In family law it is the basis for discussions of substantive limitations on marriage, and in the field of evidence the case can be cited for its relation to problems concerning the testimony of the plural wives.

More generally the case is recalled in America as a major example of persecution of a religious group by the federal government. It may also be seen as the persecution of a religious group by other religious groups and even by groups derived from the same religious tradition. In a sense, the history of the Mormons, like the history of the Quakers in the colonial period, reflects a severe limit on the assumption of an American nation built on a shared universal Christian heritage. This limit is, of course, obvious in the case of non-Christians, but the Mormon example provides a case in which even the Christian tradition was deeply divided. While the case is the judicial source of the image of the wall of separation, it is also the case that illustrates a linkage between church and state, in its insistence on a New Testament model of marriage and its rejection of other forms of marriage based on other religious beliefs.

Carol Weisbrod

Bibliography

Davis, Ray Jay, "Polygamous Prelude," 6 *American Journal of Legal History* 1–27 (1962).

Firmage, Edwin Brown, and Richard Collin Mangrum, *Zion in the Courts: A Legal History of the Church of Jesus Christ of Latter Day Saints 1830–1900* (Urbana: University of Illinois Press, 1988).

Hardy, B. Carmon, *Solemn Covenant: The Mormon Polygamous Passage* (Urbana: University of Illinois Press, 1992).

Lieber, Francis, "The Mormons: Shall Utah Be Admitted into the Union?" 5 *Putnam's Monthly* 225–236 (1855).

Linford, Orma, "Mormons and the Law: The Polygamy Cases, Parts I, II," 9 *Utah Law Review* 308–370, 543–591 (1964, 1965).

Pfeffer, Leo, *Church, State, and Freedom* (Boston: Beacon Press, 1953).

Strong, Josiah, *Our Country: Its Possible Future and Its Present Crises* (New York: Baker & Taylor, 1885).

Weisbrod, Carol, and Pamela Sheingorn, "*Reynolds v. United States* Nineteenth-Century Forms of Marriage and the Status of Women," 10 *Connecticut Law Review* 828–858 (1978).

Young, Kimball, *Isn't One Wife Enough? The Story of Mormon Polygamy* (New York: Holt, 1954).

Cases and Statutes Cited

Cleveland v. United States, 329 U.S. 14 (1946).

Davis v. Beason, 133 U.S. 333 (1890).

Employment Division, Department of Human Resources of Oregon v. Smith, 494 U.S. 872 (1990).

Everson v. Board of Education of Ewing Township, 330 U.S. 1 (1947).

Hilton v. Roylance, 69 P. 660 (Utah 1902).

Long v. State, 137 N.E. 49 (Ind. 1922).

Miles v. United States, 103 U.S. 304 (1880).

Minersville School District v. Gobitis, 310 U.S. 586 (1940).

Mormon Church (Late Corporation of the Church of Jesus Christ of Latter-Day Saints) v. United States, 136 U.S. 1 (1889).

Potter v. Murray City, 760 F. 2d 1065 (10th Cir. 1985).

Reynolds v. United States, 98 U.S. (8 Otto) 145 (1879).

Sanderson v. Tryon, 739 P. 2d 623 (Utah 1987).

Wisconsin v. Yoder, 406 U.S. 205 (1972).

Act to Admit Utah to the Union, Act of July 16, 1894, ch. 138, 28 Stat. 107, 108.

Rhode Island Charter

On July 8, 1663, Charles II of England granted a royal charter of incorporation to Rhode Island and Providence Plantations. By providing firm legal footing for the colony and essentially ratifying its ordering of political and religious institutions, the charter became a document of seminal importance in American colonial history.

Roger Williams founded Providence Plantations in 1636 after being forced to leave Massachusetts because of his views on church membership, separation from the Church of England, and the validity of settlers' claims to Indian lands. He envisioned the settlement as a refuge for "those distressed for the cause of conscience," with religious freedom as its guiding norm. In the absence of religious unity and recognized political leadership, the dissenters and adventurers who were attracted by the free air of Providence and subsequent settlements at

Portsmouth (1638), Newport (1639), and Warwick (1642) came to be characterized by social discord and faction. Additionally, in its early years the colony faced constant boundary disputes with neighboring Massachusetts and Connecticut. The colony's need for both internal order and external standing as a politically secure entity with fixed boundaries prompted it to seek incorporation. Williams opposed established religion because he thought coordination of temporal and religious authority made the latter subservient to the former. Thus, he also sought confirmation of the colony's practice of separating political and religious institutions.

Williams had secured an earlier charter in 1644, but because Charles I did not sign it—having been forced previously to flee London by Puritan leaders in Parliament—it was largely ineffective. With the Restoration of monarchy in 1660–1661, John Clarke, who labored twelve years in London trying to secure a firm charter on behalf of Williams and the colony, seized a fresh opportunity. For his part, Charles II looked to bolster monarchical authority in America by granting charters to Rhode Island and other colonies.

The charter granted legal authority, with slight variations, to existing political structures in Rhode Island, thus enabling virtual self-government among the estimated 1,500 white settlers of the colony. It called for a governor and ten assistants, as well as deputies from each town, to be elected annually by the freemen of the corporation. The deputies and assistants combined formed a general assembly that was to meet twice a year. Assemblymen were empowered to admit freemen to the corporation and to pass laws "as to them shall seem meet for the good and welfare of the said Company," so long as they were not contrary to those of England. Judicial appeals to the Crown were allowed, but without an implementing procedure this limitation on colonial authority was weak. Although boundary disputes continued for some while thereafter, they were legally settled by the charter in favor of Rhode Island.

The greatest significance of the Rhode Island Charter was the legal status it granted to the colony's "lively experiment" in religious freedom. In striking contrast to the establishmentarian practice of the day, the charter stated that "a flourishing civil state may stand and best be maintained among his Majesty's subjects with full liberty in religious concernments, and that true piety will give the greatest security for sovereignty and true loyalty." Following Rhode Island's practice, its charter extended religious freedom and legal toleration to all but atheists. "[N]o person within the said colony," it stated, "shall hereafter be any wise molested or called into question for any difference in opinion in matters of religion that does not disturb the civil peace of the colony. . . ." Toleration did not extend to the disorderly or the atheist because religious freedom was not "liberty to licentiousness and profaneness." Religious adherence in Rhode Island was to be a matter of personal conscience, not something compelled by a magistrate.

Overall, the terms of governance in the Rhode Island Charter were so favorable that it served as the fundamental law of the state until 1843. In granting legal establishment to the practices of the colony, the charter helped sunder the correlative relationship between temporal and religious authority thought necessary for civil security and well-being in the seventeenth century. More than a century before the U.S. Constitution, the Rhode Island Charter first formalized the freedom of conscience in the absence of religious uniformity that came to characterize the American experiment.

Jonathan R. Baer

Bibliography

Gaustad, Edwin S., *Liberty of Conscience: Roger Williams in America* (Grand Rapids, Mich.: Eerdmans, 1991).

———, *A Religious History of America* (New York: Harper and Row, 1966).

McLoughlin, William G., *Rhode Island: A Bicentennial History* (New York: Norton, 1978).

Noll, Mark A., *A History of Christianity in the United States and Canada* (Grand Rapids, Mich.: Eerdmans, 1992).

Sosin, J. M., *English America and the Restoration Monarchy of Charles II: Transatlantic Politics, Commerce, and Kinship* (Lincoln: University of Nebraska Press, 1980).

Valeri, Mark, "Puritanism and Civil Order in New England from the First Settlements to the Great Awakening," in John F. Wilson (ed.), *Church and State in America: A Bibliographic Guide*, vol. 1,

The Colonial and Early National Periods (New York: Glenwood, 1986), pp. 43–73.

Wilson, John F. (ed.), *Church and State in American History* (Boston: Heath, 1965).

Roemer v. Board of Public Works of Maryland 426 U.S. 736 (1976)

Roemer v. Board of Public Works of Maryland (1976) involved a First Amendment challenge to a Maryland provision for "annual noncategorical grants to . . . private colleges, including religiously affiliated institutions," as long as (1) "none of the state funds be utilized by an institution for sectarian purposes," (2) none of the institutions "award only seminarian or theological degrees," and (3) the state determines eligibility for state aid and audits institutional reports explaining the use of funds. The U.S. District Court for the District of Maryland held that the Establishment Clause of the First Amendment did not prohibit the aid statute.

The plaintiffs—"anti-aid" organizations and Maryland citizens like John C. Roemer, III—appealed to the Supreme Court, which in a 5-to-4 decision upheld the district court's finding. Justice Harry Blackmun, who announced the Court's judgment, expressed the view that the Maryland statute (1) had a secular purpose (to support higher education); (2) did not have the primary effect of advancing religion (the involved colleges were not "pervasively sectarian," and state aid was granted only for secular purposes); and (3) did not create "excessive entanglement" between church and state. The Court believed that the colleges performed "essentially secular educational functions" and that audits necessary for statutory compliance would be routine audits similar to normal college accreditation processes; aid did not pose a "substantial danger" of political divisiveness because the aided colleges, unlike church-affiliated grade schools, possessed a diverse student body and had obligations only to fiscal soundness and educational requirements, rather than to a church.

Justice Blackmun wrote the opinion of the Court, but only Chief Justice Burger and Justice Powell joined him. Justice White, joined by Justice Rehnquist, concurred in a separate opinion with the Court's result. Justice Brennan, joined by Justice Marshall, dissented in a separate opinion, as did both Justice Stewart and Justice Stevens.

Justice Blackmun began his opinion with a lecture on the necessary distinction between a scrupulous neutrality by the state "regarding religion and an impossible hermetic separation of the two." He noted the Court's past recognition that (1) "religious institutions need not be quarantined from public benefits that are neutrally available to all" and that (2) the state may sometimes "act in such a way that has the incidental effect of facilitating religious activity." He emphasized that the constitutional requirement of neutrality meant only that "the state must confine itself to secular objectives, . . . neither advance nor impede religious activity," and must avoid "such an intimate relationship with religious authority that it appears either to be sponsoring or to be excessively interfering with that authority."

These three stipulations—known as the *Lemon* test, from Chief Justice Burger's opinion in *Lemon v. Kurtzman* (1971)—determine at what point state or federal statutes violate the Establishment Clause. But this test, rather than providing a constitutional guideline, further muddied the legal waters and aroused confused debate by jurists, legislators, public groups, and citizens in the proliferating court cases involving "neutral" state aid to church-related institutions. In several other companion cases—including *Tilton v. Richardson* (1971), *Hunt v. McNair* (1973), and *Board of Education v. Allen* (1968)—the Court reached contrary results. Whereas in *Lemon* it found certain aid to church-related schools unconstitutional, the Court, on the same day it ruled in *Lemon,* held in *Tilton* that "neutral" aid to colleges for secular activities and facilities is permissible. The Court found in *Tilton, Hunt,* and *Allen* that the Constitution did not forbid all aid to religion, such as subsidies for textbooks for private or parochial grade schools or for building grants for religious colleges.

In *Roemer,* Blackmun and the dissenters (Brennan, joined by Marshall, Stewart, and Stevens) also referred, for opposite reasons and with contrasting interpretations, to three other companion cases—*Committee for Public Education and Religious Liberty v. Nyquist* (1973), *Levitt v. Committee for Public Education and Religious Liberty* (1973), and *Meek v. Pittenger* (1975)—that offered split decisions on the constitutionality of various types of state aid to church-affiliated secondary and elementary schools. The thrust of these decisions indicated the constitutionality of lending textbooks (but not instructional materials) to children attending church-related schools. In comparing cases involving colleges and grade schools, one finds that when the Supreme Court evaluates aid to colleges, there appears to be more willingness to allow aid and more flexibility in interpreting "advancement of religion," excessive entanglement, and "religiously-pervasive institutions."

In *Roemer* the Supreme Court found that the appellee Roman Catholic colleges were not "pervasively sectarian" because (1) they were institutionally autonomous, (2) they did not require compulsory chapel, (3) mandatory religion classes "only supplemented" a wide-ranging spectrum of liberal arts courses taught "without religious pressures," (4) they did not require classroom prayers, and (5) faculty and students were "chosen without regard to religion." The Court held that because the colleges were not "so permeated by religion that the secular side cannot be separated from the sectarian" and because the state statute prohibited sectarian use of funds earmarked for the colleges, state aid in this case would not serve to advance religion.

The key question for Blackmun, Burger, Powell, and the four dissenters was whether the monitoring of college compliance with the prohibition against using state funding for sectarian purposes created an "excessively entangling" church–state relationship. Blackmun, Burger, and Powell decided that there was no *excessive* entanglement, because audits to monitor compliance are no more entangling than are the inspections and audits incidental to the normal process of the colleges' accreditation by the state. In their view the risk of political divisiveness is "substantially less when the aided institution is not an elementary or secondary school, but a college, 'whose student constituency is not local but diverse and widely dispersed.'" This contrasts with the concern for the vulnerability of schoolchildren to peer and teacher influence that the Court expressed in *Lemon*.

Justice Byron White, joined by William Rehnquist, concurred with the Court's judgment in *Roemer*. White expressed his bewilderment at the "superfluous" entanglement prong of the *Lemon* test. In his view, "as long as there is a secular purpose, and as long as the primary effect of the legislation is neither to advance or inhibit religion, I see no reason—particularly in light of the sparse language of the Establishment Clause—to take the constitutional inquiry further." White's view expresses a concern about the "Catch-22" nature of the entanglement criterion, which he noted in his dissent in *Lemon:*

> The Court thus creates an insoluble paradox for the State and the parochial schools. The State cannot finance secular instruction if it permits religion to be taught in the same classroom; but if it exacts a promise that religion not be so taught—a promise the schools and its teachers are quite willing and on this record able to give—and enforces it, it is then entangled in the "no entanglement" aspect of the Court's Establishment Clause Jurisprudence.

Justice Brennan, the only Roman Catholic jurist on the Court, dissented from both the Blackmun majority position and the concurring position of White. Brennan expressed the view that the Maryland statute constituted direct aid to religion, advanced religion, and thus violated the Establishment Clause. He reminded his brethren that each of the institutions in question was church-affiliated or church-related, that state subsidies of religious activities entangled church and state, and that a public subsidy by nature requires "too close a proximity of government to the subsidized sectarian institutions and in my view creates real dangers of the 'secularization of a creed.'"

Justice John Paul Stevens agreed with Brennan, and he added his favorite homily regarding "the pernicious tendency of a state subsidy to tempt religious schools to compromise their religious mission without wholly abandoning it." Justice Potter Stewart, normally an advocate of governmental accommodation of religion, dissented in *Roemer* because of the nature of the compulsory theological courses, which were taught solely by clerics of the affiliated church and were intended to encourage religious experience in a particular faith. He agreed with the dissenting district court judge, who wrote that state money given to these religious institutions would be used to advance religion, "no matter the vigilance to avoid it."

The division of the justices over the extent to which a state may accommodate religion in its efforts to enhance education resurfaced one year later in *Wolman v. Walter* (1977), where the Court split on a wide variety of issues. In *Wolman* the Court found state provision of textbooks and health and diagnostic services to students attending church-related elementary and secondary schools constitutional, but the provision of maps and field trips was obviously impermissible. In another pass at clarifying church–state boundaries, the Court held, in *Witters v. Washington Department of Services for the Blind* (1986), that state rehabilitation aid to a blind student at a Christian college who was studying to become a pastor did not violate the Establishment Clause.

Were these landmark refinements in judicial interpretation? Or were the dissenters' calls to abandon all aid harbingers of a future turn to the principle of absolute separation of church and state? May the state aid colleges, but not grade schools? Is there a consistent pattern in church–state cases? The plethora of such cases in the 1980s and 1990s suggests a public and court system still searching for an acceptable interpretation of the religion clauses of the First Amendment. In *Lee v. Weisman* (1992) the Supreme Court decided that a nondenominational blessing at a high school ceremony violated the Constitution.

The question remains: Does government aid that crosses paths in a neutral way with the church entail government endorsement of religion? Justice Blackmun, in his exegesis on religion cases in *Roemer,* offered a useful reminder of the inevitable entanglement of church and state in America:

> A system of government that makes itself felt as pervasively as ours could hardly be expected never to cross paths with the church. In fact, our State and Federal Governments impose certain burdens on, and impact certain benefits to, virtually all our activities, and religious activity is not an exception. The Court has enforced a scrupulous neutrality by the State, as among religions, and also as between religious and other activities, but a hermetic separation of the two is an impossibility it has never required.

L. Sue Hulett

Bibliography

Eastland, Terry, *Religious Liberty in the Supreme Court: Cases That Define the Debate over Church and State* (New York: Free Press, 1992).

Levy, Leonard, *The Establishment Clause* (New York: Macmillan, 1986).

Cases Cited

Board of Education v. Allen, 392 U.S. 236 (1968).

Committee for Public Education and Religious Liberty v. Nyquist, 413 U.S. 756 (1973).

Hunt v. McNair, 413 U.S. 734 (1973).

Lee v. Weisman, 505 U.S. 577 (1992).

Lemon v. Kurtzman, 403 U.S. 602 (1971).

Levitt v. Committee for Public Education and Religious Liberty, 413 U.S. 472 (1973).

Meek v. Pittenger, 421 U.S. 349 (1975).

Roemer v. Board of Public Works of Maryland, 426 U.S. 736 (1976).

Tilton v. Richardson, 403 U.S. 672 (1971).

Witters v. Washington Department of Services for the Blind, 474 U.S. 481 (1986).

Wolman v. Walter, 433 U.S. 229 (1977).

S

Salem Witch Trials

Puritan Christianity accepted literally the writings of both the Old and New Testaments. In both books lay an implicit belief in Satan, an explicit acknowledgment that he used human beings as vehicles of evil, and a firm conviction that the punishment for his willing emissaries should be strong. Exodus 22:18 made it clear: "You shall not suffer a witch to live."

Christianity from its inception had emphasized the reality of Satan, of his nonhuman servants called devils, and of his human instruments of destruction called witches. Some humans permitted Satan to inhabit their bodies, used black powers for deviate purposes, and cast spells on their fellow humans.

Witchery in the Old World

Throughout the Middle Ages, myriad social crises brought accusations of witchery, trials of accused witches, and executions of those convicted. Most witches were women—twenty for every man so accused and convicted. According to medieval theology, women were the weaker sex mentally, physically, and even spiritually. They were, like their mother, Eve, more susceptible to temptation than men. Since they were more wanton, they were more easily seduced by Satan's promises of forbidden pleasures than men. It seemed only natural that there were to be more female witches.

There were fewer witch trials in England than in other European countries, probably because English common law forbade the use of torture to gain confessions—the chief means of making people admit to witchcraft. Torture was permitted in England only by royal prerogative, and most English kings refused to license ecclesiastical courts to use it. Although the English believed in witchcraft, they considered it a misdemeanor, and no law making it punishable by death came to England until 1563.

The first English witch law was passed during the reign of King Henry VIII (1509–1547). It was aimed primarily at confidence artists who, by claiming supernatural powers, bilked naive taxpayers of their money. Henry's law said nothing about demon possession or black magic. It assumed only that some people possessed extraordinary powers and that the powers could be used for good or evil. Henry's witch law was repealed under his son, Edward VI (1547–1553).

In 1563, during the reign of Elizabeth I (1558–1603), England adopted its first witch law suggesting a demonic threat to Christian society. Radical Protestants who had been exiled to the Continent under Queen Mary (1553–1558) had spent years in Calvinist cities where the Bible was taken literally and where belief in witchcraft was regularly confirmed by trials and executions. Calvinists, who would call themselves Puritans in England, seemed even then to be the most sensitive of all Christian groups to witchcraft; and the influence of their preaching in and around London after they returned from exile whipped the frenzy that led to the law. Puritanism would dominate Scotland from 1565, rule England from 1649 to 1660, and educate the New England mind for a decade after 1620. All three countries would fear witches. Still, Elizabeth's law was only slightly more stringent than her father's. Witchcraft was a felony only if it caused some innocent person harm; it was a capital crime only if it caused death.

King James I (1603–1625) gave witchcraft a more central, sinister place in British society and law. He brought with him from Scotland his widely read book *Demonologie,* in which he defined witchcraft as the work of Satan and called for witches to be executed. He believed that he had himself been the target in 1590 of a witches' assassination plot. By drowning a Christened cat, a group of self-admitted witches had tried to cause a storm that would sink the ship bringing James and his new bride from Denmark. James had barely survived the storm and thereafter dedicated himself to the eradication of this menace from his realm.

James's Witchcraft Act (1604) carried heavy penalties, including death, for witchery; but it also demanded strict proof of guilt. Judges were required to investigate and substantiate all accusations, and in a number of cases James himself reviewed the evidence, at times overturning convictions. He was particularly skeptical of eager witnesses for the prosecution, always demanded that their motives be examined, and was himself quick to spot deceit.

Each of James's royal Stuart descendants was less interested in and more lenient toward witchcraft than the one before, and the last execution for the crime in Britain was at Exeter in 1684. The law of 1604 was repealed in 1736.

Witchery in the New World

As witch fever declined in the Old World, it increased in the New World, particularly in Puritan New England, where over 90 percent of the American colonial witch trials were held. Most of these were conducted in Massachusetts, along what was then the western frontier, in times of social crisis.

American witchery for some reason had little of the Old World's talk of "coupling" with Satan, few instances of sexual exhibitionism, and a somewhat limited demonology. In Puritan America it was Satan himself who possessed people, used them, harmed them. Those who were possessed had convulsive seizures, exhibited superhuman strength, displayed curious patterns of speech, and gave off grunts and grimaces; but rarely did they do anything that Puritan society would find lewd. There were in America, as in Europe, more female than male witches—about 4 to 1—but the ratio here was less exaggerated, perhaps because in America women were too valuable to waste in the European fashion.

Ironically, the "signs" of demon possession in seventeenth-century New England were almost identical to the "gifts" of the Holy Spirit in eighteenth-century New England. The Great Awakening of the century following the witch trials reinterpreted the phenomena, classifying them as divine rather than satanic. Possession seems to have been a Rorschach test for religious leaders to interpret as they saw fit. It seems equally true that the witches of New England were scapegoats for a society in real trouble. Salem Village, scene of the most famous trials, serves as the prime example.

Salem Village, eight miles from the town of Salem, had become an independent parish only twenty years before the witchcraft panic of 1692. A divided and contentious church had expelled two pastors and was in a violent disagreement over the status of the current one, the Reverend Samuel Parris. Property disputes, fires, an outbreak of smallpox, and several Indian raids had left the village demoralized. The economy was changing, causing financial insecurity, with some citizens rapidly moving up and down the social ladder. England's "Bloodless Revolution" of 1688 meant that Massachusetts was about to get a new charter and governor, and there was a new tax structure that no one liked. To add spice, sermons about witchcraft had been multiplying in reaction to a witch panic in Hartford in 1662 and another in Boston in 1688, when the prominent preacher Cotton Mather had exorcised four women of the Godwin family. Mather was chief among the preachers who in 1692 were saying that Satan seemed bent on destroying God's chosen people.

In January 1692 the Reverend Parris's daughter Elizabeth and her cousin Abigail Williams began exhibiting strange behavior. They had been learning palmistry from a Carribean slave named Tituba—trying to see into the future, hoping for a glimpse of their future husbands—when in a makeshift crystal ball (an egg floating in a bowl of water) they saw what they interpreted to be a coffin and became distraught. When questioned about their emotional outbursts, they accused

Tituba and then two local women, Sarah Good and Sarah Osborne, of bewitching them. Tituba readily and dramatically confessed to familiarity with Satan, and the three women were charged with witchcraft.

In other places such arrests had ended the panic; but in Salem Village it did not. These and other girls continued to have fits and make accusations, and by June some 142 people had been arrested. At this time the newly appointed governor, William Phips, arrived to take over his duties; but he went almost immediately to western Massachusetts to oversee operations against the Indians, after appointing a court to decide the witch issue. Between June and the end of September, some nineteen men and women and two dogs were hanged as witches. Another man, Giles Corey, was "pressed" to death with weights in a futile attempt to gain a confession so that he could be tried. Fifty-five had confessed to witchcraft—many but not all of these having been found guilty and pressured to meet their God with a clear social conscience—and 150 were in jail awaiting either trial or execution.

It is possible, by looking carefully at the persons hanged for witchcraft in Massachusetts, to draw a profile of the Salem witch. She was typically an older woman. She was often not part of a patriarchal family, too abrasive to be considered a lady, and previously accused of crimes. She could either be destitute or independently wealthy—either way she was a misfit and a challenge to the Puritan order of God and man.

She was usually considered an "outsider," in the beginning merely outside polite society, then later geographically outside as well. In the end some 82 percent of the accused lived outside Salem Village, many in the hated Salem Town. Of the villagers, the accusers lived west of the Ipswich Road, and those accused lived east of it. The accused were also outside the mainstream. Recent economic reversals had shaken the social ladder; and while the destitute were considered drains on society, the newly rich were considered arrogant. Both suffered.

Finally, since Mr. Parris's relatives were among the chief accusers, those accused of being witches were mostly anti-Parris. The preacher in turn used the scare not only to be rid of his enemies but also to fill a church whose attendance had dropped off significantly in recent months. The "possessed" girls, including Elizabeth Parris, were never considered as innocent victims of a conspiracy by forces that hated God's minister and his family.

Yet even at the height of the witch fever, certain troubling questions were raised. No one doubted the reality of Satan or the fact of demon possession, and no one doubted that those who confessed were guilty. It was the ones who refused to confess and were hanged purely on the testimony of others—testimony based in large measure on "spectral" evidence of having seen in a dream or vision the accused doing witchy things—that troubled thoughtful persons. Among the first to question such testimony were Dutch Calvinists from New York.

Cotton Mather's own father, the venerable Increase, was one clergyman to call for stronger proof of guilt. In that summer of carnage in 1692, he set down guidelines for the court to follow. Confession was the strongest proof, he said, followed by the testimony of trustworthy witnesses. He divided "physical manifestation" evidence into two types: supernatural strength, the inability to recite prayers correctly, and the "tit" were all strong evidence; but mere anger, foul appearance, and a tendency to mischief were too weak to support conviction.

Increase Mather also speculated that if Satan were causing the disturbance, he should himself be on trial. Indeed, could his accessories be tried without his witness? This bit of legal and theological wit of course called into question the whole rationale of the trials. Further, he said—perhaps to shock accusers into silence—why try only the accused? Why not hold the girls at least partially responsible for their affliction?

The most telling argument against the hysteria, however, was Mather's question about the use of "spectral" evidence: dreams, visions, even sightings of the accused performing demonic acts. This had been the deciding factor in many of the convictions, and this was little more than taking one person's life on the testimony of another. Humans can lie, and they can be mistaken. Satan can take any form, even that of an innocent person, with or without the person's will. With this last point, Mather used the doctrine of Satan, which he did not doubt, to question the reality of witchery.

At the end of September Governor Phips returned from the western frontier to find

Massachusetts Colony in chaos. After studying the records, he concluded that Satan, whom he seems not to have doubted either, was using the panic to play havoc with society. On October 12 he forbade further arrests and executions. He excluded spectral evidence from the deliberations, and he dismissed the hanging court he had appointed in June. He saw to it that the forty-nine persons being held for trial were acquitted, and he gave the three already convicted reprieves. No one else was ever hanged for witchcraft in Massachusetts.

The Shadow of Salem Village

There were only a few more cases in all the colonies. The last was in Maryland in 1712. In 1697 the hanging court, including Judge Samuel Sewell and one of the accusers, admitted they had been in error and asked families of the executed to forgive them.

With the Awakening of the 1720s and the subsequent decline of Puritan hegemony in New England, interest in and obsession with witches quickly declined. New religious leaders called "possession" holy, not demonic. New England's improving economy brought a social stability that mitigated against such panics. The witch trials became a historical embarrassment, and in 1752 Salem Village changed its name to Danvers. Legally the episode lived on, not only as a lesson in excess but also in the area of evidentiary proof. We have had later "witch" trials—notably, the communist hunts of the 1950s—but the shadow of Salem Village hovers over Americans to warn them of what happens when social insecurity threatens to set aside the rules of evidence in order to rid a society of its "dangerous" citizens. It also warns, in a more general and far-reaching way, that the state runs great risks when it tries to meddle in controversies and/or prosecute "crimes" that are essentially religious in nature.

James T. Baker

Bibliography

Boyer, Paul, and Stephen Nissenbaum, *Salem Possessed* (Cambridge, Mass.: Harvard University Press, 1974).

Hole, Christina, *Witchcraft in England* (Totowa, N.J.: Rowman and Littlefield, 1977).

Karlsen, Carol, *The Devil in the Shape of a Woman* (New York: Norton, 1987).

Konig, David, *Law and Society in Puritan Massachusetts: Essex County, 1629–1692* (Chapel Hill: University of North Carolina Press, 1979).

Levin, David, *What Happened in Salem?* (New York: Harcourt, Brace, 1960).

Weisman, Richard, *Witchcraft, Magic, and Religion in 17th Century Massachusetts* (Boston: University of Massachusetts Press, 1985).

Salvation Army, Free-Speech Fights, and Religious Liberty

Between 1880 and 1900, the Salvation Army conducted one of the most widespread but little-remembered civil disobedience campaigns in American history. The issue was the right to assemble and speak in the open air. In pursuit of this right, "Salvationists" across the country willfully broke the law and went to jail. The resulting court cases were among the first in American history to ask appellate judges to decide whether the powers of city governments to regulate streets and parks outweighed the rights of citizens to assemble and speak there.

The Salvation Army, founded in England in 1865, invaded the United States in 1880. Its blend of evangelical zeal and social welfare work proved potent, and the group grew quickly. A key to the Army's rapid expansion was the open-air prayer meeting. Salvationists used these outdoor gatherings to reach the neglected classes who attended no regular church. "[W]e do not wait for them to come to us," one Army officer explained, "but we go to them."

Salvationist open-air meetings, however, often ran afoul of city rules governing the use of streets and parks. Most such measures were fairly new. Before the mid-nineteenth century, American cities exercised very little regulatory control over their public venues. Private groups and mobs, not government officials, most powerfully regulated access to open-air forums before the Civil War. But by the time the Salvation Army appeared in the 1880s, American cities had begun to ban unlicensed open-air meetings.

The Salvation Army's urge to practice its open-air ministry collided head on with the new municipal resolve to control the streets. The result was, in the Army's words, "Arrests! Arrests! Arrests!" Throughout the 1880s and 1890s, hardly an issue of the group's weekly journal passed without reporting on the most recent movement of Salvationist men and women "In and Out of the Calaboose."

Salvationists viewed the issue of street speaking as they viewed most other issues—through religious lenses. They formulated the matter in the following way: God bade them to carry out their open-air ministry; those who inhibited this work were doing the bidding of the devil; therefore, to violate open-air bans was to defy evil and to glorify God. This perspective not only left Salvation Army organizers willing to "march to prison or anywhere Jesus would call them"; it also shaped the sorts of legal arguments Army members made once they got to court. Unlike most subsequent open-air litigants, who focused on the freedoms of speech and assembly, the Salvation Army stressed the constitutional freedom of religion.

Army litigants won about half their appellate court battles. State judges in Salvationist victories agreed to strike down open-air ordinances for a variety of reasons. For instance, in *In re Frazee* (Mich., 1886) Michigan's highest court struck down an open-air ordinance from Grand Rapids on the grounds that it was unreasonably discriminatory. The Supreme Court of Kansas found in *Anderson v. Wellington* (Kans., 1888) that a similar measure, being "an abridgment of the rights of the people," illegally contravened "custom." In *Chicago v. Trotter* (Ill., 1891) Illinois judges held that Chicago's open-air ordinance unlawfully deprived Illinois citizens of their constitutional right to pursue "their own happiness."

In contrast, Salvationist arguments regarding religious liberty failed to win judicial approval. The opinion of Chief Justice Morton of Massachusetts in *Commonwealth v. Plaisted* (1889) was typical:

> The provisions of the Constitution which are relied on, securing freedom of religious worship, were not designed to prevent the adoption of reasonable rules and regulations for the use of streets and public places.

Even judges who sided with Salvationist litigants agreed with Chief Justice Morton that open-air ordinances did not infringe on constitutional freedoms of religion.

Around the turn of the twentieth century, the Salvation Army's war with the nation's municipal governments came to an end. So tenacious had the Army's open-air siege been (and so innocuous had the group in the end proved itself to be) that, after two decades of combat, American mayors, police chiefs, and city councils simply surrendered. They did not repeal their cities' open-air ordinances, as the Army wished, but they did the next best thing: They carved out enforcement loopholes through which Salvationists and, in some instances, other religious speakers could pass. Thus, in 1903, Denver added a caveat to its ban on unlicensed street meetings excusing "religious bodies" from the measure's provisions. Four years later, Minneapolis followed suit by announcing that, henceforth, permits would be required for all outdoor meetings "except those of the Salvation Army." By 1921 the American Civil Liberties Union (ACLU) reported that the Salvation Army was allowed to hold its open-air meetings "almost everywhere" without the permits required of other groups. The burden of fighting for open-air speech rights had fallen from the shoulders of the Salvation Army, to be picked up first by the Socialist Party, then by Industrial Workers of the World, and later—following World War I—by the American Civil Liberties Union, the Congress of Industrial Organizations, the Jehovah's Witnesses, and others.

John Wertheimer

Cases Cited

Anderson v. Wellington, 19 P. 719 (Kans. 1888).

Chicago v. Trotter, 26 N.E. 359 (Ill. 1891).

Commonwealth v. Plaisted, 19 N.E. 224 (Mass. 1889).

In re Frazee, 30 N.W. 72 (Mich. 1886).

Santos v. Holy Roman Catholic Apostolic Church.

See OVERSEAS POSSESSIONS OF THE UNITED STATES AND RELIGIOUS LIBERTY

Scalia, Antonin (1936–)

Justice Antonin Scalia is the first Italian American member of the Supreme Court. He was appointed to the Court by President Ronald Reagan in 1986, when Chief Justice Warren E. Burger retired and President

Reagan elevated Justice William Rehnquist to chief justice. At the time of his appointment to the Supreme Court, Justice Scalia had been a judge on the U.S. Court of Appeals for the District of Columbia since 1982. Before then he had an outstanding career in academia (professor at the University of Chicago from 1977 to 1982 and at the University of Virginia from 1967 to 1971); in government (assistant attorney general, Office of Legal Counsel, U.S. Department of Justice, from 1974 to 1977; chairman, Administrative Conference of the United States, from 1972 to 1974; general counsel, Office of Telecommunications Policy, Executive Office of the President, from 1971 to 1972); and in private practice (Jones, Day, Cockley and Reavis, from 1960 to 1967).

Although Justice Scalia authored only one majority opinion relating to religion from the time of his appointment through the 1992–1993 term, that opinion, in *Employment Division, Department of Human Resources of Oregon v. Smith* (1990), instituted a major change in free exercise jurisprudence. Moreover, in several dissents and concurrences in Establishment Clause cases, Justice Scalia has constituted a consistent voice and vote to lessen the restrictions of that clause on government action that accommodates or furthers religion.

Smith and Establishment Clause Jurisprudence

Smith was the second of two cases involving certain Native Americans in Oregon who had been fired from their jobs as drug counselors because they had ingested peyote during Native American Church religious ceremonies. When they filed for unemployment compensation, it was denied because they had been fired for cause. They challenged this denial through the state administrative and court system on the grounds that the denial of unemployment compensation under these circumstances amounted to an infringement of their free exercise rights under the First Amendment to the Constitution. They cited a line of cases overturning denials of unemployment compensation where the reason for the person's losing his or her job or not finding a new one was the result of the exercise of religious beliefs: *Sherbert v. Verner* ([1963] refusal to accept work on Saturday), *Thomas v. Review Board* ([1981] refusal to work on weapons of war), *Hobbie v. Unemployment Appeals Board* ([1987] refusal to work on Saturday), and *Frazee v. Illinois Department of Employment Security* ([1989] refusal to accept work on Sunday). Following this line of authority, the Oregon Supreme Court required payment of unemployment compensation.

In its first encounter with the case, in *Employment Division, Department of Human Resources of Oregon v. Smith* (1988), the U.S. Supreme Court distinguished Smith's claim on the ground that none of the earlier cases involved religious activity which itself was illegal. If ingestion of peyote by Native Americans during religious ceremonies was illegal in Oregon (the Court noted that there was by regulation an exception from the federal drug laws for Native American religious ceremonies), and if it was constitutionally permissible to make such activity unlawful, then the Supreme Court stated that unemployment compensation would not be required. But the Court did not wish to decide the difficult constitutional question of the state's power to make such conduct illegal until it was clear that the Oregon statute did, in fact, make it illegal. Because the Oregon court simply had not considered the criminality of the underlying conduct under Oregon law in its decision, the Supreme Court remanded the case to the Oregon court for that determination.

The Oregon Supreme Court concluded that the Oregon criminal statute contained no exception for Native American religious ceremonies, but that to fail to make such an exception violated the Free Exercise Clause of the First Amendment of the U.S. Constitution. Accordingly, again the Oregon court ordered unemployment compensation to be paid. The U.S. Supreme Court reversed in the decision authored by Justice Scalia.

Before the U.S. Supreme Court the question was squarely placed: Did the Free Exercise Clause require an exception for Native American religious ceremonies from the generally applicable criminal laws prohibiting the use of certain drugs, including peyote? At least since *Sherbert v. Verner,* (1963) the Court had articulated a test to answer that type of question. Was the state's interest in regulating the conduct in question a compelling interest, and, if so, was the regulation narrowly tailored to achieve that interest? If the answer to both questions was in the affirmative, no exception was required under the Free Exercise Clause.

Justice Scalia's opinion, in which four other members of the Court concurred, rejected this test. Justice Scalia distinguished between two different types of laws that would burden the free exercise of religion: one type would restrict certain activities *because* they were religious; the other would restrict certain activities for legitimate purposes but would also incidentally affect those religious activities within the terms of the generic restriction. Only the first, according to Justice Scalia's opinion, would implicate the Free Exercise Clause. Just as generally applicable tax and antitrust laws may be applied to newspapers despite the Press Clause of the First Amendment, Justice Scalia argued, generally applicable laws—when the object is not to burden religious activities—may be applied to persons even if they interfere with the exercise of religious beliefs. In support of this argument, the opinion asserted that in over a century of free exercise jurisprudence the Court had never held that religious beliefs excused a person from compliance with an otherwise valid law prohibiting conduct that the state is free to regulate. Scalia argued that only when a free exercise claim was combined with other constitutional claims, such as free speech or privacy rights, had the Court ever barred application of a neutral, generally applicable law to religiously motivated conduct. And in the Oregon peyote case, Scalia argued, there was no supplemental constitutional claim.

A Distaste for Balancing Tests

Moreover, Justice Scalia's opinion continued, the balancing test outlined in *Sherbert* (requiring a narrowly tailored law with a compelling government interest) had effect only in unemployment compensation cases and nowhere else. This might be explained by the fact that the unemployment compensation decision necessarily involves assessment of the particular circumstances behind someone's unemployment, thereby lending itself to individualized considerations, including individual exceptions. Whatever the explanation, the opinion held that the *Sherbert* test is no longer applicable to generally applicable criminal laws.

Justice O'Connor wrote for herself and three justices to take issue with the majority opinion. While she ultimately concluded that the First Amendment did not require an exception from Oregon's criminal law for the sacramental use of peyote, she was unwilling to abandon the traditional compelling interest test. She emphasized that the majority were acting inconsistently with precedent, and she took pains to rebut the majority's assertion to the contrary.

Justice Scalia's analysis in *Smith* is an example of his distaste for balancing tests in constitutional law. His preference is for bright-line rules. The problem with balancing tests from his perspective is that they do not adequately guide actors and judges regarding the proper outcomes. Instead, balancing tests almost invariably involve ad hoc determinations that reflect the decisionmaker's individual preferences rather than constitutionally constrained decisions. Consequently, Justice Scalia tends to favor narrowing the field of activities protected by the Constitution and then protecting more absolutely the activities that remain within the protected area. This has been particularly noticeable in the area of free speech. For example, in *Barnes v. Glen Theatre* (1991) Justice Scalia agreed that a statute prohibiting public nudity was constitutional, even as applied to nude dancing. Unlike the plurality, however, which used traditional First Amendment analysis to reach this conclusion, Justice Scalia expressed his view that the statute was a generally applicable criminal law (like the statute in *Smith*) not directed at expression and therefore simply did not raise a First Amendment issue. Nevertheless, when a statute is directed at restricting expression, Justice Scalia is most protective of speech, as his votes to overturn flag defamation laws and his majority opinion striking down a "hate speech" law (*R.A.V. v. City of St. Paul* [1992]) show. Similarly, in the case of *Church of the Lukumi Babalu Aye, Inc. and Ernesto Pichardo v. City of Hialeah* (1993), where the city had passed a series of ordinances aimed at suppressing animal sacrifices conducted by adherents of the Santería religion, Justice Scalia voted with the majority striking down the ordinances as violative of the Free Exercise Clause, because they were not neutral and generally applicable.

Relaxing the Restrictions of the Establishment Clause

Justice Scalia's jurisprudence in the Establishment Clause area is revealed in a number of dissents and concurrences. These exhibit a general tendency to relax the restrictions imposed over the last half century on government action that may further religion. This view stems from a belief that the First Amendment does not mandate government neutrality toward religion generally. Rather, the First Amendment, by singling out religious activity for particular protection, indicates a constitutional approval of governmental solicitude toward religion generally.

In *Texas Monthly, Inc. v. Bullock* (1989), for example, the Supreme Court struck down a Texas statute that provided a sales tax exemption for religious periodicals. Texas justified the exemption as an accommodation of religion either required or supported by the Free Exercise Clause, but five justices found that this religious exemption violated the Establishment Clause, and one justice found that it violated the Press Clause of the First Amendment by discriminating among publications on the basis of their content. Justice Scalia, joined by Chief Justice Rehnquist and Justice Kennedy, dissented. He noted that it was routine in America for religious organizations to be exempt from various tax laws that otherwise would be applicable. In *Walz v. Tax Commission of New York City* (1970), for example, the Supreme Court had upheld a property tax exemption for religious properties used solely for religious worship. Because the exemption did no more than accommodate religion by lifting a generally applicable burden from religious organizations, the Court argued that it did not violate the Establishment Clause.

In *Lee v. Weisman* (1992) a high school student challenged a school-sponsored graduation ceremony prayer. The Court held that the prayer, which was presented by a rabbi who had been chosen by the principal, involved official state sponsorship of a prayer under circumstances that effectively were coercive and accordingly violated the Establishment Clause. Justice Scalia dissented in an opinion joined by Chief Justice Rehnquist and Justices White and Thomas. Justice Scalia traced the history of nondenominational prayers in public ceremonies from George Washington's first inaugural address to George Bush's 1988 inaugural address. In particular, he stressed the fact that prayers and benedictions at public school graduation exercises are traditional. He took issue with the notion that the prayers here were coercive, inasmuch as the graduation ceremony itself was voluntary and no one was required to recite or participate in the prayer. Only coercion by force of law and threat of penalty, he maintained, is prohibited by the Establishment Clause. Here, to ban the ceremonial prayer frustrated "the expression of gratitude to God that a majority of the community wishes to make."

In Service of Conservative Issues

In *Lamb's Chapel v. Center Moriches Union Free School District* (1993) Justice Scalia revealed his judicial activism in service of conservative issues. He concurred in the Court's outcome, overturning the school district's refusal to allow a religious group to use the school's facilities after hours on the same basis as other community groups, but he could not join the Court's rationale, which utilized the *Lemon v. Kurtzman* (1971) three-pronged test for determining Establishment Clause violations. Rather, joined by Justice Thomas, Justice Scalia called for the explicit overruling of *Lemon.* One of Justice Scalia's complaints with *Lemon* is that its test is indeterminate, or as he put it, a "geometry of crooked lines and wavering shapes," with the result that actors and judges make ad hoc decisions. Another of Justice Scalia's objections to *Lemon* is its condemnation of governmental endorsement of religion in general.

Justice Scalia has made clear that he aligns himself with Chief Justice Rehnquist's view, most fully expressed in *Wallace v. Jaffree* (1985), that the Establishment Clause was intended to bar government from creating a national religion or from preferring one religion over another and was not intended to keep government from accommodating or furthering religion in general. Justice Scalia has also been noteworthy in his criticism of attempts to determine the *motivation* of legislators, as opposed to the purpose of a law as reflected in its language. This has come up in the area of religion when attempting to determine if a particular statute has the purpose of furthering or hindering a religion or religions. In *Edwards v. Aguillard* (1987), for example, the Court found unconstitutional a Louisiana law that prohibited the teaching of evolution in the public schools unless it was accompanied by instruction in the theory of "creation science." The Court found that the law had the primary or preeminent purpose of advancing a particular religious view about the origin of the universe.

Justice Scalia's dissent in *Edwards,* with which Chief Justice Rehnquist concurred, generally took issue with the majority's *factual* conclusion that the purpose of the law was to advance religion. Whereas the majority had reached this conclusion because they believed that the motive of the legislators had been to advance a particular religious view about the creation of the universe, Justice Scalia took issue with the conception that the subjective motivation of legislators could be discovered or, even if it could be discovered, how that might be relevant, separate from the objectively stated purpose and the actual effect of the law. Justice Scalia explored the language of the statute and found that by its terms it never referred to religion or religious beliefs. He noted that "creation science" was defined as "the scientific evidences for creation and inferences from those scientific evidences." He considered the legislative history at some length, pointing out how the testimony before the legislative committees indicated that the purpose of the law was to educate students that there was more than one *scientific* theory to account for the beginning of life. Moreover, the proponent of the legislation repeatedly denied that he was trying to advance a particular religious doctrine. He also noted that the express statement of purpose of the statute ("academic freedom") did not include any religious purpose.

Similarly, in *Church of Lukumi Babalu Aye* Justice Scalia joined in most of the majority's opinion finding that the City of Hialeah's ordinances were directed against the practice of the Santería religion, but he dissented from that portion of the Court's opinion that relied on the perceived subjective motivation of the lawmakers to conclude that the ordinances were not neutral and generally applicable.

William Funk

Bibliography

Almanac of the Federal Judiciary (Englewood Cliffs, N.J.: Prentice-Hall, published annually).

Cases Cited

Barnes v. Glen Theatre, 501 U.S. 560 (1991).

Church of the Lukumi Babalu Aye, Inc. and Ernesto Pichardo v. City of Hialeah, 508 U.S. 520 (1993).

Edwards v. Aguillard, 482 U.S. 578 (1987).

Employment Division, Department of Human Resources of Oregon v. Smith, 494 U.S. 872 (1990).

Employment Division, Department of Human Resources of Oregon v. Smith, 485 U.S. 660 (1988).

Frazee v. Illinois Department of Employment Security, 489 U.S. 829 (1989).

Hobbie v. Unemployment Appeals Board, 480 U.S. 136 (1987).

Lamb's Chapel v. Center Moriches Union Free School District, 508 U.S. 384 (1993).

Lee v. Weisman, 505 U.S. 577 (1992).

Lemon v. Kurtzman, 403 U.S. 602 (1971).

R.A.V. v. City of St. Paul, 505 U.S. 377 (1992).

Sherbert v. Verner, 374 U.S. 398 (1963).

Texas Monthly, Inc. v. Bullock, 489 U.S. 1 (1989).

Thomas v. Review Board, 450 U.S. 707 (1981).

Wallace v. Jaffree, 472 U.S. 38 (1985).

Walz v. Tax Commission of New York City, 397 U.S 664 (1970).

Schisms and Church Ownership in the Early Nineteenth Century

Under the traditional, congregational form of government there was a unity of the congregational church with the congregational society. The church concerned itself with the spiritual concerns of the parish, with the worship of God; the society concerned itself with the secular activities of the parish and the control of church property. Under congregational principles each church was also autonomous, having the power to call its own officers.

In the early years of the nineteenth century that unity began to break up under challenge from a liberal, Unitarian revolt against the conservative, Congregational churches. The religious divisions were exacerbated by parallel political divisions, with the traditionalists tending to side with the Federalists against the Jeffersonians. By 1836 more than eighty congregations had split, with almost four thousand members withdrawing from their congregations. The splits were concentrated in eastern Massachusetts, where the Unitarians had their only significant success.

Characteristic of the disputes was the controversy in the First Church of Dedham,

Massachusetts. That schism began in 1818, when the church's minister, Joshua Bates, announced his resignation to become the president of Middlebury College. Rather than follow the usual custom of allowing the church to vote first, the parish selected its new "teacher," Alvan Lamson—a recent graduate of Harvard, which was the hub of Unitarian activity. The church rejected Lamson, prompting the parish to request a special council of churches. After the council sided with the parish, the conservative members of the church withdrew and established a separate meetinghouse across the street.

With two congregations now claiming to be First Church, a dispute soon developed over the right to possess certain church property. The Supreme Judicial Court of Massachusetts decision by Chief Justice Isaac Parker in *Baker v. Fales* (Mass., 1821) was the most influential of a number of opinions dealing with similar conflicts. The court followed this precedent in *Stebbins v. Jennings* (Mass., 1830) and in *Oakes v. Hill* (Mass., 1830). For a later decision rejecting the conclusions in Massachusetts, see *Holt v. Downs* (N.H., 1877), in which Chief Justice Charles Doe of the Supreme Court of New Hampshire expressly rejected the Massachusetts precedents.

In *Baker* the members who had voted for Lamson (Unitarians) sued those who had withdrawn (Congregationalists), seeking recovery of various items of church property. Arguing the case for the Unitarian parish was Massachusetts Solicitor General Daniel Davis; opposing him was Daniel Webster, for the more conservative Congregationalists. Although the matter is subject to dispute, the court accepted that the departing members constituted a majority of the congregation.

Writing for a largely Unitarian bench, Chief Justice Parker affirmed the decision of the jury in favor of the minority, Unitarian faction. In so doing, Parker clearly wrote from within a tradition in which there was a close link between church and society. That is, nothing in the opinion suggested that there should be a separation of church and state; nothing hinted at the impropriety of a civil court's deciding a question of ecclesiastical law. Instead, Parker accepted that a local community should have the right to call its own minister, or "teacher," even over the objection of the local church congregation. In so doing, however, Parker stood on its head the earlier understanding in New England: What had once been a society in which the church governed civil organization was now becoming a society in which the civil organization—the parish—could control the church. Parker's opinion was also part of the emerging debate about a distinction between what was properly public and private. From a virtual identity between church and society was emerging a separate public society that undertook responsibilities once left to the church.

As a legal matter, the issue focused on the status of donated property. Under the relevant statutes, the church had no corporate status that would have allowed it to own property; the deacons held any property in trust. Parker took the point further to conclude that a church had no "legal character" apart from a connection with some other society, in particular, a parish. Davis had argued that the property belonged to the church in trust for the local parish; Webster argued that the property belonged to the church as an ecclesiastical body without the trust for the parish. After an examination of the various provisions in the deeds, Parker concluded that all the donors possessed a single intention: that the property was "to be used for religious purposes" and that the church itself "acquired no legal estate or personal interest therein." He accepted the historical unity of the church and the society; he thus concluded that even a donation to "the church" in earlier years meant a donation to the society with which the church was identical. To allow a particular congregation to take the donations from that society and dedicate them to a narrower group would be to destroy the original intention of the donors. In other words, a part of a congregation could not withdraw from the church and take property with it.

Parker also relied on the Massachusetts Declaration of Rights, which provided that parishes had "the exclusive right of electing their public teachers." Based on that provision, Parker concluded that there was no difference between a "public teacher" and a "minister." He conceded that the church had not called the minister; but he resorted to the declaration to shore up his point that the parish also had a right to select a person, a right that was superior to that of the church.

A decade later Parker's successor as chief justice in Massachusetts, Lemuel Shaw, faced a similar issue in *Stebbins v. Jennings* (Mass., 1830). *Stebbins* also involved a suit by remaining Unitarians, who sued to recover tankards and other property said to belong to the church in Brookfield. In *Stebbins* there was no doubt that the Unitarians were a minority; at one time only two males remained with the old church. In what was one of his first opinions as chief justice, Shaw reached the same conclusion as had Parker, although he wrote a long essay exploring the relationship between church and town, as though *Baker* did not control. Like Parker, Shaw concluded that churches could not have the powers of a corporation; indeed, churches had no independent, legal existence apart from religious societies.

Walter F. Pratt, Jr.

Bibliography

Wright, Conrad, "The Dedham Case Revisited," 100 *Proceedings of the Massachusetts Historical Society* 15–39 (1988).

Cases Cited

Baker v. Fales, 16 Mass. 488 (1821).
Holt v. Downs, 58 N.H. 170 (1877).
Oakes v. Hill, 27 Mass. (10 Pick.) 333 (1830).
Stebbins v. Jennings, 27 Mass. (10 Pick.) 172 (1830).

School District of Abington Township v. Schempp
374 U.S. 203 (1963)

Handed down the final day of the 1962 term, *School District of Abington Township v. Schempp* (1963) extended the logic of *Engel v. Vitale* (1962). If, as *Engel* had held, the First Amendment's prohibition against any "establishment of religion" barred a state from drafting and requiring recitation of its own uniform prayer for schoolchildren, *Schempp* declared that a state could not, without violating the same Establishment Clause, set aside time *during* the school day for any kind of religious prayer or for readings from the Bible.

Schempp was argued amid great fanfare. Controversy still raged over *Engel,* and the fact that Madalyn Murray—then the nation's most celebrated atheist—was one of the litigants in *Schempp* guaranteed popular attention. Although reported as a single case, *Schempp* brought together two separate cases, one from Maryland and another from Pennsylvania. In the first, Murray and her son challenged Maryland's law requiring that every school day begin with the "reading, without comment, of a chapter in the Holy Bible and/or the use of the Lord's Prayer." And in the captioned case, the Schempps, who were Unitarians, contested a Pennsylvania statute that required the reading, again without comment, of at "least ten Biblical verses at the beginning of every school day." Oral arguments clearly suggested that the justices would not approve such practices unless they were prepared to overrule *Engel*—a most unlikely prospect.

Although the justices quickly agreed to uphold *Engel,* their initial conference and subsequent negotiations over draft opinions produced divergent approaches to the school prayer issue. Justice William Brennan immediately announced that he would write his own concurring opinion, which aimed at clarifying the Establishment Clause's complex history. Chief Justice Warren assigned the majority opinion to Justice Tom Clark, widely perceived as the Court's most "conservative" member, and his draft opinion, which closely followed *Engel,* prompted two other concurrences—one by Douglas and another by Goldberg, who was joined by Harlan, and, ultimately, a dissent by Justice Potter Stewart.

Justice Clark set forth a two-part test for use in cases involving prayer and Bible reading: In order "to withstand the strictures of the Establishment Clause there must be a secular legislative purpose and a primary effect that neither advances or inhibits religion." The state, in other words, must take a "neutral" stance toward religion in the public schools. Rejecting claims by Maryland and Pennsylvania that Bible reading and prayers were simply part of the educational system's mission of instructing young people about "morals," Clark pointedly characterized the practices in both states as clearly "religious exercises" that violated the Establishment Clause's mandate of neutrality.

The three concurring opinions and the dissent stretched the Supreme Court record in *Schempp* to more than one hundred pages. In the longest of the five opinions, Justice Brennan surveyed the history of the Establishment Clause and argued that the increasing religious diversity of the American people had prompted serious doubts, especially among educators, about continuing the traditional practice of using prayers and Bible readings in public schools. Anxious to emphasize that the majority's ruling would not require purging all manifestations of religion from public life, Brennan stressed that the First Amendment "commands not official hostility toward religion, but only neutrality," and he underscored the "*particular* dangers to church and state which religious exercises in the public schools present."

The other justices were more succinct. Justice Arthur Goldberg, joined by Justice John Marshall Harlan, endorsed Brennan's historical sketch and concisely reiterated his point about the limited nature of *Schempp*'s holding. Justice William O. Douglas's brief concurrence, which seems more doctrinally expansive than any of the longer opinions, argued that the First Amendment not only forbade states from "conducting religious exercises," but also forbade the use of any public funds "to promote a religious exercise." In his dissent, Justice Stewart acknowledged that the *imposition* of prayer and Bible reading on dissenters would violate the Establishment Clause. But he argued that the records in both the Murray (*Murray v. Curlett* et al.) and *Schempp* controversies were so deficient on the question of whether or not the Maryland and Pennsylvania plans involved coercion of students that the cases should be sent to the state courts for further hearings.

Schempp has endured. Despite initial complaints—one member of Congress introduced a bill to carve the words "In God We Trust" over the Court's bench—and the continued use of Bible readings and prayers in some school districts, this decision produced far less controversy than *Engel.* Even with changes in the Supreme Court's membership and deep divisions over religious exercises in other areas of public life, the constitutional debate over prayers and Bible reading *during* school days has not been reopened. Although the issue of allowing a nonsectarian prayer at a high school graduation produced a 5-to-4 decision, in *Lee v. Weisman* (1992), even the dissenters considered *Schempp* a solidly entrenched precedent.

Norman L. Rosenberg

Bibliography

Brown, Ernest J., "Quis Custodiet Ipsos Custodes?—The School Prayer Cases," 1963 *Supreme Court Review* 1–33 (1963).

Dolbeare, Kenneth, and Philip Hammond, *The School Prayer Decisions: From Court Policy to Local Practice* (Chicago: University of Chicago Press, 1971).

Mengler, Thomas, "Public Relations in the Supreme Court: Justice Tom Clark's Opinion in the School Prayer Case," 6 *Constitutional Commentary* 331–349 (1989).

Schwartz, Bernard, *Super Chief: Earl Warren and His Supreme Court: A Judicial Biography* (New York: New York University Press, 1983).

Cases Cited

Engel v. Vitale, 370 U.S. 421 (1962).

Lee v. Weisman, 505 U.S. 577 (1992).

Murray v. Curlett et al. and Board of School Commissioners of Baltimore City, 179 A. 2d 698, 228 Md. 239 (1962).

School District of Abington Township v. Schempp, 374 U.S. 203 (1963).

School District of the City of Grand Rapids v. Ball

473 U.S. 373 (1985)

In the evolving jurisprudence of the Establishment Clause of the First Amendment the decade of the 1980s was a period of transition from the separationist approach of the preceding two decades to a more accommodationist approach by the 1990s. The majority in *School District of the City of Grand Rapids v. Ball* (1985) remained in the former tradition, but the divided Supreme Court illustrated tensions concerning the Establishment Clause guidelines enunciated in *Lemon v. Kurtzman* (1971). *Ball* and its companion, *Aguilar v. Felton* (1985), were part of the long series of Establishment Clause cases in which the Court struggled with the scope and limits of permissible aid to parochial schools. In both cases, Justice William Brennan writing for the majority—and joined by Justices Harry Blackmun, Thurgood Marshall, and John Paul Stevens—upheld taxpayers' challenges to the use of public schoolteachers to provide instruction in religious schools.

Ball involved a challenge to two programs supported by the Grand Rapids, Michigan, School District. The first was a shared-time program, in which public schoolteachers came into private schools to offer courses intended to supplement the "core curriculum." In the second, the community education program, the state funded voluntary enrichment programs after school, employing teachers whose primary employment was in the religious schools. Both programs were found constitutionally flawed under the second criterion of the *Lemon* test. Under the three-pronged guidelines enunciated in *Lemon,* to withstand Establishment Clause scrutiny, a program (1) must have a secular legislative purpose, (2) must have a principal of primary effect that neither advances nor inhibits religion, and (3) must not foster an excessive entanglement between church and state. The Court acknowledged that both programs easily passed the first prong of the test; they had a "praiseworthy" secular purpose of enriching education for the children of Grand Rapids. However, for three reasons, both programs failed the second prong, because the Court found that they had a primary effect that advanced religion.

First, both programs were found to advance religion by posing the danger of religious indoctrination by the state. The shared-time program offered secular enrichment and remedial programs during regular hours within the parochial school day, employing public schoolteachers in classrooms leased from the private schools. Although in theory the program was available to all students, in fact it served the students of the religious school, "segregated by religion, as are the schools at which they are offered." The Court feared that the religious atmosphere of the schools would—perhaps inadvertently—influence the tone of the education. "Teachers in such an atmosphere may well subtly (or overtly) conform their instruction to the environment in which they teach, while students will perceive the instruction provided in the context of the dominantly religious message of the institution, thus reinforcing the indoctrinating effect." The state, while paying for the program, might never know that this was happening because the classes were "not specifically monitored for religious content." This problem was even more likely to occur in the community education program, because the state employed teachers whose primary employment was teaching in the religious schools at which the programs were located.

Second, the Court found that the programs constituted an unconstitutional symbolic endorsement of religion. Only the "public school" sign in the classroom (placed there when the state-funded programs were in operation) distinguished the state program from the religious one—a rather subtle distinction for elementary schoolchildren, as Justice Brennan noted. Furthermore, even a student who noted the sign "would have before him a powerful symbol of state endorsement and encouragement of the religious beliefs taught in the same class at some other time during the day."

Third, both programs violated the Establishment Clause by offering impermissible financial subsidies to religious institutions. Not all financial subsidies are unconstitutional; courts must distinguish between those which are "indirect," "remote," or "incidental" and those which are "direct and substantial." The difference is one of degree, but the majority in *Ball* found that both programs fell on the impermissible side of the line. The shared-time program raised a particular concern, because it provided programs that the private schools might have provided themselves. The majority feared that approving this program would leave future courts no principled way of limiting the amount of educational program that the state might sponsor. "To let the genie out of the bottle in this case would be to permit ever larger segments of the religious school curriculum to be turned over to the public school system, thus violating the cardinal principle that the State may not in effect become the prime supporter of the religious school system."

The majority summarized its rejection of the Grand Rapids plans with the following words:

> We conclude that the challenged programs have the effect of promoting religion in three ways. The state-paid instructors, influenced by the pervasively sectarian nature of the religious schools in which they work, may subtly or overtly indoctrinate the students in particular religious tents at public expense. The symbolic union of church and state inherent in the provision of secular, state-sponsored instruction in the religious school buildings threatens to convey a message of state support for religion to students and to the general public.

Finally, the program in effect subsidizes the religious functions of the parochial schools by taking over a substantial portion of their responsibility for teaching secular subjects. For these reasons, the conclusion is inescapable that the Community Education and Shared Time programs have the "primary and principal" effect of advancing religion, and therefore violate the dictates of the Establishment Clause of the First Amendment.

Chief Justice Warren E. Burger and Justice Sandra Day O'Connor dissented in part and concurred in part. Both agreed with the Court concerning the unconstitutionality of the community education program, but they would have upheld the shared-time program. Although both judges wrote brief opinions, they referred to arguments they had developed at greater length in their dissents in *Aguilar.* Justice William Rehnquist dissented on both issues, referring to the reasoning he had provided in his dissent in *Wallace v. Jaffree* (1985). Justice White also filed a dissent.

The Court's approach in *Ball* and in *Aguilar* barely survived a decade. In 1994 the Court struck down an awkward political arrangement that New York had devised to cope with problems created by the *Aguilar* ruling, but in doing so five justices recommended that the earlier cases be reconsidered. The opportunity to do so arose in *Agostini v. Felton* (1997), decided on June 23, 1997. In this case, the Supreme Court majority determined that Establishment Clause jurisprudence during the intervening decade had changed so substantially as to undermine the rationale of *Aguilar* and *Ball.* In particular, the Court would no longer assume that a shared-time program like the one challenged in *Ball* violated the *Lemon* test by impermissibly advancing religion. Thus, *Agostini* overturned *Aguilar* specifically, along with the reasoning on which *Ball* was based.

Bette Novit Evans

Bibliography

Elfers, Thomas E., "Lead Us Not into Confusion: Michigan School Code versus United States Supreme Court Policy," 64 *University of Detroit Law Review* 225–245 (1986).

Garvey, John, "Another Way of Looking at School Aid," 1985 *Supreme Court Review* 173–193 (1985).

Keetch, Von G., "An Educational Perspective on the Evolution of *Lemon,*" 1986 *Brigham Young University Law Review* 489–503 (1986).

"The Supreme Court, 1984 Term: Establishment of Religion," 99 *Harvard Law Review* 84–193 (1985).

Cases Cited

Agostini v. Felton, 521 U.S. 203 (1997).

Aguilar v. Felton, 473 U.S. 402 (1985).

Lemon v. Kurtzman, 403 U.S. 602 (1971).

School District of the City of Grand Rapids v. Ball, 473 U.S. 373 (1985).

Wallace v. Jaffree, 472 U.S. 38 (1985).

School Prayer

Of all areas in which church and state come into conflict, there is perhaps no area that is as charged with strong feeling as school prayer.

Those who favor a strict separation of church and state are adamant in their opposition to permitting prayer or devotional practices in the public sector, except in those instances when the prayer is wholly private (e.g., a silent, unobtrusive prayer by a student asking for assistance on an exam). Opponents of public school prayer assert that it is inappropriate for government to do anything that might imply some support for or endorsement of a prayer practice. They argue that, by its nature, public religious activity has the tendency to become coercive of the rights of those who do not share the beliefs being expressed.

Proponents of prayer in schools, on the other hand, argue that to purge the public schools of all public or state-accommodated prayer constitutes discrimination against religious exercise. Particularly with the growth of the public sector in this century, they assert that the rights of the religious are denigrated when public manifestations of an individual's or group's religious identity are prohibited. They also assert that religious activity is a part of our culture and that to prohibit manifestations of that culture in the public sector is to depreciate the culture, as well. These proponents assert that, rather than endorsing religion, accommodation of religious activity in the public sector furthers the highest ideals of the Free Exercise Clause of the First Amendment and avoids discrimination against religion in the public sector. Those proponents also believe that permitting individuals to excuse themselves from such activities provides sufficient protection against any coercive effects associated with public religious exercise.

The concerns of proponents and opponents of public prayer are magnified in the school context, because impressionable young people are particularly susceptible to being influenced by the presence or absence of such practices. The U.S. Supreme Court has struggled with this maturation problem in a number of cases, without providing any firm guidelines for use in future cases.

Despite the conflict between the opponents and proponents of public prayer, particularly in the school context, very few cases were decided by federal or state courts in the nineteenth and early twentieth centuries. But as the Supreme Court began to hear religion cases in other contexts, in the 1940s, it was clear that a school prayer issue would have to be considered.

"Voluntary" Prayer Unconstitutional

In 1962, over 170 years after the ratification of the First Amendment, the Supreme Court dealt for the first time with the issue of the constitutionality of prayer in the public schools. At the time of the framing of the Bill of Rights, there were few if any public schools. It was not until the mid-nineteenth century that public schools began to be developed in significant numbers in the United States. From the mid-nineteenth century until 1962, the practice of prayer, in various forms, in the public schools was common. School prayer practices had been challenged on Establishment Clause grounds in a few states, but such practices remained largely unfettered by legal precedent until the Court heard *Engel v. Vitale* in 1962.

In 1961 a petition for certiorari was filed in the Supreme Court asking that the Court determine whether the New York Board of Regents' policy directing that a prayer be recited each day by students in the New York public school system was unconstitutional. That prayer was designed to be nondenominational, in a Judaeo-Christian sense, and read as follows: "Almighty God, we acknowledge our dependence on Thee, and we beg Thy blessings on us, our parents, our teachers and our Country." The board permitted students who desired to remain silent to leave the room during the recitation of the prayer. Parents of public schoolchildren in New York challenged the prayer practice and ultimately petitioned the Supreme Court for a writ of certiorari. Despite strong opposition from Justices Stewart and Whittaker—who believed that the Court should exercise prudence and refuse to hear the case, thereby permitting the prayer practice to stand—the Court granted the petition for certiorari on December 4, 1961, agreeing to decide whether the recitation of the regents' prayer in New York public schools violated the First Amendment.

The *Engel* case was argued on April 3, 1962, and on April 6, 1962, the Court met privately in conference regarding the case. After discussing and voting on the case, Justice Hugo L. Black was assigned the task of writing the opinion for the majority, holding that the regents' "voluntary" school prayer was unconstitutional on Establishment Clause grounds. Only Justice Potter Stewart dissented when Justice Black's opinion for the Court was delivered on June 25, 1962—although shortly before the opinion was announced, Justice Douglas expressed some concerns that he had regarding the case, in a note to Justice Black. In that note Justice Douglas wrote, "If . . . we would strike down a New York requirement that public school teachers open each day with prayer, I think we could not consistently open each of our sessions [of the Supreme Court] with prayer." Thus, even before the opinion was delivered, concerns were raised regarding the breadth of the principle being announced.

In his opinion for the Court, Justice Black held that "the constitutional prohibition against laws respecting an establishment of religion must at least mean that in this country it is not part of the business of the government to compose official prayers for any group of the American people to recite as a part of a religious program carried on by government." Justice Black acknowledged that the free exercise and Establishment Clauses of the First Amendment serve different purposes, even though they "may in certain instances overlap." Implicitly, he admitted that the purposes of the free exercise and establishment limitations may come into conflict as religious exercises or activities find their way into the public sector.

In his dissent, Justice Stewart focused largely on the concept of coercion. He argued: "The Court does not hold, nor could it, that New York has interfered with the free exercise of anybody's religion. For the state courts have made clear that those who object to reciting the prayer must be entirely free of any compulsion to do so, including any embarrassments and pressures." For Stewart, absent proof of actual coercion, the fact that students could voluntarily excuse themselves from the practice was sufficient to protect against either establishment or free exercise concerns.

Justice Stewart also expressed his concern over Justice Black's use of Jefferson's metaphor of a "wall of separation" between church and state, believing that there was no simple prescription that could resolve the complex issues arising in this context. For Justice Stewart, with the growth of the public sector, conflicts between religious exercise and public activity were inevitable, and those conflicts could not be resolved easily or fairly by invoking a metaphor of strict or absolute separation. Stewart preferred a concept of coercion, believing that it would unify the Establishment and Free Exercise Clauses in a way that would mediate fairly between free exercise and establishment concerns related to public religious activity or exercise.

The public response to the decision in *Engel* was quick and generally negative. In fact, the reported public furor that followed the decision was without equal since World War II; mail to the Court attacking the *Engel* decision exceeded the response to any other case. The legislative response was also highly critical, and several pieces of legislation that were introduced and nearly adopted in Congress would have constitutionalized school prayer or limited the jurisdiction of the Court to hear cases dealing with school prayer. Indeed, the response was so strong that Justice Clark, who joined in Justice Black's opinion, felt compelled to perform the fairly unprecedented task of speaking with the press to defend the Court's decision.

The public furor regarding the prayer issue and the disagreement between Justice Stewart and the majority in *Engel* foreshadowed much of what was to ensue regarding school prayer and related issues over the next three decades. Indeed, just one year later, on the last day of the following term of the Court, in *School District of Abington Township v. Schempp* (1963), a majority opinion by Justice Clark held that Bible reading for devotional purposes or recitation of the Lord's Prayer in the public schools constituted an unconstitutional establishment of religion, even though students who did not want to participate could be excused. Justice Clark argued that the purpose and effect of the Bible reading or recitation of the Lord's Prayer were religious and, therefore, unconstitutional under the Establishment Clause.

Justices Douglas and Brennan each wrote separate concurring opinions. Justice Douglas reiterated his concern that no state resources should ever be used to further any religious activity in the public sector. Justice Brennan wrote extensively about the historical foundations of the First Amendment and argued that permitting students to excuse themselves from the devotional exercise did not obviate free exercise concerns. Brennan believed that students who refused to participate on grounds of conscience would nevertheless feel coerced to do so; they would be conspicuous by their absence and would feel significant peer pressure to attend and participate.

Justice Stewart offered a lengthy dissent. He argued that the case should be remanded because the record before the Court was so "deficient as to make impossible an informed or responsible determination of the constitutional issues presented." In particular, Justice Stewart was concerned that there was no actual evidence in the record of official coercion. Without such a record, he asserted that it was improper for the Court to invalidate the devotional practices at issue. He also raised concerns that would be echoed for years to come, when he stated that a "compulsory state educational system so structures a child's life that if religious exercises are held to be an impermissible activity in schools, religion is placed at an artificial and state-created disadvantage." He added that "a refusal to permit religious exercises [in the public school context] thus is seen, not as a realization of state neutrality, but rather as the establishment of a religion of secularism."

Many religious and political leaders criticized the *Engel* and *Schempp* decisions by asserting that their effect was to purge the public schools of all religious activity, thereby discriminating against religion. These sentiments provided the basis for a number of legislative efforts to return prayer and Bible recitation to the public schools, but none of those efforts was successful.

A Limited Public Forum

For nearly two decades the Supreme Court did not decide another case dealing with school prayer, although such issues did arise occasionally in lower state and federal courts. During those two decades the membership of the Court changed significantly, and the justices decided to hear a case involving school prayer in the university context, *Widmar v. Vincent* (1981). On December 8, 1981, the Supreme Court, in a majority opinion written by Justice Powell, held that "a state university, which makes its facilities generally available for the activities of registered student groups, may not close its facilities to a registered student group desiring to use the facilities for religious worship and religious discussion." The lower court, which was reversed, had held that permitting such equal access for student religious groups violated the establishment provisions of the state and federal constitutions.

Justice Powell based his decision for the Court on free speech and association grounds, not on the establishment or free exercise provisions of the First Amendment. Specifically, Powell opined that the University of Missouri of Kansas City had created a limited public forum when it permitted recognized student groups to use public facilities for a wide variety of purposes. Given that a limited public forum had been established, Powell concluded that the university had discriminated against a student religious group when it refused to permit that group to use a generally open forum.

Despite having based his opinion on free speech and association grounds, Justice Powell had to face the establishment issue, because it had been asserted that, even if there was an infringement of free speech, that violation was justified on the ground that the state had a compelling interest in protecting against the establishment of religion. Justice Powell's response utilized the *Lemon* test, which requires that "the [practice at issue, which is supported or permitted by government] must have a secular legislative purpose; second, its principal or primary effect must be one that neither advances nor inhibits religion . . . ; finally, the [permitted practice] must not foster an excessive government entanglement with religion." Justice Powell quickly disposed of the first and third prongs of the *Lemon* test—the secular purpose and entanglement prongs. The first prong was satisfied by the state's secular interest in having a limited open public forum. The third prong was disposed of in a footnote, where Powell noted that the majority "agreed with the court of appeals that the university would risk greater entanglement by attempting to enforce its exclusion of religious worship and religious speech [than it would by permitting the religious group to meet on terms similar to those adhered to by other, nonreligious groups]."

The major issue for Justice Powell was whether allowing religious groups to participate in the limited public forum would have the primary effect of advancing religion. Powell concluded that it did not, because any religious benefits were merely incidental. He supported this conclusion with two arguments: (1) that an open forum in a public university does not confer the imprimatur of the state on religious sects or practices and (2) that the forum is open to a broad class of nonreligious as well as religious groups and speakers, and there is no empirical evidence in the record that religious groups would dominate the university's public forum.

Justice Powell did, however, limit his opinion for the Court. He stressed that the Court was not holding "that a campus must make all of its facilities equally available to students and nonstudents alike, or that a university must grant free access to all of its grounds or buildings." He added that the Court's decision "in no way undermines the capacity of the university to establish reasonable time, place, and manner regulations [for religious and nonreligious speech alike]." As a former member of a school board, Powell stressed that the Court did not "question the right of the university to make academic judgments as to how best to allocate scarce resources or to determine for itself on academic grounds who may teach, what may be taught, how it shall be taught, and who may be admitted to study."

The most significant limitation placed on the breadth of the opinion by Justice Powell dealt with the distinction between students at the university level and those in elementary and secondary schools. He acknowledged that elementary and even high school students are more impressionable than students at the university level. This maturation distinction is of significance in school prayer and related cases, because it has provided the basis for legitimating more regulation of religious speech and activity at the high school and elementary levels than at the college level.

While Justice Stevens concurred in the judgment of the Court in *Widmar,* Justice White was a lone dissenter. Justice White would have permitted the state of Missouri to regulate the devotional practices on the campus of the University of Missouri, arguing that the Court should defer to the state in matters of incidental aid to religion.

The Equal Access Act

After the decision in *Widmar,* Court watchers agreed that it would not be long before the Court had to decide whether such devotional practices were also constitutionally permissible at the secondary school level. The likelihood that the Court would hear such a case increased when Congress passed the Equal Access Act in 1984. That act states: "It shall be unlawful for any public secondary school which receives Federal financial assistance and which has a limited open forum to deny equal access [to] any students who wish to conduct a meeting within that limited public forum on the basis of religious, political, philosophical, or other content of the speech at such meetings." A limited public forum was said to have been created when the school permits "noncurriculum related student groups to meet on school premises during noninstructional time." A divided Court upheld the constitutionality of the Equal Access Act in *Board of Education of Westside Community Schools v. Mergens* (1990). In her plurality opinion, Justice O'Connor opined that "the logic of *Widmar* applies [to the Equal Access Act]." In their concurrence in the judgment of the Court, Justices Kennedy and Scalia argued that the act should be upheld in *Mergens* because it did not give benefits directly to a religion, nor did it coerce students to participate in activities of a religious nature. Thus, the issue of coercion, which had first been raised in the school prayer context by Justice Stewart in *Engel,* was again prominent.

Although not in the school context, the Court dealt with the maturation factor in a public prayer case when it decided *Marsh v. Chambers* (1983). In that case, the Court held, by a 6-to-3 margin, that the Nebraska legislature was permitted, as a constitutional matter, to hire a chaplain, who would open each day of the legislative session with a prayer. In upholding the prayer practice, the Court relied heavily on historical practices. Essentially, the Court asserted that, because the First Congress had hired a chaplain, after adoption of the First Amendment, the hiring of a chaplain in Nebraska was constitutional. The Court recognized that adult legislators could better insulate themselves from the proselytizing effects of the invocation practice than could impressionable schoolchildren. It was easier in this context for adult legislators to absent themselves from the morning invocation than it would be for a student attending a public school.

A Moment of Silence

Before returning in *Mergens* to the equal access issues first raised in *Widmar,* and after the *Marsh* case, the Court wrestled with the issue of whether state statutes permitting a moment of silence or silent meditation in public schools were constitutional. This issue was expressly left open when the Court decided the *Engel* case. Indeed, in *Engel,* Justice Brennan had specifically noted that the state was not necessarily prohibited from permitting "the observance of a moment of reverent silence" in the public school context. The Court faced this issue directly in *Wallace v. Jaffree* (1985).

While the facts in the *Jaffree* case were complicated by a series of actions taken by the State of Alabama to get "prayer back into the schools," the Court focused on the silent meditation issue and held that the Alabama statute authorizing a one-minute period of silence in public schools "for meditation or voluntary prayer" was unconstitutional, because it advanced an effort to endorse religion in violation of the Establishment Clause of the First Amendment. In his opinion for the Court, Justice Stevens stated that the statute was adopted in Alabama as part of an extended effort to get prayer back into the schools and was "intended to convey a message of state-approval of prayer activities in the public schools." Indeed, Stevens emphasized that the state "did not present evidence of any secular purpose" for the statute.

Despite the Court's decision in *Jaffree,* many states have statutes permitting a moment of silent meditation in the public school context. Some commentators believe that secular purposes could be asserted in support of a silent meditation statute and that such statutes are permissible, as long as they do not constitute part of an effort to endorse religion or to coerce students into participating in a religious exercise. It is likely that the Court will hear a case dealing with the silent meditation issue again in the future, particularly given that at least one state is now requiring teachers to provide such a moment of silence, despite objections to the practice.

In 1992 the Court faced the school prayer issue in another context, when it decided *Lee v. Weisman* (1992). In a 5-to-4 decision the Court held that including a cleric who offers prayer as part of an official public school graduation ceremony violates the First Amendment. Justice Kennedy, the critical fifth vote for the majority, wrote the opinion for the Court, in which he stressed the notion of coercion:

> We do not hold that every state action implicating religion is invalid if one or a few citizens find it offensive. People may take offense at all manner of religious messages, but offense alone does not in every case show a violation. We know too that sometimes to endure social isolation or even anger may be the price of conscience or nonconformity. But, by any reading of our cases, the conformity required of the student in this case was too high an exaction to withstand the test of the Establishment Clause.

Justice Kennedy also acknowledged the maturation problem, when he pointed out that, "there are heightened concerns with protecting freedom of conscience from subtle coercive pressure in the elementary and secondary public schools."

The four dissenters—Chief Justice Rehnquist and Justices Scalia, White, and Thomas—strongly disagreed with the Court's holding and reasoning in *Lee v. Weisman.* Justice Scalia chided the majority for exceeding their judicial function by using a "psychological coercion" test. He concluded that, although no one should be compelled to participate in prayer, "it is a shame to deprive our public culture of the opportunity, and indeed the encouragement, for people to do it voluntarily." He added, "To deprive our society of that important unifying mechanism, in order to spare the nonbeliever what seems to me the minimal inconvenience of standing or even sitting in respectful nonparticipation, is as senseless in policy as it is unsupported in law."

First Amendment Conflicts—and Resolutions

The Supreme Court has wrestled with school prayer issues in a variety of contexts—state-composed prayers and devotional practices, silent meditation, equal access for religious groups on campuses permitting access to nonreligious groups, graduation prayers—and it will no doubt face related issues in the future. Trying to assess how the Court will likely decide such issues is a daunting task, because the composition of the Court changes with regularity and the complexity of the issues (in school prayer cases specifically and in religion clause cases generally) has seemingly defied articulation of clear-cut principles.

In accommodating religious practices as a matter of free exercise, the Court runs directly into an apparent conflict with the Establishment Clause, which has often been interpreted to limit religious activity in the public sector. Nonetheless, the Court and constitutional commentators continue to endeavor to resolve this apparent conflict as the free exercise and Establishment Clauses relate to school prayer and similar issues.

In the Establishment Clause context, it has been suggested that there are four possible ways to resolve church–state issues: (1) government might promote a particular religion; (2) government might promote religion generally, in some nondenominational sense; (3) government might permit religious activity in the public sector on a nonpreferential basis; and (4) government might strictly separate or prohibit religious exercise in the public sector. An examination of cases relating to school prayer and other areas demonstrates that the Court has been inclined to focus on the third approach, permitting religious activity in the public sector so long as accommodation of that activity does not imply a preference for a particular religion or for religion generally.

There are three forms of nonpreferentialism, however. First, government might accommodate religion in a nonpreferential manner (i.e., no religion could be preferred over another religion, but religion generally might be preferred). Second, government might accommodate religion along with a broader group of activities that might be considered acts of conscience but might not be religious in derivation (i.e., nonpreference regarding matters of conscience). Third, government might accommodate religion along with other nonreligious activities or forms of expression (i.e., nonpreference between religion and nonreligion).

While there are justices on the Supreme Court who adopt each of these forms of nonpreference, recent decisions indicate that the middle position—nonpreference regarding matters of conscience—predominates. This is not surprising, because the Court has often stated that the Establishment Clause should limit even general religion as well as specific religious activity in the public sector. Nevertheless, given free exercise concerns, the Court has demonstrated a related uneasiness about eliminating all religious activity and expression from the public sector.

With these concerns in mind, the Court has broadened the category accommodated, from "religion" to a category that is occasionally labeled "conscience." Of course, the Court could broaden the category even further, permitting religious activity only when all other forms of activity are accommodated on similar terms, regardless of the type of activity being accommodated. This position has proved to be less desirable to most members of the Court, because it is too restrictive and would give little latitude to the exercise of religion in the public sector. Permitting religious exercise to be treated like other exercises that are motivated as a matter of conscience strikes a balance more favorable to religion, without preferring religion to other forms of conscience in the public sector.

If the Court continues to opt for the view of nonpreference regarding matters of conscience, it can deal with the apparent conflict between the free exercise and establishment values in the school prayer context without disavowing any of its prior decisions. For example, while graduation prayers would not be permissible in secondary and elementary schools, a moment of silent meditation regarding matters of conscience (or even oral statements of conscience, including prayer) would be acceptable, so long as the state refrains from preferring or endorsing a particular religion or religion generally. Similarly, the government might accommodate even readings from the Bible, if they were included as a part of a broader program that served as a call to the conscience of the students. For example, religious readings could be accommodated along with readings from Gandhi, Martin Luther King, Confucius, and Thoreau. Although such a balance will satisfy neither the strict separationist, who opposes all religion in the public sector, nor the religionist, who believes that religion should be accorded preference, it does strike what may be a viable balance between Free Exercise and Establishment Clause values in deciding school prayer and related cases in the future.

Rodney K. Smith

Bibliography

Laycock, Douglas, "Formal, Substantive, and Disaggregated Neutrality toward Religion," 39 *DePaul Law Review* 993–1018 (1990).

———, "The Origins of the Religion Clauses of the Constitution: 'Nonpreferential' Aid to Religion: A False Claim about Original Intent," 27 *William and Mary Law Review* 875–923 (1986).

Rice, Charles, *The Supreme Court and Public Prayer* (New York: Fordham University Press, 1964).

Smith, Rodney K., "Conscience, Coercion and the Establishment of Religion: The Beginning of an End to the Wanderings of a Wayward Judiciary?" 43 *Case Western Reserve Law Review* 917–961 (1993).

———, "Nonpreferentialism in Establishment Clause Analysis: A Response to Professor Laycock," 65 *St. John's Law Review* 245–271 (1991).

———, *Public Prayer and the Constitution* (Wilmington, Del.: Scholarly Resources, 1987).

Cases Cited

Board of Education of Westside Community School District v. Mergens, 496 U.S. 226 (1990).

Engel v. Vitale, 370 U.S. 421 (1962).

Lee v. Weisman, 505 U.S. 577 (1992).

Marsh v. Chambers, 463 U.S. 783 (1983).

School District of Abington Township v. Schempp, 374 U.S. 203 (1963).

Wallace v. Jaffree, 472 U.S. 38 (1985).

Widmar v. Vincent, 454 U.S. 263 (1981).

School Prayer and American Politics

Since 1962 Americans have debated whether to permit open prayer in the public schools. Despite two seemingly definitive Supreme Court rulings prohibiting prayer in public schools, this question remains divisive and unanswered. Advocates of school prayer have constantly asserted that the rulings of the Court in *Engel v. Vitale* (1962) and in *School District of Abington Township v. Schempp* (1963) violated both the Establishment and Free Exercise Clauses of the First Amendment. Opponents of school prayer argue that any type of worship in the schools would represent a form of government-supported religion. They maintain that religious practice is a private, not public, matter that should be conducted on an individual's own time. Given recent political changes in the United States, debate about school prayer will certainly reoccur.

Supporters of prayer have consistently tried to overturn the Supreme Court's rulings in *Engle* and *Schempp* at both the national and state levels. At the national level, pro-prayer forces have focused on passing a constitutional amendment that would nullify the Court's decisions. At the state level, they have attempted to negate or circumvent the Court's decisions with various laws that allow for some form of prayer in school. Under the Reagan administration supporters of school prayer won a partial victory when Congress passed the Equal Access Act of 1984, which granted public school students the right to form religious organizations and conduct religious activities on school grounds as other students can do for nonreligious clubs and activities. Despite this act's new freedoms for religious worship, many American citizens continue to fight for government-supported prayer in the public schools.

The Starting Points: *Engel* and *Schempp*

The Supreme Court's key decisions in *Engel* and in *Schempp*—along with *Murray v. Baltimore City Schools* (1962)—are the starting points for all discussion of school prayer. In *Engel* the parents of ten children attending public school on Long Island, New York, challenged the institution of a daily prayer by the New York State Board of Regents. This prayer, spoken aloud by the principal each day, stated the following: "Almighty God, we acknowledge our dependence on Thee, and we beg Thy blessings on us, our parents, our teachers and our Country." Justice Hugo Black, writing the opinion of the Court, observed that this prayer was "composed by governmental officials as a part of a governmental program to further religious beliefs." As such, it represented a violation of the First Amendment's Establishment Clause, which the Fourteenth Amendment incorporated to prohibit any state from passing a law that establishes an official religion. Justice Black rejected the New York school officials' argument that the prayer was inoffensive and constitutional because parents who did not want their children to speak the prayer could have them excused from it. Black maintained that with the "power, prestige and financial support of a government" behind the schools this type of observance would result in religious coercion. The Court therefore ruled the regents' prayer unconstitutional and by implication struck down any religious ceremonies in other state public school systems.

Only Justice Potter Stewart dissented in the Court's decision, citing historical examples of references to God in American government. He noted that both houses of Congress held prayers each morning and that the Supreme Court's crier asked for God's protection when opening Court sessions. These two examples did not represent establishment of official religion, and consequently the regents' prayer didn't either, in Stewart's view. Both examples illustrated how Americans continually have recognized "the deeply entrenched and highly cherished spiritual traditions of our nation."

After *Engel,* Republicans and Democrats in both houses of Congress announced various plans to reverse the decision by amendment. Most of these proposals declared that nothing in the Constitution could be construed as prohibiting public schools from providing nondenominational voluntary prayers for students. Despite the movement to overturn *Engel,* no such amendment was passed as the summer of 1962 came to a close. And although the *Engel* ruling implied that any state instituting an official form of school prayer was violating the Constitution, most of the nation's public schools continued to conduct prayer recitations and Bible readings when classes resumed that fall.

A year later the Court addressed the issue of such required recitation and Bible readings in Pennsylvania and Maryland when it heard the cases of *Schempp* and *Murray.* In an 8-to-1 decision the Court ruled that no state or local jurisdiction could require reading or recitation of the Bible or the Lord's Prayer in public schools. Justice Tom Clark, writing the opinion of the Court, laid the groundwork for the decision by asserting that Section 1 of the Fourteenth Amendment was the basis for applying the Establishment and Free Exercise Clauses to the states in the *Schempp* and *Murray* cases. He then discussed the Establishment Clause, concluding that the Court had historically required Congress and the states to adopt a neutral position toward religion. He maintained that the Free Exercise Clause supported this notion of neutrality because it gave the right to "every person to freely choose his own course" with regard to religion, "free of any compulsion."

In examining these two cases, Justice Clark developed a test to determine whether a law had violated the First Amendment: What was the purpose of the law, and what was its primary effect? If either the purpose or the primary effect resulted in the advancement or inhibition of religion, then the law "exceeds the scope of legislative power as circumscribed by the Constitution." Clark found that in both cases the laws of the two states had the effect of advancing religion. Thus the laws violated the First Amendment. Clark dismissed protestations by the defense, similar to those in *Engel,* that the laws passed constitutional muster because they permitted students to be excused from the exercises. He also rejected arguments that banning religious exercises from the public schools implicitly promoted a "religion of secularism." Finally, Clark refused to accept the argument that the concept of neutrality would violate the majority's right to free exercise of religion.

Justice Clark sought to reassure Americans that the *Schempp* and *Murray* decisions not be interpreted as an endorsement of atheism. He also suggested that the conclusion of the Court in the two cases did not preclude study of the Bible or of religion "when presented as part of a secular program of education." The justice praised the role of religion in America, observing that it had an "exalted place" in society "through reliance on the home, the church and the inviolable citadel of the individual heart and mind." At the same time, he stressed that only through "bitter experience" had Americans learned that the government could not "invade that citadel," regardless of the government's purpose. Instead, the government had a responsibility to remain neutral.

As in *Engel,* Justice Potter Stewart dissented, maintaining that it would be a mistake to think that the First Amendment established a "single constitutional standard . . . which can be applied in every case to delineate the required boundaries between government and religion." He went on to assert that "as a matter of history and of the imperatives of our free society religion and government must necessarily interact." Stewart also warned that a "doctrinaire reading" of the Establishment Clause could lead to conflict with the Free Exercise Clause. As an example he cited the government's long practice of spending federal money to hire chaplains for the army. This practice could certainly be construed as a violation of the Establishment Clause. However, Stewart suggested that a soldier who on this basis was denied access to a chaplain for religious guidance could effectively argue that his right of free exercise had been violated.

Justice Stewart also noted the lack of definitive proof that the students in both cases had been coerced into participating in the exercises. If they had, Stewart conceded that the prayer exercises would be unconstitutional. Without conclusive evidence that the Pennsylvania and Maryland laws violated the Constitution, Stewart told the Court that he felt the cases should be remanded to the states for further hearing.

Efforts to Amend the Constitution

Members of Congress who opposed the Court's rulings in *Schempp* and *Murray* again proposed to amend the Constitution to overturn the decisions. Numerous efforts to pass an amendment first arose in the House of Representatives. In 1964 the House Judiciary Committee deliberated on over 140 such proposals, with a bill by Frank Becker of New York drawing the most support. After several months of deliberation and testimony by dozens of witnesses the committee voted against sending any of these bills to the floor of the House. Two years later Republican Senator Everett McKinley Dirksen introduced a similar amendment in the Senate. Dirksen built a coalition of Republicans and Southern

Democrats who brought his bill to a vote in the Senate but failed to muster the two-thirds needed for passage of the amendment. Dirksen revised the amendment and reintroduced it again in 1967 but again failed to secure the necessary votes. Attempts to pass similar school prayer amendments continued, without success, in the early 1970s.

Religious organizations both praised and condemned the movements to reverse the Court's decisions. Jewish and Protestant groups tended to support the Court, while Catholics and some Southern Protestants denounced it. In 1964 representatives of the National Council of the Churches of Christ, the American Baptist Convention, and the American Jewish Congress testified before the House Judiciary Committee and urged Congress not to adopt any amendment legislation. These religious leaders argued that such an amendment would break the nation's long-entrenched tradition of separation of church and state and could establish a precedent for overturning future Supreme Court rulings. They also warned that, although school prayer laws might allow for voluntary participation, the atmosphere of a classroom would inevitably cause nonparticipating children to feel compelled to conform. Finally church officials cautioned that an amendment would harm believers as well as nonbelievers, for it "could make religion a matter of rote recitation" rather than one of study, discussion, and reflection.

At the same time, however, other American church leaders criticized the Court's stance and favored an amendment or a more lenient interpretation of the First Amendment. Catholic Cardinal James McIntyre feared that the Court's rulings signaled a shift away from "our American heritage of philosophy, of religion, of freedom" while moving toward the "atheistic, material philosophy of communism." In 1964 Bishop Fulton Sheen, of the Roman Catholic Archdiocese in New York, testified at the House Judiciary Committee hearings on passing a school prayer amendment. While Sheen felt that amending the Constitution to nullify the decision would be a mistake, he suggested that the Court had extended the Establishment Clause at the expense of the Free Exercise Clause. The bishop argued that the First Amendment gave people the right to pray as well as not pray.

During the 1970s proposals to amend the Constitution arose in both the House and the Senate but were repeatedly defeated. In 1979 Senator Jesse Helms of North Carolina attempted to pass a measure that would have prevented the Supreme Court from ruling on school prayer laws, but it was not until President Ronald Reagan's election in 1980 that pro-prayer forces had a serious opportunity to pass an amendment.

In the meantime many states made their own decisions about how to deal with the issue of school prayer. Public school districts located particularly in the Northeast and the South took steps to ensure that prayer in one form or another would continue in the classroom. In 1969 school districts in southwestern Pennsylvania and western New Jersey attempted to institute forms of daily prayer. In both states, some residents fought against these laws in court. The U.S. District Court for western Pennsylvania and the New Jersey Supreme Court ruled that the prayer measures violated the *Engel* and *Schempp* ban. Massachusetts and Alabama made similar efforts to introduce prayers into the classroom, which the courts again ruled unconstitutional.

Passage of a school prayer amendment came to the fore again by the second year of Ronald Reagan's presidency, when he made such an amendment part of his social policy. In May 1982 Reagan announced his own school prayer amendment, arguing that "the public expression through prayer of our faith in God is a fundamental part of our American heritage and a privilege which should not be excluded by law from any American school, public or private." Eight months later Reagan announced that he would make 1983 the year of the Bible, and he indicated his commitment to bringing prayer back into the public schools. Speaking before a gathering of the National Religious Broadcasters, Reagan stated that he was "determined to bring [the prayer] amendment back again and again and again and again, until we succeed in restoring religious freedom in the United States." He insisted that the First Amendment "was not written to protect the people and their laws from religious values; it was written to protect those values from Government tyranny." The president also hoped that prayer in the schools would foster religious toleration in that it would expose students to "other people's religions and [to] what other people think."

In March 1984 the Senate opened debate on a school prayer amendment. Senate Majority Leader Howard Baker proclaimed that a prayer amendment had "the best chance in decades" for passage. Public opinion polls backed up Baker's claim, indicating that approximately 80 percent of Americans supported some form of prayer in the public schools. Early in March the Supreme Court ruled that the town of Pawtucket, Rhode Island, could erect a nativity scene during the Christmas holidays. This decision also seemed to indicate a lowering of the "wall of separation between church and state" that would allow school prayer to return. In this favorable atmosphere two prayer amendments went to the floor for consideration. The first, backed by the Reagan administration, permitted vocal or silent prayer by groups or individuals. The other amendment, submitted by Democratic Senator Alan J. Dixon of Illinois, allowed only silent prayer in the schools.

Despite strong sentiment for the amendment, opposition to prayer in the schools remained stiff. Republican Senator Lowell Weicker of Connecticut, a member of Reagan's own party, led the fight against it in the Senate. Weicker argued that the *Engel* and *Schempp* decisions had never denied students the right to pray. Children could pray at any time by themselves. He also warned that although a majority of the American population might support the amendment, that did not necessarily make the amendment a wise or proper move. Playwright Arthur Miller, writing in the *New York Times,* feared that, if the United States adopted the prayer amendment, it might someday find itself a theocracy like Iran, where opposition to the government equated to opposition to God. Miller implored Americans not to destroy its two hundred years of religious freedom, which had "attracted the respect and envy of persecuted religious people everywhere in the world." *Times* columnist Anthony Lewis analyzed the prayer amendment and concluded that it would not bring religious toleration and freedom, as Reagan hoped, but would bring conflict instead as children of different faiths argued each day over which prayer should be spoken or read. James Reston, editorializing in the *Times,* denounced the amendment measure as simply a political ploy by the president in an election year.

Debate over the prayer amendments raged in the Senate throughout March, culminating in a vote on the Reagan-supported amendment late in the month. In mid-March, Senator Alan Dixon blocked efforts to vote on the Reagan amendment and instead pushed for a vote on his silent prayer amendment. The Senate overwhelmingly decided to table Senator Dixon's silent prayer amendment, setting the stage for Reagan's vocal prayer amendment, which came up for a vote a week later. Republicans and Southern Democrats mustered fifty-six votes for the amendment, but fell eleven votes shy of the two-thirds majority needed for passage. Senator Weicker commented that the amendment had failed because, he felt, many senators had come to realize that "there was no prohibition on school prayer, only organized prayer." Satisfied that this permitted students to practice their religion in the schools, these senators voted against the amendment to avoid becoming entangled in what Weicker called a "mess of speculative, political pottage."

The Equal Access Act and *Mergens*

Two months later school prayer advocates found reason for optimism again when Congress took up discussion of the Equal Access Act. Sponsored by Democrat Dan Bonker of Washington, the act allowed "student-initiated" religious groups to conduct activities on school property on the same terms as other student-organized groups. The bill prohibited any government or school sponsorship of these meetings and stipulated that school employees could attend such sessions but could not participate in them. The bill also contained several clauses designed to prevent coercion in religious activities. These precautions included a provision that disallowed federal, state, or local authorities "to influence the form or content of any prayer or other religious activity; to require any person to participate in prayer or other religious activity; to expend public funds beyond the cost of providing the meeting space for student initiated meetings, or to compel any school agent or employee to attend a student religious meeting."

The House of Representatives voted on the Equal Access Act in May 1984 and rejected it. But a version of the bill that had emerged in the Senate seemed more likely to pass. The Senate version had more flexible rules for punishing violators; it also included provisions to give students equal access to form philosophical and political groups as well as religious ones. This bill passed in the Senate, and when it went to the House for a vote in July, it won easy passage.

The Equal Access Act won the approval of the Supreme Court six years later in *Board of Education v. Mergens* (1990). In 1985 Bridget Mergens—a senior at an Omaha, Nebraska, high school—had sued her school district because it had refused to allow Mergens and fellow students to set up a Christian Bible club. The case had eventually gone to the Eighth Circuit Court of Appeals, which ruled in favor of Mergens's right to organize the club on school grounds under the Equal Access Act. In the appeal by the Omaha school district the Supreme Court, in an 8-to-1 ruling, upheld the lower court's decision. Justice Sandra Day O'Connor wrote the majority opinion, which supported the Equal Access Act: "We think that secondary school students are mature enough and are likely to understand that a school does not endorse or support student speech that it merely permits on a nondiscriminatory basis." Justice John Paul Stevens disagreed with the Court's ruling, arguing that the Court had interpreted the law in a way that failed to provide local school districts with enough discretion in such matters.

Recent Controversies and Debate

Although the Equal Access Act and the Court's ruling in *Mergens* seemed to solve, at least to some degree, the issue of prayer in the public schools, new controversies and debate arose in the 1990s over prayer at public school graduations and other ceremonies. In July 1989 a Jewish family living in Providence, Rhode Island, sued their local school district after a clergyman—who coincidentally was a rabbi—gave a nondenominational invocation at the daughter's high school graduation. A year later the American Civil Liberties Union initiated two similar suits in Utah just six weeks after the Court had heard the *Mergens* case. These cases sought to answer whether prayers—even nondenominational ones spoken at school graduations, baccalaureates, or other similar ceremonies—constituted a breach of the separation between church and state.

In the Rhode Island case, Daniel Weisman brought suit after a rabbi spoke a short prayer at the high school graduation of his daughter, Deborah, in May 1989. Although Jewish, the Weisman family objected to a graduation prayer by any clergyman, arguing that it divided students. Deborah's mother expressed concern that such prayers "cut out the minorities for whom the public school system has been a gateway for full inclusion in our society." The Weismans won their case in United States District Court, but the Providence school district appealed the case, and in 1991 the Supreme Court agreed to hear it the following year.

In *Lee v. Weisman* (1992), a narrow 5-to-4 decision, the Court ruled in favor of the Weismans and thus upheld the ban on prayer in the schools established by the *Engel* and *Schempp* cases some thirty years earlier. Justice Anthony Kennedy, writing for the Court, based the decision on the "timeless lesson" that, if American citizens are "subjected to state sponsored religious exercises," then the government has failed to perform its "duty to guard and respect that sphere of inviolable conscience and belief which is the mark of a free people." Kennedy rejected the arguments of Solicitor General Kenneth Starr and the administration of President George Bush, who had filed an amicus curiae on behalf of the Providence school board. Starr argued that "civic acknowledgments of religion in public life do not offend the establishment clause" if they do not pose the threat of establishment of religion or coerce people to participate in religious activity. Kennedy replied that "the argument lacks all persuasion." He maintained that, because American society considers high school graduation one of life's most important occasions, all Americans attend—despite the fact that no one is compelled to go.

In dissent Justice Antonin Scalia argued that the Founding Fathers knew that nothing fostered religious toleration, even affection, better than people joining together in prayer, despite religious differences. He thus angrily denounced the Court's decision, crying that the Court "with nary a mention that it is doing so" had destroyed an age-old American tradition of "nonsectarian prayer to God at public celebrations." Scalia cautioned that the Court's decisions should not be based on the "changeable philosophical predilections of the Justices of this Court" but instead on the "historic practices of our people."

Despite the decision in *Lee v. Weisman,* the issue of prayer at high school graduations remains unresolved. In March 1993 the American Center for Law and Justice, a legal organization operated by evangelist Pat Robertson, sent over fifteen thousand letters to school districts around the nation, stating that students had the right to lead their own prayers at high school graduations. The Robertson letter also offered to go to court to protect the rights of students to lead prayers. As evidence for students' rights to lead their own prayers, the legal organization cited the November 1992 decision by the U.S. Court of Appeals for the Fifth Circuit, in New Orleans, that permitted student-led prayers in spite of the Supreme Court's decision in *Weisman.* Without a definitive answer to this question, and supported by such religious organizations as Robertson's, students around the nation took the initiative and led their own prayers at graduations in 1993. Thus, despite the Court's ruling in *Weisman,* the question of prayer at public school graduations remains alive.

In addition to the school graduation issue, debate over prayer in the last year has also centered on the "moment of silence" idea. Schools, many of them in the South and Northeast, have sought to provide students with a moment of "contemplative silence" during the school day. In 1994 the State of Georgia passed a law mandating that all public schools in the state allow such a period of quiet. Although ostensibly the measure is not for religious purposes, its legality came into question when an Atlanta, Georgia, social studies teacher refused to observe the moment of silence. Brian Brown, the teacher who challenged the law, asserted that "the [Georgia] Legislature very clearly intended to make it a moment of prayer." Brown initiated a suit against the state in August 1994 on the grounds that the law violated the First Amendment. A colleague at the Atlanta school agreed with Brown, arguing that the law was advancing the agenda of fundamentalist Christians and that its intent was to "get religion into the schools through the back door."

Others, however, fail to see any connection between the moment of silence and school prayer. Jay Sekulow, a lawyer for Pat Robertson's American Center for Law and Justice, insisted that the law had nothing to do with religion, that it simply allowed students to "think for 60 seconds" before starting school. Sekulow also argued that school prayer opponents, noting that "to have a constitutional crisis over a moment of reflection shows the absurdity of how far the separation of church-and-state arguments are starting to go."

The Republican majority that was elected to Congress in November 1994 considered taking the school prayer issue to a new level. Many Republicans receive support from religious organizations interested in restoring voluntary prayer in the public schools. Now in control of both houses of Congress, the Republicans have talked about resurrecting school prayer amendments. After winning the Speaker position in November, Representative Newt Gingrich acknowledged a willingness to work with President Clinton on passing a school prayer amendment. He also argued that the Republican sweep of the congressional elections showed that Americans want to instill in themselves and their children a stronger sense of morality. Gingrich believed that school prayer would be one route toward achieving this goal. So far, however, Congress has made no serious effort to alter the status quo on this issue. In 1995 Congress passed joint resolutions favoring voluntary school prayer, but no proposed Constitutional Amendment passed the Congress.

Summary

The debate over school prayer in the United States remains divisive. In the 1962 *Engel* ruling the Supreme Court found that states requiring or permitting prayer in their public school systems represented a government-sponsored form of religion prohibited by the Establishment Clause of the First Amendment. A year later the Court reaffirmed its *Engel* decision with a concurring ruling in *Schempp,* which also developed a test for determining whether a law has breached the Establishment Clause. If the purpose of primary effect of the law either advances or inhibits religion, then it violates the Establishment Clause. The decisions in these two cases have formed the basis of the ban on school prayer in American public schools for the past three decades. The Court has remained consistent with these rulings in its decisions in later cases, such as in *Lee v. Weisman.*

Many Americans have objected to the

Supreme Court's ban on school prayer and have worked to circumvent the ban or overrule it on both the federal and the state level. In Congress efforts have routinely been made to pass a school prayer amendment that would nullify the High Court's ban and permit states to allow prayer in the public schools. With strong endorsement from President Reagan, such an amendment had solid support in the Senate in the mid-1980s. Such amendments have often cut across party lines as in the case of the Reagan amendment, which gained a majority in the Senate but failed to get the two-thirds vote needed for a constitutional amendment. Nineteen Democratic senators voted for the amendment, while eighteen Republican senators voted against it. Indeed, Senator Lowell Weicker, a member of Reagan's own party led the opposition in the Senate to the school prayer amendment.

Many states—particularly in the South, Northeast, and Midwest—have tried to take the matter into their own hands by passing laws that reinstated prayer into the schools. Some states have tried to get around the ban on prayer by allowing church groups to distribute Bibles to students before school hours or at the closing of the school day. Most of these cases have resulted in suits in which either state courts or the Supreme Court have ruled such laws unconstitutional.

Some compromise has been reached on the school prayer issue. The passage of the Equal Access Act in 1984 allowed for the return of school prayer into the schools. This law requires public school systems to grant student-led religious organizations equal opportunity to hold meetings and activities on school grounds. At the same time it forbids school employees to take part in any such meeting or activity, or in any way to endorse or disapprove of the religious function.

Rob Osberg

Bibliography

Menendez, Albert, *School Prayer and Other Religious Issues in American Public Education* (New York: Garland, 1985).

Sikorski, Robert, *Prayer in Public Schools and the Constitution, 1961–1992,* vols. 1–3 in Controversies in Constitutional Law Series, ed. Paul Finkelman (New York: Garland, 1993).

Cases Cited

Board of Education v. Mergens, 496 U.S. 226 (1990).

Engel v. Vitale, 370 U.S. 421 (1962).

Lee v. Weisman, 505 U.S. 577 (1992).

Murray v. Baltimore City Schools, 179 A. 2d 698 (1962).

School District of Abington Township v. Schempp, 374 U.S. 203 (1963).

Secular Humanism

Legal questions involving "secular humanism" have centered on (1) whether secular humanism is a religion within the context of the First Amendment's prohibition against both the establishment of a religion and the denial of the free exercise of religion and (2) whether statutes providing conscientious objector status based on religious beliefs extend to secular humanists or are limited to more traditional religions.

The term "humanism" refers to a philosophical movement with roots extending into the fourteenth century. Originally "humanitas" referred simply to an educated man—someone familiar with what we now think of as the liberal arts. Believing that the greatness of classical culture had been lost during the Middle Ages, fourteenth-century humanists sought to regain the dignity and virtue of classical Greek and Roman civilizations. In order to do this, they stressed the importance of education, including history, ethics, politics, and poetry.

Their emphasis on classical civilization and on education provides what is now regarded as the essence of secular humanism: the dignity of the individual. Distinguished from other, lower animals by the capacity to reason, human beings were seen to possess the capacity to understand nature, society, and history alike. But in addition to the capacity to gain knowledge—or perhaps in virtue of that capacity—humanists also stressed the autonomy and dignity of human beings. Restless under the authority of the Catholic Church, humanists also emphasized the importance of political and moral freedom. Humankind was thought to be the center of God's creation, entrusted with the freedom to define itself as well as to understand the natural world. In that same vein, humanists were also often ardent defenders of religious toleration; indeed, it is thought by many that religious and philosophical differences might be overcome by marrying Christian religious faith and the wisdom of ancient philosophy.

The first U.S. Supreme Court case in which secular humanism is explicitly mentioned is *Torcaso v. Watkins* (1961). The issue in *Torcaso* was whether the Establishment Clause of the First Amendment, applied to the states through the Fourteenth Amendment, allows a state to require an oath declaring belief in God as a condition of receiving a commission to serve as a notary public. In holding the requirement unconstitutional, Justice Hugo Black, writing for the Court, described secular humanism—along with Buddhism, Taoism, and Ethical Culture—as "religions" that "do not teach what would generally be considered a belief in the existence of God." Having broadly defined the term, the Court stressed that no government can force a person to "profess a belief or disbelief in any religion." Indeed, said the Court, government may not aid those religions based on a belief in the existence of God as against those religions founded on different beliefs.

In another case, *United States v. Seeger* (1965), the Supreme Court took a similar position and elaborated on the rationale behind that broad conception of "religion." The issue in *Seeger* involved a provision of the Universal Military Training and Service Act exempting conscientious objectors from military service by reason of their "religious training and belief," which the code defined as "an individual's belief in a relation to a Supreme Being involving duties superior to those arising from any human relation." Such religious beliefs specifically do not include "political, sociological, or philosophical views or a merely personal moral code." Seeger was refused conscientious objector status, based on his admitted "skepticism" about the existence of God. Seeger did not deny the existence of a "Supreme Intelligence," and indeed stated that it seemed likely based on the "cosmic order" that there may well be some "creative intelligence" behind it. The Court held that Congress had not intended to require a narrow definition of "Supreme Being" and therefore that the question to be asked is whether the claimed belief occupies "the same place in the life of the objector as an orthodox belief in God holds in the life of one clearly qualified for exemption." Thus, concluded the Court, Seeger's conviction for draft evasion should be overturned.

Extending that same reasoning a step further in *Welsh v. United States* (1970), the Supreme Court overturned Welsh's conviction for violating the same act despite the fact that he had initially told the hearing officer that his objections were not based on a "religion." Relying on *Seeger,* however, the Court held that, although Welsh's beliefs were not "religious" if the term is narrowly construed, they were religious in the sense that Congress intended by the act, because the beliefs fulfill the same role in his life as more traditional religious beliefs do for others. As in *Seeger* the Court in *Welsh* again explicitly included secular humanism among the religious beliefs that can constitute the basis of an exemption for military service under the Universal Military Training and Service Act.

Both establishment and free exercise issues were raised in, *Grove v. Mead School District No. 354* (1985). The issue in *Grove* turned on whether the use of a textbook called *The Learning Tree* violated the free exercise rights of fundamentalist Christian parents, as well as whether its use "establishes" a religion. The lower court rejected both claims, the Ninth Circuit agreed, and the Supreme Court denied certiorari.

Although it acknowledged that religious freedom includes as one of its aspects the right of parents to control the religious training of their children, the Court also stressed that the daughter in *Grove* had been assigned another textbook to read, after her parents complained, and that she had not been required to participate in classroom discussions of *The Learning Tree.* Turning to establishment issues, Judge Eugene A. Wright also held that the book in question is "religiously neutral" and therefore that its use does not constitute establishment of either religion or "anti-religion."

The central difficulty with the plaintiffs' argument, said Judge Wright, is that they divide thinking about values into only two categories: religious and antireligious. Having done that, he said, they then treat anything that is secular or "nonreligious" as "antireligious"—an inference that, he argued, is unwarranted. The Supreme Court, he pointed out, citing *Lemon v. Kurtzman* (1971), has often focused on the question whether regulations reflect a "secular purpose" and "secular effect." That means, however, that for

Establishment Clause purposes "secular" must be understood to mean religiously neutral rather than antireligious. Quoting extensively from *The Learning Tree,* Judge Wright concluded that it was neither religious nor antireligious, and so its use did not violate the Establishment Clause. (It is interesting to note, in this connection, that the Court in *Grove* also indicated its agreement with the suggestion that "religion" should be defined more broadly when, as in *Torcaso,* the issue is free exercise rather than establishment.)

The question whether secular humanism constitutes a religion for purposes of the First Amendment's free exercise and Establishment Clauses was again confronted squarely in *Smith v. Board of School Commissioners of Mobile County* (1987), although in this case the district court found that secular humanism can be a religion and that textbooks had established it. *Smith* began when a conservative religious group filed suit against the Mobile, Alabama, public school system, arguing that the state had established the "religion" of secular humanism by its selection of specific textbooks. After an extensive hearing involving numerous expert witnesses on both sides—including members of the Humanist Society—Judge Brevard Hand ruled that indeed Alabama's textbooks were an unconstitutional establishment of the religion of secular humanism.

Judge Hand's opinion in the District Court analyzed the question in terms of three related issues. The first part (and for these purposes, the most important) was devoted to demonstrating that secular humanism was, for purposes of the First Amendment, a religion. Relying on *Torcaso, Seeger,* and *Welsh,* he pointed out that the Supreme Court must consider many factors in defining religion and that the religion clauses do not protect only traditional religious beliefs. He further pointed out that the Court had often spoken of the importance of a belief's function in a person's life and had not required explicit belief in a traditional God or even membership in traditional religious institutions.

Judge Hand also pressed the analysis further than this psychofunctional approach, used by the Court in earlier cases, to distinguish four features that define religion for purposes of the First Amendment. Religions, he said, involve beliefs about (1) existence of a supernatural reality, (2) the nature of man, (3) the ultimate end or purpose of man's existence, and (4) the purpose and nature of the universe.

Turning next to the question whether secular humanism is a constitutional "religion" within the terms he had described, Judge Hand argued that it is. Secular humanism holds an official position on each of the four issues: It denies a supernatural reality, sees man as a purely biological being, defines man's purpose as seeking personal fulfillment, and denies that there is any divine purpose to the universe. Additionally, he pointed out, secular humanism has an organizational structure, like other religions, and even publishes various periodicals as well the "Humanist Manifesto"—a "platform" explaining its "belief system." He concluded that, for purposes of the First Amendment, secular humanism is a religious belief system, so that government can neither establish it nor infringe the free exercise rights of those who believe in it.

Judge Hand next considered the textbooks themselves, and, after a detailed discussion of their content—which he argued discriminate against theistic religions and preach the truths of secular humanism—he concluded that the books must be withdrawn in favor of ones that are "neutral" among all religions including secular humanism and traditional religions. Requiring students to read those books, he argued, is in reality no different from requiring them to read the Bible: Both constitute, according to the Supreme Court's definition, an unconstitutional establishment of a religion.

The Eleventh Circuit overturned Judge Hand's decision. Avoiding the question whether secular humanism is a religion, the court of appeals ruled that the textbooks would not establish it even if it were a religion. The state did not have the establishment of secular humanism as its purpose in choosing the books, nor was that an effect of its decision. Rather, said the court of appeals, the effect of the texts was to instill in children values such as "independent thought, tolerance of diverse views, self-respect, maturing, self-reliance and logical decisionmaking." This purpose, said the judges, is an "entirely appropriate secular effect."

The Supreme Court's most recent foray into issues of religion and secular humanism, *Edwards v. Aguillard* (1987), arose in response to a Louisiana "balanced treatment" law requiring those who teach evolution in public schools to also teach creationism as another account of the origins of human life. Unlike teaching evolution, which can be done without intending to advocate the "religion" of secular humanism in violation of the Establishment Clause, here the "preeminent purpose" of the legislature, in the words of Justice William Brennan, was "clearly to advance the religious viewpoint that a supernatural being created humankind."

Justice Antonin Scalia, in dissent, argued that the law was not unconstitutional, because it was at least possible that the legislature had legitimate educational and other objectives. Among the evidence Justice Scalia cited were statements by the bill's sponsor, Senator Keith, indicating that in *Torcaso* the Court had found secular humanism to be a "religion" and therefore that the balanced treatment required by the law merely brings the state back into compliance with the Establishment Clause by neutrally discussing the creationist view as well as the alternative, evolutionary theory. And, given the requirement that the Court must choose the interpretation of legislative intent that can most readily save a statute from constitutional challenge, Justice Scalia said that the equal-time law is not facially unconstitutional and should be upheld.

The question whether secular humanism constitutes a religion for purposes of constitutional interpretation has thus arisen in the context of free exercise as well as establishment. With the exception of one district court decision, judges have been reluctant to endorse the notion that secular humanism is a "religion" when the issue involves texts that do not explicitly advocate a particular religion, even if the texts are incompatible with the religious views of fundamentalists. For free exercise purposes, provisions allowing children to opt out of classes that discuss such material are an important part of the courts' overall assessment of the religious burdens that the texts impose.

So while courts have often indicated sympathy for parents whose child may be forced to confront ideas and works that tend to undermine the family's religious beliefs, that is not, by itself, a sufficiently heavy burden to justify a challenge to the material as an unconstitutional infringement of free exercise. Courts have been more willing to extend the definition of religion to include secular humanism, however, when interpreting the Selective Service Act. The question whether secular humanism is a religion also raises the possibility, as yet unresolved, that there are two constitutional definitions of religion—one, more broad, that includes secular humanism and is appropriate to free exercise; and another, more narrow, that applies to establishment.

John Arthur

Bibliography

Choper, Jesse, "Defining Religion in the First Amendment," 1982 *University of Illinois Law Review* 579–613 (1982).

Davidow, Robert P., "Secular Humanism and Its First Amendment Implications: A Response to Whitehead and Conlan," 11 *Texas Tech Law Review* 51–59 (1979).

Greenwalt, Kent, "Religion As a Concept in Constitutional Law," 72 *California Law Review* 753–816 (1984).

Sandel, Michael, "Religious Liberty: Freedom of Conscience or Freedom of Choice," 1989 *Utah Law Review* 597–615 (1989).

"Toward a Constitutional Definition of Religion," 91 *Harvard Law Review* 1056–1089 (1978).

Whitehead, John, and John Conlan, "The Establishment of the Religion of Secular Humanism," 10 *Texas Tech Law Review* 1–66 (1978).

Cases and Statutes Cited

Edwards v. Aguillard, 482 U.S. 578 (1987).

Grove v. Mead School District No. 354, 753 F. 2d 1528 (1985). 9th Circ

Lemon v. Kurtzman, 403 U.S. 602 (1971).

Smith v. Board of School Commissioners of Mobile County, 655 F. Supp. 939 (S.D. Ala., 1987).

Smith v. Board of School Commissioners of Mobile County, 827 F. 2d 684 (11th Cir., 1987).

Torcaso v. Watkins, 367 U.S. 488 (1961).

United States v. Seeger, 380 U.S. 163 (1965).

Welsh v. United States, 398 U.S. 333 (1970).

Universal Military Training and Service Act, 50 U.S.C App. 456 (j).

Sherbert v. Verner 374 U.S. 398 (1963)

For almost thirty years *Sherbert v. Verner* (1963) was the leading case interpreting the

Free Exercise Clause. *Sherbert* is generally credited with the doctrine that a law or government practice that burdens the exercise of religion may be enforced only if it is necessary to achieve a compelling governmental purpose. This meant that government was required to make exemptions or accommodations from generally applicable laws when those laws unnecessarily burdened the free exercise of religion. The Court overruled this doctrine in *Employment Division, Department of Human Resources of Oregon v. Smith* (1990).

Sherbert was decided the same day as *School District of Abington Township v. Schempp* (1963), which held that daily Bible readings in the public schools were unconstitutional. *Sherbert* and *Schempp* inaugurated an era in which the courts interpreted both the free exercise and Establishment Clauses expansively—an approach that pleased many civil libertarians but, as Justice Potter Stewart charged at the time and more critics have stated since, appeared to place the two religion clauses into direct conflict with one another. The Free Exercise Clause, as interpreted in *Sherbert,* appeared to require the government to undertake special efforts for the protection and benefit of religion; but the Establishment Clause, as interpreted in *Schempp* and later cases, appeared to forbid the government to take any action that would benefit or advance religion. This conflict between the clauses was to be the central theme of case law and scholarly criticism for the next generation.

Sherbert arose when Adele Sherbert, a Seventh-Day Adventist, was discharged from her job in a textile mill in Spartanburg, South Carolina, for refusing to work on Saturday. The mill, which previously had operated only five days a week, expanded its operations to Saturday two years after Sherbert had begun to work there. (It was stipulated in the decision that the Seventh-Day Adventist religion forbids Saturday labor.) Being unable to find five-day employment at any other textile mill in the area, or in another industry, Sherbert accordingly filed for unemployment compensation, but the state Employment Security Commission found her ineligible for jobless benefits because she had "failed, without good cause, to accept available suitable work when offered."

The Supreme Court, in an opinion by Justice William J. Brennan, Jr., held that this denial of benefits violated the free exercise Clause of the First Amendment, as applied to the states through the Fourteenth Amendment. According to the Court, the denial of unemployment compensation "forces [Mrs. Sherbert] to choose between following the precepts of her religion and forfeiting benefits, on the one hand, and abandoning one of the precepts of her religion in order to accept work, on the other hand. Government imposition of such a choice puts the same kind of burden on the free exercise of religion as would a fine imposed against appellant for her Saturday worship." The immediate significance of this holding was that it extended the logic of the unconstitutional conditions doctrine, which had already taken hold in the area of free speech, to the Free Exercise Clause. This meant that the government could not violate an individual's constitutional rights by withholding a "benefit" for constitutionally invalid reasons, any more than it could by imposing a criminal fine or penalty.

Having found that the unemployment compensation scheme constitutes a burden on the free exercise of religion (by withholding benefits because of Sherbert's exercise of a constitutionally protected right), the Court asked whether the government had a "compelling" justification for its ruling. "[I]n this highly sensitive constitutional area," the Court said, "[o]nly the gravest abuses, endangering paramount interests, give occasion for permissible limitation." The only justification asserted by the state was the difficulty of distinguishing sincere religious claims from spurious ones. This might well have been treated as a serious (even if not a "compelling") interest, because making the determination of sincerity might be thought to "entangle" the state in delicate religious judgments. This is not dissimilar to the "entanglements" that the Court, in *Lemon v. Kurtzman* (1971) and subsequent cases, has stated are involved in distinguishing between secular and religious elements in the parochial school curriculum. But in *Sherbert* the Court dismissed this interest on the ground that the record in the case did not seem to raise any doubts about sincerity.

The opinion for the majority did not appear to recognize the ambiguity in its assertion that denial of unemployment compensation to Sherbert burdened her exercise of religion. Under the South Carolina scheme, workers who refused employment or were discharged because of personal, but nonreligious, objections to the nature of the work were not generally eligible for compensation. For example, in *Judson Mills v. South Carolina Unemployment Commission* (1944) a worker was denied unemployment compensation when she refused transfer to a different shift that would make it impossible to care for her four children. It could be said, therefore, that the free exercise of religion is no more burdened by the South Carolina unemployment system than is any other personal decision.

There were two possible responses to this point, one broad and one narrow. First, the majority might have acknowledged that the unemployment compensation scheme burdened all personal decisions that conflict with work requirements but could have defended its result on the ground that the Free Exercise Clause singles out religious exercise for special protection. The Constitution does not protect against the imposition of burdens on other personal decisions, but, the Supreme Court held in *Murdock v. Pennsylvania* (1943), it does protect the exercise of religion, which is a preferred freedom under the Bill of Rights. This would result in a broad protection for religious exercise in a wide variety of contexts. This broad reading was implicitly adopted in *Wisconsin v. Yoder* (1972) and was later repudiated in *Smith*.

Alternatively, the majority could have relied on the fact that the state limits denial of benefits to those who have refused "without good cause" to accept "suitable" employment. The Court could have held that the Free Exercise Clause precludes the state from determining that adherence to a sincerely held religious tenet is not "good cause" or that work which violates such a tenet is "suitable." The effect of such a ruling would be to require states to treat adherence to sincere religious tenets with at least the same degree of respect that they accord other reasons for refusing work that may be offered. In other words, when the state has in place a system of individualized determinations based on the individual's reasons for acting or refusing to act, it may not exclude religious reasons from the protected class. This narrower explanation for the result in *Sherbert* appears to survive the decision in *Smith*.

Although the majority opinion in *Sherbert* appeared oblivious to this problem, concurring and dissenting opinions by Justices Stewart and Harlan were not. These opinions set the doctrinal stage for future debates about the relation between the two religion clauses. Both of these justices recognized that the Court's interpretation of the Free Exercise Clause (as requiring protection for religion that is not accorded to nonreligious reasons for declining employment) was in a "head-on collision" (to use Stewart's phrase) with the Court's interpretation of the Establishment Clause, which forbids preference for religion over nonreligion.

Justice Potter Stewart advocated resolving the conflict by abandoning the expansive interpretation of the Establishment Clause, which he stated was "historically unsound and constitutionally wrong." According to Stewart, "the guarantee of religious liberty embodied in the Free Exercise Clause affirmatively requires government to create an atmosphere of hospitality and accommodation to individual belief or disbelief. In short, I think our Constitution commands the positive protection by government of religious freedom, not only for a minority, however small, not only for the majority, however large, but for each of us."

In dissent, Justice Louis Harlan, joined by Justice Byron White, advocated resolving the conflict by abandoning the expansive interpretation of the Free Exercise Clause. Declaring that "[t]hose situations in which the Constitution may require special treatment on account of religion are, in my view, few and far between," he stated that he could not "subscribe to the conclusion that the State is constitutionally *compelled* to carve out an exception to its general rule of eligibility in the present case." Justice Harlan would thus resolve the conflict by leaving the accommodation of religion to the discretion of the political branches. He acknowledged that this would necessitate rejection of the expansive interpretation of the Establishment and Free Exercise Clauses, and he contended for "flexibility" in construction of both clauses. He thus adumbrated the position of the Court thirty years later in *Smith*. Seven years later, in *Welsh v. United States* (1970), Harlan "qualified" his position in *Sherbert* by specifying that any exception to a neutral law designed to accommodate religious scruples "would have to be sufficiently broad to be religiously neutral," and he voted (over dissents by

Justices Stewart and White) to hold unconstitutional a statute that exempted only religious conscientious objectors from the draft.

The various opinions in *Sherbert* thus set forth, for the first time, the interpretive options that would face the Court for years to come. The majority opinion represented the activist interpretation, reading both religion clauses expansively without seeming to recognize that this makes them mutually contradictory. Justices Harlan and White represented the position of judicial restraint, interpreting both clauses narrowly and leaving "flexibility" to the democratic branches to determine the proper treatment of religion, within wide bounds. Justice Stewart represented the accommodationist position, insisting on a vigorous enforcement of free exercise and treating the Establishment Clause as a guarantee against religious coercion or denominational favoritism. Finally, Justice Harlan hinted at, and later adopted, the secularist interpretation, under which the Free Exercise Clause does not permit, and the Establishment Clause forbids, government action that accommodates the exercise of religion. At present the Supreme Court appears to have adopted Justice Harlan's original position.

Michael W. McConnell

Bibliography

Galanter, Marc, "Religious Freedom in the United States: A Turning Point?" 1966 *Wisconsin Law Review* 217–296 (1966).

Gianella, Donald A., "Religious Liberty, Nonestablishment, and Doctrinal Development, Part I, The Religious Liberty Guarantee," 80 *Harvard Law Review* 1381–1431 (1967).

McConnell, Michael W., and Richard Posner, "An Economic Approach to Issues of Religious Freedom," 56 *University of Chicago Law Review* 1–60 (1989).

Pepper, Stephen, "Taking the Free Exercise Clause Seriously," 1986 *Brigham Young University Law Review* 299–336 (1986).

Cases Cited

Employment Division, Department of Human Resources of Oregon v. Smith, 494 U.S. 872 (1990).

Judson Mills v. South Carolina Unemployment Commission, 204 S.C. 37, 28 S.E. 2d 535 (1944).

Lemon v. Kurtzman, 403 U.S. 602 (1971).

Murdock v. Pennsylvania, 319 U.S. 105 (1943).

School District of Abington Township v. Schempp, 374 U.S. 203 (1963).

Sherbert v. Verner, 374 U.S. 398 (1963).

Welsh v. United States, 398 U.S. 333 (1970).

Wisconsin v. Yoder, 406 U.S. 205 (1972).

Sincerity and Veracity of Religious Belief

For a person to invoke the constitutional protections of religious freedom, a practice, institution, or motive must be a *religious* one. In most cases, this threshold is crossed without controversy, but occasionally it becomes the heart of the conflict. When that happens, courts may be asked to judge whether the claims are genuinely religious ones or whether the claimant is sincerely religious. Judging either the veracity of religious beliefs or the sincerity of the believer brings government perilously close to making the kinds of judgments the First Amendment seems to preclude, and yet, occasionally, such judgments are unavoidable. The most publicized instances of these controversies arise when religious figures are charged with financial fraud.

Conflicts over sincerity have also been raised in a variety of other contexts, including attempts by draftees to obtain religious exemptions from military service (*Engels v. United States ex rel. Samuels,* [1946]) attempts by prisoners to seek recognition of novel religions in prisons (*Theriault v. Silber* [5th Cir. 1974] and *Remmers v. Brewer* [S.D. Iowa 1973]), and demands by employees for religious accommodation in the workplace (*Dobkin v. District of Columbia* [D.C. 1963]).

The bitter experiences of the Mormon Church during the nineteenth century illustrate the pitfalls of making distinctions between truth and falsity in religion. These problems grew out of the conflict between the federal government's attempts to prohibit polygamy and the church's claim that polygamy was religiously mandated and hence protected by the First Amendment. In the case of *Davis v. Beason* (1890) the U.S. Supreme Court said that Mormon doctrines were not religious tenets according to "the common sense of mankind"; the church's charter was repealed, and its teaching of polygamy was declared to be a mere "pretense":

The State has a perfect right to prohibit polygamy, and all other open offenses against the enlightened sentiment of mankind, notwithstanding the pretense of religious conviction by which they may be advanced and practiced.

Implicit in this and similar decisions was that there were objectively "true" and "false" beliefs and that courts could appropriately determine which beliefs were false and could exclude them from First Amendment protection.

Fervor or Fraud?

Although courts have subsequently been more circumspect in making pronouncements about veracity, they have continued to consider sincerity. Nontraditional ministries—especially when they actively seek financial contributions—raise continual problems about the distinction between religious fervor and fraud. The case of *New v. United States* (9th Cir. 1917) illustrates one approach to making the distinction. Dr. New claimed to have supernatural powers to heal—to conquer hunger, death, poverty, and misery—which he had achieved through "righteous conduct." In prosecuting him for mail fraud, the government alleged that he had no supernatural power "but was an impostor, an heretic, a seeker of vainglory, a covertor of his neighbor's goods and his neighbor's wife, and was also a habitual indulger in each and every of the sins and practices he pretended to condemn." Hence, the government's allegations impugned both Dr. New's truth claims and his sincerity in claiming them. The Ninth Circuit made clear that Dr. New was entitled to believe anything he wanted but could not *pretend* to hold beliefs "for false and fraudulent purposes of procuring money. . . ." The evidence of Dr. New's "pretense" was his hypocrisy in failing to abide by the prescriptions of the faith he preached.

The most important and sophisticated attempt by the Supreme Court to wrestle with these problems was the fraud conviction case of *United States v. Ballard* (1944), which provided the focus for the Court's first serious reflection on the questions of religious truth and falsity. Guy Ballard experienced a religious experience in 1930; subsequently, he, his wife, and son founded a religious movement to propagate the supernatural messages he had received. After he died in 1939, his wife and son were indicted for mail fraud, charged with making false claims (specifically, having the power to heal) which "they well knew" were false. The trial judge was sensitive to the difficulty of judging "religious" beliefs. He therefore separated the question of the truth of the Ballards' religious beliefs from their sincerity, and he instructed the jury that, although the veracity of the Ballards' beliefs could not be questioned, their sincerity could. The Ballards argued that both questions violated their religious freedom rights. On appeal, the circuit court judge noted that they were originally indicted for "false" representations, not insincere ones; hence, the government had to prove that their religious representations were false. The Supreme Court granted certiorari, and a divided Court considered for the first time how to handle the difficult issue of the truth or falsity of religious belief.

The Supreme Court split three ways: Three justices (Harlan Stone, Owen Roberts, and Felix Frankfurter) argued that the Ballards could be punished for making false claims; hence, the veracity of their claims was indeed appropriate for courts. Justice Robert Jackson voted to overturn the conviction, arguing that both truth and veracity are beyond the ken of the judiciary, because they are inseparable. The majority, in an opinion written by Justice Douglas, took a middle position and found that the trial court had made the appropriate distinction between veracity and sincerity. The majority upheld the Ballards' mail fraud conviction and affirmed the trial judge's instruction that the jury may not consider the veracity of their religious claims, only their sincerity. Justice William O. Douglas's words remain a classic statement:

> Heresy trials are foreign to our Constitution. Men may believe what they cannot prove. They may not be put to the proof of their religious doctrines or beliefs. Religious experiences which are as real as life to some may be incomprehensible to others. Yet the fact that they may be beyond the ken of mortals does not mean that they can be made suspect before the law. Many take their gospel from the New Testament. But it would hardly be supposed that they could be tried before a jury charged with the duty of determin-

ing whether those teachings contained false representations. The miracles of the New Testament, the Divinity of Christ, life after death, the power of prayer are deep in the religious convictions of many. If one could be sent to jail because a jury in a hostile environment found those teachings to be false, little indeed would be left of religious freedom.

The Ballards' conviction for mail fraud was based on the Court's insistence that a person distinguish what one believes from what is believable. In his dissent, Justice Jackson raised a powerful objection to this distinction and argued that both veracity and sincerity should be beyond the ken of the judiciary. His argument is worth quoting at some length:

> . . . I do not see how we can separate an issue as to what is believed from considerations as to what is believable. The most convincing proof that one believes his statement is to show that they have been true in his experience. Likewise, that one knowingly falsified is best proved by showing that what he said happened never did happen. How can the Government prove these persons knew something to be false which it cannot prove to be false? If we try religious sincerity severed from religious verity, we isolate the dispute from the very considerations which in common experience provide its most believable answers. . . .
>
> And I do not know what degree of skepticism or disbelief in a religious representation amounts to actionable fraud. . . . Some who profess belief in the Bible read literally what others read as allegory or metaphor, as they read Aesop's fables. Religious symbolism is even used by some with the same mental reservations one has in teaching of Santa Claus or Uncle Sam or Easter bunnies or dispassionate judges. It is hard in matters so mystical to say how literally one is bound to believe the doctrine he teaches and even more difficult to say how far it is reliance on the teacher's literal belief which induces followers to give him money.

When, in cases like *Ballard,* a person's religious sincerity is in dispute, courts must confront evidence for ascertaining sincerity or its absence. As in the *New* case, disregard for one's own teachings is evidence of insincerity. In addition, commercial or other self-serving motives, evidence of criminal behavior, and frivolity have also been considered as evidence of insincerity. On the other hand, the willingness to sacrifice for one's beliefs, and long-standing commitment—especially to institutional groups that share one's faith—help establish sincerity.

Nonreligious Motives

Conflicts involving the Church of Scientology exemplify the confounding problem of commercial motive. Scientology, developed in the 1950s by the late author L. Ron Hubbard, occupies a disputed border between a profitable enterprise and a church. Scientology teaches that spiritual awareness can be enhanced and that irrational behavior can be reduced by clearing "engrams" from one's mind through intensive counseling called "auditing." During auditing a person's skin responses are measured by a galvanometer called an E-meter, which assists the auditor in determining the subject's spiritual condition. Because of the church's belief in a "doctrine of exchange," persons receiving auditing are required to pay for this service. The first of Scientology's many legal problems arose when the Food and Drug Administration declared E-meters to be mislabeled—that is, falsely represented as efficacious in treating physical illnesses. Thus, if the benefits claimed for E-meters were secular, they would be subject to FDA regulation, and quite likely a determination would be reached that they do not produce the benefits claimed. On the other hand, if the benefits promoted were *religious* ones, these claims would be beyond the reach of governmental regulators, because the issue of religious veracity is not justiciable. In *Founding Church of Scientology v. United States* (D.C. Cir. 1969) the circuit court decided that Scientology was a religion protected by the Free Exercise Clause; hence, claims made about E-meters were spiritual in nature and were not subject to prosecution for false and misleading advertising. On remand, however, the distinct court judge required the Church of Scientology to cease making medical or scientific claims for the benefits of E-meters and to situate its claims in a religious context.

Conflicts between religious practices and narcotics laws have presented another context for disputes about religious sincerity. In *People v. Woody* (Calif., 1964) the California Supreme Court ruled that traditional, ritual use of peyote by unquestionably sincere members of the Native American Church was protected by the Free Exercise Clause. But in *State v. Bullard* (N.C., 1966), this protection did not extend to drug use without evidence of religious sincerity; and in *Leary v. United States* (1969) the Fifth Circuit in 1967 had ruled that Dr. Leary's religious faith was simply insufficient to outweigh the state's interest in enforcing its narcotics laws. Perhaps the classic case in this respect is *United States v. Kuch* (D.C. Cir. 1968), in which the evidence of insincerity was frivolity. In this case, the district court upheld the conviction for illegal marijuana possession and transportation against a primate of the New American Church who claimed that marijuana and LSD were "sacraments" of her church and thus protected by the First Amendment. Examining church documents, the court found no belief in a supreme being and no religious discipline, ritual, or tenets to guide daily existence. Documents revealed that the ministers were called "Boo Hoos"; the church symbol was a three-eyed toad; the bulletin was entitled "Divine Toad Sweat"; the church anthems were "Puff the Magic Dragon" and Row, Row, Row Your Boat"; and the church motto was "Victory over Horseshit." In general, the court concluded that the church's catechism was "full of goofy nonsense."

Evidence of Sincerity

"Goofy nonsense" may disqualify a claim to religious sincerity, but a person making a religious claim need not be theologically sophisticated. Although faiths that are grounded in recognized religious groups have an easier time demonstrating their sincerity, neither individually held faiths (*Frazee v. Illinois Department of Employment Security* [1989]) nor disagreement with other members of one's faith (*Thomas v. Review Board of the Indiana Employment Security Division* [1981]) are appropriate grounds for courts to reject the sincerity of one's religious motivations. Inconsistency in religious practice may raise questions of sincerity; for example, in *Dobkin* the court was skeptical of a Saturday Sabbatarian's request for religious accommodation in the workplace when it was shown that he had been known to work in his office on Saturdays. While obvious hypocrisy and cynicism may call one's sincerity into question, occasional lapses in consistency of religious conduct do not impugn one's sincerity.

In seeking evidence of sincerity, courts may also inquire into the origins of beliefs (religious training, for example). Nevertheless, it has affirmed that recently adopted faiths are fully protected (*Hobbie v. Unemployment Appeals Commission* [1987]).

All these cases reiterate the essential disagreements that emerged in *Ballard.* The strongest advocates of religious accommodation continue to argue Justice Jackson's point that any judicial examination of religious sincerity inevitably involves scrutiny of the beliefs themselves; hence, such examination should be forbidden. Those more sympathetic to secular interests follow Justice Douglas's argument that the truth or falsity of religious doctrine can be distinguished from the sincerity of the believer and that courts may examine the latter when necessary.

Bette Novit Evans

Bibliography

Heins, Marjorie, "Other People's Faiths: The Scientology Litigation and the Justiciability of Religious Fraud," 9 *Hastings Constitutional Law Quarterly* 153–197 (1981).

Noonan, John, "How Sincere Do You Have to Be to Be Religious?" 1988 *University of Illinois Law Review* 713–724 (1988).

Riga, Peter, "Religion, Sincerity, and the Free Exercise Clause," 25 *Catholic Lawyer* 246–262 (1980).

Senn, Stephen, "The Prosecution of Religious Fraud," 17 *Florida State University Law Review* 325–352 (1990).

Cases Cited

Davis v. Beason, 133 U.S. 333 (1890).

Dobkin v. District of Columbia, 194 A. 2d 657 (D.C. 1963).

Engels v. United States ex rel. Samuels, 324 U.S. 304 (1946).

Founding Church of Scientology v. United States, 409 F. 2d 1146 (D.C. Cir.), cert. denied, 396 U.S. 963 (1969).

Frazee v. Illinois Department of Employment Security, 489 U.S. 829 (1989).
Hobbie v. Unemployment Appeals Commission, 480 U.S. 136 (1987).
Leary v. United States, 383 F. 2d 851 (5th Cir. 1967), rev'd on other grounds, 395 U.S. 6 (1969).
New v. United States, 245 F. 710 (9th Cir. 1917), cert. denied, 246 U.S. 665 (1918).
People v. Woody, 61 Cal. 2d 716, 394 P. 2d 813, 40 Cal. Rptr. 69 (1964).
Remmers v. Brewer, 361 F. Supp. 537 (S.D. Iowa 1975).
State v. Bullard, 267 N.C. 599 (1966).
Theriault v. Silber, 495 F. 2d 390 (5th Cir. 1974).
Thomas v. Review Board of the Indiana Employment Security Division, 450 U.S. 707 (1981).
United States v. Ballard, 322 U.S. 78 (1944).
United States v. Kuch, 288 F. Supp. 439 (D.D.C. 1968).

Smith

See EMPLOYMENT DIVISION, DEPARTMENT OF HUMAN RESOURCES OF OREGON V. SMITH

Snake-Handling Sects

Several small American sects have regarded the handling of snakes and consumption of poisons as a sign or confirmation of religious faith. One of the principal sects, sometimes called the Holiness Church, was founded in Tennessee in 1909 and spread to several states, where it found a number of adherents, usually in remote mountainous areas. Sect members base their beliefs and practices on Mark 16:17–18, which reads as follows in the King James Version of the Bible:

> And these signs shall follow them that believe; in my name shall they cast out devils; and shall speak with new tongues;
>
> They shall take up serpents; and if they drink any deadly thing, it shall not hurt them. . . .

Between 1940 and 1961 at least twenty members of the sects died after suffering snakebites or drinking poison, including the founder of the Holiness Church, who was fatally bitten by a diamondback rattlesnake during a Florida prayer meeting in 1955.

In response to the hazards created by the practices of the sects, several states have enacted criminal statutes to restrict or prohibit the handling of snakes. State courts have consistently upheld these laws. These courts have determined that the compelling interest of the state in protecting the safety and health of its citizens outweighs any burden that the laws impose on the free exercise of religion by the snake-handling sects.

In the most recent case, *State ex rel. Swann v. Pack* (Tenn., 1975), the Supreme Court of Tennessee unanimously held that a minister and an elder of the Holiness Church should be enjoined from handling, displaying, or exhibiting dangerous and poisonous snakes or from consuming poisons, including strychnine. The court held that a lower court had erred in confining the scope of the injunction to the display of snakes in a manner that would endanger the life or health of persons who did not consent to exposure to such danger. According to the court, "the state has a right to protect a person from himself and to demand that he protect his own life." The minister and the elder had been prosecuted by the state following 1973 church services at which two persons were killed by poison and two others were injured by snakebites. Although the defendants asked the U.S. Supreme Court to review the Tennessee decision, the Supreme Court refused to grant certiorari.

In its opinion the Tennessee court declared that the religious practices of the sect were entitled to constitutional protection since the "government must view all citizens and all religious beliefs with absolute and uncompromising neutrality. The day this Country ceases to countenance irreligion or unusual or bizarre religions, it will cease to be free for all religions." In accordance with well-established precedents laid down by the U.S. Supreme Court and lower courts, however, the Tennessee court explained that no religion "has an absolute and unbridled right to pursue any practice of its own choosing. The right to believe is absolute; the right to act is subject to reasonable regulation designed to protect a compelling state interest." Accordingly, the court declared that "a religious practice may be limited, curtailed or restrained to the point of outright prohibition, where it involves a clear and present danger to the interests of society" and that it was necessary for a court to balance "the interests between religious freedom and the preservation of the health, safety and morals of society."

The court's decision in *Swann* was consistent with an earlier decision of the Supreme Court of Tennessee, *Harden v. State* (Tenn., 1948). Decisions in other states likewise have upheld prohibitions on snake handling, even when precautions were taken to protect bystanders from snakes. In sustaining the constitutionality of a city ordinance that prohibited the display of poisonous snakes, the Supreme Court of North Carolina explained in *State v. Massey* (N.C., 1949) that "as a matter of law the case comes down to a very simple question: Which is superior, the public safety or the defendants' religious practices? The authorities are at one in holding that the safety of the public comes first." The Court of Appeals of Kentucky upheld a prohibition on snake handling in *Lawson v. Commonwealth* (Ky., 1942), as did the Court of Appeals of Alabama in *Hill v. State* (Ala., 1956).

In *Kirk v. Commonwealth* (Va., 1947) the Supreme Court of Appeals of Virginia indicated that a minister could be criminally prosecuted for involuntary manslaughter in the death of his wife, who died after suffering a snakebite during a religious service. The court held that the trial court properly instructed a jury that "while the law cannot interfere with a person's religious belief or opinion, this is no excuse for an illegal act made criminal by the law of the land, even though such act is based on conscientious religious belief."

Prohibitions against snake handling remain in force in Tennessee, North Carolina, and Virginia. Violations of the statutes are punishable by small fines in all three states and by maximum imprisonment of thirty days in Tennessee and six months in North Carolina.

William G. Ross

Bibliography

La Barre, Weston, *They Shall Take Up Serpents: Psychology of the Southern Snake-Handling Cult* (Minneapolis: University of Minnesota Press, 1962).

Penegar, Kenneth L., "Survey of Tennessee Constitutional Law in 1976–77," 1978 *University of Tennessee Law Review* 129–133 (1978).

Cases Cited

Harden v. State, 216 S.W. 2d 708 (Tn. 1948).

Hill v. State, 88 So. 2d 880 (Ala. 1956).

Kirk v. Commonwealth, 44 S.E. 2d 409 (Va. 1947).

Lawson v. Commonwealth, 164 S.W. 2d 972 (Ky. 1942).

State ex rel. Swann v. Pack, 527 S.W. 2d 99 (Tn. 1975), cert. denied, 424 U.S. 954 (1976).

State v. Massey, 51 S.E. 2d 179 (N.C. 1949).

Standing to Sue and Religion

Under Article 3 of the Constitution the power of the federal courts is limited to deciding "cases" and "controversies." There is a substantial body of case law defining what constitutes cases and controversies, much of which involves the concept of *standing.* In essence, this concept requires that, in order for a person to bring a lawsuit, the person must be suffering from or threatened with actual injury fairly traceable to the defendant's allegedly unlawful conduct and must be considered likely to be redressed by a favorable court decision.

When government takes action (such as passing a Sunday closing law) that directly affects a person (such as a Jewish shopkeeper who would close on Saturday but remain open on Sunday), standing would pose no barrier (in this example the shopkeeper could bring a suit challenging the constitutionality of the Sunday closing law as a violation of the religion clauses of the First Amendment). Similarly, if a state, locality, or public school requires a student to recite or be exposed to religious texts or instruction, the student or the student's parent, on the student's behalf, would have standing to contest that requirement.

On the other hand, when a government action benefits a religion or religious actors and does not directly injure anyone, the standing requirement may be an insuperable obstacle. For example, to allow religious officials to perform marriages that are recognized by the state does not appear to harm anyone. Consequently, if someone believed that allowing religious officials to perform marriages which are recognized by the state violated the Establishment Clause of the Constitution, that person, because he or she did not suffer a concrete injury from that law, would not have standing to challenge the law in federal courts. The Supreme Court has made clear that a citizen's interest in upholding the Constitution is not sufficient to create standing to bring a lawsuit.

Somewhere between these extremes would be the case where the government—whether federal, state, or local—expends funds that benefit a religion or religious group. The question then is whether a taxpayer is "injured" sufficiently to create standing to bring a lawsuit. In 1923 the Supreme Court answered this question in the negative in the case of *Frothingham v. Mellon* (1923), which involved a taxpayer's challenge to federal expenditures aimed at reducing maternal and infant mortality; the challenge was mounted not under the religion clauses of the First Amendment but under the Tenth Amendment, which reserves powers to the states (or to the people). The Court said that a federal taxpayer's "interest in the moneys of the Treasury . . . is comparatively minute and indeterminate" and that "the effect on future taxation, of any payment out of the funds . . . [is] remote, fluctuating and uncertain." This same case, however, in dictum stated that expenditures by a municipality have a "direct and immediate effect" on a local taxpayer.

Thus, the general rule has developed that taxpayer status is not sufficient to create standing to challenge a federal expenditure, but it may be enough to challenge a local government's expenditure. In *Doremus v. Board of Education* (1952), involving a taxpayer's challenge to Bible reading in a public school, the Supreme Court denied the taxpayer standing by analogizing state expenditures to federal expenditures, rather than to local expenditures. The Court reiterated this position concerning state expenditures in *Asarco, Inc. v. Kadish* (1989).

In *Flast v. Cohen* (1968) the Supreme Court created an exception to the general rule denying taxpayers standing to challenge federal expenditures. In *Flast,* plaintiffs were challenging as a violation of the Establishment Clause of the First Amendment elements of the Elementary and Secondary Education Act of 1965, which could be used to finance instruction in religious schools and to purchase textbooks and other instructional materials for those schools. The plaintiffs' only basis for standing was their status as federal taxpayers. The Court upheld this basis for standing where there was a logical nexus between a plaintiff's status as a taxpayer and both the government action challenged and the constitutional limitation invoked. Here, as in *Frothingham,* there was a sufficient nexus between the status of taxpayer and the government action challenged: the expenditure of government funds. Here there was also a nexus between the status of taxpayer and the constitutional challenge: in the Court's view the Establishment Clause was a specific limitation on the government's power to tax and spend. In *Frothingham,* however, the plaintiff had invoked only the Tenth Amendment, which the Court found not to be such a specific limitation on government expenditures. The Court left unclear which, if any, other constitutional provisions might constitute "specific" limitations on expenditures, but presumably they would not include the Due Process and Equal Protection Clauses.

The Court underlined the narrowness of the *Flast* exception in *Valley Forge Christian College v. Americans United for Separation of Church and State* (1982). Here the federal government had transferred surplus property to a religious institution, and an organization sued to enjoin the transfer as a violation of the Establishment Clause. The organization maintained its standing on the basis of the taxpayer status of its members. The Court, by a 5-to-4 margin, distinguished *Flast* by noting that *Flast* limited its reach to situations in which there was a nexus between the status of taxpayer and the challenged government action. In *Flast* that had been satisfied by the fact that Flast was challenging an exercise of Congress's taxing and spending power under the Constitution. Here, however, the challenged action was an administrative transfer of property pursuant to a statute based on Congress's power under Article 4 of the Constitution to "dispose of . . . property belonging to the United States." Whether the United States kept or disposed of property, or to whom the United States disposed of property, had no relationship to the payment of taxes, and so here there was an insufficient nexus between the taxpayer status and the challenged government action.

Although *Valley Forge Christian College* distinguished *Flast* rather than overruling it, the underlying basis for *Flast* seemed to have eroded. The *Flast* decision was a product of, and reflected the views of, the Court under the leadership of Chief Justice Earl Warren, who authored the opinion. These views can be characterized as removing barriers for citizens to bring suits to enforce the Constitution. Thus, in *Flast* the Court determined standing by downplaying constitutional separation-of-powers concerns in favor of ensuring that the dispute would be presented in an adversary context and in a form traditionally viewed as capable of judicial resolution. Subsequent cases, however, including *Valley Forge Christian College,* have not adopted *Flast*'s flexible and pragmatic description of standing but have instead emphasized the constitutional limitations arising out of separation-of-powers concerns. Nevertheless, as recently as 1988, in *Bowen v. Kendrick,* the Supreme Court expressly applied *Flast* without question.

Because the requirement for standing arises from a constitutional limitation on the federal judiciary, there is no constitutional limitation on state courts' entertaining lawsuits absent the standing required for a suit in federal court. Individual states, however, may have their own standing requirements.

William Funk

Bibliography

Feingenson, Neal R., "Political Standing and Governmental Endorsement of Religion: An Alternative to Current Establishment Clause Doctrine," 40 *DePaul Law Review* 53–114 (1990).

Cases Cited

Asarco, Inc. v. Kadish, 490 U.S. 605 (1989).
Bowen v. Kendrick, 487 U.S. 589 (1988).
Doremus v. Board of Education, 342 U.S. 429 (1952).
Flast v. Cohen, 392 U.S. 83 (1968).
Frothingham v. Mellon, 262 U.S. 447 (1923).
Valley Forge Christian College v. Americans United for Separation of Church and State, 454 U.S. 464 (1982).

State Constitutional Law and Religious Liberty

Reliance on state constitutional provisions for the protection of individual rights has increased significantly since the 1970s. As the Burger and Rehnquist Courts retrenched from the Warren Court's expansive view of individual liberty under the federal Constitution, many litigants were forced to turn to state courts for redress of their claims. Once a relative backwater of judicial activity, state constitutional jurisprudence has come to be recognized as a leading source in the development of contemporary standards for individual liberties.

Every state has its own constitution, which serves as the chief charter of government and the chief source of limitations on that government; a state's supreme court is the final arbiter of the meaning of its constitution. Therefore, under principles of federalism, state courts have great autonomy to define individual rights under their state constitutions. And while state courts cannot provide less protection than the federal Constitution offers, they may provide greater protection under their constitutions.

Each state's substantive constitutional law reflects the unique historical experience of that state. Accordingly, each state constitution may have unique features and provisions that are substantially different in form and degree from the U.S. Constitution or from other states' constitutions. For example, many state constitutions contain provisions that deal with the relationship of church and state in ways that differ substantially from the religion clauses of the First Amendment of the U.S. Constitution and from each other. The differences in the constitutional text and the traditions of each state provide state courts with an opportunity to interpret their constitutional guarantees independently. Indeed, because the state courts remain the final judges of the permissibility of state or individual action under their own constitutions, where a state constitution alone provides an independent and adequate basis on which to decide an issue of individual liberty, litigants often should look to state courts as the first line of defense.

Theoretically, each state's bill of rights is that state's primary and independent guarantee against oppressive action by the state. However, state courts historically were unwilling to protect individual rights under their own constitutions. In the mid–twentieth century, the U.S. Supreme Court began to respond to the failure of state courts to protect individual rights. By the end of the 1960s most provisions of the federal Bill of Rights were incorporated into the Due Process Clause under the Fourteenth Amendment and thus became binding on the states.

After the Supreme Court's incorporation doctrine decisions, most state courts relied on federal jurisprudence rather than making an independent application of their own state constitutional guarantees. However, as the federal courts became less receptive to individual liberties claims, there was a revival of state court interpretations of state constitutional law. Some of these interpretations have arisen independent of any decision of the U.S. Supreme Court, while other have been reactions to Supreme Court precedent denying claims under the U.S. Constitution. In an era of retrenchment of individual rights at the federal level, the willingness of state courts to interpret their own constitutions to grant greater protection has great significance. By 1996 there had been several hundred cases where state supreme courts had interpreted their state constitutions as being more protective of individual rights than the prevailing federal constitutional provision. Thus, in order to protect individual liberties, contemporary litigants must vigorously pursue remedies at the state level.

Every state in the Union constitutionally guarantees religious liberty, often in language which parallels that of the federal Constitution. Despite the strong commitment to religious liberty indicated by these provisions, state courts have generally relied on federal precedent in free exercise cases. State constitutions, however, often contain additional provisos that specifically address free exercise in detail. In over forty of the state constitutions, invocations of a supreme being are followed by numerous terms describing religious liberty; these provisions protect the rights of conscience, worship, and religious opinion and exercise from interference, infringement, control, discrimination, preference, persecution, or compulsion. Beyond that, approximately twenty state constitutions contain provisos that protect free exercise rights unless the exercise of such rights threatens the public peace or safety, disturbs other worshippers, or causes licentious behavior. Many state constitutions also provide for religious exemption from taxation and military service.

Until the 1960s state courts generally were unwilling to recognize religious exercise claims under the state constitutions. Instead, state courts were inclined to uphold regulations under the state police power to "limit personal liberties in the interest of the public good," even if such regulations infringed on the free exercise of religion. Requests by free exercise claimants for exemptions from general laws were denied on the basis of the state's legitimate role in preventing injury to public health, public morality, public safety, and the good order of society. For example, under their police power, states banned the unauthorized practice of medicine, required vaccinations against communicable diseases, prohibited polygamy, and prohibited the use of dangerous instrumentalities in religious ceremonies.

Sherbert, Smith, and the RFRA

State recognition of free exercise rights changed dramatically with the 1963 decision of the U.S. Supreme Court in *Sherbert v. Verner* (1963). Under *Sherbert,* all laws—even laws of general applicability—that incidentally burdened the free exercise of religion were subject to a strict scrutiny analysis. This analysis required a court to balance the law's burden on religious exercise against the government's interest in applying the law. The law was valid only if the state could demonstrate that it had a compelling interest in enacting the law and that it had no less restrictive means of effectuating that compelling interest. Because of incorporation, the *Sherbert* decision revolutionized the way states interpreted parallel provisions in their own constitutions. Indeed, most states after *Sherbert* followed the more protective federal standard.

In 1990 the U.S. Supreme Court significantly narrowed the scope of First Amendment protection for the free exercise of religion in *Employment Division, Department of Human Resources of Oregon v. Smith* (1990). In *Smith,* by a 5-to-4 vote, the Supreme Court abandoned the compelling state interest test established in *Sherbert* and its progeny, holding that the First Amendment does not protect the free exercise of religion from laws of general applicability which are facially neutral. Only when a law specifically targets a religious practice or when a government regulation involves the Free Exercise Clause in conjunction with other constitutional protections, such as freedom of speech and of the press, will the higher level of scrutiny (the compelling state interest test) be applied. Consequently, so long as a law is neutral and of general applicability, it no longer need be justified by a compelling state interest, even if the law has the incidental effect of burdening a particular religious practice.

The Supreme Court continued to adhere to the principle of the *Smith* case in *Church of the Lukumi Babalu Aye, Inc. and Ernesto Pichardo v. City of Hialeah* (1993). However, many view the *Smith* decision as the virtual repeal of the Free Exercise Clause of the First Amendment. In response to *Smith,* in 1993 Congress enacted the Religious Freedom Restoration Act (RFRA). The RFRA was specifically designed to repudiate *Smith* and restore the compelling state interest test of *Sherbert* as a matter of federal statutory law. The RFRA applied to all federal and state laws, including laws of general applicability, and it required courts to apply the compelling state interest test to any challenge of a law that substantially burdens the practice of religion. In *City of Boerne v. Flores* (1997) the Supreme Court overturned RFRA, and thus the Smith precedent prevails.

With the protection under the federal Constitution significantly narrowed by *Smith,* state constitutional law may provide the most protection against facially neutral laws that have an impact on the free exercise of religion. For many states, however, this presents a novel problem. Because the Free Exercise Clause is incorporated by the Fourteenth Amendment to apply to the states, *Sherbert* had the effect in the states of requiring the same free exercise jurisprudence at the state level as the federal standard. Because the federal standard had offered such substantial protection, most states had not conducted separate inquiries under their own constitutions. Rather, they had treated their own free exercise provisions as coextensive with the federal requirements, or they never found it necessary to reach state constitutional questions at all.

Significantly, not all states construed their constitutions as coextensive with their federal counterpart. For example, before *Smith,* state courts in Kentucky, Maine, Mississippi, and Tennessee had specifically concluded on state grounds that their state constitutional provisions required a strict scrutiny analysis. Accordingly, even after *Smith* these states will probably continue to apply the compelling state interest test.

The majority of states, however, used the *Sherbert* analysis of free exercise claims to such an extent that it is unclear whether their constitutions would independently support a compelling state interest test. In these states, it is unclear whether state constitutional interpretation will continue to match the federal standard, thereby lowering the state standard to that of *Smith,* or whether state courts will construe their constitutions independently to require the strict scrutiny level of protection.

The States and Free Exercise

The determination of whether a state will follow the lower standard of *Smith* or continue to follow the higher standard of *Sherbert* may hinge in large part on the text of that state's constitutional provisions. Although a couple of states have followed *Smith*'s lower standard, at least five states have concluded that, under the provisos of their state constitutions, a higher degree of protection for religious free exercise is required.

Since the *Smith* decision, only Oregon has explicitly stated that free exercise protection under the Oregon Constitution would mirror that federal standard established in *Smith*. Two other states, Iowa and Ohio, have indicated a willingness to adopt *Smith*'s lower standard. These states have utilized the language of *Smith* in cases that have dealt with both federal and state constitutional law, but neither state has explicitly said that the protection guaranteed under its own constitution was limited to the standard announced in *Smith*.

Some states, however, have determined that their constitution affords greater protection for the free exercise of religion than the federal standard under *Smith* does, and so they continue to apply a standard of strict scrutiny. In each of these states, the right to free religious exercise is qualified by a proviso which identifies the government interests that are capable of infringing on the protected religious exercise. Two of the states, Minnesota and Washington, have identical free exercise provisions, which state: "the liberty of conscience hereby secured shall not be construed as to excuse acts of licentiousness or justify practices inconsistent with the peace and safety of the state." Both Minnesota and Washington have construed these provisos to require continued application of the *Sherbert* analysis.

Maine and Massachusetts also have similar provisos which protect religious exercise "provided that that person does not disturb the public peace, nor obstruct others in their religious worship." Maine, consistent with its pre-*Smith* position, has interpreted this proviso to require the *Sherbert* standard of scrutiny. Massachusetts is even more protective, interpreting its constitutional language as a categorical prohibition of governmental restraints of religious worship that do not "disturb public peace or interfere with worship." Thus, in Massachusetts, if a regulation does not fall within this constitutional proviso, it is categorically struck down. If, however, a regulation does fall within the proviso, the compelling state interest test ensues, under which the state regulation still may be required to yield to the free exercise of religion.

The last state that has explicitly retained the *Sherbert* standard of strict scrutiny is Alaska—a state whose Free Exercise Clause is identical to the federal provision. Thus, even while it may be easier for states with clauses that are more detailed and more specific to justify giving more protection to free exercise than the federal standard does, Alaska's interpretation makes clear that states which have provisions identical to the federal Constitution also may interpret their state constitution to be more protective under principles of federalism.

The enactment of the RFRA, however, has begun to diminish reliance on state provisions for the protection of free exercise rights. Instead, states again are not reaching the question of state constitutional law but instead are resolving free exercise issues under the RFRA. For example, in *Smith v. Fair Employment and Housing Commission* (Cal., 1996) the California Supreme Court declined to address the standard of scrutiny that would be applied under the Free Exercise Clause of its Constitution where a free exercise plaintiff's claim failed to meet the standard required by the RFRA. Similarly, the Vermont Supreme Court, which has declared that it does not favor the expansion of free exercise rights under its own Constitution, has held that its Constitution protects religious liberty to the same extent that the RFRA restricts governmental interference with free exercise under the U.S. Constitution. Michigan also has declined to define the parameters of its Free Exercise Clause in light of the strict scrutiny standard of the RFRA.

Although several states have chosen to follow the RFRA rather than to explicate their own constitutions, it seems significant that many state courts have stepped into the void left by *Smith* and have shown themselves to be responsive to free exercise claims. Whether by applying the RFRA or by enforcing their own constitutions, state courts are, in fact, providing increased protection for their citizens.

The States and Establishment

State courts have been even more comfortable departing from federal precedent under state establishment provisions. Just as it retrenched in the free exercise area, the U.S. Supreme Court has loosened the Establishment Clause to allow for greater church–state interaction. However, under federalism principles, a state law may require stricter separation of church and state than that required under the federal standard. Indeed, although eleven states have expressly declared their church–state provisions to be no broader than the First Amendment, twenty have declared that they will not be bound by the decisions of the U.S. Supreme Court in construing their own constitutions. As a result, under state constitutional establishment clauses state courts have invalidated government practices that the U.S. Supreme Court has permitted under the First Amendment of the U.S. Constitution.

As with the free exercise cases, state courts often justify a different state standard by construing state constitutional language that is more detailed and more specific than its federal counterpart. Generally, the more precise the clause, the more likely a state supreme court is to adopt a stricter standard than that adopted by the U.S. Supreme Court.

Almost all state constitutions prohibit favoritism toward a particular religion and prohibit aid to religious groups and institutions. Indeed, twenty-five state constitutions expressly forbid the government from appropriating money or property to aid, maintain, or support a religious sect. Four of these constitutions specifically prohibit both direct and indirect aid.

Beyond general prohibitions of aid to religious institutions, many state constitutions also seek to maintain a separation of church and state in education, which is often accomplished by banning religious practices in schools receiving state funds. Twenty-one states also have sought to accomplish an educational separation of church and state by specifically proscribing state aid, maintenance, and support of religious schools. Three states also expressly ban "indirect aid" to sectarian schools.

The specific proscription against support to religious schools is a primary area where state courts have been more active in construing state establishment clauses to provide a greater "wall of separation between church and state" than the federal standard. The primary battleground in this area at the state level has been whether a state may provide textbooks and transportation to religious schools. Although the U.S. Supreme Court has construed the federal Constitution to permit states to furnish textbooks and transportation, several states have engaged in independent constitutional analysis in order to prohibit such aid.

For example, in *Gaffney v. State Department of Education* (Neb., 1974) the Nebraska Supreme Court examined the constitutionality of its state law authorizing the lending of textbooks to students attending nonpublic schools. Rather than relying on the federal establishment test of *Lemon v. Kurtzman* (1971), the Nebraska Supreme Court focused solely on Nebraska's constitutional prohibition of any "appropriation in aid of any sectarian institution or any educational institution not owned and controlled by the state," and it found the law to be unconstitutional. The court based its holding on the clarity and broad sweep of the constitutional language, as well as on the specific history of Nebraska's constitutional convention in reaching this decision. Similarly, the Alaska Supreme Court has held that, given the clarity of the state Constitution's "no aid" language, if the state's founders had wished to allow the state to provide transportation to students attending parochial schools, they would have included a provision expressly indicating such intent. Thus, state constitutions should always be examined in any establishment conflict, because their language is often more precise and more protective than the federal provision.

In the 1980s this outburst of state constitutional adjudication was referred to as "the new judicial federalism." Today this era should no longer be regarded as "new." State constitutional jurisprudence should be acknowledged as a peer of federal jurisprudence in the protection of all individual rights issues.

J. Wilson Parker

Bibliography

Antieau, Chester James, Phillip Mark Carroll, and Thomas Carroll Burke, *Religion under the State Constitutions 1965* (Brooklyn, N.Y.: Central Book Co., 1965).

Brennan, William J., "State Constitutions and the Protection of Individual Rights," 90 *Harvard Law Review* 489–504 (1977).

Carmella, Angela C., "State Constitutional Protection of Religious Exercise: An Emerging Post-*Smith* Jurisprudence," 1993 *Brigham Young University Law Review* 275–325 (1993).

Miller, Nicholas P., and Nathan Sheers, "Religious Free Exercise under State Constitutions," 34 *Journal of Church and State* 303–323 (1992).

Tarr, G. Alan, "Church and State in the States," 64 *Washington Law Review* 73–110 (1989).

———, and Mary C. Porter, *State Supreme Courts in State and Nation* (New Haven, Conn.: Yale University Press, 1988).

Cases and Statutes Cited

Church of the Lukumi Babalu Aye, Inc. and Ernesto Pichardo v. City of Hialeah, 508 U.S. 520 (1993).

Employment Division, Department of Human Resources of Oregon v. Smith, 494 U.S. 872 (1990).

Gaffney v. State Department of Education, 220 N.W. 2d 550 (1974).

Lemon v. Kurtzman, 403 U.S. 602 (1971).

Sherbert v. Verner, 374 U.S. 398 (1963).

Smith v. Fair Employment and Housing Commission, 12 Cal. 4th 1143 (1996).

Religious Freedom Restoration Act, Pub. L. 103–141, 107 Stat. 1488 (1993).

State Regulation of Religious Education

Controversies between state education officials and religious parents began with the establishment of public schools and continue today. Early battles concerned states' authority to outlaw private schooling altogether; contemporary skirmishes center on whether and how state regulations governing teacher certification, the curriculum, and the like apply to religious parents and schools.

The right of parents to send their children to private schools was established in *Pierce v. Society of Sisters* (1925). At issue in *Pierce* was an Oregon law outlawing private education. Sponsored by the Ku Klux Klan and rooted in religious hatred, the Oregon law was designed to impose Protestant values on Catholic schoolchildren. In *Pierce* the Court ruled that the state could not outlaw private schooling and that the Oregon statute would cause a state-imposed standardization that is contrary to the fundamental theory of liberty on which American government is based. For the Court, "[t]he child is not the mere creature of the State; those who nurture him and direct his destiny have the right, coupled with the high duty, to recognize and prepare him for additional obligations."

Pierce, although critically important to religious educators, was rooted in Fourteenth Amendment Due Process protections and not First Amendment religious liberty rights. That the First Amendment provides additional protections for religious parents was explicitly recognized in *Wisconsin v. Yoder* (1972), in which the Supreme Court held that the state's interest in compulsory education was not of sufficient magnitude to override a parent's interest in having her child exempted from public school for religious reasons. Although the Court in *Yoder* recognized the legitimacy of a state's interest in mandating compulsory education, it upheld the claims of members of the Old Order Amish Faith, who sought to exempt their children from high school attendance. First, the Court emphasized the diluted state interest in educating 14- and 15-year-old children who were socially acculturated and possessed basic reading, writing, and computation skills. Second, the Court accepted the proposition that the early teenage years were crucial in determining whether a child would remain part of the Old Order Amish Faith, which therefore elevated the parents' interest in removing their children from public school.

The exemption granted the Amish in *Yoder* should not be construed as an unlimited license for parents to control the education of their children. At the outset, the Court noted: "There is no doubt as to the power of a State, having a high responsibility for education of its citizens, to impose reasonable regulations for the control and duration of basic education. Providing public schools ranks at the very apex of the function of a state." The Court, therefore, would not have permitted the removal of Amish children if they were too young to have acquired basic academic skills. In addition, the Court stressed the self-contained nature of the Amish community. Apparently, the Court would not have exempted the children in *Yoder* from public school attendance if they seemed likely to become members of mainstream society. Finally, the Court suggested that it would not accord a similar right to parents who wished to remove their child from school for nonreligious reasons. The Court emphasized that "[the compulsory attendance law] carries with it precisely the kind of objective danger to the free exercise of religion that the First Amendment was designed to prevent."

The reaches and limits of *Pierce* and *Yoder* have been tested through a series of challenges by Christian educators to state laws governing private schools and home instruction. With the Supreme Court declining to resolve this dispute, the battle between education officials and religious parents takes place before state courts and legislators.

This legal battle between state regulators and religious parents and educators apparently pits intractable foes in a fight to the death. Religious interests, it seems, reject *any* state involvement in their educational ministries. State actors seem likewise unyielding in their demand that religious educators mimic their public school counterparts.

The source of the confrontation is widespread dissatisfaction both among fundamentalist Christian parents and within the state educational establishment. The main reason that fundamentalist Christian parents opt out of public schools is their perception that the schools' "secularization" (attributed to Supreme Court decisions prohibiting organized prayer, Bible reading, the teaching of biblical creationism, and the display of the Ten Commandments in classrooms) denies their right to oversee the upbringing of their children as they see fit. Many fundamentalist Christian educators also complain of the perceived "breakdown" in public education, which they associate with lack of discipline, sexual permissiveness, and drug and alcohol abuse.

In court, fundamentalist Christians attack state regulations as being antireligious and poor educational policy. They depict the state education bureaucracy as either insensitive or hostile to the religious mission of fundamentalist Christian educators. Unlike Catholic, Jewish, and other religious educators—who often embrace teacher certification requirements and other state regulations—fundamentalist Christian educators and home study proponents have greater difficulty complying with state regulations that seek to make private schools like public schools. With respect to teacher certification requirements, for example, fundamentalist educators sometimes claim that the inculcation of secular norms through state certification procedures are inconsistent with their religious beliefs. Furthermore, contending that many such regulations serve no useful educational purpose, fundamentalist Christians deem state regulatory initiatives as de facto religious harassment. To support their contention of regulatory ineffectiveness, fundamentalist Christian educators and parents point to the fact that their students generally perform as well as or better than their public school counterparts on nationally recognized achievement tests.

Weighing against these arguments is the state's paramount, compelling interest in the education of its youth, which was recognized by the Supreme Court in *Brown v. Board of Education of Topeka* (1954): "[E]ducation is perhaps the most important function of state and local governments." Not surprisingly, state education officials are reluctant to subordinate their rule-making authority and instincts to validate the deregulatory agenda of fundamentalist Christian educators and parents. The dispute between state educators and religious parents is further complicated by the extraordinary variety of regulatory regimes available to state lawmakers and regulators.

State legislators have enacted, to varying degrees, regulations that require private sectarian schools to satisfy minimal standards in the following areas: fire, health, and safety; the curriculum; textbook selection; instructional time; teacher certification; zoning; consumer protection; student reporting; testing; state licensing; community interaction; and guidance services. The most controversial of these regulations are programmatic ones that govern actual teaching practices in nonpublic schools, including the curriculum, textbook selection, and teacher certification. States contend that such regulations are necessary to ensure that all students attain certain minimal educational standards that are necessary for the welfare of the child and society.

Regulation of home education likewise is extremely varied among the states. At one extreme, some states allow parents to teach their children at home with minimal supervision. Parents need only provide the state board of education with a proposed home study program and administer a standardized achievement test at the end of each school year. At the other extreme, some states impose curriculum and teacher approval requirements. Furthermore, it is often difficult to ascertain what parents must do to have a home study program approved by the state or local education authority. The primary reason for this confusion is that twenty-one states allow home instruction by permitting "equivalent" or "comparable" instruction outside of schools. As might be expected, the determination of equivalency varies considerably from state to state and from district to district within a state.

The Supreme Court, which has not yet decided a dispute concerning state regulation of home instruction or Christian schooling, has provided limited guidance about states' authority in this area. Currently, the Supreme Court explicitly recognizes the constitutionality of reasonable state regulations of private schools that promote a compelling state interest in education. In *Board of Education v. Allen* (1968), for example, the Court observed that "[s]ince *Pierce,* a substantial body of case law has confirmed the power of the States to insist that attendance at private schools, if it is to satisfy state compulsory-attendance laws, be at institutions which provide minimum hours of instruction, employ teachers of specified training and cover prescribed subjects of instruction." In other words, because the state cannot abolish parochial schools, it must satisfy its secular interests in education via private schools. Therefore, the state must have the authority to regulate the secular educational function of private and home schools. Numerous other Supreme Court decisions have recognized the rights of a state to impose reasonable regulations on private schools. But the Supreme Court has yet to determine where it should draw the line between reasonable and unreasonable state regulations.

Needless to say, state officials and religious educators subscribe to quite different theories of what regulations are "reasonable," and judicial attempts to resolve this dispute have been truly unsatisfactory. Such cases often present courts with an apparently hopeless entanglement of fact, judgment, secular values, and religious conviction; as a result, court decisions are often at odds with one another. Some courts approve and others invalidate identical regulatory schemes. There are also great variances within a state. State and local education officials are inconsistent in applying the often vague regulatory demands, and they are selective in enforcing the law.

The variability of judicial decisionmaking is apparent in competing judicial perceptions of teacher certification requirements. Courts that rule for the state see themselves as "ill-equipped to act as school boards and determine the need for discrete aspects of a compulsory school education program"; they argue "that it goes without saying that the State has a compelling interest in the quality and ability of those who [teach] its young people" (*State v. Shauer* [N.D., 1980], *State v. Faith Baptist Church* [Neb., 1981]). Courts that side with religious interests appear equally presumptive. They find it "*difficult to imagine* . . . a state interest sufficiently substantial to sanction abrogation of [the parent's] liberty to direct the education of their children," and, although seeing a bachelor's degree as an "indicator" of competency, they nonetheless find a bachelor's requirement excessive because "it is not a *sine qua non* the absence of which establishes [incompetency]" (*State v. Whisner* [Ohio, 1976], *Kentucky State Board v. Rudasill* [Ky., 1980]).

Vagaries in judicial approaches are a result of many factors. Poor lawyering by some state prosecutors and by some attorneys for fundamentalist Christian educators offers a partial explanation for this judicial failure. Varying regulatory schemes are also at issue. More significantly, Supreme Court decisions provide ample support for each side.

Disputes between the state and fundamentalist Christian educators are ill suited to judicial resolution. These days, it is doubtful that any child may reasonably be expected to succeed in life if denied the opportunity for an education. Because of the centrality of the state's interest in ensuring the provision of good education to all youngsters, the state is vested with the authority to establish reasonable regulations governing both public and private schools. The state, however, bears a great cost when it engages in open confrontation with fundamentalist Christian educators. The chief problem is one of enforceable sanctions. Under its *parens patriae* power, the state can, on occasion, assume custody of a child if that is in the child's best interest. For example, the state may exercise this power in the face of parental neglect. While the state most frequently exercises its *parens patriae* power to prevent physical abuse and neglect of children, the state also has authority under this power to enforce truancy statutes.

Fundamentalist Christian educators have been willing to push the state to this extreme. Yet, for many reasons, states do not want to reach this degree of confrontation. The closing of churches, the jailing of individuals for practicing their religion, and the displacement of children demand a compelling justification. With fundamentalist Christian school and home study students outperforming their public school counterparts, and with increasing public awareness of problems with public school education, the state cannot offer a compelling justification for its enforcement actions. Moreover, with public attention focused on public schools, it is politically counterproductive for the state to expend scarce educational resources on the enforcement of controversial private school and home study regulations.

Deregulation of religious education—or nonenforcement of regulations—seems a sensible political solution. Confrontations between the state and fundamentalist Christian educators are politically divisive, and, if carried to their logical extreme, ultimately may force the state to jail parents and ministers and seek custody of children. Additionally, if the state feels compelled to reverse its previous policies, it may appear weak, and its interest in education will be subject to challenge. In many instances, the most expedient political course is to strike a balance favoring religious liberty and parental rights.

Massive legislative reform of both home instruction and church-affiliated schools bears this out. Some states, however, have elected to avoid conflicts with dissenting religious parents and educators by scrapping all meaningful regulations. In these states, students need not demonstrate proficiency in core subject areas. Instead, they need only take a standardized achievement test. But to mandate test taking without mandating a minimal passing score is to substitute the state's critical interest in the education of its youth with a symbolic fig leaf.

The challenge for lawmakers and regulators, as recognized by the National Association of State Boards of Education, is "to meet their obligations to assure all children receive a quality education while considering the relative rights of parents to educate their children." This challenge cannot be ignored. At the most practical level, many students participating in home study programs and attending fundamentalist Christian schools will later be "absorbed" into public school systems. More significant, the state's interest in the well-being of its children as well as its own well-being demands that these children not be discounted.

Neal Devins

Bibliography

Carper, James C., and Thomas C. Hundt (eds.), *Religious Schooling in America* (Birmingham, Ala.: Religious Education Press, 1984).

Devins, Neal, "Fundamentalist Christian Educators v. State: An Inevitable Compromise," 60 *George Washington Law Review* 818–840 (1992).

Lines, Patricia M., "Private Education Alternatives and State Regulation," 12 *Journal of Law and Education* 189–234 (1983).

Lupu, Ira C., "Home Education, Religious Liberty, and the Separation of Powers," 67 *Boston University Law Review* 971–90 (1987).

Cases Cited

Board of Education v. Allen, 392 U.S. 236 (1968).

Brown v. Board of Education of Topeka, 347 U.S. 483 (1954).

Kentucky State Board v. Rudasill, 589 S.W. 2d 877 (Ky. 1979).

Pierce v. Society of Sisters, 268 U.S. 510 (1925).

State v. Faith Baptist Church, 301 N.W. 2d 571 (Neb. 1981).

State v. Shauer, 294 N.W. 2d 883 (N.D. 1980).

State v. Whisner, 351 N.E. 2d 750 (Ohio 1976).

Wisconsin v. Yoder, 406 U.S. 205 (1972).

State Support for Religious Colleges

The Establishment Clause of the U.S. Constitution provides that "Congress shall make no law respecting an establishment of religion. . . ." Among the most important and most sensitive issues in Establishment Clause jurisprudence have been questions about the extent to which the government may give financial assistance to religious schools or to students at those schools. Since the early 1970s the U.S. Supreme Court has strictly required that no government funds which are granted to elementary and secondary schools be used to advance religion, but the Court has adopted a more tolerant position with respect to support for religious colleges and universities. This distinction stems largely from the ideas that, unlike younger children, college students are less impressionable and that, in general, colleges are committed to academic freedom. The distinction also stems from the belief that, unlike the elementary and secondary school setting (where religious instruction permeates every aspect of the educational process), it is possible in the higher education context to identify and support those aspects of the institution which are devoted to purely secular objectives.

For over twenty years, alleged violations of the Establishment Clause were analyzed under the three-pronged test set forth in *Lemon v. Kurtzman* (1971). In order for a statute to be valid under the *Lemon* test, (1) it must have a secular legislative purpose, (2) its principal or primary effect must neither advance nor inhibit religion, and (3) it must not foster an "excessive entanglement" between government and religion. To determine whether excessive entanglement exists, three factors are examined: the character of the institutions benefited, the nature of the aid provided, and the resulting relationship between government and church authorities. Additionally, the statute must not create a program or process that would cause political divisions along religious lines. In the *Lemon* case itself, the Court used this analysis to strike down state aid to nonpublic elementary and secondary schools.

The extent to which a state could provide support for religious colleges was at issue in *Tilton v. Richardson* (1971), the companion case to *Lemon.* In a narrow, 5-to-4 decision, *Tilton* indicated that aid to church-related higher education could more readily meet the three-pronged *Lemon* test than could aid to church-related elementary and secondary schools. In *Tilton* the Court upheld provisions of a federal statute providing one-time construction grants to public and private colleges, some of which were church-related. The grants were to be used for specific buildings and facilities that the applicants agreed not to use for religious instruction.

In conducting the *Lemon* analysis in *Tilton,* the Court found the federal grant program to be secular under the first prong of the *Lemon* test. Under the second prong, the Court found that, unlike aid to elementary and secondary schools, the primary effect of the grants to the colleges was not to advance religion. The Court reasoned that the primary purpose of religious colleges and universities is secular education, not religious indoctrination, and that religion did not "permeate" the secular education to the point that the religious and secular educational functions of the school were inseparable. The evidence before the Court indicated that the buildings for which grants were received were used for secular educational purposes in an atmosphere of academic freedom. Thus the Court reasoned that the risk was slight that government aid would support or advance religious activity.

The *Tilton* majority relied on the contrast between higher education and elementary and secondary schools in finding as well that the grants at issue did not violate the third prong of the *Lemon* test. In finding that the grants did not constitute an excessive entanglement between the state and the religious colleges, the Court differentiated the character of the institutions in *Tilton* from those in *Lemon* and noted that "college students are less impressionable and less susceptible to religious indoctrination" than elementary or secondary school students are. The Court also noted that "[m]any church related colleges and universities are characterized by a high degree of academic freedom." The Court reasoned that—because the risk of state aid being used for religious indoctrination or to support religious activities was substantially reduced in light of the nature of the colleges and their students—the "necessity for intensive government surveillance [was] diminished and the resulting entanglement between government and religion lessened."

The dissenters objected to the majority's excessive entanglement analysis. In their eyes the possible necessity of state surveillance to ensure only secular use of the government aid "create[d] an entanglement of government and religion which the First Amendment was designed to avoid." Thus, for the dissenters, the government aid program did represent a violation of the Establishment Clause and would fail under the third prong of the *Lemon* test.

A statute similar to the one in *Tilton* was at issue in *Hunt v. McNair* (1973), but the method of providing aid was financed through state revenue bonds rather than a direct grant. The Supreme Court relied on *Tilton* in upholding the aid, but it added a refinement to *Lemon*'s primary effect prong. In *Hunt* the Court stated that a specific aid program for church-related colleges has the primary effect of advancing religion only (1) when it flows to an institution where religion is so pervasive that a substantial portion of the institution's functions are subsumed in the religious mission or (2) when it funds a specifically religious activity in an otherwise substantially secular setting. Although the college in *Hunt* was subject to control by its sponsor, the Baptist Church, the Court found it to be similar to the colleges in *Tilton* and thus not pervasively sectarian. Moreover, as in *Tilton,* state aid went to secular facilities only, not to any specifically religious activity.

Justice Brennan wrote an opinion dissenting from the majority's analysis and was joined by Justices Douglas and Marshall. As in *Tilton,* the dissenters argued that the Establishment Clause forbade any official involvement with religion and that, because the aid scheme in *Hunt* required state surveillance and an ongoing administrative relationship, that would result in an excessive entanglement between church and state. Thus, as in *Tilton,* there were members of the Court who did not distinguish between higher education and elementary and secondary schools in analyzing the entanglement issue.

Roemer v. Board of Public Works of Maryland (1976) continued to sustain the validity of state aid to religiously affiliated colleges and universities. In *Roemer* the Supreme Court upheld a Maryland statute that granted aid in the form of subsidies to all private institutions of higher learning as long as the subsidy was not "utilized by the institution for sectarian purposes." In upholding the statute, a plurality opinion by Justice Blackmun relied on the approach set forth in *Hunt* to determine whether the aid had the primary effect of advancing religion. The opinion concluded that, unlike church-related elementary and secondary schools, the colleges at issue were not pervasively sectarian in purpose and, in fact, were characterized by a high degree of institutional autonomy from their religious affiliation. Although religion or theology courses were mandatory at these colleges and some classes began with prayer, the opinion relied heavily on the fact that decisions about faculty hiring were not made on a religious basis. Such hiring ensured professional standards and academic freedom in the classroom and relegated religious matters to the periphery of the institutional environment.

Justice Blackmun's opinion also held that no excessive entanglement existed, relying primarily on the fact that the purpose and character of the institutions was to provide secular education. Accordingly, Blackmun reasoned that Maryland's ban on the use of public subsidies for sectarian purposes could be enforced without on-site inspections or other close surveillance of a sort that might constitute excessive entanglement. Justices Brennan and Marshall dissented, again on the entanglement issue and again on grounds like those set forth in their dissents in *Tilton* and *Hunt*.

Significantly, Justice White wrote a concurring opinion that Justice Rehnquist joined. White concurred only in the judgment; he agreed that the program had a secular purpose and effect. However, White refused to apply an entanglement test, because he believed that the Establishment Clause did not mandate such a test. The analysis of Justice White was significant for its renunciation of *Lemon*'s third prong, and his continuing attack on the test revealed the fragile status of the 5-to-4 *Lemon* opinion as precedent. Since *Roemer*, the Court has moved away from the *Lemon* test to a focus on the issues of endorsement and coercion as the central factors of contemporary Establishment Clause jurisprudence.

Ten years after *Roemer*, the Court upheld a different form of aid under *Lemon*'s primary effect prong, in *Witters v. Washington Department of Services for the Blind* (1986). In *Witters* the Court upheld the validity of an assistance program that gave aid to a blind student attending a religious college to study for a career in the ministry. The Court reasoned that such aid did not have the primary effect of advancing religion, because the aid was made available to the individual, regardless of where he chose to go to school, and because it devised no financial incentive for him to choose sectarian education over secular education. Thus, the aid flowed to the religious college only as a result of the genuinely independent and private choices of aid recipients. The Court did not address entanglement because the lower courts had not reached that issue.

Although guided by the *Lemon* analysis, the majority in *Witters* nevertheless supported its decision in part by noting that "the mere circumstance that the individual [chose] to use neutrally available state aid to help pay for his religious education [did not] confer any message of state endorsement of religion." The endorsement standard that was referenced by the majority was the sole basis of Justice O'Connor's concurring opinion.

The cases involving challenges to direct aid to religious colleges as violative of the Establishment Clause were initially controversial in part because of the controversies surrounding the *Lemon* test, particularly its excessive entanglement prong. However, given the Court's shift toward the endorsement and coercion standards, the controversial nature of these cases has significantly diminished. This trend is evidenced by a recent case involving higher education and the Establishment Clause, *Rosenberger v. Rector and Visitors of the University of Virginia* (1995), which led to another 5-to-4 decision. *Rosenberger* is significant in part because neither the majority opinion nor the concurring and dissenting opinions made any reference to the once-controversial *Lemon* test.

In *Rosenberger* the Court upheld the right of a student-run religious publication to receive payment of student government funds where such funds had been made available on the same basis for secular publications. Rather than address *Lemon* at all, the majority reasoned that, where payments were made directly to a third party pursuant to a program that was neutral toward religion, no Establishment Clause violation existed, and thus the right of the publication to be free from "invidious viewpoint" discrimination prevailed. Echoing the second prong of *Lemon*'s test, the Court examined the purpose of the funding program at issue and found that, rather than seeking to advance religion, the purpose was "to open a forum for speech and to support various student enterprises, including the publication of newspapers, in recognition of the diversity and creativity of student life." Thus, the Court held that the program was neutral toward religion and did not violate the Establishment Clause. The majority, as well as Justice O'Connor in her concurrence, also opined that the program could not be construed as an endorsement of religion, especially given the extensive measures taken by the university to disassociate itself from the private speech involved. Finally, the Court noted that funds did not flow directly to the benefited organization; thus, as in *Witters,* any benefit to religion was incidental to the government's provision of secular services for a secular purpose on a religion-neutral basis.

In summary, it is unlikely that future funding efforts for higher education will be controversial so long as they have any secular purpose related to the educational mission of the institution.

J. Wilson Parker

Bibliography

Beutler, Mark J., *Public Funding of Sectarian Education: Establishment and Free Exercise Clause Implications,* 2 *George Mason Independent Law Review* 7 (1993).

Joiner, John E., Note, *A Page of History or a Volume of Logic? Reassessing the Supreme Court's Establishment Clause Jurisprudence,* 73 *Denver University Law Review* 507 (1996).

Rotunda, Ronald D., and John E. Nowak, *Treatise on Constitutional Law Substance and Procedure,* 2nd ed. (St. Paul, Minn.: West, 1992).

Cases Cited

Hunt v. McNair, 413 U.S. 734 (1973).
Lemon v. Kurtzman, 403 U.S. 602 (1971).
Roemer v. Board of Public Works of Maryland, 426 U.S. 736 (1976).
Rosenberger v. Rector and Visitors of the University of Virginia, 515 U.S. 819 (1995).
Tilton v. Richardson, 403 U.S. 672 (1971).
Witters v. Washington Department of Services for the Blind, 474 U.S. 481 (1986).

Stewart, Potter (1915–1985)

As an associate justice of the U.S. Supreme Court from 1958 to 1981, Potter Stewart figured prominently in the national debate over the appropriate place of religion in American public life. Appointed by President Dwight D. Eisenhower to replace the retiring Justice Harold Burton, Stewart developed a unique constitutional philosophy about religious issues that placed primary emphasis on the guarantees of the Free Exercise Clause rather than on the prohibitions of the Establishment Clause. In other words, Stewart emphasized religious liberty and tended to review state legislation by assessing whether laws hindered religious belief or practice, rather than focusing on the potential threat of religious establishment. In this respect Stewart differed from most of his judicial colleagues, both on the Warren and Burger Courts; indeed, over the course of his career Stewart frequently found himself defending his notion of religious liberty in dissent.

Stewart revealed his devotion to free exercise principles early in his Supreme Court career. In *Braunfeld v. Brown* (1961) the Court upheld a Pennsylvania Sunday closing law, despite the claim of Orthodox Jewish businessmen that they needed to be open on Sundays to make up for profits lost from closing on Saturday, the Jewish Sabbath. Stewart, agreeing with Justice William Brennan's lengthy dissenting opinion, argued that the law "compels an Orthodox Jew to choose between his religious faith and his economic survival," and he described the measure as "grossly violat[ing] the constitutional right to the free exercise of their religion" (p. 616). Safeguarding religious liberty, in Stewart's view, outweighed whatever interest the state may have had in promoting a day of rest.

The following year Stewart further explained his conception of the rights inherent in the Free Exercise Clause by issuing a lone dissent in the landmark school prayer case, *Engel v. Vitale* (1962). In *Engel* the majority ruled that a New York school district violated the Constitution's Establishment Clause when it ordered that a state-composed prayer be recited daily in public school classrooms. Yet, because the state had made it clear that "those who object to reciting the prayer must be entirely free of any compulsion to do so," Stewart saw no coercion on the part of the state. Instead, he viewed the majority decision as a threat to the free exercise of religion. "We deal here not with the establishment of a state church, which would, of course, be constitutionally impermissible," Stewart argued, "but with whether schoolchildren who want to begin their day by joining in prayer must be prohibited from doing so." Unlike his fellow justices, Stewart conceived of the school prayer issue as primarily a matter of free exercise, rather than as an example of religious establishment, and he vainly argued in favor of the state prayer.

In *School District of Abington Township v. Schempp* (1963), a case involving Bible reading in public schools, Stewart issued a more extensive statement on religious liberty, again in dissent. He criticized the majority for their "fallacious oversimplification" of the First Amendment's religion clauses by relying excessively on a phrase nowhere found in the Constitution: the "separation of church and state." Charging that religion and government in a free society "must necessarily interact in countless ways," Stewart argued that, although in many instances the religion clauses might complement each other, in some cases a "doctrinaire reading of the Establishment Clause leads to irreconcilable conflict with the Free Exercise Clause." When the two clauses collided, he contended, the Court ought to place the highest value on protecting the individual's right to the free exercise of religious beliefs. Because the regulations regarding school Bible reading that were at issue in *Schempp* specifically permitted students to be excused from such activity, Stewart—as he had written in *Engel*—claimed that school-sanctioned religious practice did not violate the Establishment Clause.

Later the same year, Stewart again espoused free exercise principles and warned of potential collisions between the religion clauses, in *Sherbert v. Verner* (1963). In *Sherbert* the Court decided the fate of a Seventh-Day Adventist who was fired from her job for refusing to work on Saturdays and had declined accepting other employment that forced her to do so. Because of her actions, South Carolina denied her unemployment compensation. Although Stewart agreed with the majority's ruling that the state's policy violated the woman's free exercise rights, in a concurring opinion he attacked what he conceived of as a fundamental inconsistency between the Court's decision and its recent rulings about school prayer and Bible reading. Given the Court's "broad-brushed rhetoric" forbidding any governmental aid or support for religion, Stewart argued that the majority in *Sherbert* should have upheld South Carolina's denial of unemployment compensation. Such a position would have been consistent with the Court's "positively wooden" interpretation of the Establishment Clause. Taking his notion of religious liberty a step further, Stewart argued that "the Free Exercise Clause affirmatively requires government to create an atmosphere of hospitality and accommodation to individual belief or disbelief." Thus, even when he agreed with the majority opinion, Stewart still found room to disagree with the Court's interpretation of religious liberty.

The Court fought most of the significant constitutional battles over what Stewart conceived of as free exercise issues under Chief Justice Earl Warren (1953–1969), and during the 1970s only a handful of such cases arose. *Wisconsin v. Yoder* (1972), in which the Court held that Wisconsin's compulsory high school attendance law violated the rights of Amish parents to keep their children out of school, was one of the few significant instances in which Stewart and his colleagues decided a case on the basis of the Free Exercise Clause. Moreover, only in *Stone v. Graham* (1980)—where the majority dismissed the posting of the Ten Commandments in Kentucky public school classrooms as unconstitutional in a *per curiam* opinion—did Stewart again dissent on the basis of his interpretation of the liberty guaranteed by the Free Exercise Clause.

Most religion cases heard by the Court during the 1970s involved more explicit Establishment Clause claims, and Stewart and his colleagues usually agreed on such matters. He united with his fellow justices, for example, in the landmark case of *Flast v. Cohen* (1968), where the Court held that taxpayers had standing to bring suit challenging the expenditures of federal money for the teaching of secular subjects in parochial schools. Moreover, Stewart joined majority opinions that upheld specific programs of governmental financial aid to parochial schools, in *Board of Education v. Allen* (1968), *Tilton v. Richardson* (1971), and *Walz v. Tax Commission* of the City of New York (1970).

Stewart's earlier impassioned rhetoric

about religious liberty was absent in his few written opinions in Establishment Clause cases. Assessing the appropriate degree of governmental aid to religious institutions did not lend itself to the same type of analysis as the Court's earlier cases, and Stewart's opinions regarding Establishment Clause issues neither followed an identifiable pattern nor revealed a central theme. He wrote the majority opinion invalidating an "instructional equipment loan program" in *Meek v. Pittenger* (1975), where he held that lending maps, charts, and laboratory equipment to parochial schools advanced religion "because of the predominantly religious character of the schools benefiting from the Act." A few years later, however, Stewart seemingly accepted the constitutionality of a similar program in *Wolman v. Walter* (1977), where he voted with the majority's decision to uphold the governmental aid. Stewart's only dissent on such matters came in *Roemer v. Board of Public Works of Maryland* (1976), where he challenged the constitutionality of a Maryland law that offered financial support to church-affiliated higher educational institutions.

Justice Potter Stewart's voice in interpreting the religion clauses has been significant. Early in the debate over church–state issues, Stewart astutely observed that the Free Exercise Clause and the Establishment Clause would sometimes collide with each other—that a strict separationist interpretation of the Establishment Clause would sometimes threaten the liberty guaranteed by the Free Exercise Clause. In this regard especially, Stewart's unique perspective on religious liberty, which he often articulated in dissent during the 1960s, formed the constitutional basis for the opposition to the Court's school prayer decisions. On the less controversial issues surrounding government aid to religious institutions, Stewart usually followed the majority's line of reasoning.

Timothy S. Huebner

Bibliography

Levy, Leonard W., *The Establishment Clause: Religion and the First Amendment* (New York: Macmillan, 1986).

Smith, Rodney K., "Justice Potter Stewart: A Contemporary Jurist's View of Religious Liberty," 59 *North Dakota Law Review* 183–210 (1983).

Cases Cited

Braunfeld v. Brown, 366 U.S. 599 (1961).
Board of Education v. Allen, 392 U.S. 236 (1968).
Engel v. Vitale, 370 U.S. 421 (1962).
Flast v. Cohen, 392 U.S. 83 (1968).
Meek v. Pittenger, 421 U.S. 349 (1975).
Roemer v. Board of Public Works of Maryland, 426 U.S. 736 (1976).
School District of Abington Township v. Schempp, 374 U.S. 203 (1963).
Sherbert v. Verner, 374 U.S. 398 (1963).
Stone v. Graham, 449 U.S. 39 (1980).
Tilton v. Richardson, 403 U.S. 672 (1971).
Walz v. Tax Commission of the City of New York, 397 U.S. 664 (1970).
Wisconsin v. Yoder, 406 U.S. 205 (1972).
Wolman v. Walter, 433 U.S. 229 (1977).

Sunday Closing Laws

Sunday closing laws span a long history. In 321 C.E. Emperor Constantine proscribed labor on the day of the Sun; in 691 Anglo-Saxon King Ira prohibited Sunday labor in England; and in the thirteenth and fourteenth centuries several English Kings, from Henry III to Edward III, began drafting detailed Sunday legislation. Prohibitions against myriad practices are located in the Bible, Codex Justinian, Codex Theodosian, the medieval councils, church laws and canons, statutes of English monarchs, American colonial and state law, and statutes of other countries throughout the Western World. Although Sunday laws at first were not avowedly Christian, their emergence in England, the American colonies, and the states of the Union under the U.S. Constitution clearly supported sectarian purposes.

In 1448 English King Henry VI made it unlawful to attend fairs and markets on Sunday after noting "the abominable injuries and offences done to Almighty God, and to his Saints." During the sixteenth and seventeenth centuries, Sunday law enlarged and developed numerous specific provisions and penalties. Edward VI prohibited bodily labor on Sunday for religious purposes, and he assessed injunctions for such activity; and in 1625 Charles I restricted various sports and amusements because "the holy keeping of the Lord's day [was] a principal part of the true service of God."

English Sunday laws were later introduced into the British colonies in North

America and were reified by the states of the Union. In 1610 the Colony of Virginia enacted the first Sunday law passed by British subjects on American land. Other colonies soon followed, restricting labor and retailing. A prominent theme throughout was support of the Christian Sabbath by refraining from labor, travel, and sport. In 1656, for example, Captain Kemble of Boston was jailed for kissing his wife on the Sabbath, despite his having just spent three years at sea. In 1682 Pennsylvania offered religious toleration for all people believing in a supreme being while also prohibiting labor on Sunday to encourage worship. In 1789 newly elected President George Washington was prosecuted under a Sunday law for violating a Connecticut statute that forbade travel. Other colonial laws were more severe, making failure to attend Sunday church services a criminal offense.

In the nineteenth century, Sunday closing laws began receiving challenges. In *Commonwealth v. Knox* (Mass., 1809) the Massachusetts Supreme Judicial Court held that a mail carrier could not be prosecuted for traveling on Sunday in violation of Massachusetts law, which prohibited Sunday travel except for charity or necessity. Because the U.S. Congress enacted legislation to carry out the mails, the conflicting state law fell to the Supreme Laws of the Land. Further, the court held that it was necessary to carry out a lawful contract—as here, where a mail carrier contracted with the U.S. government—and such action was therefore not prohibited. Thus, Sunday mail service continued in Massachusetts and elsewhere in the nation.

Despite *Knox,* most state courts were more deferential to Sunday-law restrictions. In *Specht v. Commonwealth* (Pa., 1848), for example, the Pennsylvania court upheld a statute prohibiting the performance of worldly business on Sunday. The court held that societal well-being demanded periods of rest at specified intervals to recover from weekly labor.

In the late nineteenth century, courts routinely upheld the laws as a proper exercise of state police power, yet they were quick to distinguish between modern closing laws and their religious-oriented ancestors. Courts encouraged worship by prohibiting labor, but they ultimately stressed more secular purposes such as a common day of rest, which benefited the public welfare. In this fashion, however, courts generally supported Sunday legislation.

In 1961 the U.S. Supreme Court proffered its view of Sunday closing laws in four concurrent cases: *McGowan v. Maryland* (1961), *Two Guys from Harrison-Allentown, Inc. v. McGinley* (1961), *Braunfeld v. Brown* (1961), and *Gallagher v. Crown Kosher Super Market* (1961). The Court decided each case on the same day but provided the bulk of its analysis in *McGowan.* Before examining *McGowan* in detail, a cursory review of the other cases is useful.

Two Guys, Braunfeld, and *Gallagher*

In *Two Guys,* Chief Justice Earl Warren, writing for the majority, upheld a Pennsylvania Sunday closing law. The regulation restricted the sale of certain commodities on Sunday and imposed fines for the statute's breach. The statute provided certain exemptions, such as works of charity, and permitted some forms of recreation. The plaintiff, a corporation that operated department stores in Pennsylvania, alleged that the statute violated both the Equal Protection Clause of the Fourteenth Amendment and myriad laws of religious freedom.

The Court rejected the equal protection argument, asserting that it was rational for the Pennsylvania legislature to permit the sale of specified commodities on Sunday and yet prohibit the sale of others. The Court asserted that distinguishing between permissive business activity was within the purview of the legislature and that, for a variety of reasons, the legislature might find that the plaintiff's business was "particularly disrupting the intended atmosphere of the day."

The Court further rejected the plaintiff's claim that the Pennsylvania statute amounted to an unconstitutional establishment of religion. Although Pennsylvania's Sunday closing laws were historically dedicated for religious reasons, the Court found that current connotations were merely secular. The statute at issue was designed to permit healthy and recreational activities on Sunday. Moreover, the legislators specifically disavowed any religious purpose in the statute's enactment and instead focused on economic necessity. After tracing the history of Pennsylvania's Sunday closing laws, the Court concluded that the state, both in its supreme court decisions and legislative motivations, did not have the purpose or effect of advancing religion.

In *Braunfeld* the Court examined a Pennsylvania statute that criminalized the retail sale of certain commodities. Relying on *Two Guys,* the Court concluded that the statute neither served to establish religion nor violated the Equal Protection Clause. The Court did consider, however, whether the statute interfered with the plaintiffs' free exercise of religion—an issue not addressed in *Two Guys.* The plaintiffs were merchants who sold clothing and home furnishings proscribed by statute from Sunday sale. The plaintiffs were also Orthodox Jews, whose faith required work stoppage from nightfall on Friday until nightfall on Saturday. The plaintiffs argued that the Pennsylvania statute, by prohibiting business operation on Sunday, would ultimately force them out of business or force them to forgo their religious beliefs.

The Court noted the sanctity of religious freedom. It further recognized, however, that current Sunday closing laws operated to improve the health, safety, and morals of citizens. Although the Constitution forbids laws that compel citizens to accept any form of religion, the *Braunfeld* Court asserted that "the freedom to act, even when the action is in accord with one's religious convictions, is not totally free from legislative restrictions." Here, the Court argued, the Pennsylvania statute does not make plaintiffs' religious practice unlawful nor does it inconvenience all members of the Orthodox Jewish faith. Rather, the statute affects only those who wish to work on Sunday. Moreover, the Court distinguished between a law that prohibits certain religion and one that makes it more expensive to practice that religion. The Court's test was clear:

> If the purpose or effect of a law is to impede the observance of one or all religions or is to discriminate invidiously between religions, that law is constitutionally invalid even though the burden may be characterized as being only indirect. But if the State regulates conduct by enacting a general law within its power, the purpose and effect of which is to advance the State's secular goals, the statute is valid despite its indirect burden on religious observance unless the State may accomplish its purpose by means which do not impose such a burden.

Although the plaintiffs argued that Pennsylvania should exempt from its Sunday prohibitions those whose religious beliefs provide a day of rest other than Sunday, the Court held that this would be a legislative decision.

Justice William Brennan dissented on the free exercise of religion claim. He argued that the majority's focus on collective goals, such as public health and safety, was misguided. Rather, he stressed the values of the First Amendment and the preservation of individual liberty.

Justice Brennan reminded the Court that religious freedom demands the most exacting scrutiny, not merely whether a statute is rationally related to a legitimate end or serves a substantial state interest but, rather, whether a statute survives a compelling interest of the state. In fact, "the Court seems to say, without so much as a deferential nod towards that high place which we have accorded religious freedom in the past, that any substantial state interest will justify encroachments on religious practice, at least if those encroachments are cloaked in the guise of some nonreligious public purpose." Justice Brennan argued that a state's purpose of having its citizens rest on a common day is far from compelling. Recognizing that Pennsylvania would face minimal burdens if the plaintiffs were allowed to operate on Sunday, Justice Brennan concluded that administrative convenience should not justify undue economic burden on their religious beliefs.

Finally, in *Gallagher* the Supreme Court considered a Massachusetts Sunday closing law. The defendant was a supermarket whose four stockholders were Orthodox Jews. The defendant sold almost exclusively kosher foods. Like the merchants in *Braunfeld,* the defendants in *Gallagher* could not work on the Sabbath without violating their faith. Moreover, other Orthodox Jews, who were required to eat only kosher food, could not shop on Saturday, their Sabbath. Thus, the Sunday closing law, combined with the religious obligation to close on Saturday, harmed both the defendants and the customers. An exemption to the Massachusetts statute allowed the supermarket to operate until 10 A.M. on Sunday; however, for economic reasons, the defendants were unable to do so.

The statute at issue in *Gallagher,* as in *Two Guys* and *Braunfeld,* provided for several exemptions concerning the sale of commodities on Sunday. The defendants argued that the arbitrary exemption provisions within the statute had no rational legislative justification and, therefore, that the statute violated the Equal Protection Clause. Starting with a presumption of constitutionality, the Court held that the defendants failed to prove the irrationality of the statutory distinctions.

The defendants next argued that the Massachusetts statutes were laws respecting the establishment of religion. The Court agreed that the Sunday legislation had a clear religious origin; however, the current statutory language and purpose were devoid of religious orientation and "the objectionable language [was] merely a relic."

For reasons stated in *Braunfeld,* the Court then rejected the defendants' argument that the Massachusetts law prohibited the free exercise of their religion because it effectively forbade the buying (or selling) of kosher foods from Friday until Monday and, consequently, put the supermarket at a serious economic disadvantage.

McGowan

With its decision in *McGowan* the Supreme Court most clearly articulated its view of Sunday closing laws. The plaintiffs in *McGowan,* employees of a large department store, were prosecuted for selling items on Sunday in violation of a Maryland statute. Maryland also had regulations restricting specific activities on Sunday or limiting them to certain hours, places, or conditions. The Supreme Court held that the Maryland statute did not violate the Equal Protection or Due Process Clauses of the Fourteenth Amendment or constitute a law establishing religion under the First Amendment.

The plaintiffs first argued that the Maryland statute violated the Equal Protection Clause because the various classifications contained within the statute were without rational and substantial relation to legislative objectives. For example, the statutes discerned which commodities could be sold on Sunday and provided exemptions to the legislation. The Court began by noting that "the Fourteenth Amendment permits the States a wide scope of discretion in enacting laws which affect some groups of citizens differently than others." To overcome a statute's presumption of constitutionality, it must be proved that classifications therein are entirely irrelevant to a state's purported objectives. The Court held that the plaintiffs had failed to suggest why such a rational basis did not exist for the disparate classifications, that the distinctions were not invidious, and that local tradition and custom might explain the legislative response.

The Court noted several reasons that would legitimize the statutory classifications. For example:

> [A]legislature could reasonably find that the Sunday sale of the exempted commodities was necessary either for the health of the populace or for the enhancement of the recreational atmosphere of the day—that a family which takes a Sunday ride into the country will need gasoline for the automobile and may find pleasant a soft drink or fresh fruit; that those who go to the beach may wish ice cream or some other item normally sold there; that some people will prefer alcoholic beverages or games of chance to add to their relaxation; that newspapers and drug products should always be available to the public.

The Court also rejected the plaintiffs' second equal protection argument: that, because the statute permitted some county retailers to sell certain items but forbade other counties from selling the same, the statute unreasonably discriminated against retailers in certain Maryland counties. The Court responded that "the Equal Protection Clause relates to equality between persons as such, rather than between areas and that territorial uniformity is not a constitutional prerequisite."

The plaintiffs' final equal protection argument contended that, because the statute permitted certain retailers within Anne Arundel County to sell items while forbidding the same by other vendors, it violated any notion of equal protection. The Court held that a legislature "could reasonably find that these commodities, necessary for the health and recreation of its citizens, should only be sold on Sunday by those vendors at the locations where the commodities are most likely to be immediately put to use." In short, the Court found no unreasonable explanation for the distinctions.

The plaintiffs' second argument contended that the language of the statute—exempting the Sunday sale of "merchandise essential to, or customarily sold at, or incidental to, the operation of" beaches, amusement parks, and so on—was unconstitutionally vague. The Court responded that a reasonable person in business could discern the meaning of the statute and, through reasonable investigation, could determine which exemptions were encompassed by the statute.

The plaintiffs further argued that Maryland's Sunday closing laws violated the constitutional protection of religious liberty. They argued that the Maryland statutes violated the free exercise of religion. However, the plaintiffs alleged only economic injury to themselves and not infringement of their religious freedom. Because a litigant may only argue a violation of his or her own constitutional rights, the Court held that the plaintiffs lacked standing to raise this issue, and thus the Court did not examine the free exercise claim.

The plaintiffs then contended that the statutes violated notions of separation of church and state because the statutes respected an establishment of religion. Because the plaintiffs' economic injury was a direct result of the statutes' restrictions based on the Christian religion, the Court held that the plaintiffs had standing to raise the establishment of religion question. The plaintiffs argued that, because Sunday is the Sabbath for the predominant Christian religions, the purpose of "the enforced stoppage of labor on that day is to facilitate and encourage church attendance; that the purpose of setting Sunday as a day of universal rest is to induce people with no religion or people with marginal religious beliefs to join the predominant Christian sects; that the purpose of the atmosphere of tranquillity created by Sunday closing is to aid the conduct of church services and religious observance of the sacred day." The Court conceded that Sunday closing laws originally had been motivated by religious forces; however, the issue here was whether Sunday legislation had changed from its early motivations or whether it still retained its religious character.

The Court traced the religious imprimatur of early Sunday closing legislation but noted that by the eighteenth century more secular justifications were used. Sunday laws began focusing on one's chance to recover from "the labors of the week just passed and may physically and mentally prepare for the week's work to come." Indeed, state Sunday closing laws were often enforced through their departments of labor. The Court then traced the history and purpose of the First Amendment to suggest that, although no state may actively support a religion, "it is equally true that the 'Establishment' Clause does not ban federal or state regulation of conduct whose reason or effect merely happens to coincide or harmonize with the tenets of some or all religions. In many instances, the Congress or state legislatures conclude that the general welfare of society, wholly apart from any religious considerations, demands such regulation." After reviewing both the history of Sunday closing legislation and the First Amendment generally, the Court noted that "recent" Sunday laws were premised on secular concerns and bore no relationship to establishment of religion.

With this review the Court then turned specifically to the Maryland statutes at issue in *McGowan*. The Court began by gleaning the religious purposes of the statutes and conceding that the predecessors of Maryland's existing Sunday laws were clearly of religious origin. The Court noted, however, that the current statutes did not provide a blanket prohibition against Sunday work or labor. In fact, the Court reminded the plaintiffs that the statute which they argued violated the Establishment Clause did, in fact, permit such things as the Sunday sale of tobacco and sweets, the playing of pinball and slot machines, and other activities that were prohibited by Maryland's earlier Sunday closing laws. The Court concluded that these provisions, "along with those which permit various sports and entertainments on Sunday, seem clearly to be fashioned for the purpose of providing a Sunday atmosphere of recreation, cheerfulness, repose and enjoyment. Coupled with the general proscription against other types of work, we believe that the air of the day is one of relaxation rather than one of religion."

The Court held that Maryland's current Sunday legislation is in opposition to its earlier Sunday laws, which were undeniably motivated by religious considerations. The Court concluded that "[a]fter engaging in the close scrutiny demanded of us when First Amendment liberties are at issue, we accept the State Supreme Court's determination that the statutes' present purpose and effect is not to aid religion but to set aside a day of rest and recreation."

The *McGowan* plaintiffs also argued that, even if the Sunday legislation was not motivated by a religious purpose, there are less restrictive means by which the state could achieve its objectives. When an alleged First Amendment right is implicated, the Court must consider both the purpose of the statute at issue and whether any less obtrusive means exists to support that purpose. Again the Court rejected the plaintiffs' argument, holding that no less restrictive alternatives exist to avoid infringing on the religious provisions of the First Amendment.

The Court did agree that if the state's primary purpose was to provide a work stoppage of one day in seven, the statute's constitutionality would be more vulnerable. The statute, however, also "seeks to set one day apart form all others as a day of rest, repose, recreation and tranquillity—a day which all members of the family and community have the opportunity to spend and enjoy together, a day on which there exists relative quiet and disassociation from the everyday intensity of commercial activities, a day on which people may visit friends and relatives who are not available during working days." Moreover, the Court noted that it would be detrimental to the general welfare and difficult to enforce a statute forcing a state to select a common day of rest other than a day that the majority of the population selected.

The Court limited its *McGowan* decision to determining the constitutionality of Maryland's statutes. Sunday legislation might violate the Establishment Clause if its purpose—evidenced by express language, legislative history, or operative effect—were to employ state assistance to religion.

In a separate opinion, Justice Frankfurter, joined by Justice Harlan, agreed with the majority yet expanded on the historical account of Sunday closing legislation. Justice Frankfurter's concurrence stressed the importance of religious freedom and warned that notions of separating church from state are not self-defining, because religion is too comprehensive an area to permit judicial line drawing. Yet, inevitably there is a point where a state's concern for its citizens and the concerns for religion overlap. Moreover, because such laws are secular in purpose, enforcement against religious beliefs that do not condemn such practices are nonetheless appropriate. Again, however, Justice Frankfurter argued that a state's secular justification does not automatically receive the imprimatur of the First Amendment. As he noted, "[i]f the value to society of achieving the object of a particular regulation is demonstrably outweighed by the impediment to which the regulation subjects those whose religious practices are curtailed by it, or if the object sought by the regulation could with equal effect be achieved by alternative means which do not substantially impede those religious practices, the regulation cannot be sustained."

The above balancing also manifests itself in distinguishing terms such as "establishment" and "free exercise." Justice Frankfurter noted that the purpose of the Establishment Clause was to ensure that neither Congress nor states would assert power toward a purely religious end. To decide whether legislation serves a religious purpose will often be unclear and will require looking to the effect of the legislation. Then, "[i]f the primary end achieved by a form of regulation is the affirmation or promotion of religious doctrine—primary, in the sense that all secular ends which it purportedly serves are derivative from, not wholly independent of, the advancement of religion—the regulation is beyond the power of the state." Similarly, if a statute furthers both religious and secular ends, yet the means are unnecessary to accomplishing the secular ends alone (i.e., the secular ends could be achieved without promoting religion), the statute will be struck down. In viewing the "purpose" of the Maryland legislature regarding the challenged statutes, Justice Frankfurter argued that the Court may not try to discern the "hidden" motives of the legislators but, instead, must examine the history of the Sunday regulations.

As did the majority opinion in *McGowan,* Justice Frankfurter traced the history of Sunday closing laws and concluded that, although Sunday legislation originally was drafted with a clear religious purpose, it evolved to entail a simple day of rest. Therefore, to Justice Frankfurter, "the English experience demonstrates the intimate relationship between civil Sunday regulation and the interest of a state in preserving to its people a recurrent time of mental and physical recuperation from the strains and pressure of their ordinary labors." For example, during World War I, committees studied industrial fatigue and recommended Sunday work stoppage. Thus, despite its historical ties to Christian churches, Sunday work stoppage became a traditional day of rest for purely secular reasons.

Justice Frankfurter then noted that forty-nine of the fifty states had some form of legislation banning various activities on Sunday that were otherwise legal during weekdays. That some language in statutes referred to "the Lord's Day" was a mere anachronism, and "the continuation of seventeenth century language does not of itself prove the continuation of the purposes for which the colonial governments enacted these laws, or that these are the purposes for which their successors of the twentieth have retained them and modified them." In somewhat more forceful language, Justice Frankfurter concluded that, "[i]n light of these considerations, can it reasonably be said that no substantial non-ecclesiastical purpose relevant to a well-ordered social life exists for Sunday restrictions?"

In his dissent in *McGowan,* Justice Douglas reminded the Court that the issue was not whether government can force one day in seven as a day of rest but, rather, whether the state can force Sunday as a day of rest because of custom and habit. In short, Justice Douglas refused to believe that Sunday closing laws could be separated from their religious motivations. He noted that both individual states and the nation are founded on a belief in a supreme being—a fact reflected in the Declaration of Independence, the Constitution, and the Bill of Rights. With this aside, Justice Douglas argued that "those who fashioned the First Amendment decided that if and when God is to be served, His service will not be motivated by coercive measures of the Government." The First Amendment limitations mean four things: "first, that the dogma, creed, scruples, or practices of no religious group or sect are to be preferred over those of any others; second, that no one shall be interfered with by government for practicing the religion of his choice; third, that the State may not require anyone to practice a religion or even any religion; and fourth, that the State cannot compel one so to conduct himself as not to offend the religious scruples of another."

Justice Douglas then traced the history of Sunday closing laws and, unlike the majority, believed that some of them still maintain clearly religious motivations. He chastised the majority's selective use of statutory language to conclude that modern Sunday laws are purely civil. To him, no matter how the laws are phrased, they clearly serve religious predispositions. Moreover, he reminded the majority that issues of religious freedom under the First Amendment demand strict judicial assessment of the regulations. The state must provide a compelling justification for its regulation and must have no less intrusive alternatives that might affect religion. For Justice Douglas, the majority decision in *McGowan* dilutes the strength of First Amendment protection, and "balances the need of the people for rest, recreation, late sleeping, family visiting and the like against the command of the First Amendment that no one need bow to the religious beliefs of another."

Agreeing that a state can require a day of rest, Justice Douglas nonetheless argued that Sunday laws operate differently. In short, they compel minorities to obey the religious majority. He posited, "[c]an there be any doubt that Christians, now aligned vigorously in favor of these laws, would be as strongly opposed if they were prosecuted under a Moslem law that forbade them from engaging in secular activities on days that violated Moslem scruples?" To him, the sanctioning of the Christian religion behind the force of law violates the Establishment Clause and is therefore unconstitutional. Moreover, any burdens placed on religion by the force of law violate the free exercise of that religion.

Thornton v. Caldor and the Limits of Sunday Laws

In 1962 the Supreme Court refused to reconsider the constitutionality of Sunday closing laws. *Arlen's Department Store v. Kentucky* (1962) involved the owners of three retail stores in Kentucky who were fined for employing persons on Sunday in violation of Kentucky law. The lower court sustained their convictions and denied that the statute violated the First Amendment. The Supreme Court dismissed the case for want of a substantial federal question.

In his dissent, Justice Douglas distinguished this case from *Braunfeld* and

Gallagher because Kentucky provided an exemption to the penal provisions for those who observe the Sabbath on a day other than Sunday. Justice Douglas, however, reiterated his dissent from *McGowan* and addressed the unconstitutionality of Sunday laws generally. He disagreed that government can legitimately compel persons to not work on Sunday simply because a majority of the state's citizens deem Sunday a "holy day." Although the Supreme Court traditionally separates any religious purpose from state Sunday laws, Justice Douglas argued that it is clearly a motivating force in the Kentucky statute. Because the statute exempts "members of a religious society" who observe the Sabbath on a day other than Sunday, "the law is plainly an aid to all organized religions, bringing to heel anyone who violates the religious scruples of the majority by seeking his salvation not through organized religion but on his own."

In *Estate of Thorton v. Caldor, Inc.* (1985) the Court recognized, albeit narrowly, the potential limits of Sunday closing laws. Donald Thorton was employed as a manager at a Connecticut store. In 1979 Thorton informed his employer (Caldor, Inc.) that he would not work on Sundays, as the employer required of its managerial employees. Thorton relied on a Connecticut statute which provided that "[n]o person who states that a particular day of the week is observed as his Sabbath may be required by his employer to work on such day. An employee's refusal to work on his Sabbath shall not constitute grounds for dismissal." Thorton rejected his employer's offer either to transfer him to a management position in Massachusetts, where the store was closed on Sundays, or to transfer him to a nonmanagerial position in the Connecticut store at a lower salary. The employer then transferred Thorton to a clerical position at the Connecticut store. Two days later Thorton resigned and filed a grievance with the Connecticut State Board of Mediation and Arbitration. The board sustained Thorton's grievance and ordered his reinstatement. The Connecticut Superior Court affirmed, concluding that the statute did not offend the Establishment Clause of the First Amendment. The Connecticut Supreme Court reversed, and the case was brought to the U.S. Supreme Court.

The Supreme Court held that the Connecticut statute, by providing Sabbath observers with an unqualified right not to work on their chosen Sabbath, violates the Establishment Clause. The Court cautioned that "[u]nder the Religion Clauses, government must guard against activity that impinges on religious freedom, and must take pains not to compel people to act in the name of any religion." Invoking the test from *Lemon v. Kurtzman* (1971), the Court stated that, to meet constitutional requirements under the religion clauses, a statute must not have a secular purpose, must not foster excessive entanglement of government with religion, and in its primary effect must not advance or inhibit religion. Because the Connecticut statute imposed on employers and employees an absolute duty to conform their business practices to the particular religious practices of an individual employee, the state thus commanded that Sabbath religious concerns trump all secular interests at the workplace. In short, "[t]he statute arms Sabbath observers with an absolute and unqualified right not to work on whatever day they designate as their Sabbath." Furthermore, the statute ignored the convenience or interests of the employer or those of other employees who do not observe the Sabbath. The Court concluded that, in granting unlimited favor of Sabbath observers over all other interests, the statute has a primary effect that impermissibly advances a particular religious practice.

In her concurrence in *Thorton,* Justice O'Connor noted that the Connecticut statute singles out Sabbath observers for special, absolute protection "without according similar accommodation to ethical and religious beliefs and practices of other private employees." In short, Justice O'Connor argued that the statute endorsed a particular religion to the detriment of those who did not share it.

Although laws requiring Sunday worship are no longer found in American codes, prohibition of Sunday labor and various amusements still survive in modified form. Some states require stores to be closed on Sunday and restrict the sale of liquor. Those affected by such restrictions have argued that these laws unreasonably interfere with their freedom of religion and freedom of enterprise. The legality of such laws has generally been sustained in American courts on the basis of implied social value, not religious implications. Secular values have been judged legally justifiable, although the designation of Sunday as a day of rest indirectly aids the religious observance of Christians.

Stephen K. Schutte

Bibliography

Antieau, Chester J., Arthur T. Downey, and Edward C. Roberts, *Freedom from Federal Establishment: Formation and Early History of the First Amendment's Religion Clauses* (Milwaukee: Bruce, 1964).

Berns, Walter, *The First Amendment and the Future of American Democracy* (New York: Basic Books, 1976).

Cord, Robert L., *Separation of Church and State: Historical Fact and Current Fiction* (New York: Lambeth Press, 1982).

Johnson, Alvin W., *Separation of Church and State in the United States* (Minneapolis: University of Minnesota Press, 1948).

Malbin, Michael J., *Religion and Politics: The Intentions of the Authors of the First Amendment* (Washington, D.C.: American Enterprise Institute, 1978).

Cases Cited

Arlen's Department Store v. Kentucky, 371 U.S. 218 (1962).

Braunfeld v. Brown, 366 U.S. 599 (1961).

Commonwealth v. Knox, 6 Mass. 76 (1809).

Estate of Thorton v. Caldor, Inc., 472 U.S. 703 (1985).

Gallagher v. Crown Kosher Super Market, 366 U.S. 617 (1961).

Lemon v. Kurtzman, 403 U.S. 602 (1971).

McGowan v. Maryland, 366 U.S. 420 (1961).

Specht v. Commonwealth, 8 Pa. 312 (1848).

Two Guys from Harrison-Allentown, Inc. v. McGinley, 366 U.S. 582 (1961).

Sunday Mails

The Sunday mails debate during the early nineteenth century was the first national controversy to focus on the meaning of the religion clauses of the First Amendment. The debate was sparked by the practice of transporting and delivering mail on Sundays. Although the subject might seem arcane today, the issues underlying the controversy reached to the very core of American constitutionalism.

To understand why the Sunday mails battle arose at all, one must first grasp the significance of Sunday (or the "Christian Sabbath") in nineteenth-century America. Many Americans regarded Sunday as a bulwark of republicanism because of its role in propagating civic morality. On this one day each week citizens were encouraged to forswear self-interest and reflect on their higher duties to both God and man. The perceived civic importance of Sunday, as well as a concern for religious liberty, led to laws closing down businesses and restricting travel on the day. Although these laws undeniably coerced those who did not observe Sunday as their Sabbath, they protected the liberty of most religious adherents by ensuring that they could not be compelled to work on their chosen day of worship.

Sunday mails constituted an exception to the general suspension of business on the first day of the week, and in 1808 Massachusetts tried to stop the practice by prosecuting a mail coach for running on Sunday. But the indictment was dropped after it was determined that mail carriers were legally exempt from the state's ban on Sunday travel. The relevant statute allowed Sunday travel if it was necessary, and in *Commonwealth v. Knox* (1809) the Massachusetts Supreme Judicial Court held that carrying the mail on Sunday under a contract with the postmaster general constituted a legitimate "necessity" arising from the federal government's constitutional authority over the mails.

The Massachusetts case was an oddity. For the most part, Sunday mails attracted little notice during the nation's early history, largely because delivery was confined to the unobtrusive operation of mail coaches. The situation changed in 1810, when Congress enacted a new postal law that dramatically expanded the scope of Sunday mails by requiring mail actually to be delivered to customers every day of the week that it arrived. In the larger towns and cities, this meant that post offices would now be open on Sundays. Suddenly the practice of Sunday mails became considerably more intrusive. In many towns and villages the post office was the only commercial establishment open on Sunday, and it invariably became the focal point for widespread Sabbath-breaking. Citizens flocked to the post office to obtain their commercial newspapers and business correspondence and to swap news with their friends. At the same time, postmasters and their clerks who believed that they must refrain from secular labor on Sunday confronted a dilemma: They either worked on Sunday, or they lost their jobs.

Almost immediately Congress began receiving petitions urging an end to both the delivery and the carrying of mail on Sundays. The petitions were respectfully received, but in the end nothing was done, and the matter was dropped.

Anti–Sunday mail efforts revived in the mid-1820s, when evangelical reformers initiated a movement to increase the voluntary observance of the Sabbath. This second campaign quickly eclipsed the first. Soon Congress was inundated with petitions, public meetings were held, and newspapers were heatedly debating the merits of the issue. From 1827 through 1830 the House of Representatives alone received more than one thousand petitions about the subject.

Critics of Sunday mails put forth several arguments, but their most compelling line of attack focused on the free exercise of religion guaranteed by the First Amendment. They claimed that Sunday mails subverted religious liberty in two ways. First, and most obviously, it forced postal workers to choose between their faith and their job. More subtly, it placed the government in the role of undercutting the religious beliefs of a large number of citizens. By requiring mail service on Sundays, the government was declaring as official policy that the Sabbath need not be respected.

Defenders of Sunday mails dismissed the religious liberty claims of postal workers, arguing that postmasters and their clerks were not really being coerced, because they could always resign. These defenders further maintained that to stop the mails on Sunday would contravene the First Amendment and establish a religion by officially sanctioning Sunday as God's Sabbath. Finally, they denounced their opponents as scheming to unify church and state and implied that they did not even have the right to petition Congress on the subject. This last attack was justly decried by the Sunday mail protestors, who pointed out that religious adherents had the same constitutional rights to become involved in politics as other citizens.

The vehemently antireligious rhetoric of many Sunday mail supporters did not mean that they were all antireligious. In fact, many were dissenting evangelicals who had never quite accepted the public role of religion that was being championed by nineteenth-century evangelical reformers like Lyman Beecher and Francis Wayland. Political coalitions do not always fit into neat categories.

The response of the federal government to this second anti–Sunday mails campaign was mixed. John McLean, later appointed to the Supreme Court, was postmaster general during part of this period. While publicly defending Sunday mails, he quietly agreed to close a few post offices on Sunday. Congressman Richard Johnson was bolder. He produced two legislative reports sharply attacking the proposed ban on Sunday mails, based on Establishment Clause grounds. Thousands of copies of these reports were distributed across the country, and they helped turn the tide against protestors. The issues finally reached the floor of Congress when Senator Theodore Frelinghuysen of New Jersey offered a bill in 1830 to abolish Sunday mails. The bill was tabled after a brief debate.

In the short term, then, the second Sunday mails campaign proved as ineffectual as the first. But the controversy continued to simmer, and eventually the anti–Sunday mail forces achieved much of their demands. By 1863 evangelical reformer Talcot Chambers could boast that the protests had "caused a reduction of Sunday-mail service to an amount scarcely one fourth of what it was when the question was first mooted." Further lobbying in the early twentieth century succeeded in shutting down all post offices on Sunday.

The Sunday mails debate remains an important episode in American constitutional history because it articulated two radically different conceptions of religious freedom. Opponents of Sunday mails championed a broad view, maintaining that government coercion of religious adherents could include far more than fines and imprisonment. They further argued that the government could inhibit free exercise by adopting policies that explicitly attacked the religious beliefs of certain groups. The other conception of religious liberty was far narrower. According to Sunday mail defenders, only the most direct forms of coercion interfered with the free exercise of religion. Both views would reappear in future debates over church and state in America.

John G. West, Jr.

Bibliography

American State Papers, Class VII: Post Office Department, Vol. 1. (Washington, D.C.: Gales and Seaton, 1834).

John, Richard, "Taking Sabbatarianism Seriously: The Postal System, the Sabbath, and the Transformation of the American Political Culture," 10 *Journal of the Early Republic* 517–567 (1990).

West, John Garret Jr., "The Politics of Revelation and Reason: Evangelicals and the Founders: Solution to the Theological-Political Problem, 1800–1835" (Ph.D.diss., Claremont Graduate School, 1992).

Case Cited

Commonwealth v. Knox, 6 Mass. 76 (1809).

Sunday Regulations in the Nineteenth Century

Nineteenth-century United States inherited the institution of restricted Sunday activities from colonial America. The colonies adopted these laws to foster religious observance by banning conduct seen as inconsistent with the religious character of the day and by compelling attendance at religious services. At a time when individual Protestant sects dominated colonial life, the connection between religious practice and moral behavior was easily seen.

When disestablishment became a widely adopted doctrine after the American Revolution, it became more difficult to justify the Sunday laws on a purely religious basis. By continuing to ban Sunday activities, states believed they could create a day of rest for the good of society. Restrictions on Sunday behavior—along with prohibitions on vice, profanity, and the use of alcohol—were given a secular justification. Since Sunday was the Christian Sabbath for the great majority of the population, its enforcement confirmed the universal belief that America was a Christian nation. Although American judges rarely doubted the authenticity of Sunday's religious nature, nineteenth-century judicial opinions gave greater weight to a secular rationale. This decline in the use of a religious justification reflected the pervasive secularization that swept nineteenth-century public life under the impact of American ideas of religious pluralism. As questions of religious belief retreated to the private world of the denomination and the individual conscience, the rationale for the enforcement of Sunday doctrines came within the wider compass of the nineteenth-century doctrine of the police power.

The earliest colonial statutes reflected the strict Sabbatarianism of seventeenth-century English Puritanism. Following the Restoration of the monarchy in 1669, the English enacted new legislation that relaxed the most stringent aspects of the Puritan Sunday. The statute of 29 Charles II (1689) banned recreational activities as well as all "worldly labor, business, or work of their ordinary callings on the Lord's day . . . works of necessity and charity only excepted." Widely followed in the American colonies, this statute resulted in two versions of Sunday legislation. The stricter one, which retained the Puritan stringencies, applied to everyone and to all activities both public and private. The more liberal version had two aspects. First, because it followed the statute of Charles II's language that banned only "ordinary callings," it thereby distinguished public behavior from private actions; the offense of Sunday activity lay in its disturbance of others. Second, liberal statutes exempted Saturday Sabbath observers. The liberal approach thus reflected the privatization of belief and the pluralist reality of American religion.

Sunday Sabbatarianism and Moral Reform

In the nineteenth century, judicial concern over Sunday regulations tracked the general movement of moral reform. Although there is little judicial evidence of post-Revolution enforcement of Sunday laws—because the laws were either generally observed or poorly enforced—by the early decades of the nineteenth century, Sunday observance became a political issue. Sunday Sabbatarianism surfaced periodically as one aspect of the moral reform movements that swept America in the early nineteenth century. Starting with a dispute over the delivery of Sunday mail in 1810, Sunday activities sparked controversies over urban travel, recreation, and commerce.

During the first wave of antebellum moral reform in the 1830s and 1840s, the courts responded with statutory interpretations sympathetic to the call for Sabbath observance. By the 1880s, however, when the second wave of Sabbatarian reform swept the country, the courts were no longer as aggressive in their support. An 1880 Massachusetts law journal called its Sunday law "almost a dead letter." By the latter part of the nineteenth century, the effects of immigration, urbanization, and changes in social attitudes weakened public support for Sunday laws and further eroded their enforcement. Liquor and business interests, also, provoked legal challenges to the existing laws.

Antebellum courts routinely upheld Sunday laws against constitutional attack. Challenged by Jews and Seventh-Day Christians who argued on religious freedom grounds against the government's sanctification of Sunday, the courts adopted a secular justification for the creation of a day of rest. As the Pennsylvania court said in *Specht v. Commonwealth* (Pa., 1848): "All agree that to the well-being of society, periods of rest are absolutely necessary. . . . In a Christian community, where a very large majority of the people celebrate the first day of the week as their chosen period of rest from labour, it is not surprising that that day should have received the legislative sanction." Despite its religious side, the court said, Sunday "is still, essentially, but a civil regulation made for government of man as a member of society." Aside from one decision in California in 1858 striking down a Sunday law (*Ex parte Newman* [Calif., 1858]), no other court struck down any nineteenth-century Sunday law on constitutional grounds. And even California's court changed its mind three years later, in *Ex parte Andrews* (Calif., 1861).

Although most state constitutions contained free exercise provisions, the courts believed that the states could legitimately enforce a religiously based morality. The courts took the position that the state bills of rights protected individual beliefs only from government coercion. Conduct, on the other hand, was always subject to regulation. As a South Carolina judge put it in *City Council of Charleston v. Benjamin* (S.C., 1846): "The day of moral virtue in which we live would, in an instant, if that standard were abolished, lapse into the dark and murky night of Pagan immorality." In 1857 constitutional scholar Theodore Sedgwick wrote, in *The Interpretation and Construction of Statutory and Constitutional Law:* "Still though Christianity is not the religion of the State . . . it is nevertheless closely interwoven into the texture of our society, and is intimately connected with all our social habits, and customs, and modes of life." Although the courts often denied that they were "establishing" a religion, their rhetoric clearly supports Mark De Wolfe Howe's conclusion in *The Garden and the Wilderness* that nineteenth-century America witnessed a de facto Protestant establishment. Those who challenged the orthodoxy of the Christian Sabbath would be tolerated, at best. Thus, when a Jew was charged with violating Charleston's ordinance, the court in *Benjamin* said that any negative impact on the defendant was "not the effect of our law. It is the result of his religion, and to enjoy its cherished benefits, living in a community who have appointed a different day of rest, he must give to its law obedience."

Sunday Contracts and Travel Injuries

Although scholarly attention has most often focused on criminal enforcement of the Sunday closing laws forbidding work and recreation on Sundays, nineteenth-century courts also addressed other private law issues arising from Sunday activities. The courts were asked to enforce contracts made on Sunday, to compensate victims of Sunday accidents, and to remunerate the owners of the horses injured in such accidents.

Before the enactment of Sunday statutes, the English common law forbade only the conduct of judicial business on Sunday. Sunday was *dies non juridicus* (literally, "a day not juridical," which means a day when courts are not open for business). Contracts made or performed on Sunday were lawful and enforceable as though made on any other day. The adoption of the statutes that barred commercial activity on Sunday, however, presented the courts with the issue of whether to enforce contracts that sprang from illegal activity. The general common-law rule was that a contract founded on an act prohibited by statute under penalty was void. Because the majority of American jurisdictions punished the transaction of business or the exercise of "worldly employment" on Sunday by fine (albeit a small one), contracts made on Sundays fell under the common-law ban. These jurisdictions made no allowance for privately negotiated Sunday contracts. In *O'Donnell v. Sweeney* (Ala., 1843) an Alabama court said that denying enforcement to Sunday contracts would "promote morality and advance the interests of religion." By mid-nineteenth century, however, some courts began having second thoughts. Sunday contracts struck some judges as falling into a special category of contracts that were illegal because of time rather than content (such as usury or gaming). Judges became more concerned about defendants' using the Sunday defense to escape liability than they were of enforcing the occasional Sunday contract or promissory note. Thus, even courts that professed a deep attachment to Sunday observance began adopting doctrines that allowed them to enforce contracts under certain circumstances.

A minority of states followed the wording of the English statute that barred only "ordinary callings" on Sundays. Following an influential early-nineteenth-century English decision, *Drury v. DeFontaine* (Eng., 1808), some American courts held that their statutes did not apply to private business dealings. New York, for example, interpreted its statute to apply only to the "public exposure of commodities." Private contracts and promissory notes signed on Sunday were enforceable. As one judge put it in 1835: "Every man is permitted, in those respects, to regulate his conduct by the dictates of his own conscience" (*Boynton v. Page* [N.Y., 1835], p. 429).

Cases from urban areas often prompted judges to reexamine their Sunday laws. In *Commonwealth v. Teamann* (Pa., 1853)—a disorderly conduct case brought against a hawker of Sunday newspapers in Philadelphia—the court noted that in earlier generations the "universal recognition of Sunday as a day of rest" had generated few cases. But now a "different spirit" prevailed. Sunday laws were being ignored. For the court it raised the question of whether Sunday would be "protected by law": "To a people whose property depends so greatly on the cultivation of a sound morality this becomes a question of vital importance." But the court wondered whether Pennsylvania's inherited "institutions and laws" were "sufficiently liberal and capacious to meet the requirements of modern advancement."

In the early nineteenth century, the northeastern states' Sunday laws specifically forbade travel on Sunday except for acts of necessity or charity. Midwestern states permitted travel by emigrants heading west. In *Commonwealth v. Knox* (Mass., 1809) Massachusetts interpreted its statute to permit the Sunday transport and delivery of the mail. Justice Theophilus Parsons interpreted the "necessity" exception to mean "moral fitness" rather than "physical necessity." Thus, carrying out a federal contract to carry the mail was justified. The driver's immunity, however, did not extend to his passengers nor to "blowing his horn . . . to the disturbance of serious people either at public worship or in their houses." Led by Protestant ministers, Sabbatarian organizations fought for strict enforcement of existing Sunday laws. In *Pearce v. Atwood* (Mass., 1816) Judge Isaac Parker noted that in the previous two to three years "a laudable zeal has appeared for a more strict observation of the day." Parker, however, objected to the vigor with which local officials were stopping travelers: "Surely, one such scene as this would do more towards injuring the public morals, and impairing a respect for the Lord's day, than the traveling of many people peaceably and quietly through a town, perhaps unnoticed by any but the officers." During the next few decades the Massachusetts courts caught up with the Sabbatarian spirit.

Tort cases involving Sunday travel began to appear more frequently in the courts in the 1840s. Massachusetts adopted the strictest position. In *Bosworth v. Inhabitants of Swansey* (Mass., 1845) its highest court heard a suit against a town for injuries suffered on Sunday as a result of a highway in disrepair. The court ruled that as a precondition to the recovery of damages the Sunday traveler had the burden of proving the lawfulness of his travel. In *Gregg v. Wyman* (Mass., 1849) the Massachusetts Supreme Judicial Court refused to allow a stable owner to sue for a damaged horse, because he had rented out the horse on Sunday. Gregg had rented his horse to Wyman, who so abused it that the horse died. But, because the rental was on Sunday, and Wyman had rented the horse solely for pleasure, the Court ruled that Gregg could not recover for his loss. The Court said that the Sunday law "is a wise and salutary law, and he who tramples on that law should fully understand that he had no right to call on the court for aid to enforce a claim founded on his unlawful act." For the next two decades Massachusetts continued to reject claims for injuries that occurred because of pleasure travel on Sundays. Most other states, however, rejected this rule and allowed negligence cases that stemmed from discretionary Sunday travel. Even the Massachusetts court began to doubt whether its principal mission was the protection of Sunday. In *Hall v. Corcoran* (Mass. 1871) the court recognized that among the New England states only Rhode Island agreed with its interpretation; moreover, the trial bar opposed its position. Finally, in *Doyle v. Lynn and Boston Railroad Co.* (Mass., 1875) the court overruled its line of horse-injury cases. The court acknowledged its increasingly secular view of Sunday when it refused to second-guess a recovery by a passenger on a street railway who had accompanied a friend to visit the sick. "Charity," the court said, includes "everything which proceeds from a sense of moral duty, or a feeling of kindness and humanity." The court no longer insisted that the plaintiff prove that his travel was for a charitable purpose. In 1877 and 1884 the legislature cast aside the remnants of the Massachusetts doctrine by adopting statutes that gave Sunday travelers the right to sue for injuries. As the justification for Sunday observance came less to rely on religious ideas, Sunday tort cases came to be seen as ordinary tort suits.

Experiences in Pennsylvania and New York also led to the normalization of Sunday tort litigation. These states were directly affected by European immigrants who imported the "Continental Sabbath," the European tradition of using Sunday not only for worship but also for relaxation and recreation. Pennsylvania's Sunday law did not bar travel. However, its ban on all forms of "worldly employment or business" allowed Sabbatarians to challenge Sunday transportation. Sunday travelers headed not only to church but also to the nearby taverns. In *Johnston v. Commonwealth* (Pa., 1853)—a case prompted by a local ministerial alliance—the city of Pittsburgh brought suit against an omnibus driver for a Sabbath violation. Affirming the driver's conviction, Judge Woodward argued that, if the court accepted the defendant's "necessity" argument, it would "throw open the tavern, the store, the workshop, and the market-house on Sunday. If we decide that *necessity* and *charity* mean convenience . . . we emasculate the statute." Woodward went on to observe that it "would be a small boon to the people of Pennsylvania to declare their indefeasible right to worship God according to the dictates of their consciences, amid the din and confusion of secular employments."

A Day of Mixed Uses

After the Civil War, things changed. In *Sparhawk v. Union Passenger Railway Co.* (Pa., 1867) Philadelphia pewholders along a trolley line sought injunctive relief against the Union Passenger Railway for running its cars on Sunday. The court threw out the case. The court said that the railway's violation of the Sunday law did not mean that the plaintiffs were entitled to an injunction. The court disconnected the day of rest from its religious basis: "Religious meditation, and devotional exercises . . . result from sentiments not universal in their demonstrations by any means, but peculiar to individuals rather than to the whole community." There was no standard to measure damages. "The injury, however, is not of a *temporal nature,*" the court said, "it is altogether of a *spiritual character for which no action lies.*" Another judge noted that people were now living in an "age of improvement" when Pennsylvania's "very illiberality should make us more desirous to extend the limits of necessity and charity, and not to confine them within narrow boundaries."

In the years following the Civil War the courts moved away from a strict view of Sunday violations. This judicial retreat paralleled the shift of Sunday from a day exclusively for worship to a day of mixed uses, increasingly focused on recreation. As Sunday attained a more secular status, the late nineteenth century witnessed the Sabbatarians' unsuccessful fight for a national day of rest. These efforts were part of a more general attempt by Protestant fundamentalists to establish the United States as a "Christian nation." Although reformers often employed secular arguments on behalf of a day of rest, their less acknowledged aim was to preserve Sunday as a day of worship.

By the early twentieth century, the retail industry had joined liquor interests in the fight to reduce or repeal Sunday legislation. These commercial interests soon joined hands with other interest groups. As the scholar Alan Racucher has noted, "Businesses and customers seeking to eliminate Sunday closing laws joined with religious minorities and civil libertarians to hoist the banner of separation of church and state." Although the U.S.

Supreme Court refused to strike down Sunday closing laws on religious freedom grounds in the 1960s, the tide of secularization was too strong. By the end of the twentieth century, few states enforced the remaining general Sunday closing laws.

Andrew King

Bibliography

Gilkeson, John S. Jr., "The Rise and Decline of the Puritan Sunday in Providence, Rhode Island, 1810–1926," 59 *New England Quarterly* 75–91 (1986).

Howe, Mark De Wolfe, *The Garden and the Wilderness* (Chicago and London: University of Chicago Press, 1965).

Raucher, Alan, "Sunday Business and the Decline of Sunday Closing Laws: An Historical Overview," 36 *Journal of Church and State* 13–33 (1994).

Sedgwick, Theodore, *The Interpretation and Construction of Statutory and Constitutional Law,* 2nd ed. (New York: Baker Voorhis, 1874).

Solberg, Winton U., *Redeem the Time: The Puritan Sabbath in Early America* (Cambridge, Mass., and London: Harvard University Press, 1977).

Cases Cited

Bosworth v. Inhabitants of Swansey, 51 Mass. 363 (1845).

Boynton v. Page, 13 Wendell 425 (N.Y. 1835).

City Council of Charleston v. Benjamin, 2 Strobhart 508 (S.C. 1846).

Commonwealth v. Knox, 6 Mass. 76 (1809).

Commonwealth v. Teamann, 10 Philadelphia Rep. 460 (1853).

Doyle v. Lynn and Boston Railroad Co., 118 Mass. 195 (1875).

Drury v. DeFontaine, 127 Eng. Rptr. 781 (1808).

Ex parte Andrews, 18 Cal. 679 (1861).

Ex Parte Newman, 9 Cal. Rptr. 502 (1858).

Gregg v. Wyman, 58 Mass. 322 (1849).

Hall v. Corcoran, 107 Mass. 251 (1871).

Johnston v. Commonwealth, 22 Pa. 102 (1853).

O'Donnell v. Sweeney, 5 Ala. 467 (1843).

Pearce v. Atwood, 13 Mass. 324 (1816).

Sparhawk v. Union Passenger Railway Co., 54 Pa. 401 (1867).

Specht v. Commonwealth, 8 Pa. 312 (1848).

Sunday Sports

In 1918 the mayor and city council of Baltimore, Maryland, passed an ordinance that would permit residents—in public parks, on Sundays—to play baseball, football, basketball, golf, lawn tennis, croquet, and other games, provided such play took place between the hours of 2 P.M. and 7 P.M. did not disturb church services, and involved no admission fees. A group calling itself the Lord's Day Alliance took legal action against the ordinance; it lost in Baltimore City Superior Court but won on appeal to the Maryland Supreme Court in *Levering v. Park Commissioners* (Md., 1919). That court found that a state law prohibited such play on Sundays. Under the state statute Marylanders were not "to profane the Lord's Day by gaming, fishing, fowling, hunting or unlawful pastime or recreation." Thus, the Maryland Supreme Court found that the City of Baltimore had no authority to pass its ordinance allowing Sunday sports.

This case pointed up one state's application of Sunday closing laws, an attempt in one city to relax the ban, and a successful attack against any such relaxation. In most states in the early twentieth century, Sunday closing laws restricted various kinds of sports activities, whether participant or spectator events.

On Sundays in the early twentieth century, no baseball fan could attend a home game played by the Boston Braves, the New York Giants, or the Philadelphia Athletics. With sports—especially professional baseball and football—subject to the Sunday closing laws, such entertainment was available in some states but not in all. In 1878 baseball's National League prohibited Sunday games, but beginning in 1892 each team could decide for itself. Cincinnati and St. Louis proceeded to schedule Sunday games, and Chicago began doing so soon after. Eastern states, however, would have none of this. In session after session, beginning in 1897, the New York legislature considered bills to relax a Sunday ban, but not until 1919 did it change the law and permit Sunday baseball—between 2 P.M. and 6 P.M., on a local-option basis. Only in 1929 was Sunday baseball no longer banned in Boston.

The final holdout among states with major league teams, Pennsylvania, made the change only in late 1933. That state, where a blue law dating from 1794 continued to be employed against Sunday sports into the twentieth century, supplies a good example of how the law operated and how it changed. In May 1919 the Philadelphia Park Commission acted to permit baseball, golf, and tennis to be played in the city's parks, and the judge in a local court dismissed a case brought by Sabbatarians to prevent the change. But the ban continued in other communities and for professional sports even in Philadelphia. In August 1926 the Philadelphia Athletics occasioned a test case of the 1794 law by playing the Chicago White Sox at Shibe Park on a Sunday. The case eventually went to the Pennsylvania Supreme Court, which, in *Commonwealth v. American Baseball Club of Philadelphia* (Pa., 1927), upheld the statute. The Court declared: "Christianity is part of the common law of Pennsylvania, and its people are Christian people. Sunday is the holy day among Christians. No one we think would contend that professional baseball partakes in any way of the nature of holiness." In 1931 the Pennsylvania House of Representatives passed legislation that would have ended the statewide prohibition and left the matter in the hands of local governments, but the measure failed in the Senate. Two years later, by contrast, such a measure became law, and in November 1933 referenda were held throughout Pennsylvania on the question: "Do you favor the . . . playing of baseball and football games . . . between the hours of two and six P.M. on Sunday?" Most urban communities voted their approval. The 1933 baseball season had already ended, but football had not, and soon the Philadelphia Eagles, playing at home on a Sunday afternoon, held the Chicago Bears to a 3-3 tie. Beginning the next spring, both the Philadelphia Athletics and the Pittsburgh Pirates scheduled some of their home games on Sundays.

These questions arose in the wider context of the cultural politics of the first third or so of the twentieth century. Natives and Protestants were more likely than immigrants, Jews, or Catholics to support enforcement of the Sunday closing laws. And rural people tended to clash with urban dwellers. Thus the legislators from Philadelphia were unanimous in their support of a change in the Pennsylvania law in 1931, when they lost, and again in 1933. In New York, downstate Democrats had to swim upstream against the system of apportionment that gave their rural, upstate, Republican foes an edge in any legislative struggle in that state. The Sunday closing laws supply a leading example of the ways in which the overlapping worlds of religion and the law supplied the framework within which various battles were fought in American life.

Such restrictions lived on in some states—particularly in the Southeast—that had professional teams only at the minor-league level. In 1925, for example, when a test case had the Richmond Colts playing at the home field of the Portsmouth Truckers, the game was called after one inning, tied 1-all, as all nine starting players on each side, plus the umpires, were taken into custody for violating the Virginia Sunday closing statute. The case went all the way to the Virginia Supreme Court of Appeals, where, in *Crook v. Commonwealth* (Va., 1927), the court ruled that a regular game could not escape the ban. In another test case in Virginia, in 1934, the visiting coach from the Greensboro (North Carolina) Patriots had occasion to explain, "This makes the sixth time I've been arrested for this 'crime.'"

Thus the application to Sunday sports of eighteenth-century statutes varied from one time to another and from one place to another. The statutes varied, and judicial construction of them did as well. If legislatures did not frame statutes clearly to permit Sunday baseball, the courts might construe them to do so, as had been hoped (or feared) in Pennsylvania and Virginia alike—and as did the Kansas Supreme Court in *State v. Prather* (Kans., 1909) and the Tennessee Supreme Court in *State v. Nashville Baseball Club* (Tenn., 1912). Nor was the story so different when it came to other sports. Cases that upheld bans against sporting events included *Bishop v. Hanna* (S.C., 1951), which held that the South Carolina statute criminalizing "public sports or pastimes" on Sundays included stock-car races in which admission fees were charged and money prizes were awarded to winners.

Not until after World War II did some states finally change their laws to permit Sunday baseball games and other professional sports events (see *Worley v. State,* [Ga., 1949]). The contrast with earlier times could be seen in the 1980s and 1900s, when few objected if, on any given Sunday, an Atlanta Braves pitcher threw a baseball, race cars roared around the Charlotte Motor Speedway, or golfers teed off at the Augusta National.

Peter Wallenstein

Bibliography

Jable, J. Thomas, "Sunday Sport Comes to Pennsylvania: Professional Baseball and Football Triumph over the Commonwealth's Archaic Blue Laws, 1919–1933." 47 *Research Quarterly* 357–365 (1976).

Lucas, John A., "The Unholy Experiment: Professional Baseball's Struggle against Pennsylvania Sunday Blue Laws, 1926–1934," 38 *Pennsylvania History* 163–175 (1971).

Riess, Steven A., "Professional Sunday Baseball: A Study in Social Reform, 1892–1934," 4 *Maryland Historian* 95–108 (1973).

Wallenstein, Peter, "'Works of Necessity and Charity Only Excepted': The Courts and the Sunday Closing Laws in Twentieth-Century Virginia." 29 *Virginia Social Science Journal* 15–30 (1994).

Cases Cited

Bishop v. Hanna, 218 S.C. 474 (1951).

Commonwealth v. American Baseball Club of Philadelphia, 290 Pa. 136 (1927).

Crook v. Commonwealth, 147 Va. 593 (1927).

Levering v. Park Commissioners, 134 Md. 48 (1919).

State v. Nashville Baseball Club, 127 Tenn. 292 (1912).

State v. Prather, 79 Kan. 513 (1909).

Worley v. State, 79 Ga. Ap. 594 (1949).

Supreme Court Justices and Their Religious Beliefs

The religious background of the U.S. Supreme Court justices only recently has begun to receive attention from scholars. The religious composition of the Court is important, however, since religious beliefs and traditions may influence judicial behavior in connection with individual legal issues, jurisprudential philosophy, and styles of adjudication. Moreover, religion sometimes has been a factor in the appointment process, and a diversity of religious experience among the justices serves as a test of the success of pluralism in American society.

The religions of American justices have been both diverse and narrow. Although justices have been drawn from most of the religions that are numerically strong in the United States, the socially elite Protestant denominations have been disproportionately represented. Of the 111 persons who have served on the Court, nearly half have been Episcopalian (thirty) or Presbyterian (seventeen), although those two denominations never have accounted for more than a small percentage of the Republic's population. Six justices have been members of the even smaller Unitarian sect. Despite the growing pluralism of American society, three of the nine justices in 1992 were Episcopalian. Twenty-four justices have been nondenominationally Protestant—a figure that generally is consistent with American society as a whole. Baptists (five justices), Methodists (four justices), and Lutherans (one justice, William H. Rehnquist) have been underrepresented on the Court. The Eastern Orthodox churches and the Church of Jesus Christ of Latter-Day Saints (Mormons) are by far the largest religious communions from which no justice has been selected.

Beginning with Louis D. Brandeis in 1916, seven Jews have served on the Court. Two Jews sat on the Court between 1932 and 1938, when Benjamin N. Cardozo served with Brandeis, and between 1965 and 1967, when Arthur J. Goldberg served with Abe Fortas. Currently, Justice Ruth Bader Ginsburg and Stephen Breyer sit on the Court.

Although only eight members of the Court have been members of the Roman Catholic Church, which now claims the allegiance of more than one-quarter of the nation, two members of the Court in 1992 were Roman Catholic. Three were Roman Catholic between the seating of Anthony M. Kennedy in 1988 and the resignation of William J. Brennan in 1990. The relatively low number of Roman Catholics who have served on the Court reflects the numerical weakness of the Roman Catholic Church during the nation's early years and its cultural isolation until recent times. Nevertheless, the first Roman Catholic (Roger B. Taney) joined the Court in 1836, and at least one Catholic has served on the Court at all times since 1894, except for the period from 1949 to 1956.

Roman Catholicism occasionally has been a factor in the appointment process, because some presidents have used the nomination of a Catholic to win political support among Catholic voters, who traditionally have been concentrated in populous and politically pivotal states. The nominations of Joseph McKenna in 1898, Edward D. White for the chief justiceship in 1910, Pierce Butler in 1922, Frank Murphy in 1940, and Brennan in 1956 may have been influenced by such political considerations. Conversely, anti-Catholicism may have detracted support from some potential nominees during earlier periods of the nation's history, because the appointment of Roman Catholic justices formerly inspired vocal protests among nativists and anti-Catholics. The assimilation of Roman Catholics into the mainstream of American society during recent years, however, largely has eliminated Catholicism as either a positive or a negative factor in the Supreme Court appointment process. Religion, for example, appears to have had little or no effect on President Reagan's decision to nominate the Roman Catholics Antonin Scalia and Anthony Kennedy.

Because the justices generally have been reticent about their religious beliefs, any assessment of their personal religious views must be speculative. Most justices, however, appear to have embraced a characteristically American attitude toward religion, insofar as they have professed a strong belief in God and have regarded religion as an important component of a moral and well-ordered society, but they have taken little interest in doctrine or liturgy.

Because religion forms an integral part of an individual's moral and intellectual character, a judge who takes his or her religion seriously cannot help but be influenced by religious considerations in ways that are not necessarily inconsistent with the objectivity required of a judge. The precise effects of such influences, however, are highly problematical and are only beginning to be studied. So many variables affect a justice that religious factors are difficult to isolate from other influences, including economics, culture, politics, and ethnicity.

The judicial career of Brandeis, for example, may suggest that Jewish justices might be particularly sympathetic to outsiders in American society. But Felix Frankfurter, another Jewish justice, demonstrated markedly less solidarity toward outsiders. The high intellectual caliber of the seven Jews who have served on the Court may reflect the rich intellectual traditions of Judaism, but then again it may reflect anti-Semitic prejudices that have made it possible for only exceptionally well qualified Jews to attain a position on the Court. The Presbyterian churches arguably are more intellectual in their approach to religion than is the Episcopal Church, but it is difficult to discern any significant difference between the intellectualism of Episcopalian and Presbyterian justices, who tend to have similar social and economic backgrounds. Hugo L. Black's literal reading of the Constitution may have reflected the biblical literalism of the Baptists, but it also may have resulted from a tenacious dedication to civil liberties that was forged in the crucible of populist politics. Rehnquist's formalistic approach toward the law may reflect the highly doctrinal character of Lutheranism, but it may be much more the result of political predilections that have little or no connection with religion.

The difficulty of correlating religion with judicial philosophy is illustrated by the disparate positions on abortion taken by the three Roman Catholic justices who have served on the Court since abortion became a leading source of constitutional controversy. Despite the Roman Catholic Church's official condemnation of abortion, Brennan strongly advocated the belief that the Constitution provides a fairly expansive right to an abortion. Scalia has taken a much more restrictive position. And Kennedy has carved out a position between Brennan and Scalia. Since all three of these justices have been described as devout Catholics, intensity of religious commitment cannot explain their differences regarding abortion.

A relationship between religious belief and adjudication likewise is difficult to discern in cases involving separation of church and state. Although some critics of the Court argued that early decisions restricting state aid to parochial schools reflected anti-Catholic biases, Brennan became one of the Court's most ardent opponents of state aid to education. Likewise, many Protestant justices have found constitutional objections to prayer and Bible reading in the public schools, even though religious exercises in the public schools arguably discriminate primarily against non-Protestants. Although Jews might be expected to be more inclined than Christians to favor a strict separation doctrine, the Court continued to expand the scope of the separation doctrine during the two decades between the resignation of Justice Fortas and the appointment of Justice Ginsburg when no Jew has sat on the Court. Support for rigid separation of church and state among devoutly Christian justices may reflect their belief that undue entanglement between church and state fails to serve the best interests of either. During the early 1960s, for example, Tom C. Clark, an active Presbyterian layman, publicly defended the Court against charges that the justices were "godless" because they opposed school prayer and Bible reading. Clark explained that the justices were personally religious and that the decisions were not intended to have any baneful impact on religion.

Much interesting work remains to be done on this subject.

William G. Ross

Bibliography

Blaustein, Albert P., and Roy M. Mersky, *The First One Hundred Justices: Statistical Studies on the Supreme Court of the United States* (Hamden, Conn.: Archon, 1978).

Burt, Robert A., *Two Jewish Justices: Outcasts in the Promised Land* (Berkeley: University of California Press, 1988).

Carter, Stephen L., "The Religiously Devout Judge," 64 *Notre Dame Law Review* 932–944 (1989).

Levinson, Sanford, "The Confrontation of Religious Faith and Civil Religion: Catholics Becoming Justices," 39 *DePaul Law Review* 1047–1081 (1990).

Perry, Barbara A., "The Life and Death of the 'Catholic Seat' on the U.S. Supreme Court," 6 *Journal of Law and Politics* 55–92 (1989).

T

Tax Law and American Religion

History of Tax Exemptions for Religious Organizations

From its foundation as a haven of religious liberty, the United States, including its laws and its tax laws, traditionally has been broadly sympathetic to religious institutions and the exercise of religious freedom. In fact, almost from the inception of the Republic formalized religions have been essentially exempt from U.S. tax laws. This is not surprising, given the colonists' collective experience before emigrating from England, where religious worship—at least with respect to the Church of England—was a part of daily life. The colonists were also no doubt quite familiar with the British law of charitable trusts and with the preamble to the Statute of Charitable Uses, which continued to have an impact in the British colonies.

In 1601 the British Parliament enacted the statute of Charitable Uses to enforce existing charitable trusts. Professor Whitehead points out that the statute's preamble, though not its actual enforcement provisions, retained continuing force in English and American common law. Although the single reference to religion in the preamble of the statute listed the repair of churches as an example of a charitable use, British decisions interpreting the statute tended to reinforce the notion of support for religion as an established charitable purpose, and it is not surprising that these notions were imported to America by the colonists.

In *Commissioner v. Pemsel* (Eng., 1891) Lord McNaghten outlined the legal definition of "charity," relying in part on the Statute of Uses, which was then almost three hundred years old. He stated: "'charity' in its legal sense comprises four principal divisions: trusts for the relief of poverty; trusts for the advancement of education; *trusts for the advancement of religion;* and trusts for other purposes beneficial to the community, not falling under any of the preceding heads" (emphasis supplied). Nine of the original thirteen colonies granted direct aid to churches through tax relief even before the American Revolution. During the colonial period, however, aid directed to a particular state-sponsored church was coupled with the prohibition of all other forms of worship. Somewhat paradoxically, the colonists who were driven to settle a new land by religious intolerance in England seemed reluctant, at first, to permit the same kind of religious tolerance that they themselves had sought only a few years earlier.

The states' adoption of Britain's approach toward religious organizations and tax exemptions was eventually reexamined and placed in historical context in *Bob Jones University v. United States* (1983). In *Bob Jones University,* federal tax-exempt status under §501(c)(3) of the Internal Revenue Code of 1986, as amended (the "code," or the "IRC"), was denied to this university because of its racially discriminatory admissions policies. The university's contention that its official religious posture required it to discriminate was given little weight by the U.S. Supreme Court. The Court looked beyond the literal requirements of IRC §501(c)(3) and concluded—in partial reliance on the Statute of Uses and subsequent cases—that an overriding congressional concern was that the organization qualify as a "charity" in harmony with public policy. Ultimately the Court found the university's racial policies to be inherently "out of synch" with U.S. public policy, and charitable status was denied. *Bob Jones University* illustrates the lasting impact that British common law has had on the U.S. definition of "charity."

In the end, however, despite common roots, the experience of the colonists proved to be much more varied than the life they had left in England. Partly because the citizenry was so heterogeneous, and given the wide variety of religious refugees seeking to find a foothold in the New World, it was recognized early in the colonial period that there was an even more compelling need for religious tolerance in America than was the case in England. The Establishment and Free Exercise Clauses of the First Amendment, therefore, were enacted to divorce religion from governmental sponsorship and promote tolerance of the divergent Christian religions, many of which had been prohibited in England.

It is not surprising that these constitutional strictures have given rise to a considerable level of controversy with regard to the granting or denial of tax exemptions. For example, the First Amendment provides, that "Congress shall make no law respecting an establishment of religion, or prohibiting the free exercise thereof; . . ." Accordingly, laws that, directly or indirectly, have an impact on religious organizations and their congregants must be "neutral"; i.e., they must neither advance nor inhibit religion. Moreover, such laws must not unduly "entangle" government with religion. These constitutional limitations, perhaps inevitably, conflict with the right of all citizens to practice (or not practice) their religions freely and without control from secular authorities.

Because the tax laws, at least facially, are to apply with equal force to all citizens, conflicts between these "freedoms" seem inevitable and raise difficult questions when it comes to applying the tax laws to religious organizations. Should the tax laws be applied pursuant to a policy of strict neutrality so that they neither favor some religions over others nor religion over atheism? Or should a more flexible standard be available so that assistance to religious organizations may be provided on the same basis as it is to secular institutions? One alternative is to completely exempt religious organizations from any form of taxation. Another option is simply to tax religious organizations like any other entities.

In practice, neither of these extreme positions is consistently applied. For one thing, granting a blanket form of tax exemption to religious organizations would, in all likelihood, be viewed as governmental advancement of religion in violation of the First Amendment's proscription against the establishment of religion. On the other hand, taxing religious organizations on the same basis as secular organizations might lead to an equally undesirable result: excessive governmental involvement with religion because of the understandable desire of the taxing authority to ensure uniform compliance with the tax laws. In this regard, it is not difficult to see that vigorous enforcement of the laws for some religious entities—coupled with relaxed standards toward others—would inevitably lead to undesirable governmental interference with a citizen's right to freely exercise, or not to exercise, his or her religion.

In *Walz v. Tax Commission of the City of New York* (1970)—the seminal case that sustained the government's grant of a tax exemption for property owned by religious organizations—the Supreme Court remarked that the two religion clauses in the First Amendment "are not the most precisely drawn portions of the Constitution." Even when viewed in a cursory fashion, they are drawn in broad, absolute terms and clearly will conflict with each other if extended to their logical extremes. For example, providing a property tax exemption could be viewed as supporting a religious organization. Conversely, the denial of the exemption could be considered, with equal plausibility, an impediment to the free exercise of that religion.

For all the controversy that these conflicting provisions of the First Amendment have generated since 1791, definitive judicial guidance has been distinctly lacking. Tax exemptions for church property and places of worship have been, and continue to be, provided by all states of the Union since the disestablishment of religion in the aftermath of the American Revolution—a period of over two centuries. Moreover, religious organizations have been exempted from federal income tax since the imposition of that tax in 1916.

Nonetheless, the Supreme Court did not directly address the constitutionality of such exemptions until 1971, in *Walz*.

In *Walz* the Court concluded that a tax exemption is the best kind of "benevolent neutrality" because, unlike a direct grant or subsidy, it does not require continued surveillance of the organization to ensure compliance with statutory requirements. Commenting generally on legislative efforts to preserve religious freedom without becoming unduly entangled in religion, the Court adopted a "course of constitutional neutrality," stating that the Constitution would not "tolerate either governmentally established religion or governmental interference with religion." Nonetheless, Chief Justice Warren Burger found "room for play in the joints of productive benevolent neutrality which will permit religious exercise to exist without sponsorship and without interference." Noted constitutional scholar Professor Laurence Tribe describes this neutrality as a "zone of permissible accommodation." A tax exemption is a form of passive preferential treatment, a method that does not breach the zone of permissible accommodation, in part, because it does not actually take funds from the state's budget for religious organizations; it simply does not ask churches to contribute directly to the state's bottom line. The Court concluded that a religious exemption "creates a minimal and remote involvement between the church and state," far less than the entanglement that taxation of religious organizations might create.

Although the tax exemption for religion is deeply rooted in this nation's history, the inherent conflicts between it and the First Amendment have created a continuing legal battle in the courts since the first challenge to a property tax exemption, in *Walz* in 1971. To minimize such involvement and to preserve a "constitutionally neutral" policy to the greatest possible extent, Congress traditionally has granted various kinds of tax relief to "valid" religious entities. The most significant of these, by far, is the broad-based exemption afforded by IRC §501(c)(3), which insulates the income of an exempt entity from taxation. However, where there is substantial doubt about the status of an entity, tax relief has been denied—usually on the grounds that the taxpayer has failed to establish the "religious" character of the organization for which the exemption has been sought.

Qualification for a tax exemption on religious grounds requires something substantially more than a mere declaration that one is practicing a "religion." Apart from problems of credibility (which are typical in the "private church" scenario, discussed later), denial of a religious exemption is usually sustained by the courts on the grounds that taxation may be imposed as a burden on rights that are protected by the First Amendment only if the burden is necessary to serve a compelling or overriding governmental interest. Tax-exempt status is granted to a religious entity only when a sufficient nexus can be established between its activities and the basis on which the exemption is claimed. Where this link is tenuous or indirect, the exemption will be denied.

In *Montana Catholic Mission v. Missoula County* (1986) the taxpayer, a mission run by the Society of Jesus (the Jesuits), owned grazing cattle which, it argued, were exempt from the imposition of a state tax. Several reasons were proposed in support of this result: (1) the income from the Mission was devoted to the education and "general improvement" of the Indians on the Flathead Reservation; (2) under local (Montana) law, the entire beneficial ownership of the cattle was in the tribal Indians; and (3) the Society of Jesus was a de facto agent of the federal government, which had permitted and approved the mission's work in satisfaction of its obligation to the Indians. Justice Rufus Peckham, writing for the Court, concluded that the claim did not raise an issue relevant to the U.S. Constitution. The mere fact that the Indians enjoyed use of the land did not entitle the plaintiff to an exemption, because at all relevant times beneficial ownership was in the plaintiff. Here the Court found that the nexus between the mission's religious activities and its cattle grazing was too tenuous to support a tax exemption.

In addition to income tax relief, benefits typically available to organizations that qualify under IRC §501(c)(3) include freedom from property taxes, sales and use tax exemptions, and, occasionally, relief from federal Social Security and unemployment taxes. Moreover, in an effort to encourage contributions to religious and other charitable entities by the public, IRC §170 affords a substantial income tax deduction for contributions made by individuals or businesses to charitable entities. A deduction is available whether an organization is exempt under IRC §501(c)(3) or under other provisions of the code that afford protected status on a more limited basis, such as IRC §509, applicable to private foundations. Finally, IRC §2055 and §2522 provide unlimited deductions against the estate and gift taxes, respectively, for contributions to charities, including religious organizations. Apart from these difficulties, the history of both federal and state tax laws demonstrates a reasonably consistent and generous grant of tax exemptions to religious organizations that began before the formal birth of the United States.

Taxation and Religious Exemptions

The First Amendment commands that "Congress shall make no law respecting an establishment of religion, or prohibiting the free exercise thereof; . . ." Although this mandate appears to be free from ambiguity, in practical application the so-called wall that separates church and state tends to operate more like a permeable screen. Notwithstanding Chief Justice Burger's admonition in *Walz* of the need to walk a constitutional "tightrope" when evaluating First Amendment issues—such as those dealing with religious exemptions—it is apparent that, rather than following the literal dictate of the First Amendment, federal and state legislatures annually enact rules and regulations that significantly affect how religious entities interact with secular citizens. Perhaps inevitably, such legislation is no doubt viewed by some as impermissible fostering of religious tenets and beliefs at the expense of atheism and agnosticism. Other citizens, not surprisingly, may consider the incidental legislation to be an unwarranted interference with the rights of adherents of the particular set of religious beliefs affected by it.

In striving to comply with the seemingly irreconcilable objectives of the First Amendment, courts are often confronted with the delicate task of balancing, on the one hand, the goal of keeping the government free from "entanglements" with religion (so as not to "establish" religion) and the need, on the other hand, for government nevertheless to become "involved" with religion (so as to ensure its free exercise). Instead of imposing a flat ban on laws affecting either the establishment or the free exercise of religion, the First Amendment works to screen out only those laws which create an impermissible level of entanglement between religion and government. Perhaps, as Chief Justice Burger suggested in *Lemon v. Kurtzman* (1971), "total separation [between church and state] is not possible in the absolute sense. Some relationship between government and religious organizations is inevitable." The intersection of tax law and religion reflects this delicate constitutional balancing act between the Establishment Clause and the Free Exercise Clause.

Legislative Power to Tax and the Religion Clauses

Experience common to all verifies that governmental power to grant, or withhold, insulation from the laws of taxation involves significantly more than a mere ability to "level the playing field." As noted earlier, an organization's status as being exempt from tax lies close to the core of its economic "vital signs." The grant of a broad-based exemption, such as that accorded to an "exempt organization" under IRC §501(c)(3), tends to significantly improve an entity's prospects for future economic success, whereas denial of exemption can permanently dim such prospects. Thus, the Free Exercise Clause requires that Congress, in granting or denying tax benefits, not place a tax burden on a religious organization so as to prohibit the organization's members from practicing their faith. At the same time, however, the Establishment Clause demands that federal and state governments not grant a tax benefit to a religious group so as to give that group a financial advantage over its nonreligious counterparts. To do so would amount to a state-sponsored religion.

The simple example of an income tax exemption serves to illustrate the competing interests of the Establishment Clause and the Free Exercise Clause. If a religious organization is denied status as an entity that is exempt from taxes, the organization may reasonably contend that the resultant tax liability is a restraint on its right to freely exercise its religious beliefs. Yet if the religious organization is granted a generous income tax exemption, a nonqualifying organization may be placed at an economic disadvantage. As the Supreme Court noted in *Bob Jones University*, every exemption amounts to a subsidy that affects nonqualifying taxpayers, forcing them to become "indirect and vicarious donors." This "favoritism" may be construed as a violation of the Establishment Clause. Denial of exempt status, in contrast, would have an opposite effect and may be seen to violate the Free Exercise Clause.

Balance of Competing Interests

In an attempt to resolve these competing interests, courts have developed a policy of neutrality similar to that embraced by the Supreme Court in *Walz.* The decisional law that has developed subsequent to *Walz* reveals a trend toward utilizing a two-step approach to ensure that neither the Establishment Clause nor the Free Exercise Clause is violated in enforcing federal or state tax law.

The first inquiry to be made is whether the grant or denial of a particular tax benefit violates the Establishment Clause. In order to make this determination, courts have employed the standard developed in 1971 by the Supreme Court in *Lemon.* If the tax benefit fails to satisfy this standard, thereby indicating a violation of the Establishment Clause, a court must proceed to the next stage. At the next level of inquiry, a court must determine whether the tax benefit violates the Free Exercise Clause: Is government "involvement" in the particular religion "necessary" to ensure its free exercise?

In *Lemon,* the Supreme Court developed a test to determine whether a statute comported with the Establishment Clause. The Court there considered statutes enacted in Rhode Island and in Pennsylvania that sought to provide financial assistance to private schools, predominantly Roman Catholic, for the teaching of secular subjects. The Rhode Island statute, for example, authorized the direct payment of a form of supplemental salary assistance to teachers in the private schools, up to a maximum of 15 percent of a teacher's salary. Courses for which the supplement could be awarded were limited to those taught in the public schools, and religious subjects were specifically prohibited. The Pennsylvania statute was somewhat similar. It authorized the reimbursement of expenses incurred by private schools in Pennsylvania for teachers' salaries, textbooks, and instructional materials in subjects taught in the public schools. Again there was a specific prohibition for any reimbursement related to a religious subject or theme.

In evaluating whether these statutes were unconstitutional, the Court, referring to its earlier decision in *Walz,* identified the "main evils" against which the Establishment Clause was intended to afford protection: "sponsorship, financial support, and active involvement of the sovereign in religious activity." It then offered the three-pronged *Lemon* test to determine whether a statute passes constitutional muster: (1) the statute must have a secular legislative purpose, (2) its principal or primary effect must be one that neither advances nor inhibits religion, and (3) it must not foster "an excessive government entanglement with religion." Even as the Court recognized that "the line of separation [between church and state], far from being a 'wall,' is a blurred, indistinct, and variable barrier," it concluded that, although both the Rhode Island and the Pennsylvania statutes had clearly secular purposes, there was a likelihood of an excessive entanglement of government and religion, involving "successive and very likely permanent appropriations [for such assistance] that benefit relatively few religious groups."

The continued vitality of the *Lemon* test is uncertain. With Justice Blackmun's retirement in 1994, none of the justices who participated in the *Lemon* decision remains on the Court today. Four justices—Rehnquist, Scalia, Kennedy, and Thomas—have expressed discontent with the standards established in *Lemon.* These justices appear to prefer a test that would permit governmental involvement in religious practices as long as nonbelievers do not feel coerced by their abstinence from religious belief. This approach emphasizes the second prong of the test: the neutrality of the legislation. Three other justices—O'Connor, Stevens, and Souter—seem to favor a test that is stricter than the coercion standard espoused by their colleagues but is more open-ended than the *Lemon* test. It is not yet clear which approach will attract Justices Ginsburg and Breyer.

A June 1994 decision that considered the creation of a special school district designed to comprise only the followers of a particular religion, *Board of Education of Kiryas Joel Village School District v. Grumet* (1994), may prove to be an important indicator of the future course the Court will take. In *Grumet,* New York's legislature had established a school district that followed the political boundaries of an incorporated village that was the exclusive enclave of members of a Hasidic sect, the Satmar Hasidim. Although the 1989 statute was neutral on its face, the village and, therefore, the school district were essentially closed to citizens who were not members of the sect. The singular school district was established so that the special education needs of children with various handicapping conditions who resided in the village could be met. Although these children were eligible to attend special education classes in the Monroe-Woodbury School District, from which the special district had been created, it was argued that mixing with children of different religious backgrounds created undue stress for the Hasidic children.

In finding the school district unconstitutional, Justice Souter—joined by Justices Blackmun, Stevens, O'Connor, and Kennedy—concluded that creation of the restricted school district violated the Establishment Clause. Rather than pursuing a neutral course, a majority of the Court's members decided that the New York legislature had improperly delegated the state's authority over public schools to a group defined by its common religion. The Court noted that this could lead to religious "favoritism," i.e., situations where special districts might be created for some religious groups but not for others. Even if this were not the case, the delegation itself constituted an impermissible fusion of governmental and religious functions in violation of the third *Lemon* standard, which prohibits excessive entanglement with religion.

Four days after *Grumet* was decided, New York's legislature, following up on a suggestion in Justice O'Connor's opinion, gave it another try. It sought to remedy the fatal defect in the earlier statute by enacting legislation that permitted a municipality to withdraw from an existing school district and to form its own district if certain specified criteria were met. The Kiryas Joel Village proceeded promptly to form its own school district along essentially the same lines as the district that had just been found to be unconstitutional!

Not surprisingly, the opponents of the newly formed district moved with comparable alacrity to challenge it. On March 9, 1995, various news organizations—including the *New York Times,* the *Albany Times Union,* the *New York Law Journal,* and Reuters—reported that Albany County (N.Y.) Supreme Court Judge Lawrence Kahn (who had determined that the first school district was in violation of the New York State Constitution) had ruled that the reformulated district was constitutional, even though it would seem to differ only superficially from the special district as originally constituted!

At this juncture, it remains to be seen whether a modification of the *Lemon* test is imminent or the grant of authority to municipalities to create school districts will lead to a new standard by which religious institutions may be judged.

In the tax arena, a free exercise claim arises—and thereby implicates the second prong of the *Lemon* test—where the particular entity's failure to qualify for an exemption leads to tax liability that interferes with behavior allegedly dictated by religious belief or compels conduct forbidden by an individual's faith. In *Murdock v. Pennsylvania* (1943), for example, the Court invalidated a city ordinance that imposed a licensing tax on any person canvassing or soliciting within the city. Application of this ban to members of religious groups unduly interfered with their right to disseminate religious information, ruled the Court, in violation of the Free Exercise Clause. In contrast, where a tax is imposed in a neutral and secular manner, the increased tax liability of a religious organization is insufficient to constitute an impediment to the free exercise of religion. Furthermore, the Court has recognized that even a substantial burden on the free exercise of religion may be justified by a "broad public interest," such as maintaining a sound tax system (*Hernandez v. Commissioner of Internal Revenue* [1989]).

After *Walz* sanctioned the federal government's and the states' widespread practice of providing tax exemptions to religious organizations for property used solely for religious purposes, the door was opened for disgruntled taxpayers to challenge other types of exemptions. Over the years, the Court has carved out a zone of neutrality determining, via the *Lemon* standard, what degree of entanglement is permissible by an exemption (or absence of an exemption) in the context of sales and use taxes, unemployment taxes, deductions for contributions to religious organizations provided by the federal income tax law, and restrictions imposed on activities of organizations seeking shelter from tax. Although exemptions from property and income taxes remained inviolable, challenges to various other tax exemptions have been somewhat more successful.

Sales Tax Exemptions

An excellent example of when an exemption from a sales and use tax may create more government entanglement than when a religious entity is subjected to the tax may be found in *Texas Monthly, Inc. v. Bullock* (1989), where the Court struck down a Texas statute that exempted from a sales and use tax "periodicals that are published or distributed by a religious faith and that consist wholly of writings promulgating the teaching of the faith and books that consist wholly of writings sacred to a religious faith." The challenger, a publisher of a general-interest magazine, argued that the exemption for *Texas Monthly* violated the Establishment Clause. By subjecting secular magazines to the tax, it was argued, such magazines were forced to "endorse" religious publications.

In deciding in favor of the secular publisher, the Court observed that if a subsidy is imposed on an array of organizations, including secular ones, there is no direct endorsement of religion. However, that was not the situation before the Court. In *Texas Monthly* the state had focused the exemption on writings that favored the teachings of religious faith. By singling out religious writings as exempt from the tax, Texas had improperly endorsed religion in violation of the Establishment Clause. Focusing on the third prong of the *Lemon* test, the Court concluded that in order to determine whether the exemption was available, government officials had to determine whether a particular message was consistent with "the teaching of the faith."

One year after *Texas Monthly* the Court decided that the Free Exercise and Establishment Clauses did not prohibit California from collecting a generally applicable sales and use tax on the distribution of religious materials by a religious organization, in *Jimmy Swaggart Ministries v. Board of Equalization* (1990). In *Jimmy Swaggart Ministries* the Court considered California's Sales and Use Tax, which required retailers to pay a sales tax "for the privilege of selling tangible personal property at retail." Jimmy Swaggart Ministries (the "Ministries") was a recognized religious organization under IRC §501(c)(3). Its charter and bylaws set forth its purpose of "establishing and maintaining evangelistic outreach," which it sought to achieve, in part, by evangelistic crusades performed through missionary endeavors and mass media methods such as audio production and reproduction of preaching, writing, printing, and publishing. California's Board of Equalization assessed sales and use taxes in the amount of $1,702,942 against the Ministries, alleged to be due from the sale of audio- and videotapes, books, and pamphlets.

The Ministries argued that application of the tax to the sale of religious items vital to its evangelical mission violated both the Free Exercise and the Establishment Clauses. In rejecting these arguments, the Court found that the sales tax itself was neutral, in that it imposed no substantial burden on the observation of a central religious belief or practice. The Court also rejected the Ministries' contention that the tax acted as a prior restraint on the free exercise of religion, distinguishing the application of this tax from free speech cases that involved municipal ordinances which required a license and a fee for permission to canvass or solicit within a city.

In contrast to these ordinances, the California Sales and Use Tax did not act as a precondition to the free exercise of religious beliefs; rather, concluded the Court, it imposed a uniformly applied tax scheme on all organizations—and thus was blind to whether the selling or purchasing organization was secular or charitable, religious or nonprofit. The religious activities of the Ministries were not singled out for special or burdensome treatment. On its face, the tax was neutral, because it was directed at the privilege of making retail sales of tangible personal property and at the storage, use, or consumption of tangible personal property. The Court also rejected the Ministries' contention that they had experienced a reduction in income because of lower demand for their merchandise, given the costs associated with administering the tax. This argument, the Court concluded, was "constitutionally insignificant." In applying the tax, the relevant question was not the religious content of the articles sold but only whether a "sale" within the meaning of the statute had occurred. Thus, the administrative entanglement found in *Texas Monthly* was absent in this case.

Unemployment Tax Exemption

In 1981 the Court considered a challenge to the tax exemption provided to the employees of churches by the Federal Unemployment Tax Act (FUTA), which imposes unemployment taxes on employers for the benefit of employees. In *St. Martin Evangelical Lutheran Church v. South Dakota* (1981) the issue was whether the term "church" referred to an individual house of worship or to an organization of worshippers. On this distinction hinged the question of whether the employees were subject to the FUTA. The Court held that the exemption granted by the FUTA was available to nonprofit, church-related primary and secondary schools. The exemption provided:

> This section shall not apply to service performed—
>
> (1) in the employ of (A) a church or convention or association of churches, or (B) an organization which is operated primarily for religious purposes and which is operated, supervised, controlled or principally supported by a church or convention or association of churches. . . .

The secretary of labor had previously interpreted the exemption as being available to a school that was operated by a church but not to "church-related" schools. Contrary to the secretary's view, the Court concluded that the statutory exemption was phrased in terms of the spiritual nature of the employer, not in terms of the specific physical place where services were provided or where the employer's works were performed. Consequently, it ruled that the exemption applied to employees of schools owned by churches, including schools that were physically separated from the place of worship. However, the exemption did not apply to schools that were separately incorporated with a separate legal existence. Deciding the issue on these narrow statutory grounds, the Court determined that it was unnecessary to consider the merits of the schools' Free Exercise Clause claim.

The following year the Court considered another case regarding the FUTA that partly clarified its stance in *St. Martin Evangelical Church* yet left an important issue open. In *California v. Grace Brethren Church* (1982) a number of California parochial schools challenged the state's refusal to grant a FUTA exemption to their employees. To clarify the discussion, the lower court divided the plaintiffs into three categories: (1) schools that were part of the corporate structure of a church; (2) schools that were separate corporations formed by a church or an association of churches; and (3) schools that were organized primarily for religious purposes but were not operated, supervised, or controlled by a church or convention of churches, i.e., independent, non-church-affiliated religious schools. As a result of the Supreme Court's decision in *St. Martin Evangelical Church,* during the pendency of *Grace Brethren Church* the secretary of labor reconsidered the department's position and concluded that both category-1 schools, such as those dealt with by the Court in *St. Martin Evangelical Church,* and category-2 schools were exempt from the tax. Thus, the decision in *Grace Brethren Church* extended the FUTA exemption to include schools that were incorporated with a separate legal existence, but it left open the question of whether independent, nonaffiliated religious schools were exempt from the tax. The Court, however, never resolved this issue, vacating and remanding the case on procedural grounds.

Income Tax Exemption under IRC §501(c)(3)

Perhaps the broadest example of a tax-favored status afforded by the Internal Revenue Code is granted to those organizations that are exempt from tax under the definition of a "charity" under IRC §501(c)(3). In fact, the exemption is even more attractive than it sounds. An exempt organization within IRC §501(c)(3) enjoys what amounts to a triad of benefits including: (1) no tax consequences to the entity when contributions are made to it; (2) depending on individual circumstances, such contributions are fully deductible to the contributor; and (3) apart from a tax imposed on unrelated business and income under IRC §511, income generated by the organization that is within the scope of its charitable activities is not subject to tax.

To qualify as exempt from federal income taxes under IRC §501(c)(3), an organization must satisfy certain criteria, which include, in part, the following:

> Corporations and any community chest, fund or foundation, organized and operated exclusively for religious, charitable, scientific, testing for public safety, literary or educational purposes, . . . no part of the net earnings of which inure to the benefit of any private shareholder or individual [and] no substantial part of the activities of which is carrying on propaganda or otherwise attempting to influence legislation . . . , [or] any political campaign on behalf of (or in opposition to) any candidate for public officials.

The various states have also adopted individual statutes which define the types of organizations that may apply for tax-exempt status for state law purposes, but such statutes do not bind the federal government in determining the federal tax status of entities purporting to be charities under the principles of *Commissioner v. Estate of Bosch* (1967).

Although a religious entity at least facially satisfies the statutory criteria of IRC §501(c)(3), it is necessary to test its proposed organizational activities for constitutional "integrity." A court must determine whether its structure or the scope of its proposed activities invite special scrutiny, either because it has the potential for undue governmental interference with the free exercise of religion or because, directly or indirectly, it tends to foster the establishment of religion.

Although IRC §501(c)(3) creates a "safe harbor" for an organization that satisfies the statutory criteria, there is a continuing obligation to comply with the statutory restrictions on its activities in order to maintain its tax-exempt status. In fact, the Internal Revenue Service (IRS) publishes an annual list of entities that formerly qualified under IRC §501(c)(3) but are no longer in compliance.

Statutory proscriptions include prohibitions against lobbying to influence legislation as well as promulgating discriminatory policies. A few years after its decision in *Walz,* the Court was afforded the opportunity to strike down a challenge to the antilobbying proscription, in *Alexander v. "Americans United," Inc.* (1974).

In *Alexander* the IRS vitiated the tax-exempt status of an organization because it determined that the organization devoted an excessive portion of its activities to influencing legislation. As a consequence, the IRS changed the status of Americans United from a nonprofit educational organization to a "social welfare" organization. This change in status subjected Americans United to liability for unemployment taxes for its employees and destroyed the basis of its eligibility to receive tax-deductible contributions under IRC §170. Americans United, in turn, sought a declaratory judgment that the lobbying restrictions of IRC §501(c)(3) were unconstitutional because they unduly limited political advocacy rights protected by the free speech component of the First Amendment. Although the Court clearly dodged the substantive issues, it eventually concluded that the proscription against lobbying was within constitutional limits. It determined that the intent and purpose of Americans United in bringing the action was to restrain the assessment or collection of the unemployment tax, which was impermissible under the Anti-Injunction Act. Thus, the antilobbying restrictions of IRC §501(c)(3) remained intact.

Although IRC §501(c)(3) does not expressly prohibit a religious organization from discriminating on the basis of race, the Court has read this restriction into the statute. In *Bob Jones University,* discussed earlier, the IRS denied tax-exempt status to a university because of its biased and racially discriminatory admissions policies. Although Bob Jones University was not affiliated with any particular religious denomination, it was (and is) dedicated to the teaching and propagation of fundamentalist Christian beliefs, which, inter alia, forbid interracial dating and marriage. To effectuate this belief, the university completely excluded African Americans from admission. Subsequently this limitation was abated somewhat, but the university, nonetheless, continued to prohibit interracial dating and marriage and denied admission to applicants engaged in an interracial marriage or known to advocate such activity. Although the Court assumed that the university's discriminatory policies were based on a genuine belief that the Bible forbade interracial dating and marriage, it nonetheless concluded that neither the Constitution nor Congress intended to protect, ensure, and "subsidize" beliefs so antithetical to fundamental principles by affording the offending organization a broad blanket of immunity from taxation as that provided by IRC §501(c)(3).

Chief Justice Burger, writing for the majority, went beyond the literal requirements of the statute and determined that tax exemptions for charitable organizations originated in the special privileges historically extended to charitable trusts by British common law. As noted, the British definition of "charity" was subsequently adopted by the states. To be exempt, therefore, an organization not only must fulfill the stated requirements of IRC §501(c)(3) but also must be "charitable" under common-law standards of "charity." Put another way, an organization that seeks the protection of exempt status must be formed for a purpose that is in harmony with public policy. Given the short history of antidiscrimination law in the United States, it was relatively easy for the Court to conclude that the racial discrimination practiced by Bob Jones University was contrary to public policy and incompatible with the concept of charity underlying the tax exemption. The university's free exercise claim was rejected on the basis of the government's overriding compelling interest in eradicating racial discrimination in education. The Court's majority concluded that this significant governmental interest substantially outweighed whatever burden the denial of tax benefits placed on the university's exercise of its religious beliefs.

In 1981 various abortion rights organizations brought a suit against the federal government in an effort to revoke the tax-exempt status of the Catholic Church. The basis for the suit was the plaintiffs' contention that the Catholic Church was in violation of the IRC §501(c)(3) antilobbying provision because of its political efforts in opposition to abortion. After eight years of litigation over whether the plaintiffs had standing to sue, the Court of Appeals for the Second Circuit denied standing to the plaintiffs and dismissed the case.

In *In re United States Catholic Conferences* (1990) plaintiffs complained of an injury allegedly resulting from the IRS's inconsistent enforcement of the antilobbying provision of IRC §501(c)(3). Such treatment, argued the plaintiffs, resulted in an "uneven playing field" that permitted the Catholic Church to engage in political campaigns without unduly endangering its tax-exempt status. Lax enforcement of the antilobbying provisions, they contended, put the federal government in the untenable position of subsidizing the political views of the Catholic Church by means of the income tax deduction for contributions to the church. The Court, apparently engaging in circular reasoning to avoid a politically dangerous issue, found that, because the plaintiffs chose not to compete with the church and thus jeopardize their own tax-exempt status, they lacked standing. Moreover, whatever injury might have resulted from inconsistent enforcement of IRC §501(c)(3) was not personal to the plaintiffs. As a consequence, the Court dismissed their claim for lack of standing without reaching a decision on the merits.

Interestingly, each plaintiff's posture in *In re United States Catholic Conferences* and *Texas Monthly* was similar, although the results were not. In *Texas Monthly,* for example, secular publishers in a defined market were competing for readers with publishers of religious magazines who were given a tax advantage—alleged to be unfair—by the state. In *In re United States Catholic Conferences,* organizations that supported a woman's right to have an abortion (the pro-choice position) were competing for supporters and political influence with the Catholic Church, which vigorously opposed this view (the right-to-life position). The plaintiffs claimed that the IRS failed to rigorously enforce the antilobbying restriction of IRC §170, because contributors to the church were allowed to deduct contributions while opponents were not. This gave the church a clear—and unfair—advantage over its competitors, argued the plaintiffs.

In *Texas Monthly* the Court struck down the tax exemption because the state had purposefully structured it to provide religious organizations with a tax advantage. In *In re United States Catholic Conferences,* in contrast, the relationship between the exemption and the tax benefit was much more tenuous. It was not the structure of the exemption itself that was alleged to be unfair, but the manner in which it was enforced. Moreover, the politically charged issue of abortion may have made the Court more reluctant to disturb the status quo, although it showed no such reluctance in deciding the issue of racial discrimination in *Bob Jones University.*

Charitable Deductions under IRC §170

Closely related to exempt status under IRC §501(c)(3) is the personal income tax deduction allowed to individuals for donations to qualified organizations. In *Hernandez* members of the Church of Scientology were assessed a deficiency for taxes related to deductions claimed in their individual tax returns for the cost of "auditing" and "training" services related to the church. These expenses were treated as gifts or contributions to charitable or religious organizations under IRC §170. At the time the issue arose, litigation was pending concerning the Church of Scientology's tax-exempt status. Accordingly, the IRS commissioner stipulated that, for purposes of the issues in *Hernandez,* the Church of Scientology would be treated as a religious organization entitled to receive tax-deductible contributions. Thus, the narrow question before the Court in *Hernandez* was whether the taxpayers' payments to the church for these services were gifts or contributions that were deductible under IRC §170 or were a quid pro quo exchange.

According to the tenets of the Church of Scientology, auditing and training services are necessary for an individual to become aware of the spiritual dimension of one's being. "Auditing" is a one-to-one encounter between a participant and a church official; the participant engages in sequential levels of auditing in order to "gain spiritual awareness." "Training" sessions are doctrinal courses for which the church charges a "fixed donation," constituting a primary source of the church's income.

In sustaining the assessment of a deficiency, the Supreme Court reasoned that under IRC §170 gifts or contributions are payments for which there is no expectation of financial return commensurate with the amount of the gift. The Court looked at the external features of the exchange that takes place in auditing and training sessions and found them to be based on a quid pro quo; in effect, the participant pays for services provided by the "auditor" or "trainer." The exchange was, therefore, reciprocal in nature and thus was not a deductible gift or contribution. In response to the taxpayers' argument that disallowance of the deduction violated the Establishment Clause, the Court responded that to allow the deduction would create an entanglement problem. The taxpayers also argued that disallowance of the deduction was an undue burden on the free exercise of their religion and an unwarranted interference with the church's doctrine. The Court rejected this argument because, as in *Jimmy Swaggart Ministries,* the taxpayers' argument that they would have less money to spend on auditing and training without the deduction was constitutionally insignificant.

In dissent, Justices O'Connor and Scalia strenuously argued that there was no discernible reason for imposing a more rigid connection between payment and services for Scientologists than with respect to the religious practices of other faiths, where an income tax deduction is allowed—such as deductions for pew rent, basket contributions, tithing, and tickets for special services. Justices O'Connor and Scalia argued that Scientologists received an "intangible benefit" of spiritual or religious worth similar to renting a pew. Additionally, even in the case of charitable contributions, the donor was permitted to receive an incidental benefit as long as the payment was not made for personal accommodation.

The Court has since adhered to its narrow interpretation of IRC §170 in *Hernandez* by rejecting a married couple's argument that they could deduct funds transferred to their sons while the sons served as full-time, unpaid missionaries for the Church of Jesus Christ of Latter-Day Saints as charitable contributions "to or for the use of the" church under IRC §170. In *Davis v. United States* (1990) the Court concluded that the meaning of the phrase "to or for the use of the" church refers to a trust or similar arrangement for the benefit of the church or a substantial portion of its members or those to whom it extended its services. No matter how worthy or noble the activity, the Court concluded, the phrase did not encompass the support of family members, even though the family members were fulfilling their duties as church missionaries. Nor was the transfer of funds to their sons a contribution "to" the church as contemplated by Treas. Reg. §1.170A-1(g), which clearly indicates that taxpayers may claim deductions only for "unreimbursed expenditures" incurred in connection with their own "rendering of services," not for those of third parties, such as their sons. Thus, a taxpayer who seeks to ensure final redemption and a tax deduction under IRC §170 by making "contributions" to religious organizations during his or her lifetime must ensure that the contribution is to the charity and not merely to particular individuals. No deduction will be allowed for payments in lieu of a support obligation or where the taxpayer receives a particular service in return.

New Religions

During the past several decades both federal and state courts have struggled with the question of whether new beliefs—sometimes shared perhaps by only a relative handful of citizens and not based on the traditional concept of a belief in a supreme deity—nonetheless have a sufficient "religious purpose" to qualify for tax-exempt status as a so-called 501(c)(3) organization. As discussed earlier, such status is critical; it not only shelters the entity's own income from taxation but also may afford generous income, estate, and gift tax deductions to donors for contributions to the entity.

With the advent of "new" religions, the courts have retrenched from an almost instinctive blanket acceptance of an organization's statement of doctrine or an individual's profession of faith and have sought to grapple with somewhat vaguely perceived notions of what a "religion" really is, since the Supreme Court has never promulgated a single, "bright-line" standard by which the religious standing of an entity, new or old, can be judged by the courts, the IRS, and taxpayers. A decision by a court or an administrative ruling by the IRS that a particular activity or group of adherents meets the requirements of "religious activity" within IRC §501(c)(3) or any other exemption for religious organizations is, in essence, a stamp of approval that the organization's primary focus is properly religious.

In making this determination, the individual or body charged with the task must have some preconceived criteria or standard of what a valid religion is, so that the particular entity under scrutiny may be judged. It must be acknowledged, however, that if the express language of the First Amendment is followed, the words "valid religion" will constitute an oxymoron.

In general, the various courts have attempted to measure the religious nature of a new entity by comparing its activities and professed objectives with those of established religions. However, the courts initially took a somewhat different view of the problem. This may be seen in *United States v. Kauten* (2nd Cir. 1943), which involved a conscientious objector who was convicted of violating the Selective Training and Service Act during World War II. In deciding the issue in favor of the government, the Second Circuit characterized a conscientious objection as a "religious impulse," thereby implying that an individual must have no choice in the matter—that a conscientious objection based on religious beliefs must, at least to some degree, be "thoughtless." Although such a view might be perceived as denigrating to religion, a perhaps not unreasonable extension of such an approach would appear to be that any such impulse must be accepted as constitutionally valid. The plaintiff's objection to serving in the military was the result of political and philosophical differences rather than a "religious impulse." Accordingly, the court affirmed his conviction under the Selective IRS and Training Act of 1940.

By the 1980s this deferential attitude toward proponents of religion and religious beliefs had been abandoned by the courts and the IRS. In 1981, for example, the Third Circuit developed a three-part test for evaluating fledgling religions. In *Africa v. Commonwealth of Pennsylvania* (3rd Cir. 1981) a prison inmate sought an injunction that would require prison officials to provide him with a special diet—consisting essentially of raw vegetables—so that he could comply with his religious principles. Although *Africa* did not involve an exemption issue, the test developed by the Third Circuit has subsequently been used to determine whether an organization is operated for a religious purpose as contemplated by IRC §501(c)(3).

According to the Third Circuit, to qualify for First Amendment protection an organization (1) must address "fundamental and ultimate" questions having to do with "deep and imponderable" matters; (2) must be comprehensive in nature, that is, must consist of a "belief system" rather than a mere isolated principle or tenet; and (3) must be recognizable by certain formal and external signs.

This test was applied by a Minnesota district court in *Church of the Chosen People v. United States* (D. Minn. 1982), where the proponent, the Church of the Chosen People, sought to recover federal income tax paid by it, claiming that the church qualified for tax-exempt status. The primary purpose and activity of this church was to preach a doctrine known as the "Gay Imperative"; that is, its fundamental goal was to convert "breeders" to a homosexual lifestyle in an effort to control population growth. After examining the church's tenets, the court concluded that the group was organized and operated for secular purposes. The church's doctrine focused on only one aspect of human existence and rested on but a single principle—sexual preference—rather than on a comprehensive belief system as required by *Africa*. Moreover, the organization lacked the external indicia, or manifestations of other, more established religions: It had no established history or literature, no regular rituals or ceremonies, and no readily identifiable members apart from its founders.

In *United States v. Jeffries* (7th Cir. 1988) the defendant, who claimed to be a "one-person church," was convicted of willfully attempting to evade income taxes and willful failure to file income tax returns. The Seventh Circuit observed that one person cannot free all his taxable income from tax liability by simply proclaiming himself a church. Significantly, the defendant did not have an established congregation served by an organized ministry, nor did he perform regular religious services or follow a doctrinal code. In *Jeffries* the appellate court, in reliance on *American Guidance Foundation, Inc. v. United States* (D.D.C. 1980), articulated factors which, if present, tend to support the conclusion that the entity is a valid religious organization. According to the Seventh Circuit, a religion ought to have:

(1) a distinct legal existence;
(2) a recognized creed and form of worship;
(3) a definite and distinct ecclesiastical government;
(4) a formal code of doctrine and discipline;
(5) a distinct religious history;
(6) a membership not associated with any other church or denomination;
(7) ordained ministers;
(8) selection of ministers after completion of prescribed studies;
(9) its own literature;
(10) established places of worship;
(11) regular congregations;
(12) regular religious services;
(13) Sunday schools for religious instruction for the young; and
(14) schools for the preparation of its ministers.

Although the very specificity of these criteria in *Jeffries* may be viewed as a reflection of the fundamental absurdity of this particular defendant's position, critics may argue that the appellate court came dangerously close to identifying these factors in such a narrow and restrictive way that they might be viewed as indispensable preconditions to a determination of what might constitute a religion. In and of themselves, then, these preconditions might be violative of the freedom guaranteed by the First Amendment to follow the principles of a "religion," no matter how obscure or bizarre its principles might be. An appropriate response to this line of argument might be that, although religious freedom is a matter of right, subsidies in the form of significant tax benefits are not. To obtain such subsidies, it appears that certain constitutional "minimums" are required.

Questions about such matters arose with increasing frequency from the late 1970s to the mid-1980s, as "tax protestor" and "Fifth Amendment" tax returns vied with those which claimed exempt status as a "private" church or other narrow form of religious entity. This latter status, it was claimed, qualified the taxpayer for the same range of tax benefits as were available to more broadly based religions and churches.

In the typical example, a "church" (frequently, though not invariably, a branch of the Universal Life Church—itself an established religious organization) was created, followed by an assignment of the taxpayer's assets to the newly created church, complete with a vow of poverty. All the taxpayer's income—including wages, dividends, and so forth—would be assigned to the church. A variation known as a "mail-order ministry" involved the taxpayer's ordination as a minister of an already-existing church and the subsequent creation of a "private" branch of the church. The taxpayer in these cases usually attempted to take a charitable deduction for the value of the assets contributed to the church and neglected to report any income earned, contending that it belonged to the church, which was tax exempt.

The IRS invariably disallowed the deductions and was regularly sustained by the courts, although the specific grounds for disallowance might vary. The taxpayer, for example, might be considered not really to have contributed anything to the church inasmuch as dominion and control of the allegedly contributed property remained in his or her hands. In other cases, the deduction was disallowed by disqualifying the recipient church, because charitable deductions are allowable only if the contributions are made to qualified recipients. The grounds for disqualification ranged from failure to meet the statutory requirement of exempt purposes to commingling of church assets and private assets. Because the burden was (and is) always on the taxpayer to show that a contribution was really made and that the recipient was qualified, failure to carry this burden would inevitably result in the court's sustaining the disallowance (see, for example, *Ruberto v. Commissioner* [2nd Cir. 1985]).

As noted, many of the reported cases involved charters, chapters, and chambers of the Universal Life Church, which is itself a tax-exempt organization. Nonetheless, the courts consistently ruled that the parent entity's exemption is insufficient to cover the activities of its various private chapters. To be entitled to exempt status, a taxpayer must establish that the specific chapter to which he or she contributed—as distinguished from its parent organization—is also tax exempt. At least in the cases decided thus far, taxpayers have usually failed abjectly to meet this requirement (see *Stephenson v. Commissioner* [6th Cir. 1984]). Substantially similar results have been obtained with respect to branches of another organization, the Basic Bible Church of America. See *McElhannon v. Commissioner* (TC, 1987) and *Jenny v. Commissioner* (TC, 1990).

Although the pace of litigation on these particular issues has fallen dramatically since the mid-1980s, the IRS continues to contest—vigorously and successfully—assignments of wages and other contributions to churches created or controlled by the taxpayer. A typical ground for sustaining the IRS position has been the taxpayer's failure to establish that his or her wages, dividends, and the like were actually turned over to the parent church, usually the Universal Life Church in Modesto, California (see, for example, *Harrison v. Commissioner* [11th Cir. 1986]), aff'g an unreported tax court decision; *Davis v. Commissioner* [1983]), aff'd by the Ninth Circuit in an unpublished opinion [June 24, 1985]; *Miedaner v. Commissioner* [1983]; and *Kiddie v. Commissioner* [1983]).

Analytically and politically, it is easier for the courts and the IRS to deny tax-exempt status to one- or two-person fledgling "religions." In recent years, however, the IRS has had to contend with two large, well-financed organizations whose memberships run into the millions. In at least one instance, the IRS eventually settled ongoing litigation rather than continuing the struggle.

In *United States v. Sun Myung Moon* (2nd Cir. 1983), for example, the Reverend Moon was convicted of a conspiracy to evade income taxes and for filing a false individual tax return. The charges resulted from a commingling of Moon's personal funds with those of the church. On appeal to the Second Circuit, the defendant argued that the trial court should have charged the jury that it had to accept the Unification Church's definition of its religious purpose without question. The court's actual instructions were that the Reverend Moon would be personally liable if the jury found that he had used church funds for his own business, investment, or personal ends rather than for religious purposes. The Second Circuit concluded that the defendant's request for jury instructions overstated the scope of First Amendment protections. The First Amendment, observed the court, does not insulate a church or its members when there is an alleged violation of a penal statute. Thus, the jury was not bound by the Unification Church's definition of "religious purpose." The court commented, "however free the exercise of religion may be, it must be subordinate to the criminal laws of the country." Under the Reverend Moon's proposed definition, any use of church funds by him would have to have been for a religious purpose.

The Unification Church's definition of religious purpose also incorporated the so-called "Messiah" defense—that Reverend Moon personifies and is indistinguishable from his church. Under this defense he argued that, inasmuch as the Unification Church could not owe any taxes on income derived from church-related activities, neither could he personally. The court, however, distinguished between Moon's identity as the spiritual leader of the church and his identity as an individual taxpayer. In rejecting this defense, the court reasoned that simply because the Reverend Moon was the head of the Unification church did not mean that he and the church did not have separate and distinct identities.

Another entity that has received close attention is the Church of Scientology. In 1987 the Supreme Court came close to ruling on its status but ultimately declined to do so, in *Church of Scientology of California v. Commissioner of the Internal Revenue* (9th Cir. 1987). Numerous other cases regarding the tax-exempt status of the "mother" church in California and its affiliate churches throughout the states have traversed both the various state and federal court systems. In *Church of Scientology of California* the IRS revoked the mother church's tax-exempt status on the ground that it failed to comply with IRC §501(c)(3)'s requirement that "no part of the net earnings [of the entity may] . . . inure[s] to the benefit of any private shareholder or individual" and that it be operated exclusively for religious or charitable purposes. The Ninth Circuit ultimately concluded that the church was operated to the personal benefit of its founder, L. Ron Hubbard, and his wife, Mary Sue Hubbard, in violation of IRC §501(c)(3). The sole beneficiary of the church's activities was not the public at large but rather its founders—in the form of excessive salaries, living expenses, and royalties. Additionally, the IRS presented evidence demonstrating alleged debt repayments to L. Ron Hubbard as well as the founder's unfettered retention of control over church assets. When discussing the self-dealing, excessive salaries and living expenses of the Hubbards, the court inevitably made a value judgment concerning how church leaders conducted its business. The Second Circuit made a similar type of judgment with respect to the Reverend Moon. The use of church funds by high-ranking Catholic, Protestant, or Jewish leaders, however, seems to go unquestioned.

In October 1993 the IRS and the church of Scientology reached a settlement that recognized the church as a valid religion. Thus ended one of the longest-running tax disputes in history, at least in this country. Details of the settlement were not made public, but the IRS finally conceded and granted tax-exempt status to the church and more than one hundred and fifty of its related corporations. Although the IRS contends that the settlement will not affect its application of the standards of IRC §501(c)(3), it seems inevitable that its compromise with the Church of Scientology will make it easier for organizations to obtain and retain tax-exempt status.

Brian E. Comerford

Bibliography

Antieau, Chester James, *Freedom from Federal Establishment: Formation and Early History of the First Amendment Religion Clauses* (Milwaukee: Bruce, 1964).

Colliton, James W., *Charitable Gifts,* 2nd ed. (Colorado Springs: Shepard's/McGraw Hill, 1993).

Cornelison, Issac Amada, *The Relation of Religion to Civil Government in the United States of America* (New York: Da Capo, 1970).

Friedland, Jerold A., "Constitutional Issues in Revoking Religious Tax Exemptions: *Church of Scientology of California v. Commissioner,*" 37 *University of Florida Law Review* 565 (1985).

Goodwin, Glenn, Note, "Would Caesar Tax God? The Constitutionality of Governmental Taxation of Churches," 35 *Drake Law Review* 383 (1986).

Hoff, Reka Potgieter, "The Financial Accountability of Churches for Federal Income Tax Purposes: Establishment or Free Exercise?" 11 *Virginia Tax Review* 71 (1991).

Levy, Leonard W., *The Establishment Clause and the First Amendment* (New York: Macmillan, 1989).

Miller, Robert T., and Ronald B. Flowers, *Toward Benevolent Neutrality: Church, State and the Supreme Court,* 4th ed. (Waco, Tex.: Markham Press Fund of Baylor University Press, 1992).

The Role of Government in Monitoring and Regulating Religion in Public Life, ed. James E. Woods and Derk Davis (Waco, Tex.: J.M. Dawson Institute of Church-State Studies, Baylor University, 1993).

The Role of Religion in the Making of Public Policy, ed. James E. Woods and Derk Davis (Waco, Tex.: J.M. Dawson Institute of Church-State Studies, Baylor University, 1991).

Thomas, Oliver S., Church and State Symposium, "The Power to Destroy: The Eroding Constitutional Arguments for Church Tax Exemptions and the Practical Effect on Churches," 22 *Cumberland Law Review* 605 (1992).

Whitehead, John W., Church and State Symposium, "Tax Exemption and Churches: A Historical and Constitutional Analysis," 22 *Cumberland Law Review* 521 (1992).

Witte, John, Jr., "Tax Exemption of Church Property: Historical Anomaly or Valid Constitutional Practice?" 64 *Southern California Law Review* 363 (1991).

Cases Cited

Africa v. Commonwealth of Pennsylvania, 662 F. 2d 1025 (3rd. Cir. 1981).

Alexander v. "Americans United," Inc., 416 U.S. 752 (1974).

American Guidance Foundation, Inc. v. United States, 490 F. Supp. 304 (D. D. C. 1980).

Board of Education of Kiryas Joel Village School District v. Grumet, 512 U.S. 687, (1994).

Bob Jones University v. United States, 461 U.S. 574 (1983).

California v. Grace Brethren Church, 457 U.S. 393 (1982).

Church of Scientology of California v. Commissioner of the Internal Revenue, 823 F. 2d 1310 (9th Cir. 1987).

Church of the Chosen People v. United States, 548 F. Supp. 1247 (D. Minn. 1982).

Commissioner v. Estate of Bosch, 387 U.S. 456 (1967).

Commissioner v. Pemsel, 1891 App. Cas. 531.

Davis v. Commissioner, 81 T.C. 806 (1983), aff'd by the 9th Cir. in an unpub'd opinion (June 24, 1985).

Davis v. United States, 495 U.S. 472 (1990).

Harrison v. Commissioner, 86-2 U.S.T.C. ¶9836 (11th Cir. 1986), aff'g an unreported tax court decision.

Hernandez v. Commissioner of Internal Revenue, 490 U.S. 680, reh'g denied, 492 U.S. 933 (1989).

In re United States Catholic Conferences, 885 F. 2d 1020 (2nd Cir. 1989), aff'd, 495 U.S. 918 (1990).

Jenny v. Commissioner, T.C. Memo. 1983-1 (1990).

Jimmy Swaggart Ministries v. Board of Equalization, 493 U.S. 378 (1990).

Kiddie v. Commissioner, T.C. Memo. 1983-582 (1983).

Lemon v. Kurtzman, 403 U.S. 602, reh'g denied, 404 U.S. 876 (1971).

McElhannon v. Commissioner, T.C. Memo. 1982-599 (1982).

Miedaner v. Commissioner, 81 T.C. 272 (1983).

Montana Catholic Mission v. Missoula County, 200 U.S. 118 (1986).

Murdock v. Pennsylvania, 319 U.S. 105 (1943).

Ruberto v. Commissioner, 774 F. 2d 61 (2nd Cir. 1985), rev'g and remanding T.C. Memo. 1984-557 (1985).

St. Martin Evangelical Lutheran Church v. South Dakota, 451 U.S. 772 (1981).

Stephenson v. Commissioner, 79 T.C. 995 (1982), aff'd per curiam, 748 F. 2d 331 (6th Cir. 1984).

Texas Monthly, Inc. v. Bullock, 489 U.S. 1 (1989).

United States v. Jeffries, 854 F. 2d 254 (7th Cir. 1988).

United States v. Kauten, 133 F. 2d 703 (2nd Cir. 1943).

United States v. Sun Myung Moon, 718 F. 2d 1210 (2nd Cir. 1983).

Walz v. Tax Commission of the City of New York, 397 U.S. 664 (1970).

Texas Monthly, Inc. v. Bullock 489 U.S. (1989)

In *Texas Monthly, Inc. v. Bullock* (1989) the U.S. Supreme Court considered whether the First Amendment requires the government to be neutral between publications that express the affirmation of religious faith and publications that express the rejection of religious faith. In their decision 5 justices said yes, 3 said no, and 1 said that the government must be neutral between discussions of religious issues and discussions of other topics (like business or sports). It was clearly a fractured Court, with a plurality opinion by Justice William Brennan, joined by Justices Thurgood Marshall and John Paul Stevens; a separate opinion concurring in the judgment by Justice Byron White; another separate opinion concerning in the judgment by Justice Harry Blackmun, joined by Justice Sandra Day O'Connor; and a dissenting opinion by Justice Antonin Scalia, joined by Chief Justice William Rehnquist and Justice Anthony Kennedy.

The case involved a Texas law that exempted from its sales tax periodicals that express the doctrines of a religious faith and books that are sacred to a faith. Because *Texas Monthly* (a general-interest magazine) was ineligible for an exemption, its publisher sued the state comptroller in state court on the ground that the discriminatory exemption violated the First Amendment. The trial court agreed, but the state appellate court did not. The U.S. Supreme Court reversed the appellate court's decision but did not produce a majority opinion.

The discord among the justices is somewhat surprising because—as the Court articulated in *Everson v. Board of Education* (1947) and has repeatedly said since—the Establishment Clause "requires the state to be neutral in its relations with groups of religious believers and non-believers." When in *Torcaso v. Watkins* (1961) the Court invalidated a Maryland law limiting eligibility for public office to citizens who would declare a belief in the existence of God, it "reaffirm[ed]" that the government has no power to "aid all religions against non-believers." And in *Wallace v. Jaffree* (1985) the Court again reiterated that the government must remain scrupulously impartial between believers and disbelievers. Given these (and similar) precedents, one might have thought that the unconstitutionality of the Texas law was obvious.

The case was complicated, however, by two pre-*Everson* decisions, *Murdock v. Pennsylvania* (1943) and *Fowlett v. McCormick* (1944), holding that taxes on the sale of religious texts by religious organizations violate the Free Exercise Clause—even though the taxes were imposed on "merchandise of any kind." In *Texas Monthly* the state relied on these decisions to argue that its tax exemption was simply an effort to comply with the Free Exercise Clause. How, asked Texas, could a tax exemption that was compelled by the Free Exercise Clause contravene the Establishment Clause?

Justice William Brennan's plurality opinion omitted this question by curtailing the scope of the free exercise precedents. As the plurality explained, *Murdock* and *Fowlett* both involved "flat" taxes (pursuant to which a fixed sum must be paid regardless of the value of the merchandise sold), whereas the Texas sales tax collected only a "small" percentage of each item's purchase price. The plurality acknowledged that the Court's reasoning in *Murdock* and *Fowlett* was broad enough to cover percentage as well as flat taxes, but the plurality "disavow[ed]" that reasoning, determining instead that percentage sales taxes (when applicable to a variety of merchandise besides religious publications) do not present any free exercise problems. And because the Free Exercise Clause does not require that religious publications receive an exemption from the Texas sales tax, the plurality found no obstacle to holding that the tax exemption violated the Establishment Clause.

The dissent disputed the plurality's contention that *Murdock* and *Fowlett,* once distinguished, were irrelevant to the Establishment Clause issue. Invoking the argument that government should be permitted to "accommodate" religious belief even if the Free Exercise Clause does not require such accommodation, the dissent asserted: "The proper lesson to be drawn from the narrow distinguishing of *Murdock* and *Fowlett* is quite different: If the exemption comes so close to being a constitutionally required accommodation, there is no doubt that it is at least a permissible one." The dissent, however, made no effort to reconcile this conclusion with such Establishment Clause precedents as *Everson, Torcaso,* and *Jaffree.*

Justice Harry Blackmun's concurrence agreed with the plurality that these Establishment Clause precedents rendered the Texas law unconstitutional. But, unlike the plurality, Justice Blackmun attempted to reach this result without restricting *Murdock* and *Fowlett.* Justice Blackmun reasoned that, because it would be possible for Texas to exempt from its sales tax publications that expressed either an affirmation or a rejection of religious faith, Texas was able to maintain the required neutrality between religious belief and disbelief even if the Free Exercise Clause required a tax exemption for religious publications. Without addressing *Fowlett* and *Murdock,* Justice Byron White's concurrence stated briefly that the Texas tax exemption violated the Press Clause of the First Amendment because it favored religion over all other topics.

In the following term, in *Jimmy Swaggart Ministries v. Board of Equalization* (1990), the Court unanimously adopted the plurality's view of *Murdock* and *Fowlett* in rejecting a Free Exercise Clause challenge to a California percentage sales tax that did not exempt religious publications. One wonders how different the opinions in *Texas Monthly* might have been had *Jimmy Swaggart Ministries* been decided first, thereby eliminating the Free Exercise Clause issue from *Texas Monthly.* Most likely, the five Justices who agreed on the Establishment Clause issue could have settled on a majority opinion, inasmuch as at the time they differed solely on the free exercise issue. Most likely, too, the dissent still would have rejected the majority's interpretation of the Establishment Clause, but in an opinion that relied less on the accommodation argument and more on the argument that the original intent of the Establishment Clause does not require government neutrality between belief and disbelief. If so, *Texas Monthly* might have been a significant precursor to the debate over first principles in *Lee v. Weisman* (1992).

But because *Texas Monthly* became mired in a free exercise dispute that was mooted the following term, the decision will never be as significant as one might have expected, given the importance of the Establishment Clause issue that the Court confronted in the case. And although the question of whether government must be neutral between religion and disbelief is central to the contemporary debate concerning the ultimate source of the government's moral legitimacy, one would hardly know this from the opinions in *Texas Monthly.*

Edward B. Foley

Bibliography

Laycock, Douglas, "Formal, Substantive, and Disaggregated Neutrality toward Religion," 39 *DePaul Law Review* 993–1018 (1990).

———, "'Nonpreferential' Aid to Religion: A False Claim about Original Intent," 27 *William and Mary Law Review* 875–892 (1986).

McConnell, Michael, "Accommodation of Religion," 1985 *Supreme Court Review* 1–59 (1985).

Cases Cited

Everson v. Board of Education, 330 U.S. 1 (1947).

Fowlett v. McCormick, 321 U.S. 573 (1944).

Jimmy Swaggart Ministries v. Board of Equalization, 493 U.S. 378 (1990).

Lee v. Weisman, 505 U.S. 577 (1992).

Murdock v. Pennsylvania, 319 U.S. 105 (1943).

Texas Monthly, Inc. v. Bullock, 489 U.S. 1 (1989).

Torcaso v. Watkins, 367 U.S. 488 (1961).

Wallace v. Jaffree, 472 U.S. 38 (1985).

Theories of Interpretation: Free Exercise Clause and Establishment Clause

Judges, scholars, and religious and political movements have offered many competing interpretations of the religion clauses of the First Amendment. These interpretations cannot be neatly distinguished and categorized. Different theories overlap or combine similar elements in different combinations; some people would apply different theories in different contexts. Some theories stated in general terms actually grow out of particular controversies and could not plausibly be applied generally. Still, it is possible to identify several principal approaches, each with quite different implications.

Free Exercise of Religion

Absolute Protection of Religious Belief

Almost everyone agrees that the Free Exercise Clause guarantees the right to believe any religion whatever. But even this bedrock principle has been violated on occasion. In *Davis v. Beason* (1890) the U.S. Supreme Court upheld a test oath that excluded Mormons from voting in federal territories. The decision has never been formally repudiated, but it was implicitly overruled in *Torcaso v. Watkins* (1961), which struck down a Maryland requirement that holders of public office declare their belief in God.

Protection of Religious Speech

There is similar consensus about the right to teach almost any religion one chooses, although some scholars would insist that this right is guaranteed only by the Free Speech Clause. The better view would seem to be that it is guaranteed by both the Free Speech and Free Exercise Clauses and that it is the Free Exercise Clause which tells us that religious speech is of special constitutional value and is entitled to the highest level of constitutional protection, generally analogous to the protection for political speech. Important affirmations of the sweeping scope of freedom of speech in religious contexts include *United States v. Ballard* (1944) and *West Virginia State Board of Education v. Barnette* (1943).

Religious speech is not absolutely protected. It is subject to content-neutral time, place, and manner regulations; and government presumably may punish deliberate incitement to inflict immediate and serious harm, although the Supreme Court has never had occasion to say so in the context of religious speech. Some contend that the Establishment Clause requires that religious speech be excluded from some public properties or from the political process. This view, which has no support in the Supreme Court's cases, is considered below.

Protection of Religiously Motivated Conduct
The principal controversy over free exercise relates to religious conduct, including worship services and ritual acts, refusal to comply with law because of religious objections, and the operation and management of religious institutions. The central question is whether religious institutions or believers should ever be exempted from generally applicable laws that interfere with the exercise of their religion.

Four major solutions to these issues have been proposed: (1) exemptions are forbidden, (2) exemptions are permitted but not required, (3) exemptions are required for matters of conscience, and (4) exemptions are required for matters of conscience and also for matters of religious autonomy.

Exemptions Are Forbidden (Mandatory Formal Neutrality)
The view that exemptions are forbidden is associated with formal neutrality interpretations of the religion clauses. It is helpful to call this theory "mandatory formal neutrality" (although that term is not in common use), to distinguish it from the variation to be discussed next. Mandatory formal neutrality theorists read the two religion clauses together to mean that religion should not be singled out for discriminatory benefits or burdens. It follows that religious conduct is fully subject to all generally applicable regulatory laws and criminal prohibitions and that religious conduct must be treated the same as analogous secular conduct.

Thus, a law forbidding the Catholic Mass or Jewish Seder would violate the Free Exercise Clause, and a law forbidding the use of wine at the Mass or Seder would violate the Free Exercise Clause. But a law forbidding the consumption of wine anywhere within a jurisdiction may and must be applied to wine at the Mass or Seder, and a law against serving wine to minors may and must be applied to First Communion or to children attending the Mass or Seder. A law permitting children to consume wine at the Mass or Seder would violate the Establishment Clause unless the state permitted children to consume equivalent amounts of wine in secular contexts. Exemptions for religiously motivated conduct are said to be a preference for religion over nonreligion.

The principal academic defender of mandatory formal neutrality was the late Philip Kurland. In *Corporation of the Presiding Bishop of the Church of Latter-Day Saints v. Amos* (1987) the Court unanimously rejected Kurland's claim that *regulatory* exemptions establish religion. But the Court appeared to adopt Kurland's claim with respect to *tax* exemptions in *Texas Monthly, Inc. v. Bullock* (1989). A divided set of opinions with no majority may be read to hold that religious institutions and activities may not be singled out for tax exemption, although they may be included in broader tax-exempt categories, such as not-for-profit organizations or religious, charitable, and educational organizations.

Exemptions Are Permitted but Not Required (Permissive Formal Neutrality)
Others argue that formal neutrality satisfies the Constitution but is not required by the Constitution. That is, generally applicable laws may be applied to religious practices, and the Free Exercise Clause does not require exemptions, but legislatures may exempt religious practices if they choose. On this view, the Constitution does not protect wine at the Mass, Seder, or First Communion, but legislatures may exempt sacramental wine from liquor laws, or prosecutors may simply look the other way and allow a de facto exemption. This view may be labeled "permissive formal neutrality" (although, again, that phrase is not in common use).

This understanding of religious liberty predates the Constitution; it appears prominently in John Locke's Letter Concerning Toleration (1689). Important academic defenders today include Mark Tushnet and William Marshall. The Supreme Court adopted permissive formal neutrality as its interpretation of the Free Exercise Clause in *Employment Division, Department of Human Resources of Oregon v. Smith* (1990). Permissive formal neutrality arguably explains many of the Court's decisions before 1963; it plainly was not the Court's interpretation from 1963 to 1990.

Important corollaries of formal neutrality are that religious conduct cannot be regulated when similar secular conduct is not and that religious conduct of one faith cannot be regulated when the similar conduct of another faith is not. The leading application of this principle in the Supreme Court is *Church of the Lukumi Babalu Aye, Inc. and Ernesto Pichardo v. City of Hialeah* (1993), holding that a city could not ban religious sacrifice of animals while permitting secular killings of animals for food, sport, and human convenience. The value of this protection for religious minorities depends on the willingness of courts to investigate government's claims that the regulated and unregulated conduct differ in some way other than religion.

Exemptions Are Required for Matters of Conscience.

A third view is that religious institutions and believers are presumptively exempt from laws that burden or prohibit compliance with conscientiously held tenets of their faith. Almost no one claims that this right to exemptions is absolute; nearly everyone concedes that government may burden or prohibit religious observances for sufficiently important reasons, examined next.

Positivist Arguments

The positivist argument for exemptions proceeds straightforwardly from the Free Exercise Clause. The Constitution says that there shall be no law "prohibiting the free exercise" of religion. If consumption of wine at the Mass or Seder or First Communion is the exercise of religion, the state cannot prohibit it, even if the state has prohibited consumption of wine in other contexts. Supporters of exemptions argue that the Free Exercise Clause on its face creates a substantive right to practice one's religion, and not merely to believe in it or be protected from discrimination because of it. From this perspective, the defect of the formal neutrality interpretation of free exercise is that it eliminates this substantive right to exercise religion, leaving a mere equality right not to be discriminated against. In a pervasively regulated society, formal equality means that religion too can be pervasively regulated, and pervasively regulated religion is not the free exercise of religion.

Supporters of formal neutrality respond that a law is not a law prohibiting the free exercise of religion unless it prohibits religious exercise deliberately, or perhaps principally, or perhaps discriminatorily. A law that also does other things and that incidentally prohibits the exercise of religion in some of its applications is not, in their view, a law prohibiting the free exercise of religion.

Religious Arguments

The theoretical arguments for the right to exemptions are varied. The principal religious argument, most prominently attributable to James Madison, is that one's duties to God are superior to one's duties to the civil society. It follows, under American theories of government, that when the people form a government and consent to be governed, they cannot delegate to government any power to regulate their duties to God.

Secular Variations

A secular version of this argument holds that the Constitution takes no view on whether humans owe duties to God or even on whether God exists. But many Americans believe they owe prior duties to God, and so in the Free Exercise Clause they reserved the right to perform those perceived duties. More generally, the secular argument for exemptions holds that exemptions are inherent in the concept of religious liberty. Religion includes religious conduct, and so religious liberty includes liberty for religious conduct. Any attempt to punish religious conduct will lead to religious conflict and persecution as surely as will attempts to punish religious belief or teaching.

Substantive Neutrality

Some supporters of exemptions agree with their opponents that the two religion clauses together require government to be neutral toward religion. But supporters of exemptions understand neutrality very differently; they say the Constitution requires substantive neutrality rather than formal neutrality.

Substantive neutrality consists of neither encouraging nor discouraging religious belief or practice. If government minimizes the extent to which it either encourages or discourages religion, government neutrality will be maximized, government influence on religion will be minimized, and religious liberty will be maximized for both believers and nonbelievers. The goal of minimizing both encouragement and discouragement requires that any challenged government policy be compared with the available alternatives. A policy may seem to benefit or encourage religion when considered in isolation, but the alternative policy may burden or discourage religion. The Constitution requires the alternative that departs least from the hypothetical baseline of neither encouraging nor discouraging religion.

Because government encourages and discourages many types of secular activity, treating religion like analogous secular activity will rarely be substantively neutral. Thus, formal neutrality and substantive neutrality have very different implications.

Substantive neutrality generally requires exemptions for religiously motivated conduct. If the state threatens to send people to jail for consuming wine at a Mass or Seder, that threat of punishment severely discourages the exercise of religion. But permitting religious use of wine in a dry district would rarely encourage anyone to become Catholic or Jewish, or even to practice their Catholic or Jewish rituals more faithfully. The small quantities of wine consumed in religious services—set in the lengthy ritual surrounding their consumption—would be little inducement to anyone attracted by the wine but not by religion.

When religious obligation aligns with secular self-interest, as in religious objections to military service or to taxation for military spending, the substantive neutrality rationale for exemptions fails. Requiring conscientious objectors to serve in the military or pay military taxes, on pain of punishment if they refuse, severely discourages their religious exercise. But exempting religious objectors from such burdens encourages people to accept the religious beliefs that would make them eligible for the exemption. It remains the case that a law requiring religious objectors to violate their conscience with respect to military service or taxes prohibits them from freely exercising their religion, but government may have compelling reasons not to exempt such self-interested behavior. Congress has sometimes dealt with dilemmas of this sort by enacting alternative service requirements that attempt to impose some equivalent burden on conscientious objectors.

Opponents of substantive neutrality deny that it is neutral even in the routine cases where religious observance does not align with self-interest. Opponents do not claim that exemptions for religious behavior often encourage religious behavior; instead, they usually deny the relevance of that standard. They view exemptions from generally applicable laws as special treatment that the Constitution does not require. Some of them view exemptions as a symbolic endorsement of religious believers and a denigration of the motives of those who would engage in analogous conduct for secular reasons.

Accommodation

Many supporters of a right to exemptions do not subscribe to substantive neutrality, principally because of its implications for the Establishment Clause, described below. These supporters of exemptions make one or more of the other arguments described above—that duties to God are superior to duties to the state or that religious liberty requires exemptions because the exercise of religion includes conduct. Exemptions from regulation are sometimes described as "accommodations of religion," a vague phrase that has been used to describe everything from regulatory exemptions to school prayer. Michael McConnell has written the principal scholarly attempt to give content to the concept of accommodation.

Compelling Government Interests

Supporters of exemptions concede that the right to exemptions can be overridden where the need is great enough. The usual formulation is that government may limit or burden the exercise of religion if the limit or burden serves a compelling interest by the least-restrictive means. But there is little consensus on what constitutes a compelling interest. Civil libertarians tend to argue that a compelling interest must be an interest of extraordinary importance, such as protecting identifiable individuals from tangible and significant harm or preventing the wholesale evasion of an important government program. They note that the constitutional text states an absolute right and that the compelling interest exception is indeed an exception, implied by necessity. Lawyers for government agencies tend to argue that most laws serve compelling interests and that every incremental violation defeats that interest. The government lawyer's understanding of compelling interest tends to eliminate the right to exemptions. That is, deference to government agencies on the issue of compelling interest tends to erode substantive neutrality back to the level of formal neutrality. The Supreme Court cases are mixed; neither courts nor scholars have developed any consistent and widely accepted understanding of compelling government interest.

Supporters of Exemptions
Supporters of a right to exemptions for matters of conscience include virtually the entire religious leadership in the United States, the major civil liberties organizations, an apparent majority of constitutional law scholars, and the Congress of the United States. In 1993 Congress enacted a statutory right to religious exemptions from all state and federal law, subject to the compelling interest test, in the Religious Freedom Restoration Act (RFRA). Douglas Laycock and Michael McConnell have written the most extensive defenses of a right to exemptions. However, the Supreme Court invalidated the RFRA in *City of Boerne v. Flores (1997),* holding that it was outside the scope of Congress' enumerated powers. Congressional leaders have indicated their desire to pass more limited legislation in response.

Exemptions Are Required for Matters of Conscience and Also for Matters of Religious Autonomy.
Those who support a right to exemptions are divided over the scope of the right. A few would confine exemptions to conduct that is religiously mandated. This approach has led at least one federal court, in *Brandon v. Board of Education* (2nd Cir. 1980), to distinguish between mandatory prayers and voluntary prayers. A more common approach is to protect conduct that is motivated by a doctrinal tenet of the claimant's religion, without inquiring whether the conduct is mandated or merely encouraged.

Some supporters of exemptions believe that religious institutions should be exempt from regulation, subject to the compelling interest test, without regard to whether the conduct at issue flows from a specific doctrinal tenet. The claim is that religious liberty protects the autonomy of religious institutions. To protect only conformity to specific doctrinal tenets is to reduce religion to a set of rules that must be obeyed—and to deny protection to all other varieties of religious experience.

Supporters of religious autonomy would presumptively exempt religious organizations from regulation of their internal affairs, such as regulation of church labor relations. Regulation of internal affairs can insert the state into the development of religious ideas and the resolution of religious disputes. Most supporters of church autonomy would also presumptively exempt religious organizations from regulation that imposes physical limits or economic burdens, such as zoning or taxation. Such regulation may limit the level of religious activity, may divert resources from missions chosen by the church to missions chosen by the state, and occasionally may drive religious organizations out of existence. Claims to religious autonomy follow from substantive neutrality; regulation that burdens or interferes with religion is a way of discouraging religion. Scholars who have argued extensively for religious autonomy include Carl Esbeck (1984) and Douglas Laycock (1981).

Scholars who have argued against exemptions for religious autonomy are generally those who have argued against exemptions for conscience as well; Mark Tushnet, and William Marshall, and Douglas C. Blomgren are principal examples. Ira Lupu supports exemptions for individual claims of conscience but opposes any exemption for religious institutions, whether for conscience or autonomy.

The Supreme Court has protected religious autonomy in certain contexts where the religious significance is especially apparent, such as in employing ministers and parochial schoolteachers and in resolving disputes over religious doctrine. In other contexts the Court has generally failed to protect religious autonomy, even during the period when it was requiring exemptions for matters of conscience. The leading case is *Jimmy Swaggart Ministries v. Board of Equalization* (1990), upholding the application of a sales tax to the dissemination of religious messages and commenting that economic burdens on churches have no constitutional significance. The comment seems to have been based on an intuitive and largely unexamined understanding of religion.

The Religious Freedom Restoration Act did not specify whether it reached religious autonomy claims. But senators and representatives repeatedly used zoning cases as one example of the problems that made the act necessary, and the act could have affected those cases only if it had protected against economic and regulatory burdens unrelated to religious doctrine. In *Amos* the Supreme Court upheld statutory exemptions that extended to matters of religious autonomy.

Establishment of Religion

It is more difficult to distinguish competing theories of the Establishment Clause and to array them on a single continuum. There are more controversial issues, more axes of disagreement, and fewer sharp divisions. Some of the theories summarized below overlap or differ in degree rather than in kind; some commentators subscribe to more than one of them.

Institutional Separation

Almost everyone agrees that the Establishment Clause requires at least institutional separation. That is, the institutions of the state should be separate from the institutions of the various religions, and neither set of institutions should control the other nor exercise the authority of the other. Religious organizations as such should have no formal role in the selection of political leaders, although they may—like any other association of citizens—attempt to persuade voters and policymakers. Similarly, government should have no role in the selection of religious leaders. No church can invoke the coercive power of the state to enforce compliance with religious norms, and the state cannot invoke the moral or theological authority of a church to demand compliance with government policy.

But institutional separation would not necessarily preclude voluntary cooperation between church and state. It would not preclude government from encouraging religious belief or providing financial support to projects with religious sponsorship or management, and it would not preclude religious organizations from voluntarily supporting or endorsing government policies. Steven Smith has published the leading academic statement of the view that the Establishment Clause requires merely institutional separation; this is also the position of some conservative Christian denominations.

Voluntarism

A widely accepted corollary of the religion clauses is that religious activity should be voluntary. Few offer voluntarism as a general theory of the religion clauses, but nearly all accept voluntarism as consistent with their preferred theory or occasionally as limiting their preferred theory. Voluntarism is principally a function of the right to freely exercise any religion one chooses. But voluntarism is also a policy of the Establishment Clause; religious institutions are to be supported voluntarily, and not through government taxation, coerced contributions, or coerced participation. There is consensus that purely religious institutions—the church itself—should be supported voluntarily. There is sharp disagreement about financial support of religious institutions that also serve secular functions, and most especially about church-affiliated elementary and secondary schools.

Noncoercion

"Noncoercion" is almost a synonym for "voluntarism," but in practice the two terms have been used in different ways. Many agree that "voluntarism" is one policy of the religion clauses but insist that it is not the only policy. "Noncoercion theory" might be understood as arguing that voluntarism is the only policy; the phrase has been associated with the claim that there can be no violation of the religion clauses without coercion. Noncoercionists believe that government may give symbolic, rhetorical, or political support to religion in general, or to preferred religions in particular, so long as it does not coerce anyone. Noncoercion theory emerged to political prominence in response to *Lynch v. Donnelly* (1984), in which the Court narrowly upheld a municipally sponsored nativity scene, and it has been focused on the narrow set of issues arising out of government-sponsored prayer and religious displays.

Noncoercion has sometimes been offered as though it were a complete theory of the Establishment Clause, but it is doubtful that its proponents so intend it. Collection of taxes is coercive, and so a rule of no coercion would seem to preclude all forms of government expenditures that benefit religious institutions. It seems likely that most noncoercion theorists subscribe to some other theory to justify some of these expenditures.

The principal academic statement of noncoercion theory is by Michael Paulsen. The Bush administration unsuccessfully urged the Supreme Court to adopt noncoercion theory in *Lee v. Weisman* (1992). The principal judicial statement is Justice Kennedy's dissent in *County of Allegheny v. American Civil Liberties Union* (1989). Justice Kennedy would add a requirement that government not proselytize, and he apparently assumes a background requirement of institutional separation.

The Endorsement Test

Justice O'Connor has repeatedly offered the endorsement test as a general theory for all Establishment Clause cases; the Supreme Court has applied it principally in cases of government prayer or government religious displays. Taken literally, the endorsement test would seem to state a clear principle that is the direct opposite of the noncoercion theory. The endorsement test holds that government should be neutral, taking no position for or against religion; the noncoercion theory responds that government may endorse religion so long as it does not coerce anyone to believe or participate.

But the endorsement test lacks this clarity in practice. Justice O'Connor proposed the test in her concurring opinion in *Lynch,* arguing that a municipal nativity scene does not endorse Christianity. This made it impossible from the beginning to predict when she would find an endorsement, even in a case where the government was deliberately communicating.

The endorsement test is not even potentially clear in other contexts. In considering an exemption for religiously motivated conduct, or government-funded math books for a religious school, or any other law or program challenged as an establishment of religion, Justice O'Connor has asked whether the program implicitly endorses religion. Endorsement has been inferred or not inferred from functional characteristics of the challenged law, from legislative history, or from both. Except in the rare case where the legislature has said it is enacting the bill because it will help a "good" religion, results have turned on specification of the functional characteristics from which Justice O'Connor would infer endorsement. In practice, lawyers and commentators from many schools of thought tend to find implied endorsements whenever they object to a government program on the basis of their own preferred theory of the Establishment Clause. Justice O'Connor and the Court would surely do better to drop talk of endorsement outside the context of religious displays and observances, and state a test directly in terms of the underlying functional characteristics. There was some suggestion in her concurring opinion in *Board of Education of Kiryas Joel School District v. Grumet* (1994) that she had come to view the endorsement test as limited to, or at least principally concerned with, "cases involving government speech on religious topics."

Leading academic commentators on the endorsement test are William Marshall, who attempted to give it meaningful content while recognizing its subjectivity, and Steven Smith, who rejected it as incoherent.

Nonpreferentialism

Nonpreferentialism is the view that government may support religion so long as it does not prefer one religion over others, that is, so long as it supports all religions equally. During the debates on disestablishment in the Revolutionary and early national periods, defenders of the old establishments unsuccessfully offered various compromises under which government would provide tax support for all churches in proportion to their support among the taxpayers. In current terminology, these proposals were nonpreferential.

Nonpreferentialism reemerged in modern times in response to the Supreme Court's decisions in *Everson v. Board of Education* (1947), announcing in unanimous dictum that government could not aid religion financially, and *Illinois ex rel. McCollum v. Board of Education* (1948), striking down a public school program that set aside time for religious instruction by the various denominations. Nonpreferentialism has been a persistent theme in criticisms of the Court ever since; the leading academic statement of nonpreferentialism is by Robert Cord.

Nonpreferentialism is a straightforward theory with respect to financial aid: Government can give money to any religious school or to any other religious program or institution, so long as it applies the same nondiscriminatory funding formula to similar programs and institutions of all faiths. Nonpreferentialism also made sense in the context of *McCollum;* any denomination could offer a class on school premises during the period set aside for religious instruction.

But nonpreferentialism also figured prominently in the argument against the Supreme Court's school prayer decisions, where the theory seems incoherent. It is impossible to pray in a form that is equally appropriate for all faiths; in this context, nonpreferentialists seem to support forms of prayer that are generically Protestant or vaguely Judeo-Christian and without references to Christ.

Taken literally, nonpreferentialism would permit government to fund the church itself, including cathedrals, synagogues, mosques, and temples; the salaries of priests, ministers, rabbis, imams, and santeros; and publication of Bibles, Talmuds, Korans, and other holy books, so long as all such programs were nonpreferential. Similarly, nonpreferentialism would permit a law requiring every person to attend religious services in the faith of his or her choice. It is doubtful that any nonpreferentialist actually supports such laws. Nonpreferentialists may believe that such laws would be constitutional but unwise. Or nonpreferentialism may be an incomplete theory that assumes some background principles, such as institutional separation or noncoercion.

Formal Neutrality

Neutrality theories differ from nonpreferentialism in one essential respect: Neutrality theories require government to be neutral as between religion and nonreligion; nonpreferentialism requires government to be neutral among religions, although it can act on the view that religion generally is a good thing.

Formal neutrality holds that government may not use religion as a basis for classification, either to confer a benefit or to impose a burden. In free exercise cases, that has the consequence that religion may not be, or at least need not be, exempted from generally applicable laws. In Establishment cases, formal neutrality has the consequence that religion may participate in the full range of government-funded programs.

The principal policy consequence of adopting formal neutrality would be that government aid to religious schools would become constitutionally unproblematic. Government could aid public education only and private education not at all; or government could aid all education, public and private, religious and secular. The only clearly unconstitutional alternatives would be to aid secular private education without aiding religious private education, or vice versa. Philip Kurland was the principal supporter of formal neutrality. Most other supporters of financial aid to religious schools have invoked nonpreferentialism or substantive neutrality rather than formal neutrality, presumably because they do not want to endorse formal neutrality's prohibition on religious exemptions from regulation and taxation.

Substantive Neutrality

Substantive neutrality holds that government should neither encourage nor discourage religious belief or practice. Thus, most supporters of substantive neutrality believe that government should not be allowed to engage in speech that is either religious or overtly antireligious; government should not sponsor prayers, or nativity scenes, or attacks on religious belief. But religious speech by private speakers should be fully protected on public property and in public debates; student prayer groups can meet on campuses without school sponsorship, and private groups can put up nativity scenes in public forums. Difficult cases for this theory sometimes arise when government speaks on a range of topics such that religion falls naturally within the range, or when government subsidizes private speech with cash, or when government creates a forum with limited capacity and then picks and chooses among potential private speakers. Such arrangements blur the line between government and private speech; sometimes silence about religion may be less neutral than including competing religious views.

Supporters of substantive neutrality generally believe that individual citizens may participate in all government programs and receive all government benefits to which they are entitled, without limiting their religious or antireligious speech or conduct. Most supporters of substantive neutrality believe that government may disburse money to or through religious institutions that perform secular functions and are not principally involved in the transmission of faith, such as hospitals and social service agencies.

This consensus breaks down with respect to schools. Some supporters of substantive neutrality believe that the same principle applies to schools and that government may fund religious schools to the extent that these schools provide education in secular subjects. Parents have a constitutionally protected choice between secular schools and religious schools; some believe that it is a classic unconstitutional condition for government to finance one of these choices and refuse to finance the alternative. The principal exploration of this argument is by Michael McConnell, who compares the debate over funding religious schools with the debate over funding abortions.

Others believe that the support of schools

is a special case, where substantive neutrality conflicts with principles of institutional separation and voluntarism or where instruction in religious and secular subjects is so commingled that it is meaningless to speak of substantively neutral financial support. Substantive neutrality theorists who believe that schools are a special case are divided. Some believe that religious schools should get no government money; some are searching for a line that will permit nondiscriminatory use at religious schools of funds appropriated for special purposes distinct from the general support of education, such as aid to the disabled, without swallowing the general rule that government should not finance religious institutions.

The National Council of churches, the Baptist Joint Committee on Public Affairs, and the Presbyterian church (U.S.A.) are major participants in church–state debates whose positions are generally consistent with substantive neutrality but who oppose government financial support for religious schools. Leading academic defenses of substantive neutrality have been written by Douglas Laycock and by Michael McConnell and Richard Posner.

Strict Separation

"Strict separation" is a vague phrase that connotes a vigorous commitment to separation of church and state that is not confined to institutional separation. In contrast to neutrality theories, the defining characteristic of strict separationists may be a willingness to discriminate against religion if necessary to avoid government aid and to achieve complete separation.

Thus, strict separationists generally oppose any use of public funds to support programs sponsored or managed by religious institutions. They especially oppose any use of public funds to directly or indirectly support religiously affiliated elementary or secondary schools, even if the money is earmarked for a part of the program that would be secular if considered in isolation. For example, strict separationists have generally opposed programs for supplying math books and other secular equipment or supplies to religious schools. They generally opposed allowing disabled students to use state educational assistance in religious schools.

Strict separationists also tend to believe that some restrictions on private religious speech are necessary to preserve separation. Thus, many strict separationists oppose any organized meeting for religious purposes on the premises of any public school or university, even if the meeting is student-initiated and not sponsored by the school. Many strict separationists oppose privately sponsored nativity scenes or menorahs on public premises, even in a public forum open to a wide range of secular speech. Some strict separationists believe that religious speech should be excluded from debates on public policy questions or, alternatively, that religious speech is inappropriate in such debates and that good religious citizens will limit their own speech and speak only in secular terms.

Strict separation is most prominently associated with the secular civil liberties organizations (such as the American Civil Liberties Union, People for the American Way, and Americans United for Separation of church and State) and with the major reform and conservative Jewish organizations (such as the American Jewish Congress, the American Jewish Committee, and the Anti-Defamation League). But none of these organizations go so far as to claim that religious speech is legally barred from public policy debates. An academic who has attempted to clearly distinguish strict separation from substantive neutrality is Ira Lupu.

Most supporters of substantive neutrality share the strict separationist belief that government should not sponsor or subsidize religion, and some supporters of substantive neutrality are as stringent as the strictest separationist in their opposition to government-sponsored prayer and religious displays. But supporters of substantive neutrality understand the no-aid principle in light of the equal and opposite principle that government should not burden religion. Consequently, they find mere neutrality in many programs where strict separationists find aid.

No Aid or Preference to Religion

Some who call themselves strict separationists oppose regulatory exemptions for religiously motivated conduct, on the ground that exemptions are a form of aid or preference to religion. "Separation" seems an especially inapt label for this view, because government regulation of religion involves more church–state contact, and hence less separation, than exempting religion. The dominant principle here is not separation but something else—sometimes formal neutrality, sometimes a belief that no government decision should give any benefit to religion. Steven Gey has stated the case against exemptions in the rhetoric of strict separation. None of the major organizations associated with strict separation interprets strict separation to preclude exemptions for religious conduct.

The Lemon *Test*

The Supreme Court's most general explanation of the Establishment Clause is the three-pronged test of *Lemon v. Kurtzman* (1971): "First, the statute must have a secular legislative purpose; second, its principal or primary effect must be one that neither advances nor inhibits religion; finally, the statute must not foster an excessive government entanglement with religion."

The first two prongs of this test are derived from an attempt to explain neutrality in a school prayer case, *School District of Abington Township v. Schempp* (1963). The facts of *Schempp* did not require the Court to distinguish formal neutrality from substantive neutrality, and inadvertent linguistic substitutions shifted the emphasis away from any form of neutrality. Thus, the first prong of the *Lemon* test has shifted from asking whether the legislative purpose is neutral to asking whether the legislative purpose is secular or religious; this question is fatally ambiguous with respect to the purpose of laws that lift burdens from churches, such as religious exemptions from regulation or laws against religious discrimination.

The second prong of the *Lemon* test literally asks whether the challenged law departs from neutrality. For emphasis, the Court specified that government can not depart from neutrality in either direction; it can neither advance nor inhibit religion. Lower courts and advocates have read that formulation to disaggregate the search for the most nearly neutral course into two separate inquiries: (1) Has government advanced religion? (2) Has government inhibited religion? It is possible to ask these two questions separately, and it is therefore possible to ask either without asking the other. And so many courts now ask whether government has advanced religion (the no-benefit-to-religion theory) instead of asking whether government has departed from neutrality.

A series of reversals in the Supreme Court suggest that the Court has never read the primary effect test to preclude exemptions for religious conduct or to preclude religious applications of generally available government benefits. In these contexts, the Court's understanding of primary effect seems generally consistent with substantive neutrality theory, and the Court has never adopted a no-benefit-to-religion position. But the Court has never clarified the language of the *Lemon* test. And the same verbal formula is used as the basis for many of the Court's tangled limitations on financial aid to religious schools.

The third prong of the *Lemon* test prohibits excessive entanglement. This use of "entanglement" first appeared in *Walz v. Tax Commission of the City of New York* (1970), as an antonym for "separation." In context, it was clear that the Court did not mean strict separation; neither did it seem to mean only institutional separation. In *Walz* the Court seemed to mean "general separation partially achieved"; separation and entanglement were matters of degree, with the acceptable degree of entanglement to be assessed in light of practicalities and an unspecified form of neutrality. This vague aspiration was not clearly defined, but it took context from the opinion's examples and repetitive explanations. It became vaguer still when the isolated phrase "excessive government entanglement" was removed from context and inserted into the *Lemon* test.

The derivation of its three prongs helps explain why the *Lemon* test has been so unsatisfactory to so many, and why the Court seems capable of reaching almost any result without abandoning its "test." The *Lemon* test is a confused amalgam of unspecified neutrality theories, unspecified separation theories, and no-benefit-to-religion theory. Its final linguistic formulation does not reflect its origins and probably does not reflect the Court's actual understanding. In the context of financial aid to religious schools, the Court often measured advancement of religion from the baseline of government inactivity, so that any aid was an unconstitutional advancement. But in all other contexts, and sometimes even in the context of religious schools, the Court measured advancement from the baseline of how government treated analogous secular activities. Efforts to reconcile cases derived from these two inconsistent definitions of neutrality account for much of the inconsistency in the Court's cases. But it appears that until quite recently, the Court did not see the inconsistency. And unlike many academic commentators, the Court did not view neutrality toward religion, however defined, as inconsistent with separationism.

The *Lemon* test's principal defenders have been strict separationists, who give it a strict separationist interpretation by arguing that any incidental benefit to religion is an advancement in violation of the second prong and that any contact between religion and government is an excessive entanglement in violation of the third prong. They sometimes win and sometimes lose with these arguments, but they fear that any change or clarification from the current Court will be less helpful to their cause.

Douglas Laycock

Bibliography

"1966 JCLI Symposium on Religion and the Constitution," 7 *Journal of Contemporary Legal Issues* 275–516 (1996).

Blomgren, Douglas C., and William P. Marshall, "Regulating Religious Organizations under the Establishment Clause," 47 *Ohio State Law Journal* 293 (1986).

Cord, Robert L., *Separation of Church and State: Historical Fact and Current Fiction* (New York: Lambeth Press, 1982).

Esbeck, Carl H., "Five Views of Church–State Relations in Contemporary American Thought," 1986 *Brigham Young University Law Review* 371 (1986).

Gey, Steven G., "Why Is Religion Special?: Reconsidering the Accommodation of Religion under the Religion Clauses of the First Amendment," 52 *University of Pittsburgh Law Review* 75 (1990).

Kurland, Philip B., "Religion and the State: The Origins of the Religion Clauses of the Constitution," 27 *William and Mary Law Review* 839 (1987).

Laycock, Douglas, "The Underlying Unity of Separation and Neutrality," 46 *Emory Law Journal* 43–74 (1997).

Laycock, Douglas, "Noncoercive Support for Religion: Another False Claim about the Establishment Clause," 26 *Valparaiso Law Review* 37 (1991).

———, "The Remnants of Free Exercise," 1990 *Supreme Court Review* 1 (1990).

———, "Formal, Substantive, and Disaggregated Neutrality toward Religion," 39 *DePaul Law Review* 993 (1990).

———, "'Nonpreferential' Aid to Religion: A False Claim about Original Intent," 27 *William and Mary Law Review* 875 (1986).

———, "Towards a General Theory of the Religion Clauses: The Case of Church Labor Relations and the Right to Church Autonomy," 81 *Columbia Law Review* 1373 (1981).

Lupu, Ira C., "The Lingering Death of Separationism," 62 *George Washington Law Review* 230 (1994).

Marshall, William P., "'We Know It When We See It': The Supreme Court and Establishment," 59 *Southern California Law Review* 495 (1986).

McConnell, Michael W., "Religious Freedom at a Crossroads," 59 *University of Chicago Law Review* 115 (1992).

McConnell, Michael W., "The Selective Funding Problem: Abortions and Religious Schools," 104 *Harvard Law Review* 989 (1991).

———, and Richard A. Posner, "An Economic Approach to Issues of Religious Freedom," 56 *University of Chicago Law Review* 1 (1989).

McConnell, Michael W., "Accommodation of Religion," 1985 *Supreme Court Review* 1.

Paulsen, Michael S., "Lemon Is Dead," 43 *Case Western Reserve Law Review* 795 (1993).

Smith, Steven D., "Symbols, Perceptions, and Doctrinal Illusions: Establishment Neutrality and the 'No Endorsement' Test," 86 *Michigan Law Review* 266 (1987).

Tushnet, Mark V., "Of Church and State and the Supreme Court: Kurland Revisited," 1989 *Supreme Court Review* 373 (1989).

Cases Cited

Board of Education of Kiryas Joel School District v. Grumet, 512 U.S. 687 (1994).

Brandon v. Board of Education, 635 F. 2d 971 (2nd Cir. 1980).

Church of the Lukumi Babalu Aye, Inc. and Ernesto Pichardo v. City of Hialeah, 508 U.S. 520 (1993).

City of Boerne v. Flutes, 521 U.S. 507 (1997).

Corporation of the Presiding Bishop of the

Church of Latter-Day Saints v. Amos, 483 U.S. 327 (1987).
County of Allegheny v. American Civil Liberties Union, 492 U.S. 573 (1989).
Davis v. Beason, 133 U.S. 333 (1890).
Employment Division, Department of Human Resources of Oregon v. Smith, 494 U.S. 872 (1990).
Everson v. Board of Education, 330 U.S. 1 (1947).
Illinois ex rel. McCollum v. Board of Education, 333 U.S. 203 (1948).
Jimmy Swaggart Ministries v. Board of Equalization, 493 U.S. 378 (1990).
Lee v. Weisman, 505 U.S. 577 (1992).
Lemon v. Kurtzman, 403 U.S. 602 (1971).
Lynch v. Donnelly, 465 U.S. 668 (1984).
School District of Abington Township v. Schempp, 374 U.S. 203 (1963).
Texas Monthly, Inc. v. Bullock, 489 U.S. 1 (1989).
Torcaso v. Watkins, 367 U.S. 488 (1961).
United States v. Ballard, 322 U.S. 78 (1944).
Walz v. Tax Commission of the City of New York, 397 U.S. 664 (1970).
West Virginia State Board of Education v. Barnette, 319 U.S. 624 (1943).

Title VII Discrimination and Religion

Consider the following case. A public school refuses to employ female teachers who have pre-school-aged children, because the principal believes that mothers should be at home with their young children. However, the school freely hires male teachers with young children, because the principal does not expect fathers to stay home with their children. Is the school liable for sex discrimination?

Absolutely, most courts would say, following *Phillips v. Martin Marietta* (1971). In that case, the Supreme Court stated that an employer may not refuse to hire women with children if the employer refuses to apply the same rule to men. Generally speaking, an employer may not apply different rules to male and female employees or job applicants. But if we change the facts slightly and suppose that the school in question is sectarian and that the principal's belief is based on religious doctrine, the question becomes problematic.

Are religious institutions bound by federal antidiscrimination laws? Does the First Amendment entitle religious employers to engage in conduct that would be illegal if committed by secular employers? These questions have perplexed the courts for decades. Resolution of the first question depends on the construction of federal antidiscrimination statutes, which contain certain exemptions and limitations available to religious employers. Resolving the second, more difficult question requires judicial construction of the religion clauses of the First Amendment.

Both the Free Exercise and Establishment Clauses of the First Amendment constrict the courts in their interpretation of federal antidiscrimination laws. For example, the Free Exercise Clause may entitle a religious employer to a more expansive exemption from antidiscrimination laws than the statutes provide. However, whenever a court grants an exemption to a religious employer, whether the exemption is based on the statute or the Constitution, the court must determine whether the exemption raises difficulties under the Establishment Clause. Each of these issues will be considered in turn.

The Civil Rights Act of 1964

The principal statute in this area is Title VII of the Civil Rights Act of 1964, the centerpiece of federal antidiscrimination law. Title VII prohibits all covered "employers" from discriminating against employees based on their race, color, religion, sex, or national origin. However, there are several exemptions available to religious employers.

Section 702 of Title VII exempts religious corporations, associations, educational institutions, and societies "with respect to the employment of individuals of a particular religion to perform work connected with" the organization's activities (42 U.S. Code 2000e-1 [1972]). As initially enacted, Section 702 was limited to employees performing work that was connected with the employer's "religious activities." However, Congress broadened the Section 702 exemption in 1972 by removing the restriction on activities.

One unresolved question is whether Section 702 entitles an employer to do more than engage in preferential hiring that favors members of a particular religion. Some religious employers contend that the exemption permits them to treat employees who are not members of the preferred religion differently with respect to compensation, promotions, and other terms and conditions of employment. However, it is clear that Section 702 does not authorize discrimination on the basis of race, color, sex, or national origin.

Section 703(e)(2) of Title VII permits certain schools, colleges, universities, and other educational institutions to "hire and employ employees of a particular religion" (42 U.S. Code 2000e-2e(1) [1964]). To invoke this exemption, the school must be largely owned, supported, controlled, or managed by a religious organization. In the alternative, the school must demonstrate that its curriculum is "directed toward the propagation of a particular religion."

Like Section 702, this provision is not limited to employees whose duties are connected with the religious activities of their employer. However, the more specific language of Section 703(e)(2) suggests that it authorizes no more than preferential hiring on the basis of religion. The Ninth Circuit ruled in *Equal Employment Opportunity Commission v. Fremont Christian School* (9th Cir. 1986) that Section 703(e)(2) would not permit discriminatory conduct toward an employee after the employment relationship had begun, or in the provision of benefits. Again, this provision would not allow an employer to engage in discrimination based on race, color, sex, or national origin.

A third and more general provision of Title VII provides a statutory defense for employers charged with unlawful discrimination. Section 703(e)(1) permits any employer, religiously affiliated or otherwise, to "hire and employ employees . . . on the basis of . . . religion, sex or national origin . . . where religion, sex or national origin is a bona fide occupational qualification reasonably necessary to the normal operation" of the employer's business (42 U.S. Code 2000e-2(e)(2) [1964]). Widely referred to as the "BFOQ defense," this provision also provides significant protection for religious employers.

A religious employer charged with unlawful discrimination may invoke more than one of these exemptions, because their coverage is overlapping. For example, in *Pime v. Loyola University of Chicago* (7th Cir. 1986) the employer reserved three tenure-track positions for Jesuits and sought to defend this practice under both Section 703(e)(2), as a religious educational institution, and under Section 703(e)(1), on the theory that being a member of the Society of Jesus was a BFOQ for teaching certain classes. The Seventh Circuit rejected the first argument, because the Society of Jesus did not exercise sufficient control over the university, but the court accepted the BFOQ defense, finding that it was necessary to maintain a "Jesuit presence" in the university's philosophy department. The BFOQ defense was also accepted in *Equal Employment Opportunity Commission v. Kamehameha Schools* (D. Haw. 1991), where the will of the school's founder specified that all teachers in the school must be Protestant. However, in 1993 the Court of Appeals reversed this decision, asserting that the Kamehameha Schools were not in fact religious schools and thus could not claim an exemption under Title VII.

The BFOQ defense has not been allowed where the employees' religious beliefs are unrelated to the performance of their job duties. Applying this rule can lead to some rather subtle distinctions. For example, in *Abrams v. Baylor College of Medicine* (5th Cir. 1986) an employer was not permitted to require doctors seeking a medical rotation in Saudi Arabia to be other than Jewish, based on the employer's concern for the safety of Jewish employees in an Arab state. However, in *Kern v. Dynalectron Corp.* (N.D. Tex. 1983) the BFOQ defense was accepted when another employer sought to hire only Muslim helicopter pilots to fly Muslim pilgrims to Mecca. Non-Muslims who are discovered in Mecca are subject to summary execution.

The BFOQ provision is a popular though difficult defense both for secular employers charged with discrimination on the basis of religion and for religious employers charged with discrimination on any of the enumerated grounds. Secular employers who are unable to invoke the BFOQ defense are not permitted to discriminate against employees based on their personal religious beliefs. For example, the Muslim owner of a grocery who has strong religious convictions is not permitted to hire only Muslims to work in the store. Employers have argued that the Free Exercise Clause permits such practices, but those claims were rejected in *Equal Employment Opportunity Commission v. Townley Engineering and Manufacturing Co.* (9th Cir. 1988).

Title VII did not initially provide a definition of religion, which led some observers to question whether the statute protected conduct based on religious beliefs or merely the right to hold religious beliefs. In 1972,

Congress added a definition of religion to Title VII that expressly included religious observance and practice as well as religious beliefs. Although Title VII now provides a more explicit definition of religion than the Constitution does, the courts and the Equal Employment Opportunity Commission continue to interpret religion in Title VII as that term has been interpreted in both clauses of the First Amendment. According to *Frazee v. Illinois Department of Employment Security* (1989), a sincere religious belief is required, but the claimant need not demonstrate membership in a particular religious sect, and the practice at issue need not be mandated by the religion so long as it is assumed as part of one's religious duties.

The 1972 amendment raises some interesting issues. If an employer discharges or penalizes, say, a Seventh-Day Adventist for refusing to work on Saturdays, is that discrimination based on the employee's religion, under Title VII? If so, then must the employer rearrange the work schedules of nonreligious employees in order to permit Seventh-Day Adventists and other religious employees to attend worship services?

Not necessarily. Congress anticipated the Establishment Clause problems inherent in such a requirement, and it limited Title VII's substantive nondiscrimination requirement with respect to an employee's religious practices. This was accomplished through Section 701(j), the definitional section of the act, which provides that: "The term 'religion' includes all aspects of religious observance and practice, as well as belief, unless an employer demonstrates that he is unable to reasonably accommodate to an employee's or prospective employee's religious observance or practice without undue hardship on the conduct of the employer's business" (42 U.S.C. 2000e(j) [1972]).

To summarize, if none of the exemptions described earlier is available, Title VII requires employers to reasonably accommodate their employees' religious practices unless the employer can demonstrate that accommodation would impose an undue hardship on the conduct of the employer's business. In *Trans World Airlines v. Hardison* (1977) the Supreme Court held that "undue hardship" is established whenever an accommodation would impose more than a *de minimis* cost on the employer. Thus, an employer who is not entitled to an exemption from Title VII need show only that accommodation would entail more than a *de minimis* cost. If the court agrees, then accommodation will not be required.

In *Ansonia Board of Education v. Philbrook* (1986) the Court took *Hardison* one step further. The Court found that an employer charged with religious discrimination under Title VII had satisfied its burden of proof by showing that a reasonable accommodation was offered to the employee. The employer was not required to show that each of the accommodations proposed by the employee would result in undue hardship. After *Philbrook,* an employer's obligation to show undue hardship will arise only where the employer contends that it is unable to offer *any* accommodation to the employee without such hardship.

Religious Exemptions from Title VII: The *McClure* Doctrine

As one might expect, *Hardison* and *Philbrook* have sharply limited the number of successful actions based on an employer's substantive obligation under Title VII to "reasonably accommodate" the religious practices of its employees. The more analytically challenging cases in this field now revolve around the scope of constitutional exemptions from Title VII that are based on the Free Exercise Clause and—the flip side of the constitutional inquiry—whether exemptions from Title VII violate the Establishment Clause.

The first case to squarely address these issues was *McClure v. Salvation Army* (5th Cir. 1972). McClure was a female officer in the Salvation Army who received less compensation than male officers did. She was terminated after complaining about the salary differential, and she filed a sex discrimination action against the Salvation Army. The Fifth Circuit denied her claim, and the Supreme Court denied certiorari.

In *McClure,* the Salvation Army was unable to invoke any of the exemptions then available under Title VII. Its differential treatment of McClure was based not on her religion but on her gender. Yet the Fifth Circuit found that McClure's pay differential could not be challenged under Title VII. The court reasoned that the Army was a religious association and that its employment of McClure was analogous to the relationship between a church and its ministers, because her duties included responsibility for the spiritual needs of those seeking assistance from the Army. The Court decided that applying Title VII to the relationship between a church and its ministers would raise serious concerns under the Free Exercise Clause. Accordingly, the court concluded that Title VII did not apply to such an employment relationship, and McClure's complaint was dismissed.

McClure can be criticized on several levels. First, as a matter of statutory interpretation, the decision is seriously flawed. Nothing in the text of the statute supports the court's holding, and the legislative history reveals no intention to permit sectarian institutions to engage in gender discrimination. By considering and rejecting a blanket exemption that would have exempted religious employers completely from the act (an approach that would have mandated the result reached in *McClure*), Congress had sent a rather clear message that religious employers continued to be bound by Title VII's prohibition on gender, race, and national origin discrimination. The Ninth Circuit so held in *Equal Employment Opportunity Commission v. Pacific Press Publishing Association* (9th Cir. 1982).

There is no evidence in the legislative history that Congress was willing to condone "incidental" discrimination based on gender or other grounds, so long as the basis for the discriminatory conduct was the employer's religious convictions. In fact, this argument was not even raised by the employer in *McClure,* and such a "layered" view of the Section 702 exemption had never been suggested by either commentators or the courts. Yet *McClure*'s formulation of an independent "church-minister" exemption to Title VII in order to "avoid" constitutional problems went a significant way toward establishing just such a "layered" reading of Section 702.

In short, although *McClure* purported to avoid the constitutional issue, the case can stand on no other footing. *McClure* thus rests, as Ira Lupu has observed, "entirely on a set of constitutional assumptions concerning the impermissibility of government intrusion into the church-minister relationship." If the Constitution did not compel the result in *McClure,* there is simply no other foundation for the decision. *McClure*'s progeny—and they are many—often repeat the sins of their predecessor. These cases blindly invoke the "church-minister exception" to Title VII without inquiring into its statutory or constitutional underpinnings. A smaller and more thoughtful group of opinions expressly ground their decisions on free exercise or establishment theories.

The Fifth Circuit subsequently declined to apply *McClure* in a case involving the entire faculty of a religiously affiliated college, in *Equal Employment Opportunity Commission v. Mississippi College* (5th Cir. 1980). In that case, a part-time psychology professor claimed that the school had refused to offer her an available full-time position because of her gender. As in *McClure,* the Fifth Circuit found that the college's actions were not protected by the Section 702 exemption to Title VII, because the school was discriminating on the basis of gender rather than religion. The court also decided that the Free Exercise Clause did not require a broader exemption than was provided by Section 702. The court noted that the college was not a church and that its faculty and staff did not function as ministers. The court also noted that the college's policy of requiring all faculty members to serve as exemplars of practicing Christians was insufficient to convert all matters involving faculty employment to matters of "purely ecclesiastical concern."

The logical next step was not long in coming. In *Equal Employment Opportunity Commission v. Southwestern Baptist Theological Seminary* (5th Cir. 1981) the Fifth Circuit applied the *McClure* doctrine to all the academic employees of a theological seminary. *Mississippi College* was distinguished on the grounds that all the teaching faculty of the seminary qualified as ministers. However, the court declined to extend the protection of the *McClure* doctrine to the seminary's relationship with its nonministerial employees, such as support staff and administrative personnel. The court decided that the Free Exercise Clause would not be offended by the application of Title VII to these employees.

Southwestern Baptist established some fundamental premises, including the right of courts to independently determine whether a given employee performs a "ministerial" function, rather than deferring to designations made by the employer. The courts also determine the extent of the burden that conformity with federal antidiscrimination laws will place on the free exercise rights of the employer. If the burden on free exercise rights is deemed "minimal," as it was in *Mississippi College* and in *Southwestern Baptist* with regard to the school's nonministerial employees, then the court will generally strike its balance in favor of the "strong national interest" in eradicating unlawful discrimination, and will refuse to extend a constitutional exemption to the religious employer.

Religious employers have generally been unable to apply the *McClure* doctrine to employees whose duties are primarily secular. Examples include *Fremont,* which refused the exemption to clerical staff at a religious school; *Pacific Press,* holding that *McClure* would not apply to an editorial secretary in a religious publishing house; *Russell v. Belmont College* (M.D. Tenn. 1982) and *Dolter v. Wahlert High School* (N.D. Iowa 1980), where teachers of secular courses at a religious school were deemed outside the scope of *McClure;* and *Whitney v. Greater New York Corp. of Seventh-Day Adventists* (S.D.N.Y. 1975), which involved a typist-receptionist in a religious organization. One contrary decision is *Little v. Wuerl* (3rd Cir. 1991), in which a teacher of secular subjects in a Catholic school was terminated for entering into a second marriage; in that case the constitutional exemption was allowed.

Two recent cases have generated substantial debate over the vitality and scope of *McClure.* In *Rayburn v. General Conference of Seventh-Day Adventists* (4th Cir. 1985) the Fourth Circuit applied *McClure* to the selection of an "associate in pastoral care" by the Seventh-Day Adventist church. A female applicant for this position had alleged discrimination based on her sex and on her association with black persons and with black-oriented religious organizations. (The courts have permitted whites who are associated with blacks or who actively pursue minority interests to bring race discrimination actions under Title VII.) The Court rejected her claim, not because it read Title VII to be inapplicable, as *McClure* had, but rather on the basis of an explicit balancing of the competing interests.

The Fourth Circuit found that both of the competing interests were of the highest order: The state had a compelling interest in ensuring equal employment opportunities for all, and the right of a church to select its own ministers was deemed essential to the survival of any religious organization. The court stated that the applicability of *McClure* should not depend on ordination but on the function of the position at issue. Reviewing the duties of a pastoral associate—which included teaching children, leading Bible study groups, counseling singles, and occasionally preaching and leading religious services—the court concluded that the position was so important to the spiritual and pastoral mission of the church that it fell within the ambit of *McClure.* Accordingly, the applicant's Title VII claim was rejected.

The broadest expansion of *McClure* was presented by *Dayton Christian Schools v. Ohio Civil Rights Commission* (6th Cir. 1985). In *Dayton Christian Schools* a religious school informed a pregnant teacher that her contract would not be renewed, because the school officials had religiously based convictions that mothers should remain home with pre-school-aged children. When the teacher consulted a lawyer to determine whether or not the school's policy violated state antidiscrimination laws, the school terminated her for failing to follow the "Biblical chain of command." The teacher then filed charges with the state civil rights agency, and the school countered with a lawsuit in federal court, raising the *McClure* defense. The Sixth Circuit enjoined the state agency from continuing its investigation. The court stated that both free exercise and establishment principles precluded the application of state antidiscrimination laws to the religious school.

At present, *Dayton Christian Schools* suggests the widest possible range of autonomy for religious employers from the application of antidiscrimination laws. The decision of the Sixth Circuit effectively immunized the school from any discrimination claim based on state law, without regard to whether the employee qualified as a "minister" under *McClure.* The Sixth Circuit based this decision on its finding that the school was a "pervasively religious institution" in which religious considerations governed all aspects of the educational program, including the teacher selection process.

Ironically, the Ohio antidiscrimination statute in *Dayton Christian Schools,* which was enacted before Title VII, contained none of Title VII's exemptions for religious employers or religious educational institutions. Thus, the school started from a weaker position, as a matter of statutory construction, than a defendant who is charged with a violation of Title VII. Yet the Sixth Circuit's decision had the effect of immunizing the school far beyond the confines of the *McClure* formulation, because the court concluded that the application of state law to such a pervasively religious school would violate both Free Exercise and Establishment Clause principles.

In *Ohio Civil Rights Commission v. Dayton Christian Schools* (1986) the Supreme Court vacated the Sixth Circuit's ruling on purely procedural grounds, finding that the Sixth Circuit should have abstained from deciding the case until pending state administrative proceedings had been resolved. The Supreme Court noted that "even religious schools cannot claim to be wholly free from some state regulation" and found that "the Commission violates no constitutional rights by merely investigating the circumstances of [the employee's] discharge. . . , if only to ascertain whether the ascribed religious-based reason was in fact the reason for the discharge." The Court also observed that the school would be entitled to raise its constitutional claims either in the administrative proceedings or in state court review of those proceedings. *Dayton Christian Schools* then settled the matter without further judicial proceedings.

Religious Exemptions and the Establishment Clause

The flip side of the Title VII problem has generated its own share of controversy: Do Section 702 and other legislative exemptions to Title VII run afoul of the Establishment Clause because they afford a preference to religious employers purely on the basis of their religious affiliation?

The Supreme Court resolved this issue with respect to the Section 702 exemption in *Corporation of the Presiding Bishop of the Church of Latter-Day Saints v. Amos* (1987). In that case, a building engineer was discharged from the Deseret Gymnasium, a nonprofit facility closely associated with the Mormon Church, because he had failed to provide his employer with a certificate attesting his conformity with various church principles. The engineer filed suit under Title VII, arguing that this was religious discrimination. The employer responded that its conduct fell within the Section 702 exemption to Title VII. The engineer then contended that if Section 702 permitted his employer to discriminate on religious grounds in hiring for nonreligious jobs, then the exemption violated the Establishment Clause.

The Supreme Court disagreed. In an opinion by Justice White, the Court found that Section 702 passed each of the three prongs of the test developed in *Lemon v. Kurtzman* (1971). Under that test, (1) a statute must have a secular purpose, (2) its primary effect may neither advance nor inhibit religion, and (3) it may not result in excessive entanglement between government and religion. Violation of any of these prongs of the *Lemon* test is deemed a sufficient basis for holding that a statute violates the Establishment Clause.

Justice White concluded that Section 702 had a secular purpose, which was to minimize governmental interference with decisionmaking in religious organizations. The Court found that, although the statute might have a beneficial effect on the ability of religious groups to advance their purposes, the effect was incidental and not a result of actions of the government. Finally, the Court concluded that the exemption actually diminished the risk of entanglement between church and state, by avoiding intrusive inquiries into religious beliefs and permitting church and state to remain separate. Thus, the Court concluded that the Section 702 exemption did not run afoul of the Establishment Clause.

The *McClure* doctrine retains its vitality, although more recent cases have begun to rest the theory on an Establishment Clause rationale. In *Scharon v. St. Luke's Episcopal Presbyterian Hospitals* (8th Cir. 1991) the court refused to hear the claim of a chaplain who had been terminated by a church-affiliated hospital. The court found that the hospital's treatment of the chaplain could not be challenged under Title VII, because application of the act would impermissably entangle law enforcement agencies with religious affairs and thereby create a problem under the Establishment Clause. The court also noted, in passing, that application of the Free Exercise Clause would require the same result.

Joanne C. Brandt

Bibliography

Bagni, Bruce, "Discrimination in the Name of the Lord: A Critical Evaluation of

Discrimination by Religious Organizations," 79 *Columbia Law Review* 1514–1549 (1979).

Brant, Joanne, "'*Our Shield Belongs to the Land': Religious Employers and a Constitutional Right to Discriminate,*" *21 Hastings Constitutional Law Quarterly* 275–321 (1994).

———, and William Marshall, "Employment Discrimination in Religious Schools: A Constitutional Analysis," in Neil Devins (ed.), *Public Values, Private Schools* (New York and London: Falmer Press, 1989).

Laycock, Douglas, "Towards a General Theory of the Religion Clauses: The Case of Church Labor Relations and the Right to Church Autonomy," 81 *Columbia Law Review* 1373–1417 (1981).

Lupu, Ira, "Free Exercise Exemption and Religious Institutions: The Case of Employment Discrimination," 67 *Boston University Law Review* 391–442 (1987).

Schlei, Barbara, and Paul Grossman, *Employment Discrimination Law* 2nd ed. (Washington: Bureau of National Affairs, 1983; Cum. Supp. 1989).

Cases and Statutes Cited

Abrams v. Baylor College of Medicine, 805 F. 2d 528 (5th Cir. 1986).

Ansonia Board of Education v. Philbrook, 479 U.S. 60 (1986).

Corporation of the Presiding Bishop of the Church of Latter-Day Saints v. Amos, 483 U.S. 327 (1987).

Dayton Christian Schools v. Ohio Civil Rights Commission, 766 F. 2d 932 (6th Cir. 1985), vacated and remanded, 477 U.S. 619 (1986).

Dolter v. Wahlert High School, 483 F. Supp. 266 (N.D. Iowa 1980).

Equal Employment Opportunity Commission v. Fremont Christian School, 781 F. 2d 1362 (9th Cir. 1986).

Equal Employment Opportunity Commission v. Kamehameha School-Bishop Estate, 780 F. Supp. 1317 (D. Haw. 1991). Rev'd 990 F.2d 458 (1993).

Equal Employment Opportunity Commission v. Mississippi College, 626 F. 2d 477 (5th Cir. 1980), cert. denied, 453 U.S. 912 (1981).

Equal Employment Opportunity Commission v. Pacific Press Publishing Association, 676 F. 2d 1272 (9th Cir. 1982).

Equal Employment Opportunity Commission v. Southwestern Baptist Theological Seminary, 651 F. 2d 277 (5th Cir. 1981), cert. denied, 456 U.S. 905 (1982).

Equal Employment Opportunity Commission v. Townley Engineering and Manufacturing Co., 859 F. 2d 610 (9th Cir. 1988). cert. denied, 489 U.S. 1077 (1989).

Frazee v. Illinois Department of Employment Security, 489 U.S. 829 (1989).

Kern v. Dynalectron Corp., 577 F. Supp. 1196 (N.D. Tex. 1983), aff'd, 746 F. 2d 810 (5th Cir. 1984).

Lemon v. Kurtzman, 403 U.S. 602 (1971).

Little v. Wuerl, 929 F. 2d 944 (3rd Cir. 1991).

McClure v. Salvation Army, 460 F. 2d 553 (5th Cir. 1972), cert. denied, 409 U.S. 896 (1972).

Ohio Civil Rights Commission v. Dayton Christian Schools, 477 U.S. 619 (1986).

Phillips v. Martin Marietta, 400 U.S. 542 (1971).

Pime v. Loyola University of Chicago, 803 F. 2d 351 (7th Cir. 1986).

Rayburn v. General Conference of Seventh-Day Adventists, 772 F. 2d 1164 (4th Cir. 1985), cert. denied, 478 U.S. 1020 (1986).

Russell v. Belmont College, 554 F. Supp. 667 (M.D. Tenn. 1982).

Scharon v. St. Luke's Episcopal Presbyterian Hospitals, 929 F. 2d 360 (8th Cir. 1991).

Trans World Airlines v. Hardison, 432 U.S. 63 (1977).

Whitney v. Greater New York Corp. of Seventh-Day Adventists, 401 F. Supp. 1363 (S.D.N.Y. 1975).

Civil Rights Act of 1964, 42 USCA, Sec. 2000; 78 Stat 241, Act of July 2, 1964, Title VII.

Tony and Susan Alamo Foundation v. Secretary of Labor 471 U.S. 290 (1985)

Both Congress and the courts have struggled with the question of the extent to which federal labor and employment statutes can regulate the treatment of employees of religious organizations and yet be consistent with the religion clauses of the First Amendment. In its decision in *Tony and Susan Alamo*

Foundation v. Secretary of Labor (1985) the U.S. Supreme Court, speaking through Justice Byron White, considered the questions of whether the federal Fair Labor Standards Act (FLSA) applies to workers engaged in the commercial activities of a religious organization as a matter of statutory interpretation and, if so, whether applying the FLSA in this manner violates the First Amendment. Consistent with lower-court rulings and Department of Labor regulations, the Court unanimously held that the FLSA did apply to the commercial activities of religious organizations and did so without violating the First Amendment. In so holding, the Court attempted to strike a balance between the policy interests that support federal regulation of the employment relationship and the constitutional concerns contained in the religion clauses of the First Amendment.

The FLSA imposes certain minimum wage, overtime, and record-keeping requirements on enterprises engaged in commerce that utilize "employees" in the conduct of their work. The "commerce" limitation of the FLSA exempts employees of religious institutions who are engaged in the noncommercial, religious work of their employer; the question in this case was whether the FLSA applies to employees of religious institutions who are engaged in commercial activities. The FLSA contains no express exemptions for commercial activities conducted by religious organizations, and the Department of Labor has consistently interpreted the act to cover such commercial activities so long as they are carried out for a "business purpose."

In this case, the Department of Labor brought suit under the FLSA against the Tony and Susan Alamo Foundation, a nonprofit religious corporation whose articulated purpose was to "establish, conduct and maintain an evangelistic church, and generally to do those things needful for the promotion of Christian faith, virtue and charity." As part of its work, the foundation operated a wide array of commercial businesses (including hog farms, service stations, restaurants, and retail stores) staffed in large measure by volunteer "associates"—most of whom were former drug addicts, derelicts, and criminals. The associates received no wages, but the foundation did provide them with food, clothing, shelter, and other benefits such as medical care. All the associates who testified at the trial of the case insisted that they were volunteers, not employees, and were engaged in evangelistic ministry through their work for the foundation.

The foundation resisted the litigation, arguing that the FLSA did not cover its activities because those activities had a religious as opposed to a business purpose; that the foundation's associates were volunteers, not employees; and that application of the FLSA to the foundation's activities violated the First Amendment.

The Supreme Court affirmed the finding of the district court that the commercial activities of the foundation did have a business purpose. Significant to the Court was the fact that the foundation's various businesses competed with nonreligious commercial enterprises. If these businesses were allowed to pay substandard wages, they would have an unfair competitive advantage over their secular competitors.

The Court further concluded that the foundation's associates were in fact employees, because they engaged in the work of the foundation with the expectation of receiving substantial in-kind benefits in exchange for their labor. Noting that none of the associates who testified claimed entitlement to wages, the Court nevertheless concluded that their testimony should not be determinative inasmuch as they could be subject to coercion by the foundation.

Finally, the Court addressed the constitutional question of whether application of the FLSA to the commercial activities of religious organizations could be squared with the First Amendment. The Court concluded that the FLSA's minimum wage requirements did not infringe the associates' free exercise rights because the associates were free to give their wages back to the foundation. Likewise, the Court concluded that the record-keeping requirements that the statute imposed on the foundation were not so onerous as to excessively entangle the government with religion.

In the years since the Supreme Court's decision in the *Alamo* case, the lower courts have continued to find the FLSA applicable to the commercial activities of religious organizations without infringing the First Amendment. For example, the U.S. Court of Appeals for the Fourth Circuit held that the FLSA covered church-operated private schools, in *Dole v. Shenandoah Baptist*

Church (4th Cir. 1990). Likewise, the Supreme Court of Nebraska found that the FLSA covered a retirement home for clergy, in *Banks v. Mercy Villa Care Center* (Neb. 1987).

At the same time, however, the lower courts have also continued to find the FLSA not applicable to the charitable, noncommercial activities of religious groups. For example, a federal district court held that the FLSA did not cover Salvation Army employees who work in homeless shelters, because those shelters are noncommercial and do not compete with secular businesses (*Wagner v. Salvation Army* [E.D. Tenn. 1986]).

Davison M. Douglas

Bibliography

Bethel, Terry A., "Recent Labor Law Decisions of the Supreme Court," 45 *Maryland Law Review* 179–239 (1986).

Cruz, David B., "Piety and Prejudice: Free Exercise Exemption from Laws Prohibiting Sexual Orientation Discrimination," 69 *New York Law Review* 1176–1237 (1994).

Marshall, William P., and Douglas C. Blomgren, "Regulating Religious Organizations under the Establishment Clause," 47 *Ohio State Law Journal* 293–331 (1986).

Cases Cited

Banks v. Mercy Villa Care Center, 407 N.W. 2d 793 (Neb. 1987).

Dole v. Shenandoah Baptist Church, 899 F. 2d 1389 (4th Cir. 1990). cert. denied, 498 U.S. 846 (1990).

Tony and Susan Alamo Foundation v. Secretary of Labor, 471 U.S. 290 (1985).

Wagner v. Salvation Army, 660 F. Supp. 466 (E.D. Tenn. 1986).

Torcaso v. Watkins 367 U.S. 488 (1961) and *McDaniel v. Paty* 435 U.S. 618 (1978)

To what extent can states prohibit a person from holding public office based on religious criteria? The U.S. Supreme Court addressed this questions in two cases. The first, *Torcaso v. Watkins* (1961), involved a First Amendment challenge to a provision of the Maryland Constitution which stated that "no religious test ought ever to be required as a qualification for any office of profit or trust in this State other than a declaration of belief in the existence of God. . . ." The provision was applied to deny Roy R. Torcaso a commission to serve as notary public, notwithstanding the fact that he had been duly appointed to that position. The second case, *McDaniel v. Paty* (1978), involved a First Amendment challenge to a Tennessee statute that made applicable to candidates for the state constitutional convention a provision of the Tennessee Constitution which disqualified ministers or priests of any denomination from serving as state legislators.

The religious oath requirement at issue in *Torcaso* was reminiscent of similar religious tests imposed in seventeenth- and eighteenth-century England. Indeed, as the Court noted, "it was largely to escape religious tests oaths and declarations that a great many of the early colonists left Europe and came here hoping to worship in their own way." But such tests reemerged in the American colonies, varying "largely on what group happened to be politically strong enough to legislate in favor of its own beliefs." By 1787, most states had provisions in their constitutions that imposed religious qualifications for public office. For example, the Delaware Constitution of 1776 required that all state officers swear a trinitarian oath, while the Georgia Constitution of 1777 required that all representatives be of "the Protestant religion." Indeed, the Constitution of New York (1777) was the only one that did not effectively impose restrictions on holding office for Jews. These provisions, combined with other laws imposing burdens or disabilities on various religious beliefs, had the formal or practical effect of "establishing" particular religious faiths in most states.

When the U.S. Constitution was written, criticism of religious oaths and similar measures had become widespread. This fact—combined perhaps with the pragmatic assessment of the difficulty of prescribing any religious requirements that would be acceptable to the entire country—led to the inclusion in Article 6 of the Constitution of a provision that "no religious Test shall ever be required as a Qualification to any Office or public Trust under the United States." This provision applied in terms only to the federal government, and so it was not explicitly relied on by the plaintiff in *Torcaso*. Instead, he claimed that Maryland's requirement that he declare his belief in God as a condition to holding office violated the First Amendment's Establishment Clause, which bans laws "respecting an establishment" of religion, and its Free Exercise Clause, which bans laws "prohibiting the free exercise" of religion.

The Supreme Court agreed, with Justice Hugo Black writing for the Court, and Justices Felix Frankfurter and John Marshall Harlan concurring in the result. Justice Black relied on several prior Supreme Court cases that had found in the First Amendment a sweeping principle of religious liberty which applied to the federal government directly and to the states through the Fourteenth Amendment. This principle, among other things, prohibited the government from punishing anyone "for entertaining or professing religious beliefs or disbeliefs." The Court also endorsed the view, attributed to Thomas Jefferson, that the First Amendment was intended to erect "a wall of separation between church and state." The Maryland law violated these requirements because it effectively punished a person whose religious (or, for that matter, nonreligious) beliefs precluded him or her from making the sort of public declaration it required, and because it effectively discriminated against persons whose religious beliefs, like Buddhism or Taoism, do not subscribe to a belief in the existence of God.

The Court's decision in *Torcaso* provided an important backdrop for the challenge to Tennessee's disqualification of clergy from holding public office in *Paty*. The appellant in *Paty*, Paul A. McDaniel, was an ordained Baptist minister of a church in Chattanooga who was a candidate for delegate to the state's constitutional convention. The appellee, Selma Cash Paty, was an opposing candidate for delegate who sued McDaniel in state court claiming that he was disqualified to serve as delegate by virtue of a provision of the Tennessee Constitution barring "minister[s] of the Gospel, or priests of any denomination whatever" from serving as delegates. The Tennessee Supreme Court upheld this state constitutional provision against McDaniel's federal constitutional challenge.

As had been the case in *Torcaso*, the Court in *Paty* examined the historical background of the law and noted that the disqualification of ministers from office was practiced in England in most of the colonies and then in some of the states. The exclusion of clergy from political office was prevalent even at the time of the ratification of the Bill of Rights; indeed, it remained common in some states until the mid-1800s. It had been endorsed by John Locke and some of the founding generation's leading thinkers, such as Thomas Jefferson, although this endorsement was not unanimous; James Madison, for example, opposed it. The principal justification for the exclusion of clergy from political office was the concern that their holding office would threaten the principle of separation of church and state and would promote religious strife.

In *Paty* it was argued that the effect of the Tennessee law was to require what the Court in *Torcaso* had suggested was absolutely forbidden by the First Amendment: the imposition of a punishment or burden on a person for their holding a religious belief. However, only two justices, William J. Brennan and Thurgood Marshall, agreed with this argument. Chief Justice Warren Burger's plurality opinion (a plurality opinion announces the judgment of the Court but is joined in by less than a majority of the justices) argued that the Tennessee constitutional provision did not directly penalize the holding of religious *beliefs*. Justices Powell, Rehnquist, and Stevens joined this opinion. Instead, the plurality concluded that the law affected religious *conduct* or *activity*—e.g., the performance of religious duties normally associated with the ministerial role. Thus, the *Torcaso* principle absolutely prohibiting the regulation of beliefs was inapplicable. The state, at least in theory, could justify its practice if it could show that the law served "interests of the highest order" which could not otherwise be served.

The plurality concluded that the clergy-disqualification law could not meet this test. The Court rejected the state's claim that the law served a compelling interest in preventing the sort of establishment of religion that the First Amendment itself prohibited. Instead, the Court found that, especially under contemporary circumstances, the state simply did not demonstrate that the dangers of clergy holding public office provided the historical rationale for such laws.

Justice Brennan's view of the prohibitory effect of the First Amendment, expressed in a concurring opinion, was significantly broader. He rejected the plurality's rigid belief–conduct distinction in favor of an approach that saw the First Amendment as absolutely prohibiting religious classifications—that is, laws conditioning access to a benefit or position on the basis of religious criteria. Because the Tennessee law punished those whose religious beliefs were so strong that they felt compelled to join the clergy, it violated the Free Exercise Clause. And because the law evidenced hostility to religion and the legitimate role that religious believers can play in political debate and policymaking, it violated the Establishment Clause.

Justice Potter Stewart wrote a brief concurrence in *Paty*, concluding that *Torcaso* and its absolute prohibition on the regulation of religious beliefs required invalidation of the Tennessee law. Justice Byron White's concurrence rejected the notion that the law violated the Free Exercise Clause; he did not believe that the law actually interfered with or burdened the plaintiff's ability to exercise his religious beliefs. Instead, Justice White found the law to violate the Fourteenth Amendment's Equal Protection Clause. In his view, the state had not offered an adequate justification for its decision to completely exclude clergy from eligibility to serve as delegates to the state's constitutional convention.

Taken together, *Torcaso* and *Paty* embody a principle that prohibits the exclusion of individuals from participation in politics—including, but not limited to, the holding of public office—on the basis of religious beliefs or religious affiliation. Of course, nothing in these cases in any way limits the right of a religious institution to condition the status of members of its own religious community on the agreement to forgo various forms of political activity, as was the case some years ago when the Catholic Church prohibited Father Robert Drinan from continuing to serve in Congress.

Richard B. Saphire

Bibliography

Borden, Morton, *Jews, Turks, and Infidels* (Chapel Hill: University of North Carolina Press, 1984).

McConnell, Michael W., "The Origins and Historical Understanding of Free Exercise of Religion," 103 *Harvard Law Review* 1409–1517 (1990).

Cases Cited

McDaniel v. Paty, 435 U.S. 618 (1978).

Torcaso v. Watkins, 367 U.S. 488 (1961).

Trial of Anne Hutchinson

Anne Hutchinson (1591–1643) was born Anne Marbury in Alford, England. She was the daughter of an English divine who, because of his Puritan sympathies, was censured by the Church of England. In 1612 Anne married William Hutchinson, son of a wealthy merchant, thereafter bearing some fourteen children.

While in England, Anne Hutchinson was attracted to the preaching of the Reverend John Cotton. In 1634 she and her family followed Cotton to Massachusetts and to Boston's First Church. Hutchinson soon assumed an active role in the religious life of the women of her community. Her advocacy of an uncompromising covenant of grace caused alarm among community leaders, however, while her attacks on leading ministers led to her arrest.

Hutchinson was accused of being an antinomian. More to the point, she opposed those who suggested that salvation could be achieved through obedience to moral law, arguing instead that once people were under the covenant of grace, or had received God's saving grace, they were absolved from the necessity of obeying moral law. Massachusetts Puritans rejected the covenant of works, as well, but they had tacitly allowed, if not encouraged, a preparationist understanding of obedience to moral law and taught that people under the covenant of grace would necessarily lead a holy life.

At first Hutchinson received the support of several prominent members of the community, including John Cotton; her brother-in-law, the Reverend John Wheelwright; and Massachusetts Governor Sir Henry Vane. As the charges grew more serious, however, Hutchinson's support waned. Cotton acquiesced in the ruling of the court against her. Wheelwright, who refused to acquiesce, was banished; and Vane, who was defeated by John Winthrop in his bid for election in the midst of the antinomian controversy, returned to England.

In November 1637 the Massachusetts authorities brought Hutchinson to trial. Presiding, as judge and prosecutor, was

Governor John Winthrop. Joining him on the bench were Deputy Governor Thomas Dudley and John Endecott. The court charged Hutchinson with disturbing the peace of the Commonwealth and its churches; harboring and countenancing those of whom the magistrates had disapproved; holding private meetings in her home, which had been condemned by the General Assembly as "a thing not tolerable nor comely in the sight of God nor fitting for [her] sex"; and speaking words that were "prejudiced" to the churches and their ministers.

Representing herself—which was common for men at that time but rare for women—Hutchinson proved to be an adept defense attorney. At one point she charged the court with having violated the law in allowing ministers to testify against her without being under oath. At another she accused some of those same ministers of violating professional rules of conduct in making public what she had said to them in confidential conversations. Because testimony about what she had said proved contradictory and because she had avoided committing her ideas to paper, Hutchinson successfully avoided conviction until she proclaimed her belief in immediate revelation, a doctrine that the Puritans held to be inimical to church and state. The state had not charged Hutchinson with belief in immediate revelation, but when Hutchinson introduced it, the court seized on it to condemn her. In the wake of her condemnation, those who had supported her or espoused similar antinomian principles (estimated to number as many as sixty in Boston, alone) and who refused to recant or leave voluntarily, were banished or disfranchised.

The court sentenced Hutchinson to banishment, but given the winter season and her pregnancy, the sentence was stayed. She was committed to the home of the Reverend Joseph Weld, where Weld, John Cotton, and the Reverend John Davenport worked to convince her of her errors. In March 1638 she received an ecclesiastical trial before First Church. Hutchinson offered a public recantation, but when she subsequently allowed that her views remained unaltered, she was accused of lying and ordered "as a leper" to withdraw from the congregation.

In the spring of 1738 Hutchinson and her family migrated to Aquidneck and, from there, to Newport, Rhode Island. She continued to preach—in the end turning to Anabaptism—and to involve herself in matters of state. In 1639 she allied herself with Samuel Gorton in leading a rebellion against Judge (Governor) William Coddington, but soon thereafter she turned to questioning "all magistracy among Christians." On the death of her husband in 1642, she and her children moved to the Pelham Bay area of Long Island (then in Dutch New Netherlands), where, in August or September 1743, she, two of her sons, and three daughters were killed by Indians.

Hutchinson is most commonly seen as one of the first in American history to be persecuted for her religious beliefs. Beyond that, however, interpretations vary. Edmund Morgan, for example, was one of the first to argue that Hutchinson's was a political trial—that rather than being banished for heresy, she was condemned for espousing a doctrine that threatened the foundation of the Bible Commonwealth. Her theology, Morgan wrote, called into question any need for the church and implied that the state should be concerned only with secular ends.

Similarly Fairfax Withington and Jack Schwartz have argued that Hutchinson's conviction was not based on any law that could properly be applied by a civil court. Her trial was not a matter of justice or an attempt to resolve the question of guilt or innocence. It was a trial of power or an effort, on the part of the state, to solve the political problem of maintaining order.

Richard Morris has drawn parallels between Hutchinson's trial and the sedition cases of the early 1950s. Moreover, as Morris has pointed out, the Massachusetts authorities denied Hutchinson modern procedural safeguards such as being formally indicted, being presented with specific charges, being provided with an attorney, and having the right of trial by jury.

Finally, Lyle Koehler has concluded that the Anne Hutchinson–antinomian debacle should be seen as a social movement that called into question the role of women in seventeenth-century Massachusetts. What attracted women to the movement, Koehler suggests, was its emphasis on the inability of the individual to effect his or her own salvation. This echoed the inability of women to achieve recognition on a sociopolitical level and extended the "feminine experience of humility" to both sexes.

Bryan F. Le Beau

Bibliography

Hall, David D. (ed.), *The Antinomian Controversy, 1636–1638: A Documentary History,* 2nd ed. (Durham, N.C.: Duke University Press, 1990; orig. pub. 1968).

Koehler, Lyle, "The Case of the American Jezebels: Anne Hutchinson and Female Agitation during the Years of Antinomian Turmoil, 1636–1640," 31 *William and Mary Quarterly* 55–78 (1974).

Morris, Richard, *Fair Trial: Fourteen Who Stood Accused: From Anne Hutchinson to Alger Hiss,* rev. ed. (New York: Harper Torchbooks, 1967; orig. pub. 1952).

Morgan, Edmund, "The Case against Anne Hutchinson," 10 New England Quarterly 549–635 (1937).

VanBurkleo, Sandra F., "'To Bee Rooted Out of Her Station': The Ordeal of Anne Hutchinson," in Michael Belknap (ed.), *American Political Trials,* rev. ed. (Westport, Conn.: Greenwood, 1994), pp. 1–24.

Withington, Fairfax, and Jack Schwartz, "The Political Trial of Anne Hutchinson," 51 *New England Quarterly* 226–240 (1978).

U

United Jewish Organizations of Williamsburgh, Inc. v. Carey
430 U.S. 144 (1977)

Initiated by Hasidic Jews in Brooklyn, *United Jewish Organizations of Williamsburgh, Inc. v. Carey* (1977) challenged a 1974 reapportionment plan adopted by the New York legislature to comply with the Voting Rights Act of 1965. The case raised important questions concerning the rights of religious groups under the Voting Rights Act and the constitutionality of using racial quotas to create electoral districts designed to allow African Americans to elect candidates of their choice.

The Voting Rights Act required jurisdictions that in 1964 had used literacy tests and had recorded low rates of voter registration to submit all changes in voting requirements and procedures to the Justice Department for preclearance. Only if the changes had neither the intent nor the effect of discriminating on the basis of race was the attorney general to permit implementation. In a series of decisions in the late 1960s and early 1970s, the U.S. Supreme Court read the preclearance requirement broadly, ruling that it was designed to prohibit changes that reduced racial minorities' opportunity to elect candidates of their choice and that it applied to reapportionment.

Although the act principally affected the South, New York had a literacy test on the books in 1964, and so several New York counties with low rates of voter registration, including Kings County (Brooklyn), came under the preclearance requirement. In 1974 the Justice Department rejected a legislative reapportionment plan creating ten senate and assembly districts in Kings County with nonwhite majorities. Several of the districts, the department ruled, had nonwhite majorities that were not sufficiently large to guarantee that a majority of voters in them would be nonwhite. After the legislature redrew these districts, ensuring that all were at least 65 percent nonwhite, the department approved the state's reapportionment plan.

A tightly knit community of Hasidic Jews in the Williamsburgh section of Brooklyn strenuously objected to the plan. Before the 1974 reapportionment, the Hasidic community of thirty thousand had been concentrated in one assembly district and a single senate district. In redrawing district lines to meet Justice Department objections, however, the legislature divided the Hasidic community into two assembly and two senate districts. Hasidic leaders sought relief in federal district court, charging that, by assigning them to electoral districts on the basis of race, the plan diluted their voting strength in violation of the Fourteenth and Fifteenth Amendments. They also charged that the plan established racial quotas in violation of the Fourteenth Amendment's Equal Protection Clause.

The district court and the Court of Appeals for the Second Circuit rejected these claims. They held that the Hasidim, although a distinct religious group, had no right under the Voting Rights Act or the Constitution to recognition as a separate community for purposes of reapportionment. The lower courts also ruled that the reapportionment plan did not deny whites equal protection or abridge their right to vote on the basis of race. Whites, they pointed out, constituted 65 percent of the county's population and were in the majority in almost 70 percent of its senate and legislative districts.

The Supreme Court affirmed the lower courts' judgment by a vote of 7 to 1, with Justice Byron White writing the opinion of the Court. White emphasized that the preclearance provisions of the Voting Rights Act necessitated the use of racial criteria in drafting reapportionment plans; only by taking race into account could legislators ensure that redistricting did not dilute the votes of racial minorities. Moreover, Justice White found that the New York reapportionment plan did not minimize whites' voting strength and therefore did not violate the Fourteenth or Fifteenth Amendments. Because the plaintiffs did not challenge the lower courts' rejection of their claim to recognition as a separate community in the reapportionment process, the Court did not address that issue.

Chief Justice Warren Burger, the lone dissenter, argued that racial quotas were impermissible under the Fourteenth and Fifteenth Amendments and could not be justified under the guise of complying with the Voting Rights Act.

Donald G. Nieman

Bibliography

Davidson, Chandler, and Bernard Grofman (eds.), *Controversies in Minority Voting: The Voting Rights Act in Perspective* (Washington, D.C.: Brookings Institution, 1992).

Lawson, Steven F., *In Pursuit of Power: Southern Blacks and Electoral Politics, 1965–1982* (New York: Columbia University Press, 1985).

Nieman, Donald G., *Promises to Keep: African-Americans and the Constitutional Order, 1776 to the Present* (New York: Oxford University Press, 1991).

Thernstrom, Abigail, *Whose Vote Counts? Affirmative Action and Minority Voting Rights* (Cambridge, Mass.: Harvard University Press, 1987).

Case Cited

United Jewish Organizations of Williamsburgh, Inc. v. Carey, 430 U.S. 144 (1977).

United States v. Aguilar
871 F. 2d 1436 (9th Cir. 1989)

During the early 1980s a number of religious groups organized a "sanctuary movement," to protest U.S. policy of tolerating human rights violations in Central America and, in particular, its immigration policy, which denied refugee status to Central Americans fleeing persecution. The sanctuary movement was active within segments of the Catholic Church, the United Methodist Church, the Presbyterian Church, and the Unitarian Universalist Association, among other organizations. By 1987 the movement included 370 churches, 19 cities, and 20 universities. Many of the activities of the movement were legal, including providing legal advocacy on behalf of persons seeking asylum. Frustrated by the failure of these efforts, some members openly declared that they would violate what they considered a discriminatory immigration law by offering shelter to refugees who were illegally in the United States. Because these activists publicly announced their intentions to violate laws in order to draw attention to injustice and seek change, they understood their act as one of civil disobedience.

In 1982 the government initiated an undercover investigation and infiltrated the movement to obtain evidence of violation of immigration laws. Its agents became active participants in the movement, and their testimony became a major part of the record in the prosecution of sanctuary activists. In 1989 Maria Socorro Pardo Viuda de Aguilar and fifteen codefendants were convicted of violating the U.S. Immigration and Nationality Act by smuggling, transporting, and harboring refugees from El Salvador, through Mexico, into the United States. Eleven defendants were ultimately convicted. Their trial raised numerous issues of immigration and criminal law, including construction of the terms of the immigration acts, questions of intent and alleged misunderstanding of the law, extraterritoriality, the fruits of illegally seized evidence, the testimony of "invited informers," and selective prosecution. This case highlights three important issues of religious free exercise under the First Amendment: (1) the question of religious-based exemptions from criminal laws, (2) the appropriateness of the "compelling state interest" standard, and (3) the constitutionality of government infiltration of religious movements.

The first free exercise issue raised in this case is whether the U.S. Constitution requires exemptions from criminal prosecution for those whose law violation is understood by the actors to be an act of religious obligation. Aguilar argued that the Constitution required religious exemptions for religiously motivated violation of the Immigration and Nationality Act by members of the sanctuary movement. Aguilar and her codefendants claimed that, because they acted with religious motives, their convictions raised First Amendment issues. In particular, defendants argued that because their motive was to perform a religiously required act of benevolence, rather than to violate the law, they lacked the requisite criminal intent. Speaking for the Ninth Circuit Court of Appeals, Judge Cynthia Holcomb Hall, rejected that argument:

> Appellants . . . argue that their religious motivation in transporting the illegal aliens would negate the requisite intent. . . . Proof that . . . transportation was not intended to further the alien's illegal presence, but to fulfill . . . religious commitments to assist those in need, would thus constitute a defense. Appellants are confusing intent and motive. So long as appellants intended directly or substantially to further the alien's illegal presence, it is irrelevant that they did so with a religious motive.

The defendants also attempted to bring testimony concerning the conditions from which the refugees were fleeing, in order to make a defense of necessity. The court precluded such testimony and ruled that a necessity defense was not appropriate, because the defendants could not show that there were no legal alternatives to law violation.

The court's arguments for rejecting Aguilar's claim for a religious exemption to immigration laws were essentially practical ones; granting widespread exemptions would vitiate any immigration policy at all, and granting limited exemptions would selectively favor some religions over others. The court noted that the sanctuary movement is supported by many religious groups and that the number of persons religiously motivated to offer assistance to those in need is incalculable. Hence, any policy of accommodating the religious convictions of these defendants would permit *every* similarly motivated group to establish its own immigration policy and, hence, would result in no immigration policy. Further, attempts to limit exemptions to this particular movement would result in violations of the Equal Protection Clause, by granting to some religious persons—and hence to some aliens—benefits that were not available to others. In short, in spite of the sincere religious motivations of members of the sanctuary movement, the court found no free exercise violation in prosecuting them for violations of immigration laws.

In this case, the courts refused to extend into criminal law the kind of accommodations typical of *Wisconsin v. Yoder* (1972). Hence, this case appears as a precursor of the kind of reasoning that the Supreme Court used during the following term in *Employment Division, Department of Human Resources of Oregon v. Smith* (1990).

The second constitutional issue raised in this case concerned whether burdens on religious exercise must meet the compelling state interest test. Aguilar argued that, because of the magnitude of the burden which immigration laws placed on her religious beliefs, the government must show a compelling interest in prosecuting each of her acts. The government argued that the compelling interest test is not required for justifying regulatory legislation. The circuit court found it unnecessary to decide on the appropriate standard, because "even applying the most exacting scrutiny appellants' first amendment claim cannot withstand analysis." Thus, the court concluded: "Even assuming that appellants have proved that the enforcement of sections 1324 and 1325 interfered with their religious beliefs, they cannot escape the government's overriding interest in policing its borders."

The third major First Amendment question raised in this case concerns government infiltration of religious institutions and the use of testimony obtained through informers. Government infiltrators not only participated in the illegal activities but also participated actively in the religious life of member churches, surreptitiously taped religious worship services, and recorded license numbers of cars in church parking lots. This evidence was obtained without a warrant. The *Aguilar* defendants argued that these methods violated both the First and Fourth Amendments and that hence the evidence was inadmissible. The court thus had to consider not only the constitutional issues concerning "invited informers" in general but also the particular problems of such informers in religious settings. The court observed:

> The critical aspect of appellants' argument is their suggestion that the first amendment and the fourth amendment are necessarily intertwined in the context of an informer's infiltration of a church. Based upon first amendment principles, appellants contend that society is prepared to recognize as reasonable churchgoers' expectations that "they could meet and worship in church free from the security of federal agents and tape recorders." A churchgoer need not "assume the risk that apparent fellow worshipers are present in church not to offer homage to God but rather to gain thirty pieces of silver."

The court noted that Aguilar and her codefendants based their argument on "the theory that the first amendment provides them with an additional expectation of privacy making the invited informer rationale inapplicable." Aguilar assumed that the First Amendment required a "heightened expectation of privacy because a 'community of trust' is the essence of a religious congregation and the ability of a person to express faith with his fellow believers 'withers and dies when monitored by the state.'" Thus, "government 'spying' on religious activities necessarily chills a person's ability to exercise freely his religious faith."

Having summarized this argument, the court rejected it. Judge Hall wrote: "While privacy, trustworthiness, and confidentiality are undoubtedly at the very heart of many instances of free association and religious expression and communication, the Court has recognized that legitimate law enforcement interests require persons to take the risk that those with whom they associate may be government agents."

Subsequent to the prosecutions in this case, several churches brought civil action against the government for violation of their religious freedoms stemming from government infiltration of churches. Thus, *Presbyterian Church (USA) v. United States* (1990) is a companion case to *Aguilar.* Although the trial court in this companion case entered summary judgment against the churches, the Ninth Circuit partly vindicated their constitutional claim. The court had no difficulty finding a compelling state interest in enforcing immigration policy, but it gave serious attention to the second prong of the compelling state interest test: whether government activities burdening religious exercise were the least-restrictive means available to achieve the government's interest. The court in this case entered a declaratory judgment limiting "invited informers" in religious institutions to the specific invitations extended to them, to investigations only with a "good faith purpose," and precluding them from "unbridled and inappropriate covert activity" aimed at abridgment of First Amendment Freedoms."

Bette Novit Evans

Bibliography

Bothwell, Mike, "Facing God or the Government: *United States v. Aguilar:* A Big Step for Big Brother," 1990 *Brigham Young University Law Review* 1003–1025 (1990).

Hoyer, Richard A., "No Haven in the Courts for the Sanctuary Movement: An Examination of the First Amendment and International Law Defenses," 27 *American Criminal Law Review* 431–455 (1989).

McCarthy, Michael F., "Expanded Fourth Amendment Coverage: Protection from Government Infiltration of Churches," 3 *Georgetown Immigration Law Journal* 163–182 (1989).

McConnell, Michael, and Renny Golden, *Sanctuary: The New Underground Railroad* (New York: Orbis, 1986).

Reidinger, Paul, "Derailing the Underground: Belief but No Asylum," 75 *American Bar Association Journal* 96 (1989).

Cases Cited

Employment Division, Department of Human Resources of Oregon v. Smith, 494 U.S. 872 (1990).

Presbyterian Church (USA) v. United States, 752 F. Supp. 1505 (D. Ariz., 1990).

United States v. Aguilar, 871 F. 2d 1436 (9th Cir. 1989) cert. denied, *Socorro Pardo Viuda de Aguilar v. United States,* 498 U.S. 1046 (1991).

Wisconsin v. Yoder, 406 U.S. 205 (1972).

United States v. Ballard
322 U.S. 78 (1944)

United States v. Ballard (1944) posed the difficult issues of whether the First Amendment permits government to inquire into the truth or falsity of religious beliefs and/or into the sincerity with which those beliefs are held. If the authorities can do neither, then they are powerless to protect the public from those who, in the name of religion, would procure money from others through fraud and misrepresentation. For government to distinguish between "true" and "false" religious beliefs is, however, inconsistent with the concept of freedom of religion.

The claims that led to the indictment of Edna and Donald Ballard for using, and conspiring to use, the mails to defraud seem rather clearly to have been untrue. The Ballards solicited money by representing themselves and Guy W. Ballard, deceased husband of Edna and father of Donald, as divine messengers. Guy, they claimed, had been selected by St. Germain (who died in 448 C.E.) to communicate his teachings to humanity; their "I Am" movement was the sole channel through which the precepts of St. Germain and other "ascended masters" would be transmitted to mankind. Edna and Donald represented that they had supernatural powers to cure diseases and other ailments, some of which the medical profession classified as incurable. They had composed form-letter testimonials from nonexistent persons affirming that the Ballards had healed them. Among the defendants' other claims were that they had a divine and supernatural ability to bring forth riches and other things necessary to mankind (powers they could transmit to others for a price), that the books they marketed had been dictated by St. Germain, and that a picture they sold was the result of a visitation by him. The Ballards had also endeavored to persuade followers of "I Am" that the end of the world was approaching and that, because followers would have no need for their money in the future, they should give it to the defendants.

Besides charging Edna and Donald Ballard with making eighteen false representations, the government alleged that they "well knew" that these representations were false. Although the defendants had not even called their system a "religion" until they were subjected to prosecution, they attacked the indictment against them as a violation of their rights under the Free Exercise Clause. In 1943 U.S. District Court for the Southern District of California refused to dismiss the charges against the Ballards, but after conferring with their attorneys and the prosecutors, the trial judge did inform the jury that "the religious beliefs of these defendants cannot be an issue in this court." The only matter for the jurors to decide, he told them, was whether the Ballards "honestly and in good faith" believed the things they had professed. Apparently thankful to avoid the issue of whether the defendants had made false representations, their attorneys acquiesced in the judge's handling of this matter. Although his charge was favorable to the defendants, the jury convicted the Ballards anyway.

The Ballards appealed their convictions and in *Ballard et al. v. United States* (9th Cir. 1943) the Ninth Circuit Court of Appeals concluded that the trial judge had been wrong to restrict the jury to considering only the issue of the defendants' good faith. The Ninth Circuit's opinion was extremely murky, but apparently the majority believed that the trial court's instruction had freed the prosecution from having to prove all the allegations contained in the indictment. In its opinion, whether the Ballards' "representations were false or true was a question which should have been submitted to the jury."

In *United States v. Ballard* (1944) the U.S. Supreme Court disagreed. "[W]e do not agree that the truth or verity of respondents' religious doctrines or beliefs should have been submitted to the jury," Justice William O. Douglas wrote in an opinion handed down on April 24, 1944. According to Douglas, the First Amendment protected "the right to maintain theories of life and death and of the hereafter which are rank heresy to followers of orthodox faiths. Heresy trials," he added, "are foreign to our Constitution." Although the Ballards' views "might seem incredible, if not preposterous, to most people," if their doctrines were "subject to trial before a jury charged with finding their truth or falsity, then the same can be done with the religious beliefs of any sect." Because the Ninth Circuit had ruled that jurors should decide that issue, Douglas concluded by reversing its decision and remanding the case to that court. He never discussed whether the trial judge had been wrong to permit the jury to pass on the Ballards' sincerity.

In dissent, Chief Justice Harlan Fiske Stone contended that the convictions should have been affirmed. While insisting that freedom of thought and worship did not include freedom to procure money by knowingly making false statements, Stone based his opinion on what he viewed as the Ballards' acquiescence in the withdrawal of the issue of the truth of their views from the jury. Justices Owen Roberts and Felix Frankfurter joined this dissent.

Justice Robert Jackson arrived at a very different conclusion—and did so on the basis of reasoning that confronted head on the issue that Douglas had avoided. As Jackson saw it, rather than remanding the case to the Ninth Circuit, the Supreme Court should have dismissed the indictments against the Ballards. In his opinion, a judicial inquiry into the sincerity with which religious beliefs were held was no more justifiable than a determination of their truth or falsehood. In the first place, the issues were not readily separable, because the believability of views was evidence from which one could infer whether a defendant did or did not believe them. "In the second place, an inquiry into intellectual honesty in religion raises profound psychological problems." Jackson purported not to "know what degree of skepticism or disbelief in a religious representation amounts to actionable fraud." Since those who gave money to preachers derived comfort from doing so even if those preachers did not really believe their own professions, these "overcredulous people" got what they paid for. Jackson feared that prosecutions for religious fraud might degenerate into religious persecution, and consequently he thought that they should not be allowed. Jackson thus concluded: "I would dismiss the indictment and have done with this business of judicially examining other people's faith."

The Supreme Court had an opportunity to address that issue two years later, when the Ballard case returned to Washington, but it declined to do so. This time the Ninth Circuit had affirmed the convictions. Justices Jackson, Frankfurter, and Burton and Chief Justice Vinson wanted the Court to decide what Frankfurter characterized as "the central issue before us, namely whether the mails may be used to obtain money by fraud when the fraud consists of a false claim of belief touching on religion." But the majority, with Douglas again acting as its spokesman, avoided that question by dismissing the charges against the Ballards because women had been excluded from the grand jury that indicted them.

Since 1946 the Supreme Court has permitted governmental inquiries into the sincerity of an individual's religious beliefs when that individual cited those beliefs in seeking special treatment from the government (such as an exemption from compulsory military service or compulsory school attendance laws). But the Court has not decided whether government may punish charlatans who trick others out of their money by persuading them to accept religious concepts that the preachers themselves do not believe. One of the two major issues posed by *Ballard* remains unresolved.

Michal R. Belknap

Bibliography

Heins, Majorie, "'Other People's Faiths': The Scientology Litigation and the Justiciability of Religious Fraud," 9 *Hastings Constitutional Law Quarterly* 153–197 (1981).

Nowak, John E., and Ronald D. Rotunda, *Constitutional Law*, 4th ed. (St. Paul, Minn.: West, 1991), pp. 1239–1242.

Tribe, Lawrence H., *American Constitutional Law*, 2nd ed. (Mineola, N.Y.: Foundation Press, 1988), pp. 1243–1246.

Cases Cited

United States v. Ballard, 138 F. 2d 540 (9th Cir. 1943).

United States v. Ballard, 322 U.S. 78 (1944).

United States v. Ballard, 329 U.S. 187 (1946).

United States v. Dwight Dion, Sr. 476 U.S. 734 (1986)

The U.S. District Court for the Southern District of South Dakota convicted Dwight Dion, Sr., a Yankton Sioux, for shooting four bald eagles on the Yankton Reservation in violation of the Endangered Species Act (1973) and for selling carcasses and parts of eagles and other birds in violation of the Bald Eagle Protection Act (1940). The Eighth Circuit Court of Appeals reversed the conviction that was based on the Endangered Species Act, holding that an 1858 treaty granted Yankton Sioux the right to hunt bald eagles on the Yankton Reservation for noncommercial purposes. In *United States v. Dwight Dion, Sr.* (1986) the Supreme Court reversed the court of appeals, stating that Congress abrogated those treaty rights when it passed the Bald Eagle Protection Act and subsequent revisions.

For a unanimous Court, Justice Thurgood Marshall wrote an opinion that dealt a blow to Indian treaty rights and religious freedom. Dion maintained that he and other Sioux had an unrestricted right to hunt eagles on their reservations because of treaty guarantees, the First Amendment, and the Indian Bill of Rights Free Exercise Clause. Eagle feathers are an important part of traditional Indian religions, and to enforce federal laws, Dion argued, amounted to restricting fundamental rights of religious free exercise.

Instead, Marshall concluded that Indians did not have unrestricted rights to hunt eagles on their reservations, because of the supremacy of federal legislation. He did so by reviewing previous case law, particularly *Lone Wolf v. Hitchcock* (1903), where the Supreme Court ruled that Congress had plenary power over all Indian issues, including the voiding of past treaties by legislation. Marshall noted the importance of Indian treaty rights, but he looked to congressional intent to understand whether treaty rights were to be retained. Because the Bald Eagle Protection Act allowed the limited taking of eagles for religious purposes, he found that Congress knew that the effect of the act would be to abrogate existing hunting treaty rights. Furthermore, records of hearings on the bill indicated congressional awareness of the potential effects the act could have on Indian culture and religion.

The *Dion* opinion is more significant for what was *not* discussed. Marshall refused to consider the religious implications of his holding, but the reality was that federal needs to preserve eagles took precedence over Indian rights to practice their religion. His opinion kept a line of case law intact that does not allow Indians to claim coverage of their traditional religious practices under the First Amendment. Moreover, Marshall ignored Indian Bill of Rights issues and the American Indian Religious Freedom Act (1978). Marshall also refused to consider the federal government's position that the treaty's right to hunt did not preclude regulation to prevent the extinction of a species—a bone of contention left over from the Pacific Northwest fishing rights cases.

John R. Wunder and Todd Kerstetter

Bibliography

Deloria, Vine, Jr., and Clifford M. Lytle, *The Nations Within: The Past and Future of American Indian Sovereignty* (New York: Pantheon, 1984).

——— and ———, *American Indians, American Justice* (Austin: University of Texas Press, 1983).

Prucha, Frances Paul, *The Great Father: The United States Government and the American Indians*, 2 vols. (Lincoln: University of Nebraska Press, 1984).

Wilkinson, Charles F., *American Indians, Time, and the Law: Native Societies in a Modern Constitutional Democracy* (New Haven, Conn.: Yale University Press, 1987).

Wunder, John R., *"Retained by the People": A History of American Indians and the Bill of Rights* (New York: Oxford University Press, 1993).

Cases Cited

Lone Wolf v. Hitchcock, 187 U.S. 553 (1903).

United States v. Dwight Dion, Sr., 476 U.S. 734 (1986).

United States v. Lee
455 U.S. 252 (1982)

United States v. Lee (1982) is one of a series of cases in the constitutional debate over whether the Free Exercise Clause of the First Amendment demands that federal and state governments exempt religiously motivated individuals from laws that burden their religious practices or convictions. A decade before this case, in the landmark decision *Wisconsin v. Yoder* (1972), the Supreme Court ruled that the Free Exercise Clause requires exemptions for religiously motivated behavior unless the state can show a compelling state interest to the contrary. In that case, the Court exempted Old Order Amish children from compulsory school laws. *Lee*, another case involving Amish plantiffs, raised a similar but unsuccessful challenge to payment of employer Social Security taxes. In this case, the Supreme Court followed the reasoning set forth in *Yoder* but unanimously refused to extend religious-based exemptions to the system of taxation. Chief Justice Warren Burger, who authored the majority opinion in *Yoder*, wrote a brief opinion here, which seven other justices joined. Justice John Paul Stevens filed a concurring opinion, taking issue with the fundamental reasoning behind constitutionally required exemptions.

Members of the Old Order Amish are religiously required to care for their own elderly and needy and therefore are religiously opposed to participating in the national Social Security system. Lee, a member of the Old Order Amish, employed several other Amish to work on his farm and in his carpentry shop. Based on his religious conviction, he refused to withhold his employees' Social Security taxes or to pay the employer's share. (Self-employed persons with religious objections have statutory exemptions from the Social Security Act; as an employer, Lee did not qualify.) Lee claimed that the imposition of Social Security taxes on him violated the free exercise rights of Old Order Amish employers and employees. The Supreme Court accepted Lee's contention that compulsory participation in the Social Security system interfered with his free exercise rights. However, the Court noted that "[n]ot all burdens on religion are unconstitutional. . . . The state may justify a limitation on religious liberty by showing that it is essential to accomplish an overriding governmental interest." Citing the "overriding interest" in the integrity of the federal system of income taxation, the Court found sufficient justification to override Lee's objections to participation.

Chief Justice Burger emphasized that the design of the Social Security system requires mandatory contributions. Making them voluntary would undermine the soundness of the program and would make a comprehensive system difficult, if not impossible, to administer. *Lee* was distinguished from *Yoder,* in which exempting the Amish from compulsory school laws did not undermine the school system as a whole. To exempt individuals from taxation because they have religious objections to the purposes for which tax money is spent would play havoc with national policy. Burger concluded that Lee, having chosen to enter into commercial activity, was obligated to abide by the generally applicable statutory scheme.

Justice John Paul Stevens's concurring opinion raised an issue that would become increasingly divisive over the next decade: the "compelling state interest" standard. This standard reverses the traditional burden of proof and requires that the government justify laws that burden religious liberty. Chief Justice Burger had accepted the compelling interest standard, although he did not apply it in any depth. In contrast, Justice Stevens rejected this reversal of burdens: "In my opinion, it is the objector who must shoulder the burden of demonstrating that there is a unique reason for allowing him a special exemption from a valid law of general applicability." In fact, he argued, seriously applying the compelling interest standard should have produced the opposite result—the social cost of accommodating the Amish would be minimal. The problem with granting Lee's exemption is not its difficulty but the fact that doing so would put government in a position of evaluating the relative merits of different religious claims, thus violating the Establishment Clause. To avoid such dangers, Stevens would find "virtually no room for a 'constitutionally required exemption' on religious grounds." Thus, he concurs with the Court and provides an argument that later courts would find persuasive in rejecting the full impact of *Yoder.*

Bette Novit Evans

Bibliography

Duthu, N. Bruce, "Note: *U.S. v. Lee:* Limitations on the Free Exercise of Religion," 28 *Loyola Law Review* 1216–1225 (1982).

Wiles, John Jamison, "Note: Has the Retreat Been Sounded for Free Exercise?" 12 *Stetson Law Review* 852–864 (1983).

Cases Cited

United States v. Lee, 455 U.S. 252 (1982).

Wisconsin v. Yoder, 406 U.S. 205 (1972).

V

Vatican and Diplomatic Recognition

American diplomatic recognition of territory governed by the Roman Catholic Church has generated controversy for more than a century. Although the United States appointed a consul to the Papal States in 1797 and established formal diplomatic relations in 1848, diplomatic ties were severed in 1867 after Congress terminated appropriations for the American legation in the wake of outcries over interference with public worship by Protestants in Rome.

In 1939, shortly after the outbreak of World War II, President Franklin D. Roosevelt appointed a personal representative to Vatican City, a 109-acre territory bounded by Rome that had been politically independent since 1929. Roosevelt's representative, Myron C. Taylor (who was not part of the diplomatic service and served without compensation) acted as a liaison between the president and the pope in mutual efforts to restore peace and alleviate the suffering caused by the war. The appointment provoked protests from various Protestant churches, which expressed fear that this would lead to more formal ties. Taylor continued to serve under President Harry S. Truman, who contended that the appointment was merely temporary.

After Taylor resigned in January 1950, Truman in 1951 proposed formal diplomatic ties with the Vatican and nominated General Mark W. Clark to serve as ambassador. Truman withdrew the nomination in the wake of opposition from the National Council of Churches (NCC), Protestants United for Separation of Church and State, and other organizations. Although Presidents Eisenhower, Kennedy, and Johnson did not appoint any representative to the Vatican, President Nixon in 1970 named Henry Cabot Lodge as his personal representative. Presidents Ford, Carter, and Reagan also appointed personal representatives to the Vatican.

In 1983 Congress opened the way for the appointment of an ambassador by repealing the 1867 prohibition on expenditures for a diplomatic mission to the papacy. Proponents of the repeal contended that the Vatican's international political role was increasingly important—particularly its efforts to promote peace and human rights. They also pointed out that most other noncommunist nations recognized the Vatican, including Great Britain since 1980. Appointment of an ambassador was opposed by a broad range of groups, including the NCC, the American Jewish Congress, and the Baptist Joint Committee on Public Affairs. The U.S. Catholic Conference remained silent on the issue. In March 1984 the Senate, by a vote of 81 to 13, confirmed the appointment of William A. Wilson as the nation's first ambassador to the Vatican.

In 1985 the government's action was challenged in a lawsuit in U.S. District Court in Pennsylvania brought by Americans United for Separation of Church and State, twenty religious organizations, and several dozen individuals including Jewish, Protestant, and Unitarian clergy. The lawsuit alleged that U.S. diplomatic relations with the Vatican violated the First Amendment's Establishment Clause, exceeded the president's constitutional powers, and resulted in special preference for one religious group over others in violation of the equal protection component of the Due Process Clause of the Fifth Amendment.

In April 1986 the U.S. Court of Appeals for the Third Circuit affirmed a federal district court's dismissal of the lawsuit in *Americans United for Separation of Church and State et al. v. Reagan* (3rd Cir. 1986). Like the district court, the court of appeals ruled that the plaintiffs lacked standing to challenge the president's action. The court explained that they lacked standing as taxpayers because the expenditures of which they complained were only incidental to the establishment of diplomatic relations and did not directly arise under the congressional taxing and spending power or exceed specific constitutional limitations on that power.

The court also held that the plaintiffs lacked standing as citizens because they failed to demonstrate that they suffered any invasion of any specific right of citizenship. It further rejected the plaintiffs' contention that they had standing because recognition of the Vatican would deny them equal access to the president, stigmatize them as "second class citizens, subscribing to religions of lesser worth," enhance the Catholic Church's ability to compete for new members, and subject non-Catholics to subtle pressures to conform to governmental policies influenced by the Vatican.

The court further held that the lawsuit would have to be dismissed even if the plaintiffs had standing, because the issue was a judicially nonreviewable "political question." The court explained that the Constitution confers on the president the sole power to recognize foreign states, which the court described as "one of the rare governmental decisions that the Constitution commits exclusively to the Executive Branch." The U.S. Supreme Court refused to hear an appeal.

In 1993 President Clinton nominated Boston Mayor Raymond Flynn to serve as ambassador to the Vatican. This nomination generated opposition from Americans United, the NCC, and various Protestant denominations, which continued to allege that diplomatic ties with the Vatican violated the Constitution. These organizations also complained that the post seemed to be reserved for Roman Catholics, inasmuch as Flynn, like the two previous ambassadors, was Catholic. Flynn generated additional controversy by insisting that he would like to actively assist the Vatican in efforts to promote peace in strife-torn areas of the world. An unauthorized peace mission by Ambassador Wilson several years earlier had led to his resignation. Despite this controversy, the Senate confirmed Flynn.

William G. Ross

Bibliography

Pfeffer, Leo, *Church and State and Freedom,* 2nd ed. (Boston: Beacon Press, 1967).

Stokes, Anson Phelps, *Church and State in the United States,* Vol. II (New York: Harper and Brothers, 1950).

Cases Cited

Americans United for Separation of Church and State et al. v. Reagan, 786 F. 2d 194 (3rd Cir. 1986), cert. denied, 479 U.S. 914 (1986).

Americans United for Separation of Church and State et al. v. Reagan, 607 F. Supp. 747 (E.D. Pa. 1985).

Vidal v. Girard's Executor 43 U.S. (2 How.) 127 (1844)

In his Opinion of the Court in *McCollum v. Board of Education* (1948), Justice Felix Frankfurter asserted that the case of *Vidal v. Girard's Executor* (1844) established that "[s]eparation in the field of education . . . was not imposed on unwilling States by [the] force of superior law," found in the Fourteenth Amendment, but rather "the prohibition of [state] furtherance . . . of religious instruction [was, as early as *Girard,*] the guiding principle, in law and feeling, of the American people." Professor James McClellan in *Justice Story and the American Constitution* draws a very different conclusion, claiming that, in fact, Justice Joseph Story "argues for . . . the no preference theory; . . . that the prohibition of laws respecting the free exercise of religion simply forbids the extension of preferential aid to a single religious sect," and that Justice Frankfurter's opinion, championing strict separation, has stood Justice Story's position on its head.

The exchange between justice and professor seems to be one of the few instances in which the case has recently entered into the debate on religious freedom. Its relative contemporary obscurity is totally in contrast to the celebrity the case enjoyed when argued before the Court in 1844. For both social and political Washington—and indeed for readers of newspapers across the country—the challenge to the will of the French-born Philadelphia financier Stephen Girard by what Story's biographer Gerald T. Dunne refers to as "the passed-over French relatives" combined Americans' enduring fascination with wealth with their interest in religion, and it consumed ten days of oral argument.

At his death, Girard, an investor in both the First and Second Banks of the United States, was worth close to seven million dollars, most of which he left to the City of Philadelphia "to provide for . . . poor male white orphan children . . . a better education, as well as more comfortable maintenance than they usually receive from . . . public funds. . . ." His exceedingly detailed will left little to chance, spelling out such things as the height of ceilings and the types of construction materials to be used in the college. More controversially it "require[d] that no . . . minister of any sect . . . , shall ever . . . be admitted . . ." to the college.

Represented by Walter Jones and Daniel Webster, the relatives claimed that Philadelphia was not authorized to administer the trust, that the beneficiaries were not clearly defined, and that the clergy prohibition was contrary to public policy because of its hostility to Christianity. Horace Binney and John Sergeant represented the city and, according to Charles Warren, performed so ably that President Tyler offered both men appointments to the Supreme Court, which both rejected. They argued that the ban was the best "way to preserve the sacred rights of conscience," given Girard's desire to admit orphans of all religious backgrounds, and that if New York could ban clergy from the legislature, Girard could ban them from his educational institution.

Speaking for a unanimous Court, Justice Joseph Story, who had presided in the absence of the unwell Chief Justice Taney, upheld the will, essentially reversing Marshall's decision in *Baptist Association v. Hart's Executors* (1819), in which he had concurred. Story explained that subsequent legal research had undermined the basis on which the earlier case had rested. As a result, he rejected the challenge to the city's power and the claim that the beneficiaries were not precisely specified. In rejecting Jones's argument against "the cruel experiment" that Girard had perpetrated, Story—who in a Harvard lecture had asserted that Christianity was part of the common law—championed self-restraint, noting that it was irrelevant "whether . . . [the will] is satisfactory to us or not . . . ," but enough that it did not mandate that "anything be taught inconsistent with Christianity." Story also emphasized that the will did not forbid laypeople from providing religious instruction and that the requirement that morality be taught would inevitably lead to reliance on the Bible, for "[w]here can the purest principles of morality be learned so clearly and so perfectly as from the New Testament?"

To his wife, Story scoffed at his friend Webster's argument and branded it "altogether an address to the prejudices of the clergy." Aside from histrionics that Carl Swisher characterized as causing "tears [to] pour from the eyes of sentimental observers [while] hardened reporters smirked about 'the Gospel according to Webster,'" Webster did raise what today would be seen as a free exercise issue by calling attention to the disadvantage caused by the clergy exclusion to those sects which did not allow lay teaching of religion.

Webster prophesied that "[i]f Girard had desired to bring trouble . . . , he could have done it in no more effectual way" than by his will. The prediction was borne out in *Pennsylvania v. Board of Directors of City Trusts of the City of Philadelphia* (1957) and *Brown v. Commonwealth of Pennsylvania* (1968), which challenged the exclusion of African Americans. The Court in *Brown* concluded that the college was sufficiently public to render its activities "state action." In light of *McDaniel v. Paty* (1978), invalidating a Tennessee ban on clergy serving in the legislature, and *Widmar v. Vincent* (1981), overturning the University of Missouri's ban on religious worship on campus—both based on the Free Exercise Clause—whether further challenges might be lodged against Girard College remains to be seen.

F. Graham Lee

Bibliography

Dunne, Gerald T., *Justice Joseph Story and the Rise of the Supreme Court* (New York: Simon and Schuster, 1970).

Keats, John, "Legacy of Stephen Girard," 29 *American Heritage* 38–47 (1978).

McClellan, James, *Justice Story and the American Constitution* (Norman: University of Oklahoma Press, 1971).

Swisher, Carl B., *The Taney Court 1836–1864: History of the Supreme Court of the United States,* Vol. V (New York: Macmillan, 1974).

Warren, Charles, *The Supreme Court in United States History,* Vol. II (Boston: Little, Brown, 1922).

Cases Cited

Baptist Association v. Hart's Executors 17 U.S. (4 Wheat) 1 (1819).

Brown v. Commonwealth of Pennsylvania, 391 U.S. 921 (1968).

McCollum v. Board of Education, 333 U.S. 203 (1948).

McDaniel v. Paty, 435 U.S. 618 (1978).

Pennsylvania v. Board of Directors of City Trusts of the City of Philadelphia, 353 U.S. 230 (1957) and 357 U.S. 570 (1958).

Vidal v. Girard's Executor, 43 U.S. (2 How.) 127 (1844).

Widmar v. Vincent, 453 U.S. 263 (1981).

Virginia Statute of Religious Liberty

Drafted by Thomas Jefferson in 1776–1777 and rejected by the Virginia Assembly in 1779, the Statute of Religious Liberty was finally enacted January 16, 1786, when Jefferson was American minister in Paris. Jefferson's friend and collaborator James Madison guided the bill to passage, overcoming growing popular support for a general, nonpreferential establishment of religion in the state. In addition to his legislative skills—first in delaying action (December 1784) and then in defeating a general assessment bill (November 1785)—Madison provided an eloquent and persuasive rationale for disestablishment in his *Memorial and Remonstrance against Religious Assessments* (May 1785). Along with Jefferson's preamble to the statute, Madison's *Memorial and Remonstrance* is a key text in defining the principles of religious liberty and the separation of church and state. The struggle for religious freedom in Virginia would in turn have a profound impact on national developments as Madison—the "Father of the Constitution" and leading advocate of a Bill of Rights in the first federal Congress—incorporated Virginian language and logic into the Establishment Clause of what would become the First Amendment.

The Virginia Statute of Religious Freedom consists of three sections: an extended preamble, setting forth the act's philosophical premises; the act itself ("no man shall be compelled to frequent or support any religious worship," nor should suffer any restraint or civil penalty for holding or freely expressing "his religious opinions and belief"); and a concluding warning to future legislatures that repeal of the act or any substantive "narrow[ing] of its operation" would be an "infringement of natural right."

Passage of the statute was made possible by an alliance of evangelical dissenters and of patriot leaders such as Jefferson and Madison who recognized the liabilities of an established church. The preamble reflected this political context, as well as Jefferson's commitment to Enlightenment principles. "To compel a man to furnish contributions of money for the propagation of opinions which he disbelieves, is sinful and tyrannical," wrote Jefferson, confident in his own belief "that truth is great and will prevail if left to itself." Such language could not conceal fundamental theological and epistemological differences between pious dissenters and Jeffersonian advocates of "natural" religion: Was "truth" revealed in Scripture, or through "free argument and debate"? But evangelicals and rationalists could agree that the Anglican establishment was incompatible with the pursuit of religious truth, whatever its sources. With a history of religious persecution by colony authorities fresh in their minds, members of the dissenting sects eagerly endorsed both the Jeffersonian principle that "our civil rights [ought to] have no dependence on our religious opinions" and his conclusion that the Anglican establishment therefore should be dismantled.

During the colonial period, state-supported churches reinforced the dominance of Virginia's first families. Parish vestrymen and justices of the county courts (often the same men) exercised all local governmental powers. Though unelected, these oligarchs took pride in their responsiveness to their humbler neighbors' demands. But the "evangelical revolt," beginning with the Presbyterian revivals of the 1760s and spreading with the Baptist insurgency of the 1770s, threatened this established order. The Anglican churches obviously failed to meet the religious needs of the common folk—and of a growing number of evangelical converts from leading families. Meanwhile, at a time when patriot leaders were mobilizing popular support against British tyranny, the use of punitive legal sanctions to stifle dissent and preserve the establishment's privileged position raised fundamental questions about gentry responsiveness.

When Independence was declared in 1776, Revolutionary leaders recognized the need to defuse evangelical discontent. But few were prepared to move beyond toleration to join Jefferson and Madison in urging disestablishment. Tension within the patriot leadership was apparent in the debate over Section 16 of the Declaration of Rights in Virginia's 1776 Constitution. The Virginia convention adopted Madison's language, guaranteeing "free exercise of religion," but rejected his proposal for disestablishment. Yet even in its adopted form, the declaration subverted the moral foundations of state support while prohibiting the use of force against religious dissenters. Section 16 thus anticipated the logic of Jefferson's Statute of Religious Liberty and Madison's *Memorial and Remonstrance,* asserting that "the duty which we owe to our creator, can be directed only by reason and conviction, not by force or violence."

Jefferson and Madison were prepared to demolish the Anglican establishment because of their confidence in the durability of Virginia's social order. Like the imperial connection itself, a legally privileged establishment was a source of unnecessary discontent and disorder. Virginia's "natural" leaders therefore had nothing to fear from the elimination of privilege and the expansion of popular political participation, particularly at the local level. But conservatives in the Revolutionary leadership balked at Jefferson's proposals for legal and constitutional reform, including the establishment of state-supported schools—and the end of state support for the Anglican establishment.

Ironically, however, the most serious obstacle to disestablishment proved to be popular politics, not conservative obstructionism. Patrick Henry—like Madison, a long-standing friend of the evangelical sects—threw his support behind a general assessment bill that would guarantee state support for all denominations. Madison's legislative legerdemain in 1784–1785 was designed to shore up his old alliance with the dissenters, particularly with the Presbyterians. Madison was disappointed in his hopes that a successful bill incorporating the Episcopal (Anglican) Church (December 1784) would abort the campaign for general assessment, but he did succeed in gaining a crucial delay. His *Memorial and Remonstrance* recurred to Section 16 and Jefferson's preamble but was framed in terms that evangelicals would find more compelling. Religious liberty was—or should be—a "right" toward other men, Madison claimed, but it was a "duty towards the Creator," a duty that was "precedent, both in order of time and in degree of obligation, to the claims of civil society."

The ultimate passage of the statute may have been a vindication of Jefferson's enlightened conception of the proper relation between state and society. But Madison's experience in pushing the bill through the legislature reinforced his own growing concerns about the dangers of majority factionalism in a democratic polity, expressed most memorably in *Federalist* No. 10. If the danger of a nonpreferential (and politically unassailable) establishment had been averted, Madison and Jefferson knew that religious freedom—and other constitutional guarantees—remained vulnerable to the changing will of the electorate. The politics of disestablishment in Virginia thus were as important for explaining Madison's enthusiastic support for national constitutional reform as would be the language of the Statute of Religious Liberty in drafting the First Amendment.

Peter S. Onuf

Bibliography

Peterson, Merrill D., and Robert C. Vaughan, *The Virginia Statute for Religious Freedom: Its Evolution and Consequences in American History* (New York: Cambridge University Press, 1988).

W

Wallace v. Jaffree
472 U.S. 38 (1985)

In *Engel v. Vitale* (1962) and *School District of Abington Township v. Schempp* (1963), the Supreme Court interpreted the Establishment Clause to prohibit spoken group prayer and similar devotional exercises in the public schools. These decisions were enormously controversial, and the controversy has not died, with many Americans continuing to believe that spoken group prayer should be permitted. Unsuccessful in their efforts to adopt a constitutional amendment to achieve this result, however, critics of the Court's decisions have pursued alternative measures. One common alternative is the "moment-of-silence law," versions of which have now been adopted by approximately half the states. In varying language, these statutes authorize moments of silence in the public schools—moments that may be used by religious students as a time for silent prayer. It was inevitable that these laws would be challenged, and the question of their constitutionality reached the Supreme Court in 1985. In a range of opinions, the justices in *Wallace v. Jaffree* (1985) confronted not only the moment-of-silence issue but also broader questions concerning the proper meaning and application of the Establishment Clause.

Wallace arose as a challenge to each of three Alabama statutes concerning the public schools, one enacted in 1978, another in 1981, and the third in 1982. The 1978 statute authorized a period of silence "for meditation." The 1981 law separately authorized a period of silence "for meditation or voluntary prayer." The 1982 enactment authorized a prescribed spoken prayer, this in direct contravention of *Engel* and *Schempp*.

The challengers ultimately abandoned their attack on the 1978 statute. The district court upheld the 1981 statute and, remarkably, the 1982 statute as well. Ignoring decades of Supreme Court precedent, Judge W. Brevard Hand concluded that the Fourteenth Amendment did not "incorporate" the Establishment Clause for application against the states and that Alabama therefore was free to ignore the Establishment Clause altogether. The court of appeals reversed, invalidating both the 1981 and the 1982 statutes, and the Supreme Court affirmed this ruling.

In accepting the case for review, the Supreme Court unanimously and summarily affirmed the court of appeals invalidation of the 1982 statute authorizing spoken prayer. When the Court later issued its decision on the 1981 statute, moreover, Justice John Paul Stevens, speaking for the Court, chastised District Judge Hand for refusing to honor the Court's incorporation decisions. Justice Stevens did not meaningfully answer Judge Hand's historical arguments concerning the original understanding of the Fourteenth Amendment, but he did resoundingly reaffirm the Court's incorporation doctrine. Even Justice William H. Rehnquist, in his dissenting opinion, accepted the incorporation issue as settled. All this suggests that, however else the Court might modify its Establishment Clause doctrine, its incorporation and spoken-prayer decisions are not likely to be overturned.

In contrast to its decisions about incorporation and spoken prayer, the Court was deeply divided on the moment-of-silence issue. It invalidated Alabama's 1981 statute by a vote of 6 to 3 but the justices' various opinions suggested that other moment-of-silence statutes were likely to survive constitutional scrutiny. Writing for a majority of five, Justice Stevens found that the Alabama statute's authorization of a moment of silence "for meditation or voluntary prayer" was "entirely motivated by a purpose to advance religion." As such, it violated the "secular purpose" requirement of *Lemon v. Kurtzman* (1971). Justice Stevens focused especially on the language and the sequence of the three enactments in Alabama. Given the 1978 law authorizing silent "meditation," Stevens argued that the 1981 statute was largely superfluous except for its "voluntary prayer" language. As a result, he concluded that the legislature had acted in 1981 with the constitutionally impermissible purpose of endorsing and promoting religion. Justice Stevens's conclusion also was supported by candid statements from the legislative sponsor of the 1981 law and by the fact that the Alabama legislature went on in 1982 to authorize a prescribed spoken prayer that was clearly unconstitutional.

In a separate opinion, Justice Sandra Day O'Connor concurred in the Court's judgment. Like Justice Stevens, she concluded that the Alabama law's peculiar legislative history rendered it infirm, but she emphasized that other moment-of-silence statutes would stand on a different footing. Justice Lewis F. Powell, Jr., who had joined the majority opinion, also submitted a concurrence in which he agreed that many moment-of-silence laws might well be constitutional. Along with Justice Rehnquist, Chief Justice Warren E. Burger and Justice Byron R. White each submitted a separate dissent.

The various opinions in *Wallace* indicate that the justices would have upheld many moment-of-silence laws. Justice Stevens's majority opinion itself suggested that a law not mentioning prayer would be constitutionally permissible. The five justices who wrote separate opinions, moreover, apparently would have approved many laws that do mention prayer. The three dissenters, of course, would have upheld even the Alabama law. Justices O'Connor and Powell would not, but they obviously regarded the Alabama legislative history as highly unusual. Absent such stark evidence of an exclusively religious motivation, Justice O'Connor clearly would have upheld a law explicitly stating that the period of silence could be used for prayer as well as for meditation or reflection, and Justice Powell probably would have joined her.

In his lengthy dissent, Justice Rehnquist argued that the *Wallace* majority was wrong not only in rejecting the Alabama law but also in their general approach to the Establishment Clause. Although he accepted incorporation, Rehnquist challenged the Court's doctrine by focusing on the original understanding of the First Amendment. He claimed that properly interpreted, the First Amendment permits the government to favor religion as long as it avoids discrimination among competing religious sects. On this view, there is no need for subtle distinctions concerning the purpose or form of moment-of-silence laws, for the government is perfectly free to "characterize prayer as a favored practice."

Daniel O. Conkle

Bibliography

Smith, Rodney K., "Now Is the Time for Reflection: *Wallace v. Jaffree* and Its Legislative Aftermath," 37 *Alabama Law Review* 345–389 (1986).

Cases Cited

Engel v. Vitale, 370 U.S. 421 (1962).
Lemon v. Kurtzman, 403 U.S. 602 (1971).
School District of Abington Township v. Schempp, 374 U.S. 203 (1963).
Wallace v. Jaffree, 472 U.S. 38 (1985).

Widmar v. Vincent
454 U.S. 263 (1981)

Can the state allow citizens to use public facilities for secular purposes but not for religious ones? *Widmar v. Vincent* (1981) is one of the most important cases in behalf of the proposition that the answer is "no." According to *Widmar,* religious speech cannot, in the name of protecting against an establishment of religion, be selected out by the state for worse treatment than secular speech when the state generally makes its facilities available for public use.

The case arose at the University of Missouri in Kansas City, which had a policy of allowing all registered student organizations to meet in university facilities and carry out their activities. One such group was Cornerstone, an organization of evangelical Christian students from a variety of denominational backgrounds. From 1973 to 1977 Cornerstone regularly conducted its meetings in university-owned buildings. This permission was, however, withdrawn in 1977, when the university decided that Cornerstone's meetings—which included prayer, hymns, and Bible commentary—violated a 1972 prohibition against the use of university buildings or grounds "for purposes of religious worship or religious teaching." Members of Cornerstone sued, claiming that the exclusion of their organization from university facilities violated their rights both to freedom of speech and to the free exercise of religion under the First Amendment. The Supreme Court, with only one dissent, agreed, though it did not reach the free exercise claim. Instead, it decided the case under existing precedents relating to regulation of freedom of speech.

The majority, in an opinion written by Justice Lewis Powell, treated the case under the branch of free-speech law relating to access to so-called public forums. The Court noted that the university had "created a forum generally open for use by student groups," which numbered more than a hundred at the time of the litigation. "The Constitution forbids a State to enforce certain exclusions from a forum generally open to the public, even if it was not required to create the forum in the first place." In the instant case the university had "discriminated against student groups and speakers based on their desire to use a generally open forum to engage in religious worship and discussion." Their desire to worship did not give them any *special* rights (which would be the brunt of a free exercise determination); but it also could not serve as the basis for treating the speech acts of worship and religious discussion in a different manner than all the other speech acts that the university freely welcomed into its buildings.

A central tenet of contemporary constitutional law is that the state cannot base exclusions from generally available forums on the *content* of the speech of those seeking access to the venue. Any such exclusions trigger the Supreme Court's most exacting standard of review, "strict scrutiny," which requires that the state demonstrate that the regulation in question "serve[s] a compelling state interest and that it is narrowly drawn to achieve that end." The university could not satisfy this test.

As noted, the primary interest asserted by the state was its duty to adhere to the Establishment Clauses of both the United States and the Missouri constitutions. Because the university facilities were maintained through public taxes, the university argued that allowing their use by groups engaged in active services of worship and religious witness would, in effect, be an illegitimate public subsidy of religion. Justice Powell responded, however, that cases had long held that "a religious organization's enjoyment of merely 'incidental' benefits does not violate the Constitution." Rather, Powell affirmed that the Constitution only prohibits the "primary advancement" of religion. He compared the assistance provided by allowing Cornerstone to meet in university facilities with the fire and police protection that is unproblematically provided to churches and other religious groups.

The Court emphasized the "narrow[ness]" of its decision. "Having created a forum generally open to student groups, the university" cannot then exclude only religious organizations from the access it freely grants any other group. Had no forum been created, Cornerstone would not have had an independent, free exercise–based right to use the facilities. Indeed, the opinion left open the possibility that a different result would have been reached if "empirical evidence" indicated "that religious groups will dominate [the university's] open forum."

Justice Stevens refused to join the Court's opinion, although he accepted the result. He was critical of what he viewed as the relatively blithe application of standard public-forum and no-content-discrimination law to a university setting. Nobody doubts, after all, that universities often properly take content into account in allocating their scarce facilities. A university could, for example, prefer a student group putting on *Hamlet* to one showing cartoons, based on its determination that Shakespeare has greater educational value than Mickey Mouse. He did agree, though, that the instant case left the university with no defense. Its policy would apparently "allow groups of young philosophers to meet to discuss their skepticism that a Supreme Being exists, or a group of political scientists to meet to debate the accuracy of the view that religion is the 'opium of the people.' If school facilities may be used to discuss anticlerical doctrine, it seems to me that comparable use by a group desiring to express a belief in God must also be permitted," and this expression of belief can include what Justice Stevens labels "ceremonial conduct."

Justice White dissented. He viewed "worship" as presenting legitimate difficulties for state institutions striving to remain faithful to the Establishment Clause. He also emphasized that there would be little cost to the legitimate free exercise interests of Cornerstone members, given their ability to meet—albeit "under conditions less comfortable than those previously available on campus"—within a couple of blocks of the campus.

Widmar has become important as an *equality* case disallowing the state from treating religious speech, including even worship, worse than it treats secular speech. Its egalitarian vision in part underlies the Equal Access Act passed by Congress in 1984, which prohibits public high schools that receive federal aid from denying religious, philosophical, or political student groups access to its facilities if it grants such access to any other "noncurriculum related" student groups. The constitutionality of the act was upheld, against an Establishment Clause challenge, in *Board of Education of the Westside Community Schools v. Mergens* (1990).

Sanford Levinson

Bibliography

Laycock, Douglas, "Equal Access and Moments of Silence: The Equal Status of Religious Speech by Private Speakers," 81 *Northwestern University Law Review* 1–67 (1986).

Strossen, Nadine, "A Framework for Evaluating Equal Access Claims by Student Religious Groups: Is There a Window for Free Speech in the Wall Separating Church and State?" 71 *Cornell Law Review* 143–183 (1985).

Cases Cited

Board of Education of the Westside Community Schools v. Mergens, 496 U.S. 226 (1990).

Widmar v. Vincent, 454 U.S. 263 (1981).

Williams, Roger (c. 1603–1683)

Among the several famous proponents of religious liberty during the seventeenth century, Roger Williams had the unique opportunity of actually applying his principles, through his role in the founding and early governance of the Rhode Island Colony. He not only served as governor, legislator, and militia leader in Rhode Island, but he also took two extended trips to England, from 1643 to 1644 and from 1651 to 1654, in order to obtain and protect a charter for the colony. On both sides of the Atlantic, he advocated religious liberty as a means to civil harmony in an era when religious pluralism was generally assumed to be one of the principal sources of social disorder. Thus, his argument for the separation of church and state as the basis for both civil peace and religious freedom—enunciated in such famous tracts as *The Bloudy Tenent of Persecution* (1644)—was fashioned in the midst of concrete activity as a public controversialist and a civic leader.

Roger Williams was an intellectual product of the Puritan movement. He shared the Puritan discontent with the doctrine and polity of the Church of England. He shared the Puritan hope for personal life renovated by the spirit of God and a church purified from the accumulated errors of the centuries. The creativity of his thought on the relation of law to religion came not from the introduction of new ideas into seventeenth-century political theory but rather from the dramatically different conclusions that he drew by rearranging the pivotal Puritan presuppositions about church and state. Although his conclusions in favor of religious liberty and the separation of church and state presaged the later course of American government, the rigid Puritan principles by which he arrived at these conclusions made it virtually impossible to assimilate his ideas directly into constitutional thought of the eighteenth century and after.

Williams was born in London to a family of the business class; his father was a citizen of the city and member of the Merchant Taylor Company, and his mother numbered a lord mayor of London among her relatives. The intellectual facility of the young Williams attracted the attention of the famed jurist Sir Edward Coke, who arranged for his education at Charterhouse School. From there, Williams attended Pembroke College, Cambridge, and earned his B.A. in 1627, to accept a call as a minister. But his Puritan religious scruples increased, and, rather than accept appointment to a parish of the Church of

England, he left Cambridge in 1629 to become private chaplain to the household of a wealthy Essex Puritan, Sir William Masham. By the autumn of 1630 Williams had associated himself with the Puritan group preparing to establish a colony in New England. He arrived in Massachusetts Bay, newly married, in February 1631.

By this time Williams had moved beyond the Puritan desire to reform the Church of England from within and had adopted, instead, the "separatist" view that the established church was so corrupt that genuinely reformed congregations must have no association with it. Almost immediately this radical view of church purity embroiled Williams in debates with the ministers and magistrates of Massachusetts Bay, who subscribed to the nonseparating view. In these debates Williams contended that magistrates had no power to coerce specifically religious duties, that the king had granted illegitimate land charters based on the false prerogative of being a "Christian prince," that civil government should not impose oaths of allegiance, and that the cross should be removed from the colonial flag.

After five years of unrelenting controversy, Williams was banished from Massachusetts and resettled in 1636 on land purchased from the Narragansett tribe, which he named Providence. Not long afterward, Williams came to espouse the still more radical ideas of the Seekers, a loose collection of the devout on the fringes of Puritanism, who believed that Christian institutions had become so thoroughly corrupted over the centuries that no authoritative or valid church now existed and would not until new apostles arrived at the millennium and reestablished the church in its pristine form. This collection of objections to Puritan politics and this ardent quest for the true church were gradually woven into a coherent position, and they mark the line along which Williams's thought would develop in his writings of the 1640s and 1650s.

Although these writings dealt largely with state policy toward religion, they were not primarily addressed to magistrates and legislators but rather to the Puritan clergy of old and New England. Indeed, Williams maintained a respectful relationship with Governor John Winthrop of Massachusetts for years after his banishment, assisting the governor in negotiations with the Indians of New England and even joining him in a modest joint venture in the pasturage of livestock. A great portion of the biographic information about Williams comes from his extensive correspondence with Governor Winthrop and his son, John Winthrop, Jr.

For the ministers of established churches, however, Williams had little patience. From his *Queries of Highest Consideration* (1644) directed at the Westminster Assembly of Divines to his polemical tract *The Hireling Ministry None of Christ's* (1652), Williams directly challenged ministers who sought to enlist the state in the promotion of their own religious beliefs and practices. This was especially true of his decade-long controversy with the New England divine John Cotton, of which Williams's *Bloudy Tenent of Persecution* was the most notable product. In part, the Williams–Cotton debate was a struggle over issues that had led to Williams's banishment, and *The Bloudy Tenent* was largely composed of documents that had circulated in manuscript in Massachusetts Bay during Williams's residence there. But during his first trip to England in 1643–1644, Williams quickly recognized that the earlier New England controversies were applicable to English debate over the freedom of preaching and the responsibility of the state of religious reform. Hence, his famous tracts on religious liberty were complex documents that both justified his position against the Massachusetts ministers and employed those debates as exhortations on behalf of "soul liberty" during the English civil wars.

Two features of Williams's idea of the church were the foundations for his political theory. The first related especially of his argument for the separation of church and state. He began with the Puritan commonplace that Christianity was the product of a spiritual rebirth. For the individuals this meant that birth in a nominally Christian land constituted no claim whatever to Christianity; as the title of one of his tracts declares, "christenings make not Christians." For the state this meant that no government could wrap its policies in the mantle of religion; "Christendom" was an illegitimate concept. From these points, Williams argued against the Puritan idea of a "godly commonwealth," in which Christian magistrates ruled and a reformed Protestant church was the established religion of the land. The ideal of the godly commonwealth, he asserted, borrowed "the state of Israel as a national state made up of spiritual and civil power" from Old Testament history and falsely applied it to the modern world in which spiritual authority belonged to the gathered church and civil authority belonged to the state. "What land, what country now is Israel's parallel," he asked rhetorically, "but that holy mystical nation the church of God, peculiar and called out to him out of every nation and country?"

Williams's second conviction about the church related especially to his advocacy of religious liberty. Although he shared the Puritan hope for a truly reformed church, he did not believe that any Christian of his time knew the authentic form of the true church or had the spiritual authority to establish a church untainted by the accumulated errors of history. The pure church of earliest Christianity had been lost during subsequent centuries of corruption and would not be recovered until new apostles restored it. In the meantime, Williams borrowed the rhetoric of Revelation to declare that humanity wandered in a spiritual "wilderness," in which the various forms of religion must be free to declare the truth as they saw it. So long as people did not disrupt the civil peace by their worship and preaching, they should be permitted the free exercise of their consciences, in the conviction that God would use the contest of religions to sift human opinion and would ultimately separate the true from the false on the Last Day.

These two principles—that the true church was a community called by God from the wider society and that the authoritative institutional formation of this church must await the millennium—provided the theological backdrop for his views on the relationship of church and state. Most emphatically, Williams opposed any form of established church, arguing not only against the Church of England in this regard but also against Puritan establishments in New England or in England during the government of Oliver Cromwell. In a recurrent analogy, Williams suggested that churches were like a guild of merchants or a college of physicians, who should be free to conduct their business as they saw fit, so long as it did not disrupt the public harmony. His scheme for handling the growing religious diversity of the seventeenth century may perhaps be delineated by distinguishing between toleration (in which an established church concedes certain rights of worship and assembly to dissenters) and religious liberty (in which no religion has a privileged status granted and maintained by the civil order).

Williams advocated a thoroughgoing extension of such liberty of conscience. Whereas most seventeenth-century English advocates of religious tolerance followed the lead of John Milton, by restricting toleration to Protestants and excluding Roman Catholics, Williams proposed that Roman Catholics, Jews, and Moslems should all be granted full liberty to practice their religions. Williams and his Rhode Island neighbors practiced this principle in their colonial government, and during the 1650s both Quakers and Jews found freedom to establish communities in the colony. But although Williams staunchly defended the civil right to liberty of conscience, he remained too much the "seeker" after truth to be personally tolerant of diverse beliefs, and in the 1670s he engaged in a fierce public debate with the Quakers, published under the whimsical title *George Fox Digg'd out of His Burrowes*. He did not believe that such debate within a religiously pluralistic society threatened civil peace, and he regularly advanced historical arguments to demonstrate that the true threat to civil order came from efforts to coerce religious uniformity.

In a famous letter to the town of Providence, Williams observed that "a true picture of a commonwealth" arose if one supposed that "both Papists and Protestants, Jews, and Turks, may be embarked into one ship." The diversity of religions represented "on board" did not affect the purpose of which it sailed or divert it from its destination. Although crew and passengers had liberty to practice "their own particular prayers or worship," it remained true that "the commander of this ship ought to command the ship's course; yea, and also to command that justice, peace and sobriety, be kept and practiced."

Did this imply that the state was purely "secular" in its nature and purposes? Williams did not think so. He distinguished sharply between religious duties on the one hand and specifically moral and civil duties on the other. Religious congregations were responsible for the former, and the state for the latter. But he derived these two forms of duties by dividing the "two tables" of the Decalogue, duties owed to God and duties owed to the neighbor. Derived in this general way from the divine will, civil duties could nonetheless be performed independent of the presence of "true religion" within the borders of a particular nation, and "a subject, a magistrate, may be a good subject, a good magistrate, in respect to civil or moral goodness," without so much as having heard of Christianity. No state and no governor had a religiously derived superiority. Civil society among native-born Americans rested on the same natural basis of morality and common purpose as the states of Europe, and Williams's *Key into the Language of America* (1643) was an extended meditation on the nature of human civility, not altogether to the advantage of the Europeans.

Roger Williams thus argued that religious diversity was compatible with civil peace, so long as the state did not display favoritism toward one of the religions, and he argued that public debate over religious ideas was the only *humanly* available means to religious truth. Thus baldly stated, his views have their parallels in the later thought of Madison, Adams, and Jefferson. Since Williams derived these principles from Puritan convictions about the particularity of revealed truth, however, his influence diminished during the eighteenth century, when political theory more often began from a general analysis of human nature, and when the civil import of religion was more often grounded in a natural religion shared by all. In such an environment, the *practice* of the old separatist and seeker might be admired, but his *argumentation* was dismissed as sectarian and contentious.

W. Clark Gilpin

Bibliography

Brockunier, Samuel Hugh, *The Irrepressible Democrat, Roger Williams* (New York: Ronald, 1940).

LaFantasie, Glenn W. (ed.), *The Correspondence of Roger Williams,* 2 vols. (Hanover, N.H., and London: University Press of New England, 1988).

Morgan, Edmund S., *Roger Williams: The Church and the State* (New York: Harcourt, 1967).

Williams, Roger, *The Complete Writings of Roger Williams,* 7 vols. (New York: Russell and Russell, 1963).

Wisconsin v. Yoder 406 U.S. 205 (1972)

In *Wisconsin v. Yoder* (1972) the U.S. Supreme Court held that a state violated the Free Exercise Clause of the First Amendment when it prosecuted parents whose religious beliefs compelled them to refuse to send their children to school beyond the eighth grade.

Wisconsin law required that all children between the ages of 7 and 16 attend school. The statute imposed the duty of ensuring compliance on "any person having under his control a child" within those ages. There was an allowance for instruction outside a school, but only if the state superintendent approved the alternate site. The prosecution of the three parents in *Yoder* began after Green County lost $18,000 in state subsidies when children began attending a newly established Amish school. Before trial, the Amish proposed a compromise that would allow students to attend vocational classes, taught by the Amish, similar to those approved in other states. The superintendent rejected the suggestions because they would not provide "substantially equivalent education."

With no compromise possible, the trial judge imposed the minimum fine of $5 on each parent. The intermediate appellate court affirmed the convictions. In *Yoder v. Wisconsin* (1971) the Wisconsin Supreme Court reversed, in one of the few American court decisions to side with the Amish. The case was also noteworthy because five of the seven justices joined a concurring opinion to emphasize that their agreement would end if the exemption of the Amish posed a "serious threat to the effective functioning" of the state's schools. The Supreme Court of the United States granted the state's petition for review but affirmed.

Yoder was the last decision by the Burger Court in favor of a free exercise claim (other than uncomplicated claims for unemployment benefits). Unlike the tenuous result in the Wisconsin Supreme Court, Chief Justice Warren E. Burger's majority opinion seemed to be a confident reaffirmation of the sweeping language of *Sherbert v. Verner* (1963). Yet the majority opinion in *Yoder* also echoed the Wisconsin concurrence, emphasizing the focus on a decidedly separate religious group whose identity ensured that it posed little threat to any social institutions. Burger's opinion, therefore, stood poised between an idyllic vision of a homogeneous past and a wary view of a fractured future. On one hand were the importance of parental control of education and the enthusiastic language of *Sherbert* in favor of religious freedom. On the other hand loomed divisiveness if children could assert rights against their parents in this and other contexts. The Court had seen the same pattern before as the right to privacy grew from a right that inhered in the family to one that set family member against family member in decisions about abortion. (Although *Roe v. Wade* [1973] was decided a year after *Yoder*, the Court first heard arguments in *Roe* on December 13, 1971—only five days after the court heard oral arguments in *Yoder*.) *Yoder* therefore marks a transition from the exuberance of *Sherbert* to the parsimony of *Employment Division, Department of Human Resources of Oregon v. Smith* (1990).

The Long Amish Tradition

That the Supreme Court found *Yoder* to be an easy decision is ironic, because the result depended on a governmental institution to protect a group's determination to be separate from the government. What appealed to the Court, nonetheless, was the long Amish tradition, rooted in the Protestant Reformation in early-sixteenth-century Switzerland. This most conservative of the Protestant groups was known at first as "Anabaptists" and later as "Mennonites," after one of their Dutch leaders. The Mennonites' aversion to any connection with the state grew out of persecutions that they had suffered at the hands of a conjoined church and state. For almost two centuries the Mennonites struggled to live a life apart. Even so, near the end of the seventeenth century, some members came to view the denomination as having compromised its principles. The most important of the disagreements concerned the practice of excommunication and shunning of members who failed to adhere to the faith's fundamental tenets. A small group that believed in the practices broke away in an attempt to cleanse the church and to live in strict accordance with biblical teaching. This breakaway group called itself "Amish" after its leader, Jacob Amman.

The Amish, like the Mennonites, were rarely welcome in any part of Europe. Rather than resist, they moved—in keeping with their opposition to disputes of any sort, even in self-defense. Thus, not long after the original schism, the Amish began to emigrate to Pennsylvania, in response to a personal invitation from William Penn. In the first half of the nineteenth century, they along with new immigrants began to move farther west, into Ohio, Indiana, and Illinois. But they continued to encounter persecution because of their beliefs. In the late twentieth century, when states began to enforce compulsory school attendance laws, their refusal to send children to public schools after the eighth grade became the most contentious point. The Amish also found their lifestyle threatened by the spread of commercial and urban life and by the consequent increase in land values, which made it increasingly difficult for young families to acquire new farms. The Amish therefore continued to move in search of an environment that was both hospitable and affordable. One destination for a few in the early 1960s was New Glarus, Green County, Wisconsin.

The Amish gave little formal structure to their religion. Groups are small because meetings are held in members' homes. All aspects of conduct are governed by the "Ordnung," an oral accumulation of locally agreed rules. For the Amish there is, therefore, no separation between belief and practice. Their religion defines their way of life. Membership in the church is based on adult baptism, a commitment that is made around age 18. To the Amish, compulsory public education threatens that way of life, especially when directed at older children. The Amish recognize the importance of the early adolescent years for determining the path of adult life. They fear that teenagers will not accept the Amish community if they are exposed to the competing ideas and lifestyles in public high schools.

State Law versus Religious Lifestyle

The Wisconsin case therefore pitted a state law and a locale in need of funds against a religious lifestyle. The National Committee for Amish Religious Freedom directed the litigation for the Amish. Started by a Lutheran pastor in Michigan in 1967, the committee retained William Ball of Harrisburg, Pennsylvania, who represented the parents from trial through the Supreme Court. With the consent of the local bishop, the parents agreed to defend the prosecution, rather than follow the usual Amish practice of paying a fine or serving a jail sentence without protest.

The appellate judges focused the issue on the state's effort to compel the final two years of education. No judge challenged the equation of lifestyle with religious belief. Each judge treated the statute as an infringement on the free exercise of religion. With the issue so formulated, the result of the balancing test was almost foreordained. Few could present a position as compelling as the Amish. The Wisconsin Supreme Court noted that "[t]he impact on the Amish of compulsory education laws is so severe that" they had chosen to move rather than send their children to public schools. Chief Justice E. Harold Hallows's opinion for the court employs even more emotive language when it describes the reason the Amish had come to Wisconsin: "[T]hey sought religious freedom, in a spirit and with a hope not unlike the Pilgrim Fathers who came to America."

Against that portrait of the Amish, the state's interest had little chance to rise to the level of "compelling." The court accepted the importance of education—it could do little else, given the centrality of education to constitutional adjudication after *Brown v. Board of Education of Topeka* (1954). Indeed, the Amish themselves accepted the state's power to require basic education. The problem the state faced was that its claim concerned only the final two years of education, not the concept itself.

The essence of the court's reasoning came from *Sherbert,* which the court read as requiring it "to ask whether an exemption of the compulsory education law for the Amish would defeat the purpose of compulsory education." Since Amish children received eight years of education, there was little doubt that exemption from two more years would not "defeat" the law's purpose. And the court so held.

Despite the Wisconsin court's confidence, it had three final points to cover—matters that implicated the ominous side of the issue. First, the court carefully limited its discussion to the rights of parents, rejecting any suggestion that the case involved an independent right of children. Second, the court was satisfied that the "uniqueness of the Amish people" made it unlikely that anyone could assert a spurious claim for exemption. Third, the court recognized that granting an exemption to the Amish could implicate the Establishment Clause. Here, though, the court described the outcome as no more than neutrality toward the religion.

The lone dissenter in Wisconsin, Justice Nathan Heffernan, rejected the conclusion that education was not a compelling state interest. He too relied on *Brown,* but he added a reference to the history of public education dating from the Northwest Ordinance of 1787, as if to suggest that the state could compete with the Amish in a battle of historical pedigrees. In addition, he argued that the court should consider the interests of the individual children. "On the basis of the religious beliefs of their parents, the Amish children are without a hearing consigned to a life of ignorance—blissful as it may seem to the author of the principal opinion, who apparently views the Amish as 'the noble savage,' uncorrupted by the world. The reader is left with a picture of idyllic agrarianism." Justice Heffernan suggested that it was possible to reach a compromise between the Amish belief and the state's interest in education.

The Supreme Court: Siding with Tradition

The Supreme Court granted the petition for certiorari even though it had refused to hear a similar case, *Garber v. Kansas* (1967), only four years earlier. Chief Justice Burger's majority opinion began with a reference to *Pierce v. Society of Sisters* (1925). *Pierce* served a dual function. First, it affirmed the importance of education; yet it also held that parents' rights were superior to the state's interest. Second, rather than cite *Brown,* it allowed Burger to reach back to what may have seemed a simpler time. As Burger wrote later in his opinion, the "history and culture of Western civilization reflect a strong tradition of parental concern for the nurture and upbringing of their children." *Pierce* stood "as a charter of the rights of parents to direct the religious upbringing of their children."

Burger was careful to point out that a way of life alone did not merit the protection of the religion clauses: "the claims must be rooted in religious belief." Even so, he had no difficulty being convinced that the Amish way of life was dictated by their literal interpretation of biblical passages. Burger's language almost glowed in its praise for the Amish "way of life in a church-oriented community, separated from the outside world and 'worldly' influences, their attachment to nature and the soil." Their proof was such that "few other religious groups or sects could make" a similar showing. Burger accepted the argument that the recent development of consolidated schools for the high school students was a clear threat to the Amish, since in those schools the children would be exposed to a variety of competing ideas. And, like the Wisconsin court, he could not resist a reference to the fact that "[f]orced migration of religious minorities was an evil that lay at the heart of the Religion Clauses."

Turning to the state's assertion of a compelling interest, Burger minimized the claim as concerning only the final two years of compulsory education. He also noted that the requirement of education beyond the eighth grade was a relatively new phenomenon. A sixty-year history of compulsory education, and even less of high school, could hardly compare with three centuries of Amish practice. He accepted the Amish argument that the education should be tested by the goal of preparation for life in the Amish community, not in the state at large. Furthermore, there was testimony in the record attesting to the success of Amish education beyond the eighth grade, again measuring success by conforming the children to the Amish lifestyle. Therefore, Burger concluded that any benefit from an additional two years of school was "at best . . . speculative."

Chief Justice Burger rejected the suggestion made by the dissent in Wisconsin and by Justice William O. Douglas—that the true issue concerned the rights of the children. Procedurally he was correct in asserting that the state had not tried the children. But he made it clear that if the state were to assert jurisdiction over the children, it would raise "grave questions of religious freedom."

Burger concluded by briefly noting that "accommodating" the Amish beliefs did not constitute an establishment of religion. "The purpose and effect of [the] exemption are not to support, favor, advance, or assist the Amish."

Justice Potter Stewart wrote a separate concurrence to emphasize that the case did not involve any question about the rights of children. Quoting from the record, he demonstrated that there was no testimony to suggest that the children involved had different religious views from their parents.

Justice Byron White also wrote a separate concurring opinion. He emphasized the almost *de minimis* nature of the dispute. The Amish accepted the need for eight years of education; the state's interest in an additional two years was therefore relatively slight. He did, however, emphasize the importance of education, pointing to *Brown* for support.

Justice Douglas joined the Court's opinion as it applied to the one Amish child who had testified that there was no difference between her beliefs and those of her parents. He dissented with respect to the other two children; he would remand the case for additional hearings concerning their religious views. Douglas pointed to recent decisions of the Court in which rights were not limited to adults. He also showed that his image of the Amish life was considerably less placid than Burger's: "If [a child] is harnessed to the Amish way of life by those in authority over him and if his education is truncated, his entire life may be stunted and deformed."

With hindsight, *Yoder* proved to be a harbinger of divisions to come—divisions rooted deeply in American society. The majority opinion found itself torn between two compelling values. On the one hand was a civic republicanism that had come to depend on public education to transmit values. On the other hand was a traditional respect for parents who had that same duty. The dissent appealed to a liberal individualism that to some seemed to flirt with the disaster of social atomism. *Yoder* sided with tradition; but the future to which it pointed did not seem as idyllic as the past it recalled.

Walter F. Pratt, Jr.

Bibliography

Hostetler, John A., *Amish Society,* 3rd ed. (Baltimore, Md.: Johns Hopkins University Press, 1980).

Keim, Albert N. (ed.), *Compulsory Education and the Amish: The Right Not to Be Modern* (Boston: Beacon Press, 1975).

Lehman, Thomas L., "The Plain People: Reluctant Parties in Litigation to Preserve a Life Style," 16 *Journal of Church and State* 287–300 (1974).

Prance, Norman, "The Amish and Compulsory School Attendance: Recent Developments," 1971 *Wisconsin Law Review* 832–853 (1971).

Cases Cited

Brown v. Board of Education of Topeka, 347 U.S. 483 (1954).

Employment Division, Department of Human Resources of Oregon v. Smith, 494 U.S. 872 (1990).

Garber v. Kansas, 389 U.S. 51 (1967).

Pierce v. Society of Sisters, 268 U.S. 510 (1925).

Roe v. Wade, 410 U.S. 113 (1973).

Sherbert v. Verner, 374 U.S. 398 (1963).

Wisconsin v. Yoder, 406 U.S. 205 (1972).

Yoder v. Wisconsin, 49 Wis. 2d 430, 182 N.W. 539 (1971).

Witters v. Washington Department of Services for the Blind

474 U.S. 481 (1986)

In a large number of cases, the Supreme Court has considered challenges to governmental programs that provide financial support for religious institutions or activities. Most of these programs have involved public funding for private religious education. Although the Court has invalidated many such programs, more recently its approach has become quite permissive. *Witters v. Washington Department of Services for the Blind* (1986) exemplifies this trend.

In preparation for a career as a pastor, missionary, or youth director, Larry Witters attended a private Christian college in Spokane, Washington. Because he suffered from progressive blindness, he was eligible for special financial aid under the terms of a Washington statute designed to "assist visually handicapped persons to overcome vocational handicaps." Noting the religious nature of his education, however, the Washington Commission for the Blind denied Witters any aid, asserting that it would be unconstitutional for the commission to use "public funds to assist an individual in the pursuit of a career or degree in theology or related areas." Witters sued for relief, but he had no success in the Washington state courts, with the Washington Supreme Court ruling that the Establishment Clause required the commission's denial of aid.

Even under a strict interpretation of the Establishment Clause, the Washington Supreme Court's decision was plainly wrong, and the U.S. Supreme Court unanimously reversed. Writing for the Court, Justice Thurgood Marshall relied on three considerations. First, Washington's program was grounded on an "unmistakably secular purpose," that of "promot[ing] the well-being of the visually handicapped." Consistent with this purpose, the aid was broadly and neutrally available to students pursuing various careers. Second, the aid was not in the form of "direct subsidies" to religious institutions. Instead, it was paid to the disabled students themselves, who transmitted it to the colleges of their choice. Thus, any aid that flowed to religious institutions did so "only as a result of the genuinely independent and private choices of aid recipients," thereby avoiding any implication that the state was sponsoring or endorsing religion. Third, even through this indirect route, "no more than a minuscule amount of the aid awarded" flowed to religious education. As Justice Marshall noted, "aid recipients have full opportunity to expend vocational rehabilitation aid on wholly secular education, and as a practical matter have rather greater prospects to do so," because "only a small handful" of the aid recipients would choose to train for a religious career.

Justice Marshall's narrowly drawn opinion was clearly supported by precedent and, taken alone, it did nothing to curtail the Court's scrutiny of governmental funding for religious institutions or activities. But through separate concurring opinions, a majority of the justices—Justices Byron White, Sandra Day O'Connor, and Lewis Powell (with Chief Justice Warren Burger and Justice William Rehnquist joining him)—indicated their support for a considerably more permissive approach. Relying on a broad interpretation of *Mueller v. Allen* (1983), these justices indicated that, although they agreed with Justice Marshall's first and second points of analysis, they believed that his third point was gratuitous, because the Washington program would properly have been upheld even if most of the funding had flowed to religious education. Justice Lewis F. Powell, Jr., expressed the basic approach of all five justices in this group: "[S]tate programs that are wholly neutral in offering educational assistance to a class defined without reference to religion" are almost certain to be upheld, "because any aid to religion results from the private choices of individual beneficiaries." Based on this view, the ultimate destination of the aid is beside the point, and neutrally drawn programs will be upheld even if a majority of recipients use the aid for religious purposes. This approach has obvious implications for various types of funding programs, including programs based on the use of educational vouchers.

Unfortunately for Mr. Witters, the Supreme Court's decision was not the end of his saga. On remand, in *Witters v. Washington Commission for the Blind* (Wash., 1989), the Washington Supreme Court again concluded that Witters could not receive aid. This time the court's ruling was based not on the Establishment Clause but rather on a "far stricter" provision in Washington's Constitution. Even after *Employment Division, Department of Human Resources of Oregon v. Smith* (1990), however, the Free Exercise Clause forbids the states from singling out religion for special disadvantage. An interesting question is whether, in denying aid to Witters, Washington thereby violated his Free Exercise right to equal treatment. Advancing just such an argument, Witters asked the U.S. Supreme Court to consider his case again, but the Court denied review.

Daniel O. Conkle

Bibliography

Rapinchuk, J. Catherine, "The Increasing Judicial Rationale for Educational Choice: *Mueller, Witters* and Vouchers," 66 *Washington University Law Quarterly* 363–387 (1988).

Cases Cited

Employment Division, Department of Human Resources of Oregon v. Smith, 494 U.S. 872 (1990).

Mueller v. Allen, 463 U.S. 388 (1983).

Witters v. Washington Commission for the Blind, 771 P. 2d 1119 (Wash. 1989).

Witters v. Washington Department of Services for the Blind, 474 U.S. 481 (1986).

Wolman v. Walter
433 U.S. 229 (1977)

Wolman v. Walter (1977) involved a First Amendment challenge to a law designed to provide nonpublic school pupils or their parents with the following: (1) secular textbooks approved for use in public schools; (2) standardized testing services used in public schools to measure progress in secular subjects; (3) speech, hearing, psychological, therapeutic, career guidance, and remedial services; (4) instructional materials of a kind "incapable of diversion to religious use"; and (5) drivers and vehicles for field trips for secular purposes. The U.S. District Court for the Southern District of Ohio found the statute constitutional. The plaintiffs—anti-aid organizations like the American Civil Liberties Union, American Humanist Association, the Unitarian Universalist Association, Americans United for Separation of Church and State, and the Coalition for Public Education and Religious Liberty—appealed to the Supreme Court, which elevated the art of splitting hairs to new heights when it divided its judgment into five amorphous and contradictory parts. Justice Harry Blackmun wrote for the Court, joined in part by Justice Potter Stewart.

First, Chief Justice Warren Burger and Justices Harry Blackmun, Lewis Powell, William Rehnquist, Potter Stewart, and Byron White concurred that state provision of books and testing services did not violate the Establishment Clause of the First Amendment. The Court rejected the plaintiffs' argument that the vagueness of the Ohio statute's language about lending books or "book substitutes" invited sectarian abuse and thus violated the principle of church–state separation. With Justices William Brennan, Thurgood Marshall, and John Paul Stevens dissenting, the Court thus upheld *Board of Education v. Allen* (1968), which allowed state provision of books to nonpublic schools. The 6-to-3 majority also dismissed the plaintiffs' complaint about providing testing services to these schools. Blackmun, writing for the majority, argued that, inasmuch as nonpublic school personnel do not draft or score the tests nor receive payment for administering them, there is no avenue for using the tests for religious teaching, no requirement of state supervision that might give rise to excessive church–state entanglement, and thus no direct aid to religion.

Second, all the justices except Brennan held that speech, hearing, and psychological diagnostic services did not violate the Establishment Clause. Third, all justices except Brennan and Marshall held that provisions of therapeutic, guidance (except guidance about course selection), and remedial services were permissible. The plaintiffs had argued against provision of diagnostic, therapeutic, or remedial services because the school staff might fail to separate religious instruction from secular responsibilities and might seek to impose a religious influence while under state subsidy. Citing *Allen*, *Roemer v. Board of Public Works of Maryland* (1976), and *Meek v. Pittenger* (1975), Blackmun noted the constitutionality of state provision of church-related schools with secular, neutral, or nonideological services, facilities, or materials.

However, this judgment contradicted, in part, the decision in *Meek,* where state authorization of remedial and diagnostic services was ruled unconstitutional because (1) teachers or counselors might fail to separate religious instruction from secular obligations and (2) efforts to guard against unneutral aid would entail state surveillance on school property and thus result in excessive church–state entanglement. In *Wolman* the Court made a distinction between diagnostic services, which have little or no educational content and entail minimal student contact, and teaching and counseling roles. Given the "clear" distinction, the Court concluded that the diagnostic staff working on private campuses would have little opportunity to proselytize. In addition, to ensure religious neutrality and nonentanglement, therapeutic, remedial, and career counseling services would be provided off campus by public officials and professionals.

Neutral accommodation of religion halted when it came to a fourth component of the decision in *Wolman,* concerning instructional materials and equipment. The Court ruled—with Burger, Rehnquist, and White dissenting—that the Establishment Clause prohibited state funds for instructional materials. Because it was presumably impossible to separate secular from sectarian educational functions in church-related schools and because maps and tape recorders (unlike books) could not be isolated to students' or parents' possession, state contributions toward such items would coincidentally and impermissibly support the religious role of the schools.

With respect to state-funded field trips, the Court—with Burger, Powell, Rehnquist, and White dissenting—noted a sharp contrast with state-funded busing for parochial schoolchildren that was found constitutional in *Everson v. Board of Education* (1947). In *Everson* "the school did not determine how often the pupil travelled . . . [and] travel was unrelated to any aspect of the curriculum." In the Ohio statute, the schools controlled the timing, frequency, destination, and purpose of trips. And, according to the Court, teachers—who give meaning to the trip—serve the nonpublic school agenda and in such a capacity might not always avoid the temptation to foster religion in their teaching role. State supervision to guarantee religious neutrality would create excessive church–state entanglement. For these reasons, the majority held funding of field trips, which presumably benefited the school more than the children, unconstitutional.

The split decisions and separate opinions in *Wolman* reveal the divided and schizophrenic character of the Court's ruling on the Establishment Clause since World War II. On the one hand, Brennan, a strict separationist who highlighted the costliness of the Ohio program, saw all provisions of the Ohio statute unconstitutional and urged overturning *Allen.* Marshall, who highlighted the danger of "reducing the high and impregnable wall between church and state erected by the First Amendment . . . to a blurred, indistinct, and variable barrier, incapable of . . . protecting both church and state," echoed the plea to overturn *Allen.* Stevens also argued that the state could only "provide public health services to children attending nonpublic schools."

From a more accommodationist position, Chief Justice Burger and Justices Rehnquist and White viewed none of the Ohio statute as unconstitutional and found continuing validity in *Allen.* This was consistent with Rehnquist's opinion in *Meek* and with Burger, Rehnquist, and White's dissents in *Committee for Public Education and Religious Life v. Nyquist* (1973) and *Roemer.* These three justices agreed, in *Nyquist,* "that the Establishment Clause does not forbid governments . . . to enact a program of general welfare under which benefits are distributed to private individuals, even though many of those individuals may elect to use those benefits in ways that 'aid' religious instruction."

Justice Powell, who often opposed aid to religion (as he did in *Roemer* but did not in *Allen*), allied with the dissenters in part in

Wolman. In the process, he acknowledged the arbitrary nature of the lines drawn by the Court between permissible and impermissible state aid to the educational role of church-related schools. Powell viewed most of the Ohio statute as constitutional, including the provision of some instructional materials "so long as the aid is incapable of diversion to religious uses" and is lent only to individuals and not the institution.

L. Sue Hulett

Bibliography

Esbeck, Carl H., "Government Regulation of Religiously Based Social Services: The First Amendment Considerations," 19 *Hastings Constitutional Law Quarterly* 343–412 (1992).

Joiner, John E., "A Page of History or a Volume of Logic? Reassessing the Supreme Court's Establishment Clause Jurisprudence," 73 *Denver University Law Review* 507–569 (1996).

Kelley, Dean M., "Religious Access to Public Programs and Government Funding," 8 *Brigham Young University Journal of Public Law* 417–438 (1994).

Laycock, Douglas, "A Survey of Religious Liberty in the United States," 47 *Ohio State Law Journal* 409–451 (1986).

Cases Cited

Board of Education v. Allen, 392 U.S. 236 (1968).

Committee for Public Education and Religious Life v. Nyquist, 413 U.S. 756 (1973).

Everson v. Board of Education, 330 U.S. 1 (1947).

Meek v. Pittenger, 421 U.S. 349 (1975).

Roemer v. Board of Public Works of Maryland, 426 U.S. 736 (1976).

Wooley v. Maynard 430 U.S. 705 (1977)

Wooley v. Maynard (1977) involved the problem of delineating the boundaries between the public domain of state ideology and the private space of individual conscience. New Hampshire required that automobile license plates issued to its citizens bear the state's motto, "Live Free or Die." Maynard considered the motto antithetical to his religious and moral convictions. As a Jehovah's Witness, he valued life above freedom, and thus he taped over the motto on his license plates.

New Hampshire, however, had made it a crime to obscure any portion of a license plate, including the motto. After being imprisoned for refusing to comply with the law, Maynard brought suit in federal court, claiming that his punishment violated the First Amendment. The court agreed, and the Supreme Court affirmed.

According to the Court, *Board of Education v. Barnette* (1943)—which held that a state may not require public school students to salute the flag—established that individuals have a constitutional right to refuse to express ideas with which they disagree. Writing for the Court, Chief Justice Warren Burger found this principle applicable because New Hampshire had forced Maynard "to be an instrument for fostering public adherence to an ideological point of view he finds unacceptable." Burger reasoned that "[I]n effect," New Hampshire law made Maynard's car "a 'mobile billboard' for the State's ideological message." The Court acknowledged that the state had a legitimate interest in fostering its ideological messages but ruled that "such interest cannot outweigh an individual's First Amendment right to avoid becoming the courier for such message."

Justice Byron White, joined by Justices Harry Blackmun and William Rehnquist, confined his dissent to jurisdictional issues. Justice William Rehnquist, in a separate dissent (which Blackmun also joined), rejected the Court's decision on the merits. While voicing no objection to the Court's interpretation of *Barnette,* he viewed it as inapplicable to Maynard's situation. He argued that requiring Maynard to display license plates with the state motto did not amount to forcing Maynard to express the message "Live Free or Die": Just because these words appear on Maynard's license plate does not mean anyone would think that Maynard himself was advocating or endorsing this message. Instead, people would assume that Maynard, like others, simply put the license plates on his cars, as required by state law, without either affirming or rejecting the state's creed.

Justice Rehnquist surmised that the First Amendment would not prohibit New Hampshire from forcing Maynard to pay taxes to support the construction of billboards proclaiming "Live Free or Die," even though Maynard's money would be instrumental to the state's effort to foster public acceptance of the state's motto. He saw no difference between the state's use of Maynard's money and its use of his car as the means of obtaining a billboard for its own ideological message. Moreover, Justice Rehnquist observed, Maynard's dollars are themselves billboards for the federal government's ideological messages: Federal law requires all U.S. currency to bear the national motto, "In God We Trust." But this requirement does not mean that atheists are forced to express faith in God whenever they carry or use U.S. currency. For this reason, Justice Rehnquist asserted, the federal law that prohibits anyone from defacing U.S. currency would not violate the First Amendment even as applied to atheists who obscure the words "In God We Trust" on all their $1 bills. Similarly, he concluded, New Hampshire does not violate the First Amendment by prohibiting Maynard from obscuring the state motto on his license plates.

Justice Rehnquist's dissent was powerful, and the Court said little in response. Regarding the comparison with currency, the Court noted that currency "passe[s] from hand to hand" and therefore is less associated with any particular individual than is an automobile. The Court added that "[c]urrency is generally carried in a purse or pocket" and thus, unlike a license plate, does not publicly advertise its ideological messages. But the Court offered no general rule for deciding whether or not a citizen has been required to display an ideological message.

Perhaps it is unfair to fault the Court's failure to articulate a general rule. This line, like so many others, is impossible to draw with precision. The best the Court could do was to exercise wise judgment in resolving the inevitable tension between the state's desire to promote its message and Maynard's desire to disassociate himself from that message. This the Court did, and New Hampshire is a freer, fairer state as a result of the Court's decision.

Edward B. Foley

Bibliography

Tribe, Lawrence H., "The Curvature of Constitutional Space," 103 *Harvard Law Review* 1–39 (1989).

———, *American Constitutional Law,* 2nd ed. (Mineola, N.Y.: Foundation Press, 1988).

Yudof, Mark, *When Government Speaks* (Berkeley: University of California Press, 1983).

Cases Cited

Board of Education v. Barnette, 319 U.S. 624 (1943).

Wooley v. Maynard, 430 U.S. 705 (1977).

Z

Zoning of Religious Uses

Zoning codes that contain provisions for "church use" or "religious use" of property may be interpreted broadly enough to include not only houses of worship but accessory facilities as well, such as sites for education, social service, and other nonworship uses. The terms may even include clergy and monastic residences. On occasion, courts employ broad interpretations of religious use to permit church-operated uses as diverse as coffeehouses, drug treatment centers, recreational facilities, and homeless shelters.

Zoning ordinances typically set forth the status of houses of worship in each district. Churches are (1) permitted as of right, (2) prohibited, or (3) conditionally permitted (i.e., permitted only after public review and discretionary grant of a special permit). These use restrictions govern new construction of a church in a given district as well as the change of use of an existing building (e.g., converting a home into a church).

Assuming that the house of worship is permitted as of right or by special permit, dimensional requirements will govern its size and spatial characteristics. Proposals for construction of a new church or for alteration of an existing building will be subject to height, setback, and bulk and density requirements in the zoning ordinance.

Inasmuch as use and dimensional controls have become standard elements of municipal zoning regulation in post–World War II America, state courts have split on their approaches to houses of worship. Many courts have chosen to give broad deference to decisions of religious communities to locate in areas of their choice, particularly in residential zones, because churches and synagogues have a constitutional status and play a major role in furthering morals and the general welfare. These state courts often found the total exclusion of churches from residential zones to be arbitrary and unreasonable, in violation of due process because such exclusion lacked substantial relation to the general welfare. This judicial analysis, typified by the decision in *Westchester Reform Temple v. Brown* (N.Y., 1968), holds the public benefit of houses of worship to outweigh their harmful effects, such as increased traffic.

On the other hand, a minority of state courts have deferred to municipal decisions to exclude churches from certain areas, so long as alternative locations were available. These courts did not consider religious property use to possess any constitutional status. They have focused instead on the similarities that churches share with other public assembly uses in the production of noise, traffic, and congestion. The exclusion of churches from residential areas is considered a reasonable method of preserving residential tranquility, and so exclusion comports with due process requirements, as was held in *Corporation of the Presiding Bishop of the Church of Jesus Christ of Latter-Day Saints v. City of Porterville* (Calif., 1949).

When federal courts of appeals began to hear constitutional challenges to restrictive zoning ordinances in the 1980s, they chose to follow the "minority" position. Many of these courts have ignored the distinctive quality of religious use of property and have refused to link land use with fundamental interests of free exercise, free speech, and free association. Footnote 2 in *Lakewood, Ohio Congregation of Jehovah's Witnesses v. City of Lakewood* (6th Cir. 1983) suggests that these trends are based on an excessively separationist Establishment Clause concern that any presumptive protection for houses of worship unconstitutionally prefers religion. In *Cohen v. City of Des Plaines* (7th Cir. 1993), however, an exemption from zoning permit requirements for religious day care and nursery schools survived an Establishment Clause challenge. The court held that the exemption removed identifiable burdens to free exercise, enabled churches to define and carry out their missions, did not require nonbeneficiaries to subsidize religious activity, and effected a more complete separation of church and state.

Religious communities bringing free exercise claims have argued that the restrictive zoning provisions burden their religion and are not justified by a compelling state interest. After *Employment Division, Department of Human Resources of Oregon v. Smith* (1990), which replaces strict scrutiny with a rational basis standard of judicial review whenever neutral laws of general applicability burden religious exercise, this compelling interest test is available only when the municipal zoning action lacks religious neutrality or violates fundamental rights to speech, association, and equal protection claims (so-called hybrid rights of free exercise claims coupled with other constitutional protections).

Use Restrictions Limiting Houses of Worship

Four circuit courts have adjudicated religious challenges to blanket exclusions of churches and denials of special permits to build. In *Lakewood,* a congregation of Jehovah's Witnesses was denied a permit to build in an exclusively residential zone. The church challenged the permit denial under the Due Process Clause of the Fourteenth Amendment; the court found the denial to be rationally related to the public welfare. The church also challenged the denial under the Free Exercise Clause of the First Amendment; the court found that constructing a church is a purely secular activity. The court reached the remarkable conclusion that, because the *construction* itself had no sacramental or religious significance to the Jehovah's Witnesses' faith, religious activity was not affected by the zoning ordinance. Exclusion from the zone constituted an "inconvenient economic burden" and "subjective aesthetic burden" on the church because it would have to find property elsewhere.

Messiah Baptist Church v. County of Jefferson (10th Cir. 1988) involved a zoning ordinance that permitted churches as conditional uses in the agricultural district. The Messiah Church, however, wanted to build a large religious complex for worship, school, recreation, and parking. The church challenged the denial of the special permit for this project. While not fully adopting *Lakewood*'s characterization of church construction as per se secular conduct, the court of appeals found no evidence that constructing a house of worship or building one in this particular location was "intimately related to the religious tenets of the church." Because the zoning restriction and a religious tenet or practice were not in direct conflict, exclusion from the zone (by permit denial) was not a violation of free exercise. As in *Lakewood,* the court concluded that when religious conduct is not being regulated, an incidental economic burden on a church is tolerable. And as in *Lakewood,* the due process challenge failed because the ordinance was found reasonable.

A crucial factor in both cases was that alternative sites existed. In *Lakewood,* houses of worship were permitted in zones that represented 10 percent of the city's land area; additionally, an existing church in any part of the city could be used (presumably by purchase or rental). In *Messiah Baptist Church,* the church could locate in any residential section of the city because in those zones churches were permitted as of right.

The absence of practical alternative sites figures prominently in *Islamic Center of Mississippi, Inc. v. City of Starkville* (5th Cir. 1988). In that case, Muslim students at Mississippi State University were denied a special permit to hold their religious services near the campus of a state university. Possible sites for another mosque within walking distance of the campus were outside the city limits; possible locations within the city limits required car transportation, which the court considered not to be a practical alternative for students. Most damaging was the evidence of religious discrimination: All Christian churches needing special permits in twenty years had received them; and a Christian church next door to the mosque site was permitted to operate, even though it created far more traffic and noise than did the mosque. Unlike *Lakewood* and *Messiah Baptist Church,* in which the standard of judicial review was the deferential rational basis test, the court here employed higher scrutiny because of the religious discrimination and the effective exclusion of a religious use from the city's borders. The zoning ordinance was found unconstitutional as applied to the Muslim students.

Another example of sensitivity to equal protection concerns can be found in *Cornerstone Bible Church v. City of Hastings* (8th Cir. 1991). This Minnesota city excluded churches from commercial and industrial zones on the grounds that they displaced commercial use and would harm the economic vitality of those districts. The church challenged the exclusion of churches from the downtown central business district on free exercise, free speech, equal protection, and due process grounds. The court held that the Free Exercise Clause was not violated, because there was no evidence of discrimination based on religious status. But, in light of the fact that secular noncommercial uses were permitted in the downtown area, the court remanded the case to the district court for trial in order to determine whether, under the Equal Protection Clause, any rational basis existed for prohibiting churches while permitting other similarly situated, noncommercial uses.

The disparate treatment of religious and secular noncommercial uses also gives rise to questions regarding the validity of time, place, and manner restrictions as well as underinclusive regulation. Therefore, the district court was instructed, on remand, to decide whether this municipal action violated free speech or the free exercise–free speech hybrid protection (available after *Smith*). The fact that churches had ample alternative locations—churches were permitted as of right in residential districts, which made up 45 percent of the city's area—was not sufficient to save this municipal action from scrutiny under equal protection, free speech, and the religion–speech hybrid.

The federal jurisprudence applies these familiar themes when faced with issues of accessory use. In *First Assembly of God of Naples, Florida v. Collier County, Florida* (11th Cir. 1994), the court found that a church's homeless shelter violated the zoning ordinance and that, because the ordinance was generally applicable and facially neutral, no free exercise interest was implicated. The shelter could be located at an alternative site. Under the Religious Freedom Restoration Act (RFRA), several courts ignored the fact that alternative sites existed and gave broad protection to accessory uses like homeless shelters and feeding programs, particularly in the case of *Western Presbyterian Church v. Board of Zoning Adjustment* (D.D.C. 1994); however, the Supreme Court held the RFRA unconstitutional in *City of Boerne v. Flores* (1997).

Zoning Impacts on Religious Uses of Private Homes

Persons desiring to convert a home into a place of worship may find that applicable zoning restrictions prevent such use. Two federal circuit courts have adjudicated disputes between such persons and municipal officials. In *Grosz v. City of Miami Beach* (11th Circuit, 1983) the zoning ordinance did not expressly permit residences to be used for organized religious services in the district in which Rabbi Grosz used his garage as a shul (a small synagogue) and conducted two daily orthodox Jewish services with at least ten men (and occasionally up to fifty). After being ordered to stop holding the larger services, the rabbi challenged the exclusion. The court decided that the municipality's interest in residential tranquility outweighed Rabbi Grosz's religious interest, because he could move his home or relocate his services to any part of the 50 percent of Miami Beach's territory that expressly permitted such religious use. Again, the availability of alternative sites mitigated the burden on free exercise of religion.

In *Christian Gospel Church v. City and County of San Francisco* (9th Cir. 1990) the Christian Gospel Church was denied a special use permit to hold worship services for up to fifty persons several times each week in a home in a residential neighborhood. The church sought permission to use the house for services because of the importance to it of "home worship." The church was found to be incompatible with residential use and detrimental to the health, safety, convenience, or general welfare of residents. The court held that the city's strong interest in protecting residential tranquility outweighed the minor inconvenience and expense to the church of finding an alternative site. Equal protection was not violated, because all assembly uses were conditional uses in this zone. The church also failed on its civil rights claims against the government and the neighborhood association (190 residents) that had opposed the permit application.

In *LeBlanc-Sternberg v. Fletcher* (2nd Cir. 1995) the court found that a zoning ordinance designed to limit the number of home synagogues also served to make dwellings unavailable to Jews. Because Orthodox Jewish communities have a high number of home synagogues to accommodate daily prayer meetings and no-car rules on the Sabbath, the exclusion of houses of worship meant the exclusion of Jews. The court held the ordinance in the violation of both the Free Exercise Clause and the federal Fair Housing Act.

In an attempt to deduce some general principles from these circuit court cases, it appears that restrictions on church location are presumptively constitutional, so long as (1) they are rationally related to the general welfare, (2) they are administered in an even-handed way and do not impose specific burdens on identifiable groups, and (3) religious activity can be conducted somewhere within the municipality's borders. Specifically, cities cannot discriminate among religions (*Starkville* and *LeBlanc*) and cannot discriminate between religious and secular uses that are similarly situated (*Hastings*).

The Supreme Court on Religion and Zoning

The Supreme Court has never adjudicated a controversy involving municipal zoning of religious uses and structures. The court mentioned land use laws only in dicta in *Boerne*, where Justice Kennedy seemed to assume that zoning laws are generally applicable and facially neutral and, under *Smith*, constitutional:

> It is a reality of the modern regulatory state that numerous state laws, such as the zoning regulations at issue here, impose a substantial burden on a large class of individuals. When the exercise of religion has been burdened in an incidental way by a law of general application, it does not follow that the persons affected have been burdened any more than other citizens, let alone burdened because of their religious beliefs.

This assumption of general applicability is incorrect. Built into zoning laws are numerous mechanisms for exceptions and special consideration. Variances, hardship exemptions, and special permits are among the many discretionary mechanisms present in land use ordinances; these are necessary to provide flexibility in an area subject to constant pressures for change. Under *Smith*, it seems that statutory regimes which contain exemption mechanisms (with government making "individualized assessments" in discretionary fashion) may continue to enjoy the highest level of judicial review, the compelling interest test. The analysis is thus not as simple as Justice Kennedy's quoted language suggests.

The only Supreme Court land use decision arose in the context of church control of uses in its surroundings. In *Larkin v. Grendel's Den* (1982) a restaurant challenged the constitutionality of a Massachusetts statute that expressly authorized churches (and schools) to veto grants of liquor licenses to establishments within a 500-foot radius of a church (or school). A church 10 feet away from Grendel's Den in Harvard Square, Cambridge, had objected to the grant of a liquor license. The Alcoholic Beverages Control Commission denied the license solely on the grounds of the church's objection. Since zoning is a legislative function, the Supreme Court found an unconstitutional delegation of governmental power to a church, in violation of the Establishment Clause of the First Amendment. The power to object was deemed to have a primary effect of advancing religion, because the churches' veto of liquor applications could be exercised at their discretion without standards to ensure a religiously neutral exercise of power. Although the law had a secular purpose (protecting churches and schools from disturbances associated with liquor establishments), this purpose could be accomplished in other ways, such as express prohibitions on liquor establishments within reasonable distances of churches and schools. Additionally, the standardless delegation of governmental powers to churches caused unacceptable levels of entanglement between church and state. Justice Rehnquist dissented, arguing that the majority failed to distinguish this unconstitutional delegation from the constitutional flat ban of liquor in the vicinity of churches and schools.

In *Church of the Lukumi Babalu Aye, Inc. v. City of Hialeah* (1993) the Supreme Court held unconstitutional city ordinances prohibiting ritual animal sacrifice because they had as their object the suppression of a central element of a particular church's worship. The ordinances were not zoning enactments; the church had, in fact, received the necessary zoning approvals. But the effect of the ordinances was to inhibit full ritual use of the site (e.g., church use was permitted so long as no animal sacrifice occurred). One of the ordinances stated that "the slaughtering of animals on the premises other than those properly zoned as a slaughterhouse, is contrary to the public health, safety and welfare of" its citizens and that it is unlawful "to slaughter any animal on any premises. . . except those properly zoned [and licensed] as a slaughterhouse." Licensed slaughterhouses operating in parts of the city zoned for such uses were specifically exempt from operation of the ordinances. Precisely for cases like this one, where government action lacks religious neutrality, *Smith* had retained the strict scrutiny standard of judicial review. The city ordinances did not survive under this standard.

Had the prohibition on ritual sacrifice come through a zoning enactment, a similar constitutional analysis would be available. The city might have enacted a blanket exclusion of buildings in which ritual sacrifice occurred, or denied a special permit to the church because of its particular practice, or granted a special permit on the condition that ritual sacrifice be abandoned. It might have refused to consider the church a "church" in the zoning code's definition and instead considered it a "slaughterhouse" forbidden at its given location. In any of these cases, the municipal action would have had as its object the suppression of a central element of a particular church's worship, just as did the public health ordinances at issue in *Church of the Lukumi Babalu.*

Angela C. Carmella

Bibliography

Carmella, Angela C. "Liberty and Equality: Paradigms for the Protection of Religious Property Use," 37 *Journal of Church and State* 573–598 (1995).

Cordes, Mark, "Where to Pray? Religious Zoning and the First Amendment," 35 *University of Kansas Law Review* 697–762 (1987).

Reynolds, Laurie, "Zoning the Church: The Police Power versus the First Amendment," 64 *Boston University Law Review* 767–816 (1984).

"Zoning Ordinances Affecting Churches: A Proposal for Expanded Free Exercise Protection," 132 *University of Pennsylvania Law Review* 1131–1162 (1984).

Cases Cited

Christian Gospel Church v. City and County of San Francisco, 896 F. 2d 1221 (9th Cir. 1990), cert. denied, 498 U.S. 999 (1990).

Church of the Lukumi Babalu Aye, Inc. v. City of Hialeah, 508 U.S. 520 (1993).

City of Boerne v. Flores, 521 U.S. 507 (1997).

Cohen v. City of Des Plaines, 8 F. 3d 484 (7th Cir. 1993), cert. denied, 512 U.S. 1236 (1994).

Cornerstone Bible Church v. City of Hastings, 948 F. 2d 464 (8th Cir. 1991).

Corporation of the Presiding Bishop of the Church of Jesus Christ of Latter-Day Saints v. Porterville, 203 P. 2d 823 (Cal. 1949), appeal dismissed, 338 U.S. 805 (1949).

Employment Division, Department of Human Resources of Oregon v. Smith, 494 U.S. 872 (1990).

First Assembly of God of Naples, Florida v. Collier County, Florida, 20 F. 3d 419 as modified by 27 F. 3d 526 (11th Cir. 1994), cert. denied, 513 U.S. 1080 (1995).

Grosz v. City of Miami Beach, 721 F. 2d 729 (11th Cir. 1983), cert. denied, 469 U.S. 827 (1984).

Islamic Center of Mississippi, Inc. v. City of Starkville, 840 F. 2d 293 (5th Cir. 1988).

Lakewood, Ohio Congregation of Jehovah's Witnesses v. City of Lakewood, 699 F. 2d 303 (6th Cir. 1983), cert. denied, 464 U.S. 815 (1983).

Larkin v. Grendel's Den, 459 U.S. 116 (1982).

LeBlanc-Stenberg v. Fletcher, 67 F. 3d 412 (2nd Cir. 1995).

Messiah Baptist Church v. County of Jefferson, 859 F. 2d 820 (10th Cir. 1988), cert. denied, 490 U.S. 1005 (1989).
Westchester Reform Temple v. Brown, 239 N.E. 2d 891 (N.Y. 1968).
Western Presbyterian Church v. Board of Zoning Adjustment, 862 F. Supp. 538 (D.D.C. 1994).

Zorach v. Clauson
343 U.S. 306 (1952)

"We are a religious people whose institutions presuppose a Supreme Being." These words from *Zorach v. Clauson* (1952), one of the Supreme Court's first important Establishment Clause cases, reflect a recurrent theme in the Court's jurisprudence: that the Establishment Clause does not require the government to be hostile to religion but, rather, permits it to accommodate the religious beliefs and practices of its citizens. Equally recurrent, however, are disputes about the meaning and the limits of this principle of accommodation. When does accommodation end and establishment begin? *Zorach* is important not only for its early articulation of the accommodation principle but also for its controversial application of that principle to uphold a program of religious "released time" for public school students.

Two cases from the late 1940s set the stage for the Supreme Court's 1952 decision in *Zorach*: *Everson v. Board of Education* (1947) and *Illinois ex rel. McCollum v. Board of Education* (1948). *Everson* was the modern Court's first significant encounter with the Establishment Clause. The Court ruled that the clause would be applied to the states as well as the federal government and that it erected "a wall of separation between Church and State." According to *Everson,* this wall of separation did not forbid neutral governmental programs that included religious as well as secular beneficiaries. As a result, the Court upheld a program of bus-fare reimbursement that was extended to students attending religious as well as secular schools. But the Court emphasized that it would not permit government to favor religion through non-neutral programs. Neither the states nor the federal government, wrote the Court, "can pass laws which aid one religion, aid all religions, or prefer one religion over another." *Everson* thus declared that government must remain neutral not only among religions but also between religion and nonreligion.

One year later *McCollum* presented the Court with an opportunity to apply the *Everson* requirement of neutrality. With only one justice, Stanley Reed, dissenting, the Court in *McCollum* invalidated an on-the-premises, religious released-time program for public school students. Under this program, classes in religious instruction were offered once a week in the school building during regular class hours. These classes, thirty or forty-five minutes in length, were taught by privately employed religious teachers who were provided by a religious council representing various faiths. The classes were not required but, rather, were offered only to those students whose parents had requested that their children attend; students not enrolled in these classes continued their secular studies.

Despite the optional nature of the religious classes and despite their largely private sponsorship, the Supreme Court in *McCollum* concluded that this scheme of instruction violated the Establishment Clause. Unlike the neutral reimbursement of bus fares to religious and nonreligious students alike, this program singled out religion for special, advantageous treatment, and it thereby violated the requirement of neutrality spelled out in *Everson*:

> Pupils compelled by law to go to school for secular education are released in part from their legal duty on the condition that they attend the religious classes. This is beyond all question a utilization of the tax-established and tax-supported public school system to aid religious groups to spread their faith. And it falls squarely under the ban of the First Amendment . . . as we interpreted it in *Everson.*

The court reaffirmed that the Establishment Clause forbids even "an impartial governmental assistance of all religions." It denied that this interpretation of the clause "manifest[ed] a governmental hostility to religion or religious teachings," noting that "both religion and government can best work to achieve their lofty aims if each is left free from the other within its respective sphere."

McCollum was a controversial decision, and it generated a large amount of academic and popular commentary. Some of this commentary was supportive of the decision, but much was critical. The released-time issue quickly was back in the courts, and it returned to the Supreme Court within the space of four years. This time, in *Zorach,* the result was different. In a 6-to-3 ruling—with dissents by Justices Hugo Black, Felix Frankfurter, and Robert Jackson—the Supreme Court upheld a released-time program in a decision that seemed at odds not only with *McCollum* but also with the reasoning of *Everson.*

The released-time program upheld in *Zorach* was in most respects similar to the program invalidated in *McCollum.* As in *McCollum,* the program offered religious instruction to public school students during regular class hours. This instruction, which lasted no more than an hour a week, was provided to students only on the request of their parents; nonparticipating students remained in their ordinary classrooms. As in *McCollum,* the religious teachers were privately employed, and the program was conducted largely under private sponsorship, but with the cooperation and assistance of the public schools.

Unlike the religious classes challenged in *McCollum,* however, the classes at issue in *Zorach* were not held in the public school building. Instead, they were conducted off the school premises, at religious centers to which participating students retreated during the period of religious instruction. And for the Court in *Zorach,* speaking through an opinion by Justice William O. Douglas, this made all the difference: "In [*McCollum*] the classrooms were turned over to religious instructors. We accordingly held that the program violated the First Amendment." But the program in *Zorach,* by contrast, was constitutionally permissible. In the view of the Court, the public schools in *Zorach* were doing "no more than accommodat[ing] their schedules to a program of outside religious instruction."

Although the Court in *McCollum* indeed had mentioned the use of the public school classrooms as partial support for its ruling, the Court had focused primarily on the impact of the compulsory education system. And as Justice Hugo L. Black observed in his dissenting opinion in *Zorach,* this impact was present to the same extent in *Zorach* as it was in *McCollum*:

> [Under the *Zorach* program, as under the program invalidated in *McCollum,*] the school authorities release some of the children on the condition that they attend the religious classes, get reports on whether they attend, and hold the other children in the school building until the religious hour is over. As we attempted to make categorically clear, the *McCollum* decision would have been the same if the religious classes had not been held in the school buildings.

Similarly, in his dissent Justice Jackson argued that the released-time program at issue in *Zorach* was "founded on a use of the State's power of coercion, which, for me, determines its unconstitutionality."

Although the cases can perhaps be distinguished, *Zorach* seemed to depart from the reasoning of *McCollum.* More generally, *Zorach* seemed to disregard the *Everson* requirement of neutrality. According to this requirement, government cannot single out religion for preferential treatment—which is, of course, precisely what a religious released-time program does, regardless of where the religious instruction is held. The public schools give special treatment to religion, and to religion alone, in an attempt to facilitate the task of religious instruction.

In defending the Court's apparent deviation from the requirement of neutrality, Justice Douglas introduced a competing principle, the principle of accommodation. According to this principle, government sometimes can single out religion for special, advantageous treatment. Such special treatment is not permissible if it involves the government in the active promotion of religion, but it is permissible when the government is merely accommodating private religious beliefs and practices.

According to Justice Douglas, this principle derives from the religious character of our society and from our commitment to religious freedom:

> We are a religious people whose institutions presuppose a Supreme Being. We guarantee the freedom to worship as one chooses. We make room for as wide a

> variety of beliefs and creeds as the spiritual needs of man deem necessary. We sponsor an attitude on the part of government that shows no partiality to any one group and that lets each flourish according to the zeal of its adherents and the appeal of its dogma. When the state encourages religious instruction or cooperates with religious authorities by adjusting the schedule of public events to sectarian needs, it follows the best of our traditions. For it then respects the religious nature of our people and accommodates the public service to their spiritual needs.

Noting the Court's differing results in *Zorach* and *McCollum*, Justice Douglas recognized that the line between permissible accommodation and impermissible promotion might be difficult to draw: "The problem, like many problems in constitutional law, is one of degree."

The strongest case for finding a permissible accommodation is when the government has treated religion specially in order to remove a burden on religious freedom that the government itself would otherwise be imposing. Thus, for example, Congress permissibly has exempted religious employers from federal nondiscrimination laws that otherwise would forbid them from making employment decisions on the basis of religious affiliation. Noting that "there is ample room for accommodation of religion under the Establishment Clause," the Supreme Court upheld this employment exemption in *Corporation of the Presiding Bishop of Church of Jesus Christ of Latter-Day Saints v. Amos* (1987). "Where, as here, government acts with the proper purpose of lifting a regulation that burdens the exercise of religion," the Court wrote in *Amos*, "we see no reason to require that the exemption come packaged with benefits to secular entities." When the burden on religious freedom is not severe, however, the Court has been reluctant to uphold religious exemptions or preferences unless they include nonreligious beneficiaries as well. In *Texas Monthly, Inc. v. Bullock* (1989), for example, the Court rejected an accommodation argument in holding that the Establishment Clause precluded a sales tax exemption that was available for religious books and periodicals but not for similarly situated nonreligious publications.

In the circumstances presented by *Zorach*, it is difficult to find a governmentally imposed burden that the released-time program was designed to relieve, much less a burden that was severe enough to justify a program that benefited religion alone. The compulsory education system does not meaningfully restrict the religious beliefs or practices of public school students, who remain free to pursue their religion during the many hours when school is not in session. They could attend religious classes after school, for example, as well as on weekends. Religious released-time programs, whether of the *Zorach* or the *McCollum* variety, seem designed less to remove a burden on religion than to confer an affirmative benefit. As such, they are not strong candidates for an accommodation analysis.

In numerous cases decided after *Zorach*, the Supreme Court seemingly has rejected *Zorach*'s broad reading of the accommodation principle. As the Court observed in *Edwards v. Aguillard* (1987), moreover, "[t]he Court has been particularly vigilant in monitoring compliance with the Establishment Clause in elementary and secondary schools," invalidating many governmental practices that seem no more constitutionally offensive than the one upheld in *Zorach*. Especially in the context of public education, the Court has been guided far less by *Zorach* than by *McCollum* and by the *Everson* requirement of neutrality, on which *McCollum* was grounded. Even so, *Zorach* has never been overruled, and off-the-premises released-time programs continue to operate in many communities around the United States.

Daniel O. Conkle

Bibliography

Alito, Samuel, "The 'Released Time' Cases Revisited: A Study of Group Decisionmaking by the Supreme Court," 83 *Yale Law Journal* 1202–1236 (1974).

Gans, A. W., "Right of School Authorities to Release Pupils during School Hours for Purpose of Attending Religious Education Classes," 2 *American Law Reports* 1371–1374 (Rochester, N.Y.: Lawyers Co-operative Publishing, 1948 and Later Case Service, 1985 and Supp. 1991).

Reed, George E., "Church–State and the Zorach Case," 27 *Notre Dame Lawyer* 529–551 (1952).

Cases Cited

Corporation of the Presiding Bishop of Church of Jesus Christ of Latter-Day Saints v. Amos, 483 U.S. 327 (1987).

Edwards v. Aguillard, 482 U.S. 578 (1987).

Everson v. Board of Education, 330 U.S. 1 (1947).

Illinois ex rel. McCollum v. Board of Education, 333 U.S. 203 (1948).

Texas Monthly, Inc. v. Bullock, 489 U.S. 1 (1989).

Zorach v. Clauson, 343 U.S. 306 (1952).

Index of Cases

D

E

F

G

H

I

J

K

L

M

Q

R

S

T

Y

Z

Subject Index

N

O

P

Q

R

S

T

U

V

W

For Product Safety Concerns and Information please contact our EU representative GPSR@taylorandfrancis.com
Taylor & Francis Verlag GmbH, Kaufingerstraße 24, 80331 München, Germany

www.ingramcontent.com/pod-product-compliance
Lightning Source LLC
LaVergne TN
LVHW080112011026
849160LV00013B/1077

* 9 7 8 0 8 1 5 3 6 5 3 5 8 *